T0398672

Handbook of Research on Effective Communication, Leadership, and Conflict Resolution

Anthony H. Normore
*California State University Dominguez Hills, USA & International Academy of
Public Safety, USA*

Larry W. Long
Illinois State University, USA & International Academy of Public Safety, USA

Mitch Javidi
*North Carolina State University, USA & International Academy of Public
Safety, USA*

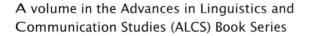

A volume in the Advances in Linguistics and
Communication Studies (ALCS) Book Series

**Information Science
REFERENCE**
An Imprint of IGI Global

Published in the United States of America by
>	Information Science Reference (an imprint of IGI Global)
>	701 E. Chocolate Avenue
>	Hershey PA, USA 17033
>	Tel: 717-533-8845
>	Fax: 717-533-8661
>	E-mail: cust@igi-global.com
>	Web site: http://www.igi-global.com

Library of Congress Cataloging-in-Publication Data

Names: Normore, Anthony H., editor. | Long, Larry W., editor. | Javidi,
	Mitch, 1958- editor.
Title: Handbook of research on effective communication, leadership, and
	conflict resolution / Anthony Normore, Mitch Javidi and Larry Long,
	editors.
Description: Hershey, PA : Information Science Reference, [2016] | Includes
	bibliographical references and index.
Identifiers: LCCN 2015050767| ISBN 9781466699700 (hardcover) | ISBN
	9781466699717 (ebook)
Subjects: LCSH: Conflict management. | Communication in organizations. |
	Communication in management. | Leadership. | Organizational effectiveness.
Classification: LCC HD42 .H366 2016 | DDC 658.4--dc23 LC record available at http://lccn.loc.gov/2015050767

This book is published in the IGI Global book series Advances in Linguistics and Communication Studies (ALCS) (ISSN: Pending; eISSN: Pending)

Advances in Linguistics and Communication Studies (ALCS) Book Series

Abigail G. Scheg
Elizabeth City State University, USA

ISSN: Pending
EISSN: Pending

MISSION

The scope of language and communication is constantly changing as society evolves, new modes of communication are developed through technological advancement, and novel words enter our lexicon as the result of cultural change. Understanding how we communicate and use language is crucial in all industries and updated research is necessary in order to promote further knowledge in this field.

The **Advances in Linguistics and Communication Studies (ALCS)** book series presents the latest research in diverse topics relating to language and communication. Interdisciplinary in its coverage, ALCS presents comprehensive research on the use of language and communication in various industries including business, education, government, and healthcare.

COVERAGE

- Computer-Mediated Communication
- Media and Public Communications
- Interpersonal Communication
- Language acquisition
- Language and Identity
- Youth Language
- Graphic Communications
- Dialectology
- Sociolinguistics
- Language in the Media

IGI Global is currently accepting manuscripts for publication within this series. To submit a proposal for a volume in this series, please contact our Acquisition Editors at Acquisitions@igi-global.com or visit: http://www.igi-global.com/publish/.

Titles in this Series

For a list of additional titles in this series, please visit: www.igi-global.com

Handbook of Research on Cross-Cultural Approaches to Language and Literacy Development
Patriann Smith (University of Illinois at Urbana-Champaign, USA) and Alex Kumi-Yeboah (University at Albany–
State University of New York, USA)
Information Science Reference • copyright 2015 • 567pp • H/C (ISBN: 9781466686687) • US $305.00 (our price)

Communication and Language Analysis in the Corporate World
Roderick P. Hart (University of Texas - Austin, USA)
Information Science Reference • copyright 2014 • 435pp • H/C (ISBN: 9781466649996) • US $215.00 (our price)

Communication and Language Analysis in the Public Sphere
Roderick P. Hart (University of Texas - Austin, USA)
Information Science Reference • copyright 2014 • 580pp • H/C (ISBN: 9781466650039) • US $190.00 (our price)

Digital Rhetoric and Global Literacies Communication Modes and Digital Practices in the Networked World
Gustav Verhulsdonck (University of Texas at El Paso, USA) and Marohang Limbu (Michigan State University, USA)
Information Science Reference • copyright 2014 • 398pp • H/C (ISBN: 9781466649163) • US $205.00 (our price)

www.igi-global.com

701 E. Chocolate Ave., Hershey, PA 17033
Order online at www.igi-global.com or call 717-533-8845 x100
To place a standing order for titles released in this series, contact: cust@igi-global.com
Mon-Fri 8:00 am - 5:00 pm (est) or fax 24 hours a day 717-533-8661

In Memory of Dr. Gwen Stowers

Dr. Gwen Stowers was Professor of Teacher Education and Program Lead for the Teaching and Learning in a Global Society concentration in the School of Education and National University in San Diego, California. Gwen began her tenure with National University in 2000, just as the University was beginning its foray into online education. By 2012, most of Gwen's work with National was online. Gwen lived with her husband and adult son in a rural, working class border town in Southern New Mexico, as well as in Tijuana, México, and in a more urban working class community in San Diego, California. Together they promoted border rights (taking pride in being called "border rats" and "horse traders"), taught English on both sides of the border, worked as real estate agents for new immigrants, published the bilingual newspaper, Las Fronteras, and worked to make aesthetic improvements on their hand sculptured adobe house. Though Gwen lost a battle with breast cancer in 2012, her legacy as a social justice advocate lives on.

List of Reviewers

Daniel Davis, *Illinois State University, USA*
Brian Ellis, *Sacramento Police Department, USA*
Christopher Hoina, *International Academy of Public Safety, USA*
Angela Jerome, *Western Kentucky University, USA*
James Klopovic, *International Academy of Public Safety, USA*
Renee Mitchell, *Cambridge University, UK, & Sacramento Police Department, USA*
Andrew Pyle, *Clemson University, USA*
Heather Rintool, *Nipissing University, Canada*
Doron Zinger, *University of California at Riverside, USA*
Kendall Zoller, *Sierra Training Associates, USA*

List of Contributors

Table of Contents

Section 1
Issues for Leaders, Organization, and Communication: Coping with Today and Planning for Tomorrow

Section 3
Improving Organization: A Focus on Teams, Engagement, and Personal Development

Section 4
Optimizing Performance: Enhancing Relational Development through Trust and Communication

Section 5
Ethic of Managerial Communication and Electronic Surveillance of Employees

Detailed Table of Contents

Section 1
Issues for Leaders, Organization, and Communication: Coping with Today and Planning for Tomorrow

This chapter introduces the scope and focus of the new book. The reader is briefly introduced to the definitions and debates about leadership and management boundaries, differences, and overlapping responsibilities in the digital age. Drawing on both theory and practice, current issues and topics are covered in depth, providing an introduction and overview of perceptible trends and scenarios relevant to the current post-Global Financial Crisis (GFC) leadership outlook for global business. The authors then provide an outline and overview of the topics and themes of each chapter and a coherent rationale for developing discussions and research from our first book "Dynamic Models of Leadership for Global Business: Enhancing digitally connected environments".

Diversity and change are key concepts facing the world, today. In the 21st century, organizational leaders recognize the importance of diverse perspectives and adaptations to changes. Globally, cultures have many definitions and difference as nations collectively strive to communicate with one another. Organizational leaders must understand the importance of cross-cultural communications in establishing trust and respect in business relationships. Doris E. Cross is an educator and researcher on diversity issues influence on organizational cultures competitive advantage. This chapter identifies factors, such as changing demographics, tumultuous economies, and workforce dynamics and effects on individual perceptions of organizational cultures.

Chapter 3

T. Ray Ruffin, University of Phoenix, USA & Colorado Technical University, USA &
University of Mount Olive, USA & Wake Technical Community College, USA
Joyce Marie Hawkins, Wake Technical Community College, USA
D. Israel Lee, Southern Illinois University, USA & University of Phoenix, USA

Policies, health, and government regulations affect various Health Care organizations and their members. One such policy, the Health Information Technology for Economic and Clinical Health (HITECH) Act, attempts to improve the performance of health care systems through the use of technology, such as Electronic Health Records (Bluementhal, 2010). The most critical task of leadership is to establish a mindset at the top of the organization and function to infuse a culture of excellence throughout the organization (Bentkover, 2012). Health organizations can only progress if their members share a set of values and are single-mindedly committed to achieving openly defined objectives (Bentkover, 2012). This chapter investigates organizational leadership in relation to health care reforms to include trends in health care leadership, Stratified Systems Theory (SST), Systems Thinking, and regulators perspectives. The chapter will consist of the following sections: background; issues controversies, and problems; solutions and recommendation; future research directions; and conclusion.

Chapter 4

Katherine P. Bergethon, Illinois State University, USA
Daniel Cochece Davis, Illinois State University, USA

Although past research readily acknowledges emotions exist in organizations, and even acknowledges that leaders benefit from having "emotional intelligence," fully understanding leadership's role in addressing the emotional dimension of organizational experience, especially during the typically high emotion situations of organizational conflicts, remains understudied. This chapter provides greater awareness of how leadership styles, especially transformational or charismatic leadership, relates with emotional intelligence to facilitate "emotional leadership" within organizations to achieve positive follower effects.

Chapter 5

Christine Clark, University of Nevada Las Vegas, USA
Gwen Stowers, National University, USA

This chapter takes a contrary view of the "meta" aspect of meta-communication (where meta is defined as "behind" or "beneath") in the online multicultural teacher education classroom, arguing that such communication inhibits learning about (content) and through (pedagogy) sociopolitically-located multicultural teacher education by enabling e-racism, e-classism, and e-sexism to operate in largely covert manners in the distance education context. Accordingly, this chapter contends that digital meta-communication on issues of race/ethnicity, socioeconomic class, and sex/gender needs to be "de-meta-ed" or made explicit in order for the kind of liberatory reflective conversation on these topics to occur that is foundational to the adequate preparation of PK-12 teachers to effectively educate all students.

There is a significant lack of documented research on Australian school improvement contextualised within business improvement model settings. This is the case, even though Australian schools have been operating within a business environment for a while now. This chapter aims at addressing this gap by discussing educational quality within schools. It will also present an adapted version for continuous school improvement within school systems in Australia. This adapted version of continuous school improvement provides a theoretical framework on how schools operating as self-managed business systems can ensure that the delivery of educational quality is strategically sustained at the organisational level and that focus remains on the important core business of student learning.

Section 2
Coping with Conflict: Dealing with Stakeholders, Culture, Competition, and Style

This chapter covers a lot of groundwork and provides and quick and through introduction to the concepts and underlying discussions on Alternative Dispute Resolution (ADR). The chapter provides a detailed discussion based on extant literature in an effort to differentiate between disputes and conflicts. Then some of the common confusions between terms commonly used in ADR are addressed. Following which various key government acts and reports that shape the state of ADR are discussed. Because of their length, therefore only those concerns within the documents that directly address ADR or are related to ADR are discussed. It remains a burden on the readers to access these documents themselves to fully appreciate their content.

Chapter 8

Social media platforms provide channels for both individuals and organizations to engage with global audiences. A successful social media message can reach millions, and shape the way publics view a particular person, group, or cause. As organizations become more engaged with publics through social media platforms, a new area of organizational risk has also developed. It is possible for an organization to create a self-inflicted crisis through the unintentional transmission of a poorly worded or ill-conceived social media message. This type of self-induced crisis event creates organizational conflict that must be managed quickly. This chapter explores three cases of organizational conflict resulting from self-inflicted crisis events. All three events caused major conversations to erupt on social media platforms. The author examines the social media-based communication practices of three organizations and draws lessons from both successes and failures for how organizations should respond to self-inflicted crises.

Chapter 9

When faced with crises organizational leaders must identify, prioritize, and communicate with organizational stakeholders. Increasingly, organizational leaders find themselves responding to crises made by persons that represent or are associated with the organization in some way. However, most case studies of image repair campaigns focus on the individual that has transgressed rather than on the often simultaneous campaigns undertaken by the organizations with which they are associated. To study these issues more closely, this chapter uses The Ohio State University's (OSU's) tattoos for memorabilia scandal as exemplar and offers meaningful insight and pragmatic considerations for practitioners dealing with similar situational constraints.

Chapter 10

This case study highlights and examines an avoidable failure of management communication and leadership in a non-governmental organization (NGO). The case study draws on a real-life example of a NGO that was established in Palestine with European Union (EU) funding and that became subsequently staffed by a team composed of local Palestinian employees and expatriate non-Palestinians who, as is commonly the case in international NGOs, were appointed to executive management and leadership roles. Overall, this case study highlights processes of cross-cultural communication between the local employees, the expatriate employees, and (indirectly) with senior executives of the EU funding agencies, whose distant yet decisive influence give a broader context to the localized communication and conflict management processes described and analyzed here. Finally, recommendations are made for future research specific to effective communication, leadership and conflict resolution in international organizations generally and in Palestinian organizations specifically.

Chapter 11

Virtual teams are increasingly common as marketplaces become more global. They offer advantages to employers, including increased time and travel savings, decreased real estate costs, and larger applicant pools. Yet, conflict is inherent in virtual teams, and leaders within virtual teams must confront debilitating conflicts due to technological issues, cultural miscommunication, and restructuring their communication. Though some elements are similar to handling conflict in any team situation, five group factors are especially subject to conflict and manifest differently in effective virtual teams: strategically selecting team members, building effective relationships, fostering trust, facilitating communication, and achieving team goals. Managing any team presents leaders with challenges regarding building relationships, facilitating communication, overcoming barriers and achieving team goals. However, adding geographic distance, cultural differences, and a lack of continuous face-to-face interaction exacerbates these challenges.

In this chapter we aim to consider both dialectical and dialogical systems, local and regional policies and practice implications for the communication and management of the creative as well as destructive conflict within networks and what else may be needed by cooperating parties as a support infrastructure to assist the development and growth of SME innovation networks. We firstly outline key terms, concepts and issues about innovation, collaboration and the goals set for business incubators by the European Union and globally, contrasting these with each other. We provide an overview of the role of key stakeholders, systems and research analyses, discussion and recommendations indicating our own. These recommendations will be informed by some case studies we have been engaged in as well as the wider research literature canon on these topics.

This chapter examines the influence of context on leadership styles in a higher education institution. Specifically, the enactment of leadership, the consequence of differing leadership styles, and the resultant interpersonal conflict. Informed by the empirical literature examining the Middle East, workplace stress and conflict, leadership and interpersonal communication, the chapter highlights the consequences of a high-conflict external context and the resultant constraints on human resource policies and practices. The recommendations include establishing a leadership development program aimed at creating an awareness of different leadership styles and the leadership of diverse groups. This includes the implementation of a cultural change program, programs to support the empowerment of minority groups, management education focusing on conflict resolution. The chapter adds to the body of literature by addressing the challenges confronting leadership in a high conflict context.

Section 3
Improving Organization: A Focus on Teams, Engagement, and Personal Development

In recent years, the interest in and development of communities of practice (CoPs) has undergone exponential growth. However, this uncontrolled expansion has, to a large extent, led to the name of community of practice being attributed to working groups or communities that are not communities of practice. The aim of this work is to shed a little light on this confusion and identify and characterise communities of practice compared with other types of groups or organizational structures. To achieve it, first of all, we are going to introduce an intuitive and agreed definition of community of practice. In a second movement, we will identify and define the principal groups or organizational structures that are used, besides communities of practice, by organizations to improve their strategies when meeting these aims that they are pursuing. We will then present a comparison between these organizational structures or groups and communities of practice. The chapter ends by offering a number of conclusions and providing some guidelines on the future development of communities of practice.

This chapter introduces the framework and causal model of organizational culture, organizational climate, knowledge management, and job performance related to business process orientation. It argues that dimensions of organizational culture, organizational climate, and knowledge management have mediated positive effect on job performance. Knowledge management positively mediates the relationships between organizational culture and job performance and between organizational climate and job performance. Organizational culture is positively related to organizational climate. Furthermore, the author hopes that understanding the theoretical constructs of organizational culture, organizational climate, knowledge management, and job performance through the use of the framework and causal model will not only inform researchers of a better design for studying organizational culture, organizational climate, knowledge management, and job performance, but also assist in the understanding of intricate relationships between different factors.

This chapter aims to explore the increasing utilization of virtual teams in the existing globally competitive and complex business environment of the 21st century. With virtual teams, companies can expand their talent pool beyond geographical barriers. Furthermore, they can incorporate a follow-the-sun process in their business strategy. Combined, this leveraged approach can better position companies to meet market demands in a more timely and cost-effective manner. To achieve this competitive advantage, business leaders must thoroughly understand the challenges associated with developing and managing virtual teams. This chapter examines the reasons for utilizing virtual teams, challenges that stem from diversity, structural and behavioral characteristics, managerial considerations for effective leadership, supporting technologies, best practices, and future implications.

This chapter examines the internal communication practices of Lenovo, a $39 billion Fortune Global 500 technology company, and the world's largest PC vendor. In particular, this study examines how this company uses social media as a form of internal marketing to foster employee engagement. Internal communications (or internal marketing) is generally led by marketing or PR professionals with expertise in human resources, public relations, marketing, social media, and/or employee engagement. One new way that companies are extending internal communication is by developing the use of their company intranets. Intranets can support an organization by sharing accurate leadership communication and company information on a timely basis to develop trust with employees and encourage them to act as brand ambassadors. This chapter describes how Lenovo has developed and uses its Lenovo Central intranet to engage employees in its mission and vision.

There is plenty of evidence on a positive influence of social relationships on work-related attitudes and behaviors. Besides, online social networks (OSNs), made possible by Web 2.0, have become a global phenomenon and have a considerable impact on the way people communicate and interact with each other. Our purpose is to evaluate the effect of using OSNs on the worker's attitudes and behaviors, particularly in the context of Higher Education. In this sense, we used a questionnaire, to evaluate the attitudes of 157 faculty members. To assess the use of OSNs, we resorted to a dichotomous variable. After analyzing and discussing the results we conclude that the use of OSNs influences the worker's performance, but not Job satisfaction, Organizational commitment or extra-role performance. The relationships we propose in what concerns the worker's attitudes are all empirically proved. Lastly, we describe the study limitations and we suggest some perspectives for future research.

Chapter 19

Principals and school leaders play a pivotal role in teacher satisfaction, retention, and learning; thus, they are uniquely positioned to help teachers improve their practice. Principals face many of the same challenges that teachers do, especially in schools serving low-income, low-performing, and ethnically diverse students. This chapter examines the extant literature concerning online professional development (OPD) and how it may hold particular promise for principals and other school leaders who work in these challenging settings, with a focus on attending to principal instructional leadership. A corollary purpose centers on how effective online communication (and the use of digital modalities) can create greater access and flexibility for participants. Establishing lines of communication and building online community may help overcome the professional isolation experienced by principals. Implications for theory and practice are discussed.

Chapter 20

Engineering Students' Communication Apprehension and Competence in Technical Oral
Presentations

Noor Raha Mohd Radzuan, Universiti Malaysia Pahang, Malaysia
Sarjit Kaur, Universiti Sains Malaysia, Malaysia

The demand for 21st century engineering graduates to be communicatively competent, particularly in English language, is increasing. Effective communication skills are one of the main competencies listed by the Malaysian Engineering Accreditation Council Policy with the expectation that all Malaysian engineering graduates will master it upon graduation. This involves skills in presenting information to technical and non technical audience through oral presentations. This chapter aims to examine engineering students' communication competence and their level of apprehension in delivering a technical oral presentation. Questionnaires, adapted from McCroskey's (1988) Self-Perceived Communication Competence and Richmond & McCroskey's (1988) Personal Report of Public Speaking Anxiety, were distributed to 193 final year Universiti Malaysia Pahang engineering students who were preparing for their Undergraduate Research presentation. The results of the study have direct and indirect implications to the teaching and learning of oral presentation skills among engineering undergraduates.

Section 4
Optimizing Performance: Enhancing Relational Development through Trust and
Communication

Chapter 21

Developing Trust within International Teams: The Impacts of Culture on Team Formation and
Process

Kurt Kirstein, City University of Seattle, USA

The widespread use of international teams has been driven by an unprecedented need to draw upon varied talents of employees from around the globe in a manner that is both organizationally and financially feasible. Despite the importance of technologies to enable such teams, their success depends largely on the levels of intra-team trust and collaboration they are able to establish throughout the life of their projects. Team members on international teams may differ substantially on a number of cultural dimensions including preferences for individualistic versus collective teamwork, power distance, uncertainty avoidance, and contextual communication. This chapter will investigate how these four cultural dimensions are likely to impact trust within an international team. Suggestions that team leaders can utilize to address these cultural dimensions are also presented.

Chapter 22

Communication: The Role of the Johari Window on Effective Leadership Communication in
Multinational Corporations

Ben Tran, Alliant International University, USA

Based on previous research, leadership appears to be enacted through communication in such a way that it contains a relational (affective) and task (content) component. Additionally, when leaders communicate effectively, their followers experience greater levels of satisfaction. Thus, the purpose of this chapter is on communication, specifically, the role of the Johari Window (JW) on effective leadership communication in multinational corporations (MNCs). In regards to the JW, many researchers did not question, and even more practitioners did not realize is that, the JW is created based on a domestic paradigm, and not necessarily applicable to a multinational environment where intercultural and multicultural communication are at play for multinational environment within MNCs. Nevertheless, the JW has continuously been applied to cross cultural studies, without a paradigm shift, utilizing a domestic paradigm (no international cultural factors at play) within a multinational environment (various international cultural factors at play), issue at hand persists.

The purpose of this chapter is to integrate credible leadership into the authors' previous work in principled negotiation. After the introduction, international negotiation is conceptualized with an in-depth description of the process. This is followed by description of negotiation styles and eight propositions for credible negotiation leadership that are predicated upon intercultural communication study. The conclusion is an application of Credible Negotiation Leadership with recommendations.

The public's perception of police legitimacy is viewed through the lens of procedural justice (Tyler, 2003). Legitimacy it is a perception held by an audience (Tankebe & Liebling, 2013). Tyler (2006, p. 375) defines legitimacy as "a psychological property of an authority, institution, or social arrangement that leads those connected to it to believe that it is appropriate, proper, and just." Four aspects of the police contact that affects a citizen's view: active participation in the decision-making, the decision-making is neutral and objective, trustworthy motives, and being treated with dignity and respect (Tyler, 2004). Accordingly an officer should act in a way that supports citizen's active participation, conveys an air of neutrality, and enhances dignity and respect. One way an officer can transmit his intent is through communicative intelligence. Communicative intelligence is a communication theory based on five capabilities (Zoller, 2015). These authors intend to link communicative intelligence to behaviors officers should engage in to enhance PJ and improve PL.

Leadership is the act of influencing others whereby power comes from things such as referent and reward bases and "have an ethical responsibility to attend to the needs and concerns of followers" (Northouse, 2010, p. 4). In this chapter, the authors highlight the extant literature on organizational leadership and its role in effective communication and engagement processes. The authors focus on first-line supervisors and the impact of communication and engagement on people under their supervision. Employee trait, state, and behavioral constructs coupled with the culture of emotional connection between police officers and the police organization are explored. Further, the authors examine the principles of empowerment including meaningfulness, competence, choice, and impact and its applicability to police leadership. The outcome of the relationship between effective leadership and employee engagement is directly linked to innovation, participation, teamwork, accountability, and the ability to face challenges. Conclusions and recommendations for future research are discussed.

Chapter 26

Today's workplace is composed of four generational groups of employees, each with varying degrees of technological expertise, career expectations, and professional experience. As such, higher education administrators need to identify differences among generations of workers and develop a strategic plan for managing and motivating across the generations. This case study addresses the following question: "How do higher education administrators lead and motivate multi-generational employees and online students?" An understanding of the common characteristics of each generational group is the first step for developing a strategy for motivating all employees and students in higher education. Communication, mentoring programs, training, respect, and opportunities for career advancement are components valued by all. It is important for higher education administrators to understand the values, work ethic, and communication style of the different generations. The implications for higher education administrators lie in establishing an organizational culture that promotes satisfaction for all individuals in the higher education setting.

This chapter explores concerns and challenges associated with the transition to online graduate instruction from the traditional face-to-face format. The author discusses several catalysts for the transition to virtual teaching; the ethics of being present; impediments to learning and communication online; and participant concerns. The chapter also considers online knowledge and meaning-making, online communities and associated uncertainties. Finally, considerations for leadership and communication moving forward are addressed.

Peter Smith, University of Liverpool, UK
Olaf Cames, University of Liverpool, UK

The majority of IT Projects are not successful and fail for non-technical reasons, despite the fact that numerous project management methodologies exist in the marketplace and are now in common use in organisations. As the CHAOS report from Standish Group documents, this remains an important and current issue (Dominguez, 2009; The Standish Group International Inc., 2013). The fact is that for more than 20 years the majority of IT projects have failed; largely as a result of human factors and communication issues. This leads to enormous economic issues for organisations in the public and private sector. This chapter proposes a new approach to project management which addresses the human factor and issues of communication. The proposed approach is novel and applies principles drawn from philosophy and action research to produce an approach which has the potential to radically change the way in which projects are managed. The approach is discussed in terms of practice and the academic literature and is applied to two project simulations.

Terje Solvoll, University Hospital of North Norway, Norway

The work setting in hospitals is communication intensive and can lead to significant difficulties related to interruptions from co-workers. Physicians often need information fast, and any delay between the decision made and the action taken could cause medical errors. One suggested solution for this problem is to implement wireless phone systems. However, psychological theory and empirical evidence, both suggest that wireless phones have the potential of creating additional problems related to interruptions, compared to traditional paging systems. The fact that hospital workers prefer interruptive communication methods before non-interruptive methods, amplifies the risk of overloading people when phones are widely deployed. This challenge causes some hospital staff to resist the diffusion of wireless phones, and one key is how to handle the balance between increased availability, and increased interruptions. In this chapter we will present solutions based on context aware communication systems which aims to reduce interruptions.

Section 5
Ethic of Managerial Communication and Electronic Surveillance of Employees

Angelo A. Camillo, Woodbury University, USA
Isabell C. Camillo, Brock University, Canada

Managerial Communication, in today's hyper communicative global business, is integral to business related disciplines such as strategic management, leadership, strategic marketing, and business ethics, etc. However, within the context of global strategic management, Managerial Communication follows under the broad umbrella of "Business Communication". Communication with internal and external stakeholders demands careful – ethical considerations, regardless of the industry. Having an inclusive – ethical strategic managerial communication policy in place, allows for strategic information dissemination as well as the protection of transmission of confidential data. This chapter discusses the topic of communication in general with emphasis on ethical managerial communication within the global context. The result of the study confirm that effective – ethical communication strategies and appropriate communications policy implementation is conducive to the firm's success. Within the framework of managerial leadership effectiveness, ethical managerial communication refers solely to managerial communication within the context of ethical global business management and not media communication.

The use of Information and Communication Technologies in the workplace is constantly increasing, but also the use of surveillance technology. Electronic monitoring of employees becomes an integral part of information systems in the workplace. The specific software which is used for monitoring electronic communications is, however, intrusive and infringes upon the employees' right to privacy. The issue of surveillance of employees' electronic communications is subject to different approaches in various jurisdictions. The most comprehensive protection to employees is afforded in the EU, and it would be enhanced once the General Data Protection Regulation is passed.

Information privacy research historically focuses on exploring individuals' concerns in the transaction environment. However, the recent growth of technology-enabled workplace surveillance is raising many concerns over employees' privacy. Employee surveillance practices are becoming increasingly prevalent, ranging from monitoring internet and email activities to capturing employees' interactions with customers and employees' personal health and fitness data using wearable health devices. Individuals may understand that employers can monitor their activities, but may not the potential uses or the repercussions of such monitoring. Moreover, employees may not feel they have the ability to opt-out of this monitoring. This chapter explores the privacy and ethical issues surrounding emerging means of workplace surveillance. The chapter considers both employee and employer perspectives and poses many questions to consider when deciding when does legitimate monitoring become an invasion of employee privacy?

Preface

INTRODUCTION

For the purposes of this book, we have focused on organizations and the intricate dynamics that make organizations tick. Among those dynamics and prevalent throughout the content are three pivotal features that can either serve as catalysts for organizational success or as a cancer that can cause an organization to crumble: leadership, communication, and orchestrating, managing and/or resolving conflict. These three pivotal concepts are crucial to all organizations. How they are utilized generally determines the sustainability and fate of the organization. These concepts will be defined as broadly as possible to encompass not only ethnic, cultural, and gender difference but all the differences protected and promoted by professional and philosophical difference. Organizations today must somehow find ways to effectively bridge, blend and lead all to be their most productive. We have searched far and wide to solicit authors who study or researched leadership, organizational health and development, or who have first-hand experiences in dealing with ways to improve organizations including communication and conflict mediation, management and orchestration. This collection of chapters is the result of numerous contributors who live and work in various non-profit and for-profit organizations throughout the world. Among the countries represented are Ireland, England, Australia, Saudi Arabia, Palestine, Unites States, Israel, Pakistan, Spain, Canada, Portugal, Malaysia, Thailand, Greece – to name a few.

As editors of this volume we realized long ago having worked globally on development, environmental, education, and other organizational projects that professionals often work at odds and in silos focused only on their restrictive professional mandate and traditional style. We have witnessed professional and organizational biases, acknowledge our own, and have at times framed issues accordingly. From our individual and collective professional experiences and multi-pronged research, we have further encountered a potpourri of professionals (e.g., economists, engineers, scientists, educators, criminal justice personnel, corporate CEOs, etc.,) who communicated the significance of individual achievement and failed to effectively partner with the communities and clientele they served. At their worst, they fight over "turf" rather than collaborate for the common good (Erbe, 2014).

Among the litany of lessons learned from our experiences we see the need to deliberately and intentionally change communication approaches (Geis & Javidi, 2015). Being aware of cultural differences is critical for any organization to be successful. We believe it is equally critical to honor and respect the integrity of cultural differences (Normore, 2009). We further believe this is best demonstrated in organizations in the way layers of leaders communicate their organizational goals and intentions. People sometimes express and communicate their particular concern that their cultural knowledge and practices are not being maintained to the extent that they would like. This concern is especially common for populations under pressure to change from forces which are seen as controlled by a dominant group.

Throughout this collection of chapters, communication will be defined broadly as well as simply to include any time and the myriad ways organizational constituencies are able to effectively bridge differences for reaching a shared goal. Consistent with our perspective, the National Communication Association (2015) succinctly and clearly defined the discipline of communication as a focus on how people use messages to generate meanings within and across various contexts, cultures, channels, and media. Within this framework, organizational communication is concerned with the symbolic act through which organizations adapt to, alter, or maintain their environment for the purpose of achieving organizational goals (Cummings, Long, Lewis, 1987). We believe it is important to differentiate between the terms "communication" and "communications." Communication is concerned with an exchange of symbols/messages/meanings among humans and is a most common method for exercising leadership. In contrast, communications is concerned with the means, technologies, channels, and media people use when communicating. Communication is a strategic message creation activity; communications is a focus on the methods and channels selected for transmitting the message. Communication, along with leadership and conflict management, are inextricably intertwined elements within organizational processes that impact on outcomes.

Although leadership has been widely studied, there is a persistent lack of agreement about what constitutes the most effective leadership styles. For example, some authors understand an effective leader as somebody who people follow, or as someone who communicates well and guides people. Others define leadership as more collaborative and include team facilitation: strong communication skills coupled with the ability to organize in order to achieve a common goal. Recent scholars in educational leadership have paid considerable attention to practices and policies that have marginalized special populations (e.g., disabilities, race, socio-economics, ethnicity, gender, aged, sexual orientation, mentally ill, homelessness, etc.,) and pose challenging questions to leaders, scholars, and the broader community to engage in discussions about leadership for social justice, global cultural literacy, and intercultural, multicultural, and cross-cultural proficiency (Erbe & Normore, 2015; Normore & Brooks, 2014; Normore & Erbe, 2013). Leadership theory and leadership practice are responding to societal changes by shifting focus from what leaders do, and how they do it, to the purpose of leadership. For our purposes, effective leadership is broadly operationalized as a process of cultural and social influence in which various people enlist the help and support of others in the accomplishment of a common task.

There is a belief by some scholars that leadership can be taught (e.g., Parks, 2005; Zoller, Normore, & Harrison, 2012). If that is true, one of the core questions might be, "What do you teach?" One of the more common approaches used to understand leadership is the study of great leaders. Others may focus on the traits and behaviors that successful leaders represent (Northouse, 2012). We argue that emphasis placed on biographies, traits, and behaviors are not the most fruitful path for one seeking to understand leadership. Rather, the key to more effective leadership lies at the end of the path that begins with considering leadership as a way of thinking about being true to the self, acting with honesty, respect, and integrity, and not following the crowd but inspiring the crowd to move toward achieving a great vision in support of holistic and life-long learning about leadership, collaboration, communication, and cross-cultural proficiency, and ways to effectively orchestrate conflict. Effective leadership encompasses an array of personal and professional elements including ethical and moral literacy, care, critique, peace, principles, morality, values, global literacy, credibility, cultural proficiency and authenticity—to name a few. Diverse groups solve problems and manage conflict better than very similar groups by drawing on wider range of experiences. What is also clear from research is that serving diverse communities requires a unique set of leadership skills and knowledge reflective of and responsive to the cultural and linguistic diversity of populations (Erbe & Normore, 2015).

The Handbook of Effective Communication, Leadership, and Conflict Resolution is inherently and potently transformative for organizational leaders who encourage the most innovative form of managing and solving conflict, and who foster the most effective forms of internal and external communication, in support of the local, national and global communities served. If organizations lack even the basics of what is being advocated throughout this book, they may benefit from investigating the contemporary role of organizational leadership. Such organizational conflict resolution experts are prepared to coach leadership in impartial inclusive process, mediate across difference and otherwise assist all members of organizations develop the skills and consciousness needed to effectively communicate, negotiate, and collaborate across differences.

THE STRUCTURE OF THIS BOOK

This book is comprised of 32 chapters organized into 5 sections: " Issues for leaders, organization, and communication: Coping with today and planning for tomorrow", "Coping with conflict: Dealing with stakeholders, culture, competition, and style", Improving organization: A focus on teams, engagement, and personal development", Optimizing performance: Enhancing relational development through trust and communication", and "Ethics of managerial communication and electronic surveillance of employees".

Section 1: Issues for Leaders, Organization, and Communication– Coping with Today and Planning for Tomorrow

This section features six chapters. In chapter 1, *Leadership in the Digital Age: Rhythms and the Beat of Change,* authors Peter A. C. Smith and Tom Cockburn (The Leadership Alliance, Inc., Ontario, Canada) introduces definitions and debates about leadership and management boundaries, differences, and over-lapping responsibilities in the digital age. Drawing on both theory and practice, current issues and topics are covered in-depth, providing an overview of perceptible trends and scenarios relevant to the current post-Global Financial Crisis (GFC) leadership outlook for global business. In chapter 2, *Globalization and Media's Impact on Cross Cultural Communication: Managing Organizational Change*, Doris E. Cross (Organizational Change and Development Company, USA) contends that in order to effectively manage market changes, organizational leaders are encouraged to examine the inclusion of diverse perspectives to capture both employees and consumers' loyalty. She argues that diverse perceptions in organizational cultures encourage new ideas and innovative approaches to meeting the needs of diverse customers. Authors Tony Ray Ruffin (University of Phoenix, USA),

Joyce Marie Hawkins (Wake Tech Community College, USA) and Israel Lee (University of Phoenix, USA) introduce the reader to the dynamics of a changing health care system in chapter 3, *Organizational Leadership and Health Care Reform*. These authors investigate organizational leadership in relation to health care reforms to include stratified theory and systems thinking. They argue that health organizations can only progress if their members share a set of values and are single-mindedly committed to achieving openly defined objectives.

Chapter 4, *Emotional Leadership: Leadership Styles, Emotional Intelligence, Conflict Management and Followers' Effects* is presented by Katherine Bergethon (Illinois State University, USA) and Daniel Cochece Davis (Illinois State University, USA). These authors highlight greater awareness of how leadership styles, especially transformational or charismatic leadership, relates with emotional intelligence to facilitate "emotional leadership" within organizations to achieve positive follower effects. Chapter 5 shifts the focus a bit in *Speaking with Trunks, Dancing with the 'Pink Elephants': Troubling e-Racism, e-Classism, and e-Sexism in Teaching Multicultural Teacher Education.* Author Christine Clark (University of Nevada Las Vegas, USA) takes a contrary view of the "meta" aspect of meta-communication (where meta is defined as "behind" or "beneath") in the online multicultural teacher education classroom. The author contends that digital meta-communication on issues of race/ethnicity, socioeconomic class, and sex/gender needs to be "de-meta-ed" or made explicit in order for the kind of liberatory reflective conversation on these topics to occur that is foundational to the adequate preparation of PK-12 teachers to effectively educate all students. In chapter 6, *Reframing Continuous School Improvement in Australian Schools,* author Venesser Fernandes (Monash University, Australia) discusses the school improvement process. Fernandez discusses educational quality within Australian schools and follows up with an adapted version for continuous school improvement within school systems in Australia.

Section 2: Coping with Conflict – Dealing with Stakeholders, Culture, Competition, and Style

This section features seven chapters. In chapter 7, *Alternative Dispute Resolution: A Legal Perspective,* author Saleem Gul (Institute of Management Sciences, Pakistan) discusses Alternative Dispute Resolution (ADR). Gul provides a detailed overview in an effort to differentiate between disputes and conflicts and identifies common confusions between terms commonly used in ADR. In chapter 8, *Surviving the Conflict of Self-Inflicted Organizational Crises,* Andrew Pyle (Clemson University, USA) examines the social media-based communication practices of three organizations and draws lessons from both successes and failures for how organizations should respond to self-inflicted crises. Authors Lauren J. Keil (Advisory Board Consulting and Management, USA) and Angela M. Jerome (Western Kentucky University, USA)) introduce the reader to the dynamics surrounding the expulsion of an American Senator in chapter 9, *Leadership in a Time of Crisis: Jim Tressel's Ousting from the Ohio State University.* Keil and Jerome discuss how the intertwined, complicated relationship between the NCAA, college/university leadership, coaches, student-athletes, alumni, and fans often places college/university administrators in precarious rhetorical positions. The authors use The Ohio State University's (OSU's) tattoos for memorabilia scandal as an exemplar and offers meaningful insight and pragmatic considerations for practitioners dealing with similar situational constraints.

Chapter 10, *Communication, Culture, and Discord: A Lesson in Leadership Failure,* authors Reema Rasheed (ESDC, Palestine) and Keith Jackson (SOAS, University of London, UK) examine an avoidable failure of management communication and leadership in a Non-Governmental Organization (NGO). They demonstrate how timely and effective leadership interventions might prevent conflict becoming both ingrained and detrimental to the health of the organization, thereby undermining its potential to fulfil its mission. In chapter 11, *Leading Virtual Teams: Conflict and Communication Challenges for Leaders*, authors Daniel Cochece Davis (Illinois State University, USA) and Nancy M. Scaffidi-Clarke (Mount Saint Mary College) argue that managing any team presents leaders with challenges and that adding geographic distance, cultural differences, and a lack of continuous face-to-face interaction exacerbates these challenges. Authors Peter A. C. Smith and Tom Cockburn (The Leadership Alliance, Inc., Ontario, Canada), Blanca Maria Martins (Universitat Politécnica de Catalunya, Spain), and Ramon Salvador Valles (Universitat Politecnica de Catalunya, Spain) present chapter 12, *Conflict of Interest or Community of Collaboration? Leadership, Dialectics and Dialog Issues in Community Renewal and SME Collaboration Process in the EU.* The authors consider various systems that range from local and regional policies and practice implications for the communication and management of the creative as well as destructive conflict within networks and what else may be needed by cooperating parties as a support infrastructure to assist the development and growth of SME innovation networks. In chapter 13, *Role of Leadership Style in Creating Conflict and Tension in a Higher Education Institution,* authors Grace Khoury (Birzeit University, Palestine) and Beverley McNally (Prince Mohammad Bin Fahd University, Saudi Arabia) examine the role of context on the development of human resource policies and practices, the consequence of differing leadership and management styles, and the resultant interpersonal conflict that occurs.

Section 3: Improving Organizations – A Focus on Teams, Engagement, and Personal Development

This section features seven chapters. In chapter 14, *Communities of Practice in Organizational Learning Strategies*, authors Sandra Sanz (Universitat Oberta de Catalunya, Spain) and Mario Pérez-Montoro (University of Barcelona, Spain) identify and characterize communities of practice compared with other types of groups or organizational structures. They identify the principal groups or organizational structures that are used by organizations to improve their strategies when meeting these aims, and offer guidance on the future development of communities of practice. In chapter 15, *A Unified Framework of Organizational Perspectives and Knowledge Management and their Impact on Job Performance,* author Kijpokin Kasemsap (Suan Sunandha Rajabhat University, Thailand) argues that dimensions of organizational culture, organizational climate, and knowledge management have mediated positive effect on job performance. Author Edward T. Chen (University of Massachusetts Lowell, Massachusetts, USA) presents chapter 16, *Virtual Team Management for Higher Performance.* Chen discusses ways for business leaders to meet fast-paced market demands is by utilizing virtual teams. He examines the reasons for utilizing virtual teams, challenges that stem from diversity, structural and behavioral characteristics, and managerial considerations for effective leadership, supporting technologies, best practices, and future implications.

Chapter 17, *Leadership Communication, Internal Marketing and Employee Engagement: A Recipe to Create Brand Ambassadors* is presented by authors Karen Mishra, (Meredith College School of Business, USA), Aneil Mishra (East Carolina University, USA), and Khaner Walker (Lenovo Consulting, USA). These authors examine the internal communication practices of a multi-billion dollar Fortune Global 500 technology company. In particular, the authors share how this company uses social media as a method of internal communications in fostering employee engagement through the use of their company intranets. In chapter 18, *The use of Online Social Networks in Higher Education and its influence on Job performance,* authors Vera Silva Carlos and Ricardo Gouveia Rodrigues (University of Beira Interior, Portugal) discuss the effects that the use of Online Social Networks (OSNs) have on the worker's attitudes and behaviors. The authors used a questionnaire to evaluate the attitudes of 157 faculty members in Higher Education Institutions and concluded that the use of OSNs influences the workers' performance traits. In chapter 19, *Developing Instructional Leadership and Communication skills through Online Professional*

Development: Focusing on Rural and Urban Principals, Doron Zinger (University of Riverside, USA) highlights the promise for principals and other school leaders who work in online challenging settings, with a focus on attending to principal instructional leadership. Zinger asserts that lines of communication and building online community may help overcome the professional isolation experienced by principals. Chapter 20, *Engineering Students' Communication Apprehension and Competence in Technical Oral Presentations,* authors Noor Raha Mohd Radzuan (Universiti Malaysia Pahang, Malaysia) and Sarjit Kaur (Universiti Sains Malaysia, Malaysia) discuss the anxieties of non-English speaking engineering graduates who are expected to master formal and informal presentation skills in order be competent in effective professional communication in today's global market place. These authors examine the correlation of engineering students' perceived communication competence and their level of apprehension in giving a technical presentation.

Section 4: Optimizing Performance – Enhancing Relational Development through Trust and Communication

The section features nine chapters. In chapter 21, *Developing Trust within International Teams: The Impacts of Culture on Team Formation and Process,* author Kurt D. Kirstein (City University of Seattle, USA) argues that the success of global virtual teams depends largely on the levels of intra-team trust and collaboration they are able to establish throughout the life of their projects. The author explores how cultural dimensions including preferences for individualistic versus collective teamwork, power distance, uncertainty avoidance, and contextual communication are likely to impact intra-team trust within a global virtual team, and offers suggestion to team leaders about how to address these cultural dimensions. In chapter 22, *Communication: The Role of the Johari Window on Effective Leadership Communication in Multinational Corporations (MNCs),* Ben Tran (Alliant International University, USA) articulates the role of the Johari Window (JW) on effective leadership communication in multinational corporations (MNCs). The author clarifies that the JW was created based on a domestic paradigm, and not necessarily applicable to a multinational environment where intercultural and multicultural communication are at play for multinational environment within MNCs. Authors Larry W. Long (Illinois State University, and International Academy of Public Safety, USA) Mitch Javidi (North Carolina State University, and the International Academy of Public Safety, USA) L. Brooks Hill (Trinity University, USA), and Anthony H. Normore (California State University Dominguez Hills and International Academy of Public Safety, USA) introduce chapter 23, *Credible Negotiation Leadership: Applying Communication Theory to Enhance Leadership and Manage Conflict while Achieving Productive Outcomes during International Negotiations.* These authors infuse the concept of credible leadership into their previous work in principled negotiation. They conceptualize international negotiation with an in-depth description of negotiation styles and propositions for credible negotiation leadership that are predicated upon intercultural communication study. In chapter 24, *Empowering Police, Empowering Citizens: The Influence of Communicative Intelligence on Procedural Justice and Police Legitimacy,* authors Renee Mitchell (Cambridge University, UK and Sacramento Police Department, USA) and Kendall Zoller (Sierra Training Associates, USA) assert that the foundation of policing and procedural justice is communication and link communicative intelligence to the verbal and physical behaviors officers should be engaging in to enhance procedural justice and improve police legitimacy. In chapter 25, *Effective Engagement: Police Supervisor and Police Officers,* authors Brian Ellis (Sacramento Police Department, USA) and Anthony H. Normore (California State University Dominguez Hills and International Academy of Public Safety,

USA) provide a comprehensive overview of organizational leadership and its role in effective communication and engagement processes. They argue that the relationship between effective leadership and employee engagement is directly linked to innovation, participation, teamwork, accountability, and the ability to face challenges.

Chapter 26, *Communicating across the Generations: Implications for Higher Education Leadership* is presented by author Carolyn N. Stevenson (Kaplan University, USA). Stevenson examines why higher education administrators need to identify differences among generations of workers and develop a strategic plan for managing and motivating across the generations. She asserts that communication, mentoring programs, training, respect, and opportunities for career advancement are components valued by all. In chapter 27, *The Role of Leadership and Communication: (Re)-Conceptualizing Graduate Instruction Online,* author Heather Rintool, Nipissing University, Canada) explores concerns and challenges associated with the transition to online graduate instruction from the traditional face-to-face format. The author discusses several catalysts for the transition to virtual teaching; the ethics of being present; impediments to learning and communication online; and participant concerns. Rintool suggests considerations for leadership and communication moving forward are addressed. Peter Smith (University of Liverpool, UK) and Olaf Cames (University of Liverpool, USA) present chapter 28, *CAMES - An Approach to Project Management Based on Action Science and the Ideal Speech Situation.* These authors propose a novel approach to project management that addresses the human factor and issues of communication. The proposed approach is novel and applies action science to radically change the way in which projects are managed. This section concludes with chapter 29, *Mobile Communication in Hospitals: Is it Still a Problem?* Author Terje Solvoll (Norwegian Centre for Integrated Care and Telemedicine, Tromsø Telemedicine Laboratory, University Hospital of North Norway & Department of Computer Science, University of Tromsø, Norway) argues that work setting in hospitals is communication intensive, and can lead to significant difficulties related to interruptions from co-workers. The key is how to handle the balance between increased availability, and increased interruptions. Solutions are offered based on context aware communication systems, aiming to reduce interruptions.

Section 5: Ethics of Managerial Communication and Electronic Surveillance of Employees

The final section contains three chapters. Chapter 30, *The Ethics of Strategic Managerial Communication in the Global Context* is presented by authors Angelo Camillo (Woodbury University, USA) and Isabella Carolina Camillo (Brock University, Canada). These authors argue that managerial communication today is an integral component of many business related disciplines (strategic management, leadership, strategic marketing, business ethics, etc.). These authors contend that having a managerial communication policy in place allows for strategic information dissemination as well as the protection of transmission of confidential data within the context of global business management. In chapter 31, *Surveillance of Electronic Communications in the Workplace and the Protection of Employees' Privacy*, author Ioannis Iglezakis (Aristotle University of Thessaloniki, Greece) highlights issues with the use of surveillance technology in organizations. Electronic monitoring of employees is an integral part of information systems in the workplace and is evident in the European Union (EU). The author argues, however, that it is sometimes intrusive and infringes upon the employees' right to privacy. He distills ambiguities and ethics concerning the balancing of interests between employers and employees. Chapter 32, *Dataveillance and Information Privacy Concerns: Ethical and Organizational Considerations*, author Regina

Connolly (Dublin City University, Ireland) and Grace Kenny (Dublin City University, Ireland) presents numerous emerging issues concerning technology-enabled workplace surveillance and considers whether the privacy concerns of employees can be successfully balanced against managements' justification for the employment of such technologies in the workplace.

Anthony H. Normore
California State University Dominguez Hills, USA & International Academy of Public Safety, USA

Larry W. Long
Illinois State University, USA & International Academy of Public Safety, USA

Mitch Javidi
North Carolina State University, USA & International Academy of Public Safety, USA

REFERENCES

Cummings, H., Long, L., & Lewis, M. (1987). *Managing communication in organizations* (2nd ed.). Scottsdale, AZ: Gorsuch Scarisbrick Publishers.

Erbe, N. (2014). *Approaches to managing organizational diversity and innovation.* Hershey, PA: IGI Global Publishers. doi:10.4018/978-1-4666-6006-9

Erbe, N., & Normore, A. H. (2015). *Cross-cultural collaboration and leadership in modern organizations.* Hershey, PA: IGI Global Publishers. doi:10.4018/978-1-4666-8376-1

Geis, K., & Javidi, M. (2015). *Deliberate leadership.* Academic Press.

National Communication Association. (2015). *What is communication?* Retrieved from https://www.natcom.org/discipline/

Normore, A., & Erbe, N. (2013). *Collective efficacy: Interdisciplinary perspectives on international leadership.* Bingley, UK: Emerald Group Publishing.

Normore, A. H. (2009). Culturally relevant leadership for social justice: Honoring the integrity of First Nations communities in Northeast Canada. In J. Collard & A. H. Normore (Eds.), *Leadership and intercultural dynamics* (pp. 47–68). Charlotte, NC: Information Age Publishing.

Normore, A. H., & Brooks, J. S. (2014). *Educational leadership for social justice: Views from the social sciences.* Charlotte, NC: Information Age Publishing.

Normore, A. H., Javidi, M., Anderson, T., Normand, N., Hoina, C., & Scott, W. (2014). *Moral compass for law enforcement professionals.* Holly Springs, NC: International Academy of Public Safety.

Northouse, P. G. (2012). *Leadership: Theory and practice.* Thousand Oaks, CA: SAGE.

Parks, S. D. (2005). *Leadership can be taught: A bold approach for a complex world.* Boston, MA: Harvard Business Review Press.

Acknowledgment

As editors and authors we aspire to courageously examine issues that deal with a plethora of challenges in our appreciation of the pivotal role of leadership in organizations and its essential role in communication and conflict management. The contributors push the reader to tackle these issues found in organizations and their impact on our global society as a whole. They challenge us to consider the changes we need to make, conduct personal examination of how we lead and pose difficult questions about why we engage the ways we do. Our hope is that these chapters will serve as catalysts for further discourse and research on collaboration within and across disciplines so these disciplines can appreciate of what each brings to table in support of organizational health and success. We wish to acknowledge a myriad of people who have influenced our lives and our professional work. Our sincere gratitude goes to our families and friends, and to IGI Global Publishers, particularly Eleana Wehr and the other staff who supported us, for the opportunity to disseminate our work, and to all the contributing authors and to reviewers who reviewed the original manuscripts. In particular we wish to acknowledge Renee Mitchell, Kendall Zoller, Andrew Pyle, Heather Rintool, Doron Zinger, Daniel Davis, Brian Ellis, Christopher Hoina, Angela Jerome, and James Klopovic who willingly gave their time to review chapters and provide feedback accordingly. They share in our passion for organizational leadership, horizontal, vertical, and lateral communication, and the importance of understanding and appreciating how best to mediate, negotiate, manage, and resolve various forms of conflict.

Section 1

Issues for Leaders, Organization, and Communication:
Coping with Today and Planning for Tomorrow

Chapter 1
Leadership in the Digital Age:
Rhythms and the Beat of Change

Tom Cockburn
Center for Dynamic Leadership Models in Global Business, Canada

Peter A. C. Smith
Center for Dynamic Leadership Models in Global Business, Canada

ABSTRACT

This chapter introduces the scope and focus of the new book. The reader is briefly introduced to the definitions and debates about leadership and management boundaries, differences, and overlapping responsibilities in the digital age. Drawing on both theory and practice, current issues and topics are covered in depth, providing an introduction and overview of perceptible trends and scenarios relevant to the current post-Global Financial Crisis (GFC) leadership outlook for global business. The authors then provide an outline and overview of the topics and themes of each chapter and a coherent rationale for developing discussions and research from our first book "Dynamic Models of Leadership for Global Business: Enhancing digitally connected environments".

INTRODUCTION

It's a new era of business and consumerism—and we all play a role in defining it. Today's biggest trends - the mobile web; social media; and a younger digital-savvy demographic; have produced a new interactive landscape. Such emerging digital resources have brought demands for changes in many societies, which go beyond simply increasing access to the technology per se for consumers. For example recent research by Pew Global Researchers (2014) has noted that 20% of the world has mobile and online access and this has reinforced other social demands in particular from the younger generation who are usually the first to take up the newer technologies and access the web. As the report states:

Majorities in 22 of 24 countries surveyed say it is important that people have access to the internet without government censorship. In 12 nations, at least seven-in-ten hold this view. Support for internet freedom is especially strong in countries where a large percentage of the population is online. And, in most of the countries polled, young people are particularly likely to consider internet freedom a priority. (Pew Global Research Center, March 19, 2014)

DOI: 10.4018/978-1-4666-9970-0.ch001

This democratization of information is not limited to the customer sphere, but also has a significant impact on internal organizational processes. There is a well-researched and growing recognition that in consequence 'Business as usual' is no longer a viable option, and it is not logical to continue applying models of leadership founded in traditional 'best practice' experience. These and other changes beg many questions about what leaders must do to succeed and what new 'psychological contracts' need to be negotiated between citizens, followers, employees and the formal and informal leaders in all organizations in order to sensibly and practically define what is allowable, acceptable, desirable, possible and mandatory in the workplace today. As a consequence, we live today in a world rich in digital resources, but as yet we share a poverty of leadership competence in exploration and exploitation of these resources. Solis (2011) and Smith and Cockburn (2013; 2014) explore this complex information revolution, explaining how it has changed the future of business; media; culture; and leadership; and detail what leaders can do to address these changes.

At the time of writing the leaders of many nations and businesses are under threat and are failing. As many as 40% of all new leaders fail within the first 18 months according to recent surveys, thus the leadership crisis continues to grow more threatening and as leaders' world of work grows more complex each year, the leaders' own self-doubt about their skills is magnified (Newhall, 2011, Smith & Cockburn, 2013, xii). As noted above, both organizations and leaders at all levels today have to work hard and strive to continuously maintain a sharp, cutting-edge profile within their organizations (Pretorius & Roux, 2011), as well as reinvent themselves to address the constantly shifting unpredictable opportunities and constraints of operating in a global business environment. There is as pressing need to search for more effective, dynamic leadership models in order to keep pace intellectually and

practically with the heady pace and complex swirl of new socio digital media, devices and applications bubbling to the surface of our lives each day. The practical drawback here is that many current definitions of leadership continue to be much contested in an often confused area of academic research; practitioner debate; and often lagging public perceptions fuelled by the popular media (Kets de Vries, 1993; Higgs, 2003; Ruettimann, 2011; Krohe, 2011).

In this chapter the authors provide a very brief overview of traditionally accepted definitions of leadership in organizations as discussed in detail in Smith and Cockburn (2013; 2014). We also acquaint the reader with the new up-to-date flexible, gender-neutral leadership model presented in Smith and Cockburn (2013; 2014) that we believe will successfully address current and future leadership demands in digitally defined contexts.

In general, as we have noted before, many leadership definitions are either so broad that they become bland; so narrow that little of any practical significance can be elicited; or in the case of public perceptions, tend to refer to historic or military metaphors of heroic leaders (Smith & Cockburn, 2013). In addition, many of these definitions often seem to be based on versions of leadership activities and competences that are out of touch with a globalized world of cloud computing, viral marketing, ecological disasters, and the Volatile, Uncertain Complex and Ambiguous ('VUCA') world of today (Smith & Cockburn, 2013, pp.6-7, Lawrence, 2013). The older certainties of the more stable and less disrupted 'best practice' world are gone.

That there is some appreciation of the nature of today's VUCA world, is indicated by the current academic consensus that best leadership practice does revolve more closely around the transformational leadership styles than the older transactional or traits-based models. So, although there is debate about the character of it, or how it impacts on the leader or followers, there is at least some implicit or explicit recognition that change is a major factor in the leaders' world. Therefore transformational leadership is probably the style with which most readers of this book will be familiar, and most importantly, this style is in harmony with the learning approach that is foundational to the leadership process model we set out in detail in Smith and Cockburn (2013).

The changes we see today are often based around efficiency and effectiveness gains linked to greater automation, artificial intelligence systems installation, or the trawling of big data from social media and customer feedback. For instance, the amount of autonomous Internet-connected devices is growing and is expected to reach 200 billion in 2020, so radically altering the Industrial sector. So this sort of change begs the question: What are the strategic risks associated with organizations' increasing dependence on integrated and embedded information and communications systems and technologies that underpin all of that? For instance the risks posed by these systems in that they enable every facet of the organization, impacting customers, employees and trading partners? What metrics allow leaders to quantify, evaluate and cover the risks of not updating systems or alternatively the risks inherent in system failure, hacking, failed installation or poor integration of new or linked IT systems? Some systems for stock exchange trading work with millions of dollars in transaction every second of the business day, so a system 'meltdown' can be very costly to organizations, clients, and the wider community. More generally, although providing the world with many advantages these technologies are reliant on many finite resources to produce them, so there is an underlying question about complexity, sustainability and environmental impact.

We have noted and taken heed of the changes to modern organizations, their technologies, their emerging cultures, as well as associated risks at various levels and in different markets. All these factors indicate the need for greater leader-awareness of these matters. These risks as well as the potential benefits to leaders and the stakeholder

communities are amply described, analysed and discussed in Smith and Cockburn (2014).

A process of structural and cultural change to organizations, which also continue evolving today, preceded the above-mentioned socio-digital changes. The internal layers of organisations have been stripped down during the last 15-20 years of downsizing and de-layering prior to the post-Global Financial Crisis (GFC) restructuring. Other hitherto pre-existing boundaries within and between organisation and environment have in some senses now become more permeable as the global socio-digital networks expand because of the greater *interactivity* of such networks. In pursuing strategic alliances or local operational networking, at both the *internal-internal* and the *internal-external* systems of organizational states and systems, those engaged in global business at all levels and types of organizations seek greater collaboration.

A number of years ago, Kauffman (1995) related this rapid change process to an evolutionary theory of business development, and described it as technological co-evolution: one business creating niches for another in the ecological landscape of the new technology market or the "technosphere" as he dubbed it. However, he also describes two core evolutionary strategies. The first is what he calls the "Red Queen" effect, which he links to organizations selfishly competing. Over time, as the business landscape gets harder with increasing competition, shortened product and supply lead times, and higher expectations of customers, these companies end up having to run faster just to stand still relative to the general pace of change. Crucially however, the new technology developed by one firm often provides a niche for another firm's product or service to enter. There are symbiotic developments as well as competitive developments, similar to the kinds of co-evolutionary developments seen in "predator" and "prey" species in the animal world (Kauffman, 1995, p125).

Globally, this model often also applies to big businesses today, as they inhabit similarly turbulent and chaotic markets with increasing diversity and redundancy leading to high numbers of fatalities. This co-evolutionary model contrasts with the evolutionarily stable strategy often found in large, hierarchical organisations that have frozen too readily into compromise solutions. The leader in all sizes of organization in the era of emerging web 3.0,Facebook, Twitter and Wikileaks now faces a different global market, public, regulatory, and employee community, than previously. So leaders must change their approach to address the current and imminent challenges they face today or else watch as their organizations fall behind in the race for business; or they will drop so far behind they cannot catch up. Leadership as we have said elsewhere (Smith & Cockburn, 2013), has previously always been equated with authority and 'power over' – in Smith & Cockburn (2014) we equate leadership with planning, performance-related learning, and 'power to'.

We have drawn on the research and practical expertise of authorities from across the world in Smith & Cockburn (2014). That is fitting since the changes that are emerging continue to widen their application and impact across even the most remote and seemingly inaccessible societies, businesses, governments and cultures, albeit in different ways and at different speeds. As mentioned above, the evolving web and emergent Smart technologies presaging the 'Internet of Things' has opened up the world and increasingly; mobile technology has diminished distances and expanded communication as we pointed out in our previous book (Smith & Cockburn, 2013).

Therefore, in order to thrive and survive in today's precarious and 'edgy' global economic environment organizations of all kinds have to strive to continuously reinvent themselves to address rapidly developing or emerging digital technologies which continue to disrupt or demolish markets for many goods and services. However, leaders and managers have new tools and techniques to deploy to increase interest and engagement for staff as well as improve effectiveness and efficiency of operations, including such aspects as sustainable growth, reduced environmental impact, andr staff wellbeing and safety.

Writers and bloggers are presenting ideas to their online audiences on various related topics. For example, drawing from relevant consulting experience Marr(2014) presents a few current instances that illustrate current digital technology applications. One case relates to a construction company whose staff work in hazardous environments and which is now using wearable devices to collect and analyze data on employee's body functions whilst working. Their aim is to identify ways to detect fatigue and stress levels from the analytics data retrieved and to put systems in place to withdraw people from dangerous jobs if fatigue and stress levels are too high. Other companies are looking for socio-digital tools that can analyze data on staff engagement via employees' posts on Facebook or Twitter, or may recruit based upon information which browsers or potential candidates' job apps utilize.

Digitial technologies are increasingly now being embedded in various transdisciplinary applications (Smith & Cockburn, 2013). As Ulla de Stricker (2014, p4) notes "The increasing sophistication and scale of the systems organizations use to manage information objects and to amass, manipulate, visualize, and extract data have added to the stresses the organizations experience in dealing with their knowledge." In parallel, yet another layer of complexity is added by the changing social mores in mainstream cultures in many societies and leaders face the related dilemma of constantly shifting economic vistas as these and other factors change the character and relative global influence of advanced and emerging markets. For instance, these changes include such fundamental areas of life as 'dining'. Reflecting not only the availability of fast food but the pace of life today and the availability of the cheaper travel, the internet, mobile communications and social networking media have contributed to changes in eating habits in the USA (Hartman, 2014). As one commentator has remarked, "The time it takes the average American to prepare dinner is now less than half the length of a Hell's Kitchen episode. Cooking has become a spectator sport, with people watching TV chefs battle it out while they grow ever-distant from the farmers who produce their food. The loss of culinary skills and regular meal times mean 40% of American meals are solitary, and eating with friends and family has become the exception rather than the norm" (Nierenberg, 2014).

However, these changes are not just because people are too busy to stop and cook dinner but as the Hartman (2014) report makes clear it reflects the spread of information on food as well as its preparation. "Research shows people consume social media content far more than they create it, which means many are mainly exploring. As a result, one person's online suggestion to try a Korean hamburger or a peppermint mocha latte—or more powerful, one person posting an appetizing-looking photo of the same—can reach thousands of people in a day." The report suggests that the growth in Internet access and use has also promoted the growth in cyber-explorations of food with one site Allrecipes.com already in the global top 10 sites. This is now a trans-generational growth phenomenon as older users have begun to catch up with the younger generation of early adopters of social media, helped by retailers like Starbucks, McDonalds, IKEA and others whose online presence on sites such as Twitter, Facebook, allied to their physical locations have been transformed into "Wifi" hotspots operating as online as well as offline "community anchors" (Hartman, 2014, pp2-3).

Globally the upcoming generations of consumers and staff fall into the category of 'digital natives'; that is, they are frequent and enthusiastic users of social media and new technology. As Dan Schawbel (2013) stated in a Forbes article "By 2025, millennials will account for 75% of the global workforce and by next year, they will account for 36% of the American workforce. This group is the future and they expect digital media to form part of their future whether they are at work or socialising and frequently they make fewer distinctions. They often expect the same amount of functionality in their workplace technology as in their personal devices, hence the growth of the BYOD (Bring Your Own Device) phenomenon. Clearly digital natives will significantly increase the impact of socio digital technology on all individual behaviors and expectations.

However, the BYOD growth rate and complexity is not evenly distributed between continents or populations. As has been noted in a survey of 3,796 consumers in countries as diverse as Brazil, Russia, India, South Africa, United Arab Emirates, Malaysia, Singapore, Japan, Australia, Belgium, France, Germany, Italy, Spain, Sweden, UK, US, there is a marked difference between emerging, rapidly-growing markets and others. The survey indicated different orientations to work and to using your own devices. It showed that 75 per cent of respondents in the emerging markets (including Brazil, Russia, India, UAE, and Malaysia) as compared to 44 per cent in more mature markets would prefer to use their own devices at work. (*Logicalis* White paper, 2014). As has been previously indicated there is an Eastward shift occurring and the newer markets are building up to a new business 'attractor' in complexity terms. That is, forces driving global business and investment are creating an alternative center of gravity to Western markets of the 'old' and the 'new' world (Smith and Cockburn, 2013)

Under these circumstances of emergent change in a VUCA environment where changes in the political, social, financial, technological and business practice fields are all dynamically interlinked approaches to leadership must be reviewed to ensure the requisite variety and resilience to cope with the 'surprises' to come. That is, leadership is best conceived as "a process of continuous optimization and adaption, where the next leadership action is based on what is happening now. In other words leadership is emergent, and is co-developed with the context in which the leadership is taking place"(Smith & Cockburn, 2013). In *Dynamic Leadership Models for Global Business: Enhancing Digitally Connected Environments* we proposed a dynamic foundation for understanding and practicing leadership based on proven ways to deal with complexity as outlined in chapter 2.

New macro trends and incipient strategic webs of cooperation, new joint ventures, and market co-alitions are presenting potential future challenges for the current first world powers such as the US (Saddi, et al., 2011, Pew report, 2014). Some of these trends are exemplified by recent actions of countries in the Gulf Cooperation Council (GCC), Brazil, Russia, India and China (BRIC) and the so-called, 'next 11' group (Bangladesh, Indonesia, Iran, Mexico, Nigeria, Pakistan, Philippines, South Korea, Vietnam and Turkey). In the next decade there will be a massive power shift in corporations with over 50% of Fortune 500 CEOs coming from outside of the EU and USA. Entropy has also appeared as a result of mega-communities, such as the fragile monetary zone of the EURO threatened with "Grexit" (Greece's exit from the Euro zone of currencies) and rising tides of migrants from Africa and the middle east landing in Greece and Italy, countries least able to afford to address their needs. The 'unity' of the UK is under threat from a rising tide of nationalism in Scotland and the UK government is required to hold a referendum on exit from the EU in 2017.

Elsewhere, in BRICS other streams of socio-political as well as business change are bubbling up to the top. The Chinese output and expansive growth has faltered this quarter (June, 2015) and the leadership contest between India and China, the economy of the USA, Japan and emerging Corporate identities as well as popular uprisings and social unrest such as presently occurring in Syria, Iraq and the Ukraine pose further serious issues (Khanna, 2011, Pew, 2014). The conflicts in the Islamic states of the Middle East has exposed

some of the internal issues such as tribal rivalries in the Yemen as well as a burgeoning security issue for western states through the radicalization of young Muslims in the EU, UK, USA and elsewhere who not only leave their homes in the West to join ISIL as volunteers but in some cases foment violent terrorist protest actions such as bombings and shootings as seen in France, Canada and UK. The government and business local and international liaison and security measures to forestall, to contain, to degrade or to destroy such threats add costs and strains to the burdens of the national administrations involved.

In our previous book we outlined the emerging contexts and domains where we saw relevant issues, concerns and applications of our model. We recognised that some issues needed to be resolved in order to enable greater access and participation in the emerging era for all. Prejudices and stereotypes lingered and hindered growth and development or productive engagement such as age-based stereotypes which, according to Blauth et al (2011) severely restrict or constrain productivity and collabration between the four or five generations working in organizations today. These authors also sugegst that an 'age-blind' workplace may not be the answeer to such issues of collaboration between generations in the workplace (Blauth et al, 2011, p.10).

The editors and authors of this book have also recognised that things were moving fast and further changes were imminent in a diverse array of fields and professional disciplines and that our initial chapter topics were by no means exhaustive or mutually-exclusive but instead are often interconnected in many ways. So the context for this book has emerged and evolved further as currents of change have escalated in line with the general predictions of exponential acceleration in "Moore's law".

The chapters in book one are described in figure 1 below for your information and in order to locate the new book as an extension and advance on the previous research. We would again stress

Figure 1.

the dynamic interrelationships and the connectedness between the various chapter topics since these continue to be major features of work and life to day that we all have to deal with and have if anything grown since last year in some ways. Consequently such aspects must form part of the leaders' reflections,understanding and actions to enable organizational as well as career survival.

As the world of demand and supply continues to shift and some of these fields are now beginning to overlap or the demarcation of roles are becoming blurred in many ways as consumers become or are emerging into embryonic 'prosumers' in many sectors (Toffler, 2006). A McKinsey Global Lifestyle brief in May 2013 stated that advances in analytics and pricing algorithms are now giving companies the opportunity to deliver personalized pricing to their customers. The aspirations and implications of human-machine efficiency and 'algorithmic governance' (technology-controlled systems to ensure law abiding behavior of citizens) include use of devices and systems to remotely control automobile speeds on motorways. The issue has been raised in the past but as we get nearer to 'intelligent' robots some research has been initiated into the dynamics of robot-human teams (Schuster et al, 2011a/b, Cockburn et al, 2015). The rise of the robots has not yet reached its peak and there are still problems and constraints on how far it will drive out human involvement.

This emergent world is increasingly technology-driven with exciting new opportunities which demolish older 'forcefields' and frames of reference on what is possible in the production of goods and services. However, without becoming too "technologically intoxicated" the latter drivers also unveil the tantalisingly dynamic global business complexity that imposes new demands and new limits as peoples' interconnected, social,cultural and economic lives evolve within expanding and increasingly global technological frameworks (Cockburn and McKie, 2004). Currently robotics is constrained to certain manufacturing operations for commodities that are relatively unchanging such as cars as compared to those which are more frequently updated or upgraded such as cellphones and some which are in the luxury services and goods domain. Rus (2015) indicates that the technology is still mainly used to augment rather than to replace humans in production facilities due to such limitations.

The B2C world is being transformed by the array of increasingly diverse digital devices enabling more customisation as well as sharing, crowd-sourcing of resources, ideas and new products and services such as venture capital, building, fashion and furniture design. The same innovations have also simultaneously impacted on B2B suppliers and potentially weakened some intellectual property rights. With the increasing functionality the impact of Big data provides the opportunity to outsource not only product evaluation or market pilots but product design to the 'crowd'. Potentially at least, the organization has a global talent pool to draw from. This goes beyond the older ideas such as initiating a consumer prize competition to get new ideas.

The other side of this 'coin' is the impact on the careers of some of those professions such as that of designers (as well as design courses and education). Some companies now see the world-wideweb and the promise of untapped reserves of global 'crowd' creativity as a valuable form of customer feedback and a cheaper, more effective option than hiring a trained designer ('Click' technology updates on BBC). Frey and Osborne (2013) estimate around 47% of US jobs fall into their 'at risk' of computerisation and automation. As these authors state: "While computerisation has been historically confined to routine tasks involving explicit rule-based activities (Autor et al, 2003; Goos, *et al.*, 2009; Autor and Dorn, 2013), algorithms for big data are now rapidly entering domains reliant upon pattern recognition and can readily substitute for labour in a wide range of non-routine cognitive tasks (Brynjolfsson and McAfee, 2011; McKinsey Global Institute, 2013). In addition, advanced robots are gaining enhanced senses and dexterity, allowing them to perform a broader scope of manual tasks (IFR, 2012b; Robotics-VO, 2013; McKinsey Global Institute, 2013). This is likely to change the nature of work across industries and occupations."

In addition, a recent report suggests some possible social media backlash is developing as shown by studies purporting to demonstrate the need for "tech breaks" and warnings that social media can also make people lonely, so there are now "Digital Detox" camps for adults as well as some children (Hartman, 2014, p5). So, the future is, as usual, ambiguous for forecasting outcomes. So, although the research survey has generally been positive (since 8 of the 15 theses presented are positive with respect to how the changes in society and economy enacted through the new technology are seen), some of the expert commentators consulted for the Pew research report on "Digital Life 2025", also point to privacy and surveillance issues, distinctions forming between classes of users and access to sites (Pew 2014).

In other words, organizations, leaders, and all the stakeholders are in a situation where they are co-evolving at an accelerating rate. Leadership is no longer a matter of setting a direction and ensuring it is being followed - leadership for the future is all about having a vision with an uncertain path to its achievement that may only be attempted through awareness, flexibility, agility, and adaptability in the collaborative company of fellow stakeholders.

As we commented elsewhere,

Leadership today and in the future must be achieved in face of organizational complexity, whereas Yeo (2009, p. 67) states "If anything can go wrong, it will (Murphy's Law)". Now and in the future leadership is all about having a vision with an uncertain path to its achievement that may normally only be navigated through flexibility and agility based on the collaborative wisdom of fellow stakeholders. (Dynamic Leadership Models for Global Business: Enhancing Digitally Connected Environments, Smith and Cockburn, 2013)

In global contexts, the sustainable strength of integral business transformation lies in the capability to continuously create, connect, and execute strategy throughout the entire business system. Leaders must be conscious of the repercussions of their role as context creators in which a collaborative nexus of customer/employee emotional and creative engagement occurs. However, many leaders are not aware and there are also other tensions and conflicts in workplaces generated from cultural roadblocks to building and maintaining trustful collaboration between employees in different professional specialisms as well as between coworkers and their leaders. Some problems exist precisely because of 'creative' or crowd fixes applied locally that have masked conflicts or other issues, embodied some local tacit knowledge or cultural bias. Often that sort of knowledge is not part of the wider knowledge management structure in an organization, or reflects demarcations of 'ownership' of problems and responsibilities for investigating issues.

For yet other organizations there is a reluctance in the hearts and minds of some leaders with 'getting their hands dirty' or doing tasks they feel are boring or beneath them even if such activities are vital to the future of that organization. The sorts of areas resisted are diverse but include corporate PR or fundraising in the case of some NGOs or Not-for-profits. Thus, according to the BoardSource 2012 Governance Index, 46% of not-for-profit CEOs gave their boards "D" or "F" grades for their fundraising efforts and fundraising is the lowest ranked of 10 board responsibilities. Consequently, in practical terms that often means managing and funding necessary changes become too 'political' and are in the 'too hard to fix' file or are locked into particular operations, or specific regions (Smith & Cockburn, 2013, de Stricker, 2014).

Thus as the EU's business innovation observatory report indicates with respect to Artificial Intelligence (AI) work especially: " development of AI for big data in Europe has a number of drivers and faces several obstacles. These drivers and obstacles impact both technology companies developing solutions and companies looking to implement AI. Drivers include a highly educated workforce, scalability of developed solutions and public support programmes fostering innovation. Obstacles include the difficulty of attracting funds both for company set up and early financier divestment, high administrative burdens for small companies and unfavourable tax environments" (EU, 2013, p4).

Global leadership models therefore must be continuously reviewed and enhanced to keep pace with these complex, dynamic forcefields. Further, leaders seek a practical and sustainable approach that helps build effective personal leadership, whilst also leveraging organizational capabilities with action plans that take account of the complexity of emergent problems, learning

and reciprocal unlearning to harvest technological potential. These include factors such as the professional silos, time pressure, change management, influence and cultural change.

If we accept the premise that a critical success factor for achieving global competitive business advantage today and in the foreseeable future involves networking and collaboration between webs of consumers, individual organizations and/or networks of allied organizations, then today's business environments demand updated leadership and managerial attitudes towards understanding the tools and practices at both organizational and network levels, focusing on knowledge sharing, collaborative leadership, and more inclusive managerial procedures and systems (Hyypia & Pekkola, 2011). With relevance particularly to globalized environments, Harris (2011) has drawn attention to the work of Spillane (2006) claiming that this research has sparked renewed interest in distributed leadership practice, focusing particularly on the interactions between leaders, followers and their evolving workplace situation.

Our first book was unique in treating current leadership challenges that are not amenable to leadership approaches of the past, recognised complexity in global business exceeded the merely technically-complicated and now our newly composed book brings this objective up to date. The first book attempted to provide an emergent viewpoint derived from the dynamics of interconnected contexts, learning and activities, where the reader is both the systems architect of his/her own leadership (the system) and an optimal, generalized, gender-neutral process through which the reader's style of leadership might be built up in an ongoing manner. It is our intention that this book is also written in an accessible manner that effectively empowers the reader to develop their leadership aptitudes, and sustainably mature their organization and staff for the kinds of challenges they face now and will encounter in the future.

Nevertheless this new book is distinctly separate from our previous book as it builds upon and extends its central thrust, setting out important new approaches to leaders' orientations towards digital technologies, and a much needed comprehensive overview of these various newly emerging elements that are driving the ever increasing complexity in our global environments. This book extends the discussion to encompass impacts in the socio-digital sphere across all business functions and includes reviews of emerging roles, responsibilities, and the redefined rights that accompany them in diverse organization types, sectors, consumers and organizational structures as the millennial generation comes to the fore in the domain of leadership. The book also includes case histories and examples reflecting issues and models in chapters therefore providing a useful reflective reference tool for leaders in any organization to better analyze and review their strategic situation, available decisions options, resources and outcomes, to enhance or construct flexible action plans.

The approach of authors in the new book does not entail any assumptions as to skills or expertise of users, and is adaptable for all organizations, being comprehensible for both technical and non-technical readers, and so enabling all readers to readily apply the book's content to their own evolving situations and emerging roles and responsibilities.

Objectives for this chapter:

- Introduce and review leadership impacts of digital technology;
- Discuss the authors' perspective on impacts and issues of digital technology leadership;
- Present concluding remarks and explore emerging trends;
- Detail the relevant references.

BACKGROUND

Research on leadership in general or what leadership is, what leaders do and what it takes to be a great leader is reportedly the most researched area of human behavior in the social sciences (Dulewicz & Higgs, 2005) dating back to the 19th century. Before the nineteenth century there were commentaries and observations about leaders and leadership; many of the so-called 'Great man' theories that underpinned some of the research. They were, as the name implies mainly biased towards a gender-specific, traits based perspective, namely that leadership was the sole preserve of great men with inherited traits of leadership (Zaccaro, 2007). Often these traits based models are aligned with popular perceptions of leaders.

Yukl (2002, 2009, 2010) has suggested 5 broad categories of research on leadership: as trait theories, behavioral models, power-influence, situational and a blended type of integrative models. Bolden et al., (2003) proposed seven theory types: 'Great Man' theories, trait theories, behaviorist theories, situational leadership theories, contingency theory, transactional theory and transformational theory. More recently, a review article lists 29 different types of leadership theories (Gardner et al., 2010).

Spicker (2012) has now succinctly summarized this into a set of six principal classes of leadership theories as follows:

- **Leadership as Motivation and Influence:** For example, Yukl (2010, p. 21) suggests that leadership reflects "... the assumption that it involves a process whereby intentional influence is exerted over people to guide, structure and facilitate activities and relationships in a group or organization", and Northhouse (2007, p. 3) asserts that leadership is "a process of influencing the activities of an individual or group in efforts toward accomplishing goals in a given situation".
- **Leadership as a Set of Personal Attributes or Traits:** Leadership may be understood as describing someone who motivates or influences others through for

example charisma, emotional intelligence, and on and on!

- **Leadership as a System of Authority:** Leaders 'run things' and are 'in charge' or 'take charge'.
- **Leadership as a Relationship with Subordinates:** Many definitions of leadership assume that leaders have followers, and leadership can be seen as a relationship where the leader(s) mold(s) the behaviors of the followers in order to influence them to perform in certain ways or produce certain results.
- **Leadership as a Set of Roles:** A leader might act as a pioneer, working in a different way as an example for others to follow.
- **Leadership as Management:** A number of authorities assert that leadership is quite different from management, where management is said to be about the status quo and leadership about change (Kotter, 2001).

However, many of these theories and models are often underpinned by, or premised upon traditional, rationalist, economic models that often seem to ignore the effects of complexity by assuming a relatively stable, though complicated global socioeconomic system. Others propose that there is a clear dichotomy between management skills and leadership skills. We propose no such dichotomies are present, recognising that management skills and leadership skills form a continuum and both ideally can exist in the same person but are used for different but interdependent ends (Smith & Cockburn, 2013).

We have therefore outlined an alternative to the traditional academic models in our previous book. Our proposed model attends to complexity and emergence as an endemic feature of global business today yet requiring a manageable approach from those with leadership responsibilities. Our model is both practical and realistic, embodies the academic research consensus supporting

transformational leadership styles and is in the form of a simple 4-step model. The model entails leaders learning to cope with complexity using an iterative, gender-free, collaborative methodology (Smith & Cockburn, 2013) that is briefly summarised in chapter two of the new book.

MAIN FOCUS OF THE CHAPTER

The current chapter has opened the book by locating leadership and management of global and local operations within often turbulent and always dynamically intersecting dimensions of complexity evident in an increasingly technology-dominated social and market environment. The pace of the shift online will continue to "...accelerate as global Internet traffic, which has expanded 18-fold since 2005, surges an additional 8-fold by 2025" according to Hirt and Wilmott (2014).

Part of the digitization processes are beneath the surface part of the "Industrial Internet" of machines talking to other machines and a component of the largely unknown 'second economy' outlined in a McKinsey paper by Arthur (2011). The 'second economy' operates beneath the visible structures and processes of the usual model of the 'first economy' systems of production, manufacturing and consumption dynamics. Although referring to technological co-evolution, it also seems reasonable to infer organizational and leadership co-evolution too as a concomitant structural development. The technology-driven networks in the second economy could add $10 to $15 trillion to global GDP in the coming years it is suggested (GE reports, cited in M. van Rijmenam, http://www.bigdata-startups.com/big-data-trends-2014/). Much of the second economy involves automated processes such as Big data capture used to inform other technological systems and trigger various responses directed at production, consumption or regulation of these and of ancillary systems to smooth, improve and grow the economic functioning of global business.

Nor is 'Big data', from trawling the Internet solely available to big organisations' marketing or production functions, as there is a plethora of open source tools becoming available to all. Big data analytics have been used in a variety of ways by different organizations globally. These applications range from the advanced deployment of the techniques to relatively simple uses of social media. KLM the Dutch airline has a 'meet and seat' program which enables passengers who wish to do so, to select compatible seat partners based upon their online profile in order to make travel more interesting. Elsewhere, Australian retailer "Shoes of Prey", have an analytics system allowing them to begin upselling based on the fashion tastes of its clients derived from analysis of individual customer-spend and profitability data they capture (M. van Rijmenam, http://www.bigdata-startups.com/big-data-trends-2014/).
The Brazilian fashion outlet *C&A* on the other hand simply uses Facebook 'likes' displayed on coat hangers in their store displays to encourage purchases, *Y&R* Dubai's marketing campaign for the UAE-based 'Gulf News' employed an adapted coffee cup sleeve that displays headlines tweeted by the paper in the previous hour (http://www.springwise.com, 2014). These and other examples of rich and diversely intersecting domains of technology, society and market are increasingly ubiquitous and make the former distinctions between online and offline less tenable.

In short, unless we relapse into a socio-digital ice age, the evolution and integration of the online and offline bridging, using various interface or augmentation technologies and systems and spanning diverse fields or disciplines such as BNIC and GRIN are where the sources of major changes will be spawned. These are often transdisciplinary projects. Diverse applications are being developed integrating technologies from one field into another to produce innovative and beneficial devices such as non-invasive Brain-to-computer interfaces allowing partial or wholly paralysed or injured patients to carry out tasks they otherwise

could not achieve and also potentially transforming surgery and medicine. Some research is into varieties of wearable devices and yet others are harnessing Big data to social media and attempting to personalise consumption which, at the same time is transforming business disciplines such as marketing and HR.It is also worth noting that these synergies from transdisciplinary research also contain the potential for conflict as well as collaboration.

Clearly there are costs and risks associated with collaboration in much the same way as there are risks associated with conflict and such risks or fears must be managed as far as possible. Collaborators may fear loss of intellectual property either deliberately or through lax security by one or other of their collaborators. Other fears include potential reputational or share price damage by their collaboration on a project that gets 'tainted' by scandal or generates a lot of controversy such as 'fracking' has done in the USA and elsewhere for instance. Some such fears are about power asymmetries of collaborating on unequal terms. For instance where an SME supplying services or goods to a big corporation depends heavily on the corporation's goodwill and is thus vulnerable to costcutting tactics such as a profit squeeze on SME suppliers' margins in order to improve the corporation's bottom line. In line with the old saying 'once bitten twice shy', mutual trust is the casualty.

This is also the territory the authors of the chapters in this book have begun to navigate and to map. The map is by no means complete and it is still likely to change in the course of time as some areas expand and others decline or mutate. Nevertheless, researchers already predict that around one-third of Fortune 500 organizations will be encountering major problems with their business intelligence by 2017 (Vladimir, 2014). So the message has yet to penetrate to all sectors of the global business community.

Excluding our editors' introductory and short concluding chapters setting the book in context now and looking to some possible future scenarios and research directions, there are 13 other chapters in this our new book. The 13 chapters are each written by authorities in leadership and/or in a particular digital technology area and address the significance of the developmental impact in that field whether that impact is positive or negative. These include chapters on conceptual and practical models, research and data about Big data Analytics, digital collaboration technology, personal pr collaboration privacy, IT and gender relations, empowerment, innovation, competitive intelligence, social and developmental networks and strategic use of IT in organizations.

Such topics surely apply amongst global leaders in public and private organizations, including NGOs, hospitals and commerce today. The chapters cover other impacts on leadership in sectors as diverse as healthcare, pharmaceuticals, data security, work reorganization, business risks and corporate financial flows as well as social media usage, in functions such as marketing, Human Resources and product design. The question is how best to organize these diverse chapters to reflect the themes of the book?

The arrangement and ordering of the chapters has emerged as the book progressed beyond the initial 'drawing board'; our book proposal and topic list proffered to the publisher for review and consideration. As with leadership and global business complexities and 'life' events intervened and seemed to conspire to make work difficult as in the expression of 'Murphy's law' –anything that can go wrong is likely to do so at some point during the project. Equally we had some good fortune and things turned out well; better than expected in a few cases. Some of the chapter proposals we received were unexpected or 'left field' ones we had not really anticipated and even those covering topics we had anticipated in our discussions, often drew on diverse and interesting ideas, concepts, models, case materials and particular research of the authors with which we have only now become familiar.

Others were a mixed bag and a few had to be rejected. The book compilation process and editing was also much impacted by surprises and extra complexity due to unforeseen eventualities and spirals of complexity with both editors' computers crashing, thankfully at different times but with our data having to be retrieved. On another occasion one of the editors became seriously ill and hospitalized (although now recovered). Nevertheless and perhaps because of these surprises and trials, we have an interesting and insightful book for the reader to engage with. We offer a number of chapters, which hold both theoretical as well a practical benefits that we believe will enrich the readers' work and study goals.

Following the initial context setting and the chapter outlining and refreshing readers about our model in our previous book, the chapters move from 'broadbrush', contextual discussions and framing chapters outlining the fluid new global business and action landscapes organizations inhabit and vistas leaders see before them to more narrowly focused, detailed analyses and descriptions of particular technologies entering leaders' fields of vision and action. Others add data and outcome discussions drawn from emerging professional and research domains such as Big data Analytics, Social networking media, BYOD and Healthcare or focus on particular aspects such as cyber crime and privacy.

Chapter 2 in the new book brings the reader up to date with an overview of the leadership models, learning processes and practical applications drawn from the research and consulting work carried out and developed by Peter A.C. Smith and Dr Tom Cockburn over time in the course of research or discussions with our academic and practitioner colleagues or clients in the Center for Dynamic Leadership Models in Global Business. The model outlines a simple, iterative process incorporating learning new, effective and relevant ways of working in the current and future environments as leaders. The latter learning process for leaders may also incorporate some unlearning of inappropriate habits or customary ways of working that are no longer appropriate in the organization or in the business world today. The model is free of gender or cultural biases, simple to apply and humanistic since it involves enhanced communication and openness, captures creative input and empowers 'voice' of actors whilst reducing negative conflicts in teams.

Chapter 3 is by Prof Akhilesh,, Kalyan Banerjee and Uma Maheshvari, titled *Leading in the Era of Digital Abundance* These authors have taken the theme of growing recognition of the potential global abundance and availability of digital and information resources as their core topic, albeit in a context of finite physical resources and issues of environmental degradation. They discuss the emerging skills development drivers and how these task leaders to undertake personal growth to enable their organizational growth as well as simply keeping pace with the sociodigital technology exponential growth rate. These authors outline a specific program they have developed for leaders, drawing conclusions about applicability globally as business and academic thinking turns to explorations of transdisciplinary synergies in the development of products and services for all types of organizations, professions and industry sectors.

Chapter 4 is by Dr Janel Smith and is titled *Leadership in the Age of Social Media: The 'Social Media Uprisings' and Implications for Global Business Leadership*. In this chapter Dr Smith discusses her research on use of digital and mobile technologies in social movements and what these incipient currents may mean for businesses and leaders. In her own words, "This Chapter asserts that the social media mobilizations have inherently, and to some degree inadvertently, taken up the emergent potentialities of social media technologies in redefining the scope of leadership." Dr Smith examines the "nexus between social media technologies and business leadership by analyzing the roles and influence of social media in shaping leadership processes within the 'social media

uprisings' associated with the Arab Spring and reflecting on how these insights can be applied to global business leadership". This emerging area is of increasing importance in the fluid global dynamics of the 21st century and how a study of the interplay between informal and formal networks, leaders and their actions in an evolving social context can provide lessons for leaders of corporate or government agencies. The influence of socio digital media in shaping how leaders thinks and act suggests their role has transformed to become more than that of merely ubiquitously convenient communication conduits between parties. Since the so-called 'practical' turn in academic research literature and especially since the Tahrir Square occupation and Arab Spring, the significance and effectiveness of the co-evolving leadership exercised through organizing of 'flash mobs' has become a popular topic of debate.

Chapter 5, is by Sampath S.Windsor and Dr Carol Royal, and is titled *A new breed of socio-cultural leaders and how they use CSR in ICT for development as a tool of sustainability: A case study of telecentres in a South Asian developing country.* In this chapter the authors describe and discuss their research and the chapter gives a practical, pragmatic and focused look at how the broader perspectives of other authors are enacted in situ. They use a case analysis of for-profit and not-for-profit telecenters in emerging countries and how these may potentially become an adjunct to sustainability and community development and Corporate Social responsibility. They uncovered fusion of Socio-Cultural Leaders (SCL) that perpetuated CSR synergies within Nenasala telecenters to successfully enhance sustainability, community focus, and competitive advantage against their non-Nenasala, for-profit telecenter counterparts.

Chapter 6 is by James Blaisdell, Michael Kelly, Kieran Muldoon, Joe Toner & Dr Michael Lang and titled *The Use of Personal Mobile Devices by Employees: Balancing the Risks of Security Breaches with the Benefits of Flexible Work*

Practices. The team of authors here consider another facet of the new workplace and the new demographic brought up with social media and one or more devices of their own with which they are both familiar and very comfortable and so wish to see as part of their work roles. There are a number of security and potential management issues associated with organizations and leaders allowing this BYOD approach to proliferate. These are discussed and debated by the authors.

Chapter 7 is by Rahul Saxena and is titled *Analytics.* In this chapter Rahul outlines the historical convergence of the techniques and tools or methodologies drawn from the fields of statistics, operations research, industrial engineering and computer science and he describes the emergence of the discipline of Data analytics. Rahul not only discusses Analytics as a discipline but as an increasingly important, emerging profession within the evolving landscape forming around the network of the digitally informed global business ecosystem. He then elaborates on how the tools and techniques of this discipline are an asset for business decision-making in practical ways, relating this to the current perceived deficiencies in the levels of leadership awareness or interest as well as the need to inform and build leaders' confidence and skills development to enable them to more astutely explore its potential or exploit this technological domain now and in future.

Chapter 8 is by Matthew Kolakowski and Paul Bishop and titled *Principles of Effective E-Learning.* In this chapter the authors describe and discuss the research on digital technology systems applied to learning. As the two authors state: "… primary principles of effective e-learning and the subsequent impact on leadership in global business as digital technologies mediums continue to emerge within academia and the workplace" This is an important and continually developing socioeducational and cultural field as MooCs begin to become more accepted in some parts of academe and some are getting credentialized and ICT is effectively mainstreamed now and a

part of Educational policy development in many western countries. The currents of streaming and 'pop up', 'just-in-time', 'anywhere, anytime' are reflected in the social fabric of many countries and especially amongst the younger millennial and their younger siblings who have only known the digital era. For these demographics there is no looking back to earlier didactic models and 'old style' learning media minus devices or as part of a historical project.

Chapter 9, by Dr Peter Johansson, Dr Tomas Backström and Dr Marianne Döös is titled *Visualizations of relatonics. A management tool to support managers' (re-) organizing of work?* In their abstract they concisely outline the chapter as "This chapter is based on theorising and analysis from an ongoing research and development project exploring the use of visualisations in task-based development; specifically, the potential of new types of organisational images that may support understanding about work-integrated learning. Thus, the aim of the chapter is to explore the possibilities of visualising work-integrated competence networks – here referred to as *relatonics* – and contribute to the understanding of how such visualisations can support efforts of organising change when organisational boundary-crossing cooperation is needed for a significant task. "So, as is readily evident to the reader this too is a chapter with both a practical focus on implementation of this methodology within a business environment as well as a research or academic model building description and discussion.

Chapter 10 is by Kijpokin Kasemsap and is titled *The Role of Social Networking in Global Business Environments.* The topic of social networking has received much publicity from a variety of commentators in business and academe to date and Dr Kasemsap reviews and analyzes emerging trends in the field and points to some lessons that apply for business leaders. This chapter points to specific training for business leaders in order to enable them to become more conversant and proficient in the use and deployment of social media and the networking potentialities these systems exhibit or enable.

Chapter 11 is by Prof Javanthi Ranjan and is titled *Application of Analytics to better target physicians.* Professor Ranjan tackles the thorny subject of how Big Pharma garners analytic data on physicians prescribing practices and how this material is used in the marketing of pharmaceutical products. In this chapter Professor Ranjan discusses the differences between hype and reality about big data and places the emerging analytics movement into perspctive whilst discussing the opportunities, scale and limitations of the application of the tools of decision-collection and analysis by the the analytics professionals with respect to the pharmaceutical and healthcare industry speifically.

Chapter 12 is by Sue Milton and is titled *Data Privacy versus Data Security.* This chapter employs case material and the author's own experience as a CEO to give an overview of how concerns about balancing privacy and security impact on business systems, processes and reputation. The chapter author uses a pair of anonymous case organization descriptions, each one with a different set of priorities, constraints and expectations of Information technology and of the associated costs and benefits, to help elucidate for readers the issues affecting each and the sorts of outcomes that they experience.

Chapter 13, by Michael Anton Geodeker, titled *Cyber Security: Future IT Security Challenges to tomorrow's leaders and businesses*, encompasses empirical research on raising employees' growing concerns about protecting organizations increasingly reliant on ICT, the protection of data and of confidentiality of clients as well as intellectual property from hackers as well as viruses. These and other cyber challenges of cyber crime and cyber warfare are set to rise exponentially as increased uses of transdisciplinary digital technologies spread the areas and domains where we are increasingly dependent ranging from false credentials in E-learning derived from hacking into online learning bodies, through to industrial espionage carried out by accessing staff development files in organizations to see what ways companies are training and developing their engineers, scientists and others as a means to determine strategic directions, markets targeted and attempts to 'steal a march' on rivals to get there first (Innovaro, 2014).

Chapter 14, is authored by Dr Carlos Eduardo Pereira, and is titled ICT, gender and empowerment at the emerging digitized workplace. Eduardo takes up the debate about technology and women's opportunities in the workplace where brains rather than brawn prevails. Nevertheless, there is still an apparent glass ceiling in the IT industry leadership area in particular. In this chapter the author seeks to explore to what extent the use of emerging digital technologies can contribute to contesting gender inequalities and assist in the expansion of social justice in the workplace and enactment of women's leadership in business.

Chapter 15 is a short reflective concluding commentary by Peter A.C. Smith and Tom Cockburn and is titled *Epilog: Retrospective and Prospective reflections.* This chapter briefly outlines some of the emerging challenges observed, notable themes and perspectives described and discussed in the book and some ways we see these moving forward in the global business context leaders face in future. We do not have any 'crystal ball' and prophesying the future in our complex world is always a fraught endeavor but one which leaders attempt each day in their working lives, even with the benefit of Big Data analytics.

REFERENCES

Arthur, W. B. (2011, October). The Second Economy. *McKinsey Quarterly.* Retrieved 11/10/2011, at https://www.McKinseyquarterly.com/The_second_economy_2853

Autor, D. H., & Dorn, D. (2013). The Growth of Low-Skill Service Jobs and the Polarization of the US Labor Market. *American Economic Review, 103*(5), 1553-97. Retrieved on 03/17/2014 from http://ideas.repec.org/s/aea/aecrev.html

Blauth, C., McDaniel, J., Perrin, C., & Perrin, P. B. (2011). *Age-Based Stereotypes: Silent Killer of Collaboration and Productivity*. Tampa, FL: AcheiveGlobal.

Brynjolfsson, E., & McAfee, A. (2011). *Race against the machine: How the digital revolution is accelerating innovation, driving productivity, and irreversibly transforming employment and the economy*. Digital Frontier Press.

Cockburn, T., Jahdi, K., & Wilson, E. (Eds.). (2015). *Responsible governance: International perspectives for the new era*. New York, NY: Business Expert Press.

Cockburn, T., & McKie, D. (2004). Imagining uncertainty: Creative tales of corporate and global futures. *Global Business & Economic Review Journal, 6*(1), 92–106. doi:10.1504/GBER.2004.006222

De Stricker, U. (2014). *Knowledge management Practice in Organizations*. Hershey, PA: IGI Global. doi:10.4018/978-1-4666-5186-9

Dervojeda, K., Verzijl, D., Nagtegaal, F., Lengton, M. & Rouwmaat, E. (2013). *Big Data -Artificial Intelligence*. Business Innovation Observatory.

Drury, A., & Absolom, R. (2012). *Multi-market BYOD Survey Results: The Management gap*. Retrieved on 03/22/2014 from *http://ovum.com/research/multi-market-byod-survey-results-the-byod-management-gap/*

Du Rausis, M. P., Manyika, J., Hazan, E., Bughin, J., Chui, M., & Said, R. (2011). *Internet matters: The net's sweeping impact on growth, jobs and prosperity*. McKinsey Global Institute.

Dulewicz, V., & Higgs, M. (2005). Assessing leadership dimensions, styles and organizational context. *Journal of Managerial Psychology, 20*(2), 105–123. doi:10.1108/02683940510579759

Frey, C. B., & Osborne, M. A. (2013). *The Future of Employment: How susceptible are jobs to computerisation?* Academic Press.

Gardner, W. L., Lowe, K. B., Moss, T. W., Mahoney, K. T., & Cogliser, C. C. (2010). Scholarly leadership of the study of leadership: A review of The Leadership Quarterly's second decade, 2000–2009. *The Leadership Quarterly, 21*, 922–958.

Goos, M., Manning, A., & Salomons, A. (2009). Job polarization in Europe. *The American Economic Review, 99*(2), 58–63. doi:10.1257/aer.99.2.58

Harris, A. (2011). Distributed leadership: Implications for the role of the principal. *Journal of Management Development, 31*(1), 7–17. doi:10.1108/02621711211190961

Hartman, H. (2014). *Food & the New Community, How the Internet changes Food Culture*. Retrieved on 03/14/2014 from http://www.hartman-group.com/news/press-releases/eating-alone-is-the-new-norma-reports-the-hartman-group

Higgs, M. J. (2003). How can we make sense of leadership in the 21st century? *Leadership and Organization Development Journal, 24*(5), 273–284. doi:10.1108/01437730310485798

Hirt, M., & Willmott, P. (2014). Strategic principles for competing in the digital age. *McKinsey Quarterly*. Retrieved from http://www.mckinsey.com/insights/strategy/strategic_principles_for_competing_in_the_digital_age

Hyypiä, M., & Pekkola, S. (2011). Interaction challenges in leadership and performance management in developing a network environment. *Journal of Advances in Management Research, 8*(1), 85–98. doi:10.1108/09727981111129318

I F R. (2012). *World robotics 2012*. Tech. Rep. International Federation of Robotics.

Index, B. G. (n.d.). Retrieved from https://www.boardsource.org/eweb/dynamicpage.aspx?webcode=GovernanceIndex

Innovaro. (2014). *Technology Foresight*. Retrieved from http://www.trendsandforesight.com/uploads/TF%202013%2039%20Experience%20API.pdf

Kauffman, S. (1995). *At home in the universe - the search for laws of self-organization and complexity*. New York, NY: Oxford University Press.

Kets de Vries, M. F. R. (1993). *Leaders, fools and imposters: Essays on the psychology of leadership*. San Francisco, CA: Jossey-Bass.

Khanna, P. (2011). *How to run the world: Charting a course to the next renaissance*. New York, NY: Random House.

Krohe, J. (2011). How much do you know? Too much and not enough. *The Conference Board Review*. Retrieved November 10, 2011, from http://www.tcbreview.com/summer_2011.aspx

Logicalis. (2014). Compilation of reports and white papers. *Employee Behaviour and Attitudes toward Mobile Device Usage at Work*. Logicalis.

Marr, B. (2013). *How Big Data Will Change People Management Forever*. Retrieved from http://smartdatacollective.com

McKinsey Global Institute. (2013). *Disruptive technologies: Advances that will transform life, business, and the global economy*. Technical Report.

Newhall, S. (2011). Preparing our leaders for the future. *Strategic HR Review*, *11*(1), 5–12. doi:10.1108/14754391211186250

Nierenberg, D. (2014). *Article*. Retrieved on Monday 10 March 2014 from http://www.the-guardian.com/

Northhouse, P. (2007). *Leadership: Theory and practice*. Thousand Oaks, CA: Sage Publications.

Pew Global Research Report. (2014). *Emerging and Developing Nations Want Freedom on the Internet-Young Especially Opposed to Censorship*. Retrieved 03/21/2014 from http://www.pewglobal.org/2014/03/19/emerging-and-developing-nations-want-freedom-on-the-internet/

Pretorius, M., & le Roux, I. (2011). A reality check for corporate leaders: When managers don't respect their bosses. *Strategy and Leadership*, *40*(1), 40–44. doi:10.1108/10878571211191693

Robotics-VO. (2013). *A Roadmap for US Robotics. From Internet to Robotics*. Robotics in the United States of America.

Ruettimann, L. (2011). HR: You're doing it wrong. The culture myth. *The Conference Board Review*. Retrieved November 19, 2011 from http://www.tcbreview.com/summer_2011.aspx

Rus, D. (2015). The Robots Are Coming. How Technological Breakthroughs Will Transform Everyday Life. *Foreign Affairs*. Retrieved from https://www.foreignaffairs.com/articles/2015-06-16/robots-are-coming

Saddi, J., Sabbagh, K., & Sheddiac, R. (2011). Measures of Leadership. *Strategy + Business*. Retrieved October 20, 2011 at http://www.strategy-business.com/article/10203?gko=64f7f&cid=enews20100720

Schawbel, D. (2013). 10 Ways Millennials Are Creating The Future Of Work. *Forbes*. Retrieved from http://onforb.es/18QL7p3

Schuster, D., Jentsch, F., & Shumaker, R. (2011, May). *Robots as team members*. In Information Systems and Technology Panel Symposium on Emerged and Emerging "disruptive" Technologies. Symposium conducted at the meeting of the North Atlantic Treaty Organization (NATO), Madrid, Spain.

Schuster, D., Ososky, S., Jentsch, F., Phillips, E., Lebiere, C., & Evans, A. W. (2011). A research approach to shared mental models and situation assessment in future robot teams. *Proceedings of the Human Factors and Ergonomics Society Annual Meeting*. Santa Monica, CA: Human Factors and Ergonomics Society. doi:10.1177/1071181311551094

Smith, P., & Cockburn, T. (2013). *Dynamic Leadership Models for Global Business: Enhancing Digitally Connected Environments*. IGI Global. doi:10.4018/978-1-4666-2836-6

Solis, B. (2011). *The end of business as usual: Rewire the way you work to succeed in the consumer revolution*. New York: John Wiley & Sons.

Spicker, P. (2012). Leadership: A perniciously vague concept. *International Journal of Public Sector Management*, 25(1), 34–47. doi:10.1108/09513551211200276

Spillane, J. P. (2006). *Distributed leadership*. San Francisco, CA: Jossey-Bass.

Toffler, A., & Toffler, H. (2006). *Revolutionary wealth*. New York, NY: Knopf.

Van Rijmenam, M. (2014). *Is Artificial Intelligence About To Change Doing Business Forever?* Retrieved from http://www.bigdata-startups.com/the-big-data-trends/

Van Rijmenam, M. (2014). *How Big Data Analytics Will Affect Your Company Culture*. Retrieved from http://smartdatacollective.com/bigdatastart-ups/180176/how-big-data-analytics-will-affect-your-company-culture

Vladimirov, R. (2014). *Website*. Retrieved from http://www.technologyreview.com/news/519051/is-samsungs-galaxy-gear-the-first-truly-smart-watch/

Yukl, G. (2002). *Leadership in organizations* (5th ed.). Upper Saddle River, NJ: Prentice Hall.

Yukl, G. (2009). Leading organizational learning: Reflections on theory and research. *The Leadership Quarterly*, 20(1), 49–53. doi:10.1016/j.leaqua.2008.11.006

Yukl, G. (2010). *Leadership in organizations* (6th ed.). Upper Saddle River, NJ: Pearson.

Zaccaro, S. J. (2007). Trait-based perspectives of leadership. *The American Psychologist*, 62(1), 6–16. doi:10.1037/0003-066X.62.1.6 PMID:17209675

ADDITIONAL READING

Burghin, J., Livingston, J., & Marwaha, S. (2011). Seizing the potential of 'big data'. *McKinsey Quarterly*. Retrieved November 4, 2013, from https:// www. mckinseyquarterly. com/ Seizing_the_potential_of_big_data_2870

Cockburn, T., & Jahdi, K. S. (2010). Leveraging organizational learning in NGO-business collaboration. *Interface, 10*(5)

Economist Intelligence Unit (2011) *Big Data: Harnessing a game-changing asse*t

Eijkman, H. (2010b). Dancing with postmodernity: Web 2.0 as a new epistemic learning space. In Lee, M. W., & McLoughlin, C. (Eds.), Web 2.0-based e-learning: Applying social informatics for tertiary teaching (pp. 343–364). Hershey, PA: IGI Global. doi:. ch018 doi:10.4018/978-1-60566-294-7

Kelly, J. (2013). *Big Data Market Size and Vendor Revenues*. Wikibon Article.

Prensky, M. (2001). Digital Natives, Digital Immigrants, *On the Horizon*, MCB University Press, Vol. 9: 5, retrieved on 03/21/2014 from http://www.hfmboces.org/HFMDistrictServices/TechYES/ PrenskyDigitalNatives.pdf

Stone, B. (2010). *The Children of Cyberspace: Old Fogies by Their 20s*, The New York Times, January 9, retrieved on 02/23/2014 from? pagewanted=all

Beveridge, C., Brooks, J., Chang, J., et al (2011) *Transitioning to Workforce 2020*, Cisco White paper

Twenge, J. M., Campbell, S. M., Hoffman, B. R., & Lance, C. E. (2010). Generational differences in work values: Leisure and extrinsic values increasing, social and intrinsic values decreasing. *Journal of Management*, *36*(5), 1117–1142. doi:10.1177/0149206309352246

Chapter 2
Globalization and Media's Impact on Cross Cultural Communication:
Managing Organizational Change

Doris Cross
Organizational Change and Development Company (OCDC), USA

ABSTRACT

Diversity and change are key concepts facing the world, today. In the 21st century, organizational leaders recognize the importance of diverse perspectives and adaptations to changes. Globally, cultures have many definitions and difference as nations collectively strive to communicate with one another. Organizational leaders must understand the importance of cross-cultural communications in establishing trust and respect in business relationships. Doris E. Cross is an educator and researcher on diversity issues influence on organizational cultures competitive advantage. This chapter identifies factors, such as changing demographics, tumultuous economies, and workforce dynamics and effects on individual perceptions of organizational cultures.

INTRODUCTION

In an increasingly global environment the ability to communicate effectively becomes a challenge for business leaders. Although, a common language may is shared among cultures misunderstandings may exist due to ethnic, cultural, and differential levels of understanding. For the last decade, business sectors have experienced declining organizational performance due to poor communication or a lack of understanding or information about their employees and clients. Understanding the impact of globalization on cross-culture communication is imperative for organizations aspiring to capitalize from a competitive advantage in the global market. Today's economic challenges further highlight the need for organizational leaders to develop and obtain accurate information on to control, understand, and monitor economic markets. As nations becomes more globally connected their ability to communicate across cultures has established itself as a primary focal point. Global businesses must

DOI: 10.4018/978-1-4666-9970-0.ch002

understand how to communicate with employees and customers from different cultures in order to increase performances and increase their values to stakeholders.

In the 21st century, America faces a tumultuous environment that challenges its economic stability. Demographic shifts and workforce changes have impacted businesses performance requirements and this nation's ability to compete on a global level. Currently, a worldwide market has evolved with representation from diverse groups that include race, ethnicity, gender, national origin and age. This global market of distinct consumers creates opportunities for businesses to increase performance levels by tapping into the priceless contributions of its constituents.

Creativity is a highly prized commodity in an expanding global economy. Diversity among global workforces and consumers serves as a pivotal force for leaders to develop strong world-wide partnerships and teams for economic survival and prosperity. Business and education leaders strive to understand and embrace difference to develop a highly competitive and skilled workforce. In a global community, economic survival motivates the increased reliance on the entrepreneurial spirits of diverse populations. Individuals from different cultures, backgrounds, genders and personal preferences stimulate innovation and creativity through their communications and differences (Driskilll & Brenton, 2005). Bok (2006) contend that in today's global economy, universities in Europe, Asia, and America focus on individuals' education, skills development, ability to communicate, and performance approaches to develop a highly skilled and diversified workforce.

GLOBAL PERSPECTIVES ON RACE AND ETHNICITY

Globally, definitions of race and ethnicity are based on varying factors such as heredity, genetics, and socio-economic statuses. In the United States and other nations, the issue of race and ethnicity heightens the interest of demographic realities. The two concepts remain vague, wide-ranging, and misused by many. In the literature, the concept of race is ascribed to a person's group based on their biological and physical appearances. These characteristics are considered inherent, heritable, persistent, or predictive in nature. Yet, this notion is considered unverifiable based on scientific conjectures on pure phenotype origins and social and cultural traits. Biological blending among groups with different prototypes makes it difficult to substantiate this premise. In some countries, social and cultural traits are often used to classify race among groups with identical phenotypes (Chang & Dodd, 2001; Perez & Hirschman, 2009). For example, Brazil's racial classifications based on skin shades vary from South Africa's black-white-colored paradigms (Deng, 1996, 1997; Stam, 1997). Koreans and Japanese who are classified in the same racial category are considered two different "races" primarily by Japanese's notion of blood affinities (Dikkster, 1997; Min, 1992). Racial classifications are often influenced by a group's socio-economic status. Brazilians social-economic statuses affect racial identifications or assignments. Also, research scholars state that in the Mexican society it is difficult to distinguish between Indians and Mestizos phenotypes. However, both groups are identified by their social and cultural traits (Hanchard, 1994; Reichmann, 1999; Twine, 1998). Nutini (1997) confirms that Indians "become" Mestizos by the acquisition of social and cultural traits irrelevant to phenotypes.

On the other hand, ethnicity is a culturally derived term that embodies the values, institutions and patterns of behavior of a group (Chang & Dodd, 2001; Perez & Hirschman, 2010). Ethnicity is considered a composite whole of the group that represents its holistic experiences, world views, and aspirations. Research studies indicate that ethnicity defines people's membership in a group, its centrality to the human experience and identity; and a sense of oneness that incorporates languages, religion, and demarcations (Bottaffi, Bacalentri, Braham, Gindro, 2002).

According to Unander (2000), genetic differences among groups with different phenotype attributes are minor and minimally account for differences in human behavior. Overall, these findings are summarized as: Racial differences are more in the mind than genes; racial and ethnic categories are neither fixed across or within a society but fluid and changing depending on social and political contexts; and ethnic and racial differences do not inherently lead to conflict but a struggle for a balance in power (Unander, 2000).

Dynamic Forces Impacting America's Future and Competitive Edge

For much of America's history, race has been the greatest barrier to a common vision for its community (Perez & Hirschman, 2009; Chang & Dodd, 2001). It raises major concerns over managing diversity in an increasing diverse nation and global economy. As the global market unfurls, the United State is challenged to compete with a highly skilled workforce prepared to interact with diverse populations. The 2007 report of Kirsch, Brown, and Yamamoto, entitled *America's Perfect Storm*, identifies powerful social and contextual forces and influences that are changing the future of our nation. Researchers predict that dynamic interactions between three economic factors will influence the nation for 25 years into the future. These three forces changing the U.S. include substantial disparities in skills distributions, economic restructuring, and changing demographic trends.

Divergent Skill's Distributions

The United States has the largest number of ethnically diverse populations in the world, while 21 other nations consist of predominantly non-white populations (cite). Immigrants entering the United States have increased and are projected to reach 1.5 million annually (Kirsch et al., 2007, Cox & Blake, 1991).

A major contributing force to this nation's dilemma is the "wide disparity in literacy and numeracy skills among school age and adult populations" (Kirsch et al., 2007, p. 4). Researchers determined that U.S. high school graduation rates peaked in 1969 at 77%, declined to 70% in 1995, and remained in this range into the current decade (Kirsch et al., 2007). The graduation rate of under-represented minorities (URM) and immigrant students was projected closer to a 50% rate. Additionally, international surveys (adult and student populations) indicate that the United States is behind world leaders in educational achievement. In a report issued by the Organization for Economic Co-operation and Development (OECD comprised of 30 countries), the United States ranked 16th out of 21 OECD countries with comparable high school graduation rates (Orfield, 2004, as cited Kirsch et al., 2007). America's diminished lead in education has diminished among OECD countries listed the U.S. as a nation where its young adults are less educated than previous generations. More than 88 million U. S. adults were cited to have at least one educational barrier with either no high school diploma, college degree, or a proficiency in English (NCAL, 2008).

Between 1992 and 2007, NAEP, 2009, 2011 reported large gaps in reading and mathematics gaps existed among diverse groups. The size of achievement gaps among diverse populations had remained large, stable, and unchanged (Kirsch et al., 2007). Critical literacy skills required to compete in today's businesses economic climate are identified as critical thinking, creativity, problem solving, innovation and effective oral and written communications skills (Gordon, Particelli, & Morgan, 2009).

A large number of America's youth (13 to 17 years old) did not possess adequate literacy and/or language skills. As a result, they are unable to compete in an increasingly complex and technologically advanced society. More than one-half of America's adult population lacked the literacy skills required to compete globally (NAEP, 2009, 2011). These skill deficits reflect an uneven distribution that reflects students' educational performances by gender, race, and ethnicity (Vanneman, Hamilton, Baldwin-Anderson, & Rahman, 2009). The under-represented minorities (URM) and immigrant numbers are increasing but some groups remain at the lower end of educational attainment.

However, the 2012 National Assessment of Educational Progress (NAEP) long term assessment results indicate some progress in narrowing the gaps among diverse groups: racial, ethnic and gender. Female students scored higher in reading than male students. However, male students scored higher than females in mathematics. The gaps between White-Black and White-Hispanic students have narrowed which reflect larger gains among Black and Hispanic than White students. In contrast, Asian students' scores do not reflect a large gap between White-Asians academic performance. Asian immigrants are noted to have increased by 45% into the U.S within the last ten years. Yet nearly 30% of Asians 25 and older are projected to have higher education degrees compared with the remaining U. S. population (Shrestha & Heisler, 2011).

Research studies indicate that America's average students performances are noted as "mediocre" (Vanneman, Hamilton, Baldwin-Anderson & Rahman, 2009; NCAL, 2008). The gap between the United States' best and least proficient is higher than other OECD countries. An increase in global diversity requires Americans to acquire diverse perspectives that differ from its major culture. The United States dominant culture is primarily comprised of individuals from European ancestry. Anglo Americans constitute over 70% of America's demographic population. Today, economic challenges faced by U. S. leaders include effectively working with a multi-cultural, multi-racial, two-gender, and older workforce to insure America's prosperity and sustainability. Global workforces require diverse groups develop their innovative and creative skills to manage global markets around the world. Organizational leaders are encouraged to foster a genuine desire to un-

derstand diverse cultures, to work collaboratively, recognize our cultural interdependence and work in synergy, at home and abroad.

Changing Economy

The continuous evolution of America's economy and workforce job requirements presents intense changes in today's global market. Jobs in the area of professional, management, technical, and higher skill levels have increased within the college labor market clusters (Kirsch et al., 2007, Lermam & Schmidt, 1999). Additionally, Kirsch et al., 2007 contends changes generated through technological advancements and global competitions establish new sources of wealth, novel patterns of international trade, and balance shifts between capital and labor. America's manufacturing employment decreased over four decades while the number of employees 16 years and older increased significantly. The number of employed persons (16 years and older) grew by 29% or 30 million from 1984 to 2000 (Kirsch et al., 2007). Labor studies show job opportunities have increased by 20 million for college level employees (Lerman & Schmidt, 1999; NCAL, 2008; Shrestina & Hesler, 2011). Over 2/3rds of America's employment growth is attributable to individuals with higher level skills. Within the next decade, jobs will require higher levels of education, training and skills which will account for close to one-half of America's employment growth (U.S. Census 2013, Hemphill, Vanneman, Rahmin (2011).

Research studies further report that America's job compositions have increased the economic returns on higher skill levels. For example, the lifetime earnings of males with bachelor's degrees in 1979 were 51% higher than those with high school diplomas. In 2004, the earnings of males with higher education widened to 96%. Women have entered the workforce, over the last 50 years, in greater numbers. Women constitute almost half (44.95%) American workers and earn almost 60% of university degrees in America and Europe.

The changing dynamics of America's economy indicates that the earning power for those with higher skills levels are substantially larger and provide better opportunities for advancement. The prospect of a higher education has enhanced job prospects for women. Today, over half of the students enrolled in higher education institutions are women. Over 80% of American women are in the workforce compared to lesser numbers of those with high school diplomas (Economist, 2013. Dramatic increases in the number of women workers reflect their economic value and growth in the workplace for many countries. Research studies indicate that women comprise the majority of professional workers in the U. S. and countries such as Spain, Italy, Japan, Denmark and Sweden. Increases in the number of diverse groups and women entering the workforce presents challenges for global markets.

Demographic Shifts

According to 2012 U. S. Census data, Asians and Hispanics are this nation's fastest growing races. The 2011-2012 growth among under-represented minority (URM) groups reflects the following percents and totals as follows: Asians increased by 2.9% (18.9 million); Hispanics by 2.2% (53 million); African-Americans/Blacks by 1.3% (44.5 million); Native Hawaiians & Pacific Islanders by 2.2% (1.4 million); and American Indians and Alaskan Natives increased by 1.5% (6.3 million).

The United States' demographic shifts have profound effects on its workforce's composition and requirements. An increase in global diversity for organizations worldwide requires diverse perspectives that differ from America's dominant culture (Schauber, 1999; Perez & Hirschman, 2009; U.S. Census, 2013).

Lertman & Schmidt (1999) report the dynamics of the global economy and indicate the need for well managed, diverse workforces which hold competitive advantages world-wide. Within the next forty years, the U.S. is projected to increase

in size by 100 million people reaching a total of close to 400 million inhabitants. America will grow larger in size with an older workforce with increasing numbers of diverse racial and ethnic populations (U.S. Census, 2013; Shrestha & Hesler, 2011, Kotlin, 2010). Additionally, researchers forecast that America's labor force will grow more slowly, with limited growth predicted to occur from its current residents. Immigration is anticipated to account for more than one-half of America's population growth, with entries from diverse backgrounds and varying educational backgrounds. These projections were made based on the projected economic growth of the United States, prior to its recession.

Within the next 20–30 years Driskall and Brenton (2005) contend that organizations' ability to create cultures that embrace diversity is crucial to America's performance, innovation, and ultimate economic viability. U.S. Census (2013) statistics predict that America's shifting demographics will demonstrate an increase in racial and ethnic groups by 2040. A large portion of America's growth will occur in its racial minorities particularly Hispanics and Asians. Presently Caucasian-American residents comprise 69.1% of the U.S. population but will decrease in 2040 to 53.7%. Currently the Hispanic population is 12.4% but predicted to significantly increase to 22.2%. African-Americans are at 12.4% but anticipated to increase more slowly to 14%. Simultaneously, the Asian American population will almost double from 3.5% to 7.2% (U.S. Census. 2013). Yet, America's workforce is projected to face current trends that will affect its composition for example, the age composition will reflect an older workforce; women workers will continue to occupy a large portion; the number of diverse groups will expand; and an increase in the number of unskilled workers (Lerman & Schmidt, 1999).

Research studies reveal America's current policies and practices, social and political polarizations and income and wealth inequities further affect the nation's economic well-being (Kirsch et al., 2007).In the last decade, the dramatic shifts' that has occurred are a growth in diverse populations; an increase in the number of women, older workers, and immigrants in the workforce. As a result, organizational leaders are key driving forces in developing change efforts that confront the challenges (nationally and internationally of a changing workforce which includes age, skill level, religious, gender, ability and racial and ethnic diversity (Lerman & Schmidt, 1999, Kirsch et. al, 2007, Kotkin, 2011, Shrestina & Hesler, 2011). In the context of the current shift in the U. S. job market, current demographic trends will affect the current and future composition of the workforce (Lerman & Schmidt, 1999).

Implications for U.S. and Global Competition

America's demographic shifts have prompted organizational leaders to explore the benefits of increased diversity (Hudson Highland, 2004; Senge, 2005; Dervisiotis, 2007; MOR Barack, 2010). Organizational leaders aspire to develop flexible and dynamic teams of trained individuals to address current needs of a global market place. Multiple perspectives with differing cultural value sets, synergy created from increased communications, and collaborations between different ethnic and cultural groups have begun to influence market values (Harris & Moran, 2000; Moran & Harris, 1982, as cited in Driskill & Brenton, 2005). Multicultural and multiracial global workforces within the U.S. serve as a testing ground for business leaders to heighten their abilities to effectively manage on an international level.

In the 21st century, research findings indicate that diversity is the greatest challenge faced by this nation (Varner & Beamer, 1995; NACE, 2008; Mor Barack, 2010; Reed, 2011). Opposing environmental forces such as poverty, intolerance, unemployment and low-skilled workers are equivalent threats to America's domestic and international sustainability (NAS, 2007). Research

findings predict that, by 2030, average literacy ratings will decline by 5%, but economic demands will increase. As better-educated individuals leave the current workforce and the number of less prepared immigrants increase, those who have lower levels of education and skills will replace them. Job requirements will increase and the available number of qualified adults for high-paying jobs will decrease. On an international front, competitors for U.S. jobs will include its current residents, as well as its global competitors.

The United States must develop its human resources to effectively manage its domestic and international investments. In a time of ever-expanding world markets and opportunities, U.S. organizational leaders are encouraged to embrace the core issue of diversity and its competitive advantage. America's relationship with nations across the globe is contingent upon the effective management of demographic changes at home and abroad.

ORGANIZATIONAL CULTURES AND CHANGE

An essential challenge for leaders is to intertwine the value of innovation with organizational cultures. Societal changes, generated by the dynamics of the 21st century, have encouraged organizational leaders to re-examine ways for developing a viable workforce. Bolman and Deal (2003) contend that the world is more complex today than 50 years ago due to technological developments. America's reliance on a strong workforce is reliant on meeting the needs of its national and international clientele. Future projections of researchers predict the United States will rely on its technological advancement, cultural innovation, and the dynamics of its diverse society (Kotin, 2010). As a result, an increase in global competition and market risk has become a primary concern for organizations. Globally, leaders embrace agreements and partnerships to cope with narrowing market shares and growing competition (Freidman, 2006). Innovations among countries (such as China, Japan, India, and Eastern Europe) assist nations to achieve higher real incomes (Eckel & Hartley, 2008; Hudson Highland Group, 2004, Mor Barack, 2010). Simultaneously, competition among global markets sets in motion organizational leaders' interest in adapting cultural structures to embrace changes from different perspectives.

Creative adaptation can occur by reframing organizational cultures to embrace diversity and develop the contributions of all its members (Bolman & Deal, 2003). With diversity in ethnicity, gender, age and other groups in the workforce we must create an inclusive culture that values and uses the talents of all its employees. For example, we must be prepared to manage, motivate and communicate with teams that span continents. We must also be prepared to enact cultural changes that meet the needs of diverse consumers, employees and business constituents.

Research studies reveal that the most common failure in implementing organizational change is a disregard for changes within the culture (Cameron & Quinn, 2006); while other empirical studies indicate that a positive relationship exists between dimensions of an organization's culture and its performance levels (Cameron & Ettington, 1988; Denison, 1990; and Trice and Beyer, 1993, as cited in Cameron & Quinn, 2006). The organizational culture determines how an organization operates. Hesslelbein, Goldsmith, and Beckhard (1997) cited in Champy (1997) state that the forces of change cause "fundamental industry restructuring" (p. 10). An organization's fundamental goals are governed by an established culture which is difficult to change without systemic changes to its values, beliefs, and assumptions (Senge, 2005,) At the same time, Cameron and Quinn (2006) contend that "unremitting, unpredictable, and sometimes alarming change makes it difficult for any organizational leader to remain a constancy of direction" (p. 10).

Organizational Culture

Organizational theorists vary on definitions of what constitutes an organizational culture, its definitive characteristics, and potential for change (Smirich, 1983). Similar to national cultures or civilizations, all organizations have their unique way of doing things (Driskill and Brenton, 2005). For this chapter, definitions of organizational cultures were reviewed, from varying perspectives, to identify a common agreement on the definition of an organizational culture. Some research studies indicate that an organization's culture is reflected by its valued beliefs and assumptions, dominant leadership styles, language and symbols, procedures and routines, and definitions of success that make an organization unique (Cameron & Quinn, 2006).

Gertz, 1973; Cameron & Quinn, 2006; Ouchi, 1981; denotes culture as a historically transmitted pattern of meanings embodied in symbols by which employees communicate through their behavior. Employees communicate, perpetuate, and develop their knowledge through shared values. Scott and Davis, 2007; Louis, 1983; Robbins, 1991 contends that employees share common beliefs and norms that participants employ to orient and govern their contributions" (p. 6). Lorsch (1985) argues culture is a hidden yet unifying theme that provides meaning, direction and mobilization" (p. 84). An organizational culture consists of "the beliefs that organizational members share on how they manage themselves, other employees, and conduct their business (Tierney, 1988; Bolman and Deal, 2003 Senge, 1995). From this perspective, culture is considered both a product and a process a fairly stable set of assumptions and ideologies that forms behaviors (Smirch, 1985; Trice & Beyer. 1993, Driskiall & Brenton, 2005).

In reviewing these characterizations of an organization's culture, some strands of similarities and commonalities exist. Schein's (1982, 1992) definition of culture will guide this chapter. Schein states that an organizational culture is a pattern of shared basic assumptions that a group has learned as it solved its problems of external adaptation and internal integration that has worked well enough to be considered valid and is therefore taught to new members as the correct way to perceive, think, and feel in relation to those problems (Bolman & Deal, 2003; Schein, p. 16; Scott & Deal, 2007). Schein's (1982, 1992) reference to adaptation and integration describes external influences that guide and direct internal operations and decisions made by an organization's leadership. When an organization faces a crisis, Schein contends that "the manner, in which a leader responds to it, creates new norms, values, and procedures which reveal underlying assumptions" (p.254). Organizational cultures are interdependently linked with the leadership of an institution (Burke, 2010; Schein, 1985, 1992; Driskill & Brenton 2005).

Organizational Change Theories

Environmental changes have inspired organizational leaders to examine change efforts from different perspectives. Similar to the concept of "culture" theories, "change" theories are numerous in numbers and differ in their approach and implementation. According to Dumpry (1996) (as cited in Moldenhauser-Salazaar, 1999) "there is no all embracing widely accepted theory of organizational change and no agreed upon guidelines for action by change agents" (p.69). Numerous research studies on organizational change have attempted to characterize the change process that occurs within entities (Van de Ven & Poole, 1995; Lewin, 1951; Senge, 2005; Marx, 1954). Organizations are considered complex systems, operating from a systemic approach and an open system perspective. Open systems are systems that operate from an exchange of environment resources. Symbiotic relationships of influence and change exist between organizational and environments (Robert & Davis, 2007). As a result, the processes and events sequences that occur

within these changes are difficult to explain for organizational leaders and, at times, difficult to manage (Van de Ven & Poole, 1995).

According to Burke (2008), the most comprehensive typology of organizational change is provided by Van de Ven and Poole (1995) in Table 1. These scholars attempt to explain and understand organizational change processes derived from theories and metaphors associated with different fields of study. Van de Ven and Poole contend that the interchange between interdisciplinary perspectives serves to provide a more comprehensive understanding of organizational life. These conflicting perspectives are an avenue by which new theories are formulated and developed to further explain a complex phenomenon. Based on interdisciplinary perspectives from disciplines such as biology, business management, geography, psychology, education and sociology, Van de Ven & Poole (1995) formulate this change process typology

Van de Ven and Poole introduce four types of process theories to explain the "how and why" organizational change occurs - life-cycle, teleological, dialectical, and evolutionary theories. These following process theories conceptualize theories followed by the American Association of State Colleges and Universities (ASCU) (2003) and also introduce two additional theories. Association for the Study of Higher Education (ASHE, (2003) indicates that Van de Ven & Poole's theoretical models are credible and presents social cognition and cultural changes as adaptive approaches to change. Many of the theories have been tested within business organizations (Driskall & Brenton, 2005; Cameron & Quinn, 2006). However, the learning organization theory, another cultural approach to change, has not been tested in higher education institutions (Senge, 2005).

Life Cycle Theory

According to Van de Ven & Poole (1995, 2004), life cycle theories are the most common type of

Table 1: Breakdown and Remedies in Process Models of Organizational Change

	Teleology (Planned Change)	Life Cycle (Regulated Change)	Dialectic (Conflictive Change)	Evolution (Competitive Change)
Process Cycle	Dissatisfaction, search, goal setting, and implementation	Prescribed sequence of steps or stages of development	Confrontation, conflict, and synthesis between opposing interests	Variation, selection, and retention among competing units
Situations when model applies (generating mechanism)	Social construction of desired end state; goal consensus	Prefigured program regulated by nature, logic, or rules	Conflict between opposing forces	Competition for scarce resources
Typical breakdowns	Lack of recognition Decision biases Groupthink Lack of consensus	Resistance to change Lack of compliance Monitoring and control	Destructive conflict Power imbalance Irresolvable differences	Requisite variety Lack of scarcity
Remedies	Triggering attention Critical thinking Consensus building	Responding to complaints Local adaptation Internalizing mandates	Conflict management Negotiation Skills Political savvy	Niche development Marketing Strategies for competitive advantage

Note Adapted from: Van de Ven, A. H. & Sun, K. (August, 2011).

organizational change typology. The resultant model was derived from a psychology rather than a biology based discipline. The theory purports that organizations are entities that share processes similar to those of any human's psycho-social development. An analogy is drawn between human and organizational development. Life cycle models evolved from studies of human organisms and their developmental stages of birth, growth, maturity, and decline (as cited in Levy & Merry, 1986. p. 36, cited in Van de Ven & Poole). Van de Ven & Poole (1997) analogize and contend that organizational events similarly progress in linear and sequential manners in which change can be anticipated in a logical way. Moldenhauer-Salazar (1999) likewise contends that organizations' life cycle stages parallel those of human development assumptions. Thus, life-cycle theories progress towards organizational decline and death. Similar to human organisms, organizational life cycle theories develop in a linear and irreversible progression regulated by nature, logic or intuition (Van de Ven & Poole, 1995). Collins (2009) pinpoints Freddie Mae, a major financial institution, and its progression through organizational life stages as one noteworthy example. Freddie Mae, like many organizations, was formed, experienced unprecedented growth and success but later experienced an equally noteworthy decline.

Research studies cite the benefits of a life cycle approach as confirmable because of its empirical validation (Cohen & Sproull, 1996m Feldman & Pentland, 2003, Rogers, 2003 cited in Van de Ven & Sun, 2012). ASHE (2003) contends the drawbacks of a life cycle approach are its predetermined life stages. Within this approach, human elements of change are of minimal consideration. The life cycle theories do not address the unpredictable elements present in today's tumultuous business climate (Moldenhauser-Salazar, 1999). Most successful change initiatives have a training element, this approach does not. Adherence of organizations to a prescribed sequence of life stages, does not account for the out of sequence changes that occur today. Yet, the company's decline was not necessarily predictable. It was attributed to low performance due to an unpredictable economic climate. Collins (2009) further counters that companies' progressions can be restored with effective change management approaches.

Evolutionary Theory

Evolutionary theorists operate on the assumption that change proceeds according to a continuing cycle of variation, selection and retention (Burke, 2008). Variations are the creation of innovative forms of organizations developed through unexpected or random challenges. Organizational leaders make selections based on the competition for scarce resources. Survival is based on available resources and the best matches within an environmental niche. The Association for the Study of Higher Education (ASHE, 2003) contends that evolutionary theories operate from the assumption that "change is dependent on circumstances, situational variables, and the forces faced by each environment" (p. 28). In accord with Darwin's evolution theory, this approach indicates that change occurs because of environment demands for survival (ASHE, 2003).

Demographic changes may influence an organization's management approach to insure its survival and success. For example, America's population growth of Hispanic-Americans has generated environmental market conditions which require diversification in both products and services.

Teleological Theory

A planned or teleological change theory, Burke (2008) contends, operates from a prevailing assumption that an organization is purposeful and adaptive. An organization develops a goal or end state in which repetitive actions occur in an effort to formalize its vision. The American Association of State Colleges and Universities (AASCU) further contends that this approach is the foundation for many business related change efforts; specifically, models of strategic planning and goal setting (Chakravarthy & Lorange, 1991; Etzioni, 1963; March & Olsen, 1976; March & Simon, 1958; Parsons, 1951 cited by Merton, 1968, in AASCU, 2003). Van de Ven and Pool argues

that proponents of this theory focus on what is required to fulfill an organization's goals and the social practices that drive them.

In contrast to life cycle theories, teleological theories view organizations primarily as single entities with each possessing a set of goals indicative of its behavior (Moldenhauser-Salazar, 1999). Teleological theories pinpoint the role of organizational leaders in leading the change that occurs in organizations. Leaders determine an organization's response to established goals and, subsequently, the strategic plans to enact change. ASHE (2003) contends that change occurs over time and it is driven by leaders and other organizational constituents' recognition of the need for change.

Teleological theories are the most researched approaches with the largest number of models (Burke, Lake, & Paine, 2009; Nutt & Wilson, 2010 cited in Van de Ven & Sun, 2012). The most common types of teleological approaches are organizational development (Golembiewski, 1989: Goodman, 1982, cited in ASHE, 2006)) and total quality management (Freed, Klugman, & Fife, 1997, cited in ASHE, 2006). Rosabeth Kanter (1983) compares the metaphor of a leader with that of a "change master." An organizational leader is at the center of aligning goals, establishing expectations, modeling behavior, enhancing communications among its members, engaging employees, and assigning rewards (ASHE, 2003).

Duffy (1980), as cited in ASHE, 2003) disparages this approach as an overly rational and linear process of change with overemphasis on human creativity, thought, and problem-solving. Duffy (1988) notes that among varying change theories, human behavior can create problems rather than assist in the change process. Teleological models assume compliance, stable conditions, and the ability to address radical or transformational change (Burnes, 1996; Collins, 1998; Levy & Merry, 1986; Schein, 1985; Senge, 1990, as cited in American Association of State Colleges and Universities (AASCU), 2003). Teleological approaches often collapse because participants fail to recognize the need for change or reach agreements on their change approach (Van de Ven and Sun, 2011). Some teleological approaches require a large commitment of time and resources from an organization. Total Quality Management programs, a key teleological approach, focuses on the transformation of leaders and teams to alter personal philosophies and create a new organizational culture (Van de Ven & Sung, 2011).

Dialectic Theory

Simultaneously, a fourth school of thought is represented by dialectical theories, which operate from the assumption that organizations exist in a pluralistic world of colliding events, forces, or contradictory values that compete with each other for domination and control (Burke, 2008). These opposing or contradictory viewpoints can be internal or external to the organization. Change is noted to occur, particularly in businesses, when the opposing values of an organization replace what is considered the status quo. Moldenhauser-Salazar (1993) contends that dialectic theoretical approaches are widely used for understanding organizational change. This approach "distinguishes itself from the other three schools by viewing organizations as politically negotiated orders of individuals, subcultures, and coalitions" (p. 7). The complexity of organizational change is characterized by variations of power and access to critical resources available from constituents of the organization. The interdependence among stakeholders creates an interest in overcoming barriers to fulfill interests through ongoing bargaining and compromise that facilitate organizational change (Pfeffer, 1982, as cited in Moldenhauser-Salazar, 1999).

According to ASHE (2003), the primary focus of dialectical models is collective action rather than actions spearheaded by a leader. Bolman and Deal (2003) indicate that within this model the dominant change processes include bargaining, consciousness-raising, persuasion, influence and power, and social movements. For example, in higher education institutions a polarization occurs between opposing perspectives of faculty members and administrators. These two forces serve to influence each other and create organizational change.

Research studies indicate that evolutionary, life cycle, and teleological models specify that change is a rational and progressive process that enhances conditions (Van de Ven & Sung, 2012; Burke, 2010; Van de Ven & Poole, 1995). In contrast, the dialectical deterministic approach lacks emphasis on the environment and provides minimum assistance to organizational leaders or change agents. Van de Ven and Poole further state that the interplay between established theories and nascent theories provide a stronger and broader explanation for organizational change.

Emerging Theories

Three emerging change models, not included in Van de Ven and Poole's (1995) typology, are the social cognition, and cultural theories and learning organizations cited in ASHE (2003). The theories of social cognition, organizational cultures, as learning organizations offer alternative models to circumvent breakdowns in managing organizational change.

Social Cognition

Recently, this cognitive model evolved from the life cycle model through further examination of "how learning occurs" and by connecting learning with change (Argyris, 1982). Knowledge associated with cognition and changes are noted to occur when organization values and behaviors clash and create cognitive conflict (Bushe & Shani, 1991; Morgan, 1986, as cited in ASHE, 2003). Leaders shape the change process through framing and interpreting changes for individuals to understand the need for change (ASHE, 2003; Van de Ven & Sun 2011).

The major benefits attributed to the social cognitive model are expansions on the interpersonal and human aspects of change. Similar to the dialectical model, cognitive change is not always progressive or positive. Nevis, Lancourt, and Vassallo (1996, as cited in ASHE, 2003) indicate that the cognitive model focuses on mental processes as opposed to affective aspects of human nature. Criticisms on social cognitive approaches further include the perspectives that the theory deemphasizes the effects of environmental and external forces on change; suggests that individuals are pliable (Bolman & Deal, 1991; Morgan, 1996); and over emphasizes people's ability to change their fundamental identity and reality.

Cultural Change.

According to ASHE (2003), cultural models blend the assumptions of the social cognition theory and those of the dialectical model with irrationality, spirit, unconscious, fluidity, and complexity of organizations. According to Smirich (1983), change from a cultural perspective can occur as a result of planned or unplanned events, be progressive or regressive, and contain intended or unintended outcomes and actions. Change can be nonlinear, irrational, non-predictable, ongoing and dynamic (Smirich, 1983). Change occurs naturally as a response to changes in the human environment: both intimate, or cultural, and external, or political (Morgan, 1986).

One of the best known theorists of cultural change, Schein (1985) contends organizational change occurs when different parts of its culture are altered. He further states organizational leaders promote change by re-creating aspects of the symbolic system and culture and certain cultures are more prone to change. He further contends that change is a long term and slow process involving modifications to an organization's values, beliefs,

myths, and rituals; in short, it's culture. An organization's history and traditions are important elements of change because they represent the change processes that occurred over time.

The benefits and criticisms of a cultural change model are noted in ASHE (2003) as follows. The cultural model's strengths include considering the full range of human behavior, re-emphasizing the temporal dimension of change, and revealing the relationship between institutional change and culture (Collins, 1998; Schein, 1985). Theorists have raised serious concerns on the over-simplification of the notion of culture. Collins notes Schein's portrayal of individuals or groups' flexibility to change is a misnomer in reference to creating a culture of change. According to Van de Ven and Poole (1995), the combination of varying theoretical organizational change perspectives constitute a mechanism whereby the opportunity to develop new perspectives or theories emerge.

Organizational Learning (Cultural)

According to Morgan,1986; Rajagopalan & Spreitzer, 1996; Bolman & Deal, 1991; cited in ASHE (2003), Senge's model of learning organizations blends the evolutionary, social cognition, cultural, and teleological approaches to change, but primarily focuses on cultural. Organizational change theorists posit that change has to occur at all levels of an organization to create sustainable change (Schein, 1985; Senge, 2005).

Researchers contend a learning organization is "a place where people are continually discovering how they create their reality and how they can change it" (Senge, 2005, p. 140). Senge proposes five learning disciplines that converge in changing organizations and create effective learning organizations. They are as follows: systems thinking—a conceptual framework to make patterns clearer, personal mastery (defined as the discipline of continually clarifying and deepening personal vision), mental model examination (defined as deeply scrutinizing ingrained assumptions, generalizations, or images that influence how researchers understand the world and take action and often described as reflective practice by other scholars), team learning (defined as the processes of producing extraordinary results starting with dialogue and using teams as the fundamental learning unit in changing modern organizations), and shared vision building (defined as the processes of creating a genuine vision in which people excel and are creative and innovative because of their desire to do so). The role of organizational leaders in implementing change is the use of the dialectical approach to encourage stakeholders' participation in the change process.

Dever (1997) endorses Senge's theory on learning organizations and its potential impact on organizations. Dever contends that the five disciplines (systems thinking, personal mastery, mental models, shared vision, and team learning) identified for learning organizations are compatible with the traditional values of higher education institutions (HEIs). Yet the learning organization theory has minimal research presented on higher education institutions (Cameron & Quinn, 2006). Dever questions whether strong leadership is compatible with the organizational learning theory. He argues that Senge's learning organization theory places the role of the CEOs into the role of providing steward or servant leadership. In this role, the leader is responsible for taking risks, meeting challenges, empowering others, being accountable, and leading an organization in a change effort. ASHE (2003); Edmondson & Moingeon, 2013; Popper & Lipshitz, 2013 contend that Senge's approach is popular because it draws from and integrates multiple approaches, although some argue that Senge's (1999, 2005, 2006) model primarily reflects the teleological model that provides organizations with a rational approach that leaders can follow.

In today's economic climate, leaders must decide whether to remain "as is" with a diminished capacity to adapt to change or transform their organizations to meet the demands of their workforce and stakeholders through a continuous adaptation to change (Eckel, 2008). Across the nation and the world, organizations are optimally persuaded to transform organizational cultures in response to a world-wide shifting of priorities (Eckel, 2008). Several overlapping forces are prompting organizations to re-examine their cultural structures to embrace diversity.

Diversity, Leadership, Communication and Organizational Culture Change

Conversely, change has been an essential element of human existence since the beginning of time. Today's ever-changing tumultuous economic profile fueled with a multi-racial and multicultural global market has accelerated the pace of change in the 21st century (Dervitsiotis, 2007). Due to technological and scientific advancements, organizations compete from a larger playing field and for higher stakes. Learning the skills to work with diversity in domestic multicultural and international groups are no longer an option but a necessity (University of the Pacific, 2014). Organizational leaders in numerous business environments are under duress to cultivate sensitivity to the role cross cultural communication plays in obtaining performance goals. As nations become more globally interdependent, it becomes imperative for individuals to understand one another's cultures

In today's economic climate, organizational leaders must decide whether to remain "as is" without a sensitivity to cross-cultural communications. However, this approach diminishes a business's capacity to adapt to change. Or, leaders must transform their organizations to meet the demands of culturally different workforces and stakeholders. By continuously updating of a sensitivity to communication approaches among other groups.). Across the nation and the world, organizations are persuaded to transform organizational cultures in response to human interactions (Eckel, 2008). Several overlapping forces have prompted organizations to re-examine companies' communication styles to embrace diversity.

Media Influences Perceptions of Diversity and Cross-Communications

Although technology has contributed greatly to advancements in global markets, the media has gained increased influence on the perceptions of different cultures. The media has become a trusted authority that is relied upon for information. However, media can be helpful and harmful in facilitating communication across cultures. Without, individuals viewing cultures or things from different perspectives or from opposing versions of another's experiences (Jimenez, 2014). In America, ethnic groups have long recognized how powerful the media has been in shaping their popular images and, therefore, influencing their destinies. Resultantly, diverse groups have become more proactive in creating their own media images (Cortes, 2000). In order for American businesses to succeed on both a domestic and international front, they must be cognizant of changing global demographics. These changes not only determine their clientele but their workforce composition, as well.

Cross-Cultural Perceptions, Communications and Change

People's perceptions and attributions influence how they behave in their organization. Perception describes the way people filter, organize and interpret sensory information. Attribution explains how people act, determining how people react to the actions of others as well. Accurate perception allows employees to interpret what they see and hear, effectively make decisions, complete tasks and act in an ethical manner. Faulty perceptions lead to problems in the organization, such as stereotyping, that lead people to erroneous assumptions (Duggan. 2013)

Leaders' Role in Confronting Prejudice and Discrimination

Organizational leaders are confronted with minimizing biases from distorted perceptions of different ethnic groups. For organizational leader's consideration, this chapter has recognized he interdependence of global competition, diverse groups within that context - the potential for change; forces influencing change; and organizational leaders' responsibility to manage change.

Six Patterns of Cultural Differences

In a global world, we are more connected and interdependent that ever before. Each of us our tier to behavior, value, interest that are shaped by our cultures. In organizational cultures, culture is the most difficult to change but the most powerful force to facilitate change. In summary. Culture is central to what we see, what we make of what we see, and how we express this interpretation.

Dupraw & Axner (2012) contend that as people from different cultural groups take on the challenge of working together, cultural values sometimes conflict. We can misunderstand each other, and react in ways that can hinder what are otherwise promising partnerships. The authors suggest there are 6 fundamental patterns of cultural differences -- ways in which cultures, as a whole, tend to vary from one another -- are described below. The descriptions point out some of the recurring causes of cross-cultural communication difficulties. As organizational leaders enter into multicultural dialogues or collaborations, keep these generalized differences in mind. They are:

1. Different Communication Styles: The way people communicate varies widely between, and even within, cultures. One aspect of communication style is language usage. Across cultures, some words and phrases are used in different ways. For example, even in countries that share the English language,

the meaning of "yes" varies from "maybe, I'll consider it" to "definitely so," with many shades in between. Another major aspect of communication style is the degree of importance given to non-verbal communication. Non-verbal communication includes not only facial expressions and gestures; it also involves seating arrangements, personal distance, and sense of time.

2.   Different Attitudes toward Conflict: Some cultures view conflict as a positive thing, while others view it as something to be avoided. Differences are best worked out quietly. A written exchange might be the favored means to address the conflict.

3.   Different Approaches to Completing Tasks: From culture to culture, there are different ways that people move toward completing tasks. Some reasons include different access to resources, different judgments of the rewards associated with task completion, different notions of time, and varied ideas about how relationship-building and task-oriented work should go together. When it comes to working together effectively on a task, cultures differ with respect to the importance placed on establishing relationships early on in the collaboration.

4.   Different Decision-Making Styles: The roles individuals play in decision-making vary widely from culture to culture. For example, in the U.S., decisions are frequently delegated -- that is, an official assigns responsibility for a particular matter to a subordinate. In many Southern European and Latin American countries, there is a strong value placed on holding decision-making responsibilities oneself. When decisions are made by groups of people, majority rule is a common approach in the U.S.; in Japan consensus is the preferred mode. Be aware that individuals' expectations about their own roles in shaping a decision may be influenced by their cultural frame of reference.

5.   Different Attitudes Toward Disclosure: In some cultures, it is not appropriate to be frank about emotions, about the reasons behind a conflict or a misunderstanding, or about personal information. Keep this in mind when you are in a dialogue or when you are working with others. When you are dealing with a conflict, be mindful that people may differ in what they feel comfortable revealing. Questions that may seem natural to you -- What was the conflict about? What was your role in the conflict? What was the sequence of events? -- may seem intrusive to others. The variation among cultures in attitudes toward disclosure is also something to consider before you conclude that you have an accurate reading of the views, experiences, and goals of the people with whom you are working.

6.   Different Approaches to Knowing: Notable differences occur among cultural groups when it comes to epistemologies -- that is, the ways people come to know things. European cultures tend to consider information acquired through cognitive means, such as counting and measuring, more valid than other ways of coming to know things. Compare that to African cultures' preference for affective ways of knowing, including symbolic imagery and rhythm. Asian cultures' epistemologies tend to emphasize the validity of knowledge gained through striving toward transcendence (Direaw, 2014).

Solutions and Recommendations

Research studies covered in this chapter uncovered emerging trends that may influence our current economic climate. Environmental changes are occurring at a faster rate than ever before. International trade among the U.S. and other countries continue to advance at high speeds with companies competing for the best and brightest across the globe. Organizational leaders are called upon to interact with individuals with values, beliefs, and cultures that differ from their own. Technological advancements, demographic shifts, and workforce changes continue to influence the transformation of this global community. Diversity has become an integral factor as well. The U. S. has the largest number of diverse groups in the world. As a result, the U.S. is situated to establish the leadership role in developing organizations that are most effective in embracing diversity. At the same time, it has much work to do within.

The U.S. must form partnerships between businesses, schools, governments, and communities to educate students to develop skill levels for contributions at home and abroad. Advanced colleges and universities should develop cultures that embrace and acknowledge the potential contributions of diverse groups. The author contends that the Senge (2005) theory has the most potential implications for the requisite cultural changes identified in this chapter.

Organizational change approaches are varied. Research studies are needed to better understand the interacting complexities, interdependencies and interactions among various change models. More definitive measures of change models that are most effective in real world organizations will guide leaders in adapting more readily to change.

FUTURE TRENDS

In today's global economy, we have to develop strategies to deal with diversity on all levels. According to Friedman, the world is growing increasingly flat and will continue to do so. Greater pressures exist within the workforce due to changing markets, demographic shifts, high level skill demands, and technological advancements. Even more salient is the changing composition of the workforce with differences of ethnicity. gender, age, religion, disability and social orientation. The future prognosis challenges business leaders to develop diverse workplaces that encourage

inclusive cultures that values and uses the talents of all its employees. On the other hand, education leaders are challenged to provide a quality education to students so that they obtain the skills required to compete in global economy. Education and business leaders must build partnerships to adequately prepare American citizens to compete and manage businesses globally. According to Friedman, Companies, large or small, increasingly are operating at an international level. At home and abroad, companies face a change in demographics that include differences in language, nationality, religion, gender and race. Many of those individuals from diverse groups have become consumers, employers, and stake holders with diverse expectations about the way the company should work and their stake in its operations. Business leaders must find the best way to gain acceptance of its customers, employees, and stakeholders by reflecting their stake in businesses. For example, providing multilingual service and support for customer and employee satisfaction and opens up opportunities in different sectors of the market.

CONCLUSION

Change has been an essential element of human existence since the beginning of time. Today's ever-changing tumultuous economic profile of a multi-racial and multicultural global market has accelerated the pace of change in the 21st century (Dervitsiotis, 2007). Due to technological and scientific advancements, organizations compete from a larger playing field and for higher stakes. Contemporary organizations have moved from a stable economic market to a volatile and unpredictable global market. Dervitsiotis contends that human organizations in a stable environment operate under a "business as usual" mindset (citation). Organizational leaders operating in an unstable environment are challenged to adapt new strategies to meet the needs of their constituents. In today's economic climate, leaders must decide whether to remain "as is" with a diminished capacity to adapt to change or transform their organizations to meet the demands of their workforce and stakeholders through a continuous adaptation to change (Eckel, 2008). Across the nation and the world, organizations are optimally persuaded to transform organizational cultures in response to a world-wide shifting of priorities (Eckel, 2008). Several overlapping forces are prompting organizations to re-examine their cultural structures to embrace diversity.

This chapter explores environmental forces that challenge United States future economic sustainability and growth in an expanding global market. Six organizational change models were examined as potential approaches for organizational leaders to embrace diversity and aspire to create organizations that effectively manage divergent populations. Key areas to consider when fostering change within and between organizations include: 1) determining what constitutes relevant diversity and 2) examining that diversity's values and how they differ in and between organizational cultures. Research studies indicate that the assumptions of similarities among organizational cultures and national culture are inaccurate (Hudson Highland, 2004, Mor Barack, 2010, Cox & Blake, 1991)). An organizational culture neither dominates nor erases national cultures. However, organizational cultures within multinational corporations can shape and influence national cultures. In order to effectively plan to create cultural synergy and inspire innovation among and within multicultural organizations, we must understand and accept certain cultural values. The author contends that large scale transformation efforts will be successful in proportion or relative to the amount of understanding that organization and its leaders have about the cultures within.

We have introduced six major change models and cross-cultural communications for leaders to consider in implementing change on a national and international level. The six models (teleological, evolutionary, life-cycle, dialectical, culture, social

cognition and learning organizations) present a repertoire of organizational change approaches. Leaders can develop their skills in diagnosing and managing organizational change can occur through reflecting trying and testing these myriad approaches based on their needs and situations.

REFERENCES

Adler, M. J., & Ghadar, E. (2003). Strategic human resource management. New York: Routledge Publications.

Association for the Study of Higher Education. (2001). *Theories and models of organizational change (ASHE--ERIC Higher Education Report)*. Washington, DC: John Wiley Inc.; doi:10.1002/ache.2804

ASHE-ERIC. (2003). Understanding and facilitating organizational change in the 21st century: Recent research and conceptualizations. Washington, DC: John Wiley Inc.

American Association State Colleges and Universities (AASCU). (2005). *Strengthening the science and mathematics pipeline for a better America.* Washington, DC: American Association of State Colleges and Universities. Retrieved from http://www.aascu.org

Aud, S., Rathburn, A., Flicker-Wilkinson, S., & Kristapovich, P. Wang, Zhang, J., & Notter, L. (2013). The Condition of Education. Annual Report for the National Center for Education Statistics (NCES), Institute of Education Sciences. Washington, DC: U.S. Department of Education.

Bok, D. (2006). *Our underachieving colleges: A candid look at how much students learn and why they should be learning more.* Princeton, NJ: Princeton University Press.

Bolman, L. G., & Deal, T. E. (2003). *Reframing organizations: Artistry, choice and leadership.* San Francisco, CA: Jossey Bass, Inc.

Bottaffi, G., Bacalentri, R., Braham, P., & Gindro, S. (2002). *Dictionary of race ethnicity, & culture.* New York, NY: Sage Publications.

Burke, W. W. (2010). *Organization change: Theory and practice. Foundations for Organizational Science.* Thousand Oaks, CA: Sage Publications, Inc.

Cameron, K. S., & Quinn, R. E. (2006). *Diagnosing and changing organizational culture.* San Francisco, CA: John Wiley Inc.

Cortes, C. E. (2000). Minorities Insinuating Images Influence Perceptions. Making the Media Work for You. *Media & Values.*

Chang, H., & Dodd, T. (2001). International perspectives on race & ethnicity: An annotated bibliography. *Electronic Magazine of Multicultural Education.*

Cox, T. H., & Blake, S. (1991). Managing cultural diversity: Implications for organization competitiveness. *Journal of Management Executive, 5*(3).

Deng, F. M. (1996). Identity in Africa's internal conflicts. *The American Behavioral Scientist, 40*(1), 45–46. doi:10.1177/0002764296040001007

Deng, F. M. (1997). Ethnicity: An African predicament. *The Brookings Review, 15*(3), 28–31. doi:10.2307/20080749

Dervitsiotis, K. N. (2007). On becoming adaptive: The new imperative for survival and success in the 21st century. *Total Quality Management, 18*(1-2), 21–38. doi:10.1080/14783360601043005

Dever, J. T. (1997). Reconciling educational leadership in the learning organization. *Community College Review, 25*(2), 37–63. doi:10.1177/009155219702500205

Driskill, G. W., & Brenton, A. L. (2005). *Organizational culture in action: A cultural analysis workbook.* Sage Publications, Inc.

Eckel, P., & Hartley, M. (2008). Developing academic strategic alliances: Reconciling multiple institutional cultures, policies and practice. American Council on Education. *The Journal of Higher Education, 79*(6), 613–637. doi:10.1353/jhe.0.0023

Freidman, T. L. (2006). *The world is flat: A brief history of the 21st century.* New York, NY: Farrar, Straus and Giroux.

Gordon, E., Ponticelli, R., Morgan, R. R., & Donaldson, C. (2009). *Closing the literacy gap in American business.* Westport, CT: Qutarum Books.

Hemphill, C. F., & Vanneman, A. (2011). *Achievement gaps: How Hispanic and White students in public schools perform in mathematics & reading on the National Assessment of Educational Progress (NCES 2011-459), National Center for Educational Statistics, Institute of Education Sciences.* Washington, D. C: U.S. Department of Education.

Hudson Highland Group. (2004). *The Case for diversity: Attaining global competitive advantage.* The Hudson Highland Group Thought Series.

Jimenez, L. (2014). Media, Diversity and Negative Perceptions and Assumptions. *Diversity Journal.*

Kanter, R. B. (1983). *The change masters: Innovation and entrepreneurship in the American corporations.* New York, NY: Simon and Schuster.

Kirsch, I., Brown, H., & Yanamoto, K. (2007). *America's perfect storm: Three forces changing our nation's future. Education Testing Service.* Washington, DC: U. S. Department of Education.

Kotkin, J. (2010). *The Next hundred million: American 2050.* New York, NY: Penguin Press.

Latham, J., & Vinyard, J. (2008). *Organization, diagnosis, design, and transformation.* Monfort Institute: University of North Carolina.

Levine, T. R., Sun Park, H. S., & Kim, R. K. (2007). Some Conceptual and Theoretical Challenges for Cross Cultural Communication Research in the 21st Century. *Journal of Intercultural Communication Research, 36*(3), 205–221. doi:10.1080/17475750701737140

Lerman, R. I., & Schmidt, S. R. (1999). *An overview of economic social and demographic trends affecting the U. S. labor market*. Report J-9-M-0048 prepared for the US Department of Labor, Office of the Assistant Secretary for Policy. Washington, DC: Urban Institute.

Min, P. G. (1992). A comparison of the Korean minorities in China and Japan. *International Migration Review, 26*(1), 4–21. doi:10.2307/2546934 PMID:12285045

Moldenhauser-Salazar, R. (1999). *Visions and missions: A case study of organizational change and diversity in higher education* (Doctoral Dissertation, University of Michigan). Retrieved from ProQuest Dissertations and Theses Databases (UMI: 9959824).

Mor Barack, M. E. (2010). *Managing diversity toward a global Inclusive workplace* (2nd ed.). Thousand Oaks, CA: Sage Publications.

National Academies of Science (NAS). (2007). *Rising Above the Gathering Storm: Energizing and Employing America for a Brighter Economic Future*. Retrieved from http://books.nap.edu/catalog/11613.html

National Commission on Adult Literacy. (2008, June). *Reach Higher America: Overcome Crisis in the U. S. Workforce. Report of the national Commission on Adult Literacy*. Retrieved from Council of Advancement for Adult Literary: www.nationalcommissionadultliterarcy.org

Nutini, H. G. (1997). Class and ethnicity in Mexico: Somatic and racial considerations. *Ethnology, 36*(3), 227–238. doi:10.2307/3773987

Ouchi, W. G. (1981). *Theory Z: How American business can meet the Japanese Challenge*. Reading, MA: Addison-Wesley Publishing Co.

Perez, A. D., & Hirschman, C. (2009). The changing racial and ethnic composition of the US population: Emerging American identities. *National Institutes of Health, 35*(1), 1-51. doi:10.1111/j.1728-4457.2009.00260.x

Reed, S. E. (2011). *The Diversity Index: The Alarming Truth about Diversity in Corporate America*. New York, NY: American Management Association.

Schacful, P. (2008). Cultural diversity, information, and communication: Today's impact on global virtual teams: An explanatory study. *Journal of Global Information Management, 45*(2), 131–142. doi:10.1016/j.im.2007.12.003

Schauber, A. C. (1999). *Assessing organizational climate: First step in diversifying an organization*. Doctoral Dissertation, Union Institute, UMI: 9945517

Schein, E. H. (1992). *Organizational culture and leadership: A dynamic view* (2nd ed.). San Francisco, CA: Jossey-Bass Publishers.

Schein, E. H. (1992). The role of the CEO in the management of change. In T. A. Kochan & M. Usteem (Eds.), *Transforming Organizations*. New York, NY: Oxford University Press.

Schein, E. H. (1985). How culture forms develops and changes. In R. H. Kilmann & M. J. Saxton (Eds.), *Gaining Control of Corporate Structure*. San Francisco, CA: Jossey Bass.

Scott, W. R., & Davis, G. F. (2007). *Organizations and organizing: Rational, natural and open system perspectives*. Upper Saddle, NJ: Pearson Prentice Hall.

Senge, P. M., & Drucker, P. (2006). Strategies for change leaders. Executive Forum. *Leadership Institute*. Retrieved from http://www.mendeley.com

Senge, P. M. (2006). *The fifth discipline: The art and practice of the learning organization.* New York, NY: Doubleday, Random House Inc.

Senge, P. M. (2005). *The fifth discipline: The art and practice of the learning organization.* New York, NY: Doubleday, Random House Inc.

Shrestina, L. B., & Hesler, E. J. (2011). *The Changing Demographic Profile of the United States.* CRS Report #RL32701 for United States Congress.

Smirich, L. (1985). Concepts of culture and organizational analysis. *Science Quarterly, 28,* 39-58. Retrieved from http://www.jstor.org/stable/2392246

Stam, R. (1997). *Tropical multiculturalism: A comparative history of race in Brazilian cinema and culture.* Durham, NC: Duke University Press.

Trice, H. M., & Beyer, M. R. (1993). *The culture of work organizations.* Upper Saddle, NJ: Prentice Hall.

Census, U. S. (2013). *Profile on America's workforce demographics.* Retrieved September 6, 2013, from http://quickfacts.census.html.

Van de Ven, A. H., & Poole, M. S. (1995). Explaining development and change in organizations. *Academy of Management Review, 20*(3), 510. doi:10.2307/258786

Van de Ven, A. H., & Sun, K. (2012). Breakdowns in Implementing Models of Organizational Change. *Academy of Management Journal, 50*(58-63).

Vanneman, A., Hamilton, L., Baldwin-Anderson, J., & Rahman, T. (2009). *Achievement Gaps: How Black and White Students in Public Schools Perform in Mathematics and Reading on the National Assessment of Educational Progress, (NCES 2009-455). National Center for Education Statistics, Institute of Education Sciences.* Washington, DC: U.S. Department of Education.

Varner, I., & Beamer, L. (1995). *Intercultural Communication in the Global Workplace.* Chicago, IL: Irwin Publishing Co.

KEY TERMS AND DEFINITIONS

Adaptation: The process of absorption of people from different countries and different cultures brought together as the consequences of the migration process.

Cross-Cultural Communication: Is not limited to learning other languages, but includes understanding how cultural patterns and core values impact the communication process—even when everyone is speaking English.

Culture: The body of knowledge of and manners acquired by an individual; the shared customs, values, and beliefs which characterize a given social group, and which characterize a given social group, and passed down from generation to generation.

Diversity: In the context of work/organizations, diversity is a business/employment term originating in the late 1900s, referring to the quality of a workforce (and potentially a group of users/customers or audience) as defined by its mixture of people according to ethnicity, race, religion, disability, gender, sexuality, age, etc.

Enculturation: The assimilation of the contents, practices, and values of the cultural traditions of a group by the individual belonging to the group.

Equality: The need to insure that the interests and desires of all have equal rights and opportunities.

Ethnicity: Defines people's membership in a group, its centrality to the human experience and identity; and a sense of oneness that incorporates languages, religion, and demarcations.

Innovation: The introduction of new ideas, goods, etc., or new methods of production - a new way of doing something. To be called an innovation, an idea must be replicable at an economical cost and must satisfy a specific need.

Leadership: A person or number of people responsible for leading a team or group of people, usually in some sort of organized body or company, or the direction of a smaller team in a specific project or situation.

Organization: An established place of business whose products or services are developed for profit for the organization.

Organizational Culture: Organizations that has its unique language, artifacts, values, celebrations, heroes, history and norms.

Performance: A scheme set up in the workplace in which the organization obtains revenue according to how well its members perform in their job.

Race: A person's physical appearance, such as skin color, eye color, hair color, bone/jaw structure etc. linked to the scientific notion of a phenotype.

Chapter 3
Organizational Leadership and Health Care Reform

T. Ray Ruffin
University of Phoenix, USA & Colorado Technical University, USA & University of Mount Olive, USA & Wake Technical Community College, USA

Joyce Marie Hawkins
Wake Technical Community College, USA

D. Israel Lee
Southern Illinois University, USA & University of Phoenix, USA

ABSTRACT

Policies, health, and government regulations affect various Health Care organizations and their members. One such policy, the Health Information Technology for Economic and Clinical Health (HITECH) Act, attempts to improve the performance of health care systems through the use of technology, such as Electronic Health Records (Bluementhal, 2010). The most critical task of leadership is to establish a mindset at the top of the organization and function to infuse a culture of excellence throughout the organization (Bentkover, 2012). Health organizations can only progress if their members share a set of values and are single-mindedly committed to achieving openly defined objectives (Bentkover, 2012). This chapter investigates organizational leadership in relation to health care reforms to include trends in health care leadership, Stratified Systems Theory (SST), Systems Thinking, and regulators perspectives. The chapter will consist of the following sections: background; issues controversies, and problems; solutions and recommendation; future research directions; and conclusion.

INTRODUCTION

Researchers emphasize the significance of organizational leadership. Others talk about being central to the fulfillment of firms especially for industries such as health care that are international and vibrant worldwide (Chathoth & Olsen, 2002). Policies, health, and government regulations affect various Health Care organizations and their members. The Health Information Technology for Economic and Clinical Health (HITECH) Act of 2009, attempts to improve the performance of

DOI: 10.4018/978-1-4666-9970-0.ch003

health care systems through the use of technology, such as Electronic Health Records (EHRs) (Bluementhal, 2010). Technology is an important tool for health plans to provide better care and quality assurance. Regulators closely monitor health plans, such as the Department of Managed Health Care (DMHC), the Centers for Medicare & Medicaid Services (CMS), Independent Medical Reviewers (IMR), and the National Committee of Quality Assurance (NCQA), and other independent entities (IMRhelp & DMCH, 2015). These regulators are constantly looking at electronic data and regulating health plans' performance. Based in health care reports and audits results, the outcomes reflect quality assurance for members to assure overall compliance. The HITECH Act is focused on health organizations using certified EHRs. The HITECH Act was enacted to expand the federal government's ability to establish a national electronic patient records system by 2014 (APA Practice Organization, 2014). According to the requirements of the Patient Protection and Affordable Care Act (PPACA), this deadline not been met. Therefore, organizations are to comply with the Act and are in a situation of influx that has to be addressed (ACA, 2015).

The HITECH Act of 2009 has the ability to involve health consumers, hospitals in their own care, and connect entire communities into more patient self-awareness. Leadership is critical for transforming these challenges into opportunities. Some of the opportunities would promote preventive care at an affordable price, rather than paying higher premiums, depending in an individual's health care needs. The most critical task of leadership is establishing a mindset at the top of the organization and functioning to infuse a culture of excellence throughout the organization (Bentkover, 2012). Health care organizations progress if they treat their members with integrity, value, and are single-mindedly committed to achieve openly a defined objective for better health (Bentkover,

2012). This chapter investigates organizational leadership in relation to health care reforms to include trends in health care leadership, Stratified Systems Theory (SST), Systems Thinking, and regulators perspectives. The chapter will consist of the following sections: background; issues controversies, and problems; solutions and recommendation; future research directions; and conclusion. This will enhance the field of research on effective communication, leadership and conflict resolution and society in general.

BACKGROUND

Prior to 1994, the standards were comprised of chapters on management, governance, regulators, medical staff, and nursing services. Basically, each division in the health organization essentially had their own standards. These standards were based on individual divisions; and all related policies and procedures complied with that division (Schyve, 2009). Essentially each division was operating as an organizational silo for the good of that individual division's, governance, accountability, ethical conduct. These regulators have their own threshold languages (SB853) that cover about 20 different languages. However, the languages covered are primarily Spanish and Chinese in health care (Wu, 2015). These threshold languages are anticipated to guarantee the success of the division and better patient understanding (Schyve, 2009).

The Joint Commission pursued the guidance from the country's foremost healthcare management experts and clinical leaders to redesign this division-by-division. One of the main themes discovered was that healthcare organization should not be viewed as a corporation of divisions and should be considered a system that provide quality of care among patient care (Schyve, 2009). A system is a mixture of internal policies, national policies, federal policies, procedures, individuals, and assets that work together to accomplish the common goal for better patient care and HITECH 2009 (Schyve, 2009).

With this in mind, information management in health organizations use of oral, electronic, and written communications to connect health care providers, patients, and family members. As organizations move into a patient and family-centered approach to health care, effective communication will prove to be the best approach for patient and family members. Schyve (2007) suggests it is essential to recognize the patient's standpoint and to include the patient in the management plan in order for it to be effective. However, in order for a provider and/or a family member to act as a legal representative for a patient, an Appointment of Representation (AOR) form must be complete and on file. The AOR must have the patient's signature to act on his or her behalf (DMHC, 2015). Senate Bill 853 (SB 853) was enacted to bolster improved patient care through active discussion with patients' for better patient communication and translation in different languages at no cost (Wu, 2015). Without this provision, attempting to provide health care could be problematic for the patient, precluding access to, and interfering with quality of care.

Evidence-based practice must be merged into a restructure of the work processes of the system or subsystem of which it is to be a part. Case in point, it is more operationally effective to integrate a language clarification service into a restructured work processes in the Emergency Room (ER) to ensure a language barrier does not impede providing necessary services to a person whose primary or only language is Chinese. Here, it is clear, using the SB853 is better than using existing system of operations. This integration will be smooth and efficient without disturbing others' work processes (Schyve, 2007). In the absence of this process, patients use the Urgent Care services to save money and higher hospital co-payments, also saving money to health plans. Creating a systems approach to generating patient

safety is a major goal of health organizations, which allows leadership to be involved and make better profit decisions (Schyve, 2009). The need for efficiency in the processes facing health organizations is substantial pressure to implement Health Information Technology (HIT) systems.

Health organizations, such as larger hospitals located in urban and rural areas, are constantly coaching their provider affiliates, urgent care facilities, and other vendors in the implementation of EHRs (Jha, DesRoches, Campbell, Donelan, Rao, Ferris, Shields, Rosebaun, & Blumental, 2009). The EHR applications have to be certified to fulfill the federal government's definition of "meaningful use" or risk significant financial penalties. To offset the pressure and cut the cost of every hospital in the United States, the government has provided avenues for access to the additional finances for larger facilities. Making hospitals eligible for more funds to purchase and incorporate EHRs works to increase the viability of the institution (Bau, 2011).

Utilization of HIT technology would signal efficient, safe, and higher quality of care. There are no reliable estimates of the occurrences of adoption of EHRs of hospital in the United States (Jha et al, 2009). In 2014, research found approximately 38% of eligible hospitals achieved meaningful use EHR implementation by the end of 2012 (Diana, Harle, Huerta, Ford, & Menachemi, 2014). Concurrently, 61% of the facilities provided some type of EHR status in the 2012 survey. According to Diana, Harle, Huerta, Ford, and Menachemi (2014), 38% of these facilities still remain with meaningful use EHRs. Hospital adopting incentives were different and had unique characteristics for profits status, and better techniques in membership. The facilities receiving incentives were located in urban areas, joint Commission-accredited for teaching, and larger facilities.

The HITECH Act of 2009 is driving fundamental market and industry changes that health organizations need to be strategically poised to implement health care reforms. It is essential to health organizations' leaderships to have characteristics that support nourishing a competitive advantage in an international and vibrant atmosphere. The responsibility of scale and complexity is necessary for changes and leadership demands to occur. Using robotic facility care and a robotic quality assurance monitoring plan will be essential to embrace change and holding everyone accountable. Technology can only assist in the necessary changes to the health care system; it does not initiate large scale change.

MAIN FOCUS OF ORGANIZATIONAL LEADERSHIP AND HEALTH CARE REFORM

Organizational leadership is a two-fold management tactic—one that works in the direction of what is best for individuals; the other for what is best for a group as a whole (TDK Technologies, 2015). It is also an approach and a work ethic that enables an individual to lead from the top, middle, or bottom of a health care organization (TDK Technologies, 2015). When describing and discussing leadership requirements are to lead an effective organization, it is imperative to look at leadership competencies. It is also the opportunity to look for potential challenges of the organization's innovations. Leadership competencies are talents and activities that lends to greater performance (Society for Human Resource Management, 2015). These competencies are crafting a distinctive leadership brand via capabilities that yield results for stakeholders. These processes can also be used by organizations to gain a competitive advantage and strategic innovation for patient care (SHRM, 2015). Investigators at the Center for Creative Leadership have recognized vital leadership competencies that are constant among organizations. They split the total structure into competencies for leading the organization, leading the self and leading others in the organization (Society for Human Resource Management, 2015) and DMHC, NCQA, IMR (IMRhelp & DMHC, 2015), regulators. These are shown in the Table 1:

At its staple, performance improvement processes spawn Quality Improvement (QI), a team process. In the correct conditions, a team couples the knowledge, skills, experience, and viewpoints

Table 1., Developmental assignments: Creating learning experiences without changing jobs. Greensboro, N.C.: Center for Creative Leadership Press Adapted from (McCauley, 2006)

Leading the Organization:	Leading the Self:	Leading Others:
Managing Change	Demonstrating ethics and integrity	Communicating effectively
Solving problems and decision making	Displaying drive and purpose	Developing others
Managing politics and influencing others	Exhibiting leadership stature	Valuing diversity and difference
Taking risks and innovating	Increasing your capacity to learn	Building and maintaining relationships
Setting vision and strategy	Managing yourself	Managing effective teams and work groups
Managing the work	Increasing self-awareness	Leading with efficiency
Enhancing business skills and adding knowledge	Developing adaptability	Implementing new government and cultural strategies
Understanding and navigating the organization	Practicing ethical standards	Leading with integrity

of different individuals within the team to make lasting improvements. A team approach is most effective when:

1. The process or system is complex.
2. No one person in an organization knows all the dimensions of an issue.
3. The process involves more than one discipline or work area.
4. Solutions require creativity.

The role of a health care organization and the leadership implementations are to sustain continuous performance improvement, as it is essential to patient-centered care. Leadership and change-management strategies, comprised of patient, staff, chair-side chats, and clinician board engagement are effective ways to reinforce the foundation for patient-centered care (Frampton, Guastell, Brady, Hale, Horowitz, Bennett Smith, et al., 2008). The purpose of these communication approaches are the direct contacts they afford between management, frontline staff, regulators, and patients (Australian Commission on Safety and Quality in Health Care, 2010). Continuous improvement necessitates a transformation from the way health care organizations have customarily provided care. Health care Organization leadership must improve and devise strategies and processes for connecting patients. This is especially important for families and health care professionals in their own care and, at a best service level, in procedure, program, and quality improvement/assurance. Leadership has to be involved with patient safety inventiveness and healthcare strategy (Australian Commission on Safety and Quality in Health Care, 2010).

Trends in Health Care Leadership

The current health care trends have changed; they tend to be more complex, unpredictable, and volatile. The leadership skills have also changed and require leaders to adapt to change and possess critical thinking abilities for organizational decision making. The "methods currently used to change leadership have not changed much" (Petrie, 2014, p. 5). Management strategies such as mentoring, coaching, and training remain important. Leaders have a major challenge in these areas, as they are not developing quickly enough to adapt to the new environment. The future challenge is not simply leading, but how to grow bigger in the leadership role. Managers seem to become more adaptive to a leadership role of their own development.

Leadership needs to concentrate on the current challenges and environments in building leadership in an unpredictable world. More developed "exploration of leadership development trends and emerging applications of leadership that could shape the basis of subsequent developmental programs" (Petrie, 2014. p. 5). Therefore, a leadership style that focuses more in common goals, rather than a single leadership development style, will prove to be of greater value and utility. Simple programs or existing models appear to be insufficient for providing high-level leadership to address the unpredictable requirements of leadership demands. A fast pace innovative methodology will be needed for health care organizations to meet needs the culturally diverse and inclusive environment of the workplace. Petrie (2014) suggested under normal circumstances "businesses that embrace change are better prepared for the future, than those that avoid or resist change" (p. 5). Kahn (2015) stated that the 21st century requires a paradigm shift in healthcare. Leaders and professionals need to prepare to lead with empathy, work in teams, and apply emotional intelligence in the workplace. Petrie (2014) posits thinking out of the box for new improvements and to build programs based on critical thinking and assumptions. When making assumptions one must consider the following questions:

1. What are the current healthcare strategies that could be most effective in this field?
2. What needs to be done regarding the development emphasis in health care leadership?

3. What a health plan needs to minimize, do more, or stop doing?

4. What is the goal/ vision for health care leadership development in the future?

Petrie (2014) explains "technology is a huge infrastructure and a driven change in this case" (p. 5). Normally, businesses that embrace change will do great in the future, than those that avoid the change (p. 5). Nevertheless, leadership is not a "one size fits all" approach; frequently, leaders must become accustomed to their approach to fit the circumstances (Mind Tools Ltd, 2015). Therefore, a fast pace innovation demand will be needed in health care organizations. Organizations need to be prepared to try new approaches that will create a cultural and diverse change to share with subordinates and clients. Kahn (2015) stated that the 21st century calls for a healthcare paradigm shift and innovation demands. Leaders and professionals need to prepare to lead with empathy, work with teams, and apply emotional intelligence in the workplace. Staff commitment and buy-in are needed (U.S. Department of Health and Human Services, 2011).

Whether a health care organization is attempting to improve patient wait times or telephone service, it helps a team strengthen an organization to attain enduring improvements (U.S. Department of Health and Human Services, 2011). Leadership stereotypically delivers inspiration, objectives, operational oversight, and other administrative services to a health organizational business. This leaves the prospect of the United States being reliant to an extent to its leadership capabilities. History reveals that empires have been erected and crumbled due to inoperative and fragile leadership respectively (Rao, 1991). To investigate organizational leadership in relations to health care reforms it is imperative to understand and include Stratified Systems Thinking and Systems Thinking.

Stratified Systems Theory (SST)

Stratified Systems Theory (SST) is a formative theory associated to strategic leadership and organizational hierarchy. This involves a bureaucracy that serves as a vital structure for understanding the prominence of cognitive capability of strategic leaders (Browning Leadership Model, 2013). Established by Elliott Jaques, SST concentrates on a person's cognitive ability and capacity to reason over an explicit period of time. The SST is designed to deliberate through multifaceted and collaborative structures of cause and effect (Browning Leadership Model, 2013). A fundamental concept in the development of executive-level leaders is the changing nature of performance requirements at the organizational level of leadership (National Defense University, 1997).

There are three broadly defined strata of leaders in most large-scale organizations: the top-level (strategic), the mid-level (organizational), and the lower-level (production or action-oriented). Relatively inexperienced leaders are at the lower level of responsibility; their responsibility for the success of the organization is limited; therefore, they are action-oriented. They have little latitude in the decisions they make, procedures they use, and the degree of innovation they can employ. Lower-level leaders may improvise, but rarely innovate because, at their level of leadership, consistency of action is important. The mid-level leader is responsible for establishing intermediate goals, directing and developing plans, procedures, and processes used by the lower-level leaders. Plans, policies and procedures, and specified processes are major tools for coordinating effort, particularly in large-scale organizations with many independent parts. The mid-level leaders are also responsible for prioritizing missions and allocating resources to tailor capability at the lower levels. This includes supervising resource allocation plans that implement concepts developed at higher levels, as in the Department of Defense's Planning, Programming, Budgeting, and Execution Systems. The term "strategic" implies broad scale and scope, to a vision extending over very long time spans-in some cases out to fifty years or more. Strategic leadership and decision making is a process by which those responsible for large scale organizations. The set long-term directions and obtain, through consensus building, the support of constituencies necessary f or the commitment of resources. The following regulators are involved in any strategic change in patient care, the DMHC, IMR, NCQA, and CMS. These regulators have a common goal to improve lives in health care, employment, child care, and to manage innovative health. In which allow human service programs to strength communities, and transform lives in a better healthy environment (IMRhelp & DMHC, 2015).

These regulators are focused on research accomplished with senior Army officers and government (Zaccaro, 2001). Elliot Jaques and Owen Jacobs argued that leadership in enormous portion necessitates a greater cognitive ability and creative problem-solving process (Zaccaro, 2001). Through the use of SST, the research available supports this assertion. Understanding that as a person moves up in an organizational leadership hierarchy, problem types and resolutions selection becomes complicated and ambiguous. This organizational leadership environment necessitates a multifaceted cognitive capacity at each level of leadership and a more profound need at the higher levels of leadership. Jaques and Jacobs recognized seven stages or strata of organizational work. As a leader moves to an advanced level, the leader added novel value at that level (Browning Leadership Model, 2013). They clustered these seven stages in three stratums, reflecting strategic, organizational or general management, and tactical supervision (Browning Leadership Model, 2013). The top two stratums reflected ancillary leadership and the bottom layer reflected direct

leadership. Table 2 displays an overview of SST for a large -scale organization.

If there is a single, "most important" theme in SST, it is that "cognitive power" is astonishingly important. The critical tasks associated with higher organizational levels are simply more difficult than those experienced at lower organizational levels. Mastering them necessitates a threshold of proficiency to understand complexity, and that threshold level increases by level. This has significant implications for succession planning and leader development (Jacobs & Clemet, 2013). Presently, health care organization should not anticipate a competitive advantage, unless it can recognizes fledgling leaders with advanced leadership potential and provide them with responsible and opportunity before they are needed (Jacobs & Clemet, 2013). An assessment process pioneered by Gillian Stamp at Brunel University enables early identification of high potential in future leaders (Jacobs & Clemet, 2013). As part of the assessment process at one of the Joint/Senior Service Colleges, Jacobs and Clement (2013) developed:

1. **Concept Formation:** One part of the assessment is a concept formation task. People differ in how they approach the task. Some strategies are more effective than others. Rapid trial and error is much less effective than stopping to think more holistically about the task. This is a self-awareness dimension that appears critical to successful performance at the highest organizational levels.

2. **Curiosity and Openness to New Experience:** A second key part of the assessment is a measure of attraction to complexity and innovation. Most of our high-capacity general officers were interested in a broader range of topics beyond the military. They spent a lot of time "exploring" and their enhanced awareness frequently aided the performance of primary tasks.

Table 2. Level of Organizational Stratification Proposed by Stratified Systems Theory (SST) Adapted from (Zaccaro, 2001)

| | | | Type of Unit with Civil Service an Business Correlates | | | Task Requirements and Characteristics | | | |
| | | | | | | | Scope of Work | | SST Time Span of work |
Stratum	Domain	Rank/Grade	Military	Civil Service	Business	System Resources and Policy Task Requirement	Number of Subordinates	Sphere of Influence	
VII	Indirect	General	Unified or Specified Command	Cabinet Secretary	C-Level	Creates integrate complex systems; organize acquisition of major resources; create policy	500,0000-1,000,000	International	20+ Years
VI	Strategic Systems	Lieutenant General	Corps	Deputy Secretary	Group	Oversee directly operation of subordinate divisions; allocate resource; apply policy	50,000-60,000	National	10-20 Years
V	Organizational/ Operational	Major General	Division	Under Secretary	Full DMS	Direct operation of complex systems; allocate assigned resources; implement policy	11,000-12,000	Regional	5-10Years
IV		Brigadier General	Separate Brigade	Assistant Secretary	Medium Sized Business	Direct operation of systems; organize resources allocations to interdependent subordinate, programs and subsystems policy	5000	Sector	4-7 Years
		Colonel	Division Brigade				2,500	10-15 KM	
III	Direct	Lieutenant Colonel/ Sergeant Major	Battalion	Principal Staff	One-Man Business or Unit	Develop execute plans and tasks; organize subsystems; priorities, resources ; translate and implement policy and assigned missions	500-600	4,000-5,000 M	1+ Years
		Major	Battalion ORT Level				100-200	1500 M	
II	Tactical/ Command	Captain First Sergeant	Company Platoon	Assistant Principal	Section	Supervise direct performance of subsystems; anticipate solve real time problems; shift resources; translate and implement policy	3-40		3+ Months
I		Lieutenant NCO	NCO's And Ors	Office Supervisor	Supervisor	Direct performance of work; use practical judgement to solve ongoing problems			Less than 5 Months

3. **Reflective Awareness:** This is fundamental to learning from experience. The top-level generals were more reflective than the others. The Center for Creative Leadership at Greensboro, NC, found much the same thing in their study of executives. The developmental implication is that organizations should "grow" managers and leaders by encouraging reflective analysis of experience. (p. 203-204).

Systems Thinking

According to Rouse (2015) system thinking can be defined as an approach that contrasts with traditional analysis, which study systems by breaking them down into their separate elements (para 1). System thinking is used in any area of research and to the study of medical, environmental, political, cultural, religious, economic, and educational systems (para. 1). Leaders maneuver in an environment of ambiguity and overwhelming density. Problems are no longer simple; they are complex and at times with no clear answers. These types of problems have required a novel approach to the thinking process for effective leaders to maintain success (Reed, 2006), problems have to be viewed differently. From this perspective, it is easier to introduce a new system, rather than attempting to retrofit an existing system into the situation for which the approach may initiate inefficient, ineffective, and frustratingly slow processes. Sociologist Robert K. Merton coined the phrase "goal displacement" to define conforming to rigid procedures becoming the goal, rather than looking at the whole organization (Reed, 2006). The world was imagined by theorists such as Isaac Newton, as having the features of a clock. The mechanisms of the clock could be understood by the progression of exploration and the methodical method (Reed, 2006).

According to Reed (2006) the fundamental premise is: Identify a system. After all, not all things are systems. Some systems are simple and predictable, while others are complex and dynamic. A common indication of a non-system thinking leader is one who takes unwise risks, and demands ease and certainty in a difficult situation. The effective systems thinker leader maintains focus on the organization as a whole, and at the same time understands the interworking's of the systems of that constitute the organization. Effective leaders using "system thinking" is essential to the success of a healthcare organization (Schyve, 2009).

Regulatory Perspectives

Regulations are orders prescribed by authority to regulate conduct (Meriam Webster.com, 2014). The correlation of relations in health care, are health care reforms (e.g., PPACA and Health Care and Education Reconciliation Act of 2010). These regulations are the most extensive change in the United States healthcare system, since the passage of the Medicare and Medicaid in the mid-1960s (Penno, 2014). The HITEACH Act gives Health and Human Services (HHS) the authority to write regulations (U.S. Department of Health & Human Services, 2014). The HHS has a Regulatory Agenda that is published in the Autum and Spring of each year; its purpose is to regulate the development of a national health information technology infrastructure. Areas under the regulatory control of the HHS include the Affordable Care Act, Health Information Privacy, and Human Research protection regulations (HHS.gov, 2014).

The Affordable Care Act works as a conditional tax for Americans who do not purchase insurance coverage. Under this provision, those who do not have coverage will be taxed approximately $60 per month for Bronze coverage—the minimal and least expensive coverage under the act. If this insurance plan is not affordable, exemptions are built into the provision to assist individual in unique financial circumstances (Friedman & Becker, 2012). The Centers for Medicare and Medicaid Services (CMS) created the "Duals Program" to assist patients with chronic illnesses, and who have low income. The Duals Program is designed for patents in need of specialty services that other Medicare members do not need. The program is a combination of Medicare-Medicaid and Prescription Drug. The benefits include a number of services such as home services, cleaning, grooming, self-care, cooking, and other great services to improve someone's life (Centers for Medicare and Medicaid Services [CMS.GOV], 2013). Therefore, the PPACA may be advantageous for members who do not have insurance and low income. The Duals Program may be advantageous for those who are in the need of unique critical care, limited income, and no another means for financial assistance.

ORGANIZATIONAL LEADERSHIP AND HEALTH CARE REFORM ISSUES, CONTROVERSIES, PROBLEMS

Governments, societies, and actions with the major intent to endorse, renovate, or uphold health as defined by the World Health Organization (WHO) is a health system (Bloland, Simone, Burkholder, Slutsker, & De Cock, 2012). Public health is a hazardous part of the grander concept of health systems. Public health and has been defined as "what we as a society do collectively to assure the conditions in which people can be healthy" (Committee for the Study of the Future of Public Health IoM, 1988, para. 1). The United States (U.S.) health care system can be said to have numerous systems that operate independently and collaboratively as the situation dictates (Rice, 2013). To appreciate this concept, it is imperative to understand the U.S. public health infrastructure. The infrastructure includes three key goals: A capable and qualified workforce, up-to-date data and information systems, and public health agencies capable of assessing and responding to public health needs (HealthyPeople.gov, 2010).

By the year 2020, there is expected to be a deficit of 250,000 public health workers, a significant number of this population will be retiring members of the corporate suite. These executives will take with them experience, knowledge, and work ethic that is sorely needed in the workplace. According to Grimm, Johansson, Nayar, Apenteng, Opoku, and Nguyen (2015), the average age of a state public employee is 47 years; the average age of a health department executive is 53 years. Critical to this discussion understands that individuals in each of the aforementioned instances are at or past the age to retire from their current position. The Association of Schools and Programs of Public Health (ASPPH) suggests that colleges and universities, which graduate learners from the schools of Public Health and Human Services, would have to graduate and train "three times the current graduate to meet the projected shortfalls" of public health workers (para. 3). An additional challenge for the health care system will be ensuring the incoming executive structure is culturally adapted to deal with the inclusive nature of the future. With the largest population of the U.S. being Hispanic/Latino and Asian, the leadership will have to be bi-lingual, preferably, multi-lingual, and culturally aware and sensitive to the needs of this demographic. Concomitantly, leaders, technicians, and general labor workers in mid-level positions in the health care system will require a level of proficiency to meet the needs of the patients "at the door". To meet this need, health care practitioners will be required to possess leadership skills for the required disciplines (e.g., respiratory therapy, phlebotomy, dental hygienist...etc.) and linguistic prowess to help the target clients.

In every area the health care system there is mid-level of responsibility critical the success of the health care organizations. McLarty and McCartney (2009) reported, "discretionary decision-making is common at the point of care on matters that impact day-to-day operations" (para. 13). Therefore, it is essential that personnel who may be making decisions be optimally trained and equally functioning in this mid-level position of responsibility. Unfortunately, the person or people normally situated to provide the training may be absent or retired. Concurrently, there are other traits needed for mid-level leadership that cannot be taught, but must be modeled—empathy, approachability, and emotional intelligence. These affective habits are indispensable when providing services for the public, especially in health care. Many of the people coming into the health care system of Spanish-speaking and Asian in origin who's English mastery is under-developed; in this case, patience, empathy, and emotional intelligence are a priori.

Title VI of the Civil Rights Act of 1964 requires personnel in Health and Human Services to provide services for all people regardless of race, color, or national origin. Consistent with this requirement, state governments are mandating cultural competency training and education in medical and nursing schools (Hoffman, 2011). Ensuring that mid-level leaders and supervisors are equipped with these essential tools, allow the health care facility the opportunity to meet the needs of the patients, boost the morale of service providers, and enhance the work performance of all employees (Hoffman, 2011).

The quantum advancement in information technology has allowed the health care industry to make significant improvements in the type and quality of care that facility may provide. Nano-technology allows physicians to access patient information at the blink of an eye, translate prescriptions measures and doses with a few keystrokes, and reach other colleagues for operations without breaking the stride of an operation. Tactical and strategic enterprises of the health care industry using IT stand the probability of making substantial change in the way business is conducted in the health care space (Wager, Lee, & Glaser, 2013). However, wisdom warns, when introducing "new" technology into an organization, caution, and humility is required.

In introducing "new" technology into a health organization, it is imperative to remember that until the technology is relatively interwoven into the infrastructure of the organization, it could be problematic. Wager, Lee, and Glaser (2013) suggest that when introducing new technology into an environment, micro-projects should be undertaken. Through this process, the learning curve of familiarization with the technology can occur without far-reaching negative impacts of mistakes (that are a part of the learning process) will be frustrating for the patients and equally frustrating and embarrassing for the practitioners. As technology has becomes normalized in the workplace, comfort with processes, and changes will coalesce into a high functioning facility.

SOLUTIONS AND RECOMMENDATIONS

There is a necessity for collective approaches encompassing health care for patients and their family members. This is including but not limited to managing care, accentuating value, and monitoring quality of care outcomes. This is digitally linked so that patient-provider-caregiver teams have complete, shared patient information and access to pertinent medical research and care protocols (Bentkover, 2012). Research increasingly associates patient learning and engagement to improved health outcomes, lower costs and an enriched care experience. Patient associations include reduced cost and better quality of care. The HITECH Act of 2009 supports health care quality improvement and cost reductions. This falls in line with the Patient Protection and Affordable Care Act (PPACA). The PPACA was designed to reduce the large number of under and uninsured people in the U. S. by mandating that individuals obtain health insurance.

An example is the required functions of EHRs being aligned to requirements for emerging models of health care delivery improvement, including patient-centered medical homes. According to Bau (2011) Accountable Care Organizations (ACO) is a term "used for health care providers, who emphasize partnerships between patients and their physicians" (p. 1). The HITECH Act of 2009 has the ability to involve patients and health consumers in their own care, even enthuse entire communities into more patient self-awareness. Campbell (2000) denotes the organization's external atmosphere as being the source in terms of the actions taken by leadership, while setting standards of performance. Expectations are a direct result of the influence of the external environment on the health organization.

The leadership must have "alignment of expectations around a small set of core values and ideals that define the organization's culture, such as service, innovation, teamwork, and achievement" (Campbell, 2000, p. 63). Public Health Institutes (PHIs) are non-profit organizations that increase the public's health by modernization. Public health Institutes are leveraging resources, and building partnerships across sectors, including government agencies, communities (National Network of Public Health Institutes, 2010). Health System Strengthening (HSS) has become a major focus of the U. S. (Bloland, et al, 2012). The Role of Public Health Institutions in Global Health System Strengthening is critical in achieving major health goals in preventive care in the community. Health care can be provided through public and private sectors and providers.

Public health care is usually provided by the government through national healthcare systems. Private health care can be provided through "for profit" hospitals and self-employed practitioners, and "not for profit" non-government providers, including faith-based organizations (Basu, Andrews, Kishore, Panjabi, Stuckler, 2012). The financial impact can be severe for uninsured families that struggle financially to meet basic needs and medical bills can quickly lead to medical debt (Kaiser Family Foundation, 2013). Normally, health care services would be offered through

employers. Conversely, not everyone can afford health care market coverage. Many companies have amended hours to permit them not to have to offer health insurance to full time employees. This has made some Americans unable to afford coverage on their own through the market. Since, some American have not bought their insurance, they have been penalized by the government yearly for not signing up through PPACA (Kaiser Family Foundation, 2013).

The scale and density of compulsory changes demands for leaders, who are able to identify weaknesses. Leaders need to articulate a vision for the future, lay out a path, enthuse change and embrace the overall health organization responsibility (Bentkover, 2012). Adopt new technologies for accumulating and employing clinical data to advance performance at the point of care. Technology can only expedite enormous scale changes. Organizational leadership is an essential agent for transforming these challenges into opportunities. Incremental changes are deficient to achieve the goal of delivering higher quality care at a reasonable rate. It is clear that citizens need health care's stakeholders to commit to forming a cohesive, patient-centered system that embraces continuous improvement, promotes teamwork and transparency (Bentkover, 2012).

Due to the complexity of health care, multidisciplinary teams and strategies are essential. Multidisciplinary teams from participating centers/units need to work closely together, taking advantage of communication strategies such as face-to-face meetings, conference calls, and dedicated e-mail, List- Serv applications, and utilize the guidance of trained facilitators and expert faculty throughout the process of implementing change initiatives when possible (R. Bucci, personal communication, April, 15, 2015). Leaders in the health care industry must be able to balance governance and accountability and use a common language, when instilling a culture of quality and safety. Health organizations can capture a plethora of wisdom and talent through systems thinking and use it to solve complex issues and reduce risk factors in health care sectors (R. Bucci, personal communication, April, 15, 2015).

For instance, the CCL works with numerous organizations and over 20,000 leaders from roughly 100 countries yearly (CCL, 2015). Through researching the needs of the health care organization business needs, CCL strategizes and provides wide-ranging leadership strategy and execution (CCL, 2015). Through the use of state-of-the-art strategy design and cutting-edge development programs to ongoing support and evaluation resources, CCL offers proven solutions for an all-inclusive range of individual and health organizational challenges (CCL, 2015).

FUTURE RESEARCH DIRECTIONS

There needs to be further research into the area of Emotional Intelligence (EI) and the role it plays in the decision making process for health care. According to Mayer, Caruso and Salovey (2004), EI is the capacity to reason about emotions, and of emotions to enhance thinking. Emotional Intelligence "includes the abilities to accurately perceive emotions, to access emotions, and generate emotions" (p. 267). Based on the assumption that EI is "to assist thought, to understand emotions and emotional knowledge, and to reflectively regulate emotions so as to promote emotional and intellectual growth" (p. 267).

Intelligence "refers to the capacity to reason validly about information" (University of New Hampshire, 2012, p. 1). The term emotional intelligence in this fashion is consistent with scientific literature in the fields of intelligence, personality psychology, and emotions presented by Sternberg (2000). The four branch model of emotional intelligence designates four zones of abilities that together style numerous areas of emotional intelligence (Mayer & Salovey, 1997). More specifically, this model defines emotional intelligence as involving the abilities to:

- Accurately perceive emotions in one-self and others.
- Use emotions to facilitate thinking.
- Understand emotional meanings.
- Manage emotions.

The four-branch model represents what today is called the ability model of emotional intelligence. The branches are organized from the areas explicitly connected to the emotions-area (perceiving emotions) to the area's general to personality (managing emotions) (University of New Hampshire, 2015). Inside each branch, abilities can be recognized that are early-developing (e.g., in childhood) and abilities that await more development (University of New Hampshire, 2015). University of Toronto (2013) study suggested "an emotionally intelligent approach to making decisions is if one is feeling anxious, because of something unrelated to the decisions, to not make the decisions right away" (p. 1). Based on the study by University of Toronto (2013) found that "learning to pay attention only to those feelings that are relevant to the decisions being made is what counts" (p. 1).

National Defense University (1997) research led to a vital question: "Is the leader of the future going to control technology or is the technology going to control the leader?" (p. 1).

What will be the new demands and pressures placed on senior leaders of the future?

- How can leaders hope to cope with this "permanent white water" environment?
- How can leaders absorb and use the vast amounts of information needed for the complex, fast moving, decision making environment?
- Do leaders know that they have the cognitive skills required to process massive amounts of information for competent decision making in the strategic environment (National Defense University, 1997, p. 1 Chapter 3)?

Leading Continuous Change explains the "4Ds" (Discovering, Deciding, Doing, and Discerning) structure for a new mindset that assists leaders with leading continuous change more successfully. Keen leaders know that today's pressures for change come from all directions and rarely come from one direction at a time (CCL, 2015). Leaders need to understand:

- Understand how leading complex, continuous change is different and therefore requires a different approach than leading one simple change at a time.
- Apply the "4D" framework that lays out the four actions and four accompanying mindsets that must be adopted to lead continuous change more successfully.
- Point to examples of organizations that have succeeded or failed at undertaking complex change.
- Help prepare their organization to lead complex change successfully by using a comprehensive checklist that will be provided in the session. (CCL, 2015 para. 1).

Effective leadership builds a bridge between hope and sustainable, relevant impact. Leadership is required at all levels of society. Confronting the world's most tenacious problems in health care necessitates work at all levels, not just from at the top of the most powerful health organizations (CCL, 2015). Leadership development can meet each person where they are and open the door for transformative change (CCL, 2015. Transformational leaders have reliability and elevated emotional intelligence (EI). They motivate individuals with a collective vision of the future and they communicate well (Mind Tools Ltd, 2015). Transformational leaders normally are self-aware, genuine, and compassionate (Mind Tools Ltd, 2015). Transformational leaders convince members be responsible, because they anticipate the best in individuals, and hold themselves responsible for their actions, while simultaneously treating their members with respect and integrity (Mind Tools Ltd, 2015). This leads to high efficiency and commitment towards patient care and communication (Mind Tools Ltd, 2015). Nevertheless, leadership is not a "one size fits all" concept; frequently, leaders must adapt to their approach to fit the circumstances and must make rational decisions (Mind Tools Ltd, 2015).

CONCLUSION

This chapter investigated organizational leadership in relations to health care reforms to include trends in health care leadership. The Stratified Systems Theory (SST), Systems Thinking, and regulators perspectives are included to provide different perspectives of leadership in health care. The chapter consisted of the following sections: background; main focus of the chapter, issues controversies, and problems; solutions and recommendation; and future research directions. Prior to 1994, the standards were comprised of chapters on Management, Governance, Medical Staff and Nursing Services. Basically each division in the health organization essentially had their own standards, based on the division itself (Schyve, 2009). Essentially, each division was operating as an organizational silo. The main strategies were: division, governance, accountability and their own languages of SB853 that were anticipated to guarantee the success of the division (Schyve, 2009). The Joint Commission pursued the guidance from the country's foremost healthcare management experts and clinical leaders to redesign this division by a by-division approach. One of the main themes discovered was that healthcare organization should not be viewed as a corporation of divisions and should be considered a system (Schyve, 2009). A system is a mixture of procedures, individuals, and assets that, work together, to accomplish one goal (Schyve, 2009).

Petrie (2014) explains "technology is a huge infrastructure and a driven change in this case"

(p. 5). Normally, businesses that embrace change will do great in the future, than those that avoid the changes (Petrie, 2014, p. 5). Nevertheless, leadership is not a "one size fits all" thing; frequently, leaders must become accustomed to their approach to fit the circumstances (Mind Tools Ltd, 2015). Therefore, a fast pace innovation demand will be needed in health care organizations. Organizations need to be prepared to try new approaches that will create a cultural and diverse change to share with subordinates and clients. Kahn, (2015), stated that 21st century calls for a healthcare paradigm shift and innovation demands. Leaders and professionals need to prepare to lead with empathy, work with teams, and apply emotional intelligence in the workplace. Staff commitment and buy-in are needed (U.S. Department of Health and Human Services [HRSA], 2011).

SST is a formative theory associated to strategic leadership and organizational hierarchy. This involves a bureaucracy that serves as a vital structure for understanding the prominence of cognitive capability of strategic leaders (Browning Leadership Model, 2013). Established by Elliott Jaques, SST concentrates on a person's cognitive ability and capacity to reason over an explicit period of time. The SST is designed to deliberate through multifaceted and collaborative structures of cause and effect (Browning Leadership Model, 2013). Leaders maneuver in an environment of ambiguity and overwhelming density. Problems are no longer simple they are complex and at times with no clear cut answers. This has created a new thinking process for effective leaders to maintain success (Reed, 2006).

The problem has to be viewed differently. From the system view, which have a habit of enduring, even when everything else changes. With this view it is easier to create a new system, than fixing or eliminating an old system. Sociologist Robert K. Merton devised the phrase "goal displacement" to define conforming to rigid procedures becoming the goal, rather than looking at the whole organization (Reed, 2006). The world was imagined by theorists such as Isaac Newton, as having the features of a clock. The mechanisms of the clock could be understood by the progression of exploration and the methodical method (Reed, 2006).

A fundamental concept in the development of executive-level leaders is the changing nature of performance requirements as a utility of the organizational level (National Defense University, 1997). Leaders maneuver in an environment of ambiguity and overwhelming density. Problems are no longer simply they are complex and at times with no clear cut answers. This has created a new thinking process for effective leaders to maintain success (Reed, 2006). The problem has to be viewed differently, from the system view which have a habit of enduring, even when everything else changes. With this view it is easier to create a new system, than fixing or eliminating an old system. Sociologist Robert K. Merton devised the phrase "goal displacement" to define conforming rigid procedures becoming the goal, rather than looking at the whole organization (Reed, 2006).

Regulations are orders prescribed by authority to regulate conduct (Meriam Webster.com, 2014). When it relates to health care, they are also called health care reforms. An example is the Patient Protection and Affordable Care Act (PPAC) and Health Care and Education Reconciliation Act of 2010. These are the most extensive changes of the U. S. healthcare system, since the passage of the Medicare and Medicaid in the mid-1960s (Penno, 2014). For example the HITEACH Act gives Health and Human Services (HHS) the authority to write regulations (HHS.gov, 2014). The purpose of the regulations is to regulate the development of a national health information technology infrastructure. The HHS has a Regulatory Agenda that is published each fall and spring. In the fall a regulatory plan that condenses main concerns for the year. The HHS has regulatory authority that includes: the ACA, Health Information Privacy (HIPPA) and Human Research protection regulations (HHS.gov, 2014).

Governments, societies, and actions with the major intent to endorse, renovate, or uphold health as defined by the World Health Organization (WHO) is a health system (Bloland, Simone, Burkholder, Slutsker, & De Cock, 2012). This has been defined as "what we as a society do collectively to assure the conditions in which people can be healthy" (Committee for the Study of the Future of Public Health IoM, 1988, para. 1)". The U.S. health care system can be said to have numerous systems that operate independently and collaboratively at times (Rice, 2013). It is imperative to understand the U.S. public health infrastructure, which includes 3 key goals: improvement of health. Health care creation of environments promotes good health, and promotion of healthy developments, and behaviors (HealthyPeople.gov, 2010).

There is a necessity for collective approaches encompassing patients and their family members. Involve patients and families in managing care, accentuate value and care outcomes that are digitally linked so that patient-provider-caregiver teams have complete. The shared patient information and access to pertinent medical research, and care protocols (Bentkover, 2012). Research increasingly associates patient learning and engagement to improved health outcomes, lower costs and an enriched care experience. Patient associations include reduced cost and better quality of care. The HITECH Act of 2009 supports health care quality improvement and cost reductions. This is consistent with the Patient Protection and Affordable Care Act and Duals (PPACA). The PPACA was designed to reduce the large number of under and uninsured people in the U. S. by mandating that individuals obtain health insurance. The Duals programs are for patients with chronic illnesses that may require personal aid beyond typical assistance.

Further research is needed in the area of Emotional Intelligence (EI) and the role it plays in the decision making process for providing health care. According to Mayer, Caruso and Salovey (2004), EI is the capacity to reason about emotions, and

how emotions to enhance or inhibit thinking. EI includes the "abilities to accurately perceive emotions, to access and generate emotions" (p. 267). Based on that assumption EI is "to assist thought, to understand emotions and emotional knowledge, and to reflectively regulate emotions so as to promote emotional and intellectual growth" (p. 267). The four-branch model represents what today is called the ability model of emotional intelligence. The branches are organized from the areas explicitly connected to the emotions-area (perceiving emotions) to the area's general to personality (managing emotions) (Meyers, 2012). Inside each branch, abilities can be recognized that are early-developing (e.g., in childhood) and abilities that await more development (e.g., adulthood) (Meyers, 2012).

Leading continuous change focuses on the "4Ds" (Discovering, Deciding, Doing, and Discerning) structure for a new mindset that assists leaders with leading continuous change more successfully. Keen leaders know that today's pressures for change come from all directions and rarely come from one at a time (CCL, 2015). Suggestions alone cannot initiate change. Effective leadership must build a bridge between hope and sustainable, relevant impact. Leadership is required at all levels of society. Confronting the world's most tenacious problems in health care necessitates work at all levels, not just from at the top of the most powerful health organizations (CCL, 2015). Leadership development can meet each person where they are and open the door for transformative change (CCL, 2015.

Transformational leaders have reliability and elevated emotional intelligence. They motivate individuals with a collective vision of the future, and they communicate well (Mind Tools Ltd, 2015). Transformational leaders normally are self-aware, genuine, compassionate, and unpretentious (Mind Tools Ltd, 2015). Transformational leaders motivate members because they anticipate the best in individuals; concomitantly, they hold themselves responsible for their actions (Mind

Tools Ltd, 2015). These types of leaders set vibrant goals and have equally adroit conflict-resolution skills. These leaders, mindsets, and high expectations lead to highly efficient and committed organizational environments (Mind Tools Ltd, 2015).

REFERENCES

ACA. (2015). *Affordable Care Act and Title X Program*. Retrieved October 8, 2015, from http://www.hhs.gov/opa/affordable-care-act/index.html

APA Practice Organization. (2014). *The Health Information Technology For Economic and Clinical Health Act* (HITECH Act). Retrieved September 1, 2015, from http://www.apapracticecentral.org/advocacy/technology/hitech-act.aspx

Australian Commission on Safety and Quality in Health Care (ACSQHC). (2010). *Patient-Centered Care: Improving Quality and Safety by Focusing Care on Patients and Consumers*. Discussion Paper. Retrieved September 2, 2015, from http://www.safetyandquality.gov.au/wp-content/uploads/2012/01/PCCC-DiscussPaper.pdf

Basu, S., Andrews, J., Kishore, S., Panjabi, R., & Stuckler, D. (2012). Comparative Performance of Private and Public Healthcare Systems in Low- and Middle-Income Countries: A Systematic Review. *PLoS Medicine, 9*(6), e1001244. doi:10.1371/journal.pmed.1001244 PMID:22723748

Bau, I. (2011). Connected for health: The potential of health information and communications technologies to reduce health care disparities. *National Civic Review, 100*(3), 15-18. doi:10.1002/ncr.20064

Bentkover, J. D. (2012). *Leadership is Central to Healthcare System Reform*. Retrieved September 2, 2015, from http://www.beckershospitalreview.com/hospital-management-administration/leadership-is-central-to-healthcare-system-reform.html

Bloland, P., Simone, P., Burkholder, B., Slutsker, L., & De Cock K. M. (2012). The Role of Public Health Institutions in Global Health System Strengthening Efforts. *PLoS Med, 9*(4), e1001199. doi:10.1371/journal.pmed.1001199

Blumenthal, D. (2010). Launching HITECH. *The New England Journal of Medicine*.

Browning Leadership Model. (2013). Leading at the Strategic Level: The Browning Leadership Model. Designed by Jen Russell for The Browning Strategic Leadership Model. *Stratified Systems Theory*. Retrieved September 2, 2015, from http://www.browningleadershipmodel.org/Stratified_Systems_Theory.pdf

Campbell, D. J. (2000). The proactive employee: Managing workplace initiative. *The Academy of Management Executive, 14*(3), 52–66. Retrieved from http://amp.aom.org/content/14/3/52.short

Center for Creative Leadership. (2015). *Nearly 70% of all change efforts fail. We can do better.* Retrieved October 14, 2015, from http://www.ccl.org/leadership/landing/leadingContinousChange.aspx?gclid=CjwKEAjw1_KwBRDEz_Wvn-cL4jGwSJAAEym0dYf9Q_XkbWnD4Nod-hy-8vtzE_yQDuk0gEf6Kio6uPnBoC7kTw_wcBhttp://www.ldihealtheconomist.com/he000023.shtml

Center for Health Leadership. (2015). *Developing public health leaders, creating change, and reducing health inequities*. Retrieved October 7, 2015, from http://www.healthleadership.org/

Centers for Medicare and Medicaid Services. (2013). *Medicare Data for Dual Eligible for States*. Retrieved October 1, 2015, from https://www.cms.gov/Medicare-Medicaid-Coordination/Medicare-and-Medicaid-Coordination/Medicare-Medicaid-Coordination-Office/MedicareDataforStates.html

Chathoth, P. K., & Olsen, M. D. (2002, April-September). Organizational Leadership and Strategy in the Hospitality Industry. *Journal of Service Research, 2*(1).

Cohn, J. (2012 June 13). Obamacare, Good for the Economy. *The New Republic*. Retrieved October 10, 2015, from http://www.newrepublic.com/article/104035/romney-republicans-say-affordable-care-act-will-kill-jobs-best-available-evidence

Committee for the Study of the Future of Public Health IoM. (1988). *The future of public health*. Washington, DC: National Academy Press.

Diana, M. L., Harle, C. A., Huerta, T. R., Ford, E. W., & Menachemi, N. (2014). Hospital Characteristics Associated With Achievement of Meaningful Use. *Journal of Healthcare Management, 59*(4), 272–284. PMID:25154125

DMHC. (2015). *DMHC regulates Health Plans and Helps health plan members and providers*. Retrieved October 6, 2015, from http://www.dmhc.ca.gov/

Ford, E. W., Menachemi, N., Huerta, T. R., & Yu, F. (2010). Hospital IT Adoption Strategies Associated with Implementation Success: Implications for Achieving Meaningful Use. *Journal of Healthcare Management, 55*(3), 175–188. PMID:20565034

Frampton, S., Guastello, S., Brady, C., Hale, M., Horowitz, S., & Bennett-Smith, S. (2008). *The Patient-Centered Care Improvement Guide*. The Planetree Association and The Picker Institute.

Friedman, A., & Becker, N. (2012). *Understanding the Individual Mandate's SCOTUS Pivot Points*. Retrieved September 2, 2015, from http://www.ldihealtheconomist.com/he000023.shtml

Grimm, B. L., Johansson, P., Nayar, P., Apenteng, B. A., Opoku, S., & Nguyen, A. (2015). *Assessing the Education and Training Needs of Nebraska's Public Health Workforce*. doi:10.3389/fpubh.2015.00161

HealthyPeople.gov. (2010). *Public Health Infrastructure*. Retrieved September 2, 2015, from http://www.healthypeople.gov/2020/topics-objectives/topic/public-health-infrastructure

HHS.gov. (2014). *Regulations*. Retrieved September 22, 2015, from: http://www.hhs.gov/regulations

Hoffman, N. A. (2011). The Requirements for Culturally and Linguistically Appropriate Services in Health Care. *Journal of Nursing Law, 14*(2), 49–57.

IMRhelp. (2015). *Independent medical review*. Retrieved October 8, 2015, from http://www.dir.ca.gov/dwc/IMR.htm

Jackson, B., & Robertson, L. (2011 January 7). *A 'Job-Killing' Law?*. FactCheck. Retrieved October 10, 2015, from http://www.factcheck.org/spindetectors/about/

Jacobs, T., & Clement, D. (2013). *Contributions of Stratified Systems Theory to Military Leader Development and Organization Redesign in the US Army*. Retrieved September 2, 2015, from http://dmcodyssey.org/wp-content/uploads/2013/09/part-three-chapter-4-p197-209.pdf

Jha, A. K., DesRoches, C. M., Campbell, E. G., Donelan, K., Rao, S. R., Ferris, T. G., & Blumental, D. et al. (2009). Use of electronic health records in U.S. hospitals. *The New England Journal of Medicine, 360*(16), 1628–1638. doi:10.1056/NEJMsa0900592 PMID:19321858

Kahn, L. (2015). *Leadership in Health Care for the 21st Century*. Retrieved September 2, 2015, from http://www.amjmed.com/article/S002-9343(14)00287-3/pdf

Kaiser Family Foundation. (2013). *The Uninsured: A Primer - Key Facts about Health Insurance on the Eve of Coverage Expansions*. Retrieved September 2, 2015, from http://kff.org/uninsured/report/the-uninsured-a-primer-key-facts-about-health-insurance-on-the-eve-of-coverage-expansions/

Mayer, J. D., & Salovey, P. (1997). *What is Emotional Intelligence?*. Retrieved September 2, 2015, from http://www.unh.edu/emotional_intelligence/EI%20Assets/Reprints...EI%20Proper/EI1997MSWhatIsEI.pdf

Mayer, M. D., Caruso, C. R., & Salovey, P. (2004). Emotional Intelligence Meets Traditional Standards for an Intelligence. *Intelligence, 27*(4), 267-298.

McCauley, C. (2006). *Developmental assignments: Creating learning experiences without changing jobs*. Greensboro, NC: N.C. Center for Creative Leadership Press.

McLarty, J., & McCartney, D. (2009). The nurse manager the neglected middle. *Healthc Financ, 63*(8), 74.

McNamara, R. S. (1995). *In Retrospect: The Tragedy and Lessons of Vietnam*. New York: Random House, Inc.

Meyers, J. D. (2012). *What Is Emotional Intelligence (EI)?* Retrieved September 2, 2015, from http://www.unh.edu/emotional_intelligence/ei%20What%20is%20EI/ei%20fourbranch.htm

Mind Tools Ltd. (2015). *Leadership Styles: Choosing the Right Approach for the Situation*. Retrieved September 2, 2015, from http://www.mindtools.com/pages/article/newLDR_84.htm

National Defense University. (1997). *Strategic Leadership and Decision Making Part One: The Environment of Strategic Leadership and Decision Making*. Retrieved September 21, 2015, from http://www.au.af.mil/au/awc/awcgate/ndu/strat-ldr-dm/pt1ch1.html

National Network of Public Health Institutes. (2010). *What is a Public Health Institute?* Retrieved September 21, 2015, from http://www.nnphi.org/about/what-is-a-public-health-institute

Panning, R. (2014). Healthcare Reform 101. *Clinical Laboratory Science, 27*(2), 107–111. Retrieved from http://www.bing.com/search?q=Panning,+R.+(2014).+Healthcare+Reform+101&form=MSSEDF&pc=MSE1 PMID:25000654

Petrie, N. (2014). *Future Leadership Trends*. Retrieved September 21, 2015, from http://insights.ccl.org/wp-content/uploads/2015/04/futureTrends.pdf

Reed, G. E. (2006 May-June). *Leadership and Systems Thinking*. Defense AT&L. Retrieved September 2, 2015, from http://www.au.af.mil/au/awc/awcgate/dau/ree_mj06.pdf

Rice, T., Rosenau, P., Unruh, L. Y., Barnes, A. J., Saltman, R. B., & van Ginneken, E. (2013). United States of America: Health system review. *Health Systems in Transition, 15*(3), 1–431. PMID:24025796

Rouse, M. (2015). *Systems Thinking Definition*. Retrieved September 22, 2015, from http://searchcio.techtarget.com/definition/systems-thinking

Schyve, P., M. (2007). Language Differences as a Barrier to Quality and Safety in Health Care: The Joint Commission Perspective. *Journal of General Internal Medicine, 22*(Suppl 2), 360–361. doi:10.1007/s11606-007-0365-3

Schyve, P. M. (2009, Winter). *Leadership in healthcare organizations: A Guide to Joint Commission Leadership Standards*. San Diego, CA: A Governance Institute White Paper.

Shepard, K., Gray, J. L., Hunt, J. G., & McArthur, S. (2005-2007). *Senior Fellow of the Global Organization Design Society Former GO Society Board Member.* Retrieved October 10, 2015, from http://globalro.org/index.php/sig/1619-julian-fairfield-page

Society for Human Resource Management (SHRM). (2015). *Leadership Competencies.* Retrieved September 2, 2015, from http://www.shrm.org/research/articles/articles/pages/leadershipcompetencies.aspx

Sternberg, R. (2000). *Handbook of Intelligence.* Cambridge, UK: Cambridge University Press. doi:10.1017/CBO9780511807947

Tacit. (2014). *The Impact of Tacit Knowledge on Perceived Performance of Doctors in a Chinese Hospital.* Retrieved October 8, 2015, from http://trap.ncirl.ie/1793/contactsatnocost

Technologies, T. D. K. (2015). *Key Components of Organizational Leadership.* Retrieved September 2, 2015, from http://www.tdktech.com/tech-talks/key-components-of-organizational-leadership

University of Toronto. (2013). *Higher Emotional Intelligence leads to better decision-making.* Retrieved September 2, 2015, from https://www.rotman.utoronto.ca/Connect/MediaCentre/News-Releases/20131119.aspx

U.S. Department of Health and Human Services. (2011). *Quality Improvement.* Retrieved September 2, 2015, from http://www.hrsa.gov/quality/toolbox/508pdfs/qualityimprovement.pdf

U.S. Department of Health and Human Services. (2014). *Regulations.* Retrieved September 2, 2015, from http://www.hhs.gov/regulations

Wager, K. A., Lee, F. W., & Glaser, J. P. (2013). *Health Care Information Systems: A Practical Approach for Health Care Management.* Hoboken, NJ: John Wiley & Sons.

Webster, M. (2014). *Regulation.* Retrieved September 2, 2015, from http://www.merriam-webster.com/dictionary/regulation

Wu, E. (2015). *SB853 Bill Health care language assistance.* Retrieved October 6, 2015, from: http://cpehn.org/policy-center/cultural-and-linguistic-competency/sb-853-health-care-language-assistance-act

Zaccaro, S. (2001). The Nature of Executive Leadership: A Conceptual and Empirical Analysis of Success. Washington, DC: American Psychological Association

KEY TERMS AND DEFINITIONS

Appointment of Representation (AOR): A form of power of attorney.

Australian Commission on Safety and Quality in Health Care (ACSQHC): A commissioner agency that leads and coordinates health care improvements across Australia.

Centers for Medicare & Medicaid Services (CMS): Medicare and Medicaid Services.

Department of Management Health Care (DMHC): A health plan regulator for High Maintenance Organizations plans.

Emotional Intelligence (EI): Motivates individuals with a collective vision of the future to communicate well.

Health Insurance Portability and Accountability Act (HIPAA): Makes the ability to transfer and continue health insurance coverage for patient care to millions of citizens and families that lose their jobs, and protects the patients' privacy.

Independent Medical Reviewers (IMR): An Independent Medical Reviewer that works along with the DMC to regulate health plans.

Medicare Urban (MU): A program that covers hospitals in urban areas.

National Committee of Quality Assurance (NCQA): A non-profit organization to improve quality in health plans.

Patient Protection and Affordable Care Act (PPACA): This is an act created by Obama Care to maximize quality and affordability of insurance plans.

Quality Improvement (QI): The main goal is to make sure that all policies and regulations are implemented in health plans.

Senate Bill 853 (SB853): This Senate Bill provides various threshold languages and making language barriers to more understandable.

Systems Thinking: A holistic approach analysis to leadership and decision making.

TDK Technologies: Vendor for Technology and Management for e-commerce.

World Health Organization WHO: A health system for profit and non-profit organizations.

Chapter 4
Emotional Leadership:
Leadership Styles and Emotional Intelligence

Katherine P. Bergethon
Illinois State University, USA

Daniel Cochece Davis
Illinois State University, USA

ABSTRACT

Although past research readily acknowledges emotions exist in organizations, and even acknowledges that leaders benefit from having "emotional intelligence," fully understanding leadership's role in addressing the emotional dimension of organizational experience, especially during the typically high emotion situations of organizational conflicts, remains understudied. This chapter provides greater awareness of how leadership styles, especially transformational or charismatic leadership, relates with emotional intelligence to facilitate "emotional leadership" within organizations to achieve positive follower effects.

INTRODUCTION

Leadership is a significant topic in management fields, and many researchers found leadership style an influential variable in organizations' functions (Wu, 2009). There are many different leadership styles and theories made popular through contemporary research (e.g., Almintisir, Akeel, & Devi Subramainiam, 2013; Ayoko & Konrad, 2012; Hansbrough, 2012; Hemsworth, Muterera, & Baregheh, 2013; Sahaya, 2012). Numerous previous studies meaningfully contributed to the known concept of "leadership" (e.g., Bass, 1997;

Burns, 1978; Goleman, 1995; Maritz, 1995; Tracey & Hinkin, 1998). Goleman (1998) defined leadership as, "the art of persuading people to work towards a common goal" (p. 12). Leadership is also viewed as an essential component in the success or failure of an organization (e.g., Bass, 1997; Maritz, 1995).

This chapter focuses on transformational leadership, emotional intelligence, and a new combination of these concepts called "emotional leadership." Some of the most challenging situations for any leader are those involving conflicts or stress, where emotions run high, and an emo-

DOI: 10.4018/978-1-4666-9970-0.ch004

tional intelligence is needed. These are the times when transformational and charismatic leadership styles may best address the situation's challenges. Yet, while many studies focus on such things as "emotional intelligence," still limited information pertains to the emotional dimensions of leadership. A comprehensive review of transformational leadership, emotional intelligence, and the combinative concept of emotional leadership are presented, followed by the positive impact of emotional leadership on followers.

EMOTIONAL LEADERSHIP

Recently, leadership theorists have urged the exploration of leaders' personalities or inner emotions (e.g., Campbell, 2007). Emotional management is being described as a crucial component of leadership. Boal and Hooijberg (2001) proposed that managerial wisdom is mandatory for successful strategic leadership: a component called social intelligence or emotional intelligence, or the ability to understand others' emotions and to act fittingly in context.

Transformational Leadership

Transformational leadership has received substantial research attention over the last two decades (Pawar, 2003). Transformational leadership theories focus around leaders as instruments of change, by motivating others toward valuable change (Antonakis, Cianciolo, & Sternberg, 2004). Transformative leaders are able to balance both rewards and leadership requirements, while simultaneously motivating followers, and forsaking self-interest for the good of the organization (Abeysekera & Jayakody, 2011; Bass, 1985; Sahaya, 2012). Additionally, this orientation seeks to move other organizational members beyond their personal goals and specific conflicts with other organizational members, and focuses them toward macro organizational-level goals. Burns

(1978) characterized transformational leadership as an approach that encourages followers by appealing to higher ideals and moral values (Burns, 1978; Tracey & Hinkin, 1998). By empowering followers, transformational leaders can gain higher personal investment from those individuals, which will then create better organizational cohesion and success (Thompson, 2012; Tracey & Hinkin, 1998). Thompson (2012) outlined how transformational leadership can improve workforce competencies using Kouzes and Posner's (1995) practices (i.e., challenging the process, enabling the other to act, modeling the way and encouraging the heart). Thompson (2012) proffered that these practices can improve issues in staffing and training areas.

Components of Transformational Leadership

Transformational Leadership (TL) is commonly defined by four basic components (Bass, 1985; 2007; Costley & Howell, 2006; Hansbrough, 2012; Lassey & Sashkin, 1983): idealized influence (attributed and behavioral), inspirational motivation, intellectual stimulation, and individual consideration. Further examining of these individual concepts enables a better understanding of the overall transformational leadership approach.

Idealized Influence

Idealized influence is behavior resulting in follower admiration, respect, and trust (Bass & Avolio, 1994; Tracey & Hinkin, 1998). It requires risk-sharing from leaders, a consideration of followers' needs over personal needs, and ethical and moral conduct (Bass & Avolio, 1994; Tracey & Hinkin, 1998). Idealized influence (attributed) is viewing a leader as being competent, self-confident and committed to higher-order ideals and ethics (Costley & Howell, 2006). A leader with high levels of idealized influence or charisma would have the ability to encourage followers' trust, admiration, loyalty and respect (Bass, 1985). Idealized Influence Attributes (IIA) refers to followers' perceptions of a leader's characteristics (Bass, 1985; Bass & Avolio, 1995; Hemsworth, Muterera, & Baregheh, 2013). IIA defines a leader who is an exemplary role model and is admired and respected by followers (Bass & Avolio, 1995).

Idealized influence behaviors (IIB) included followers' perceptions of a leader's observable behavior, and describes a leader who can be trusted and possesses high moral and ethical standards (Bass & Avolio, 1995). Bass (1985) theorized a leader's ability to influence supports the subsequent concept: inspirational motivation.

Inspirational Motivation

Bass (1985) characterized inspirational motivation as a subset of influence; the leader will motivate followers by expressing a clear desired vision with enthusiasm and confidence. Bass and Avolio (1990) described inspirational motivation as the leaders' ability to inspire and motivate followers via providing examples through symbols, images, emotional appeals, and effective communication of expectations. The inspirational motivation dimension includes leader behaviors specifying clear expectations and a commitment to overall organizational goals (Almintisir, Akeel, & Devi Subramainiam, 2013; Bass & Avolio, 1994; Tracey & Hinkin, 1998). Inspirational motivation also creates team enthusiasm and optimism. Bass (1985) proposed that followers could be further motivated through the next concept: intellectual stimulation.

Intellectual Stimulation

The third component, intellectual stimulation, occurs when leaders help and motivate followers to view and solve problems from a new perspective by stimulating imaginations (Costley & Howell, 2006). Bass (1985) argued that intellectually stimulating leaders inspire followers to recog-

nize personal beliefs and values. Intellectually stimulating leaders encourage differing ideas and motivate followers to think individually for the sake of innovation (Avolio, Waldman, & Einstein, 1988; Hemsworth et al., 2013). Collectively, this can be referred to as "divergent thinking" (Guilford, 1967).

Individual Consideration

The last of the four components, individual consideration, is when leaders support, encourage and compliment follower's wants and needs in order to improve self-confidence, facilitating development (Bass, 1985; Costley & Howell, 2006). Both transformational and charismatic leaders will exhibit interest and provide personal attention to each individual follower (Avolio et al., 1988), allowing leaders to foster respect through continuous feedback. Leaders using individual consideration listen attentively and encourage follower achievement and growth (Tracey & Hinkin, 1998).

Antonikas et al. (2004) outlined five other shared factors within the transformational leadership and charismatic leadership theories: *meaning-making* (leaders' engagement with followers interpretations of organizational events); *appeals to higher-order needs* (leaders' focus on intrinsic rewards instead of extrinsic rewards); *empowerment* (leaders consider relationships with followers as mutually influential); *setting of high expectations* (leaders challenge followers to meet high performance expectations and shared idealized goals); and *fostering of collective identity* (leaders' encouragement of followers to forsake individual self-interests for the betterment of the organization as a whole). Conversely, "pseudo-transformational leadership is defined by self-serving, yet highly inspirational leadership behaviors, unwillingness to encourage independent thought in subordinates, and little caring for one's subordinates more generally" (Christie, Turner, & Barling, 2011, p. 2943). Christie, Turner and Barling's (2011) work focuses on the meaning of leader charisma and the negative impacts pseudo-transformational leadership has on positive outcomes and followers' satisfaction.

Like individual followers and leaders, organizations and organizational leaders will need to share a common goal. Mahalinga Shiva and Suar's (2012) research investigated transformational leadership's influence on organizational effectiveness and obtained mixed outcomes. Organizational effectiveness refers to the success of an organization in meeting set goals (Hsin-Kuang, Chun-Hsiung, & Dorjgotov, 2012).

Emotional Intelligence

Emotional intelligence is the basic ability to manage one's own emotions, resulting in one's emotional quotient (EQ). This is similar to an intelligence quotient (IQ), defined as one's brainpower, except EQ is defined as one's emotional control power (Clawson, 2012; Elizabeth & Wolff, 2008; Goleman, 1995; Service & Fekula, 2008). Singh (2013) views it as "a form of intelligence that comprises a set of non-cognitive abilities in the affective domain that influences one's ability to perceive or sense and understand the emotions of others…" (p. 1290). Emotional intelligence has become a concept associated with effective leadership (Hayashi & Ewert, 2006). Bass (1999) stated, "leadership is as much emotional and subjective as rational and objective in effect" (p. 18). Service and Fekula (2008) stated, "Leaders must be able to motivate, guide, inspire, listen and persuade" (p. 28). Successful leaders understand emotional impacts made on followers; such leaders possess high EQ abilities helping impart goal orientation, the importance of the task, enthusiasm, organizational commitment and success (Service & Fekula, 2008) onto their followers. Emotions that have been connected with effective leadership are positive emotions (e.g., hope), which engage followers through depictions of positive future outcomes (Campbell, 2007; Salovey and Mayer, 1990). Empathy and caring, or the ability

to understand and consider others' feelings, are also emotions associated with effective leadership abilities (Campbell, 2007; Goleman, 1998; Humphrey, 2002; Salovey & Mayer, 1990).

Goleman (1995) asserted that emotional intelligence engages individuals' abilities of self-awareness, emotional management, personal motivation, empathy, and relationship management. Goleman (1995) also described EI as an individual's ability to "motivate oneself and persist in the face of frustrations; to control impulses and delay gratification; to regulate one's moods and keep distress from swamping the ability to think; to empathize and to hope" (p. 34). Singh (2013) characterized emotional intelligence as a major predictor of leadership success, and Sterrett (2000) stated that EI is what differentiates exceptional performance from mediocre performance. Emotional intelligence affects both physical and mental health (Goleman, 1995), and is linked to job performance enhancement, as well as leadership effectiveness (Elizabeth & Wolff, 2008; Yung-Shui & Tung-Chun, 2009). Research confirms that EI contributes to improved individual and organizational performance (e.g., Turner & Lloyd-Walker, 2008). Barthwal and Som (2012) agreed: "In an office setting, emotions can lead to team camaraderie and increased productivity" (p. 141).

Emotional Intelligence and Transformational Leadership

Gardner and Stough (2002) predicted that there is a strong correlation between high EI and strength of leadership. Roush and Atwater (1992) found transformational leadership was connected with a "feeling" instead of a "thinking" style (see also Kupers & Weibler, 2006; Roush & Atwater, 1992). Transformational leadership is considered more emotion-based than transactional leadership, and involves higher emotional skills (Palmer, Wallis, Burgess, & Stough, 2001; Vrba, 2007; Yammarino & Dubinsky, 1994). Vrba (2007) found the relationship between TL and EI skills to be stronger than the relationship between EI and transactional leadership.

Duckett and Macfarlane's (2003) study explored the relationship between emotional intelligence and transformational leadership by testing store managers' EQ level and transformational leadership qualities using the tripartite performance scoring system (i.e., annual appraisal scores; sales to target figures; and directors ranking) and store managers' EQ profile scores. Their findings showed transformational leadership and managers' emotional intelligence levels could be positively linked to the store managers' performance levels.

Anand and UdayaSuriyan (2010) examined connections between emotional intelligence and leadership, noting the value and effects of emotional intelligence on leadership and organizational success. They reinforced the relevance of emotional intelligence and leadership practice in public sector organizations, concluding that "emotional intelligence contributes to the magnetic and engaging qualities of the mangers who possess exceptional abilities of the leaders" (p. 71). Similarly, Sunindijo (2012) explored the value of emotional intelligence and transformational leadership in construction organizations. Relationships between emotional intelligence and political skill were investigated, with conclusions that all three (i.e., emotional intelligence, political skill and transformational leadership) were valuable within organizations.

Finally, Goleman, Boyatzis, and Mckee (2002) suggested that the presence of empathy in visionary leadership matters most when considering emotional intelligence, and that this mode "comes naturally to 'transformational' leaders" (p. 59).

Summary of Emotional Leadership/ TL + EI= EL

House, Spangler, and Woycke (1991) see one of the distinguishing features of charismatic or *emotional leaders* is engaging followers at an emotional level,

while non-charismatic leaders only engage followers at a rational level. Humphrey (2002) suggested that managing followers' emotions is one of the core responsibilities of leaders. Jin's (2010) study used the *emotional leadership* theory to measure the core emotional traits and skills in effective public relations leadership. An emotional leader is able to understand emotions of followers and that understanding enables a leader's influence. When a leader combines transformational leadership and emotional intelligence competencies, an emotional leader is formed. Managing followers' emotions is a crucial component of leadership. This is especially true in organizational situations of transition, when competing expectations and goals often breed emotionally-charged conflicts. As such, situations where transformational leadership is most needed are *also* typically highly conflict and emotionally-ridden. Bringing together organizational factions is, in large part, the effective outcome of transformational leadership, but this is most often accomplished through emotional and conflict management. An important aspect of *emotional leadership* is support for, or showing concern for, the welfare of followers, and expressing appreciation for their efforts (Casmir & Yong Ngee, 2010). *Emotional leadership* encompasses a wide range of behaviors including providing encouragement to followers and maintaining pleasant leader-follower relationships characterized by mutual trust, respect for followers' ideas, and consideration for followers' feelings. Collectively, then, previous literature suggests that leaders will benefit from an emotional leadership approach.

Emotional Leadership Effects on Followers

Leadership characteristics create meaningful effects on organizational performance because of leadership characteristics' influence on followers (Bass & Avolio, 1990; Chemers, 1997; Sahaya, 2012), including how leadership styles can affect followers' job performance and job satisfaction (e.g., Almintisir et al., 2013; Chung-Kai & Chia-Hung, 2009; Robbins, 2001; Sahaya, 2012; Wu, 2009).

A key element in any leader/ follower relationship is the personality of the follower: "The needs, attitudes, values, and feelings of the follower determine the kinds of stimuli produced by the leader to which the follower will respond" (Tannenbaum, Weschler, & Massarik, 1961, p. 31). The leader/follower roles and goals vary, depending on the group; tensions may often arise if goals of the leader are in conflict with the group's objective (Gardner, 1990). A leader would be considered successful if the needs of the followers are properly identified and addressed (Bass, 1990; Sims & Quatro, 2005). The TL leader/ follower relationship is one with continuing moral purpose and is fundamentally driven by the followers' aspirations and values (Wan Ismail & Al-Taee, 2012). Hansbrough (2012) explores the connection between attachment anxiety and the follower's perceptions of transformational leadership. Attachment anxiety's presence in followers can cause them to report transformational leadership traits in a leader, even when those traits are not present (Hansrough, 2012).

Job Satisfaction and Job Performance

Bass (1990) defined job satisfaction as "attitudes and feelings about one's job" (p. 919). The concept of job satisfaction can expand to include the attitude toward one's job based on feelings, beliefs, and behaviors (Omar & Hussin, 2013). Tan and Quek (2001) noted that one's internal values and work environment are keys to job satisfaction. Yang (2012) suggests two dimensions of job satisfaction: *intrinsic* (the level of satisfaction connected to one's actual job) and *extrinsic* (the level of satisfaction associated with the atmosphere where the work takes place). Emotional leadership characteristics significantly impact organizational commitment and job satisfaction (Abraham, 2000;

Chung-Kai & Chia-Hung, 2009; Garg & Ramjee, 2013; Hong, Catano & Liao, 2011; Singh, 2013; Weinberger, 2002). Satisfied employees will more likely exhibit greater work responsiveness, as well as consistency and quality, which positively influence organizational success (Yi-Feng, 2009). Therefore, organizations would benefit from increasing each individual's job satisfaction.

Shooshtarian, Ameli, and Aminilari (2013) explored the influence of emotional intelligence and emotional leadership on job satisfaction, job performance and organizational commitment. Employees were measured on emotional intelligence and job satisfaction, with findings showing emotional intelligence to be positively correlated with job satisfaction, finding individuals "with higher EI and skills in emotions control, have more job satisfaction and desirable job performance, because they are more adept at appraising and regulating their own emotions and aware about the influence of emotions on behavior and outcomes" (Shooshtarian et al., 2013, p. 42).

Moorman (1991) found connections between job satisfaction, job performance, and emotional intelligence (see also Aryee, Walumbwa, Zhou, & Hartnell, 2012; Dunn, Dastoor & Sims, 2012; Moorman, 1991; Turner & Lloyd-Walker, 2008). Emotional intelligence has emerged as an important aspect of management and closely linked to job performance (Shahhosseini et al., 2013). Job performance, sometimes termed "task performance" (Chung-Kai & Chia-Hung, 2009), is the action of completing required job assignments with the intention of receiving a formal reward (Chung-Kai & Chia-Hung, 2009; Yuan, Wan-Lung, Jia-Horng & Kuang-Pin, 2012). Yuan, Wan-Lung, Jia-Horng, and Kuang-Pin (2012) note that emotional intelligence has been previously linked to research involving job performance, but state there is no empirical research focusing on EI's influence on follower task performance competencies, leading them to suggest "the development of emotionally intelligent behavior will lead to development of increased task performance behavior over time"

(p. 1717). Chung-Kai and Chia-Hung (2009) found that TL positively impacts leader-member exchange quality (LMX), and that LMX has a strong influence on an employee's task performance. Leader-member exchange is characterized by a leader's relationship with a follower that has mutual trust, respect, loyalty and obligation (Chung-Kai & Chia-Hung, 2009). Kuppusamy, Ganesan, and Rosada (2010) also found transformational characteristics positively impacting organizational performance through TL factors fostering employee self-awareness, and creating organizational commitment. Abeysekera and Jayakody (2011) examined the impact of TL behavior on leadership in Sri Lankan marketing. They found all four TL factors positively impacting the leader/follower relationship and the companies' campaign successes (based on predefined company goals). Similarly, Andreescu and Vito (2010) explored the two leadership orientations: worker-centered leadership and task-centered leadership. Worker-centered leadership aims to help employees trust in the leader, and task-centered leadership emphasizes good communication. Andreescu and Vito (2010) proffered a positive relationship between these leadership behaviors: TL leadership characteristics and job performance.

Followers' Well-Being

Well-being could be stated simply as feeling good or feeling bad (Warr, 2006). Employee well-being is commonly connected with job satisfaction (Bass, 1990). Higher levels of negative organizational conflict are often associated with lower job satisfaction, while higher levels of positive conflict are often associated with higher job satisfaction. Both Kelloway, Turner, Barling, and Loughlin (2012) and Liu, Siu, and Shi (2010) focus on TL's influence on employees' well-being, and these studies purport that employers and leaders should consider the well-being of employees/subordinates because contented workers positively impact their organizations (Kelloway et al., 2012; Liu et al., 2010).

Liu et al.'s (2010) research concentrated on three parts "of individual employees' well-being: positive affective well-being (job satisfaction), negative affective well-being (perceived work stress), and physiological well-being (stress symptoms)" (p. 457). Liu et al. (2010) found TL positively affected job satisfaction and lessened employee's perceived work stress and stress symptoms. Emotional leadership positively affects followers' well-being, which strengthens follower organizational commitment (Garg & Ramjee, 2013). Effective TL can actually contribute to followers' physical well-being, especially when utilized in organizations' safety training practices (Mullen & Kelloway, 2009). Kelloway et al. (2012) had similar findings, but concluded that leaders committed to empowering, motivating and encouraging employees through ethical role model behaviors will gain followers trust. Additionally, they found that employee well-being was positively impacted because TL facilitated employees' trust in the leader.

Nielsen, Randall, Yarker, and Brenner (2008) acknowledged the relationship between TL and well-being by purporting: "there are three work characteristics that may mediate the relationship between transformational leadership behavior and well-being in followers: increased role clarity, increased meaningfulness, and increased opportunities for development" (p. 18). An example statement of role clarification would be, "My boss gives vague explanations of what is expected of me" (Hunt, Sekaran, & Schriesheim, 1982, p. 142). Role clarification is one of the dimensions used in one version of the Leader Behavior Description Questionnaire (LBDQ- Form XII), a questionnaire usually used in the measure of discretionary leadership (Hunt et al., 1982).

Organizational Commitment

Organizational commitment also positively affects motivation, organizational citizenship and job performance (Garg & Ramjee, 2013; Meyer, Stanley, Hescovitch & Topolnytsky, 2002; Mowday, Porter & Dubin, 1974). Garg and Ramjee (2013) surveyed the relationship between leadership style and employee commitment of South African Parastatal companies, finding positive relationships between emotional leadership behaviors (e.g. building trust, inspiring a shared vision, encouraging creativity development) and employee commitment. Employee commitment is an employee's emotional attachment to, identification with, and involvement in, the organization (see also Andreescu &Vitio, 2010; Meyer & Allen, 1997). The employee's commitment alludes to an individual's attitude toward, belief in, and acceptance of, the organization's goals (Garg & Ramjee, 2013; Meyer & Allen, 1997), as opposed to being in conflict or disagreement with them.

Innovation

The transformational part of TL illustrates the leader's ability to transform followers into leaders, which, in turn, transforms leaders into agents of change (Chemers, 1997). Kouzes and Posner (1995) refer to innovation as change, and then emphasizes the importance of leadership's role within change and innovation. Hyypia and Parajanen (2013) found "TL behavior can be applied to creativity and innovation processes, especially if related to actions when leadership is seen as different roles during a process, instead of as actions or characteristics of a certain individual role" (p. 36). The study focused on how to support staff creativity in order to bring about innovative opportunities (Hyypia & Parajanen, 2013).

Giberson and Miklos (2013) concentrated on innovation in team settings, supporting the idea that transformational leadership creates "stronger support for innovation within the work team, which was subsequently related to team innovation" (p. 160). Aryee, Walumbwa, Zhou and Hartnell (2012) presented evidence positively linking employee's work engagement to innovative behaviors. Aryee et al. (2012) found "Transformational leadership is positively related to followers' experienced mean-

ingfulness of work" (p. 6). Similarly, Aryee et al. (2012) also discovered followers' experience of "meaningfulness of work" positively contributed to work engagement, and that "Work engagement is positively related to innovative behavior" (p. 8). Innovative climate mediates transformational leadership factors' association with innovative behavior (Naami & Asadi, 2011). Naami and Asadi (2011) used three questionnaires as measuring tools: the innovative behavior questionnaire, the innovative organizational climate questionnaire, and the Multi factorial leadership style questionnaire (MLQ), finding that innovative organizational climate equalizes the relationship between one of the four TL factors (i.e. intellectual stimulation, inspirational motivation, individual consideration, and idealized influence) and innovative behavior.

Conflict Management

Researchers (e.g. Berlew, 1974; Locke, 1976; Motowidlo & Borman, 1978; Peterson, Park, Hall, & Seligman, 2009; Shamir, Zakay, Breinin, & Popper, 1998) assert that transformational leadership improves followers' morale, which increases the group sense of collective purpose and goals. Ayoko and Konrad's (2012) posited that leadership was an important factor for maintaining successful group performance and morale under conditions of conflict. Conflict often results from team member diversity. Leaders' emotional management, conflict management and transformational behaviors largely determine the impact positive and negative conflict has on team outcomes. Gibson and Vermeulen (2003) found leader performance management behaviors could improve learning in diverse teams, suggesting transformational leadership was significant for generating positive outcomes (Ayoko & Konrad, 2012; Gibson & Vermeulen, 2003). Additionally, findings suggest that transformational leadership behaviors reduced the affect of conflict in group performance (e.g., Ayoko & Korad, 2012). Ayoko and Konrad (2012) learned that in order to avoid the negative emotions associated with task and relationship conflict from damaging group performance, leaders of diverse groups should act to manage emotions among group members. The authors concluded that leaders should not try to diminish the conflicts arising from team diversity, but, instead, utilize conflict management strategies to manage intra-group conflicts effectively to produce positive results. Transformational leadership improves followers' morale, which increases the group sense of collective purpose and goals.

DISCUSSION AND IMPLICATIONS

Overall, the collective research illustrates positive influences of both transformational leadership characteristics and emotional intelligence capabilities, impacting job satisfaction, job performance, followers' well-being, organizational commitment and conflict management. Although much research exists, collectively, on emotional intelligence and transformational leadership as separate concepts, there has been far less research focusing on the synthetic idea of "emotional leadership." In theory, the combination of high emotional intelligence and TL characteristics should produce positive leader/follower relationship, with emotional leadership facilitating success and well-being for followers, leaders, and their organizations.

This chapter proposes a simple synthetic composition of transformational leadership and emotional intelligence skills to create an effective emotional leadership theory. Emotional leaders would display both EI and TL characteristics (i.e., engage followers on an emotional level, influence moral and ethical behavior, intellectually stimulate innovation, and treat followers as individuals). Leaders looking to influence organizational commitment and success could cultivate EQ and TL traits; organizations would benefit from hiring emotionally-developed leaders.

Subsequent research and theorizing is needed in order to complete the proposed emotional leadership concept, but this review serves as a foundation for future scholarship to move in that fruitful direction. As the global market continues to expand, research on emotional leadership within diverse group settings and the resultant conflict management processes could be tremendously valuable (Ayoko & Konrad, 2012; Berlew, 1974; Gibson & Vermeulen, 2003; Locke, 1976; Motowidlo &Borman, 1978; Peterson et al, 2009; Shamir et al. 1998). Although this review found no specific negative outcomes from utilizing emotional leadership tactics, there are potential risks when considering emotional connections between leaders and followers, and the negative impacts such emotional leadership could have (e.g., the possibility of inappropriate or codependent leader/follower relationships).

REFERENCES

Abeysekera, N., & Jayakody, J. K. (2011). Relationship marketing perspective in salesperson's transformational leadership behavior effect. *Contemporary Management Research*, 7(2), 143–156. doi:10.7903/cmr.3602

Abraham, R. (2000). The role of job control as a moderator of emotional dissonance and emotional intelligence-outcome relationships. *The Journal of Psychology*, *134*(2), 169–184. doi:10.1080/00223980009600860 PMID:10766109

Almintisir, A., Akeel, A., & Devi Subramainiam, I. (2013). The role of transformational leadership style in motivating public sector employees in Libya. *Australian Journal of Basic & Applied Sciences*, 7(2), 99–108.

Anand, R., & UdayaSuriyan, G. (2010). Emotional intelligence and its relationship with leadership practices. *International Journal of Business and Management*, 5(2), 65–76.

Andreescu, V., & Vitio, G. F. (2010). An exploratory study on ideal leadership behavior: The opinions of American police managers. *International Journal of Police Science & Management, 12*(4), 567–583. doi:10.1350/ijps.2010.12.4.207

Antonakis, J., Cianciolo, A. T., & Sternberg, R. J. (Eds.). (2004). *The nature of leadership.* Thousand Oaks, CA: Sage Publications.

Aryee, S., Walumbwa, F. O., Zhou, Q., & Hartnell, C. A. (2012). Transformational leadership, innovative behavior, and task performance: Test mediation and moderation processes. *Human Performance, 25*(1), 1–25. doi:10.1080/089592 85.2011.631648

Avolio, B. J., Waldman, D. A., & Einstein, W. O. (1988). Transformational leadership in a management game simulation: Impacting the bottom line. *Group & Organization Studies, 13*(1), 59–80. doi:10.1177/105960118801300109

Ayoko, O. B., & Konrad, A. M. (2012). Leaders' transformational, conflict, and emotion management behaviors in culturally diverse workgroups. *Equality, Diversity and Inclusion. International Journal (Toronto, Ont.), 31,* 694–724. doi:10.1108/02610151211277581

Barthwal, S., & Som, A. J. (2012). Emotional intelligence as a measure of an employee's overall effectiveness. *Drishtikon: A Management Journal, 3,* 140-176.

Bass, B. M. (1985). *Leadership and performance beyond expectations.* New York: Free Press.

Bass, B. M. (1990). *Bass & Stogdill's handbook of leadership: Theory, research & managerial applications.* New York, NY: The Free Press.

Bass, B. M. (1997). Does the transactional-transformational leadership paradigm transcend organizational and national boundaries? *Journal of American Psychologist, 52*(2), 130–139. doi:10.1037/0003-066X.52.2.130

Bass, B. M. (1999). On the taming of charisma: A reply to Janice Beyer. *The Leadership Quarterly, 10*(4), 541–554. doi:10.1016/S1048-9843(99)00030-2

Bass, B. M. (2007). From transactional to transformative leadership: Learning to share the vision. In R. P. Vecchio (Ed.), *Leadership: Understanding the dynamics of power and influence in organizations* (pp. 302–317). Notre Dame, IN: University of Notre Dame Press.

Bass, B. M., & Avolio, B. J. (1990). *Manual: The multifactor leadership questionnaire.* Palo Alto, CA: Consulting Psychologists Press.

Bass, B. M., & Avolio, B. J. (1994). *Improving organizational effectiveness through transformational leadership.* Thousand Oaks, CA: Sage.

Bass, B. M., & Avolio, B. J. (1995). *The multifactor leadership questionnaire.* Palo Alto, CA: Mind Garden.

Berlew, D. E. (1974). Leadership and organizational excitement. In D. A. Kolb, I. M. Rubin, & J. Mc Intyre (Eds.), *Organizational psychology: A book of readings* (2nd ed., pp. 265–277). Englewood Cliffs, NJ: Prentice Hall.

Boal, K., & Hooijberg, R. (2001). Strategic leadership research: Moving on. *The Leadership Quarterly, 11*(4), 515–549. doi:10.1016/S1048-9843(00)00057-6

Burns, J. M. (1978). *Leadership.* New York, NY: Harper & Row; doi:10.1177/1742715005049347

Campbell, C. R. (2007). On the journey toward wholeness in leader theories. *Leadership and Organization Development Journal, 28*(2), 137–153. doi:10.1108/01437730710726831

Casimir, G., & Yong Ngee, K. N. (2010). Combinative aspects of leadership style and the interaction between leadership behaviors. *Leadership and Organization Development Journal, 31*(6), 501–517. doi:10.1108/01437731011070005

Chemers, M. M. (1997). *An integrative theory of leadership*. Mahwah, NJ: Lawrence Erlbaum Associates.

Christie, A., Barling, J., & Turner, N. (2011). Pseudo-transformational leadership: Model specification and outcomes. *Journal of Applied Social Psychology, 41,* 2943-2984. doi:10.1111/j.1559-1816.2011.00858.x

Chung-Kai, L., & Chia-Hung, H. (2009). The influence of transformational leadership on workplace relationships and job performance. *Social Behavior & Personality: An International Journal, 37*(8), 1129–1142. doi:10.2224/sbp.2009.37.8.1129

Clawson, J. G. (2012). *Level three leadership: Getting below the surface*. Upper Saddle River, NJ: Pearson Education.

Costley, D. L., & Howell, J. P. (2006). *Understanding behaviors for effective leadership*. Upper Saddle River, NJ: Pearson Education.

Duckett, H., & Macfarlane, E. (2003). Emotional intelligence and transformational leadership in retailing. *Leadership and Organization Development Journal, 24*(6), 309–317. doi:10.1108/01437730310494284

Dunn, M. W., Dastoor, B., & Sims, R. L. (2012). Transformational leadership and organizational commitment: A cross-cultural perspective. *Journal of Multidisciplinary Research, 4,* 45–60.

Elizabeth, S. K., & Wolff, S. B. (2008). Emotional intelligence competencies in the team and team leader. *Journal of Management Development, 27*(1), 55–75. doi:10.1108/02621710810840767

Gardner, J. W. (1990). *On leadership*. New York, NY: The Free Press.

Gardner, L., & Stough, C. (2002). Examining the relationship between leadership and emotional intelligence in senior level managers. *Leadership and Organization Development Journal, 23*(2), 68–78. doi:10.1108/01437730210419198

Garg, A. K., & Ramjee, D. (2013). The relationship between leadership styles and employee commitment at a Parastatal company in South Africa. *The International Business & Economics Research Journal, 12,* 1411–1472.

Gibson, C. B., & Vermeulen, F. (2003). A healthy divide: Subgroups as a stimulus for team learning behavior. *Administrative Science Quarterly, 48*(2), 202–239. doi:10.2307/3556657

Goleman, D. (1995). *Emotional intelligence: Why EQ can matter more than IQ*. New York: Bantam Books.

Goleman, D. (1998). *Working with emotional intelligence*. New York, NY: Bantam.

Goleman, D., Boyatzis, R., & McKee, A. (2002). *Primal leadership: Realizing the power of emotional intelligence*. Boston, MA: Harvard Business School Press.

Hansbrough, T. (2012). The construction of a transformational leader: Follower attachment and leadership perceptions. *Journal of Applied Social Psychology, 42*(6), 1533–1549. doi:10.1111/j.1559-1816.2012.00913.x

Hayashi, A., & Ewert, A. (2006). Outdoor leaders' emotional intelligence and transformational leadership. *Journal of Experimental Education, 28*(3), 222–242. doi:10.1177/105382590602800305

Hemsworth, D., Muterera, J., & Baregheh, A. (2013). Examining Bass's transformational leadership in public sector executives: A psychometric properties review. *Journal of Applied Business Research, 29,* 853–862.

Hong, Y., Catano, V. M., & Liao, H. (2011). Leader emergence: The role of emotional intelligence and motivation to lead. *Leadership and Organization Development Journal, 32*(4), 320–343. doi:10.1108/01437731111134625

House, R. J., Spangler, W. D., & Woycke, J. (1991). Personality and charisma in the US presidency: A psychological theory of leadership effectiveness. *Administrative Science Quarterly, 36*(3), 374–396. doi:10.2307/2393201

Hsin-Kuang, C., Chun-Hsiung, L., & Dorjgotov, B. (2012). The moderating effect of transformational leadership on knowledge management and organizational effectiveness. *Social Behavior & Personality: An International Journal, 40*(6), 1015–1024. doi:10.2224/sbp.2012.40.6.1015

Humphrey, R. H. (2002). The many faces of emotional leadership. *The Leadership Quarterly, 13*(5), 493–504. doi:10.1016/S1048-9843(02)00140-6

Hunt, J. G., Schriescheim, C. A., & Sekaran, U. (Eds.). (1982). *Leadership: Beyond establishment views*. Carbondale, IL: Southern Illinois University Press.

Hyypia, M., & Parajanen, S. (2013). Boosting creativity with transformational leadership in fuzzy front-end innovation processes. *Interdisciplinary Journal of Information. Knowledge & Management, 8*, 821–841.

Jackson, B., & Parry, K. (2011). *A very short, fairly interesting and reasonably cheap book about studying leadership*. Los Angeles, CA: Sage Publications.

Jin, Y. (2010). Emotional leadership as a key dimension of public relations leadership: A national survey of public relations leaders. *Journal of Public Relations Research, 22*(2), 159–172. doi:10.1080/10627261003601622

Kelloway, E., Turner, N., Barling, J., & Loughlin, C. (2012). Transformational leadership and employee psychological well-being: The mediating role employee trust in leadership. *Work and Stress, 26*(1), 39–55. doi:10.1080/02678373.2012.660774

Kouzes, J. M., & Posner, B. Z. (1995). *The leadership challenge: How to keep getting extraordinary things done in organizations*. San Francisco, CA: Jossey-Bass Publishers.

Küpers, W., & Weibler, J. (2006). How emotional is transformational leadership really? *Leadership and Organization Development Journal, 27*(5), 368–383. doi:10.1108/01437730610677972

Kuppusamy, J., Ganesan, J., & Rosada, S. (2010). Leadership styles and management techniques: An analysis of Malaysian women entrepreneurs. *Communications of the IBIMA,* 1-10. doi:.10.5171/2010.817881

Lassey, W. R., & Sashkin, M. (1983). Theories of leadership: A review of useful research. In W. R. Lassey & M. Sashkin (Eds.), *Leadership and social change* (pp. 91–106). San Diego, CA: United Associates.

Liu, J., Siu, O., & Shi, K. (2010). Transformational leadership and employee well-being: The mediating role of trust in the leader and self-efficacy. *Applied Psychology, 59*(3), 454–479. doi:10.1111/j.1464-0597.2009.00407.x

Locke, E. A. (1976). The nature and causes of job satisfaction. In M. D. Dunnette (Ed.), *Handbook of Industrial and Organizational Psychology* (pp. 297–350). Chicago, IL: Prentice Hall.

Mahalinga Shiva, M. M., & Suar, D. (2012). Transformational leadership, organizational culture, organizational effectiveness, and programme outcomes in non-governmental organizations. *Voluntas: International Journal of Voluntary & Nonprofit Organizations, 23*(3), 684–710. doi:10.1007/s11266-011-9230-4

Maritz, D. (1995). Leadership and mobilizing potential. *Human Resource Management, 10*(1), 8–16.

Meyer, J. P., & Allen, N. J. (1997). *Commitment in the workplace*. Thousand Oaks, CA: Sage.

Meyer, J. P., Stanley, D. J., Hescovitch, L., & Topolnytsky, L. (2002). Affective continuance and normative commitment to the organization: A meta-analysis of antecedents, correlates and consequences. *Journal of Vocational Behavior, 61*(1), 20–52. doi:10.1006/jvbe.2001.1842

Moorman, R. H. (1991). Relationship between organizational justice and organizational citizenship behaviors: Do fairness perceptions influence employee citizenship? *The Journal of Applied Psychology, 76*(6), 759–776. doi:10.1037/0021-9010.76.6.845

Motowidlo, S. J., & Borman, W. C. (1978). Relationships between military morale, motivation, satisfaction, and unit effectiveness. *The Journal of Applied Psychology, 63*(1), 47–52. doi:10.1037/0021-9010.63.1.47

Mowday, R. T., Porter, L. W., & Dubin, R. (1974). Unit performance, situational factors and employee attitudes in spatially separate work units. *Organizational Behavior and Human Performance, 12*(2), 231–248. doi:10.1016/0030-5073(74)90048-8

Mullen, J. E., & Kelloway, E. (2009). Safety leadership: A longitudinal study of the effects of transformational leadership on safety outcomes. *Journal of Occupational and Organizational Psychology, 82*(2), 253–272. doi:10.1348/096317908X325313

Naami, A., & Asadi, P. (2011). Study on the mediating role of innovative climate in the relationship between transformational leadership style and innovative behavior of an industrial company workers in Khoozestan. *Australian Journal of Basic & Applied Sciences, 5*, 861–866.

Nielsen, K., Randall, R., Yarker, J., & Brenner, S. (2008). The effects of transformational leadership on followers' perceived work characteristics and psychological well-being: A longitudinal study. *Work and Stress, 22*(1), 16–32. doi:10.1080/02678370801979430

Omar, W., & Hussin, F. (2013). Transformational leadership style and job satisfaction relationship: A study of structural equation modeling (SEM). *International Journal of Academic Research In Business & Social Sciences, 3*, 346–365.

Palmer, B., Wallis, M., Burgess, Z., & Stough, C. (2001). Emotional intelligence and effective leadership. *Leadership and Organization Development Journal, 22*(1), 5–10. doi:10.1108/01437730110380174

Pawar, B. S. (2003). Central conceptual issues in transformational leadership research. *Leadership and Organization Development Journal, 24*(7), 397–406. doi:10.1108/01437730310498596

Peterson, P., Park, N., Hall, N., & Seligman, M. E. P. (2009). Zest at work. *Journal of Organizational Behavior, 30*(2), 161–172. doi:10.1002/job.584

Robbins, S. P. (2001). *Organizational behavior* (9th ed.). Upper Saddle River, NJ: Prentice-Hall.

Roush, P. E., & Atwater, L. E. (1992). Using the MBTI to understand transformational leadership and self perception accuracy. *Military Psychology, 4*(1), 17–34. doi:10.1207/s15327876mp0401_2

Sahaya, N. (2012). A learning organization as a mediator of leadership style and firms' financial performance. *International Journal of Business and Management, 7*(14), 96–113. doi:10.5539/ijbm.v7n14p96

Salovey, P., & Mayer, J. D. (1990). Emotional intelligence. *Imagination, Cognition and Personality, 9*(3), 185–211. doi:10.2190/DUGG-P24E-52WK-6CDG

Service, R. W., & Fekula, M. J. (2008). Beyond emotional intelligence: The EQ matrix as a leadership imperative. *Business Renaissance Quarterly, 3*(2), 23–57.

Shahhosseini, M., Daud Silong, A., & Arif Ismaill, I. (2013). Relationship between transactional, transformational leadership styles, emotional intelligence and job performance. *Researchers World: Journal of Arts. Science & Commerce, 4*(1), 15–22.

Shamir, B., Zakay, E., Breinin, E., & Popper, M. (1998). Correlates of charismatic leader behavior in military units: Subordinates' attitudes, unit characteristics and superior's appraisal of leader performance. *Academy of Management Journal, 41*(4), 387–438. doi:10.2307/257080

Shooshtarian, Z., Ameli, F., & Aminilari, M. (2013). The effect of labor's emotional intelligence on their job satisfaction, job performance and commitment. *Iranian Journal of Management Studies, 6*(1), 29–45A.

Sims, R. R., & Quatro, S. A. (2005). *Leadership: Succeeding in the private, public and not-for-profit sectors*. Armonk, NY: M.E. Sharpe.

Singh, P. (2013). Influence of leaders' intrapersonal competencies on employee job satisfaction. *The International Business & Economics Research Journal, 12*, 1289–1302.

Sterrett, A. S. (2000). *The manager's pocket guide to emotional intelligence*. Boston, MA: HRD Press.

Sunindijo, R. Y. (2012). Integrating emotional intelligence, political skill, and transformational leadership in construction. *Civil Engineering Dimension, 14*, 182–189. doi:10.9744/CED.14.3.182-189

Tan, H. H., & Quek, B. C. (2001). An exploratory study on the career anchors of educators in Singapore. *The Journal of Psychology, 135*(5), 527–545. doi:10.1080/00223980109603717 PMID:11804006

Tannenbaum, R., Weschler, I. R., & Massarik, F. (1961). *Leadership and organization: A behavioral science approach*. New York, NY: McGraw-Hill Book Company.

The Power of Transformational Leadership. (2013). *Professional Safety, 58*(1), 19.

Thompson, J. (2012). Transformational leadership can improve workforce competencies. *Nursing Management-UK, 18*(10), 21-24. doi: 10.7748/nm2012.03.18.10.21.c8958

Tracey, J. B., & Hinkin, T. R. (1998). Transformational leadership or effective managerial practices? *Group & Organization Studies, 23*(3), 220–236. doi:10.1177/1059601198233002

Turner, R., & Lloyd-Walker, B. (2008). Emotional intelligence (EI) capabilities training: Can it develop EI in project teams? *International Journal of Managing Projects in Business, 1*(4), 512–534. doi:10.1108/17538370810906237

Vrba, M. (2007). Emotional intelligence skills and leadership behaviour in a sample of South African first-line managers. *Management Dynamics, 16*(2), 25–35.

Wan Ismail, W., & Al-Taee, F. (2012). Integrating gender, traits and transformational leadership style as viewed from human resource management. *International Journal of Academic Research, 4*, 16–20.

Warr, P. (2006). Differential activation of judgments in employee well-being. *Journal of Occupational and Organizational Psychology, 79*(2), 225–244. doi:10.1348/096317905X52652

Weinberger, L. A. (2002). Emotional intelligence: Its connection to HRD theory and practice. *Human Resource Development Review*, *1*(2), 215–243. doi:10.1177/15384302001002005

Wu, F. Y. (2009). The relationship between leadership styles and foreign English teachers' job satisfaction in adult English cram schools: Evidences in Taiwan. *Journal of American Academy of Business, Cambridge*, *14*(2), 75–82.

Yammarino, F. J., & Dubinsky, A. J. (1994). Transformational leadership theory: Using levels of analysis to determine boundary conditions. *Personnel Psychology*, *47*(4), 787–811. doi:10.1111/j.1744-6570.1994.tb01576.x

Yang, M. (2012). Transformational leadership and Taiwanese public relations practitioners' job satisfaction and organizational commitment. *Social Behavior & Personality: An International Journal*, *40*(1), 31–46. doi:10.2224/sbp.2012.40.1.31

Yi-Feng, Y. (2009). An investigation of group interaction functioning stimulated by transformational leadership on employee intrinsic and extrinsic job satisfaction: An extension of the resource-based theory perspective. *Social Behavior & Personality: An International Journal*, *37*(9), 1259–1277. doi:10.2224/sbp.2009.37.9.1259

Yuan, B. C., Wan-Lung, H., Jia-Horng, S., & Kuang-Pin, L. (2012). Increasing emotional intelligence of employees: Evidence from research and development teams in Taiwan. *Social Behavior & Personality: An International Journal*, *40*(10), 1713–1724. doi:10.2224/sbp.2012.40.10.1713

Yung-Shui, W., & Tung-Chun, H. (2009). The relationship of transformational leadership with group cohesiveness and emotional intelligence. *Social Behavior & Personality: An International Journal*, *37*(3), 379–392. doi:10.2224/sbp.2009.37.3.379

Chapter 5

Speaking with Trunks, Dancing with the "Pink Elephants":
Troubling E–Racism, E–Classism, and E–Sexism in Teaching Multicultural Teacher Education

Christine Clark
University of Nevada Las Vegas, USA

Gwen Stowers
National University, USA

ABSTRACT

This chapter takes a contrary view of the "meta" aspect of meta-communication (where meta is defined as "behind" or "beneath") in the online multicultural teacher education classroom, arguing that such communication inhibits learning about (content) and through (pedagogy) sociopolitically-located multicultural teacher education by enabling e-racism, e-classism, and e-sexism to operate in largely covert manners in the distance education context. Accordingly, this chapter contends that digital meta-communication on issues of race/ethnicity, socioeconomic class, and sex/gender needs to be "de-meta-ed" or made explicit in order for the kind of liberatory reflective conversation on these topics to occur that is foundational to the adequate preparation of PK-12 teachers to effectively educate all students.

INTRODUCTION

In this chapter, we will discuss how race/ethnicity, socioeconomic class, and sex/gender come up or come "through" in online communication. We examine the "appearances" of these dimensions of identity from the lens of how we, as online faculty, "see" them, and how they manifest in online course discussions in student-to-student communication.

More specifically, we define the problem of e- or electronic racism, e-classism, and e-sexism as a meta-communicative (less than fully conscious), yet "dancing pink elephant" (figure 1) (blatant) in the online multicultural education classroom from the perspectives of how faculty perceive students' race/ethnicity, socioeconomic class, and sex/gender identities, as well how these identities become "transparent" in student e-conversation.

DOI: 10.4018/978-1-4666-9970-0.ch005

Figure 1. Dancing pink elephants

BACKGROUND

This chapter draws from/builds on three meta-communicative concepts. First, it engages Charles Lawrence's view that race and class are meta-communicative or covert conversational topics because they are "forbidden" (2005). Second, it connects to Mark Lawrence McPhail's notion that direct or non-meta-communicative dialogue about race is "(im)possible" or exceedingly difficult to meaningfully realize (2003). Third, it intertwines Paulo Freire's idea of "false generosity" in exploring the extent to which the meta-communicative aspects of e-racism, e-classism, and e-sexism can be surfaced in order to effectively and consistently develop PK-12 teacher disposition to teach from an ever-deepening critically conscious, sociopolitically-located multicultural educational point of entry across the curriculum (1970).

In "Forbidden Conversations: On Race, Privacy, and Community" (2005), Lawrence, an African American, describes a conversation he had with a white colleague about public schools. The conversation took place shortly after Lawrence's colleague moved to the Washington, D.C. area, where Lawrence already lived. The colleague asked Lawrence to recommend a "good" school for his children. Lawrence uses this conversation to illustrate the meta- or forbidden nature of

conversation about race and class even between Blacks and Whites from the same socioeconomic class background, in this case the upper middle class. Lawrence argues that in asking for such a recommendation, his colleague was *really* asking him to tell him where the predominantly white, upper middle class schools in Washington, D.C. were, but without expressly stating so. Accordingly, Lawrence answers his colleague's question by referring him to areas of the District where all the public schools were predominantly white and upper middle class, instead of directly engaging him in a conversation about how he defines what a "good" school is and why. Lawrence analyzes this conversational exchange as a pre-choreographed conversational dance that he and his colleague had been conditioned to do with one another when issues of race and class emerged. Lawrence goes on to articulate that dancing this dance is the normative manner of communication between people from different racial groups in the United States when issues of race, and class as it pertains to race, emerge.

In essence, Lawrence is describing what Gloria Anzaldúa (1999) has characterized as a form of "border patrol"-like behavior that emerges when people approach situations (borders) in which honest engagement with each other might lead them to meaningfully bridge-the-gap between them (border cross). Avoiding these situations—staying on one's own side of the border—preserves the status quo social order that privileges Whites and, disproportionately, the rich, which is exactly why borders are policed and border crossing is "forbidden." But, Anzaldúa argues, because we have all been so thoroughly socially conditioned—pre-choreographed—to avoid the forbidden, we all operate as less-than-fully-conscious or meta border patrol agents in going about our own everyday lives. In this way, Michel Foucault (1995) suggests the "panopticon" becomes the people—we, all of us, learn to perform surveillance on others and, further, to even internalize this surveillance function in assessing ourselves. Applying Foucault's idea to the current political landscape in the United States, Michael Moore (2010) argues that as a consequence of this panopticonal self-assessment, working and middle-class Whites tend not to vote in their own economic self-interest (including not voting at all) because, at least at a meta-cognitive level, they have, once again, been socially conditioned—pre-choreographed—to avoid acting (forbidden to act) against the interest of the mostly White rich. They do this on one hand because racial borders (constructed around myths of biological superiority and inferiority based largely on skin color) have taught them to see these Whites as they see themselves (as sharing an identity), and on another hand because economic borders (constructed around the myth of class mobility) have taught them to believe that one day they will also be rich.

In "Race and the (Im)Possibility of Dialogue" (2003), McPhail expresses seeing the same meta or forbidden communicative dynamics that Lawrence describes. But for McPhail, at least initially, through a dialogic form of communication the meta- can be surfaced and meaningfully engaged such that the forbidden is not only eroded, it becomes the aspirational. Fortified by this belief, McPhail dedicates many years of his life to facilitating and/or co-facilitating (with a white co-facilitator) race-based intergroup dialogue

(sustained, open and honest conversation about race and racism between people of color (especially black people) and white people). Over time, McPhail's belief begins to wane as a result of the prevailing nature of engagement—or rather, non-engagement—of Whites in these dialogues. Time and time again, no matter the care that McPhail (and/or his co-facilitator) takes to establish a unilaterally supportive framework for race-based intergroup dialogue for *all* the participants in it, the white participants repeatedly resist engaging as members of a racial group (as Whites versus as individuals) and, therefore, reject understanding the experiences of people of color as a function of racial group membership in relationship to structural inequalities in society, rather than simply as a function of individual capacity and/or effort. To add insult to injury, when this white resistance is met with expressions of pain, frustration, and anger from participants of color, white participants emotionally retreat in the dialogue (become hostilely silent) or physically run away from the dialogue (opt out), rather than directly engage with the counter-perspectives and related emotions offered to them by their co-participants of color. The cumulative effect of this repetitive cycle of withdrawl from race-based intergroup dialogue on the part of Whites leaves McPhail wondering if such dialogue is, in fact, possible. He does not extinguish all hope of its possibility, but he does lay the burden for its possibility at the feet of white people's willingness to not only join such a dialogue, but finish one.

In *Pedagogy of the Oppressed* (1970), Freire discusses the path to liberation from conditions of oppression (on the basis of race, class, sex, etc.) for both the oppressed and the oppressors. In the course of this discussion, Freire argues that the nature of oppression is such that seeking liberation from it for the oppressors is more contradictory than it is for the oppressed, precisely because while the oppressors are dehumanized by oppression, they also benefit from it. This is precisely why Whites initially join race-based intergroup dialogues, but ultimately retreat in and run from them. As a result of this contradiction, Freire argues that the oppressors are not "strong enough" to liberate themselves nor the oppressed from oppression, because attempts to do so will necessarily be compromised by "false generosity," or the desire to do justice (be generous) mitigated by the desire to maintain an unfair advantage in society (be false) through the systemic power and control that in race-based intergroup dialogue they deny exists. For this reason, Freire argues that only the oppressed are "strong enough" to liberate themselves and the oppressors from oppression, in part because their strength is not compromised by benefits derived from oppression, and in part because in being oppressed their strength is informed by consciousness of the utter inhumanity of oppression such that they will not seek to simply reverse the terms of oppression (i.e., to oppress the oppressor).

This chapter seeks to surface the meta-manner in which Lawrence's concept of the "forbidden," McPhail's concept of the "(im)possible," and Freire's concept of "false generosity" emerge in online multicultural education classroom dynamics. Only by surfacing or de-meta-ing these concepts, can the teacher education students in these classrooms learn to chart a path from liberatory reflective conversation to liberation from oppression for themselves and their future PK-12 students.

MAIN FOCUS OF THE CHAPTER

With this conceptual framework in mind, this chapter will explore student names, technical writing skills, and conversational content as race/ethnicity-, socioeconomic class-, and sex/gender-related online meta-communicative devices.

What's in a Name? Names as Meta-Communicative Devices Online

In this section, the discussion of student names will examine the manners in which sex/gender and gender identity/gender expression manifest in intra- and inter-cultural and androgynous names, as well as the ways in which primarily race, ethnicity, first language, geographic origin, and immigration status emerge in given and taken names in online conversation in the online multicultural educational classroom. Concomitantly it will examine the exacerbating/mitigating effects that cross-race (also often cross-class) marriages (and, domestic partnerships) have on the compounding advantages/challenges of students' PK-12 schooling.

In almost every online classroom, regardless of its content focus, various social identity group membership dimensions of faculty and students are revealed—both explicitly (known) and implicitly (assumed). For example, in the first week of an online course, the professor and students generally introduce themselves to one another by posting and responding to each other's introductory biographies. It is common in the biographies for marital status, parental responsibilities, and other sex/gender-related information to be disclosed. As a result, faculty and student sex/gender is often known early on in a course. However, this is not always the case, and, even when it is, it is not uncommon for faculty and students to forget personal details shared only at one point in (e.g., at the outset) and/or in one area of (e.g., in a specific discussion forum) the course. As a result, when the professor's or a student's name is cross-culturally gender ambiguous (e.g., "Chris") and/or the gendered nature of the name is not understood and, therefore, not recognized cross-culturally (e.g., "Sivagami"), course discussion can reveal default and/or erroneous gender-based assumptions that faculty and students make. For example, assuming—unintentionally or intentionally—that all names are male unless expressly informed to the contrary, and/or unconsciously or consciously interpreting the gender of a culturally unfamiliar name from the lens of one's own culturally influenced gender norms. But, professor and student sex/gender identity emerges in the online classroom in ways that have little to do with names. Research shows that how men and women communicate online mirrors their patterns of communication in the three-dimensional world (Clark & Gorski, 2002). Accordingly, women tend to engage in online communication with greater equivocation, qualification, and disclamation, use more descriptive language, and are more attentive to conversational exchanges (to being responsive to others, especially those who have engaged them directly) than men. Typically, in non-multiculturally conscious online courses, when these dimensions of identity and related reactions emerge in the classroom they are not attended to with deliberation—they are not considered important enough to either try to tie to the instructional focus of the course, or to engender taking time away from that focus. As result, student engagement with issues of difference remains largely at a "meta" level.

As alluded to in the preceding paragraph, cultural identity dimensions also emerge in the online classroom, perhaps intentionally through explicit disclosure in introducing oneself, and perhaps surreptitiously based on the assumptions made about one's name. In the online multicultural education classroom, it is not uncommon, precisely because of the explicit content focus of the course, for students to deliberately disclose things about themselves in their self-introductions that they might typically want to share in other contexts but are reluctant to for any number of reasons, not the least of which has to do with concern about whether the

disclosure will have the effect of marginalizing them in the classroom community. One common unsolicited disclosure comes from white female students, from a variety of class locations, about their being married to, usually, working class Latino men, who often speak English as a second language. This disclosure serves many different purposes.

For some students this disclosure is a way of being racially authentic in the classroom, to interrupt assumptions classmates might make about their cultural identities based on their Spanish surnames, and to "claim" their whiteness/"own" their white privilege (as an unearned advantage), rather than simply "passing" for Latina. In these instances, these students are challenging the "forbidden," charging directly at it in order to deliberately "de-meta" it.

For some students this disclosure is predicated on the belief that if they are assumed to be Latina, the perception of their academic prowess could be negatively impacted by faculty racial/linguistic prejudice, and/or their immigration status could be called into question by the racial/linguistic prejudices of both the professor and/or their classmates. In these instances, the disclosure clearly reveals an awareness of the reality of prejudice (and the corresponding connections between this prejudice and their assumed and actual *or* erroneously assumed PK-12 schooling experiences), at the same time it reveals a willingness to invoke white privilege to avoid being the target of such prejudice. When this occurs, these students, perhaps unintentionally, contribute to the "(*im*)possible" nature of cross-race intergroup dialogue. Peter McLaren (2000) characterizes this behavior in Whites as follows: "To choose blackness or brownness merely as a way to escape the stigma of whiteness and to avoid responsibility for owning whiteness is still very much an act of whiteness. To choose blackness or brownness as a way of politically disidentifying with white privilege and instead identifying and participating in the struggles of non-white [sic] peoples is an act of transgression, a traitorous act that reveals a fidelity to the struggle for justice" (p. 43).

And, for some students this disclosure is an attempt to present oneself as "less White" or as "a good white person" or as "not prejudiced." In these instances, the disclosure reveals a desire to run away from recognition of one's unearned race privilege, as well as a lack of awareness of the reality that one's racial prejudices do not disappear simply because one marries someone from another racial group. Here students exhibit "false generosity" in seeking to appear committed to issues of equality but only to the extent these issues are unconnected to issues of equity—that is, only to the extent that such commitment does not cost them something personally.

It is important to acknowledge that the very same racial, ethnic, linguistic, geographic, immigration status-related, and/or class dynamics can and do manifest in white female-Latina or white male-Latino domestic partnerships, they just do so less often because these relationships are statistically less common, and because disclosure of this dimension of these relationships is also less common as a result of the added "forbidden" dimension associated with "coming out" as lesbian or gay given the larger heterosexist and homophobic societal context. While such added disclosure is, as discussed above, more likely in the multicultural education classroom, and even more likely in the online multicultural education classroom given the at least somewhat "anonymous" and "distant" nature of online learning (discussed further below) it is still quite rare (Clark, 2005b).

In the online multicultural education classroom, the revelation of cultural identity, especially dimensions of it based on race, ethnicity, first language, geographic origin, and immigration status, does not only emerge by chance (as it would in any online course), or merely as a function of student assumptions about what will be welcomed or expected (because of the multicultural content focus of the course), it is explicitly cultivated by—structured into—the course design. One of the most common ways that such revelation is scripted is through course discussion prompts that ask students to "tell a story" about one or more of their names—how they got it, what it means and/or means to them, what they feel or think of it, experiences they have had because of it, etc. While not expressly stated in the name story prompt, it is virtually impossible to tell a name story without referencing some aspect of one's race, ethnicity, religion, class background, caste, first language, geographic origin, or immigration status.

Facilitated with skill (expressed as faculty responses to and questions about students' stories), this activity has the potential to: 1) foster the development of interpersonal, cross-cultural relationships between students; 2) support the establishment of group norms in drawing out areas of common ground across student experiences based on their individual identities; 3) create the context for student engagement with issues of conflict in highlighting areas of difference across student experiences based on their group identities; and, 4) encourage students to come together to act against injustice, instead of acting oppositionally toward each another as a consequence/in unconscious or sub-conscious reaction to injustice (Boler & Zembylas, 2013; Chubbuck, 2010; Clark & O'Donnell, 1999; Cochran-Smith, 2010; Enterline, Cochran-Smith, Ludlow, Mitescu, 2008; Nagda, Gurin, & López, 2003; Nagda, Kim & Truelove, 2004; Nagda & Zúñiga, 2003; Paris, 2012; Zúñiga & Nagda, 1993; Zúñiga, Nagda & Sevig, 2002; Zúñiga & Sevig, 1997). As a result, this activity can, at once, walk through the forbidden, the (im)possible, and the falsely generous, enabling student engagement in liberatory reflective conversation.

It's Not What You E-say, it's How You E-say it: Technical Writing Skills and Online Meta-communication

In this section, the discussion of technical writing skills will examine how the compounding advantages/challenges of students' PK-12 school experiences show up in their written communication online through their first and, where relevant, second language literacy and fluency, as well as through their command of grammar and American Psychological Association (APA) formatting.

The section will also examine the role of race and class issues in the development of student critical consciousness online. More specifically, this examination will explore how student critical consciousness is often facilitated by their membership in marginalized groups and impeded by their membership in dominant ones. Correlations between the presence and/or absence of this consciousness and the compounding advantages/challenges of students' PK-12 school experiences discussed in the preceding section will be drawn.

Because online education makes pursuing higher education more accessible to students who are working and/or parenting full-time, it is an option that, perhaps, disproportionately, working class students engage.

As a result, several trends in online communication based largely on race, first language, and class emerge.

The first trend is that working class, domestic (e.g., African American, Native American, Puerto Rican, Chicana/Chicano, among others) students of color tend to demonstrate high levels of critical consciousness related to multicultural content in the *content* of their online discussion posts, coupled with significant technical writing challenges in the *structure* of these posts. Both post characteristics here can be attributed to these students' experiences of marginalization in society based on race and class. Students live with the reality of their own experiences as working class people of color (including their sub-standard PK-12 schooling experiences) as in utter opposition to the masternarrative that the United States is a race and class "neutral" society. For these students, knowledge of the "forbidden" is a part of their "everyday." To the extent these students hold this knowledge covertly, and/or in ways (through shame, defensiveness, or pride, or as a function of exhaustion (in coping with racism and classism)) that preclude them from seeking and/or accepting academic support to improve their writing, the "forbidden" will persist uninterrupted.

Skilled facilitation of these (and other) students' learning in the multicultural classroom (again, expressed as faculty responses to and questions about students' shared ideas and experiences) must expressly connect their consciousness and lived reality in the discussion area of the classroom. But skilled facilitation of *only* these students' learning must also be expressed in the form of direct, honest, supportive, timely, detailed, and comprehensively constructive feedback on their technical writing skills in the gradebook area of the course. Connection of this feedback to their consciousness and to their lived reality can engender a reduction in student shame, defensiveness, and pride. Further, connection of this feedback to the reduction of time spent on assignments as writing skills improve can help students muster the energy to take advantage of writing tutors and/or academic writing courses. Many faculty, especially white faculty, avoid giving this kind of private feedback to students, especially to working class students of color, in part because it is time-consuming to do so, and in part because it is simply easier to be "falsely generous" in the evaluation of student work. Giving and receiving compassionately truthful feedback is painful to both parties, especially when doing so crosses race and class lines—in it's own way it is a form of cross-race, cross-class dialogue and, therefore, carries with it the burden of both the "forbidden" and the "(im)possible."

The second trend is that working class white students tend to embrace "English only" and "Standard English" educational policies and benchmarks in the *content* of their online discussion posts, coupled with the same significant technical writing challenges in the *structure* of these posts that their of color classmates do. For these students, the development of critical consciousness based on their own experiences as working class people (including their sub-standard PK-12 schooling experiences) is retarded and/or impeded by their race privilege. As a result, these students, again perhaps unintentionally, contribute to the "(*im*) possible" nature of not only cross-race intergroup dialogue, but specifically cross-race, intra-class intergroup dialogue, as well as, simply, intra-class intergroup dialogue. While these students share more in common with their working class student of color classmates (and therefore stand to gain more from forging "forbidden" alliances with these classmates to act against class-based injustices in society), they, instead, aspirationally identify with middle and upper class white students who express reactionary ideals and, therefore, forge the type of alliances with these classmates that preclude social action of any kind.

Skilled facilitation of these (and other) students' learning in the multicultural classroom (again, expressed as faculty responses to and questions about students' shared ideas and experiences) must expressly connect their *lack of* consciousness and lived reality in the discussion area of the classroom. But, again, skilled facilitation of *only* these students' learning must likewise be expressed in the form of direct, honest, supportive, timely, detailed, and comprehensively constructive feedback on their technical writing skills in the gradebook area of the course. Connection of this feedback to their *lack of* consciousness and to their lived reality can *engender* shame, defensiveness, and pride, as well as pain and anger. For many of these students, being faced with the contradiction of their racist, meritocratic political philosophy in relationship to their own lack of meritocratic performance can be initially emotionally and intellectually overwhelming. Further, connection of this feedback to the need for them to spend the time to take advantage of writing tutors and/or academic writing courses in order to, in fact, merit good grades can be very off-putting to these students. Again, many faculty, especially white faculty, avoid giving this kind of private feedback to students, especially to working class white students, in part because it is time-consuming to do so, and in part because it is simply easier to be "falsely generous" in the evaluation of student work, especially when students perceive the quality of their work through similarly, though self-directed, "falsely generous" lenses—that is, when student self-evaluation is based on the myth of their merit that is, at once, predicated on race privilege and class oppression and a denial that such privilege and oppression exist. Once again, giving and receiving compassionately truthful feedback is painful to both parties, especially when doing so forces examination of race and class dynamics in relationship to a students conflicting race and class locations and corresponding, now compromised, political philosophy. Again, developing and delivering this kind of feedback carries with it the burden of both the "forbidden" and the "(im)possible," making it an emotionally and intellectually "heavy lift" for faculty, especially white faculty, day in and day out. White, at least middle class faculty are typically unaccustomed to the exhaustion that direct engagement with racism and classism—even in only in academic contexts—can cause; accordingly, they also typically lack the coping skills for so doing and, for this reason as well, avoid constructing and conveying such feedback.

The third trend is a bifurcated one. This trend is that middle and upper class white students tend to either express progressive *or* reactionary ideals in the *content* of their online discussion posts, coupled with technical writing prowess in the *structural* expression of this these ideals in their posts. For these students, the development *or* lack of development of critical consciousness cannot be linked with marginalization on the basis of race or class. Sometimes the development of such consciousness can be linked to experiences of marginalization on the basis of another dimension of social group membership (e.g., first language, geographic origin, immigration status, as well as sex/gender, gender identity or expression, sexual orientation, religion, and (dis)ability status, among others). Other times the development or lack of development of this consciousness is a function of how these students have come to see and understand oppression in society. Students who have been taught to think critically about social issues (taught to confront the "forbidden") in their privileged PK-12 schooling experiences, recognize and understand that oppression exists in society, largely as a function of the differential access to full participation in democracy afforded to people based on their race- and class-based social identity group memberships. Students who have not been taught to think critically about social issues (taught to avoid the "forbidden") in their privileged PK-12 schooling experiences, do not recognize that oppression exists in society, and, therefore attribute differential access to full participation in democracy that accrues to people based on their race- and class-based social identity group memberships to be a function of individual and/or group capacity (intelligence and/or ability), coupled with individual effort and discipline.

Finally, skilled facilitation of these (and other) students' learning in the multicultural classroom (again, expressed as faculty responses to and questions about students' shared ideas and experiences) must expressly connect their *consciousness or lack thereof* and lived reality in the discussion area of the classroom. But, once again, skilled facilitation of *only* these students' learning must likewise be expressed in the form of direct, honest, supportive, timely, detailed, and comprehensively constructive feedback *on their consciousness or lack thereof.* Too often, faculty spend less time engaging students through such feedback whose intellectual and/or technical skill sets are already strong, regardless of the ideals they express.

In the multicultural education classroom, all students must be supported and challenged in equitable ways, that is, in relationship to where their learning edges are—supported to stay engaged (to make the "(im)*possible*"), and challenged to grow in the ways their discussion posts and other assignments indicate are necessary based on the goals and objectives of the course (to confront and learn to move with diligence through the "forbidden") (Anyon, 2014; Clark, 2005a; Nagda, Gurin, & López, 2003; Nagda, Kim & Truelove, 2004; Nagda & Zúñiga, 2003; Palos, 2011). This is, perhaps, the most difficult to accomplish in the multicultural education classroom with technically proficient students, regardless of race, who express progressive ideals. With these students, as well as all other students, it is paramount to search for points of contention in their consciousnesses (for example, an expressed belief in the fundamental oneness of all humanity juxtaposed with opposition to same sex marriage) and some area for improvement, however small, in their technical skill development.

It's Not How You E-say it, it's What You E-say if You E-say it: Content and Online Meta-Communication

In this section, the discussion of student conversation content in the online multicultural education classroom will focus examination in two areas. The first area will examine how students express, if at all, what they feel, think, believe, experience, know, and understand in relationship to race/ethnicity, socioeconomic class, and sex/gender in online conversation. This examination will pay particular attention to how, if it all, students differentiate and/or learn to differentiate conjecture from actuality. The second area will examine the ways in which student internalized oppression can manifest as fidelity to racism, classism, and sexism, and how the "cover" provided by the relative anonymity of e-communication context can deepen this oppression and the manifestations of the e-versions of these isms.

Conjecture and Actuality

One of the unique benefits of online education is that students who might typically be less inclined to participate (based on personality (e.g., shyness) and/or internalized messages related social identity group membership (e.g., English language prowess, self-perceived validity of ideas based on sex, race, etc.)) in face-to-face education, are not only more inclined to participate in the online classroom; they *have* to because they simply cannot rely on the participation and/or overparticipation of their classmates to take up all the class discussion time. (While the asynchronous nature of online class discussion time means it technically never ends, it is usually internally structured to end at a certain point each week.) Similarly, students who might commonly have more difficulty in attempting to enter into class discussion (i.e., who are reluctant to "jump in," are used to raising their hands to get faculty or classmate attention before speaking, and/or who wait to be called on to speak) in face-to-face education, do not experience these challenges in the online classroom; there is less "air time" competition in online class discussion, and the "call" to discussion or discussion prompt greets all students in the same manner whenever they opt into the discussion (though some students do still compete to post their responses to discussion prompts first or most robustly). As a result, engendering equitable student participation online is somewhat less of a challenge than it is in the face-to-face setting.

But, while the question of *if* students participate may be a less challenging one in online education, precisely because students—all students—are participating (and often participating more) in such educational contexts, facilitating all of

what they say (the sheer volume of it) is quite challenging. In the online multicultural education classroom, facilitating all of what students say (the sheer volume of it *as well as* the nature of it) is even more challenging because of the a priori-perceived politicized focus of the course content. What is most challenging in this regard is working with students to help them differentiate what they *feel*, from what they *believe*, from what they *think* (opinion), from what they *experience*, from what they *understand*, from what they *know* (fact), from what they can *prove* (based on rigorous academic research).

Because multicultural education focuses study on dimensions of differences based on all human social identity group memberships, it is, in fact, about everyone, and about us in very personal ways. Consequently, it is hard for students to suspend judgment for almost any length of time (hence the tendency toward immediate, knee-jerk response) or to defer judgment about the accurateness of the subject matter to the professor and/or course materials in the same what they might be customarily inclined to do, for example, in a physics classroom.

Hence, skilled facilitation of student learning in this area requires faculty deliberate and staid attention to the issue of "positionality," broadly conceptualized, in all that is said (written). Responding to student posts by asking positionality-focused problem-posing questions such as: Who benefits from this picture of reality and how? Whose interests does this idea serve and why? How did you come to believe this, by what process? Can you prove what you are saying here if you had to? How do you understand or make sense of this and why? What would it mean for you if what you think in this regard could be proven to be absolutely wrong and why? Why do you feel this way? How do you know this is true/false? Have you ever had this experience? Indeed these are "forbidden" questions, yet they are the only kind of questions, that when answers to them are crafted, have the potential to make cross-group dialogue (across all dimensions of difference) "(im)*possible.*"

Further, the attention to the technical aspects of academic writing, again through individuated feedback in the gradebook area of the course, can be facilitative in building student learning in this area as well. While academic writing can be overly formulaic and dispassionate in ways that promote Eurocentric (and other) norms (and that should be acknowledged with students to do so), it can also be instructive in helping students learn how to construct and communicate their ideas in manners that require them and, therefore, reflect their ability, to situate these ideas: 1) relative to like ideas that have preceded and could follow theirs; 2) relative to ideas that both support and challenges theirs; 3) in a manner of organization that ensures that others can follow them; and, 4) in a tone of communication that encourages others to take them seriously. This dimension of skilled facilitation in the multicultural education classroom pushes past "false generosity" in seeking to prepare all students to succeed in the world as it currently exists (e.g., a world in which APA formatting is a measure of academic excellence), as well as to inspire them to change it for the better for all (e.g. a world in which multiple ways of knowing have equal value as indicators of learnedness).

Internalized Oppression

As previously alluded to, the relative anonymity of online education can have the effect of encouraging student participation in general, and online multicultural education can further this effect by engendering student disclosures relating to their social identity group memberships. But the online nature of education also has the effect of providing students "cover" in expressing their feelings, beliefs, and thoughts/opinions, as well as in describing their experiences, and demonstrating their understandings and knowledge in relationship to the course subject matter. In the online multicultural education classroom this can mean that students are not only more willing to share negative characterizations of people who are different from themselves, but also of people who are like them. While such characterizations can be and are also shared in face-to-face multicultural educational settings, in the online setting this sharing is often more cavalier and callous.

Discussed previously in relationship to working class white students' characterizations of people of color (different from themselves) and of poor people (like them), the latter aspect of this phenomenon also emanates from women about women, and people of color about people of the same color. This phenomenon is discussed in the social justice education literature (broadly conceived) as "internalized oppression" (Adams, Bell, & Griffin, 2007; Adams, et. al., 2010; Clark & O'Donnell, 1999; Moll, Amanti, Neff, & González, 1991; Yosso, 2005). Such oppression manifests when people from non-dominant social identity groups internalize the negative messages about their own groups that are promoted by members of dominant groups both individually and systemically and then apply them to themselves, others in their group, and/or the group as a whole to explain their own, another person's, and/or the group's perceived lack of ability, value, and/or academic and/or economic progress. Alice Walker (2010) has commented on this phenomenon among African Americans arguing that it is not difficult to understand why black America might not want to identify with Africa (or Africans) when the vast majority of images of it portrayed in the U.S. media paints it as a poor and dirty place where people are suffering from starvation and disease. Henry Giroux (1996) has suggested that when what you are is made negative on a grand scale, the tendency is to run away from yourself, to disassociate yourself from your organic history and culture, to, in essence, develop a "fugitive identity." Adding insult to injury, Toni Morrison (2007) contends that in developing a fugitive identity, black Americans have also developed "images of whiteness" in their "black imagination." Said another way, the internalized oppression that many black Americans experience may be so profound that they no longer need to run from who they are, because their mind's eye has been permeated by white supremacy to such an extent that an authentic sense of who they were, are, and/or, could be apart from that supremacy may no longer exist, not even in their souls. Other people of color and women (as well as members of other non-dominant groups based on other dimensions of social identity group membership) experience and exhibit parallel identity conflicts, many of which show up in their discussion posts in the online multicultural education classroom.

Skilled facilitation of student learning in this area requires tremendous faculty empathy as differentiated from sympathy—that is, faculty must express "feeling *with*" the student whose posts demonstrate internalized oppression, not "feeling *for*" him or her. In "feeling *with*," faculty place themselves in the same position as the student, alongside her or him, instead of in a position apart from, outside, above, at a distance from, etc., that of the student. While there is the potential to fall into the trap of "false generosity" in expressing empathy as well as sympathy, not only is the potential greater with expressions of sympathy, the consequences of so doing are as well. As discussed previously in relationship to the "positionality" manifest in student posts, here the "positionality" of faculty responses to students' posts is likewise key.

When faculty express feeling *for* a student experiencing internalized oppression, it can have the effect of deepening that oppression by communicating to the student that what she or he is experiencing is emotionally and/or intellectually unfamiliar to the faculty member, making dialogue about the "forbidden" nature of the experience "(*im*)possible." If the faculty member is from the non-dominant group relative to the student's

internalized oppression, the student can interpret the faculty member's sympathy as evidence that she or he is unaware of her or his own "inferiority." And, if the faculty member is from a dominant group relative to the student's internalized oppression, the expression of sympathy can signal to the student that their internalized oppression is warranted precisely because members of the dominant group do not experience it. Regardless of faculty identity relative to the student's internalized oppression, expressions of sympathy are ineffective in facilitating all students' learning in this area.

On the other hand, when faculty express feeling *with* a student experiencing internalized oppression, it can have the effect of mitigating that oppression by communicating to the student that what she or he is experiencing is emotionally and/or intellectually familiar to the faculty member, making dialogue about the "forbidden" nature of the experience "(im)*possible*." If the faculty member is from the non-dominant group relative to the student's internalized oppression, the student might be inclined to engage the faculty member's empathy further in an effort to discover overtly (by asking outright) or covertly (by asking tangentially related and/or indirect questions) how she or he copes with, responds to, manages, etc., her or his experience of this oppression. And, if the faculty member is from a dominant group relative to the student's internalized oppression, the expression of empathy can signal to the student that their internalized oppression is unjustified because members of the dominant group not only recognize it, recognize it as something warranting solidarity, allyship, and *leaning in toward*, not d-i-s-t-a-n-c-i-n-g a-w-a-y f-r-o-m. Regardless of faculty identity relative to the student's internalized oppression, expressions of empathy are effective in facilitating all students' learning in this area. These expressions of empathy should continue in individuated feedback to students in the gradebook area of the course.

It is important to note that, in contrast to sympathy, empathy does not necessarily imply kindness in the traditional sense of this word. Reverend James H. Cone describes the type of non-traditional kindness that often uniquely exemplifies empathy in this way: "G-d has a way of pointing you to the right thing if you remain open and listen to people who mean you well; *and, remember, the people who mean you well are not always those who say nice things…*" (2002). So, in empathizing with students experiencing internalized oppression, it may be necessary to "mean them well" by responding to their posts with commentary that may not always be nice. This is especially the case when the expression of internalized oppression is directed outward—at other members of the non-dominant group relative to the student's internalized oppression, as opposed to inward—at the student her or himself (that is self-directed) as a member of the non-dominant group relative to her or his internalized oppression. In these instances it is important not only for the student at focus, but for all students (from every identity group), to "e-see" and "e-hear" faculty interrogate, challenge, cite the erroneous origins of, provide counter perspectives to, identify weaknesses in, offer alternative understandings of, analyze from more comprehensive points of entry into, etc., manifestations of internalized oppression based on the research in multicultural education.

FUTURE RESEARCH DIRECTIONS

This chapter points to two key areas for future research. The first key area relates to developmental sequencing, and the second key area pertains to instructor readiness.

In thinking about how to predictably achieve the overarching multicultural educational instructional goal of preparing all teacher education students (but especially white middle class females) to effectively teach all students (but

especially working class youth of color), it is clear that having a single multicultural education course in a teacher licensing program of study, while helpful, is not adequate. Further, where multiple such courses—either that contain multicultural educational components or are wholly multiculturally educationally focused—exist in a program, if attention is not paid to how the multicultural components and/or foci are sequenced, while student exposure may be robust, their cumulative knowledge, skills, abilities, and dispositions may be scant, spotty, and/or superficial. Accordingly, future research in multicultural teacher education needs to attend to the development of carefully reasoned scaffolds that are expressly designed to help students build progressively more comprehensive, insightful, and complex multicultural educational knowledge, skills, abilities, and dispositions from the beginning of a course to the end of it, and from one course to the next. With respect to the multicultural educational foci in this chapter, this would mean that students would, over time, develop reliably and demonstrably: 1) increased skill for and comfort with engagement with the "forbidden" and "(im)possible" aspects of especially cross-race intergroup dialogue; 2) greater critical awareness of the how the propensity for "false generosity" on the part of white participants in cross-race intergroup dialogue can threaten the dialogue's efficacy; and, 3) amplified strategic capacity for preventing "false generosity" from manifesting (in self and others) in cross-race intergroup dialogue, and for preserving the dialogue if it does. While there is emerging research in this area, it is not yet broadly, deeply, and differentially well developed enough to be meaningfully instructive in this regard (Clark & O'Donnell, 1999; Gurin, Dey, Hurtado, & Gurin, 2002; Hurtado, 2001).

Throughout this chapter there is an implicit assumption that the people who teach multicultural education courses possess the academic foundation and practical experience necessary to support students learning in the manners discussed. While this assumption is reasonable, it is also largely erroneous. While the literature on the nature of teacher and/or professor preparation required to accomplish these multicultural educational goals is growing, because it is an area of study typified by tremendous political economic conflict, much more research in this area is needed (Anderson & Stillman, 2913; Boler & Zembylas, 2013; Castro, 2010; Chubbuck, 2010; Cochran-Smith, 2010; Delpit, 2006; Domine, 2011; Enterline, Cochran-Smith, Ludlow, Mitescu, 2008; Garmon, 2005; Hughes, 2010; Mowry, 2005; Paris, 2012; Powers, 2006; Picower, 2011; Quinn & Meiners, 2007; Whipp, 2013). Such research should seek to: 1) document the political and economic conflicts related to the development of multicultural educational prowess; 2) find areas of common ground between the parties engaged in the conflict, and articulate, to the extent possible, collaborative pathways forward for establishing constructivist "good practice" (*not* positivist "best practice") benchmarks for multicultural education; and ultimately, 3) explicate what multicultural educational

knowledge bases and skill sets are needed and how they can be reliably developed and assessed.

CONCLUSION

This chapter undertook a critical examination of the myth of online communication/education as race-, class-, and sex-"blind" and, therefore, "bias free." In so doing, this examination uncovered meta-manners by which prejudice, discrimination, and oppression on the basis of social identity group membership—especially those related to race, class, and sex—emerge in and permeate conversation even in the multicultural education e-classroom. Once uncovered, this examination brought to light that the key to eroding and (hopefully) eradicating e-racism, e-classism, and e-sexism (among other forms of e-discrimination and e-oppression) lies in de-meta-ing the conversation on these topics—in short, in learning to dance *with* the pink elephants (figure 2) in the e-classroom, instead of acting as though these elephants are not only not, pink and not dancing, but not even there.

Figure 2. People dancing with pink elephant

REFERENCES

Adams, M., Bell, L. A., & Griffin, P. (Eds.). (2007). *Teaching for diversity and social justice* (2nd ed.). New York, NY: Routledge.

Adams, M., Blumenfeld, W., Casteñeda, C. R., Hackman, H., Peters, M., & Zúñiga, X. (2010). *Readings for diversity and social justice* (2nd ed.). New York, NY: Routledge.

Anderson, L., & Stillman, J. (2013). Student teaching's contribution to preservice teacher development: A review of research focused on the preparation of teachers for urban and high-needs contexts. *Review of Educational Research, 83*(1), 3–69. doi:10.3102/0034654312468619

Anyon, J. (2014). *Radical possibilities: Public policy, urban education, and a new social movement*. New York, NY: Routledge.

Anzaldúa, G. (1999). *Borderlands/la frontera: The new Mestiza* (2nd ed.). San Francisco, CA: Aunt Lute Books.

Boler, M., & Zembylas, M. (2003). Discomforting truths: The emotional terrain of understanding difference. In P. Trifonas (Ed.), *Pedagogies of difference: Rethinking education for social change* (pp. 110–136). New York, NY: Routledge.

Castro, A. J. (2010). Themes in the research on preservice teachers' views of cultural diversity: Implications for researching millennial preservice teachers. *Educational Researcher, 39*(3), 198–210. doi:10.3102/0013189X10363819

Chubbuck, S. (2010). Individual and structural orientations in socially just teaching: Conceptualization, implementation and collaborative effort. *Journal of Teacher Education, 61*(3), 197–210. doi:10.1177/0022487109359777

Clark, C. (2005a, Spring). Intergroup dialogue as pedagogy across the curriculum. *Multicultural Education, 12*(3), 51–61.

Clark, C. (2005b, Fall). People of color coming "out" and being "out" on campus: A conversation with Mark Brimhall-Vargas, Sivagami Subbaraman, and Robert Waters. *Multicultural Education, 13*(1), 45–59.

Clark, C., & Gorski, P. (2002). Multicultural education and the digital divide: Focus on gender. *Multicultural Perspectives, 4*(1), 30–40. doi:10.1207/S15327892MCP0401_6

Clark, C., & O'Donnell, J. (Eds.). (1999). *Becoming and unbecoming white: Owning and disowning a racial identity*. Westport, CT: Greenwood Publishing Group, Inc., Bergin & Garvey.

Cochran-Smith, M. (2010). Toward a theory of teacher education for social justice. In M. Fullan, A. Hargreaves, D. Hopkins, & A. Lieberman (Eds.), *The international handbook of educational change* (2nd ed., pp. 445–467). New York, NY: Springer. doi:10.1007/978-90-481-2660-6_27

Cone, J. H. (2002). Liberation theology and multicultural community. Border Crossing Speaker Series Keynote Address. University of Maryland, College Park, MD.

Delpit, L. (2006). *Other people's children: Cultural conflict in the classroom*. New York, NY: The New Press.

Domine, V. (2011). Building 21st century teachers: An intentional pedagogy of media literacy education. *Action in Teacher Education, 33*(2), 194–205. doi:10.1080/01626620.2011.569457

Enterline, S., Cochran-Smith, M., Ludlow, L., & Mitescu, E. (2008). Learning to teach for social justice: Measuring change in the beliefs of teacher candidates. *New Educator, 4*(4), 267–290. doi:10.1080/15476880802430361

Foucault, M. (1995). *Discipline and punish: The birth of the prison* (2nd ed.). New York, NY: Vintage.

Freire, P. (1970). *Pedagogy of the oppressed*. New York, NY: Continuum.

Garmon, M. A. (2005). Six key factors for changing preservice teachers' attitudes/beliefs about diversity. *Educational Studies*, *38*(3), 275–286. doi:10.1207/s15326993es3803_7

Giroux, H. A. (1996). *Fugitive cultures: Race, violence, and youth*. New York, NY: Routledge.

Gurin, P., Dey, E. L., Hurtado, S., & Gurin, G. (2002). Diversity and higher education: Theory and impact on educational outcomes. *Harvard Educational Review*, *72*(3), 330–366. doi:10.17763/haer.72.3.01151786u134n051

Hughes, J. (2010). What teacher education programs can do to better prepare teachers to meet the challenges of educating students living in poverty. *Action in Teacher Education*, *32*(1), 54–64. doi:10.1080/01626620.2010.10463542

Hurtado, S. (2001). Linking diversity with educational purpose: How the diversity impacts the classroom environment and student development. In G. Orfield (Ed.), *Diversity challenged: Legal crisis and new evidence* (pp. 143–174). Cambridge, MA: Harvard Publishing Group.

Lawrence, C. R. III. (2005). Forbidden conversations: On race, privacy, and community (A continuing conversation with John Ely on racism and democracy). *The Yale Law Journal*, *114*, 1353–1403.

McLaren, P. (2000). *Ché Guevara, Paulo Freire, and the pedagogy of revolution*. Lanham, MD: Rowman & Littlefield.

McPhail, M. L. (2003). Race and the (im)possibility of dialogue. In R. Anderson, L. Baxter, & K. Cisna (Eds.), *Dialogue: Theorizing difference in communication studies* (pp. 209–224). Thousand Oaks, CA: Sage Publications.

Moll, L., Amanti, C., Neff, D., & González, N. (1992). Funds of knowledge for teaching: Using a qualitative approach to connect homes and classrooms. *Theory into Practice*, *31*(2), 132–141. doi:10.1080/00405849209543534

Moore, M. (2010). *Capitalism: A love story*. Beverly Hills, CA: Anchor Bay Entertainment.

Morrison, T. (2007). *The bluest eye*. New York, NY: Vintage International.

Mowry, D. (2005, December 2). Cultural competence: Oregon style. *Oregon Catalyst.com*. Retrieved October 11, 2009, from http://www.oregoncatalyst.com/index.php/archives/20-Cultural-Competence;-Oregon-Style.html

Nagda, B. A., Gurin, P., & López, G. E. (2003). Transformative pedagogy for democracy and social justice. *Race, Ethnicity and Education*, *6*(2), 165–191. doi:10.1080/13613320308199

Nagda, B. A., Kim, C. W., & Truelove, Y. (2004). Learning about difference, learning with others, learning to transgress. *The Journal of Social Issues*, *60*(1), 195–214. doi:10.1111/j.0022-4537.2004.00106.x

Nagda, B. A., & Zúñiga, X. (2003). Fostering meaningful racial engagement through intergroup dialogues. *Group Processes & Intergroup Relations*, *6*(1), 111–128. doi:10.1177/1368430203006001015

Palos, A. (Dir.) (2011). *Precious knowledge* [DVD]. United States: Dos Vatos Films.

Paris, J. (2012). Culturally sustaining pedagogy: A needed stance, terminology, and practice. *Educational Researcher*, *41*(3), 93–97.

Picower, B. (2011). Learning to teach and learning to learn: Supporting the development of new social justice educators. *Teacher Education Quarterly*, *38*(4), 7–24.

Powers, E. (2006, June 6). A spirited disposition debate. *Inside Higher Ed*. Retrieved November 10, 2009, from http://www.insidehighered.com/news/2006/06/06/disposition

Quinn, T., & Meiners, E. (2007). Do ask, do tell: What's professional about taking social justice and sexual orientation out of classrooms? *Rethinking Schools Online*. Retrieved September 30, 2009, from http://www.rethinkingschools.org/archive/21_04/ask214.shtml

Walker, A., & Byrd, R. (2010). *The world has changed: Conversations with Alice Walker*. New York, NY: The New Press.

Whipp, J. L. (2013). Developing socially just teachers: The interaction of experiences before, during, and after teacher preparation in beginning urban teachers. *Journal of Teacher Education*, *64*(5), 454–467. doi:10.1177/0022487113494845

Yosso, T. J. (2005). Whose culture has capital? A critical race theory discussion of community cultural wealth. *Race, Ethnicity and Education*, *8*(1), 69–91. doi:10.1080/1361332052000341006

Zúñiga, X., & Nagda, B. A. (1993). Dialogue groups: An innovative approach to multicultural learning. In D. Schoem, L. Frankel, X. Zúñiga, & E. Lewis (Eds.), *Multicultural teaching in the university* (pp. 233–248). Westport, CT: Praeger.

Zúñiga, X., Nagda, B. A., & Sevig, T. D. (2002). Intergroup dialogues: An educational model for cultivating engagement across differences. *Equity & Excellence in Education*, *35*(1), 7–17. doi:10.1080/713845248

Zuñiga, X., & Sevig, T. D. (1997). Bridging the "us/them" divide through intergroup dialogues and peer leadership. *Diversity Factor*, *6*(2), 23–28.

ADDITIONAL READING

Alimo, C., Kelly, R., & Clark, C. (2002, Fall). Intergroup dialogue program student outcomes and implications for campus racial climate: A case study. *Multicultural Education*, *10*(1), 49–53.

Banks, J. (Ed.). (2009). *The Routledge international companion to multicultural education*. New York: Routledge.

Banks, J., & Banks, C. (Eds.). (2004). *Handbook of research on multicultural education* (2nd ed.). San Francisco: Jossey-Bass.

Bigelow, B. (2006). *The line between us: Teaching about the border and Mexican immigration (paperback)*. Milwaukee, WI: Rethinking Schools.

Clark, C. (2002). Effective multicultural curriculum transformation across disciplines. *Multicultural Perspectives*, *4*(3), 37–46. doi:10.1207/S15327892MCP0403_7

Clark, C. (2002, Summer). Intergroup dialogue on campus. *Multicultural Education*, *9*(4), 30–31.

Clark, C. (2004, Spring). Multicultural education as a tool for reclaiming schools organized as breeding grounds for prisons. *Multicultural Education*, *11*(3), 50–53.

Clark, C., & Gorski, P. (2001). Multicultural education and the digital divide: Focus on race, language, socioeconomic class, gender, and disability. *Multicultural Perspectives*, *3*(3), 39–44. doi:10.1207/S15327892MCP0303_7

Clark, C., & Gorski, P. (2002). Multicultural education and the digital divide: Focus on class. *Multicultural Perspectives*, *4*(3), 25–36. doi:10.1207/S15327892MCP0403_6

Clark, C., Jabonete-Bouis, G., Subbaraman, S., & Balón, D. (2004, Winter). Social justice from classroom to community. *Multicultural Education*, *12*(2), 55–59.

Freire, P. (2005). *Education for critical consciousness*. London, England: Continuum International Publishing Group.

Gorski, P., & Clark, C. (2001). Multicultural education and the digital divide: Focus on race. *Multicultural Perspectives*, *3*(4), 15–25. doi:10.1207/S15327892MCP0304_5

Gorski, P., & Clark, C. (2002). Multicultural education and the digital divide: Focus on disability. *Multicultural Perspectives*, *4*(4), 28–36. doi:10.1207/S15327892MCP0404_6

Gorski, P., & Clark, C. (2002). Multicultural education and the digital divide: Focus on language. *Multicultural Perspectives*, *4*(2), 30–34. doi:10.1207/S15327892MCP0402_7

Gorski, P., & Clark, C. (2003). Turning the tide of the digital divide: Multicultural education and the politics of surfing. *Multicultural Perspectives*, *5*(1), 29–32. doi:10.1207/S15327892MCP0501_6

Gurin, P., Gurin, G., Dey, E. L., & Hurtado, S. (2004a). The educational value of diversity. In P. Gurin, J. Lehman, & E. Lewis (Eds.), *Defending diversity: Affirmative Action at the University of Michigan* (pp. 97–188). Ann Arbor, MI: University of Michigan Press.

Gurin, P., Nagda, R., & Lopez, G. (2004b). The benefits of diversity in education for democratic citizenship. *The Journal of Social Issues*, *60*(1), 17–34. doi:10.1111/j.0022-4537.2004.00097.x

hooks, b. (1994). *Teaching to transgress: Education as the practice of freedom*. New York: Routledge.

Horton, M., & Freire, P. (1990). Conversations on education and social change. In B. Bell, J. Gaventa, & J. Peters (Eds.), *We make the road by walking* (pp. 1–296). Philadelphia, PA: Temple University Press.

Hurtado, S., Dey, E. L., Gurin, P., & Gurin, G. (2003). The college environment, diversity, and student learning. In J. S. Smart (Ed.), *Higher education: Handbook of theory and research* (Vol. 18, pp. 145–189). Amsterdam: Luwer Academic Press.

Karno, D. (2008, April). *NCLB, Standardized curriculum, & privatization: Where does democratic education fit in?* Paper presented at the annual meeting of the Midwest Political Science Association (MPSA) Annual National Conference, Chicago, IL.

Ladson-Billings, G. (2006, October). From the achievement gap to the education debt: Understanding Achievement in U.S. schools. *Educational Researcher*, *35*(7), 3–12. doi:10.3102/0013189X035007003

Limburg, F., & Clark, C. (2006, Spring). Teaching multicultural education online. *Multicultural Education*, *13*(3), 49–55.

Lui, M., & Robles, B. Leondar-Wright, B., Brewer, R., Adamson, R., with United for a Fair Economy. (2006). The color of wealth: The story behind the U.S. racial wealth divide (paperback). New York: The New Press.

McLaren, P. (1997). *Revolutionary multiculturalism: Pedagogies of dissent for the new millennium*. Boulder, CO: Westview.

Milem, J., & Hakuta, K. (2000). The benefits of racial and ethnic diversity in higher education. In D. Wilds (Ed.), *Minorities in higher education, 1999-2000: Seventeenth annual status report* (pp. 39–67). Washington, DC: American Council on Education.

Nieto, S. (1998). From claiming hegemony to sharing space: Creating community in multicultural courses. In R. Chávez Chávez & J. O'Donnell (Eds.), *Speaking the unpleasant: The politics of non-engagement in the multicultural education terrain* (pp. 16–31). Albany: State University of New York Press.

Nieto, S., & Bode, P. (2008). Affirming diversity: The sociopolitical context of multicultural education (fifth edition) (paperback). Upper Saddle River, NJ: Pearson Education/Allyn & Bacon.

Olson, C., Evans, R., & Shoenberg, R. (2007). At home in the world: Bridging the gap between internationalization and multicultural education. Washington, DC: American Council on Education (ACE).

Sleeter, C. E. (1996). *Multicultural education as social activism*. Albany, NY: State University of New York Press.

Tannen, D. (1999). Fighting for our lives. In D. Tannen (Ed.), *The argument culture: Stopping America's war of words* (pp. 3–26). New York: Random House Publishing Group.

Thompson, M. C., Brett, T. G., & Behling, C. (2001). Educating for social justice: The program on intergroup relations, conflict, and community at the University of Michigan. In D. Schoem & S. Hurtado (Eds.), *Intergroup dialogue: Deliberative democracy in school, college, community and workplace* (pp. 99–114). Ann Arbor, MI: University of Michigan.

KEY TERMS AND DEFINITIONS

Critical Consciousness: Awareness developed through critical thought that enables one to see beyond the superficial to what is typically controversial because it threatens the hegemony or status quo.

e-Classism: The manifestations of prejudice and discrimination on the basis of socioeconomic class background (and/or employment status) in the electronic (or "e-"), online, and/or virtual realm.

e-Discrimination: The manifestations of unfair or unjust treatment, especially that which violates policy and law, on the basis of any dimension of social group identity (e.g., race, class, sex, etc.), especially toward members of "protected class," marginalized, and historically underrepresented groups in the electronic (or "e-"), online, and/or virtual realm.

e-Oppression: The manifestations of systemic discrimination—via overtly and covertly coercive mechanisms that operate in the political, economic, psychological, and physical spheres of society—from members of one or more dominant social identity groups (e.g., upper class, white, men, etc.), toward members of one or more non-dominant social identity groups (e.g., poor, of color, women, etc.) in the electronic (or "e-"), online, and/or virtual realm.

e-Racism: The manifestations of prejudice and discrimination on the basis of race (and/or ethnicity, tribe, religion, creed, color, and caste) in the electronic (or "e-"), online, and/or virtual realm.

e-Sexism: The manifestations of prejudice and discrimination on the basis of sex (and/or gender, gender identity, and gender expression) in the electronic (or "e-"), online, and/or virtual realm.

De-Meta-Ed: The process by which a covert phenomenon was made overt.

False Generosity: The inherently conflicted, and ultimately compromised, nature of commitment to equity expressed by members of dominant social identity groups who, on one hand seek social justice for all peoples, but on the other hand seek to maintain their unjust advantage over members of non-dominant social identity groups.

Internalized Oppression: The un- or subconsciously absorbed: 1) negative and/or inferior feelings, opinions, or beliefs about one's own non-dominant social identity group(s), and/or, 2) positive and/or superior feelings, opinions, or beliefs about dominant social identity groups of which one is *not* a member; both sets of ideas emerge in reaction to prolonged exposure to manifestations of systemic discrimination—via overtly and covertly coercive mechanisms that operate in the political, economic, psychological, and physical spheres of society—and that are actively promoted by members of dominant social identity groups.

Meta: Behind or beneath.

Meta-Communication: Hidden and/or covertly underlying meaning; the deeper, alternative, and/or opposite meaning behind or beneath what is actually expressed.

Panopticon: A higher or strategic vantage point from which covert and/or overt surveillance can be conducted; the rifle tower in a prison; a prison or prison-like environment in which occupants are under constant scrutiny and, therefore, have no personal refuge and/or privacy.

Transparency: Openness, straightforwardness, directness; the absence of deception, coercion, duplicity; the skill, ability, and will to be honest even when honesty may compromise one's image, reputation, standing, etc., because it is the right thing to be.

Voice: Oral agency; the skill, ability, and will to express critically conscious—counterhegemonic or anti-status quo—feelings, opinion, beliefs, *and factual knowledge* about issues of oppression manifest in society at large and/or expressed by specific members of society.

Chapter 6
Reframing Continuous School Improvement in Australian Schools

Venesser Fernandes
Monash University, Australia

ABSTRACT

There is a significant lack of documented research on Australian school improvement contextualised within business improvement model settings. This is the case, even though Australian schools have been operating within a business environment for a while now. This chapter aims at addressing this gap by discussing educational quality within schools. It will also present an adapted version for continuous school improvement within school systems in Australia. This adapted version of continuous school improvement provides a theoretical framework on how schools operating as self-managed business systems can ensure that the delivery of educational quality is strategically sustained at the organisational level and that focus remains on the important core business of student learning.

INTRODUCTION: THE KALEIDOSCOPIC LANDSCAPE OF CONTINUOUS SCHOOL IMPROVEMENT

Making any more mistakes in the "How to" of delivering a quality education will be disastrous to us as a nation, we cannot afford to delay having a world-class education system that builds a stronger future and a fairer Australia that can face the challenges of a globally competitive world (Commonwealth Of Australia, 2008, p. 34).

For decades there has been a concerted effort at the international and national level to improve educational quality as part of both international and national educational reform agendas. However defining and coming to an understanding of what educational quality is, has been an ambiguous and difficult journey. There is in fact no universal agreement on its definition, its processes, its methods for measurement, and the complexity of many simultaneously interacting relevant variables that would need to be analysed. This ambiguity in itself provides credence to the fact that educational quality is not a universally defined phenomenon but something that has to be understood at its point of action albeit having a universally accepted notional framework of understanding that nations strive to achieve. As seen over the years, some of

DOI: 10.4018/978-1-4666-9970-0.ch006

the problems endemic to studies of educational effectiveness have been attributed to a lack of empirical evidence, a lack of longitudinal studies modelling change, the issue of data analysis methods, problems in the choice of measures for the outcomes, the issue of sample size, and statistical adjustments (Hill, Rowe, Holmes-Smith & Russell, 1996).

In a rapidly changing environment of social and economic globalisation, education is identified as a primary centrepiece and a requisite for fulfilling many individual, familial and national aspirations (Adams et al., 2012, p. 6). Hill, Rowe, Holmes-Smith and Russell (1996) suggest that, "The provision of schooling is one of the most massive and ubiquitous undertakings of the modern state. Schools account for a substantial proportion of public and private expenditure and are universally regarded as vital instruments of social and economic policy aimed at promoting individual fulfilment, social progress and national prosperity" (p. 1). In this environment, understandings around educational quality have become very much complex and comprehensive.

Schools are open systems where people work together to achieve a common purpose. As open systems, schools are always interacting with their environments and therefore structure themselves to deal with forces within these environments. Betts (1992) suggests that, "The improvement of quality involves the design of an educational system that not only optimises the relationship among the elements but also between the educational system and its environment. In general, this means designing a system that is more open, organic, pluralistic, and complex" (p.40). Adams et al. (2012, p. 2) suggest that there are three major implications that should be considered in improvement efforts across education policy, planning and practice which include: (a) increased centrality of education in national development policy and planning; (b) increased focus and priority on decentralisation and localisation with further empowerment of teachers and administrators; and, (c) the trend

towards an emphasis on, and assessment of education quality at all levels. Brooks and Normore (2010) further suggest that "a more glocalised (a meaningful integration of local and global forces) approach to education by the discrete agency of educational leaders is imperative" (p. 52) in being able to develop a deeper understanding of educational quality. As they suggest, "the implications of glocalisation are profound, and the consequences of not understanding the way that the local and global are interconnected will increase over time" (p. 73). Torres and Antikainen (2003) similarly identify that "the presence of globalisation makes the study of education even more complex. Traditional preoccupation with the intersection of classes, race, gender, and the state become magnified with the dialectics of the global and the local" (p. 5).

Thus, it seems obvious that school improvement initiatives taken to improve educational quality continue to be required at all levels: international, national, state, regional and organisational (see Figure 1). Having a conscious and agentic understanding of the importance of this continuous change for improvement in educational quality is required by stakeholders at every level. Using a strong glocalised approach, educational quality becomes decentralised and localised being situated around continuous and improved educational effectiveness at the individual level as well as at the organisational, regional, national and international levels of educational development. Also, as Figure 1 suggests, it is imperative that whatever the level of improvement, the effect is felt at the individual level – the student learner. The individual learner is central to all educational improvements going on at each of these levels.

Banathy (1991, p.80) describes such an educational system as one that interacts with constantly changing, multiple environments and coordinates with many other systems in the environment. In essence, the question then is how can this dynamic glocalised educational system be understood? Engeström & Glaveanu (2012) use the third

Figure 1. A Glocalised Framework of Continuous School Improvement

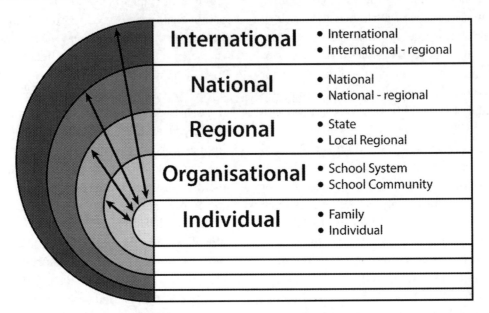

generation activity theory as a systems model for theorizing and for empirical studies which expand the unit of analysis from a single activity system to multiple, interacting activity systems. Daniels and Warmington (2007) in discussing Engeström's (2001) third generation activity theory identify the importance of extending beyond a singular activity system such as a school organisation and to examine and work towards the transformation of networks of interacting activity systems such as the school community or other similar schools and multi-organisational fields of activity such as regional departments of education as well as national and international education bodies. Daniels and Warmington (2007) contend that through the interactions of these interacting activity systems and their relative subjects and objects, the transformation of practice, in this case, educational practice, grows and improves itself.

Australian schools have been engaged in school improvement for a number of decades with many theoretical models and frameworks outlining the importance of good practice and good organisation to deliver quality education (Drysdale, Goode & Gurr, 2009; Masters, 2012; Mulford, 2008; Reid,

Cranston, Keating & Mulford, 2010; Silins, Zarins & Mulford, 2002). Gammage (2008) suggests that, "since the mid-seventies, the Australian systems of education showed a keen interest towards decentralisation and that evidence of school-based management as a strategy and a major vehicle in introducing education reforms became evident" (p. 665). At the national level, looking at the dominant discourse in Australian education, Reid et al. (2010, p. 27) suggest that there is a public purpose of education that must be maintained in Australian schools over the individual or economic purposes of education and state that, "in a globalising world where the role of the nation state is changing and societies are becoming increasingly culturally diverse, schools are necessary for the public purpose of forming active citizens for democratic publics – people with the will and commitment to shape, and participate in an inclusive and democratic civil society and polity that is responsive to the new environment." Goddard (2010) further suggests that, at the organisational level, "strategies such as democratic governance, a culture of collaboration, a commitment to professional growth, strong leadership, and concern for the equity, success, and well-being of individual students" (p. 47) must be implemented by school administrators and educational leaders. As Gammage (2008) further elaborates, "when the private sector embraced a more decentralised, high-involvement management approach, public education systems too started to focus on reforms to provide more flexible, autonomous and responsive, high-performing schools which are able to meet the complexities of a global knowledge economy" (p. 664). Currently, this is the *modus operandi* within schools, be it in the public, independent or catholic school systems with primary, secondary or K-12 levels, or localised in the urban or regional landscape of Australia (Caldwell, 2005; 2007; Cranston, 2000; 2001; Dellar, 1998; Leithwood & Menzies, 1998; Thomas et al., 2011). De Grauwe's (2005) research into school-based management informs of five common reasons for this being so widely accepted: a democratic system; more relevant with local solutions to local problems; less bureaucratic; allows greater responsibility; and, allows greater mobilisation of resources. Interestingly, there is little documented research written at length about Australian school improvement in terms of business improvement (Kovacs, 2009; Robinson, 1996) even though after decentralisation, Australian schools have been operating within a business environment. The objectives of this chapter are as follows:

1.   To introduce a new perspective on educational quality that has been framed using a business improvement vernacular geared towards school improvement.
2.   To discuss an adapted version of continuous school improvement where schools operate as self-managed business systems and develop themselves as strategically-oriented learning organisations.

BACKGROUND: FRAMING A PROGRESSIVE-REFLECTIVE APPROACH TO EDUCATIONAL QUALITY WITHIN SCHOOLS

The term *Quality* continues to remain hard to define because the concept of quality in itself can mean many things to many people (Cheng & Tam, 1997; Weick, 2000). The understanding of quality has been found to be different for each individual due to the unique existence of a person with their own particular set of life experiences. Hence quality is undefined (Pfeffer & Coote, 1991) and the indicators used to measure quality for one individual may not be the same for another (Fuller, 1986; Hughes, 1988). Uselac (1993) states that "Quality is an attribute of a product or a service. Quality is not [restricted to] products and services but includes processes, environment and people" (p. 20). Sallis (1993) defines quality as both an absolute and relative concept leading to a *consumer definition for quality*. As an absolute, quality relates to rank, demonstrating that it is mainly concerned with performing to the highest standards. Greenwood and Gaunt (1994) define quality as "a product or service delivered to a very high specification at a very high price, only accessible to customers or clients who have high incomes and wealth" (p. 26). Quality as a relative concept is not an end in itself; but the means by which the end product is judged to be up to standard. Thus, quality products must do what they claim to do, and do what their customers expect of them (Sallis, 1993). This definition of quality deals with measuring up to specification by meeting pre-set standards and is known as the producer definition of quality – *fitness for purpose or use* (Murgatroyd & Morgan, 1993). Here a quality assurance system is established to ensure that there is a consistent production of goods or services to a particular standard or specification. Quality Assurance systems such as the ISO 9000 series, the Malcolm Baldrige National Quality Award (MBNQA), the former British Standards (BS5750), European Quality Award (EQA), the Deming Prize (Japanese) or the Australian Quality Award (AQA) which later changed to the Australian Business Excellence Framework (ABEF) are examples of this definition of quality. The last concept of quality integrates the other two, and is commonly known as the customer-driven concept of quality – *quality in perception*. It identifies the *results aspect* (Goetsch & Davis, 2000) of quality. This quality is defined as that which satisfies best and exceeds customer's expectations.

The American National Standards Institute (ANSI) and the American Society for Quality (ASQ) have standardised an official definition for this quality (ANSI/ASQC A3-1978, 1978) which states that "Quality is the totality of features and characteristics of an entity bearing on its ability to satisfy stated and implied needs [of customers or clients]" (p. 3). In short, quality is dynamic – associated with various factors such as: products, services, people, processes and environments that meet or exceed client/customer expectations. For some, this totality perspective has also been defined as Total Quality Management (TQM). When extended to educational systems, a TQM-based educational organisation will work on developing systems and processes that satisfy the expectations of both internal and external stakeholders within that system to ensure that educational quality is maintained. Thus, within the context of education, two central issues for educational quality are: 'Quality of what?' and 'Quality for whom?' The first question, 'Quality of what?' refers to those aspects of educational performance which relate to the overall quality specifications. The second question, 'Quality for whom?' refers to different stakeholders involved within the school. As indicated by Reddy (2007):

[educational] quality is a multifaceted concept viewed from different perspectives by different stakeholders ... though its meaning is not a settled matter, there is consensus on the fact that a high quality of education should facilitate the attainment of knowledge, skills and attitudes that have intrinsic value, for all students, and contributes to economic and social development (p. 18).

Due to these different concepts, concerns and stakeholders in education, educational quality is assessed using diverse indicators as well as wide-ranging strategies (Cheng & Tam, 1997). In addition, expectations of different stakeholders within education can be different or even contradictory (Hughes, 1988), making the notion of *achieving educational quality* more complex. To unravel this complexity and coming from a business improvement perspective that is grounded in a progressive-reflective approach, the author proposes that two aspects of educational quality need to be considered, i.e. *Quality Assurance* and *Quality Enhancement*.

Defining Quality Assurance within Educational Quality

Quality Assurance refers to the policies, processes and actions through which the quality of a system is developed and maintained (McKimm, 2003 as cited in Hodgkinson & Kelly, 2007, p. 78). *Quality Assurance* ensures fitness of purpose (Hodgkinson & Kelly, 2007) or use (Murgatroyd & Morgan, 1993). In a *Quality Assurance* educational system two inter-related activities would typically be found (see Figure 2), i.e. one that is concerned with *Management for Quality* (doing the right job) and the other with *Quality Management* (doing the job right) (Hodgkinson & Brown, 2003 as cited in Hodgkinson & Kelly, 2007, p. 78).

The first inter-related activity: *Management for Quality* includes those school improvement processes where the quality of an educational program or service is achieved through certain set goals (Hodgkinson & Kelly, 2007). Looking at the processes involved within the delivery of quality education, Deming's philosophy of

Figure 2. A Schematic Diagram of Quality Assurance Mechanisms Implemented within School Organisations
Source: Adapted from Hodgkinson & Kelly (2007, pp. 78-79)

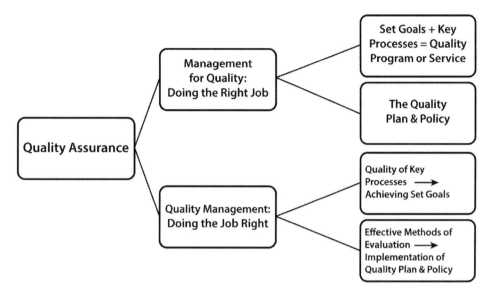

profound knowledge and his fourteen principles provide a plausible route for the management of an educational institution to ensure that they are able to deliver good service quality in education (Redmond, Curtis, Noone, & Keenan, 2008). According to Schultz's (2014) discussion of Deming's philosophy, the leader drives this *Management for Quality* where "The system of profound knowledge … requires the leader…to consider all organisational aspects when making decisions. This means recognising how processes are interconnected and how they function as a whole within the larger environment so that the organisation can reach intended expectations" (p. 6). Hodgkinson and Kelly (2007) suggest *Management for Quality* implies that "there is a tacit understanding of the prescribed quality of the [program] or service that has to be delivered. To be effective, this tacit understanding requires articulation, strategies and actions" (p. 78). Hence, the educational organisation uses a focused and dynamic approach to implement a quality plan and policy. Thus, the activities that come under *Management for Quality* within an educational

organisation assist it in staying competitive and having new thinking linked with the challenges of a global economy, new technologies, environmental and social diversity, and customer-oriented management (Lee & Lazarus, 1993).

The second inter-related activity: *Quality Management* has been defined as the quality of the processes whereby an educational institution works towards achieving its goals (Hodgkinson & Kelly, 2007). It is that aspect of the overall management function that determines and implements the quality policy which in effect is the collective intentions and directions of the organisation (Van Vught & Westerheijden, 1992). *Quality Management* within an educational organisation is framed within the context of planned cultural change. As Hodgkinson and Kelly (2007, pp.78-79) suggest, "It is dependent upon an understanding of how people learn, how they interact, and how they sustain, develop, or even destroy, a culture… It [involves] well-articulated methods of evaluation of the management processes involved. These methods are often referred to as quality audits or annual monitoring and review" or school accountability frameworks (Montecinos et al., 2014). Furthermore, Montecinos et al. (2014) suggest that school leadership plays a significant role in mediating the emotional and motivational effects that arise from these mandated internal and external accountability processes integrated within the school organisational culture (p. 256). Elaborating on this, Emstad (2011) highlights that school leadership plays a central role in building this organisational culture through coordination of problem-solving processes among teachers, organisation of teacher teams and the holding of the entire school accountable for school improvement.

Such a quality culture has been defined by Saraph and Sebastian (1993) as, "the total collective and shared learning of quality-related values as the [educational] organisation develops its capacity to survive in its external environment and to manage its own internal affairs" (p. 73). *Quality Management* is a cultural transformation within an educational organisation. It upholds the organisational goals (*Management for Quality*) as it sustains processes for continuation of a shared organisational vision, a proactive leadership, an effective professional development program, provision of services that satisfy customer needs, and a continuous improvement process of review and evaluation within an educational organisation (Berry, 1997). *Quality Management* provides an organisational culture characterised by increased satisfaction brought about through continuous improvements in educational processes and the proactive participation of all educational stakeholders in these improvement processes (Dahlgaard, Kristensen, & Kanji, 1995; Ngware et al., 2006). These two inter-related activities: *Management for Quality* and *Quality Management* provide schools a comprehensive framework for monitoring *Quality Assurance* mechanisms through a progressive-reflective approach of looking from the inside outwards and looking from the outside inwards.

Defining Quality Enhancement within Educational Quality

Quality Enhancement refers to the improvement of educational quality brought about through cycles of continuous improvement and innovation that becomes the culture of the educational organisation (Hodgkinson & Kelly, 2007). Through *Quality Enhancement*, services provided are more responsive to stakeholder needs established through processes of continual improvement existing through the understanding and improving of systems (DiPietro, 1993), such as school organisations.

Due to the transformative nature of these continual improvement processes a deliberate change process is put in place that is directly concerned with adding value through improved educational quality and through the implementation of subsequent cycles of on-going transformative change within the educational organisation (Hodgkinson & Kelly, 2007). Under *Quality Assurance* the '*Management for Quality*' and '*Quality Management*' are primary activities for a quality system incorporated within an educational organisation, while *Quality Enhancement* provides the systemic processes required to sustain changes so that long term objectives can be achieved. These systemic processes were first identified as a '*Continuous Quality Improvement approach*' and were proposed by Walter Shewart (1931). Later, Deming's famous continuous quality improvement cycle of Plan, Do, Study and Act became more widely used and known for this approach (see Figure 3). Svensson and Klefsjö (2006, p. 303) in their TQM-based self-assessment model identify four phases to self-assessment that closely resembled Deming's Continuous Improvement Cycle, which include: Plan, Describe, Analyse and Act.

Svensson and Klefsjö (2006, p. 304) suggest that within an educational organisation self-assessment tasks (PDSA cycles in Figure 4) and continuous improvement tasks (future projects in

Figure 3. A Modified Version of Deming's PDSA Cycle
Source: Adapted from Brown & Marshall (2008, p. 206)

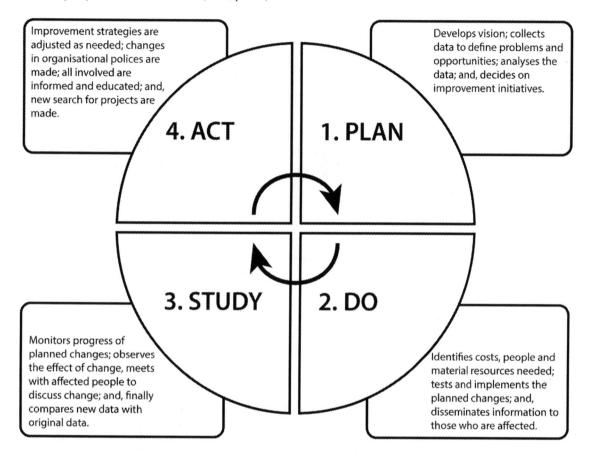

Figure 4) are two interdependent and consecutive cycles. In most instances, the self-assessment task is followed by continuous improvement tasks. Fernandes (2013, p. 59) suggests that the combination of both these tasks: self-assessment tasks and continuous improvement tasks, working interdependently and consecutively in a continuous improvement system leads to a quality-enhanced educational organisation (see Figure 4). In this dynamic continuous improvement system, after the first initial self-assessment task the educational organisation leads itself into a set of continuous improvement tasks (future projects) that are inbuilt with their own self-assessment tasks. These continuous improvement tasks are the first stage of organisational continuous improvement tasks. However, as indicated in Figure 4, each

of the first stage continuous improvement tasks, as future projects, follow their cycles of inbuilt self-assessment tasks (PDSA cycles) which then leads the organisation to a second stage of continuous improvement tasks also having inbuilt self-assessment tasks. These stages then continue to move on and ahead in these interdependent and consecutive cycles. The rationale behind this progressive-reflective approach is that system self-assessments are done at each stage to analyse the effect the continuous improvement tasks are having on the whole organisation. This multiple-stage continuous improvement with inbuilt self-assessment tasks allows the organisation to closely look at the efficiency of the project and to ensure that it is moving to its next desired state of improvement. Thus future projects are in fact but

Figure 4. The Two Interdependent and Consecutive Cycles of Organisational Self-Assessment and Organisational Continuous Improvement Tasks
Source: Adapted from Svensson, M. & Klefsjö, B. (2006, p. 304)

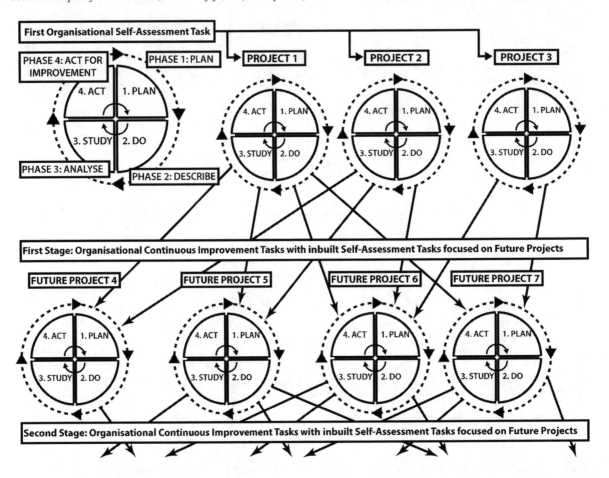

desired states of improvement developed after an organisation has assessed itself on the previous state of improvement.

Svensson and Klefsjö's (2006) study also suggests that for any continuous quality improvement project to succeed it requires the following: 1) a common understanding by all stakeholders on what quality is in their context; 2) a common and shared understanding of what the purpose and core values of the project are; 3) sufficient time and resources spent on planning the self-assessment tasks and continual improvement tasks; and, 4) effective communication within the organisation during the planning, execution and evaluation stages of the project. Brown and Marshall (2008, pp. 206-

207) suggest that in using Deming's approach in education, three assumptions must be held: (1) Decisions should be facts-based, evident through the collection and analysis of objective data. (2) People performing the work know it best hence stakeholder involvement at all levels is critical. (3) Teams have more success in problem-solving than individuals. Hence, teams must be trained in the continuous improvement approach. Hodgkinson and Kelly (2007) suggest that, "*Quality Enhancement* is given practical expression through staff appraisal and development, and the fostering of a culture of continuous improvement and innovation" (p. 79). Its successful implementation requires a cultural change and the willingness of

stakeholders to participate in a variety of reflective activities or programs (Bone, 1996, p. 44). These organisations have a collegiate management style, allowing the development of school values and providing it with necessary quality enhancement processes that ensure these values are reviewed periodically so that they do not become 'hidden resistors to change'.

In framing educational quality through *Quality Enhancement* approaches, the educational organisation will determine, define and develop its people and its processes based on a system of continuous quality improvements involving a number of self-assessment tasks as well as continuous improvement projects working in consecutive cycles. The educational organisation thus bases its quality policies, processes and actions (*Quality Assurance*) around the approach of systemic continuous improvement (*Quality Enhancement*). Hence there is a symbiotic relationship between *Quality Assurance* and *Quality Enhancement* evident within the educational organisation where they use a progressive-reflective approach with a business improvement perspective that allows them to take a 360 degree view of the continuous improvement path being taken by them at each stage of improvement and ensuring that this path leads them ahead.

MAIN FOCUS OF THIS CHAPTER: REFRAMING EDUCATIONAL QUALITY WITHIN CONTINUOUS SCHOOL IMPROVEMENT

Referring to Reddy's (2007) definition given earlier in this chapter, educational quality is a multi-faceted concept that draws its strength from the consensus that an educational institution delivers a high quality of education which adds value to its students as well as contributes towards the overall economic and social development of the nation. In framing educational quality within school contexts, it is important to consider the

school as a social system. Banathy and Jenks (1990) suggest that, "Systems thinking helps us to understand the nature of education as a complex and dynamic system that operates in ever changing environments and interacts with a variety of other societal systems" (p. 7). A system is most commonly defined as a set of elements, principles or procedures that function as a whole in order to meet a common purpose. The system is based on synergy where the parts that make up the system cannot function on their own but instead the whole system is greater than the sum of its parts, i.e. the elements, principles or procedures. This is because the relationship between the parts adds value to the overall system. Betts (1992) suggests, "The improvement of quality involves the design of an educational system that not only optimises the relationship among the elements but also between the educational system and its environment... this means designing a system that is more open, organic, pluralistic, and complex" (p. 40). Similarly, Cheng (2003) suggests that "Educational quality is the set of elements in the input, output and process sections of educational institutions that provide services which completely satisfy internal and external strategic constituencies by meeting their explicit and implicit expectations" (p. 207). Schools are often described as open systems that have a number of complexities and pluralities embedded within their organic nature therefore making the task of leading school improvement processes within schools today, more complex than it has been in the past.

Sallis (1996) in focusing upon a systems approach to school improvement processes suggests that Total Quality Management (TQM) provides "a philosophy of continuous improvement, which can provide an educational institution with a set of practical tools for meeting and exceeding present and future customer needs, wants and expectations" (p. 27). This would indicate that business improvement models relying on continuous improvement philosophies and practices could make use of a TQM philosophy to provide the internal and external strategic constituencies with a set of practical tools and processes that help drive the school improvement processes and meet the expectations of stakeholders within that organisation. Betts (1992) advocates a need for using TQM in education as it is 'a total systems approach' and is needed in current times to address the issues surrounding educational quality. As Betts (1992) suggests, "Nearly a century of change has left schools playing catch-up, and it will take a whole-system approach to meet society's evolving needs" (p. 38). There is sufficient evidence to show that schools using TQM approaches have had both positive as well as negative outcomes and while some have managed to sustain the improvement effort put in place, others have not. A closer analysis of this dilemma raises an interesting argument on what type of TQM should be deployed within an educational organisation.

Total Quality Management (TQM) in the educational context of teaching and learning (Chizmar, 2000) has been defined as "a collaborative and holistic implementation of ideas derived from the industrial TQM model" (p. 1). In some ways this definition perpetuates the misconceptions that have been associated with TQM and its application in education. Due to the strong overtones of the industrial model, TQM has found many barriers since the eighties in being implemented within educational institutions such as schools as compared to higher education institutions. Reservations about the use of quality models have been due to their association initially with industry (Hodgkinson & Kelly, 2007) and business (Desjardins & Obara, 1993) where earlier models have strong overtones of industrial language (Kohn, 1993) and business processes (Walpole & Noeth, 2002). Others feel that the application of TQM programs within educational systems can be challenging, costly and time-consuming (Kwan, 1996; Rampa, 2005; Temponi, 2005; Terry, 1996). Successful implementation of quality systems has required a complete commitment from various stakeholders in the organisation, especially the leadership,

as well as a large degree of re-engineering and change (Weller, 1998), involving a huge amount of time and resources (Hernandez, 2001; Rampa, 2005). TQM programs can sometimes be met with opposition and reluctance by conservative school teachers (Crawford & Shutler, 1999) and academics in higher education sector who have reservations about students being considered as customers and related processes of customer satisfaction (Eagle & Brennan, 2007; Idrus, 1995; Kwan, 1996).

Also, in education there are many types of "customers" and defining each of them is difficult (Kohn, 1993). While the student is the primary beneficiary of education, other stakeholders ranging from parents, prospective employers and society as a whole, have an interest in what they see as the extent of a successful and appropriate education that meets the needs of the student (Madu & Kuei, 1993). Some researchers define students as customers (Brandt, 1993; Holt, 1993b), while others believe there is a huge difference between students' wants and needs (Chickering & Potter, 1993) to be able to put in satisfactory standards or benchmarks. Some have compared the student to a worker (Schmoker & Wilson, 1993; Siegel, 2000), student knowledge to the product, and education (teaching and learning) to the core operating process (Bonstingl, 1993). However, in education, this "product" is not as tangible as it is in business or industry. The teaching and learning process cannot be mass-produced; instead it is an individual, student-centred process (Kohn, 1993; Sztajn, 1992). TQM critics fear that educators using TQM programs may focus solely on visible and measurable outcomes such as measurable performance indicators, because implementing quality requires data and data-driven decisions. In doing so, they feel that this will inhibit important outcomes of education such as creativity and non-measurable factors such as the love of learning and the enhancement of curiosity (Holt, 1993a). Another concern raised in the use of quality programs is the confusion of many packaged programs being available and the lack of clarity on what would be best-suited for a particular setting. Within educational organisations, there is a wide diversity in what is perceived as quality products or services due to a number of factors such as leadership, teaching staff and their competencies and methods, students enrolled, team building and teamwork, or geographic location of the school (Garbutt, 1996). As such, it becomes difficult to determine which quality program will work best within a particular educational organisation. There are also many misconceptions that seem to be driven by the lack of information about the scope of quality programs and the larger impact of the continuous improvement programs within educational systems (Temponi, 2005). Even when TQM programs have been taken on board and run successfully in schools and school systems, a lack of sufficient research on their impact has left an imbalance in the overall perspective around the effectiveness of TQM in school contexts and has led to a more negative one.

Though all has not been lost and some have suggested that, when managed correctly, TQM is a way of thinking or a philosophy that focuses attention on the management functions that transform learning into 'quality learning' (Rampa, 2005). In success stories, the contribution of quality pioneers such as Edward Deming and the application of his principles through TQM programs within educational organisations have assisted in the provision of a quality service to a diverse group of stakeholders (Redmond et al., 2008). Also, when looking further into this situation, there is sufficient evidence to suggest that TQM has provided a set of guiding principles focused entirely on meeting the needs and expectations of stakeholders within an educational institution with in-built mechanisms of continuous improvement (Steyn, 2000). As Murgatroyd and Morgan (1993) suggest, this is brought through by "the systematic management of an organisation's customer-supplier (or more appropriately stakeholder) relationships" (p. 59) that ensures

sustainable, steep-slope improvement in quality performance. The KEYS Initiative developed and run by the National Education Association in USA examined the relationship between organisational characteristics of schools and student learning and found that schools that consistently displayed six key factors of total quality in education directly promoted high student achievement (Hawley & Rollie, 2007). Bernhardt's (2013) work on continuous school improvement underpinned by TQM theory, presents a strong case for educators to understand the impact data can make on educational quality, especially in times of high-stakes accountability, where educators are required to gather, analyse, and use data to improve teaching and learning within schools.

Examples of success in TQM initiatives can be obtained from descriptive reports on cases at Fox Valley Technical College, U.S. (Spanbauer, 1989) and Mt. Edgecumbe High School, Alaska (Hubbard & Menzel, 1995); Oregon State University, U.S. (Coate, 1990); Texas State District, U.S. (Hernandez, 2001); Wolverhampton University, U.K. (Doherty, 1993); Aston University, U.K. (Clayton, 1995); University of Central Queensland, Australia (Idrus, 1995); the Departments of Education in South Australia and Victoria, Australia (Kovacs, 2009; Kovacs & King, 2005); Southwest School, New South Wales, Australia (Robinson, 1996); the Swedish National Agency for School Improvement (Svensson & Klefsjö, 2006); the Kenya Education Master Plan for Education and Training 1997-2010 (Ngware, Wamukuru, & Odebero, 2006); and Otago Polytechnic, New Zealand (Idrus, 1996).

Hence, in effect, TQM has had mixed effects since its inception and integration into educational contexts. As discussed earlier on, it cannot be implemented successfully if an industrial version is used within a school context, although sometimes it has worked to a certain degree in higher education. TQM models need to be adapted to fit into school contexts. Fernandes (2013) provides an adapted version of TQM in school contexts, where the influence of both *Quality Assurance* mechanisms and a *Quality Enhancement* approach provides schools with a more approachable and convenient deployment of TQM within their school improvement processes and a better position for achieving educational quality. This progressive-reflective concept of implementing *Quality Assurance* mechanisms through quality enhancement approaches has been termed in literature as *Strategic TQM* (Combe & Bostchen, 2004; Mehra, Hoffman, & Sirias, 2001; Sousa, 2003). In combining *Quality Assurance* and *Quality Enhancement* together, an educational organisation will be using Strategic TQM, not TQM within their continuous improvement systems. This relationship can also be interpreted and called the Strategic TQM equation (see Figure 5).

Holness (2001) suggests that having a synergistic *Quality Assurance* system as well as a continuous improvement system, i.e. *Quality Enhancement* approach provides an effective and sustainable approach towards educational quality. As Holness (2001) identifies, when a continuous improvement program is used in conjunction with a meaningful *Quality Assurance* program, significant improvements are felt within the organisation. Holness (2001) finds that the results of these are seen over time as a culture for quality is developed. Findings from the study by Hallinger and Heck (2011) suggest that improvements made within schools lead to changes in the school over a period of time having strong links found between the school context, its collaborative learning-directed leadership, and the academic capacity of school personnel. Ngware et al. (2006) also found that, a successful *Quality Enhancement* approach is found when the school management

provides leadership that promotes TQM practices resulting in empowered employees participating in decision-making leading to quality student learning. As Ngware et al. (2006) put it, "school leadership [should] put in place mechanisms to ensure that quality assurance practices are being followed and are being sustained and continuously improved upon" (p. 342). Strategic quality planning becomes increasingly important for the provision of quality services to be sustained over time. Ngware et al. (2006) further discuss that, "*Quality Assurance* is an integral part of TQM in educational organisations. Developing strategic quality plans through continuous improvement systems provides a way of actualising quality assurance in a systematic and performance-oriented way" (p. 352). Holness (2001) and Ngware et al. (2006) have identified the importance of *Quality Assurance* mechanisms and *Quality Enhancement* programs working together and have identified common elements such as mechanisms for systematic and informed strategic planning, group decision-making, logical and results-oriented performance and on-going evaluation.

Bilich and Neto (Bilich & Neto, 1997, S.88) state that, "An organisation that uses *Strategic TQM* incorporates constant evaluation of its concepts of management and of its administrative practices through the use of innovative strategies applied within a strategic culture." *Strategic TQM* identifies four elements that make a quality management system more integrated: the environment, leadership, method and a systems view (Pruett & Thomas, 1996). *Strategic TQM* is an aspirational model of TQM over its predecessor – the benchmarking deficit model of TQM found in the eighties and

Figure 5. The Strategic TQM Equation for Educational Organisations

nineties. The deficit model of TQM focused on benchmarking and quality control, advocating innovation but firmly fixed in standardisation, encouraging cultural change through open communication and collaborative teamwork but institutionalising managerial control and work place accountability. In *Strategic TQM*, *Quality Assurance* and *Quality Enhancement* work together to develop a thinking framework that aligns with the strategic intent of the school physically embodied through its mission. Various levels of self-assessment and continuous improvement allows school members to ascertain the value of the improvements being made and the strategic direction being taken. It provides a sense of community where an emphasis is placed on a progressive-reflective approach in the drive for continuous improvement. The question however arises as to whether *Strategic TQM* is a suitable frame for continuous quality improvement within schools? Fernandes (2013) suggests that "educational quality cannot be easily assessed by a single indicator…the achievement of satisfactory quality involves considering all stages of the quality loop as a whole within an educational organisation" (p. 40). *Strategic TQM* assists an organisation in addressing this complexity by measuring educational quality through its *Quality Assurance* mechanisms and its *Quality Enhancement* approach. In fact, referring back to the initial discussion in this chapter, the aspect of glocalisation and decentralisation lends itself to the notion that self-managing schools need to develop sustainable improvement processes that allow them to follow the quality loop of Plan, Do, Study and Act in their journey towards educational effectiveness. Schools today are becoming complex organisations of change where all those who participate in the process of schooling are in effect preparing citizens for tomorrow's glocalised world, hence, schools need to be able to intelligently sustain and continuously improve their school systems through a progressive-reflective approach such as *Strategic TQM*.

SOLUTIONS AND RECOMMENDATIONS: THE RELATIVE GAIN OF AUSTRALIAN SELF-MANAGING SCHOOLS TRANSFORMING INTO STRATEGICALLY-ORIENTED LEARNING ORGANISATIONS

Strategic TQM provides schools with a substantial philosophy, tools and processes to meet and sustain change and improve continuously. It offers a transformative framework for school improvement that creates a school culture where the drive for educational quality is critically important. It is best understood as 'a proactive posture' incorporated by school organisations using a quality approach. Grumdahl (2010) states that in effect it is "a valuable [improvement] tool when used in combination with creating a culture in which staff and students experience a sense of belonging, where differences and creativity are valued and celebrated, and where the pursuit of excellence in learning applies to all" (p. 144). In other words, schools work towards improving their quality, and focus on improving their school culture by transforming into learning organisations as this continuously effects the improvements in the quality of their educational offerings. Bilich and Neto (1997, S.88-89) suggest that, "An organisation that administers quality in a strategic way takes advantage of any and every information supplied in order to perfect itself; on the other hand, an organisation that is not preoccupied with quality, considers all and any complaints as more of a nuisance, deriding this important source of information." In further discussing the transformative nature of *Strategic TQM*, Madu, Aheto, Kuei and Winokur (1996) have found that strategically oriented organisations focus upon four critical transformations which include:

1. Structural transformation,
2. Cultural transformation,

3. Organisational transformation, and
4. Process transformation

However, a fifth and equally important transformation being proposed in line with the philosophy of *Strategic TQM* is that of an *Environmental transformation*. These five transformations more appropriately known as 'the SCOPE improvement cycle' provide schools with the tools for ensuring that they have successful, sustained and continuous improvements within their school improvement processes (see Figure 6).

While *Quality Assurance* and *Quality Enhancement* provide an educational organisation with leadership as well as strategic methods, the role of *Strategic TQM* helps to recognise the environmental forces that influence the organisation since it is part of a larger system (Fernandes, 2013). Instead of having its quality improvement strategies limited to quasi-static audited mechanisms, *Strategic TQM* allows organisations to become dynamically responsive to changing trends in society, making them more environmentally proactive (Leonard & McAdam, 2003; McAdam, Leonard, Henderson, & Hazlett, 2006). The *Stra-*

tegic TQM approach uses a contingency approach which allows educational organisations to cope with complex and dynamic phenomena associated with rapidly changing internal and external environments (McAdam, Leonard, Henderson, & Hazlett, 2006). It focuses on developing closer ties between all stakeholders inside and outside the educational organisation through its proactive position towards improvement (DiPietro, 1993; Mehra & Ranganathan, 2008). This works in strengthening the environmental influence and capability of the organisation. Self-managing schools make effective use of *Quality Assurance* mechanisms and a *Quality Enhancement* approach to assist them in formulating and translating their strategy planning (Mehra et al., 2001; Sousa & Voss, 2002) into effective business and operational plans (Currie, 1999; Sousa, 2003). Herein lies the answer as to why the author supports the notion that while TQM has had mixed results in educational institutions such as schools, *Strategic TQM* is different and works more in sync with the complexity currently faced by school leadership.

As discussed by Bilich and Neto (1997), this transformative nature of Strategic TQM provides

Figure 6. The SCOPE Improvement Cycle: Five Critical Transformations in Strategically Oriented Educational Organisations

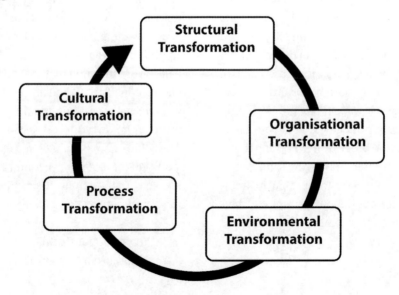

an organisation with the advantage of working strategically and becoming a learning organisation in its own right. Peter Senge (1990) suggests that organisations capable of surviving and prospering are indeed learning organisations where people, processes, and systems are all dedicated to continuous learning and improvement. According to Bonstingl (1992), a school that is a *strategically-oriented learning organisation* will have: committed leadership, reflective teaching and learning processes, informed and participative roles of stakeholders and allocation of sufficient human, material, time, and financial resources. Research also indicates that within these schools, the level of organisational learning directly impacts on student participation and engagement with the school, subsequently improving their learning outcomes (Silins & Mulford, 2002). In effect, a *strategically-oriented learning organisation* will be committed to a continuous, progressive-reflective approach of self-evaluation and action.

Fernandes (2013) suggests that when applied within a school setting, the school is transformed into a *strategically-oriented learning organisation* where each stakeholder in effect becomes a participant in transforming the school and improving its current state. In discussing this further, Fernandes (2013) identifies four key aspects of a *strategically-oriented learning organisation.* These include: (1) Leadership, (2) Teamwork, (3) Bundling Strategies, and (4) Contextual Influences (see Figure 7). Since *Strategic TQM* involves an educational organisation in transformative and continuous quality improvement, it stands to reason that transformative leadership will be an essential enabler for this to happen. In fact, leadership is a central factor in the transformation of schools into *strategically-oriented learning organisations* (Leithwood, 1994; Silins, 1994; Silins, Mulford, Zarins, & Bishop, 2000; Montecinos, et al., 2014)). Leaders who aspire to transform their schools into learning communities are visionary and life-long learners themselves (Cocklin, 1999; Diggins, 1997; Hale & Whitlam, 1997; Kotter,

1996). Hayes, Christie, Mills and Lingard (2004) found that elements of productive leadership were evident in such schools where a supportive culture works towards collective responsibility. Leadership diffuses throughout the organisation by its transformation from being an individual capacity located in the principal into a group attribute of school improvement teams and finally into an overall organisational property (Hallinger & Heck, 2011). School leaders give away their leadership authority by inducting and coaching others within the school and by actively building up organisational leadership capacity (Johnson, 2000). Through this distribution of leadership, the focus remains on the interactions of leadership practice by those who are both in formal as well as informal leadership roles within the organisation (Harris & Spillane, 2008). Through an integrated leadership model using both transformational as well as instructional leadership in improving school performance the principal elicits a high level of commitment and professionalism from their teacher leaders and works at developing their leadership capacity and as well as working interactively with them (Marks & Printy, 2003; Printy, Marks & Bowers, 2009). The results of this approach are stakeholder improved involvement and satisfaction, improved communication, increased productivity, improved quality and less rework, (Sim & Rogers, 2009).

Redmond et al. (2008) identify that teamwork breaks down organisational and professional barriers allowing the creation of opportunities amongst school stakeholders to generate new insights and ideas for improving the educational quality. Kovacs (2009) suggests that, the team approach builds a critical mass of knowledge where, "embedding the approach throughout the school takes place by 'osmosis' as the experience of the team grows by applying improved practices to their area of responsibility and then supportively informing the efforts of others." (p.260) Robinson (1996) suggests that coupled with a visionary and collaborative leadership style other strategies found in these

Figure 7. Four Key Aspects of a Strategically-Oriented Learning Organisation

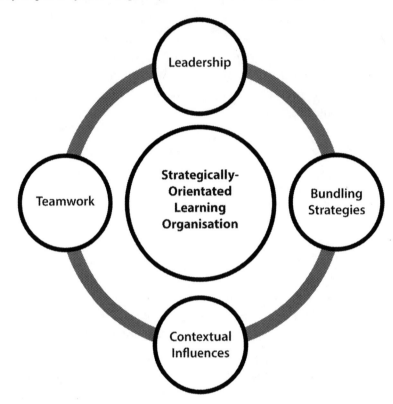

schools include: a problem-solving approach; collaborative decision-making; trust; empowerment for all stakeholders; delegation of roles and responsibilities; the provision of opportunities of leadership; continuous improvement of processes; effective communication channels; and, training and development programs for staff, parents and members of the community. The shift is from a controlling culture into a learning organisation culture with a nurturing and coaching leadership function.

Many quality systems have evolved into comprehensive management systems that have coupled a number of innovations together depending upon the needs and structure of the individual organisation. Modell (2009) has defined this organisational evolution as a 'bundling phenomenon' where organisations go through a diffusing process of innovations, using a reflective-managerial approach, as they map out their own goals and targets over

a period of time and make contextually-based adjustments in line with the overall purpose of the organisation. Finally, an important aspect of a *strategically-oriented learning organisation* is that any quality initiative implemented within the organisation is unique to it. Effective implementation of *Strategic TQM* within a learning organisation requires being able to discern what would be the best initiative for a particular organisation (Jones & Seraphim, 2008; Temtime, 2003). While the knowledge and understanding quotient of *Strategic TQM* must be high for successful implementation, each organisation develops its own subset of *Strategic TQM* characteristics and activities that are contextually unique (Jones & Seraphim, 2008). Navaratnam (1997) outlines the metaphor of 'a never-ending journey' of continuous improvement where educational quality can be designed, developed, implemented, achieved, measured and improved incrementally and continuously, through an integrated process view and continuous management practice within the educational organisation. Navaratnam defines this as, 'total quality in education' (1997, p. 19).

FUTURE RESEARCH DIRECTIONS

This chapter has discussed an adapted version of continuous school improvement where schools operate as self-managed business systems and develop themselves as strategically-oriented learning organisations. This concept of *Strategic TQM* (Figure 5) needs to be further investigated within different types of school settings making use of the five critical transformations of the SCOPE Improvement Cycle (Figure 6) and the four key aspects of a strategically-oriented learning organisation (Figure 7).

CONCLUSION: AN ADAPTED FRAME FOR CONTINUOUS SCHOOL IMPROVEMENT IN AUSTRALIAN SCHOOLS

This chapter discussed the importance and need for Australian schools today to understand the complexity and ever-changing landscape of school improvement as they frame educational quality within their own school contexts. Using a progressive-reflective approach, this chapter focused on how schools can use the proposed continuous school improvement frame based on business improvement and consisting of two main aspects: *Quality Assurance* and *Quality Enhancement,* to develop a system of *Strategic TQM*. The relative gain of this adapted version of TQM known as *Strategic TQM* over earlier industrial TQM models indicates that this model will better assist self-managed Australian schools in their achievement of educational quality. In describing the "what" and "how" of Strategic TQM, the author ends the chapter propounding

that *Strategic TQM* leads schools through transformative change that results in them becoming *strategically-oriented learning organisations*. Through the actual embodiment of the philosophy and practice of *Strategic TQM*, Australian self-managing schools can work towards transforming into strategically-oriented learning organisations using a system of continuous school improvement that effectively drives all school processes towards the attainment of educational quality and where quality student learning is the core educational service being provided.

REFERENCES

Adams, D., Acedo, C., & Popa, S. (2012). In Search of Quality Education. In C. Acedo, D. Adams, & S. Popa (Eds.), *Quality and Qualities: Tensions in Higher Education* (pp. 1–22). Rotterdam: Sense Publishers. doi:10.1007/978-94-6091-951-0_1

American National Standard ANSI/ASQC A3-1978. (1978). *Quality Systems Terminology*. Milwaukee, WI: American Society for Quality Control.

Banathy, B. H. (1991). *Systems Design of Education: A Journey to Create the Future*. Englewood Cliffs, NJ: Educational Technology Publications.

Banathy, B. H., & Jenks, C. L. (1990, April). *The transformation of education: By design.* Paper presented at the Annual Meeting of the American Educational Research Association, Boston, MA. Retrieved from http://files.eric.ed.gov/fulltext/ED323660.pdf

Bernhardt, V. (2013). *Translating data into information to improve teaching and learning*. New York: Routledge.

Berry, G. (1997). Leadership and the development of quality culture in schools. *International Journal of Educational Management, 11*(2), 52–65. doi:10.1108/09513549710163943

Betts, F. (1992, November). How Systems Thinking Applies to Education. *Educational Leadership*, *50*(3), 38–41. Retrieved from http://search.proquest.com/docview/224857527?accountid=12528

Bilich, F., & Neto, A. A. (1997). Strategic total quality management. *Total Quality Management*, *8*(2-3), 88–89. doi:10.1080/0954412979767

Bone, D. (1996). Quality management is collegiate management: Improving practice in a special school. In P. Lomax (Ed.), *Quality Management in education: Sustaining the vision through Action Research* (pp. 19–46). London: Routledge and Hyde Publications.

Bonstingl, J. J. (1992). The quality revolution in education. *Educational Leadership*, *50*(3), 4–9.

Bonstingl, J. J. (1993). The quality movement: What's it really about? *Educational Leadership*, *51*(1), 66–70.

Brandt, R. (2003). Is this school a learning organization? 10 ways to tell. *Journal of Staff Development*, *24*(1), 10–16. Retrieved from http://search.proquest.com/docview/211520094?accountid=12528

Brooks, J., & Normore, A. (2010). Educational leadership and globalization: Literacy for a glocal perspective. *Educational Policy*, *24*(1), 52–82. doi:10.1177/0895904809354070

Brown, J. F., & Marshall, B. L. (2008). Continuous quality improvement: An effective strategy for improvement of program outcomes in a higher education setting. *Nursing Education Perspectives*, *29*(4), 205–211. PMID:18770948

Caldwell, B. (2005). *School-based management. Education Policy Series. International Academy of Education and International Institute for Educational Planning*. UNESCO.

Caldwell, B. (2007). *Self managing schools and improved learning outcomes*. Canberra: Department of Employment, Education, Training and Youth Affairs.

Cheng, Y. C. (2003). Quality assurance in education: Internal, interface, and future. *Quality Assurance in Education*, *11*(4), 202–213. doi:10.1108/09684880310501386

Cheng, Y. C., & Tam, W. M. (1997). Multi-models of quality in education. *Quality Assurance in Education*, *5*(1), 22–31. doi:10.1108/09684889710156558

Chickering, A. W., & Potter, D. (1993). TQM and quality education: Fast food or fitness center. *The Educational Record*, *74*(2), 35–36.

Chizmar, J. F. (2000). Total quality management of teaching and learning. *The Journal of Economic Education*, *25*(2), 1–8. doi:10.1080/00220485.1994.10844828

Clayton, M. (1995). Encouraging the kaizen approach to quality in a university. *Total Quality Management*, *6*(5/6), 593–601. doi:10.1080/09544129550035242

Coate, L. E. (1990). TQM on campus: Implementing total quality management in a university setting. *Business Officer*, *24*(5), 26–35.

Cocklin, B. (1999). Gumly Gumly Public School as a learning community. In J. Retallick, B. Cocklin, & K. Coombe (Eds.), *Learning Communities in Education* (pp. 265–286). London: Routledge.

Combe, I., & Bostchen, G. (2004). Strategy paradigms for the management of quality: Dealing with complexity. *European Journal of Marketing*, *38*(5), 500–523. doi:10.1108/03090560410529187

Commonwealth Of Australia. (2008). *Quality education: The case for an education revolution in our schools* Retrieved from http://apo.org.au/files/Resource/deewar_quality-education_2008.pdf

Cranston, N. (2000). The impact of school-based management on primary school principals: An Australian Perspective. *Journal of School Leadership, 10*(3), 214–232.

Cranston, N. C. (2001). Collaborative decision-making and school-based management: Challenges, rhetoric and reality. *Journal of Educational Enquiry, 2*(2), 1–26.

Crawford, L. E. D., & Shutler, P. (1999). Total quality management in education: Problems and issues for the classroom teacher. *International Journal of Educational Management, 13*(2), 67–72. doi:10.1108/09513549910261122

Currie, W. (1999). Revisiting management innovation and change programmes: Strategic vision or tunnel vision? *Omega, 27*(6), 647–660. doi:10.1016/S0305-0483(99)00023-7

Dahlgaard, J. J., Kristensen, K., & Kanji, G. K. (1995). Total quality management and education. *Total Quality Management, 6*(5), 445–456. doi:10.1080/09544129550035116

Daniels, H., & Warmington, P. (2007). Analyzing third generation activity systems: Labour power, subject, position and personal transformation. *Journal of Workplace Learning, 19*(6), 377–391. doi:10.1108/13665620710777110

De Grauwe, A. (2005). Improving quality of education through school-based management: Learning from international experiences. *International Review of Education, 51*(4), 269–287. doi:10.1007/s11159-005-7733-1

Dellar, G. B. (1998). School Climate, School Improvement and Site-based Management. *Learning Environments Research, 1*(3), 353–367. doi:10.1023/A:1009970210393

Desjardins, C., & Obara, Y. (1993). From Québec to Tokyo: Perspectives on TQM. *Educational Leadership, 51*(1), 68–69.

Diggins, P. B. (1997). Reflections on leadership characteristics necessary to develop and sustain learning school communities. *School Leadership & Management, 17*(3), 413–425. doi:10.1080/13632439769953

DiPietro, R. A. (1993). TQM: Evolution, scope and strategic significance for management development. *Journal of Management Development, 12*(7), 11–18. doi:10.1108/02621719310044910

Doherty, G. D. (1993). Towards total quality management in higher education: A case study of the University of Wolverhampton. *Higher Education, 25*(3), 321–339. doi:10.1007/BF01383857

Drysdale, L., Goode, H., & Gurr, D. (2009). An Australian model of successful school leadership. *Journal of Educational Administration, 47*(6), 697–708. doi:10.1108/09578230910993087

Eagle, L., & Brennan, R. (2007). Are students customers? TQM and marketing perspectives. *Quality Assurance in Education, 15*(1), 44–60. doi:10.1108/09684880710723025

Emstad, A. B. (2011). The principal's role in the post-evaluation process. How does the principal engage in the work carried out after the schools self-evaluation? *Educational Assessment, Evaluation and Accountability, 23*(4), 271–288. doi:10.1007/s11092-011-9128-0

Engeström, Y. (2001). Expansive learning at work: Toward an activity theoretical reconceptualization. *Journal of Education and Work, 14*(1), 133–156. doi:10.1080/13639080020028747

Engeström, Y., & Glaveanu, V. (2012). On third generation activity theory: Interview with Yrjö Engeström. *Europe's Journal of Psychology, 8*(4), 515–518. doi:10.5964/ejop.v8i4.555

Fernandes, V. M. (2013) *The Effectiveness of Total Quality Management as a School Improvement Process.* (Doctoral dissertation). Monash University Theses Collection, Melbourne, Australia. Retrieved from http://arrow.monash.edu. au/hdl/1959.1/871750

Gammage, D. T. (2008). Three decades of implementation of school-based management in the Australian Capital Territory and Victoria in Australia. *International Journal of Educational Management, 22*(7), 664–675. doi:10.1108/09513540810908575

Garbutt, S. (1996). The transfer of TQM from industry to education. *Education + Training, 38*(7), 16–22. doi:10.1108/00400919610130736

Goetsch, D. L., & Davis, S. B. (2000). *Quality management: Introduction to total quality management for production, processing and services* (3rd ed.). Prentice-Hall International Inc.

Goodard, J. T. (2010). Toward Glocality: Facilitating leadership in an age of diversity. *Journal of School Leadership, 20*, 37–56.

Greenwood, M. S., & Gaunt, H. J. (1994). *Total quality management for schools.* London: Cassell.

Grumdahl, C. R. (2010). *How schools can effectively plan to meet the goal of improving student learning.* (Doctoral dissertation). University of Minnesota. Retrieved from:https://conservancy. umn.edu/bitstream/handle/11299/59567/Grumdahl_umn_0130E_10969.pdf?sequence=1

Hale, R., & Whitlam, P. (1997). *Towards the virtual organization.* London: The McGraw-Hill Co.

Hallinger, P., & Heck, R. H. (2011). Exploring the journey of school improvement: Classifying and analyzing patterns of change in school improvement processes and learning outcomes. *School Effectiveness and School Improvement, 22*(1), 1–27. doi:10.1080/09243453.2010.536322

Harris, A., & Spillane, J. (2008). Distributed leadership through the looking glass. *Management in Education, 22*(1), 31–34. doi:10.1177/0892020607085623

Hayes, D., Christie, P., Mills, M., & Lingard, B. (2004). Productive leaders and productive leadership: Schools as learning organisations. *Journal of Educational Administration, 42*(4/5), 520–538. doi:10.1108/09578230410554043

Hernandez, J. R., Jr. (2001). *Total quality management in education: The application of TQM in a Texas school district.* (Unpublished doctoral dissertation). University of Texas, Austin, TX. Retrieved November 3, 2008, from Dissertations & Theses: Full Text (Publication No. AAT 3034546).

Hill, P. W., Rowe, K. J., Holmes-Smith, P., & Russell, V. J. (1996). The Victorian Quality Schools Project: A study of school and teacher effectiveness (Report, Volume 1). Centre for Applied Educational Research: University of Melbourne.

Hodgkinson, M., & Brown, G. (2003). Enhancing the quality of education: A case study and some emerging principles. *Higher Education, 45*(3), 337–352. doi:10.1023/A:1022680504729

Hodgkinson, M., & Kelly, M. (2007). Quality management and enhancement processes in UK business schools: A review. *Quality Assurance in Education, 15*(1), 77–91. doi:10.1108/09684880710723043

Holness, G. V. R. (2001). Achieving quality using TQM and ISO. *ASHRAE Journal, 43*(1), 195–199.

Holt, M. (1993a). Dr. Deming and the improvement of schooling: No instant pudding. *Journal of Curriculum and Supervision, 9*(1), 6–23.

Holt, M. (1993b). The educational consequences of W. Edwards Deming. *Phi Delta Kappan, 74*(5), 382–388.

Hubbard, S., & Menzel, S. (1995). Mt. Edgecumbe High School case study report. In S. Hubbard & S. Menzel (Eds.), *The Study of School-to-Work Reform Initiatives. Volume II: Case Studies* (pp. 5-55). Studies of Education Reform Series. Academy for Educational Development, Washington, DC. National Inst. for Work and Learning. Retrieved from http://files.eric.ed.gov/fulltext/ED397551.pdf

Hughes, P. (Ed.). (1988). *The challenge of identifying and marketing quality in education.* Sydney, Australia: The Australian Association of Senior Educational Administrators.

Idrus, N. (1995). Empowerment as a manifestation of total quality: A study in three countries. *Total Quality Management, 6*(5 & 6), 603–612. doi:10.1080/09544129550035251

Idrus, N. (1996). Towards total quality management in academia. *Quality Assurance in Education, 4*(3), 34–40. doi:10.1108/09684889610125850

Jackson, D. S. (2000). The School Improvement Journey: Perspectives on leadership. *School Leadership & Management Development, 20*(1), 61–78. doi:10.1080/13632430068888

Jones, J. P., & Seraphim, D. (2008). TQM implementation and change management in an unfavourable environment. *Journal of Management Development, 27*(3), 291–306. doi:10.1108/02621710810858614

Kohn, A. (1993). Turning learning into a business: Concerns about total quality management. *Educational Leadership, 51*(1), 58–61.

Kovacs, J. (2009). Facilitating Change in Australian Schools: Applying a Business Quality Improvement Model. Unpublished Doctoral dissertation. Melbourne, Australia: Swinburne University of Technology. Retrieved from http://researchbank.swinburne.edu.au/vital/access/manager/Repository/swin:14100

Kovacs, J., & King, M. (2005). Studying the Impact of the Quality in Schools and Quality and Improvement in Schools and Preschools Initiatives: 1997-2003. *Quality Learning and Improvement in Schools and Preschools Summary Report*, November 2005 [Electronic Version]. Melbourne: Quality Learning Australia Pty Ltd. Retrieved from http://www.qla.com.au/pathtoitems/QLA_QISP_Report.pdf

Kwan, P. Y. K. (1996). Application of total quality management in education: Retrospect and prospect. *International Journal of Educational Management, 10*(5), 25–35. doi:10.1108/09513549610146114

Lee, Y. R., & Lazarus, H. (1993). Uses and criticisms of total quality management. *Journal of Management Development, 12*(7), 5–10. doi:10.1108/02621719310044901

Leithwood, K. (1994). Leadership for school restructuring. *Educational Administration Quarterly, 30*(4), 498–518. doi:10.1177/0013161X94030004006

Leithwood, K., & Menzies, T. (1998). A review of research concerning the implementation of site-based management. *School Effectiveness and School Improvement, 9*(3), 233–285. doi:10.1080/0924345980090301

Leonard, D., & McAdam, R. (2003). An evaluative framework for TQM dynamics in organisations. *International Journal of Operations & Production Management, 23*(5/6), 652–677. doi:10.1108/01443570310476663

Madu, C. N., Aheto, J., Kuei, C., & Winokur, D. (1994). Adoption of strategic total quality management philosophies: Multi-criteria decision analysis model. *International Journal of Quality & Reliability Management, 13*(3), 57–72. doi:10.1108/02656719610116081

Madu, C. N., & Kuei, C. (1993). Dimensions of quality teaching in higher institutions. *Total Quality Management, 4*(3), 325–338. doi:10.1080/09544129300000046

Marks, H. M., & Printy, S. M. (2003). Principal leadership and school performance: An Integration of Transformational and Instructional Leadership. *Educational Administration Quarterly, 39*(3), 370–397. doi:10.1177/0013161X03253412

Masters, G. N. (2010). *Teaching and learning school improvement framework. Melbourne: Australian Council for Educational Research (ACER).* Brisbane: Department of Education and Training.

McAdam, R., Leonard, D., Henderson, J., & Hazlett, S. A. (2006). A grounded theory research approach to building and testing TQM theory in operations management. *International Journal of Management Sciences, 36*, 825–837. doi:10.1016/j.omega.2006.04.005

McKimm, J. (2003). Assuring quality and standards in teaching. In H. Fry, S. M. Ketteridge, & S. Marshall (Eds.), *A Handbook for Teaching and Learning in Higher Education* (2nd ed., pp. 182–199). London: Kogan Page.

Mehra, S., Hoffman, J., & Sirias, D. (2001). TQM as a management strategy for the next millenia. *International Journal of Operations & Production Management, 21*(6), 855–877. doi:10.1108/01443570110390534

Mehra, S., & Ranganathan, S. (2008). Implementing total quality management with a focus on enhancing customer satisfaction. *International Journal of Quality & Reliability Management, 25*(9), 913-927. doi: 02656710810908070

Modell, S. (2009). Bundling management control innovations: A field study of organisational experimenting with total quality management and the balanced scorecard. *Accounting, Auditing & Accountability Journal, 22*(1), 59-90. doi: 09513570910923015

Montecinos, C., Madrid, R., Fernández, M. B., & Ahumada, L. (2014). A goal orientation analysis of teachers' motivations to participate in the school self-assessment processes of a quality assurance system in Chile. *Educational Assessment, Evaluation and Accountability, 26*(3), 241–261. doi:10.1007/s11092-014-9190-5

Mulford, B. (2008) The leadership challenge improving learning in schools. Australian Education Review. Melbourne: Australian Council for Educational Research (ACER).

Murgatroyd, S., & Morgan, C. (1993). *Total quality management and the school.* Buckingham, UK: Open University Press.

Navaratnam, K. K. (1997). Quality management in education must be a never-ending journey. In K. Watson & S. Modgol (Eds.), *Educational dilemma: Debate and diversity; VI: Quality in education.* London: Cassell.

Ngware, M. W., Wamukuru, D. K., & Odebero, S. O. (2006). Total quality management in secondary schools in Kenya: Extent of practice. *Quality Assurance in Education, 14*(4), 339–362. doi:10.1108/09684880610703947

Pfeffer, N., & Coote, A. (1991). Is Quality Good for You? A Critical Review of Quality Assurance. In *Welfare Services. Social Policy Paper No. 5.* London: Institute for Public Policy Research.

Printy, S. M., Marks, H. M., & Bowers, A. J. (2009). Integrated Leadership: How Principals and Teachers Share Transformational and Instructional Influence. *Journal of School Leadership, 19*(5), 504–532.

Pruett, M., & Thomas, H. (1996). Thinking About Quality and its Links with Strategic Management. *European Management Journal, 14*(1), 37–46. doi:10.1016/0263-2373(95)00045-3

Rampa, S. H. (2005). The Relationship between Total Quality Management and School Improvement. Unpublished doctoral dissertation. Pretoria, South Africa: University of Pretoria; Retrieved from http://repository.up.ac.za/bitstream/handle/2263/23595/Complete.pdf?sequence=5

Reddy, S. (2007). *SCHOOL QUALITY: Perspectives from the Developed and Developing Countries.* Azim Premji Foundation. Retrieved from http://www.azimpremjifoundation.org/pdf/ConsolidatedSchoolQualityreport.pdf

Redmond, R., Curtis, E., Noone, T., & Keenan, P. (2008). Quality in higher education: The contribution of Edward Deming's principles. *International Journal of Educational Management, 22*(5), 432–441. doi:10.1108/09513540810883168

Reid, A., Cranston, N., Keating, J., & Mulford, B. (2010). *Exploring the Public Purposes of Education in Australian Primary Schools.* Report on an ARC-Linkage Project conducted in partnership with the Australian Government Primary Principals Association (AGPPA) and the Foundation for Young Australians. Retrieved from: http://www.agppa.asn.au/index.php?option=com_content&view=article&id=28&Itemid=18

Robinson, B. M. (1996). *Total quality management in education: The empowerment of a school community.* (Unpublished doctoral dissertation). University of Nebraska, Lincoln, NE.

Sallis, E. (1993). *Total quality management in education.* London: Kogan Page Ltd. doi:10.4324/9780203417010

Sallis, E. (1996). *Total quality management in education* (2nd ed.). London: Kogan Page Ltd.

Saraph, J. V., & Sebastian, R. J. (1993). Developing a quality culture. *Quality Progress, 26*(9), 73–78.

Schmoker, M., & Wilson, R. B. (1993). Adapting total quality doesn't mean "turning learning into a business". *Educational Leadership, 51*(1), 62–63.

Schultz, J. R. (2014). *Four-cornered Leadership: A Framework for Making Decisions.* CRC Press, Taylor & Francis Group.

Senge, P. (1990). *The Fifth Discipline: The Art and Practice of the Learning Organisation.* New York: Doubleday.

Shewart, W. A. (1931). *Economic Control of Quality of Manufactured Product.* New York: Van Nostrand.

Siegel, P. (2000). Using Baldridge to improve education: A rationale based on results. *Training & Development, 54*(2), 66–67.

Silins, H. (1994). Leadership Characteristics and School Improvement. *Australian Journal of Education, 38*(3), 268–281. doi:10.1177/000494419403800306

Silins, H., & Mulford, B. (2002). Schools as learning organisations: The case for system, teacher and student learning. *Journal of Educational Administration, 40*(5), 425–446. doi:10.1108/09578230210440285

Silins, H., Mulford, B., Zarins, S., & Bishop, P. (2000). Leadership for Organizational Learning in Australian Secondary Schools. In K. Leithwood (Ed.), *Understanding Schools as Intelligent Systems* (pp. 267–291). Stamford, CT: JAI Press; doi:10.1080/03057640302041

Silins, H., Zarins, S., & Mulford, B. (2002). What characteristics and processes define a school as a learning organisation? Is this a useful concept to apply to schools? *International Education Journal, 3*(1), 24–32.

Sim, K. L., & Rogers, J. W. (2009). Implementing lean production systems: Barriers to change. *Management Research News, 32*(1), 37–49. doi:10.1108/01409170910922014

Sousa, R. (2003). Linking Quality Management to Manufacturing Strategy: An Empirical Investigation of Customer Focus Practices. *Journal of Operations Management, 21*(1), 1–18. doi:10.1016/S0272-6963(02)00055-4

Sousa, R., & Voss, C. (2002). Quality Management Re-visited: A Reflective Review and Agenda for Future Research. *Journal of Operations Management, 20*(1), 91–109. doi:10.1016/S0272-6963(01)00088-2

Spanbauer, S. J. (1989). *Measuring and Costing Quality in Education*. Appleton, WI: Fox Valley Technical College Foundation.

Steyn, G. M. (2000). Applying Principles of TQM to a learning process: a case study. *SAJHE/SATHO, 14*(1), 11-14. Retrieved from http://hdl.handle.net/10500/242

Svensson, M., & Klefsjö, B. (2006). TQM-based self-assessment in the education sector: Experiences from a Swedish Upper Secondary School Project. *Quality Assurance in Education, 14*(4), 299–323. doi:10.1108/09684880610703929

Sztajn, P. (1992). A matter of metaphors: Education as a handmade process. *Educational Leadership, 50*(3), 35–37.

Temponi, C. (2005). Continuous improvement framework: Implications for academia. *Quality Assurance in Education, 13*(1), 17–36. doi:10.1108/09684880510578632

Temtime, Z. T. (2003). The Moderating Impacts of Business Planning and Firm Size on the Total Quality Management Practices. *The TQM Magazine, 15*(1), 52–60. doi:10.1108/09544780310454457

Terry, P. M. (1996). *Using Total Quality Management Principles to Implement School-Based Management*. Paper presented at the 14th Annual International Conference of the International Association of Management, Toronto, Canada. Retrieved from http://files.eric.ed.gov/fulltext/ED412590.pdf

Thomas, M., Hawkins, A., Christian, F., Merlene, M., & de Meyrick, C. (2011). *Independent Review of the School Based Management Report. Summary Report (October 2011)*. Department of Education and Communities, NSW: ARTD Consultants. Retrieved from: https://www.det.nsw.edu.au/media/downloads/about-us/statistics-and-research/key-statistics-and-reports/irsb-management-pilot-sr.pdf

Torres, C. A., & Antikainen, A. (2003). Introduction to a sociology of education: Old dilemmas in a new century? In C. A. Torres & A. Antikainen (Eds.), *The International Handbook on the Sociology of Education: An International Assessment of New Research and Theory* (pp. 1–18). Lanham, MD: Rowman & Littlefield.

Uselac, S. (1993). *Zen Leadership: The Human Side of Total Quality Team Management*. Loudonville, OH: Mohican.

Van Vught, F. A., & Westerheijden, D. F. (1992). *Quality Management and Quality Assurance in European Higher Education: Methods and Mechanics*. Center for Higher Education Policy Studies, University of Twente.

Walpole, M., & Noeth, R. J. (2002). *The Promise of Baldrige for K-12 Education*. ACT Policy Report: ACT Policy Research Inc. Retrieved from https://www.act.org/research/policymakers/pdf/baldrige.pdf

Weick, K. E. (2000). Quality Improvement: A Sensemaking Perspective. In R. E. Cole & W. R. Scott (Eds.), *The Quality Movement & Organization Theory* (pp. 155–172). Thousand Oaks, CA: Sage Publications Inc.

Weller, L. D. (1998). Unlocking the culture for quality schools: Reengineering. *International Journal of Educational Management, 12*(6), 250–259. doi:10.1108/09513549810237959

ADDITIONAL READING

Bass, B. M., & Riggio, R. E. (2006). *Transformational Leadership* (2nd ed.). New Jersey: Lawrence Erlbaum Associates.

Cheng, Y. C., & Mok, M. M. C. (2007). School-based management and paradigm shift in education: An empirical Study. *International Journal of Educational Management, 21*(6), 517–542. doi:10.1108/09513540710780046

Day, C., Sammons, P., Hopkins, D., Harris, A., Leithwood, K., Gu, Q.,.... (2009). The impact of school leadership on pupil outcomes. Research Report DCSF-RR108. London: Department for Children, Schools and Families; Retrieved from http://webarchive.nationalarchives.gov.uk/20130401151715/http://www.education.gov.uk/publications/eOrderingDownload/DCSF-RR018.pdf

Hargreaves, D. (2007). *System re-design – 1: The road to transformation*. London: SSAT.

Harris, A. (2011). Distributed leadership friend or foe? *Educational Management Administration & Leadership, 41*(5), 545–554. doi:10.1177/1741143213497635

Leithwood, K. (2001). School leadership in the context of accountability policies. *International Journal of Leadership in Education, 4*(3), 217–235. doi:10.1080/13603120110057082

Leithwood, K., Mascall, B., Strauss, T., Sacks, R., Memon, N., & Yashkina, A. (2007). Distributing leadership to make schools smarter: Taking the ego out of the system. *Leadership and Policy in Schools, 6*(1), 37–67. doi:10.1080/15700760601091267

Lingard, B., Hayes, D., & Mills, M. (2002). Developments in school-based management: The specific case of Queensland, Australia. *Journal of Educational Administration, 40*(1), 6–30. doi:10.1108/09578230210415625

Mulford, B. (2011). Teacher and school leader quality and sustainability. Resource sheet no. 5. January 2011. Canberra, ACT: Closing the Gap Clearinghouse; Retrieved from http://www.aihw.gov.au/uploadedFiles/ClosingTheGap/Content/Publications/2011/ctgc-rs05.pdf

Senge, P. M. (1990). *The Fifth Discipline: The Art and Practice of the Learning Organization*. New York: Doubleday.

Stoll, L., & Timperley, J. (2009). *OECD: Improving School Leadership – the toolkit*. OECD Publishing.

Zammit, K. Sinclair, C., Cole, B., Singh, M., Costley, D., a'Court, L.B. & Rushton, K. (2007). Teaching and Leading for Quality Australian Schools: A review and synthesis of research-based knowledge. February, 2007 Report prepared by University of Western Sydney for Teaching Australia. Retrieved from: http://www.aitsl.edu.au/docs/default-source/default-document-library/teaching_and_leading_for_quality_australian_schools

KEY TERMS AND DEFINITIONS

Continuous Improvement: Refers to a long-term approach towards improvement that systematically seeks to achieve small, incremental changes in the organisational processes that lead towards improvements in efficiency and quality. It is also known as Kaizen and is the responsibility of every person in the organisation, not just a selected few.

Quality Assurance: Refers to the policies, processes and actions through which the quality of a system is developed and maintained.

Quality Enhancement: Refers to the improvement of educational quality brought about through cycles of continuous improvement and innovation so that it becomes the culture of the educational organisation.

Strategic TQM: It provides schools with a substantial philosophy, tools and processes to organise themselves to meet and sustain change and improve themselves continuously.

Total Quality Management: Refers to a systematic approach to the practice of management within an organisation. At the organisational level it requires changes in organisational processes, and strategic priorities; and at the individual level, it requires changes in the beliefs, attitudes, and behaviours of individuals working within that organisation. It is considered both as a philosophy and a set of guiding principles for organisational management.

Section 2

Coping with Conflict:
Dealing with Stakeholders, Culture, Competition, and Style

Chapter 7
Alternative Dispute Resolution:
A Legal Perspective

Saleem Gul
Institute of Management Sciences, Pakistan

ABSTRACT

This chapter covers a lot of groundwork and provides and quick and through introduction to the concepts and underlying discussions on Alternative Dispute Resolution (ADR). The chapter provides a detailed discussion based on extant literature in an effort to differentiate between disputes and conflicts. Then some of the common confusions between terms commonly used in ADR are addressed. Following which various key government acts and reports that shape the state of ADR are discussed. Because of their length, therefore only those concerns within the documents that directly address ADR or are related to ADR are discussed. It remains a burden on the readers to access these documents themselves to fully appreciate their content.

INTRODUCTION

Disputes are common amongst today's organizations. It is therefore important to understand how to resolve them and to appreciate the law and regulations defining the canvas of dispute resolution. This chapter focuses on disputes in general and Alternative Dispute Resolution mechanisms and processes in particular. We begin with a background discussion on dispute resolution and make the case for studying this topic further. Then the discussion presents a critical review of the literature pertaining to disputes. The purpose of this is to arrive at a common understanding and definition of a dispute and to differentiate between disputes and conflicts. Although, this chapter is about the alternative methods of resolving organizational conflicts and disputes. However, because of the close relationship of Alternative Dispute Resolution (ADR) to conventional dispute resolution and to establish the context for further discussion on ADR some of the discussion focuses on the conventional methods of resolving disputes. After providing a background to dispute resolution and differentiating between disputes and conflicts and defining disputes the chapter then follows with a discussion detailing the processes of mediation and arbitration. In this section the focus is on the ADR techniques, however because of ADR's close association with the litigation process

DOI: 10.4018/978-1-4666-9970-0.ch007

some elements of the legal system (as it relates to ADR) are also discussion. For all, purposes the adjudication process seems to be an anomaly process because it resides on the boundary of the standard legal system and the alternative system. The process of mediation, adjudication, and arbitration are discussed and the reader is provided with an overview of the process. Then our focus turns to alleviating common misunderstandings between the various methods used in ADR. This includes a discussion on: mediation vs. arbitration and arbitration vs. adjudication. The discussion then focuses on various acts passes by the UK government and other important acts and reports that have had a significant impact in defining the state of ADR as we know it today. Areas where the UK legal system differs from that of the USA are also pointed out. The documents and acts covered in this chapter include: The Housing Grants, Construction and Regeneration Act (HGCRA) and the Right to Adjudication, Admissibility of hearsay Evidence and the Civil Evidence Act of 1995, The Human Rights Act of 1998 and its Relevance to Adjudication, The Arbitration Act of 1996, United Nations Commission International Trade Law (UNCITRAL) Model Law on International Commercial Arbitration, Alternative Dispute Resolution and the Civil Procedures Rules 1998 (including the new legal terminology that replaced the one in effect prior to 1999), and the Access to Justice Act of 1999. These were chosen for inclusion in the chapter because of their explicit relevance to the topic of discussion and the significant impact that they have had on ADR. In this discussion the genesis of ADR is outlined and the present state of ADR is clarified. Finally, future research directions are provided before the chapter is concluded.

BACKGROUND

Conflicts and disputes are nothing new, we as humankind have been experiencing conflicts and disputes from the onset. The oldest conflicts that we read or hear about are mostly biblical, some examples include the conflicts between God and the devil, followed by conflicts between brothers Caine and Abel, and between God and the Babylonians. Needless to state, the cause, nature, and durations of conflicts have varied over the times and so have their outcomes. Conflicts and disputes if managed or resolved lead to stronger and longer-lasting relationships (Jehn, 1994), to an expedited and judicious conclusion (Fenn, 2006), and to a greater readiness to work together in the future (Rahim, 2001). Conversely, if not managed properly, they can wreak havoc and may lead to actions causing impairment or death, and destruction as seen in the case of wars.

Although, in general usage the terms conflict and dispute are used interchangeably, however they are two markedly distinct concepts. Each consisting of its own unique life-cycle, management and resolution mechanisms, tools of analysis, etc. (Fenn, 2006). It is therefore important to differentiate between them. The term conflict, it so happens, is in wider use compared to the term dispute (Fenn, Lowe, & Speck, 1997). Conflicts are interest driven (Burton, 1993), and as interests often vary conflicts therefore are pandemic. Disputes on the other hand are distinctly associated with issues of justice, and although not as prevalent as conflicts, require immediate and serious efforts to achieve resolve (Fenn, Lowe, & Speck, 1997). These concepts will be discussed in more detail in section 3.

The terms management and resolution may be used as suffixes to both conflict and resolutions. However, the intent of management and resolution would vary depending on whether it is associated with a conflict or a dispute. In the case of conflict management, the concern is the management of the interests of the parties involved and ensuring that agreed interests continue to be maintained (Rahim, 2001). Whereas, conflict resolution is concerned with resolving concerns arising from any perceived or actual disparity of interests (Fenn, 2006). In the case of dispute management the focus is on ensuring that injustices do not arise (Fenn, Lowe & Speck, 1997). While, in dispute resolution the concern is the provision of expedient and equitable justice (ibid), as and when lapses occur (although, this is easier said than done). Conflicts may be, and often are, resolved by the parties involved in the conflict. Disputes on the other hand require the intervention of a neutral third party (Moffitt & Bordone, 2005).

Some conflicts and disputes are short-run, lasting perhaps hours or days, whereas more serious breaches of interest or injustice can be extremely protracted (Fenn, 2006). For example, cases dealing with small claims are resolved quickly but property disputes can take a long time to settle. Various thoughts exist on how to deal with such issues. We can classify these into two categories: the preventive and the corrective (Rahim, 2001). In the preventive mode the focus is on managing the situation so that it does not escalate, become protracted, or lead to a loss of property or life. While, in the corrective mode the focus is on de-escalating an escalated scenario and on achieving some sort of resolution that may be amicable or not (as in the case of lose-lose negotiation techniques, see Blake and Mouton (1964)). And at times when a resolution is not possible to leave the negotiation table in such a state that future deliberations and negotiations may eventually be possible (e.g. when the 'withdrawing' style is adopted).

It should be clear from the discussion so far that conflict and dispute are two very interesting but distinct concepts. However, focusing on both in a single chapter would only lead to a topical discussion of both and would be unfair. Therefore, to do justice to the topic and to provide a detailed discussion this chapter focuses only on disputes and their resolution. We will, revisit disputes in contrast to conflicts and disagreements in section 3, to begin to comprehend the concept of a dispute more fully.

Over the years many alternatives to resolving disputes have emerged. Although, the nomenclatures of these mechanisms vary, they may essentially be classified into two broad categories: the formal and the informal (Fenn, 2006). The informal category of dispute resolution is also termed Alternate Dispute Resolution (ADR). The formal mechanisms of resolving disputes would include any legally available remedies, these include: litigation and adjudication. The informal mechanisms of resolving conflicts include mediation and arbitration. Mediations and arbitration pervade all sorts of disputes from the commercial and contracts to the personal. As discussed above, the underlying factor binding the formal and ADR methods of dispute resolution is a struggle for rights. ADR also extends to personal or tribal involvements such as a dispute between a couple (Rands, Levinger, & Mellinger, 1981) or a dispute between a tribe and one of its members.

In certain places the ADR dispute resolutions mechanism however, are used as 'the' formal mechanism. This is because certain geographic regions are provided unique constitutional statuses. Case in point would be the tribal belt in the North West of Pakistan. Here, the 'jirga' [lit. a gather of elders] (or more formally an 'administrative jirga') is the only legally available remedy for disputes between the tribes and the government. In the same spirit, an example of an informal dispute resolution method would be the 'panchayat' [lit. gathering of five], which prevails in the provinces of the Punjab across the Indian-subcontinent. The 'panchayat' is a mechanism similar to a 'jirga' but used solely for disputes between families, neighbors, and at times communities i.e. in a non-administrative manner. An administrative jirga may be classifiable as a method of arbitration. However, the non-administrative 'jirga' and the 'panchayat' are open to public attendance and therefore violate the confidentiality requirement of arbitration. For a more comprehensive discussion on both these concepts the reader is referred to read Wardak (2003).

The next section (section 3) presents a discussion aimed at differentiating between the concepts of a conflict, dispute, and a disagreement. This will enable us to have a common understanding of the concept of a dispute and will aide in forwarding the discussion towards dispute resolution processes.

DIFFERENTIATING BETWEEN CONFLICTS, DISPUTES, AND DISAGREEMENTS

As indicated in the introduction section of this chapter, the conflict body of literature provides evidence of an entanglement between the notions of: conflict, dispute, and disagreement. The discussion contained in this section therefore, seeks to differentiate between the three.

Burton (1993) envisions conflicts and disputes to be different temporally. For him, conflicts are long-term, while disputes are short-term. Burton (ibid) goes on to argue that conflicts are unavoidable, yet manageable (Kolb & Bartunek, 1992; Lax & Sebenius, 1986). While disputes are avoidable, occurring only when conflicts are not managed and resolved. Fenn's (2006) definition of a conflict takes a similar stance and envisages disputes as existing within larger, long-term conflicts.

On the other hand, a disagreement is considered to be a bargaining impasse, which in Schelling's (1957) view is a struggle between bargainers to commit themselves to their preferred bargaining positions. Thus, disagreements or bargaining impasses are resolved through a process of negotiation. If such impasses are not overcome, the disagreements become protracted. Frustrations run high during such cases, many examples exist from around the world where loss of human life occurred as a result of the pain and suffering experienced by the parties involved. Similarly, Carneval and Pruitt (1992) identify the resolution of disagreements as an occurrence of mediation. Such agreements could be explicit (where both parties actively participate in reaching a decision) or 'tacit' (where both parties move towards

a decision without discussion) (ibid). Explicit agreements are normally written down so that the parties involved do not back out. The existence of disagreements is a positive phenomenon as it generates reasoning and alternatives (Jehn & Mannix, 2001). Interestingly, disagreements vanish as soon as full-disclosure is made by both parties (Sosa, 2010), perhaps because there is no longer any hidden agenda or imperfect information left.

In further clarifying the difference between conflicts and disputes, Burton (1990, 1997) considers a conflict as a serious challenge to existing norms, relationships, and rules of decision-making, and a dispute as the control of discontent stemming from the implementation of specific policies. Later, Burton (1998) categorizes disputes as occurring over material and physical resources, whereas conflicts occur over human needs and aspirations. Examples of conflicts include the conflict between Isreal and Palestine and between India and Pakistan regarding Kashmir. While Fenn et al. (1997) consider a conflict as an incompatibility of interest and a dispute as associated with distinct justiciable issues (such as injury or claims for equitable relief). Hence, both disputes and conflicts are 'affective' i.e. relational in nature but have different causes. It is important to note that conflicts have both positive and negative aspects, while disputes are solely afflictive (ibid).

Interestingly, disputes are classified into two categories 'litigated' (i.e. where a court's verdict is reached) and 'settled' i.e. those that settle prior to trial or prior to verdict pronouncement during a trial (Priest & Klein, 1984). Although, litigation is not the only mechanism for dispute resolution, it is not favored because a trial is considered to be a failure of reaching a decision socially (Gross & Syverud, 1992). Furthermore, litigations involving trial by jury, also refereed to as a 'legal lottery' for their inconsistent outcomes, are favored even less than those involving trial by judge. Additionally, within the legal circles, there are arguments that too many disputes are settled out-of-court (either pre-trial or pre-verdict) and mediated or arbitrated. Whereas, the focus incase of litigation should be on adjudication and not settlement.

Disputes emerge and are transformed through a process in which 'unperceived injurious experiences are, or are not, perceived (naming), do or do not become grievances (blaming), and ultimately emerge as disputes (claiming)' (Felstiner, Abel, & Sarat, 1980). Work by Harrisson (2003) identifies seven different categorizations of disputants: information seekers, exception seekers, victims, enforcers, protectors, targets, and destroyers. These differences point at the motivation of the disputants involved and explains why each dispute is unique and is resolved differently.

Conflict too has been envisioned as forming a continuum, ranging from conflict avoidance to violence (C. Moore, 1989). Alternatively, Fenn at al., (1997) proposes a continuum ranging from conflicts to disputes, where the former requires conflict management and the latter dispute resolution (Fenn, 2006) i.e. arbitration or litigation. Moreover, conflict management usually makes use of non-binding techniques, while dispute resolution makes use of a combination of binding and non-binding methods (ibid).

Envisioning conflict, settlement, and lack of conflict or peace as disjoined events is certainly valid in many contexts and can aid our understanding. For example, knowing what state a party is in could signal their intent or commitment and could also serve as a deterrent to the other party (Kahn, 1964; Schelling, 1957). However, in reality contending parties are simultaneously 'in conflict' or 'at peace' i.e. the intensity of the conflict varies along a spectrum. Conditions of absolute conflict or absolute peace do no exist. These moments can be explained as productive and 'appropriative activities', where the former is concerned with doing productive work and the latter focused on seizing resources controlled by other defending against invasions. Interestingly, appropriative activities may also include profiteering through

robbery, confiscation, redistribution, or coercive encroachment.

To avoid any confusion between a conflict and a dispute, we accept Fenn's (2006) differentiation and consider conflicts to be longer lasting, having both positive and negative aspects, whereas disputes are short-term, afflictive, and arising within conflictual conditions. Etiologically, therefore conflict management is accepted as a means of preventing the occurrence of disputes (i.e. a preventive measure), while dispute resolution is considered as a corrective measure. In agreeing with Burton (1990) we accept conflicts to be related to issues of human needs and aspirations, while disputes are related to material and physical resources. Conflicts are managed throughout the period where two parties are engaged, while disputes require resolution through external input in the form of mediation, arbitration, judge, or jury. Several disputes could arise during a conflict, while the intensity of conflict during the period of engagement between parties varies.

Now that we have a clearer understanding of the difference between conflicts, disputes, and disagreements it would aide our understanding further to say a few words about the choice of methods available for resolving disputes.

PATHWAYS TO RESOLVING DISPUTES

As mentioned earlier there are two distinct pathways to resolving a dispute: the formal and the informal (Fenn, 2006). First let us have a look at the formal path. The origin of the formal methods of resolving disputes lies in the concept of a 'sovereign', where a hereditary leader (or one gaining power over the people after deposing a sovereign) would wield powers of resolving disputes between their subjects. As societies progressed and the power of the sovereigns' were culled, and in many countries replaced by elected

Table 1. Dispute Triggers, adapted from Fenn (1997)

Triggers of Disputes	Focus	Identified by
Unrealistic expectation, contract documents, communications, lack of team spririt, and changes	Construction general	Bristow and Vasilopoulous (1995)
Payments, performance, delay, negligence, quality, and administration	Construction procurement and contracts	Conlin, Langford, and Kennedy (1996)
People, process, and product	Construction contracts	Diekmann, Girard, and Abdul-Hadi (1994)
Contract terms, payment, variation, time, nomination, re-nomination, and information	Construction general	Heath, Hills, and Berry (1994)
Root causes and proximate causes	Construction general	Kumaraswamy (1997)
Management, culture, communications, design, economics, tendering pressures, law, unrealistic expectation, contracts, and workmanship	Construction law	Rhys Jones (1994)
Acceleration, access, weather, and changes	Construction claims	Semple, Hartman, and Jergas (1994)
Misunderstanding and unpredictability	Construction claims	Sykes (1996)

governments, that power was transferred to the legislative bodies. Presently, the formal methods of resolving disputes fall under the domain of such bodies. Where, disputes between the subjects of a nation are resolved using litigation (Rahim, 1986).

However, the legislative bodies have been slow to respond in providing expeditious justice, perhaps because of a lack of competence, resources or will. Some possible arguments for the lethargy prevailing in the legislative systems include the ever-increasing population (which puts a sever burden on the legislative bodies) and the inherent complexity found in society that is giving rise to an ever increasing number of unexplored issues (Semple et al., 1994). As an example, the Internet and World Wide Web have given rise to a diverse set of issues that have required major changes in the legislative process e.g. see (Blavin & Cohen, 2002). The intricate and changing nature of society and business is also a cause of many disputes that burdens the legislative systems further (Forst, 1984), for example: disputes related to discrimination, gender, racism, etc. have been instrumental in laying the foundation for previously unseen types of disputes. The process of litigation is costly and many perceive that the

judgments that are issued often are one-sided and do not cater to the mutual benefit of the parties involved (Hylton, 1990). Lastly, some countries, such as those in the Third World, face the added dynamic of corruption that further complexify's the litigation process (E. Buscaglia, 1996).

There are various types of costs associated with litigation, such as: court fees, retainer fees payable to the lawyer, and the cost of the judgment in case of losing the case (Kritzer, Sarat, Trubek, Bumiller, & McNichol, 1984). Because of the exorbitant cost of the litigation process and unpredictability of outcomes, and the emotional drain it places on those involved this mode of dispute resolution has been termed a "legal lottery" (Bowers, 1996). Interestingly, in some industries both the formal and the informal methods of disputes resolution are problematic, e.g. according to Lord Denning (in "Dawnays Ltd v FG Minter Ltd," 1971) "One of the greatest threats to cash flow is the incidence of disputes. Resolving them by litigation is frequently lengthy and expensive. Arbitration in the construction industry is often as bad or worse".

Alternatively, disputes may be resolved using informal methods. These methods perhaps predate the formal mechanism and are more prevalent because of their accessibility, discretion, and swiftness in resolution. Such methods are regaining popularity owing to the issues plaguing the formal mechanism and are increasingly being used as an alternative to litigation, see as an example (E. Buscaglia & Stephan, 2005). In very simple terms, the informal methods to dispute resolution, also known as alternative dispute resolution (ADR), consist of three key parties: the disputants and a mediator or an arbitrator (Fenn, 2006). Both parties in a dispute are provided equal opportunity to present their case (including providing testimony and evidence) and the arbitrator or mediator is tasked with playing their role in the dispute (Cheung, Suen, & Lam, 2002). The mediator's role is that of a facilitator, while the arbitrator's role is that of a judge and jury. Alternative Dispute Resolution (ADR) is now increasingly being used as the favored method of dispute resolution (ibid). Additionally, the Construction Round Table, a group of main contractors and major sub-contractors, in their voluntary Code of Conduct commit themselves, *inter alia*, to: fair dealings with subcontractors, taking the team lead in the interest of the project, and accepting prompt third party dispute resolution – thus, paving the ground for ADR.

Mediation, arbitration, and adjudication are terms used in the law, to refer to the process of alternative dispute resolution that aims to resolve a dispute between two parties with concrete effects. The role of the mediator or arbitrator is of a third party, who facilitates the disputants to negotiate a settlement (Smith, 1962). This is in contrast to the role of a 'conciliator', who is an expert in the subject area surrounding the dispute and may offer advice during the dispute resolution process (Wenying, 2005). It may be argued that all conciliators take the role of mediators, but not all mediators are conciliators.

The terms mediator, arbitrator, and adjudicator are broad references to instances where a third party helps others reach a settlement. When used in the context of business, the process of mediation has a structure, timetable, and dynamics that 'ordinary' negotiations do not (Bühring-Uhle, Kirchhoff, & Scherer, 2006). The law ensures privacy and confidentiality during ADR and participation is voluntary. It should be noted that mediators facilitate rather than direct the mediation process using a variety of techniques during an ADR to open or improve dialogue and empathy between the disputants (McGovern, 1996).

The cost of using a mediator includes a retainer fee comparable to that of an attorney. However, the time required to complete the mediation process is significantly less than the time it takes to resolve a dispute in litigation. Additionally, mediation increases the control that the disputants have over the resolution process (McGovern, 1996). Whereas, control in the case of litigation or adjudication, resides with a judge or the jury. Therefore, mediation is likely to produce a result that both parties accept. In order to ensure that the agreements reached as a result of the mediation process are not violated, the mediated agreement is fully enforceable in a court of law. In order for mediation to be successful, both the parties must be willing to work together towards a resolution. By virtue of the fact, that if the parties agree to mediation we get a sense that they are willing to negotiate.

Mediation is one of the key techniques in ADR and will therefore be discussed in some detail. For those interested in knowing more about Mediation, please see C. W. Moore (2014). The mediation process may have disclosure requirements if stipulated by the courts. Disclosure pertains to documents, reports or other material. In litigations the disputants are required to exchange such material gathered through a process of discovery or disclosure and the same is true in the case of arbitration or mitigation (Ponte, 2001). The mitigation clauses may require the parties to attend in person; participation at one stage may compensate for the absence in another. Parties choosing to go into mitigation may be required by a judge to make a summary of the dispute and then bring the summary to the mitigation table. Although there are no formal compulsory elements to a mitigation process, the following elements are found in most mitigation scenarios: ground rules of the mitigation process, parties detailing their stories, identification officials, clarifying and indicating respective interests and objectives, search for objective criteria, identification of options, discussion and analysis of solutions, adjustment and refinement of proposed solutions, and a record of the agreement in writing.

The process of ratification provides safeguards for mediating parties. This could alleviate any opportunities for a third party to undermine the mediation result. As an example, in some cases the court must explicitly endorse the mediation agreement. A mediator at his discretion may refer a party to a dispute to specialist for further assistance at the end of the mediation, such as to: psychologists, counselors, social workers, etc. There are special codes of conduct binding the mediator, common elements of which consist of: informing participants of the process, adopting a neutral stance, explicating potential conflicts of interest, maintaining confidentiality, ensuring well being, directing participants to appropriate sources for legal advice, and practicing within their fields of experience. The parties involved in a dispute may choose mediation through consensus, or it may be stipulated by contract. At times the mediator may be liable for misleading the parties or for breaching confidentiality. However, follow-on court action is rare.

Mediator liabilities can arise in several forms including:

- Liability of contract
- Liability and tort
- Liability for breach of fiduciary obligations

Liability in contract arises if the mediator breaches the contract, written or verbal, between the parties. The two most common forms of breach are *failure to perform* and *anticipatory breach*. The limitation of liability includes a requirement to show actual cause. Liability in tort arises when a mediator influences a party (thereby, compromising the integrity of the decision), defames a party, breaches confidentiality, or is negligent. To claim damages, the party must show actual damage, and must exhibit that the mediator's action was the direct cause of the damage. Liability of breach of fiduciary obligations arises if the parties misconceive their relationship with the mediator as anything other than that of neutrality. Court action in such cases is unlikely to succeed since such liability relies on misconception.

There are varieties of mediation, including:

1. Evaluative mediation
2. Facilitative mediation
3. Transformative mediation
4. Narrative mediation
5. Mediation with arbitration
6. Online mediation, and
7. Biased mediation

These are explained in brief next. In the evaluative mediation process the mediator evaluates the fortitude of the arguments presented by both parties and predicts the outcome of a court decision if litigation were to take place. During a facilitative mediation, the mediator is concerned with the mediation process and not its outcome. The mediator as facilitator helps the parties find resolution to their dispute. In the transformative mediation, the mediator as a transformer is concerned with encouraging some sort of transformation to occur during the mediation process. Transformations may include: a change is perspective of a party, improved communication, arriving at a mutually defined agreement, etc. The mediator in the narrative mediation seeks to extract examples and stories constituting a lived experience of the disputants. These allow the parties to see the problem(s) a new and to come up with new and unique solutions. The mediator's role here is to emphasize on helping the party realize that the dispute is not people centric, rather it is problem centric (Winslade & Monk, 2000). In mediation with arbitration, preference is towards reaching settlement through mediation but if that fails the process of arbitration is employed. The arbitration results are binding on the parties. Online mediation simply refers to medium of technology used during mediation. Lastly, biased mediation would be one where the mediator takes the side of one party against another.

ADR TERMS IN COMMON USE

The term ADR is an umbrella term encompassing four popular processes that sound quite similar. In an order to alleviate any confusion between these concepts each is compared against its closest rival below.

Mediation vs. Arbitration

The terms mediation and arbitration are used synonymously, but they are slightly different. Although, mediation and arbitration are alternatives to litigation, they are sometimes used in conjunction with litigation. Both mediation and arbitration necessitate the involvement of an independent third party to oversee the process, and they both may be binding. However, it is common practice to use mediation in a non-binding manner and arbitration as a binding process. Binding arbitration leads to the replacement of the trial process with arbitration.

Moving from mediation to arbitration is not a thoughtless process. Although, mediation may cause some anxiety in that a party or both the parties may feel that mediation is slow or they may not be happy with its outcome. However, in the *The Channel Tunnel Group Ltd. V. Balfour Beatty*

Construction Ltd ("The Channel Tunnel Group Ltd v. Balfour Beatty Construction Ltd," 1993) the House of Lords held that the courts have the jurisdiction to refuse to hear proceedings brought into breach of an agreed dispute resolution. The court ruled that "… those who make agreements for the resolution of disputes must show good reasons for departing from them…". It was besides the point that a party seeking payment found their "… chosen method too slow to suit their purpose."

Arbitration can involve a single arbitrator or consists of a panel of arbitrators who act as judge(s). In case panel-arbitration is used, the panel consists of an arbitrator chosen by each party and a third arbitrator chosen by both the parties together. Decisions in such a case are made by majority vote. In the case of construction disputes the third member of the arbitration panel is chosen from the International Chamber of Commerce (following industry rules). Alternatively, a singe mediator (whose role is that of a facilitator rather than a judge) generally conducts mediation.

Over the years ADR in the form of mediation and arbitration has gained some favor. As an example, taking cues from the access to justice movement in the UK, the Philippines have served as a roll-model for many countries in establishing mobile courts. These courts travel around the country resolving disputes using mediation and arbitration. However, success of the mobile courts has been hindered by the lack of proper law making. In that, parties to mediation had the option to pursue litigation if they were not content with the decision rendered by the mobile courts. Later changes in the laws have resolved this issue, whereby once the parties choose to go to mediation they cannot exercise litigation. Another pathway to justice has also made significant ground, such as the Federal Ombudsman office in Pakistan that allow for non-litigious resolution of disputes between civil citizens and federal and provincial offices.

Arbitration vs. Adjudication

Although, arbitration and adjudication are different processes for resolving disputes, they are similar in a few respects. They both are:

1. Alternatives to the litigation process
2. Confidential processes, and
3. Binding (although to different degrees)

Arbitration is a more generally used process spanning disputes falling in the domain of employment law, international trade, contracts, construction, intellectual property, and sports. The process of arbitration has already been explained in sub-section (A) above.

Adjudication is a process used mostly in the construction industry. The use of adjudication is provisioned as a right during construction disputes through the HGCRA (discussed in section 6.1). It is also used as a process to resolve tenant disputes.

Adjudication is a legal process in which an arbiter or judge listens to arguments, views evidence, and comes to a decision determining the rights and obligations between the parties involved. The process of adjudication is also described as a 'mini-trial' that results in a fairly quick decision, as compared to a full-trial that tend to be protracted (Washington State Office of Administrative Hearings, 2015). In the case of construction disputes the time allowed for adjudication to reach a decision is 28 days.

Adjudication can go severely wrong. As an example, in the case of *Bouygues UK Ltd v. Dahl Jensen UK Ltd (In Liquidation) ("Bouygues UK Ltd v. Dahl Jensen UK Ltd," 1999)* £250,000 were patently awarded to the wrong party. When Bouygues failed to honor the decision, Jensen won an enforcement order from the court. Bouygues had contended that the figures did not add up, and that if the adjudicator was correct it could only be because he was releasing the final moiety of retention, which neither party had requested.

Thus, the adjudicator had exceeded his authority and the decision was null and void. Jensen on the other had argued that it was part of his remit, but because he had made a mistake, thus the decision was valid. The adjudicator invited both claimants to reconsider but to no avail. Eventually, a decision was passed in favor of Jensen with the argument by the adjudicator that he "… was doing precisely what he had been asked to do, and was answering the right question, but he was doing it in the wrong way".

ADR A LEGAL PERSPECTIVE

This section presents the key Acts and Model Laws that shape the ADR landscape. Specific sections of the acts that are relevant to the topic of ADR are reproduced, where necessary, or discussed in detail. This section is meant to bring to fore the key developments founding the basic constructs of ADR and the boundary within which it is enacted. Understanding these constructs will enable the reader to not only understand the landscape of ADR as it is at the moment but also to develop the necessary comprehension of where it is headed. Although, the topics discussed below may not on their surface seem to relate with each other. However, each deals with a specific but essential element of ADR.

The Housing Grants, Construction and Regeneration Act (HGCRA) and the Right to Adjudication

The HGCRA is an omnibus act that extends to housing grants, laws pertaining to construction contracts and architects, regeneration of sites, energy efficient construction, and dissolution or formulation of new townships. In simpler terms, it could be considered as the defining act pertaining to construction. This section focuses on the HCGRA's implication in ADR.

Adjudication is a statutory right of any party involved in a contract dispute falling in the domain of the HGCRA (Housing Grants, 1996). The key sections of the act are 108(1) to (5). These are reproduced below:

1. A party to a construction contract has the right to refer a dispute arising under the contract for adjudication under a procedure complying with this section. For this purpose 'dispute' includes any difference.

2. The contract shall:
    a. Enable a party to give notice at any time of his intention to refer a dispute to adjudication.
    b. Provide a timetable with the object of securing the appointment of the adjudicator and referral of the dispute to him within 7 days of such notice.
    c. Require the adjudicator to read a decision within 28 days of referral or such longer period as agreed by the parties after the dispute has been referred.
    d. Allow the adjudicator to extend the period of 28 days by up to 14 days, with the consent of the party by whom the dispute was referred.
    e. Impose a duty on the adjudicator to act impartially.
    f. Enable the adjudicator to take the initiative in ascertaining the facts and the law.

3. The contract shall provide that the decision of the adjudicator is binding until the dispute is finally determined by legal proceedings, by arbitration... or by agreement.

4. The contract shall also provide that the adjudicator is not liable for anything done or omitted in the discharge or purported discharge of his functions as adjudicator unless the act or omission is in bad faith, and that any employee or agent of the adjudicator is similarly protected for liability.

5. If the contract does not comply with the requirements of subsection (I) to (4), the adjudication provisions of the Scheme for Contraction Contracts apply.

Clause 5 above, of the HGCRA resulted in the Joint Contracts Tribunal (JCT) to reconstitute their form JCT SFBC 98 by including some of the recommendations of the Latham Report and by making it compliant to the HGCRA via the introduction of Cause 41(A) (Pickavance, 2007).

Adjudication is increasingly being suggested as a binding or non-binding method of potentially unlocking disputes. Aside from the jurisdiction of the HGCRA, adjudication is finding its way into activities that fall outside the domain of construction.

Admissibility of Hearsay Evidence and the Civil Evidence Act of 1995

Before the introduction of the Civil Evidence Act of ("Civil Evidence Act," 1995) 'hearsay' evidence was inadmissible in the cases of litigation and arbitration. The only way to include key evidence was to call in a hostile witness. This caused significant issues in the case of Rent Review disputes, where the key witness could not participate as they would either be bound by confidentiality agreement or ineligible because of conflict of interest (Hackett, 2000). A somewhat similar problem often arises in construction disputes as well. Where, a sub-contractor X pursuing a main contractor would obtain evidence from another sub-contractor Y in an informal and free manner. However, sub-contractor Y may be hopeful for a favorable outcome of the case, or is expectant of future business and therefore may not be willing to provide testimony, or appear on behalf of sub-contractor X.

The Civil Evidence Act of 1995 relaxes the previous position on 'hearsay' evidence, and gives discretionary powers to judges and arbitrators, contingent on six tests (Hackett, 2000):

1. Is it really unrealistic to include the original source of the evidence now being relied upon?
2. Was the original statement made contemporaneously?
3. Does the evidence involve multiple 'hearsay'?
4. Do the parties involved have motive to conceal or misrepresent matters?
5. Was the original statement an edited account, made in collusion or made for a particular purpose?
6. Do the circumstances, in which the 'hearsay' evidence is mentioned, suggest an attempt to prevent proper evaluation of its importance?

It is recommended that 'hearsay' evidence be accepted with care keeping in mind the motives and credibility of the person of source. The best type of evidence would be actual factual accounts presented by either of the parties.

The Human Rights Act 1998 and its Relevance to Adjudication

The Human Rights Act of 1998 came about as a result of acceding to the European Convention on Human Rights. This act seeks to provision individuals with the right of protection against the state or its system lead (alleged) oppressions. The act mandates 'public authorities' to provide a fair and public hearing for those with grievances. The term 'public authorities' is an umbrella term that encompasses both: (1) a court of tribunal or (2) any person who is a public functionary.

This act is relevant to dispute resolution as arbitration falls under the concept of a 'tribunal'. However, arbitration is not a public hearing, thus the consequences of this act are significant. Latter interpretations of the act led to the conclusion that this act applies directly in the cases of forced arbitration. However, the courts determined that 'voluntary arbitration' does not fall under the term 'tribunal' and thus arbitration in such a case does not have to be public. However, it should be noted that voluntary arbitration is subject indirectly to the act by the following (a) the general duty of arbitrators to apply English Law and (b) it is obligatory for the Commercial Court under the Act to apply Convention rights albeit to the extent required of an appellate court (Robinson, 2002)

The Arbitration Act of 1996

Arbitrations (local and domestic) in the UK and Great Britain are governed by the Arbitration Act 1996, which is a successor of three acts dating back to the 1950. As discussed earlier in this chapter arbitration is the preferred mechanism of dispute resolution over litigation. The key reason for this, courtesy of Lord Woolf, is that arbitration offers better case management and early trial dates. However, arbitration is under threat from section 9 of the Arbitration Act 1996, which allows for the courts to retain action where an arbitration clause exists. As many solicitors are amending construction contracts in favor of litigation, arbitration may possibly be completely replaced with adjudication. However, this does not imply that arbitration is losing favor as a dispute resolution process involving other types of disputes. In fact, a survey by Price Waterhouse Coopers (2013) reveals that arbitration was still the preferred mode of dispute resolution in the construction sector.

Although, the Arbitration Act 1996 takes influence from the UNCITRAL Model Law (discussed in section 6.5), the UK government's refusal to adopt it has been a cause of some criticism. The Arbitration Act 1996 applies to disputes both domestic and international, outlines the principles underlying the legislation (e.g. fairness, anonymity, and bounding court intervention), and provides for appeals in the case of point of law.

UNCITRAL Model Law on International Commercial Arbitration

The United Nations Commission on International Trade Law (UNCITRAL) adopted the Model Law on International Commercial Arbitration in 1985. Last amendments to the Model Law were made in 2006. The UNCITRAL Model Law is a detailed guideline for legislators for the purpose of adoption, or for formulating arbitration acts of their own pertaining to disputes in light of the particular needs of international arbitrations. The model law has been adopted by 66 countries in 99 different jurisdictions (United Nations Commission on International Trade Law, 2015).

There are two key parts to the UNCITRAL, the Model Law and the Arbitration Rule. The arbitration rules are a comprehensive set of procedures that disputing parties may agree to follow during an arbitration. There are three versions of the UNCITRAL Arbitration Rules, the latest of which was introduced in 2013 and includes transparency clauses pertaining to investor-state arbitrations (United Nations Commission on International Trade Law, 2015).

Alternative Dispute Resolution and the Civil Procedure Rules 1998

Civil procedures in the UK went through major reforms as a result of Lord Woolf's (the then Lord Chief Justice) Access to Justice reports of 1995 and 1996 (Lord Woolf, 1998). Problems haunting the legal system as identified in the Woolf Report that necessitated the reforms include: high expense, slowness, and complexity. Since its introduction all court procedures in the UK now follow the Civil Procedure Rules 1998.

ADR is not mentioned in the 1995 Woolf Report but features prominently in the 1996 report. This is not to say that Alternative Dispute Resolution (ADR) was not a part of the legal framework prior to the Woolf reports. On the contrary, ADR was being encouraged since the

early 1990s by the Commercial Courts that went on to issue its *Practice Note: Commercial Courts; Alternative Dispute Resolution* in 1994. This note mandates that legal advisors council their clients to resolve disputes using mediation, conciliation, or otherwise; and to inform the parties of the most cost-effective modes of resolving disputes. These recommendations were adopted by the High Courts in 1995 though the issuance of a *Practical Note: Civil Litigation; Case Management*.

The Civil Procedure Rules in sections 1.4(2) encourages cooperative behavior from both parties and *inter alia* encourages the use of ADR procedures (in para 1.4(2)(e)) whenever deemed appropriate by the courts. Since its introduction the Civil Procedure Rules has been amended 60 times with the last major amendment occurring in 2013. Further, as of 2009 the pre-action protocols also formally began encouraging ADR via the letter of claim, mandating that it should 'state (if this is so) that the claimant wishes to enter into mediation or another alternative method of dispute resolution, and draw attention to the court's power to impose sanctions for failure to comply with this practice direction'. This gave rise to a reciprocal requirement in the letter of response, which states '...Both the Claimant and Defendant may be required by the Court to provide evidence that alternative means of resolving their disputes were considered. The Courts take the view that litigation should be a last resort...' (41st amendment to the CPR). It is quite confusing to note that ADR is recommended but not compulsory (i.e. other methods may also be used) as specified in the *Practice Direction: Pre-action Conduct* issued April 2009. Other methods would include: mediation, arbitration, early neutral evaluation, and ombudsmen schemes.

The Woolf Report and amended Civil Procedure Rules have given rise to a New Legal Dictionary. A comparison of the 'old' vs. 'new' legal terms is provided in table 2. Terminology specific to arbitration is identified in parenthesis.

Table 2. Glossary of New vs. Old Legal Terminology

New Terms	Old Terms
Claimant	Plaintiff (Litigations)
Claimant	Claimant (Arbitration)
Defendant	Defendant (Litigation)
Respondent	Respondent (Arbitration)
Claim Form	Summons or Writ
Defence	Defence
Application Notice	Interlocutory Summons
Statement of Case	Pleadings
Disclosure	Discovery
Further Information	Further and Better / Particulars & Interrogatories
Permission	Leave
Assessment	Taxation of Costs

Access to Justice Act 1999

The Access to Justice Act 1999 goes beyond the recommendations of Lord Woolf's Report *Access to Justice* that addressed how civil procedures could be made more user friendly. The Access to Justice Act 1999 sets out to update procedures for obtaining financial assistance in bringing or defending legal actions in civil or criminal courts. Further, it reviews the procedures for challenging decisions passed by the lower courts and allowing cases that touch on particular points of law touching on public policy to go all the way to the House of Lords. Although the Access to Justice Act 1999 does not make any direct references to ADR in the context of commercial disputes, it does mention in Section 8(3) that mediation is appropriate for many family disputes than court proceedings. However, impact of the Access to Justice Act pervades the legal system.

One of the concerns of the Access to Justice Act 1999 (AJA) is Conditional Fee Arrangements (CFA). Prior to 1990 the general rule that prevailed prevented anyone from acting on other than full fee basis. Since, the introduction of the Access

to Justice Act 1999 CFA is now allowed. It is important to note that the CFA allows for Conditional Fee but does not allow Contingency Fee. Contingency Fee is where the legal team agrees to represent a client based on speculation of the case's success. Contingency Fee's are allowed in the USA but not in the UK.

Contractors and sub-contractors can safeguard themselves financially by opting for 'Pre-event' litigation insurance and 'after-the-event' litigation cost insurance. The pre-event litigation insurance is a bolt-on option to the main policy for the prudent contractors. Such policies are tremendously useful incase some unforeseen litigious scenarios arise. Having such a policy aids in the least amount of disruption to the cash flows of the insured contractors and sub-contractors.

After-the-event litigation cost insurance policies are only available to the claimants and not to the defendants. An exception would be where the defendant in the main action is also the claimant in the counterclaim. Such insurance policies take the form of after-the-event litigation costs and respond only in the event of the Claimant losing the case. Such insurance add-ons enable claimants, whether individual or companies, to afford justice. That is, they can seek to enforce their perceived legal rights under a contract, and avoid the previous uncertainty of financial risks of losing – specifically, doubling the costs of litigation incase of loss.

FUTURE RESEARCH DIRECTIONS

Future research can focus on qualitative explorations of the role of ADR on the relationships between parties. Additionally, regional and tribal ADR methods can be explored in more detail and compared against more traditional ADR methods. Other issues of interest would include exploring the role of trust and power during ADR proceedings. From a quantitative perspective the effectiveness of ADR can be explored and a case for the more effective ADR methods can be built. There is also potential for case studies and longitudinal studies that can aim to explore ADR in action and provide for more thicker and *in situ* descriptions of what goes on when ADR is being practiced.

CONCLUDING REMARKS

This chapter has covered a lot of groundwork and provides and quick and through introduction to the concepts and underlying discussions on Alternative Dispute Resolution (ADR). The chapter provided a detailed discussion based on extant literature in an effort to differentiate between disputes and conflicts. Then some of the common confusions between terms commonly used in ADR were addressed. Following which various key government acts and reports that shape the state of ADR as we know it were touched upon. The reader will appreciate that these acts and documents themselves are far too lengthy to be sufficiently described in a single chapter, therefore only those concerns within the documents that directly address ADR or are related to ADR are discussed. It remains a burden on the readers to access these documents themselves to fully appreciate their content.

REFERENCES

Blake, R. R., & Mouton, J. S. (1964). *The Managerial Grid*. Houston: Gulf Publishing Company.

Blavin, J. H., & Cohen, L. G. (2002). Gore, Gibson, and Goldsmith: The Evolution of Internet Metaphors in Law and Commentary. *Harvard Journal of Law & Technology*, 16.

Bouygues UK Ltd v. Dahl Jensen UK Ltd, (1999).

Bowers, C. P. (1996). Courts, Contracts, and the Appropriate Discount Rate: A Quick Fix for the Legal Lottery. *The University of Chicago Law Review. University of Chicago. Law School*, *63*(3), 1099–1137. doi:10.2307/1600250

Bristow, D., & Vasilopoulous, R. (1995). The New CCDC 2: Facilitating Dispute Resolution of Construction Projects. *Constitutional Law Journal (Newark, N.J.)*, *11*(2), 95–117.

Bühring-Uhle, C., Kirchhoff, L., & Scherer, G. (2006). *Arbitration and mediation in international business*. New York: Kluwer Law International.

Burton, J. W. (1990). *Conflict Resolution and Prevention*. New York: St. Martin's Press.

Burton, J. W. (1993). Conflict Resolution as Political Philosophy. In H. van der Merwe & D. J. Sandole (Eds.), *Conflict Resolution Theory and Practice: Integration and Application* (pp. 55–64). Manchester, UK: Manchester University Press.

Burton, J. W. (1997). *Violence Explained: The Sources of Conflict, Violence and Crime and Their Prevention*. Manchester, UK: Mancherster University Press.

Burton, J. W. (1998). Conflict Resolution: The Human Dimension. *International Journal of Peace Studies*, *3*(1), 4.

Buscaglia, E. (1996). Corruption and Judicial Reform in Latin America. *Policy Studies*, *17*(4), 273–285. doi:10.1080/01442879608423713

Buscaglia, E., & Stephan, P. B. (2005). An Empirical Assessment of the Impact of Formal Versus Informal Dispute Resolution on Poverty: A Governance-Based Approach. *International Review of Law and Economics*, *25*(1), 89–106. doi:10.1016/j.irle.2004.06.004

Carnevale, P. J., & Pruitt, D. G. (1992). Negotiation and Mediation. *Annual Review of Psychology*, *43*(1), 531–582. doi:10.1146/annurev.ps.43.020192.002531

Cheung, S. O., Suen, H. C., & Lam, T. I. (2002). Fundamentals of Alternative Dispute Resolution Processes in Construction. *Journal of Construction Engineering and Management, 128*(5), 409–417. doi:10.1061/(ASCE)0733-9364(2002)128:5(409)

Civil Evidence Act, (1995).

Conlin, J., Langford, D., & Kennedy, P. (1996). *The Relationship Between Construciton Procurement Strategies and Construction Contract Disputes.* Paper presented at the CIB W92 North Meets South, Durban, South Africa.

Coopers, P. W. (2013). *Corporate Choices in International Arbitration.* Academic Press.

Dawnays Ltd v FG Minter Ltd (2 All ER 1389; [1971] 1 WLR 1205 1971).

Diekmann, J., Girard, M., & Abdul-Hadi, N. (1994). *Disputes Potential Index: A study into the Predictability of Contract Disputes.* Academic Press.

Felstiner, W. L., Abel, R. L., & Sarat, A. (1980). The Emergence and Transformation of Disputes: Naming, Blaming, Claiming..... *Law & Society Review, 15*, 631.

Fenn, P. (2006). Conflict Management and Dispute Resolution. In D. Lowe & R. Leiringer (Eds.), *Commercial Management of Projects: Defining the Discipline* (pp. 234–269). Blackwell Publishing. doi:10.1002/9780470759509.ch11

Fenn, P., Lowe, D., & Speck, C. (1997). Conflict and Dispute in Construction. *Construction Management and Economics, 15*(6), 513–518. doi:10.1080/014461997372719

Forst, B. (1984). Overburdened Courts and Underutilized Information Technology: A Modern Prescription for a Chronic Disorder. *Judicature, 68*, 30.

Gross, S. R., & Syverud, K. D. (1992). Getting to No: A Study of Settlement Negotiations and the Selection of Cases for Trial. *Michigan Law Review, 90*, 323–373. PMID:10115793

Hackett, J. (2000). *Construction Claims: Current Practice and Case Management.* London: LLP Professional Publishing.

Harrisson, T. R. (2003). Victims, Targets, Protectors, and Destroyers: Using Disputant Accounts to Develop a Grounded Taxonomy of Disputant Orientations. *Conflict Resolution Quarterly, 20*(3), 307–329. doi:10.1002/crq.27

Heath, B., Hills, B., & Berry, M. (1994). *The Origin of Conflict within the Construction Process.* Paper presented at the First Plenary Meeting of TG15, The Netherlands.

Hylton, K. N. (1990). The influence of litigation costs on deterrence under strict liability and under negligence. *International Review of Law and Economics, 10*(2), 161–171. doi:10.1016/0144-8188(90)90021-K

Jehn, K. A. (1994). Enhancing effectivenes: An investigation of advantages and disadvantages of value-based intragroup conflict. *The International Journal of Conflict Management, 5*(3), 223–238. doi:10.1108/eb022744

Jehn, K. A., & Mannix, E. A. (2001). The dynamic nature of conflict: A longitudinal study of intragroup conflict and group performance. *Academy of Management Journal, 44*(2), 238–251. doi:10.2307/3069453

Kahn, R. L. (1964). Introduction. In R. L. Kahn & E. Boulding (Eds.), *Power and Conflict in Organizations* (pp. 1–7). Basic Books.

Kolb, D., & Bartunek, J. M. (Eds.). (1992). *Hidden Conflict in Organizations: Uncovering Behind-the-Scenes Disputes.* Newbury Park, CA: Sage. doi:10.4135/9781483325897

Kritzer, H. M., Sarat, A., Trubek, D. M., Bumiller, K., & McNichol, E. (1984). Understanding the Costs of Litigation: The Case of the Hourly-Fee Lawyer. *Law & Social Inquiry, 9*(3), 559–581. doi:10.1111/j.1747-4469.1984.tb00020.x

Kumaraswamy, M. M. (1997). Conflicts, Claims and Disputes in Construction. *Engineering Construction & Architectural Management, 4*(2), 95-111. 10.1046/j.1365-232X.1997.00087.x

Lax, D., & Sebenius, J. (1986). *The Manager as Negotiator*. New York: Free Press.

McGovern, F. E. (1996). *Beyond efficiency: A bevy of ADR justifications (An unfootnoted summary)*. Dispute Resolution Magazine, 3.

Moffitt, M. L., & Bordone, R. C. (Eds.). (2005). *The Handbook of Dispute Resolution*. San Francisco, CA: Jossey-Bass.

Moore, C. (1989). *The Mediation Process*. San Francisco: Jossey Bass.

Moore, C. W. (2014). *The mediation process: Practical strategies for resolving conflict*. New York, NY: John Wiley & Sons.

Pickavance, K. (2007). *Construction Law and Management*. London: Routledge.

Ponte, L. M. (2001). Broadening traditional ADR notions of disclosure: Special considerations for posting conflict resolution policies and programs on e-business Web sites. *Ohio State Journal of Dispute Resolution, 17*, 321.

Priest, G. L., & Klein, B. (1984). The Selection of Disputes for Litigation. *The Journal of Legal Studies, 12*, 1–55.

Rahim, M. A. (1986). *Managing Conflict in Organizations*. New York, NY: Praeger.

Rahim, M. A. (2001). *Managing Conflict in Organizations* (3rd ed.). Westport, CT: Quorum Books.

Rands, M., Levinger, G., & Mellinger, G. D. (1981). Patterns of Conflict Resolution and Marital Satisfaction. *Journal of Family Issues, 2*, 297–321.

Rhys Jones, S. (1994). How Constructive is Construction Law? *Constitutional Law Journal (Newark, N.J.), 10*(1), 28–38.

Robinson, W. (2002). The Effects of the Human Rights Act 1998 on Arbitration. *Amicus Curiae*, (42).

Schelling, T. C. (1957). Bargaining, Communication, and Limited War. *The Journal of Conflict Resolution, 1*(1), 19–36. doi:10.1177/002200275700100104

Semple, C., Hartman, F., & Jergas, G. (1994). Construction Claims and Disputes: Causes and Cost/Time Overruns. *Journal of Construction Engineering and Management, 120*(4), 785–795. doi:10.1061/(ASCE)0733-9364(1994)120:4(785)

Smith, R. A. (1962). Question of Arbitrability-The Role of the Arbitrator, the Court, and the Parties. *Southwestern Law Journal, 16*(1).

Sosa, E. (2010). The Epistemology of Disagreement. *His Armchair Philosophy*.

Sykes, J. (1996). Claims and Disputes in Construction. *Constitutional Law Journal (Newark, N.J.), 12*(1), 3–13.

The Channel Tunnel Group Ltd v. Balfour Beatty Construction Ltd, (1993).

United Nations Commission on International Trade Law. (2015). *UNCITRAL Model Law on International Commercial Arbitration*. Retrieved from http://www.uncitral.org/uncitral/en/uncitral_texts/arbitration/1985Model_arbitration_status.html

Wardak, A. (2003). *Jirga: a traditional mechanism of conflict resolution in Afghanistan*. Retrieved from Glamorgan: http://unpan1.un.org/intradoc/groups/public/documents/apcity/umpan017434.pdf

Washington State Office of Administrative Hearings. (2015). Glossary for Administrative Hearings.

Wenying, W. (2005). Role of Conciliation in Resolving Disputes: A PRC Perspective. *The Ohio State Journal on Dispute Resolution, 20*(421).

Winslade, J., & Monk, G. (2000). *Narrative Mediation: A New Approach to Conflict Resolution*. San Francisco: Jossey-Bass Publishers.

Woolf, L. (1998). *Access to Justice: Interim and Final Reports by Lord Woolf to the Lord Chancellor*. Academic Press.

KEY TERMS AND DEFINITIONS

ADR: Alternative Dispute Resolution.

AJA: Access to Justice Act 1999.

Anticipatory Breach: Also called anticipatory repudiation, is a term in the law of contracts that describes a declaration by the promising party to a contract, that he or she does not intend to live up to his or her obligation under the contract.

CFA: Conditional Fee Arrangement.

Fiduciary Duty: A relationship between a trustee and beneficiary based on trust.

Hearsay Evidence: The report of another person's words by a witness, usually disallowed as evidence in a court of law.

HGCRA: Housing Grants, Construction and Regeneration Act.

Jirga: Literally defined as a gathering of elders. It is a term used in the Pashto language of the North Western region of Pakistan and in the Pastho speaking areas of Afghanistan. A jirga is a conflict / dispute resolution process where the disputing parties after agreeing to the jirga process plead their case in front of elders from within their community. The outcome of the jirga is based on either party achieving a two-thirds majority or via a decision recommended by the elders. The higher courts of Pakistan have ruled that jirga's for criminal cases are illegal because their decisions have often proved to be counter to the constitutional rights of the persons in dispute. However, administrative jirga's are allowed within the Federally Administered Tribal Areas of Pakistan and within rural and urban areas to resolve small claims and disputes.

Panchayat: Literally defined as a gathering of five. It is a term used within the rural Punjab provinces of Pakistan and India to define a dispute resolution process similar to the 'jirga'.

Tort: A wrongful act or an infringement of a right (other than under contract) leading to civil legal liability.

UNCITRAL: United Nations Commission International Trade Law Model Law on International Commercial Arbitration.

Chapter 8
Surviving the Conflict of Self-Inflicted Organizational Crises

Andrew S. Pyle
Clemson University, USA

ABSTRACT

Social media platforms provide channels for both individuals and organizations to engage with global audiences. A successful social media message can reach millions, and shape the way publics view a particular person, group, or cause. As organizations become more engaged with publics through social media platforms, a new area of organizational risk has also developed. It is possible for an organization to create a self-inflicted crisis through the unintentional transmission of a poorly worded or ill-conceived social media message. This type of self-induced crisis event creates organizational conflict that must be managed quickly. This chapter explores three cases of organizational conflict resulting from self-inflicted crisis events. All three events caused major conversations to erupt on social media platforms. The author examines the social media-based communication practices of three organizations and draws lessons from both successes and failures for how organizations should respond to self-inflicted crises.

INTRODUCTION

In recent years, social media platforms have provided channels for both individuals and organizations to engage with vast global audiences. It is not an overstatement to say that a successful social media message can reach millions and shape the way publics view a particular person, group, or cause. For example, the "ALS Ice Bucket Challenge" went viral in the summer of 2014 and raised more than $115 million by November of the same year (Worland, 2014). The challenge consisted of a bucket of ice water being dumped over a person's head, and then challenging other people to do the same within 24 hours. If the

challenged individual did not comply, they were expected to donate money to a charity (Worland, 2014). The specific charity that made the challenge go viral was for research into amyotrophic lateral sclerosis (ALS), also known as Lou Gehrig's disease (ALS Association, 2015). The ALS Ice Bucket Challenge began to gain major traction when former Boston College baseball player Pete Frates, diagnosed with ALS in 2012, decided to challenge some friends via Facebook (Keyes, 2014). Frates was not the first to use the challenge with the hashtag "#StrikeOutALS," but he appears to be the person whose social network launched the challenge beyond a local fad to an international phenomenon.

DOI: 10.4018/978-1-4666-9970-0.ch008

Another dimension of the power of social media messages is the case of Justine Sacco, former senior communication director for media company IAC, whose thoughtless and insensitive tweet went viral and caused international outrage. Shortly before boarding a flight from London to South Africa, Sacco tweeted, "Going to Africa. Hope I don't get AIDS. Just kidding. I'm white!" Sacco was not concerned about the influence of her tweet – with only 170 followers on Twitter she tended to use her account as a personal space for venting frustration; she likely did not think anyone would read the tweet (Ronson, 2015). Instead, the tweet was noticed, was passed along via Twitter, and eventually became the "No. 1 worldwide trend on Twitter" (Ronson, 2015, para. 5). Before Justine Sacco landed in South Africa she had already lost her job, become the subject of international disdain and ridicule, and sparked a global conversation about race, class, and the influence of social media.

As organizations become more engaged with publics through social media platforms, a new area of organizational risk has also developed. One of the greatest strengths of social media messaging is also one of its greatest weaknesses. It is possible for an organization to create a self-inflicted crisis through the unintentional transmission of a poorly worded or ill-conceived social media message (Bhasin, 2012). This type of self-induced crisis event creates organizational conflict that must be managed quickly.

This chapter consists of three parts. The author begins by reviewing relevant literature. Next, the author conducts a comparative case study of three distinct self-inflicted crisis events: the Starbucks "Race Together" campaign (Hensley & Blau, 2015); the ineffective response from Urban Outfitters following the production of offensive products (The Week, 2015); and the mistaken tweet sent by the DiGiorno account which misused the "#WhyIStayed" hashtag (Griner, 2014). Finally, the chapter concludes with lessons learned from the case studies, as well as a set of principles to inform organizations managing this type of organizational conflict.

REVIEW OF LITERATURE

Social Networking Sites

Social Network Sites (SNSs) as they are currently conceived have existed in some form since 1997 (boyd & Ellison, 2007). SNSs, such as Facebook, MySpace, or Twitter, are:

web-based services that allow individuals to (1) construct a public or semi-public profile within a bounded system, (2) articulate a list of other users with whom they share a connection, and (3) view and traverse their list of connections and those made by others within the system (p. 211).

These sites exist to serve a variety of functions, from maintaining connections with existing friendship networks, to finding other individuals who share a particular interest (boyd & Ellison, 2007). In addition to these functions, SNSs exist as a space for engaging in dialogic communication.

Micro-Blogs

Within the context of social media and SNSs exists a subset of platforms called "micro-blogs" (Edwards, Edwards, Spence, & Shelton, 2013; Kaplan & Haenlein, 2011). These types of sites, such as Twitter or Tumblr, "allow users to exchange small elements of content such as short sentences, individual images, or video links" (Kaplan & Haenlein, 2011, p. 106). Zhao and Rosson (2009) found that people tend to use micro-blogs to share information they might not otherwise share on existing channels, such as a real-time update on their actions, or for pervasive access to information in a format that requires brevity.

Consider the micro-blogging site Twitter, which is currently the largest micro-blogging site on the Internet, with over 302 million active monthly users (Twitter, 2015). Since its inception in 2006, Twitter has become a massive, international, web-based system for interpersonal and organizational interaction (Kaplan & Haenlein, 2011). A large piece of Twitter's designed purpose is to be a dialogic tool for businesses to engage with stakeholders in new, dynamic ways. However, recent research into organizational use of SNSs indicates that organizations are not using these sites dialogically (Bortree & Seltzer, 2009; Park & Reber, 2008). For example, Linvill, McGee, and Hicks (2012) found that "colleges and universities primarily employed Twitter as an institutional news feed to a general population" (p. 637), rather than as a tool for two-way communication.

The tendency to use Twitter as a broadcasting tool rather than for meaningful interaction is evident in other organizational contexts as well. While studying non-profit organizations' use of Twitter, Lovejoy, Waters, and Saxton (2012), and Waters and Jamal (2011) found that non-profit organizations tend to rely on one-way, asymmetrical communication practices for engaging with stakeholders. Similarly, Rybalko and Seltzer (2010) found that *Fortune 500* companies also underutilize the dialogic capabilities of Twitter and similar social resources. Organizations are sending out links to articles, updates about upcoming events, and informing customers about sales. However, they are generally not effectively engaging in two-way communication. This is not only a missed opportunity for connecting with organizational stakeholders, but also a failure to employ a tool that could greatly assist in managing organizational conflict.

Organizational Conflict

Conflict is part of all relationships. Organizations are, by most definitions, networks of interconnected relationships. As Tjosvold (2008) asserts,

"to work in an organization is to be in conflict" (p. 19). Roloff (1987) defines organizational conflict as "activities that are incompatible with those of colleagues within their network, members of other collectivities, or unaffiliated individuals who utilize the services or products of the organization" (p. 496). Rahim (2002) adds that conflict is "an interactive process" (p. 207). Accepting that conflict is a regular and accepted part of life in an organization, there are perhaps two ways that organizational members can approach and respond to conflict as it arises. On the one hand, people can view conflict as a debilitating, overwhelming, or detrimental event, or series of events. Taking this view can lead to the deterioration of the organization (Aula & Siira, 2010). More specifically, a negative view of conflict can result in accidents, absenteeism, and a general decrease in overall health and well-being (De Dreu, C.K.W., van Dierendonck, D., & Dijkstra, M.T.M., 2004; Meyer, 2004).

From the other perspective, one can view conflict as an opportunity for growth or renewal. Rather than thinking of the negative, organizational members can move toward a conflict-positive perspective (Tjosvold, 2008). From this perspective individuals can see conflict as an opportunity for improvement and positive change in the organization, seeking to grow from conflicting perspectives and ideas. With this concept of conflict, organizational members should pursue three key goals for effective conflict management: pursue organizational learning, meet the needs of organizational stakeholders, and communicate ethically throughout the process (Mitroff, 1998; Rahim, 2002; Tompkins, 1995). By seeking to learn from the events that led up to the conflict, the conflict itself, and how it was resolved (whether successfully or not), organizational members can help the organization function more effectively and avoid similar conflict in the future. By meeting the needs of stakeholders, organizations can help those in conflict to feel heard and appreciated, and can also foster an environment where stakeholders shape the organization by assessing and potentially revising outdated policies and unclear organizational goals. Lastly, while pursuing ethical communication practices, both organizational members and organizational leaders are more likely to make decisions and perform actions that will benefit the organization and the larger community. This also benefits stakeholders, and helps those in conflict trust the organization and its leaders.

While conflict in organizations is a regular occurrence, there are times when it can escalate to the level of crisis. In the current social media context, social-mediated communication has created a context where conflict can become a crisis in moments.

Organizational Crisis

An organizational crisis is defined "as a specific, unexpected, and non-routine event or series of events that create high levels of uncertainty and simultaneously present an organization with both opportunities for and threats to its high priority goals" (Ulmer, Sellnow, & Seeger, 2015, p. 7). This definition is good for the cases evaluated in this chapter, with one small caveat. The crises that develop as a result of social media errors or misstatements are generally self-inflicted crisis events. These crises, therefore, should be preventable events. Although they should be preventable, it does not alter how organizations should respond to and manage these crises.

While many organizational leaders, and most legal teams, will immediately want to save face and engage in reputation management following a crisis, this may not be the best option for the organization. Much of the extant literature on crisis communication indicates that engaging in open, honest communication and developing strong stakeholder relationships is a healthier option that will lead to renewal and to stronger organizational relationships in the future (Botan, 1993, 1997; Olaniran, Scholl, Williams, & Boyer,

2012; Olaniran & Williams, 2001; Ulmer, et al., 2015, 2009, 2007). A theoretical perspective that captures this concept is the discourse of renewal (Ulmer et al., 2015).

The discourse of renewal theory argues for organizations (members and leaders) to pursue four key communication goals before, during, and after crisis. First, organizational learning is vital. Organizations should learn from past successes and failures and from those of other organizations (Ulmer et al., 2015). Second is effective organizational rhetoric. Organizational leaders should communicate early and often during a crisis, and should work to help organizational members and other key stakeholders look toward a "new normal," rather than trying to get "back to normal" (Ulmer et al., 2015). The third communication goal is ethical communication. Organizational members and leaders should strive to communicate ethically in crisis situations. This is perhaps best represented by Nilsen's (1974) concept of significant choice. Nilsen argues that stakeholders must be provided with the information they need so that they can be equipped to make choices based on all available, relevant information, rather than on partial or cherry-picked information. Ulmer et al. (2015) apply the concept of significant choice to crisis response situations. The final goal is for organizational members to maintain a prospective vision, looking forward for ways to achieve renewal after the crisis, rather than dwelling on the past and fixating on what might have been done differently (Ulmer et al., 2015).

The tenets of the discourse of renewal align well with the recommendations found in the literature on organizational conflict management. Both bodies of literature argue for the value of open, honest, ethical communication. There is also a call for key stakeholders to be involved in the process of managing the event. Importantly, both call for a focus on renewal, growth, and vision for the future, rather than dwelling on who is to blame and what might have been done differently leading up to the conflict or crisis. While it is useful to learn from past mistakes, it is detrimental to allow those mistakes to be the sole focus, preventing growth and forward movement. There are several recent cases that support these perspectives.

Self-Inflicted Crisis Events

A quick review of headlines over the past few years would show a consistent trend of organizations sparking conflicts on social media. Sometimes, the conflicts are caused by small mistakes and are easily managed. For example, an American Red Cross employee inadvertently tweeted from the official Red Cross account instead of his own private account: "Ryan found two more 4 bottle packs of Dogfish Head's Midas Touch beer... when we drink we do it right #gettingslizzerd" (Bhasin, 2012). In this case, the Red Cross responded well: "We've deleted the rogue tweet but rest assured the Red Cross is sober and we've confiscated the keys" (Bhasin, 2012). The brewing company, Dogfish Head, immediately jumped in on the conversation by encouraging Twitter followers to use the "#gettingslizzerd" hashtag as a rallying point for donating to disaster relief (Bhasin, 2012).

This quick response minimized the public backlash by acknowledging the error, while also appropriately maintaining levity with what could have been a very sensitive matter. The Red Cross acknowledged the tweet was unprofessional, and ensured the public that they were addressing the situation. In other situations, this type of unintentional conflict turns into a self-induced crisis event for the organization involved. This chapter presents and analyzes three such self-inflicted crisis events.

CASE DESCRIPTIONS AND ANALYSES

This chapter is built around a comparative case study of three specific self-induced organizational crises that required some level of conflict management. A comparative case study is useful as a tool for analyzing individual, organizational, social, and group dynamics (Flick, 2004; Yin, 2014). The following three cases were chosen because they are recent exemplars of organizations that either effectively or ineffectively managed conflict after a self-induced crisis. The cases were selected as part of a purposeful maximal sample, as they demonstrate different perspectives on the problem the author wishes to study and address (Creswell, 2013). Data for the cases were gathered from organizational websites, reports from news media, and from Twitter through the use of Salesforce Radian6 social media listening software. Each section begins with a summary paragraph of the overall case, followed by the full case description and analysis.

Starbucks

The first case is an example of a campaign that seemed to be a good idea, but was unfortunately poorly executed. In March of 2015, Starbucks attempted to launch a campaign designed to encourage conversations about race in the U.S. The company announced the campaign following a series of successful town hall meetings with employees and community members across the U.S. (Starbucks, 2015). Following the series of well-received, well-publicized town hall meetings, Starbucks attempted to launch their "#RaceTogether" campaign by having baristas talk to customers about race relations in the United States. The backlash they faced on social media was damaging to the organization as a whole (Hensley & Blau, 2015). After one week, the company had baristas stop writing "Race Together" on cups and allowed the program to quickly die out (Sanders, 2015). The conversation on social media around the campaign was fairly limited, so the case study will examine how the company might have engaged more effectively with stakeholders on social media platforms.

When Starbucks CEO Howard Schultz announced the launch of a series of programs for employees and local communities in 2014 they were generally well received. For example, the Starbucks College Achievement Plan is a program where Starbucks partnered with Arizona State University to provide free tuition to their baristas (Molinet, 2015; Starbucks, 2014). The other two programs launched in 2014 were called "SolutionsCity" and the Retail Excellence Training Program. Solutions City is designed to engage local leaders across the United States about civic challenges "on three key issues: providing access to education, supporting veterans, and empowering youth" (Starbucks, 2014, para. 12). The Retail Excellence Training Program was targeted at offering young people in areas associated with low access to education a chance to gain professional experience and training (Starbucks, 2014). Starbucks continued to gain ground when, in December of 2014, CEO Howard Schultz hosted an impromptu meeting about race relations in the United States at the Seattle headquarters (Starbucks, 2014). This meeting turned into a series of talks with partners and employees over the course of several weeks.

Entering 2015, Starbucks continued to tap into programs that were building social capital and improving the public image of a company already known for service to local communities (Mirabella, 2014; QSR, 2014). The company also continued to push forward with efforts to spur on conversations about race in the United States. In March of 2015 Mellody Hobson, Starbucks board member and president of Ariel Investments, spoke to the annual meeting of Starbucks shareholders about being "color brave" (Hobson, 2015). She challenged those in attendance to set aside the misconception that being "color blind" means they are solving problems related to race. She argued, "color blindness means we are ignoring the problem" (Hobson, 2015, para. 14). Schultz then took this idea and ran with it, announcing to the shareholders at the annual meeting in 2015 that Starbucks would be continuing the mission of advancing racial equality in the United States by launching a campaign to start a conversation. Schultz called for employees to begin conversations in individual stores by engaging with customers and writing "Race Together" on customers' cups. This was paired with an 8-page spread in USA Today on March 20, 2015, with content designed to highlight injustice and challenges related to racism in the United States today (Starbucks, 2015). With this announcement, Schultz launched Starbucks into a weeklong social media crisis that may have yielded more criticism than conversation.

Soon after the campaign was announced, Starbucks started to receive feedback on social media. Over the course of two weeks there were more than 22,000 tweets about the campaign (Twitter data were collected via Radian6 software). The tone of the tweets had a broad spectrum. Some were simply snarky: "'Iced tea please.' (customer pays, barista slowly makes change). (customer waits anxiously hoping to get change before barista mentions race)" (@bendreyfuss, 2015, March 15), "yesterday: talk about Love at McDonalds. today: talk about race at starbucks. tmrw: psychoanalysis from guy who makes blizzards at dairy queen" (@MikeIsaac, 2015, March 16). Others attacked the campaign: "Despite our difference all of us -- left or right, black or white -- can agree that this Starbucks race talk idea is really stupid" (@HeerJeet, 2015, March 17); "The only thing worse than Starbucks is discussing sensitive cultural topics with strangers at Starbucks" (@joshpetri, 2015, March 16). Some ignored the campaign and instead bashed Starbucks' leadership: "The only folks happy about Starbucks baristas discussing race with customers are the suits who run it. Feel-good liberalism at its worst" (@JamilSmith, 2015, March 16). Some of the conversation around the campaign acknowledged that the idea behind Race Together was probably well-intentioned, but was perhaps not the best way to encourage a legitimate discussion: "I get what Starbucks is trying to do, but nah. I'm just in there trying to get a caramel macchiato" (@kokofasho, 2015, March 17). With rare exception, the Twitter conversation around the Race Together campaign was negative and cynical.

While Twitter users were exploring inventive ways to insult Starbucks' campaign, the campaign looked very different to people who were viewing it on a day-to-day basis in specific Starbucks stores. Over the course of a few days, NPR's Kelly McEvers and Karen Grigsby Bates visited eleven different Starbucks locations (McEvers, 2015). Bates found no one among the baristas looking to talk about race, and she had nothing written on or added to her cup to indicate there was any kind of campaign going on. McEvers, on the other hand, found one location (out of the five she visited) where baristas were talking about race.

As the conversation around the campaign grew online and in stores, Starbucks' leadership seemed absent from the conversation. From the time the campaign was launched through a week after it ended there were a total of ten tweets from Starbucks that had anything to do with the Race Together campaign. All of those tweets were either links to articles that Starbucks had written for their own public relations web portal, or were retweets from people congratulating them for launching the campaign. There was more interaction between Twitter users and Corey duBrowa, the Senior Vice President of Global Communications for Starbucks. However, by March 17 the conversation turned from supportive tweets or general disapproval to specific, pointed questions for duBrowa about the campaign and what Starbucks would be doing for its employees, especially people of color. Some of the tweets were clearly intended to attack or "troll" duBrowa: "So was this your idea? Because it's really bad. @coreydu @CNN" (@GRIMALKINRN, 2015, March 17). Others offered serious questions. For example, one user asked the following and was promptly blocked by duBrowa: "@coreydu Are you going to educate your workers on race relations and racism in America? Will you compensate them for this?" (@BartoszScheller, 2015, March 17). Before long,

duBrowa was blocking users who were critical of him or the campaign.

By the evening of Wednesday, March 18, duBrowa had deactivated his Twitter account. The response to his account deactivation is fairly predictable: "Laughing hysterically at the fact @ coreydu deleted his account after PoC [Persons of Color] engaged him on race. Starbucks going to close its doors too?" (@jskylerinc, 2015, March 17); "not sure it's not a good look for @coreydu to be blocking all these black women the same day starbucks rolls this #racetogether thing out" (@local_maxima, 2015, March 17); "@Starbucks your PR Rep @coreydu quit Twitter over #RaceTogether. Might wanna shut that [expletive] down before it becomes an even BIGGER disaster" (@ Jskylerinc, 2015, March 17). On Thursday, March 19, duBrowa reopened his account and posted a blog addressing his absence while sharing that he "felt personally attacked…" and "overwhelmed" (Geier, 2015).

On March 22, 2015, Starbucks CEO Howard Schultz published an "open letter" to partners (Starbucks employees are called partners) about the Race Together initiative. He indicated that the initiative to have baristas talk about race with customers had ended, and that they would continue as an organization to pursue conversations about race in other ways and other venues. Over the week that the initiative was ongoing, Starbucks largely ignored the conversation that was happening on Twitter. While it is true that there were individuals whose interests seemed to end at attacking or belittling Starbucks, there were many who offered real concerns and sincere critiques. While Starbucks did not see lasting harm to their credibility or to their business, it is perhaps a testament to the multiple initiatives they already have in process designed to support local communities, national groups, and their own employees, rather than a reflection on how successful their campaign was. This was a missed opportunity for Starbucks, whose leadership seems to have remained silent on social media during what could have been a chance for growth and to accomplish organizational goals.

Urban Outfitters

An exemplar of unsuccessful organizational conflict management is the recurring poor decision making of Urban Outfitters. In May of 2011, Urban Outfitters was accused of stealing art from independent artists to use in their product designs (Bhasin, 2012). Urban Outfitters responded they were "looking into this," but did not enact any type of measurable response. Within three hours, Urban Outfitters lost 17,000 followers on Twitter and both #urbanoutfitters and #thieves were trending topics (Bhasin, 2012). Urban Outfitters ended up in hot water again in 2014 by running a "vintage sweatshirt" line that included a Kent State sweatshirt with what appeared to be bloodstains and bullet holes, a clear allusion to the 1970 campus shootings which resulted in the deaths of four students (Winchel, 2014). Urban Outfitters offered no apology and responded simply that everyone misunderstood the purpose of the sweatshirt (Wilson, 2014). On multiple occasions, Urban Outfitters produced offensive materials and then proceeded to offer no apology for their actions. While each of these events was ongoing, there was a sizeable conversation happening about the organization on social media platforms. Rather than engaging with key publics to address their concerns, Urban Outfitters remained silent and ignored the conversation. This repeated mismanagement of self-induced crisis events has created discontent with the company (Huddleston, 2014). The case study will examine how Urban Outfitters could have responded differently, and will explore how its communication practices could be more effective.

As a clothing company apparently seeking an image as edgy and different, Urban Outfitters has an unfortunate history of developing offensive products. Complaints about Urban Outfitters' products go back more than a decade, with the 2003 launch of the game "Ghettopoly," a Monopoly knockoff with content like "Cheap Trick Avenue" and "Smitty's XXX Peep Show" (Controversies, 2015). The complaints continued unabated over the following years, as Urban Outfitters released products such as a shirt with a Palestinian boy carrying an AK-47 assault rifle and the word "victimized," which produced backlash from members of the Jewish community who felt it was an open endorsement of terroristic activities (Controversies, 2015). In 2010 the company came under fire after selling a shirt marketed for young girls with the words "Eat Less" emblazoned across the front. That same year there was outrage when a clothing item was offered with the color options of "White/Charcoal" or "Obama/Black." Urban Outfitters was sued by the Navajo nation in 2012 after ignoring a cease and desist order for using the name "Navajo" on a product line without first asking for permission from the Navajo nation (Fonseca, 2012). In addition to the problematic products listed here, there were a dozen different offensive or tactless products produced for and sold by Urban Outfitters from 2003 to 2015. Unlike the practices of Starbucks, mentioned previously, Urban Outfitters seemed to have no sense of the value of or need for developing social capital.

By September of 2014 Urban Outfitters had been out of the spotlight for producing offensive products for a few months and it seemed like the organization had, perhaps, turned a corner. Then, on September 15, 2014, they launched a line of "vintage college sweatshirts," one of which was from Kent State University – and appeared to have blood stains and bullet holes (Ohlheiser, 2014). The Kent State sweatshirt seemed to be an intentional allusion to the mass shooting at the university often referred to as the "Kent State Massacre," in which four students were killed and others were injured by National Guard troops responding to violent protests (Ohlheiser, 2014). Shortly after the sweatshirt was posted to the website, Urban Outfitters experienced strong negative responses from the public, as well as a statement from Kent State indicating that the product was "beyond poor taste and trivializes a loss of life that still hurts the Kent State community today" (Ohlheiser, 2014, para. 5). Urban Outfitters responded to the negative publicity by releasing the following statement on Twitter (@UrbanOutfitters, 2014, September 15):

Urban Outfitters sincerely apologizes for any offense our Vintage Kent State Sweatshirt may have caused. It was never our intention to allude to the tragic events that took place at Kent State in 1970 and we are extremely saddened that this item was perceived as such. The one-of-a-kind item was purchased as part of our sun-faded vintage collection. There is no blood on this shirt nor has this item been altered in any way. The red stains are discoloration from the original shade of the shirt and the holes are from natural wear and fray. Again, we deeply regret that this item was perceived negatively and we have removed it immediately from our website to avoid further upset.

Disgruntled consumers went to Twitter to express their displeasure with this apology. On September 15 alone, @UrbanOutfitters was mentioned in more than 24,000 tweets – most of them negative. The sentiments of the tweets ranged from disbelief in the sincerity of the apology, to outright attacks on the company and the individuals responsible for the sweatshirt and the apology.

Recognizing their apology was not well received, Urban Outfitters released a follow-up apology on September 16 via TIME (Rothman, 2014):

Urban Outfitters would like to extend our sincerest apologies to Kent State University and the Kent State community. We are deeply saddened by the recent uproar our Vintage Kent State sweatshirt has caused. Though it was never our intention to offend anyone, we understand how the item could have been perceived negatively. The tragic events that took place in 1970 are not forgotten

and our company regrets that people believe we would intentionally make light of such a horrific part of our nation's history. To promote such an event is disgraceful, insensitive and in poor taste. To further clarify, despite what has been reported, this is a vintage item and there is only one. Once the negative feedback was brought to our attention we removed the item immediately from sale. Urban Outfitters purchased the one-of-a-kind sweatshirt from the Rose Bowl Flea Market as part of our sun-faded vintage collection. There is no blood on the sweatshirt nor did we ever promote it as such. The discoloration that has been mistaken for blood is from natural fading and sun exposure. With all of that said, this truth does not excuse us from our failure to identify potential controversial products head on. We, as a company who caters to a college-age demographic, have a responsibility to uphold to our customers. Given our history of controversial issues, we understand how our sincerity may be questioned. We can only prove our commitment to improving our product-screening process through our actions and by holding ourselves accountable. Again, we sincerely apologize for this unfortunate misunderstanding and are dedicated to perfecting our internal processes to help avoid these issues in the future. (para. 5)

While the first apology was poorly received and not well thought out, the second apology is empathic and thoughtful. Urban Outfitters acknowledges that their credibility is at almost zero, especially because of their history of inappropriate, offensive products.

After this event one might think that Urban Outfitters had changed their policy on vetting potentially offensive products. On the contrary, in February of 2015 the company came under fire once again for producing a tapestry that was "'eerily reminiscent' of the holocaust" and of the clothing homosexual individuals were required to wear in concentration camps (Controversies, 2015, para. 2). Once again the company received criticism and backlash. In the short-term, Urban

Outfitters lost followers on social media sites and received continued complaints about the products they were selling. On a more tangible scale, following the most recent rounds of product scandals Urban Outfitters' sales were down 7% (Huddleston, 2014). By continuing to pursue courses of action that yield short-term (and consistently negative) publicity, Urban Outfitters has sacrificed credibility, popularity, and profitability. The company has subjected itself to multiple crisis events, though each one was on a fairly small scale. Rather than addressing the conflict of these crises, Urban Outfitters offered token apologies and continued to act in a manner consistent with an organization uninterested in changing its practices. In this case, organizational communication related to the ongoing conflict is not only ineffective, but also nearly non-existent.

DiGiorno

In September of 2014, a video was released of Baltimore Ravens linebacker Ray Rice assaulting his then-fiancée, Janay Palmer, and dragging her out of an elevator (Kaplan, 2014). Once the video was made public, a woman named Beverly Gooden inadvertently started a social media activism campaign around the hashtag "#WhyIStayed." She shared stories of her own abusive relationship as a show of support for women currently trapped in such a setting, and it quickly became an internationally trending topic, drawing stories from hundreds of supporters (Kaplan, 2014). A member of the DiGiorno Pizza social media team saw "#WhyIStayed" trending on Twitter and, without researching the meaning behind it, tweeted "#WhyIStayed because you had pizza." The public outcry was immediate and intensely negative. Within four minutes of posting the tweet, DiGiorno had pulled the offending tweet and begun responding with a personalized apology to each person who tweeted about the event. The case study analysis will focus on DiGiorno's

personalized, thoughtful responses to each person who reached out to them, and lessons will be drawn to explore how other organizations can learn from DiGiorno's apologies.

Secrets are difficult to keep in today's society. People are under surveillance most of the time, especially in urban areas where businesses have security cameras, traffic lights have cameras, and almost every person walking down the street has a phone with a built in high-quality camera. It should have been no surprise to Ray Rice, then, that video of his assault on his then-fiancée (now wife) Janay Palmer would eventually be released. In February of 2014 Rice and Palmer were arrested on assault charges as the two had a public physical altercation (Bien, 2014). What was not known until September of 2014 was that while in an elevator, before they were arrested, Rice knocked Palmer unconscious then dragged her by her hair from the elevator (Bien, 2014). The video of the assault was shared widely over social media and traditional media outlets. Quickly, the conversation around the assault began to focus around the question, "Why did she [Palmer] stay?" (Kaplan, 2014). This message was troubling to Beverly Gooden, a woman who survived and eventually escaped from an abusive relationship (Kaplan, 2014). On September 8, the day the video of Rice's assault in the elevator was released, Gooden was so frustrated by the rhetoric suggesting Palmer "should have just left" that she went to Twitter and started sharing her own story using the hashtag "#WhyIStayed" (Kaplan, 2014). Gooden's tweets were as follows (@bevtgooden, 2014, September 8):

Domestic violence victims often find it difficult to leave abusers http://www.blueridgenow.com/ article/20120108/ARTICLES/120109857 … #WhyIStayed

All these folks trashing women for staying in abusive situations have NO clue what happens the moment you reach for a door handle.

I tried to leave the house once after an abusive episode, and he blocked me. He slept in front of the door that entire night. #WhyIStayed

Gooden went on to list more than a dozen reasons why she stayed in the relationship, including "he said he would change," and "my pastor told me God hates divorce" (@bevtgooden, 2014; Kaplan, 2014). Once Gooden began sharing her experiences, other people began to share their own stories using "#WhyIStayed." Over the time that the hashtag was trending, thousands of abused individuals shared their stories of why they stayed in abusive relationships, offering support and encouragement to one another and to those similarly trapped.

Late in the day on September 8, someone on the DiGiorno Pizza social media team noticed that "Why I Stayed" was a trending topic. DiGiorno runs a humorous twitter account (@DiGiornoPizza) and often tweets about trending topics in order to connect with new Twitter users. In this instance, someone on the DiGiorno team jumped on board without first researching the purpose of the hashtag. They tweeted "#WhyIStayed you had pizza" (@DiGiorno, 2014, September 8 [tweet has been removed from the account]). Within a few minutes there were dozens of angry tweets targeting DiGiorno and the company's apparent decision to try to sell pizza by capitalizing on a tragic event. A hashtag that was developed to support individuals in abusive relationships was now being coopted for free advertising.

Except, it seems that DiGiorno was not intentionally making light of the event. Four minutes after the #WhyIStayed tweet went out it was deleted and this follow up was broadcast: "A million apologies. Did not read what the hashtag was about before posting" (@DiGiornoPizza, 2014, September 8). Their response might seem disingenuous, but the apology did not stop at one tweet. Over the course of 24 hours there were hundreds of tweets. DiGiorno's social media team went into high gear, apologizing by name to each

person who tweeted about DiGiorno's mistake. Each apology was both personalized and targeted. The apology tweets did not use a copy-and-paste template or the same repeated verbiage. The apologies seemed heartfelt:

@Posietron I'm so sorry - I made the mistake of not investigating before posting. I saw it trending and participated. Never again.

@Starkman88 @Stareagle agreed. I made a mistake and couldn't be more embarrassed or sorry.

@AllisonRockey Me either. It was a terrible lapse in judgment to not investigate the conversation before participating. I'm so sorry Allison

@ejbrooks @jordanbks It was. And I couldn't be more sorry about it, Emma. Please accept my deepest apologies.

The apologies continued at the rate of a couple of apologies per minute from 11:15 pm until after one o'clock the following morning. Six hours later the apologies picked back up and continued all day on September 9. The DiGiorno account would apologize when someone tweeted about the offensive tweet, and then would apologize a second time if the person expressed further anger, dismay, disappointment, or concern.

Perhaps the most fascinating aspect of the DiGiorno #WhyIStayed case is that within a few hours of the initial apology, individuals who were the first to criticize DiGiorno became DiGiorno's champions, defending them against attacks by individuals who learned about the tweet well after the fact. One individual indicated they have made the same kind of mistake and appreciated DiGiorno owning their mistake: "@ DiGiornoPizza apology ACCEPTED, #digiornopizza ! I never check hashtags before using them. #ApologyAccepted others need to #GetOverIt" (@allychat, 2014, September 11). Another person applauded the personalized apologies: "Props to

@DiGiornoPizza on personally apologize (sic) for a mistake. adweek.com/adfreak/digior…" (@The_Raheel, 2014, September 9). Other users went directly to countering attacks from other users: "@emitoms @DiGiornoPizza seriously? It's the most apologetic acct ever. Never seen such remorse over an honest mistake. Leave the pizza alone" (@RealMikeWelch, 2014, September 9). Although this situation developed because of an insensitive and thoughtless action, Digiorno's leadership and social media team seems to have grasped the value of building social capital in the wake of the social media fallout.

The discussion on social media continued in this way for several days. While DiGiorno's apologies to users who expressed their anger consisted of a few hundred tweets, the larger conversation over three days comprised more than 8,000 tweets. Much of the tweet traffic over that time was from users defending DiGiorno for their personalized apologies. By September 11, many outlets had published stories about the event with titles such as: *3 Ways DiGiorno Reacted Well to Their Twitter Crisis*; and *The Perfect Response to Social Media Crisis*. In this instance, DiGiorno's self-inflicted crisis turned into an opportunity for effective communication and growth. The social media team was able to manage the ongoing conflict with upset Twitter users, all potential consumers of DiGiorno's products, and was able to come through the event in a healthy and respectable position.

LESSONS FROM SUCCESS AND FAILURE

There is much to be learned from studying prior successes and failures, so that organizations can communicate more effectively in the future. As social media use spreads and consumers expect information more and more quickly, organizations will continue to create self-induced crisis events. By learning from organizations that have

weathered such events, both successfully and unsuccessfully, other organizations can prevent such events – and manage them more effectively when they occur. By drawing on the three case studies presented in this chapter, the author draws three major lessons from which organizations can learn and adapt. First, when a problem arises, organizations should respond quickly and openly. Second, organizations should acknowledge when they have done something wrong. Last, it is important for organizations to be part of the conversation when a conflict or crisis is ongoing, rather than ignoring the conversation and attempting to remain aloof.

Respond Quickly and Openly

When organizations encounter conflict with stakeholders during self-induced crisis events, the first lesson they should apply for managing the conflict is to respond quickly and openly. As Ulmer et al. (2015) demonstrate, stakeholders respond positively to being provided with relevant information in the midst of an uncertain situation. By responding quickly and providing the information stakeholders are seeking, organizations can maintain their credibility with their publics. Urban Outfitters damaged their credibility with key publics by communicating in a way that seemed obfuscating and less than genuine. Their first apology seemed hollow, referred to by many Twitter users as a "non-apology apology." Had Urban Outfitters taken a more open, apologetic stance from the outset, they likely would not have needed to issue a second, follow-up apology.

Acknowledge Mistakes

The initial tendency when faced with an unexpected challenge or organizational error is often for the organization to distance itself from the event and seek firm footing for legal defense. Starbucks appeared to seek distance from negative reactions to the Race Together campaign by choosing not to engage in dialogue on social media platforms.

Urban Outfitters attempted to distance itself from public outrage over the sale of the Kent State sweatshirt by insisting that their intent had been misinterpreted. DiGiorno's approach of quickly acknowledging their mistake and working for several days to express their regrets is an effective model for responding to this type of event. One need only look to past crisis events to see that this approach has proven effective.

Consider the oil spill that took place off the coast of Huntington Beach, California, in 1990. The spill happened a few months after the Exxon Valdez spill at a time when "oil spill fervor was at its height" (Sandman, 2012). The ship was leased by British Petroleum, but was operated by a contract shipper. The CEO of BP America was asked in a press conference whether the spill was BP's fault. The CEO responded, "Our lawyers tell us it is not our fault. But we feel like it is our fault, and we are going to act like it is our fault" (Sandman, 2012, p. 67). As a result of their forthright response and quick cleanup "BP's image in the vicinity of the spill is higher today than it was before the spill" (Sandman, 2012, p. 67). The response by BP was so successful that the Huntington Beach spill has nearly disappeared from popular memory, while the Exxon Valdez spill the year before remains a well-known and oft-discussed piece of history. Acknowledging mistakes on the front end creates time and space for organizations to rebuild credibility, and allows key publics time to forgive the mistake and move on.

Participate in Relevant Conversations

In an increasingly high-speed communication environment, one of the most damaging moves an organization can make is to simply avoid being part of the conversation. For example, airline customers use Twitter and Facebook to express complaints or to get up-to-date information on arrival times and gate changes. Airline representatives acknowledge that social media platforms, such as Twitter, are becoming more and more relevant (Carrington, 2013).

When the Kent State sweatshirt was put up for sale Urban Outfitters remained aloof from the social media conversation, implicitly indicating that the company could not be bothered to respond to the criticism and complaints of its customers. While the Race Together campaign was ongoing, the official Starbucks and Starbucks News Twitter accounts were largely silent. Frustrated or disgruntled customers went to social media to engage with the company and ask legitimate questions about the campaign. In the best-case scenario, these individuals were ignored. In the worst-case scenario, many of the people asking questions were blocked by Starbucks' leadership and were therefore unable to receive a clear answer to their questions. DiGiorno, following a major social media gaffe, moved quickly to take part in the rapidly developing conversation around its message. DiGiorno's decision to remain engaged in the conversation resulted in acceptance from a large portion of the individuals who were angered by their tweet, as well as eventual positive press for how they handled the event.

Organizations using social media to connect with stakeholders must remember the power of social-media messaging to benefit as well as to damage credibility and organizational relationships. Organizations should utilize social media platforms to engage with stakeholders in meaningful ways. Specifically, social media platforms should be used to engage in effective conflict management with internal and external stakeholders. The flexibility and unprecedented reach of social media can be used to connect with key publics at an incredible pace. Engaging in productive dialogue that once would have required town hall meetings or similar face-to-face interactions can now, in part, be managed in an online forum. While press releases, email Listservs, and newsletters allow for only one-way communication, social media platforms now allow organizational members to effectively engage in dialogue with key publics.

FUTURE RESEARCH DIRECTIONS

This chapter explores how organizations can prepare for, respond to, and manage the conflict of self-induced crisis events. This study is far from exhaustive, and should serve as a launching point for research in related areas. First, further studies should be conducted of other organizations that have undergone similar events and faced similar crises. Studying a larger sample of organizations will enhance the understanding researchers have of these phenomena and how they can be managed effectively. Additionally, it would be helpful to connect with social media users who have taken part in the conversation around social-media based responses to organizational conflict and self-induced crises. By surveying users who have been involved in these events researchers can determine whether preliminary findings are consistent over a much larger population than can be determined in an interview or case study. Future research should seek to expand both the breadth and depth of the current study.

CONCLUSION

This chapter consisted of three parts. First, the author reviewed relevant literature. Next, the author conducted a comparative case study of three distinct self-inflicted crisis events: first, the Starbucks "Race Together" campaign (Hensley & Blau, 2015); second, the ineffective response from Urban Outfitters following the production of offensive products (The Week, 2015); and finally, the mistaken tweet sent by the DiGiorno account which misused the "#WhyIStayed" hashtag (Griner, 2014). Lastly, the chapter concluded with lessons learned from the case studies, a set of principles to inform organizations managing this type of organizational conflict, and proposed directions for future research.

A new area of organizational risk has developed as a direct result of increased organizational engagement on social media platforms. The possibility for organizations to create a self-inflicted crisis through the unintentional transmission of a poorly worded or ill-conceived social media message is one that should not be ignored or minimized. Self-induced crisis events create organizational conflict that must be managed quickly. As was witnessed with the Starbucks case, and somewhat after the fact in the DiGiorno case, there is much to be said for organizations developing social capital and a "reservoir of goodwill" (Ulmer et al., 2015) with their publics. As was made clear by the Urban Outfitters case, and to a lesser extent by Starbucks, it is vital that organizations not leave a communication void. When there is a void it will tend to be filled, and in the midst of a developing crisis that void could be filled by misinformation and speculation. It is important for organizations to steer the conversation as much as possible. By adopting the practices suggested in this chapter, organizations can pursue a more engaged, connected relationship with key stakeholders.

REFERENCES

ALS Association. (2015). *What is ALS?* Retrieved from http://www.alsa.org/about-als/what-is-als.html

Bhasin, K. (2012, February). 13 epic Twitter fails by big brands. *Business insider*. Retrieved from http://www.businessinsider.com/13-epic-twitter-fails-by-big-brands-2012-2?op=1

Bien, L. (2014, November). A complete timeline of the Ray Rice assault case. *SB Nation*. Retrieved from http://www.sbnation.com/nfl/2014/5/23/5744964/ray-rice-arrest-assault-statement-apology-ravens

Bortree, D. S., & Seltzer, T. (2009). Dialogic strategies and outcomes: An analysis of environmental advocacy groups' Facebook profiles. *Public Relations Review*, *35*(3), 317–319. doi:10.1016/j.pubrev.2009.05.002

Botan, C. (1993). A human nature approach to image and ethics in international public relations. *Journal of Public Relations Research, 5*(2), 71–81. doi:10.1207/s1532754xjprr0502_02

Botan, C. (1997). Ethics in strategic communication campaigns: The case for a new approach to public relations. *Journal of Business Communication, 34*(2), 188–202. doi:10.1177/002194369703400205

boyd, d. m., & Ellison, N. B. (2007). Social network sites: Definition, history, and scholarship. *Journal of Computer-Mediated Communication, 13*(1), 210-230.

Creswell, J. W. (2013). *Qualitative inquiry & research design: Choosing among five approaches* (3rd ed.). Thousand Oaks, CA: Sage.

Edwards, C., Edwards, A., Spence, P. R., & Shelton, A. K. (2014). Is that a bot running the social media feed? Testing the differences in perceptions of communication quality for a human agent and a bot agent on Twitter. *Computers in Human Behavior, 33*, 372–376. doi:10.1016/j.chb.2013.08.013

Flick, U. (2004). Design and process in qualitative research. In U. Flick, E. von Kardorff, & I. Steinke (Eds.), *A companion to qualitative research* (pp. 146–152). Thousand Oaks, CA: Sage.

Fonseca, F. (2012, February). Navajo nation sues Urban Outfitters over goods. *Associated Press*. Retrieved from http://www.nbcnews.com/id/46574519/ns/business-retail/t/navajo-nation-sues-urban-outfitters-over-goods/#.Vd-wTLS_uTA

Geier, B. (2015, March). Why this Starbucks PR exec deleted his Twitter account. *Fortune*. Retrieved from http://fortune.com/2015/03/19/starbucks-vp-twitter-delete/

Hensley, N., & Blau, R. (2015, March). Starbucks ends 'Race Together' coffee cup campaign, continues push for forums and new stories. *NY Daily News*. Retrieved from http://www.nydailynews.com/news/national/starbucks-ends-race-coffee-cup-campaign-article-1.2158755

Hobson, M. (2015, March). Starbucks board member Mellody Hobson: Let's be color brave. *Starbucks Newsroom*. Retrieved from https://news.starbucks.com/news/starbucks-board-member-mellody-hobson-lets-be-color-brave

Huddleston, T. (2014, November). Urban Outfitters' profits and shares tumble. *Fortune*. Retrieved from http://fortune.com/2014/11/17/urban-outfitters-shares-dip-as-namesake-brand-weighs-down-same-store-sales/

Kaplan, A. M., & Haenlein, M. (2011). The early bird catches the news: Nine things you should know about micro-blogging. *Business Horizons, 54*(2), 105–113. doi:10.1016/j.bushor.2010.09.004

Kaplan, S. (2014, September). #WhyIStayed: She saw herself in Ray Rice's wife, Janay, and tweeted about it. So did thousands of others. *The Washington Post*. Retrieved from http://www.washingtonpost.com/news/morning-mix/wp/2014/09/09/whyistayed-she-saw-herself-in-ray-rices-wife-janay-and-tweeted-about-it-so-did-thousands-of-others/

Keyes, A. (2014). Striking out ALS: Ice Bucket Challenge brings floods of donations. *NBC News*. Retrieved from http://www.nbcnews.com/feature/making-a-difference/striking-out-als-ice-bucket-challenge-brings-flood-donations-n177896

Linvill, D. L., McGee, S. E., & Hicks, L. K. (2012). Colleges' and universities' use of Twitter: A content analysis. *Public Relations Review, 38*(4), 636–638. doi:10.1016/j.pubrev.2012.05.010

Lovejoy, K., Waters, R. D., & Saxton, G. D. (2012). Engaging stakeholders through Twitter: How non-profit organizations are getting more out of 140 characters or less. *Public Relations Review*, *38*(2), 313–318. doi:10.1016/j.pubrev.2012.01.005

Making Light of Domestic Violence. (n.d.). *Adweek*. Retrieved from http://www.adweek.com/adfreak/digiorno-really-really-sorry-about-its-tweet-accidentally-making-light-domestic-violence-159998

McEvers, K. (2015, March). Starbucks' 'Race Together' campaign begins. *NPR*. Retrieved from http://www.npr.org/2015/03/21/394517431/starbucks-race-together-campaign-begins

Mirabella, L. (2014, October). Starbucks teams with city to address community problems. *Baltimore Sun*. Retrieved from http://www.baltimoresun.com/business/bs-bz-starbucks-baltimore-youth-employment-20141020-story.html

Mitroff, I. I. (1998). *Smart thinking for crazy times: The art of solving the right problems*. San Francisco: Berrett-Koehler.

Molinet, J. (2015, April). Back to school! Starbucks offers baristas free college tuition in landmark deal with Arizona State University. *New York Daily News*. Retrieved from http://www.nydailynews.com/news/national/starbucks-offers-baristas-free-college-tuition-article-1.2175742

Nilsen, T. R. (1974). *Ethics of speech communication* (2nd ed.). Indianapolis, IN: Bobbs-Merrill.

Ohlheiser, A. (2014, September). Urban Outfitters apologizes for its blood-red-stained Kent State sweatshirt. *The Washington Post*. Retrieved from http://www.washingtonpost.com/news/morning-mix/wp/2014/09/15/urban-outfitters-red-stained-vintage-kent-state-sweatshirt-is-not-a-smart-look-this-fall/

Olaniran, B., & Williams, D. (2001). Anticipatory model of crisis management. In R. Heath (Ed.), *Handbook of public relations* (pp. 487–500). Thousand Oaks, CA: Sage. doi:10.4135/9781452220727.n41

Olaniran, B. A., Scholl, J. C., Williams, D. E., & Boyer, L. (2012). Johnson and Johnson phantom recall: A fall from grace or a re-visit of the ghost of the past. *Public Relations Review*, *38*(1), 153–155. doi:10.1016/j.pubrev.2011.08.001

Park, H., & Reber, B. (2008). Relationship building and the use of Websites: How Fortune 500 companies use their Websites to build relationships. *Public Relations Review*, *34*(4), 409–411. doi:10.1016/j.pubrev.2008.06.006

QSR. (2014, April). *Starbucks kicks off 4th annual global month of service*. Retrieved from http://www.qsrmagazine.com/news/starbucks-kicks-4th-annual-global-month-service-0

Rahim, M. A. (2002). Toward a theory of managing organizational conflict. *The International Journal of Conflict Management*, *13*(3), 206–235. doi:10.1108/eb022874

Ronson, J. (2015, February). How one stupid tweet blew up Justine Sacco's life. *The New York Times*.

Rothman, L. (2014, September). Urban Outfitters: 'We understand how our sincerity may be questioned'. *TIME*. Retrieved from http://time.com/3387566/urban-outfitters-sweatshirt-apology/

Rybalko, S., & Seltzer, T. (2010). Dialogic communication in 140 characters or less: How Fortune 500 companies engage stakeholders using Twitter. *Public Relations Review*, *36*(4), 336–341. doi:10.1016/j.pubrev.2010.08.004

Sanders, S. (2015, March). Starbucks will stop putting the words "race together" on cups. *The two-way: Breaking news from NPR*. Retrieved from http://www.npr.org/sections/thetwoway/2015/03/22/394710277/starbucks-will-stop-writing-race-together-on-coffee-cups

Sandman, P. (2012). *Responding to community outrage: Strategies for effective risk communication*. American Industrial Hygiene Association.

Starbucks. (2014, December). *A conversation with Starbucks partners about race in America*. Retrieved from https://news.starbucks.com/news/schultz-begins-a-conversation-with-starbucks-partners-about-racial-issues

Starbucks. (2015a, March 16). *What race together means for Starbucks partners and customers*. Retrieved from https://news.starbucks.com/news/what-race-together-means-for-starbucks-partners-and-customers

Starbucks. (2015b, March 20). *Video of the 2015 annual shareholders meeting*. Retrieved from https://news.starbucks.com/news/an-unprecedented-conversation-about-race-in-America

The Week. (2015, February). 14 Urban Outfitters controversies. Retrieved from http://theweek.com/articles/480961/14-urban-outfitters-controversies

Tjosvold, D. (2008). The conflict-positive organization: It depends upon us. *Journal of Organizational Behavior*, *29*(1), 19–28. doi:10.1002/job.473

Tompkins, T. C. (1995). Role of diffusion in collective learning. *The International Journal of Organizational Analysis*, *3*(1), 69–85. doi:10.1108/eb028824

Twitter. (2015). *About Twitter: Fact sheet*. Retrieved from https://about.twitter.com/company

Ulmer, R. R., Seeger, M. W., & Sellnow, T. L. (2007). Post-crisis communication and renewal: Expanding the parameters of post-crisis discourse. *Public Relations Review*, *33*(2), 130–134. doi:10.1016/j.pubrev.2006.11.015

Ulmer, R. R., Sellnow, T. L., & Seeger, M. W. (2009). Post-crisis communication and renewal: Understanding the potential for positive outcomes in crisis communication. In R. L. Heath & D. H. O'Hair (Eds.), *Handbook of Risk and Crisis Communication*. New York: Routledge.

Ulmer, R. R., Sellnow, T. L., & Seeger, M. W. (2015). *Effective crisis communication: Moving from crisis to opportunity* (3rd ed.). Thousand Oaks, CA: Sage.

14. Urban Outfitters Controversies. (2015, February). *The Week*. Retrieved from http://theweek.com/articles/480961/14-urban-outfitters-controversies

Waters, R. D., & Jamal, J. Y. (2011). Tweet, tweet, tweet: A content analysis of nonprofit organizations' Twitter updates. *Public Relations Review*, *37*(3), 321–324. doi:10.1016/j.pubrev.2011.03.002

Wilson, M. (2014, September). Urban Outfitters CEO to employees: Kent State sweatshirt sale an 'unfortunate occurrence'. *PR Daily*. Retrieved from http://www.prdaily.com/Main/Articles/Urban_Outfitters_CEO_to_employees_Kent_State_sweat_17280.aspx

Winchel, B. (2014, September). Urban Outfitters offends with red-stained 'vintage' Kent State sweatshirt. *PR Daily*. Retrieved from http://www.prdaily.com/Main/Articles/17261.aspx

Worland, J. (2014, November). Here's what's happening with the Ice Bucket Challenge money. *TIME*. Retrieved from http://time.com/topic/als-ice-bucket-challenge-2/

Yin, R. K. (2014). *Case study research: Design and methods* (5th ed.). Thousand Oaks, CA: Sage.

Zhao, D., & Rosson, M. B. (2009, May). How and why people Twitter: the role that micro-blogging plays in informal communication at work. In *Proceedings of the ACM 2009 international conference on supporting group work* (pp. 243-252). New York: ACM. doi:10.1145/1531674.1531710

ADDITIONAL READING

Levine, R., Locke, C., & Searls, D. (2009). *The cluetrain manifesto*. Basic books.

Seeger, M. W. (2006). Best practices in crisis communication: An expert panel process. *Journal of Applied Communication Research, 34*(3), 232–244. doi:10.1080/00909880600769944

Sellnow, T. L., & Seeger, M. W. (2013). *Theorizing crisis communication*. Malden, MA: Wiley-Blackwell.

Senge, P. M. (2006). *The fifth discipline: The art and practice of the learning organization*. Broadway Business.

Ulmer, R. R., Sellnow, T. L., & Seeger, M. W. (2015). *Effective crisis communication: Moving from crisis to opportunity* (3rd ed.). Thousand Oaks, CA: Sage.

Van den Hurk, A. M. (2013). *Social Media Crisis Communications: Surviving a Public Relations Fail*. UK: Pearson Education.

White, C. M. (2011). *Social media, crisis communication, and emergency management: Leveraging Web 2.0 technologies*. CRC press. doi:10.1201/b11251

KEY TERMS AND DEFINITIONS

Conflict: A state of discord caused by the actual or perceived opposition of needs, values and interests between people working together.

Crisis: A specific, unexpected, and non-routine event or series of events that create high levels of uncertainty and simultaneously present an organization with both opportunities for and threats to its high priority goals.

Hashtag: (On social media sites such as Twitter) a word or phrase preceded by a hash or pound sign (#) and used to identify messages on a specific topic.

Micro-Blog: Social networking sites that allow users to exchange small elements of content such as short sentences, individual images, or video links.

Social Media: Websites and applications that enable users to create and share content or to participate in social networking.

Social Networking Sites: Web-based services that allow individuals to (1) construct a public or semi-public profile within a bounded system, (2) articulate a list of other users with whom they share a connection, and (3) view and traverse their list of connections and those made by others within the system.

Twitter: The largest micro-blogging site on the Internet, with over 302 million active monthly users.

Chapter 9
Leadership in a Time of Crisis:
Jim Tressel's Ousting from
The Ohio State University

Lauren J. Keil
Advisory Board Consulting and Management, USA

Angela M. Jerome
Western Kentucky University, USA

ABSTRACT

When faced with crises organizational leaders must identify, prioritize, and communicate with organizational stakeholders. Increasingly, organizational leaders find themselves responding to crises made by persons that represent or are associated with the organization in some way. However, most case studies of image repair campaigns focus on the individual that has transgressed rather than on the often simultaneous campaigns undertaken by the organizations with which they are associated. To study these issues more closely, this chapter uses The Ohio State University's (OSU's) tattoos for memorabilia scandal as exemplar and offers meaningful insight and pragmatic considerations for practitioners dealing with similar situational constraints.

INTRODUCTION

Image repair[1] undeniably operates at the intersection of organizational leadership, conflict resolution, and conflict management. In times of crisis organizational leaders must identify, prioritize, and communicate with stakeholders. As Rawlins (2006) asserted, stakeholder prioritization, regardless of public relations task, is most often based on audiences' legitimacy, power, and urgency. Research indicates that post-crisis audience prioritization can be particularly troubling

for organizational leaders for a number of reasons. For example, Benoit (2014) warned:

It is important to keep in mind that a person or organization accused of wrongdoing may want to persuade more than one audience; we must also realize that the individuals in one specific audience can have varied attitudes. These situations can make image repair more challenging, but it is a mistake to ignore these realities when they arise. (p. 123)

DOI: 10.4018/978-1-4666-9970-0.ch009

Jerome's (2008) case study of NASCAR driver Tony Stewart's image repair campaign demonstrated the nuanced care that must be taken by organizational leaders to successfully respond to diverse audiences following a crisis. She observed that Home Depot's (Stewart's primary sponsor) decision to fine Stewart for his transgression, rather than suspend/fire him, before stakeholder reactions to the crisis could be accurately gauged, functioned to signal Home Depot's derision with Stewart for stakeholders who felt some punishment was warranted while, at the same time, allowing it to avoid backlash from stakeholders who felt suspension/termination was not warranted.

While case studies do not produce generalizable results, Seeger (2006) argued that one may generate a list of best practices by generalizing "from other forms of communication" and extrapolating "from the now considerable body of largely case-based research in crisis communication" (p. 233-234). For example, he asserted that multiple case studies illustrate the value of communicating with honesty, candor, and openness in post-crisis messages. Likewise, Benoit (2014) concluded that lying is never an effective image repair strategy because, "if the truth emerges and the original accusations are shown to be true, the accused now has an additional problem" (p. 124).

Benoit (2014) illustrated the lessons that may be learned from case studies of image repair in five areas: sports/entertainment, corporate, political, international, and third party. The studies appearing in Blaney, Lippert, and Smith's (2013) collection, *Repairing the Athlete's Image,* also focus on the lessons that can be learned from image repair campaigns conducted in a sports context. However, most case studies done in this area focus on the image repair campaigns of individuals who have transgressed rather than on the, often simultaneous, campaigns undertaken by the organizations that the transgressor represents or with which he/she is associated. For example, when student-athletes/coaches violate NCAA rules, laws, and ethical mores, the colleges/universities that govern them often have to mount their own image repair campaigns. In doing so, the colleges/universities often face complex stakeholder dichotomies. When this occurs, the organization has to decide whether it should fine/suspend/terminate the, often beloved, coach or student-athlete(s) accused. Further, the organization must evaluate how its decisions may help/harm the institution's image in the eyes of its fans and NCAA officials that often have differing opinions on the issue.

A few studies (e.g., Fortunato, 2008; Sisler, 2015) illuminate the value of inquiry that places primacy on the image repair campaigns of organizational leaders who are forced to mount image repair campaigns resulting from actions perpetrated by the athletes representing their organizations. However, additional studies are warranted. The current study examines the image repair campaign undertaken by the leadership of The Ohio State University (OSU) following its tattoos for memorabilia scandal. Further, it offers pragmatic considerations and recommendations for practitioners dealing with similar situational constraints.

BACKGROUND

Before delving into the case analysis, it is necessary to provide background in three different areas. First, this crisis has an intricate backstory that warrants telling. Second, an outline of the relevant scholarship on which the arguments herein are based is needed. Third, the methodology undertaken by the authors is discussed.

Case Background

On April 2, 2010, former OSU football player, Chris Cicero, and head football coach, Jim Tressel, exchanged emails about tattoo parlor owner, Ed Rife, who was under investigation for drug trafficking by the U.S. Department of Justice. Cicero informed Tressel that Rife had purchased autographed memorabilia from OSU football players; Tressel thanked him for the information (Associated Press, 2011a; Farrey, 2011). This was a problem because NCAA policy does not allow student-athletes to sell "institutionally issued athletic awards, apparel, and/or equipment" for personal gain (as cited in Farrey, 2011, n.p.). Tressel did not relay this information to anyone on OSU's leadership team (Associated Press, 2011a). Two weeks later, Cicero again initiated an email exchange with Tressel, providing specific details about what types of memorabilia had been traded and sold to Rife (Associated Press, 2011a; Farrey, 2011). Again, no member of OSU's leadership team was informed (Farrey, 2011). On September 13, 2010, Tressel signed the NCAA's annual certificate of compliance signifying he knew of no violations and/or had reported all possible violations to school officials (Associated Press, 2011a).

The OSU crisis came to a boiling point on December 7, 2010 when OSU officials were informed by the Office of the U.S. Attorney that government raids on the home and business of Rife unearthed OSU memorabilia traded for tattoos and/or cash by six OSU football players, a list that included OSU's star quarterback, Terrelle Pryor (Associated Press, 2011a; Dohrmann & Epstein, 2011; Farrey, 2011). The raid turned up 36 items of Buckeye memorabilia, including a $7,000 Bowl Championship Series ring from 2002 (Farrey, 2011).

Interestingly, OSU leaders knew before they hired Tressel that he had a questionable performance history. He was accused of providing the Youngstown State University (YSU) quarterback with $10,000 in cash and cars in 1998 during his tenure as YSU's head football coach. However, Tressel denied any knowledge of the activity and received no punishment for it (Farrey, 2011). Such accusations were not a one-time occurrence. After leaving OSU in 2002, star running back, Maurice Clarett, alleged Tressel assisted him in acquiring the use of vehicles from a Columbus car dealership while an OSU student-athlete (Farrey, 2011; Friend, 2011). In 2008, Pryor received a ticket while driving a car owned by a Columbus, OH car salesman, Aaron Kniffin; two similar instances subsequently occurred (Farrey, 2011). In July 2010, OSU looked into the relationship between its athletes and Kniffin after receiving an anonymous letter accusing student-athletes of trading autographed memorabilia for the use of cars with employees of the new car dealership at which Kniffin was employed. Doug Archie, OSU's NCAA Compliance Officer, found no violation of NCAA rules (Farrey, 2011).

Through all this Tressel remained one of the most respected coaches in college football (See Dohrmann & Epstein, 2011). Beyond his admirable reputation, Tressel had the most successful 10-year career in OSU history and an overall winning record in the Big Ten, including his 9-1 record against rival and fellow football powerhouse the University of Michigan ("Ohio State players," 2011).

Literature Review

To analyze the image repair strategies used by OSU's leadership team in this case, the authors used Benoit's (1995, 2014) typology because it is, without question, the most used to analyze image repair campaigns from a rhetorical perspective. Having spawned a plethora of case studies, it offers an aggregate of findings from which to offer practical recommendations.

Benoit's typology outlines five categories for image restoration: denial, evading responsibility, reducing offensiveness, corrective action, and mortification. Each category also includes subcategories that further elaborate on the strategy and its uses. The first strategy identified is *denial*, which includes *simple denial* and *shifting the blame*. When utilizing simple denial, an actor simply denies that the act occurred, that he/she performed it, or, as suggested by Brinson and Benoit (1999), that the act was not harmful to others or the public. In using shifting the blame, the accused actor points to another actor as the transgressor. *Separation*, developed from shifting the blame, involves not just blaming another actor but also trying to distance oneself from the other (Brinson & Benoit, 1999).

The second overarching strategy, *evasion of responsibility*, may be selected by actors who were involved in the performance of the act in question, but hope to reduce the perceived responsibility. In using the first sub-strategy of evasion of responsibility, *provocation*, an actor acknowledges commission of the offensive act but attempts to justify the act by claiming another actor provoked the act. The second subcategory, *defeasibility*, is used when the accused claims a "lack of information about or control over important factors in the situation" (Benoit, 2014, p. 23). The third subcategory under evading responsibility is *accident*, in which the accused blames the situation on forces beyond his or her control. The last subcategory, *good intentions*, as the name implies, is utilized when the accused wants to show the public that the act was committed with good intentions.

The third category, *reducing offensiveness,* is comprised of six subcategories. The first of these subcategories, *bolstering*, "may be used to mitigate the negative effects of the act on the actor by strengthening the audience's positive affect for the rhetor" (Benoit, 2014, p. 24). This is a common strategy used when actors know they cannot deny the accusations but still attempt to alter the audience's opinion about the situation, person, or organization by highlighting positive traits. *Minimization* focuses on decreasing "the amount of negative affect associated with the offensive act" (Benoit, 2014, p. 24). *Differentiation* is used by an accused to compare the act to other more offensive or harmful acts in an effort reduce the public's negative perception of the accused's act. The difference between the two is further explained by Benoit (2014) with exemplars. Minimization is represented by the statement "I broke your vase, but it was not an expensive one," while differentiation is represented by the statement "I borrowed your laptop without asking; I didn't steal it" (p. 28).

The fourth subcategory of reducing offensiveness is *transcendence*. This strategy is best explained in the context of the current study by Brinson and Benoit (1999) who describe it as placing "the act in a broad, positive context to help improve the offender's image and includes appeals to other persons, values, or group loyalties" (p. 488). The fifth subcategory, *attacking the accuser*, is used when an actor calls into question the credibility of the person or persons behind negative accusations, such as general publics, media outlets, or competitors (Brinson & Benoit, 1999). Finally, *compensation* is used to reimburse those who have experienced physical, emotional, or material harm as a result of the event/act in question.

The fourth major category is *corrective action*. In using this strategy, the accused vows to repair any harm done by his or her act and ensure the act will not occur again. The last major image restoration strategy identified by Benoit is *mortification*, which requires the accused to apologize to those harmed and ask for forgiveness.

While space does not allow for a comprehensive overview of case studies done using this typology, the following demonstrates how case studies using Benoit's typology to conduct studies in the sports realm provide insight for organizational leaders. Before proceeding, it is integral to acknowledge Kruse's (1981) stance regarding apologia in team sport. She argued that sports is a "sphere of social reality separate from the sociopolitical world" (p. 271). Building on the work of Edwards (1973), Novak (1976), and others, she asserted that because athletic teams, players, fans, and all others associated with the organization form a "family," members may temporarily set aside ethical norms if the option to win is present. Thus, an act that may be considered unethical or be disapproved of in the regular world may be viewed as acceptable in the sports world because the end goal is to win, regardless of the means to achieve it

(Kruse, 1981). She noted, however, that there are cases in which an unethical act is seen as morally reprehensible enough to surpass the need to win such as when a player places his/her own selfish needs above those of the team, when a vital team member leaves the team or does not play to the best of their ability, or simply when individual members display "behaviors that indicate an overly casual or frivolous attitude toward the team or the game" (Kruse, 1981, p. 276). In such cases, family members will allow for a punishment that fits the crime.

Looking at Terrell Owens' image repair campaign following a failed contract negotiation with the Philadelphia Eagles, Brazeal (2008) demonstrated the value in using the works of both Benoit and Kruse in case study analysis. She noted that for much of his NFL career there had been "coaches, players, and fans willing to overlook Owens' boorish behavior because of his remarkable talent" (p.145). That was until the Eagles' refusal to renegotiate was met by Owens' belligerent interactions with coaches and public criticism of the team's quarterback, Donovan McNabb. In the end, the Eagles chose to deactivate Owens, which led to his immediate need for image repair. Brazeal asserted that Owens' campaign was flawed from the outset because he did not provide direct mortification for his actions or offer examples of how he would change as a result of the crisis. Further, his agent erroneously sought to paint Owens as a victim.

Brazeal concluded the image repair campaign failed because,

Even though American culture also values individualism and free enterprise, athletes should also show "loyalty, unity, affiliation, and the ability to place the good of the group above one's own interests" (Kruse, 1981, pp. 273–274). From the beginning, Owens appeared to place himself (and his paycheck) above the team. Additionally, Owens did not recognize that athletes are expected to present a "public display of absolute devotion and commitment toward the team, the game, and the world of sport" (Kruse, 1981, p. 274) and "[o] ne should never criticize the team with which one is associated" (p. 274, emphasis added). (p.149)

She also observed that Owens and his representative tried to recover from their early, failed attempts at image repair by making an effort to "rhetorically re-engage" the audience by "giving lip service to its values," contending "that Owens had been a loyal team player…that other players had done 'worse things'" and "that Owens had merely "agreed with a statement" about McNabb." (p. 149). However, Brazeal argued that these strategies failed as well because "by downplaying the importance of these incidents, they actually devalued the culture. Most importantly, they failed to argue that Owens would conform to the culture in the future" (p. 149). Brazeal also offered broader implications for her study. Drawing on the work of Hearit (2006), for example, she documented the pitfalls of relying on "surrogate speakers" (p. 149) following a crisis response, as well as the tenuous choice of attacking the media during an image repair campaign.

In the case outlined above, Jerome (2008) found that Stewart used a well-received rhetoric of atonement in his image repair campaign by immediately and publicly acknowledging wrongdoing, focusing on the lessons he learned from the incident, and focusing on corrective action. She also argued that the wronged photographer publicly acknowledging that he had accepted Stewart's apology aided Stewart in his efforts. Drawing on Kruse's assertions, Jerome remarked that Stewart's status as one of the winningest competitors in the sport also may have offered him leeway that would not have been afforded a weaker competitor. Though she does not make the claim, there is reason to believe such situational factors may also aid other entities in their image repair campaigns. For example, Coombs (1995) noted the effect performance history has on organizations responding to crises. Winning, whether on the field, politically, or in the stock market, shapes stakeholders' perceptions.

Using the case of an Australian rugby team that broke the salary cap rule set by its governing body as exemplar, Bruce and Tini (2008) also offered lessons for organizational leaders; the key lesson concerns framing. They argue the successful use of a diversion strategy in which the organization framed its most popular members, players and coaches, as innocent led to organizational rebuilding. Even though team managers initially lied about their transgression, game attendance actually doubled the following year. Bruce and Tini argued fans' wishes to support the players and coach to whom they had the "strongest emotional connection" likely led to the increased attendance and, in turn, organizational rebuilding (p. 113). In essence, fans were willing to support the players and coaches because they believed them to be innocent victims in the crisis. Thus, sacrificing management to maintain this key stakeholder relationship worked in the team's favor. Though Bruce and Tini acknowledged a diversion strategy may not have much use outside of sports and entertainment, they offered other conclusions that may aid organizations in a broader context. For example, once its lies were exposed, the organization attempted to use provocation and mortification strategies; but, those were met with "increasingly negative and unsympathetic coverage" (Bruce & Tini, 2008, p.11). In fact, some of its claims, such as that salary caps were unfair, were barely covered in media reports. Eventually, the organization attempted to scapegoat its CEO, but subsequent media articles placed blame on the entire management team. In the end, the team received the harshest penalty ever handed down by the league and the entire management team had to resign. In summarizing the lessons learned, Bruce and Tini (2008) asserted,

In this case, although the organisation's blatant premeditated dishonesty did not result in wholesale rejection of the team, its poor crisis management alienated other key stakeholders such as the media and turned fans against the management team. The result was that the print and broadcast news media in both Australia and New Zealand clearly constructed a limited and negative representation of the Bulldogs' organization as 'cheaters'. (p. 113)

They concluded this line of argument by acknowledging that although honesty from the beginning may not have lessened the punishment received, it may have curtailed image loss with the media. The value of media support is also highlighted by Nelson (1984), who outlined how the media aided Billie Jean King in her image repair campaign by refusing to frame homosexuality as distasteful.

Studying a crisis faced by Formula One racing, Pfahl and Bates (2008) also cultivated lessons that have applicability far beyond the athletic arena. For example, they found that the crisis in question was exacerbated by the fact that multiple organizations were involved in the crisis. While Formula One was the governing body for the car race in question, Michelin provided the tires and Indianapolis Motor Speedway owned the track on which the race took place. Pfahl and Bates (2008) found that "meta-organizational unity can be sacrificed for individual organizational purposes" (p. 141). This same image repair constraint is noted by Rowland and Jerome (2004) and Jerome and Rowland (2009). Specifically, Jerome and Rowland (2009) note the damage done to the images of both Firestone and Ford as a result of each organization trying to repair its own image at the expense of the other in their tread separation crisis.

Fortunato's (2008) study of Duke University's (Duke) lacrosse scandal parallels the current study better than any other published study. In 2006, three Duke Lacrosse players were indicted for physically and sexually abusing an exotic dancer hired for a team party (Fortunato, 2008). In its response to the crisis, Duke did not try to deny the acts had occurred; rather its President, Richard Brodhead, "consistently described the behavior as inappropriate for Duke students" (Fortunato, 2008, p. 120). The university also cancelled the lacrosse team's season and vowed stricter oversight in subsequent years. It also took responsibility for creating an environment where such an incident could occur, but bolstered its value as an organization and its commitment to corrective action where it could (Fortunato, 2008). For example, Brodhead announced the university's establishment of five different committees to examine the history of the lacrosse team's behavior, analyze Duke's response to the scandal, audit the student judicial process at Duke, investigate the campus culture, and guide university administrators (Fortunato, 2008). He also noted that Duke should be a national leader in dealing with such issues. In statements specifically aimed at alumni and parents of undergraduate students, he reiterated his position by noting that Duke should use this incident as an opportunity to become a better institution (Fortunato, 2008). Months later, when the district attorney resigned from the case amid ethical questions, two of the accused students were allowed to return to Duke; the third had graduated before he was charged. All charges against all three men were eventually dropped (Fortunato, 2008). Therefore, Duke's need for image repair was significantly diminished as the dropped charges indicated judicial officials' belief that the players were innocent.

Fortunato's (2008) main focus was on how Duke framed the crisis, but he identified points of congruity between Duke's chosen strategies and public relations theory. For example, he noted, "Duke's overall response was to accept responsibility for the incident and take corrective action, both identified by Benoit (1995, 2000) and Coombs (1999, 2006) as strategies that can help in restoring the reputation of an organization in a crisis" (p. 120). However, he made no attempt to evaluate the success of Duke's chosen strategies or how the media framed the story in its reports. Rowland and Jerome (2004) noted that organizations wishing to maintain a positive image in the face of a crisis should show concern

for victims, bolster organizational values, deny intent to do harm, and seek the root cause of the crisis. It appears that Duke's response embodied all of those strategies.

Last, Ulmer, Sellnow, and Seeger's (2015) discourse of renewal adds insight for the current study. They argued that crises provide organizations an opportunity for positive post-crisis discourse. According to Ulmer et al. (2015) a discourse of renewal requires four elements: organizational learning, ethical communication, prospective vs. retrospective vision, and effective organizational rhetoric. In an earlier work, Ulmer, Seeger, and Sellnow (2007) noted that a discourse of renewal should focus on the provisional rather than the strategic, be rooted in the values of the organizational leader, and focus on corrective action and change. Further, they noted that organizational leaders should be the model for renewal and that renewal strategies will work best with stakeholder groups with which the organization has a positive relationship pre-crisis.

Method

For this analysis, a variety of articles and websites relating to OSU, Tressel, and the tattoos-for-memorabilia scandal were analyzed. These included articles and videos from websites such as *Sports Illustrated, ESPN, Fox Sports, the Columbus Dispatch, the OSU newsroom,* and *YouTube.* While it was impossible to gather all existing information on the scandal from all possible sources, artifacts collected from these sources were representative of the overall campaign. News websites such as *ESPN.com* and *Sportsillustrated.com* were the first websites accessed for potential information because these sports news outlets contained detailed information about the scandal. Other articles and videos were also found, as needed for clarification/detail, by typing key words from the scandal into the Google search engine. The first round of data for this study was retrieved and analyzed between June and August 2011.

A critical analysis was the chosen procedure to analyze the collected data for this study. Once the initial data was collected, the first author began the process of analysis by organizing the information chronologically to understand the rhetorical trajectory of the image repair strategies used by both Tressel and OSU's leaders. After these artifacts were organized, Benoit's (1995) image restoration typology was used as the primary framework for initial message analysis. Linkages were drawn between strategy use and function to compose a first draft of this text.

Then, the second author took the first draft and necessary texts and reexamined the rhetoric to expand/clarify the arguments made and to better situate the arguments made herein within the broader scholarly context, focusing specifically on the rhetoric of OSU Athletic Director, Gene Smith, and President, Gordon Gee, as they were the organizational leaders most prominent in the organization's image repair campaign. Further, she collected texts and literature between July and October 2015 that allowed for a more nuanced discussion of the rhetorical success of OSU's leadership post-scandal and the pragmatic considerations for practitioners dealing with similar situational constraints as those faced by OSU in this crisis. Further, the second author ensured the analysis was in line with Benoit's (2014) updated typology.

ANALYSIS

This analysis is laid out in five sections. These are: Initial Responses, Emails Discovered, Separation, Attempting Renewal, and Returning to the Top.

Initial Responses

On December 7, 2010, the U.S. Attorney's office notified OSU leadership that a raid of Rife's home and office uncovered the OSU memorabilia described above (Farrey, 2011). On December 16, OSU officials spoke with the six players cited in the Rife scandal. Three days later, OSU self-reported to the NCAA and declared all student-athletes involved ineligible (Associated Press, 2011a; "OSU athletic director," 2010). On December 23, Smith and Tressel held a press conference. In his statement, Tressel combine *denial, corrective action,* and *bolstering* strategies. In essence, he denied prior knowledge of the incidents, but accepted responsibility for their occurrence (See Farrey, 2011; "OSU coach," 2010). Smith provided a timeline of events from December 7 forward and explained the NCAA's initial decision on student-athlete suspensions (their suspensions would be served during the following season, allowing them eligibility for the quickly approaching Sugar Bowl) (Associated Press, 2011a; "OSU athletic director," 2010). Further, he *bolstered* the character of the student-athletes involved when asserting that they were "honest," "forthright," and "remorseful" in their interviews "which allowed us to move expeditiously" ("OSU athletic director," 2010, n.p.).

The most substantive part of Smith's statement focused on *denial and minimization;* he stated,

There are no other NCAA violations around this case. We're very fortunate we do not have a systemic problem in our program. This is isolated to these young men, isolated to this particular incident. There are no other violations that exist. (as cited in Staples, 2011, para. 16)

Around this same time, Smith also stated that OSU hoped the players involved would receive reduced penalties through the NCAA appeals process because some of the cash received in the transactions went to help the student-athletes' family members who were struggling financially ("Ohio State football," 2010).

In another statement Smith demonstrated OSU's continued commitment to *corrective action* stating,

We were not as explicit with our student-athlete education as we should have been in the 2007-08 and 2008-09 academic years regarding the sale of apparel, awards and gifts issued by the athletics department. We began to significantly improve our education in November of 2009 to address these issues. After going through this experience, we will further enhance our education for all our student-athletes as we move forward. (as cited in NCAA, 2010, para. 12)

These strategies allowed OSU to navigate the dichotomy noted above smoothly at this point in the crisis. College sports fans and media commentators are notoriously critical of the NCAA; a great deal of that criticism arises from the double standard inherent in the NCAA's impermissible benefits policy (See Jenkins, 2013; Solomon, 2013). The NCAA and its member institutions make millions of dollars each year (Berkowitz, 2013) while student-athletes may not benefit from their athletic prowess beyond scholarships. The NCAA's choice to allow the student-athletes in question to play in the 2010 Sugar Bowl and serve their suspensions during the 2011 season demonstrates this double standard. The NCAA said its decision was based on the fact that the student-athletes had not received proper education concerning NCAA rules on such issues (Walker, 2010). However many, like Dave Walker, a correspondent for *The Bleacher Report*, felt it was based on the NCAA's potential loss in television revenue if the student-athletes in question were ruled ineligible for the game. He wrote, "So what will the penalty against them be? All are suspended for five games next year. Not this year. Not in a big money BCS game…" (Walker, 2010, para. 5-6). Though Walker felt the suspensions should start immediately, he argued the violations were "tacky at best" and the sentiment of his piece suggests he believed the punishment far harsher than the crime (Walker, 2010, para. 19).

Given the above, Kruse's work indicates that most fans would not even see the violations as ethical violations. Though the team might lose the games for which the players would be suspended, the team had a whole year to plan for that, and the NCAA and its oft-criticized rules were an easy scapegoat. While OSU leaders needed to reassure fans, the situation afforded Smith the opportunity to prioritize the NCAA as the primary audience for his rhetoric. To avoid lack of institutional control penalties from the NCAA which come with harsh punishments, OSU leaders needed to convince the NCAA that these were isolated incidents, that they had no prior knowledge of them, that they were telling the truth, and that they were committed to correcting the problem. The strategies chosen served that purpose, but the crisis was far from over.

Emails Discovered

A little less than a month later, OSU's legal affairs office uncovered the Tressel/Cicero emails (Associated Press, 2011a; Farrey, 2011; "Tressel resignation," 2011) and what could have been a blip on the NCAA violations radar became a full blown NCAA compliance and image repair nightmare for OSU. OSU officials questioned Tressel mid-January 2011, and he admitted to committing a major NCAA violation on February 8, 2011 (Associated Press, 2011a; Farrey, 2011; "Tressel resignation," 2011). The dichotomy would now get more treacherous for OSU leaders to navigate.

In his response, Tressel used *bolstering, good intentions, minimization, differentiation, defeasibility,* and *corrective action* strategies. For example, his statements indicated the student-athletes were his first priority and implied he felt compliance with NCAA rules was less important than potential disruption of a confidential federal investigation. Further, he noted that none of the student-athletes were named in the drug trafficking allegations and that he should have asked OSU legal counsel how to handle the situation. Last, he remarked on the personal growth that would come from the scandal (See Tressel, 2011).

While OSU knew people continued to defend Tressel as "an otherwise perfect coach who made one little mistake" (Staples, 2011, para. 5), it also knew that Tressel broke at least one of the two unforgiveable NCAA violations: allowing players impermissible benefits and lying to the NCAA (Staples, 2011). For these reasons, appeasing both stakeholder groups would be virtually impossible.

It is not surprising that OSU leaders mirrored Home Depot's strategy at this stage; they handed Tressel a two-game suspension and fined him $250,000, which would be used to pay for OSU's defense of itself to the NCAA (Farrey, 2011; Marshall, 2011). However, OSU officials continued to support Tressel. A March 11, 2011, statement sent to the NCAA and signed by Smith, Gee, and faculty athletics representative, John Bruno, stated that Tressel's "behavior in this situation is out of character for him and is contrary to his proven history of promoting an atmosphere of NCAA compliance within the football program" and noted, "Since his hiring as the head football coach in 2001, he and his staff have attended NCAA rules education sessions on a consistent basis, regularly sought interpretations and self-reported secondary violations" (as cited in Boren, 2011, para. 5). In its public response to Tressel's admission OSU stated, "The institution is very surprised and disappointed in Coach Tressel's lack of action in this matter" (as cited in Associated Press, 2011a, para. 22). However, Smith reiterated OSU had self-reported Tressel's violation to the NCAA in the hopes that "the governing body of college sports will agree with the sanctions handed out by the Buckeyes officials" (as cited in Marshall, 2011, para. 4). Smith went as far as to say, "Wherever we end up at the end of the day, Jim Tressel is our football coach. He is our coach and we trust him implicitly. There is no question in my mind that his decision was from the heart" (as cited in Marshall, 2011, para. 5).

Further, when Gee was asked whether he had considered terminating Tressel, he replied, "No,

are you kidding?" (as cited in Marshall, 2011, para. 7). Gee then quipped the now infamous statement: "I hope he doesn't fire me" (as cited in Forde, 2011, para. 6). Gee's reluctance to terminate Tressel indicated his keen awareness of the ethic of team sport outlined by Kruse. However, he failed to realize the perception his joke created.

Of the statements, Shaw (2011) jested, "It was hard to tell if Tressel were being disciplined or enshrined in The Hall of Fame at The Ohio State University" (para. 9). Because of this, Shaw argued that Gee's statements significantly harmed OSU's case with the NCAA because they insinuated that he believed Tressel was "invulnerable" (para. 3). In a retrospective of the case Lesmerises (2014a) stated, "Gee's involvement with Ohio State's NCAA issues always will be remembered with eight words: "I'm just hopeful the coach doesn't dismiss me." (para. 1). In hindsight, Gee also noted the affect this statement had on the case (Lesmerises, 20014a).

OSU Separation

On April 19, OSU announced that Tressel's fine may not cover its investigative costs, and it released the compliance form on which Tressel lied (Associated Press, 2011a). On April 21, the NCAA's Notice of Allegations was released and alleged that Tressel "knew or should have known that at least two football student-athletes received preferential treatment from and sold institutionally issued athletic awards, apparel, and/or equipment to Rife, but he failed to report" the violations to school authorities (as cited in Farrey, 2011, n.p.). In early May, OSU and the Ohio Bureau of Motor Vehicles (OBMV) announced its second investigation into questionable used-car purchases made by student-athletes (Boren, 2011; Farrey, 2011). The investigation by the OBMV found the car dealer's paperwork to be in order, but examining NCAA violations was not part of its job. Yet, OSU "dropped its plan to hire experts to conduct an independent investigation of vehicle purchases by players and their family members" (as cited in Boren, 2011, para. 12).

In late May 2011, OSU's campaign fell apart for two reasons. First, former OSU wide receiver, Ray Small, publicly admitted that he sold two of his Big Ten Championship rings (around 2008) for approximately $2,000 to pay rent and a car payment on a car he had purchased from Kniffin; however, he claimed no one in OSU's program was aware of his actions (Farrey, 2011; Meisel & Oldham, 2011). Second, *Sports Illustrated* informed OSU officials that its problems were far worse than first thought. *Sports Illustrated* learned that similar incidents had occurred as far back as 2002 and involved at least 28 current and former players (Dohrmann & Epstein, 2011). OSU's problems were not isolated; they were systemic.

In response, Gee wrote in a letter to OSU's Board of Trustees that stated,

As you all know I appointed a special committee to analyze and provide advice to me regarding issues attendant to our football program. In consultation with the senior leadership of the university and the senior leadership of the board, I have been actively reviewing the matter and have accepted coach Tressel's resignation. (as cited in Associated Press, 2011b, para. 12)

For his part, Smith delivered a video statement to "Buckeye Nation" (as cited in "Smith: Tressel's," 2011, para. 2). He first laid out the steps in the resignation process, including information regarding Tressel and Fickell's speeches to the team. He then moved into *bolstering* and a form of *transcendence* with this statement about Fickell's meeting with the team, "This happens to be finals week; they obviously need to focus on finishing their classes, which is really what we're all about—making sure they get their education and their degree" (as cited in "Smith: Tressel's," 2011, para 5). Further, he went on to argue that

Fickell had his priorities straight and would keep the team and the university on the right track:

We are coming off of a time frame where the football program achieved it highest academic rating ever, so we are proud of the accomplishment of those young men and we want to stay on that trajectory and Luke and his staff are committed to surrounding them with the support that they need to stay focused in that regard. (as cited in "Smith: Tressel's," 2011, para. 5)

Smith also noted,

As you all know, we are under NCAA investigation. We will not discuss any of the matters around that case or any further accusations that may emerge. We will do what we always do. We respond to them, we collaborate with the NCAA and try and find the truth. (para. 6)

In another statement Smith said,

We look forward to refocusing the football program on doing what we do best-representing this extraordinary university and its values on the field, in the classroom, and in life. We look forward to supporting Luke Fickell in his role as our football coach. We have full confidence in his ability to lead our football program. (as cited in "Tressel resignation," 2011, n.p.)

Though Smith could not use transcendence as it was conceptualized by Benoit (1995, 2014) or his predecessors (Ware & Linkugel, 1973; Scott & Lyman, 1968), who argued transcendence places the scandal in a broader context such that it may viewed as less egregious or justified, he did argue that the scandal was secondary to the central mission of the university, educating students and preparing them for life beyond the university.

While OSU had previously supported the coach through the allegations, it is not surprising it turned to *separation* as a strategy.

Staples (2011) explains it best. Before his admitted transgression,

Tressel was packaged and sold as a paragon of virtue in a college football universe teaming with schemers and bloodsuckers. As long as he beat Michigan and won the Big Ten, most people seemed more than happy to swallow that narrative. (Staples, 2011, para. 9)

However,

They want you to think this is all a Jim Tressel problem and not an Ohio State problem. A Jim Tressel problem means Ohio State needs a new coach. An Ohio State problem means brutal NCAA sanctions that could cripple the program for years. (Staples, 2011, para. 8)

Though OSU players and alumni continued to support Tressel (see "Ohio State players," 2011), the looming NCAA investigation left administrators little choice but to separate OSU from Tressel if it hoped to escape lack of institutional control charges from the NCAA (Staples, 2011). Staples notes,

What infuriates Ohio State fans most is that other head coaches have sailed along with no personal punishment or a mere wrist slap. Those fans fail to understand that those coaches wore the armor of plausible deniability...The moment Tressel responded to a Cicero e-mail—thereby acknowledging its receipt—he stripped himself of his armor. (para. 13)

He goes on,

If it ever emerged that Smith or anyone in that athletic administration knew of the e-mails and didn't report them, they could be charged with the same unethical conduct violation as Tressel, and the Committee on Infractions almost certainly

would blast the program for a lack of institutional control. (para. 19)

Eight days later, Gee responded to allegations that Tressel's resignation was forced (Lesmerises, 2011). He noted that early decisions were based on the facts as OSU leaders knew them at the time and on Tressel's "incredible body of work as the football coach and as a university citizen," but continued,

We have a process at the university in which we do not immediately make decisions. We try to be deliberate and that was the process. Two months later, I think there were a lot of additional facts, and I think there was also the reality that were are facing serious issues. And the coach realized that and made what I think is the best decision on behalf of the university, which was to resign. (as cited in Lesmerises, 2011, para. 3-4)

He argued that OSU had allowed Tressel to stay so long after admitting his participation in the emails with Cicero in order to give him a chance to "make his case" and "engage in appropriate conversation about the mistakes he had made" (as cited in Lesmerises, 2011, para. 11). Even though Gee claimed OSU had acted correctly in immediately reporting and investigating the allegations, he remarked, "We as an institution have to be appropriately humble and contrite about the mistakes we've made, and then move on from there" (as cited in Lesmerises, 2011, para. 9). Interestingly, he never enumerated to what mistakes he was referring, but noted that the scandal had not affected fundraising or student applications (Lesmerises, 2011).

Though no one ever proved OSU leadership knew about the e-mails or any of the other incidences in this case, a July 2011 article in the *Columbus Dispatch* publicly called the integrity and practices of both Tressel and OSU leadership into question (Pyle & Ludlow, 2011). Through an open records request, Pyle and Ludlow (2011) found that prior to Smith's hiring in 2005, Tressel's performance evaluations indicated a problem. The previous Athletic Director, Andy Geiger, had warned Tressel six times that there was a need to "improve his compliance with NCAA regulations;" these warnings were documented in writing (Pyle & Ludlow, 2011, n.p.). Further, for 2005-2006, the compliance office noted that the speed with which Tressel reported violations was "unacceptable" (Pyle & Ludlow, 2011, n.p.). One review, written in 2003, specifically asked him to pay attention the vehicles his players were driving and to report any "unusual circumstances" to the compliance office (as cited in Boren, 2011, para. 3). Mysteriously, once Smith was hired, no written documents about compliance were placed in Tressel's personnel file even though OSU football had 10 violations from 2008-2010. This was not the evaluation process for any other high-profile employee at OSU, including its President or its men's basketball coach (Pyle & Ludlow, 2011).

Given Tressel's admission, what OSU leaders knew of his compliance record, and the fact that there was no written record of his compliance evaluations under Smith, OSU no longer had hope of satisfying both its fans and the NCAA with Tressel at the helm. While OSU officials might have wanted to spare Tressel to appease fans, concern about NCAA sanctions left them with little choice but to focus on image repair with the NCAA at this juncture because of the legitimate power it had over the future of OSU football. Essentially, the university found it easier to replace one person, Tressel, than rebuild an entire football program from the ground up.

Attempting Renewal

While the NCAA had to take primacy, OSU could not ignore its fans. It needed fan support to thrive if it was to remain a strong program long-term. Not surprisingly, it would make a move to do that in notable style.

Following Fickell's year as Interim Head Coach, OSU announced the hiring of former Florida Head Football Coach, Urban Meyer, a proven championship-caliber coach. Such a hire likely went a long way to repairing OSU's image with disgruntled fans. Shortly thereafter, the NCAA handed down a one-year bowl ban for OSU based on its violations. The NCAA also banned OSU from Big Ten Championship eligibility for one year, placed it on three years of probation, and forced it to forfeit nine scholarships over a three-year period (Smith, 2011; The Ohio State University, 2011). OSU was not, however, charged with lack of institutional control, a violation which would have all but killed the OSU football program. On the decision, Smith stated,

We are surprised and disappointed with the NCAA's decision. However, we have decided not to appeal the decision because we need to move forward as an institution. We recognize that this is a challenging time in intercollegiate athletics. Institutions of higher education must move to higher ground, and Ohio State embraces its leadership responsibilities and affirms its long-standing commitment to excellence in education and integrity in all it does. My primary concern, as always, is for our students, and this decision punishes future students for the actions of others in the past. Knowing our student-athletes, however, I have no doubt in their capacity to turn this into something positive – for themselves and for the institution. I am grateful to our entire Buckeye community for their continued support. (as cited in The Ohio State University, 2011, para. 2)

He closed by touting the academic and athletic accolades won by OSU student-athletes (The Ohio State University, 2011). This statement depicts a discourse focused on renewal. Spoken by an organizational leader at the center of the crisis, it privileges a prospective vision for the future; a future in which OSU would be a leader. Though some may have questioned the ethical communication of OSU's leadership to this point, Smith demonstrated organizational learning in his words by focusing on corrective action and reaffirming OSU's core values.

Both Gee and Smith survived the crisis unscathed. Gee remained the President of OSU for two years after the crisis, leaving in 2013 after "jokingly referring to 'those damn Catholics' at Notre Dame and poking fun at the academic quality of other schools" (Welsh-Huggins, 2013, para. 1). However, he was granted President Emeritus status at OSU (Lesmerises, 2014a). Smith remains at OSU and was promoted to Vice President (Lesmerises, 2014c).

Returning to the Top

Meyer led the team to an undefeated season his first year, but was left unable to play for a national championship because of the bowl ban (Lesmerises, 2014b). Further, Meyer's recruiting classes have ranked seventh or above nationally each year since he took over the team (Axelrod, 2015). Most notably, the Buckeyes became the 2015 College Football Playoff National Champions by defeating the University of Oregon 42-20 with a third-string quarterback ("Ohio State Buckeyes," 2014). As Kruse's work indicates, such success likely healed old wounds with fans who did not agree with the statements and actions of OSU leaders during the tattoos-for-memorabilia scandal.

SOLUTIONS AND RECOMMENDATIONS

This essay adds meaningful insight into the study of image repair campaigns and addresses pragmatic considerations central to the issues at the heart of this text. It clearly illustrates the unique rhetorical intricacies faced by colleges/universities when their coaches/student-athletes violate NCAA rules. However, the lessons learned herein may benefit practitioners in a variety of contexts.

First, this case calls into question the decision to hire someone whose performance history is questionable. Sports organizations are notorious for such hires. However, the potential for such hires crosses organizational contexts. Second, if such a hire is made, this case highlights the value of written performance evaluations. In an interview, Paul McConnell, President and CEO of Orlando-based McConnell & Co., who works in higher education, contended, "It's highly unusual not to require a written evaluation, especially for someone so prominent" (Pyle & Ludlow, 2011, n.p.). The authors could find no evidence that OSU officials ever explained the reason for the switch to oral evaluations for Tressel. One has to wonder if it was done to offer OSU leaders the protection of *defeasibility* should another set of violations arise. After all, documentation demonstrates Tressel and/or his players were connected to shady dealings on at least three occasions prior to 2010. However, it left them with no way to prove their own innocence. During Lesmerises' (2014a) retrospective interview, Gee revealed,

As a university president...I always felt I spent relatively minute amounts of time on athletics... You have great athletic directors, you let them run it, you keep yourself informed, but I'm not the athletic director, I'm the president of the university. But all of the sudden this whole thing overwhelmed us... (para. 26-27)

Had Gee put the checks and balances in place to make sure rigorous, documented reviews of Tressel continued under Smith, as they had under Geiger, this crisis may have been avoided altogether.

Third, given what organizational leaders knew of Smith's performance history, the use of denial and minimization strategies in the initial stages of the campaign was a mistake. Even though Tressel initially denied prior knowledge of this particular set of violations, taking the word of Tressel and the players was tenuous given Tressel's troubled past. Further, the raid uncovered memorabilia from as far back at 2002, but the university insisted this was a contained incident. While the 2002 players had long-since left OSU, it still indicated a systemic problem. The authors cannot know why OSU administrators chose to use these strategies. Did they do so because they put too much trust in Tressel and his players or did they do so because they knew they had a systemic problem and chose to lie to the NCAA in the hopes warding off harsher penalties?

Regardless of the answer, this case adds support for existing research, such as that of Benoit (2014), Fortunato (2008), and Rowland and Jerome (2004), which indicates OSU officials may have been better served by telling the truth if they knew it or seeking the root cause of the issue through an exhaustive investigation and providing an extensive corrective plan once the investigation was complete. Smith did mention corrective action in his early statements, but they lacked detail. Further, though Gee mentioned a thorough review in the latter stages of the case, OSU leaders claimed these were isolated events a mere eight days after the Office of the U.S. Attorney apprised them of the situation. Gee's own statements (See Lesmerises, 2011) indicated they made an error in making definitive statements before all facts were gathered. Drawing harried, definitive conclusions early in a crisis or lying likely will not be beneficial to any type of organization.

This case also teaches practitioners a great deal about managing stakeholders during crises of this nature. At the outset, OSU's leadership was able to focus almost solely on repairing its image with the NCAA because, as Kruse (1981) notes, highly dedicated fans and other organizational members that consider the team a family are willing to forgive a variety of transgressions. However, it also reveals that organizational/leader survival may call forth the need to sacrifice a beloved organizational member. Though fan support was important to OSU, the ability to continue its football program had to take primacy. This is in line with the work of Rawlins (2006)

who noted, "the enabling and functional linkages have the greatest priority as stakeholders because their power/dependency/influence relationship is frequent and critical to the regular operations of the organizations" (p. 8). Further, he argued that prioritization will change based on situation and other stakeholder characteristics such as likelihood they will be outspoken about an issue and whether that activism will be supportive or adversarial. Key publics, he contended, are those "whose participation and cooperation are required to accomplish organizational goals" (p. 12) and should be those that receive the highest priority. Benoit's (2014) final chapter echoes these assertions.

However, because fan support would be important to the long-term future of OSU, its leaders needed to renew their faith. While Smith did move to a discourse of renewal toward the end of the crisis, OSU's hiring of Meyer and the team's continued winning performances likely did more to repair OSU's image with fans than any focus on academics or corrective action campaign could have done. Smith echoed this sentiment in his retrospective interview when saying of Meyer, "He's perfect for the situation we had. He's perfect for The Ohio State University, being from Ohio, being here before, his wife being from Ohio. It was a little bit of a Camelot from that perspective." (as cited in Lesmerises, 2014c, para. 28). Once more, this strategy is not unique to NCAA violations crises. Winning transcends sports. Just as sports organizations want to win games, organizations of all other varieties seek wins (e.g., in sales numbers, membership).

Some may wonder why OSU did not attack its accuser, the NCAA. After all, media commentators and fans continually note their distaste for the NCAA's regulatory decisions on a number of fronts. Nevertheless, the authors argue that such a strategy would rarely be beneficial for OSU or any other college/university given the NCAA's position as ultimate arbiter of all things college sports. Again, this factor is not unique to colleges and universities. All organizations have to contend with regulatory agencies daily (e.g., the SEC, the EPA). While there have been occasions where decisions made by governing bodies have been met with so much public ire as to goad the body into overturning its original decision, such occasions are rare. Thus, it is not surprising, given Kruse's (1981) assertions, that as the actions taken by Tressel caused excessive strife for the university, OSU administrators' dedication to Tressel dwindled.

FUTURE RESEARCH DIRECTIONS

As with any study, limitations exist. These include the obvious limitation that this study was based on only one case. Further, this study is completely dependent on press statements and media reports. Thus, the authors had no ability to assess the closed-door decision making processes of OSU administrators that would have undoubtedly added insight to strategy choice. Also, it is impossible to know what would have happened if OSU had made different rhetorical choices. Along with these limitations, some areas of future research deserve mention. Ideally, future studies could include other cases where different NCAA rules have been violated and/or where similar rules have been violated but other image repair strategies were chosen. Further, in the interest of contributing to the broader context of organizational image repair, leadership, and conflict research, the claims made herein should be tested on other types of organizational image repair campaigns.

CONCLUSION

This study extends the study of sports rhetoric in important ways. However, it also clearly contributes to the ever-growing body of knowledge about image repair, organizational leadership, and conflict management. Last, it offers insights beneficial to all organizations dealing with dichotomous situational constraints.

REFERENCES

Associated Press. (2011a, April 19). A timeline of Tressel's NCAA troubles. *USA Today.* Retrieved August 28, 2015 from http://usatoday30. usatoday.com/sports/college/football/2011-04-19-2215755358_x.htm

Associated Press. (2011b, May 30). Jim Tressel resigns as Ohio State's coach. *CBS News.* Retrieved August 28, 2015 from http://www.cbsnews.com/news/jim-tressel-resigns-as-ohio-states-coach/

Axelrod, B. (2015, July 28). How Urban Meyer has Ohio State set up for a long-term dynasty. *The Bleacher Report.* Retrieved July 29, 2015 from http://bleacherreport.com/articles/2533002-how-urban-meyer-has-ohio-state-set-up-for-a-long-term-dynasty

Benoit, W. (1995). *Accounts, excuses, and apologies: A theory of image restoration.* State University of New York Press.

Benoit, W. (2014). *Accounts, excuses, and apologies: Image repair theory and research.* State University of New York Press.

Berkowitz, S. (2013, May 2). NCAA had record $71 million surplus in fiscal 2012. *USA Today.* Retrieved March 17, 2014 from http://www.usatoday.com/story/sports/college/2013/05/02/ncaa-financial-statement-surplus/2128431/

Blaney, J. R., Lippert, L. R., & Smith, J. S. (2013). Repairing the athlete's image. Lanham, MD: Lexington Books (Rowman & Littlefield).

Boren, C. (2011, July 15). Report: Ohio State's Jim Tressel had history of compliance violations. *The Washington Post.* Retrieved October 18, 2015 from https://www.washingtonpost.com/blogs/early-lead/post/report-ohio-states-jim-tressel-had-history-of-compliance-violations/2011/07/15/gIQAJjbFGI_blog.html

Brazeal, L. M. (2008). The image repair strategies of Terrell Owens. *Public Relations Review, 34*(2), 145–150. doi:10.1016/j.pubrev.2008.03.021

Brinson, S. L., & Benoit, W. L. (1999). The tarnished star: Restoring Texaco's damaged public image. *Management Communication Quarterly, 12*(4), 483–519. doi:10.1177/0893318999124001

Bruce, T., & Tini, T. (2008). Unique crisis response strategies in sports public relations: Rugby league and the case for diversion. *Public Relations Review, 34*(2), 108–115. doi:10.1016/j.pubrev.2008.03.015

Coombs, W. T. (1995). Choosing the right words: The development of guidelines for the selection of "appropriate" crisis response strategies. *Management Communication Quarterly, 8*(4), 447–476. doi:10.1177/0893318995008004003

Dohrmann, G., & Epstein, D. [2] (2011, May 30). SI investigation reveals eight-year pattern of violations under Tressel. *Sportsillustrated.com.* Retrieved June 14, 2011 from http://www.si.com/more-sports/2011/05/30/jim-tressel

Farrey, T.[3] (2011, May 30). Timeline: Jim Tressel's fall. *ESPN.com.* Retrieved July 19, 2011 from http://sports.espn.go.com/ncf/news/story?id=6607982

Forde, P. (2011, May 30). Tressel's end fits with saga's pattern. *ESPN.com.* Retrieved June 14, 2011 from http://espn.go.com/espn/print?id=6607408&type=story

Fortunato, J. A. (2008). Restoring a reputation: The Duke University lacrosse scandal. *Public Relations Review, 34*(2), 116–123. doi:10.1016/j.pubrev.2008.03.006

Friend, T. (2011, May). Maurice Clarett tells his side. *ESPN.com.* Retrieved October 24, 2015 from http://sports.espn.go.com/ncf/news/story?id=1919246

Jenkins, S. (2013, January 20). NCAA touts amateurism rules over open market, but which is more corrupt. *The Washington Post.* Retrieved January 22, 2014 from http://www.washingtonpost.com/sports/colleges/ncaa-touts-amateurism-rules-over-open-market-but-which-is-more-corrupt/2013/09/20/511e18ea-2204-11e3-a358-1144dee636dd_story.html

Jerome, A. M. (2008). Toward prescription: Testing the rhetoric of atonement's applicability in the athletic arena. *Public Relations Review, 34*(2), 124–134. doi:10.1016/j.pubrev.2008.03.007

Jerome, A. M., & Rowland, R. C. (2009). Organizational apologia: The rhetoric of inter-organizational conflict. *Western Journal of Communication, 73*, 395–417. doi:10.1080/10570310903279059

Kruse, N. W. (1981). Apologia in team sport. *The Quarterly Journal of Speech, 67*(3), 270–283. doi:10.1080/00335638109383572

Lesmerises, D. (2011, June 7). Ohio State President Gordon Gee: "Flurry of activity" led to Jim Tressel resignation. *Cleveland.com.* Retrieved October 27 from http://www.cleveland.com/osu/index.ssf/2011/06/ohio_state_president_gordon_ge.html

Lesmerises, D. (2014a, June 3). Gordon Gee: 'I think everyone won'-closing the book on the Ohio State tattoo scandal. *Cleveland.com.* Retrieved October 27 from http://www.cleveland.com/osu/index.ssf/2014/06/gordon_gee_i_think_everyone_wo.html

Lesmerises, D. (2014b, June 5). Urban Meyer: 'I can tell you there is nothing behind door no. 2'-Closing the book on the Ohio State football scandal. *Cleveland.com.* Retrieved October 28, 2015, 2015 http://www.cleveland.com/osu/index.ssf/2014/06/urban_meyer_i_can_tell_you_the.html

Lesmerises, D. (2014c, June 11). Gene Smith: 'We moved forward a long time ago"- Closing the book on the Ohio State football scandal. *Cleveland.com*. Retrieved October 27 from http://www.cleveland.com/osu/index.ssf/2014/06/gene_smith_our_kids_are_much_f.html

Marshall, A. (2011, March 8). Ohio State football coach Jim Tressel suspended 2 games, fined $250,000 in aftermath of Yahoo report. *Cleveland.com*. Retrieved June 14, 2011 from http://www.cleveland.com/osu/index.ssf/2011/03/post_36.html

Meisel, Z., & Oldham, J. (2011, May 24). Ray Small tells all: Ex-Buckeye says he sold memorabilia, some players don't 'think about' rules. *The Lantern*. Retrieved October 14, 2015 from http://thelantern.com/2011/05/ray-small-tells-all-ex-buckeye-says-he-sold-memorabilia-some-players-dont-think-about-rules/

NCAA. (2010, December 23). *NCAA Requires Loss of Contests for Six Ohio State Football Student-Athletes*. Retrieved August 29, 2015 from http://www.dispatch.com/content/stories/sports/2010/12/23/text-of-ncaa-press-release.html?sid=101

Nelson, J. (1984). The defense of Billie Jean King. *Western Journal of Speech Communication*, *48*(1), 92–102. doi:10.1080/10570318409374144

Ohio State Buckeyes-2014 NCAA Football Champions. (2014). Retrieved July 29, 2015 from http://www.ohiostatebuckeyes.com/sports/m-footbl/2014-championship.html

Ohio State football players sanctioned. (2010, December 26). *ESPN.com News Service*. Retrieved August 29, 2015 from http://sports.espn.go.com/ncf/news/story?id=5950873

Ohio State players, alums stand behind Tressel. (2011, May 31). *Sportsillustrated.com*. Retrieved June 1, 2011 http://sportsillustrated.cnn.com/2011/football/ncaa/05/30/tressel-reaction.ap/index.html

OSU Athletic Director Gene Smith on timeline of events. (2010, December 23). *WEWSNewsChannel5*. Retrieved August 29, 2015 from https://www.youtube.com/watch?v=aJ3z7_oM5W0

OSU coach Jim Tressel on suspensions. (2010, December 23). *WEWSNewsChannel5*. Retrieved August 29, 2015 from https://www.youtube.com/watch?v=OuqH3PVQJAg

Pfahl, M. E., & Bates, B. R. (2008). This is not a race, this is a farce: Formula One and the Indianapolis Motor Speedway tire crisis. *Public Relations Review*, *34*, 135–144.

Pyle, E., & Ludlow, R. (2011, July 16). *Ohio State football: Tressel had early history of warnings*. Retrieved October 14, 2015 from http://www.dispatch.com/content/stories/local/2011/07/16/tressel-had-early-history-of-warnings.html

Rawlins, B. (2006). Prioritizing stakeholders for public relations. *Institute for Public Relations*. Retrieved October 18, 2015 from http://pdfcast.org/pdf/prioritizing-stakeholders-for-public-relations

Rowland, R. C., & Jerome, A. M. (2004). On organizational apologia: A reconceptualization. *Communication Theory*, *14*(3), 191–211. doi:10.1111/j.1468-2885.2004.tb00311.x

Scott, M. B., & Lyman, S. M. (1968). Accounts. *American Sociological Review*, *33*(1), 46–62. doi:10.2307/2092239 PMID:5644339

Seeger, M. W. (2006). Best practices in crisis communication: An expert panel process. *Journal of Applied Communication Research*, *34*(3), 232–244. doi:10.1080/00909880600769944

Shaw, B. (2001, March 9). What, Gee worry? OSU president's lack of concern over the Tressel scandal will likely raise some with the NCAA: Bud Shaw's sports spin. *Cleveland.com*. Retrieved October 27, 2015 from http://www.cleveland.com/budshaw/index.ssf/2011/03/what_gee_worry_osu_presidents.html

Sisler, H. E. (2015). Crisis of man to crisis of men: Ray Rice and the NFL's transition from crisis of image to crisis of ethics. *TopSCHOLAR*. Retrieved October 18, 2015 from http://digitalcommons.wku.edu/theses/1520/

Smith, E. (2011, December 20). Ohio State hit with bowl ban, Tressel gets show-cause penalty. *USA Today*. Retrieved March 8, 2011 from USA-Today.com.

Smith: Tressel's speech to team "eloquent". (2011, May 30). *USA Today*. Retrieved August 28, 2015 from http://usatoday30.usatoday.com/sports/college/football/2011-05-30-4107396395_x.htm

Solomon, J. (2013, August 6). Jay Bilas uses NCAA store to highlight Johnny Manziel scandal. *AL.com*. Retrieved September 16, 2014 from www.al.com

Staples, A. (2011, May 30). Tressel tries to take brunt of NCAA wrath with Ohio State resignation. *Sportsillustrated.com*. Retrieved June 1, 2011 from http://www.si.com/more-sports/2011/05/30/jim-tresselosu

The Ohio State University. (2011, December 20). *Statement on NCAA sanctions*. Retrieved August 28, 2015 from http://www.ohiostatebuckeyes.com/genrel/122011aab.html

Tressel, J. (2011, March 8). Jim Tressel press conference 3/8/11. *Eleven Warriors*. Retrieved from http://www.youtube.com/watch?v=_wy-QwtXvCC4

Tressel Resignation: A Timeline of Quotes. (2011, May 30). *The Columbus Dispatch*. Retrieved August 28, 2015 from http://www.dispatch.com/content/stories/sports/2011/05/30/timeline-in-quotes.html

Ulmer, R. R., Seeger, M. W., & Sellnow, T. L. (2007). Post-crisis communication and renewal: Expanding the parameters of post-crisis discourse. *Public Relations Review*, *33*(2), 130–134. doi:10.1016/j.pubrev.2006.11.015

Ulmer, R. R., Sellnow, T. L., & Seeger, M. W. (2015). *Effective crisis communication: Moving from crisis to opportunity*. Thousand Oaks, CA: Sage.

Walker, D. (2010, December 23). Ohio State Buckeyes: Why Terrelle Pryor and others should sit out the Sugar Bowl. *The Bleacher Report*. Retrieved October 27, 2015 from http://bleacherreport.com/articles/551973-bad-buckeyes-why-terrell-pryor-and-others-should-sit-out-the-sugar-bowl

Ware, B. L., & Linkugel, W. A. (1973). They spoke on defense of themselves: On the generic criticism of apologia. *The Quarterly Journal of Speech*, *59*(3), 273–283. doi:10.1080/00335637309383176

Welsh-Huggins, A. (2013, June 5). Ohio State President Gordon Gee resigns. *The Boston Globe*. Retrieved October 25, 2015 from https://www.bostonglobe.com/sports/2013/06/05/ohio-president-gee-resigns/ifaooLYgKU6YAiqkjzOaSK/story.html

ADDITIONAL READING

Benoit, W. L., & Hanczor, R. S. (1994). The Tonya Harding controversy: An analysis of image restoration strategies. *Communication Quarterly*, *42*(4), 416–433. doi:10.1080/01463379409369947

Coombs, W. T. (2015). *Ongoing crisis communication: Planning, managing, and responding*. Thousand Oaks, CA: Sage.

Edwards, H. (1973) Sociology of sport (rpt. Homewood, III.: The Dorsey Press, 1977).

Hearit, K. M. (2006). *Crisis management by apology: Corporate responses to allegations of wrongdoing*. Mahwah, NJ: Lawrence Erlbaum.

Millar, D. P., & Heath, R. L. (2004). *Responding to crisis: A rhetorical approach to crisis communication*. Mahwah, NJ: Lawrence Erlbaum.

Novak, M. (1976). *The joy of sports: End zones, bases, baskets, balls, and the consecration of the American spirit*. New York: Basic Books.

Reirson, J. L., Sellnow, T. L., & Ulmer, R. R. (2009). Complexities of crisis renewal over time: Learning from the tainted Odwalla Apple Juice case. *Communication Studies*, *60*(2), 114–129. doi:10.1080/10510970902834841

Smart, B. (2005). *The sport star: Modern sport and the cultural economy of sporting celebrity*. London: Sage.

Varma, T. M. (2011). Crisis communication in higher education: The use of "negotiation" as a strategy to manage crisis. *Public Relations Review*, *37*(4), 373–375. doi:10.1016/j.pubrev.2011.08.006

Walsh, J., & McAllister-Spooner, S. M. (2011). Analysis of the image repair discourse in the Michael Phelps controversy. *Public Relations Review*, *37*(2), 157–162. doi:10.1016/j.pubrev.2011.01.001

KEY TERMS AND DEFINITIONS

Apologia: The act of rhetorical defense undertaken following an event that threatens one's image.

Bolstering: Listing the positive actions of actors in a crisis.

Corrective Action: Taking steps to ensure similar events/acts will not take place in the future.

Crisis: An event that threatens the image of an actor with key stakeholders.

Defeasibility: An argument made by an actor that focuses on his/her ignorance of the event/act pre-crisis.

Differentiation: A statement showing the difference between the current crisis and one that could have been much worse.

Good Intentions: An attempt to decrease the egregiousness of an act by arguing that it was undertaken with goodwill.

Image Repair: An attempt to restore or transform one's image following a crisis.

Minimization: A strategy used by those in crisis that attempts to decrease the perceived harm done.

NCAA: The National Collegiate Athletic Association, governing body of Division 1-3 collegiate athletics programs.

Renewal: A rhetorical strategy undertaken to capitalized on the lessons learned from a crisis.

Separation: An attempt to both shift blame onto another and place distance between the the blame shifter and the blamed.

Transcendence: An attempt to move past a crisis by appealing to higher values.

ENDNOTES

[1] Image repair studies were born out of earlier studies on apologia. For this reason, the terms are used interchangeably in this essay.

[2] In 2011, Dohrmann and Epstein were listed as the authors of this piece. As of August 30, 2015 no authors are listed. The current web address is used here, but the original retrieval date remains. The title of the piece has not changed.

[3] Tom Farrey was listed as the author of this piece in 2011. Though he is still acknowledged at the bottom of the piece, the web address for the piece has changed, and Chris Low was listed as the author as of August 30, 2015. The current web address is used here, but the original retrieval date remains. The title of the piece has not changed.

Chapter 10
Communication, Culture, and Discord:
A Lesson in Leadership Failure

Keith Jackson
University of London, UK

Reema Rasheed
Economic and Social Development Center of Palestine, Palestine

ABSTRACT

This case study highlights and examines an avoidable failure of management communication and leadership in a non-governmental organization (NGO). The case study draws on a real-life example of a NGO that was established in Palestine with European Union (EU) funding and that became subsequently staffed by a team composed of local Palestinian employees and expatriate non-Palestinians who, as is commonly the case in international NGOs, were appointed to executive management and leadership roles. Overall, this case study highlights processes of cross-cultural communication between the local employees, the expatriate employees, and (indirectly) with senior executives of the EU funding agencies, whose distant yet decisive influence give a broader context to the localized communication and conflict management processes described and analyzed here. Finally, recommendations are made for future research specific to effective communication, leadership and conflict resolution in international organizations generally and in Palestinian organizations specifically.

CONTEXT

The European-Palestinian Project Office (EPPO) was opened in Palestine in the mid-1990s as a non-profit-making and non-governmental organization (NGO). EPPO was funded initially by the European Union and was designed to provide legal advice and skills training support to the newly founded Palestinian Authority (PA). Specifically, EPPO's stated mission was to *contribute to a sustainable and democratic rule of law within the Palestinian Authority.*

Funded from a European Union (EU) office located in Brussels (Belgium), the first Director appointed to EPPO was a Swedish man (Yanne) who brought in a Spanish man (Miguel) as his Deputy. A senior official in Brussels had recommended Miguel, explaining to Yanne that Miguel would bring a keen strategic edge to the operation: 'He's tough', the official told him. 'Not always

DOI: 10.4018/978-1-4666-9970-0.ch010

easy to get on with, I hear, but you'll need some-one with a hard edge in such a difficult business environment'. Perhaps in order to balance the promised 'hard' with a softer and more familiar 'edge', Yanne persuaded the EU office to allow him to bring another Spanish colleague, a woman named Clara, as Yanne had admired her work in financial and administrative support on previous NGO projects. Yanne's first Palestinian or local appointment was Ahmed, whom he hired to act both as EPPO's logistics officer and as a source of local knowledge: none of the Europeans had worked in Palestine before, and none spoke or understood Arabic. From the outset, the spon-sors required the working language of EPPO to be English, though Yanne soon discovered that Miguel and Clara occasionally chatted and joked in Spanish. Yanne didn't understand Spanish, and neither did Ahmed; but Yanne decided to let this continue until everyone at EPPO had settled into their work. He decided to insist on "English only" at EPPO later.

As the PA's activities became more diversified, so the requests for EPPO support increased. After two years of stop-start operations, Yanne and Miguel found themselves increasingly involved in managing relationships to external stakehold-ers across Palestine. Simultaneously, Yanne was spending more time negotiating EPPO's position with various donor and regulatory agencies in Europe. Unfortunately, it was around this time that Yanne's daughter - who had remained in Sweden with his wife - became seriously ill, meaning he started taking increasing periods of leave away from the office. As a consequence, another local employee (Eman) was hired as 'Office Manager' with general responsibility for the running of the office in Palestine and specifically to support Clara. Clara welcomed this support because the responsibility for balancing and accounting for budgets had increased exponentially as EPPO took on new projects while simultaneously clos-ing others. The budgeting responsibility was becoming too too much for one person (Clara) and so Eman was brought in as the second local hire specifically in order to work under Clara on this core strategic and operational function. For reasons that we explain later, the story of this case study – and the conflict that forms its core - is told from Eman's perspective. But first we should define what we mean by 'conflict', and particu-larly where 'culture' along with 'cross-cultural communication' – or '*mis*-communication' - ap-pear key factors towards describing the context for the possible causes and potential solutions to organization-specific conflict.

CONFLICT

In contexts for organizational behavior and man-agement Robbins (2005:422) defines 'conflict' as:

A process that begins when one party perceives that another party has negatively affected, or is about to negatively affect, something that the first party cares about

The emphasis Robbins gives here to perception is vital; for here we can recognize perception as a natural human propensity to process and interpret information coming though the senses, notably sight, hearing, touch, taste and the elusive fifth sense of intuition (Gleitman, 2001). In relation to conflict, perception works intuitively as a survival mechanism, guiding human beings and animals towards choosing to meet conflict head on or flee (Sperber, 1995). As individuals, we are each socialized into one or other cultures: for example, within the family, at school. It is through the ex-perience of socialization that our perceptions of what is 'normal' or 'right' or 'wrong' are formed.

In the context of our current discussion this emphasis on perception becomes of practical relevance to managers tasked with working in and communicating across organizations characterized by the diverse cultural perspectives and experiences of members, as in the case of EPPO. Here, the local social, cultural political an economic context is vital towards shaping each actor's perception of how or when 'conflict' arises, and how or at what point in its emergence becomes perceived as threatening and / or as an opportunity for effective leadership (cf. Muna, 2011). In short, the realization that teach member of the organization, and consequently each potential actor in the conflict that arose at EPPO, is also a member of a community seeking to survive and prosper under certain conditions is key towards becoming at first sensitive to how each actor / team member might respond once 'conflict' becomes perceived as reality. What organization theorists and define as 'occupational' or work-related 'stress in its many forms can be expected to ensue, therefore potentially further skewing the interaction between EPPO employees towards conflict (cf. Khoury & Analoui, 2010).

To illustrate, we might assume that Eman - born, raised and educated as a young woman in the United States of America, married with family, and now working in Palestine in an office headed by non-Arab men - is likely to bring different perceptions of what might lead to 'conflict' and how it might be avoided. For example, Ahmed was raised under occupation, and while committed and eager to see an independent Palestinian state, tended to analyze actions and words with an underlying meaning more so than Eman. Given that he openly confessed to carrying through life a 'heightened political sensitivity', Eman noticed both inside and outside the EPPO office that Ahmed's response to any perception of anti-Palestine sentiment or comment tended to be both immediate and sharp. Eman wondered whether this attitude and behavior arose out of Ahmed's personality or from his experience of growing up in what Yanne and his colleagues might term Palestinian 'culture'

CULTURE

According to Hofstede, 'culture' is 'the collective programming of the mind which distinguishes the members of one human group from another' (1984:21). Where 'culture' is perceived as a key factor in how conflicts arise, Avruch (2002) reminds us that 'conflict' is a feature of all societies and of all relationships: potentially, conflict can generate both positive and negative outcomes. Some people can experience change and gain by being challenged; others perceive change or challenge to be a source of potential loss. As stated above, individual and group perceptions of what is 'normal' behavior - for example, in respect of what might be perceived as leading to interpersonal conflict - is shaped to a significant degree by socialization into local cultures and subcultures: e.g. at home, school, and during initial training into one or other workplace. Correspondingly, we might choose to echo Eman's reflection that Ahmed's overtly pro-Palestine sensibilities had been shaped by his political activism during his younger years.

Expanding our attention from societies to 'nations' or, as in the case of Palestine currently, 'territories', a dominant paradigm in the international management literature emanating from western business schools remains the multi-dimensional model for defining and comparing 'national cultures' developed by the aforementioned Dutch researcher, Geert Hofstede (cf. Hofstede, 1984, 2001). As academic attention has gradually shifted from a focus on 'management' to a focus on 'leadership' (cf. Western, 2013), the influence of the so-called 'Hofstede model' has become one of the most cited and thereby influential models available to international management research for the definition and comparison of culture-specific contexts for leadership (cf. Yukl, 2012; Jackson, 2013).

However, applying such general etic ('outsider-looking-in') macro-level comparisons to locally-situated emic ('insider-looking-in') level real-life experiences and perceptions should be done with caution, critical balance, and (not least) respect (cf. Muna & Khoury, 2012). For such sweeping scholarly analyses can appear over-generalized in terms both of research reliability and validity when applied to individuals or what to cultural insiders might be identified as 'non-typical' behaviors and other expressions of 'collective programming'. To illustrate, McSweeney (2002) challenges Hofstede's prior confidence in describing 'Yugoslavian culture' before that country declined into bitter inter-ethnic conflict in the 1990s. Specifically in reference to cultures for cross-cultural management and leadership in Palestinian organizations, such macro-level analyses can appear grossly oversimplified in term of helping to describe, explain and compare management styles relevant to local social, ethnic and (not least) political contexts (cf. Muna & Khoury, 2012).

Correspondingly, when linking culture to conflict Avruch reminds us (2002:5) that individual variables beyond nationality and notions of 'national culture' are relevant when attempting to define 'cross-cultural conflict':

By definition, conflict occurring between individuals or social groups that are separated by cultural boundaries can be considered 'cross-cultural conflict'. But individuals, even in the same society, are potentially members of many different groups, organized in different ways by different criteria: for example, by kinship into families or clans; by language, religion, ethnicity, or nationality; by socioeconomic characteristics into social classes; by geographical region into political interest groups; and by education, occupation, or institutional memberships into professions, trade unions, organizations, industries, bureaucracies, political parties, or militaries.

Specific to our case of EPPO as an international NGO and thereby a likely context for cross-cultural communication and conflict, we can look beyond questionable notions of 'national culture' and work to definitions of 'organizational culture', such as the following offered by Schein (1992:12):

A pattern of shared basic assumptions that the group learned as it solved its problems of external adaptation and internal integration, that has worked well enough to be considered valid and, therefore, to be taught to new members as the correct way to perceive, think, and feel in relation to those problems.

Again we can try to imagine Eman's experience of joining EPPO after the four initial members had over two years established patterns of working together that might be perceived as 'valid' or normal to them but which Eman might at first perceive as confusing and, over time, questionable in terms of their relative effectiveness and ethical credibility.

For example, as we develop Eman's perspective on patterns of assumption and behavior - including expressions of cultural ignorance or prejudice - that form the story-line of this case study and which you, the reader, might initially understand as leading to negative or destructive conflict in that it rendered EPPO less able to fulfill its stated mission. Correspondingly, we should note how Eman soon recognized that Ahmed appeared more open in expressing his concerns about this perceived threat to EPPO's mission to her than to other office colleagues, thereby expressing (perhaps) something of the 'kinship' highlighted by Avruch (2002) cited above together with its echoes of 'community' defined by culture-specific, historical, geographical or even ethnic boundaries of perception and self-identity (cf. Giddens, 2009). In the particular case of Palestine and the context describing EPPO's strategic mission, we should give mention to the geographical combined with the political along with potential problems of 'internal integration' (cf. Schein, 1992) in relation to the organizational culture and subcultures created and shared by EPPO employees. Building on previous interpretations of this concept, Schein (2012) recognizes how attempts to manage processes of 'internal integration' can generate opportunities for effective business leadership generally and for leadership towards conflict identification and resolution specifically.

LEADERSHIP

In one widely accepted definition, Gary Yukl (2005:8) interprets 'leadership' as 'the process of influencing others to understand and agree about what needs to be done and how to do it' combined with 'facilitating individual and collective efforts to accomplish shared objectives'. Against the background of our earlier discussion questioning boundaries set by academics between culture-specific (group) attitudes and behaviors in relation to individuals, it is relevant to begin this part of our discussion by distinguishing between 'leadership' as a process and 'leaders' as individuals (cf. Northouse, 2015). For, emphasizing the opportunities that conflict generates for individual leaders is relevant towards raising questions as to the extent that individual personalities might play a decisive role in the how the 'conflict' itself defined and, by extension, how its potential resolution might be envisaged.

To illustrate, we might already now begin to suspect that Eman and Miguel will 'get on' like 'oil and water', as the common phrase goes. Such images translate vividly across culture-specific contexts. To illustrate, in East Asian cultures 'discord' is commonly conceptualized as 'fire-water' Across Middle Eastern cultures, one side's 'apple of opportunity' can too readily become an 'apple of discord' when members of ethnically or religiously defined group lay claim to the apple and, indeed, seek to define said apple in line with their own narrowly defined interests (cf. Said, 1978): from a leadership perspective, whose influence should prevail, and why? In short, business leaders who fail to take account and demonstrate sensitivity or empathy towards competing local (emic) per-

ceptions and expectations of 'normal' behavior are likely eventually to appear to organizational members as a potential source of conflict, as part of 'the problem' rather than of 'the solution' (cf. Jackson, et.al. *forthcoming*).

To the mix of conceptual definitions stirred thus far we can bring the observations made over years by Drucker (2001:40-41) of management in not-for-profit organizations (including NGOs) where attention to 'the mission' tends to be a primary factor determining how effectively the organization and its staff sense they are 'gelling' together as a team where members are 'all pulling' in the same (often altruistic) direction – what Schein (above) terms 'internal integration' – and achieving a positive impact on the communities that they are dedicated – often for little financial reward – to support and serve: i.e. the 'external adaptation' highlighted by Schein (1992, 2012). Re-connecting with the definition of conflict proposed by Robbins (2005), we can expect members of NGOs such as EPPO to assess their own and each other's performance and motivation by reference to how much they appear to 'care about' what the organization stands for and has been set up to achieve in and for society.

To illustrate, we can expect (for example) Miguel and Ahmed to approach any attempt to operationalize EPPO's stated mission to 'contribute to a sustainable and democratic rule of law within the Palestinian Authority' from distinctly different although not necessarily opposing directions: as a conscience, their perception with regard to any conflict that might arise on the pathway towards fulfilling this mission is likely to be sensitized *a priori* differently: echoing Schein (1992:12), each is likely to bring differing sets of assumptions about what constitutes 'the correct way to perceive, think, and feel' in relation to the 'problems' and about what might be perceived, individually and / or collectively, 'threats' and 'opportunities' that any organization and its business leaders encounter in pursuit of their strategic objectives.

Looking ahead now specifically to our case study, we might emphasize here how leaders as individuals – Yanne, for example - might prepare to enter each organizational context, and thus a context for potential discord and conflict, much as actors prepare to enter the stage: analogous to our case, bringing with them a rehearsed awareness of their individual potential to predict and even resolve conflict before it arises and begins to threaten the organization's strategic health and, ultimately, the interests of their intended audience: for example, the Palestinian communities that EPPO was set up to serve. Taking culture as key element defining such contexts, leaders might prepare themselves by perceiving themselves as 'cultural avatars' or, as Western (2013:111) has it:

Leaders have a certain amount of agency and influence; they can be powerful, yet they are better understood as skilled cultural 'avatars' […]. Like avatars in a computer game, leaders act (often unconsciously) on behalf of other interests, they carry and transmit cultures on behalf of wider forces.

Consequently, and as we now begin to detail and explore the rise of interpersonal and cross-cultural conflict at EPPO, we can already imagine that Eman and other members of EPPO might perceive conflict that threatens the organization's ability to fulfill its mission as something to be avoided, for their own sake and on behalf of their respective families and communities 'and other forces': that is to say, if we assume that each individual member of EPPO shares a personal and professional 'mission' to work collaboratively towards this purpose - an assessment either way that might only appear convincing or persuasive by taking into account the broader strategic context (cf. HDR, 2014). In other words, we can predict already now how, within the confines of this case study as of any similar 'case study' about leadership, the consequences of leadership failure are likely to impact on the perceptions, experiences

and expectations not only of the actors directly involved but also of those indirectly affected such as the families and communities of the individual employees of EPPO, currently and in future.

CONFLICT AT EPPO: BEGINNINGS

Developing on the stage set above we can begin to explore the beginnings of conflict at EPPO. As stated previously, we choose to do this from the perspective of Eman, the newest and youngest member of the organization and thus the one (we might assume) to be the most open and sensitive in terms of how she might perceive potential sources of conflict between members of the organization that might turn negatively destructive, thereby threatening EPPO's ability to fulfill its mission in Palestine and, more immediately, restrict each member's opportunities to perform professionally as individuals and effectively as a team. Echoing the Robbins (2005) definition of 'conflict' cited above, and taking note of the different perceptions of EPPO's mission that – as in any NGO – might act as sources of conflict, we choose Eman to be the 'first party' whose perceptions can guide us through a critical series of events that led to open and negative conflict at EPPO.

As outlined previously, Eman was hired initially to support Clara as the accounting duties became more complex in terms of the quantity and quality of work required. A tipping point came during one of Yanne's ever more frequent periods of absence in Sweden: unexpectedly – to Yanne, at least – Clara handed in her notice. As soon as Yanne heard the news, he phoned Clara from Sweden. Eman had already heard how Clara claimed to prefer furthering her career in Europe where she, like Yanne could be closer to her family. Eman had already noted how Yanne tended to defer to Clara when it came to operational decisions at EPPO. She had wondered why Miguel was not central to these and had come to assume that Miguel regarded himself as having a more strategic role, and particular when she heard him use terms such as 'stakeholders' for local people and organisations she knew by name. Unsurprisingly (to Eman, at least), Yanne persuaded Clara to stay in post until his return to Palestine from Sweden. She also agreed to 'train up' a successor. She even offered to help find a successor using her contacts in Europe. Eman noted that neither Yanne, Clara nor Miguel approached her to ask whether she felt able to succeed Clara. It was not that she particularly wanted the job, although more pay would be useful. She believed in her own competence and thought that she'd demonstrated enough of this during her short time at EPPO. "It would be fair if they at least asked me', she confided to Ahmed. Ahmed assured her that although Yanne is 'sympathetic', he would hesitate to appoint 'a local' to such a strategically sensitive position. Eman sensed some expression of thwarted ambition on Ahmed's part in the manner he chose to explain this to her.

It was during this period of uncertainty caused by Clara's impending departure that Eman came to work one afternoon to find that the drawer of her desk had been broken open. Sensing a potential security breach, she reported the incident to Miguel, as he was the most senior EPPO manager on site. Miguel replied that he, in fact, had broken open her desk because 'I was looking for the company stamp and I couldn't wait till you got here'. Eman felt both disappointed and furious. Later that same week Ahmed reported that his desk had been broken into. This time, however, Miguel had left a note saying 'Sorry, I was looking for the spare keys to the office'. Ahmed spoke to Eman about this. They recognized how Miguel always kept his own office securely locked, but appeared not to respect their wish or need to do the same. They decided to wait until Yanne's return before taking the issue further. In the end, they agreed not to, given Yanne's obvious concern about the deterioration of his daughter's health at home together with the stress of finding a replacement for Clara. Ahmed expressed the view that 'anyway', no action would

be taken against Miguel and it might appear that Eman and Ahmed had something to hide should they voice their concerns to Yanne: 'You know how much Miguel's been going on to us all about "security issues" recently', Ahmed said.

A further incident involving Miguel and Ahmed occurred sometime later when Yanne was absent again. Ahmed came into the general office one afternoon excited by the news that he had secured a procurement agreement with a local provider that would create both a financial saving for EPPO in addition to promoting the NGO's status more widely in the local community. Miguel appeared unimpressed: 'So how much commission is this provider offering to give *you*?' he asked Ahmed. The response was stunned silence. Talking about the incident some time later with Eman, Miguel asked her: 'Don't you ever get tired of being a Palestinian, always being treated like a second class species?' Eman felt too shocked and disgusted to answer. Almost immediately afterwards Eman was furious at herself for not having responded to Miguel. 'If he'd said such a thing to Ahmed', she thought, 'he'd have got a different response'. Eman felt disappointed in her own lack of challenge to Miguel's comments.

Reflecting on her reaction later, Eman recognized that part of her shock came from the way Miguel spoke English to her. Was it just his Spanish accent, or did he really mean to communicate disrespect or disdain to her? She recalled having overheard Miguel speaking to Ahmed in the same way, and having recognised the expression of controlled anger in Ahmed's face at the time. Although English remained officially the operational language of EPPO, a casual visitor to the office would notice that Eman and Ahmed occasionally exchanged words in Arabic while Miguel and Clara spoke Spanish and English interchangeably. When Yanne was around, everyone returned to using English as normal. So, it was in English that Eman learned of Clara's replacement: Esther.

Esther is Belgian and had worked as an accountant at the EU in Brussels. Yanne admitted he 'wasn't sure' whether Esther would be a permanent replacement or not: a rumor circulated from somewhere that Esther had just recently divorced and was looking to get away from Brussels for a while. Yanne did mention, though, that apart from fluent English and French, Esther also spoke some Spanish. ('And not Arabic', thought Eman).

At the appointed time, Esther arrived and received only two weeks of induction with Clara rather than the intended four weeks. This was because Clara had decided to take two weeks of paid leave to attend her grandmother who had 'fallen ill suddenly' - at least, this is what Clara said. Eman noticed that Clara had become much quieter than usual during her final days in the office: even the jokes in Spanish with Miguel appeared to have dried up. Eman focused her attention on Esther and perceived her at first as being confident about the hand-over. She certainly appeared experienced in this type of work, although questioned some of the details about how the projects were being financed: 'We couldn't do it this way in Brussels', she announced, half-smilingly. Soon after Clara had finally left, Esther appeared to become suddenly anxious and disorganized. Her attitude towards Miguel also appeared to change dramatically. Ahmed and Eman had heard another rumor that Esther had initially shared Miguel's two-bedroom apartment in Ramallah while she settled in to the new job. This 'rumor' only gained in credibility when Clara publicly announced her new address to everyone in the office, including Miguel.

It was during this period that Eman was called to work with Esther much as she had with Clara: they needed to keep balancing the accounts and increasingly their work involved checking and issuing contracts for clients and other stakeholders of EPPO projects. Further pressure fell on Eman as Esther began trying to impose 'Brussels standards' on the work they did. One day Miguel walked past as they were both trying to compare a contract previously drafted by Clara with one

they needed to draft afresh. Esther asked Miguel if he could remember how Clara had drafted new contracts: 'Why should I know, it's not my job', he said with a dismissive gesture of his hand. Esther explained how she had previously asked Yanne the same question, but he also claimed not to know how Clara had done this task. Reflecting on this lack of shared knowledge in the organization, Eman heard Miguel say to Esther: 'And be sure to lock that contract back into the archive once you've finished with it'. ('Why did he say that in front of me, and in English not French or Spanish?' Eman asked herself). Ahmed interrupted her thoughts with the whispered comment (in Arabic): 'So, it looks like he's got a new lock to break open next time he's alone in the office', which caused both of them to laugh and Miguel to look across to them sharply.

The next day Miguel announced a new 'need to know' policy for the office. 'I've cleared it with Brussels', he said. 'And what about Yanne?' Esther asked. 'Yes, he's on my side, too' Miguel replied. This new policy was explained with reference to 'security reasons' and further that 'EPPO is going through a vital strategic phase: we need to ensure that interests and integrity of our key stakeholders are maintained.' Eman noticed that the policy was never precisely formulated or formally written. Yanne appeared too distracted to comment on it. However, Eman did notice how the policy became a constant point of reference used by Miguel to explain his (to her) increasingly erratic and aggressive behaviour in the office. For example, Eman felt Miguel made her particularly and increasingly an object of suspicion when Esther came under pressure to draw up and sign off the end of year accounts. Esther appeared anxious that her former colleagues in Brussels might question her work, saying that if 'the books look bad' the budget for the next financial year would be under threat. Again, Miguel appeared to offer Esther no help, guidance, or even encouragement with closing the current year's budget: for example, by giving her a template used previously by Clara: 'It's your job, not mine', was a common response to Esther's requests for help: 'why don't you just do it *the Brussels way*?', he added with what appeared to be a fake smile. Whatever positive relationship these two had before (Eman thought) has well and truly broken down.

Again Eman did what she could to help Esther, often neglecting her own family duties to work late at the office in support – a choice that, when Miguel heard about it, appeared to prompt more frequent and aggressive reminders to Esther about the 'right need to know policy' and the ever present 'security threat' when working with 'confidential' or 'strategically sensitive information'. 'I hope you both lock away all documents securely each evening', Miguel warned them. Eman noticed how Esther started appearing increasingly anxious, unraveled, and even ill under the stress of Miguel's repeated 'security' warnings.

Esther appeared to reach a breaking point one day when checking details of the closing budget in relation to the drafting of next year's budget. Only Eman was in the office when she heard Esther on the phone to project headquarters in Brussels. She was talking in French, but Eman could recognize that Esther was concerned with a set of figures she had sketched onto a piece of notepaper she held in one hand; she appeared to ask repeatedly for confirmation that the figures were 'correct'. When it appeared they were, Esther screwed up the paper, threw it across her desk, stood up, and then said: 'Eman, can you take care of things? I need to go home right now. Probably I see you tomorrow.' Eman noticed Esther's lapse in grammar – the Spanish-English 'I see you tomorrow'. 'Poor Esther really is upset about something', Eman thought. Eman just said 'OK', realizing with almost sisterly concern that Esther's distress appeared to have reached breaking point. Without thinking Eman picked up the notepaper Esther had thrown away. She glanced at it and quickly realized what the problem had been. She thought of Miguel and his 'need to know' policy. She sighed wondering what she would or should do

now. The truth was that she – and Ahmed, too, for that matter – need the income from this job in order to complete their studies and, hopefully with a good reference from Yanne, get a more responsible and better paid job when EPPO closed – which it would do sooner or later. She perceived that what she had just read on Esther's notepaper as a sudden threat to these ambitions.

Eman sighed and reflected on a lifetime's experience of working with people from various cultures. She recognized that this breakdown of communication – or (thinking again of Miguel) the current style of communication apparently designed to cause conflict - would spell the end of the EPPO 'team' in its current form. 'Where is Yanne?' she thought. 'Is there anything he can do to repair this breakdown before it's too late?'

CONFLICT AT EPPO: CLIMAX

All in all, the news was good. Yanne and his wife had been advised by doctors in Sweden that their daughter would make a full recovery. On his way back to Palestine Yanne had stopped by the Head Office in Brussels to learn that EPPO had been receiving positive feedback from local stakeholders and that this feedback had been escalated to the diplomatic level. Particular mention was given to the way in which EPPO appeared 'effectively led'. Consequently, EPPO received further funding in order to expand its operations. Meanwhile, Yanne was informed he should start looking for a successor, as he was in line for a promotion and a re-assignment to a post closer to Sweden, and perhaps even to the EU's project office in Sweden.

The situation that Yanne found on his arrival was 'not as expected', he said. 'I'd come back to congratulate everyone on doing a good job, and no one is here to welcome me'. In fact, only Eman was there to welcome him back to the EPPO office, and one of her first tasks was to inform Yanne that Esther had taken indefinite leave 'on health grounds', while Miguel had taken to 'working from home'. Ahmed had decided to take some of the holiday leave he had owing to him: he had stacked up a huge amount of overtime during the past few months and wanted to spend some time with his family, Eman explained. 'Why all this now?' Yanne asked. 'I'm not sure', Eman replied, 'but perhaps this has something to do with it'.

Eman handed Yanne the notepaper that Esther had thrown away after her conversation with people in Head Office. In both neat and (in places) clearly angry handwriting - including repeat underlining of Miguel's name - the figures that Esther had been querying with Brussels appeared to confirm that over the last year Miguel had been receiving 12% more than his budgeted salary. Ahmed was getting pretty much what was due to him, while Eman was getting more than 60% less of her budgeted salary. Esther herself was getting around 25% less than was budgeted for her. Both Eman and Ahmed received their salary in a combination of local currencies and EURO, while Miguel and Esther received EURO, as did Yanne, along with Swedish Crowns. Yanne's salary did not appear on the notepaper as this came out of a separate budget at Head Office. 'My apologies for breaking the "need to know" policy', Eman said with an ironic smile.

Yanne appeared agitated. 'Clara never told me anything about this,' he said. 'And Miguel?' asked Eman. 'Let me think about this', said Yanne. He then turned and walked to unlock the door of his office. Before entering he looked back and said: 'We need to get everyone together to discuss a few things. Try to arrange a meeting, please, Eman, and today or tomorrow, if possible.' 'I'll do my best', Eman replied. 'I'm sure you will', Yanne said, visibly shaken.

CONFLICT AT EPPO: RESOLUTION?

In the event it took several days to get all five EPPO members in the same room together. They held their meeting. Yanne led the discussion (such that

it was) before announcing the 'good news' that the view from Brussels that EPPO had been 'fulfilling its mission successfully' and would continue to receive funding 'for three or five years, at least'. Finally, Yanne congratulated staff on their 'hard work' and 'team spirit' before finally stating his view that 'lessons have been learned' and 'we have all now got to move on'.

Eman nearly smiled when she heard Yanne's words, as she knew that Esther was using office time and (in hearing distance of Eman) EPPO phone lines to search for a new job. Perhaps in anticipation of leaving, Esther appeared to have become much more efficient and assertive in her work. She no longer asked for information, she demanded it. If she did not receive answers, she wrote and filed a note for the attention of Miguel and Yanne – 'and perhaps eventually Brussels', thought Eman, Gradually, Yanne, Miguel and Ahmed learned to give Esther what she needed when she demanded it; either this, or they avoided her.

Both Eman and Ahmed agreed that this was a better way of working together: clear, consistent and objective communication was the solution. Both also agreed about feeling more able and encouraged to work as a team, and confided more openly with each other than before. Although both Eman and Ahmed need to work at EPPO in order to support their respective families, they are each anxiously awaiting the closing of the office so that they have the necessary experience and their new degrees to find jobs in a more satisfying working environment. However, they each need to find a better-paid alternative before leaving EPPO.

Meanwhile, Eman suspects that Miguel still does not inform Yanne about all details of the NGO's live and prospective projects along with his own 'consultations with key stakeholders'. Yanne began spending more time in Ramallah. He became more proactive in asking for details: he even started learning some Arabic and began practicing it (light-heartedly) on Eman. The staff meetings are now more regular and more designed as opportunities to share information. At each staff meeting each member of staff is asked to report on their activities and account for the resources they use, including Miguel. Frequently at these meetings Miguel cites 'issues of security' as a reason not to give full disclosure. Eman and her colleagues are aware that Yanne and Miguel have separate meetings before and after the full staff meetings. Apart from at meetings, Miguel is seldom seen in the office, preferring to represent EPPO 'in the field' or 'at the business end of our mission'. For Eman, not having Miguel around so often comes as a relief. However, she is anxious about the prospect of Miguel becoming Director of EPPO after Yanne leaves.

CONFLICT AT EPPO: IMPLICATIONS

This case study first appeared as Rasheed and Jackson (2014). Since that time, we co-authors have been working (teaching, researching, consulting), travelling for family and business reasons, reflecting on what 'cross-cultural communication' and 'leadership' might mean in both theory and practice. From our reflections we can re-affirm that, when working with business and management case studies, it is important to work with questions of the 'Who did what when, how and why' variety in order to construct a narrative or story that outlines the key series of events: in this case. Of the type and consequence of leadership interventions defined in general terms in the academic literature and, by comparing what really happened in one case to what might have happened in similar cases, we might come to some recognition of relative successes, failures and, as we emphasize here, 'missed opportunities' for effective leadership. By further asking questions such as 'what if?' we can begin to subject case studies to the aforementioned human powers of meta-representations and thereby as an opportunity to learn more about effective business leadership across organizational, national, cultural and

other pre-defined and yet future-oriented contexts for business leadership practice and research. In other words, working with case studies offers an opportunity to *generalize* from specific cases – which, by definition, describe past events - and learn from these relevant to future opportunities for business research and practice (cf. Yin, 2013). Using case studies in this way is how processes of 'management education' and 'leadership development' might be structured (cf. Poon & Rowley, 2011; Jackson, *forthcoming*).

To illustrate briefly, we believe that this case illustrates how models of leadership that emphasize that leaders need followers in order to be effective in practice deserve further critical attention; that conflict might best be avoided and contained where there is some sustained degree of harmony between effective leadership and effective followership (cf. Northouse, 2015). We propose that this view might communicate readily across organizational, national, regional and any other contexts for business leadership and followership defined with specific reference to 'cultures'. As the world becomes increasingly globalized and interdependent, we might learn from a mix of 'Western' and 'non-Western' sources of wisdom in begin to equate effective or 'successful' leadership increasingly with 'multicultural leadership' (cf. Muna & Zennie, 2011). Correspondingly, Western business schools might look beyond established mainstream management literature and do more to embrace the insight that *effective* leadership can be found and assessed primarily in assessing the quality of the relationships forged by leader and followers, and this regardless of context-specific variables such as nationality, gender, age or ethnicity (cf. Kanai, 2000; Muna & Khoury, 2012; Gupta, 2014; Ren, 2015).

As we have attempted to illustrate throughout this discussion, we hope that by working critically with this case study as a 'lesson in leadership failure', individuals of whatever background might become better placed to communicate and otherwise act as effective leaders in future contexts

EPPO Staff Members (Before the Arrival of Esther)

Yanne: Founding Director of EPPO in Palestine. Male, 58 years old, married, two daughters (family remains in Sweden). Yanne is fluent in Swedish and English and has a Masters degree in Law. Takes a paternalistic approach to management: makes a point of marking each staff member's birthday with a small gift; ends each working day with the words 'best regards to the family' to Ahmed and Eman, for whom he also allows time for urgent family matters and (see below) for self-development.

Miguel: Arrived with Yanne as Deputy Director. Male, 35 years old, single. Miguel grew up to Spanish-British and so is fluent in both Spanish and English along with the French he learned while working as a clerical officer with the European Commission in Brussels. He was selected by senior EU officials in Brussels to support Yanne when establishing the EPPO in Palestine. Unknown to his colleagues at EPPO, Miguel regards this appointment as the gateway to an executive level career in the international NGO sector. Also unknown to his colleagues, he is using his time in Palestine to study part-time for an MBA (by distance) from Brussels.

Clara: Brought in by Yanne to administer the budgets – a vital role of accountability in respect of the Brussels office and in terms of controlling the resources available to provide legal advice and skills training to the PA and other local stakeholders. Clara is Spanish, female, aged 27, a qualified accountant, and fluent in Spanish and English, with some French. Yanne relies on her to manage the details of the operation, reminding him and other staff members about the limits of their responsibilities and capacities. Although not qualified to give legal advice to clients, Clara has proved herself capable of running the EPPO office singlehandedly whenever Yanne or Miguel are absent.

Ahmed: Hired soon after the office opened to provide logistical expertise along with local knowledge. A 34-year-old Palestinian fluent in English, Arabic and Hebrew, he is married with two children. Ahmed spends a lot of time liaising with the local community and so has little direct involvement with the working of the office. Regarded as someone who 'gets jobs done', Yanne supports Ahmed's part-time studies towards a degree in business at a local community college.

Eman: Hired after EPPO had been operating for two years as 'Office Manager', primarily to support Clara. Eman is slightly younger than Clara (25) and married. As a Palestinian born and raised in the USA she is fluent in English and Arabic. When she joined EPPO she already had a degree in Business Administration and soon became regarded as a quick learner under Clara. With Yanne's support, Eman is studying part-time towards a Masters degree.

Esther: Hired as a replacement for Clara and on a contract with an unspecified term. Rumoured to have been brought in as a replacement for Clara in order to work through a divorce that threatened to interrupt her career progression in Brussels: her former husband also works in some branch of the EU. Esther is Belgian, a qualified accountant, and before EPPO had worked as an accountant at the EU in Brussels for several years. (She chooses not to talk about this period to her EPPO colleagues). When she joins EFPO she is 33 years old, 'single', and fluent in French and English with some Spanish.

REFERENCES

Avruch, K. (2002). *Culture and negotiation pedagogy*. Available at www.pon.harvard.edu

Barmeyer, C., & Franklin, P. (Eds.). (forthcoming). *Intercultural Management: European Case Studies - Achieving Synergy from Diversity*. London: Palgrave McMillan.

Brockman, J., & Matson, K. (Eds.). (1995). How Things Are: a Science Tool-Kit for the Mind. London: Phoenix.

Buchanan, D., & Huczynski, A. (1997). *Organizational Behaviour*. Harlow: Prentice Hall.

Drucker, P. (2001). *The Essential Drucker*. London: Harper.

Dunnette, M. (Ed.). (1976). *Handbook of Industrial and Organizational Psychology*. Chicago: Rand McNally.

Giddens, A. (2009). *Sociology* (6th ed.). Cambridge: Polity Press.

Gleitman, H. (1981). *Basic Psychology*. New York: Norton.

Gupta, V. (2014). The Business System of India. Academic Press.

Handy, C. (1993). *Understanding Organisations*. Harmondsworth: Penguin.

Hasegawa, H., & Noronha, C. (Eds.). (2014). *Asian Business And Management Systems: Theory, Practice and Perspectives* (2nd ed.). Basingstoke: Palgrave Macmillan.

HDR. (2014). Sustaining Human Progress: Reducing Vulnerabilities and Building Resilience. In *United Nations Development Report, explanatory note on the 2014 Human Development Report composite indices: Palestine, State of*. New York: United Nations.

Hofstede, G. (1984). *Culture's consequences: International differences in Work-related Values*. London: Sage.

Hofstede, G. (2001). *Culture's Consequences*. London: Sage.

Jackson, K. (2013). East Asian Management: An Overview. Academic Press.

Jackson, K. (forthcoming). Education. In *The Encyclopedia of Social Theory*. New York: John Wiley. doi:10.7208/chicago/9780226389394.001.0001

Jackson, K., Arshynnikova, O., Gasser, N., & Harasyuk, R. (forthcoming) Lynchpin: from diversity to discord and synergy to (near) derailment of a Japanese-Ukrainian infrastructure project. Academic Press.

Kanai, T. (2000). Shin no leadership wa leader to follower no aida ni aru [The real leadership lies between the leader and the followers]. *Hanbai no Hito*, (109), 8-12.

Khoury, G., & Analoui, F. (2010). How Palestinian managers cope with stress. *Journal of Management Development*, 29(3), 282–291. doi:10.1108/02621711011025795

Khoury, G., & Khoury, M. (Eds.), *Cases on Management and Organizational Behavior in An Arab Context*. Hershey, PA: IGI Global. doi:10.4018/978-1-4666-5067-1

McSweeney, B. (2002). Hofstede's model of national cultural differences and their consequences: A triumph of faith - a failure of analysis. *Human Relations*, 55(1), 89–118. doi:10.1177/0018726702055001602

Muna, F. A. (2011). Contextual Leadership: A Study of Lebanese Executives Working in the Lebanon, the GCC Countries, and the United States. *Journal of Management Development*, 30(9), 865–881. doi:10.1108/02621711111164349

Muna, F. A., & Khoury, G. C. (2012). *The Palestinian Executive: Leadership Under Challenging Conditions*. Farnham: Gower.

Muna, F. A., & Zennie, Z. A. (2011). *Developing Multicultural Leaders: The Journey to Leadership*. Basingstoke: Palgrave Macmillan. doi:10.1057/9781137104649

Northouse, P. G. (2015). *Leadership: Theory and Practice*. New York: Sage.

Poon, I., & Rowley, C. (2011). Leadership Development. Academic Press.

Rasheed, R. K. J. (2014). Communication, culture and discord: A case study of avoidable leadership failure in a European-Palestinian NGO. Academic Press.

Ren, S., Wood, R., & Zhu, Y. (2015). *Business Leadership Development in China*. Abingdon: Routledge.

Robbins, S. (2005). Organizational Behavior. Eaglewood Cliffs: Prentice Hall.

Robbins, S. (2012). *Organizational Behavior*. New York: Pearson.

Rowley, C., & Jackson, K. (Eds.). (2011). *Human Resource Management: The Key Concepts*. Abingdon: Routledge.

Rowley, C., & Ulrich, D. (2012). *Leadership in the Asia Pacific, Asia Pacific Business Review Special Issue*. Abingdon: Routledge.

Said, E. (1978). *Orientalism: Western Conceptions of the Orient*. Harmondsworth: Penguin.

Schein, E. (1992). *Organizational Culture and Leadership*. New York: Jossey Bass.

Schein, E. (2012). *Organizational Culture and Leadership*. New York: Jossey Bass.

Senior, B., & Swailes, S. (2012). *Organizational Change*. London: FT-Pearson.

Sperber, D. (1995). How do we communicate? Academic Press.

Sperber, D. (Ed.). (2000). *Metarepresentations*. Oxford: Oxford University Press.

Thomas, K. (1976). Conflict and conflict management. In *Managing Across Diverse Cultures in Asia: Issues and Challenges in a Changing World*. London: Routledge.

Western, S. (2013). *Leadership. A Critical Text* (2nd ed.). London: Sage.

Wilson, D. (2000). Metarepresentation in linguistic communication. Academic Press.

Yin, R. K. (2013). *Case Study Research: Design and Methods* (5th ed.). London: Sage.

Yukl, G. (2005). *Leadership in Organizations* (6th ed.). New York: Pearson.

Yukl, G. (2012). *Leadership in Organizations* (8th ed.). New York: Pearson.

Chapter 11
Leading Virtual Teams:
Conflict and Communication Challenges for Leaders

Daniel Cochece Davis
Illinois State University, USA

Nancy M. Scaffidi-Clarke
Mount Saint Mary College, USA

ABSTRACT

Virtual teams are increasingly common as marketplaces become more global. They offer advantages to employers, including increased time and travel savings, decreased real estate costs, and larger applicant pools. Yet, conflict is inherent in virtual teams, and leaders within virtual teams must confront debilitating conflicts due to technological issues, cultural miscommunication, and restructuring their communication. Though some elements are similar to handling conflict in any team situation, five group factors are especially subject to conflict and manifest differently in effective virtual teams: strategically selecting team members, building effective relationships, fostering trust, facilitating communication, and achieving team goals. Managing any team presents leaders with challenges regarding building relationships, facilitating communication, overcoming barriers and achieving team goals. However, adding geographic distance, cultural differences, and a lack of continuous face-to-face interaction exacerbates these challenges.

INTRODUCTION

Virtual teams are increasingly common as marketplaces become more dynamic, as well as global. Virtual teams offer advantages to employers, including increased time and travel savings, decreased real estate costs, and larger applicant pools. However, with these benefits come new challenges. Conflict is inherent in virtual teams, and leaders within virtual teams must confront debilitating conflicts due to technological issues, cultural miscommunication, and restructuring their communication to include both local and distanced staff. Though some elements are similar to handling conflict in any team situation, five group factors are especially subject to conflict and manifest differently in *effective* virtual teams: strategically selecting team members, building effective relationships, fostering trust, facilitating communication, and achieving team goals.

DOI: 10.4018/978-1-4666-9970-0.ch011

This chapter melds together several traditional elements of team-building, leadership and group communication/dynamics, as well as emerging elements pertaining to how technology impacts each of these traditional elements within a virtual team milieu. Managing any team presents leaders with challenges regarding building relationships, facilitating communication, overcoming barriers and achieving team goals. However, adding geographic distance, cultural differences, and a lack of continuous face-to-face interaction exacerbates these challenges. Virtual team leaders must do everything traditional leaders do, but at a distance. If leaders are going to succeed in virtual environments, they must learn to anticipate the needs and potential problems of the virtual employee and act accordingly. The technological advances of the late twentieth and early twenty-first centuries have made the global community more accessible, expanding the sphere of influence, and bringing together diverse groups. The geographically-situated workplace became non-essential through computer networking, the Internet and other communication aides. Managers are exploring new ways of organizing and efficiently running their companies as a result. Virtual teams are rapidly becoming a commonplace reality by facilitating various groups of people into uniform factions sharing common goals. The key to leading virtual teams, however, is to effectively formulate the groups and then practice routine maintenance to ensure their success.

BACKGROUND

A "virtual team" can be defined as "a collection of individuals who are geographically and/or organizationally or otherwise dispersed and who collaborate via communication and information technologies in order to accomplish a specific goal" (Zigurs, 2003, p. 340). Organizations benefit greatly from the use of virtual teams by enjoying a larger applicant pool, lower real estate costs (e.g., smaller office space to lease), as well as savings from time and lower travel costs (Cascio & Shurygailo, 2003). Conversely, virtual employees receive greater flexibility in work schedules. Although there are benefits for both parties, with increased geographic distance come unique challenges for virtual teams and traditional team leadership (Maruping & Agarwal, 2004).

In order to look at how to *lead* virtual teams, one must first look at definitions of "leadership:" "Leadership is a process used by an individual to influence group members toward the achievement of group goals, where the group members review the influence as legitimate" (Howell & Costley, 2001, p. 4). Clawson (2002) defines "leadership as the ability and the willingness to influence others so that they can respond willingly" (p. 34). These definitions can help delineate "leaders" from "managers," who hold specific organizational positions and help coordinate resources. Clearly, an individual could be both a leader and a manager, but group leaders are not always found in an organization's management positions. With that said, in order to meet the demands of leading teams in virtual environments, virtual team leaders must have a clear understanding of not only how to lead others effectively, but also the unique circumstances associated with communicating in a computer-mediated environment. In this new environment, leaders must overcome typical challenges such as building group cohesion, facilitating communication and achieving team objectives. However, they must accomplish these feats at a distance.

Member Selection

Leading an effective virtual team begins with careful member selection (Bradley & Vozikis, 2004). Blackburn, Furst and Rosen (2003) compare a virtual leader selecting team members to a basketball coach recruiting her/his players. Continuing with this analogy, a coach recruits the most talented players, who have the ability, knowledge, and tenacity to enhance team performance to assure success. When recruiting virtual team members, a good team leader will seek individuals who often possess these same attributes.

More importantly, a successful virtual team needs members who are experts in their field. One of the benefits of virtual teams is that locale does not drive member selection. Virtual team leaders can choose members based on expertise, not geographic proximity (DeRosa, Hantula, Kock & D'Arcy, 2004).

Additionally, Potter and Balthazard (2004) found that while expertise is important in member selection, one should consider individual interaction styles as well. Potter and Balthazard found that negative interaction styles between virtual team members impact satisfaction, thus driving down group performance. In addition, they researched the influence individual personality type had on group productivity. Results indicated that although extroverted (e.g., outgoing) personalities were a great addition to virtual teams, too many extroverted individuals on one team negatively impacted productivity (Potter & Balthazard, 2004). Also, Potter and Balthazard's (2002) earlier research indicated similarities among more traditional face-to-face teams and virtual teams concerning the relationship between interaction style and performance.

Working in a virtual team requires a certain amount of trust among its members (Gibson & Manuel, 2003; Handy, 1995; Hossain & Wigand, 2004); therefore, team leaders must develop that trust within the virtual team and strive to maintain it (Krebs, Hobman, & Bordia, 2006). An easy method of doing this is to ensure the team's goals are met by recruiting only the most skilled members. This competence can help create fertile internal group trust, as individual group members feel more comfortable handing off work when they feel the other members are competent.

Cuevas, Fiore, Salas and Bowers (2004) found that because there are little to no virtual cues in electronic communication, team members are

judged on expertise and other task-related attributes, rather than on their physical and nonverbal characteristics. For this reason, having only the most skilled staff serve on virtual teams is imperative, as less skilled members can jeopardize trust levels within the team.

Although virtual team members must possess a high degree of knowledge in their field, team members must also be extremely comfortable in virtual environments, as learning and understanding can be difficult, depending on how familiar the team member is with the technological system/platform. This is especially the case for new team members, joining an existing virtual team. For this reason, team members should be engaged in their task, but also comfortable in the environment (Kirschner & Van Bruggen, 2004). If a team member does not feel comfortable working virtually, her/his insecurity can negatively impact the team's morale and the project's outcome.

Succinct communication skills are an absolute necessity for any member of virtual teams. Individuals working virtually must be experienced in selecting the appropriate computer mediated communication (CMC) method necessary to convey their ideas, thoughts, or issues. For example, a team can utilize audio or visual conferencing in an effort to provide a natural social presence. The use of newsgroup forums is another resourceful way to provide communication between members. Understanding how to interpret virtual team members' feedback proves invaluable at keeping the team on task, overcoming cultural barriers or clarifying misinformation (Blackburn et al., 2003).

Virtual teams are often comprised of a diverse group of individuals who are different in terms of their competencies, perspectives, organizational affiliation, cultural background, nationality, education, age, and gender (Staples, Wong, & Cameron, 2004). Diversity is one of the many benefits of utilizing a virtual team. In addition, if these individuals are located closer to the customer base, chances are great that they have a better chance of connecting with them

(Staples et al., 2004). Diversity also gives team members a chance to learn about other cultures. However, virtual team leaders must ensure that team members are culturally sensitive to these differences. Further, virtual leaders must realize and share how these differences might positively or negatively impact team communication, norms, and task completion.

A key attribute of a virtual team member is self-motivation. Since there is little opportunity for team leaders to monitor virtual employees' time management, individual performance and work ethic, team members should be self-motivated and autonomous. In addition, since virtual employees do not adhere to traditional United States' 9 am to 5 pm corporate time structure, virtual team members need to manage their schedules efficiently. As a team, this includes consideration of time zones. For example, the United States uses six different winter and seven different summer time zones (USA Time Zones Map, 2009), with the states in each time zone functioning on different times, yet existing simultaneously. While most states shift their clocks to "daylight savings time," some states do not.

Further, virtual team members must motivate themselves accordingly to complete task deadlines and take initiative to communicate with other team members or the leader when necessary. If a team member is having trouble (e.g., technological issues, project deadline, conflict with team member, etc.) and does not communicate it to the team, it could significantly affect the result of the project and impact the group as a whole.

Virtual team leaders must also be aware of situational factors potentially affecting team efficiency. Lee-Kelley (2002) found that certain variables like team size or project duration influenced project managers' perception of project difficulties, more so than communication challenges such as the lack of face-to-face interaction between co-workers or team members.

Organizational culture also has a role in a virtual team's success. Davis (2004) uses Tao-ism, an Asian philosophy, to assess leadership in virtual teams. Davis discusses the principle of Macrocosm/Microcosm, explaining that the same principles hold true for both large and small systems. He uses this Tao principle to analyze the role an organization plays in a virtual team, in that the organizational systems at all levels must support the needs of virtual teams. This includes promoting a culture of trust and effective organizational leadership at each level, as well as removing barriers such as unsupportive top managers.

Building Relationships and Trust

Solid relationships are critical for any team; however, in a virtual environment, establishing relationships between team members is often a predictor of the team's success. Pauleen (2003-2004) found that global leaders consider it essential to develop personal relationships with virtual team members as personal relationships lead to understanding, trust, motivation, and familiarity; all of which contribute to a better working relationship. In traditional office environments, relationships grow more intimate through constant face-to-face interaction over time or "propinquity." For those working virtually, stopping by a co-worker's office to "chit chat" is a non-existent luxury when their co-workers are located all over the world. For this reason, virtual team leaders must be intentional and creative in fostering personal relationships with their virtual team.

Trust is a key component in creating an effective working relationship. This is true in any collaboration, since in order to be a successful team, each member has to feel confident in the team as an entity, but also in each member's individual ability. However, in virtual teams, group trust is often a predictor of success (Zaccaro & Bader, 2003). In virtual environments, establishing trust is sometimes difficult as these teams often live abroad, collaborate often via technological interaction for short-term projects, and do not always have the opportunity to form strong bonds

(Pauleen & Yoong, 2001a; Powell, Piccoli, & Ives, 2004; Roebuck, Brock & Moodie, 2004; Qureshi & Vogel, 2001; Zaccaro & Bader, 2003). Further, technological interaction provides very little nonverbal communication; without these nonverbal cues, teammates may find it difficult to assess the dependability of another, thus leading to potential trust issues (Tyran, Tyran, & Shepherd, 2003). Without trust, team members may try to avoid interaction with other team members. Zigurs (2003) also points out that, without trust, team effectiveness, satisfaction, and commitment decrease. This can undermine the team and serve as a barrier for goal attainment (Bradley & Vozikis, 2004). However, Jarvenpaa, Knoll, and Leidner (1998) found evidence of "swift trust," which was a term originally developed to refer to the early establishment of trust in temporary face-to-face teams. Jarvenpaa et al. found that in global virtual teams, trust was associated with the perception of team members' integrity, ability, and benevolence. Although in Jarvenpaa, Shaw, and Staples' (2004) research, trust had the greatest impact in situations with weak structure and little impact in strongly structured conditions. This implies that when there is less uncertainty in the team, the role of trust weakens. Thus, one can infer that trust is most important when there are unclear roles or expectations.

Creating a sense of community within a team helps to strengthen relationships and positively reinforces group performance. Kayworth and Leider (2001-2002) found that there was a significant relationship between the perceived leadership ability of a virtual team leader and her/his ability to mentor her/his team. As such, building relationships is a key component of an effective distance leader.

Research indicates that face-to-face interaction, used strategically at the beginning of a relationship, as well as during key points throughout (e.g., to establish a shared vision, to overcome anxiety, tend to a potential crisis), is optimal in creating a sense of community (Bradley & Vozikis, 2004;

Connaughton & Daly, 2004; Thompsen, 2000; Zakaria, Amelinckx, & Wilemon, 2004). While this may not always be feasible for all virtual teams, virtual leaders should strive to visit all team members in the beginning of the relationship. This helps leaders establish an extended presence and get to know her/his staff (Qureshi & Vogel, 2001). By getting to know the people involved on one's team, the leader has a better chance of foreseeing potential issues, learning what motivates and empowers team members, and demonstrates the leader's accessibility: all of which are crucial in succeeding in a virtual environment. If face-to-face interaction is not feasible, personalized electronic interactions are another way to build successful online relationships.

Although many leaders assume that communication with virtual team members should always relate to the project task, virtual team leaders must take advantage of every opportunity to build personal relationships with virtual team members (Connnaughton & Daly, 2004). Hart and McLeod (2003) found that co-workers with strong personal relationships sent more task-related messages than those with weaker relationships. Further, they found that the messages exchanged between those with stronger relationships were more concise than those with weaker relationships. Thus, stronger personal relationships facilitate productive work relationships (Hart & McLeod, 2003).

Although email is not the most effective way to facilitate virtual team relationships (Pauleen & Yoong, 2001a), Connaughton and Daly (2004) found instances where email was effective at establishing a relationship between a distance *leader* and virtual team members. As part of their research, Connnaughton and Daly interviewed several senior managers, project leaders, and global organization executives. They note an interview, where "Vincent" sends weekly updates via email to all virtual team members. These updates contain pertinent business information to help keep them connected to each other and the project. However, at the end of each update,

Vincent speaks of something that happened to him personally during the week. Vincent explains that these personal stories help connect him to his team members even though they are located across the globe. Moreover, when Vincent visits his team members at remote locations, they can have both formal and informal conversations, which create a more relaxed environment for business. This serves to minimize the perceived distance and may help combat the feeling of isolation often occurring while working at a distance. Leonardi, Jackson, and Marsh (2004) found that there was almost a double-edged sword of distance in that many virtual workers were pleased to be out of the office environment and felt able to accomplish more work, but the lack of office interaction contributed to their feelings of isolation.

In order to enhance the feeling of community in virtual teams, members must feel motivated and supported by their team, leader, and organization. Electronic communication methods can be successful in lending support and motivating a virtual team. Kostner (2001) found that sharing organizational success stories across locations served as a motivational tool for both local and distance employees. Staples and Cameron's (2004) findings suggest that motivation is positively associated with the perception of the significance of a team member's task. This serves as a reminder to virtual leaders that they must consistently remind team members of the importance of each task assigned. When employees feel the tasks they perform are significant, and contribute to the overall success of the team, company or society, both the team and the organization are positively influenced (Staples & Cameron, 2004). In addition, based on Whitehead's (2001) findings, virtual leaders should allot time at the end of project for team reflection. Whitehead suggests that recognizing each member's contribution gives team members a sense of accomplishment and empowers them to succeed. Project reflection also serves as a learning tool and adds to member accountability. However, project management also gives team members a sense of empowerment. Having a sense of empowerment is more central in a virtual environment than in a traditional face-to-face office environment: Kikrman, Rosen, Tesluk and Gibson (2004) found that increased empowerment correlates to an increase in both process improvement and job satisfaction in virtual teams.

Creating an atmosphere where virtual team members feel like they are a vital part of their team and the organization, positively contributes to the overall feeling of community within the team. Virtual leaders must strive to create a sense of team spirit both within their team and within the organization as a whole: "Virtual teams are hungry for the warmth and glue that [the] sense of team messages create" (Kostner, 2001, p. 127). When virtual team members feel connected to the team and identify with the organization's vision and purpose, virtual team members are likely to be more committed to the organization and thus more productive (Solomon, 2001).

Choosing the Right Communication Method

Although there are many benefits to using virtual teams, there are also unique challenges. When team members are from all parts of the world and work at a distance, communication becomes a primary issue. Distance, cultural differences, and time zone issues will always interfere with smooth communication between group members (Olaniran, 2004): "Successful virtual team facilitators must be able to manage the whole spectrum of communication strategies via new technologies as well as human and social processes, and often do it across cultures" (Pauleen & Yoong, 2001a, p. 190). Further, because of the absence of nonverbal cues (e.g., a smile, nodding of the head, or a perplexed look), computer mediated communication (CMC) does not reveal signals showing that one understands (Driskell, Radtke, & Salas, 2003). For this reason, although there may be many CMC methods available to them, virtual leaders must always consider the appropriate CMC method, as well the particular audience to which it is targeted (Clutterbuck, 2004; Martins, Gilson, & Maynard, 2004). In addition, virtual team members need to dedicate more effort and time to ensure the message sent was understood by teammates (Driskell et al., 2003).

In a virtual environment, ascertaining the appropriate CMC channel to deliver a message is a frequent, but important, task. Many virtual team leaders become so entranced with the benefits of email that the team corresponds only through email. However, successful virtual leaders realize that each method of CMC is valuable for the appropriate situation (Pauleen & Yoong, 2001a).

Although email is an asset to virtual teams, it is not as useful for building relationships, fostering trust, creating group cohesion or communicating potential crisis situations (Pauleen & Yoong, 2001a). However, email is essential for coordinating business processes (e.g., relaying of information) and corresponding with team members. Because email gives the sender/receiver more time to construct their thoughts using appropriate words/phrases, email is more beneficial to non-native English speakers than communicating via phone (Grosse, 2002). However, Carlson, George, Burgoon, Adkins, and White's (2004) research indicates that for the same reason text-based messages help overcome language barriers, it is also the easiest form of communication in which to deceive others.

Although a more conventional communication method, telephones are still a reliable way in which to establish relationships, or to communicate issues of a sensitive nature (Pauleen & Yoong, 2001a). In Pauleen and Yoong's (2001a) study, participants were able to establish rapport via phone early in the team's relationship and, after the relationship was established, utilize email for daily/weekly communication. Participants relying solely on email for creating rapport, as well as maintaining communication, experienced many

miscommunications attributable to the lack of early relationship-building.

Desktop conferencing is relatively new in comparison with other communication methods, allowing a group of individuals to dial into a conference call while also providing visual pictures of each attendee in addition to audio functions; these features can be somewhat problematic. The technological infrastructure of other countries may not be equipped to handle such technology, potentially resulting in slow connections and high connection costs for some conference attendees.

Another CMC is synchronous chat or instant message. Synchronous chat can be a valuable tool to establish informal dialogue with team members. Pauleen and Yoong (2001a) found that synchronous chat was a preferable way to fortify relationships with virtual team members, as it allowed facilitators to create spontaneous, informal conversation. Further, Pauleen and Yoong (2001b) found having a variety of communication media available to virtual facilitators may increase inventiveness as well as relationship-building, but may also lead to confusion and further difficulties. Kayworth and Leidner (2001-2002) found virtual facilitators using many different methods of CMC were more satisfied with their ability to communicate with their team.

Understanding Culture

Although understanding that each communication medium works best under different circumstances is essential in communicating effectively in virtual environments, one must also consider the audiences. In virtual teams, specifically global virtual teams, members can reside in any country, speak a variety of different languages, can be any age, ethnicity, or religion. While this presents many opportunities for creativity, it also introduces unique challenges (Kayworth & Leidner, 2001-2002). Culture dictates how an individual processes and interprets the environment around them. However, one's culture may also account for many of the misinterpretations suffered when communicating (Bell & Kozlowski, 2002; Pauleen & Yoong, 2001b); distance and lack of nonverbal cues (i.e., body language) exacerbates this situation. As a result, communication becomes more complex and opportunities for misunderstandings increase.

Culture determines an individual's communication style, but also how they relate to others. Zakaria, Amelinckx, and Wilemon (2004) reference Edward Hall's Contextual Theory (1976) in their study regarding global virtual teams. Contextual Theory posits that to understand communication and behavioral differences concerning culture, one must first examine the context in which it occurs. Different cultures fall into one of two categories: high context or low context. Cultures with a high context receive their behavioral cues from their external environment, whereas those with a low context rely less on their environment for cues on how to behave. Individuals from high context cultures tend to use more indirect or understated communication styles, whereas individuals from low context cultures prefer more direct communication with less uncertainty (Zakaria et al., 2004). This information helps those facilitating global virtual teams, as individuals from low context cultures will need information presented in a more direct manner, whereas individuals from high context cultures may be less comfortable with such direct communication, though they may also be more aware of the subtleties expressed through indirect communication.

Effective virtual leaders must also understand that different cultures have their own value system. Being aware of the cultural values of team members, and communicating with them appropriately, not only demonstrates a mutual understanding within the team, but also aids in accomplishing project goals more efficiently. Lee (2002) found that email is not a popular communication method in East Asia. Those in Lee's study explained that email was a disrespectable method of communication as it demonstrates a lack of regard for the person to which you are communicating. Further, East Asian individuals were not responding to emails in a timely fashion. Lee discovered that this was due to them taking time to construct an appropriate response and get additional feedback on the document prior to sending it. Those in Lee's study were taking extra care to be diligent in their response; however, this delay in response time can lead to serious miscommunication, and negatively affect trust between teammates (Lee, 2002).

Lee's (2002) study begets another common cultural miscommunication: collectivism versus individualism. Cultures valuing collectivism recognize the importance of working as a team and relationship-building. Individuals from these cultures may find it particularly challenging to work at a distance. Feelings of isolation, more common to those who work at a distance, may interfere with project goals. In addition, there may be further miscommunications within the team, as those from individualistic cultures may view their collectivist teammates as needy; whereas those from collectivist cultures may view their individualistic team members as non-team players or discourteous (Zakaria et al., 2004). Virtual leaders need to recognize these cultural differences as potential issues early on in the team-building process, and implement appropriate solutions that work for the group. Connaughton and Daly (2003) suggest that prior to working with those from another country, the individual should learn about the culture and communication behaviors so s/he can communicate more effectively.

Virtual team leaders must also be aware of communication issues associated with these intra-organizational and inter-organizational boundaries, in addition to cultural and geographic boundaries (Fernandez, 2003). Crossing organizational boundaries may include individuals working virtually with different departments within the same organization, different branches of the same organization or different organizations entirely. Communication is usually less problematic between peers or teammates, but more difficult when different levels of seniority are introduced into the group (Grosse, 2002). Pauleen and Yoong (2001b) found that when different organizations were collaborating on virtual projects, organizational culture and policy issues were most prominent as potential problems.

SOLUTIONS AND RECOMMENDATIONS

The scholarship concerning virtual team organizations has numerous suggestions for the establishment of successful teams. The research overwhelmingly indicates that, if all possible, face-to-face interaction is essential in the early stages of virtual team formation and at key points throughout the team's relationship. In addition, utilizing personal messages to build relationships and group trust proves to be beneficial for mutual understanding, trust, motivation, and familiarity; all of which lead to more productive working relationships (Pauleen, 2003-2004). Further, Pauleen (2003-2004) suggests that virtual leaders should maintain relationships with virtual team members after task completion, for future team needs and opportunities. Kayworth and Leidner (2001-2002) found that out of many different perceived leadership traits, one's ability to mentor was most related to perceived leadership ability. Those interviewed also mentioned communication effectiveness and role clarity as perceived leadership behavior.

Accessibility is important for all leaders, but even more so in a virtual environment. Virtual leaders should establish a presence at the beginning of a relationship/project. This helps build relationships, but also supports the thought of the leader being accessible to answer questions, articulate goals and expectations, as well as provide guidance and feedback. Hertel, Konradt, and Orlikowski (2004) found positive correlations between team effectiveness and management practices associated with goal, task and outcome mutual dependence. In addition, quick and accurate responses to team questions avoid team members feeling isolated (Bell & Kozlowski, 2002; Bradley & Vozikis, 2004; Zigurs, 2003).

When establishing a presence, virtual leaders should use this time to set clear goals and define team member roles. Carlson et al. (2004) found that discrepancy in team member roles was the main cause of electronic communication deception in virtual teams. In addition, by setting clear expectations for projects, as well as team communication, workers can be more autonomous (Bell & Kozlowski, 2002).

Low levels of group trust can potentially lead to misinterpretation of information by group members, increasing the possibility for conflict. For this reason, virtual leaders must successfully predict and manage group conflict. Although some level of conflict is necessary for groups to achieve their goals, this conflict must be managed (Griffith, Mannix, & Neale, 2003). Montoya-Weiss, Massey, and Song's (2001) research indicated that successful virtual teams managed conflict using either competitive or collaborative management style. Paul, Samarah, Seetharaman, and Mykytyn (2004) found similar results regarding collaborative conflict management style. Collaborative style was found to positively influence satisfaction and member participation.

FUTURE RESEARCH DIRECTIONS

The scholarship concerning virtual team organizations is consistent. However, moving further into the world of virtual teaming, additional research is necessary on the use of spyware software programs, and the outsourcing of jobs. As a way to protect confidential information, block derogatory content, and monitor employee efficiency and activities, virtual groups can utilize software programs such as *Proxy* and *Superscout*. These programs allow project leaders or group administrators to act as virtual moderators, isolating and intercepting any team policy violations. Although this software may increase employee productivity, it may also damage the virtual team morale, as it indicates a lack of trust between the management and staff. Aside from low morale, the lack of trust may also manifest itself into insubordination and disrespect for the principles of the company as well as the team.

Because building virtual teams broadens the pool of qualified candidates for team positions, outsourcing to a foreign market has become a low-cost solution to an employment crisis. However, it is also a derisive issue. Outsourcing causes consternation among local employees over the potential lack of jobs. Because foreign workers from second or third world countries generally cost less to employ than staff from developed nations, workers in the U.S. fear the loss of jobs abroad. Creating a virtual team with both foreign and domestic employees may cause consternation and conflict between the teammates. The managers of a virtual team must ensure an equal playing field between all employees, regardless of socio-economic condition or geographic location.

CONCLUSION

This chapter melds together several traditional elements of team-building, leadership and group communication/dynamics, as well as emerging elements pertaining to how technology impacts each of these traditional elements within a team milieu. Managing any team presents leaders with challenges regarding building relationships, facilitating communication, overcoming barriers and achieving team goals. However, adding geographic distance, cultural differences, and a lack of continuous face-to-face interaction exacerbates these challenges. Virtual team leaders must do everything traditional leaders do, but at a distance. If leaders are going to succeed in virtual environments, they must learn to anticipate the needs and potential problems of the virtual employee and act accordingly.

REFERENCES

Bell, B. S., & Kozlowski, S. W. J. (2002). A typology of virtual teams: Implications for effective leadership. *Group & Organization Management*, *27*(1), 14–49. doi:10.1177/1059601102027001003

Blackburn, R., Furst, S., & Rosen, B. (2003). Building a winning virtual team. In C. B. Gibson & S. Cohen (Eds.), *Virtual teams that work: Creating conditions for virtual team effectiveness* (pp. 95–120). San Francisco, CA: Jossey-Bass.

Bradley, W. E., & Vozikis, G. S. (2004). Trust in virtual teams. In S. H. Godar & S. P. Ferris (Eds.), *Virtual and collaborative teams: Process, technologies, and practice* (pp. 99–113). Hershey, PA: Idea Group Publishing. doi:10.4018/978-1-59140-204-6.ch006

Carlson, J. R., George, J. F., Burgoon, J. K., Adkins, M., & White, C. H. (2004). Deception in computer-mediated communication. *Group Decision and Negotiation*, *13*(1), 5–28. doi:10.1023/B:GRUP.0000011942.31158.d8

Cascio, W. F., & Shurygailo, S. (2003). E-leadership and virtual teams. *Organizational Dynamics*, *31*(4), 362–376. doi:10.1016/S0090-2616(02)00130-4

Clawson, J. G. (2003). *Level three leadership: Getting below the surface* (2nd ed.). Upper Saddle River, NJ: Prentice Hall.

Clutterbuck, D. (2004). *The challenge of the virtual team*. Training Journal.

Connaughton, S. L., & Daly, J. A. (2003). Long distance leadership: Communicative strategies for leading virtual teams. In D. Pauleen (Ed.), *Virtual teams: Projects, protocols and processes* (pp. 116–144). Hershey, PA: Idea Group.

Connaughton, S. L., & Daly, J. A. (2004). Leading from afar: Strategies for effectively leading in virtual teams. In S. Godar & S. P. Ferris (Eds.), *Virtual and collaborative teams: Projects, protocols and processes* (pp. 49–75). Hershey, PA: Idea Group. doi:10.4018/978-1-59140-204-6.ch004

Cuevas, H. M., Fiore, S. M., Salas, E., & Bowers, C. A. (2004). Virtual teams as sociotechnical systems. In S. Godar (Ed.), *Virtual and collaborative teams* (pp. 1–16). Hershey, PA: Idea Group. doi:10.4018/978-1-59140-204-6.ch001

Davis, D. D. (2004). The Tao of leadership in virtual teams. *Organizational Dynamics*, *33*(1), 47–62. doi:10.1016/j.orgdyn.2003.11.004

DeRosa, D. M., Hantula, D. A., Kock, N., & D'Arcy, J. (2004). Trust and leadership in virtual teamwork: A media naturalness perspective. *Human Resource Management*, *43*(2-3), 219–232. doi:10.1002/hrm.20016

Driskell, J. E., Radtke, P. H., & Salas, E. (2003). Virtual teams: Effects of technological mediation on team performance. *Group Dynamics*, *7*(4), 297–323. doi:10.1037/1089-2699.7.4.297

Fernandez, W. D. (2003). Trust and the trust placement process in metateam projects. In D. Pauleen (Ed.), *Virtual teams: Projects, protocols and processes* (pp. 57–69). Hershey, PA: Idea Group.

Griffith, T. L., Mannix, E. A., & Neale, M. A. (2003). Conflict in virtual teams. In C. Gibson & S. Cohen (Eds.), *Virtual teams that work: Creating conditions for virtual team effectiveness* (pp. 335–352). San Francisco, CA: Jossey-Bass.

Grosse, C. U. (2002). Managing communication within virtual intercultural teams. *Business Communication Quarterly*, *65*(4), 22–38. doi:10.1177/108056990206500404

Handy, C. (1995). Trust and virtual organization: How do you manage people whom you do not see. *Harvard Business Review*, *73*(3), 40–50.

Hart, R. K., & McLeod, P. L. (2003). Rethinking team building in geographically dispersed teams: One message at a time. *Organizational Dynamics*, *31*(4), 352–361. doi:10.1016/S0090-2616(02)00131-6

Hertel, G., Konradt, U., & Orlikowski, B. (2004). Managing distance by interdependence: Goal setting, task interdependence, and team-based rewards in virtual teams. *European Journal of Work and Organizational Psychology*, *13*(1), 1–28. doi:10.1080/13594320344000228

Hossain, L. W., & Wigand, R. T. (2004). ICT enabled virtual collaboration through trust. *Journal of Computer-Mediated Communication*, *10*(1). Retrieved from http://jcmc.indiana.edu/vol10/issue1/hossain_wigand.html

Howell, J. P., & Costley, D. L. (2001). *Understanding behaviors for effective leadership*. Upper Saddle River, NJ: Prentice Hall.

Jarvenpaa, S. L., Knoll, K., & Leidner, D. E. (1998). Is anybody out there? Antecedents of trust in global virtual teams. *Journal of Management Information Systems*, *14*(4), 29–64. doi:10.1080/07421222.1998.11518185

Jarvenpaa, S. L., Shaw, T. R., & Staples, D. S. (2004). Toward contextualized theories of trust: The role of trust in global virtual teams. *Information Systems Research*, *15*(3), 250–267. doi:10.1287/isre.1040.0028

Kayworth, T. R., & Leidner, D. E. (2001-2002). Leadership effectiveness in global virtual teams. *Journal of Management Information Systems*, *18*(3), 7–41.

Kikrman, B. L., Rosen, B., Tesluk, P. E., & Gibson, C. B. (2004). The impact of team empowerment on virtual team performance: The moderating role of face-to-face interaction. *Academy of Management Journal*, *47*(2), 175–192. doi:10.2307/20159571

Kirschner, P. A., & Van Bruggen, J. (2004). Learning and understanding in virtual teams. *Cyberpsychology & Behavior, 7*(2), 135–139. doi:10.1089/109493104323024401 PMID:15140357

Kostner, J. (2001). *Bionic e-teamwork: How to build collaborative virtual teams at hyperspeed.* Chicago, IL: Dearborn Trade.

Krebs, S., Hobman, E. V., & Bordia, P. (2006). Virtual team and group member dissimilarity: Consequences for the development of trust. *Small Group Research, 37,* 721–741. doi:10.1177/1046496406294886

Lee, O. (2002). Cultural differences in e-mail use of virtual teams: A critical social theory perspective. *Cyberpsychology & Behavior, 5,* 227–232. doi:10.1089/109493102760147222 PMID:12123245

Lee-Kelley, L. (2002). Situational leadership: Managing the virtual project team. *Journal of Management Development, 21,* 461–476. doi:10.1108/02621710210430623

Leonardi, P. M., Jackson, M., & Marsh, N. (2004). The strategic use of "distance" among virtual team members: A multi-dimensional communication model. In S. Godar (Ed.), *Virtual and collaborative teams* (pp. 156–171). Hershey, PA: Idea Group. doi:10.4018/978-1-59140-204-6.ch009

Martins, L. L., Gilson, L. L., & Maynard, M. T. (2004). Virtual teams: What do we know and where do we go from here? *Journal of Management, 30,* 805–835. doi:10.1016/j.jm.2004.05.002

Maruping, L. M., & Agarwal, R. (2004). Managing team interpersonal processes through technology: A task–technology fit perspective. *The Journal of Applied Psychology, 89,* 975–990. doi:10.1037/0021-9010.89.6.975 PMID:15584836

Montoya-Wiess, M. M., Massey, A. P., & Song, M. (2001). Getting it together: Temporal coordination and conflict management in global virtual teams. *Academy of Management Journal, 44,* 1251–1263. doi:10.2307/3069399

Olaniran, B. (2004). Computer-mediated communication in cross-cultural virtual teams. *International and Intercultural Communication Annual, 27,* 142–166.

Paul, S., Samarah, I. M., Seetharaman, P., & Mykytyn, P. P. (2004-2005). An empirical investigation of collaborative conflict management style in group support system- based global virtual teams. *Journal of Management Information Systems, 21,* 185–222.

Pauleen, D. J. (2003-2004). An inductively derived model of leader-initiated relationship building with virtual team members. *Journal of Management Information Systems, 20,* 227–256.

Pauleen, D. J., & Yoong, P. (2001a). Facilitating virtual team relationships via internet and conventional communication channels. *Internet Research, 11,* 190–202. doi:10.1108/10662240110396450

Pauleen, D. J., & Yoong, P. (2001b). Relationship building and the use of ICT in boundary-crossing virtual teams: A facilitator's perspective. *Journal of Information Technology, 16,* 205–220. doi:10.1080/02683960110100391

Potter, R. E., & Balthazard, P. A. (2002). Virtual team interaction styles: Assessment and effects. *International Journal of Human-Computer Studies, 56,* 423–443. doi:10.1006/ijhc.2002.1001

Potter, R. E., & Balthazard, P. A. (2004). Understanding composition and conflict in virtual teams. In S. Godar (Ed.), *Virtual and collaborative teams* (pp. 35–47). Hershey, PA: Idea Group. doi:10.4018/978-1-59140-204-6.ch003

Powell, A., Piccoli, G., & Ives, B. (2004). Virtual teams: A review of current literature and directions for future research. *The Data Base for Advances in Information Systems, 35*(1), 6–36. doi:10.1145/968464.968467

Qureshi, S., & Vogel, D. (2001). Adaptiveness in virtual teams: Organisational challenges and research directions. *Group Decision and Negotiation, 10*(1), 27–46. doi:10.1023/A:1008756811139

Roebuck, D., Brock, S., & Moodie, D. (2004). Using a simulation to explore the challenges of communicating in a virtual team. *Business Communication Quarterly, 67*, 359–367. doi:10.1177/1080569904268083

Solomon, C. M. (2001). Managing virtual teams. *Workforce, 80*(6), 60–64.

Staples, D. S., & Cameron, A. F. (2004). Creating positive attitudes in virtual team members. In S. Godar (Ed.), *Virtual and collaborative teams* (pp. 76–113). Hershey, PA: Idea Group. doi:10.4018/978-1-59140-204-6.ch005

Staples, D. S., Wong, I. K., & Cameron, A. F. (2004). Best practices for virtual team effectiveness. In S. Godar (Ed.), *Virtual and collaborative teams* (pp. 160–185). Hershey, PA: Idea Group. doi:10.4018/978-1-59140-166-7.ch007

Thompsen, J. A. (2000). Effective leadership of virtual project teams. *Futurics, 24*(3/4), 85–91.

Tyran, K. L., Tyran, C. K., & Shepherd, M. (2003). Exploring emerging leadership in virtual teams. In C. Gibson & S. Cohen (Eds.), *Virtual teams that work: Creating conditions for virtual team effectiveness* (pp. 183–195). San Francisco, CA: Jossey-Bass.

USA Time Zones Map with Current Local Time. (2009). Retrieved August 11, 2009, from http://www.worldtimezone.com/time-usa12.php

Whitehead, P. (2001). Team building and culture change: Well–trained and committed teams can successfully roll out culture change programs. *Journal of Change Management, 2*, 184–193. doi:10.1080/714042495

Zaccaro, S. L., & Bader, P. (2003). E-leadership and the challenges of leading e-teams: Minimizing the bad and maximizing the good. *Organizational Dynamics, 31*, 377–387. doi:10.1016/S0090-2616(02)00129-8

Zakaria, N., Amelinckx, A., & Wilemon, D. (2004). Working together apart? Building a knowledge–sharing culture for global virtual teams. *Creativity and Innovation Management, 13*(1), 15–29. doi:10.1111/j.1467-8691.2004.00290.x

Zigurs, I. (2003). Leadership in virtual teams: Oxymoron or opportunity? *Organizational Dynamics, 31*, 339–351. doi:10.1016/S0090-2616(02)00132-8

ADDITIONAL READING

Duarte, D. L., & Tennant Snyder, N. (2006). *Mastering Virtual Teams: Strategies, Tools, and Techniques That Succeed.* Jossey Bass Business and Management Series.

Fisher, K., & Fisher, M. (2001). *The Distance Manager: A Hands On Guide to Managing Off-Site Employees and Virtual Teams.* McGraw-Hill.

Gerke, S. K., & Berens, L. V. (2003). *Quick Guide to Interaction Styles and Working Remotely: Strategies for Leading and Working in Virtual Teams.* Huntington Beach, CA: Telos Publications.

Gibbs, J. L., Nekrassova, D., Grushina, S. V., & Wahab, S. A. (2008). Reconceptualizing virtual teaming from a constitutive perspective: Review, redirection, and research agenda. In C. S. Beck (Ed.), *Communication Yearbook 32* (pp. 187–230). New York: Routledge.

Gibson, C. B., & Cohen, S. (Eds.). (2003). *Virtual teams that work: Creating conditions for virtual team effectiveness.* San Francisco, CA: Jossey-Bass.

Kostner, J. (1994). *Virtual Leadership: Secrets from the Round Table for the Multi-Site Manager.* New York: Warner Books.

Nemiro, J., Beyerlein, M. M., Bradley, L., & Beyerlein, S. (Eds.). (2008). *The Handbook of High Performance Virtual Teams: A Toolkit for Collaborating Across Boundaries.* San Francisco, CA: Jossey Bass.

KEY TERMS AND DEFINITIONS

Virtual Team: Any team where at least one team member participates through an electronically facilitated presence, rather than a physical face-to-face presence.

Virtual Team Communication: The communication facilitating a virtual team's activities.

Chapter 12
Conflict of Interest or Community of Collaboration?
Leadership, SME Network Dialectics, and Dialogs

Tom Cockburn
The Leadership Alliance, Inc., Canada

Blanca Maria Martins
Universitat Politécnica de Catalunya, Spain

Peter A. C. Smith
The Leadership Alliance, Inc., Canada

Ramon Salvador Valles
Universitat Politécnica de Catalunya, Spain

ABSTRACT

In this chapter we aim to consider both dialectical and dialogical systems, local and regional policies and practice implications for the communication and management of the creative as well as destructive conflict within networks and what else may be needed by cooperating parties as a support infrastructure to assist the development and growth of SME innovation networks. We firstly outline key terms, concepts and issues about innovation, collaboration and the goals set for business incubators by the European Union and globally, contrasting these with each other. We provide an overview of the role of key stakeholders, systems and research analyses, discussion and recommendations indicating our own. These recommendations will be informed by some case studies we have been engaged in as well as the wider research literature canon on these topics.

INTRODUCTION: DIALECTICS AND DIALOGS IN BUSINESS INNOVATION PRACTICE

National and global business environments are in a constant state of complex, evolutionary flux, although there are times when such change is faster or more radical than others. The global business environment has been described as a Volatile Uncertain Complex and Ambiguous (VUCA) context (Smith & Cockburn, 2013, pp.6-7, Lawrence, 2013). Whatever the complexity dynamics and speed of change, countries, businesses and individual organizations must match or exceed their external environment's rate of change in order to maintain or develop their position. In such turbulent times there is a greater likelihood of conflict and fractures in professional or com-

DOI: 10.4018/978-1-4666-9970-0.ch012

mercial networks especially where debate is stifled or it is simply assumed by leaders that there is only 'one best way' to achieve success. However the process is a complex one rather than an inevitable linear or 'unidirectional' one and 'surprise' is the key feature of global business complexity (Smith and Cockburn, 2014).

This chapter seeks to briefly describe and discuss key debates concerning public and private sector policy-making efforts geared to 'scaffolding' the growth of innovation clusters or networks for supporting collaboration between local or regional groups of Small to Medium Enterprises (SME). The discussion here includes examining the policy development, implementation and practices aimed at sustainable management of potential conflict between the parties and individuals involved. The avowed aims of such policies for funded networking efforts are to help the SMEs individually and within the network, to 'stand on their own feet' as commercial businesses with marketable goods and services generating employment in their area.

We do not use the term dialectics here in the strict, deterministic Hegelian manner of rising contradictions inevitably leading to struggle, contention and ultimate synthesis at a new, higher level of praxis. We refer to dialectics as rational debate, argumentation, conflict or contention between parties that may be overt or may exist latent within the interplay of dialog between them and erupt or evolve from discussions concerning the best way forward or the allocation of resources. Such conflict may not always be deemed wholly destructive if it leads to positive change.

Open and frank dialog incorporating dialectics and challenges is a means to promote greater collaboration and harmony by attempting to clarify potential or actual misunderstandings, anticipate, forestall or otherwise 'surface' and address unspoken or latent forms of tension in the network. However, we also recognize that collaboration may pose problems for some or all parties from time to time. The interplay of dialog and dialectics is a multidimensional and multispiral process over

time as Kodama (2005, pp. 49-51) suggests when describing the concept of 'dialectical dialog'. Target audiences for this chapter therefore include academics, policymakers, consultants and students studying management, Politics and Government, Communication, business strategy, information systems and knowledge management.

Three cases are used to illustrate key aspects of the need to creatively balance dialog and dialectics and aim for a balance of forces and drivers promoting collaboration between businesses in networks of Small to Medium Enterprises (S.M.Es). We provide some broad guidelines for improving policy development and implementation including some relevant Human Resource Management policies and training points.

Success for a country's economy, as for a business company or network within the country, comes from policies and practices that provide it with the necessary competencies and freedom to permit the maintenance and appropriate development of products for their business environments - this is termed Right to Market (R2M) (Koudal & Coleman (2005). For a business organization, R2M means introducing the right products and/ or services at the right time in the right contexts with the right supply chains, and then continually updating, optimizing, and retiring them as necessary. For a country the same principles apply except that governments aim for beneficial policies and regulations such as international trade treaties, import-export business support, monetary policies, internal market regulations and the like. R2M involves the complex, dynamic interplay of dialog and dialectics at various points in the supply chain.

Business organizations must also maintain their economic, social and ecological policies consistent with those of the country in which they operate and with countries where they do business, or where they have impact. Thus for a business organization or country to be classified as operating "sustainably" care must be exercised to make sure that R2M does not negatively impact relevant ecological or social systems – this is termed Right for Market (R4M) (Coakes, Smith and Dee, 2011). Such competent national and company management collaborative dialog in action then provides the fundamentals and stimulus necessary for the country's citizens to prosper and maintain high social and environmental standards and to reduce dialectical frictions or fissures developing.

Market advantage is increasingly located for firms, regions and countries in 'intangibles' such as intellectual resources and capabilities within the employees or population skill-base, business systems and intellectual property. To address the challenges and opportunities presented by today's complex and often unpredictable markets, a country, innovation network or individual firm must be able to combine resources in novel ways to develop new products and services, dispose of, or reconfigure, resources that are no longer relevant, and acquire new resources. The ability to manipulate resources continuously and rapidly - to innovate - becomes an adaptive capability that is not easily imitated by competitors which enables a country or its in-country firms to maintain, or improve, their current market positions.

Innovation then can be defined as the process of bringing new problem-solving ideas into use (Amabile, 1988; Glynn, 1996; Kanter, 1983). The emphasis here is on the phrase bringing new ideas '*into use*'. Tidd (2001) argues that the mere invention of new knowledge is insufficient and Sullivan (1998) and Teece (1998) both say that innovation has only occurred if the new knowledge has been implemented or commercialized in some way. A number of other authors echo that viewpoint (Pinchot, 1985; Thornberry, 2001; Zahra, 1985) asserting that without some form of entrepreneurial activity to exploit opportunities as they arise, innovation remains little more than an 'aspirational' destination, rather than a tangible one.

The above interpretations imply that entrepreneurship and innovation both add value, and that the entrepreneur's role is to manage the risky in-

novation process such that it will lead to sustained competitive advantage and viability. McFadzean et al. (2005) quote Amit et al. (1993, pp. 816) saying that the two concepts should be linked together, and McFadzean et al. (2005) and Shaw et al. (2005) make a strong case for considering these concepts systemically.

Innovation predominantly occurs as a result of interactions between various actors, rather than as a result of an isolated individual's efforts (Håkansson, 1987; von Hippel, 1988; Lundvall, 1992). Hargadon (2003) provides numerous examples of collaborative dialogs of the latter sort (2003) based on ten years of research. He demonstrates that revolutionary innovations result from the creative combination of ideas, people and objects rather than flashes of brilliance by lone inventors. This fits with Schumpeter's view of innovation as new combinations of already existing knowledge, ideas, and artifacts (Schumpeter, 1942).

Leonard-Barton and Sensiper (1998) argue that innovation depends upon the collective expertise of individuals in a community characterized by an iterative process of people working together building on the creative ideas of one another. Stacey (2001) places self-organizing human interaction, with its ability for emergent creativity, at the center of the knowledge creating process, and suggests that organizational knowledge depends on the qualities of the relationships between people. In other words, successful national innovation networks must be based in co-ordination mechanisms that support the problem-solving efforts of the nation's Human Capital, and the dynamic processes of 'sensemaking' within it. Sensemaking is the collaborative dialog involving the network members freely sharing their ' sense' of ideas and concepts about 'how things work' or could work, in an open manner whilst remaining open to consideration of others' views and contributions to that discussion.

Sensemaking dialogs and dialectics may reside in how individuals frame their discussions. Glynn (1996) points to the existence of "innovation champions" who have the social, political or interpersonal knowledge to influence the acceptance of innovative change. Smith (2005) describes the personal characteristics of these "opinion leaders" and the means by which innovations are diffused, adopted, or rejected. Some such champions find themselves isolated in their organization or country, and one may expect that a country's geography and culture will have an influence on interactive learning and innovation processes. These processes are not space-less or global, but on the contrary are mediated by the roles geographical and cultural spaces play. For example, spatial proximity to empowerment drivers such as universities, research centers, new venture capital, etc., carries with it, among other things, the potential for intensified face-to-face interaction, trustful relations between various actors including female leaders and professionals, easy observations, and immediate benchmarks (Malmberg & Maskell, 2002; Smith and Cockburn, 2013). In short, spatial proximity seems to enhance the processes of interactive learning and value creation; the more so the society in question enables female creativity to play a role.

An implication of the above is that there is reason to believe that the knowledge structures of a given geographical territory are more important than other characteristics, such as general factor supply, production costs, etc., when it comes to determining where we should expect economic growth and prosperity in today's world economy. Regional innovation also tends to align with national innovation status. As the distribution of EU regional innovation is skewed this poses some questions about the efficacy and efficiency of EU innovation policy and how programs engender conflicts of interest between policy goals and EU global/regional resource allocation.

Background: Policy Goals

The European Union aspires to become the most competitive economy in the world and envisages

reaching that pinnacle of success by becoming more innovative than other areas. However, it is clear that the EU today still has many challenges ahead to rival the top innovating nations such as the United States of America and Japan (Commission of the European Communities, 2004a). For example, as we mentioned earlier knowledge structures of regions matter and the 2014 regional innovation survey, which scores regions for leadership, followership and moderate or modest innovation status, states: " All the EU regional innovation leaders (27 regions) are located in only eight EU Member States: Denmark, Germany, Finland, France, Ireland, Netherlands, Sweden and United Kingdom."

At a macro level in the EU there is a perceived global challenge to local integration in the scientific, innovation and R&D policy and practice arenas developed as part of the concept of the (ERA) European Research Area (Mali, 2005, p.151). As Mali states,

Following the rationales of co-ordination and harmonisation in scientific, technological and innovation activities, the key factor for Europe is to compete with other major global 'players', e.g. the United States and Japan. (Mali, 2005, p. 152)

Others such as Sorge (2005) have also highlighted such global-local dialectics within the business community although these are not wholly reflected in current innovation policy as discussed below. Three core reasons governments use to justify investing in support of R&D and innovative firms paradoxically reflect the challenges of curbing conflict dialectics and building integration and collaboration.

The three core rationales for EU innovation policy focus are:

1. **Improving EU Employment Figures:** Evidence suggests that innovating firms are both more profitable and grow faster than non-innovators (Freel, 2000; Geroski &

Machin, 1992). The EU Regional Policy was developed with the view that "intangibles" are gradually becoming a priority for regional policy in those less-developed regions successfully overcoming their shortage of infrastructures. The emphasis is therefore increasingly placed on those conditions that will most directly and immediately affect the capacity of businesses, particularly SMEs, to develop new job-creating activities. This necessarily involves policies for the promotion of innovation that are more regionalized as the Regional Innovation Strategies (RIS)/RIS+ experience has clearly shown." (European Commission Report, 2002, p.12). There are still some counter tendencies and dialectic tensions, e.g. job-creating elements may act as a brake on some new high tech businesses.

2. **Improving Firms' Competitiveness:** As Triebs et al. (2012a/b) later pointed out, there is a positive correlation between firms' R&D investment and productivity – driven by both technological progress and higher technical efficiency – which was found to be particularly acute in high-tech sectors. Accordingly, engaging in R&D activities – via technological advancement and by reducing inefficiency and waste – helps to increase productivity and ensure competitiveness.

3. **Structural Changes:** Shifting into R&D intensive knowledge industries to 'future-proof' the EU economies does not mean ignoring other sectors. Although there is evidence to suggest that a broad range of SMEs and other companies are needed for a fully-fledged socio-economic regeneration, the literature on the dynamics of industrial structures and the growth of innovative companies indicates that the EU's economy is less knowledge-intensive than its main competing regions –i.e. Europe is rather more specialized on medium than on highly knowledge-intensive sectors (see Moncada-Paternò-Castello and Cincera, 2012).

So the policymakers' decisions revolve around how best to ensure they meet the above core goals. Which sectors and what types of organizations should be supported and in what ways for a sustainable and optimum taxpayer Return on Investment (ROI)?

There are different routes to achieve these goals and this is also an area of challenge and dialectics relating to values of politicians or other proponents within the multi-state EU. One way is to support the growth of large businesses that are in the high-tech sector and try to stimulate some spillover or synergistic effects so that a scientific and economic 'multiplier effect' will eventuate and permeate society as part of the 'trickle-down effect' from fiscal and other policies. The rationale has often been that large-size enterprises account for a major part of the value added of the EU business sector despite representing a very small share of the total population of businesses (OECD, 2012). Moreover, the share of business enterprise expenditures on R&D (BERD) in terms of Gross Value Added (GVA) of EU large-size enterprises is around five times bigger than that of SMEs (EC, 2013). However, there are some contra-indications coming from recent research.

Attracting inward investment to an area is presumed to be the result in part, of knowledge spillovers and other synergies emanating from the act of co-locating high tech firms in the vicinity of each other. Contrarily however, Belderbos and Somers suggest dominant players in the field are effectively limiting such 'knowledge spillovers' in various ways in order to maintain their dominance and so often also discourage investors. They refer to research indicating that the larger firms which are dominant in specific fields and which fail to reduce knowledge outflows to neighboring organizations may be 'shooting themselves in the foot' and under-capitalizing on their technology dominance. They further assert that firms seeking to avert potential loss of Intellectual Property will likely thereby have a detrimental effect upon the regional attempts at increasing innovation (ibid, p.21) by discouraging inward investment.

Others look beyond big corporations and see potential for more national and local economic as well as social regeneration by opening up avenues of funding and technical, mentoring or other resource support for entrepreneurs in S.M.Es. SMEs currently represent more than 98% of all businesses in the EU and hold 67% of the total employment in the EU (EC, 2012). This SME economic participation has been a feature of many economies for many years. Schumpeter asserted decades ago that economies (and ultimately societies) depend upon their entrepreneurs for renewal and survival so they must be supported and encouraged to keep following the path of continuous innovation (Schumpeter, 1942).

Other research results have reinforced Schumpeter's view of entrepreneurs and unambiguously show that young innovative companies tend to grow more than other types of organizations. An increase in R&D expenditure by 1% generally stimulates employment in the business sector by about 0.15% (Bogliaccino, Piva, & Vivarelli, 2012). In addition, 3 other aspects strengthen the SME case. These are, 1) smaller firms tend to produce better-quality innovations than others, 2) R&D subsidy policies based upon size of the firm generally perform better than size- independent policies and 3) supporting small firms' investment in R&D often leads to more growth than subsidising large firms' (Akcigit, 2009; Coad & Hölzl, 2010; Moncada- Paternò-Castello, 2011). Such fast-growing, innovative SMEs can also play a fundamental role in accelerating the EU's economic performance and assist greatly with regeneration and renewal dialog about EU industrial structure (Moncada- Paternò-Castello, 2011; Cincera & Veugelers, 2012; Czarnitzki & Delanote, 2013; Ciriaci, Moncada-Paternò, & Voigt, 2013).

However despite the fact that approximately 30% of EU business expenditures on R&D are by firms with less than 500 employees, Europe is still lagging behind in the numbers of such R&D-investing companies compared to places such as the USA. In fact, evidence suggests that the average size of R&D intensive firms can explain the overall R&D intensity gap between the EU and the US. These kinds of US companies are concentrated in sectors that are intrinsically R&D-intensive, so thereby raising the US's overall R&D performance compared to that of the EU (Moncada-Paternò-Castello, Ciupagea, Smith, Tübke, & Tubbs, 2010; Ortega-Argilés & Brandsma, 2010). Nevertheless, the SME/start-up failure rate remains high.

On average, 1 in 3 new European enterprises fail before they reach their second year of trading. 50 to 60% never survive beyond the seventh year. Moreover, the post- Global Financial Crisis (GFC) period makes potential investors wary of engaging in the risky business of establishing new companies (Sauner-Leroy, 2004). So it is within this uncertain and complex international and local environment that the EU policy has been developed.

Scaffolding SME Success

For EU policymakers, the objective of 'Innovation in SMEs' is to optimize the Research, Development & Innovation environment for SMEs, including through the establishment and facilitation of support services, with the aim of scaffolding and strengthening the innovation capacity of SMEs and creating value in the market and/or society, thus underpinning the "Europe2020" strategy for smart, inclusive and sustainable growth. (European Commission: Horizon 2020 webpage http://ec.europa.eu/programmes/horizon2020/)

Although less sanguine about future policy success in closing the gap between the EU and the USA or Japan, Moncada-Paternò-Castello and Voigt (2013), point out that two of the five targets of the Europe 2020 strategy are to increase employment and shift towards increased growth of innovative R&D- intensive SMEs to speed up the development of knowledge based economies in the EU. They see this as fostering innovation and requiring increased R&D investment in the EU to 3% of countries' GDP. Horizon 2020 defines innovation management capacity building as a core element of their support. They define innovation management as systematically covering all the steps in the process of generating innovative concepts, screening them for viability and on to putting them on the market and making a profit.

Thus the EU innovation policy makers and planners have aligned the goals with the three core reasons mentioned in the previous section and give EU funding or support aiming to improve:

1.   European Firms' competitiveness;
2.   Begin Structural change in the economy and types of industries;
3.   Improve employment rates.

There remains a number of conflicting areas at different levels of analysis such as the contest between community orientation, collaboration and the business dividend for owners as well as taxpayers and the wider community in the EU (Moulaert & Nussbaumer, 2005, pp. 89-90).

In one of the two key competitor countries (Japan) recent case study research has indicated that community engagement is vital to success. Kodama (2005, p.31) states: "Community leaders serve an important function in creating networked strategic communities. The case study shows how community leaders have created networked strategic communities in which the central government, regional governments, universities, hospitals, private businesses and non-profit organizations take part in the advancement of regional electronic networking." Given the intrinsic tendencies of large firms to protect IP and for Big Firm clustering to be a detrimental impact on funds invested, in promoting the innovation cluster policy it might seem that further consideration is needed. There are still ongoing debates regarding how best to advance the overall regeneration and support growth of fledgling High tech businesses

in national and transnational markets in Europe and elsewhere. Kodama's version of 'dialectical dialog' envisions a network both challenging each member's innovations for robustness as well as engaging in a constructive dialog about collaboration and integration of the innovation into the network's New Product Development (NPD) (Kodama, 2005, pp. 49-51).

Any major transformations such as researching and developing new services and products or systems for delivery in an industrial system often has some delay before reaching anticipated or optimum levels of sales, production, market penetration and so on. So targeting support at critical moments in the SME lifecycle and orienting them towards scaffolding for success are important to overcome or reduce the dialectical tensions inherent in the R&D capital building and know-how generation processes. In an industrial context, these interactions often follow the value-chain and the supply-chain management. An enterprise facing a particular problem turns to a supplier, a customer, a competitor, or some other related actor such as research centers or financial tools, to get assistance in specifying the problem and defining the terms for the solution. From this it follows that the level of analysis for understanding the processes of industrial innovation and change in a country is some notion of an industrial system or network of organizations with their entrepreneurs and innovators, carrying out similar and related economic activity; however, the above discussion confirms that organizations in a country can not compete as isolated agents.

In today's complex and dynamic environments, national and corporate entrepreneurship and innovation capabilities must also be allied with macro level environmental and social concerns if R4M and long-term sustainability are to be successfully achieved. Even though many businesses and governments are now moving towards more sustainable practices, the overall impact of these efforts still seems much less than optimal. Most methodologies and practices are not holistic enough, and display significant problems in implementation- for example, due to their individualized or piecemeal implementation, their deficient structures, and their inadequate communication channels.

Added to the above there is the perceived need to research the physical/technical and cultural means to scaffold and build dialogs encouraging more SME networking locally, nationally and between or across regions in the EU in order to capture and apply organizational innovations and learning for SMEs collectively in the European Union as well as individually. Problems of continuity of support are also important as illustrated by one case referred to below, where a support network suffered a setback because one of two universities providing technical and other support first reduced then withdrew staff as the institution repositioned itself and restructured departments.

We intend therefore to narrow our focus for the chapter somewhat in order to keep things manageable and simply to present case-illustrated overviews and comparisons or contrasts of the processes involved and the dialectics and dialogs in relationships amongst regional, national and internationally networked SMEs and between them and others in the wider community of actors involved in implementation and monitoring policy and practice. We will draw upon global indicators and comparisons of best practice where available to support current empirical research with SMEs in the EU and so will briefly review an international network from another continent-Latin America for lessons learned as well as EU cases.

MAIN FOCUS OF CHAPTER

Remarks on Illustrative Network Case Examples

The approach that has become widely implemented in both academic as well as in policy circles since the publication in 1990 of Michael Porter's book,

The Competitive Advantage of Nations, is the notion of "clusters". For our purposes we define a cluster as a "spatial agglomeration of similar and related economic and knowledge creating activities." As Scheel (2007) asserts, in today's knowledge based economy, the ability to innovate is more important than cost efficiency in determining the long-term ability of enterprises to flourish. This does not mean that cost considerations are irrelevant, but simply that the combined forces of the globalization of markets and the deepening divisions of labor make it increasingly difficult to base a competitive position on cost-advantages only.

As an example of an attempt to build a clustering structure where things have gone wrong outside of the EU and where we may learn things to avoid, we briefly examine the Latin American environment where this acceleration of value due to industrial clustering is not occurring. After analyzing more than twenty projects in the last 15 years, dedicated to the clustering of SMEs and supporting organizations, in different countries of the Latin American region, we have arrived at some very discouraging conclusions. Although some exceptional successes can be found, they are more the outcome of corporate successes, but not of regional competitive clusters of SMEs and industries, according to world-class best practices. In summary, we claim that the Latin American region can show very few cases of true clustering synergies policymakers and others expected to see among all the main players of this industrial organization framework, i.e. the entrepreneurial community, academia, the government and the social communities.

The reasons for this dysfunction are multiple and complex. Most business leaders blame local and federal governments and their politicians. Others cite financial costs; the cultural isolation of the companies; the total misalignment of the public policies and industrial strategies; the poor competitiveness and innovation of most SMEs. Principally due to the lack of research and development and a poor system of transferring the results to industry made worse by the poor connectivity infrastructures and e-readiness and also the great nuisance affecting most countries of the region; the insufficient technical, technological and innovation training systems, obsolete regulatory frameworks with obscure and biased 'rule of law.'

Porter (1990) showed that competitive advantages of enterprises are not solely characterized by intra-organizational conditions but by the important environment drivers outside the enterprises which characterize the co-operation and dialog between the enterprises and between support agencies or 'meso- institutions' such as chambers of commerce and industry, technology centers, new venture capitalists (i.e. those institutions operating between micro-level of the firm and wider macro of public sector and nationalized organizations). This standpoint led to a shift in the priorities of national regional development policy. Today, individual enterprises are no longer at the center, but rather participating in a networking of enterprises, strengthening their relationships between each other and to suppliers and customers as well as to public bodies.

Lundvall (1992) and Nelson (1993) carried out pioneering research in this area. The newer approaches in innovation theory no longer describe innovation as a linear process. Instead it is argued that innovations represent the result of interactions and feedback processes by various different players (firms, knowledge producers, technology transfer institutions) in so-called innovation systems. The development potential of a region (of a country) from this perspective is based on the innovation strength of networks, which are characterized, by self-steered processes, co-operative exchange structures and a great dynamism.

In addition to a large number of studies and analysis, numerous cluster initiatives in the EU bear witness to the popularity of the cluster concept. "Triple Helix" in Sweden, "Clusterland" in Upper Austria or "Pôle de compétitive" in France, are representative of this popularity. Clusters

are regarded as features of successful economic regions which are in position to improve regional competitiveness through innovations whereby the different interpretations of cluster concepts reflect individual regional – and partly also national – peculiarities.

Therefore, the support of networks of enterprises promises to be an efficient instrument in terms of structural, SME-oriented innovation policies. However, empirical experience with these approaches to date shows that cluster policy is no panacea as a regional policy. Particularly the skill of identifying and initiating clusters which promise success as well as of motivating enterprises, meso-institutions, public players and possibly research organizations to work together must often first be developed by those responsible for clusters and monitored to sustain their engagement and support as illustrated in the next case of the network discussed below.

The aforementioned analysis clearly shows the success of innovation occurs precisely in the complex dynamic interactions and sustained positive reinforcement between global and local processes. The competitiveness of the regions themselves depends to an increasing degree on their innovation capabilities. Successful regions generally understand how to network intelligently local and regional players such as enterprises, universities, research institutions, associations, policy makers and administration in order to bundle and augment the knowledge distributed over individual heads and to transfer it into new products, processes and services (clusters).

The experience of an National Innovation System (NIS) in Chile is typical. For example, in 1999 James Mullin, Robert M. Adam, Janet E. Halliwell, and Larry P. Milligan working for IDRC in Chile proposed a number of initiatives for better public-sector coordination; however, seven years later, the National Council for Innovation and Competitiveness of Chile (2006,p.56) stated in its final report, "The best international practices show that an efficient National Innovation System needs at the top, an institutional framework to drive, coordinate and provide it of direction. In that sense, foreign specialists had agreed that our National Innovation System is underdeveloped, ill coordinated, lacking guidelines and an integral and coherent approach."

A brief outline of history of three projects is given in the rest of the chapter. An overview and outline of each case study is first detailed, fol-lowed by a case study summary template. The template is used for ease of comparison, contrast and reflection for readers (see Table 1).

Summary of Table 1 Case

Poor coordination, lack of systems integration of business, government, universities and meso-insti-tutions and external agencies like the World bank.

Table 1. NIS Case study summary template

Case Study Field/Topic/Issue/Problem	National Innovation System (Chile) Case Example 1
Context: Where it took place Organization background Who was involved?	IDRC advisors to the (2006) Chile Chilean government, businesses and National Council for Innovation and Competitiveness of Chile
Change Drivers: What prompted the change? Who sponsored it? Management/owners/others? Why/ did you choose Action Learning? Who led the change?	Lack of a National Innovation System framework and agenda as well as limited influential change and action learning champions pushing the message and securing local 'buy in' and sustainability. Not applicable Government ministers, World bank, International Development Bank with technical advisors from universities
Change Narrative: What did you do? What resources were needed? Policy change/support? Enabling technologies? Other support?	In terms of the '3 dimensional strategy' model of Gratton & Truss (2003), The policy and strategy were in place but the systems and action dimensions were weak. The latter strategic weaknesses impacted on the leadership focus, capability and will to follow-through and follow up success or failures with remedial actions. NIS plus innovation champions of suitable stature and influence to activate the changes and follow through and Information Technology capability
Key Outcomes: What was achieved? Goals/targets missed or deferred? Advantages? Disadvantages? Lessons learned?	Failed network project Surfaced government concerns about potential corruption and distrust of more business involvement in NIS (then 18% funding but only 3% performance) but lack of data as R&D not a tax write-off so not recorded separately to general business costs. Issues of perceived equity and targeting of rewards for participants. Learned that networks need better, more proactive than reactive forms of governance, supervision, coordination, plus a wider practical and conceptual research base and technology infrastructure and 'know how' about differences between teams and networks and communities and the relevant leadership styles for their involvement and development within funding limits, action and research timeframes
Transformability/Sustainability: Could this case example and learning from it be transferred To other business/industry contexts? Considering resources and achievements is this achievable?	EU context seems quite distinct and overall project coordination exists but has some similarities in terms of diverse national cultures, social and behavioral norms. Include incentives for SMEs in high tech areas to cluster and engage the community where social regeneration is at stake. It is achievable with more open and dialectical dialog arrangements such as action learning cultivating enhanced regional knowledge structures and within better infrastructures such as are recommended in the IRDC report, by Mullin et al., *Science, Technology, and Innovation in Chile* (1999)
Where to Next: What is envisaged or planned as a next step? For organization, team, staff member/members etc.	Train academic and SME teams in Action learning principles and practices. Build the Economic, Human Resource, Technological and Administrative co-ordination infrastructures and relevant rewards systems to enhance 'bottom-up' decision-making, 'buy in' and engagement from all stakeholders, ensuring ongoing review of goals and actions such as increasing business involvement and possible fiscal incentives, R&D funding via 'integrative' projects looking at applying science and technology to business

At a macro, level this can be considered a failure of the learning capacity of the society, as well as the business organizations and network itself inasmuch as poor collaboration and lack of inclusive networking among the components of the NIS resulted in the fragmentation of the necessary learning loops in business, governance and societal domains.

The idea of fragmentation of learning loops as a major cause of societal failures have been discussed by Senge and Kim (1997/2013) and applied to NIS by Ramirez (2008). In its most elementary form it refers to chronic incapacity to generate shared inter-institutional visions and the necessary commitment to carry them out but may also be due to the Volatile Uncertain Complex and Ambiguous (VUCA) context where political and other factors amplify negative loops reinforcing the status quo or powerful elites' and entrenched interests.

Case 2 Outline

The Giving Real Opportunities with Technological Help (GROWTH) SME networking project funded by the European Union (EU) was initiated as a regenerative project for the small to medium enterprises (SMEs). It was originally formed in 2001 in South Wales and "housed" and supported by staff from two schools in the then University of Wales Institute. The aim was to facilitate a self-organizing, stakeholder-community of SMEs committed to economic and social regeneration and to anchor the indigenous capital in the region.

The GROWTH project aimed to increase networking amongst SMEs to initiate a Welsh small business electronic community. The project also sought to promote and support the incubation of new businesses and generate tacit as well as explicit knowledge within the network to stimulate the regeneration of the regional economy.

The main objectives were for the development of an online business club for SMEs, particularly those linked to the light manufacturing and sports product and leisure service sectors in South-east Wales and linking SMEs to other major business networking forums. It also sought to create an information network and a business support and guidance service for entrepreneurs and their co-workers in these and other sectors (Cockburn et al, 2001).

The network grew rapidly and the project team was working with 25-30 local companies and beginning to establish company "clusters" helping to secure their development and growth both in economic terms and in terms of growth as sociable communities of practice or "learning organizations" working with their peers from diverse industry sectors locally as well as some international connections such as Sweden and the USA.

Some showcase events were organized in Cardiff with speakers from industry and from the universities involved. Educational programs were organized for some in management, health and safety, business finance and other topics. The largest single event was held at the Cardiff International Arena –a large entertainment and exposition center. That event showcased success stories for VIPs including members of the Welsh Assembly, Cardiff Chamber of Commerce, National Quality Assurance body and representatives of various professional bodies such as UKAIS, CIPD. Other smaller events were held in local venues and members of the public as well as network SME staff were encouraged to attend. Many also attended regional social 'get togethers' and online seminars. Over time, as intended there were some parts of the network which merged with larger mainstream networks in the relevant business sectors such as Information technology, engineering and Medical laboratory Services. In parallel with the above evolutionary changes, some of the organizations merged with or were acquired by other larger businesses.

However, a number of other significant changes in the network infrastructure support and it's leadership structure occurred in ensuing decade as the founding universities restructured and refocused their support to more specific or niche areas such as Sport, Tourism, Hospitality, Design and Media Arts and correspondingly reduced their previous collaboration as they moved closer to partner with other institutions their leadership preferred or they were obliged to do so by government funding changes and redesignations of their missions and strengths (see Table 2).

The following case (case #3, below) draws on the pilot experience of a group of Spanish SMEs in the chemical sector on their way to setting up

Table 2. GROWTH SME network Case study summary template

Case Study Field/Topic/Issue/Problem	GROWTH Case Example 2
Context: Where it took place Organization background Who was involved?	Growth Network of 25-35 SMEs collaborating with two schools at UWIC UK to develop an online forum and action learning groups of SMEs, 2 university schools initially in one university and expanded later to collaborate with another university as managing agents and researchers
Change Drivers: What prompted the change? Who sponsored it? Management/owners/others? Why did you choose Action Learning? Who led the change?	Network grew well and was forming clusters of SMEs from sectors/market niche. Action learning was well-received in the network as company gains and contributions from action learning set members were visible and practical. Macro changes impacted the lifecycle as well as clusters deciding to join other major established business organization forums, some left GROWTH then thus reducing the size of the network. Local Funding issues, Higher Education restructuring and 'brand' repositioning of the respective universities in light of changes in national educational priorities as well as institutional 'politics' and anticipated 'status' changes eroded gains and support internally at universities whilst community support waned in ethnic businesses when a key local leader was ousted from a senior role in the network. This was perceived as increasing risks in their markets and communities for many of the hospitality –based SMEs.
Change Narrative: What did you do? What resources were needed? Policy change/support? Enabling technologies? Other support?	One Head of School left to work abroad and his replacement changed strategic direction to better align to the changed national situation and basically allowed the school's contribution to the project to 'wither on the vine' through lack of support. Technologies employed were mainly email and mobile telephony. University computing department staff running programs on specific system technological problems identified at face-to-face meetings provided support. Issues identified in reporting results to community as well as SME teams and focus of rewards as they were perceived as variable for some of the non-academics involved especially.
Key Outcomes: What was achieved? Goals/targets missed or deferred? Advantages? Disadvantages? Lessons learned?	Network and clusters initiated several action learning projects to enhance effectiveness or efficiency in the SMEs were completed and target numbers reached in the first few years. Rewards for SMEs were thus clear at first. Disadvantages were too much reliance on university experts and Action Learning so that there was a skills gap when one left and was not replaced. That hiatus was made worse as the 'searching' was delegated to some 'administrators' in the first instance instead of being seen as an urgent and important task for more senior 'experts' and academics who could have sought assistance from within their own academic expert network in that field of learning. Some SMEs began to see themselves as 'research fodder' for the academics and thus felt that the business rewards were reduced over time in favor of publications and research ratings for lecturers.
Transformability/Sustainability: Could this case example and learning from it be transferred To other business/industry contexts? Considering resources and achievements is this achievable?	Yes-build in extra cover for loss of experts by training action learning set members trained as they work on problem solving and networking. The idea of clusters and networks has transferability for most contexts except for very highly specialized skill sets in high demand/short supply which may also be overcome if funding is made available to recruit replacements or some 'standby' technical help staff are available online.
Where to Next: What is envisaged or planned as a next step? For organization, team, staff member/members etc.	Network has since disbanded and there is a self-organized revamped action-learning network attached to one other university in the region as part of their part-time, distance learning MBA program. It gets company support but not EU funding.

a cluster within the context of the European FP7 project CADIC-Cross-organizational Assessment and Development of Intellectual Capital (Jul.2010-Mar.2013). Assuming a situation where an SME (the catalyst of the cluster building process) invites some of its peers in the industry to create a cluster, it focuses on the factors that might have caused the cluster to face and overcome its early degeneration.

Before embarking into the specifics of CADIC and the practical SME case – we should make clear that CADIC adopts a rather loose definition of cluster, as those network arrangements that, *though embedded in, transcend geographical location, focus on global markets, operate as ad-hoc and/or long term business networks, are ICT enabled, and are based on dynamic aggregations of capabilities of different SMEs* (Damaskopoulos, Gatautis, & Vitkauskaitë, 2008, p.1). Within this purview, clusters are no longer seen as regionally bound, top-down built constellations nurtured by regional (and strongly public funded) economic systems but rather as bottom-up driven and dynamic hubs operating in a global system of flows of Intellectual Capital (IC) and economic activity.

CADIC was conceived to help SMEs to set up and strengthen own clusters (or collaborative networks) on a much easier and more cost-efficient basis. It believes the enterprise itself to be the key to successful clustering; thus, supporting mechanisms need to be designed to tackle the challenges and activities which are most important within the different cluster phases in order to help the cluster (and the SME) to muddle through and develop. The starting point of the CADIC idea of bottom-up cluster is supporting the dynamics of clustering from an individual SME level by enhancing capabilities leading to successful networking and learning. Accordingly so, the cluster level is regarded as a result of the companies' capabilities to collaborate, learn and actively engage in the cluster.

In late 2009, the Engineering Business Unit of SIDASA (hereinafter Sidasa-EBU) decided to join CADIC as an opportunity to leverage its vision and promote and professionalize its collaborations. The EBU has a relatively small structure so the search for development and management of partnerships has always been at the core of its strategy. Sidasa-EBU is the engineering arm of SIDASA, a company of the Units Coating Group with headquarters in Barcelona, created in 1952 and currently managed by the second generation of the family founders. The EBU had at the moment 11 employees and a turnover of nearly 16 M EUR.

By Dec.2010, still at the outset of the formation stage, the cluster consisted of six SMEs, all knowledge-intensive and representing the whole value chain of the industry of aluminum anodizing mainly for cosmetics, cans and packaging. All six companies knew each other and had strong ties built along more than twelve years of doing business together; the same applied for the individuals involved. The research and technological centers AIMME and AFAPIC, the Catalan research association of the manufacturers of aluminum for the cosmetic industry, completed the initial core group that would master the CADIC journey. The partners' selection process underwent several stages as the topic became more clearly targeted.

Except for one of the SMEs, the rest of the partners were at the moment involved in a common project. Three of them were clients of the catalyst SIDASA-EBU and eventually competed in markets different from the cluster's core, so we knew coopetition might be an issue. Leaving out AIMME and one SME partner, which had their offices in Valencia, the rest of the companies were located in Barcelona. Considering different geographical markets (spatial separation) would pre-empt the risk of collusion within the cluster (Gnyawali & Park, 2006). Most of the companies were family owned with hierarchical structure and centralized governance. Although laissez-faire in appearance, their management style reproduced on average "the-owner-seizes-it-all" type of management–under tight control of the owners and predominantly financially and short-term focused.

The catalyst CM, pretty aware of the rather conservative and close-minded character of the industry, feared that this would turn into a major setback when attempting to urge the cluster forward. Thus, in successive idea exchanges with the CFT, it was agreed that an organization from outside the industry would be involved –a 'disruptive satellite' partner with the specific role of 'disrupting' or breaking the potential inertia within the core group, contributing its experience, new ways of thinking and view about doing business in a network environment. Eventually, it would support the SME sense and make sense of the 'cluster', so enabling the creation of a shared vision and common goals. H&C SL, an IT passionate and visionary, assumed this role.

The vision and values for the cluster were agreed in a central workshop on Jan.2011. This was followed by two other workshops intended to identify the IC strengths of the cluster companies and to introduce the online platform that would enable knowledge sharing and IC to flow. To lay the pillars of a secure and flexible learning environment (FLE) that would affect trust and collaboration was of major concern.

Several initiatives were brought to the table– from Best Available Techniques (BATs) for surface treatment of metals/plastics to augmented reality and energy audits; but one by one they were smothered. The lack of external funding, the uneven level of commitment of the partners, and also loss of trust, in addition to the very difficult circumstances of the Spanish economy, converged to make these obstacles insurmountable. In a last effort to ignite the cluster the catalyst CM set forth the idea to create a European association of green anodizing companies. With the pressure for sustainability increasing, the creation of a 'green alliance' of SMEs and research centers would not only confer a competitive advantage to the company partners but would contribute to the institutionalization of the cluster's shared goals and values, and ultimately to its legitimacy as a separate and embracing entity.

In the Spring of 2011 the catalyst CM initiated contacts with four French companies, strong players in the anodizing sector and comparatively more aggressive than the Spanish ones. The differentiation, sustainability and value creation power of this strategy was apparent. Whether the new association would supersede the cluster or the two would remain independent institutions, meant that high potential existed for generating 'buzz' and action-ideas as the result of the joint exploration and exploitation of IC synergies, knowledge spillovers, and symbiotic dynamics. Everything was ready for the launch of GrInnANet-the European Green Innovation Anodizing Network; with this objective, a first meeting was planned in the midst of LuxePack, in Oct.2011. Attending the fair was also a third company, not a partner in the cluster but with strong relationships with some of the cluster companies and significant weight in the Spanish market of anodizing, product of recent M&A moves. The fears and mistrust of this 'intruder' company was enough of an argument for the other partners –with the exception of the catalyst – to step back. If had been successful, this new group would have pooled close to 90% of the world market of anodizing.

The failure of LuxePack signalled the end of GrInnANet and with it the early degeneration of the Sidasa-EBU cluster as formerly conceived. With no alternative projects in sight, the shadow of mistrust about *who would really benefit* from this partnership, in addition to the stifling financial situation of some of the cluster companies, left the cluster breathless. In Jan.2012 the team of Sidasa-EBU in a joint meeting with the CFT agreed on a complete turnaround. A month later, the Transport Systems-STL cluster saw the light. With the Sidasa-EBU team, in command, and five to six SMEs, traditional suppliers of the EBU, integrated the initial core. The aim was to innovate and standardize the line transport system of the surfaces treatment equipment. By July, a total of five workshops had taken place and several technical innovations and management changes were introduced. In the meantime, Albert, a recently graduated engineer and son of Sidasa's CEO, an enthusiast and passionate about his job, had joined the group and together with the CM assumed the leadership of the cluster (see Table 3).

FUTURE TRENDS

Networks are here to stay for the foreseeable future. The ability to utilize 'Big data' responsibly comes with the drivers for 'democratization' of leader-

Table 3. CADIC Spanish cluster Case study summary template

Case Study Field/Topic/ Issue/Problem	CADIC (Spanish Cluster) Case Example 3
Context: Where it took place Organization background Who was involved?	CADIC pilot SME located in Catalonia to build a cluster from bottom-up, co-innovate and create networking management capacity. Sidasa-EBU, the catalyst, having a small structure of 11 employees that can grow up to 100, with more than 90% of its turnover coming from exports. *Context*: Financial strangle, pressure for internationalization; collaborative networks to M&A and staying in market. Sidasa-EBU, a core group of 6 SME, research centers AIMME /AFAPIC; UPC and Cecot-SME Innovation Foundation as supportive institutions.
Change Drivers: What prompted the change? Who sponsored it? Management/ owners/ others? Why did you choose Action Learning? Who led the change?	The vision, conviction about the importance of networks for SME growth/innovation and the commitment of the CM (esp. of the son of the CEO during the STL stage) was key. Motivation unevenly distributed across members. Action learning readily introduced within Cluster Management Framework methodology; best option given self-generative nature/ dynamics of bottom-up clusters and practical action-based approach of CADIC. Macro/business changes; catalyst's foreign markets moved from Europe to Brazil /US /SE Asia taking the CM away from headquarters for longer periods, difficult situation of some SMEs –negatively affects cluster; lack the necessary systematic for action-based collaborative learning.
Change Narrative: What did you do? What resources were needed? Policy change/support? Enabling technologies? Other support?	GrInnANet, a good try to re-ignite cluster but not equally understood by all members –French SMEs seen more as threat rather than an opportunity. The lack of action-based involvement of the SME Association along the cluster building preempted the emergence of its assumed brokering role –no impact on policy /territory.
Key Outcomes: What was achieved? Goals/targets missed or deferred? Advantages? Disadvantages? Lessons learned?	GrInnANet initiatives (energy audits, etc.) waned as public funds were cut off. The alliance with the French never saw the light. Meanwhile, for the STL network gains were visible and value-adding: standardization of coating equipment with co-innovations introduced on the way; IC skills and NW management capacity enhanced –SME domain. Too much reliance on the catalyst, and particularly on the role of the catalyst CM –unleashed wrong perceptions about win-wins / power unbalances. This particular issue solved (partially) within the STL by promoting shared leadership. Addressing the network challenge suggests that each SME joining the cluster be determined to reboot and relearn the ways it apprehends and interacts with its ecosystem and does business. The SME IC base –and not only its RC– will probably have to be reconfigured and upgraded for constructive collaboration. Past experience in common projects might not be as important for NW success as suggests the literature on partners' selection. Introducing competitors too early at the formation stage might hamper the quick transition from calculus to affective trust, withering the cluster until its final end or degeneration –coopetition matters. Communication lies at the center of bottom-up clustering processes, enabling the translation of cluster goals to the SME's (appropriation), and vice versa, while affecting trust and collaboration. Such appropriation process is critical for the legitimacy of the cluster. In the absence of effective and meaningful communication there is no emergence (IC flows / shared leadership). Social-IT readiness also fundamental Leading in bottom-up clusters is conversational (a knowledge and IC-conversation towards a shared goal) Ability of CM to create psychological safety (people feel free to express relevant thoughts and feelings) is key. Roles CM and CFT are pivotal in the phase of startup -- > 'sense making'/ adaptive capacity/pollination
Transformability/Sustainability: Could this case example and learning from it be transferred To other business/industry contexts? Considering resources and achievements is this achievable?	Yes –but with caution; more in-depth qualitative research needed. The bottom-up character of the cluster make that the building process be highly emergent and sensitive to interventions from CM/CFT. Not only the SME context but beliefs and perceptions of individuals assume a salient role in the translation of the cluster vision to the company's, and vice versa, affecting the trajectory of the cluster and the duration of the life-cycle stages –trust being a key driver. Type of knowledge created (analytical vs. synthetic) is an important moderator, making it difficult to figure out the outcomes. Supportive and facilitating role of the CFT is critical for the success of bottom-up SME clusters –esp. at formation stage; this role should be externally funded.
Where to Next: What is envisaged or planned as a next step? For organization, team, staff member/members etc.	GrInnANet is in stand-by. If it ever flourishes will be with new members, possibly from dyadic relationships –e.g. French company-Sidasa-EBU. STL reconfigured and expanded to fulfil competencies/technology gaps. The challenge will be to develop other projects that would allow NW management skills and learning to be integrated into the mainstream business activities of the SMEs and the cluster. Systematic support of CFT until more mature stages of cluster seems key.

ship and governance through forms of collective decision-making using digital social media is rising as the next generation of leaders in business emerges and 'taking the pulse' or 'canvassing opinions' becomes easier (Smith and Cockburn, 2013, Cockburn, Jahdi and Wilson, 2015). However, this also reinforces the rising digital accessibility of 'leaders' and organizations by the wider community including 'whistleblowing', hacking/cyber threats as well as opportunities. Thus cyber security and cyber business opportunities are critical areas for leaders and managers to be aware of and to raise their capabilities in. As a corollary, the R4M aspects must take on greater significance in leaders' and Boards' agendas for risk management and evaluation of potential for conflict and/or collaboration within and between networks.

CONCLUSION

Research supports the view that networking boosts the innovation and competitiveness output of firms in diverse industries in the EU and globally-if there is a strong and stable infrastructural framework for coordination, support and community engagement at a micro as well as a macro level. That will require seed funding and cultural support in some of the newer members states as they adjust to post-Soviet systems and begin to climb the 'technological development' ladder. The support must continue and extend to management and leadership development not simply to new technologies but to owner/manager 'upskilling' which has been shown to lead to more adoption of best practice systems in the business community, to greater emotional resilience, enhanced organizational agility and coping skills when the competition is high or the economy flags.

The EU has grown from the original 7 and now numbers 28 countries. With that growth comes increasing social, cultural, economic and scientific complexities to add to the larger global market complexity the EU faces. As two of the current authors have stated previously, (Smith & Cockburn, 2013, 2014) in order to successfully operate in conditions of complexity in a VUCA environment, W. Ross Ashby's principle of requisite variety applies. That principle suggests that the internal diversity of any self-regulating system must match that of its environment if the organization and in this case the policies are to be successful in dealing with the challenges posed by that kind of business environment. This is the polar opposite of the bureaucracy and the tight control that characterizes the approach adopted by so many organizations today.

To address the demands of the principle of requisite variety, most organizations encourage networks as a basis for their necessary knowledge sharing in their operations and organization and to developing an organizational culture that supports strong social capital (Smith and Cockburn, 2013, pp. 272-278). Such networks need both intellectual capital and skills and action plans to resolve potential problems (e.g. to avoid the problem seen in the Growth network). Social, ethical and emotional capital consists of the stock of active connections among people, and is founded upon the emotional regimes exhibiting high levels of trust, mutual understanding, commitment along with shared values and pro-social behaviors that bind the members of such networks and communities thereby enabling knowledge sharing and cooperative action (Cohen & Prusak, 2001, Cockburn et al, 2012). This approach has been accelerated by the ability to support and extend network communication and knowledge sharing through digital connectivity (Smith & Cockburn, 2013, pp. 278-287).

SUMMARY LESSONS FOR POLICYMAKERS, NETWORK AND TEAM LEADERS

- Networks differ from communities and from small teams.

- Network relationships and emotional bonds are looser than team relationships generally so strengthening social capital including emotional bonds is (both within SMEs and across the network) vital.
- Teams are generally more focused and more tightly knit.
- Networks and teams both require leadership styles which motivate and promote team focus, capability and the will to complete as well as helping clarify expectations and goals at each stage of a project or Network lifecycle.
- One form of Network leadership is exemplified by Cadic leadership, coaching and advisory roles as summarized in the chapter Endnotes (below) and may greatly assist building regional knowledge structures and learning in the Network.
- Network and teams require 'scaffolding' support structures and resources.
- Managers must encourage and develop action-learning processes including learning from failure.
- The key to a collaborative work environment is that many individuals at *all levels* are responsible for achieving success.
- Voluntarism is important in network formation and effectiveness so willing, keen and capable members or SME representatives are best.
- Network management must also ensure dialectical dialog and action learning occurs within the Network in order to capture and strengthen knowledge transfer, 'buy in' to decision-making and improved regional knowledge structures as discussed above.
- Lack of equitable incentives and rewards for all collaborators is a barrier to network development. Restrictions on many contributors sharing in the rewards and recognition is another barrier.

- No transparency and candor in communication about problems as well as successes will hamper collaboration and dilute trust.
- Insufficient employee input and utilization restricts efficacy of networking actions.
- Limitations in effective allocation of resources allied to ineffective technology, legacy systems, bureaucratic processes and procedures also limit agility and responsiveness.
- Trust is often much diluted in networks compared to teams so network managers and sponsors must focus on building trust and 'trustworthiness' in managers and leaders as well as capability and will to complete or follow through without neglecting dialectical dialog.
- Top down corporate direction rather than the informal social, professional or technical linkages autonomously developed between peers may be less effective overall without significant HR input as above (Bakker, Et al., 2006).

REFERENCES

Akcigit, U. (2009). *Firm Size, Innovation Dynamics and Growth. In 2009 Meeting Papers (No. 1267).* Society for Economic Dynamics.

Amabile, T. M. (1988). A model of creativity and innovation in organizations. In B. M. Stew & L. L. Cummings (Eds.), *Research in organizational behavior* (pp. 123–167). Greenwich, CT: JAI.

Amit, R., Glosten, L., & Muller, E. (1993). Challenges to theory development in entrepreneurship research. *Journal of Management Studies, 30*(5), 815–834. doi:10.1111/j.1467-6486.1993.tb00327.x

Bakker, M., Leenders, R. T. A. J., Gabbay, S. M., Kratzer, J., & Van Engelen, J. M. L. (2006). Is trust really social capital? Knowledge sharing in product development projects. *The Learning Organization*, *13*(6), 594–605. doi:10.1108/09696470610705479

Belderbos, R., & Somers, D. (2015). Do Technology Leaders Deter Inward R&D Investments? Evidence from regional R & D location Decisions in Europe. In Regional Studies. Carfax.

Bogliacino, F., Piva, M., & Vivarelli, M. (2012). R&D and Employment: An application of the LSDVC Estimator using European Microdata. *Economics Letters*, *116*, 56–59.

Cincera, M., & Veugelers, R. (2012). Young leading innovators and the EU's R&D intensity gap. *Economics of Innovation and New Technology*, 1-22.

Ciriaci, D., Moncada-Paternò-Castello, P., & Voigt, P. (2013). *Innovation and Employment: A sustainable relation?*. IPTS Working Papers on Corporate R&D and Innovation series - European Commission – No. 01/2013 – EUR 25807.

Coad, A., & Hölzl, W. (2010). *Firm growth: empirical analysis (No. 1002)*. Papers on Economics and Evolution.

Coakes, E., Smith, P. A. C., & Alwis, D. (2011). Sustainable innovation and right to market. *Information Systems Management*, *28*(1), 30–42. doi: 10.1080/10580530.2011.536110

Cockburn, T., Jahdi, K., & Wilson, E. (Eds.). (2015). *Responsible governance: International perspectives for the new era*. New York, NY: Business Expert Press.

Cockburn, T., Jahdi, K. S., & Wilson, E. (2012). Ethical capital and the culture of integrity: 3 cases in UK and NZ. In W. Amann & A. Stachowicz-Stanusch (Eds.), *Business Integrity in Practice – insights from international case Studies*. New York, NY: Business Expert Press.

Cockburn, T., Treadwell, P., & Wootten, C. (2001). The politics of community: Challenges in digital education. *Campus-Wide Information Systems*, *18*(5), 187–194. doi:10.1108/10650740110408517

Cohen, D., & Prusak, L. (2001). In Good Company: How Social Capital Makes Organizations Work. Harvard Business Press.

Commission of the European Communities. (2004). *European Innovation Scoreboard 2004: comparative analysis of innovation performance.* Author.

Commission of the European Communities. (2005). *Report on the implementation of the European Charter for Small Enterprises, (COM(2005) 30 final)*. Author.

Czarnitzki, D., & Delanote, J. (2012). *Young innovative companies: The new high-growth firms?* ZEW Discussion.

Czarnitzki, D., & Delanote, J. (2013). Young innovative companies: The new high-growth firms? *Industrial and Corporate Change*, *22*(5), 1315–1340. doi:10.1093/icc/dts039

Damaskopoulos, T., Gatautis, R., & Vitkauskaitė, E. (2008). Extended and dynamic clustering of SMEs. *Engineering Economics*, *1*(56), 11–21.

European Commission. (2013). *Share of Business enterprise expenditures on R&D (BERD) to the gross value added (GVA) – Unpublished calculations by DG Research and Innovation/Economic Analysis Unit based on OECD*. Eurostat and DG Enterprise and Industry.

European Commission. (2002). *Regional Innovation Strategies under the European Regional Development Fund Innovative Actions 2000-2002*. Author.

Freel, M. S. (2000). Strategy and structure in innovative manufacturing SMEs: The case of an English region. *Small Business Economics*, *15*(1), 27–45. doi:10.1023/A:1012087912632

Geroski, P., & Machin, S. (1992). Do Innovating Firms Outperform Non-Innovators? *Business Strategy Review*, *3*(2), 79–90. doi:10.1111/j.1467-8616.1992.tb00030.x

Glynn, M. A. (1996). Innovative genius: A framework for relating individual and organisational intelligences to innovation. *Academy of Management Review*, *21*(4), 1081–1111.

Gnyawali, D. R., & Park, B.-J. R. (2006). Impact of co-opetition on firm competitive behavior: An empirical examination. *Journal of Management*, *32*(4), 507–530. doi:10.1177/0149206305284550

Gratton, L., & Truss, C. (2003). The three-dimensional people strategy: Putting human resources policies into action. *The Academy of Management Executive*, *17*(3), 74–86. doi:10.5465/AME.2003.10954760

Håkansson, H. (1987). Product development in networks. In H. Håkansson (Ed.), *Technological development: A network approach* (pp. 84–128). New York: Croom Helm.

Hargadon, A. (2003). *How Breakthroughs Happen*. Boston, MA: Harvard Business School Press.

Kanter, R. M. (1983). *The change masters: Innovation for productivity in the American corporation*. New York: Simon & Schuster.

Kodama, M. (2005). New knowledge creation through dialectical leadership: A case of IT and multimedia business in Japan. *European Journal of Innovation Management*, *8*(1), 31–55. doi:10.1108/14601060510578565

Koudal, P., & Coleman, G. C. (2005). coordinating operations to enhance innovation in the global corporation. *Strategy and Leadership*, *33*(4), 20–32. doi:10.1108/10878570510608013

Lawrence, K. (2013). *Developing Leaders in a VUCA environment*. UNC-Kenan-Flagler Business School Whitepaper.

Leonard-Barton, D., & Sensiper, S. (1998). The role of tacit knowledge in group innovation. *California Management Review*, *40*(3), 112–132. doi:10.2307/41165946

Lundvall, B.-Å. (1992). *National Systems of Innovation: Towards a Theory of Innovation and Interactive Learning*. London: Pinter.

Mali, F. (2005). Global-Local Dialectics in the Process of European Scientific Integration. Institute for Advanced Studies on Science, Technology and Society.

Malmberg, A., & Maskell, P. (2002). The elusive concept of localization economies: Towards a knowledge-based theory of spatial clustering. *Environment & Planning A*, *34*(3), 429–449. doi:10.1068/a3457

McFadzean, E., O'Loughlin, A., & Shaw, E. (2005). Corporate entrepreneurship and innovation part 1: The missing link. *European Journal of Innovation Management*, *8*(3), 350–372. doi:10.1108/14601060510610207

Moncada-Paternò-Castello, P. (2011). The growth of companies in the EU: the case for a more sophisticated research and innovation policy. IPTS Policy Briefs Series.

Moncada-Paternò-Castello, P., Ciupagea, C., Smith, K., Tübke, A., & Tubbs, M. (2010, April). Does Europe perform too little corporate R&D? A comparison of EU and non-EU corporate R&D performance. *Research Policy*, *39*(4), 523–536. doi:10.1016/j.respol.2010.02.012

Moncada-Paternò-Castello, P., & Voigt, P. (2013). *The effect of innovative SMEs' growth to the structural renewal of the EU economy-a projection to 2020*. Academic Press.

Moulaert, F., & Nussbaumer, J. (2005). Beyond the Learning Region: the Dialectics of Innovation and Culture in Territorial Development. In R. A. Boschma & R. C. Kloosterman (Eds.), *Learning from Clusters: A Critical Assessment* (pp. 89–109). Netherlands: Springer. doi:10.1007/1-4020-3679-5_5

Mullin, J., Adam, R. M., Halliwell, J. E., & Milligan, L. P. (1999). *Science, technology, and Innovation in Chile, International Development Research Centre*. Canada: IDRC Books.

Nelson, R. R. (Ed.). (1993). *National Innovation Systems: A Comparative Study*. Oxford: Oxford University Press.

OECD. (2012). *Entrepreneurship at a Glance 2012*. OECD Publishing; doi:10.1787/entrepreneur_aag-2012-en

Ortega-Argilés, R., & Brandsma, A. (2010). EU-US differences in the size of R&D intensive firms: Do they explain the overall R&D intensity gap? *Science & Public Policy*, *37*(6), 429–441. doi:10.3152/030234210X508633

Pinchot, G. (1985). *Intrapreneuring*. New York: Harper & Row.

Ramirez, J. C., & Silva Lira, I. (2008). Globalization and regional development: The economic performance of Chile's regions, 1990-2002. *CEPAL Review*, *95*(Aug), 103–123.

Sauner-Leroy, J. B. (2004). Managers and productive investment decisions: The impact of uncertainty and risk aversion. *Journal of Small Business Management*, *42*(1), 1–18. doi:10.1111/j.1540-627X.2004.00094.x

Scheel, C. (2007). Why the Latin American region has not succeeded in building world-class industrial clusters. In *KGCM Proceedings*. Winter Garden, FL: International Institute of Informatics and Systems.

Schumpeter, J. A. (1942). Capitalism, Socialism and Democracy. Harper & Brothers.

Shaw, E., O'Loughlin, A., & McFadzean, E. (2005). Corporate entrepreneurship and innovation part 2: A role- and process-based approach. *European Journal of Innovation Management*, *8*(4), 393–408. doi:10.1108/14601060510627786

Smith, P., & Cockburn, T. (2013). *Dynamic Leadership Models for Global Business: Enhancing Digitally Connected Environments*. IGI Global. doi:10.4018/978-1-4666-2836-6

Smith, P., & Cockburn, T. (Eds.). (2014). *Impact of Emerging Digital Technologies on Leadership in Global Business*. IGI Global. doi:10.4018/978-1-4666-6134-9

Smith, P.A.C. (2005). Knowledge Sharing and Strategic Capital: The Importance and Identification of Opinion Leaders. *The Learning Organization*, *12*(6), 563 – 574.

Sorge, A. (2005). *The Global and the Local: Understanding the Dialectics of Business Systems*. Oxford: Oxford University Press. doi:10.1093/acprof:oso/9780199278909.001.0001

Stacey, R. D. (2001). *Complex Responsive Processes in Organizations*. London: Routledge.

Sullivan, P. (1998). *Profiting from intellectual capital: Extracting value from innovation*. New York: John Wiley and Sons Inc.

Teece, D. J. (1998). Capturing value from knowledge assets: The new economy, markets for know-how and intangible assets. *California Management Review*, *40*(3), 55–79. doi:10.2307/41165943

Thornberry, N. (2001). Corporate entrepreneurship: Antidote or oxymoron? *European Management Journal, 19*(5), 526–533. doi:10.1016/S0263-2373(01)00066-4

Tidd, J. (2001). Innovation management in context: Environment, organization and performance. *International Journal of Management Reviews, 3*(3), 169–183. doi:10.1111/1468-2370.00062

Triebs, T., & Kumbhakar, S. (2012b). *Management Practice in Production.* Ifo Working Paper Series Ifo Working Paper No. 129. Ifo Institute for Economic Research at the University of Munich.

Triebs, T., Saal, D. S., Arocena, P., & Kumbhakar, S. C. (2012a). *Estimating Economies of Scale and Scope with Flexible Technology.* Ifo Working Paper Series Ifo Working Paper No. 142. Ifo Institute for Economic Research at the University of Munich.

Von Hippel, E. (1988). *The Sources of Innovation.* New York: Oxford University Press.

Willmott, H., & Alvesson, M. (Eds.). (1994). *Critical Management Studies.* London: Sage.

Zahra, S. A. (1985). Corporate entrepreneurship and financial performance: The case of management leveraged buyouts. *Journal of Business Venturing, 10*(3), 225–24. doi:10.1016/0883-9026(94)00024-O

ADDITIONAL READING

Extension of the European Cluster Observatory: Promoting better policies to develop world-class clusters in Europe. Retrieved August 7, 2015, from http://www.emergingindustries.eu/Upload/CMS/Docs/Policy_roadmap.pdf

Helping SMEs to grow and internationalize, see "For a European Industrial Renaissance", COM(2014) 14 final. Retrieved August 2, 2015, from http://eur-lex.europa.eu/legal-content/EN/TXT/PDF/?uri=CELEX:52014DC0014&from=EN

Innovation Union Scoreboard. annex H-Performance per indicator last accessed July 18th,2015 http://ec.europa.eu/eip/raw-materials/ en/community/ document/european-commission-innovation-union-scoreboard-2013

White Paper on Emerging of European World-Class Clusters (2010, July 14). Retrieved July 10, 2015, from http://www.tci-network.org/news/91

KEY TERMS AND DEFINITIONS:

Action Learning: Is a form of learning by using 'learning sets' composed of problem-holders who assist each other to work on issues faced by each party.

Dialectical-Dialog: Refers to a concept by Kodama whereby Networks seek rational balance between challenge and collaboration enabling constructively-critical evaluation of and 'sensemaking' about options with the purpose of getting the best way forward that gets "buy in" from all parties.

Dialectics: Is conflicts between proponents of opposing views which may eventuate in a communication breakdown or a new synthesis and understanding between parties.

Dialog: Is a collaborative discussion where parties seek a consensus.

Sensemaking: Concerns ways that Network participants understand and 'make sense' of their circumstances and options.

S.M.E.: Is defined as a Small to Medium Enterprise.

S.M.E. Networks: Or clusters are interconnected, collaborating collectives composed of SMEs, advisors, government or funding body representatives and relevant others such as researchers.

ENDNOTES

[1]   For further information about the CADIC project, http://www.cadic-europe.org/, and more specifically, access the CADIC Guideline, http://www.cadic-guideline.eu/home/.

[2]   Within CADIC, there are two fundamental roles: the Cluster Manager (CM) and the Cluster Facilitator Team (CFT). The CMs are located in the single SMEs and have the key function of driving the cluster activities to success, considering both, the interests of the single SME and the interests of the cluster. The CFT has primarily an advisory role. Usually a professional from an SME Association, a senior member of the cluster's Catalyst SME or an independent consultant, supported by a 'country coach' from a CADIC RTD partner.

APPENDIX

Study Questions

Overall, movement through the life-cycle in bottom-up clusters seems wave-like: with new projects, coming on line to provide fresh insights informed by, and capitalizing on the achievements (and problems discovered) of previous projects. However, successful progression depends, crucially, upon being able to set the cluster development process in a reflective frame. Failing to achieve this reflective frame means that wave-like development process will cycle between the initial stages of 'learning the ropes' and projectism, consuming increasingly additional resources and undermining motivation. Trapped in this cycle, a growing series of separate projects (most likely with local success) may be implemented, so long as additional funds can be found, but rarely does the cluster emerge and nor network management capacity enhanced, having no or little impact on the territory. Given this assumption,

- What type of methodologies and tools, and roles, are assumed to support the development and leverage of clusters/networks' generative dynamics towards IC-based growth and renewal?
- The aforementioned examples suggest there might be a networking or collaboration readiness level in the SME, pre-existent to bottom-up clustering. Assessing such level may draw the line between the cluster's failure and success, also along the life-cycle. How is this readiness level defined? What are the elements of the business environment that are most likely to have influence on it? (Consider both the SME and the cluster action domains)
- How does the cluster /network organization help other partner companies achieve their business strategies and objectives?
- Given that about two-thirds of European clusters are essentially top-down,
- How can bottom-up initiatives be integrated into top-down managed clusters to make clusters *and* cluster SMEs more agile and resilient? Where in the life-cycle would these interventions have the highest impact?
- Recent emphasis of EU programs on the creation of emergent industries as a way to reduce Europe's innovation and competitiveness gap with the US and boost growth and employment, has turned the attention to clusters as supportive mechanisms to unlock innovation potential of SMEs on a large scale, promoting the smart use of resources.
- Under which circumstances clusters would clusters/networks be able to play such role, and how? What should this 'supportive' role be and what it may encompass?

Chapter 13
The Role of the Leadership Style in Creating Conflict and Tension in a Higher Education Institution

Grace C. Khoury
Birzeit University, Palestine

Beverley McNally
Prince Mohammad Bin Fahd University, Saudi Arabia

ABSTRACT

This chapter examines the influence of context on leadership styles in a higher education institution. Specifically, the enactment of leadership, the consequence of differing leadership styles, and the resultant interpersonal conflict. Informed by the empirical literature examining the Middle East, workplace stress and conflict, leadership and interpersonal communication, the chapter highlights the consequences of a high-conflict external context and the resultant constraints on human resource policies and practices. The recommendations include establishing a leadership development program aimed at creating an awareness of different leadership styles and the leadership of diverse groups. This includes the implementation of a cultural change program, programs to support the empowerment of minority groups, management education focusing on conflict resolution. The chapter adds to the body of literature by addressing the challenges confronting leadership in a high conflict context.

ORGANIZATION BACKGROUND

As Metcalfe (2009) argues, the Middle East, specifically the Arab region, is growing in importance to the world economy. Increasingly, the region is being seen as a lucrative market for multinational companies. Consequently, there is a growing requirement for Arab businesses to

expand into new markets in order to become part of the international economy (Metcalfe, 2009). In order for this to occur, and more importantly, for Arab businesses to be successful, there has been an increased priority placed on the provision of higher education. Thus, there has been an almost exponential increase in the establishment of higher education institutions in the Middle East (Abu

DOI: 10.4018/978-1-4666-9970-0.ch013

Lughod, 2000). However, these higher-education institutions have confronted numerous challenges in their attempts to deliver high-quality programs. Challenges, that have arisen, primarily from, the on-going internal conflict, war, and sectarian violence, that besets the region. Consequently, a major test facing these institutions is to overcome these challenges while at the same time ensuring that their academic reputations continue to grow.

Therefore, the aim of this chapter is to examine the influence of leadership and leadership styles on communication and conflict resolution in a Palestinian higher education institution. In doing so it provides an alternate perspective to the work of Khoury and McNally (2014) who explored the role of external context on human resource policies and practices. Specifically, the chapter examines the influence of differing leadership styles and their impact on interpersonal relationships in a high-conflict transitioning society.

The National Public University (NPU) is situated in one of the more high-conflict zones in the Middle East – Palestine. Palestine is considered to be a transitioning society, that is one that is moving from a high dependency on international aid to one of development and self-reliance (Paprock, 2006). Not only has the country experienced the presence of an occupying force, internal conflict and war, it also faces the considerable internal challenges. The two areas comprising the country, Gaza and the West Bank, are geographically separated and there has been a lack of unity within the political structure. This creates difficulties for institutions that are reliant on external funding and governmental support in order to carry out their core functions.

As with all other universities within Palestine, NPU has been established under the most trying social, political, and economic circumstances (Abu Lughod, 2000) and initially offered two year associate degrees in Arts and Sciences. The establishment of additional academic departments

followed, with the Faculty of Business being established in the late 1970's. In the mid 1990's the Faculty of Graduate Studies was established. The University has grown to include Faculties of Law and Public Administration, Information Technology, Nursing and Allied Health Sciences. In addition, to the seven current faculties, NPU has eleven institutes and research centres that focus primarily on community development and research.

The University is governed by a Board of Trustees comprising prominent community, business and political leaders. This feature is a source of pride for the University as many of the country's leaders and prominent business people are graduates of the University. This willingness to contribute is common in the region, as alumni recognize that they have received a unique opportunity under somewhat trying circumstances, to contribute to the economic wellbeing of the Palestinian people. In doing so they wish to ensure that future generations receive the same opportunities as they did. The role of the Board of Trustees is to set the strategic direction, participate in the formulation of the strategic plan and to build relationships with the wider community, with the purpose of raising funds for the university. At the time of writing the gender representation on the Board of Trustees comprises six females and fifteen males.

The University Council is the statutory body that approves regulations and policies of the University. The Council is comprised of the University President, the Vice Presidents and Deans. The gender representation of this body comprises one female and thirteen males. Historically, there have only been two females that have held a Vice-President position which has led to representation on the University Council. Reporting to the University Council is an Academic Council which consists of twenty-seven members, two representatives from each faculty plus all deans and the Vice-President of Academic Council and his assistant. Currently, there are only two female faculty members of the twenty-seven member council.

NPU has approximately nine hundred faculty and staff members and has a student body of nine thousand. One of the foremost challenges confronting the university is the recruitment and retention of qualified, competent faculty and staff. As stated previously the University is situated in a high-conflict region and there are considerable constraints and potential dangers confronting faculty from their external environment. This places considerable stressors on employees going about their everyday life. Therefore, it could argued that one leadership responsibility is to ensure that the internal environment is as stress free as possible.

As with the majority of Palestinian universities funding is limited. Moreover, the current political situation makes it virtually impossible to obtain alternative funding (Abu Lughod, 2000). This has led to all areas of NPU, for example, the library, research centres and teaching and learning, being severely constrained in their activities. More importantly, the University has to pay levies and taxes on books and similar resources. Baramki (2009) provides the example of a main-frame computer costing around $50,000 in the 1980s incurring almost the same amount again in levies and taxes. The situation has not changed significantly in the intervening period. Accordingly, there is a growing awareness within NPU that it is imperative that all resources, financial, physical and human are utilized to the maximum.

The Business School of NPU

The Business School of NPU in its structure is typical of the majority of business schools in the region. The Business School is one of the largest in the University, with fifty faculty and staff and approximately two thousand students. The school offers five undergraduate majors, business administration, finance, accounting, marketing, economics and business economics. A 2004 decision led

to the graduate programs being accommodated within their subject discipline faculty. Two postgraduate programs, specifically the Masters in Business Administration (MBA) and the Masters in Economics are under the direct control of the Dean of the Business School. The MBA is the largest master's program at NPU. The co-ordinator for each of the masters programs is selected from the Business School faculty and appointed for a two year term with the right of extension for an additional two years. In some instances the co-ordinator may hold dual roles, for example, head of department and co-ordinator of a specific program. The events contained within this case occurred within the Business School of NPU.

Setting the Stage

The Middle East can lay claim to having a long-standing tradition in the provision of higher education with one of the first universities (Azhar) founded in Cairo 972 A.D (Abu Lughod, 2000). Moreover, it can also be argued that the universities in the Arab region are recognized as making significant contributions to the development of European institutions of higher learning, specifically the Universities of Paris and Padua (Abu Lughod, 2000). Abu Lughod (2000) goes on to contend that the decline of the Arab world from the sixteenth century onwards also led to the decline in the influence of the traditional institutions of higher education in the Arab world. However, the current resurgence and expansion of higher education in the Middle East has led to the development of institutions that are significantly removed from the traditional model. Accordingly, the models that have been adopted for these new and emerging institutions are based primarily on European and American systems of higher education. This is in response to the identified need for Arab countries to become a successful part of the global economy and therefore these educational systems are deemed more relevant to meeting the needs of the region. Consequently, governments and ruling authorities in the region have tasked these institutions with ensuring the provision of a quality of education that compares favorably with their counterparts in the West.

The relative early stage of development of these higher education institutions means that the management and human resource policies and processes are also in their infancy. While it is possible to draw from the experiences of fellow higher education establishments especially those in the West, this is not always practicable. The unique context in which Palestinian institutions are situated creates its own set of challenges – challenges, for which solutions are not easily transferable or readily available. For example, the external context contributes high levels of stress for, faculty, staff and students of all universities in the region. Ramon, Campbell, Lindsay, McCrystal, and Baidoun (2006) found that emotional stress, fear and competing national and religious identities are common within the Arab world. They go on to state that this stress is created by the most simple of tasks such as difficulties in travelling to work, negotiating security checkpoints and at times, fear during encounters with security forces. This reality, when combined with high levels of stress within the internal context, can make an employment situation untenable for some. There is a universal acceptance that workplace stress is present in the majority of workplaces (Khoury & Analoui, 2009). Research in the USA indicates that one-third of the American workforce reports that their jobs are 'often' or 'always' stressful (Murphy & Sauter, 2003) as cited in (Khoury & Analoui, 2009). Consequently, given the political tensions of the region, it can be reasoned that higher-educational institutions in the Middle East have an equally high, if not greater propensity for workplace stress to occur. Therefore, the context within which NPU is situated is deemed to have considerable influence on the behaviors of individuals and consequently on their responses to the interactions that occur within the internal context of the University. As Heminway and Smith (1999)

assert when examining workplace stress it is important that the stressor exist within a specific occupational group are identified. Therefore, this chapter attempts to identify the role of context and culture in creating stressful situations in Higher Education Institutions.

Garrison (1998) contends that the behaviors and attitudes within a specific context are developed from the historical, political, economic and religious traditions that exist within that society. Moreover, these behaviors and attitudes are often indiscernible and yet have a significant impact on that society and its business culture. Furthermore, they are difficult, if not impossible, to study empirically. Therefore, the authors argue by giving voice to the incidents highlighted in this case we are better able to come to understand the challenges within the context of NPU that must overcome if it is to be successful in achieving a world class academic reputation. This will ensure a supply of talented graduates in order to meet the needs of the Palestinian business community.

CASE DESCRIPTION

As with most new organizations the development of HR policies and practices has been somewhat reactive. They have focused primarily on the needs of the organization as they have arisen as opposed to a more planned proactive approach. The demands of an extremely volatile context have frequently diverted management's attention from the on-going daily needs of the organization. As Baramki (2009) writes much of Palestinian university leadership energies have been focused on protecting employees and students from interference and frequent closures of the University by the military. Consequently, there has been a lesser level of attention paid to the development of HRM policies and practices for NPU. Specifically the, internal policies and processes with respect to recruitment and selection, and the development of policies and opportunities designed to upgrade the skills and qualifications of talented young people in order for them to take on leadership roles successfully. According to Avery (2005), skilled knowledgeable leadership is critical to ensuring organizational sustainability. Therefore, the inability to appoint and develop leaders with the required capabilities may adversely impact on the ability of NPU to provide quality education.

The Role of Context

The external context within which NPU is situated is considered to have played a significant role in creating the issues discussed in this case. For example, the on-going media representation of strife in the Middle East has created a perception that the region is an extremely unsafe place to work. Consequently, the region is not seen as an attractive option for career academics. Moreover, when international employees have been recruited, they were often denied residence permits by the Israeli government. In addition to citizens of the USA, Britain and France these prospective employees included Palestinians wishing to return home. As Baramki (2009) wrote many of these Palestinians had been educated at international universities and wished to return home to contribute to the success of Palestinian universities yet were denied entry by the Israeli authorities. NPU found this situation particularly stressful, as when the institution did attract high-quality employees, they were often thwarted in finalizing the appointment because of an inability to attain the appropriate visas. In addition, foreign faculty resident permits were repeatedly not renewed or if employees had left Palestine on vacation they were not permitted to return (Baramki, 2009).

As a result, this situation has led to the development of what could only be termed 'work-arounds' in an effort to overcome these issues. One such practice has been the employment of post-graduate alumni in an internal recruitment process. This practice was a response on the part of the deans throughout NPU to resolve the issues created by the inability to attract and confirm the appointment of suitably qualified PhD holders as faculty. However, even this practice was fraught with difficulty as, those post-graduate students who did complete their qualifications at NPU frequently sought further education, teaching and research opportunities outside Palestine. Moreover, often those post-graduates remaining at NPU had not had the opportunity to develop the level of skills and experience necessary to carry out a junior faculty role, let alone take on a leadership or position of responsibility.

The volatile external context has also created a high level of insecurity with respect to employment. A consequence of which has resulted in some faculty engaging in income-generating practices that allowed them to establish a secure financial base. This has included taking on extra duties that paid overtime, undertaking part-time work at other higher education facilities, and external consulting roles, all in addition to full-time teaching commitments. There is evidence to suggest that some faculty staff held full-time positions at two different institutions simultaneously. The extra work engaged in by faculty has also included delivery of training sessions on behalf of independent training organizations, management consulting roles within the business environment.

In addition, the limited financial resources caused some individuals to develop close relationships with different departments/centers within the university. While this may be considered collegial behavior in an academic environment, in reality, the converse was the case. These relationships were primarily seen as a means for the individual to source funding for conference travel and to generate additional personal income. However, while, the administration of NPU was aware of these practices, they were loath to act upon this knowledge given the difficulties faced in providing competitive remuneration and the retention of suitably qualified staff.

It was noted that often these relationships created a conflict of interest. The consequence was divided loyalties, role conflict and on occasions the 'home' department not being able to rely on the availability of staff. The outcome was over-committed faculty many of whom subsequently developed health issues that were diagnosed as resulting from high levels of stress. One example provided to the authors was about one individual, Dr. Bassem, who always looked tired and rarely smiled as he was always rushing from one organization to another. Dr. Kamelia, one of the few women in the Business School who had held a position of responsibility, reported that another faculty member had died a premature death from a heart attack – this individual had been appointed to the Head of the Business Administration Department and had died prior to taking up the role. He was relatively young and his death was unexpected.

The Relationship between Context, Recruitment and Selection

As stated earlier, NPU has experienced considerable difficulty in attracting suitable faculty and when they did, it was difficult to gain travel and resident permits. Accordingly, a myriad of practices have developed within the different departments and colleges and away from the sphere of influence of the HR department. Nor has a system of 'checks and balances' been developed in order to ensure that the recruitment process was equitable and people being recruited into faculty positions were appropriately qualified. As a result there has been a lack of consistency and best practice evident in a number of internal recruitment situations within the Business School.

One such situation was that appointment of individuals to academic leadership positions. One example is the appointment of the Dean of the Business School. The position of Dean has been unadvertised and the faculty member with the highest academic qualifications was appointed to the role. The Dean's term is three years with a right of extension for an additional three years. Consequently, some individuals have had their

term extended more than once as there was a lack of suitably qualified staff to take on the position. Hence, the Dean of the Business School in this case study, Dr. Saeed, held the position of Dean in excess of twelve years. Dr. Saeed was a very conservative traditional male who had been reappointed for four terms during his tenure. He had also achieved full professor status, and is well published in his field. Therefore, he had achieved a high level of academic credibility. He had also gained considerable political power through the various networks he had established during this period. However, as Kisamore, Jawahar, Liguori, Mharapara, and Stone (2010) identified, politically skilled individuals are more likely to engage in the use of negative power-laden behaviors. This is because they often encounter resistance from those who have a different working or communication style. Consequently, situations of interpersonal conflict arise, which, in turn, can be devastating to the organizational culture.

Over a period of time, Dr. Saeed had developed a sense of ownership and entitlement to the position. Moreover, it is perceived that he has paternalistic hierarchical authoritative management style. This combined with the longevity of Dr. Saeed in the Dean's role has led to the principal management style of the Business School becoming one of conflict or forcing. That is, individuals approach situations in an aggressive competitive manner in order to assert themselves and to achieve their goals. This may include the use of coercive power in the form of threats in order to achieve their objective (Grodnitzky, 2005). This situation was complicated still further by the fact that Dr. Saeed, in his position as Dean, had established a power-based network both within the Business School and the wider University. This has permitted him to implement many decisions despite the objections of the Business School Faculty.

One example provided to the authors was a challenge he made that related to the internal appointment of a young woman the Dean preferred but whom the then Chairman had reservations about appointing. The statement being made by the Dean "*I am going to help her get the faculty appointment – even if I have to manipulate the roles and positions in the department so I outrank you.*"

This situation arose as a result of the application and subsequent appointment of Jane to the Business School. Jane was in her mid-thirties and was a graduate of NPU. Holding two master's degrees, she had worked as an academic assistant for approximately three years and as a project manager elsewhere in NPU. She had been given some business courses to teach on a part-time basis or in summer school. Subsequently, she had applied for a faculty position in the Business School but had been unsuccessful. The reason, provided by the Chairman at the time, related to concerns about Jane's level of professionalism in some areas. However, the Dean, Dr. Saeed supported her renewed application for a faculty role. The selection panel felt that the concerns that prevented her appointment previously were still evident. However, despite the reservations of the selection committee, chaired by Dr. Kamelia, Jane was appointed to a faculty role and within a very short period of time to a position of responsibility. Those who held reservations about the appointment felt powerless and disenfranchised and there was a resultant impact on commitment and morale amongst these members of the selection panel.

In addition, the practices associated with the recruitment of NPU graduates into faculty roles has led to a perception that these alumni are not academic colleagues in the true sense of the word. Rather they are students that teach or purely teaching assistants. In addition there was a perception that they had been appointed into their role because of a shortage of faculty as opposed to their appointment being based on qualifications and experience. This, despite some of them having published in peer reviewed journals and held positions of responsibility within academia.

The practice of rotating the head of department, while on the surface appears to provide faculty with management experience, has the unintended consequence where often a faculty member has found themselves in a position of having to evaluate the performance of a more senior member of staff. This then caused conflict, particularly when a faculty member of lower academic standing found themselves in a position of authority over a more senior, experienced member of staff. Given the patriarchal hierarchical nature of Palestinian society (Muna & Khoury, 2012; Rought-Brooks, Duaibis, & Hussein, 2010) the consequence has been situations of interpersonal conflict where the more junior faculty member has been over-ruled by the more senior faculty, this regardless of the 'rightness' of the decision.

Probably one of the more concerning incidents occurred as a result of the Dean's interference in the recruitment processes where he was later found to have a conflict of interest. One such incident reported to the authors arose when the Dean attempted to appoint an associate professor who had previously been employed by NPU. The majority of the recruitment committee did not approve the application. The committee members had been the applicant's colleagues in the past and knew that he had been implicated in a sexual harassment case involving a student. Dr. Saeed, the Dean, called Dr. Kamelia, chair of the selection panel, into his office with the express purpose of informing her of the applicant's innocence and berating her about her decision. Despite Dr. Kamelia trying to explain that it was the committee's decision, not hers alone, the Dean appeared to blame her personally. During the conversation it transpired that the applicant was related by marriage to the Dean. Although the applicant was never appointed to a full-time permanent position he was given a contract by the Dean to teach part-time at both under-graduate and post-graduate level.

Equally, concerning was the application for appointment of Mr. A., a previous faculty member. Mr. A had just resigned from his job in a government ministry for unknown reasons. He was seeking re-employment at NPU. After careful consideration the committee declined to appoint him, despite the Dean, proactively lobbying the committee to rehire this individual. The reason given was that there was evidence to suggest that Mr. A would only remain at NPU until he found a more lucrative position. The Dean was angered by this decision. His action in response to the decision was to establish a new recruitment committee consisting of members who were considered to be loyal to the Dean and his wishes. Subsequently, the appointment of this candidate was ratified by the new committee. Unsurprisingly, the applicant found a more lucrative position and resigned within a year. However, as a result of his relationship with the Dean, he was permitted to continue to teach MBA courses when he desired. However, as he works full-time in another organization he has become overcommitted and consequently failed to show up to class on frequent occasions.

Conflicting Management and Leadership Styles

There are many sources of conflict within an organization; these include structural factors which arise from the nature of the organization, work design and those personal factors that arise from individual differences (Quick & Nelson, 2013). Within the Middle East (Arab) there are a set of social conventions that create perceptions and values with respect to the role of women in society. This, in turn, is deemed to create a set of structural issues with respect to women's roles in general, and in leadership roles specifically. This has led to what Metcalfe (2009) contends is an under representation of Arab women in senior management and leadership positions. Yet, as Al Dabbagh (2009) asserts many Arab states have made considerable strides in establishing developmental opportunities in both the public and private sectors for women. Al Dabbagh (2009) goes on to argue, that one of the major challenges is to provide educational opportunities that support the development and provision of women's rights in the Middle East. This will include the establishment of the frameworks that support the development of women into academic leadership roles. Therefore, it can be expected that there will be a corresponding increase in participation of women in the decision-making arena in organizations such as NPU.

However, it can be argued that the level of gender representation in management and governance roles within NPU could be considered typical of an Arab society. Moreover, many of the traditional patriarchal Palestinian attitudes towards women, as identified by Rought-Brooks et al. (2010), are still evident in the Business School at NPU. This, in turn, has led to high levels of interpersonal conflict in the department. According to (Ting-Toomey, 1994, p. 360) as cited in (Oetzel and Ting-Toomey (2003) conflict can be defined as "the perceived and/or between two or more parties over substantive and/or relational issues." In this case, the interpersonal conflict arose as a result of the difference in management and leadership styles between Dr. Saeed, the Dean and the female faculty members, specifically, those female faculty members who held leadership positions within the Business School. The specific incidents in the case relate directly to the interpersonal relationship between the Dean and the female Director of the MBA, Dr. Kamelia. When asked to reflect on why the interpersonal conflict developed in the manner it did, it was suggested by one respondent that, it may have had its origins in the fact that Dr. Kamelia had been nominated for the position of dean prior to Dr. Saeed. It was subsequently discovered, that unknown to Dr. Kamelia, Dr. Saeed had approached the university president to advise him that Dr. Kamelia did not want the role.

It has been reported to the authors that the Dean's management style was autocratic. In addition, he was perceived to have a paternalistic, somewhat patronising attitude towards the female faculty members. Rought-Brooks et al. (2010) write that Palestinian society is highly patriarchal and that many of the laws do not offer sufficient protection to women and are often discriminatory against them. This situation acts to support and embed the patriarchal, paternalistic behaviors within organizations. In addition, Dr. Saeed also taught many of the current female faculty while they were undergraduates. Many of whom held a master's degree but who did not have the additional qualifications, publications or experience that would be expected of a faculty member. It was not uncommon for him to assign nicknames to female faculty – for example, of famous singers, or 'Barbie' and another 'Butterfly.' Not only did this practice serve to depersonalize the professional female faculty, it unfortunately encountered little if any opposition from within the business school. While there is evidence that the female faculty are uncomfortable with this labelling and considered it sexist, there were no formal HR structures to support them in dealing with this difficult situation.

These behaviors can be considered a form of harassment and can result in those affected experiencing stress as a consequence of their personal self-worth being insulted (Greenberg & Baron, 2003). The situation was exacerbated because the majority of these young women were appointed by the Dean during his last term in the role. His justification being that the chronic shortage of qualified faculty with PhD's necessitated the appointments of non-Ph.D holders. Therefore, it could be considered that they were disempowered as they perceived they owed their current roles within academia to Dr. Saeed.

In addition, the interpersonal communication between the Dean and those women in positions of responsibility has also been fraught. In particular, with the head of the MBA program, Dr Kamelia. As discussed earlier positions of responsibility were appointed for two years with right of renewal. Dr. Kamelia took over the role from Dr. Saeed on his initial appointment as Dean. The MBA program was an important program for NPU and generated significant income for the university. Dr. Kamelia had worked hard to improve the MBA program and had introduced many new initiatives. This in-

cludes an admissions test to assist in the screening of applicants to the program prior to acceptance. Similar to the GMAT, the test was approved by the MBA program committee for use in addition to undergraduate GPA, work experience and high school grades and personal references. Also, Dr. Kamelia obtained permission for international faculty from the USA and Europe to travel to NPU and act as visiting scholars to enhance the program. A very significant achievement given the past difficulties experienced in obtaining the appropriate visas for faculty. Dr. Kamelia was also successful in obtaining permission from NPU's Academic Council to amend course descriptions and course plans to improve the offerings to graduates enrolled in the program. Dr. Kamelia had also received public recognition from the Vice-President of the Academic Affairs for these initiatives and at this point she felt that her efforts to improve the offerings in the NPU Business School were valued.

Unfortunately, the improvements angered the previous director of the MBA Dr. Saeed, the current Dean. Of particular significance was the introduction of an admissions test as part of the screening process for MBA students. It is the conflict over the use of this test that is perceived to have escalated the interpersonal conflict between Dr. Saeed and Dr. Kamelia. The Dean did not agree with the admissions criteria and sent a letter to the MBA admissions committee asking them to revert to the criteria that was in place while he was MBA Director. It was during the meeting called to discuss the Dean's letter that the Dean forced himself into the meeting. At this stage, the majority of the committee were in favor of retaining the new criteria. What resulted was an incident of verbal abuse with the Dean screaming at Dr. Kamelia, in front of the other committee members, that she had prepared a "garbage test". Following this stressful encounter, the Dean actively began undermining the work of the MBA committee at the Business School Council meeting. Again a verbal exchange took place with Dr. Kamelia asking the Dean not to undermine the MBA committee's decision and not to consider everything they do as wrong just because it is different.

Advice received from colleagues of Dr. Kamelia is that they consider her to have a participative decision making style, is accepting of criticism, enjoys a challenge and is highly professional in all aspects of her role. All those responding to the request for commentary on Dr. Kamelia's style spoke of her passion for education, her visionary approach and the ability to convey this vision. One quote is as follows: *"most importantly, is the fact that she pursued to change us, to change our culture, our behavior. She is literally a transformational leader ... I also would like to mention that I feel satisfied with her managerial style because as opposed to other supervisors she is democratic, ethical and caring".*

This management style is significantly different to the autocratic, paternalistic style exhibited by the Dean. It was evident that the difference in management leadership styles was at the base of the majority of interpersonal conflict between the two parties. After a period of time the interpersonal conflict reached such a level that Dr. Kamelia began to display symptoms of stress related illnesses, for example, stomach ulcers, irregular heart rhythms, in addition to muscular pain. Consequently, the medical advice Dr. Kamelia received recommended to reduce her workload as it was believed that over-work and stress were the reason for her medical aliments. However, there is evidence to indicate that Palestinian organizations are not fully conscious of the negative impact of stress on workplace culture and productivity. Therefore, the human and financial consequences of the high-conflict, context, specifically the external context and its relationship to stress in the internal environment are not addressed (Khoury & Analoui, 2009).

Unfortunately, Dr Kamelia found that to reduce her workload was not a solution that was easily implemented. The interpersonal conflict had escalated to the level of intensity where Dr. Kamelia felt her position was untenable. In the absence of a formalized disputes resolution process there appeared to be only one solution and that was to discuss the matter with the President of NPU. The subsequent conversation with the President was wide-ranging covering a number of issues with relevance to the MBA program. After this meeting Dr. Kamelia reported that she felt that she had been listened to and that her concerns, where possible, would be addressed. Approximately, one month later, Dr. Kamelia received an invitation, via a third party, to meet with the Dean in his office in an effort to 'put an end to this conflict' between them. Unfortunately, when she went to the meeting she found that the Dean was extremely upset and angry. The situation was particularly heated and his comments referred to how, after thirty years of being respected and admired amongst the administration staff she had decided to 'stab him in the back' and report him to the president. It was clear that he perceived her behavior as professionally harmful to him.

From this point on, in the absence of any form of mediation service being available, the situation was left to fester on its own. The level of communication between the two parties was such that their interaction did not extend beyond a curt hello in the corridor. Despite this conflict, Dr. Kamelia felt that based on her success with the MBA program she would have her term as director extended at the end of her two year term. Therefore, it came as somewhat of a surprise to find out that her term was not being renewed. More importantly, it was the manner in which this decision was conveyed that was more of a shock. It was during lunch with a visiting professor from the USA that she first received an inkling of what was to happen. The question was asked *"do they have someone better than you to head the (MBA) program? I heard you were stepping down."* Naturally Dr. Kamelia was somewhat devastated. Not only that she was not going to be reappointed but the means by which she found out only served to make the situation worse. Between this comment and the farewell lunch for the visiting professor there was no formal communication from the Dean with respect to the decision. However, she did manage to convey to the Dean her disquiet with respect as to how she heard about the decision. The Dean did promise to meet with her and explain the decision – this meeting never occurred. In seeking clarification, Dr. Kamelia approached both President of the University and the Vice-President of Academic Affairs. The former was out of the country, however, in a meeting with the Vice-President, he informed her that her appointment was not extended because the Dean could not work with her personally. However, the following comment was made, "*if you can handle the aggravation then your appointment can be extended.*" It was clear that the situation was not going to improve and that senior management were either powerless or disinclined to have any further involvement in the matter.

Upon further reflection, Dr. Kamelia realized that she should not have been so surprised by the decision. However, she felt that her accomplishments did warrant some recognition. None was forthcoming. Reflecting on these events it became evident that not only was there a clash of management/leadership styles, it appeared that a situation of workplace envy was present. Envy as described by Klein (1957) is the "angry feeling that another person possesses and enjoys something desirable – the envious impulse is to take it away or to spoil it" (p212), as cited in Mouly and Sankaran (2002). This includes the denial of promotion or renewing of positions of responsibility. Both of which had occurred in the case of Dr. Kamelia. Mouly and Sankaran (2002) go on to contend that in order to prevent the negative effects of workplace envy then preventive intervention must occur at the highest levels of the organizations. This in turn emphasizes the importance of robust HR systems and processes in supporting this intervention.

CURRENT CHALLENGES FACING THE ORGANIZATION

The scarcity of resources in Palestine is not a situation that is going to be resolved quickly. It is an unfortunate fact of life that the paucity of resources leads to competition. This in turn can create a negative culture – one which may have adverse consequences for the organization.

The events in this study indicate that there is an issue around the abuse of power within the Business School at NPU. This is not surprising as a recent study conducted by Muna and Khoury (2012) revealed that there was a noticeable lack of power sharing among executives in Palestine. The study revealed that the dominant style was the autocratic-consultative style of management. Muna and Khoury (2012) go on to write that in their study, Palestinian executives, stressed the importance of the familial role they had – similar to that of a father or older brother. The events in this case suggest that this view was held by the Dean and to some extent upper management at NPU. However, this paternalistic role is gradually becoming less relevant or appropriate in the eyes of the new generation of academics, particularly, the women. Therefore, a challenge confronting NPU is to ensure that the clash of styles and belief systems do not negatively impact the operation of academic units such as the Business School.

The events in the external context – events that are difficult to control –create high levels of stress for both employees and students of NPU. Therefore it is imperative that the stress levels in the internal context are minimised to the greatest degree. Consequently, the challenge for NPU is to develop and implement robust relevant human resource development (HRD) policies with the aim of creating politically skilled leaders who are better able to negotiate the dynamics present within the university. Kisamore et al. (2010) argue that organizational leaders have to be responsive to behaviors in the workplace that create high levels of stress. A responsive leadership is critical to the creation of a positive workplace environment.

Moreover, the distortion of perceptions around the appropriate use of resources, level of skills, ability and qualifications of the more junior faculty need to be modified. In addition, the engaging in destructive criticism, envy and holding of 'grudges' that have led to a negative culture needs to be halted. The evidence suggested that these behaviors manifest themselves in actions, where those who feel threatened, try to 'get even' with the individuals who were perceived to have wronged them or threatened their authority. Research shows that politically skilled individuals are more likely to engage in abusive behaviors as a result of interpersonal conflict, which can damage the organizational culture (Kisamore et al., 2010). This also supports the argument of Greenberg and Baron (2003) who state that this may extend to an individual going as far as to deliberately harm a co-worker. The presence of workplace envy requires intervention from the senior management team – yet as discussed earlier in the case – their attention has been diverted by the challenges and pressure present in the external context.

This then leads to the greatest challenge of all – how to find a balance between the events in the external context that create a negative living environment for the employees and students of NPU and the importance of growing a positive healthy internal organizational culture.

SOLUTIONS AND RECOMMENDATIONS

Subsequent to the events outlined in this case, NPU has become more aware of the 'work-around' practices that have been occurring and the resultant negative impact on the delivery of quality educational services. Consequently, there are now more proactive efforts to restrict such practices. This includes the prohibition on the undertaking of secondary employment outside the university.

The university policies include, the requirement for post-graduate students appointed to a teaching role to be enrolled in a PhD program within two years. The tenure of these appointments is also restricted to two years.

The first recommendation concerns the implementation of a cultural change program with the aim of eliminating existing power-structures based on gender, position and authority. Integral to any cultural change program is an examination of the role of leadership in boosting the development of an ethical multicultural organization (Canen & Canen, 2008). The desired outcome of such a program is the development of a more collegial, team-based, workplace where rewards are based on merit. This is in keeping with Baehler and Bryson's (2008) argument that practical interventions that concentrate on culture, work organization and relationship management may be the most effective means by which to address internal workplace discord.

Canen and Canen (2008) contend that acknowledging diversity is a theoretical, practical and political framework that values diversity, seeks routes to translate such value into actual responses to cultural plurality, and challenges prejudices and stereotyping against cultural, ethnic, racial, gender, religious and other identities. They go to argue that multiculturalism can assist in conflict management and in changing institutions into ethical, multicultural organizations.

The research revealed the need for a comprehensive leadership development program to be implemented with some urgency. One form of development that is recommended is education in conflict management and resolution. Specifically, as recommended by Lakis (2009) that this includes the use of collaborative interest-based approaches. The aim of such education is to contribute to a culture of co-operation as opposed to the divisive culture that currently exists.

In addition, in-service development programs should be designed and implemented with the aim of assisting leaders to develop a more sensitive approach to all forms of diversity (Canen & Canen, 2008). Not only would this contribution be to the reduction of conflict, it would also support the development of employees from minority groups to a point where they are capable of being promoted into academic leadership positions. As recommended by Abu Elanain (2014) these programs should also emphasize the importance of mentoring young faculty, the development of interpersonal communication and human relations skills.

During the study it became obvious that the Human Resource Department was significantly under-resourced. The consequence was that the HR Department was not empowered to develop quality HR policies that improve the issues as outlined in this case. These include policies aimed to ensure that discrimination based on gender is eradicated. That the recruitment and selection polices are reviewed and amended so there is greater transparency and accountability, especially with respect to the internal recruitment processes. This includes ensuring that all internal vacancies are advertized and that recruitment panels are independent and their decisions are upheld without interference from those who may have a vested interest in the result. One example is that an HR representative be invited to the recruitment and selection committee's meetings to observe the proceedings.

It is important to have guidelines with regard to appointment panels and monitoring of hiring decisions. The people who are likely to be part of a hiring panel should be provided with appropriate training and development experiences with the aim to reduce the level of bias in hiring decisions. The difficulties experienced by NPU in recruiting qualified staff highlights the importance of everyone, who is qualified and applies for a position, is treated equitably. It is imperative to the well-being of NPU that they do not lose talented qualified people because of bias and discrimination in the hiring process or in the workplace. This would include ensuring individuals being selected into

leadership positions are evaluated on the basis of diversity awareness leadership competence.

It is recommended that a system of 'check and balances' should be implemented and a means of appeal and arbitration established in the event of a dispute arising. It is considered that this policy will make deans and senior managers more accountable for their decisions in the promotion and recruitment processes. Consequently, the establishment of an alternative disputes resolution or mediation service to support the resolution of interpersonal conflict is recommended. The aim of this service would be to provide impartial advice and guidance in resolving grievances. This service would also act as an intermediary for employees who raise issues with respect to inappropriate behavior and decision-making. It could also involve the use of trained facilitators to work with individuals who are experiencing interpersonal conflict in the workplace

It is recommended that specific criteria be developed for promotion between academic ranks. This will help clarify the process and provide transparency especially with respect to the promotion of faculty from minority groups. To support the transparency of the promotion process some universities in the West have developed 'promotion monitoring teams' for example, the Association of University Women, of that specific university to monitor the internal appointment processes. These interest groups also provide mentoring support for those preparing their promotion portfolio.

CONCLUSION

This chapter examined the impact of the external context on the internal culture of a large Palestinian organization. Specifically, the creation of workplace stress, the miscommunication that occurred as a result of differing leadership styles and the resultant conflict that created a negative culture. NPU does not have the power to change the political, military and conflict issues that exist within its external environment. However, it does have the power to change its internal context. To achieve this, the level of communication must be improved, leadership development enhanced and the issues that create high levels of conflict must be addressed.

REFERENCES

Abu Elanain, H. M. (2014). Leader-member exchange and intent to turnover. *Management Research Review*, 37(2), 110–129. doi:10.1108/MRR-09-2012-0197

Abu Lughod, A. (2000). Palestinian higher educaion: National identity, liberation and globalization. *Boundary*, 27(1), 75–95. doi:10.1215/01903659-27-1-75

Al Dabbagh, M. (2009). The context for intergroup leadership: Women's groups in Saudi Arabia. In T. Pittinsky (Ed.), *Crossing the divide: Intergroup leadership in a world of difference*. Boston, MA: Harvard Business School Publishing Corporation.

Avery, G. C. (2005). *Understanding leadership*. London: Sage Publications.

Baehler, K., & Bryson, J. (2008). Stress, Minister: Government policy advisors and work stress. *International Journal of Public Sector Management*, 21(3), 257–270. doi:10.1108/09513550810863169

Baramki, G. (2009). Peaceful Resistance: Building a Palestinian University under Occupation. London: Pluto Press.

Canen, A. G., & Canen, A. (2008). Multicultural leadership. *The International Journal of Conflict Management*, 19(1), 4–19. doi:10.1108/10444060810849155

Greenberg, J., & Baron, R. A. (2003). *Behavior in organizations* (8th ed.). Upper Saddle River, NJ: Prentice Hall.

Grodnitzky, G. (2005, March). Forcing conflict as a leadership style. *Leaders, Teams, Profits*. Retrieved 29 May 2013, from http://www.drgustavo.com/LTP/Issue34.pdf

Heminway, M. A., & Smith, C. A. (1999). Organizational climate and occupational stressors as predictors of withdrawal behaviors and injuries in nurses. *Journal of Organizational Psychology*, 72(3), 285–299. doi:10.1348/096317999166680

Khoury, G., & Analoui, F. (2009). How Palestinian managers cope with stress. *Journal of Management Development*, 29(3), 282–291. doi:10.1108/02621711011025795

Khoury, G., & McNally, B. (2014). Under pressure: The role of the external context in creating internal tensions - A case study of a Palestinian University. In G. C. Khoury & M. C. Khoury (Eds.), *Cases on Management and Organizational Behavior in an Arab Context* (pp. 128–145). Hershey, PA, USA: IGI Global. doi:10.4018/978-1-4666-5067-1.ch008

Kisamore, J. L., Jawahar, I. M., Liguori, E. W., Mharapara, T. L., & Stone, T. H. (2010). Conflict and abusive workplace behaviors: The moderating effects of social competencies. *Career Development International*, 15(6), 583–600. doi:10.1108/13620431011084420

Klein, M. (1957). *Envy and gratitude: A study of unconcious sources*. London: Tavistock.

Lakis, J. (2009). Social conflicts and the culture of co-operation in transitional society. *Baltic Journal of Management*, 4(2), 206–220. doi:10.1108/17465260910958818

Metcalfe, B. (2009). *Developing women's capability in the public sector in Middle East*. Paper presented at the International Conference on Administrative Development: Towards Excellence in the Public Sector, Riyadh, Saudi Arabia.

Mouly, S., & Sankaran, J. (2002). The enactment of envy within organizations. Insights from a New Zealand academic department. *The Journal of Applied Behavioral Science, 38*(1), 36–56. doi:10.1177/0021886302381003

Muna, F., & Khoury, G. (2012). *The Palestianian executive: Leadership under challenging conditions*. Farnham, UK: Gower Publishing Ltd.

Murphy, L. R., & Sauter, S. L. (2003). The USA perspective: Current issues and trends in the management of work stress. *Australian Psychologist, 38*(2), 151–158. doi:10.1080/00050060310 001707157

Oetzel, J., & Ting-Toomey, S. (2003). Face concerns in interpersonal conflict: A cross-cultural empirical test of the face negotiation theory. *Communication Research, 30*(6), 599–624. doi:10.1177/0093650203257841

Paprock, K. E. (2006). National human resource development in transitioning societies in the developing world: Introductory overview. *Advances in Developing Human Resources, 8*(1), 12 -27.

Quick, J. C., & Nelson, D. L. (2013). *Principles of organizational behavior: Realities and challenges* (International ed.). South Western Cengage Publishing.

Ramon, S., Campbell, J., Lindsay, J., McCrystal, P., & Baidoun, N. (2006). The impact of political conflict on social work: Experiences from Northern Ireland, Israel and Palestine. *British Journal of Social Work, 36*(3), 435–450. doi:10.1093/bjsw/bcl009

Rought-Brooks, H., Duaibis, S., & Hussein, S. (2010). Palestinian women: Caught in the crossfire between occupation and patriarchy. *Feminist Formations, 22*(3), 124–145. doi:10.1353/ff.2010.0018

Ting-Toomey, S. (1994). Managing intercultural conflicts effectively. In L. Samovar & R. Porter (Eds.), *Intercultural communication: A reader* (7th ed.; pp. 360–372). Belmont, CA: Wadsworth.

KEY TERMS AND DEFINITIONS

Effective Communication: Transferring information through a medium in a clear way to avoid misunderstanding and develop relations.

Interpersonal Conflict: A dissimilarity between two individuals or subgroups of an organization relating to considerable umbrage and restlessness.

Leadership Styles: The exhibited behavior of a leader in directing and motivating people to achieve organizational objectives.

Perceptions: Impressions people have and the way they interpret and comprehend something.

Use of Power: Capability to influence.

Workplace Envy: Jealousy and resentment feelings towards colleagues who possesses the skills and capabilities one desires.

Workplace Stress: The perceived imbalance between the demands made of people and their capabilities to handle those demands.

Section 3

Improving Organization:
A Focus on Teams, Engagement, and Personal Development

Chapter 14
Communities of Practice in Organizational Learning Strategies

Mario Perez-Montoro
University of Barcelona, Spain

Sandra Sanz
Open University of Catalonia, Spain

ABSTRACT

In recent years, the interest in and development of communities of practice (CoPs) has undergone exponential growth. However, this uncontrolled expansion has, to a large extent, led to the name of community of practice being attributed to working groups or communities that are not communities of practice. The aim of this work is to shed a little light on this confusion and identify and characterise communities of practice compared with other types of groups or organizational structures. To achieve it, first of all, we are going to introduce an intuitive and agreed definition of community of practice. In a second movement, we will identify and define the principal groups or organizational structures that are used, besides communities of practice, by organizations to improve their strategies when meeting these aims that they are pursuing. We will then present a comparison between these organizational structures or groups and communities of practice. The chapter ends by offering a number of conclusions and providing some guidelines on the future development of communities of practice.

INTRODUCTION

In recent years, we have been witnessing the appearance of a new scenario in organizations in which information and knowledge have become benchmark economic assets.

There are many interpretative proposals that attempt to identify the reasons that justify this new situation. In any event, and even though the whole is very wide, there are two variables, one of a technological nature and the other of a more directly economic nature, that may justify these changes.

On the one hand, a series of new information and communication technologies have permitted the access, management and intensive use of in-

DOI: 10.4018/978-1-4666-9970-0.ch014

formation and knowledge to previously unknown levels. Furthermore, we find that the evolution of the market of these technologies has ended up allowing their costs now to be accessible to the majority of medium and small companies.

On the other hand, a new economic panorama, presided over by the globalization of markets and a new culture of competitiveness, has also been consolidated. In this new economic scenario, companies design new policies of alliances and of organizational culture that may serve as a strategy of adaptation to this new and changing environment. The intangible – and not just the material – assets of companies begin to be understood as that added value that can ensure their correct operation and survival in globalized markets.

Within this economic perspective, and motivated in part by the need to look for new organizational strategies to tackle and survive the phenomenon of the globalization of markets, a new discipline is emerging: Knowledge Management. This new management strategy can be understood as the discipline responsible for designing and implementing systems aimed at systematically identifying, capturing and sharing the knowledge involved in an organization so that it can be converted into a value for the organization.

In this new organizational context, the interest in and development of communities of practice (CoPs) has undergone exponential growth caused in many cases – although not all – by knowledge management itself. The need to manage that part of the professional experiences and practices of the members of an organization where conventional knowledge management systems do not reach has led to its spreading like wildfire. The words of Richard McDermott, "the key to driving change towards sharing knowledge probably lies in communities of practice" (McDermott 1999), have in some way become the *abracadabra* of many entrepreneurs who have seen in communities of practice the solution to many of their problems. From being a term very much restricted to university spheres and just a few organizations, it has

spread unstoppably to all environments: professional or otherwise. This uncontrolled expansion has, to a large extent, led to the name of community of practice being attributed to working groups or communities that are not.

The aim of this work is to shed a little light on this confusion and identify and characterise communities of practice compared with other working teams or groups, and compared with other types of communities such as communities of learning and communities of interest.

In order to achieve these aims, we will be pursuing the following strategy. We are first of all going to introduce an intuitive, and to some extent agreed, definition of community of practice. This definition will enable us to be aware of the principal characteristics that describe this type of community. In a second movement, we will identify and define the principal organizational groups that, besides communities of practice, are used by organizations to improve their strategies when meeting the aims that they are pursuing. We will then present a comparison between these organizational structures or groups and communities of practice. The chapter ends by offering a number of conclusions and providing some guidelines on the future development of communities of practice.

COMMUNITIES OF PRACTICE

No one now doubts that the subject of communities of practice arouses increasingly more interest in the academic field and in that of professional consultancy. Also, this subject is related to the emergent field of social knowledge (Gallo & Yan, 2015; Gurteen, 2012).

However, this widespread interest is simultaneously bringing about a curious and, to some extent, perverse phenomenon. As occurred with the term "information" in the 1980s and 1990s, in recent years the expression "Community of Practice" has become a clear example of a buzzword. In other words, it has become an expression that more and more people are using but which, sadly, very few people know exactly what they are referring to when they use it. Endless companies, consultants, e-learning specialists, Human Resources department managers, among many others, state that they are currently working with this type of strategy. None of them, each with their particular focus, has the slightest hesitation in declaring their unconditional submission to this new enterprise when, often regrettably, they are not at all certain of what it consists or the extent of this type of community.

Amid this sea of confusion, the term Communities of Practice ends up being continuously applied to other types of groups or communities or even work activities that very often have nothing to do with them. Probably one of the reasons that led Wenger and Snyder, two of the most prestigious authors who have theorized about the universe of this special type of community, to write their article "Communities of practice: the organizational frontier" (Wenger and Snyder, 2000) was the desire to try to put an end to this. However, the confusion and the application of the concept continues to rise. The more known the term becomes, the worse the use that is made of it in the non-specialist environments.

Despite the fact that in the scientific literature, the authors coincide in defining communities of practice in very similar terms (although always with small nuances), when transferred to organizational environments or seminars, and even more so to the Internet, we have been able to detect that the application of the concept of community of practice is very often incorrect. In this sense, it should be no surprise that, for example, in many of the workshops on communities of practice that are given to those in charge of knowledge management in companies, cases that are very far from being CoPs may be presented as examples to illustrate the sessions. Or that in talks or lectures, participants can hurry to identify initiatives for the creation of working groups of a different nature in their companies as genuine Communities of

Practice. Or that texts appear on the Internet on supposed experiences that are christened as CoPs without they really being so.

Yet, what really is a community of practice? Ever since Etienne Wenger coined the term in the book published with Jane Lave entitled *Situated learning. Legitimate peripheral participation* (Cambridge University Press, 1991), many authors have defined the concept.

Consequently, for example, Wenger himself, along with Snyder (2000), later defined it as "a group of people who meet informally to share their experience and passion for a common enterprise." In 2002, he extended and improved this definition in the book that he published with McDermott and Snyder (*Cultivating Communities of practice*) as follows: "groups of people that share a concern, a set of problems, or a passion about a topic, and who deepen their knowledge and expertise in this area by interacting on an ongoing basis." According to Sergio Vásquez (2002) "a community of practice is a group of people linked by a common, recurring and stable practice whereby they learn in this common practice." Also, Lesser and Storck (2003) defined it as follows: "a community of practice is a group whose members regularly engage in sharing and learning, based on their common interests." While John Seely Brown (2003) in the 5th Annual Braintrust Knowledge Management Summit in San Francisco defined CoPs as "a group of people with different functions and viewpoints, committed to joint work over a significant period of time during which they construct objects, solve problems, learn, invent and negotiate meanings and develop a way of reading mutually."

We could extend this list of definitions and ascertain that they can reach considerable dimensions. In any event, it is clear that two defining aspects concur in all of them: commitment and common interest. In short, communities of practice are a group of people who carry out the same professional activity or responsibility and who, concerned with a common problem or moved by a common interest, expand their knowledge and expertise in this matter through ongoing interaction (Sanz, 2008).

However, despite the best efforts of these authors to offer a comprehensive definition of them, it is clear that CoPs continue to be confused with other types of communities such as learning communities (Hydle at al., 2014) or interest and with other organisation-related groups such as formal or informal groups and working teams: problem-solving, multidisciplinary or virtual.

OTHER ORGANISATIONAL STRUCTURES

In the context of organisations, it is often the custom to create and develop small groups or communities (in short, organisational structures) to improve internal operations and so meet the desired aims more adequately.

Communities of Practice constitute a special type of these organisational structures. However, if we put this type of community to one side and take another look at the different strategies commonly implemented in organisations, we can identify three large types of groupings or organisational structures: groups, working groups and communities.

Broadly speaking, and in intuitive terms and for any context, communities can be defined as sets, groupings or congregations of people who live together under certain constitutions and rules. However, if we are talking about groups and teams, we need to understand them as groups of people brought together for specific research or a specific service.

The element that certainly most clearly differentiates groups and teams from communities is that the former work to achieve an aim, which is what binds them together and is their *raison d'être*. However, in communities the fact of sharing is what defines them. They share things: zones, services or interests. For example, in the case of a community of owners, this is the common use of

the shared building; and in an educational community, the services and interests of the training centre. There is no specific aim other than that they form part of something that is common to others or that is of interest to everyone. You may be chosen to become part of a group or team, but not to become part of a community. You will be part of a community simply by being in it, by sharing things with it, by being governed by its more or less explicit rules.

If we now turn our attention to the context of organisations, we can identify a series of different types of groups, working teams and communities. Among the main group types, we can identify formal and informal working groups. Among the working teams, we can identify problem-solving working teams, self-managed teams, multidisciplinary teams and virtual teams. However, for communities we can identify communities of interest, learning communities and communities of practice.

Groups

In most cases, communities of practice develop at the very heart of the organisation. It is not difficult therefore to confuse them with the groups that are deployed within this context.

In the context of organisations, groups should be seen as organisational structures that comprise two or more individuals, who interact, are inter-dependent and who have combined to meet specific aims.

In this type of context, groups are usually allocated a series of functions and are used to carry out certain organisational strategies. As a result, they are particularly suited to modifying behaviour, attitudes and values and to disciplining their members. They can in fact be used to exert pressure on members who fail to comply with the rules to make them do so. In addition to this, they are also useful in decision-making and negotiation. Members with different backgrounds can contribute different perspectives to the decision-making process. However, this does not mean that group decisions are always better than individual decisions.

There is a nucleus of common characteristics that, in part at least, define the groups in organisational contexts. These include the fact that they tend to present certain internal communication patterns. This communication can be channelled through a key member or flow freely among all the members of a group. On the other hand, another typical characteristic is that when group interactions are efficient they can influence motivation. If, for example, the members of a group take part in establishing objectives, they will probably make a greater commitment to meeting group goals. Leadership also plays an important role in the context of group processes. Understanding the concepts that refer to groups helps understand the interactions between leaders and followers and also the interactions between all group members. Finally, groups also offer clear advantages to the individuals that comprise them. They offer social satisfaction to their members, the same as a sense of belonging and support for the needs of individuals, they promote communication and they provide security.

We should stress that a wide variety of groups, whose composition, functions and other properties differ significantly, coexist within the organisational context. In this sense, groups in organisational contexts can be classified in many ways and according to different criteria. The general criteria (that are not exclusive in nature) that are most commonly used to classify them are temporality, purpose, hierarchy and activity.

According to the time criterion, two different types of groups can be identified based on the type of stability in the relationships that bind their members together: permanent and temporary groups. Permanent groups are seen as being stable in time and are responsible for the everyday operating and maintenance tasks of the organisation. The time permanency of these groups does not prevent changes being made to their composition. A good

example of this is the different departments that make up a company. However, temporary groups (created *ad hoc*) are designed to carry out transitory tasks, projects or activities. The group has a limited duration and breaks up once its function is complete or it has achieved its aim. This could be a research and development group, a study commission, an advisory committee, etc.

In addition, according to the purpose criterion, and based on the aims to be achieved, four different types of groups can be identified in these contexts: production groups, problem-solving groups, conflict-resolution groups and organisational change and development groups. In production groups, their members undertake specific work together. These are the departments and units of the organisation. Problem-solving groups focus on specific problems of the organisation. Quality circles or project study groups are clear examples of these types of groups. Conflict-resolution groups tackle situations of confrontation between the different parts of the organisation or the organisation with the outside world. Essentially, they are negotiation groups. Finally, organisational change and development groups include different groups and group techniques. These include training groups, team development groups and awareness groups.

According to a hierarchical criterion, two different types of groups can also be identified based on the location within the organisational structure: vertical differentiation and horizontal differentiation groups. Vertical differentiation groups comprise members, who, in turn, belong to different organisation structures ranging from senior management ("strategic apex"), through middle management groups ("middle line") to non-managerial groups ("operating core"). Horizontal differentiation groups, however, coincide with the different functional groups. These are groups that provide specialist services (in terms of production, research, etc.), based on specific skills, and temporary committees, created with different missions, which are essentially to advise and take decisions.

Finally, according to the activity, two different types of working groups can be identified: group activity groups and individual activity groups. Group activity groups are team groups with interdependent tasks, group aims and incentives, stable relationships, etc. However, individual activity groups are dominated by individual activity and values. Members are linked together by little more than sharing a space, a task, professional speciality or reporting to the same boss. A "sales team" in which, among other conditions, individual commissions are awarded (which generates competition among its members), could be seen as a clear example of this final type.

Putting these general criteria of temporality, purpose, hierarchy and activities to one side, the specialist literature contains a certain consensus for accepting and arranging organisational groups according to the degree of formality that characterises them. This classification has been suggested by Robbins (2008) and also coincides with the classification also suggested by authors Hellriegel & Slocum (2008). According to this classification, groups can be arranged by two large categories: formal and informal groups.

Formal groups are defined by the organisational structure, with a number of work allocations designed that establish tasks. In these groups, the behaviour that members should commit to is stipulated by and aimed at organisational goals. The six members of a flight crew are an example of a formal group. These groups are defined and planned to achieve the aims of the organisation. Departments or commissions, for example, irrespective of other criteria, share their formal character. Command and task groups are stipulated in these departments or commissions. Command groups are determined by the company organisation chart. This comprises subordinates who report directly to an appointed manager. Task groups are also determined by the organisation and represent employees who carry out specific types of work. These are also known as functional groups.

In contrast, informal groups are presented as alliances that are not formally structured, nor are they determined by the organisation. These groups are natural formations within the work environment that appear in response to the need for social contact. Three employees from different departments who almost always have lunch together are an example of an informal group. Spontaneous relationships occur between the members of the organisation and are geared towards meeting the personal and social needs of its components. Groups that are created through friendship or attraction, groups of people who share the same problem, can be examples of this type. Interest groups and friends groups can be identified in informal groups. Interest groups are members of the organisation who may join together to achieve a specific aim of common interest (such as exchanging holidays or improving their salary conditions). In friends groups, however, their members share specific characteristics, such as similar age or origins, and they frequently go beyond the work context.

Working Teams

Stephen P. Robbins (2004) places special interest on differentiating working teams from working groups. According to this author, a working group is one where its members primarily interrelate to share information and to take decisions in such a way as to be able to help each member to develop in their area of responsibility. Its performance is merely the sum of the contribution of each member of the group. There is not the necessary positive synergy to create a general level of performance greater than that of the sum of its contributions. However, in the case of teams, this positive synergy is created through a coordinated effort, whereby the sum of its individual efforts is greater. Management seeks this positive synergy that will enable their organisations to increase performance. The extensive use of teams creates the potential for an organisation to generate greater results without an increase in contributions.

Teams can be classed on the basis of their objectives. The three most common forms of team that are found in an organisation are problem-solving teams, self-managed teams and multidisciplinary teams.

In problem-solving teams, members share ideas or offer suggestions on how to improve work processes and methods. Rarely, however, do they have the authority to put any of their suggested actions into practice. One example of problem-solving teams are quality circles. Self-managed teams, in contrast, are groups of employees (normally between 10 and 15) who take on the responsibilities of their former supervisors. Generally speaking, this includes work planning and scheduling, collective control over work pace, taking operational decisions and the execution of the actions on the problems. Completely self-managed working teams even select their own members and make them assess each other's performance. Finally, multidisciplinary teams are made up of employees of the same hierarchical level but from different work divisions, who meet to carry out a task. Multidisciplinary teams are an efficient means of allowing people from different divisions in an organisation (or even between organisations) to exchange information, develop new ideas and solve problems, and coordinate complex projects.

It is also important to point out that Robbins (2004) distinguishes a fourth a kind of team that he calls virtual teams, which use computational technology to bring together physically dispersed members with the aim of achieving a common objective. These teams may do the same as the other teams, such as exchange information, take decisions, complete tasks and also include other members from the same organisation or connect them with employees from other organisations, e.g. suppliers or partners. They may meet for a few days to solve a problem, for a few months to complete a project or they may exist permanently.

Communities

As we mentioned, communities can be identified as the third type of organisational structure, along with working groups and working teams, which are usually developed to improve the correct operation of organisations. If we leave communities of practice to one side, we can distinguish two large types of community: learning communities and communities of interest.

We will begin by describing learning communities. Learning communities are contexts in which the students learn thanks to their participation and involvement, in collaboration with other students, the teacher and other adults, in genuine processes of research and collective construction of knowledge on personal and socially relevant questions (Onrubia 2004).

The premise on which the idea of classrooms as learning communities is based is the consideration that individual learning is, to a large extent, inseparable from the collective construction of knowledge, and that this collective construction constitutes the context, the platform and the basic support so that each student can advance in their own knowledge. In line with this, the activity of the classrooms that are structured as learning communities is not organised, as in traditional classrooms, around the teacher conveying specific pre-established content, but around research processes on specific subjects previously agreed between teacher and students, and which teacher and students tackle jointly and collaboratively.

These processes can take diverse specific forms, such as the creation of projects, case analysis, situation-problem solving or preparing products which will be presented in public. The true and relevant nature of the situations, activities and tasks based on collaborative knowledge-construction processes that are carried out in the classrooms that are structured as learning communities are specified in a whole series of traits that radically define the traits that typically characterise the activity in traditional classrooms (Onrubia 2004). Consequently, in a classroom organised as a learning community, teacher and students commonly tackle global and complex tasks, the resolution of which demands the combined use of knowledge and skills of various types. Considering within this framework the diversity of the students as an essential resource for favouring learning and benefitting somewhat, traditional teaching could never enable students to acquire the same knowledge in the same way and at the same time.

This way, for example, students in a subject such as physics learn to resolve the exercises together and share the way of understanding the concepts in such a way that the ones who find it more difficult to reason and understand the process of how to solve a problem can solve them by listening to their classmates. And this way, they all learn at the same time.

Within this educational context, it is also important to note that it is not possible to obviate the influence of e-learning on the growing interest in communities. In training platform classrooms conceived by some large companies or on the forums of some intranets it is relatively frequent to share the process of assimilation of new skills or new knowledge. In the sphere of secondary education, the use of learning communities as a training resource is becoming increasingly more frequent.

To conclude this characterisation, we should make it clear that learning communities are not reserved exclusively for teaching classrooms and education but can clearly be exported to organisational contexts. However, we should not forget that in these contexts too, the knowledge that is conveyed continues to be linked to concepts or subjects and not to "ways of doing". For example, the case may arise that a learning community emerges around a new IT tool that an organisation has acquired, and that a number of colleagues decide to help each other to learn how it works more quickly. It is clear that we are not speaking of communities of practice because there is not

the desire to share experience or to tackle or solve some task or other, but the process of learning how to use new software. The learning community will end when all the members know how to use the new tool. If we remember the Wenger and Snyder article (2000), communities of practice are not bound to the end of a project or specific objective.

We will now go on to describe communities of interest. Just as the learning communities are largely linked to e-learning, the communities of interest are part of the heart of the Internet. Scientists were the first to use the Internet to share data, cooperate in research and exchange information. However, as of the second half of the 1990s, this use has extended to other interests. Certainly, without looking any further, the "fan" phenomenon has also been one of its greatest driving forces: rock fans, film buffs, avid readers, and so on. Today, the casuistries are infinite. From cancer patients who share how to face the effects of chemotherapy (the Hospital Clínico in Barcelona, Spain) is running an initiative that is as brilliant as it is valuable in this sense) to mothers' groups who share breastfeeding and ante-natal preparation techniques or information about nurseries and schools (as is the case, for example, on the forum of the *Crianza Natural Spanish* website), besides being able to buy childcare, breastfeeding, etc. products online.

Communities of interest share a common interest or passion. The interests may be as varied as the hobbies or casuistries of people. However, the common interest is not the professional practice and although they share techniques or ways of doing things, the common focus does not revolve around learning a specific aspect. Another of their distinctive characteristics, as defended by Amstrong, A. & Hagel, J. (2000), is the mutual lack of acquaintance between their members. Although face-to-face meetings of small groups between members belonging to the community are relatively frequent, it is more common for a member not to know the majority of their colleagues personally. It is even highly probable that they do not know any of them.

COMMUNITIES OF PRACTICE COMPARED WITH OTHER ORGANISATIONAL STRUCTURES

Up to now, we have introduced a general and intuitive definition of communities of practice and we have made a characterisation of some of the principal structures or groups, besides communities of practice, that are used by organisations to improve their strategies when meeting the objectives that they are pursuing. We will now make a comparative analysis between some of these organisational structures and communities of practice.

However, we are not going to make a comparative analysis between every single one of the structures described and communities of practice, but we are going to limit ourselves to comparing only those groups that, due to their special nature, may be confused with communities of practice: formal task groups, problem-solving teams, multidisciplinary teams, virtual teams, learning communities and communities of interest.

In order to complete this analysis, we are first going to extract a series of characterisation elements that will allow us to make a synthetic characterisation of all the organisational structures chosen and then present, in a more experiential form, a comparative analysis.

The characterisation elements that we will be using can be classed in two large general groups or categories: organisational elements (type of leadership, connection with the organisation's processes and cohesion factor) and practical implementation elements (size, virtuality, calendar of meetings, time limitation). All of these elements, with the occasional aid of some illustrative cases, will allow us later to identify clearly the differences and similarities between each one and so complete our comparative analysis.

SYNTHETIC CHARACTERISATION OF SOME ORGANISATIONAL STRUCTURES

We will begin by defining the formal group. These groups need conventional, recognised and active leadership. The task to be carried out is what keeps them together. It is one of the most numerous of the working groups, with between 13 and 16 people, because it is felt that the more members the better and the quicker they can complete the task if each member specialises in one thing. Virtuality is minimal in these groups and the pace of meetings is frequent. The groups will be kept together until the next company reorganisation.

On the other hand, the problem-solving team works more autonomously, and the leader delegates in the team or a team member. The team works until the problem is solved. To ensure its ability to solve and its agility, it is a good idea for these groups not to exceed 12 people, although 10 or fewer members is advised. Virtuality may be partial, yet at the same time it will be necessary to meet frequently, at least twice a week.

In the multidisciplinary team, as in the case of the problem-solving team, leadership is delegated in the actual team. The desirable number of members should be around 10 people. They can work virtually although they will need the face-to-face characteristic to meet frequently. And the achievement of the proposed objective, to solve a process, will be the end of the team.

On the other hand, in the virtual team, the project commissioned is the cohesion factor of its members, which they themselves lead. Virtuality enables communication with a larger number of people, overcoming space-time limitations, so virtual teams are usually bigger. Although it is probable that they need to meet from time to time, they can operate almost exclusively virtually. Its members will be affected by the next reorganisation, although virtuality fosters long-lasting work relationships.

For a learning community to work, by contrast, it is suitable to have the figure of an animator or moderator, as in the case of the communities of practice (Rubin, J. At al., 2014). What keeps its members together is the learning object and this disappears when they have learned what they were seeking to learn. The ideal number of members is between 20 and 25, which ensures that the contents are assimilated at more or less the same pace. It is not necessary to meet, as the community can work perfectly without the need for meetings

By contrast, communities of interest do not need any type of leadership, as it is the interest that moves their members. Each one gets out what they have come looking for, exchanges information, acquires the articles they need, etc. Moderation/animation makes no sense in this context. This type of community is very big in terms of number of members, they work entirely virtually and their members are a part of it for as long as they find a reason to be connected with it.

Finally, within this same synthetic layout, in communities of practice the role of the moderator/animator is vital to ensure their success. It is necessary for a member respected by the rest to control the interventions and the subjects proposed and to urge all the members to participate. In addition, in virtual communities of practice, moderators have an even more valuable role as they are responsible for organising the knowledge that is exchanged, saving the files that have been provided, summarising the contributions made, etc. It is a very similar mission to that of the moderator of learning communities. The cohesion factor is the desire to share professional practice, share their experience with other colleagues and benefit from the expertise of the others. This interest can last a lifetime because there will always be new things to learn and share, and the commitment of their members is too strong a bond. In order for the exchange of knowledge to be sufficiently

rich, it is desirable for the number of participants to be considerable, between a minimum of 50 and a maximum of 80. Neither is it desirable for the number to be too big as it would then become an unmanageable community. If the CoPs are virtual, and it is desirable for them to be so – although we should not forget that there are also face-to-face communities of practice that are absolutely valid – they do not need face-to-face meetings at all.

Table 1. offers a synthesis of the characterisation of all the organisational structures analysed.

Once the synthetic characterisation of the organisational structures is complete, we are going to offer a comparative analysis of all of them and the communities of practice.

We will start with the similarities and differences between the formal task group and the communities of practice. As we have already said, these groups have an assigned fixed, highly specific task that they have to carry out. For example, a company's Human Resources Department will probably have more than one formal task group in operation: selection, hiring, payrolls, risk prevention, training. This very specific factor which may probably lead to a high level of specialisation is at the heart of a possible confusion between these groups and communities of practice, perhaps due to the level of skill that they may achieve. But not even these teams' own synergy, which will perhaps lead to confusion that is more difficult to untangle with regard to CoPs, occurs in this type of groups. This is because they are simply a group of people who work together every day on a set of continuous and interdependent tasks. Their duration as a team is totally dependent on the coming reorganisation and there is no commitment among them.

We will now compare problem-solving groups with communities of practice. One of the most common applications for problem-solving teams during the 1980s was quality circles. These are teams of 8 to 10 employees and supervisors who have a shared area of responsibility and who meet regularly to discuss problems, recommend solu-

Table 1. Synthetic characterisation of some organisational structures Comparative Analysis

	Type of Leadership	Cohesion Factor	Size	Virtuality	Calendar of Meetings	Time Limitation
Formal Task Group (or functional team)	Formal	Task to carry out	13-16 per.	Minimal	Frequent	Until the next reorganisation
Problem-Solving Team	Delegated	Problem to solve	8-12 per.	Partial	Very frequent	Until the problem is solved
Multidisciplinary Team	Delegated	Processes to improve	8-12 per.	Partial	Very frequent	Until the process is improved
Virtual Team	Delegated	Task to carry out	15-30 per.	Total	Practically non-existent	Until the next reorganisation
Learning Community	Moderator/animator	Learning	20- 25 per.	Total	Non-existent	Until the knowledge has been acquired
Community of Interest	_____	Interest	100-500 per.	Total	Non-existent	While the interest lasts
Community of Practice	Moderator/animator	Sharing professional practice	50-80 per.	Total	Non-existent	While the interest and the commitment of its members last

tions and take corrective actions. Described like this, many would consider this a CoP, as their respective definitions seem to coincide. But that is not the case. There are a number of clear characteristics, which we have described above that at first glance would not fit in: they have fewer members than CoPs, there is no clear leader which, unlike the communities of practice, these teams do not need and the time limitation that depends on problems being solved. However, the clearest element that sets them apart is the cohesion factor: the aim of the team is to solve one or more problems, in short, to achieve their aim. To do this, they meet as many times as necessary, but there is no desire to share their expertise nor is there any commitment with regard to other members of the group. The group's purpose is to solve the problem posed to them and once solved they will not maintain contact nor will they exchange information until there is a new problem to solve.

We will now look at the comparison between multidisciplinary teams and communities of practice. Many companies have used horizontal teams without frontiers for decades. For example, IBM created a huge temporary multidisciplinary team in the 1960s, which included employees from the different departments in the company to develop its highly successful *360 System*. Similarly, committees made up of members from all departmental lines are another example of a multidisciplinary team. These teams are clearly distinguished from communities of practice – as well as from the key factor of being a team they are motivated by a specific aim – in that their members do not belong to the same area of speciality. This makes it impossible to share their professional practice and, therefore in this sense, for an exchange of expertise to occur (Bashouri and Duncan, 2014).

The similarities and differences between learning communities and communities of practice, although fewer, are also clear. The frontier between communities of practice and learning communities is diffuse, but we feel that there is a factor that distinguishes them clearly. The former occur and are understood in the context of organisations or professions. In other words, they belong to everyday work, to everyday professional practice, hence the name community of practice. However, learning communities are confined to the teaching profession and the process of assimilating concepts and subjects, but there are a number of additional features that help us differentiate between them. As a result, for example, the difference in the number of members in learning communities is less than for CoPs and also, unlike communities of practice, learning communities come to an end when the target knowledge of the learning process has been acquired. Besides this, they coincide fully in the possibility of a total virtuality should there be a preference for face-to-face and also the need for a moderator/animator. As in the case of CoPs, this figure is vitally important to ensure the functioning of learning communities.

We will conclude this analysis by comparing communities of interest and communities of practice. Communities of interest share information and experiences and these may or may not be connected with professional practice. For example, at http://cnx.org professionals associated with education collaborate to share open educational resources and share news information concerning these resources. Also, http://eprints.reclis.org contains the first open content repository, specifically for libraries. These two examples are closely associated with the profession, but at no point do they go deeply into its knowledge or skill, but they do share information, news and resources. As we said above, communities of interest are clearly an Internet-derived product. This type of community only exists in a virtual sense and what usually occurs is that a members does not personally know the majority of their colleagues. It is even highly likely that they do not know any of them. This is in contrast to learning communities and communities of practice, where their members do know each other prior to the start of the community. However, one characteristic that communities of interest and communities of practice have in common is that the time limitation of these two types of community constitutes the end of the interest.

Although these characteristics are long-lasting in the case of communities of interest, and interest is renewed. When one member stops connecting, it is very easy for a new member to appear.

SOME ILLUSTRATIVE CASES

Our exposition would be incomplete were we not to offer some cases that illustrate the ideas set out so far. To meet this objective, we are going to give a brief presentation of two Spanish cases that we feel to be paradigmatic with regard to the promotion and development of a community of practice: the cases of *La Caixa* and of *Repsol YPF*.

As we will see below, the case of "La Caixa" and the case of Repsol YPF are very different. In one, CoPs appear completely spontaneously from a good melting pot while in the other they are implemented in a much more guided way under a controlled system of objectives and associated incentives. It is clear that both cases are a success as we are speaking of two of the most powerful companies in Spain. However, in the case of Repsol YPF, we run the risk that by working by objectives we are losing sight of one of the principles that define communities of practice. What happens when these objectives have been attained? Does the CoP disappear? Should this be the case, we would surely no longer be speaking of a community of practice. It would be something else, perfectly valid and useful – just look at the results – but if we take into account all of the arguments that we have been defending throughout this chapter, the examples of communities shown by Repsol YPF are on a rather diffuse border.

La Caixa

The "Caixa d'Estalvis i Pensions de Barcelona" bank, known as "La Caixa", has undergone exponential growth over the last ten years, making it Spain's third largest bank.

In 2000, this bank found itself in the position of having to train a large number of employees to replace workers who had retired and to ensure expansion.

To carry out this training, it commissioned an expert e-learning company to create a virtual training platform. As a result, *VirtaulaCaixa* began offering training, with two trial virtual classrooms and 25 new employees. The model proved so successful that in 2004 more than 5,800 recent employees had received training through this new e-learning model.

As well as pedagogical innovation and participatory design methods, a determining factor of the success of the VirtaulaCaixa was the student support system, which was implemented using different media that had been specifically designed for the different communities taking part in VirtaulaCaixa: new employees, service managers, trainers and many more.

Students are, in fact, arranged into communities. New employees have two levels of participation in the community: their virtual classroom and the total community of new employees. In their virtual classroom, they have the support of two trainers, who are in charge of guiding them through the learning process. These new employees, however, also participate socially in VirtaulaCaixa enabling them to communicate with other work colleagues at the bank who are in the same situation (e.g. they have recently joined) and to share problems, opportunities and worries. In other words, participation in VirtaulaCaixa creates a community of new employees.

On many occasions, this community of new employees functions as a learning community depending on which point in the training they have reached. This outstanding custom of sharing the learning process, and overcoming difficulties together, creates an excellent melting pot from where future communities of practice can originate. By this, we do not mean that these learning communities become CoPs once these new em-

ployees are working to full capacity. Nowadays, this is impossible because once they have completed their training, they stop being part of the community of new employees and their reference framework becomes the area of business to which they belong. However, they retain that spirit of sharing and of community which favoured the growth of incipient communities of practice, as we shall explain below.

VirtaulaCaixa currently comprises four communities: Virtaula (the permanent training community for all "la Caixa" employees), New Employees (the online training environment for first-year employees), Trainers (the community of practice and learning for all "la Caixa" trainers) and Financial Services Manager (the training environment associated with the professional development programme for Financial Services Advisors).

The first community, Virtaula, is divided into different DANs (Business Area Management). Each DAN brings together a group of branches that belong to the same zone (county, district, neighbourhood, etc.). In each DAN there may be between 60 and 80 workers. Each business area manager has available the training actions that their employees receive. These actions are carried out through a forum where the different topics for discussion are proposed. A number of initiatives are created here by the area managers – in this particular case, women managers – who choose to promote and encourage employees to share their experiences. This is the case of the Hortaleza-Canillas DAN and the Aljarafe I DAN, where, under the slogan "we all learn from everyone", incipient CoPs have come into being.

Alongside the DANs are the E-groups. These are groups that do not correspond directly to a DAN and where knowledge about specialist subjects is exchanged. Both the DAN and the e-groups comment and discuss concepts related to professional banking practice. These concepts originate from small deliveries of teaching material called "pills" which are specific doses of training content. All employees have access to these pills through the library. This is a highly useful formula that is closer to the learning community than the community of practice. Whatever shape it takes, what is clear is that the spirit of mixing with others and of sharing, so creating a true social fabric of knowledge, flows through the Virtaula.

Repsol YPF

Repsol YPF is an oil company that is on the list of the world's 100 biggest companies. After the two original companies, Repsol and YPF, merged, its growth and expansion has been unstoppable, which has led to an exponential increase in workers who need to be trained and integrated. A lot of employees working on the same things on opposite sides of the world.

The oil company also has an award that is hard to achieve: that of recognition of the transparency of its website. For the third year running, the Repsol YPF website, www.repsolypf.com, has been the most valued of the Spanish Ibex-35 companies thanks to its transparency in the management of the contents of its European corporate website. It is evident that this points to a clear desire to systematise and standardise processes to the utmost. On it, one can find a huge amount of information about the company's structure, organisation and results.

Part of this desire to systematise and standardise is shown in the Knowledge Management model with the aim of knowing who does what and how they do it. Benefitting from the experience of so many employees and sharing it with the others. Combining both efforts and criteria. All of this is achieved through the communities of practice that they implement.

The Knowledge Management Model has two basic components: the human and organisational component (introduction of new organisational structures such as the Communities of Practice where objectives, indicators, Knowledge Maps,

etc. are associated) and the processes / technology component (introduction of processes and technology that aid collaboration, enabling knowledge management).

The Knowledge Management programme is based on the operation of Communities of Practice. The main objective of the Communities of Practice is to generate mechanisms to share and collaborate in the acquisition, publication, search, retrieval and reuse of knowledge, improving the company's operating and general results.

Each of these communities brings together the specialists and people interested in a specific subject, based on a site in the company intranet, where they have information about the subjects relating to their activity (Canavan, Scott and Mangematin, 2013).

The Communities of Practice belonging to this knowledge management system are: Geosciences, Acquisition, quality control and log evaluation. (E-log), Safety and Environment (SyMA), Drilling and workover (Drilling), Well Stimulation (EP), Surface facilities (ISUP), Production, Maintenance of facilities (Maintenance) and Reservoirs

Each community is coordinated by a Manager, who is responsible for the community being formed, developing and continuing. They would be the equivalent of the moderator/animator. They lead the definition of objectives and organise and lead the general activities. Working with them is a Motor Team (which would be the equivalent of what we call animator/moderator), which helps the manager in defining the objectives and plans, and assumes the leadership in various functions of the community: communication, organisation of workshops, updating the site, leading teams in specific subjects or initiatives, etc. The remaining members participate as the Active Community, contributing their knowledge and reusing that of the others. The sponsor of the community is a management-level person, who keeps the community's initiatives in line with the interest of the business.

They also have face-to-face activities in the form of workshops, which bring together the active community, the motor group and the managers with the aim of sharing experiences, knowledge, problems solved and good practices, based on a predetermined subject area / problem.

There is a team in the Systems Department devoted exclusively to the requirements of the managers of the Communities of Practice and of the Knowledge Management Team. The Knowledge Management Team is interdisciplinary in nature, comprised of technology, humanistic careers and specific business professionals (Borzillo, Schmitt, Antino, 2012).

Besides this, Repsol YPF has a programme called Management by Commitment, which regulates the commitments undertaken by the employees, monitors their fulfilment and awards recognition. Knowledge Management is integrated with the Management by Commitment Programme, annually defining objectives related to knowledge management. This integration offers the opportunity to the people in charge of the communities of practice of being able to devote more time to them, empowering the results currently obtained.

The members of the communities (motors and managers) take part and undertake commitments with their day-to-day work voluntarily, becoming clear benchmarks of the behaviours of collaboration, cooperation, proactivity and excellence fostered and rewarded by Repsol YPF through Management by Commitment. They even receive recommendations on the percentage of time to devote to the CoP (15%) and to the motor teams (10%).

Participation and collaboration in the knowledge management initiatives are rewarded by the management through its Annual Recognitions Plan. In this plan, the behaviours that are rewarded are as follows: 1) Active participation in the community. 2) The contribution of experts and benchmarks. 3) Innovation and excellence in professional practice.

Actions to communicate the recognition to the whole of the company are carried out through letters to directors, publications on the intranet, newsletters and Technical Information Newsletter. The prizes range from attendance at congresses or on courses, suitcases up to objects of tangible value.

CONCLUSION

Throughout this paper, our aim has been to achieve two main objectives. On the one hand, to characterise communities of practice. And, on the other, highlight and pinpoint what they have in common and what differentiates them from other groups or structures used as strategies for improving the internal functioning or organisations. And, on the basis of these aims, we are able to reach a number of interesting conclusions and indicate certain directions regarding the future evolution of this type of organisational structure.

The first conclusion is obvious and follows on from the content of this paper: communities of practice can be characterised so that we do not confuse them or assimilate them into other groups or organisational structures. This characterisation may help us establish at all times whether we have a genuine community of practice or, to the contrary, whether what is being undertaken is another type of group strategy.

The second conclusion focuses on the possibility of being able to identify the elements that they may share and, in turn, those that may differentiate communities of practice from the other organisational structures or groups analysed.

The third conclusion centres on the fact that, probably due to the confusion that the term itself entails, promoting communities of practice as a strategy for introducing improvements to the internal functioning of organisations is not that widespread and generalised. However, there are other reasons, apart from the confusion that the term itself involves, that may justify the low level of integration of this type of strategies in company processes. Of these, we would like to highlight the significant difficulty of comfortably allocating organisation costs for these types of projects, the lack of indicators that enable their efficiency to be assessed, low investment to accompany their development or the limited involvement of senior management in this type of project.

However, in terms of the future short- and medium-term scenario, the consolidation and expansion of the creation of communities of practice in organisational contexts may depend on a range of factors. It is therefore important to associate and secure the managerial support of the organisations to accompany projects of this type. Without this support, these projects are heading for failure. One example of this type of support could be translated into a context where Human Resources Departments included the promotion of communities of practice in their training programmes as an additional action. A clear case of this strategy could be the communities of practice that are being developed at the RACC (Royal Automobile Club of Catalonia), where communities of practice are used to train new workers. Due to the huge expansion experienced over the last 6 years, it is a quick and efficient system for beginners to get up to speed reliably and without delay in their work post.

Besides this, development of the communities should also be accompanied by training strategies for their members. Training needs to be given in animation and group management techniques for the moderator and in informational literacy so that all participants can enjoy the benefits and flexibility of the online implementation of the communities.

No less important is the creation of a stable and open circuit in which to disseminate the successful developments, and also the failures, of the experiences related to the communities of practice. This would allow the refinement and improvement of the strategies to foster and accompany the imple-

mentation of these organisational structures. In short: fostering with this stable circuit a form of "metacommunity" of practices on the subject of the development of the communities of practice themselves.

Finally, in the technological sphere, the challenges are also important. The expansion and consolidation of this type of strategy necessarily involves, in the first place, correcting this false dominant perception that fostering and accompanying a community of practice is summarised solely and exclusively in a technological implementation. Having corrected this perception, it is also critical to develop adequate software that meets the following conditions: that meets the needs of the community of practice (easy-to-use tools as near as possible to the usual work interface of the members of the CoP), that becomes a technological standard in the field of the implementation and that is open source, so its development does not depend on the investment of an IT multinational. Without the development of this kind of software, the future of the communities and their potential benefits become significantly gloomy.

REFERENCES

Amstrong, A., & Hagel, J. (2000). The real value of online communities. In E. L. Lesser & M. Fontaine (Eds.), *Knowledge and communities* (pp. 85–98). Boston: Butterworth-Heinemann. doi:10.1016/B978-0-7506-7293-1.50009-3

Bashouri, J., & Duncan, G. (2014). Communities of practice: Linking knowledge management and strategy in creative firms. *The Journal of Business Strategy*, *35*(6), 49–57. doi:10.1108/JBS-08-2013-0072

Borzillo, S., Schmitt, A., & Antino, M. (2012). Communities of practice: Keeping the company agile. *Journal of Business Strategy*, *33*(6), 22-30.

Bronfman, V. S. (2002). Comunidades de práctica. Paper presented at the Workshop GEC S.A., Barcelona, Spain.

Brown, J. S., & Duguid, P. (1991). Organizational learning and communities of practice: Towards a Unified View of working, learning and innovation. *Organization Science*, *2*(1), 40–57. doi:10.1287/orsc.2.1.40

Canavan, D., Scott, P. S., & Mangematin, V. (2013). Creative professional service firms: Aligning strategy and talent. *The Journal of Business Strategy*, *34*(3), 24–32. doi:10.1108/JBS-10-2012-0058

Coll, C. (2001). Las comunidades de aprendizaje y el futuro de la educación: el punto de vista del forum universal de las culturas. Simposio Internacional Sobre Comunidades de Aprendizaje, Barcelona, Spain.

Coll, C. (2004). Una experiencia educativa con futuro. *Trabajadores de la enseñanza*, 249, enero 2004, 12-13. Retrieved February 2, 2009, from http://www.fe.ccoo.es/publicaciones/TE/249/249pdf

Else, S. (2003). Practicing Knowledge Communities. *Knowledge Management*. Retrieved February 2, 2009, from http://www.destinationkm.com/articles/default.asp?ArticleID=1044

Fisher, G. (2001). Communities of interest: learning through the Interaction of Multiple Knowledge Systems. *Proceedings of the 24th IRIS Conference*. Ulvik, Department of Information Science, Bergen.

Gallo, G., & Yan, Ch. (2015). The Effects of Reputational and Social Knowledge on Cooperation. *Proceedings of the National Academy of Sciences of the United States of America*, *112*(12), 3647–3652. PMID:25775544

Glueck, M. (Ed.). (2006). *Work the Net: a Management Guide for Formal Networks*. New Delhi: GTZ.

Gurteen, D. (2012). *Leading Issues in Social Knowledge Management. A collection of important Social Knowledge Management papers*. Academic Publishing International.

Hellriegel, D., & Slocum, J. W. (2008). Organizational Behavior (12th ed.). Cincinnati, OH: South-Western College Publishing (Thomson Learning).

Hydle, K., Kvalshaugen, R., & Breuning, K. (2014). Transnational practices in communities of task and communities learning. *Management Learning*, *45*(5), 609–629. doi:10.1177/1350507613500881

Lave, J., & Wenger, E. (1991). *Situated Learning: Legitimate Peripheral Participation*. Cambridge, UK: Cambridge University Press. doi:10.1017/CBO9780511815355

Lesser, E. L., & Storck, J. (2001). Communities of practice and organizational performance. *IBM Systems Journal*, *40*, 4. Retrieved February 2, 2009, from http://www.research.ibm.com/journal/sj/404lesser.html

Mc Dermott, R. (1999). Nurturing Three Dimensional communities of Practice: How to get the most out of human networks. *Knowledge management Review*. Retrieved February 2, 2009, from http://www.co-i-l.com/coil/knowledge-garden/cop/dimensional.shtml

McDermott, R. (1999). Why Information Technology Inspired But Cannot Deliver Knowledge Management. *California Management Review*, *41*(3), 103–117. doi:10.2307/41166012

Onrubia, J. (2004). Las aulas como comunidades de aprendizaje. *Trabajadores de la enseñanza, 249*, 14-15. Retrieved February 2, 2009, from http://www.fe.ccoo.es/publicaciones/TE/249/249pdf

Robbins, S. P. (2008). *Organizational Behavior* (13th ed.). Prentice Hall.

Rubin, J. (2014). The learning strategy prism: Perspectives of learning strategy experts. *System*, *43*(1).

Sanz, S. (2009). Comunitats de pràctica o l'aprenentatge compartit. *Revista Guix*.

Wenger, E. (1998). *Communities of practice: Learning, meaning, and identity*. Cambridge, UK: Cambridge University Press. doi:10.1017/CBO9780511803932

Wenger, E., McDemortt, R., & Snyder, W. (2002). Cultivating Communities of practice. Boston: Harvard Business Scholl Press.

Wenger, E., & Snyder, W. (2000). Communities of practice: The organizational frontier. *Harvard Business Review*, (January-February), 139–145.

KEY TERMS AND DEFINITIONS

Communities of Practice: Group of people who perform the same professional activity or responsibility who, concerned with a common problem or moved by a common interest, expand their knowledge and expertise in this subject through ongoing interaction.

Communities of Interest: Group of people who share a common interest or passion and exchange information, news and products with regard to it.

Learning Communities: Contexts in which the students learn thanks to their participation and involvement, in collaboration with other students, the teacher and other adults, in genuine processes of research and collective construction of knowledge on personal and socially relevant questions.

Formal Task Group: Group formed by workers responsible for a specific work task.

Problem-Solving Team: Organisational structure formed by workers who share ideas or offer suggestions on how to improve working processes and methods.

Multidisciplinary Team: Organisational structure formed by employees of the same hierarchical level but from different work divisions, who meet to carry out a task.

Virtual Team: Organisational structure formed by employees who use computational technology to bring together physically dispersed members with the aim of achieving a common objective.

Chapter 15
A Unified Framework of Organizational Perspectives and Knowledge Management and Their Impact on Job Performance

Kijpokin Kasemsap
Suan Sunandha Rajabhat University, Thailand

ABSTRACT

This chapter introduces the framework and causal model of organizational culture, organizational climate, knowledge management, and job performance related to business process orientation. It argues that dimensions of organizational culture, organizational climate, and knowledge management have mediated positive effect on job performance. Knowledge management positively mediates the relationships between organizational culture and job performance and between organizational climate and job performance. Organizational culture is positively related to organizational climate. Furthermore, the author hopes that understanding the theoretical constructs of organizational culture, organizational climate, knowledge management, and job performance through the use of the framework and causal model will not only inform researchers of a better design for studying organizational culture, organizational climate, knowledge management, and job performance, but also assist in the understanding of intricate relationships between different factors.

INTRODUCTION

Globalization has resulted in the use of knowledge as competitive weapon in modern organizations (Chu, Kumar, Kumar, & Khosla, 2014). Organizational culture is a strategic resource that influences a range of activities within firms, and empirical evidence from management and mar-keting demonstrates that it impacts performance (Wei, Samiee, & Lee, 2014). Organizational culture is found to contribute to knowledge sharing and learning within project-based organizations, playing an important role in establishing organizational context and foundation for social interaction (Wiewiora, Murphy, Trigunarsyah, & Brown, 2014). A strong organizational culture that aligns

DOI: 10.4018/978-1-4666-9970-0.ch015

members' behavior with organizational objectives boosts financial performance (Chatman, Caldwell, O'Reilly, & Doerr, 2014). Organizational climate is associated with a variety of positive outcomes (e.g., increased organizational success, lower employee turnover, higher job satisfaction, and enhanced overall firm performance) (Koles & Kondath, 2015). Organizational climate is linked to employee commitment toward gaining improved job performance (Neelam, Bhattacharya, Sinha, & Tanksale, 2015).

With the advances in information technology and its increasing impact on humans and society, there has been an expanding need to spread knowledge from domain to domain (Hvannberg, 2015). The success of knowledge processes often relates to organizational cultural characteristics (Mueller, 2015). Effective knowledge management leads to organizational success (Kim, 2014) and organizational performance (Cho & Korte, 2014). The reuse of knowledge and information arising from the different phases of a product's lifecycle is crucial for a company in order to achieve competitive advantage (Ahmed-Kristensen & Vianello, 2015). To leverage their knowledge resources, many organizations deploy knowledge management systems, which contain at their core a knowledge repository (Ravindran & Iyer, 2014).

The integration of business process management and knowledge management helps companies to improve temporal, qualitative and cost aspects of the provision of goods and services and to increase their innovative capacities (Schmid & Kern, 2014). Practices of knowledge sharing relate to communication, observation, artifacts, and human resource practices (Mueller, 2015). Communication plays an important role in these practices, as individuals share a considerable amount of knowledge in conversations and in written communication, such as documents, guidelines, and handbooks (Renzl, 2007). Research objectives are to unify a framework and a causal model of organizational culture, organizational climate,

knowledge management, and job performance related to business process orientation of software manufacturing plant employees in Thailand.

BACKGROUND

Organizational effectiveness (e.g., job performance and productivity) depends on business processes designed from a stakeholder perspective (Siemieniuch & Sinclair, 2002). Consequently, improvement of the process design is the key to improve business performance (Hammer, 2007a). Business process orientation is defined as a process oriented thinking and management of organization emphasizing process outputs and customer satisfaction (Hinterhuber, 1995; McCormack, 2007). The concept of business process orientation involves seven components (i.e., design and documentation of business processes, management commitment toward process orientation, process ownership, process performance measurement, corporate culture in line with the process approach, application of continuous process improvement methodologies, and process-oriented organizational structure) (Kohlbacher & Gruenwald, 2011). Business process orientation introduces transparency in the organization (Kohlbacher, 2009). Furthermore, the more business process oriented an organization is, the better it performs both from an overall perspective as well as from the perspective of the employees (McCormack, Johnson, & Walker, 2003).

Likewise, there is a strong relationship between business process orientation and organizational performance (McCormack & Johnson, 2001). The effects of business process orientation on organizational performance are the speed improvements, increasing of customer satisfaction, improvement of quality, reduction of cost, and improvement of financial performance, respectively (Kohlbacher, 2010). By discovering and analyzing an organization's business processes, non-value adding activities are easily detected (Kohlbacher, 2009). The elimination of non-value adding activities should lead to cost reductions which in turn should lead to improved job performance (Kohlbacher, 2009). Furthermore, Hammer (2007b) stated that business process orientation leads to better financial performance. The results of the empirical study of McCormack and Johnson (2001) provided evidence that business process orientation helps companies to improve business performance and reduce inter-functional conflict. Business process orientation also involves cultural aspects (Hinterhuber, 1995). The cultural fit is an important issue since people and processes must combine to produce output (Armistead & Machin, 1997).

Only an organizational culture based on teamwork, willingness to change, customer orientation, personal accountability, and a cooperative leadership style goes hand in hand with the process approach (Hammer, 2007b). Hammer (2007b) and Hinterhuber (1995) indicated that the business process orientation leads to higher product quality. A focus on organizational processes has increased in managerial practice (Benner & Veloso, 2008). Business process orientation can be interpreted as the organizational effort required to make business processes the platform for organizational structure and strategic planning (Reijers, 2006; Sabherwal, Hirschheim, & Goles, 2001). Furthermore, the aspect of business process orientation is to help firms gain competitive advantage, and, as such, managers facing organizational problems may adopt process management practices as a response to these problems (Kohlbacher & Gruenwald, 2011). The empirical study of Ittner and Larcker (1997) revealed that certain business process management methods improve profitability. Case study research, carried out by Kung and Hagen (2007), uncovers a positive relationship between business process orientation and product quality.

It is widely accepted that shifting to business process orientation can help firms yield extraordinary performance improvements, as quality increase, satisfaction enhancement, procedure optimization and cross-functional connectedness increment, through the rethinking and reengineering of their core businesses (Hammer, 2007b; Kohlbacher, 2010; McCormack & Johnson, 2001). Extensive literature showed that business process orientation consists of a change in structure, focus, management, and culture of a company (Hammer, 2007b; Kohlbacher, 2010; McCormack & Johnson, 2001), which in turn effects the way and environment of employee's work. In process-oriented organizations, employees are able to make the improvement and innovation decision through their group works (Axtell et al., 2000). According to Avery (2004), leaders can affect followers and performance indirectly by actions such as creating an environment in which employees can work effectively, developing an appropriate culture that helps employees build commitment to organizational goals, and formulating strategy. Furthermore, job performance of organization has a strong impact of organization culture as it leads to enhance productivity (Awadh & Saad, 2013).

Kess and Haapasalo (2002) stated that software processes are related to knowledge processes, structured within a knowledge management framework. Aurum et al. (2003) pointed out that software development can be improved by recognizing related to knowledge content and structure, as well as appropriate knowledge and engaging in planning activities. Kess and Haapasalo (2002) advocated the use of project reviews to improve software quality. The results of a case study into a telecommunication organization are indicated, thus revealing the centrality of knowledge creation and sharing to improving the software development process (Kess & Haapasalo, 2002). Rus and Lindvall (2002) stated that organizations must facilitate both formal and informal knowledge sharing among software developers. Furthermore, Rus and Lindvall (2002) asserted that knowledge management complements existing approaches to software process improvement, rather than seeking to replace them. In 2003, the book of Managing Software Engineering Knowledge (Aurum et al., 2003) was published, focusing on a range of topics, from identifying why knowledge management is important in software engineering, to supporting structures for knowledge management applications in software engineering, and to offering practical guidelines for managing knowledge.

Dingsoyr and Conradi (2002) surveyed the literature for studies of knowledge management initiatives in software engineering. Furthermore, Dingsoyr and Conradi (2002) found eight reports on lessons learned, which are formulated with respect to what actions that companies took, what the effects of the actions were, what benefits were reported, and what kinds of strategy for managing knowledge were used. Knowledge is widely recognized as a strategic asset in improving organizational performance (Sharma & Djiaw, 2011). The goal of knowledge management is to deliver the right knowledge to the right members at the right time which can help members take the right actions and further improve the performance of circulation processes in an organization (Milton, Shadbolt, Cottman, & Hammersley, 1999; O'Dell & Grayson, 1999). The critical issue in the stage of product planning to the stage of getting on the market is on how to integrate all of the knowledge from different individuals in order to reach effective and efficient creation and knowledge management (Madhavan & Griver, 1998).

Knowledge management implementation contributes to the improvement of product processes and yields, decreases mistakes, accelerates product processes, and further increases process efficiency, accordingly, to evaluate process performances, such as yield, product quality, process flexibility, and reduces process circulation time (Boomer, 2004; Hollander & Mihaliak, 2002). Organizational culture is generally seen as a set of key values, assumptions, understandings, and norms shared by members of an organization and taught to new members as correct (Daft, 2005). It

is argued that organizational culture may be the critical key that managers can use to direct the course of their firms (Smircich, 1983). Furthermore, Selamat et al. (2013) stated that organizational climate is a crucial factor in enhancing job performance. The culture of cooperative norms has a significant influence on the ability to apply knowledge (Ahmad, Mohamad, & Ibrahim, 2013).

Overview of Organizational Culture

According to Ravasi and Schultz (2006), organizational culture is a set of shared mental assumptions that guide interpretation and action in organizations by defining appropriate behavior for various situations. Deal and Kennedy (1982) defined organizational culture as the way things get done around here. According to Schein (1992), organizational culture is the most difficult organizational attribute to change, thus outlasting organizational products, services, founders and leadership and all other physical attributes of the organization. Denison (1990) defined artifacts as the tangible aspects of culture shared by members of an organization. Verbal, behavioral, and physical artifacts are the surface manifestations of organizational culture.

According to Schein (1992), the two main reasons why cultures develop in organizations are due to external adaptation and internal integration. External adaptation reflects an evolutionary approach to organizational culture and suggests that organizational cultures develop and persist because they help an organization to survive and flourish (Schein, 1992). If the organizational culture is valuable, then it holds the potential for generating sustained competitive advantages (Schein, 1992). Additionally, internal integration is an important function since social structures are required for organizations to exist (Schein, 1992). Organizational practices are learned through socialization at the workplace. Work environments reinforce organizational culture on a daily basis by encouraging employees to exercise cultural values (Schein, 1992). Furthermore, innovativeness, productivity through people, and the other cultural factors have positive economic consequences (Peters & Waterman, 1982).

An organizational culture that is an adhocracy is most effective in advancing entrepreneurial orientation, especially in national cultures that are characterized by strong individualism and low power distance, whereas a hierarchical organizational culture is generally a barrier to entrepreneurial orientation (Engelen, Flatten, Thalmann, & Brettel, 2014). Managers and employees differ in their perception of organizational culture (Campbell & Göritz, 2014). Bhalla and Nazneen (2013) stated that the most dominant components of organizational culture are confrontation, openness, and experimentation. All relations describing enterprise architecture mechanisms and their effects are significantly moderated by organizational culture (Aier, 2014). Huhtala et al. (2015) indicated that organizations should support ethical practices at the work-unit level, to enhance work engagement, and should also pay special attention to work units with a low ethical culture because these work environments can expose employees to burnout.

Overview of Organizational Climate

Originally, the term of organizational climate was used to refer to a range of environmental influences such as the psychological environment; and social, organizational, and situational influences on behavior (Forehand & Gilmer, 1964; Guetzkow, Forehand, & James, 1962). Organizational climate is the process of quantifying the organizational culture (John, Robert, & Konopaske, 2008). Organizational climate precedes the notion of organizational culture (John et al., 2008). It is a set of properties of work environment, perceived directly or indirectly by the employees, that is assumed to be a major force in influencing employee

behavior (John et al., 2008). Organizational climate is often defined as the recurring patterns of behavior, attitudes, and feelings that characterize the individual's life in the organization (Isaksen & Ekvall, 2007) while an organizational culture tends to be deep and stable.

Although organizational culture and organizational climate are related, organizational climate often proves easier to assess and change. These individual perceptions are often aggregated or collected for analysis and understanding at the team or group level, or the divisional, functional, or overall organizational level. Research on organizational climate in organizations has attracted a lot of attention in the last decade (James et al., 2008). Organizational climate research began with analysis at the individual level, concentrating on what is termed psychological work climate. In this approach, individual co-workers are asked to indicate the organizational climate at their workplace (Tordera, Gonzalez-Roma, & Peiro, 2008). Furthermore, there is a relationship between organizational climate and the various measures of organizational outcomes such as productivity and innovation (Patterson et al., 2005), knowledge management (Chen & Huang, 2007), and innovative performance (Bengtson & Solvell, 2004).

Overview of Knowledge Management

Knowledge management capabilities are divided into two types (i.e., knowledge infrastructure and process capabilities) (Cho & Korte, 2014). Effective knowledge management should be coherent and based on organizational strategy (Bagnoli & Vedovato, 2014). Kasemsap (2014a) explained that knowledge management, strategic orientation, and organizational innovation have a positive impact on organizational performance. Organizational learning is systematically correlated with knowledge management in global business (Kasemsap, 2014b). Human resource management, organizational learning, and knowledge management capability lead to improved organizational performance in global business (Kasemsap, 2015a). Using data mining methods for business intelligence makes it easier for the users to promote its overall contribution to the knowledge management process (Kasemsap, 2015b).

While knowledge management-related business strategy is important, the knowledge-sharing behavior of knowledge workers is a critical enabler of effective knowledge management and organizational performance (Chu et al., 2014). Recent knowledge management research focuses on promoting the knowledge sharing and reusing among the people (Liu & Wang, 2015). Supporting inter-team knowledge sharing is fundamental in scaling agility across the entire organization, and is regarded as the new horizon for agile software development (Santos, Goldman, & de Souza, 2015). The analytic hierarchy process (AHP) can be a useful guide in the decision-making process of knowledge management implementation (Anand, Kant, Patel, & Singh, 2015). Introducing knowledge sharing to an organization must address blockages in the learning flows caused by fragmentation within the community of action research (Massingham, 2015). The main value of knowledge is its usefulness in solving problems (Gillberg & Vo, 2014).

According to Penrose (1959), knowledge of an employee is based on his or her skills and experiences and ability to absorb new knowledge. Therefore, while knowledge is a resource in its own right, the way in which knowledge is managed and used will affect the quality of services that can be leveraged from each resource owned by the firm. Knowledge management is placed in an important supporting role within the firm (Penrose, 1959). An alternative way of viewing knowledge management is to consider it as a coordinating mechanism that enables organizational resources to be converted into capabilities (Nelson & Winter, 1982). Nelson and Winter (1982) stated that coordinating mechanisms are required to

ensure people not only know their own jobs but are also able to interpret and respond to information flowing into the organization. Thus, effective knowledge management, a capability in its own right, is also critical to the firm survival because it underpins the development of other capabilities. Knowledge management has been considered to be an important resource in competitive advantage of organization (Nahapiet & Ghoshal, 1998).

Overview of Job Performance

Job performance referred to an act of accomplishing or executing a given task (Griffin, 2012). Coming from a psychological perspective, Campbell (1990) defined job performance as an individual level variable. Likewise, job performance is something a single person does (Campbell, 1990). First, Campbell (1990) defined job performance as behavior. It is something done by the employee. This concept differentiates performance from outcomes. Outcomes are the result of an individual's performance, but they are also the result of other influences. In other words, there are more factors that determine outcomes than just an employee's behaviors and actions (Campbell, 1990).

Campbell (1990) allowed for exceptions when defining performance as behavior. For instance, Campbell (1990) clarified that performance does not have to be the directly observable actions of an individual. It can consist of mental productions such as answers or decisions. However, performance needs to be under the individual's control, regardless of whether the performance of interest is mental or behavioral (Campbell, 1990). The related construct of performance is productivity (Campbell & Campbell, 1988). This can be considered as a comparison of the amount of effectiveness that results from a certain level of cost associated with the effectiveness. In other words, effectiveness is the ratio of outputs to inputs (Campbell & Campbell, 1988).

A UNIFIED FRAMEWORK OF ORGANIZATIONAL PERSPECTIVES AND KNOWLEDGE MANAGEMENT AND THEIR IMPACT ON JOB PERFORMANCE

Research Objectives

1. To unify a framework of organizational culture, organizational climate, knowledge management, and job performance related to business process orientation.
2. To unify a causal model of organizational culture, organizational climate, knowledge management, and job performance related to business process orientation.

Research Questions

1. What is a framework of organizational culture, organizational climate, knowledge management, and job performance related to business process orientation?
2. What is a causal model of organizational culture, organizational climate, knowledge management, and job performance related to business process orientation?

Relationships among Organizational Variables

In the context of projects, certain cultural attributes have been found to promote, whereas others to hoard, knowledge sharing in a context of projects (Wiewiora, Trigunarsyah, Murphy, & Coffey, 2013). Wiewiora et al. (2013) indicated that cultural values related to informality, teamwork, collaboration, employee involvement, and non-competitive environment promoted sharing of any kinds of knowledge, whereas values related to competitiveness, achievement, and focus on winning led to knowledge hoarding. The type of culture in which organizations operate has a strong influence on their knowledge-sharing behaviors (Wiewiora et al., 2014). Ghorbanhosseini (2013) found that organizational culture, teamwork, and organizational development have a direct and significant impact on human capital, and that human capital has a positive effect on organizational commitment. Guerci et al. (2015) indicated that the increasing challenges faced by organizations have led to numerous studies examining human resource management practices, organizational ethical climates, and sustainability. Top management ethical leadership enhances organizational performance (Shin, Sung, Choi, & Kim, 2015).

The impact of organizational climate on firm performance has interested both academicians and practitioners (Clark, 2002; Koene, Vogelaar, & Soeters, 2002; Patterson, 2005). Competitive globalization pressures and rapid technology advances increase the need for firms to continuously adapt, improve, and innovate (Brown & Eisenhardt, 1995; Gilson & Shalley, 2004). Firms with greater innovativeness will be more successful in responding to changing environments and developing new capacities to achieve better performance (Montes, Moreno, & Fernandez, 2004). Organizational culture can be defined as a pattern of basic assumptions (Schein, 1984). These assumptions may facilitate or hinder information flow between various organizational stakeholders both inside and outside the organization (De Long & Fahey, 2000). Furthermore, organizational culture creates organizational climate (Reichers & Schneider, 1990), and it endures longer than their climatic counterparts (Denison, 1996; Moran & Volkwein, 1992). Knowledge-sharing activities are highly influenced by organizational culture (De Long & Fahey, 2000) and exhibit a strong relationship with organizational values (McDermott & O'Dell, 2001).

Furthermore, organizational values influence knowledge-sharing activities of employees in positive or negative ways (Alavi, Kayworth, & Leidner, 2005). Companies must develop knowledge management activities that fit with their organizational cultures rather than trying to change their cultures to fit their knowledge management programs (McDermott & O'Dell, 2001). Organizational climate denotes the way things are around here (Reichers & Schneider, 1990). Organizational climate may exist at two distinct levels: the psychological climate of the individual referring to perceptions of the work environment; and organizational climate constituting shared perceptions of employees about the organizational environment (Ostroff, 1993). Organizational climate implies the personality of the organization (Forehand & Vonhallergilmer, 1964). Organizational climate affects employee attitudes, employee behavior and organizational effectiveness (Ferris et al., 1996). Whereas organizational climate is observable and held in workers' minds at a conscious level, culture abides within the subconscious of employees (Moran & Volkwein, 1992; Reichers & Schneider, 1990; Sparrow & Gaston, 1996).

Organizational climate research considers perceptions related to psychological fields at the individual and organizational levels, while organizational culture research is concerned with a collectivist emphasis involving understandings at the group level (Sparrow & Gaston, 1996). There is a model containing climatic factors of ownership of ideas, openness, risk taking, and trust (Golembliewski, 1993). Knowledge is widely recognized as a strategic asset that enables firms to sustain distinctive competencies and discover innovation opportunities (Chen, 2004; Grant, 1996). Some previous studies have revealed the important role of knowledge management in the innovation processes and outcomes (Argote, McEvily, & Reagan, 2003; Nonaka & Takeuchi, 1995). Effective knowledge management provides individuals and groups with the opportunities to create, retain, and share knowledge (Argote et al., 2003). Knowledge management activities may need appropriate organizational climate for tacit knowledge embedded in individual employees (Dougherty & Hardy, 1996) and utilize the knowledge to develop new products. Organizational climate is the shared perception among organizational members about organizational common practices, procedures, and value systems (De Long & Fahey, 2000).

Employees rely on shared climate to interpret events, develop appropriate attitudes, and understand expectations concerning their behaviors and consequences (Wasko & Faraj, 2005). Organizational climate can shape the context for organizations to influence employees' perception of knowledge management and innovations (Chen & Lin, 2004). Supportive climate can be considered as the force that holds people together and lets them share and contribute their knowledge to help achieve their mutual goals. The existence of a supportive climate sends a clear signal to employees that certain aspects of behaviors and initiatives in innovation activities are expected and supported in organizations. Supportive climate indicates that the work environment is sociable, encouraging, open, relationship-oriented, and collaborative (Wallach, 1983). The positive effect of knowledge management on innovativeness may be contingent on the extent of supportive climate. Individual knowledge is tacit, specific, and highly personal, and therefore is not easy to be translated into collective organizational knowledge (Szulanski, 1996).

Furthermore, a supportive climate would help promote shared representations, interpretations, and systems of meaning among people and therefore would enhance teamwork through creating an atmosphere of cooperation and openness (Nahapiet & Ghoshal, 1998; Shadur, Kienzle, & Rodwell, 1999). If firms have a higher level of supportive atmosphere, organizational barriers will be reduced to foster interpersonal relationships among members. Employees can develop a common mental code to transfer tacit knowledge into practical use (Simonin, 1999). Such supportive climate can attract employees to involve in the activities of transforming knowledge into innovations, and increase the necessary resources and funding invested in the process (Brown &

Eisenhardt, 1995). Organizational climate may play an essential role in shaping employees' behaviors and influencing their perceptions of knowledge management. From the social capital perspective, firms can mobilize different aspects of organizational climate such as supportive climate and innovative climate (Bock, Zmud, Kim, & Lee, 2005) to provide employees with common practices, shared beliefs, and value systems to be engaged in knowledge management.

Employees can be mobilized to create and exchange knowledge when they work in a continuously innovative atmosphere (Norrgren & Schaller, 1999). Under an innovative climate, the work environment is challenging, stimulating, creative, and risk-taking (Wallach, 1983). Firms can encourage employees to think freely, to share their opinions and ideas openly, and to explore new knowledge and skills through formulating an innovative climate (Oliver & Anderson, 1994). When firms possess a higher level of innovative climate, employees may enact to exchange and share knowledge for insightful and innovative ideas. An innovative climate would encourage employees to contribute their knowledge and devote their effects to create knowledge within the firm. When employees perceive a higher degree of supportive atmosphere, they are more inclined to working together and sharing knowledge (Janz & Prasarnphanich, 2003). Such collaborative behaviors among employees enable them to get more involved in knowledge management activities. Thus, a supportive climate would have a positive impact on knowledge management. Employees learn collectively to develop and exchange knowledge and skills when implementing their work and try to promote each other's performance (Janz & Prasarnphanich, 2003).

Leaders can affect followers and performance indirectly by actions such as creating an environment in which employees build commitment to organizational goals, and formulating strategy (Avery, 2004). Successful leaders tend to create an organizational climate within work environment where they are able to assist employees to set and achieve individual, team, and organizational objectives (Perryer & Jordan, 2005). Previous research suggested that organizational climate can positively affect performance, although the components of organizational climate vary across studies. Organizational climate includes leader-member communication (e.g., the provision of information by the manager, organizational efficiency, and the clarity of tasks) (Koene et al., 2002). Organizational climate can be categorized and subdivided into the five key themes (i.e., structure, rewards and recognition, cohesion, warmth and support, and customer care) (Clark, 2002). There is a positive link between organizational climate and customer retention rates at a micro-organizational level in a UK bank (Clark, 2002). A warm and supportive climate increases the employees' job satisfaction and performance at the organizational level (Griffith, 2006).

Moreover, employee perceptions of a positive organizational climate are associated with intentions to remain with that employer in retail grocery employees (Cooil, Aksoy, Keiningham, & Maryott, 2009), in women in the IT sector (Trauth, Beehr, & Haiyan, 2009), and in hospital nurses (Stone et al., 2006). Organizational climate perceptions are positively associated with individual performance (Brown & Leigh, 1996; Pritchard & Karasick, 1973) and organizational performance (Lawler, Hall, & Oldman, 1974; Patterson, 2005). Based on published reports of the positive influence of supportive climates on organizational performance (Clark, 2002; Griffith, 2006; Koene et al., 2002), small businesses with supportive climates are predicted to be associated with the enhanced performance. Openness within an organization is supportive of the generation of new ideas and innovation during activities such as brainstorming (Gold, Malhora, & Segars, 2001) as employees share their knowledge with others (Alavi et al., 2005). Furthermore, when employees fear that their ideas will be credited to others, it is unlikely that new knowledge will flourish in an organization (De Long & Fahey, 2000).

Possible consequences of effective knowledge management include competitive advantage (Connor & Prahalad, 1996; Hall, 1993), improved financial performance (Teece, 1998; Wiig, 1997), innovation (Antonelli, 1999; Carneiro, 2000), the anticipation of problems (Carneiro, 2000), enhanced organizational learning (Buckley & Carter, 2000), and the superior use of information (Carneiro, 2000). According to Hemmelgarn et al. (2006), organizational culture and organizational climate mold the work attitudes and behavior of the organizational member and, as a result, affect the organizational performance. Employees working in organizations with more positive cultures and climates are more likely to be satisfied with their jobs and more committed to their organizations (Aarons & Sawitzky, 2006). The behavioral norms and expectations that exist within an organizational culture explain, in part, differences in the quality of care across organizations and the extent to which service providers report the high levels of commitment and satisfaction with their work (Mallak, Lyth, Olson, Ulshafer, & Sardone, 2003). Organizational culture and organizational climate shape the nature, tone and focus of the relationships and interactions between the service provider and service recipient (Hemmelgarn, Glisson, & Dukes, 2001).

Organizational culture is described as the way things are done around here, referring to the shared norms, beliefs, and behavioral expectations that drive behavior and communicate what is valued in organizations (Hemmelgarn et al., 2001). Glisson and James (2002) indicated that positive climates describe higher levels of job satisfaction and commitment to the goals of their organization. For those reasons, effective employee relationships are more likely to occur in organizations where employees report lower depersonalization, emotional exhaustion, role conflict, and role overload, all of which are the key indicators of organizational

climate (Hemmelgarn et al., 2006). Organizations have recognized that knowledge constitutes a valuable intangible asset for creating and sustaining competitive advantages (Miller & Shamsie, 1996). Knowledge-sharing activities are generally supported by knowledge management system. However, technology constitutes only one of the many factors that affect the sharing of knowledge in organizations such as organizational culture, trust, and incentives (Cabrera & Cabrera, 2005).

The sharing of knowledge constitutes a major challenge in the field of knowledge management because some employees tend to resist sharing their knowledge with the rest of the organization (Bock & Kim, 2002). One prominent obstacle is the notion that knowledge is the important property and ownership (Dalkir, 2005). In order to counteract this, individuals must be reassured that they will receive some type of incentives for what they create (Dalkir, 2005). Furthermore, individuals are most commonly rewarded for what they know, not what they share (Dalkir, 2005). If knowledge is not shared, negative consequences such as isolation and resistance to ideas occur. Shared knowledge offers different viewpoints and possible solutions to problems. To promote knowledge sharing and remove knowledge-sharing obstacles, the organizational culture should encourage discovery and innovation (Dalkir, 2005). According to Denison et al. (2004), organizational culture contributes to the success of the organization. The study on organizational culture can take on a multitude of aspects, including levels, strength, and adaptation (Denison et al., 2004).

Organizational cultures can be assessed along many dimensions, resulting in different models and theories. For example, organizational culture can be categorized as adaptability, achievement, clan, and bureaucracy (Daft, 2005), as clan, adhocracy, hierarchy, and market (Cameron & Freeman, 1991; Quinn & Cameron, 1983). According to Wallach (1983), an organizational culture can be a combination of three categories (i.e., bureaucratic, innovative, and supportive cultures).

Wallach (1983) stated that the Organizational Culture Index (OCI) profiles an organizational culture on the three stereotypical dimensions, and the flavor of an organization can be derived from the combination of these three dimensions. A bureaucratic culture is hierarchical, compartmentalized, organized, systematic, and has the clear lines of responsibility and authority (Wallach, 1983). An innovative culture refers to a creative, results-oriented, challenging work environment (Wallach, 1983). A supportive culture exhibits teamwork and a people-oriented, encouraging, trusting work environment (Wallach, 1983). An employee can be more effective in his or her current job, and realize his or her best potentials, when there is a match between individual's motivation and organizational culture. This has significant implications in recruitment, management, motivation, development and retention of employees (Shadur et al., 1999).

Organizational culture is a critical factor that influences knowledge management or the effectiveness of knowledge sharing (Gold et al., 2001). Organizational culture involves the combination of artifacts, values, and beliefs underlying assumptions that organizational members share about appropriate behavior (Gordon & DiTomaso, 1992; Schein, 1992). Organizational culture involves beliefs and behavior, thus manifesting itself in a wide range of features of organizational life (Hofstede, Neuijen, Ohayv, & Sanders, 1990). As such, organizational culture refers to a set of shared values, belief, assumptions, and practices that shape and guide members' attitudes and behavior in the organization (O'Reilly & Chatman, 1996; Wilson, 2001). Long (1997) suggested that organizational culture defines the value of knowledge, and also explains the existence of the advantage of knowledge innovation in an organization. This kind of advantage further affects the willingness of employees to share and be involved. Therefore, building a knowledge culture in a process that embraces knowledge management is very important. Alavi and Leidner (1999) indicated that the

knowledge-sharing experience in an organization is mostly related to organizational culture.

The concept of organizational climate emerged, which is shared among the members of the work or organizational unit. It is measured by averaging the individual scores of psychological work climate (Gillespie, Denison, Haaland, Smerek, & Neale, 2008). According to Bliese (2000), aggregating values of climate should only be used if there is a sufficient agreement in the individual climate ratings. Differences in variance in organizational climate ratings from one unit to another unit may be relevant for explaining outcomes. This variance is known as organizational climate strength (Dawson, Gonzalez-Roma, Davis, & West, 2008; Schneider, Salvaggio, & Subirats, 2002). A high variance indicates that members of an organization differ in how they view the organizational climate. Using the organizational climate mean and variance at the aggregate level has sometimes shown to be ineffective in progressing the understanding (Dickson, Resick, & Hanges, 2006; Lindell & Brandt, 2000). However, other researchers report substantial findings for aggregate level climate strength on employee outcomes (Colquitt, Noe, & Jackson, 2002; Moliner, Martinez-Tur, Peiro, Ramos, & Cropanzano, 2005). Many studies emphasized the importance of a particular kind of organizational climate, such as having the correct type of climate (Argyris, 1958), creating a climate, and allowing for employee participation and control (McGregor, 1967). Perryer and Jordan (2005) argued that successful leaders tend to create an organizational climate within work environment where they are able to assist employees to set and achieve individual, team, and organizational objectives (Perryer & Jordan, 2005).

Drucker (1993) stated that knowledge management is different from general management activities since it focuses on the perspective of knowledge, and is eventually aimed at applying this knowledge in a systematic and organized manner to further create knowledge. Arthur Anderson Business Consulting (1999) noted that the knowledge management improves the quality and quantity of innovative knowledge in an organization. According to Arthur Andersen Business Consulting and APQC (1996), there are seven processes (i.e., create, identify, collect, adapt, organize, apply, and share). Tang (1999) mentioned that knowledge and skills affect organizational innovative research capability. When knowledge is delivered and distributed freely in an organization, its potential values will appear eventually. If knowledge can be applied appropriately or new knowledge can be created substantially, it does not only improve productivity, but it also inspires creativity (Davenport & Prusak, 1998). Furthermore, Johannessen et al. (1999) combined knowledge vision with knowledge management. Johannessen et al. (1999) indicated that organizational vision leads to knowledge creation, and knowledge creation leads to organizational creation and integrates knowledge utilization.

A successful knowledge management must depend on the cooperation of domains of culture, management, and organization (Alavi & Leidner, 1999). Davenport et al. (1998) introduced the eight factors of successful knowledge management projects, and most of them are influenced by organizational culture. Aside from this, Davenport and Prusak (1998) indicated that in addition to the characteristics of knowledge, the components of an organizational culture are the keys for successful knowledge control and transference. Furthermore, the culture of knowledge sharing in an organization is a criterion for successful knowledge management (Davenport et al., 1998; Hauschild, Licht, & Stein, 2001). Once the knowledge is efficiently integrated and utilized, it can improve organizational innovation as well as strengthen visions (Johannessen et al., 1999). Knowledge management is seen as an enabler of organizational learning (Sanchez, 1996). Knowledge management efforts typically focus on organizational objectives such as the improved performance, competitive advantage innovation, the sharing of lessons learned, the organizational integration, and the continuous improvement of the organization (Sanchez, 1996).

Knowledge management efforts overlap with organizational learning and may be distinguished from that by a greater focus on the management of knowledge as a strategic asset and a focus on encouraging the sharing of knowledge (Sanchez, 1996). Knowledge is easily stored because it may be codified, while the relational perspective recognizes the contextual and relational aspects of knowledge which can make knowledge difficult to share outside of the specific location where the knowledge is developed (Hayes & Walsham, 2003). A successful knowledge management effort needs to convert internalized tacit knowledge into explicit knowledge in order to share it, but the same effort must also permit individuals to internalize and make personally meaningful (Serenko & Bontis, 2004). Furthermore, knowledge management systems can be categorized as falling into one or more of the following groups (i.e., groupware, document management systems, expert systems, semantic networks, relational and object-oriented databases, simulation tools, and artificial intelligence) (Gupta & Sharma, 2004).

There are two forms of work performance (i.e., in-role performance and extra-role performance) (Morrison, 1994; Williams & Anderson, 1991). In-role performance refers to an employee's action to fulfill the requirements of his/her job description (Williams & Anderson, 1991), whereas extra-role performance refers to actions outside the formal role requirements and are at the employee's discretion (George & Brief, 1992). Performance measurement systems play an important role in developing strategic plans and evaluating the achievement of organizational objectives. An effective performance measurement system should cover all aspects of performance that are relevant to the existence of an organization and the means by which it achieves success and viability (Hillman & Keim, 2001; Kaplan & Norton, 1996). Furthermore, performance indicators involve the financial, strategic, and operating business measures to estimate how well a company meets its targets. Organizational performance enables the management to evaluate the position of the organization, thus translating the needs for performance improvement. Organizational performance management research has defined performance from a variety of perspectives (Venkatraman & Ramanujam, 1986). In this study, job performance was measured using questionnaire developed by Stevens et al. (1978), comprising two dimensions of job performance (i.e., quality of performance and productivity).

Material and Methods

Data of this study were collected from 560 operational employees from 5,419 operational employees working in the 64 software manufacturing plants in Thailand by using the Yamane formula (Yamane, 1970) for a 96% confidence level with a 4% margin of error by the proportional random sampling method. All the constructs were operationalized using seven-point Likert scales ranging from 1 (strongly disagree) to 7 (strongly agree) conformed to the questionnaires to be evaluated by software manufacturing plant employees on factory sites. Data were analyzed with descriptive statistics using SPSS (version 20) and assessed with confirmatory factor analysis (CFA) to confirm the heterogeneity of all constructs and path analysis (Joreskog & Sorborn, 1993) to detect the cause-effect relationships among various dimensions of main constructs of the study using LISREL (version 8.8) on a structured questionnaire containing standard scales of organizational culture, organizational climate, knowledge management, and job performance, besides some demographic details like age, education, and tenure with the organization.

Organizational culture was measured using the 24-item organizational culture questionnaire developed by Wasko and Faraj (2005) to assess three cultural facets of bureaucratic, innovative, and supportive culture. Organizational climate was measured as a multidimensional construct reflecting the shared patterns of understanding and norms of behaviors within the organization using the questionnaire developed by Oliver and Anderson (1994), Shadur et al. (1999), and Wallach (1983) comprising two dimensions of innovative climate and supportive climate. Innovative climate was measured by asking the respondents three questions about incentive environment, stimulation, and active commitment on innovation. Two indicators measuring supportive climate reflect whether the firm provides employees needed support and sense of security. Knowledge management was measured using questionnaire developed by Darroch (2003) comprising three elements of knowledge acquisition, knowledge dissemination, and responsiveness to knowledge.

Knowledge acquisition is captured by six factors: valuing employees attitudes and opinions and encouraging employees to up-skill; having a well-developed financial reporting system; being market focused by actively obtaining customer and industry information; being sensitive to information about changes in the marketplace; employing and retaining a large number of people trained in science, engineering or math; working in partnership with international customers; and getting information from market surveys. Five factors describe the knowledge dissemination construct: readily disseminating market information around the organization; disseminating knowledge on-the-job; using techniques such as quality circles, case notes, mentoring and coaching to disseminate knowledge; using technology to facilitate communication; and preferring written communication to disseminate knowledge. Responsiveness to knowledge was described by five factors: responding to knowledge about customers, competitors and technology; being flexible and opportunistic by readily changing products, processes and strategies; and having a well-developed marketing function. Job performance was measured using questionnaire developed by Stevens et al. (1978) comprising two dimensions of job performance (i.e., quality of performance and productivity).

SOLUTIONS AND RECOMMENDATIONS

A framework and a causal model are unified relevant to the research objectives and research questions. The framework and the causal model show that dimensions of organizational culture, organizational climate, and knowledge management have mediated positive effect on job performance. Organizational culture and organizational climate are positively linked to knowledge management. Knowledge management positively mediates the relationships between organizational culture and job performance and between organizational climate and job performance. Furthermore, organizational culture is positively related to organizational climate. The unified framework is positively compatible with the following research findings. Organizational culture, organizational climate, and knowledge management are positively linked to job performance related to business process orientation conformed to the review of literature. Therefore, firms should take consideration of their organizational culture and organizational climate in the transition process of knowledge management to increase job performance linked to the practical application of business process orientation shown on the review of literature.

Business process orientation is positive with inter-departmental connectedness and negative with inter-functional conflict because of the high frequent cross-functional interact and co-operation at daily work in the process-oriented organizations (McCormack, 2001), therefore business process orientation provides a good organizational culture to support organizational innovation collaboration. Likewise, McCormack and Johnson (2001) conducted an empirical study to explore the relationship between the business process orientation and the enhanced business performance. Consequently, business process orientation is critical in reducing conflict and encouraging greater connectedness within an organization, while improving business perfor-

mance (McCormack & Johnson, 2001). Moreover, organizations with strong measures of business process orientation shows better overall business performance (McCormack & Johnson, 2001). Furthermore, high business process orientation levels within organizations provide a more positive corporate climate illustrated through better organizational connectedness and less internal conflict (McCormack & Johnson, 2001).

According to the result, organizational climate and knowledge management act as intervening variables between organizational culture and job performance. When firms adopt knowledge management activities to promote job performance related to business process orientation, the role of organizational culture and organizational climate becomes more evident and critical. Therefore, the strength of knowledge management affecting job performance related to business process orientation will be influenced by what kinds of organizational culture and organizational climate that firms adopted. If firms possess a higher degree of innovative and supportive climate, the degrees of knowledge management would be more enhanced.

These finding show that organizational culture and organizational climate can promote a higher degree of knowledge creation and sharing within firms. In addition, the present results are also quite instructive in helping to explain the effects of organizational culture and organizational climate on knowledge management related to business process orientation conformed to the review of literature. In general, if the characteristics of organizational culture are less centralized, less formalized, and more integrated, the levels of knowledge management by utilizing software processes would be more enhanced relevant to the study of Kess and Haapasalo (2002) stating that software processes are related to knowledge processes, structured within a knowledge management framework.

Therefore, firms should carefully design and nurture appropriate organizational contexts to facilitate knowledge management to improve job performance by utilizing software processes. Likewise, firms need to cultivate an innovative and supportive atmosphere to enhance knowledge creation and sharing to improve job performance related to business process orientation. In addition, firms need to design their organizational culture as less formalized, more centralized, and more integrated to provide employees more autonomy and make them feel honored to participate in their work. The appropriate organizational contexts would result in a more satisfied level of knowledge management and job performance related to business process orientation within firms.

Organizational climate helps employees in firms become more productive and assists them in achieving individual objectives, enhancing organizational performance, as well as improving both staff and customer satisfaction (Perryer & Jordan, 2005). Organizational climate increases the ability of leaders and employees to work together, and can enhance performance in terms of effectiveness and efficiency (Griffith, 2006). Effectiveness may improve via employee-leader cooperation and the motivation to work effectively, which in turn may improve the organization's execution of its tasks. Efficiency is also expected to increase as a supportive climate reduces the need for controls (such as rules and monitoring) and increases the ability to confront performance problems. Both of these factors help maximize the use of organizational resources (Griffith, 2006). It is important that the other organizations implementing large-scale manufacturing reformations need to pay great attention to organizational culture, organizational climate, knowledge management, and job performance in order to effectively achieve business success.

FUTURE RESEARCH DIRECTIONS

The author indicates some limitations in this study and suggests possible directions for future research. This study is based on self-report data

Figure 1. Unified Framework and Causal Model
Key: OCT = Organizational Culture, BRC = Bureaucratic Culture, INC = Innovative Culture, SPC = Supportive Culture, OCM = Organizational Climate, IC = Innovative Climate, SC = Supportive Climate, KM = Knowledge Management, JP = Job Performance, QP = Quality of Performance, PD = Productivity

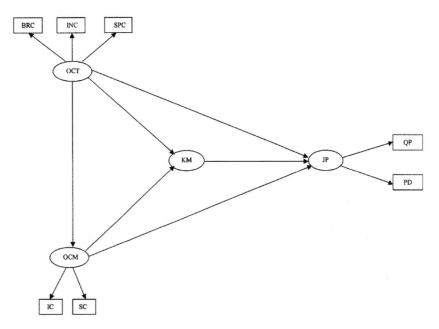

that may have the possibility of common method variance. Future research is suggested to benefit from using objective measures for job performance that can be independently verified. The low return rate of the survey is still noted as a potential limitation in this study. Future research can benefit from a larger sample to bring more statistical power and a higher degree of representation. This study was done by empirically investigating software manufacturing companies.

Potential cultural limitation should be noted and it is suggested that future research be done in different cultural contexts to generalize or modify the concepts. Furthermore, this study mainly concerns the effects of organizational culture and organizational climate on knowledge management and job performance related to business process orientation within software manufacturing companies. Other variables (e.g., organizational citizenship behavior, organizational commitment, organizational justice, job satisfaction, job involvement, and employee engagement) may potentially affect knowledge management and job performance as well. Future research may work on examining their impacts on knowledge management and job performance.

CONCLUSION

The purposes of this study were to unify a framework and a causal model of organizational culture, organizational climate, knowledge management, and job performance related to business process orientation for software manufacturing plant employees in Thailand. The findings show that the organizational culture, organizational climate, and knowledge management have strengths to moderate positive effects on job performance. In relation to the unified framework, that is the extent to which organizational culture, organizational climate, and knowledge management have mediated positive effect on job performance. Given the need for knowledge and performance as a

solution to the complex challenges, firms need to be aware of the implications of organizational contexts that may affect knowledge management and job performance. Firms should recognize the importance of knowledge management and need to put more efforts in building up the effective knowledge creation and sharing mechanisms to promote their job performance. Firms should pay special attentions to organization contexts in which knowledge creation and sharing are most likely to enhance job performance, and those in which such enhancement is less likely to occur.

Firms may create a positively supportive and innovative climate to encourage employees not only behave in interactive ways, but share their different perspectives and to manifest creative and innovative behaviors. In addition, firms should recognize and shape organizational culture favorable to knowledge management and job performance related to business process orientation. Managers in firms also need to emphasize the development of an open climate to permit tacit knowledge sharing (Seidler-de Alwis & Hartmann, 2008) and informally to encourage creativity through knowledge sharing (Taminiau, Smit, & De Lange, 2009). Managers need to promote frequent interaction among employees to enhance the creation of team-based knowledge (Donnelly, 2008) and the sharing of tacit knowledge (Cavusgil, Calantone, & Zhao, 2003). When organizations tolerate mistakes in the knowledge development process, the barriers to knowledge creation and knowledge sharing diminish (McLaughlin, Paton, & Macbeth, 2008). Organizational climates that feature openness enhance the sharing of tacit knowledge (Seidler-de Alwis & Hartmann, 2008). Informality of knowledge sharing within an organizational climate encourages creativity (Taminiau et al., 2009).

Organizations aiming to increase job performance and achieve business goals should focus on developing organizational culture, organizational climate, and knowledge management. In terms of managerial implications, the results suggest that managers desiring to enhance their business performance related to business process orientation should consider creating organizational culture, organizational climate, knowledge management, and job performance. For example, by encouraging employees to try out new approaches, and recognizing and rewarding those that work well; practicing transparent and honest communication between the managers and employees about what is happening and about changes that could be important for staff; striving for cohesion through a clearly enunciated vision, by building commitment to organizational goals, fostering cooperation and collaboration, and allowing employees to participate in formulating strategy; and building warm interpersonal relationships by expressing concern for the employees' well-being, helping employees to set and achieve individual goals, caring about their opinions, and making an effort to show the warmth and kindness to them.

Organizations are realizing that intellectual capital or corporate knowledge is a valuable asset that can be managed as effectively as physical assets in order to improve performance. The focus on the impact of knowledge management on job performance by utilizing software processes based on the practical application of organizational culture and organizational climate conformed to business process orientation is to connect people, processes, and technology for the purpose of maximizing corporate knowledge management to achieve the business goal and better job performance.

REFERENCES

Aarons, G., & Sawitzky, A. (2006). Organizational climate partially mediates the effect of culture on work attitudes and staff turnover in mental health services. *Administration and Policy in Mental Health*, *33*(3), 289–301. doi:10.1007/s10488-006-0039-1 PMID:16544205

Ahmad, F., Mohamad, O., & Ibrahim, H. (2013). Effect of organizational culture on individual absorptive capacity: Evidence from Malaysian electrical and electronic sector. *Researchers World –Journal of Arts, Science & Commerce*, *4*(1), 66–76.

Ahmed-Kristensen, S., & Vianello, G. (2015). A model for reusing service knowledge based on an empirical case. *Research in Engineering Design*, *26*(1), 57–76. doi:10.1007/s00163-014-0184-6

Aier, S. (2014). The role of organizational culture for grounding, management, guidance and effectiveness of enterprise architecture principles. *Information Systems and e-Business Management*, *12*(1), 43–70.

Alavi, M., Kayworth, T. R., & Leidner, D. E. (2005). An empirical examination of the influence of organizational culture on knowledge management practices. *Journal of Management Information Systems*, *22*(3), 191–224. doi:10.2753/MIS0742-1222220307

Alavi, M., & Leidner, D. E. (1999). Knowledge management system: Issues, challenges, and benefits. *Communications of the AIS*, *1*(7), 1–37.

Anand, A., Kant, R., Patel, D. P., & Singh, M. D. (2015). Knowledge management implementation: A predictive model using an analytical hierarchical process. *Journal of the Knowledge Economy*, *6*(1), 48–71. doi:10.1007/s13132-012-0110-y

Antonelli, C. (1999). The evolution of the industrial organization of the production of knowledge. *Cambridge Journal of Economics*, *23*(2), 243–260. doi:10.1093/cje/23.2.243

Argote, L., McEvily, B., & Reagan, R. (2003). Managing knowledge in organizations: An integrative framework and review of emerging themes. Management Science, 49(4), 571–582.

Argyris, C. (1958). Some problems in conceptualizing organizational climate: A case study of a bank. *Administrative Science Quarterly, 2*(4), 501–520. doi:10.2307/2390797

Armistead, C., & Machin, S. (1997). Implications of business process management for operations management. *International Journal of Operations & Production Management, 17*(9), 886–898. doi:10.1108/01443579710171217

Arthur Andersen Business Consulting. (1999). *Zukai knowledge management*. Tokyo, Japan: Keizai Inc.

Arthur Andersen Business Consulting and APQC. (1996). *The knowledge management assessment tool: External benchmarking version*. Houston, TX: The American Productivity and Quality Center.

Aurum, A., Jeffery, R., Wohlin, C., & Handzic, M. (2003). *Managing software engineering knowledge*. Berlin, Germany: Springer–Verlag. doi:10.1007/978-3-662-05129-0

Avery, G. C. (2004). *Understanding leadership: Paradigms and cases*. London, UK: Sage.

Awadh, A. M., & Saad, A. M. (2013). Impact of organizational culture on employee performance. *International Review of Management and Business Research, 2*(1), 168–175.

Axtell, C. M., Holman, D. J., Unsworth, K. L., Wall, T. D., Waterson, P. E., & Harrington, E. (2000). Shopfloor innovation: Facilitating the suggestion and implementation of ideas. *Journal of Occupational and Organizational Psychology, 73*(3), 265–285. doi:10.1348/096317900167029

Bagnoli, C., & Vedovato, M. (2014). The impact of knowledge management and strategy configuration coherence on SME performance. *Journal of Management & Governance, 18*(2), 615–647. doi:10.1007/s10997-012-9211-z

Bengtson, M., & Solvell, O. (2004). Climate of competition, clusters, and innovative performance. *Scandinavian Journal of Management, 20*(3), 225–244. doi:10.1016/j.scaman.2004.06.003

Benner, M. J., & Veloso, F. M. (2008). ISO 9000 practices and financial performance: A technology coherence perspective. *Journal of Operations Management, 26*(5), 611–629. doi:10.1016/j.jom.2007.10.005

Bhalla, P., & Nazneen, A. (2013). A study of organizational culture in Indian organized retail sectors. *International Journal of Retail Management and Research, 3*(1), 1–6.

Bliese, P. D. (2000). Within-group agreement, non-independence, and reliability: Implications for data aggregation and analysis. In K. Klein & S. Kozlowski (Eds.), *Multilevel theory, research, and method in organizations* (pp. 349–381). San Francisco, CA: Jossey–Bass.

Bock, G. W., & Kim, Y. G. (2002). Breaking the myths of rewards: An exploratory study of attitudes about knowledge sharing. *Information Resources Management Journal, 15*(2), 14–21. doi:10.4018/irmj.2002040102

Bock, G. W., Zmud, R. W., Kim, Y. G., & Lee, J. N. (2005). Behavioral intention formation in knowledge sharing: Examining the roles of extrinsic motivators, social-psychological factors, and organizational climate. *Management Information Systems Quarterly, 29*(1), 87–111.

Boomer, J. (2004). Finding out what knowledge management is – and isn't. *Accounting Today, 18*(14), 9–22.

Brown, S. L., & Eisenhardt, K. M. (1995). Product development: Past research, present findings, and future directions. Academy of Management Review, 20(2), 343–378. doi: 10.2307/258850

Brown, S. P., & Leigh, T. W. (1996). A new look at psychological climate and its relationship to job involvement, effort, and performance. Journal of Applied Psychology, 81(4), 358–368. doi:10.1037/0021-9010.81.4.358 PMID:8751453 doi:10.1037/0021-9010.81.4.358 PMID:8751453

Buckley, P. J., & Carter, M. J. (2000). Knowledge management in global technology markets. *Long Range Planning*, *33*(1), 55–71. doi:10.1016/S0024-6301(99)00102-8

Cabrera, E. F., & Cabrera, A. (2005). Fostering knowledge sharing through people management practices. *International Journal of Human Resource Management*, *16*(5), 720–735. doi:10.1080/09585190500083020

Cameron, K. S., & Freeman, S. J. (1991). Cultural congruence, strength, and type: Relationships to effectiveness. *Research in Organizational Change and Development*, *5*(2), 23–58.

Campbell, J. L., & Göritz, A. S. (2014). Culture corrupts! A qualitative study of organizational culture in corrupt organizations. *Journal of Business Ethics*, *120*(3), 291–311. doi:10.1007/s10551-013-1665-7

Campbell, J. P. (1990). Modeling the performance prediction problem in industrial and organizational psychology. In M. Dunnette & L. Hough (Eds.), *Handbook of industrial and organizational psychology* (pp. 687–732). Palo Alto, CA: Consulting Psychologists Press.

Campbell, J. P., & Campbell, R. J. (1988). *Productivity in organizations: New perspectives from industrial and organizational psychology*. San Francisco, CA: Jossey–Bass.

Carneiro, A. (2000). How does knowledge management influence innovation and competitiveness? *Journal of Knowledge Management*, *4*(2), 87–98. doi:10.1108/13673270010372242

Cavusgil, S. T., Calantone, R. J., & Zhao, Y. (2003). Tacit knowledge transfer and firm innovation capability. *Journal of Business and Industrial Marketing*, *18*(1), 6–21. doi:10.1108/08858620310458615

Chatman, J. A., Caldwell, D. F., O'Reilly, C. A., & Doerr, B. (2014). Parsing organizational culture: How the norm for adaptability influences the relationship between culture consensus and financial performance in high-technology firms. *Journal of Organizational Behavior*, *35*(6), 785–808. doi:10.1002/job.1928

Chen, C. J. (2004). The effects of knowledge attribute, alliance characteristics, and absorptive capacity on knowledge transfer performance. *R & D Management*, *34*(3), 311–321. doi:10.1111/j.1467-9310.2004.00341.x

Chen, C. J., & Huang, J. W. (2007). How organizational climate and structure affect knowledge management: The social interaction perspective. *International Journal of Information Management*, *27*(2), 104–118. doi:10.1016/j.ijinfomgt.2006.11.001

Chen, C. J., & Lin, B. W. (2004). The effects of environment, knowledge attribute, organizational climate, and firm characteristics on knowledge sourcing decisions. *R & D Management*, *34*(2), 137–146. doi:10.1111/j.1467-9310.2004.00329.x

Cho, T., & Korte, R. (2014). Managing knowledge performance: Testing the components of a knowledge management system on organizational performance. *Asia Pacific Education Review*, *15*(2), 313–327. doi:10.1007/s12564-014-9333-x

Chu, M. T., Kumar, P., Kumar, K., & Khosla, R. (2014). Mapping knowledge sharing traits to business strategy in knowledge based organization. *Journal of Intelligent Manufacturing*, *25*(1), 55–65. doi:10.1007/s10845-012-0674-1

Clark, M. (2002). The relationship between employees' perceptions of organizational climate and customer retention rates in a major UK retail bank. *Journal of Strategic Marketing, 10*(2), 93–113. doi:10.1080/09652540210125260

Colquitt, J. A., Noe, R. A., & Jackson, C. L. (2002). Justice in teams: Antecedents and consequences of procedural justice climate. *Personnel Psychology, 55*(1), 83–109. doi:10.1111/j.1744-6570.2002. tb00104.x

Connor, K. R., & Prahalad, C. K. (1996). A resource-based theory of the firm: Knowledge versus opportunism. *Organization Science, 7*(5), 477–501. doi:10.1287/orsc.7.5.477

Cooil, B., Aksoy, L., Keiningham, T. M., & Maryott, K. M. (2009). The relationship of employee perceptions of organizational climate to business-unit outcomes: An MPLS approach. *Journal of Service Research, 11*(3), 277–294. doi:10.1177/1094670508328984

Daft, R. L. (2005). *The leadership experience.* Vancouver, Canada: Thomson–Southwestern.

Dalkir, K. (2005). *Knowledge management in theory and practice.* Oxford, UK: Elsevier Butterworth–Heinemann.

Darroch, J. (2003). Developing a measure of knowledge management behaviors and practices. *Journal of Knowledge Management, 7*(5), 41–54. doi:10.1108/13673270310505377

Davenport, T. H., De Long, D. W., & Beers, M. C. (1998). Successful knowledge management projects. *MIT Sloan Management Review, 39*(2), 43–57.

Davenport, T. H., & Prusak, L. (1998). *Working knowledge: Managing what your organization knows.* Boston, MA: Harvard Business Review Press.

Dawson, J. F., Gonzalez-Roma, V., Davis, A., & West, M. A. (2008). Organizational climate and climate strength in UK hospitals. *European Journal of Work and Organizational Psychology, 17*(1), 89–111. doi:10.1080/13594320601046664

De Long, D. W., & Fahey, L. (2000). Diagnosing cultural barriers to knowledge management. The Academy of Management Executive, 14(4),

Deal, T. E., & Kennedy, A. A. (1982). *Corporate cultures: The rites and rituals of corporate life.* Harmondsworth, UK: Penguin Books.

Denison, D. R. (1996). What is the difference between organizational culture and organizational climate? A native's point of view on a decade of paradigm wars. *Academy of Management Review, 21*(3), 619–654. doi:10.2307/258997

Denison, D. R. (1996). What is the difference between organizational culture and organizational climate? A native's point of view on a decade of paradigm wars. *Academy of Management Review, 21*(3), 619–654.

Denison, D. R., Haaland, S., & Goelzer, P. (2004). Corporate culture and organizational effectiveness: Is Asia different from the rest of the world? *Organizational Dynamics, 33*(1), 98–109. doi:10.1016/j.orgdyn.2003.11.008

Dickson, M. W., Resick, C. J., & Hanges, P. J. (2006). When organizational climate is unambiguous, it is also strong. *The Journal of Applied Psychology, 91*(2), 351–364. doi:10.1037/0021-9010.91.2.351

Dingsoyr, T., & Conradi, R. (2002). A survey of case studies of the use of knowledge management in software engineering. *International Journal of Software Engineering and Knowledge Engineering, 12*(4), 391–414. doi:10.1142/S0218194002000962

Donnelly, R. (2008). The management of consultancy knowledge: An internationally comparative analysis. *Journal of Knowledge Management, 12*(6), 71–83. doi:10.1108/13673270810875877

Dougherty, D., & Hardy, C. (1996). Sustained product innovation in large, mature organizations: Overcoming innovation-to-organization problems. *Academy of Management Journal, 39*(5), 1120–1153. doi:10.2307/256994

Drucker, P. F. (1993). *Post-capitalist society.* New York, NY: Harper Business.

Engelen, A., Flatten, T. C., Thalmann, J., & Brettel, M. (2014). The effect of organizational culture on entrepreneurial orientation: A comparison between Germany and Thailand. *Journal of Small Business Management, 52*(4), 732–752. doi:10.1111/jsbm.12052

Ferris, G. R., Frink, D. D., Galang, M. C., Zhou, J., Kacmar, M. K., & Howard, J. L. (1996). Perceptions of organizational politics: Prediction, stress-related implications, and outcomes. *Human Relations, 49*(2), 233–266. doi:10.1177/001872679604900206

Forehand, G. A., & Gilmer, B. V. (1964). Environmental variation in studies of organizational behavior. *Psychological Bulletin, 62*(6), 228–240. doi:10.1037/h0045960 PMID:14242590

Forehand, G. A., & Vonhallergilmer, B. (1964). Environmental variation in studies of organizational behavior. *Psychological Bulletin, 62*(6), 361–382. doi:10.1037/h0045960 PMID:14242590

George, J. M., & Brief, A. P. (1992). Feeling good-doing good: A conceptual analysis of the mood at work-organizational spontaneity relationship. *Psychological Bulletin, 112*(2), 310–329. doi:10.1037/0033-2909.112.2.310 PMID:1454897

Ghorbanhosseini, M. (2013). The effect of organizational culture, teamwork and organizational development on organizational commitment: The mediating role of human capital. *Tehnički vjesnik, 20*(6), 1019–1025.

Gillberg, C., & Vo, L. C. (2014). Contributions from pragmatist perspectives towards an understanding of knowledge and learning in organisations. *Philosophy of Management, 13*(2), 33–51. doi:10.5840/pom201413210

Gillespie, M. A., Denison, D. R., Haaland, S., Smerek, R. E., & Neale, W. S. (2008). Linking organizational culture and customer satisfaction: Results from two companies in different industries. *European Journal of Work and Organizational Psychology, 17*(1), 112–132. doi:10.1080/13594320701560820

Gilson, L. L., & Shalley, C. E. (2004). A little creativity goes a long way: An examination of teams' engagement in creative processes. *Journal of Management, 30*(4), 453–470. doi:10.1016/j.jm.2003.07.001

Glisson, C., & James, L. R. (2002). The cross-level effects of culture and climate in human service teams. *Journal of Organizational Behavior, 23*(6), 767–794. doi:10.1002/job.162

Gold, A. H., Malhora, A., & Segars, A. H. (2001). Knowledge management: An organizational capabilities perspective. *Journal of Management Information Systems, 18*(1), 185–214.

Golembliewski, R. T. (1993). *Approaches to planned change: Orienting perspectives and micro-level interventions.* New Brunswick, NJ: Transaction Publishers.

Gordon, G. G., & DiTomaso, N. (1992). Predicting corporate performance from organizational culture. *Journal of Management Studies, 29*(6), 783–798. doi:10.1111/j.1467-6486.1992.tb00689.x

Grant, R. M. (1996). Toward a knowledge-based theory of the firm. *Strategic Management Journal, 17*(7), 109–122. doi:10.1002/smj.4250171110

Griffin, R. W. (2012). *Fundamentals of Management*. Mason, OH: South–Western Cengage Learning.

Griffith, J. (2006). A compositional analysis of organizational climate-performance relation: Public schools as organizations. *Journal of Applied Social Psychology, 36*(8), 1848–1880. doi:10.1111/j.0021-9029.2006.00085.x

Guerci, M., Radaelli, G., Siletti, E., Cirella, S., & Shani, A. B. R. (2015). The impact of human resource management practices and corporate sustainability on organizational ethical climates: An employee perspective. *Journal of Business Ethics, 126*(2), 325–342. doi:10.1007/s10551-013-1946-1

Guetzkow, H., Forehand, G. A., & James, B. J. (1962). An evaluation of educational influence on executive judgment. *Administrative Science Quarterly, 6*(4), 483–500. doi:10.2307/2390727

Gupta, J., & Sharma, S. (2004). *Creating knowledge based organization*. Boston, MA: Idea Group Publishing. doi:10.4018/978-1-59140-162-9

Hall, R. (1993). A framework linking intangible resources and capabilities to sustainable competitive advantage. *Strategic Management Journal, 14*(8), 607–618. doi:10.1002/smj.4250140804

Hammer, M. (2007a). The 7 deadly sins of performance measurement. *MIT Sloan Management Review, 48*(3), 19–28.

Hammer, M. (2007b). The process audit. *Harvard Business Review, 85*(4), 111–123. PMID:17432158

Hauschild, S., Licht, T., & Stein, W. (2001). Creating a knowledge culture. *The McKinsey Quarterly, 74*(1), 74–82.

Hayes, M., & Walsham, G. (2003). Knowledge sharing and ICTs: A relational perspective. In M. Easterby-Smith & M. Lyles (Eds.), *The Blackwell handbook of organizational learning and knowledge management* (pp. 54–27). Malden, MA: Blackwell.

Hemmelgarn, A. L., Glisson, C., & Dukes, D. (2001). Emergency room culture and the emotional support component of family-centered care. *Children's Health Care, 30*(2), 93–110. doi:10.1207/S15326888CHC3002_2

Hemmelgarn, A. L., Glisson, C., & James, L. (2006). Organizational culture and climate: Implications for services and interventions research. *Clinical Psychology: Science and Practice, 13*(1), 73–89. doi:10.1111/j.1468-2850.2006.00008.x

Hillman, A. J., & Keim, G. D. (2001). Shareholder value, stakeholder management and social issues: What's the bottom line? *Strategic Management Journal, 22*(2), 125–139. doi:10.1002/1097-0266(200101)22:2<125::AID-SMJ150>3.0.CO;2-H

Hinterhuber, H. H. (1995). Business process management: The European approach. *Business Change & Re-engineering, 2*(4), 63–73.

Hofstede, G., Neuijen, B., Ohayv, D. D., & Sanders, G. (1990). Measuring organizational cultures: A qualitative and quantitative study across twenty cases. *Administrative Science Quarterly, 35*(2), 286–316. doi:10.2307/2393392

Hollander, D. P., & Mihaliak, C. E. (2002). Tech helps deliver innovation in claims. *National Underwriter, 106*(48), 26–27.

Huhtala, M., Tolvanen, A., Mauno, S., & Feldt, T. (2015). The associations between ethical organizational culture, burnout, and engagement: A multilevel study. *Journal of Business and Psychology, 30*(2), 399–414. doi:10.1007/s10869-014-9369-2

Hvannberg, E. T. (2015). Identifying and explicating knowledge on method transfer: A sectoral system of innovation approach. *Universal Access in the Information Society, 14*(2), 187–202. doi:10.1007/s10209-013-0340-1

Isaksen, S. G., & Ekvall, G. (2007). *Assessing the context for change: A technical manual for the situational outlook questionnaire.* Orchard Park, NY: The Creative Problem Solving Group.

Ittner, C. D., & Larcker, D. F. (1997). The performance effects of process management techniques. *Management Science, 43*(4), 522–534. doi:10.1287/mnsc.43.4.522

James, J. R., Choi, C. C., Ko, C. H., McNeil, P. K., Minton, M. K., Wright, M. A., & Kim, K. (2008). Organizational and psychological climate: A review of theory and research. *European Journal of Work and Organizational Psychology, 17*(1), 5–32. doi:10.1080/13594320701662550

Janz, B. D., & Prasarnphanich, P. (2003). Understanding the antecedents of effective knowledge management: The importance of a knowledge-centered culture. *Decision Sciences, 34*(2), 351–384. doi:10.1111/1540-5915.02328

Johannessen, J. A., Olsen, B., & Olaisen, J. (1999). Aspects of innovation theory based knowledge management. *Journal of International Management, 19*(2), 121–139.

John, M. I., Robert, K., & Konopaske, M. T. (2008). *Organizational behavior and management.* Boston, MA: McGraw–Hill/Irwin.

Joreskog, K. G., & Sorbom, D. (1993). *LISREL 8: User's reference guide.* Chicago, IL: Scientific Software International.

Kaplan, R. S., & Norton, D. P. (1996). Linking the balanced scorecard to strategy. *California Management Review, 39*(1), 53–79. doi:10.2307/41165876

Kasemsap, K. (2014a). Strategic innovation management: An integrative framework and causal model of knowledge management, strategic orientation, organizational innovation, and organizational performance. In P. Ordóñez de Pablos & R. Tennyson (Eds.), *Strategic approaches for human capital management and development in a turbulent economy* (pp. 102–116). Hershey, PA: IGI Global. doi:10.4018/978-1-4666-4530-1.ch007

Kasemsap, K. (2014b). The role of knowledge sharing on organisational innovation: An integrated framework. In L. Al-Hakim & C. Jin (Eds.), *Quality innovation: Knowledge, theory, and practices* (pp. 247–271). Hershey, PA: IGI Global. doi:10.4018/978-1-4666-4769-5.ch012

Kasemsap, K. (2015a). Developing a framework of human resource management, organizational learning, knowledge management capability, and organizational performance. In P. Ordoñez de Pablos, L. Turró, R. Tennyson, & J. Zhao (Eds.), *Knowledge management for competitive advantage during economic crisis* (pp. 164–193). Hershey, PA: IGI Global. doi:10.4018/978-1-4666-6457-9.ch010

Kasemsap, K. (2015b). The role of data mining for business intelligence in knowledge management. In A. Azevedo & M. Santos (Eds.), *Integration of data mining in business intelligence systems* (pp. 12–33). Hershey, PA: IGI Global. doi:10.4018/978-1-4666-6477-7.ch002

Kess, P., & Haapasalo, H. (2002). Knowledge creation through a project review process in software production. *International Journal of Production Economics, 80*(1), 49–55. doi:10.1016/S0925-5273(02)00242-6

Kim, S. B. (2014). Impacts of knowledge management on the organizational success. *KSCE Journal of Civil Engineering, 18*(6), 1609–1617. doi:10.1007/s12205-014-0243-6

Koene, B. A., Vogelaar, A. L., & Soeters, J. L. (2002). Leadership effects on organizational climate and financial performance: Local leadership effect in chain organizations. *The Leadership Quarterly*, *13*(3), 193–215. doi:10.1016/S1048-9843(02)00103-0

Kohlbacher, M. (2009). *The perceived effects of business process management.* Paper presented at the IEEE Toronto International Conference, Toronto, Canada. doi:10.1109/TIC-STH.2009.5444467

Kohlbacher, M. (2010). The effects of process orientation: A literature review. *Business Process Management Journal*, *16*(1), 135–152. doi:10.1108/14637151011017985

Kohlbacher, M., & Gruenwald, S. (2011). Process ownership, process performance measurement and firm performance. *International Journal of Productivity and Performance Management*, *60*(7), 709–720. doi:10.1108/17410401111167799

Koles, B., & Kondath, B. (2015). Organizational climate in Hungary, Portugal, and India: A cultural perspective. *AI & Society*, *30*(2), 251–259. doi:10.1007/s00146-013-0507-6

Kung, P., & Hagen, C. (2007). The fruits of business process management: An experience report from a Swiss bank. *Business Process Management Journal*, *13*(4), 477–487. doi:10.1108/14637150710763522

Lawler, E. E., Hall, D. T., & Oldman, G. R. (1974). Organizational climate: Relationship to organizational structure, process and performance. *Organizational Behavior and Performance*, *11*(1), 139–155. doi:10.1016/0030-5073(74)90010-5

Lindell, M. K., & Brandt, C. J. (2000). Climate quality and climate consensus as mediators of the relationship between organizational antecedents and outcomes. *The Journal of Applied Psychology*, *85*(3), 331–348. doi:10.1037/0021-9010.85.3.331

Liu, X. J., & Wang, Y. L. (2015). Semantic-based knowledge categorization and organization for product design enterprises. *Journal of Shanghai Jiaotong University (Science)*, *20*(1), 106–112. doi:10.1007/s12204-015-1596-9

Long, D. D. (1997). *Building the knowledge-based organizations: How culture drives knowledge behaviors.* Cambridge, MA: Center for Business Innovation, Ernst & Young LLP.

Madhavan, R., & Griver, R. (1998). From embedded knowledge to embodied knowledge: New product development as knowledge management. *Journal of Marketing*, *62*(4), 1–12. doi:10.2307/1252283

Mallak, L. A., Lyth, D. M., Olson, S. D., Ulshafer, S. M., & Sardone, F. J. (2003). Culture, the built environment, and healthcare organizational performance. *Managing Service Quality*, *13*(1), 27–38. doi:10.1108/09604520310456690

Massingham, P. (2015). Knowledge sharing: What works and what doesn't work: A critical systems thinking perspective. *Systemic Practice and Action Research*, *28*(3), 197–228. doi:10.1007/s11213-014-9330-3

McCormack, K. P. (2001). Business process orientation: Do you have it? *Quality Progress*, *34*(1), 51–60.

McCormack, K. P. (2007). *Business process maturity: Theory and application.* Raleigh, NC: DRK Research.

McCormack, K. P., & Johnson, W. C. (2001). *Business process orientation: Gaining the e-business competitive advantage.* Boca Raton, FL: St. Lucie Press. doi:10.1201/9781420025569

McCormack, K. P., Johnson, W. C., & Walker, W. T. (2003). *Supply chain networks and business process orientation.* Boca Raton, FL: St. Lucie Press.

McDermott, R., & O'Dell, C. (2001). Overcoming cultural barriers to sharing knowledge. *Journal of Knowledge Management, 5*(1), 76–85. doi:10.1108/13673270110384428

McGregor, D. (1967). *The professional manager.* New York, NY: McGraw–Hill.

McLaughlin, S., Paton, R. A., & Macbeth, D. K. (2008). Barrier impact on organizational learning within complex organizations. *Journal of Knowledge Management, 12*(2), 107–123. doi:10.1108/13673270810859550

Miller, D., & Shamsie, J. (1996). The resource-based view of the firm in two environments: The Hollywood firm studios from 1936 to 1965. *Academy of Management Journal, 39*(3), 519–543. doi:10.2307/256654

Milton, N., Shadbolt, N., Cottman, H., & Hammersley, M. (1999). Towards a knowledge technology for knowledge management. *International Journal of Human-Computer Studies, 51*(3), 615–641. doi:10.1006/ijhc.1999.0278

Moliner, C., Martinez-Tur, V., Peiro, J. M., Ramos, J., & Cropanzano, R. (2005). Relationships between organizational justice and burnout at the work-unit level. *International Journal of Stress Management, 12*(2), 99–116. doi:10.1037/1072-5245.12.2.99

Montes, F. J., Moreno, A. R., & Fernandez, L. M. (2004). Assessing the organizational climate and contractual relationship for perceptions of support for innovation. *International Journal of Manpower, 25*(2), 167–180. doi:10.1108/01437720410535972

Moran, E. T., & Volkwein, J. F. (1992). The cultural approach to the formation of organizational climate. *Human Relations, 45*(1), 19–47. doi:10.1177/001872679204500102

Morrison, E. W. (1994). Role definitions and organizational citizenship behavior: The importance of the employee's perspective. *Academy of Management Journal, 37*(6), 1543–1567. doi:10.2307/256798

Mueller, J. (2015). Formal and informal practices of knowledge sharing between project teams and enacted cultural characteristics. *Project Management Journal, 46*(1), 53–68. doi:10.1002/pmj.21471

Nahapiet, J., & Ghoshal, S. (1998). Social capital, intellectual capital, and organizational advantage. *Academy of Management Review, 23*(2), 242–266. doi:10.2307/259373

Neelam, N., Bhattacharya, S., Sinha, V., & Tanksale, D. (2015). Organizational culture as a determinant of organizational commitment: What drives IT employees in India? *Global Business and Organizational Excellence, 34*(2), 62–74. doi:10.1002/joe.21594

Nelson, R. R., & Winter, S. G. (1982). *An evolutionary theory of economic change.* Cambridge, MA: Harvard Business School Press.

Nonaka, I., & Takeuchi, H. (1995). *The knowledge-creating company.* New York, NY: Oxford University Press.

Norrgren, F., & Schaller, J. (1999). Leadership style: Its impact on cross-functional product development. *Journal of Product Innovation Management, 16*(4), 377–384. doi:10.1016/S0737-6782(98)00065-4

O'Dell, C., & Grayson, J. (1999). Knowledge transfer: Discover your value proposition. *Strategy and Leadership, 27*(2), 10–15. doi:10.1108/eb054630

O'Reilly, C. A., & Chatman, J. A. (1996). Culture as social control: Corporation, cults, and commitment. In B. Staw & L. Cummings (Eds.), *Research in organizational behavior* (pp. 157–200). Greenwich, CT: JAI Press.

Oliver, R. L., & Anderson, E. (1994). An empirical test of the consequences of behavior-and outcome-based sales control systems. *Journal of Marketing*, *58*(4), 53–67. doi:10.2307/1251916

Ostroff, C. (1993). The effects of climate and personal influences on dividual behavior and attitudes in organizations. *Organizational Behavior and Human Decision*, *56*(1), 56–90. doi:10.1006/obhd.1993.1045

Patterson, K. A. (2005). *Leadership practices.* Virginia Beach, VA: Regent University Law School Admissions.

Patterson, M. G., West, M. A., Schackleton, V. J., Dawson, J. F., Lawthom, R., Maitlis, S., & Wallsace, A. M. et al. (2005). Validating the organizational climate measure: Links to managerial practices, productivity and innovation. *Journal of Organizational Behavior*, *26*(4), 379–408. doi:10.1002/job.312

Penrose, E. (1959). *The theory of the growth of the firm.* Oxford, UK: Oxford University Press.

Perryer, C., & Jordan, C. (2005). The influence of leader behaviors on organizational commitment: A study in the Australian public sector. *International Journal of Public Administration*, *28*(5/6), 379–396. doi:10.1081/PAD-200055193

Peters, T. J., & Waterman, R. H. (1982). *In search of excellence – Lessons from America's best run company.* New York, NY: Harper & Row.

Pritchard, R. D., & Karasick, B. W. (1973). The effect of organizational climate on managerial job performance and job satisfaction. *Organizational Behavior and Human Performance*, *9*(1), 126–146. doi:10.1016/0030-5073(73)90042-1

Quinn, R. E., & Cameron, K. (1983). Organizational life cycles and sifting criteria of effectiveness: Some preliminary evidence. *Management Science*, *29*(1), 33–51. doi:10.1287/mnsc.29.1.33

Ravasi, D., & Schultz, M. (2006). Responding to organizational identity threats: Exploring the role of organizational culture. *Academy of Management Journal*, *49*(3), 433–458. doi:10.5465/AMJ.2006.21794663

Ravindran, S., & Iyer, G. S. (2014). Organizational and knowledge management related antecedents of knowledge use: The moderating effect of ambiguity tolerance. *Information Technology Management*, *15*(4), 271–290. doi:10.1007/s10799-014-0190-4

Reichers, A. E., & Schneider, B. (1990). Climate and culture: An evolution of constructs. In B. Schneider (Ed.), *Organizational climate and culture* (pp. 5–39). San Francisco, CA: Jossey–Bass.

Reijers, H. A. (2006). Implementing BPM systems: The role of process orientation. *Business Process Management Journal*, *12*(4), 389–409. doi:10.1108/14637150610678041

Renzl, B. (2007). Language as a vehicle of knowing: The role of language and meaning in constructing knowledge. *Knowledge Management Research & Practice*, *5*(1), 44–53. doi:10.1057/palgrave.kmrp.8500126

Rus, I., & Lindvall, M. (2002). Knowledge management in software engineering. *IEEE Software*, *19*(3), 26–38. doi:10.1109/MS.2002.1003450

Sabherwal, R., Hirschheim, R., & Goles, T. (2001). The dynamics of alignment: Insights from a punctuated equilibrium model. *Organization Science*, *12*(2), 179–197. doi:10.1287/orsc.12.2.179.10113

Sanchez, R. (1996). *Strategic learning and knowledge management.* Chichester, UK: John Wiley & Sons.

Santos, V., Goldman, A., & de Souza, C. R. B. (2015). Fostering effective inter-team knowledge sharing in agile software development. *Empirical Software Engineering*, *20*(4), 1006–1051. doi:10.1007/s10664-014-9307-y

Schein, E. H. (1984). Coming to a new awareness of organizational culture. *MIT Sloan Management Review*, *25*(2), 3–16.

Schein, E. H. (1992). *Organizational culture and leadership: A dynamic view*. San Francisco, CA: Jossey–Bass.

Schmid, W., & Kern, E. M. (2014). Integration of business process management and knowledge management: State of the art, current research and future prospects. *Journal of Business Economics*, *84*(2), 191–231. doi:10.1007/s11573-013-0683-3

Schneider, B., Salvaggio, A. N., & Subirats, M. (2002). Climate strength: A new direction for climate research. *The Journal of Applied Psychology*, *87*(2), 220–229. doi:10.1037/0021-9010.87.2.220

Seidler-de Alwis, R., & Hartmann, E. (2008). The use of tacit knowledge within innovative companies: Knowledge management in innovative enterprises. *Journal of Knowledge Management*, *12*(1), 133–147. doi:10.1108/13673270810852449

Selamat, N., Samsu, N. Z., & Kamalu, N. S. (2013). The impact of organizational climate on teachers' job performance. *Educational Research*, *2*(1), 71–82.

Serenko, A., & Bontis, N. (2004). Meta-review of knowledge management and intellectual capital literature: Citation impact and research productivity rankings. *Knowledge and Process Management*, *11*(3), 185–198. doi:10.1002/kpm.203

Shadur, M. A., Kienzle, R., & Rodwell, J.J. (1999). The relationship between organizational climate and employee perceptions of involvement. *Group & Organization Management*, *24*(4), 479–503. doi:10.1177/1059601199244005

Sharma, R. S., & Djiaw, V. (2011). Realising the strategic impact of business intelligence tools. *VINE: The Journal of Information and Knowledge Management Systems*, *41*(2), 113–131. doi:10.1108/03055721111134772

Shin, Y., Sung, S. Y., Choi, J. N., & Kim, M. S. (2015). Top management ethical leadership and firm performance: Mediating role of ethical and procedural justice climate. *Journal of Business Ethics*, *129*(1), 43–57. doi:10.1007/s10551-014-2144-5 PMID:26430288

Siemieniuch, C., & Sinclair, M. (2002). On complexity, process ownership and organizational learning in manufacturing organizations, from an ergonomics perspective. *Applied Ergonomics*, *33*(5), 449–462. doi:10.1016/S0003-6870(02)00025-X PMID:12236654

Simonin, B.L. (1999). Ambiguity and the process of knowledge transfer in strategic alliances. *Strategic Management Journal*, *20*(7), 595–623. doi:10.1002/(SICI)1097-0266(199907)20:7<595::AID-SMJ47>3.0.CO;2-5

Smircich, L. (1983). Concepts of culture and organizational effectiveness. *Administrative Science Quarterly*, *28*(3), 339–358. doi:10.2307/2392246

Sparrow, P. R., & Gaston, K. (1996). Generic climate maps: A strategic application of climate survey data. *Journal of Organizational Behavior*, *17*(6), 679–698. doi:10.1002/(SICI)1099-1379(199611)17:6<679::AID-JOB786>3.0.CO;2-M

Stevens, J., Beyer, J., & Trice, H. (1978). Assessing personal role and organizational predictors of managerial commitment. *Academy of Management Journal*, *21*(3), 380–396. doi:10.2307/255721 PMID:10246524

Stone, P. W., Larson, E. L., Mooney-Kane, C., Smolowitz, J., Lin, S. X., & Dick, A. W. (2006). Organizational climate and intensive care unit nurses' intention to leave. *Critical Care Medicine*, *34*(7), 1907–1912. doi:10.1097/01.CCM.0000218411.53557.29 PMID:16625126

Szulanski, G. (1996). Exploring internal stickiness: Impediments to the transfer of best practice within the firm. *Strategic Management Journal,* *17*(S2), 27–43. doi:10.1002/smj.4250171105

Taminiau, Y., Smit, W., & De Lange, A. (2009). Innovation in management consulting firms through informal knowledge sharing. *Journal of Knowledge Management,* *43*(1), 42–55. doi:10.1108/13673270910931152

Tang, H. K. (1999). An inventory of organizational innovativeness. *Technovation,* *19*(1), 41–51. doi:10.1016/S0166-4972(98)00077-7

Teece, D. J. (1998). Capturing value from knowledge assets: The new economy, markets for know-how and intangible assets. *California Management Review,* *40*(3), 55–79. doi:10.2307/41165943

Tordera, N., Gonzalez-Roma, V., & Peiro, J. M. (2008). The moderator effect of psychological climate on the relationship between leader-member exchange (LMX) quality and role overload. *European Journal of Work and Organizational Psychology,* *17*(1), 55–72. doi:10.1080/13594320701392059

Trauth, E. M., Beehr, T. A., & Haiyan, H. (2009). Retaining women in the US IT workforce: Theorizing the influence of organizational factors. *European Journal of Information Systems,* *18*(5), 476–497. doi:10.1057/ejis.2009.31

Venkatraman, N., & Ramanujam, V. (1986). Measurement of business performance in strategy research: A comparison of approaches. *Academy of Management Review,* *11*(4), 801–814. doi:10.5465/AMR.1986.4283976

Wallach, E. (1983). Individuals and organizations: The cultural match. *Training and Development Journal,* *37*(2), 29–36.

Wasko, M. M., & Faraj, S. (2005). Why should I share? Examining social capital and knowledge contribution in electronic networks of practice. *Management Information Systems Quarterly,* *29*(1), 35–57.

Wei, Y., Samiee, S., & Lee, R. P. (2014). The influence of organic organizational cultures, market responsiveness, and product strategy on firm performance in an emerging market. *Journal of the Academy of Marketing Science,* *42*(1), 49–70. doi:10.1007/s11747-013-0337-6

Wiewiora, A., Murphy, G., Trigunarsyah, B., & Brown, K. (2014). Interactions between organizational culture, trustworthiness, and mechanisms for inter-project knowledge sharing. *Project Management Journal,* *45*(2), 48–65. doi:10.1002/pmj.21407

Wiewiora, A., Trigunarsyah, B., Murphy, G., & Coffey, V. (2013). Organizational culture and willingness to share knowledge: A competing values perspective in Australian context. *International Journal of Project Management,* *31*(8), 1163–1174. doi:10.1016/j.ijproman.2012.12.014

Wiig, K. M. (1997). Knowledge management: An introduction and perspective. *Journal of Knowledge Management,* *1*(1), 6–14. doi:10.1108/13673279710800682

Williams, L. J., & Anderson, S. E. (1991). Job satisfaction and organizational commitment as predictors of organizational citizenship and in-role behaviors. *Journal of Management,* *17*(3), 601–617. doi:10.1177/014920639101700305

Wilson, A. M. (2001). Understanding organizational culture and the implication for corporate marketing. *European Journal of Marketing,* *35*(3/4), 353–367. doi:10.1108/03090560110382066

Yamane, T. (1970). *Statistics: An introductory analysis.* Tokyo, Japan: John Weatherhill.

ADDITIONAL READING

Berson, Y., Da'as, R., & Waldman, D. A. (2015). How do leaders and their teams bring about organizational learning and outcomes? *Personnel Psychology, 68*(1), 79–108. doi:10.1111/peps.12071

Blackburn, R. A., Hart, M., & Wainwright, T. (2013). Small business performance: Business, strategy and owner-manager characteristics. *Journal of Small Business and Enterprise Development, 20*(1), 8–27. doi:10.1108/14626001311298394

Borges, R. (2013). Tacit knowledge sharing between IT workers: The role of organizational culture, personality, and social environment. *Management Research Review, 36*(1), 89–108. doi:10.1108/01409171311284602

Bowling, N. A., Khazon, S., Meyer, R. D., & Burrus, C. J. (2015). Situational strength as a moderator of the relationship between job satisfaction and job performance: A meta-analytic examination. *Journal of Business and Psychology, 30*(1), 89–104. doi:10.1007/s10869-013-9340-7

Boyce, A. S., Nieminen, L. R. G., Gillespie, M. A., Ryan, A. M., & Denison, D. R. (2015). Which comes first, organizational culture or performance? A longitudinal study of causal priority with automobile dealerships. *Journal of Organizational Behavior, 36*(3), 339–359. doi:10.1002/job.1985

Clossey, L., & Rheinheimer, D. (2014). Exploring the effect of organizational culture on consumer perceptions of agency support for mental health recovery. *Community Mental Health Journal, 50*(4), 427–434. doi:10.1007/s10597-013-9681-8 PMID:24343525

Connell, J., & Voola, R. (2013). Knowledge integration and competitiveness: A longitudinal study of an industry cluster. *Journal of Knowledge Management, 17*(2), 208–225. doi:10.1108/13673271311315178

Denford, J. S. (2013). Building knowledge: Developing a knowledge-based dynamic capabilities typology. *Journal of Knowledge Management, 17*(2), 175–194. doi:10.1108/13673271311315150

Faust, M. (2014). How to facilitate organizational transformation with a turnaround mindset and an innovation culture. *Silicon, 6*(1), 1–4. doi:10.1007/s12633-013-9167-x

Guan, J., & Zhu, W. (2014). How knowledge diffuses across countries: A case study in the field of management. *Scientometrics, 98*(3), 2129–2144. doi:10.1007/s11192-013-1134-1

Huyghe, A., & Knockaert, M. (2015). The influence of organizational culture and climate on entrepreneurial intentions among research scientists. *The Journal of Technology Transfer, 40*(1), 138–160. doi:10.1007/s10961-014-9333-3

Khan, A., Ramzan, M., & Butt, M. S. (2013). Is job satisfaction of Islamic banks operational staff determined through organizational climate, occupational stress, age and gender. *Journal of Business Studies Quarterly, 4*(3), 13–26.

Lam, C. K., Walter, F., & Ouyang, K. (2014). Display rule perceptions and job performance in a Chinese retail firm: The moderating role of employees' affect at work. *Asia Pacific Journal of Management, 31*(2), 575–597. doi:10.1007/s10490-013-9348-6

Lee, C., Rahayu, W., & Nguyen, U. T. (2014). Knowledge management technologies for semantic multimedia services. *Multimedia Tools and Applications, 71*(1), 195–198. doi:10.1007/s11042-013-1740-1

Maes, J., & Sels, L. (2014). SMEs' radical product innovation: The role of internally and externally oriented knowledge capabilities. *Journal of Small Business Management, 52*(1), 141–163. doi:10.1111/jsbm.12037

Manroop, L. (2015). Human resource systems and competitive advantage: An ethical climate perspective. *Business Ethics (Oxford, England)*, *24*(2), 186–204. doi:10.1111/beer.12069

Manroop, L., Singh, P., & Ezzedeen, S. (2014). Human resource systems and ethical climates: A resource-based perspective. *Human Resource Management*, *53*(5), 795–816. doi:10.1002/hrm.21593

Markus, K., & Hajo, A. R. (2013). The effects of process-oriented organizational design on firm performance. *Business Process Management Journal*, *19*(2), 245–262. doi:10.1108/14637151311308303

Matayong, S., & Mahmood, A. K. (2013). The review of approaches to knowledge management system studies. *Journal of Knowledge Management*, *17*(3), 472–490. doi:10.1108/JKM-10-2012-0316

Moon, H., & Lee, C. (2014). The mediating effect of knowledge-sharing processes on organizational cultural factors and knowledge management effectiveness. *Performance Improvement Quarterly*, *26*(4), 25–52. doi:10.1002/piq.21161

Oehler, A., Höfer, A., & Schalkowski, H. (2015). Entrepreneurial education and knowledge: Empirical evidence on a sample of German undergraduate students. *The Journal of Technology Transfer*, *40*(3), 536–557. doi:10.1007/s10961-014-9350-2

Purcarea, I., Espinosa, M., & Apetrei, A. (2013). Innovation and knowledge creation: Perspectives on the SMEs sector. *Management Decision*, *51*(5), 1096–1107. doi:10.1108/MD-08-2012-0590

Rabeh, H. A. D., Jimenéz-Jimenéz, D., & Martínez-Costa, M. (2013). Managing knowledge for a successful competence exploration. *Journal of Knowledge Management*, *17*(2), 195–207. doi:10.1108/13673271311315169

Roch, G., Dubois, C. A., & Clarke, S. P. (2014). Organizational climate and hospital nurses' caring practices: A mixed-methods study. *Research in Nursing & Health*, *37*(3), 229–240. doi:10.1002/nur.21596 PMID:24729389

Singh, A., Singh, K., & Sharma, N. (2014). Agile knowledge management: A survey of Indian perceptions. *Innovations in Systems and Software Engineering*, *10*(4), 297–315. doi:10.1007/s11334-014-0237-z

Tzortzaki, A. M., & Mihiotis, A. (2014). A review of knowledge management theory and future directions. *Knowledge and Process Management*, *21*(1), 29–41. doi:10.1002/kpm.1429

Zhang, L., & Zhang, Z. (2014). The effects of incentive mechanism on knowledge management performance in China: The moderating role of knowledge attributes. *Project Management Journal*, *45*(2), 34–47. doi:10.1002/pmj.21403

KEY TERMS AND DEFINITIONS

Business Process Orientation: A business approach in which whatever an organization makes related to business activities performed together to produce a defined set of results.

Framework: The broad overview, outline, or skeleton of interlinked items which supports a particular approach to a specific objective of the study.

Job Performance: The work-related activities expected of an employee and how well those activities are executed.

Knowledge Management: The strategies and processes designed to identify, capture, structure, value, leverage, and share an organization's intellectual assets to enhance its performance and competitiveness.

Organizational Climate: The properties of the business environment in a workplace observed by employee that strongly influence their actions and job performance.

Organizational Culture: The values and behaviors that contribute to the unique social and psychological environment of an organization.

Productivity: A measure of the efficiency of a person, machine, factory, and system in converting inputs into useful outputs.

Quality of Performance: A numerical measurement of the performance of an organization or process assessed through measurement of physical products and statistical sampling of the output of processes.

Chapter 16
Virtual Team Management for Higher Performance

Edward T. Chen
University of Massachusetts – Lowell, USA

ABSTRACT

This chapter aims to explore the increasing utilization of virtual teams in the existing globally competitive and complex business environment of the 21st century. With virtual teams, companies can expand their talent pool beyond geographical barriers. Furthermore, they can incorporate a follow-the-sun process in their business strategy. Combined, this leveraged approach can better position companies to meet market demands in a more timely and cost-effective manner. To achieve this competitive advantage, business leaders must thoroughly understand the challenges associated with developing and managing virtual teams. This chapter examines the reasons for utilizing virtual teams, challenges that stem from diversity, structural and behavioral characteristics, managerial considerations for effective leadership, supporting technologies, best practices, and future implications.

INTRODUCTION

Virtual teams are becoming a necessity in the globalization of the economy. While there are several benefits to virtual teams, they will not be realized if managers do not minimize the challenges. The management of project teams is an important part of a manager's job. Today's managers need to understand the various forms that a project team can take on and the best way to manage those teams. The traditional project team is made up of a group of people, most likely from different departments, working in the same location who is working to achieve a goal. The team members

will meet in a conference room to discuss the project and assign tasks. These tasks may be done independently by team members but because they are located in the same office, they can easily and discuss the project outside of the formal meetings (Barnwell, Nedrick, Rudolph, Sesay, & Wellen, 2014; Schlenkrich & Upfold, 2009).

Information systems and the growth of high speed Internet across the globe have enabled companies to implement a global virtual team structure (Piccoli, Powell, & Ives, 2004). Companies implementing virtual teams have seen a reduction in costs, greater utilization, increased access to new markets, and a larger pool of resources with

DOI: 10.4018/978-1-4666-9970-0.ch016

a greater variation in skill sets (Olson, Appunn, McAllister, Walters, & Grinnell, 2014). However, working virtually does come with challenges. Virtual teams need to navigate communication difficulties, the effects of culturally diverse membership, and the technical difficulties involved in linking regions across large distances (Grosse, 2002; Jarvenpaa & Leidner, 1999; Jones, 2009; Lisak & Erez, 2015). In order to maximize the benefits and minimize the weaknesses from virtual teams, managers need to be more involved than they are with local teams. Virtual teams require the manager to establish and closely monitor organizational design within the team, with an eye toward encouraging an environment of trust and open, effective communication (Henderson & Lee, 1992; Gaan, 2012; Krebs, Hobman, & Bordia, 2006; Morgan, Paucar-caceres, & Wright, 2014; Zolin & Hinds, 2004). A manager must also mitigate conflict that arises. He or she must function in multiple roles, including administrator, coach, and advisor, throughout the lifespan of the team. The objective of this chapter is to explore the challenges of virtual teams and identify how to manage them in order to maximize performance (Brunelle, 2012).

Research for this chapter is comprised of several journal articles, corporate white papers, and trade magazines that revealed overlapping coverage of reasons to build virtual teams, limitations, challenges that team members encounter, managerial tactics, and the future outlook for virtual teams in a variety of settings. These articles contained empirical evidence of claims; however, to date it appears more research is needed to support virtual team best practices. Thus, this chapter is written for both IS researchers and IT practitioners.

VIRTUAL TEAMS

A singular, unifying definition of virtual teams is difficult to find. This is largely due to the fact virtual teams vary in many ways (Curseu, Schalk, & Wessel, 2008). Some definitions differentiate global virtual teams from local virtual teams. A local virtual team refers to a team of people that are located in a common geographic area and share the same culture. A local virtual team can also include personnel that work out of home or remote offices. On the other hand, global virtual team members are separated by larger distances and differ in cultural backgrounds between members (Lisak & Erez, 2015; Magnusson, Schuster, & Taras, 2014). The other area in which there is some debate is on the longevity of the team. In other words, some definitions classify a virtual team with an expectation that the team has a specific end date. Lastly, there is a difference in how these team members interact with one another. Some definitions indicate that virtual teams have no face-to-face interaction, whereas other definitions state that the face-to-face interaction time is limited. Despite these differences, there are some common aspects of virtual teams in which there seems to be some consensus. These common aspects include that: (1) virtual teams work remotely, (2) there are multiple members on the team, (3) the members work together on a common project or focused goal, and (4) the communication among team members is through electronic means (Curseu, Schalk, & Wessel, 2008; Magnusson, Schuster, & Taras, 2014; Morgan, Paucar-caceres, & Wright, 2014;).

In recent years, there have been unprecedented technological advancements, which have made virtual teams more viable than ever before. Businesses sometimes prefer virtual teams for numerous organizational advantages, as they look to expand beyond their traditional boundaries. This expansion can allow companies to access a vast pool of previously unattainable resources (Eissa, Fox, Webster, & Kim, 2012). In addition to the enhanced skills of these personnel, many companies find benefits in reduced cost and increased utilization (Horwitz, Bravington & Silvis 2006). Although there are many benefits to virtual teams, there are weaknesses to address. The major challenge of virtual teams is ensuring proper communication. The lack of face-to-face communication limits the effectiveness, due to the inability to pick up on important nonverbal cues (Kayworth & Leidener, 2002). There are methods and techniques used by managers of virtual teams to minimize these weaknesses and provide an environment suited for maximizing success and performance (Morgan, Paucar-caceres, & Wright, 2014).

Virtual teams are defined as groups of employees with unique skills, situated in distant locations, whose members must collaborate using technology across space and time to accomplish important organizational tasks (Lipnack & Stamps, 2000). Modern virtual teams are assembled with individuals from all areas of the world based on their expertise and fit with the virtual team being assembled. Coupled with their unique talents, they can bring experiences and perspectives to complement other team members. More importantly, when configured and managed appropriately, virtual teams can be more productive than traditional face-to-face teams (Siebdrat, Hoegl & Ernst, 2009).

In 2011, Deloitte published a paper on how virtual teams successfully support the implementation of information technology projects. They first examined the impact of cost, time and quality on performance. These three elements are the forces that shape the need for and goals of virtual teams, regardless of the industry or task. Cost, for example, can be significantly reduced by limiting travel expenses and hiring lower-cost, high-talent labor that meet specific goals set forth for a project. Looking at time as the second key element, companies can shorten cycle-time by operating around the clock with team members located in different time zones. Lastly, quality improvements can be gained by assembling a virtual team that represents the highest caliber employees based on value, experience, and specialization. Thus, the virtual team bypasses geographical barriers in conventional business strategies. Combined,

these three elements represent the primary levers of competitive advantage. To realize this advantage, however, we must first examine the details of virtual teams, beginning with the challenges they face (Beck, et al., 2011).

CHALLENGES

Compared to traditional face-to-face teams, virtual teams present some unique challenges for companies, team managers, and members. Stemming from vast differences in culture and communication, diversity is evident and often the most significant challenge for virtual teams (Pearlson & Saunders, 2010; Staples & Zhao, 2006). Also, the degree of virtualization, say 25% versus 100% dispersion, dictates the severity of challenges that virtual teams may face (Schlenkrich & Upfold, 2009).

To gain a better understanding of these challenges, managers must look at the different components of virtual team diversity to include culture, communication, technology, and logistics. If a virtual team is comprised of members from multiple countries such as the U.S., China, India, and Germany, cultural differences will inevitably exist. Differences can include varying expectations, biases, and communication skills and habits (Iles & Hayers, 1997). When communicating via email, phone, or even video, important intricacies such as facial expressions, vocal modulations, verbal signals, and body gestures can be altered or lost in translation. As a medium to facilitate communication amongst the virtual team, the very technologies used can also present several challenges. For example, team members may be afraid of or lack skills necessary to operate technologies such as video teleconferencing equipment. Furthermore, some virtual team members may have a strong preference for one technology over another, say email versus phone. Lastly, logistical challenges exist for team members spread across multiple time zones. While this enables teams to work around the clock and follow-the-sun, shift overlap may be necessary for day-to-day communication and team meetings (Kayworth & Leidner, 2002).

STRUCTURE

If managers decide to use a virtual team in their organization, they must look at it from a complete and comprehensive perspective. Structurally, virtual team success is dependent on the successive construction of three critical layers (Piccoli, Powell, & Ives, 2004). Beck, et al. (2011) view these as the infrastructure, tactical, and strategic layers.

Infrastructure Layer

Beginning with the infrastructure layer, it sets up the foundation for how the virtual team will operate. This includes various types of hardware, software, remote access applications, networks, standard documents, operating procedures, and clearly defined roles, expectations, and meeting schedules. Unlike traditional face-to-face teams located in the same building or office, virtual teams must ensure that information flows despite the challenges associated with being physically separated, albeit in different time zones.

Tactical Layer

Once the infrastructure layer is established and team members are deployed, managers must begin to facilitate the communication and collaboration necessary for daily and efficient operations. This can be accomplished by designing a schedule with overlapping shifts and onsite visits, identifying virtual team leaders and scheduling headquarters visits, training members to be technologically proficient and culturally cognizant, and creating an environment that encourages frequent collaboration, as it could be with traditional teams.

Strategic Layer

Finally, after the infrastructure and tactical layers are set up and working well, managers must now consider ways to optimize the performance of the virtual team by making strategic refinements. This includes monitoring and adjusting the balance of onsite and offsite resources and tasks, fine-tuning the flow of knowledge and information between clients and off/onsite locations, and finding areas for additional cost savings (Beck, et al., 2011).

STEPS

Once the virtual team structure is established, it is important for managers to know that virtual teams will go through different steps of development (Orlikowski, 2000; Piccoli, Powell, & Ives, 2004). Furst, Reeves, Benson and Blackburn (2007) summarize these steps using Tuckman's four steps of team development: forming, storming, norming, and performing.

Forming Step

During the forming step, team members become acquainted with each other by sharing basic information about themselves and their duties. This is when team trust begins to build and where goals and expectations are made clear. With limited opportunities for virtual team member conversations, other than work related topics, trust builds slowly (Krebs, Hobman, & Bordia, 2006). It is possible that members will incorrectly stereotype each other during this step.

Storming Step

In the storming step, the group will work toward identifying key roles and responsibilities. However, conflict is likely as the team contends with points of parity and differentiation. The situation can be further complicated by the use of virtual team communication technologies. Consequently, team members may withdraw from the group or increase their dependence on the virtual team leader to resolve their concerns.

Norming Step

Moving to the norming step, team members work through their interpersonal conflicts and begin to focus on efficient information flow and collaboration. Professional bonds develop and their actions become aligned with their distinct roles and the overarching strategy. It is during this time that members are challenged with best practices for communication and collaboration using the technologies provided by leadership.

Performing Step

Finally, in the performing step, the virtual team begins to work as a cohesive unit, providing support for one another and focusing on completion of project deliverables. Still, it is possible during this step that communication and collaboration will suffer from side conversations and meetings among certain team members (Furst et al., 2004).

INTERVENTIONS

Given the inherent nature of these steps, it is possible for mangers guide the team using a variety of well-timed interventions. During the forming step, virtual team managers can strive to provide clarity for individual and group goals, encourage knowledgeable and experienced virtual members to help mentor other team members, and begin to foster a team culture by establishing common ground.

When conflict arises during the storming step, managers can organize in-person meetings to alleviate tension from misunderstandings, train employees on how to resolve conflict, and if needed, help team members develop, and agree on alternative solutions to their issues.

In the norming step, virtual team members can spend less time on building relationships and resolving interpersonal conflicts, and focus more on the task at hand. Managers can accelerate this process by refining schedules and task deadlines, improving the use of virtual team communication technologies, and leveraging a team member to perform some of the virtual team management duties.

Lastly, in the performing step, managers and senior leadership can focus on more global issues by further developing a company culture that understands and fully supports virtual teams. For team members with existing on-site responsibilities, support from managers and senior leadership is pivotal to sustaining on-site and off-site workloads that fluctuate in volume and importance (Furst, et al., 2004; Pinar, Zehir, Kitapçi, & Tanriverdi, 2014).

BEST PRACTICES

Beyond the layers of virtual team organizational structure and the predictable nature of the steps of development, it is vital for managers to understand some of the intricacies of successfully managing virtual teams (Hoch & Kozlowski, 2014). A review of virtual team literature highlights some key areas of concern.

Leadership Characteristics

Research indicates four key characteristic dimensions of effective virtual team leaders: communication, understanding, role clarity, and leadership attitude. Similar to traditional teams, and perhaps even more important with virtual teams, communication is key to success. With virtual teams, successful managers offer regular and constructive feedback to team members and present tasks in a detailed and clear manner. To build effective relationships that encourage collaboration, managers must be perceived as understanding and supportive on a personal level. They can achieve this by remaining open to team member concerns, encouraging the two-way flow of constructive feedback, and by demonstrating a genuine interest in the personal and professional endeavors of the virtual team members (Chang, Hung, & Hsieh, 2014).

Once lines of communication are open and relationships have formed, effective virtual team leaders must: clearly define and deliver roles and responsibilities for the team, influence members and hold them accountable for tasks, and be able to roll their sleeves up for a hands-on approach to mentoring. Finally, leadership attitude will help shape the culture of the virtual team and keep it on track for deliverables. Depending on the situation, managers must strike a balance between controlling the team, but yet giving them freedom to consistently maintain virtual team member relationships (Graham, Daniel, & Doore, 2015; Kayworth & Leidner, 2002; Pinar, et al., 2014).

Managing Dispersion

There are varying degrees of dispersion, from different floors in the same building to different continents. To a certain extent, many traditional teams operate as virtual teams do, for example, with frequent email and phone interactions.

Interestingly, an MIT study on virtual teams working in partnership with global software developer SAP to evaluate 80 teams across 28 locations, including Brazil, China, Germany and the United States, indicates that team performance varies with degrees of dispersion among traditional and virtual teams. Those correlations are not in a straight line manner. Barriers for collaboration exist in all levels of dispersion, but they may be misjudged in settings with smaller separations such as working in the same building. The authors

demonstrate that team performance, effectiveness and efficiency, can actually be higher for a team dispersed around a country as compared to being in the same building. Companies and virtual team managers can improve performance by designing tools to increase "socio-emotional and task-related" processes in a "dispersed team" environment (Magnusson, Schuster, & Taras, 2014; Orlikowski, 2000; Siebdrat et al., 2009).

First, to emphasize teamwork skills, managers must hire virtual team members with both technical and social skills to foster the efficient exchange of valuable information through communication and collaboration. This allows virtual teams to capitalize on the very reason they have been assembled – having performance advantages over traditional teams for the assigned tasks.

Second, managers must train and encourage virtual team members to identify and resolve issues on their own. Without the level of interaction and intervention commonly seen in traditional teams, virtual team members must have the maturity and social skills to work through indifferences so they can continue to collaborate, regardless of the challenges associated with dispersion (Orlikowski, 2000).

Next, an effective way to foster virtual team culture and social interactions is by organizing periodic face-to-face meetings, particularly at the beginning steps of the virtual team project. This ice-breaker helps the team establish a foundation for team relationships and trust (Chang, Hung, & Hsieh, 2014; Zolin & Hinds, 2004). Siebdrat, et al. (2009) even state that projects should start with a simple, yet important step: "to go out for a beer with all team members in order to establish a common ground before starting the collaboration"(p. 68)

Lastly, to sew these efforts together, it is helpful to foster a global culture. In fact, the MIT research concluded that virtual team members thrive in an environment where they see themselves as part of a larger and supportive network, beyond the walls of the dispersed virtual team. Companies employ various tactics such as rotating assignments and cultural training to accomplish this goal. This helps virtual team members expand their skill set and knowledge of diverse cultures. Thus, fostering a global culture environment enables employees to better adapt to the demand of working with a dispersed group of individuals on a virtual team project (Siebdrat, et al., 2009).

BUILDING VIRTUAL TEAMS

In 2009, the Economist Intelligence Unit conducted a survey of 407 participants from $100m plus annual companies in various industries. With 318 respondents, the survey found that virtual teams range from five to twenty people. Designed primarily for project-based work, respondents indicated that they spend nearly 50% of the total time on off-site virtual team projects. 16% of the respondents indicated they spent more than 80% of their time on virtual team projects. The report also indicated that only 14% of managers use face-to-face interviews and only 7% use technologies such as video conferencing to conduct remote interviews (*Economist*, 2009). Therefore, managers are faced with the challenge of assembling a team of members who can work together, virtually, to meet the project goals.

Ironically, face-to-face meetings can serve as a litmus test for how knowledgeable and comfortable potential team members are with the technologies they may be using in the virtual team. However, Furst's research indicated that although technology savvy team members are valuable assets for communication and collaboration, interpersonal and teamwork skills may be of higher importance (Furst, et al., 2009). Furthermore, Kirkman, et al. (2004) state that extrinsic motivators are often absent in virtual teams, therefore, building a team with a high level of intrinsic motivation is also key to high virtual team performance (Fan, Chen, Wang, & Chen, 2014).

TRUST

Team member and leadership trust can be lacking in a virtual team. In traditional teams, many people can instinctively assess how much they should trust an individual based on body language observations such as eye contact, hand movements, and tone of voice. Conversely, virtual teams do not have an opportunity to screen for body signs unless they have periodic face-to-face meetings. Meyer (2010) notes that trust is primarily measured in terms of reliability. If team members consistently deliver on promises in a timely and accurate manner, trust will follow. For virtual team managers, this implies that they should build distinct processes to ensure that team members have a template for consistently delivering results. This will help build trust among virtual team members and leadership (Chang, Hung, & Hsieh, 2014; Jarvenpaa & Leidner, 1999; Krebs, Hobman, & Bordia, 2006; and Meyer, 2010).

DECISION PROCESS

Culture impacts the way teams communicate, collaborate, and arrive at decisions. In a traditional setting, this process may be simple. In a virtual team environment; managers must consider how culture fits into the mix. For example, U.S. managers may have a style that favors formal group input and rapid decision making and solution implementation. In some European countries such as France or Sweden, team members may default to lengthy debates and even confrontation when making a decision. On the other hand, decisions are made in more formal, one-on-one settings prior to meeting with a larger group in Japan. Managers of diverse virtual teams should realize that the decision making process to which they are accustomed may not be useful with their team. Therefore, virtual team leaders may need to explicitly outline how the decision process will work for the team. They may need to test different types of decision making processes to fit the diverse cultural backgrounds of the virtual team (Baker, 2002; and Meyer, 2010).

LEADERSHIP ROLES

Effective leadership is an essential component for virtual teams, not just for the team manager, but also for the team members. Since the group members are often times dispersed and operating independently, communication barriers and collaboration problems may exist. Virtual team members need to self-manage to ensure that the team continues to perform despite the challenges they encounter as a result of their diversity and distance from one another (Arnison & Miller, 2002; Magnusson, Schuster, & Taras, 2014; Staples & Zhao, 2006).

Furst, et al., (2004) speak from their own experiences as actual virtual team managers that managers should clarify the "fuzzy front end." It is frequently described as having ambiguous roles and responsibility, unclear goals, and limited guidance for obtaining resources and support for projects. To deal with this issue, virtual team managers should lead with collocated teams, starting with clearly defined expectations, directions, and a centralized approach to collaboration. Unlike traditional teams where loose job descriptions and flexible schedules are permissible, virtual teams need the structure, support, and clarity to counter the innate challenges they face from being dispersed and culturally diverse (Chang, Hung, & Hsieh, 2014; Meyer, 2010).

EMPOWERMENT AND PERFORMANCE

In addition to gaining competitive advantage, virtual teams are designed to capitalize on efficient processes by dispersing their human resources.

The intent for virtual teams is to be more effective than their collocated counterparts at delivering products and services to customers. To do this, managers should consider how virtual teams can be empowered and which performance aspects to focus on.

Empowerment studies have typically revolved around individuals. However, recent research indicates that empowerment plays a critical role in virtual teams as well (Klidas, & van den Berg, 2007; and Kirkman, Rosen, Tesluk, & Gibson, 2004). Collectively, teams can be empowered when they have positive feelings about their duties. This empowerment is derived from four dimensions: potency, meaningfulness, autonomy, and impact. Potency refers to how teams assess their overall effectiveness, meaningfulness expresses the degree of intrinsic care for team tasks, autonomy relates to how much flexibility team members have to make decisions, and impact refers to how teams see their efforts impacting the organization. Even if one of these areas is lacking, it is still possible for team to feel empowered (Kirkman, Rosen, Tesluk, & Gibson, 2004). Furthermore, virtual team empowerment is a dynamic state that is closely related to the collective level of team motivation throughout the project (Fan, et al., 2014; Klein, Noe & Wang, 2006).

Due to the nature of virtual teams, it appears that team empowerment is more critical to success than it is in traditional collocated teams. Theories suggest that this is vitally important for day-to-day operations as well as the end goal of customer satisfaction (Curseu, Schalk, & Wessel, 2008; and Piccoli, Powell, & Ives, 2004). Process improvement for virtual teams includes high levels of planning, collaboration, resource distribution, and performance improvements. Virtual teams are significantly involved in these areas. It is believed that high levels of potency, meaningfulness, autonomy, and impact will have positive impacts on virtual team process improvement.

Additionally, virtual teams must meet or exceed the goals of internal stakeholders and external customers. Studies indicate that if the four dimensions of empowerment are high, virtual teams will be able to satisfy customers. This assumption is based on the study that intrinsically motivated, self-sufficient, and knowledgeable team members are positively positioned to promptly handle a variety of customer concerns, regardless of the level of dispersion from team members or the organization (Fan, et al., 2014; Kirkman et al., 2004).

FUTURE OUTLOOK AND RESEARCH DIRECTIONS

The future outlook for virtual teams looks promising in a variety of settings. With the growing global use of the Internet, consumers are better equipped with technologies to accurately price and choose the products and services they need. Consequently, companies are under pressure to deliver innovative solutions to market needs in a timely and cost effective manner. Virtual teams are one tool companies can use to meet these needs by tapping into the global market for talented labor. It is improbable that traditional face-to-face teams will be completely replaced by virtual teams. It is likely that the use of virtual teams will increase in the coming years as an enhancement to traditional teams and conventional business strategy (Arnison & Miller, 2002).

In addition to virtual teams in corporations, there are three considerations for future research in regards to virtual teams: medical, military, and educational applications. To keep medical costs low and provide comfort for cancer patients, Pitsillides, et al. (2001) suggest that virtual medical teams should be a viable option for patient home care. With the growing cost of medical care and virtual team technologies available, further research should be conducted to reveal that virtual teams can benefit healthcare providers and improve patient care, particularly at the end of life.

Virtual teams, to a certain extent, have been used for decades in military applications. It is becoming increasingly common for military leadership to lead combat operations from remote locations in a decentralized and on-the-fly manner (Jones, 2009). Virtual teams will continue to present opportunities for the military to reduce the cost of operations and deliver faster and more accurate results for military tasks. Furthermore, it is believed that the use of virtual teams in the military will lead to new and improved technologies for the civilian sector (Hyllengren, Larsson, Fors, Sjöberg, Eid, & Olsen, 2011; and Pierce, 2012).

Finally, with the emerging e-learning technologies, there are opportunities to improve all levels of education for people both in the U.S. and abroad. Funded by donations, and with substantial support from the Bill and Melinda Gates Foundation, the Khan Academy is a non-profit organization that offers free education, mostly math and sciences, for anyone with Internet access and a desire to learn (Khan Academy, 2012). Educators will work more as facilitators of self-disciplined virtual learner teams in both the public and private sectors (Cater, Michel & Varela, 2012).

CONCLUSION

Virtual teams are going to continue to rise in popularity in the global economy and today's leaders must ensure that they have the skill set to lead these teams. There are several challenges to virtual teams but they are not insurmountable and the benefits outweigh the challenges. Conventional wisdom suggests that performance of team's decreases as the level of dispersion increases, causing management to view virtual teams as a risk to delivering success. However, the use of virtual teams is becoming more of a commonality rather than a rarity in our existing global, competitive corporate environments. With the rapid innovations of the Internet and various computer-mediated communication systems companies are quickly hopping on the virtual team band wagon. Virtual teams give companies the ability to work globally, gain entrance into new markets and address staffing needs while promoting corporate social responsibility. Recent studies show that that if the appropriate tools and leadership are in place, and executed properly, virtual teams can actually outperform teams that are co-located if they are set up and managed properly.

In conclusion, virtual teams can provide great corporate strategic benefits. These benefits include reducing costs, enhancing team perspective through diversity, entering new global markets, and increasing productivity. These benefits are not gained by just setting up virtual teams. The organization, as a whole, needs to be designed such that it provides a framework that integrates virtual teams. Managers need to be cognizant of the effects of distance and culture to team performance. Building trust and ensuring open communication among the team members should be high priorities. The manager also needs to be a leader to the team; encapsulating the administrator, coach, and advisor functions. In the end, managing virtual teams is more challenging than local teams and requires constant interaction in order to maximize effectiveness.

Virtual teams present a unique opportunity for businesses to respond to market needs. By tapping into the global talent pool and dispersing team members, companies can improve their position to provide quality, cost effective, and valuable products and services in a timely manner. Key to this process is the successful construction and management of virtual teams. Understanding the difference between traditional and virtual teams is the first step, followed by a deeper understanding of how diversity creates challenges for virtual teams. With proper structure and planning, managers can use various tactics to sustain a highly functional level of communication and collaboration among dispersed team members. Furthermore, by utilizing communication and collaboration products, virtual teams can increase their productivity resulting in greater competitive advantage.

Managers shall set up a plan to gradually build the virtual team from infrastructure layer, to tactical layer, to strategic layer. Once the team structure is constructed, managers can follow Tuckman's four-step model to develop a robust and productive virtual team. As mentioned earlier, the future of human achievement will be driven by the leverage of talented groups of people, not individuals. If utilized properly, virtual teams can significantly contribute to this achievement on a global scale.

REFERENCES

Arnison, L., & Miller, P. (2002). Virtual teams: A virtue for the conventional team. *Journal of Workplace Learning*, *14*(4), 166–173. doi:10.1108/13665620210427294

Baker, G. (2002). The effects of synchronous collaborative technologies on decision making: A study of virtual teams. *Information Resources Management Journal*, *15*(4), 79–93. doi:10.4018/irmj.2002100106

Barnwell, D., Nedrick, S., Rudolph, E., Sesay, M., & Wellen, W. (2014). Leadership of international and virtual project teams. *International Journal of Global Business*, *7*(2), 1–8.

Beck, M., Brannon, S., Dracos, G., Junnarkar, P., Katz, R., Malik, A.,... Sonavane, S. (2011). Working in a virtual world: Establishing highly effective virtual teams on information technology projects. *Deloitte*. Retrieved September 15, 2012 from http://www.deloitte.com/assets/Dcom-UnitedStates/Local%20Assets/Documents/us_consulting_WorkingwithaVirtualWorld_080911.pdf

Brunelle, E. (2012). Virtuality in work arrangements and affective organizational commitment. *International Journal of Business and Social Science*, *3*(2), 56–62.

Cater, J. J., Michel, N., & Varela, O. E. (2012). Challenges of online learning in management education: An empirical study. *Journal of Applied Management and Entrepreneurship*, *17*(4), 76–96.

Chang, H. H., Hung, C. J., & Hsieh, H. W. (2014). Virtual teams: Cultural adaptation, communication quality, and interpersonal trust. *Total Quality Management & Business Excellence*, *25*(11/12), 1318–1335. doi:10.1080/14783363.2012.704274

Curseu, P. L., Schalk, R., & Wessel, I. (2008). How do virtual teams process information? A literature review and implications for management. *Journal of Managerial Psychology*, *23*(6), 628–652. doi:10.1108/02683940810894729

Economist Intelligence Unit. (2009). Managing virtual team: Taking a more strategic approach. *The Economist*. Retrieved September 15, 2012 from http://graphics.eiu.com/upload/eb/NEC_Managing_virtual_teams_WEB.pdf

Eissa, G., Fox, C., Webster, B. D., & Kim, J. (2012). A framework for leader effectiveness in virtual teams. *Journal of Leadership. Accountability and Ethics*, *9*(2), 11–22.

Fan, K. T., Chen, Y. H., Wang, C. W., & Chen, M. (2014). E-leadership effectiveness in virtual teams: Motivating language perspective. *Industrial Management & Data Systems*, *114*(3), 421–437. doi:10.1108/IMDS-07-2013-0294

Furst, S. A., Reeves, M., Benson, R., & Blackburn, R. S. (2004). Managing the life cycle of virtual teams. *The Academy of Management Executive*, *18*(2), 6–20. doi:10.5465/AME.2004.13837468

Gaan, N. (2012). Collaborative tools and virtual team effectiveness: An inductively derived approach in India's software sector. *Decision*, *39*(1), 5–27.

Graham, C. M., Daniel, H., & Doore, B. (2015). Millennial leadership: The Oppositional relationship between leadership type and the quality of database system's development in virtual environments. *International Journal of e-Collaboration*, *11*(3), 29–48. doi:10.4018/ijec.2015070103

Grosse, C. U. (2002). Managing communication within virtual intercultural teams. *Business Communication Quarterly*, *65*(4), 22–38. doi:10.1177/108056990206500404

Henderson, J. C., & Lee, S. (1992). Managing I/S design teams: A control theories perspective. *Management Science*, *38*(6), 757–777. doi:10.1287/mnsc.38.6.757

Hoch, J. E., & Kozlowski, S. W. J. (2014). Leading virtual teams: Hierarchical leadership, structural supports, and shared team leadership. *The Journal of Applied Psychology*, *99*(3), 390–403. doi:10.1037/a0030264 PMID:23205494

Horwitz, F. M., Bravington, D., & Silvis, U. (2006). The promise of virtual teams: Identifying key factors in effectiveness and failure. *Journal of European Industrial Training*, *30*(6), 472–494. doi:10.1108/03090590610688843

Iles, P., & Hayers, P. K. (1997). Managing diversity in transnational project teams: A tentative model and case study. *Journal of Managerial Psychology*, *12*(2), 95–117. doi:10.1108/02683949710164190

Jarvenpaa, S. L., & Leidner, L. E. (1999). Communication and trust in global virtual teams. *Organization Science*, *10*(6), 791–815. doi:10.1287/orsc.10.6.791

Jones, T. L. (2009). *Virtual team communication and collaboration in Army and corporate applications*. Retrieved September 15, 2012 from http://www.dtic.mil/cgi-bin/GetTRDoc?AD=ADA502091

Kankanhalli, A., Tan, B. C. Y., & Wei, K.-K. (2007). Conflict and performance in global virtual teams. *Journal of Management Information Systems, 23*(3), 237–274. doi:10.2753/MIS0742-1222230309

Kayworth, T. R., & Leidner, D. E. (2002). Leadership effectiveness in global virtual teams. *Journal of Management Information Systems, 18*(3), 7–40.

Khan Academy. (2012). *A free world class education for anyone anywhere.* Retrieved September 15, 2012 from http://www.khanacademy.org/about

Kirkman, B. L., Rosen, B., Tesluk, P. E., & Gibson, C. B. (2004). The impact of team empowerment on virtual team performance: The moderating role of face-to-face interaction. *Academy of Management Journal, 47*(2), 175–192. doi:10.2307/20159571

Klein, H. J., Noe, R., & Wang, C. (2006). Motivation to learn and course outcomes: The impact of delivery mode, learning goal orientation, and perceived barriers and enablers. *Personnel Psychology, 59*(3), 665–702. doi:10.1111/j.1744-6570.2006.00050.x

Klidas, A., van den Berg, P. T., & Wilderom, C. P. M. (2007). Managing employee empowerment in luxury hotels in Europe. *International Journal of Service Industry Management, 18*(1), 70–88. doi:10.1108/09564230710732902

Krebs, S. A., Hobman, E. V., & Bordia, P. (2006). Virtual teams and group member dissimilarity: Consequences for the development of trust. *Small Group Research, 37*(6), 721–741. doi:10.1177/1046496406294886

Lipnack, J., & Stamps, J. (2000). *Virtual teams: People working across boundaries with technology* (2nd ed.). New York: Wiley.

Lisak, A., & Erez, M. (2015). Leadership emergence in multicultural teams: The power of global characteristics. *Journal of World Business, 50*(1), 3–14. doi:10.1016/j.jwb.2014.01.002

Magnusson, P., Schuster, A., & Taras, V. (2014). A process-based explanation of the psychic distance paradox: Evidence from global virtual teams. *Management International Review, 54*(3), 283–306. doi:10.1007/s11575-014-0208-5

Meyer, E. (2010). Leadership: The four keys to success with virtual teams. *Forbes.* Retrieved August 1, 2012 from http://www.forbes.com/2010/08/19/virtual-teams-meetings-leadership-managing-cooperation.html

Morgan, L., Paucar-caceres, A., & Wright, G. (2014). Leading effective global virtual teams: The consequences of methods of communication. *Systemic Practice and Action Research, 27*(6), 607–624. doi:10.1007/s11213-014-9315-2

Olson, J. D., Appunn, F. D., McAllister, C. A., Walters, K. K., & Grinnell, L. (2014). Webcams and virtual teams: An impact model. *Team Performance Management, 20*(3/4), 148–177. doi:10.1108/TPM-05-2013-0013

Orlikowski, W. J. (2000). Using technology and constituting structures: A practice lens for studying technology in organizations. *Organization Science, 11*(4), 404–428. doi:10.1287/orsc.11.4.404.14600

Pearlson, K. E., & Saunders, C. S. (2010). *Managing and Using Information Systems.* Hoboken, NJ: John Wiley & Sons, Inc.

Piccoli, G., Powell, A., & Ives, B. (2004). Virtual teams: Team control structure, work processes, and team effectiveness. *Information Technology & People, 17*(4), 359–379. doi:10.1108/09593840410570258

Pinar, T., Zehir, C., Kitapçi, H., & Tanriverdi, H. (2014). The relationships between leadership behaviors team learning and performance among the virtual teams. *International Business Research, 7*(5), 68–79. doi:10.5539/ibr.v7n5p68

Pitsillides, A., Pitsillides, B., Dikaiakos, M., Christodoulou, E., Andreou, P., & Georgiadis, D. (2006). DITIS: A collaborate virtual medical team for home healthcare of cancer patients. *Topics in Biomedical Engineering, II*, 247–266. doi:10.1007/0-387-26559-7_18

Schlenkrich, L., & Upfold, C. (2009). A guideline for virtual team managers: The key to effective social interaction and communication. *The Electronic Journal of Information Systems Evaluation, 12*(1), 109–118.

Siebdrat, F., Hoegl, M., & Ernst, H. (2009). How to manage virtual teams. *MIT Sloan Management Review, 50*(4), 63–68.

Staples, D. S., & Zhao, L. (2006). The effects of cultural diversity in virtual teams versus face-to-face teams. *Group Decision and Negotiation, 15*(4), 389–406. doi:10.1007/s10726-006-9042-x

Zivick, J. (2012). Mapping global virtual team leadership actions to organizational roles. *Business Review (Federal Reserve Bank of Philadelphia), 19*(2), 18–25.

Zolin, R., Hinds, P. J., Fruchter, R., & Levitt, R. E. (2004). Interpersonal trust in cross-functional, geographically distributed work: A longitudinal study. *Information and Organization, 14*(1), 1–26. doi:10.1016/j.infoandorg.2003.09.002

Chapter 17

Leadership Communication, Internal Marketing, and Employee Engagement:
A Recipe to Create Brand Ambassadors

Karen E. Mishra
Meredith College, USA

Aneil K. Mishra
East Carolina University, USA

Khaner Walker
Lenovo, USA

ABSTRACT

This chapter examines the internal communication practices of Lenovo, a $39 billion Fortune Global 500 technology company, and the world's largest PC vendor. In particular, this study examines how this company uses social media as a form of internal marketing to foster employee engagement. Internal communications (or internal marketing) is generally led by marketing or PR professionals with expertise in human resources, public relations, marketing, social media, and/or employee engagement. One new way that companies are extending internal communication is by developing the use of their company intranets. Intranets can support an organization by sharing accurate leadership communication and company information on a timely basis to develop trust with employees and encourage them to act as brand ambassadors. This chapter describes how Lenovo has developed and uses its Lenovo Central intranet to engage employees in its mission and vision.

INTRODUCTION

This chapter examines the internal communication practices of a Lenovo, a $39 billion multinational technology company. This case study examines the intent, development, and use of *Lenovo Cen-* *tral*, its company intranet. The case study also analyzes how it uses social media to publish internal communications with employees in ways that enhance employee engagement. This chapter will introduce the role of internal communication (or internal marketing), how leadership commu-

DOI: 10.4018/978-1-4666-9970-0.ch017

nication through social media can support such communication, the path to employee engagement, and Lenovo's success with *Lenovo Central* (Mishra, Walker, Mishra, 2014). The chapter also discusses the managerial implications for other firms interested in implementing an intranet in order to improve internal communication and foster employee engagement.

LITERATURE REVIEW

The Role of Internal Communication

The practice of internal communication can enhance an organizational culture by promoting employee engagement through open communication (Cahill, 1995; Deloitte, 2013; Harrison, 2013; Men & Stacks, 2014). Employees typically prefer to receive more communication from their superiors as it promotes their willingness to be involved in solving problems in the organization. Research has consistently argued for and empirically found that greater sharing of information by the organization serves to enhance employee empowerment, including a greater sense of impact on the organization and a greater sense of meaning (Mishra, & Spreitzer, 1998; Spreitzer & Mishra, 1999; Siegall & Gardner, 2000; Mills & Ungson 2003). Similar arguments and findings exist for the positive effect of communication within an organization on employee engagement (Kress, 2006; Saks, 2006; Rockland, 2014). In fact, a recent survey by PWC found that 20% of engagement by employees occurs as a result of the company's internal communications (Rockland, 2014). Welch & Jackson (2007) also identified internal communication as crucial for achieving employee engagement. A 2007/2008 Watson Wyatt study found that "Firms that communicate effectively are four times as likely to report high levels of employee engagement as firms that communicate less effectively."

Most recently, a Deloitte culture survey (2013) found that 50% of employees feel that "regular and candid communication" leads to a "culture of meaningful purpose." In addition, internal marketing "enables the firm to serve the needs of the customer (DeBussy, Ewing & Pitt, 2003: p. 150)." As reported in the Deloitte survey on culture and beliefs (2013), only 57% of employees who are happy at work said that their bosses talked about culture with them. Saks (2006) emphasized the need for clear and consistent communications with employees in order to achieve employee engagement, and suggested that employees who are more engaged will have a more positive relationship with their employer. Yet, managers seem to have less time to communicate, due to their demanding jobs (Robson & Tourish, 2005).

The Role of Leadership Communication

It has long been thought that leaders play an important role in communicating the brand promise to all stakeholders, including employees (Vallaster & de Chernatony, 2002). A Watson Wyatt (2008-2009) study found that those strategies that engage employees include communication from managers, leadership communication, and a focus on internal communication. In fact, the most effective brand building efforts emphasize the importance of employees in transmitting information from company leadership to external stakeholders (Vallaster & de Chernatony, 2002). D'Aprix (2009) concluded that organizational leaders have lost credibility with external stakeholders because they have not been truthful with employees about a variety of issues that impact the company and its customers. However, employees are more willing to take on the role of brand ambassador when they understand and trust brand information from the top (Vallaster & de Chernatony, 2002).

In fact, recent research confirms that authentic and transparent leadership communication leads to employee engagement, trust, and collaboration (Men & Stacks, 2014). In particular, employees consider communication more transparent when they perceive their leaders as more ethical (Men & Stacks, 2014). Employees are also more engaged when they feel like the communication they receive from their company leadership is honest, able to withstand scrutiny, and focused on their best interests (Men & Stacks, 2014).

The Role of Trust

Effective internal communication can improve the trust between employees and management within an organization (DeBussy, Ewing & Pitt, 2003; Gavin & Mayer, 2005; Zeffane, Tipu, & Ryan, 2011) by widely sharing information, and by building engagement and commitment. In one study (Robson & Tourish, 2005), employees identified a need for more internal communications, including face-to-face meetings, more openness, greater listening, improved email communication, more appreciation, an improved newsletter, and communications training in order to empower and engage employees. Often, however, top managers feel that communication with external constituents is more important than communication with internal ones (Therkelsen & Fiebich, 2003). A more recent study of retail employees (Mishra & Boynton, 2009) found that those managers that take time for face-to-face meetings, to listen, and to provide feedback for employees on a regular basis, build strong trusting relationships with those employees who in turn have feelings of loyalty to both the local retail establishment and the larger corporate entity, as well.

Research has confirmed this strong link between trust and open communication within an organization because such communication resolves ambiguities and promote interdependence (Mishra, 1996; Mishra, Schwartz & Mishra, 2011). Chia (2005) argued that "trust and commitment are byproducts of processes and policies which are designed to make the relationship satisfactory for both parties, such as open, appropriate, clear and timely communication" (p. 7). Trust between leaders and their employees, in terms of openness and concern, can be conveyed through empathic communication (Mishra & Mishra, 1994; 2013). Mishra (1996) found that "the extent to which the trusted person engages in undistorted communication then reinforces the trust (in terms of openness) placed in him or her" (p. 276). More generally, Dolphin (2005) argued that "sound relationships can only be developed on the basis of trust and reliable information (p. 185)."

Employee Engagement

Employee engagement is defined as "the degree to which an individual is attentive and absorbed in the performance of his or her role (Saks, 2006, p. 602)". In the management literature, this "discretionary effort" is also known as organizational citizenship behavior (OCB), behavior that is both non-rewarded and discretionary, or above and beyond what is expected of the employee (Yankelovich & Immerwahr, 1983; Organ, 1988). A recent study found that employee engagement is positively impacted by employer branding, leading to greater employee discretionary effort (Piyachat, Chanongkorn & Panisa, 2014). In fact, a greater emphasis on internal branding can lead to creating highly engaged employees, or brand ambassadors within a company (Asha & Jyothi, 2013). To ensure maximum success in the organization, the values of both the organization and the employee should match (Asha & Jyothi, 2013). In fact, 72.5% of discretionary effort was explained by such a match (Asha & Jyothi, 2013). Engaged employees as brand ambassadors can positively influence the reputation of the company through their use of social media (Dreher, 2014). Customers trust that employees are credible and authentic spokesmen (and women) of their companies, which allows their messages to gain traction (Dreher, 2014).

The Role of Social Media at Work

In addition to employees' use of social media to interact with customers, companies can use it to develop relationships with their employees. A recent study examined how social media can enhance the way companies build an engaged workforce (Towers Watson, 2013). It found that only 56% of companies are using social media to build a sense of community with its workforce, such as sharing information with employees about culture, teambuilding or innovation (Towers Watson, 2013). Many more companies place an importance in using social media with external stakeholders (Lipiainen, Karjaluoto & Nevalainen, 2014). The Towers Watson study also found that only 23% of organizations are effective at building a shared experience with their remote workforce (Towers Watson, 2013). Collaboration sites, such as a company intranet, are one way to build a shared experience. Web 2.0 technologies, such as an intranet, allow a firm to connect employees, customers, and partners (Lee, 2011). Only 45% of companies surveyed actually use such a site and of those, just less than 35% found them effective (Towers Watson, 2013).

Increasingly, companies are developing intranets and other types of internal social media in order to keep employees apprised of the internal communications of the organization (Nakata, Zhu & Izberk-Bilgin, 2011). This is occurring as marketing and IT are increasingly working together to improve the communication networks of the organization (Nakata, Zhu & Izberk-Bilgin, 2011). Griffith & Harvey (2001) advised that "To reap the benefits of strong relational networks in the global marketplace, effective inter-organizational communications need to be established among members of the network (p. 88)." As internal communications executive Heather Lowe of Lenovo noted, "I made the conscious decision to come back into internal communication after having always worked in external, because I believe that the message should start with internal (H. Lowe, personal communication, May 5, 2013)." The Deloitte survey (2013) found that 45% of executives feel social media will enhance culture, yet only 27% of employees agree. Some Gen Y employees actually prefer to use social media for personal use, instead of company use (Lipiainen, Karjaluoto & Nevalainen, 2014). One of the reasons executives feel positively about social media is that 38% of them believe it increases transparency in the organization, but again, only 17% of employees agree (Deloitte, 2013). The reason for this discrepancy between executives and employees needs to be better understood.

Heather Lowe, Senior Manager Internal Communications, said that the most pressing challenge for her team is to "build a social media hub that can be used internally in an effective way, because then people can check it any time no matter where they are on the globe." She believes that the focus should be on short messages, such as using a video, so that when there are employees who speak many languages, it is easier for them to understand. In addition, it is critical to make sure that the internal messages mesh with the external messages about the brand. In fact, the internal communication team noted that several years ago, *Lenovo Central* was weak and people didn't think of it as a first resource of information. People didn't believe information about the company unless it was in their inbox or hand-delivered to them. Using the social media functionality of the redesigned *Lenovo Central* allowed the internal communications team to draw more people to that resource.

The Role of a Company's Intranet

One benefit of an intranet is to allow for two-way communication with employees (Lipiainen, Karjaluoto & Nevalainen, 2014), such as getting and giving feedback and ideas. In addition, a global company has the added challenge of communicating with employees regardless of their location

(Lipiainen, Karjaluoto & Nevalainen, 2014) in a way that respects not only corporate culture, but ethnic culture. One reason global communications fail, is that managers are not aware of "local sensitivities" (Mounter, 2003: p. 268). Khaner Walker, Sr. Manager of Communications at Lenovo, also found this, noting that in the eastern part of the world, an employee values honor, so they want updates from their direct manager in order to show respect, but some managers aren't equipped to deliver updates. This is where the intranet can help augment a manager's ability to share information across the organization (Lee, 2011). In addition, when communicating with non-native English speakers, it is critical to listen, be sensitive to organizational needs, and promote a dialogue with global stakeholders (Mounter, 2003).

Marketing communications departments typically rely on a variety of channels to share company information, including intranets (internet services specifically for employee use) in order to share corporate and employee knowledge (Ruppel & Harrington, 2002; DeBussy, Ewing & Pitt, 2003; Lipiainen, Karjaluoto & Nevalainen, 2014). These intranets are also presumed to influence and be influenced by corporate culture as they develop and are adopted throughout the organization (Su & Contractor, 2011). Ruppel & Harrington (2002) found that "intranet implementation is facilitated by a culture that emphasizes an atmosphere of trust and concern for other people (ethical culture), flexibility and innovation (developmental culture), and policies, procedures and information management (hierarchical culture)". Lee (2011) noted that companies can "enhance the value of existing traditional businesses (p.9)" by using Web 2.0 "to complement existing company capabilities by integrating multiple Web 2.0 platforms (p. 11)" with social networks that connect employees, such as a company intranet. "The survival of emerging Web 2.0-based business models depends on attracting existing businesses as customers, contributors, and users (Lee, 2011, p. 13)."

Skok & Goldstein (2007) advocated for using a knowledge management (KM) strategy that focuses on expert, knowledge activities and group activities. In addition, they thought a champion would best "motivate management and staff, and to overcome possible barriers to management buy-in and a knowledge silo culture (p. 327)." One study found that new media, particularly the introduction of intranets, do positively impact internal marketing communications in the workplace (DeBussy, Ewing & Pitt, 2004) by increasing transparency and enhancing information flows. In addition, this study confirmed that intranets contribute toward two-way communication in the workplace, resulting in a more democratized workplace. Lipiainen, Karjaluoto & Nevalainen (2014) also found these benefits of an intranet, and advocated for company guidelines to help employees manage the tools better.

Employees as Brand Ambassadors

Finally, the intranet signals that employees are important stakeholders with equal access to information. A study of consultants by Su & Contractor (2011) found that "the organizational intranets contained both tacit (e.g., skill learning, sales and marketing) as well as explicit (e.g., articles, deliverables, and policies) information." When employees are encouraged to participate in that communication, they are more committed to their brand (Gelb & Rangarajan, 2014). Those networks build trust, which in turn build trust and credibility for the brand (Gelb & Rangarajan, 2014). The Towers Watson study (2013) concurred, finding that "remote workers are looking for clear communication, integrity and coaching from their managers."

In addition to improving information sharing, intranets are also ways to improve social capital as well. One recent study found that intranets are especially important for socializing new employees into an organization as well as serving as an organizational knowledge tool to retain employees (Chu & Chu, 2011). Specifically, Chu & Chu (2011) found that "the newcomers' adoption of intranet techniques has significant effects on socialization regarding how well they master their job, define their role, learn about their organization's culture and goals, and become socially integrated (p. 1175)." Radick (2011) noted a change in the use of intranets, "Whereas the intranet used to be focused on connecting people to information, it's now about connecting people to people."

Heather noted that their internal communications efforts, both electronic and face-to-face, should be transparent and trustworthy:

People can see through corporate BS. If it's got that tone, (then) they're not really saying what they mean, – so it's just important to be as plainspoken as you can and to be as transparent as you can. I know a lot of organizations try to hold information back and think 'oh, we're not ready to say that', but to the extent that you can give away as much as you know, it will go a long way towards creating that climate of trust.

In addition, it is not just Heather's team that has this responsibility, but the executive leadership, such as Chairman Yang Yuanqing (or YY, as he is called) at Lenovo that has this responsibility: "That's how you gain trust: your leaders go out there face-to-face, and be as visible and as open to taking questions as they can. They should provide as much information as they feel they can without compromising the business (H. Lowe, personal communication, May 5, 2013)."

Finally, when employees feel committed to the brand, they are more likely to positively engage with customers, which also builds brand equity (Gelb & Rangarajan, 2014). Employees have a wide reach beyond customers, however, and can positively impact prospective customers, prospective employees, and the general public (Gelb & Rangarajan, 2014).

RESEARCH QUESTION

This exploratory study of internal communication professionals and their internal customers seeks to understand the role of internal communications in a multinational technology company with locations around the globe. This study focuses on the role of the company intranet in its internal communications strategy to share information, foster employee engagement, and facilitate brand ambassadorship for Lenovo. This study used exploratory, semi-structured interviews conducted with managers responsible for public relations and/or internal communication at their firm (see interview questions in Appendix 1), as well as employees who utilize the company intranet on a daily basis (see interview questions sin Appendix 2).

METHOD

The first author and a research assistant conducted all interviews in person. Each conversation was recorded, transcribed, and analyzed to understand how and what executives think about internal communications at Lenovo. Eight Lenovo executives participated in this study. Four of the participants work in internal communications for Lenovo at the headquarters in Morrisville, North Carolina. Four executives, also located at the North American headquarters in Morrisville, North Carolina, use the intranet on a daily basis; two from the accounting department and two from inside sales. A snowball technique was used in obtaining interview subjects for this study. One of the accountants is an MBA student of the first author and referred the first author to the second accountant. The inside sales executives were both alumni of the first author's university. This was appropriate for this study because some degree of trust is helpful between the researcher and the interviewee to understand their role in internal communication (Atkinson & Flint, 2001).

The interview questions for the internal communications staff specifically asked how they execute internal communications at Lenovo (see appendix I). The interview questions for the accounting and sales executives asked how they feel internal communications are accessible and useful to them at Lenovo (see appendix II).

The interviews were conducted asking about internal communications in general, to understand Lenovo's best practices. At the completion of the interviews, the dominant theme of each interview was how *Lenovo Central* was such an important source of information to each employee on a daily basis, as well as how much *Lenovo Central* dominated the time and effort of the internal communications executives. *Lenovo Central* became the most important internal communication vehicle for the Lenovo internal communication team, and thus, the focus of this study.

INTERVIEW FINDINGS

The internal communication executives interviewed for this study are:

1. Nancy Liang, Executive Director - Executive Assistant to Chairman & CEO
2. Khaner Walker, Senior Manager Communications
3. Kelly Reid, Senior Global Communications & Content Strategist
4. Heather Lowe, Senior Communications Manager

The accounting and inside sales executives interviewed for this study are:

1. Kim Marut, North America Balance Sheet Lead Accountant
2. Marian Lakin, Monetization Controller
3. Joanna Still, Inside Sales Rep
4. Stephanie Mack, Inside Account Manager

The primary theme that emerged from these interviews on internal communications practices was the importance of *Lenovo Central*, the company's intranet, in their daily work lives.

RESULTS

Lenovo's Success with its Intranet, *Lenovo Central*

Khaner Walker is the Senior Manager of Communications at Lenovo in Raleigh, North Carolina. One of his primary roles is to support many different departments via *Lenovo Central*, the company intranet. Through his extensive background and work experience in journalism and public relations, Khaner has a unique vision for how *Lenovo Central* can provide timely, accurate, and critical content for employees across the globe. His goal is "to grow *Lenovo Central's* reach and usefulness for employees, along with enabling more interaction with employees (social postings on their own "wall," creating their own image galleries, etc.)." He has found that the more *Lenovo Central* grows, the more competitive and creative each department head becomes in getting out the most interesting content on their particular site within *Lenovo Central*. Khaner's previous work experience has proven to be an extremely effective preparation for seeking out important information for Lenovo employees to know about and then translate that information in a way that is timely, accurate, and compelling (K. Walker, personal communication, January 18, 2013).

Khaner's boss, Nancy Liang, is *Executive Director - Executive Assistant to Chairman & CEO* at Lenovo (N. Liang, personal communication, June 28, 2013). She came to Lenovo with a Harvard MBA and six years of experience at Cummins, where she was Director of Internal Communications. At the time of the study, she lead the team of six employees for the $39 billion company, who do most of the work in communicating news to all Lenovo employees around the globe, including *Lenovo Central*. Nancy has since been promoted to *Executive Director - Executive Assistant to Chairman & CEO* at Lenovo. Her personal philosophy for internal communications at Lenovo is PCPC: People, Content, Process, Channel.

In terms of People, it is important to Nancy that 1) messages are sent to the right set of stakeholders; and that 2) messages are sent from the correct manager. When it has been decided that a message will come directly from the top, Nancy is insistent that decisions are deliberately made to send messages from either Chairman and CEO Yang Yuanqing's company email or his personal email, depending on the message and the target audience. This is critical, as research has found that CEOs believe that communication coming directly from the top positively influence "employees' feelings towards work and the organization's bottom line (Pincus, Rayfield & Cozzens, 1991, p. 27)." The most recent research by the Edelman Trust Barometer (2014) confirms that "trust in the person leading the company is inextricably linked with trust in the company itself."

Nancy confirmed that this is true for Lenovo and for Chairman and CEO Yang Yuanqing, as well. When speaking to a class of MBA students at Meredith College in Raleigh, North Carolina (N. Liang, personal communication, October 28, 2013), she remarked that "YY", as she calls him, "reads everything that is on *Lenovo Central*". She said that this confirms for her and for her team that what they do is of utmost importance for the company. In addition, any new information or announcement coming from one of his senior vice presidents, YY wants on *Lenovo Central* within 24 hours of them speaking or writing about it (N. Liang, personal communication, October 28, 2013).

One of her team members, Kelly Reid, is senior manager of global internal communications. Kelly's job is to manage and curate content for *Lenovo Central* (K. Reid, personal communication, May 5, 2013). As far as **Content**, Kelly said

that, "we know who our audience is for the most part. It's the 30,000 Lenovo employees around the world." Nancy feels, however, that it is important to craft the message in just the right way for the audience it is intended for. For instance, it is critical to know your audience and whether the message should be in English or Chinese or both. Kelly agreed, saying that "the most effective way to communicate a message to people of many languages is by combining art and copy, so it's in a poster form." Kelly added that, "I think the biggest challenge because it's the most important challenge is asking the question 'why are we sending this. Why are we communicating this to the audience?'"

When Nancy is strategizing about Process, her team gathers, curates, writes, produces, and monitors the information that is posted on *Lenovo Central*. This includes financial information, interviews, photos from events, links to articles written about Lenovo, and monitoring the mechanism to encourage employees to co-create content, as well. Her team also works with each department at Lenovo to make sure that their own portals are up-to-date and useful for their own teams. Khaner mentioned that he is finding that department heads are becoming more competitive with each other in the content that they publish, wanting to make sure that they are putting forth their best effort.

The most important Channel her team communicates through is *Lenovo Central*, where information is available 24/7. This channel comes complete with a new news banner that changes each day, a photo gallery, a video gallery from around the world, and a place on *Lenovo Central* for events, such as a recent London fashion show or the Chairman's CCTV award. There is also a spot on the front page of *Lenovo Central* where employees can co-create content by updating news themselves and share it with fellow employees. This is critical for helping employees feel like they are an important part of creating and building the Lenovo culture. Heather, Senior Manager Internal Communications mentioned that ideally, they are looking for employees to contribute more to this social media presence: "We're moving towards a social media-based system, where no one person has the burden of creating content. It's crowd-sourced, meaning everybody is feeding in their view of the organization into one central hub. It's built piece by piece instead of a team of five or seven people churning out masses of content for the rest." Kelly also stressed the importance of adding content to *Lenovo Central* for employees:

The most effective way to create a lasting message is by putting it on Lenovo Central, which has the news section and the community section, and having the person go and find it and read it. Because they discovered it on their own…we're trying to move away from email communications and start to build a sense of discovery on Lenovo Central.

This social media aspect of *Lenovo Central* allows employees to share information internally. They can post to their "wall" and share news and updates, which also helps fellow employees see how users are connected back to the up-to-date HR directory so that everyone can see who they are, who they work for, and where they work in the organization.

One other important channel Lenovo uses is its annual Kickoff event in April where Chairman and CEO Yang lays out the strategic plan for the year so that employees are kept informed on the mission and vision of the company. Chairman and CEO Yang and his top executives meet with employees in three places around the world to make sure that everyone has an opportunity to be involved. Top managers share messages about the strategic plan, the Lenovo brand, and the new Lenovo products.

It is important to understand how *Lenovo Central* impacts its intended audience, as well. For example, the accounting employees use *Lenovo Central* to get up-to-date information they need on employees from all over the world. When Kim, an accounting manager, needs an organizational chart for a group in China, she knows she can count on *Lenovo Central* to have the most current information (K. Marut, personal communication, February 26, 2013). This was particularly critical for her during a restructuring when people were moving to new positions, or especially in China, where people frequently leave the company for new positions. Toni, an accounting manager, also noted that this is critical because then she can rely on *Lenovo Central* to give her the most up-to-date

Figure 1. Lenovo Central Homepage
Note. Screenshots from "Lenovo Central". Copyright 2014 by Copyright Holder. Reprinted with permission.

Figure 2. Lenovo Central Employee Wall
Note. Screenshots from "Lenovo Central". Copyright 2014 by Copyright Holder. Reprinted with permission.

information rather than rely on rumors, which are not necessarily accurate (A. Lakin, personal communication, March 15, 2013). Toni noted that *Lenovo Central* is also very good at keeping her apprised of senior level changes in the organization. The one thing Toni would change about *Lenovo Central* would be for it to keep better track of lower-level moves, as her department regularly deals with folks from all levels of the organization, all over the world.

The sales function also values *Lenovo Central*. Joanna and Stephanie are both inside sales reps at Lenovo. They value this as something that helps keep them "in-the-loop". They find it up-to-date and organized. While they don't know who is behind *Lenovo Central*, they are impressed nonetheless at how timely the information is that they can rely on. This is especially important for them because their bosses are not always available onsite to provide them with this timely information in a face-to-face manner. They know that they have access to company information regardless of whether or not they are able to meet with their

supervisor on a regular basis to get company and employee information directly (J. Still, personal communication, March 15, 2013; S. Mack personal communication, March 20, 2013).

Challenges with *Lenovo Central*

Some of the employees noted that while they appreciate Lenovo Central, they have no idea who is in charge of it. This might be a problem if those employees need to utilize the intranet to share information throughout the company and don't know the official channels and/or people to go through to share that information. While the internal communications staff works hard behind the scenes, there might be an opportunity to be more visible to the employees whom they are there to help.

Another challenge is communicating ethnic and/or cultural teachings through *Lenovo Central*. A couple of the employees interviewed expressed a desire for more exposure and communication around global culture to help them better understand how different cultures operate in the locations where Lenovo operates. They noted that since people are the core of the company, working all over the globe, it is important to understand those cultures because of who they are and where they're from.

The Larger Role of *Lenovo Central*

Khaner Walker, Senior Manager of Communications, summed up what he thinks is the role that *Lenovo Central* ultimately plays within Lenovo and in evangelizing the Lenovo brand.

I think our Intranet has had a key role in Lenovo's transformation from a PC company, to what we call a PC+ company (tablets, smartphones, smart TVs, etc.). This has been a major, substantive shift for Lenovo, considering our deep legacy in PCs from both Lenovo and IBM PC, and how our employees have enjoyed a considerable amount of success just from Lenovo's growing PC business (indeed we became the world's #1 PC company in early July 2013).

But we realize the world is changing. The PC market as a whole is slowing down, and while Lenovo has been able to avoid this trend, we must innovate and push beyond our norms to realize our vision of becoming a lasting technology leader.

We use the Intranet on almost a daily basis to highlight Lenovo's PC+ strategy and expand upon what it means, what the company is doing, where we are launching new PC+ products, and where we will be launching.

Consider the viewpoint of an IBM employee who has been with the company for 15-20 years, or a Lenovo employee in China where they have enjoyed considerable PC success. This is more than introducing a new type of computer – this is a major, tremendously important shift in our company's strategy, which Lenovo Central has been the frontlines for internally. We use the

Intranet to go beyond the strategy Yuanqing (our CEO) lays out on a PowerPoint slide – we bring it to life in a way employees can understand, see for themselves, and ultimately embrace.

A quick glance at yesterday's headlines from our Q1 earnings announcement highlights the success of this shift: "Lenovo Sells More Tablets and Phones than PCs, and That's Important" – Fast Co. "Lenovo, the world's largest PC maker, now sells more smartphones and tablets than computers." – NY Times.

The world's largest PC company now sells more phones and tablets than computers...an amazing shift – one that has happened much, much faster than we anticipated, and perhaps in large part due to a rapid, enthusiastic adoption internally.

I would argue that Lenovo Central's growing readership (more than 60,000 visits a month), increased views on videos that focus on PC+ products (compared to videos that focus on PCs), and my team's non-stop coverage of PC+ news plays a vital role in the company's successful transformation.

DISCUSSION AND CONTRIBUTIONS

Lenovo is a global company: is it possible for other multi-national corporations to incorporate its best practices in internal communication? There are some key takeaways.

1. *Make daily communication a priority.* Even though top executives are busy, lower level employees crave information about the company, the strategy, and their fellow employees. Making information available (such as on a company intranet) prevents rumors and false information from taking over. Even when you as the manager don't have time to spend in daily face-to-face conversations

with employees, an intranet can help fill in the information gaps. In addition, the more positive information employees have at their disposal, the better brand ambassadors they can be for the company when friends and neighbors ask about your brands and services.

2. *Establish one global language* for the company to use so that everyone knows what to expect and how to receive internal communication messages. This helps to create a consistent message and delivery, as well. However, organizations should be flexible in their use of language, and consider incorporating a second key language, to keep all employees engaged in other parts of the world to avoid any major misunderstandings

3. *Share cultural information as well as company information.* As organizations become more global in its employees and operations, it should find ways to help employees learn about what is culturally important and relevant about all employees in order to them in order to increase their personal understanding of each other. This will help employees learn to appreciate the background and experience of fellow team members who work in other locations.

4. *Create a dynamic communications vehicle* (such as a company intranet or daily email digest) to disseminate messages in a timely and interesting way to all employees. Make sure that this is a two-way communications vehicle, not just a one-way tool. Employees will feel more engaged if they have the opportunity to participate in and co-create communication efforts. If this is a two-way communications vehicle, employees will be more likely to remain engaged and utilize this as much as or more than email.

5. *Partner with HR* to make sure that the HR directory is up-to-date and is tied into the communications system. This can help facilitate the exchange of timely and accurate information among a directory of global employees, as well as help build important relationships across cultural and country boundaries.

6. *Let employees know who the internal communications team is.* The team should be accessible to all employees so that they know who they can go to for up-to-date information as well as who can help them share new information with their colleagues.

7. *Share brand strategy.* By sharing strategic information with your employees, you can engage them in the vision of the company, its products, and the future direction of the company so that they become brand ambassadors for your company. Year after year, the Edelman Trust Barometer (2013; 2014) finds that consumers trust information from "someone like me" more than they trust information from traditional advertising. If your employees share brand information that they learn from the intranet, it will be much more powerful than any advertising campaign.

FUTURE RESEARCH DIRECTIONS

Companies like Lenovo using its intranet, *Lenovo Central*, represent a "best practice" in internal communications. Future research should study how many other Fortune Global 500 companies are actually using such an intranet in their own firms to allow employees to be kept up-to-date on all internal and external matters about their firm. In addition, future research should consider whether colleges are preparing future executives for this role in companies. Internal communications is a relatively new role in corporate communications, which may be why there are relatively few executives suited to take on this new challenge. Finally, future research should address whether or not Fortune Global 500 intranets are doing what Lenovo Central is doing, hosting its intranet in two languages, when this company has headquarters in both Beijing and North Carolina. The former Director of Global Internal Communications, who is now *Executive Director - Executive Assistant to Chairman & CEO*, speaks both Mandarin and English, which makes her uniquely qualified to manage an internet in both languages. How many other companies are thinking globally when they are developing their internal communications department and their intranets? Or is English the dominant language of business?

CONCLUSION

As a global technology leader, Lenovo is also leading the way in developing a world-class employee intranet, *Lenovo Central*. Designed to bridge cultures and languages, *Lenovo Central* is the place that employees state that they go to get up-to-date information about their colleagues and their company. Lenovo also uses its company intranet as a social media site to engage its employees with information about the company, to instill a sense of pride about the Lenovo brand, and to foster brand ambassadorship among its employees.

As companies grow and become more global in scope, this form of social media will be critical for crossing both geographic and socio-cultural boundaries, as well as engaging employees in acting as brand ambassadors, and sharing critical information about their company to their customers, neighbors, colleagues, and friends.

REFERENCES

Asha, C. S., & Jyothi, P. (2013). Internal branding: A determining element of organizational citizenship behavior. *The Journal of Contemporary Management Research*, 7(1), 37–57.

Atkinson, R., & Flint, J. (2001). Accessing hidden and hard-to-reach populations: Snowball research strategies. *Social Research Update*, *33*. Retrieved from http://sru.soc.surrey.ac.uk/SRU33.pdf

Cahill, D. (1995). The managerial implications of the learning organization: A new tool for internal marketing. *Journal of Services Marketing*, 9(4), 43–51. doi:10.1108/08876049510094513

Chia, J. (2005). *Measuring the immeasurable*. Retrieved from http://praxis.massey.ac.nz/fileadmin/Praxis/Files/Journal_Files/Evaluation_Issue/CHIA_ARTICLE.pdf#search=%22%20joy%20chia%20measuring%20the%20immeasurable%22

Chu, A., & Chu, R. (2011). The intranet's role in newcomer socialization in the hotel industry in Taiwan – technology acceptance model analysis. *International Journal of Human Resource Management*, 22(5), 1163–1179. doi:10.1080/09585192.2011.556795

D'Aprix, R. (2009). *The Credible Company*. San Francisco: Jossey-Bass.

De Bussy, N., Ewing, M., & Pitt, L. (2004). Stakeholder theory and internal marketing communications: A framework for analyzing the influence of new media. *Journal of Marketing Communications*, 9(3), 147–161. doi:10.1080/1352726032000129890

Deloitte Core Beliefs and Culture Survey. (2013). Retrieved from http://www.deloitte.com/assets/Dcom-UnitedStates/Local%20Assets/Documents/us_leadership_2013corebeliefs&culturesurvey_051613.pdf, August 6, 2013.

Dolphin, R. R. (2005). Internal communications: Today's strategic imperative. *Journal of Marketing Communications*, 11(3), 171–190. doi:10.1080/1352726042000315414

Dreher, S. (2014). Social media and the world of work. *Corporate Communications. International Journal (Toronto, Ont.)*, 19(4), 344–356.

Edelman Trust Barometer. (2013). Retrieved on 8/21/13 from http://www.edelman.com/insights/intellectual-property/trust-2013/

Edelman Trust Barometer. (2014). Retrieved on 1/22/14 from http://www.edelman.com/insights/intellectual-property/2014-edelman-trust-barometer/

Gelb, B. D., & Rengarajan, D. (2014). Employee contributions to brand equity. *California Management Review*, *56*(2), 95–112. doi:10.1525/cmr.2014.56.2.95

Griffith, D. A., & Harvey, M. G. (2001). Executive insights: An intercultural communication model for use in global interorganizational networks. *Journal of International Marketing*, *9*(3), 87–103. doi:10.1509/jimk.9.3.87.19924

Harrison, A. G. (2013). Engagement Ring: Building connections between employees and strategy. *Public Relations Tactics*, *20*(5), 16.

Kalla, H. K. (2005). Integrated internal communications: A multidisciplinary perspective. *Corporate Communications*, *10*(4), 302–314. doi:10.1108/13563280510630106

Kelemen, M., & Papasolomou, I. (2007). Internal Marketing: A Qualitative Study of Culture Change in the UK Banking Sector. *Journal of Marketing Management*, *23*(7-8), 745–767. doi:10.1362/026725707X230027

Kress, N. (2005). Engaging your employees through the power of communication. *Workspan*, *48*(5), 26–36.

Lee, I. (2011). Overview of emerging Web 2.0-based business models and web 2.0 applications in business: An ecological perspective. *International Journal of E-Business Research*, *7*(4), 1–16. doi:10.4018/jebr.2011100101

Lipiainen, H., Karjaluoto, H., & Nevalainen, M. (2014). Digital channels in the internal communication of a multinational corporation. *Corporate Communications. International Journal (Toronto, Ont.)*, *19*(3), 275–286.

Mangold, W. G., & Faulds, D. J. (2009). Social media: The new hybrid element of the promotion mix. *Business Horizons*, *52*(4), 357–365. doi:10.1016/j.bushor.2009.03.002

Men, L. R., & Stacks, D. (2014). The effects of authentic leadership on strategic internal communication and employee-organization relationships. *Journal of Public Relations Research*, *26*(4), 301–324. doi:10.1080/1062726X.2014.908720

Mills, P. K., & Ungson, G. (2003). Reassessing the limits of structural empowerment: Organizational constitution and trust as controls. *Academy of Management Review*, *28*(1), 143–153.

Mishra, A. K. (1996). Organizational responses to crisis: The centrality of trust. In R. Kramer & T. Tyler (Eds.), *Trust in organizations* (pp. 261–287). Newbury Park, CA: Sage. doi:10.4135/9781452243610.n13

Mishra, A. K., & Mishra, K. E. (1994). The role of mutual trust in effective downsizing strategies. *Human Resource Management*, *33*(2), 261–279. doi:10.1002/hrm.3930330207

Mishra, A. K., & Mishra, K. E. (2013). *Becoming a Trustworthy Leader: Psychology & Practice*. Routledge Press.

Mishra, K. E., & Boynton, L. (2009). *Talk-the-Talk: Using Internal Communication to Build Trust with Employees*. International Public Relations Research Conference, Miami, FL.

Mishra, K. E., Boynton, L., & Mishra, A. K. (2014). Driving Employee Engagement: The Expanded Role of Internal Communications. *Journal of Business Communication*, *51*(2), 183–202. doi:10.1177/2329488414525399

Mishra, K. E., & Schwarz, G. M. (2011). The Evolution of Trust and Control as Seen through an Organization's Human Resources Practices. In R. Searle (Eds.), Trust and Human Resource Management. Cheltenham, UK: Edward Elgar.

Mishra, K. E., Walker, K., & Mishra, A. K. (2014). Employee Use of Social Media in the Workplace: How "Lenovo Central" brings employees together. In I. Lee (Ed.), Integrating Social Media into Business Practice, Applications, Management, and Models. Academic Press.

Mishra, A. K., & Spreitzer, G. M. (1998). Explaining How Survivors Respond to Downsizing: The Roles of Trust, Empowerment, Justice and Work Redesign. *Academy of Management Review*, *23*(3), 567-588.

Mounter, P. (2003). Global internal communication: A model. *Journal of Communication Management*, *7*(3), 3. doi:10.1108/13632540310807412

Nakata, C., Zhu, Z., & Izberk-Bilgin, E. (2011). Integrating marketing and information services functions: A complementarity and competence perspective. *Journal of the Academy of Marketing Science*, *39*(5), 700–716. doi:10.1007/s11747-010-0236-z

Organ, D. W. (1988). *Organizational citizenship behavior: The good soldier syndrome*. Lexington, MA: Lexington Books.

Pincus, D. J., Rayfield, R. E., & Cozzens, M. D. (1991). The Chief Executive Officer's internal communications role: A benchmark program of research. In L. A. Grunig & J. E. Grunig (Eds.), *Public Relations Research Annual* (Vol. 3, pp. 1–36). Hillsdale, NJ: Lawrence Earlbaum Associates.

Piyachat, B., Chanongkorn, K., & Panisa, M. (2014). The mediate effect of employee engagement on the relationship between perceived employer branding and discretionary effort. *DLSU Business & Economics Review*, *24*(1), 59–72.

Quirke, B. (2008). *Making the connections: Using internal communication to turn strategy into action*. Burlington, VT: Gower.

Radick, S. (2011). *The power of social networks: Reviving the intranet*. Public Relations Tactics.

Robson, P., & Tourish, D. (2005). Managing internal communication: An organizational case study. *Corporate Communications*, *10*(3), 213–222. doi:10.1108/13563280510614474

Rockland, D. B. (2014). *Why internal communications is a business driver*. Tactics.

Ruppel, C. P., & Harrington, S. J. (2001). Sharing knowledge through intranets: A study of organizational culture and intranet implementation. *Professional Communication*, *44*(1), 37–52. doi:10.1109/47.911131

Saks, A. M. (2006). Antecedents and consequences of employee engagement. *Journal of Managerial Psychology*, *21*(7), 600–619. doi:10.1108/02683940610690169

Siegall, M., & Gardner, S. (2000). Contextual factors of psychological empowerment. *Personnel Review*, *29*(6), 703–722. doi:10.1108/00483480010296474

Skok, W., & Goldstein, B. (2007). Managing organizational knowledge: Developing a strategy for a professional services company. *Strategic Change*, *16*(7), 327–339. doi:10.1002/jsc.805

Spreitzer, G. M., & Mishra, A. K. (1999). Giving Up Control Without Losing Control: Trust and Its Substitutes' Effects on Managers' Involving Employees in Decision Making. *Group & Organization Management*, *14*(2), 155–187. doi:10.1177/1059601199242003

Su, C., & Contractor, N. (2011). A Multidimensional Network Approach to Studying Team Members' Information Seeking From Human and Digital Knowledge Sources in Consulting Firms. *Journal of the American Society for Information Science and Technology*, *62*(7), 1257–1275. doi:10.1002/asi.21526

Therkelsen, D. J., & Fiebich, C. L. (2003). The supervisor: The linchpin of employee relations. *Journal of Communication Management*, *8*(2), 120–129. doi:10.1108/13632540410807592

Towers Watson Study. (2013). Retrieved from http://www.towerswatson.com/en/Insights/IC-Types/Survey-Research-Results/2013/05/Infographic-2013-Change-and-Communication-ROI-Study

Vallaster, C., & deChernatony, L. (2004). Internal brand building and structuration: The role of leadership. *European Journal of Marketing*, *40*(7/8), 761–784.

Watson Wyatt White Paper. (2008/2009). *Driving business results through continuous engagement*. Retrieved on 29 August from http://www.watsonwyatt.com/research/pdfs/2008-US-0232.pdf

Welch, M., & Jackson, P. R. (2007). Rethinking internal communication: A stakeholder approach. *Corporate Communications*, *12*(2), 177–198. doi:10.1108/13563280710744847

Yankelovich, D., & Immerwahr, J. (1983). *Putting the work ethic to work*. New York: Public Agenda Foundation.

Zeffane, R., Tipu, S. A., & Ryan, J. C. (2011). Communication, Commitment & Trust: Exploring the Triad. *International Journal of Business and Management*, *6*(6), 77–87. doi:10.5539/ijbm.v6n6p77

ADDITIONAL READING

Brown, B., Sikes, J., & Willmott, P. (2013). *Bullish on digital: McKinsey Global Survey Results*. McKinsey & Company.

Burgess, C. (2013). *The Social Employee: How Great Companies Make Social Media Work*. McGraw-Hill.

KEY TERMS AND DEFINITIONS

Employee Engagement: Employee engagement is "the degree to which an individual is attentive and absorbed in the performance of their roles" (Saks, 2006, p. 602).

Internal Communication: Internal communication (or internal marketing) is communication between the organization's leaders and one of its key publics: the employees (Dolphin, 2005). It is "social interaction through messages" (Kalla, 2005, p. 303) and reflects management's ability to build relationships between internal stakeholders at all levels within an organization (Welch & Jackson, 2007). Quirke (2008) noted that the role of internal communication is to "illuminate the connections between different pieces of information" (p. x), and its job is "to provide employees with the information they need to do their job" (p. x).

Intranet: internet services specifically for employee use in order to share corporate and employee knowledge (Ruppel & Harrington, 2002; DeBussy, Ewing & Pitt, 2003).

Lenovo: Lenovo is not just another technology company. We make the technology that powers the world's best ideas. We design tools for those who are driven by accomplishment. We are the company that powers the people who Do. The engine that helps them Do more. Do better. Do what's never been done. And we are united in the quest to help our users defy the impossible.

Lenovo Central: The company Intranet for Lenovo.

Social Media: Social media is also referred to as consumer-generated media. It includes online information created and/or shared by consumers about their favorite products and/or brands.

"Social media encompasses a wide range of online, word-of-mouth forums including blogs, company-sponsored discussion boards and chat rooms, consumer-to-consumer e-mail, consumer product or service ratings websites and forums, Internet discussion boards and forums, moblogs (sites containing digital audio, images, movies, or photographs), and social networking websites, to name a few" (Mangold & Faulds, 2009).

Trust: Trust is defined as a willingness to be vulnerable to another person or party based on some positive expectations regarding the other party's intentions and/or behaviors (Mishra & Mishra, 1994).

APPENDIX 1

Interview Questions for Internal Communication Executives

1. Tell me about your role in communications at Lenovo
2. What is your biggest challenge in developing relevant and timely communications in a global company?
3. What is the most effective way to share one message to people in different places?
4. What is the most effective way to share one message to people who speak different languages?
5. How does Lenovo's culture affect the way you choose to communicate across departmental or business borders?
6. How do marketing, communications and public relations work together to create organizational messages?
7. How do your organizational messages mesh with your external advertising messages?
8. Which come first, the external brand messages or the internal ones?
9. What role does the internet play in the way you communicate with employees?
10. What role does face-to-face communication play in the way you share messages about the company and the brand with employees?
11. What role does the immediate supervisor play in disseminating your messages?
12. If you could design an ideal communications system, what would it look like?
13. If you could design a new undergraduate communications class, what would it include?
14. What is the role does trust play in building open and transparent communications systems?
15. What is the role of the leader in building open and transparent communication systems?
16. As a recipient of those messages, what do you like about the communication process?
17. Is there anything you would change, if you could? Please elaborate.
18. Is there anything else you would like to share about this process?

APPENDIX 2

Interview Questions for Lenovo Employees

1. Tell me about how internal communications work at Lenovo
2. How does Lenovo's culture affect the way you see that messages work across departmental or business borders?
3. Do you feel that your organizational messages mesh with your external advertising messages?
4. What role does the internet play in the way the organization communicates with employees?
5. What role does face-to-face communication play in the way your manager shares messages about the company and the brand with employees?
6. If you could design an ideal communications system, what would it look like?
7. What is the role does trust play in building open and transparent communications systems?
8. What is the role of the leader in building open and transparent communication systems?
9. As a recipient of those messages, what do you like about the communication process?

10. Is there anything you would change, if you could? Please elaborate.
11. Is there anything else you would like to share about this process?

Chapter 18
The Use of Online Social Networks in Higher Education and Its Influence on Job Performance

Vera Silva Carlos
University of Aveiro, Portugal

Ricardo Gouveia Rodrigues
University of Beira Interior, Portugal

ABSTRACT

There is plenty of evidence on a positive influence of social relationships on work-related attitudes and behaviors. Besides, online social networks (OSNs), made possible by Web 2.0, have become a global phenomenon and have a considerable impact on the way people communicate and interact with each other. Our purpose is to evaluate the effect of using OSNs on the worker's attitudes and behaviors, particularly in the context of Higher Education. In this sense, we used a questionnaire, to evaluate the attitudes of 157 faculty members. To assess the use of OSNs, we resorted to a dichotomous variable. After analyzing and discussing the results we conclude that the use of OSNs influences the worker's performance, but not Job satisfaction, Organizational commitment or extra-role performance. The relationships we propose in what concerns the worker's attitudes are all empirically proved. Lastly, we describe the study limitations and we suggest some perspectives for future research.

INTRODUCTION

The development and popularity of online social networks (OSNs) has shaped a new world of collaboration and communication. More than a billion individuals worldwide are connected and networked together, creating, collaborating and contributing with their knowledge (Cheung, Chiu & Lee, 2011). OSNs, the so called Web 2.0, have

also taken on a high role and importance in the relationships between people and organizations. Castilla (2005) mentions that social relationships are an important tool for the understanding of the workers' outcomes in the organizations and that it is necessary to understand the dynamics of these interactions. In this perspective, the main purpose of this study consists of evaluating the influence of OSNs on the workers' attitudes and behaviors.

DOI: 10.4018/978-1-4666-9970-0.ch018

Specifically, it is intended to evaluate to what extent the use of OSNs to maintain contact with co-workers influences job satisfaction, organizational commitment, organizational citizenship behaviors and individual performance. On the other hand, the intention is to verify whether there are positive relationships between the workers' attitudes and behaviors – some of them already proved in previous studies -, specifically between satisfaction and commitment, satisfaction and organizational citizenship behaviors, satisfaction and performance, commitment and organizational citizenship behaviors, commitment and performance and organizational citizenship behaviors and performance. If the proposed relations are proved, it will be possible to broaden the understanding of each of the concepts being studied, and increase their importance in the organizational context.

More than organizations in most sectors, Higher Education Institutions (HEI) know a great deal about facilitating environments in which people collaborate to create, share and advance knowledge. HEI should, in this sense, be very well prepared to reap value from the new online tools (Barnatt, 2008). In this scenario, it seems adequate to resort to the Higher Education (HE) context to investigate the proposed relations. HEI are characterized as community service providers, specifically of transference and economic value increase of the scientific and technological knowledge, which are autonomous and should define good management practice codes. The transference and knowledge increase, as well as the fact that HE teachers ought to cooperate, justify the choice of context and the answering of a questionnaire given to the Lecturing staff as an instrument to gather data.

Firstly, the concepts that are being studied are briefly summarized. Then, two research models, based on 10 hypotheses, are proposed. After explaining and stating the hypotheses, the methodology is described and the results are presented and discussed. Finally, we describe the findings, the limitations of the study are explained and some guiding lines for future research are suggested. The methods used to analyze the results are the *t-student* test and the PLS method. It is possible to conclude that the use of OSNs to maintain contact with co-workers. We also verify that satisfaction positively influences commitment, organizational citizenship behaviors and performance, that commitment has a positive impact on organizational citizenship behaviors and on performance, and that organizational citizenship behaviors have a positive effect on performance.

THE WEB 2.0

Web 2.0 refers to the appearance of the Internet as an interpersonal resource and a service delivery platform (Barnatt, 2008). The term Web 2.0 is used to describe applications that distinguish themselves from preceding generations of software by a number of principles (Ullrich et al., 2008).

The second incarnation of the Web (Web 2.0) has been called the 'social Web', because, in contrast to Web 1.0, its content can be more easily generated and published by users, and because the collective intelligence of users encourages its more democratic utilization. Originally, the World Wide Web (WWW) was intended to be used to share ideas and encourage discussion within a scientific community. Web 2.0 heralds a return to these original uses, and prompts important changes in the ways the World Wide Web is being handled in Education. In this context, there is a need to raise awareness of Web 2.0 tools and the possibilities they offer, and an imperative need to carry out quality research to inform better use of Web 2.0 applications (Boulos & Wheeler, 2007).

The development of social media has transformed the ways in which the Internet is experienced by most users. Nowadays, the Internet is no longer a one-way broadcast distribution system where the user downloads data, information and other resources created by a relatively small number of content providers. Instead, it is driven by (and to some level determined through) the activities of its ordinary users - what has been described as many-to-many rather than one-to-many connectivity. The Web 2.0 is, then, substantially different from the cyberspace-era Internet of the 1990s and 2000s (Selwyn, 2011).

Online Social Networks (OSNs)

Over the last decade, social media technologies have altered our thinking about relationships, connections with and empathy to others, and the effect and influential power of online communities on how we think, organize, and act politically. Since the origin of the Internet and the incorporation of email technology in our personal and work lives, our ways of communicating started to change. Nevertheless, it was not until the creation of social media interfaces like Facebook, MySpace, Friendster, LinkedIn, YouTube, Twitter, among others, that have we seen the immense harnessing of the potential of the online connectivity in our lives. We are now able to create, maintain, and access communities online, while also using the social media technology as a tool to transition between online and face-to-face contact via friendships, planned activities, and formal organizational affiliations (Davis III, Deil-Amen, Rios-Aguilar & Canche, 2012).

Social media usually refer to media used to enable social interaction. Social media technology is defined as Web-based and mobile applications that allow individuals and organizations to create, participate, and share new user-generated or existing content in digital settings, through multi-way communication. It is important to underline the difference between user-generated content, which is non-traditional media developed and produced by individual users, and existing content, which usually consists of traditional media (news, magazines, radio, and television) reproduced for the Web. The broad definition of social media technology includes the totality of digital products and services enabling online, user generated social behavior and exchanges around user-generated content. This definition, however, does not comprise educational learning and content management systems, such as Blackboard, eLearning Suite, WebCT, Desire2Learn (Davis III et al., 2012).

Therefore, Web 2.0 technology has progressively transformed social interactions among people. Media such as blogs, instant messaging and social networking Websites are becoming universal, and they all provide a 'map' of communication pathways among their users (Sledgianowski & Kulviwat, 2009).

Regarding the *network* concept, Hoang and Antoncic (2003) state that there are three components that characterize a network: the content of relationships, its regulation and the structure or pattern that results from it. As to what the content is concerned, the relationships are seen as a means through which one of the parts has access to a variety of resources that the other part has. Regarding the regulation of relationships, the authors refer that there are several mechanisms that coordinate the exchanges in a relationship. The trust among the parts involved in the relationship, for example, constitutes a critical element, which improves the quality of the flow of resources in the relationship of exchange. The regulation of the networks can also be defined as the trust in implicit open contracts, which are based on social mechanisms, and not legally imposed. The structure of the network is defined as a pattern of relationships that are formed from the direct and indirect bonds among the organizational actors.

According to Bunt, Wittek and Klepper (2005), that there are two types of motives in the evolution of a network: expressive and instrumental. Many intra-organizational networks models postulate that relational dynamics are directed, primarily, by expressive motives. In this case, the reduction of cognitive dissonance in affective triads and the tendency that the individual has to bind with the ones he considers similar act as the main mechanisms for the formation of relationships. So, individual cognitions and attributes are the main factors that contribute to the evolution of networks. Other models have suggested that the work environment creates specific restrictions to the formation of social ties, which may limit or impede the mechanisms underlying the evolution of networks in 'natural' groups. There are two instrumental perspectives. One of them emphasizes the impact of the formal structures of the organizations, particularly the functional interdependences and the formal control strategies associated to the individuals' hierarchic position. At this rate, the interpersonal trust is modeled as a function of formally defined interdependence and power patterns. Individuals adapt to their formal work environment and manage critical dependences, incorporating them into social exchanges. Therefore, the dynamics of the informal networks is contingent to the formal organizational structure. The second instrumental perspective suggests that the interpersonal trust is a result of the individual's effort to optimize the benefits that his/her personal networks may generate, independently of his/her position in the formal structure. Based on these models, and after an empirical test, the authors conclude that both types of motives influence the evolution of networks, specifically organizational networks.

When it comes to organizational networks, it is relevant to mention that they function as communication channels and make the existence of resources exchange possible to several levels, including to the ideological level, as a form of spreading and sharing ideas. The formal transmission of knowledge among work groups, as well as the exchange of information that occurs in the organization, are fundamental aspects for the success of the network (Barbeira & Franco, 2009).

Web 2.0 sociable technologies and social software also work as enablers for organizations. They include social networking services, collaborative filtering, social bookmarking, social search engines, file sharing and tagging, instant messaging and online multi-player games. The more popular Web 2.0 applications in Education, namely wikis, blogs and podcasts, are but the tip of the social software iceberg. Web 2.0 technologies represent, then, a revolutionary way of managing and repurposing online information and knowledge repositories – including research information –, in comparison with the traditional Web 1.0 model (Boulos & Wheeler, 2007)

OSNs may also function as tools to help individuals in the workforce organize their workload and life. When appropriately used and integrated into an organization's business plan and model they enable the organization and its workers to:

1. Increase customer satisfaction\timely responses to customer inquiries;
2. Facilitate communication between customers and experts to share knowledge in areas of interest;
3. Find experts within the organization as well as those outside with similar interests;
4. Provide the whole product to fully meet the customer's needs, since customers can easily reveal their needs;
5. Understand and visualize real communication paths within an organization an entire business process transaction; and
6. Extend the shelf life of conferences and organization meetings with an online network of attendees and databases (Asunda, 2010).

OSNs have, then, become a global phenomenon (Sledgianowski & Kulviwat, 2009; Benson, Filippaios & Morgan, 2010; Heidemann, Klier & Probst, 2012), with enormous social and economic impact within a few years (Heidemann, Klier & Probst, 2012). They have been shown to facilitate business relationships (Benson, Filippaios & Morgan, 2010), as described above, and to build social capital (Benson, Filippaios & Morgan, 2010; Young, 2011).

Regarding the social perspective, OSNs have a great impact on the way people communicate and interact with each other (Grabner-Kraeuter &

Waiguny, 2011), providing an efficient and user-friendly way to maintain social relationships and share information. Particularly, they play a major role in the spread of information at very large scale (Guille, Hacid, Favre & Zighed, 2013).

OSNs enable individuals to simultaneously share information with several peers. Measuring the causal effect of these mediums on the diffusion of information involves identifying who influences whom, and also whether individuals would still spread information in the lack of social signals about that information. Although stronger ties are individually more significant, it is the more abundant weak ties who are responsible for the propagation of new information, which suggests that weak ties may play a more prevailing role in the diffusion of online information than currently believed (Bakshy, Rosenn, Marlow & Adamic, 2012).

Though OSNs may influence an individual's behavior, they also reflect the individual's personal activities, interests, and opinions. These commonalities make it practically impossible to determine from observational data whether any specific interaction, method of communication, or social environment is responsible for the apparent spread of a behavior through a network. There are three possible mechanisms that may clarify diffusion-like phenomena, specifically on Facebook: (1) An individual shares a link and contact with this information on the news feed leads a friend to re-share that link; (2) Friends visit the same Web page and share a link to that Web page, independently of one another; (3) An individual shares a link within and external to Facebook, and contact with the externally shared information leads a friend to share the link (Bakshy et al., 2012).

The use of social media interfaces through computer and mobile devices has become widespread and, presently, the two most noticeable interfaces are Facebook and Twitter. Facebook enables users to create profiles, allows those user-operated profiles to interact with each other, allows the expression of interests and the discovery of commonalities among users, and allows users to create and maintain connections and invite other users to join a community. By contrast, Twitter is a social media interface that allows users to share a restricted amount of user-generated content, rapidly and easily, to a broad number of other users. In this interface, the communication exchange is crucial, and the conception and sharing of user profiles is not required. However, Twitter can link to profiles that exist on other social media interfaces (Davis III et al., 2012).

Social networking sites are, thus, interesting examples of 'maps' of communication paths among their users, because they represent rich and popular communication interfaces for hundreds of millions of users (Sledgianowski & Kulviwat, 2009). Also, according to Young (2011), OSNs like Facebook strengthen existing friendships by supplementing traditional forms of communication (like face to face or telephone). On the other hand, participation in the Facebook community enables efficient and convenient contact to be maintained with a larger and more varied group of acquaintances, thus, as mentioned, extending potential social capital, that is a sociological concept related to the connections between social networks.

SOCIAL MEDIA ON THE EDUCATION SECTOR

Education likes to explore emerging technologies as new or improved tools to enhance instruction and learning (Tess, 2013). Though, regardless of the widespread use of social media technologies, little is known about the benefits of its use in post-secondary contexts and for specific purposes, such as marketing, recruitment, learning, and/or student engagement. Hence, it is essential to begin to examine if and how Higher Education Institutions (HEI) are integrating the use of such technologies (Davis III et al., 2012).

Many HEI and educators now find themselves expected to catch up with social media applications and users (Selwyn, 2011). In a time of change, Higher Education has to adapt to external circumstances created by the prevalent adoption of popular technologies such as social media, online social networking and mobile devices. Therefore, faculty members need opportunities for concrete practices which are capable of creating a personal belief that a particular technology is worth using and an understanding of the settings in which it is best applied (Kukulska-Hulme, 2012). It is known that Web 2.0 technologies are becoming more prevalent in the daily lives of students (Bennett, Bishop, Dalgarno, Waycott & Kennedy, 2012) and they are progressively evident in the Higher Education setting as many instructors resort to technology in order to mediate and enhance their instruction as well as stimulate active learning for students (Tess, 2013). Within this framework, instructors and designers have begun to explore their use in formal education (Bennett, Bishop, Dalgarno, Waycott & Kennedy, 2012).

According to Forkosh-Baruch and Hershkovitz (2012), the use of OSNs in Higher Education promotes knowledge sharing, hence facilitating informal learning within the community and opening academic institutes to the community altogether. OSNs can also be used as an indirect support for learning, providing an emotional outlet for school-related stress, validation of creative work, peer-alumni support for school-life transitions, assistance with school-related tasks and stimulating social and civic benefits, online and offline, which have repercussions in education (Greenhow, 2011).

One of the dominant social media platforms is Facebook. Initially, it was privately conceived within and navigated through the social networks of students at Harvard University and, later, at other elite universities, like Princeton, Yale, and Stanford. If we consider the birth of this particular OSN at Harvard, we can distinguish it as an example of how mechanisms of a university's

social 'community' were quickly transferred onto this online platform. Since its foundation, this interface has enlarged across numerous Higher Education communities and, then, rapidly covered a broader range of linked networks of individuals and groups all over the world. Nowadays, the adoption of social media technology stretches across the world, integrating into the lives of individuals of varied social, national, racial and ethnic, cultural and socioeconomic backgrounds (Davis III et al., 2012).

Although the potential of OSNs as means of sharing academic knowledge in Higher Education has not been actualized yet, it is now being explored by these organizations, as well as by the community (Forkosh-Baruch & Hershkovitz, 2012). Nevertheless, there is a lot of tension between Web 2.0 and educational practices (Bennett, Bishop, Dalgarno, Waycott & Kennedy, 2012). Many scholars debate for the integration of social media as an instructive tool. However, most of the current research on the usefulness and efficiency of social media in the Higher Education class is restricted to self-reported data and content analysis (Tess, 2013), being, therefore, insufficient. It is claimed that there is a technological delay between Higher Education and the rest of society, which can be traced back to the insertion of film and radio throughout the first decades of the 20th century. Undeniably, as with most of the preceding waves of new technology, social media persist as an area of great expectation and exaggeration. It is vital, then, that the higher educators are able to approach social media in an objective way (Selwyn, 2011).

Although the infrastructure to support the presence of social media exists in most HEI, instructors have been slow in accepting the tool as an educational one. Though social media has been prevalent on Higher Education its viability as a learning medium has only been considered recently. On the other hand, the incorporation of OSNs in Higher Education is a choice made at the instructor level rather than an institutional determination. Consequently, the implementation may be more of a test that leads to the need of developing research and, eventually, to more questions (Tess, 2013).

Regarding the awareness and use of OSNs by Higher Education faculty members, they are very familiar with social media (Moran, Seaman & Tinti-Kane, 2011), using these media either for professional purposes (Moran, Seaman & Tinti-Kane, 2011; Veletsianos, 2011) or in their classes - or both (Moran, Seaman & Tinti-Kane, 2011).

In such networks, learning takes the form of participation and identity formation through commitment and contribution to networked practices. Specifically on Twitter, scholars: 1) share information, resources and media related to their professional practice, 2) share information about their class and students, 3) request help from and offer recommendations to others, 4) engage in social comments, 5) engage in digital identity and impression administration, 6) seek to network and create connections with others, and 7) highlight their involvement in online networks other than Twitter (Veletsianos, 2011).

Moran, Seaman and Tinti-Kane (2011) concluded that most of faculty members report using at least one social media site in support of their professional career. However, in their research, 19% of faculty members who state they use social media in support of their professional careers do it rarely. Over one-quarter of faculty members report using blogs, LinkedIn and Wikis and just over 10% refers Twitter or Flickr. Professional use of SlideShare and Myspace is under 10%, and daily use of Facebook, at 11%, surpassed that of other social media sites, followed by blogs (5% daily use), YouTube (4%) and Wikis (3%). Also, 70% of faculty members mention privacy concerns as an 'important' or 'very important' barrier to using OSNs.

Foster, Francescucci and West (2010) stress the importance of privacy in OSNs, as some participants who have privacy concerns may not have developed the confidence to contribute to new communities. Increasingly, people are sharing sensitive personal information via OSNs. While such networks do permit users to control what they share with whom, access to control policies are notoriously difficult to configure correctly, and this raises the question of whether OSN users' privacy settings match their sharing intentions (Madjeski, Johnson & Bellovin, 2011). Within this framework, privacy concerns should be accounted for when analyzing the use of OSNs in every context, even in the context of Higher Education.

Thus, it is important that technology designers consider how to add information about privacy settings into their website, as well as to define better options, in order to ensure that participants feel comfortable and that their privacy is protected. Having appropriate protection of privacy and personal information will develop and enhance trust within the community, so that participants increase their confidence level to contribute in relevant and meaningful ways to a conversation (Foster, Francescucci and West, 2010).

WORK-RELATED ATTITUDES AND BEHAVIORS

Considering our goal is to better understand the effect of using OSNs to maintain contact with co-workers on the Lecturing staff's attitudes and behaviors, we briefly describe below two work-related attitudes – job satisfaction and organizational commitment – and two behaviors – organizational citizenship behaviors and individual performance.

Job Satisfaction (JS)

There are few, if any, more central concepts for organizational psychology than for job satisfaction. (Judge et al., 2001, pp. 25)

JS began to gather the interest of theorists, researchers and managers since the Taylorist model was compromised and the human factor in the company was given more importance (Vala et al.,

1995). The concept has been originating some controversy (Staw, 1986), since it is characterized as a "*complex emotional reaction to work*" (Locke, 1968, pp. 9) or as an attitude (Saari e Judge, 2004). Either way, satisfaction consists of a positive emotional state or a positive attitude towards work and the experiences that occur in the work environment (Vala et *al.*, 1995).

In an effort to characterize and explain JS, several theories emerged. These theories are categorized in agreement with the two perspectives mentioned before: satisfaction as an emotional state, feelings and affective responses, and satisfaction as a generalized attitude towards work. There are also two distinct dimensions in what concerns JS: the global approach, based on the attitude towards work in general, not being a result of the sum of different aspects related to work, but depending on them, and the multidimensional approach, which is described as the satisfaction that reverses from a number of factors associated with work, and it is possible to measure satisfaction for each one of them (Alcobia, 2001).

JS theories may also be divided according to the following classification: (1) situational theories, which support that satisfaction is a result of the nature of work and environmental factors, (2) dispositional theories, according to which satisfaction results from personal and personality factors, (3) interactive theories, which suggest that JS derives from the interaction between personality factors and factors inherent to the situation. Dispositional theories are the most recent, but also the less developed ones. However, individual differences have been considered since investigation related to JS began (Judge et *al.*, 2001).

The job characteristics model was suggested by Hackman and Oldham (1976) to measure three classes of variables: work objective characteristics, mediator psychological stages and individual needs of growth. According to this model, the central characteristics of each task – like the variety of competencies, the identity and the meaning of the tasks, the autonomy, the level of information provided to the worker about his/her performance, that is, the feedback – influence the individual's psychological stage. The function characteristics and satisfaction are also regulated by the worker's need for growth. The model can be used as a concept basis to identify the potential of job motivation, the workers' availability to respond positively to work improvement and to redesign specific characteristics of the jobs that need to be modified. Judge et *al.* (2001) state that, in this perspective, the jobs that have intrinsically motivating characteristics will lead to higher levels of motivation and even to a better performance. However, it is necessary to keep in mind that the individuals that want greater challenges and reveal a greater interest for work are, generally, more motivated and happier (Hackman e Oldham, 1976).

Organizational Commitment (OC)

Meyer and Herscovitch (2001) argue that the OC definitions, presented in the literature, have two common aspects: (1) commitment consists of a force of connection – a psychological or attitude stage, and (2) commitment determines a direction at the level of the individual's behavior.

From the previous definitions of OC, Allen and Meyer (1990) created a commitment model, according to which the concept is composed of three dimensions: (1) *affective,* which consists of a connection, identification and involvement with the organization; (2) *continuance*, referring to the commitment based on the cost that the individual associates with leaving the organization and (3) *normative*, related to the feelings of obligation to stay in the organization.

The perspective that will be adopted in this research is the one proposed by Cook and Wall (1980), who defend that the OC refers to the affective reactions to the characteristics of the employer organization. It is related to the worker's feelings of connection with the goals and values of the organization; to the role that he adopts in relation to them and to the connection with the organization with the aim of benefitting it, and not just for its instrumental value. Since this is a positive result of the experience of quality work, the concept can be considered a contributing factor to the well-being at work.

Organizational Citizenship Behaviors (OCB)

The OCB are defined as 'extra-role' behaviors (Rego, 2002). The concept has different origins: (1) in Barnard's proposal (1938), according to which, the workers' will to cooperate is indispensable for the organization, (2) in the Katz and Khan (1970, 1974, 1987) distinctions in behavioral typologies facing the organizations, (3) in Organ's essay, which states that people can adopt a cooperative behavior in order to respond reciprocally to the work experiences that provide satisfaction, as opposed to the behaviors inherent to the role, which depend on certain restrictions. Based on Organ's work (1977), Bateman and Organ (1983) measured this new kind of performance. From then on, several definitions and dimensions were proposed for the concept (Williams & Anderson, 1991; Graham, 1991; Van Dyne, Graham & Dienesch, 1994; Organ & Moorman, 1993; Konovsky & Organ, 1996; Podsakoff et *al.*, 2000).

According to Rego (2002) and González and Garazo (2006), there are five dimensions of OCB that are more frequently used, which is in agreement with the literature:

1. *Altruism* (Podsakoff, MacKenzie & Fetter, 1993; Organ & Lingl, 1995; Konovsky & Organ, 1996; Podsakoff & Mackenzie, 1997; Rego, Ribeiro & Cunha, 2009*)* – that is defined as 'helping behavior' (Lo & Ramayah, 2009);
2. *Civic Virtue* (Podsakoff, MacKenzie & Fetter, 1993; Organ & Lingl, 1995; Konovsky & Organ, 1996; Podsakoff & Mackenzie,

1997*;* Rego, Ribeiro & Cunha, 2010*)* – the responsibility of the subordinates to participate in the life of the organization (Podsakoff et *al.*, 2000);
3. *Sportsmanship* (Podsakoff, MacKenzie & Fetter, 1993; Organ and Lingl, 1995; Konovsky & Organ, 1996; Podsakoff & Mackenzie, *1997*; Rego, Ribeiro & Cunha, 2009*)* – behavior of warmly tolerating unavoidable irritations. Workers will assume new responsibilities and learn (Podsakoff & MacKenzie, 1997);
4. *Conscientiousness* (Podsakoff, MacKenzie & Fetter, 1993; Rego, Ribeiro & Cunha, 2010) – based on how organized, hardworking and responsible the worker is (Lo & Ramayah, 2009);
5. *Courtesy* (Organ & Lingl, 1995; Konovsky & Organ, 1996; Rego, Ribeiro & Cunha, 2009) – related to the prevention of problems at the work place (Lo & Ramayah, 2009).

Lo and Ramayah (2009) adopted Organ's conceptualization, according to which the OCB are 'extra-role' behaviors that arise as a way of acting beyond what is defined by work requirements, which means that the workers do non-mandatory tasks without expecting any rewards or recognition. The authors developed an instrument which contained the five dimensions more frequently found in literature, as it was mentioned before. The perspective of OCB adopted by these authors will be the one used in this study.

Individual Performance (IP)

Viswesvaran (2001) defines IP as behaviors that can be evaluated, but he points out that the difference between behaviors and results is not clear, since IP is composed of several behavioral manifestations, that are identifiable only through operational measures and that differ depending on the context in which they are applied.

In agreement with the theory of social capital, according to which the organizational theories focused on costs and on human capital are not adequate to respond to rapid changes on the nature of work, on the organizational structures and on the inter-organizational competitiveness (Dess & Shaw, 2001), a worker, fundamental for the organization, may be recognized for his/her capacity to have a high performance, as well as for his/her capacity to create value for the organization. In this way, the fundamental workers are those who have an influence on the other workers, who have knowledge and whose performance is characterized by the following aspects: (1) Skills to deal with organizational networks; (2) Skills to transmit organizational memory; (3) Flexible confidence; (4) Skills to energetically act in a team; (5) Influence in the performance chain/net; (6) Difficulty in being replaced; (7) Innovation traits (Xiaowei, 2006).

RESEARCH MODELS AND HYPOTHESES

Literature points out the existence of positive relations among the social relationships established at work and:

1. Job satisfaction (JS) (Castilla, 2005; Hurlbert, 2001);
2. Organizational commitment (OC) (Donaldson, Ensher & Grant-Vallone, 2000);
3. Organizational citizenship behaviors (OCB) (Donaldson, Ensher & Grant-Vallone, 2000); and
4. Individual performance (IP) (Castilla, 2000).

Considering that Higher Education faculty members are very familiar with social media, and that many use social media for professional purposes (Moran, Seaman and Tinti-Kane, 2011), it seems plausible to assume that social relationships developed online, specifically with co-workers,

influence the worker's job-related attitudes and behaviors. Thus, we formulate the following research hypotheses:

H_1: *The use of OSNs to maintain contact with co-workers (OSN) influences JS.*
H_2: *OSN influences OC.*
H_3: *OSN influences OCB.*
H_4: *OSN influences IP.*

The hypotheses can be summarily represented by the research model in Figure 1.

According to some authors (Chang & Chang, 2007; Eker, Eker & Pala, 2008; Malik, Nawab & Naeem, 2010), satisfaction has a positive influence on commitment. In an attempt to assert these studies we propose H_5.

H_5: *JS has a positive impact on OC.*

Literature also points out that satisfaction is positively related to OCB (Donavan, Brown, & Mowen, 2004; González & Garazo, 2006; Jones, 2006). Thus, we formulate the following hypothesis:

H_6: *JS has a positive impact on OCB.*

Samad (2005) and Jones (2006) refer that performance is positively influenced by satisfaction. These studies allow the formulation of the following hypothesis:

H_7: *JS has a positive impact on IP.*

According to Donavan, Brown and Mowen (2004), commitment has a positive impact on OCB, specifically on the 'altruism' dimension. Lavelle et al. (2008) also investigated the relationship between OC and OCB and concluded that affective commitment has an impact on OCB, characterized by the authors as the participation in meetings or events related to the organization. These studies allow the formulation of the following hypothesis:

Figure 1. Model 1

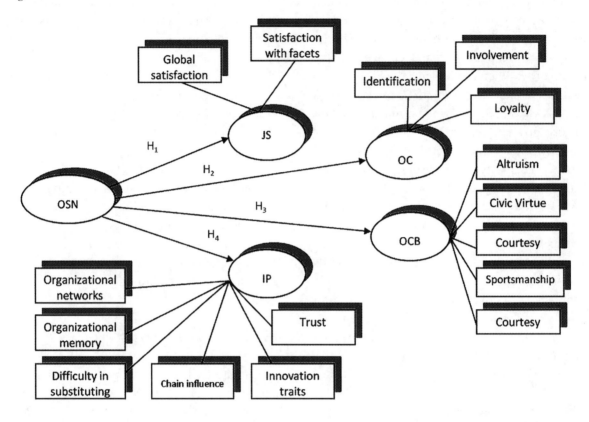

H₈: *OC has a positive impact on OCB.*

Samad (2005) found a positive impact of commitment on performance. The author adopts the perspective of Mowday et *al.* (1982), in which OC is defined as (1) the belief in the organization and the acceptance of its values and goals, (2) the will to make an effort to the well-being of the organization and (3) the will/wish to stay in the organization. Locke, Latham and Erez (1988) argue that the strength of this relationship will depend on the amount of variance in commitment. According to Meyer et *al.* (2002) commitment has an impact on performance, being this impact positive for affective and normative commitment, and negative for continued commitment. In an attempt to assert these studies we propose H₉.

H₉: *OC has a positive impact on IP.*

Following Podsakoff and MacKenzie (1997), there is a positive relationship between OCB, in the perspective as helping behaviors, and the effectiveness of the organizations. Consequently, a relationship between OCB and IP is supposed to exist, so the following hypothesis is formulated:

H₁₀: *OCB has a positive impact on IP.*

The six hypotheses can be summarily represented by the research model in Figure 2.

METHODOLOGY

Sample and Data Collection

This research, descriptive in nature and quantitative, is carried out through the deductive method (Ciribelli, 2003) and is based on a model that

Figure 2. Model 2

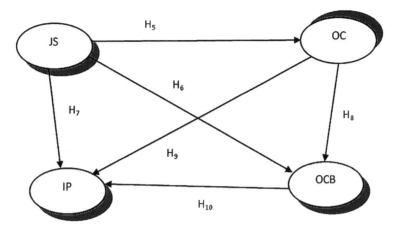

tries to relate the following variables: the use of OSNs to maintain contact with co-workers (OSN), job satisfaction (JS), organizational commitment (OC), organizational citizenship behaviors (OCB) and individual performance (IP).

The HE system in Portugal includes (1) the public higher education system, constituted by the institutions belonging to the State, (2) the private higher education system, composed of institutions belonging to private and cooperative entities. According to article 5, HEI integrate (1) the university institutions, incorporating the universities and the non-integrated university institutions, (2) the polytechnic institutes, incorporating the polytechnic institutes and the non-integrated polytechnic institutes. [1]

Following the information of the National Institute of Statistics[2], updated on the 31st May, 2007, the number of Professors in Higher Education was 37,281, both in the public sector (26,098) and in the private sector (11,183). The sample in this study is composed by 157 Professors, of which 137 work in public HEI and 20 in privately-held ones; 101 teach at universities and 56 at polytechnic institutions.

We built a questionnaire in order to assess the use of OSNs. To evaluate work-related attitudes and behaviors, four instruments were gathered on 7 points *Likert* type scale, where 1 means

'completely disagree' and 7 means 'completely agree'. This scale allows a wide appreciation of the worker's perception about the variables under study. It was necessary to validate the instruments for the Portuguese population by translating them into Portuguese and converting them back into English. The second translations were compared to the original instruments and some mistakes corrected. Because we were dealing with HEI, it was necessary to replace the expressions 'firm' and 'organization' for the expression 'teaching institution', or just 'institution'. A pre-test was given to 6 individuals, which led to the need to make some changes. After these changes were made, the questionnaires were revised. Then, the final questionnaire, divided in five parts, was made available online and all the Portuguese HEI, public and private, were requested, via e-mail, to invite the Professors to participate in this study.

Development of Measures and Scales

Online Social Networks (OSN)

To evaluate the use of OSNs, we built a questionnaire that contained the following questions: (1) Do you use OSNs? (Yes/No), (2) If you answered 'yes', indicate which ones you use, (3) If you answered 'yes', indicate the how often you use OSNs, (4) If you answered 'yes', indicate whomyou maintain contact with on OSNs (friends/family/co-workers/unknown people/other), (5) If you answered 'no', indicate why you do not use OSNs (lack of time/lack of interest/high personal exposure/other). OSN is assessed using a 0-1 variable. Since our purpose is to evaluate the influence of OSNs on work-related attitudes, we'll consider the use of OSNs to contact with the co-workers as the independent variable for model 1.

Job Satisfaction (JS)

Job Diagnostic Survey (JDS) was developed to measure three classes of variables: objective characteristics of work, critical psychological states and individual needs for growth. This measurement evaluates the global satisfaction and the satisfaction with job facets. Global satisfaction is measured through three dimensions, which include general satisfaction (5 items), internal work motivation (6 items) and satisfaction with growth (4 items). JDS also measures satisfaction with the following job facets: job security (2 items), pay (2 items), social (3 items) and supervision (3 items). The scores of items 3, 5 and 9 have to be reversed for statistical analysis (Hackman and Oldham, 1975).

Organizational Commitment (OC)

This measure, developed by Cook and Wall (1980), describes, in general, the worker's commitment towards the organization he/she works for. It contains nine items, three of them measuring the identification with the organization, other three the involvement with the organization and, the remaining, loyalty. Three of the items are written in the negative form and their score has to be reversed for statistical analysis purposes.

Organizational Citizenship Behaviors (OCB)

The scale used to evaluate the OCB was developed by Lo and Ramayah (2009). The instrument is composed of 20 items, which describe five dimensions of OCB: (1) civic virtue, (2) conscientiousness, (3) altruism, (4) courtesy and (5) sportsmanship. Four of the items were withdrawn from the scale by the authors, since they did not apply to the cultural context in which they used the instrument. However, those items were used in this study. One item is written in the negative form, so the score was reversed for statistical analysis purposes.

Individual Performance (IP)

In this study, the concept of 'individual performance' is measured using the performance traits that characterize the worker. Xiaowei (2006) developed a self-assessment measure of the performance traits, based on the revision of other authors' work. Seven dimensions were considered: the relationship among organizational networks (3 items), the transmission of organizational memory (2 items), trust (4 items), group synergy (2 items), chain influence on performance (2 items), difficulty in substituting (2 items) and innovation traits (3 items). On the whole, the measure is made up of 18 items. Seven of the items are written in the negative form, so their score has to be reversed for statistical analysis purposes.

Apart from the use of three scales to assess these variables, the respondents were requested to provide further information, such as age, gender and nature of the HEI where they work (public/private and university/polytechnic).

Data Analysis Methods

To analyze the results we used the statistical package *SPSS,* version 18.0.

In this study, among other objectives, we intend to verify whether the means, for each variable, are statistically different depending on the use of OSNs to maintain contact with co-workers. In this case, the method used was the t-student test, for independent samples, which makes it possible to test whether the means of two populations are significantly different (Maroco, 2007).

To test model 2, we used the PLS method. This method has been increasingly applied because of its ability to shape latent constructs under conditions of non-normality and small to medium samples. As a technique to create models based in components of structural equations, it is similar to the regression, but it models simultaneously the structural paths, i.e., the theoretical relationships among the latent variables, and it measures the paths, i.e., the relationships among a latent variable and its indicators (Chin, Marcolin, e Newsted, 2003). This method was used to study the relationships when the independent variables were not solely 0-1 variables.

FINDINGS AND DISCUSSION

Sample Characterization

The sample is composed mostly by female individuals (62.4%). In what concerns age, the majority of the individuals is 30 to 49 years old (73.8%). A larger number of individuals belong to polytechnic institutions (64.3%) and to public HEI (87.3%).

Utilization of OSNs

The majority of the sample uses OSNs (72.6%), but out of 157 individuals only 29.9% uses OSNs on a daily basis and only 10.8% uses three or more OSNs. 65,5%, use Facebook. Most of the individuals (57.2%) use OSNs to maintain contact with co-workers, although some of them also use

it to contact friends, family or unknown people. However, only 29,3% uses OSNs at work.

The reason most often identified by faculty members not to use OSNs is 'high personal exposure', followed by 'lack of interest' (19), 'lack of time' (15) and, finally, 'unawareness' (1).

The concerns shown by faculty members that do not use OSNs suggest that there may be a lack of trust on OSNs, especially with respect to the reason 'high personal exposure'. According to Foster, Francescucci and West (2010), even some individuals that use OSNs have privacy concerns and do not have the confidence to contribute to new communities.

Group Comparisons (Model 1)

In order to evaluate the influence of the use of OSNs to contact with co-workers on work-related attitudes and behaviors, we used, as mentioned before, the t-student test for independent samples.

It is possible to check, regarding the variable 'OCB', that $p = .177 > .05$, so we do not reject H_0, which means that there is no significant statistical difference between the means for the individuals that use OSN to maintain contact with co-workers and the ones that do not, in what concerns OCB.

For the variables JS and OC, $p > .05$, and so H_0 is not rejected, which means there is no significant difference between the means for individuals that use OSN to maintain contact with co-workers and the ones that do not. It is possible to check, regarding the variable 'IP', that $p = .032 < .05$, so we reject H_0, which means that there is a significant statistical difference between the means for the individuals that use OSN to maintain contact with co-workers and the ones that do not.

The results described above lead to and the rejection of H_1, H_2 and H_3. H_4 is supported. The use of OSN to maintain contact with co-workers influences IP, but not JS, OC or OCB. In what concerns commitment, the results found may be due to the fact that the definition of OC is directed towards the employer organization and not to co-workers.

Considering that the results were not significant for JS, OC and OCB, we also evaluated the influence of OSN on the different dimensions that constitute these concepts. The variable OSN has a significant positive influence on satisfaction with job facets (p =.048). This means that the individuals that use OSN are more satisfied in what concerns job facets, such as job security, pay, social and supervision, in comparison to those who do not use OSN. The variable OSN also has a significant positive influence on civic virtue (p =.006), one of the dimensions of OCB, which means that the individuals that use OSN demonstrate more OCB related to the dimension 'civic virtue', that is behaviors that reveal the responsibility to participate in the life of the organization, in comparison to those who do not use OSN.

These results partially corroborate H_1 and H_3.

PLS Method (Model 2)

We used the PLS method to test the relations among the worker's attitudes and behaviors.

The results show that there are positive correlations among all the variables, although the correlations among JS and OCB, JS and IP, OC and OCB, OCB and IP are low. The correlations among the other variables are moderate.

To test the significance of the relationships, we utilized the bootstrapping method, which is used to create a high number of samples (in this case, 1000) from the original sample, through systematic eliminations of observations. When $\alpha > .05$, in what concerns a certain relationship between variables, that is, when the relationship is not supported by the data, we eliminate it from the model. In this study, there was no need to eliminate any of the relationship, since they are all significant.

In what concerns the Cross loadings, there were some problems with the correlations among certain indicators, but we did not consider they were important enough to alter the model, also because that could imply the loss of validity of the scale contents.

In what concerns the direct effects of the model, JS has a direct positive impact of .724 on OC (H_5), an impact of .070 on OCB (H_6) and it has a negative impact of -.042 on IP. When considering the direct effects between the variables, OC explains 49.5% of OCB (H_8), but only 6.8% of IP (H_9). Finally, OCB explains 70.1% of IP (H_{10}).

There are also indirect positive effects between JS and OCB (.358) – mediated by OC –, between JS and IP (.251) – mediated by OC and OCB –, and between OC and IP (.347) – mediated by OCB.

According to the results shown on table 2, JS has a positive impact of .724 on OC (H_5), a positive impact of .429 on OCB (H_6) and it explains 30.9% of IP (H_7). OC explains 49.5% of OCB (H_8) and

Figure 3. Final model and direct effects

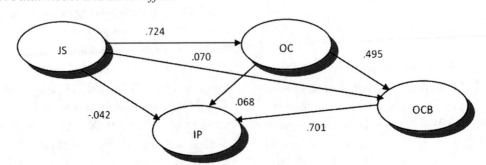

Table 1. Indirect effects for model 2

	JS	OC	OCB	IP
JS			.358	.251
OC				.347
OCB				
IP				

JS – Job satisfaction; OC – Organizational commitment; OCB – Organizational citizenship behaviors; IP – Individual performance

Table 2. Total effects for model 2

	JS	OC	OCB	IP
JS		.724	.429	.309
OC			.495	.416
OCB				.701
IP				

JS – Job satisfaction; OC – Organizational commitment; OCB – Organizational citizenship behaviors; IP – Individual performance

41.6% of IP (H_9). Finally, OCB explains 70.1% of IP (H_{10}). Using another explanation, when, for example, OCB raises one unit, IP raises .701. These results are in agreement with the studies we identified in the literature review, so all the hypotheses included in model 2 are supported.

Explanatory Capacity of the Model and Internal Consistency of the Measures

In order to complete the analysis of the model, it is necessary to verify its explanatory capacity. The R^2 allows verifying what proportion of the variation of Y is explained by the variable X (Manso, 1996). The variable 'OC' explains 52.5% of the model, OCB explains 30.1% and IP explains 52.1% of the variation in the model. The variable 'JS' does not explain any variation in the model because it appears as the predictive variable.

A high composite reliability is a necessary condition to obtain a high validity and it is an important pre-requisite in the application of measures used to evaluate behaviors (Raykov & Grayson, 2003). The value for IP is moderate, while the values for the other variables are high.

Cronbach's alpha allows us to analyze the internal consistency of a measure and provides a sub-estimate of the real credibility of the analyzed instrument (Marôco & Garcia-Marques, 2006). The alpha values of Cronbach for the scale that measures JS (.88), OC (.85) and OCB (.88) are relatively high, suggesting that these theoretical constructs exhibit appropriate psychometric properties (Cronbach, 1951). However, the value

for the scale of IP is somewhat low (.61), which means that further improvement of the scale may be needed.

As we can see on figure 4, the use of OSNs to maintain contact with co-workers only has an effect on IP, if we do not consider the dimensions of the concepts. When considering the dimensions of JS, OC and OCB, we find that OSN influences the dimension 'satisfaction with facets' (JS) and the dimension 'civic virtue' (OCB). The results show that the use of OSNs to maintain contact with co-workers does not influence, at all, commitment.

In what concerns satisfaction with facets (job security, pay, social and supervision) the results make sense, since the variable OSN is related to the use of OSNs to maintain contact with co-workers, and so this may have a positive effect on social relationships at work, including with supervisors.

We explain the influence of 'OSN' on 'civic virtue' by the fact that OCB are also related to the worker's performance, and specifically this dimension of OCB could easily be confused with in-role behaviors. On the other hand, the contact that the worker maintains on OSNs with the co-workers could enhance the worker's will to participate actively in the organization's life due to a possible exchange of information regarding the organization on OSNs.

In what concerns the relationships among work-related attitudes and behaviors, we verify that IP is also influenced by JS, OC and OCB. OC is positively influenced by JS and OCB is positively influenced by JS and OC.

Figure 4. Combination of model 1 and model 2

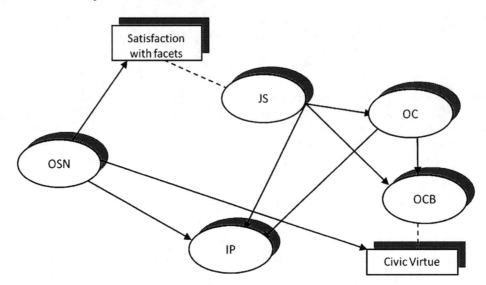

CONCLUSION

The results allow us to conclude that the individuals who maintain contact with co-workers on OSNs show a higher performance that lead to a higher performance, when compared to those that do not use OSNs. Curiously, some of the dimensions that compose the performance measure are directly connected to concepts related to networks, such as 'relationship among organizational networks', 'transmission of organizational memory/knowledge', 'trust' and 'chain influence on performance'.

Although we found that the use of OSNs does not influence commitment, in what concerns JS and OCB, we found that the individuals that maintain contact with co-workers on OSNs show more satisfaction with job facets – job security, pay, social and supervision –, which may be explained by the fact that the variable OSN is related to the use of OSNs to maintain contact with co-workers, and so this may have a positive effect on the worker's social relationships at work, including with supervisors.

The fact that no significant relation between the use of OSNs to contact co-workers and commitment was found may be due to the fact that

commitment is related to the affective reactions to the characteristics of the employer organization, and not to the interpersonal relationships established in the work environment. However, the use of OSNs to maintain contact with co-workers has a positive influence on the participation in the life of the organization (OCB), which may seem contradictory. Nevertheless, OCB refer to extra-role performance but, as mentioned before, 'civic virtue' behaviors could easily be confused with in-role performance. On the other hand, there might be an exchange of information regarding the organization on OSNs that may raise the worker's will to actively participate on the organization's life.

It seems important to mention that the motive 'high personal exposure' identified more often by the workers as the reason they do not use OSNs, reveals a lack of trust on OSNs, a fact that is in agreement with one study we found, that refers that even the individuals who use OSNs do not contribute as much as they could to online communities due to privacy concerns.

With respect to the worker's attitudes and behaviors, we've empirically supported all the proposed relations, which had already been found in previous studies. This way, we assure their value for HEI and we reaffirm their importance in the organizational context, which is particularly relevant nowadays, if we consider the current worldwide crisis.

Besides OSNs, one other concept that is central in this study is performance. The concepts of satisfaction and OCB, as a whole, and the concept of commitment were not found to be significantly influenced by the use of OSNs to maintain contact with co-workers. However, performance was. On the other hand, we found that performance is also positively influenced by satisfaction, commitment and ortogonaliza citizenship behaviors.

The results found in this study allow us to conclude that, in order to keep workers that show a high performance in HEI, the use of OSNs to maintain contact with co-workers should be encouraged. Our conclusion is in agreement with the study carried out by Boulos and Wheeler (2007). The authors mention the need to raise awareness of Web 2.0 tools and the possibilities they offer in the educational context. Moreover, HEI know a great deal about facilitating environments in which people join forces to create, share and advance knowledge, so they should be prepared to reap value from the new online tools (Barnatt, 2008). Furthermore, HEI should assure that their workers are satisfied, thus enhancing commitment and, consequently, organizational citizenship behaviors and performance.

FUTURE RESEARCH DIRECTIONS

The use of OSNs to maintain contact with co-workers could have been more deeply evaluated. We slate the replication of the study considering the types of exchanges made with co-workers on OSNs.

The relationship between the use of OSNs to maintain contact with co-workers and OCB should be studied in more depth, using a different instrument and/or resorting to a different context. We suggest asking respondents what type of information they exchange with co-workers, in order to allow to draw more deep conclusions in what concerns the influence of 'OSN' on the dimension 'civic virtue'.

We also propose the evaluation of the quality of interpersonal relationships at work. This way, it will be possible to understand the effect that the use of OSNs to maintain contact with co-workers has on the relationships that workers maintain in the work environment.

In the future, this investigation should be enlarged, to include other organizational variables, such as motivation or work-related stress, so the understanding of the concepts used in this study can be enhanced.

One very important aspect identified in this study is the need of deepening the understanding about how to use OSNs as an educational tool, and the effects of their integration in this particular context.

Moreover, considering our results, it would be interesting to examine the effects of using OSNs on the amount and quality of research carried out by academics, as well as on the amount and quality of research developed in cooperation with academics from different HEI, particularly regarding the effects of professional OSNs, such as LinkedIn.

We also propose the use of other measures to evaluate the variables, particularly performance, as well as the replication of the study in other contexts, such as service or sales companies, with the aim of making comparisons and extending the empirical evidence of the proposed relations.

REFERENCES

Alcobia, P. (2001). Atitudes e satisfação no trabalho. In J. M. Ferreira, J. Neves, & A. Caetano (Eds.), *Manual de psicossociologia das organizações*. Lisboa: McGraw-Hill.

Allen, N., & Meyer, P. (1990). Organizational socialization tactics: A longitudinal analysis of links to newcomers' commitment and role orientation. *Academy of Management Journal, 33*(4), 1–18. doi:10.2307/256294

Asunda, P. (2010). Productivity, social networks and net communities in the workplace. *Techniques: Connecting Education and Careers, 85*(5), 38–41.

Bakshy, E., Rosenn, I., Marlow, C., & Adamic, L. (2012). The Role of Social Networks in Information Diffusion. *International World Wide Web Conference*, Lyon, France. doi:10.1145/2187836.2187907

Barbeira, M. R., & Franco, M. J. (2009). Um sistema de gestão do conhecimento como fomentador de redes estratégicas interorganizacionais. *Revista Ibero-Americana de Estratégia, 8*(2), 5–29.

Barnard, C. (1938). *The functions of the executive* (2nd ed.). Harvard University Press.

Barnatt, C. (2008). Higher Education 2.0. *International Journal of Management Education, 7*(3), 47–56.

Bennett, S., Bishop, A., Dalgarno, B., Waycott, J., & Kennedy, G. (2012). Implementing Web 2.0 technologies in higher education: A collective case study. *Computers & Education, 59*(2), 524–534. doi:10.1016/j.compedu.2011.12.022

Benson, V., Filippaios, F., & Morgan, S. (2010). Online social networks: Changing the face of business education and career planning. *International Journal of Business and Management, 4*(1), 20–33.

Boulos, M. N., & Wheeler, S. (2007). The emerging Web 2.0 social software: An enabling suite of sociable technologies in health and health care education. *Health Information and Libraries Journal, 24*(1), 2–23. doi:10.1111/j.1471-1842.2007.00701.x PMID:17331140

Bunt, G. G., Wittek, R. P., & Klepper, M. C. (2005). The evolution of intra-organizational trust networks. *International Sociological Association, 20*(3), 339–369. doi:10.1177/0268580905055480

Castilla, E. J. (2005). Social networks and employee performance in a call center. *American Journal of Sociology, 110*(5), 1243–1283.

Chang, C.-S., & Chang, H.-H. (2007). Effects of internal marketing on nurse job satisfaction and organizational commitment: Example of medical centers in southern Taiwan. *The Journal of Nursing Research, 15*(4), 265–274. doi:10.1097/01.JNR.0000387623.02931.a3 PMID:18080971

Cheung, M. K. C., Chiu, P.-Y., & Lee, M. K. O. (2011). Online social networks: Why do students use facebook? *Computers in Human Behavior, 27*(4), 1337–1343. doi:10.1016/j.chb.2010.07.028

Chin, W., Marcolin, B., & Newsted, P. (2003). A partial least squares latent variable modeling approach for measuring interaction effects: Results from a Monte Carlo simulation study and an electronic-mail emotion/adoption study. *Information Systems Research, 14*(2), 189–217. doi:10.1287/isre.14.2.189.16018

Cook, J., & Wall, T. (1980). New work attitude measures of trust, organizational commitment and personal need non-fulfillment. *Journal of Occupational Psychology, 53*(1), 39–52. doi:10.1111/j.2044-8325.1980.tb00005.x

Ciribelli, M. (2003). *Como realizar uma dissertação de mestrado através da pesquisa científica*. Rio de Janeiro: Viveiros de Castro Editora.

Davis, C. H. F. III, Deil-Amen, R., Rios-Aguilar, C., & Canche, M. S. G. (n.d.). Social Media in Higher Education: A literature review and research directions. *The Center for the Study of Higher Education at The University of Arizona And Claremont Graduate University*.

Dess, G., & Shaw, J. (2001). Voluntary turnover, social capital and organizational performance. *Academy of Management Review, 26*(3), 446–456.

Donavan, D., Brown, T., & Mowen, J. (2004). Internal benefits of service-worker customer orientation: Job satisfaction, commitment and organizational citizenship behaviors. *Journal of Marketing, 68*(1), 128–146. doi:10.1509/jmkg.68.1.128.24034

Donaldson, E., Ensher, E. A., & Grant-Vallone, E. J. (2000). Longitudinal examination of mentoring relationships on organizational commitment and citizenship behavior. *Journal of Career Development, 26*(4), 233–248. doi:10.1177/089484530002600401

Eker, M., Eker, S., & Pala, F. (2008). The effects of job satisfaction on organizational commitment among Turkish health care staff: An empirical study. *Journal of Academic Studies, 10*(36), 46–68.

Forkosh-Baruch, A., & Hershkovitz, A. (2012). A Case Study of Israeli Higher-Education Institutes Sharing Scholarly Information with the Community via Social Networks. *The Internet and Higher Education, 15*(1), 56–68. doi:10.1016/j.iheduc.2011.08.003

Foster, M. K., Francescucci, A., & West, B. C. (2010). Why users participate in online social networks. *International Journal of Business and Management, 4*(1), 3–19.

González, J., & Garazo, T. (2006). Structural relationships between organizational service orientation, contact employee job satisfaction and citizenship behavior. *International Journal of Service Industry Management, 17*(1), 23–50. doi:10.1108/09564230610651561

Grabner-Kraeuter, S. & Waiguny, M. (2011). Why users stay in online social networks: perceptions of value, trust, subjective norm and the moderating influence of duration of use. *American Marketing Association, 22*(1), 240-249.

Graham, J. (1991). An essay on organizational citizenship behavior. *Employee Responsibilities and Rights Journal, 4*(4), 249–270. doi:10.1007/BF01385031

Greenhow, C. (2011). Online social networks and learning. *On the Horizon, 19*(1), 4–12. doi:10.1108/10748121111107663

Guille, A., Hacid, H., Favre, C., & Zighed, D. A. (2013). Information Difusion in Online Social Networks: A Survey. *Association for Computing Machinery, 42*(2), 17–28.

Hackman, R., & Oldham, G. (1975). Development of the Job Diagnostic Survey. *The Journal of Applied Psychology, 60*(2), 150–170. doi:10.1037/h0076546

Hackman, R., & Oldham, G. (1976). Motivation through the design of work: A test of a theory. *Organizational Behavior and Human Performance, 16*(2), 250–279. doi:10.1016/0030-5073(76)90016-7

Heidemann, J., Klier, M., & Probst, F. (2012). Online social networks: A survey of a global phenomenon. *Computer Networks, 56*(18), 3866–3878. doi:10.1016/j.comnet.2012.08.009

Hoang, H., & Antoncic, B. (2003). Network-based research in entrepreneurship: A critical review. *Journal of Business Venturing, 18*(2), 165–187. doi:10.1016/S0883-9026(02)00081-2

Hurlbert, J. S. (2001). Social networks, social circles and job satisfaction. *Work and Occupations, 18*(4), 415–430. doi:10.1177/0730888491018004003

Jones, M. (2006). Which is a better predictor of job performance: Job satisfaction or life satisfaction? *Journal of Behavioral and Applied Management, 8*(1), 20–42.

Judge, T., Parker, S., Colbert, A., Heller, D., & Remus, I. (2001). Job satisfaction: a cross-cultural review. In N. Anderson, D. Ones, H. Sinangil, & C. Viswesvaran (Eds.), *Handbook of Industrial, Work and Organizational Psychology* (Vol. 2, pp. 25–52). London: Sage Publications.

Katz, D., & Kahn, R. (1987). Psicologia social das organizações (3ª ed.). São Paulo: Editora Atlas.

Konovsky, M., & Organ, D. (1996). Dispositional and contextual determinants of organizational citizenship behavior. *Journal of Organizational Behavior, 17*(3), 253–266. doi:10.1002/(SICI)1099-1379(199605)17:3<253::AID-JOB747>3.0.CO;2-Q

Kukulska-Hulme, A. (2012). How should the higher education workforce adapt to advancements in technology for teaching and learning? *The Internet and Higher Education, 15*(4), 247–254. doi:10.1016/j.iheduc.2011.12.002

Lavelle, J., Brockner, J., Konovsky, M., Price, K., Henley, A., Taneja, A., & Vinekar, V. (2008). Commitment, procedural fairness, and organizational citizenship behavior: A multifoci analysis. *Journal of Organizational Behavior, 30*(3), 337–357. doi:10.1002/job.518

Lo, M.-C., & Ramayah, T. (2009). Dimensionality of organizational citizenship behavior (OCB) in a multicultural society: The case of Malaysia. *International Business Research, 2*(1), 48–55. doi:10.5539/ibr.v2n1p48

Locke, E., Latham, G., & Erez, M. (1988). The determinants of goal commitment. *Academy of Management Review, 13*(1), 23–39.

Locke, E. (1968). *What is job satisfaction?* Washington, DC: American Psychological Association.

Malik, M., Nawab, S., Naeem, B., & Danish, R. Q. (2010). Job satisfaction and organizational commitment of University teachers in public sector of Pakistan. *International Journal of Business and Management, 5*(6), 17–26. doi:10.5539/ijbm.v5n6p17

Manso, J. (1996). Estatística descritiva e previsão (2ª ed.). Covilhã: Universidade da Beira Interior.

Maroco, J. (2007). Análise Estatística com utilização do SPSS (3ª ed.). Lisboa: Edições Sílabo.

Maroco, J., & Garcia-Marques, T. (2006). Qual a fiabilidade do alfa de Cronbach? Questões antigas e soluções modernas? *Laboratório de Psicologia, 4*(1), 65–90.

Marshall, B., Choi, J., El-Shinnaway, M. M., North, M., Svensson, L., Wang, S., & Valenzuala, J. P. et al. (2009). Online and offline social ties of social network website users: An exploratory study in eleven societies. *Journal of Computer Information Systems, 50*(1), 54–64.

Madjeski, M., Johnson, M., & Bellovin, S. M. (2011). *The Failure of Online Social Network Privacy Settings.* Columbia University Computer Science Technical Reports.

Meyer, J., & Herscovitch, L. (2001). Commitment in the workplace: Toward a general model. *Human Resource Management Review, 11*(3), 299–326. doi:10.1016/S1053-4822(00)00053-X

Meyer, P., Stanley, D., Herscovitch, L., & Topolnytsky, L. (2002). Affective, continuance, and normative commitment to theorganization: A meta-analysis of antecedents, correlates, and consequences. *Journal of Vocational Behavior, 61*(1), 20–52. doi:10.1006/jvbe.2001.1842

Moran, M., Seaman, J., & Tinti-Kane, H. (2011). *Teaching, Learning, and Sharing: How Today's Higher Education.* Boston: Pearson Learning Solutions.

Organ, D. (1977). A reappraisal and reinterpretation of the satisfaction-causes-performance hypothesis. *Academy of Management Review*, *2*(1), 46–53.

Organ, D., & Lingl, A. (1995). Personality, satisfaction and organizational citizenship behaviors. *The Journal of Social Psychology*, *135*(3), 339–250. doi:10.1080/00224545.1995.9713963

Organ, D., & Moorman, R. (1993). Fairness and organizational citizenship behavior: What are the connections? *Social Justice Research*, *6*(1), 5–18. doi:10.1007/BF01048730

Podsakoff, P., & MacKenzie, S. (1997). Impact of organizational citizenship behavior on organizational performance: A review and suggestions for future research. *Human Performance*, *10*(2), 133–151. doi:10.1207/s15327043hup1002_5

Podsakoff, P., & MacKenzie, S. (1993). Citizenship behavior and fairness in organizations: Issues and directions for future research. *Employee Responsibilities and Rights Journal*, *6*(3), 257–269. doi:10.1007/BF01419449

Podsakoff, P., MacKenzie, S., Paine, J., & Bachrach, D. (2000). Organizational citizenship behaviors: A critical review of the theoretical and empirical literature and suggestions for future research. *Journal of Management*, *26*(3), 513–563. doi:10.1177/014920630002600307

Raykov, T., & Grayson, D. (2003). A test for change of composite reliability in scale development. *Multivariate Behavioral Research*, *38*(2), 143–159. doi:10.1207/S15327906MBR3802_1

Rego, A. (2002). *Comportamentos de cidadania nas organizações*. Lisboa: McGraw-Hill.

Rego, A., Ribeiro, N., & Cunha, M. (2010). Perceptions of organizational virtuousness and happiness as predictors of organizational citizenship behaviors. *Journal of Business Ethics*, *93*(1), 215–235. doi:10.1007/s10551-009-0197-7

Saari, L., & Judge, T. (2004). Employee attitudes and job satisfaction. *Human Resource Management*, *43*(4), 395–407. doi:10.1002/hrm.20032

Samad, S. (2005). Unraveling the organizational commitment and job performance relationship: Exploring the moderating effect of job satisfaction. *Business Review (Federal Reserve Bank of Philadelphia)*, *4*(2), 79–84.

Selwyn, N. (2012). Social Media in Higher Education. In *The Europa World of Learning* (62nd ed.). Routledge.

Staw, B. (1986). Organizational psychology and the pursuit of the happy/productive worker. *California Management Review*, *28*(4), 40–53. doi:10.2307/41165214

Sledgianowski, D., & Kulviwat, S. (2009). Using social network sites: The effects of playfulness, critical mass and trust in a hedonic context. *Journal of Computer Information Systems*, *49*(4), 74–83.

Tess, P. A. (2013). The role of social media in higher education classes (real and virtual) – A literature review. *Computers in Human Behavior*, *29*(5), A60–A68. doi:10.1016/j.chb.2012.12.032

Ullrich, C., Tan, X., Borau, K., Shen, L., Luo, H., & Shen, R. (2008). Why Web 2.0 is good for learning and for research: principles and prototypes. *Proceedings of the 17th International World Wide Web Conference*. doi:10.1145/1367497.1367593

Vala, J., Monteiro, M., Lima, L., & Caetano, A. (1995). *Psicologia social das organizações: estudos em empresas portuguesas*. Oeiras: Celta Editora.

Van Dyne, L., Graham, J., & Dienesch, R. (1994). Organizational citizenship behavior: Construct redefinition, measurement and validation. *Academy of Management Journal*, *37*(4), 765–802. doi:10.2307/256600

Viswesvaran, C. (2001). Assessment of individual job performance: a review of the past century and a look ahead. In N. Anderson, D. Ones, H. Sinangil, & C. Viswesvaran (Eds.), *Handbook of Industrial, Work and Organizational Psychology* (Vol. 1, pp. 110–126). London: SAGE Publications. doi:10.4135/9781848608320.n7

Williams, L., & Anderson, S. (1991). Job satisfaction and organizational commitment as predictors of organizational citizenship and in-role behaviors. *Journal of Management*, *17*(3), 601–617. doi:10.1177/014920639101700305

Xiaowei, L. (2006). A test on the systematic fuzzy measures of the key degree for the core employees' performance traits. *Canadian Social Science*, *2*(5), 38–43.

Young, K. (2011). Social ties, social networks and the Facebook experience. *International Journal of Emerging Technologies and Society*, *9*(1), 20–34.

Veletsianos, G. (2011). Higher education scholars' participation and practices on Twitter. *Journal of Computer Assisted Learning*, *28*(4), 336–349. doi:10.1111/j.1365-2729.2011.00449.x

KEY TERMS AND DEFINITIONS

Attitude: Describes an internal arrangement of the individual in relation to an element of the social world, which guides the conduct they adopt in the presence, real or symbolic, of that element.

Behavior: It is the activity of an organism interacting with its environment.

Higher Education Institutions: Community service providers, specifically of transference and economic value increase of the scientific and technological knowledge, which have as main goals to facilitate environments in which people collaborate to create, share and advance knowledge.

Individual Performance: Defined as behaviors that can be evaluated, that is, behaviors that are identifiable only through operational measures.

Job Satisfaction: A positive emotional state – feelings and affective responses –, or a generalized positive attitude towards work and the experiences that occur in the work environment, that depends on situational factors and/or on personality and personal factors, and that can be measured according to a global approach – based on the attitude towards work in general, not being a result of the sum of different aspects related to work, but depending on them –, or to a multidimensional approach – satisfaction that reverses from a number of factors associated with work, being possible to measure satisfaction for each one of them.

Online Social Networks: They function as communication interfaces between millions of users, providing an efficient and user-friendly way to maintain social connections and to easily create and share information.

Organizational Citizenship Behaviors: Characterized as extra-role behaviors, that is, behaviors that arise as a way of acting beyond what is defined by work requirements (in-role behaviors), which means that the workers do non-mandatory tasks without expecting any rewards or recognition.

Organizational Commitment: It is a force of connection – a psychological or attitude stage – with the goals and values of the organization, which determines a direction at the level of the individual's behavior towards the employer organization, with the aim of benefiting it.

Social Networks: They function as communication channels and allow the exchange of resources to several levels, as a form of spreading and sharing ideas. The social relationships established at work are an important tool for the understanding of the workers' outcomes in the organizations.

ENDNOTES

[1]   Diário da República, 1st series, N. 174, 10, September, 2007, Law n. 62/2007

[2]   Indicators of the teaching staff of HEI in Portugal. Accessed on the 24th May, 2011, on http://www.ine.pt/xportal/xmain?xpid=INE&xpgid=ine_indicadores&indOcorrCod=0000887&contexto=pi&selTab=tab0

Chapter 19
Developing Instructional Leadership and Communication Skills through Online Professional Development:
Focusing on Rural and Urban Principals

Doron Zinger
University of California Irvine, USA

ABSTRACT

Principals and school leaders play a pivotal role in teacher satisfaction, retention, and learning; thus, they are uniquely positioned to help teachers improve their practice. Principals face many of the same challenges that teachers do, especially in schools serving low-income, low-performing, and ethnically diverse students. This chapter examines the extant literature concerning online professional development (OPD) and how it may hold particular promise for principals and other school leaders who work in these challenging settings, with a focus on attending to principal instructional leadership. A corollary purpose centers on how effective online communication (and the use of digital modalities) can create greater access and flexibility for participants. Establishing lines of communication and building online community may help overcome the professional isolation experienced by principals. Implications for theory and practice are discussed.

INTRODUCTION

Schools in the Unites States are tasked with educating an increasingly diverse population of students in a rapidly changing world. Schools are dynamic communities and environments where the roles of their leaders are complex and challenging. Supporting and equipping these leaders to succeed may be one of the most important factors impacting student learning and improving student outcomes. Furthermore, the capacity of principals serving schools comprised of large numbers of ethnically diverse is doubly important due to high teacher turnover and additional difficulties present in predominantly urban and rural school settings. Upon completion of their credentialing programs, principals often have much to learn, and in the age of high stakes testing and accountability, they

DOI: 10.4018/978-1-4666-9970-0.ch019

may have little time to learn what they will need to survive and then thrive at their school sites. This chapter will explore online professional development (OPD) focused on developing principal instructional leadership and communication skills in urban and rural settings. Additionally, how OPD may provide a new avenue to support principals' development and build their leadership capacity will be examined.

BACKGROUND

The Roles of Principals

It can be argued that a principal, more than any other individual, can move a school forward and impact student learning. Indeed, high performing school leaders have long been associated with high performing schools (Barth, 1986; Marks & Printy, 2003), and although teachers play a critical role in and have significant impact on student learning (Hawley & Valli, 2000), principals have a significant and direct impact on teacher learning and performance (Hallinger, 2005; Youngs & King, 2002). Broadly, principals have significant influence on teacher retention, teacher learning and teaching, and subsequently, student learning (Johnson, Kraft, & Papay, 2012). For example, lack of administrative support is responsible for 40% of teacher turnover, more than double the rate of turnover due to teacher concerns about student behavioral issues (Boyd et al., 2011).

Urban School Leadership

Principals in urban settings face a number of challenges that do not exist (or that exist to a lesser extent) in suburban schools (Markow, Macia, & Lee, 2013). These challenges include staffing schools with effective teachers, engaging parents and the community, and coping with greater levels of stress (Markow et al., 2013). Teacher turnover in urban schools serving large percentages of students from ethnically diverse backgrounds is particularly problematic (Grissom, 2011); however, in urban settings principals can have a greater impact on teacher satisfaction and retention. The financial cost, time, and effort of having to hire, train, and support teachers only to see them leave can be daunting. Grissom found that high-performing principals had the same teacher turnover rates at urban and suburban schools. Average-performing principals however; had higher turnover rates in urban schools when compared with suburban schools. Thus, focusing on supporting urban school principals and increasing their effectiveness can have a significant impact on teacher satisfaction, retention, and performance. As high rates of teacher turnover are associated with poor student performance (Grissom, 2011), reducing these rates in urban settings is especially critical for the growing population of students from ethnically diverse backgrounds. Additionally, as principals can often be unprepared for leading schools when they complete their initial accreditation process (Barnett, 2004) and their schools may be under-resourced (Grissom, 2011), they, themselves, may be at a higher risk of burnout and susceptible to turnover. Indeed, Grissom calls for a policy change to promote finding and hiring the best principals into these schools. Nevertheless, even the best principals are unlikely to excel in challenging urban schools without subsequent. Thus, supporting principals' capacity to directly impact teacher performance and satisfaction may be the top priority for principal development.

Rural School Leadership

Principals in rural settings face many of the same challenges that urban principals do. These shared challenges include school infrastructure and finances, as well as attracting and keeping qualified teachers (Theobald, 2005). Like their urban counterparts, many new principals in rural schools are unprepared for the demands of leading their schools in the age of accountability (Salazar, 2007). In some cases, the challenges in rural settings are greater than in urban settings. Rural districts are typically smaller than urban districts and, subsequently, they often cannot leverage resources as larger districts can (Jacob, 2007). For example, when it comes to teacher recruiting efforts and negotiations with vendors, rural districts are often at a disadvantage when compared with urban or suburban districts (Jacob, 2007). Geographic isolation is also especially challenging in rural settings, where schools may be separated by great distances (Howley, Chadwick, & Howley, 2002). Although face-to-face PD has been shown to improve rural principal leadership practice, principals may be leery of engaging in PD that keeps them away from the demands of their school sites (Salazar, 2007). The shared challenges faced by rural and urban school leaders may make a learning partnership between them mutually beneficial (Theobald, 2005). Providing rural and urban school leaders opportunities to build learning communities with their peers may lead to innovative approaches to addressing their shared and individual challenges.

Instructional Leadership

A great deal has been learned about the challenges principals face given the central role they play in schools. Having to juggle multiple responsibilities and shifting priorities are frequent challenges for principals. Challenges including curriculum and standards reforms, school academic outcomes, student instruction, and parental and community expectations are nearly universal, transcending states and countries (Walker & Qian, 2015). It often seems as if a principal's job is never done, and like many middle managers in industry, time limitations are a constant challenge (Hallinger & Murphy, 2013). Time constraints subsequently influence principal decision making within the

context of policy mandates, individual school priorities and issues, and their personal educational vision, background, and training. Within these complexities of school leadership, instructional leadership has emerged as a key priority for principals and school leaders (Marks & Printy, 2003) and has shaped and defined the conceptions of what effective school leadership is (Grissom & Loeb, 2011).

Instructional leadership contrasts with transformational leadership. Where transformational leadership is based on a principal's charisma and ability to inspire and motivate, instructional leadership has been operationalized as activity focused on instruction and learning (Grissom & Loeb, 2011). Instructional leadership is challenging and multifaceted, requiring exceptional perception and communication skills. Instructional leadership encompasses a wide range of areas including curriculum implementation, teacher support and supervision, teacher coaching, and classroom observations. Hallinger (2005) suggested that principals often tend to avoid the instructional leadership role and that those who could function as effective instructional leaders by supporting teacher practice are in the minority. Indeed, despite the focus on instructional leadership and importance of administrative support of teachers, the average principal only spends about 13% of their time on instructional tasks (Grissom, Loeb, & Master, 2013). Less than half of that time (about 5%) is spent in walkthroughs. Classroom walkthroughs produced mixed results in terms of teacher perceptions and student outcomes primarily due to lack of cohesion with a larger PD program or a lack of feedback to teachers (Grissom et al., 2013). Generally, teachers who had walkthroughs but did not receive feedback had negative perceptions of walkthroughs. Despite the challenging nature of this landscape, addressing and supporting principal development as instructional leaders can yield substantial positive results for teacher and students (Marks & Printy, 2003).

Principal's Needs for PD

Within instructional leadership, a principal's capacity and ability to support teacher learning depends heavily on his or her communicative and interpersonal skills. The introduction of the Interstate School Leaders Licensure Consortium (ISLLC) Leadership Standards in 1996 helped formalize standards for school leaders. These standards have since been revised and updated to address the changing vision of schools. Though a number of the standards address teachers and instruction, one of the seven standards explicitly addresses teacher development (Standard 3 of the 2015 ISLLC standards); however, the standards are broad and offer little specific support on how to attain the standards. For example: "Provide high-quality, actionable, and salient feedback to all staff members, and facilitate collegial exchanges of feedback" (ISLLC standards 2015) is one of the actions described under standard three. Feedback can be provided through numerous modalities and using different approaches. Additionally, teachers may have individual and different preferences for the types of feedback they receive. Subsequently, effective communication skills underpin any feedback approach that a principal may provide. As part of the communicative basis for teacher development and support, Youngs and King (2002) point to the importance of building rapport with teachers. Blase & Blase (2000) additionally found that effective principals focus on process rather than a prescriptive outcome and promote reflective practice when working with teachers. Principals may lack the skills and practice to successfully coach and support teachers upon completing their administrative certification. Indeed, the effectiveness and quality of principal preparation programs is unclear (Murphy & Vriesenga, 2006). Therefore, identifying or developing effective PD focused on principals' communication skills ought to be a priority.

The very nature of their positions makes finding professional development difficult for principals. PD opportunities are fewer for principals, when compared with teachers for example. Furthermore, unlike teachers, who can form peer communities on their school campus, principals are isolated from their administrative peers as there is typically only one principal on a school site (Howley, Chadwick, & Howley, 2002). This is especially challenging in rural settings where principals have to overcome geographic isolation to attend face-to-face PD. Nonetheless, engaging in face-to-face PD can reduce principals' feelings of isolation (Howley, Chadwick, & Howley, 2002). Furthermore, Howley and colleagues found that interacting with peers and mentors could promote early career principal's reflective practice. It is not surprising that promoting reflective practice can improve principal practice (Boerema, 2011; Drago-Severson, 2012) much like it can improve teacher practice. Yet the immediate needs of the school site can limit a principal's ability and willingness to participate in PD (Salazar, 2007). Thus, OPD may provide principals with flexibility to engage with peers, develop peer and mentor networks, and have a positive impact on principals' skills and practice.

ONLINE PROFESSIONAL DEVELOPMENT

Technology Alone Will Not Suffice

Technology and the internet hold great promise for learning. The flexibility and access created by the internet can indeed transform learning. Notions that the digital age and digital access can revolutionize and democratize learning (Mitra & Dangwal, 2010) and be "harmonizing and empowering" (Negroponte, 1996) have become popularized in education. Yet, proliferation of internet, connected devices and the bandwidth to support them have not resulted in universal learning in places where access is now available. To the contrary, simply providing students with technology such as laptops has, at times, produced disappointing results for students (Warschauer, Cotten, & Ames, 2011). In some empirical studies, no changes in student outcomes were found when students were provided with access to computers and the internet (Fairlie & Robinson, 2012). It is somewhat odd that in the field of education, expectations have persisted that simply providing technology will improve learning. To be sure, technical support and training on the use of technologies are prerequisites to successful implementation and deployment of programs (Warschauer, 2011). Technology should be viewed as a tool that can promote or impede learning depending on how it is used, leveraged, and supported. It is this premise, and that learning is a complex and social endeavor (Greeno, 1998; Lave & Wenger, 1991), that guide this conversation about online environments for principal learning.

Considerations for Transitioning from PD to OPD

OPD may hold a promising approach to alleviating some of the challenges raised by face-to-face PD, especially for principals and school leaders who are often constrained by both time and physical location. Flexibility in time and space is perhaps the greatest benefit of OPD, as participants can access and interact with curriculum and other participants around their work schedule (Duncan-Howell, 2010). Yet, the use of online tools and the internet are subject to the same pitfalls as face-to-face PD. Lessons learned from face-to-face PD and research-based best practices must be considered when designing and evaluating OPD. To begin with, simply using technology or placing PD online does not guarantee that learning will occur, nor is PD likely to be effective without proper support in place (Vrasidas & Zembylas, 2004). Furthermore, new practices are unlikely to make it back to the school site without additional support (Barth, 1986). Thus, ongoing support is likely to significantly improve programmatic implementation on a school site.

Most educations PD literature centers on teacher and teaching, and this may serve as a good starting point for designing PD and OPD for principals. Desimone (2009) points to five characteristics of effective PD on which there is consensus in the research "(a) content focus, (b) active learning, (c) coherence, (d) duration, and (e) collective participation" (p.183). Though focused on teacher PD, these characteristics should hold true to other OPD practitioners such as principals. A number of approaches have been taken and investigated to address the characteristics presented by Desimone. Content design, instructor or facilitator training, relevant and individualized content, online communities, active learning environments, and technical support are all components critical to effective OPD design (Duncan-Howell, 2010). With the proliferation of OPD, it has become accepted by teachers and other educators who now generally perceive OPD to be as effective as face-to-face PD when technical support is in place (Reeves & Li, 2012). This acceptance of online learning as a viable modality is an import first step for OPD implementation. Communicating online thus becomes the key to effective OPD, where building community and addressing the needs of individual participants can mitigate the attrition rates often seen in online learning.

OPD Technological and Digital Literacy Considerations

Online tools provide flexibility and access, which are rarely available in face-to-face professional development; however, attrition rates are significantly higher in online courses than in courses taken face-to-face (Angelino, Williams, & Natvig, 2007). Though potentially powerful, successful online learning is more dependent on *how* technology is implemented, not simply *what* technology is implemented; in addition, technical support and technological infrastructure is important to ensure user accessibility and content functionality (Warschauer, 2011). It is also important to ensure that participants who have limited or no experience with the technologies involved in online learning are supported and prepared to use online tools (Reeves & Li, 2012). Thus, the need for a technical support component adds an additional layer of complexity to OPD which is not usually needed in traditional face-to-face PD. Furthermore, designers of OPDs simply cannot assume that students who enroll in an online course are literate in the modality or tools used within the course.

Orienting students to online learning environments may be a key first step in designing successful online courses. Mandated online learning orientation courses have been shown to improve student perceptions of and increased persistence in online courses (Jones, 2013). Other promising approaches include orientation classes prior to the first content class (Dash, Magidin de Kramer, O'Dwyer, Masters, & Russell, 2012). Orientations of the learning management system (LMS), message boards or blogs, access to course content, and how to turn in assignments are important technical components for students to learn. It is interesting to note that Bozarth et al. (2004) found that most students reported that they did not feel they needed an orientation course prior to taking their first online class yet reported that they benefited from the orientation program. This finding highlights the benefits that may be derived from making orientation for online courses mandatory.

When it comes to principals in online learning environments, special care may be needed in avoiding assumptions that may derail OPD prior to its beginning. Though principals hold positions of leadership and often manage and oversee large campuses, assumptions should not be made about their digital literacy or knowledge of online learning environments. It may be wise to survey or poll participants ahead of the PD to get a better sense of their backgrounds as they relate to the content of the course as well as experience and use of online learning environments. The same consideration should be given to instructors or facilitators of principal OPD. As these facilitators can often be practitioners themselves, their knowledge of OPD pedagogies and technology may be limited.

OPD Structure

Successful online learning programs are well thought out in their implementation and are subsequently responsive to participant needs (Means, Bakia, & Murphy 2014). OPD design that is purposeful in its structures and processes to promote individual participant needs is more likely to succeed (Lock, 2006). New routines, practices, and a cultural shift are often required to take place for participants as they move from face-to-face interactions to online interactions and as they build communities of learners (Lock, 2006). Learning needs to be structured so that content is directly relevant to participants and collaboration is promoted online (Duncan-Howell, 2010). How the facilitator communicates with participants is also critical for student engagement and OPD success. An instructor or facilitator must be sufficiently prepared to support participants, both in use of the online tools and in the content of the PD (Derry, Seymour, Steinkuehler, Lee, & Siegel, 2004). Through a 3-year evolution of an OPD, Derry and colleagues found that a "structured socio-technical design" had to be implemented to include instructional materials, communication technology, and social activities. These elements were necessary to guide participants. Key findings from this body of research point to the importance of user-centered structured design that finds a balance between individual participant interest, reflection, and growth, and a focus on the overall goals of the OPD and its community.

In practice, these findings paint a complex and shifting landscape of learners and instructor. One can imagine a participating principal whose time is constantly in short supply asking how attending OPD will help them improve their practice and meet the challenges they face daily. OPD programs that can clearly and affirmatively answer these questions are more likely to initially engage, and ultimately be successful, with principals.

Facilitating OPD

Much like in face-to-face environments, instructors and facilitators can promote or impede participant learning through digital modalities. The role of the instructor or facilitator is perhaps more critical online, where students do not interact with teachers on as regular a basis as they do in a classroom setting. Whereas in a classroom, students can raise their hands when they have a question, online students need to rely on email, blogs, or message boards for communication. Indeed, facilitators are key to the development and success of communication in online discussion forums (Lowes, Lin, & Wang, 2007). Additionally, it is important not to assume that instructors are familiar with these technologies.

Instructors should be supported and oriented with how the online environment works. Furthermore, instructors who are accustomed to teaching face-to-face may expect that instructional approaches that work in that environment will translate directly to online learning. Bozarth et al. (2004) found a mismatch between instructor and student technical expectations, and addressing these during an orientation could resolve many of potential disconnects before content instruction ever begins. Bozarth et al. (2015) also found that clarity about expectations and course specific protocols were important to elucidate by the instructor. Clearly articulating expectations of timeliness and frequency of instructor feedback, for example, are important to establish early in an online course. These early steps are critical in facilitating the development of community between the instructor and participants, and among participants themselves. Facilitators who are effective in developing a community with participants can bring a greater sense of stability to the online learning environment (Carter, 2004).

Communication

Communication is at the heart of PD interaction and participant growth. While face-to-face interaction offers immediate responses and greater interaction, online interactions through asynchronous computer mediated communication (CMC) can offer more reflective communication (Hawkes & Romiszowski, 2001). Blogs have emerged as a leading form of CMC, and they encourage reflection as well as provide a forum for peer support (Hall & Davison, 2007). Blogs, however, are susceptible to the same concerns as other instructional tools in that they should be used purposefully and with participants in mind. In OPD, a balance must be struck in blogs between openness and a focus (Byington, 2011). Here again, the designers and facilitators may play a critical role in shaping user experience and promoting user engagement, vesture, and motivation. For example, facilitators have been found to impede and promote constructive discussion on blogs and message boards, directly impacting student satisfaction with online courses and their subsequent desire to continue taking online courses (Lowes et al., 2007).

Green (2011), in a study of school librarians, found that a follow-up program coupled with OPD had a significant impact on participant program completion rates. To highlight the importance of online communication, practices such as peer interaction through discussion and online questions, emails with other course participants, as well as instructor interaction lead to nearly doubling the completion rates of the OPD when compared with OPD without follow-up support. Although Green's study focused on school librarians, her findings nevertheless have important implications for principals given that principals and librarians work under similar conditions. This study reinforces the importance of the need for not just high quality OPD, but effective online communication through ongoing feedback, follow-up, and professional peer interaction to support participants.

LEARNER-CENTERED PD

OPD Tensions between Individual and Community Goals

Online environments present new challenges and tensions that need to be addressed in order to engage participants and meet individual and group goals. Social engagement is at the heart of both individual participation as well as the online community as a whole (Henderson, 2007). The importance of community is echoed by others (Wenger, White, & Smith, 2009), who present the challenges and potential solutions posed by online community. First, "a community implies an experience of togetherness that extends through time and space.... separation in time and space then creates a dilemma for communities" (p.2). Second, Wenger and colleagues point to the relationship between an individual and their community as a source of tension. As communities promote togetherness, individuals need to balance their own identities with their participation in the community. These tensions need to be addressed in order to provide participants with a constructive online learning environment. Wenger and colleagues suggest that communication tools such as blogs, trackback, and RSS feeds may bridge gaps between individuals within a community. OPD community also needs to be fostered by a teacher or facilitator to promote individual participation and development. The processes can begin with individual introductions and, when effectively guided, develop into interaction, involvement, and inquiry (Waltonen-Moore, Stuart, Newton, Oswald, & Varonis, 2006). Therefore, the development of community should be fostered by structures that promote productive and focused discourse, feedback and, reflection and should be guided by a facilitator who helps individuals and the community navigate towards meeting their individual and collective course goals.

OPD Duration

Desimone (2009) and others have pointed to the importance of the duration of PD. In surveying participants in OPD, Duncan-Howell (2010) found that teachers preferred ongoing PD lasting 2-3 months over single sessions of PD lasting 1-2 hours and over ongoing PDs lasting longer than 6 months. Participants in OPD have the opportunity to build rapport, trust and community. Additionally, time to reflect on practice and interact with peers through learning cycles are also affordances of OPD, which cannot be experienced through a single session, one time PD. Duncan-Howell's findings echo those of Penuel, Fishman, Yamaguchi, and Gallagher (2007), who also argue that there may be an interaction between more reform-minded approaches to instruction and PD of longer duration. That is, more reform-minded approaches to PD or OPD that focus on participant reflective practice require longer duration. In addition, Heller, Daehler, Wong, Shinohara, and Miratrix (2012) conducted a PD course totaling 24 hours, taking place over approximately 3 months, and found that the PD produced significant teacher learning outcomes. Though there does not appear to be an exact duration of time associated with producing the best participant learning outcomes, a range of 2-3 months appears to be the most effective for participants. The range of 2-3 months provides sufficient time for participants to enact and reflect on practices they learn through the course. In the case of principals and OPD focused on instructional leadership, a 2-3 month span would afford enough time for them to apply skills and practices learned in their daily work with teachers. The time span would also allow them to solicit feedback from other OPD participants and facilitators, reflect on their practice, and enact what they have learned. At 2-3 months, a course would take less than a semester of school time and could be aligned with the principal's schedule to maximize course effectiveness.

THE CASE OF AN EVOLVING, PRINCIPAL-FOCUSED OPD PROGRAM

There are few principal-focused OPDs currently being implemented, and even fewer have been examined. In the Los Angeles area, a number of innovative urban school leadership programs have been developed to meet the needs of school leaders serving in the country's second largest school district. One of these schools, California State University, Dominguez Hills (CSUDH), has been developing and implementing principal-focused OPD for nearly three years. Faculty at CSUDH focused on school leadership and administration have deliberately developed a program that prepares aspiring principals to lead urban schools (Issa Lahera, Holzman, & Robinson, 2014). The program emphasizes instructional leadership and relationship building and has responsively evolved over a number of iterations (Issa Lahera, Author, Mendoza, & McManus, 2015). To meet the individual needs of graduates, create greater access, and provide additional and deeper opportunities for principals to build skills and competencies, leaders of the program began developing OPD in 2012. The extreme time demands placed on new principals in challenging urban schools was a primary drive of the program. The OPD program was designed to supplement, identify, and address gaps in principals' skills upon their completion of credentialing programs. The first course launched as a hybrid class, where students met face-to-face with the instructor during the first and last weeks of the eight-week course. Students were screened and selected for the course based on criteria created by the instructor in order to align instruction and students. The hybrid nature of the course however, created cost and access issues.

Cost ultimately drove many of the initial OPD design decisions. Specifically, the intent of the OPD program was to offer low or no-cost OPD that was entirely online, thereby dramatically increasing access to courses. Subsequently, the program leaders at CSUDH found and utilized resources that could be obtained for little to no-cost so that the program could be sustained long term. The underlying approach to design was to provide principals with an OPD where they could receive feedback, access resources and tools, and build a professional network. A certificate approach was initially adopted by OPD designers, whereby participating principals would earn digital badges for completion of individual courses and certificates could be earned for completion of specific course sequences. These certifications could then be applied to digital resumes and endorsed by course instructors. This model was adopted from the business world, where many tech companies have employed a badge and certification system in lieu of college and university courses. The certifications were additionally designed to provide participating principals with a sense of accomplishment and achievement. OPD course duration was set-up to be between six and eight weeks, depending on the depth and breadth of content.

As the program was initially piloted, two significant challenges were initially identified. First, the OPD quickly began taking on the characteristics of a massive open online course (MOOC). Specifically, the early OPDs had very high attrition rates, and students often logged in initially, looked at various components of the course but did not complete it. This "MOOC'ing" of the course worked counter to the goals of the OPD, where persistence and completion were key goals for participating principals. Subsequently, the OPD designers began to incentivize beta testers of the courses with stipends to promote course completion and feedback from participants. Secondly, concerns were raised by OPD instructors about the quality and rigor of work produced by participants. Specifically, instructors argued that if they were to pass students and students were to earn a certification, those students must meet the same rigor expectations of face-to-face courses. In looking more deeply at this issue, two other concerns were identified. First, course expectations were not clearly articulated to students. That is, the time commitment expectations, work quality expectations, and scope of assignments were not explained clearly to participants. Subsequently, for the following iterations of the OPD, a formal commitment document was created and signed by participants where expectations of time commitment, participation, and quality of work were clearly stated. Second, when course designers looked at instructor responsiveness, they found that some instructors did not provide timely feedback to students. Thus, a policy for instructor feedback was created, such that instructors were expected to respond to students within 48 hours. Both of these changes then lead to greater student persistence in OPD courses.

Prior to the launch of the second iteration of the certificate OPDs, principals who were likely to enroll in the courses were surveyed to identify desired topics and areas of interest for courses. Once course content was identified and the initial courses were designed, three cycles of pilot testing with a diverse group of principals took place to provide feedback from multiple perspectives on course design and implementation. This feedback was then used to refine the courses. A total of 156 students enrolled in the initial courses offered as part of the second iteration of the certificate OPD. Courses included a variety of topics including developing a collaborative culture, administration of teacher classroom management, and effective use of data. A total of 38 participants completed the courses, representing a 24% completion rate. All students who completed their course evaluation either agreed or strongly agreed (on a five point strongly disagree to strongly agree Likert scale) that they course met their learning needs (16 of the 38 students who finished the course completed the end of course surveys). Students were also surveyed about their takeaways from the OPD, and those responses were used to inform refinements in the courses.

As the leaders of the principal preparation program and OPD designers at CSUDH move forward, they continue to focus on increasing student persistence through courses, as well as accessibility and sustainability of the OPD program. With each iteration of the OPD courses, they refine content, delivery method, instructional approaches, and assignments based on feedback from instructors and participants. They continue to expand the range of courses available to meet the diverse needs of principals and aspiring principals with a focus on supporting and developing principals who are ready to lead. The iterative process which the faculty and support staff at CSUDH have undertaken over the last three years sheds light on the complexities of designing and implementing principal focused OPD designed to increase leadership capacity. The case of CSUDH's OPD program highlights challenges in facilitation, engagement, communication, and curriculum design of OPD targeting urban principals, as well as the iterative process that will likely be required to address challenges over the course of years in order to achieve a program that is rigorous, relevant, and engaging to participating principals.

SOLUTIONS AND RECOMMENDATIONS

The intersection of principal instructional leadership and OPD is complex. Numerous considerations have to be weighed in the planning and development of OPD. Designing OPD to improve principal instructional leadership is contingent on developing principals' online communication skills in an effort to develop their face-to-face communication skills. Taking a systematic approach to the design and evolution of OPD should lead to positive outcomes initially and should continue to improve in later iterations of the OPD. Furthermore, the professional community that develops through OPD may require several iteration of PD content to mature and develop. Patience and responsiveness may be pre-requisites to fostering online community in the context of OPD.

Based on existing literature, when considering the design and evolution of OPD, a three staged approach is suggested (see figure 1). The backgrounds of the OPD's target audience should be examined and considered before PD is designed or implemented. What are the participants' beliefs and values related to the use of technology and OPD? Do their beliefs and values align with the goals and vision of the PD and its content? Additional attention should be paid to school-specific factors. The challenges previously mentioned regarding urban schools should lend context to how OPD should be designed. If an OPD is designed to address a topic or concern that is of little interest or value to potential participants, it is unlikely to succeed. Conversely, if an OPD is designed to address an area of need, participants may be more likely to engage and participate in the course. With a focus on instructional leadership, numerous areas relating to communication could be identified as potential starting points. These could include how to coach, mentor, supervise, observe, evaluate, and provide feedback to teachers. It would be helpful to survey or interview potential participants so that specific course content could be tailored more closely to their collective and individual needs

With participants' considerations taken into account, the design and implementation of the OPD is more likely to succeed. To promote participant engagement and learning, numerous design considerations need to be addressed prior to the launch of the course. A decision should be made on the types of technologies to be integrated into the OPD, and based on participant backgrounds, how much instruction and preparation will be

Figure 1. Principal OPD design framework

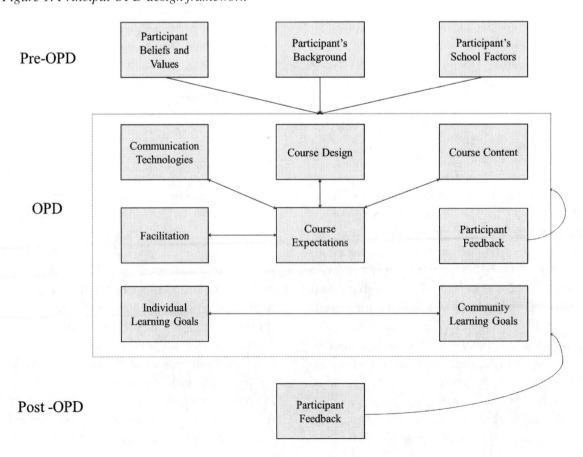

needed to ensure that they are comfortable with and able to navigate the specific technologies. Though the use of email has become ubiquitous, the use of message boards, audio and video tools, and LMSs are far from universal. As such, providing users with individual or collective support to ensure digital literacy in those modalities may be a pre-requisite to their engagement with an online community. Beyond the technical aspect of the online tools, etiquette and norms across those technologies should be established to minimize miscommunication and unmet expectations.

The course design itself plays an important role in what participants may get out of an OPD. How long the course is, the types of assignments, and due dates are all important factors to consider. Though, ideally, OPD evolves into an ongoing professional community, the time dedicated to a topic, especially initially, is an important consideration. Principals should have clear expectations of the time they are expected to commit and for how long they are expected to commit it. It is also important to provide clear workload and deadline expectations of any assignments or other participant work that is to be turned in or posted. Learning cycles and feedback loops should be established to promote reflection and closure to specific topics. That is, the design should allow for participants to learn new content, discuss, reflect, collaborate, and plan as they navigate through cycles of the course. Design should take into consideration that principals are professionals and have very limited time, so assignments and activities should be clear, and resources should be readily available to support principals. Establishing weekly routines and cycles, for example, may help create a more predictable and comfortable environment for participants that is more conducive to learning. How often participants have to post and respond to others on message boards and the type and frequency of feedback they receive are other important considerations for design.

Beyond design, the content of the course should align with individual learning goals and the overall goals of the course. Ideally, the content should offer flexibility to address individual interests and need while still encompass the overarching topic and goal of the OPD. For example, the topic of teacher coaching as a component of instructional leadership may contain numerous aspects. First, different modalities such as articles, book chapters, websites, and videos may all be used as instructional material to support principal learning. Secondly, subtopics may provide participants with content that is more relevant to their lived experience, such as how to approach teachers who are resistant or how to help teachers identify their own challenges through coaching. In terms of modality and specific content, providing participants with choice and allowing them to take greater ownership of their own learning should contribute to increased engagement. For example, principals could be given a choice of specific subtopic they would like to explore and discuss in a given week, and then select a number of relevant resources as a starting point, followed by message board discussion and reflection.

Design and content also intersect in activities, projects, and assignments from an OPD. Assignments and projects should involve the principals' practice and tie in with instructional leadership activities they carry out on a daily basis. In the example of coaching as a course topic, assignments and projects, both short and long term, should involve the principal working with teachers and coaching them. The PD should function to inform, support, and promote principal reflection as they negotiate the complexities of coaching. Assignments that are disconnected from the principal's personal experience are less likely to engage them or support their learning.

As mentioned above, facilitation is a critical component of the OPD. The facilitator needs to be adept with the technology used in the OPD, an expert in the course content, and an excellent communicator. Communication skills would include using online modalities ranging from email to video conferencing, as well as being able to read and interpret communication from and among participants. Thus, providing facilitators with the training and support they need to be successful is likely a prerequisite to participant success in OPD. Facilitators hold the key to supporting individual participants and building a learning community. Initially, facilitators have to establish the norms and expectations for participants. Miscommunication and misalignment of expectations can quickly derail the OPD and discourage individual participants. After initially setting the expectations, the facilitator needs to "read the room" frequently to get a sense of where individual participants are and be responsive as well as proactive. Emails and questions directed at the facilitator should be answered within one business day, and the feedback on student work should be prompt and meaningful. Facilitators themselves should also solicit feedback on a regular basis to inform their approach and course design.

Feedback from participants provides insights that may be missed by the facilitators and OPD designers. Furthermore, OPDs should continually evolve based on the participants' needs. If an instructional leadership OPD program is to grow and last, content will need to change periodically, and instructional approaches may need to change over time. Though feedback at the completion of a course is important, responding to participant feedback during a course may be equally important. If participants have concerns or issues that are not addressed during the course, they may opt to drop out of the course, never providing potentially critical feedback, and ultimately sour on the idea of OPD. Responsiveness to participants during an OPD course is likely to increase their engagement in the course and build a stronger relationship between facilitator and participant, ultimately creating a better learning experience for the participating principal improving their learning and likelihood of enrolling in subsequent courses.

Feedback after the completion of a course can be used to promote principal reflection and shape future iterations of the OPD, as well as provide insight into the design of new OPDs that address principals' needs. A survey or reflective assignment designed to solicit feedback can also provide closure and help demonstrate participant growth and learning. How did their practice change? What did they see as their biggest challenges? What challenges did they overcome? And what challenges do they see ahead? Answers to these questions, as well as course content specific questions, can provide valuable information. The feedback collected can also support reflection by OPD facilitators and designers, promoting discussion and thinking around how to best address the needs of the participants.

FUTURE RESEARCH DIRECTIONS

There have been calls for closer examination of leadership preparation, and for connecting the ISLLC standards to specific curriculum designed to prepare school leaders for the challenges they face daily in schools (Barnett, 2004; Murphy & Vriesenga, 2006). Though some structures for administrative credential programs have been established, there appears to be little framework for effective in-service ongoing PD or OPD for principals. Developing a framework is important, but is also doubly challenging as participants in administrative credentialing programs are, in effect, a captive audience enrolled in classes they must complete. Pre-service programs may better lend themselves to investigation of participant learning and development than OPD programs, which are less common, though very important. Exploratory studies soliciting feedback from principals to identify areas of need (Spanneut, Tobin, & Ayers, 2012) have already been conducted. Taking Spanneut and colleagues' approach to guide content in OPD may create an OPD environment that can be examined and assessed. Examining OPD designed for rural and urban principals may be especially important. Subsequently, Identifying and testing approaches to principal OPD may offer practical insight and theory on how to best address the instructional leadership needs of principals.

CONCLUSION

Well designed and supported OPD may provide important learning opportunities for principals serving in the most challenging and isolated environments. Learning outcomes of the OPD are more likely to be reached when participants are engaged in discourse and feel they are a part of a learning community. Thus, with increased accessibility to OPD, principals have the opportunity to develop skills and practices that they otherwise would not have. Furthermore, the sharing of experiences, ideas, and peer-support in OPD promote communication that transcends geographic and temporal limitations, allowing for sharing of more diverse views and learning by participants. Designing, assessing, and evolving OPD focused on addressing principal's instructional leadership could improve their skills and practices and lead to improved classroom instruction. Considering the complex school and OPD landscapes in the design of OPD, along with the lived experience of participating principals can set the stage for meaningful learning and school improvement.

REFERENCES

Angelino, L. M., Williams, F. K., & Natvig, D. (2007). Strategies to engage online students and reduce attrition rates. *The Journal of Educators Online*, *4*(2), 1–14.

Barnett, D. (2004). School leadership preparation programs: Are they preparing tomorrow's leaders? *Education*, *125*, 121–129.

Barth, R. S. (1986). Principal centered professional development. *Theory into Practice*, *25*(3), 156–160. doi:10.1080/00405848609543218

Blase, J., & Blase, J. (2000). Effective instructional leadership. *Journal of Educational Administration*, *38*(2), 130–141. doi:10.1108/09578230010320082

Boerema, A. J. (2011). Challenging and supporting new leader development. *Educational Management Administration & Leadership*, *39*(5), 554–567. doi:10.1177/1741143211408451

Boyd, D., Grossman, P., Ing, M., Lankford, H., Loeb, S., & Wyckoff, J. (2011). The influence of school administrators on teacher retention decisions. *American Educational Research Journal*, *48*(2), 303–333. doi:10.3102/0002831210380788

Bozarth, J., Chapman, D. D., & LaMonica, L. (2004). Preparing for distance learning: Designing an online student orientation course. *Journal of Educational Technology & Society*, *7*, 87–106.

Carter, K. (2004). Online training: What's really working? *Technology & Learning*, *24*(10), 32–36.

Dash, S., Magidin de Kramer, R., O'Dwyer, L. M., Masters, J., & Russell, M. (2012). Impact of online professional development or teacher quality and student achievement in fifth grade mathematics. *Journal of Research on Technology in Education*, *45*(1), 1–26. doi:10.1080/15391523.2012.10782595

Desimone, L. M. (2009). Improving impact studies of teachers' professional development: Toward better conceptualizations and measures. *Educational Researcher*, *38*(3), 181–199. doi:10.3102/0013189X08331140

Drago-Severson, E. (2012). The need for principal renewal: The promise of sustaining principals through principal-to-principal reflective practice. *Teachers College Record*, *114*, 1–56. PMID:24013958

Duncan-Howell, J. (2010). Teachers making connections: Online communities as a source of professional learning. *British Journal of Educational Technology*, *41*(2), 324–340. doi:10.1111/j.1467-8535.2009.00953.x

Fairlie, R. W., & Robinson, J. (2012). *Experimental evidence on the effects of home computers on academic achievement among schoolchildren* (No. w19060). National Bureau of Economic Research. Retrieved from http://www.sole-jole.org/12192.pdf

Green, M., & Cifuentes, L. (2011). The effects of follow-up and peer interaction on quality of performance and completion of online professional development. *Journal of Interactive Learning Research, 22*, 85–109.

Greeno, J. G. (1998). The situativity of knowing, learning, and research. *The American Psychologist, 53*(1), 5–26. doi:10.1037/0003-066X.53.1.5

Grissom, J. (2011). Can good principals keep teachers in disadvantaged schools? Linking principal effectiveness to teacher satisfaction and turnover in hard-to-staff environments. *Teachers College Record, 113*, 2552–2585.

Grissom, J. A., & Loeb, S. (2011). Triangulating principal effectiveness: How perspectives of parents, teachers, and assistant principals identify the central importance of managerial skills. *American Educational Research Journal, 48*(5), 1091–1123. doi:10.3102/0002831211402663

Grissom, J. A., Loeb, S., & Master, B. (2013). Effective instructional time use for school leaders: Longitudinal evidence from observations of principals. *Educational Researcher, 42*(8), 433–444. doi:10.3102/0013189X13510020

Hallinger, P. (2005). Instructional leadership and the school principal: A passing fancy that refuses to fade away. *Leadership and Policy in Schools, 4*(3), 221–239. doi:10.1080/15700760500244793

Hallinger, P., & Murphy, J. F. (2013). Running on empty? Finding the time and capacity to lead learning. *NASSP Bulletin, 97*(1), 5–21. doi:10.1177/0192636512469288

Hawley, W. D., & Valli, L. (2000). Learner-centered professional development. *Phi Delta Kappa Center for Evaluation, Development, and Research, 27*, 7–10.

Heller, J. I., Daehler, K. R., Wong, N., Shinohara, M., & Miratrix, L. W. (2012). Differential effects of three professional development models on teacher knowledge and student achievement in elementary science. *Journal of Research in Science Teaching, 49*(3), 333–362. doi:10.1002/tea.21004

Howley, A., Chadwick, K., & Howley, C. (2002*). Networking for the nuts and bolts: The ironies of professional development for rural principals.* Paper presented at the Annual Meeting of the American Educational Research Association, New Orleans, LA.

Issa Lahera, A., Mendoza, M., & McManus, H. (2015). Developing authentic non-traditional principals to lead underserved student populations: The case of charter and autonomous school leadership academy. Journal of Authentic Leadership in Education, 4(2), 1-8.

Issa Lahera, A., Holzman, S., & Robinson, P. (2014). Ready to lead: Creating a pathway that ensures readiness. In A. H. Normore, K. Hamdan, & A. I. Lahera (Eds.), *Pathways to excellence: Developing and cultivating leaders for the cassroom and beyond* (pp. 117–137). Bingley, UK: Emerald Group Publishing. doi:10.1108/S1479-366020140000021017

Jacob, B. A. (2007). The challenges of staffing urban schools with effective teachers. *The Future of Children, 17*(1), 129–153. doi:10.1353/foc.2007.0005 PMID:17407926

Jones, K. R. (2013). Developing and implementing a mandatory online student orientation. *Journal of Asynchronous Learning Networks, 17*, 43–45.

Lave, J., & Wenger, E. (1991). *Situated learning: Legitimate peripheral participation*. Cambridge, UK: Cambridge University Press. doi:10.1017/CBO9780511815355

Lowes, S., Lin, P., & Wang, Y. (2007). Studying the effectiveness of the discussion forum in online professional development courses. *Journal of Interactive Online Learning, 6*(3), 181–210.

Markow, D., Macia, L., & Lee, H. (2013). *The MetLife survey of the American teacher: Challenges for school leadership*. New York, NY: Metropolitan Life Insurance Company.

Marks, H. M., & Printy, S. M. (2003). Principal leadership and school performance: An integration of transformational and instructional leadership. *Educational Administration Quarterly, 39*(3), 370–397. doi:10.1177/0013161X03253412

Means, B., Bakia, M., & Murphy, R. (2014). *Learning online: What research tells us about whether, when and how*. New York, NY: Routledge.

Mitra, S., & Dangwal, R. (2010). Limits to self-organising systems of learning - The Kalikuppam experiment. *British Journal of Educational Technology, 41*(5), 672–688. doi:10.1111/j.1467-8535.2010.01077.x

Murphy, J., & Vriesenga, M. (2006). Research on school leadership preparation in the United States: An analysis. *School Leadership & Management, 26*(2), 183–195. doi:10.1080/13634230600589758

Negroponte, N. (1996). *Being Digital*. New York, NY: Vintage.

Penuel, W. R., Fishman, B. J., Yamaguchi, R., & Gallagher, L. P. (2007). What makes professional development effective? Strategies that foster curriculum implementation. *American Educational Research Journal, 44*(4), 921–958. doi:10.3102/0002831207308221

Reeves, T. D., & Li, Z. (2012). Teachers' technological readiness for online professional development: Evidence from the US e-Learning for Educators initiative. *Journal of Education for Teaching, 38*, 389–406.

Salazar, P. S. (2007). The professional development needs of rural high school principals: A seven-state study. *Rural Educator, 28*(3), 20–27.

Spanneut, G., Tobin, J., & Ayers, S. (2012). Identifying the professional development needs of public school principals based on the interstate school leader licensure consortium standards. *NASSP Bulletin, 96*, 67–88. doi:10.1177/0192636512439230

Theobald, P. (2005). Urban and rural schools: Overcoming lingering obstacles. *Phi Delta Kappan, 87*(2), 116–122. doi:10.1177/003172170508700207

Vrasidas, C., & Zembylas, M. (2004). Online professional development: Lessons from the field. *Education + Training, 46*, 326–334. doi:10.1108/00400910410555231

Walker, A., & Qian, H. (2015). Review of research on school principal leadership in mainland China, 1998-2013: Continuity and change. *Journal of Educational Administration, 53*(4), 467–491. doi:10.1108/JEA-05-2014-0063

Warschauer, M. (2011). *Learning in the Cloud*. New York, NY: Teachers College Press.

Warschauer, M., Cotten, S. R., & Ames, M. G. (2011). One laptop per child birmingham: Case study of a radical experiment. *International Journal of Learning, 3*(2), 61–76. doi:10.1162/ijlm_a_00069

Youngs, P., & King, M. B. (2002). Principal leadership for professional development to build school capacity. *Educational Administration Quarterly, 38*(5), 643–670. doi:10.1177/0013161X02239642

ADDITIONAL READING

Anderson, T. (2008). *The theory and practice of online learning*. Athabasca, Alberta, Canada: Athabasca University Press.

Dede, C., Ketelhut, D. J., Whitehouse, P., Breit, L., & McCloskey, E. (2008). A research agenda for online teacher professional development. *Journal of Teacher Education*, *60*(1), 8–19. doi:10.1177/0022487108327554

Drago-severson, E. (2012). New Opportunities for Principal Leadership : Shaping School Climates for Enhanced Teacher Development. *Teachers College Record*, *114*, 1–44. PMID:24013958

Salmon, G. (2013). *E-tivities: The key to active online learning*. New York, NY: Routledge.

Spillane, J. P., Halverson, R., & Diamond, J. B. (2001). Investigating school leadership practice : A distributed perspective. *Educational Researcher*, *30*(3), 23–28. doi:10.3102/0013189X030003023

Tschannen-Moran, M. (2009). Fostering teacher professionalism in schools. *Educational Administration Quarterly*, *45*(2), 217–247. doi:10.1177/0013161X08330501

KEY TERMS AND DEFINITIONS

Asynchronous Communication: Communication that does not happen in real time, for example e-mail, or blogs, where messages are sent, and responded to at a later time.

Computer Mediated Communication: Any communication, synchronous or asynchronous that occurs over a computer, but now extending to other devices capable of communication over the internet including tablets, and phones.

Digital Literacy: Literacy across computerized devices and technologies, as well as programs, software. The ability to effectively navigate and communicate over the internet through various digital modalities.

Instructional Leadership: School leadership activities and focus on instruction. These activities include teacher instructional support, curriculum development and implementation, and assessment of instruction.

Online Professional Development (OPD): Professional development that is conducted over the internet. OPD can be synchronous or asynchronous, completely self-guided or guided by an instruction, facilitator, or participant, and can include a variety of instructional approaches, and communication technologies including video conferencing, videos, blogs, and group projects.

Rural Schools: Schools located significant distances away from urban centers that are often geographically isolated. Rural schools often serve large populations of poorer students. Rural schools are characterized by lower academic achievement than suburban schools, and many have high rates of student mobility.

Suburban Schools: Schools located away from urban centers that primarily serve more affluent, white and Asian students.

Synchronous Communication: Communication that takes place in real time, for example a phone conversation or video conference.

Transformational Leadership: Leadership approach or style characterized by inspiring and motivating followers.

Urban Schools: Schools located in or near urban centers, primarily serving poor and ethnically diverse students in densely populated areas. Urban schools are often characterized by lower academic achievement than suburban schools, and high rates of mobility by students.

Chapter 20
Engineering Students' Communication Apprehension and Competence in Technical Oral Presentations

Noor Raha Mohd Radzuan
Universiti Malaysia Pahang, Malaysia

Sarjit Kaur
Universiti Sains Malaysia, Malaysia

ABSTRACT

The demand for 21st century engineering graduates to be communicatively competent, particularly in English language, is increasing. Effective communication skills are one of the main competencies listed by the Malaysian Engineering Accreditation Council Policy with the expectation that all Malaysian engineering graduates will master it upon graduation. This involves skills in presenting information to technical and non technical audience through oral presentations. This chapter aims to examine engineering students' communication competence and their level of apprehension in delivering a technical oral presentation. Questionnaires, adapted from McCroskey's (1988) Self-Perceived Communication Competence and Richmond & McCroskey's (1988) Personal Report of Public Speaking Anxiety, were distributed to 193 final year Universiti Malaysia Pahang engineering students who were preparing for their Undergraduate Research presentation. The results of the study have direct and indirect implications to the teaching and learning of oral presentation skills among engineering undergraduates.

INTRODUCTION

In coping with rapid transformations in the fields of technology brought about by the effects of globalization and internationalization, Malaysia is focused on progressing and advancing actively towards extensive economic transformation towards achieving developed nation status by the year 2020. Having a dynamic business environment, technological advancements and well-developed infrastructure, Malaysia is indeed well positioned to play a role in today's competitive world. With current Malaysian strategic economic planning emphasizing on a knowledge-based economy, grooming human capital has become the major concern of the Malaysian government. Further-

DOI: 10.4018/978-1-4666-9970-0.ch020

more, as quality human capital is one of Malaysia's greatest assets, great emphasis has been accorded towards ensuring demands from expanding manufacturing and services sectors are met. In order to cater for the needs of these sectors, workforce supplied must not only be technically skillful, they must also be competent in using the global language, English. With the current emphasis on progressive knowledge economies, having sound technical knowledge and being highly proficient in English (especially in oral communication) have become critical skills for Malaysian employees to attain in today's increasingly globalized workplace contexts. Such crucial assets in the workforce will go a long way in helping Malaysia to play a more competitive role in ensuring that we do not get left out in the current social and economic environment.

BACKGROUND

Educational Policy on English Language in Malaysia

Realizing the importance of workforce to be highly proficient and competent in written and oral English, some changes to the educational policy regarding English language have been made by the Malaysian Ministry of Education such as the introduction of the Malaysian University English Test (MUET) in 2000 which aimed to enhance pre-university students' level of English language proficiency. Then, in 2003, English was used as the medium of instruction for Mathematics and Science subjects in secondary schools with the main intention of enhancing students' English language ability as part of their preparation before they enrolled in local universities in preparation to join the future workforce. However, the use of English to learn Math and Science was reverted in 2012 in all schools. Instead, more hours have been allocated to the teaching of English in an effort to strengthen mastery of the language. The

hotly debated issue of the declining standards of English proficiency among Malaysian students and university graduates has captured the attention of the Ministry of Education. Recently, the Education Minister, Tan Sri Muhyiddin Yassin announced that all Form Five students will need to obtain a compulsory pass in the English subject in the national examination (Sijil Pelajaran Malaysia; equivalent to the British 'O' level) in 2016. This policy implementation is seen as being vital in ensuring and encouraging Malaysian students to be bilingually proficient in Bahasa Malaysia and English (Singh, 2013).

To date, many studies attempting to establish the level of English proficiency among Malaysian undergraduates have been conducted. For instance, Pawanchik (2006) surveyed 120 matriculation students' English language proficiency levels. The findings show that almost 60% of the students achieved Band 1 (extremely limited user), Band 2 (limited user) or Band 3 (modest user) in their MUET scores. In another study conducted by Yasin et al. (2010) among 169 diploma and certificate students in one Malaysian Polytechnic found that more than 70% of the students only obtained low scores in the English subject in the Malaysian Certificate of Education (SPM) examination. Besides results in national examinations which signify the low level of English among Malaysian graduates, the students themselves reported that they encounterd problems in speaking English confidently as well as experiencing English communication apprehension (Sarudin, Zubairi & Ali, 2009; Radzuan, 2008). Despite the realization of the importance of good English language ability, many findings on Malaysian students' English ability raise much concern about the readiness of our graduates for the workplace. Research shows that the rate of unemployment among Malaysian graduates is attributed to their lack of technical skills and poor employability skills (Hanapi and Nordin, 2014; Ismail, Yussof, and Lai, 2011). They defined employability skills as "the quality and personal insights which a graduate should have"

(p. 1058) and it includes English communication skills and problem solving skills (Ismail, Yussof, and Lai, 2011). They further reported that employers demand highly competent English language communicators.

Oral English Communication Skills in the Workplace: Malaysian Context

The concept of today's increasingly borderless world makes it necessary for Malaysian graduates to be well exposed to a wide range of abilities as well as being highly proficient in English. English is the lingua franca or the global official language in both business and other corporate sectors in ASEAN countries, and it includes Malaysia (Kickpatrick, 2010). Azizan and Lee (2011) reported that most Malaysian employers demand that employees be proficient in the English language, both in oral and written communication. The findings were reported from a survey conducted by the Malaysian Employers Federation (MEF) in 2010. The data also shows that English communication skills are at the top list of requirements in job applicants followed by working experience, interpersonal skills and working commitment. Having high English language proficiency undoubtedly benefits both employees-to-be and current employees (Mavender and Shamsudin, 2012) and eventually helps uplift the companies' reputation and success.

Many research studies have been conducted to investigate English communicative needs in Malaysian professional contexts which emphasize on oral communication competence. In the business world for example, marketing personnel play important roles in developing the company especially in the areas of product promotions and product selling. A research study by Subramaniama and Harun (2012) reported that in a business environment, English is widely used in all spoken and written communication. For marketing personnel, having high proficiency in spoken English is an expected skill as they are required to carry out their job efficiently as they

need to explain clearly and convince their clients in product promotions and product selling. Kaur & Lee (2006) who investigated the oral communication needs of Information Technology (IT) personnel at the workplace found that majority IT personnel used English language to communicate with their co-workers. They further posited that English language is highly important in areas such as recruitment, promotion and professional development.

Similar findings were reported by Kassim and Ali (2010) and Radzuan et al. (2008) whereby it was found that being highly proficient in English not only helps engineering graduates to be recruited but also helps engineering professionals in future job promotions. Besides such functions, English is also used for internal and external communication as reported by Buang et al. (2003). They posited that English is frequently used by Malaysian engineers for various purposes and with different levels of staff. According to them, it includes activities such as giving oral reports to supervisors, communicating with colleagues and taking part in conferences. Another study that demonstrated the use of English among engineers in the workplace was conducted by Kassim and Ali (2010). The researchers gathered data from engineers who were in private and joint-venture multinational engineering companies in Malaysia. The findings illustrate the English is mostly used in communicative events such as teleconferencing, informal-related work discussions and meetings, giving oral presentations and networking.

Oral English Communication Competence

McCroskey and McCroskey (1988, p. 109) define communication competence as the 'adequate ability to pass along or give information; the ability to make known by talking or writing'. It is the ability of one person to transfer messages effectively in detail through both forms: speaking and writing. In the context of this study, the message is transformed using English as a second language (ESL hereafter). Salleh (2008, p. 305) summarizes communication competence as "one's adaptation of a communication situation by demonstrating skills in appropriating knowledge relevant to the communication situation and context". In most situations, people evaluate other persons' competency (for example, in teacher and students' relationship) through various assessment methods, but in some cases which are related to communication, the decision to communicate with other people is made based on the individual's perceptions of their own competency (McCroskey & McCroskey, 1988). Hence, to comprehend communication behaviour in detail, self-report measures were developed.

Several studies have been conducted to discover the elements of communication competence. A study by Grant (2004) shows that students perceived 'effectiveness', 'appropriateness' and 'confidence' as the main criteria for effective communication competence, while the 'quality of performance' reflected one's competency in communication (Almeida, 2004). Communication competence also is empirically proven to affect students' college success. A longitudinal study by Rubin, Graham and Mignerey (1990) on college students' communication competence discovered that during sophomore years, students' communication competence was rated low, but it increased when they were in junior and senior years. Results also indicated that communication competence was positively related to college success, where higher GPA scores were reported among students who claimed to be competent communicators.

Research studies on communication competence among second language (L2) students are limited. Recently, Yousef, Jamil and Razak (2013) studied the relationship between ESL learners' language learning communication strategies and communication competence, willingness to communicate, communication apprehension and motivation. Using Critical Factor Analysis (CFA), it was found that learners' motivation and the strategies used in their language learning

directly influence communication competence. Replicating Rojo-Laurilla's study (2007), Devi and Shahnaz (2008) conducted a study on communication competence and communication apprehension of ESL electrical engineering students in a public university in Malaysia. They found that students reported to have moderate communicative competence in all communication contexts such as public, dyad and groups as well as in communicating with strangers, acquaintances and friends and moderate communication apprehension and the results were similar to Rojo-Laurilla's (2007) findings. Another related study which aimed to discover Malaysian engineering students' communication competence found that despite facing communication and presentation skills challenges, the 23 engineering undergraduates were still highly motivated in delivering project presentations during their Industrial training period (Yusoff, 2010).

Engineering Communication

While there have been many research studies conducted on establishing a positive relationship between technical knowledge and an ability to communicate that knowledge, there has been less research done on the synergy among written, oral and visual communication in engineering. Similarly, fewer studies focus on the role of reflection about communication as part of engineering practice. Offering engineering education in today's globalized contexts require a re-examination of various curricular goals and practices in response to each country's social, economic and political change. There is now increasing diversity within the student population in many higher education settings in terms of 'cultural capital' especially in relation to "educational preparedness – linguistic competencies, numeracy, and visual and conceptual analytical competencies" (Archer, 2006, p. 452).

English has now become the chosen medium for communication in view of the fact that it is an international global language that is used in most economic transactions, including international engineering projects (Sharma, 2014). Idrus and Salleh (2008, p. 62) define oral communication as "communicating orally in a manner which is clear, fluent, and to the point, and which holds the audience attention, both in groups and one-to-one situations". Crosling and Ward (2002, p. 45) posited that "oral communication is as integral to and as powerful in the workplace as it is in the societal life of humans". They further claim that "the success of oral communication depends on the parties sharing background knowledge and assumptions, and miscommunication can result if there is a mismatch". Therefore, it is of utmost important that the message delivered, both through oral or written, is well understood by the audience.

Challenges in Delivering Effective Oral English Presentations

In a presentation, the speaker is presenting information and communicating meaning to audience and it is vital that the information is understood and appreciated (Morell, 2015). This clearly shows that being highly competent in English language helps the presenter to successfully deliver his/her message across.

One of the critical success factors for 21st century business to flourish and for an individual worker to be successful in his career is being highly competent in oral presentations (Sharma, 2014; Evans, 2013; Berjano, Sales-Nebot & Lozano-Nietoc, 2013). From Evan's (2013) survey with professionals in the business sector in Hong Kong, it was highlighted that they faced several challenges in giving effective oral English presentations. They include mainly the structuring of the presentation, specifically the part in engaging the interest of the audience. Besides that, they also faced problems in the Question and Answer session, particularly in handling questions promptly and sounding authoritative and surprisingly, they also encountered problems in communicating informally during the presentations. In addition,

designing proper and effective slides for presentation was another challenge faced by these business professionals. However, in most instances students find oral presentation tasks crucial and demanding (Berjano, Sales-Nebot and Lozano-Nietoc, 2013). Radzuan (2013) reported that among the dominant factors for engineering undergraduates to be highly anxious in delivering oral presentations are lack of presentation skills and low level of English proficiency.

The delivery of an oral presentation can be a source of extreme anxiety (King, 2002). Woodrow (2006) investigated second language speaking anxiety as experienced by English learners studying in Australia. Findings showed that the major stressor in-class situation by respondents who were mainly from Asian countries was delivering oral presentations. Most of them (51.1%) reported having physiological reactions (e.g. sweating, racing heart, blushing) and cognitive reactions (e.g. worrying about performance and mind going blank) (48.9%), followed by behavioural reactions (fidgeting, stuttering and talking too much) (34%) when delivering oral presentations.

Kakepoto et. al. (2012) conducted a study to investigate the factors that influence ineffective oral presentations. A total of 25 engineering students in Pakistan universities were involved in the study where their presentations were recorded and assessed based on specific rubrics. It was found that majority students (53%) possessed low level of self-confidence and 87% of them experienced anxiety when delivering presentations. The other factor that contributed to ineffective oral presentations was students' knowledge in presentation skills. Majority students (64%) were found to possess limited presentation skills that hindered them in presenting effective oral presentations.

Research in foreign/second language learning reported that deficiency in the target language has eminently contributed to learners' anxiety and apprehension (Horwitz et al., 1986). This is supported by a study conducted by Radzuan and Kaur (2011) which revealed that one of the factors affecting engineering students' ability to deliver technical oral presentations in English was their English language proficiency. From the interviews carried out with the final year engineering students, it was reported that these students had insufficient English vocabulary and they feared that their messages were not conveyed clearly to the audience. These factors heightened their level of apprehension in delivering technical oral presentations.

Similar findings were reported in a study carried out by Mustafa and Zain (2009). They found that students' lack of confidence in speaking in English (L2) was attributed to insufficient vocabulary and fear of making mistakes in front of their peers. In the investigation of L2 learners' anxiety during oral presentations, a study conducted by Hizwari et al. (2008) among diploma students in a Malaysian technical university revealed that factors such as fear of negative evaluation and classroom anxiety hindered the learners intention to communicate orally and hence, their unwillingness adversely affected their performance ability.

As anxiety in giving oral presentation has become the focus of concern among many L2 learners and instructors, many research studies propose alternative approaches to further develop and enhance both L2 learners' oral communication skills and oral presentation skills (Webster, 2002; King, 2002). Bulca and Safaei (2013) reported that the step-by-step approach introduced to the management and arts students who were taking a public presentation course helped the students to eliminate their feeling of anxiousness in delivering public presentations. Furthermore, students' familiarization with the tasks was improved, learners were able to build rapport with their audience and they enjoyed their presentations with their team members. In addition to that, to deliver an effective presentation at an international conference, Hashemi and Hokmabadi (2011) posited that certain presentation structures and strategies need to be followed by the presenter. These include all the phases namely introduction phase, information phase, persuasion phase and conclusion phase. Also, conference presenters need to place emphasis on elements of non-verbal communication such as eye contact, body gestures and voice projection.

The use of technology such as Microsoft Powerpoint can also aid students' technical presentations to be more effective due to increased self confidence in the students (Rose, 2002). With some insights and strategies from communication scholars to overcome public speaking anxieties and reduce nervousness, instructors can certainly better prepare students for oral presentations.

This chapter aims to examine the relationship between engineering students' self-perceived communication competence and anxiety in delivering technical oral presentations. The term technical oral presentation in this paper refers to engineering undergraduates' final year project presentations which are mandatory for graduation. According to DiSanza and Legge (2003, p. 198; cited in Bhattacharyya & Sargunan, 2009), a technical presentation refers to "a prepared formal presentation on scientific, engineering, technological, business types, regulatory, legal, managerial, or social scientific information topics to non-expert audience". A variety of common presentations that fit under the rubric of technical communication include laboratory presentations, feasibility reports, progress/status reports, survey presentations, training lectures, and business reports (2003, p. 198). Hence, the oral presentations in this study are a form of technical oral presentation in technical communication.

MAIN FOCUS OF THE CHAPTER

The Study

This study aims to investigate engineering students' perceived communication competence and their level of apprehension in delivering technical oral presentations. Two sets of questionnaires were administered to 193 final year chemical engineering students in a public technical university in the East Coast of Malaysia. Prior to answering the questionnaires, the students were briefed on the purpose of the study and instructions were given on how to complete the two sets of questionnaires.

The Sample

The participants were the final year students from the Faculty of Chemical Engineering and Natural Resources (FCENR), Universiti Malaysia Pahang (UMP hereafter), the first public technical university in the East Coast of Malaysia. In the faculty, there are 3 different Bachelor programs offered: Bachelor in Chemical Engineering (Chemical), Bachelor in Chemical Engineering (Biotechnology) and Bachelor in Chemical Engineering (Gas). Chemical engineering and biotechnology are the two niche areas which are given attention by UMP. A total of 193 students were registered in the Undergraduate Research Project 2 (BKB4944) course. In order for engineering undergraduates to graduate in UMP, they need to complete a research project which requires them to report technical content in written and spoken form. They were given two semesters to complete the project. In the first semester, the students will work on their proposal, and at the end of the semester, they are required to submit a proposal consisting of Chapter 1 (Introduction), Chapter 2 (Literature Review) and Chapter 3 (Methodology) and present their proposal orally to their lecturers and fellow friends. In the second semester, the students will work on their project and write a full report which consists of Chapter 1 (Introduction), Chapter 2 (Literature Review), Chapter 3 (Methodology), Chapter 4 (Data analysis) and Chapter 5 (Conclusion) and later in Week 13, present their findings to their lecturers.

Measurement Instruments

Communication Competence

The *Self-Perceived Communication Competence* (SPCC hereafter) survey developed by McCroskey & McCroskey (1988) assesses self-perceived competence in four contexts: dyadic, meeting, group and public – and with respect to three targets – stranger, acquaintance, and friend. This instrument has strong content validity (Rosenfeld, Grant III & McCroskey, 1995) and there is evidence for construct validity as well (Chesebro et al., 1992). McCroskey & McCroskey (1988, p. 110) posited that "in the case of communication competence, self-report scales may be very useful if we want to know how competent the person thinks he/she is". In this study, the participants completed the questionnaires by indicating their level of competence in each given context, with 0 as the lowest score and 100 as the highest. Each communication context indicates a possible range of level of competence.

Presentation Anxiety

The second instrument used in this study is the Personal Report of Public Speaking Anxiety (PRPSA hereafter). Richmond & McCroskey (1988) developed the PRPSA as a self assessment on the level of anxiety in delivering public speaking. For the purpose of this study, some amendments have been made to the instrument, that is all "public speaking" or "speech" words were replaced with "technical presentations" which closely denote the type of presentation the students are delivering.

This instrument consists of 34 statements gauging participants' feelings associated with giving a presentation. In this study, the participants were asked to complete 34 statements using the following five-point rating scale: *(1) strongly agree, (2) agree (3) undecided (4) disagree, and (5) strongly disagree.* According to Richmond and McCroskey (1998), the PRPSA scores fall into five categories with a minimum score of 34 and maximum score of 170. Below is the range of scores and their indication:

- 34–84 = low anxiety (5%);
- 85–92 = moderately low anxiety (5%);
- 93–110 = moderate anxiety (20%);
- 111–119 = moderately high anxiety (30%); and
- 120–170 = high anxiety (40%).

Total scores are calculated by adding the 22 positive items, then summing the scores of the other 12 reversed items and finally substracting the total from 132. For example, if the scores range from 120 to 170, it indicates high anxiety in the student when delivering a presentation. This instrument is highly reliable (alpha estimates >.90). The reliability of the scale in this investigation is.89.

Data Collection Procedures and Data Analysis

The data collection procedures started with the selection of participants. A total of 193 questionnaires were administered to the final year chemical engineering students, but only 140 questionnaires were returned and analyzed. The gender breakdown was 49.3% males and 50.7% females. The subjects in the sample represented three different programs offered by FCENR, with 49.3% from Pure Chemical programme and the rest were from Biotechnology (37.1%) and Gas Technology (13.6%) respectively.

Descriptive Analysis

Table 1 displays the number and percentage of respondents who were classified as possessing high, moderate and low presentation anxiety and

self-perceived communication competence based on the PRPSA and SPCC respectively. The data illustrate that although 24 respondents believed they had good communication competence, only 12 respondents (8.6%) reported having low anxiety in giving presentations. The results also show that 28.5% of the respondents reported having moderately high and high anxiety during giving presentations. About 13.5% of respondents who reported having 'high' levels of anxiety during oral technical presentations also perceived themselves as having poor communication competence. The data also revealed that majority of the respondents rated themselves as having 'moderate' anxiety and 'moderate' levels of communication competence.

Table 2 displays the mean and the standard deviation of the students' perceived communication competence. The mean total SPCC score is 72.6929 which is moderate with a standard deviation of 13.56360. The minimum total SPCC is 27.67 and the maximum total SPCC is 100.00. It indicates that the respondents rated themselves as being moderately competent communicators.

Table 1. Number and percentage of respondents classified as high, moderate or low on PRPSA and SPCC total scores

Scale	Respondents
PRPSA	
Low anxiety	12 (8.6%)
Moderately low anxiety	18 (12.9%)
Moderate anxiety	70 (50%)
Moderately high anxiety	21 (15%)
High anxiety	19 (13.5%)
SPCC	
Good self-perceived communication competence	24 (17.1%)
Moderate self-perceived communication competence	98 (70.0%)
Poor self-perceived communication competence	18 (12.9%)

Table 2. SPCC scores

	N	Minimum	Maximum	Mean	Std. Deviation
SPCC	140	27.67	100.00	72.6929	13.56360
Valid N (listwise)	140				

Table 3 displays the mean and the standard deviation of the students' oral technical presentation anxiety. The mean technical presentation anxiety score among the students is 103.15 (moderate) with a standard deviation of 15.43. The minimum technical presentation anxiety score is 57 (low) whereas the maximum score is 142 (high). Thus, we can conclude that technical presentation anxiety does exist among the students but at a moderate level.

Table 4 illustrates the correlation analysis between SPCC and PRPSA. The Pearson Correlation Coefficient is significant at the 0.01 level. This shows that there is a linear relationship between SPCC and PRPSA. The Pearson Correlation Coefficient is -0.424, indicating moderate strength of association and at the same time indicating that PRPSA and SPCC are inversely related. Thus, we can conclude that the higher the students' perception of their communication competence, there is a possibility of a lower score for technical oral presentation anxiety. Therefore, it is apparent that when students have more confidence on competence, they have less presentation anxiety.

FUTURE RESEARCH DIRECTIONS

This study was conducted with several limitations. Firstly, this study did not empirically examine the relationship between presentation anxiety, self-perceived communication competence and students' grades in Undergraduate Research Project oral presentations. It is believed that such a study would be valuable to better clarify the findings of this study. Secondly, this study applied the quantitative approach; therefore, better data would have been yielded if the qualitative approach was systematically combined in this study.

CONCLUSION

The extant literature on engineering students' language and skills repertoires indicate that good language proficiency and effective presentation skills are inextricably intertwined in engineering students' repertoires. Arising from the findings of this case study, there is scope for overall improvements among final year technical oral presentations. The findings suggest that engineering lecturers and language teachers can collaborate and work with students in making them aware of the ways in which they can construct effective scientific academic discourse, and the ways they can use their oral technical presentation skills to insert their own voice into their presentations. The findings of this study clearly show that presentation anxiety exists among engineering students

Table 3. PRPSA scores

	N	Minimum	Maximum	Mean	Std. Deviation
PRPSA	140	57.00	142.00	103.1571	15.43483
Valid N (listwise)	140				

Table 4. Correlations between SPCC and PRPSA

		SPCC	PRPSA
SPCC	Pearson Correlation	1	-.424(**)
	Sig. (2-tailed)	.	.000
	N	140	140
PRPSA	Pearson Correlation	-.424(**)	1
	Sig. (2-tailed)	.000	.
	N	140	140

** Correlation is significant at the 0.01 level (2-tailed).

but at a moderate level. Similar findings were reported on engineering students' self-perceived communication competence in English language where most of them perceived themselves to be 'moderately' competent. Furthermore, it was established that students with high communication competence usually experience low presentation anxiety. Notwithstanding related concerns, fluency in English language and adequate technical knowledge could influence students' level of confidence in delivering technical oral presentations. Effective oral communication assessments can be designed so that such assessments are part of the engineering course. Indeed, a combination of both oral and visual elements in technical oral presentations can aid engineering students towards presenting technical problems and solutions that mirror workplace scenarios.

The fact that English is a lingua franca in most professional fields such as engineering and IT, being proficient English communicators is indeed necessary in today's globalized workplaces. Therefore, more effective English communication instructions for Malaysian engineering students should be developed and improved to further enhance students' quality and competitiveness in the global job market.

REFERENCES

Archer, A. (2006). A Multimodal Approach to Academic 'Literacies': Problematising the Visual/Verbal Divide. *Language and Education*, *20*(6), 449–462. doi:10.2167/le677.0

Azizan, H., & Lee, Y. M. (2011, April 12). Minding our language. *The Star*.

Berjano, E., Sales-Nebot, L., & Lozano-Nietoc, A. (2013). Improving professionalism in the engineering curriculum through a novel use of oral presentations. *European Journal of Engineering Education*, *38*(2), 121–130. doi:10.1080/03043797.2012.745829

Bhattacharyya, E., & Sargunan, R. A. (2009). *The technical oral presentation skills and attributes in engineering education: Stakeholder perceptions and university preparation in a Malaysian context*. Paper presented at the 20th Australasian Association for Engineering Education Conference, University of Adelaide.

Buang, Z., Elangsegaran, R., Jano, Z., Ahmad, S., & Husain, K. (2003). *An investigation on the nature of spoken English among engineers in Malaysian industry*. Kolej Universiti Teknikal Kebangsaan Malaysia.

Bulca, M., & Safaeib, L. A. (2013). Public presentation: Who fears? *Procedia: Social and Behavioral Sciences*, *70*, 574–579. doi:10.1016/j.sbspro.2013.01.095

Chesebro, J. W., McCroskey, J. C., Atwater, D. F., Bahrenfuss, R. M., Cawelti, G., Gaudino, J. L., & Hodges, H. (1992). Communication apprehension and self-perceived communication competence of at-risk students. *Communication Education*, *41*(4), 345–360. doi:10.1080/03634529209378897

Crosling, G., & Ward, I. (2002). Oral communication: Workplace needs and uses of business graduates employees. *English for Specific Purposes*, *21*(1), 41–57. doi:10.1016/S0889-4906(00)00031-4

Devi, S. I., & Shahnaz, F. F. (2008). Oral communication apprehension and communicative competence among electrical engineering undergraduate in UTeM. *Journal of Human Capital Development*, *1*(1), 1–10.

DiSanza, J. R., & Legge, N. J. (2003). *Business and Professional Communication: Plans, Processes and Performance*. Boston, MA: Allyn & Bacon.

Engineering Accreditation Council. (2007). *Engineering Programme Accreditation Manual*. Kuala Lumpur: Board of Engineers Malaysia.

Evans, S. (2013). ''Just wanna give you guys a bit of an update'': Insider perspectives on business presentations in Hong Kong. *English for Specific Purposes*, *32*(4), 195–207. doi:10.1016/j.esp.2013.05.003

Hanapi, Z., & Nordin, M. S. (2014). Unemployment among Malaysia graduates: Graduates' attributes, lecturers' competency and quality of education. *Procedia: Social and Behavioral Sciences*, *112*, 1056–1063. doi:10.1016/j.sbspro.2014.01.1269

Hashemi, M., & Hokmabadi, M. (2011). Effective English Presentation and Communication in an International Conference. *Procedia: Social and Behavioral Sciences*, *30*, 2104–2111. doi:10.1016/j.sbspro.2011.10.409

Hizwari, S., Ahmad, I., Hifzurrahman, A., & NorHaizar, W. (2008). *Second language anxiety among diploma students in Technical University (Universiti Malaysia Perlis)*. Paper presented at the International Conference on the Roles of the Humanities and Social Sciences in Engineering 2008 (ICOHSE08). Accessed online on 10 March 2014 from http://hdl.handle.net/123456789/5831

Horwitz, E. K., Horwitz, M. B., & Cope, J. (1986). Foreign language classroom anxiety. *Modern Language Journal*, *70*(2), 125–132. doi:10.1111/j.1540-4781.1986.tb05256.x

Idrus, H., & Salleh, R. (2008). Perceived self-efficacy of Malaysian ESL Engineering and Technology students on their speaking ability and its pedagogical implications. In B. H. Tan, K. E. Tan & P. Nair (Eds.), The English Teacher (Vol. 31, pp. 61-75). Selangor: Malaysian English Language Teaching Association (MELTA).

Ismail, R., Yussof, I., & Lai, W. S. (2011). Employers' perceptions on graduates in Malaysian services sector. *International Business Management*, *5*(3), 184–193. doi:10.3923/ibm.2011.184.193

Kakepoto, I., Habil, H., Omar, N. A. M., & Said, H. (2012). Factors that Influence Oral Presentations of Engineering Students of Pakistan for Workplace Environment. *Information and Knowledge Management*, *2*(7), 70–78.

Kassim, H., & Ali, F. (2010). English communicative events and skills needed at the workplace: Feedback from the industry. *English for Specific Purposes*, *29*(3), 168–182. doi:10.1016/j.esp.2009.10.002

Kaur, S., & Lee, S. H. (2006). Analysing workplace oral communication needs in English among IT graduates. *English for Specific Purposes World*. Accessed online on 20 April 2010 from http://www.esp-world/info

King, J. (2002). Preparing EFL learners for oral presentations. *Dong Hwa Journal of Humanistic Studies*, *4*, 401–418.

Kirkpatrick, A. (2010). *English as a lingua franca in ASEAN. A multilingual model*. Hong Kong, China: Hong Kong University Press. doi:10.5790/hongkong/9789888028795.001.0001

Mavender, K., & Shamsudin, S. (2012). Writing professional discourse: The challenges faced by Malaysian engineers. *The Asian ESP Journal*, *8*(4), 125–161.

McCroskey, J. C., & McCroskey, L. L. (1988). Self-report as an approach to measuring communication competence. *Communication Research Reports*, *5*(2), 108–113. doi:10.1080/08824098809359810

Morell, T. (2015). International conference paper presentations: A multimodal analysis to determine effectiveness. *English for Specific Purposes*, *37*, 137–150. doi:10.1016/j.esp.2014.10.002

Mustafa, R., & Zain, S. N. M. (2009). Language anxiety in a remedial English language course: What teachers need to know. *Journal of Linguistics Studies*, *2*(1), 56–68.

Pawanchik, S. (2006). Improving Students Proficiency in English. In The 2006 European College Teaching & Learning Conference, Florence, Italy.

Radzuan, N. R. M. (2013). *An analysis of technical oral presentation anxiety among engineering students in Universiti Malaysia Pahang.* (Unpublished PhD Thesis).

Radzuan, N. R. M., Ali, F., Kassim, H., Hashim, H., Osman, N., & Abid, R. (2008). Developing Speaking Skills Module for Engineering Students. *The International Journal of Learning.*, *14*(11), 61–70.

Radzuan, N. R. M., & Kaur, S. (2011). Technical Oral Presentations in English: Qualitative Analysis of Engineering Students' Sources of Anxiety. *Procedia: Social and Behavioral Sciences, 29*, 1436–1445. doi:10.1016/j.sbspro.2011.11.383

Richmond, V. P., & McCroskey, J. C. (1998). *Communication: Apprehension, Avoidance and Effectiveness* (5th ed.). Boston: Allyn and Bacon.

Rojo-Laurilla, M. A. (2007). English for maritime purposes: Communication apprehension and communicative competence among maritime students in the Philippines. *Reflections on English Language Teaching, 6*(2), 39–58.

Rose, A. T. (2002, November). Improving student skills in multimedia presentations. In *Frontiers in Education Conference* (Vol. 2, pp. F1F-8). doi:10.1109/FIE.2002.1158134

Rosenfeld, L. B., Grant, C. H. III, & McCroskey, J. C. (1995). Communication apprehension and self-perceived communication competence of academically gifted students. *Communication Education, 44*(1), 79–89. doi:10.1080/03634529509378999

Rubin, R. B., Graham, E. E., & Mignerey, J. T. (1990). A longitudinal study of college students' communication competence. *Communication Education, 39*(1), 1–14. doi:10.1080/03634529009378783

Salleh, L. M. (2008). Communication competence: A Malaysian perspective. *Human Communication A Journal of the Pacific and Asian Communication Association, 11*(3), 303-312.

Sarudin, I., Zubairi, A. M., & Ali, A. M. (2009). *A comparative analysis of engineering students' problem in speaking and writing.* Paper presented at the 2nd International Conference of Teaching and Learning, INTI University College, Malaysia.

Sharma, M. (2014). English and Communication Skills for the 21st Century Engineers. *International Journal of Research in Advent Technology,* 86-89.

Singh, S. (2013, March 8). Muhyiddin: English a compulsory pass subject as early as 2016. *The Star.*

Subramaniama, G. K. J., & Harun, R. N. S. R. (2012). Marketing students' perceptions and their experiences during industrial training on English oral communication skills. *Procedia: Social and Behavioral Sciences, 66*, 283–289. doi:10.1016/j.sbspro.2012.11.270

Webster, F. (2002). A genre approach to oral presentation. *The Internet TESL Journal, 8*(7), 1-5. Retrieved online on 13 March 2010 from http://iteslj.org/Techniques/Webster-OralPresentation.html

Woodrow, L. (2006). Anxiety and speaking English as a second language. *RELC Journal, 37*(3), 308–328. doi:10.1177/0033688206071315

Yasin, A. Y. M., Shaupil, W. M. H. W. M., Mukhtar, A. M., Ab Ghani, N. I., & Rashid, F. (2010). The Englisg Proficiency of Civil Engineering Students at a Malaysian Polytechnic. *Asian Social Science, 6*(6), 161. doi:10.5539/ass.v6n6p161

Yousef, R., Jamil, H., & Razak, N. (2013). Willingness to Communicate in English: A Study of Malaysian Pre-Service English Teachers. *English Language Teaching, 6*(9), 205–216. doi:10.5539/elt.v6n9p205

Yusoff, M. (2010). Analysing communication competence in oral presentations: Engineering students' experiences. *Journal of Human Capital Development*, *3*(1), 99–117.

KEY TERMS AND DEFINITIONS

Engineering Students: Final year chemical engineering students who are currently working on Final Year Project (FYP) and studying in Universiti Malaysia Pahang, Malaysia.

Perception: A belief or opinion held by one person on a matter.

Presentation Skills: Skills that are needed to deliver presentations effectively for instance, eye contact and body language.

Self-Perceived Communication Competence: A person's perception on how competent he/ she thinks is in communicating in English language.

Technical Oral Presentation Anxiety: The feeling of fear and worry in delivering technical oral presentations.

Technical Oral Presentation: A prepared formal oral presentation on Final Year Project delivered by final year undergraduate engineering students.

Undergraduate Research Project: A two-semester course which requires engineering students to work on a project individually as part of the fulfilment of graduation requirements.

Section 4

Optimizing Performance:
Enhancing Relational Development
through Trust and Communication

Chapter 21
Developing Trust within International Teams:
The Impacts of Culture on Team Formation and Process

Kurt Kirstein
City University of Seattle, USA

ABSTRACT

The widespread use of international teams has been driven by an unprecedented need to draw upon varied talents of employees from around the globe in a manner that is both organizationally and financially feasible. Despite the importance of technologies to enable such teams, their success depends largely on the levels of intra-team trust and collaboration they are able to establish throughout the life of their projects. Team members on international teams may differ substantially on a number of cultural dimensions including preferences for individualistic versus collective teamwork, power distance, uncertainty avoidance, and contextual communication. This chapter will investigate how these four cultural dimensions are likely to impact trust within an international team. Suggestions that team leaders can utilize to address these cultural dimensions are also presented.

INTRODUCTION

Given the increasing globalization of business practices, and the difficulties associated with international and even domestic travel, organizations are seeking ways to realize the benefits of multinational collaboration without the undue inconvenience and expense that have typically been associated with globalization efforts. Improving information and communication technologies have provided the means by which multinational companies can move beyond the geographic constraints that were formerly associated with

traditional face-to-face business models. Such technologies enable companies to draw upon the contributions of employees or associates from around the world as they develop creative products for a global market. These advances have opened the door to new and evolving levels of collaboration though the use of international teams, which can be understood as a group of people who work together, via technology, toward a shared purpose despite space, time, and organization boundaries (Lipnack & Stamps, 2000). International teams cross multiple domains to streamline a company's operations by maximizing personnel efficiency

DOI: 10.4018/978-1-4666-9970-0.ch021

and adding flexibility (Hanover Research Council, 2008). The complexity of international teams is increasing steadily as the structure of global organizations shift. What was formerly a dual or tri-nation organizational hierarchy has now evolved into truly globally networked organization. What was formerly an arrangement of organizations, each with its own national identity, has shifted into new entities that create and employ novel transnational strategies (Harvey, Mcintyre, Moeller & Sloan III, 2012).

Certainly, international teams could not exist, or be effective, without the proper technology infrastructure to support them. Yet, as important as technology is to an international team, it is merely a tool to carry forward the team's purpose. What is more important is that the team is clearly organized, with a unified purpose, and that it is capable of drawing upon the strengths of all its members. Given the international variances of these teams, cultural considerations become a significant concern and may even be a more important factor in the team's success than its chosen technologies or working processes.

The ways in which team members communicate and contribute ideas will, to a large part, be driven by their cultural orientation toward interpersonal interactions (Sosik & Jung, 2002). The level of initiative demonstrated by team members may have much more to do with their attitudes toward authority and power than anything related to personal motivation (Hofstede & Hofstede, 2005). Even the content and completeness of communication are impacted by norms that vary widely from one culture to the next. Failure to understand culturally-based differences toward key activities that will be encountered in team formation and process can pose a serious threat to the generation and maintenance of intra-team trust which is critical to the success of international teams (Dubé & Paré, 2001; Gibson & Manuel, 2003).

This chapter will review key considerations of cultural relevance to intra-team trust on international teams. Specifically, this chapter will ad-

dress how a team's development and maintenance of intra-team trust is impacted by its members' views on individualism versus collectivism, power distance, uncertainty avoidance, and contextually based communication. Each of these cultural dimensions is presented in the sections that follow along with a list of suggestions that team leaders and members can utilize to minimize the adverse impacts that these dimensions can bring to a team.

BACKGROUND

Team formation can be a challenging process and one that takes time. Often, the process of forming the team and bringing its members together to accomplish a difficult task can take longer than the actual task itself (Wallace, 2001). Peck (1987) used the term pseudocommunity to refer to the ways in which a team interacts when it is first formed. The team will attempt to become an instant community through cordial interactions and the denial of differences. Yet, Peck points out that such reticence toward the recognition of individual differences does not support the development of novel solutions to pressing problems. The team must progress beyond its pseudocommunity stage and this requires the acknowledgement of different traits, attitudes, experience, and cultural norms.

Increasingly, large numbers of employees serve on teams with members whose locations, work processes, and collaboration technologies differ from their own. Teams are assembled and most complete the bulk of their work using communication and information technologies such as email, audio and video conferencing, and other technologies that allow information exchange across distances and time zones. International teams differ in the range of communication technologies used and their purposes for using them. Some tools may be for cohesiveness, some are used to facilitate the building of trust through social interaction and development, some are used to demonstrate that team members are meeting goals, and others are utilized to ensure satisfactory team communication (Timmerman & Scott, 2006).

International teams bring benefits and challenges (Dubé & Paré, 2001). The advantages of such teams are that they can create culturally synergistic solutions, enhance creativity and cohesion among team members, promote a greater acceptance of new ideas, and, hence, provide a competitive advantage for multinational companies. The disadvantages are that they tend to have more time-consuming decision-making processes and when miscommunication and misunderstandings occur, stress and conflicts among team members are heightened and less easily dispelled (De Pillis & Furumo, 2007; Zakaria, Amelinckx, & Wilemon, 2004).

It is important to note that virtualness of an international team is a matter of degree - not a distinct category (Timmerman & Scott, 2006). This creates the possibility for substantial differences in the ways that international teams are structured and managed. There are also vast differences in the processes and technologies that are used and the purposes for using them. Ideally, the methods selected will be those best suited to the needs of the team. In many cases, the chances of an International team reaching a positive outcome are dependent upon the team's ability to establish a sense of community and doing so requires that each team member feels a sense of belonging to and trust in the team (Gibson & Manuel, 2003).

Serving as a member of an international team needs to be an intentional activity; it requires team members to overcome challenges that are not present in proximal, local teams (Cohen & Gibson, 2003). Much has been written about the communication challenges that arise when team members do not have facial or physical cues to depend on when interpreting messages from their distant colleagues (Gibson & Manuel, 2003; Nunamaker, Reinig, & Briggs, 2009; De Pillis & Furumo, 2007).

A further complication to communication has to do with language. Despite the fact that English is often the default language used by all team members, there remain a number of problems resulting from language nuances, subtleties, and even the use of colloquialisms that are not universally understood. Additionally, international team members face competing demands for their attention from their international team, from their immediate workplace, and from the practical challenges of assimilating new technologies into their daily routines (Numaker, Reinig, & Briggs, 2009).

In a global workplace, managers face increasing difficulties due, in part, to the nature of globalized work. Increasingly, complex and subtle differences among employees caused by cultural differences are appearing in the function of teams, business units, and corporate identities. According to Early and Mosakowski (2004), "our need to understand how work differs across cultures, how diverse teams function, and how deals are negotiated across corporate and national boundaries has exploded in recent years" (p. 151). And while many look toward emerging and expanding communication and information technologies as the mechanisms that make such collaboration possible, others would argue that technological tools are not nearly as important as the human element of international teams. In fact, most would argue that "while technology is important, the human component of [international] teams is the most important piece of a functioning group regardless of institutional profile" (Hanover Research Council, 2008, p. 2). An important way in which these human components impact team performance relates to the interpersonal and cultural dimensions that each member brings to the team.

Hofstede and Hofstede (2005) identified a number of dimensions that differ between cultures and are important considerations for international teams. Their lists includes dimensions that address collective versus individualistic orientations, power distance, uncertainty avoidance, masculine versus feminine approaches to team interaction, and differences in short term versus long term focus. They argued that cultures tend to differ on these five dimensions in predictable patterns although it was acknowledged that these differences are general patterns and do not serve to define the specific behaviors of individuals. Yet, the patterns are consistent enough that predictions can be made about the likely behaviors of team members from specific cultural backgrounds.

Hofstede and Hofstede (2005) also argue that, from a very young age, individuals develop their values and worldviews through frameworks that are culturally specific. All future knowledge, skills, and experiences are based upon these foundations. The extent to which individuals will be successful in their interactions with those of differing cultural backgrounds may be determined by their ability to look beyond their own foundations in order to recognize alternative worldviews which are as deeply rooted as their own (Leinonen, Järvelä, & Häkkinen, 2005). Chen, Chittoor, and Vissa (2015) highlighted the importance and impact of traditional social structures upon commonly accepted western approaches to business that are often employed by multinationals. They pointed out the importance of acknowledging the subtle, yet significant differences that social and cultural patterns can make.

Hall (1976) contributed to the examination of the impact of cultural dimensions in his discussion of high and low context communication. Individuals from high context cultures rely on unstated or connotative information as a key part of any message. Those from low context cultures attempt to embed all meaning into the message itself. When considering the varying communication styles of international team members from around the world, the relevance of the use of context becomes clear. It is even more important to consider context when nonverbal cues are absent (De Pillis & Furumo, 2007; Clapp-Smith, Vogelgesand, & Avey, 2009).

The remaining sections of this chapter will examine, in depth, the possible impacts of four cultural dimensions on international teams. Three dimensions are from Hofstede and Hof-

stede (2005). These include collectivism versus individualism, power distance, and uncertainty avoidance. From Hall (1976), the dimension of contextual communication will be examined.

Hofstede and Hofstede's (2005) dimension regarding a masculine versus feminine orientation is not reviewed in this chapter in relation to intra-team trust in international teams not because it is not relevant but because the manner in which "feminine" behaviors may manifest themselves in an international team would make them difficult to distinguish from behaviors that are founded in cultural norms related to high power distance or collective orientations. For example, the reserved nature of a collectivist approach may appear, in a virtual context, indistinguishable from the modesty that is associated with a feminine orientation (Hofstede, 1985). The differing yet intermingled nuances of collective practices, high power distance, and feminine orientations are a possible area of future exploration but are outside the scope of this chapter. Likewise, it can be assumed that the dimension regarding a short term versus a long-term view of time would have complex impacts on team member interaction. Yet, given that teamwork is often short term in nature, this dimension would be much more important and difficult to track. This topic, too, deserves exploration that is outside the scope of this chapter.

INTRA-TEAM TRUST IN INTERNATIONAL TEAMS

As Zakaria, et al. (2004) point out, many organizations that use international teams consider human factors, such as trust and a defined purpose, to be the elements most critical to long term success and are careful to avoid an overreliance on technology. These human factors include, but are not limited to, the existence and maintenance of intra-team respect, mutual trust, reciprocity, and positive individual and group relationships. Establishing an initial level of trust among group members is crucial to a team's evolution (Gibson & Manuel, 2003). Trust develops gradually over time (Crossman & Lee-Kelley, 2004). Thus, low to medium trust at the beginning of a team's construction is usually present. Ideally, trust grows, leading to a steady expansion as the team evolves.

Gunderson, Hellesøy, and Raeder (2012) stated that that need for team members to trust in the team leader is a necessary but insufficient condition for team performance and success; the team members must also trust in each other. Thus it is important for the team leader to employ strategies that expand the level of trust within the team. In their study of transformational leadership among international teams, they found that trust amongst the team members had a significant effect on team performance; the higher the level of trust, the better the performance. This further highlights the importance of trust in international teams.

The process of intra-team trust development may differ between proximal and international teams. In international teams, members are physically located in different areas that often cross national, cultural, racial, and economic boundaries, complicating the creation of primary trust levels (Cogburn & Levinson, 2008; Leinonen, Järvelä, & Häkkinen, 2005). Evans (2007) found that successful leaders need to attend to the level of trust, respect, empowerment, communication and personal commitment as the key factors in international operations and that trust plays a key role in developing successful international leaders. Furthermore, it is trust that is such a critical requisite for the level of collaboration necessary to allow an international team to succeed (Temple & Wragg, 2000).

Collaboration in teams requires a significant amount of shared interaction, decision-making, and responsibility for the project's success. These collaborative activities are strongly influenced by the level of trust among team members, especially when the completion of one's own work depends on the ongoing cooperation of another person or group. Thus, trust is a key factor for interdependent

team members to work together effectively (Liu et al., 2008). Additionally, lack of trust can lead to increased costs and decreased team member satisfaction. It can impact a team member's willingness to even remain on the team. Lack of trust may ultimately become a self-fulfilling prophecy, as individuals who feel that they are not trusted may see no reason to behave in a trustworthy manner (Crossman & Lee-Kelley, 2004).

The formation of trust in any team, including those that are global, involves two key attributes. The first is competence. Team members must believe that each of their fellow teammates is capable of completing the task that he/she has been assigned. Initially, this competence may have to be taken on faith, but over time, each member will get the chance to demonstrate his/her competence, hopefully on an increasing basis, as he/she becomes an integral part of the team. This becomes evident in the individual contributions of each team member and, ultimately, the outcomes of the team. The second attribute is benevolence, or good will. Each team member must believe that all of the other team members are acting in the best interests of, and displaying good will toward, the team (Zakaria et al., 2004). This is harder to detect and it can be complicated when cultural norms and work processes differ among team members. When the team is virtual, the problems are exacerbated by the lack of physical and verbal cues (De Pillis & Furumo, 2007).

Doney, Cannon, and Mullen (1998) indicated that, to a certain extent, trust is likely to be founded on shared social norms, values, and underlying behavioral assumptions all of which may result from some form of shared cultural history. However, participating members within an international team may be culturally diverse with no previous working or collaborative history and, therefore, do not share a common past. They may also not share a common approach to teamwork or work in general and these differences may be founded in cultural attributes that were infused into them from a very early age (Hofstede & Hofstede, 2005;

Barkema, et al., 2015). In order to fully understand the process of trust creation, maintenance, and evolution, it is necessary to examine the various cultural dimensions that may differ, primarily between nationalities, and determine the extent to which they may have a positive or negative impact on the trust, cohesion, and ultimate success of an international team.

CULTURAL DIMENSIONS OF INTERNATIONAL TEAMS

The most distinctive feature of international teams lies in the differing context of its members. This context can involve an individual's way of life and work within a specific geographical area that has its own culturally based conditions and assumptions that relate to business. This context will also be impacted by each individual's unique history (Gluesing, et al., 2003). Thus, international team members from different cultures will, in all probability, describe a team's objectives, membership criteria, and activities in very different terms. Team members will have different understandings of the concept of teamwork and may have a lack of awareness of other team members' working processes (Zakaria et al., 2004; Barkema et al., 2015). This may be one of the biggest challenges that a virtual team is likely to face while attempting to collaborate on a shared task.

Cultural diversity may represent a substantial challenge to the success of an international team, but it may also bring to its members richness that they may not have experienced before. Experiencing national, cultural, or even organizational differences can be useful to all team members regardless of their previous experience in globalized business practices and, managed properly, this experience can help fulfill the promise that virtual teams were intended to fill, which, according to Dubé and Paré (2001), is a virtual team that is enhanced and not paralyzed by cultural differences.

National and organizational cultures are likely to have a significant impact on the ways that employees conduct themselves in any organization and their perceptions of effective leadership (Resnic et al., 2011). In an international team, cultures, working styles, and even management styles may conflict. For example, people from different cultural backgrounds may have different notions regarding what constitutes acceptable or good performance (Dubé & Paré, 2001; Resnic, et al., 2011). Communication styles are also likely to differ across cultures. Furthermore, notions of ownership and accountability can vary according to whether a culture is more collective or more individualistic. Team leaders should be mindful of these issues and understand their own cultural biases and how they may affect their judgments (Dubé & Paré, 2001).

To this end, the sections that follow contain a review of four cultural dimensions that are likely to impact the formation, processes, and maintenance of intra-team trust on international teams. These sections will be presented with the intention of offering success strategies to team members and leaders regardless of their national or cultural identities. By investigating the subtle nuances of these four dimensions, team members from around the world can begin to understand a portion of what contributes to the development of intra-team trust and ultimately the success of international teams.

Collective and Individual Approaches to International Teams

An important factor in team success is team communication. The way in which a team interacts will be impacted by the cultural orientation of its members in regards to the individual versus collective dichotomy. According to Hofstede and Hofstede (2005), the members of varying cultures tend to lean either toward a collective orientation, where members view themselves as part of a group and work to support the needs of the group, or toward an individual orientation, where members are conditioned to focus on their own individual needs. "In a collective culture the self is defined in terms of in-group memberships in which shared values and norms, common goals and utilitarian relationships are highly regarded" (Sosik & Jung, 2002, p. 7). On the other end of this dichotomy, members of individualist cultures tend to define themselves in terms of personal needs, individual liberties, and a belief that self-interest is more important than the needs of the group (Sosik & Jung, 2002; Combs, Milosevic, Jeung, & Griffith, 2012). Hofstede and Hofstede identified general regions of the world as being more individualistic or more collective. In very general terms, the "West," which encompasses Europe and North America, tended to be more individualistic whereas Asia, Latin-America, Africa, and the Middle East tended to be more collective.

When assembling an international team consisting of members from countries that might be expected to vary along the individual – collective continuum, the cultural mindsets of both the team members and the team leader are significant (Combs, Milosevic, Jeung, & Griffith, 2012). In an individualistic society, management is the management of individuals. In a collective society, management is the management of groups (Hofstede & Hofstede, 2005). Additionally, collectivists tend to make a sharp distinction between in-group and out-group members leading to different reactions to those outside the team whereas the individualists tend to treat everyone the same. Collectivists tend to be distrustful of those outside the team until a relationship has been established. Individualists tend to not wait for the relationship to begin the work of the team (Barkema, et al., 2015).

Once relationships are established, members of collective societies are, initially, more likely to come together, embrace teamwork and be comfortable being part of a team, even for extended periods, whereas those from individualistic cultures tend to maintain an individual focus and also tend to view teams as temporary working relationships to be dissolved over time (Sosik & Jung, 2002; Molinsky & Hahn, 2015b). Within international teams that may be geographically distributed, team members from collective societies may feel a sense of isolation, as there are fewer opportunities to build relationships and less direct group input. This may be seen as a strength to the individualistic team member who will tend to focus on the work and may regard building relationships only as a means to an end.

The composition of the team may be a factor as well. Individualistic team members will value a wide array of skills and talents among the various team members whereas collectivists may see this as a threat to team harmony (Hofstede & Hofstede, 2005; Combs, Milosevic, Jeung, & Griffin, 2012). Once the team has formed and has begun its work, individualistic team members are more likely to assume a competitive or aggressive approach to the completion of the team's goals whereas members from collective cultures may emphasize relationship building and collaboration as the best way to ensure the team's outcomes. Additionally, team members from individualistic cultures tend to place more emphasis on what can be accomplished in the short term and may push for immediate results leading to short-term successes. Members from collective societies may prefer to focus on long-term results and may value relationships, persistence and tenacity over immediate gratification (Sosik & Jung, 2002; Molinsky & Hahn, 2015b).

Perhaps the clearest statement of difference between the two types of cultures is that collectivist team members work to support the needs of the team whereas individualistic members are more motivated to pursue their own needs. This has the potential to lead to conflict, which is another area where the cultural types differ. Collective cultures may tend to avoid conflict whereas individualistic cultures are more likely to be direct and confrontational (Zakaria, et al., 2004).

Given all of these differences in preferred working styles, potential problems may arise in regards to how members of one culture type view another. Those from individual cultures may see members from collective cultures as overly needy, demanding, and unwilling to take proactive, independent action. Individualistic team members may be perceived as cold and not true team players by those from collective cultures who may question their willingness, or even ability, to collaborate (Hofstede & Hofstede, 2005).

These views, and the wide array of differences that led to them, can be a significant threat to intra-team trust. During the team's formation stage (Tuckman, 1965) it is natural that each member will expect all other members to think, act, and perform in a consistent manner. When inconsistent and unexpected behaviors are encountered, the level of trust that team members hold for one another can be significantly compromised, directly impacting team performance (Crossman & Lee-Kelley, 2004). In order to avoid this, a number of steps can be taken by team leaders, or even by team members, to account for and to counteract the impact of these cultural differences. These include:

- Establish relationships among team members. Members from both types of cultures can benefit from this although the individualistic team members may not see it at first. The best way to establish relationships in an international team is to have the team meet face-to-face, during its formation, for a brief period (Hanover Research Council, 2008). If that is not possible, video conferencing can be a good alternative.
- During the formation of the team, set clear rules governing expectations for communication and participation in meetings. This is intended to curb the individualists who may dominate meetings and help bring out the collectivists who, because of their fo-

cus on collective group process and consensus, may tend to be more reserved.

- Utilize a mix of technologies that could appeal to the needs of both types of cultures. Some tools, such as video conferencing and other technologies that support synchronous communication, are more likely to appeal to those team members attempting to work as a group. The individualistic members may prefer more solitary, asynchronous forms of communication but they may also see the additional benefits of tools that enable group collaboration if they enable them to achieve their personal goals more quickly.

Team leaders will need to recognize that they are likely to have varying relationships with each of the team members. Leading the individualistic members will mean helping them to see how the goals of the team are aligned with their own, how participation in the team can further their own careers, and how feedback on team process is intended to sharpen individual skills. Conversely, the collectivist members will prefer to interact with a team leader who they will regard as the head of a group and who they will expect to preserve the balance and harmony of the team as it works collaboratively toward its goals (Hofstede & Hofstede, 2005; Combs, Milosevic, Jeung, & Griffith, 2012). Balancing these two sets of demands becomes a challenge for the team leader. What further complicates this balance are other cultural dimensions that tend to be associated with the individual versus collective dichotomy. How team members view leadership and power can have a significant impact on how they interact with their teammates or the team leader.

Power Distance in International Teams

One of the primary benefits of teamwork and a significant driver behind the widespread adoption of teams in recent years is the ability to draw upon the skills and knowledge of a wide group of individuals, all of whom can collectively produce results that are likely to have stronger and wider appeal to a global marketplace. The ability to capitalize on the skills of all team members depends on clearly established communication parameters both on the part of the team members and the team leader. However, cultural approaches to communication can get in the way, especially when communication needs to span multiple levels of a perceived hierarchy. Thus, a team leader cannot assume that members of an international team will consistently communicate in a singular, consistent manner with each other and with the team leader.

An important consideration in International teams that may impact communication is power distance. Power distance is defined as "the extent to which the less powerful members of institutions and organizations within a country expect and accept that power is distributed unequally" (Hofstede as cited in Paulus, Bichelmeyer, Malopinsky, Pereira, & Rastogi, 2005, p.44). Some cultures can be described as having lower power distance where leaders and subordinates share much of the privilege, power, and decision making authority; there is less distance in the functions and positions of leaders and followers. However, in higher distance cultures, those in authority are expected to maintain a higher level of privilege and power and they are looked to for all significant decisions. Paulus et al. (2005) described the differences in the following way:

In low power distance groups, individuals generally believe that inequalities between levels of the hierarchy should be minimized, that subordinates in the hierarchy should be consulted by those at higher levels, and that the ideal leader believes power resides in the people. In contrast, in high power distance groups, inequalities between hierarchy levels are expected and even desired, subordinates expect to be told what to do and the

ideal leader has absolute undisputed authority yet uses it for the good of the people. (p. 44)

According to Hofstede and Hofstede (2005), the power dimension breaks down geographically very much like the differences in the individualism collectivism dimension, however there are some notable differences. Cultures in the East, Middle East, Latin-America and Africa tend to accept higher power distance. Those in the West have adapted to less power distance. The difference between the power distance and the individualism – collectivism dimension is that a number of European countries, mostly in the eastern and southern region, tend to utilize a higher power distance structure.

How this plays out is an important consideration for team leaders especially when considering how team members across multiple cultures are likely to communicate. According to Hofstede and Hofstede (2005), those in higher power distance situations see superiors and subordinates as existentially unequal. Subordinates expect to work for superiors with higher levels of authority who will tell them what to do. Conversely, those in lower power distance cultures see superiors and subordinates as essentially equal, and subordinates expect to be consulted on important decisions.

Managing a team of individuals where there is a mix of views on the dimension of power sharing presents a number of challenges, many of which will involve perceptions of initiative, motivation, and team commitment. Those in high power distance situations may expect team leaders to clearly spell out directions and expectations. They may not step forward and take action independently, as to do so would be disrespectful of the position of the team leader or other team members who they may regard as holding a superior position on the corporate hierarchy. As a result, they may be regarded as uncommitted and unmotivated by those who do not share their cultural perspective. Conversely, those from lower power distance cultures are more likely to take independent action in an effort to drive the team toward its goals. Those holding a high power distance perspective may view these members as disrespectful toward the leaders to the point of being demanding or arrogant.

Two other areas where differences in power distance become relevant are decision-making processes and approaches to conflict. Those who have been conditioned to look to superiors to make all-important decisions may be reluctant to depart from that practice when serving on an international team. This becomes even more challenging with the lack of familiarity and personal contact as individuals from high power distance countries are more likely to depend on rules and structure to take the place of relationships. This will reinforce the need to respect hierarchy. Additionally, with different attitudes toward authority, there are likely to be different attitudes toward conflict and its resolution. Lower power distance individuals are likely to be more comfortable with direct confrontation and rapid conflict resolution whereas those individuals from higher power distance cultures would see conflict as potentially disrespectful and something to be avoided (Paulus et al., 2005; Molinsky & Hahn, 2015a).

Thus, when forming and leading a team of individuals from countries that tend to view power distance differently, a number of steps can be taken to minimize the problems that may result. These include:

- The team needs to establish a set of operational rules that can be adopted by both power distance styles. These rules should clarify the roles, expectations, and contributions of each team member.
- The team leader should make an effort to establish clear communication patterns and expectations in a way that limits any perceived positional barriers that may inhibit team process.
- It is important to ensure that individuals know that they will be expected to contribute to the team. It may be useful to set up a regular process that follows a set schedule, where each team member is expected to report his/her contributions on a regular basis.
- The team leader should be proactive in providing opportunities to ensure that each team member is clear about his/her role and responsibilities. The team manager should not assume that silence from team members is meant to imply that they understand the tasks that they are responsible for.
- The team leader should be watchful for team members who may be seen as reserved or holding back due primarily to cultural conditioning (Molinsky & Hahn, 2015a). Failure on their part to match the working styles of the lower power distance team members may lead to issues regarding intra-team trust (Sosik &Jung, 2002). It is best for the team leader to head these off before they lead to conflict.

It is important to note that the team leader cannot expect that his or her global team members are going to abandon years of cultural conditioning and change overnight. However, clear rules regarding expectations and communication patterns might allow team members from different cultures to temporarily adapt to alternative working styles, but these adaptations may last only as long as the team lasts. Views on power distance and the manner in which this drives an individual's communication styles are ingrained and reinforced by the norms of his or her culture, and given the nature of international teams, team members are prone to continue to be influenced by these norms throughout their team participation.

Tolerance for Uncertainty in International Teams

To a certain extent, ambiguity and uncertainty are found in all types of work. Hofstede and Hofstede (2005) pointed out that both could be found in every human society and, through the use of technology, law, and religion, each society has constructed its own ways of alleviating the resultant anxiety that is associated with uncertainty. Yet, "the essence of uncertainty is that it is a subjective experience" (Hofstede & Hofstede, 2005, p. 165) and, being such, it means different things to different people. This level of variation extends to cultures as well. Not only is the perception of uncertainty culturally subjective, but the collective manner in which members of a culture face uncertainty may also be specific to that culture. Some cultures may tolerate uncertainty and accept it as a societal norm whereas other cultures may be less comfortable with uncertainty and may seek to develop or adopt structures to minimize it. The extent to which the members of a culture take steps in response to their need for uncertainty avoidance is an important consideration when forming international teams.

In short, uncertainty avoidance can be defined as "the extent to which the members of a culture feel threatened by uncertain or unknown situations" (as cited by Hofstede in Paulus et al., p. 44). Members from cultures that tend to avoid uncertainty may feel anxious when working on tasks or with people who are new, unfamiliar, technologically challenging, or virtual, unless clear procedures and rules have been established. (Zakaria et al., 2004). These feelings of anxiety may appear in the form of nervous stress that is likely to create a need for predictability and written rules (Hofstede & Hofstede, 2005).

As stated before, uncertainty and its associated anxiety are subjective. It is the needs of the individual that will define the level of clarity necessary with regard to work assignments. And, according to Workman (2007), there tend to be increased levels of ambiguity in terms of tasks and interpersonal relationships when individuals seek levels of clarity that have not been provided. The use of technology, as opposed to face-to-face interactions, may complicate and increase the level of task and relationship ambiguity, which is likely to be complicated by time zones, distance,

and lack of team structure. The higher the levels of separation, the more opportunities there are for ambiguity and uncertainty. This is especially true on international teams. Workman (2007) stated that as the level of separation on an international team increases:

Both formal and informal interaction decreases and it becomes increasingly difficult to model team members' approaches to tasks or monitor work progress or convey nonverbal information that establishes normative or structural expectations, which constrict shared meaning, social identification and cooperation. (p. 356)

The isolated work structures that are often associated with international teams limit the opportunities for members to learn from each other or to obtain tacit understanding of team process through their associations with other team members. The clarity that comes from merely observing the activities within the team is often minimized or absent. Some team members will adapt to this lack of clarity with less anxiety than others and the determinant in regards to the level of stress experienced by a team member is closely tied to the manner in which his/her culture is tolerant of uncertainty. Gibson and Manuel (2003) argue that intra-team trust is tied to risk and interdependence, both of which face additional complications that relate to the nature of international teams where members do not share the same approach to uncertainty. Risk, in a limited form, becomes the driver for intra-team trust; if there is no risk, there is no need to establish trust. Interdependence, and the level of comfort that is required to sustain it, is impacted by the extent to which team members believe there is cause to depend on one another. Varying approaches to uncertainty and the anxiety it may produce will result in different assessments of risk and interdependence, both of which impact trust (Gibson & Manuel, 2003).

In an international team, uncertainty intolerance can present itself through members' anxiety that is the result of a lack of formal structure. To help compensate for this lack of structure and the elevated ambiguity created by separation, team members may turn to formal structures such as written rules and procedures (Workman, 2007). To the extent that it is possible, team leaders should have explicit rules available to answer all questions that surface, however it may be a challenge to anticipate the myriad concerns that can arise especially if the team leader's tolerance for uncertainty is different than that of the team members. It is important to note that in the absence of formalized rules, those who seek clarification of roles or tasks may look to the organizational structure, including higher levels of leadership, to provide it.

In addition to the suggestion of providing formal structure, other strategies to address uncertainty tolerance include:

- Team leaders should be able to provide clarity regarding roles. This may include the need for formal, written job descriptions that detail what is to be expected of a team member. This is especially important when the complexity of the team members' roles begins to increase.
- The team needs to provide to its members an appropriate level of precision and formalization regarding how it will function. While clarity of roles is important, it is also important for the team to establish clarity around the functions and processes that the team will adopt to get its work done. Such steps can be taken during the formation of the team.
- The team should be able to clearly establish what it expects to achieve and what the outcomes of the team will be. All members of the team should be able to clearly describe what success will look like when the team's work has been completed (Hofstede & Hofstede, 2005).

Given that risk-taking is likely to introduce uncertainty (Gibson & Manuel, 2003), there may be challenges with uncertainty intolerant team members who may be reluctant to think in new and innovative ways. This may have to be encouraged through coaching on the part of the team leader who will help team members find ways to minimize the anxiety associated with such risks. Another factor that is likely to result in uncertainty is conflict, as those that are less tolerant of uncertainty may be inclined to avoid situations that may lead to conflict or not confront conflict once it occurs. Lastly, another factor that often introduces uncertainty is the adoption of new technology platforms. Given the dependence on communication and information technologies to support the work of an international team, it will be key that all team members feel confident in their use of these technologies and this may require a careful approach to implementation of any new or unfamiliar tools (Hofstede & Hofstede, 2005).

Individuals that are less tolerant of uncertainty are going to have a more difficult time engaging with their teams if they do not trust the team's processes because they do not have enough details, precision, and clarity to alleviate the anxiety they feel as a result of being a member of an international team. It will be a challenge for all members of the team to establish an appropriate level of clarity in its processes, one that strikes a balance between the need for structure and the need for action.

The Contextual Dimension of Communication in International Teams

Cultural context in regards to communication relates to the amount of information that is directly encoded and communicated in a message. It specifies the extent to which explicit communication is required to share information and make decisions (Cole, 2015). It differentiates between messages where meaning is implied or culturally based as opposed to messages where meaning is nothing more than a construct of straight facts. (Massey, Montoya- Weiss, Hung, & Ramesh, 2001).

Context differs from culture to culture and this can have a significant impact on the ways that international team members communicate. Hall (1976) distinguished between low-context and high-context cultures and used the differences between them to describe the amount of information that needs to be "coded and explicitly transmitted in a message" in order for communication to be efficient within and across different cultures (Hall as cited in Koeszegi, Vetschera, & Kersten, 2004, p. 85).

In low-context cultures like the US or Northern Europe, communication is dependent primarily on the message itself with little regard for any culturally based connotations. One does not have to be familiar with the culture in order to fully understand its messages. There is only a small amount of shared and implicit information carried in the context of an event and the need to interpret the cultural significance of such messages is not expected. This creates a need for communication in such cultures to be clear, concise, and direct (Cole, 2015; Hall as cited in Koeszegi et al., 2004).

However, in high context cultures, like those in Latin-American or eastern Asian countries, much of the information that is part of a message is either contained in the physical context of an event or internalized by the persons involved in the event. High context cultures prefer indirect and circular communication patterns. There is a significant amount of cultural connotation that is applied to the formulation and interpretation of messages. As a result, less information needs to be coded explicitly in each message because a substantial amount of meaning can be implied from the context (Hall as cited in Koeszegi et al., 2004). Additionally, it may be the intent of the high-context communicator to convey the message over time meaning that the full message may not be communicated in a single exchange (Cole, 2015).

This difference in communication styles can present substantial challenges when communicating across different contextual and cultural styles. "In order to understand the behavioral priorities of those from a particular culture, one must understand the context in which they occur" (Hall as cited in Zakaria et al., 2004, p. 7). In high context cultures, messages may not be clear when received and interpreted by those who do not share an understanding of the nuances or connotations that make up part of that message. This may be further complicated by language differences. Yet, it is the shared information that allows members of high-context cultures to communicate in a preferred style where they are not required to provide information that is redundant, overly direct, or unpleasant; this information is communicated in the context of the message. However, those from low context cultures do not assume any meaning that is derived from a contextual setting. Thus, their communication may be more direct, less formal, and could be perceived as discourteous by high-context group members (Molinsky & Hahn, 2015a). A further complication comes from the fact that those who are high-context team members can communicate with low-context team members but the opposite is not always true. It is important to analyze the context of the communication and ask for prompts to get at the true meaning. This is a skill that develops over time with practice (Cole, 2015).

The contextually based challenges for international teams are many. Team members from high-context cultures may be less direct in their communication styles and may use more formality in initial contact as the relationships between team members and with the team leader will be unclear (Hall in Zakaria et al., 2004; Molinsky & Hahn, 2015a). Team members from lower-context cultures are likely to depend less on context to formulate complete, direct communication, which they are conditioned to relay in a manner that may seem to be aggressive or overbearing to their high-context colleagues. These differences may extend beyond the initial formation of the team and can impact team trust and harmony if a commonly accepted and respectful method of information exchange is not found.

Contextually based communication is also likely to impact team operations in regards to intra-team conflict. Members from low-context cultures are more likely to perceive disagreements as an integral part of the team's process. Not only is conflict acceptable, but it can even be positive when it encourages creativity and innovation. However, high-context team members could perceive open disagreement and confrontation as a violation of culturally based communication norms that may not be apparent to those outside a particular culture. It might even be viewed as highly insulting and something that would cause both parties to lose face (Molinsky & Hahn, 2015a). Additionally, team members from low-context cultures are more likely to separate issues related to conflict from the people involved in the conflict, while those from high-text cultures are less likely to separate the two and may take personal offense to the disagreement permanently impacting intra-team trust (Zakariaet al., 2004).

Another issue relevant to contextual communication is the amount of information that is conveyed once a conflict has occurred. International teams, with their limitations on direct contact and physical cues, make even direct communication more difficult. When the team involves individuals who rely on context to communicate a message, it may be harder to detect when conflict is occurring, and when it does occur, it may be difficult to resolve. Those in high-context cultures may respond to conflict in an evasive, non-confrontational manner, which may cause the conflict to remain in place unresolved. Those in a low-context culture may respond in a direct, confrontational way and expect a quick resolution (Zakaria et al., 2004). Both approaches to conflict have the potential to impact ongoing communication patterns, if they are not facilitated to a resolution that is acceptable by all parties.

In order to better facilitate communication among members of an international team, there are a few tasks that a team leader can attend to. These include:

- The team leader needs to be ready to facilitate communication among team members making certain that messages are clearly understood by all recipients regardless of whether they have an understanding of the cultural context in which the message originated.
- The low-context team members, including the team manager, may need to practice the use of queues or probes to ensure that they are getting the full message from the high-context communicators. This involves asking follow-up questions and analyzing the replies for what is and what is not included thereby helping to refine further follow-up questions.
- The team leader may need to take steps to ensure that communication patterns are respectful, courteous, and supportive of the team's goals.
- The team leader and members need to be vigilant about detecting any potential areas of conflict. When conflict is found, it will be important to resolve it in a manner that is respectful of both communication styles.

Contextually-based communication patterns have been shown to be related to the cultural dimensions that have been mentioned previously in this chapter. Collectivist cultures tend to lean toward high context communication in the majority of social interactions. Individualist cultures tend to be more direct and utilize low-context communication (Massey et al., 2001). Additionally, both collectivist and high-context cultures tend to be higher in uncertainty avoidance and demonstrate a lower tolerance for ambiguity, conflict avoidance, and a strong desire for consensus (Massey et al.).

CONCLUSION: LEADERSHIP CONSIDERATIONS FOR INTERNATIONAL TEAMS

The establishment of protocols, or norms, at the inception of a team or project is essential for an international team's development of intra-team trust that supports effective collaboration. It helps establish clarity about what is acceptable and/or unacceptable behavior for team members. Most international teams that do not reach their intended goals attribute their failures to a lack of communication and trust between team members (Hanover Research Council, 2008).

According to Zakaria, et al. (2004),

International team members need to possess both appropriate information technology skills and intercultural communication competence in order to be effective. They must possess global communication skills that enable them to collaborate, address conflict, sustain intra-team relations and create an effective knowledge-sharing culture. (p. 23)

Members on an international team must "develop a global mindset which means that they are open minded, maintain appropriate behaviors, and are sensitive to the differences they encounter during the communication and collaboration process" (p. 23). The team leader can influence much of the success for the outcomes of an international team. In addition to overseeing the function of the team, leaders can also be communication facilitators, ready to assist in the event people face difficulties in sending and receiving the intended messages across cultures and borders.

Since information and communication technologies eliminate the verbal and social cues that are prerequisite to certain cultures, leaders must help team members build and maintain trust, ease the transition process, select and use appropriate electronic communication and collaboration technologies, and coach and manage performance without the traditional forms of feedback. (Zakaria et al., 2004, p. 25)

A comprehensive approach to cultural differences needs to be negotiated, agreed upon, and integrated into the team's process early in the formation stage. Once adopted, these operational rules guide the work of the team and can become common ground in the event of conflict. Yet, establishing such guidelines does not occur by itself but must be actively developed and maintained by team leaders along with team members.

During the team formation process, leaders and members can work together to:

- Ensure that they are definite and specific in their expectations, particularly when defining measures and milestones.
- Make assumptions, expectations, roles, procedures, standards, norms, and processes explicit.
- Develop a clear team purpose statement to clarify expectations and responsibilities.
- Set goals that are measurable and obtainable while specifying the actions and activities needed to obtain the results (Hanover Research Council, 2008).

Furthermore, efforts should be made to ensure that team members' cultural differences in work emphasis, deadline adherence, and project management style become transparent to the team (Zakaria, et al. 2004).

Lastly, much of the research on cultural differences on work styles has been focused on differences between countries or regions. This leads to what Earley and Mosakowski (2004, p. 152) referred to as the "ecological fallacy," which they use to refer to a tendency to assume that culturally based trends can be generalized to all members of that culture. It is important to remember that not all members of a culture will embrace cultural dimensions in the same manner. In fact, two people from the same culture can have very different approaches to cultural dimensions. Thus, it is important to further the skills of international team members to include the ability to dynamically assess cultural differences and adapt behaviors on an individual basis. "Rather than training business managers to adapt to cultures, we need to provide them with dynamic skills to interpret and react to individual differences" (Earley & Mosakowski, 2004, p. 152). It is also important to note that as cultures merge through globalization and technology, that some of these cultural dimensions may shift. These may also be impacted as local and global business expectations begin to change. Resnick, et al. (2011) found that the differences between the collectivists and individualists could be diminishing as cultures who have traditionally been individualistic in their approach begin to embrace organizational trends such as self-organizing teams and shared-vision leadership. These may cause them to shift their overall approach to the ways that international teams are formed and led.

FUTURE RESEARCH DIRECTIONS

This chapter has focused on four cultural dimensions that impact international teams, but there are additional areas of consideration that are worthy of attention. An examination of each of these areas will highlight a number of opportunities for further research.

First, English language proficiency, both at the overt and subtle levels, is likely to have a substantial impact on the differences in cultural dimensions. On an international team, one cannot assume a uniform level of understanding regarding a language that is shared by native and non-native speakers. Many of the communication challenges attributed to differences in cultural dimensions may be heightened by variances in English language proficiency. This becomes even more of an issue as team members attempt to interact solely through the use of communication and information technologies. The extent to which cultural differences can be attributed to variances in levels of English language proficiency as opposed to differences in cultural dimensions is an area for further exploration.

Second, technology is ever changing and new or better tools are likely to have a substantial impact on how international teams operate. Both asynchronous and synchronous technologies to facilitate meetings, host videoconferences, share documents, and track team process from location around the world are commonplace today. It is reasonable to expect additional technologies or improvements in existing tools to impact international teams. Thus, a significant area of further research could look at how new trends in both asynchronous and synchronous technologies are likely to impact an organization's adoption and use of international teams. Additionally, not all team members will have access to the same types of technology. Even Internet bandwidth remains widely varied from location to location. Thus, another research opportunity is the variance in technology skills and access, as well as the extent to which this variance is likely to impact the processes and outcomes of an international team.

A third possible area of future research would be to examine how the differences in cultural dimensions related to masculine versus feminine and long-term versus short-term time orientations might impact the formation of intra-team trust on international teams. Both dimensions were excluded from this analysis due to complexities that were likely to result from their combination with other aspects of international teams. Yet a more masculine orientation, possibly in combination with a short-term time focus, could have a significant impact on the formation of intra-team trust on international teams especially when the actions that may result from such an orientation would run counter to the trends associated with other cultural dimensions. These various combinations and their interactions are areas worthy of further examination.

Lastly, team leadership has received a great deal of attention in the literature, however most of the research in this area has been conducted on proximal teams. It will be useful to continue to examine best practices in team leadership for international teams. Specifically, how a team leader helps the team in its efforts to establish and maintain intra-team trust, mediate conflict, and successfully achieve its outcomes are areas that warrant further investigation as globalization and technology impact international teams into the future.

REFERENCES

Barkema, H. G., Chen, X. P., George, G., Luo, Y., & Tsui, A. (2015). West meets east: New concepts and theories. *Academy of Management Journal, 58*(2), 460–479. doi:10.5465/amj.2015.4021

Chen, G., Chittoor, R., & Vissa, B. (2015). Modernizing without westernizing: Social structure and economic actions in the Indian financial sector. *Academy of Management Journal, 58*(2), 511–537. doi:10.5465/amj.2012.1039

Clapp-Smith, R., Vogelgesang, G. R., & Avey, J. B. (2009). Authentic leadership and positive psychological capital: The mediating role of trust at the group level of analysis. *Journal of Leadership & Organizational Studies, 15*(3), 227–240. doi:10.1177/1548051808326596

Cogburn, D. L., & Levinson, N. S. (2008). Teaching globalization globally: A 7-year case study of South Africa – U.S. virtual teams. *Informational Technologies and International Development, 4*(3), 75–89. doi:10.1162/itid.2008.00018

Cohen, S. G., & Gibson, C. B. (2003). Introduction. In C. B. Gibson & S. G. Cohen (Eds.), *Virtual teams that work: Creating conditions for virtual team effectiveness* (pp. 59–86). San Francisco: Jossey-Bass.

Cole, B. M. (2015). Lessons from a martial arts dojo: A prolonged process model of high-context communication. *Academy of Management Journal, 58*(2), 567–591. doi:10.5465/amj.2012.0986

Combs, G. M., Milosevic, I., Jeung, W., & Griffith, J. (2012). Ethnic identity and job attribute preferences: The role of collectivism and psychological capital. *Journal of Leadership & Organizational Studies, 19*(1), 5–16. doi:10.1177/1548051811433359

Crossman, A., & Lee-Kelley, L. (2004). Trust, commitment and team working: The paradox of virtual organizations. *Global Networks, 4*(4), 375–390. doi:10.1111/j.1471-0374.2004.00099.x

De Pillis, E., & Furumo, K. (2007). Counting the cost of virtual teams: Studying the performance, satisfaction, and group dynamics of virtual and face-to-face teams. *Communications of the ACM, 50*(12), 93–95. doi:10.1145/1323688.1323714

Doney, P. M., Cannon, J. P., & Mullen, M. R. (1998). Understanding the influence of national culture on the development of trust. *Academy of Management Review, 23*, 491–512. doi:10.2307/259297

Dube, L., & Pare, G. (2001). International teams: Recent interviews with GVT leaders and members offer critical advice from the trenches regarding the challenges and coping strategies for collaborating on a global scale. *Communications of the ACM, 44*(12), 71–73.

Earley, P. C., & Mosakowski, E. (2004). Toward culture intelligence: Turning cultural differences into a workplace advantage. *The Academy of Management Executive, 18*(3), 151–157.

Evans, D. (2007). An exploratory review of global leadership: The example of French and British leadership styles. *The Journal of Leadership Studies, 1*(1), 28–33. doi:10.1002/jls.20005

Gibson, C. B., & Manuel, J. A. (2003). Building trust: Effective multicultural communication process in virtual teams. In C. B. Gibson & S. G. Cohen (Eds.), *Virtual teams that work: Creating conditions for virtual team effectiveness* (pp. 59–86). San Francisco: Jossey-Bass.

Gluesing, J. C., Alcordo, T. C., Baba, M. L., Britt, D., Wagner, K. H., & McKether, W. (2003). The development of International teams. In C. B. Gibson & S. G. Cohen (Eds.), *Virtual teams that work: Creating conditions for virtual team effectiveness* (pp. 95–120). San Francisco: Jossey Bass.

Gunderson, G., Hellesøy, B. T., & Raeder, S. (2012). Leading international project teams: The effectiveness of transformational leadership in dynamic work environments. *Journal of Leadership & Organizational Studies, 19*(1), 46–57. doi:10.1177/1548051811429573

Hall, J. T. (1976). *Beyond culture*. New York: Doubleday.

Harvey, M., Mcintyre, N., Moeller, M., & Sloan, H. Hanover Research Council. (2012). Managerial self-concept in a global context: An integral component of cross-cultural competencies. *Journal of Leadership & Organizational Studies, 19*(1), 115–125. doi:10.1177/1548051811431826

Hofstede, G. H. (1985). The interaction between national and organizational value systems. *Journal of Management Studies, 22*(4), 347–357. doi:10.1111/j.1467-6486.1985.tb00001.x

Hofstede, G. H., & Hofstede, G. J. (2005). *Cultures and organizations: Software of the mind* (2nd ed.). New York: McGraw Hill.

Koeszegi, S., Vetschera, R., & Kersten, G. (2004). National cultural differences in the use and perception of Internet-based NSS: Does high or low context matter? *International Negotiation, 9*(79), 79–109. doi:10.1163/1571806041262070

Leinonen, P., Järvelä, S., & Häkkinen, P. (2005). Conceptualizing the awareness of collaboration: A qualitative study of a International team. *Computer Supported Cooperative Work, 14*(4), 301–322. doi:10.1007/s10606-005-9002-z

Lipnack, J., & Stamps, J. (2000). *Virtual teams: People working across boundaries with technology* (2nd ed.). New York: John Wiley and Sons.

Liu, X., Magjuka, R. J., & Lee, S. L. (2008). The effects of cognitive thinking styles, trust, conflict management on online students' learning and virtual team performance. *British Journal of Educational Technology, 39*(5), 829–846. doi:10.1111/j.1467-8535.2007.00775.x

Massey, A. P., Montoya-Weiss, M., Hung, C., & Ramesh, V. (2001). Cultural perceptions of task-technology fit: Acknowledging cultural differences helps companies build the strongest International teams and determine the strongest tool they need. *Communications of the ACM, 44*(12), 83–84. doi:10.1145/501317.501353

Molinsky, A., & Hahn, M. (2015a, April 6). Learning the language of indirectness. *Harvard Business Review*.

Molinsky, A., & Hahn, M. (2015b, April 8). Building relationships in cultures that don't do small talk. *Harvard Business Review*.

Nunamaker, J. F. Jr, Reinig, B. A., & Briggs, R. O. (2009). Principles for effective virtual teamwork. *Communications of the ACM, 52*(4), 113–117. doi:10.1145/1498765.1498797

Paulus, T. M., Bichelmeyer, B., Malopinsky, L., Pereira, M., & Rastogi, P. (2005). Power distance and group dynamics of an international project team: A case study. *Teaching in Higher Education, 10*(1), 43–55. doi:10.1080/1356251052000305525

Peck, M. S. (1987). *A different drum: Community making and peace*. New York: Touchstone.

Resick, C. J., Gillian, S. M., Keating, M. A., Dickson, M. W., Kwan, H. K., & Peng, C. (2011). What ethical leadership means to me: Asian, American, and European perspectives. *Journal of Business Ethics, 101*(3), 435–457. doi:10.1007/s10551-010-0730-8

Sosik, J. J., & Jung, D. I. (2002). Workgroup characteristics and performance in collectivistic and individualistic cultures. *The Journal of Social Psychology, 142*(1), 5–23. doi:10.1080/00224540209603881 PMID:11913835

Temple, P., & Wragg, C. (2000). Virtual teamwork (or the magnificent seven ride again). *Perspectives, 4*(2), 1–3.

Timmerman, C. E., & Scott, C. R. (2006). Virtually working: Communicative and structural predictors of media use and key outcomes in virtual work teams. *Communication Monographs, 73*(1), 108–136. doi:10.1080/03637750500534396

Tuckman, B. W. (1965). Developmental sequence in small groups. *Psychological Bulletin, 63*(6), 384–399. doi:10.1037/h0022100 PMID:14314073

Wallace, R. W. (2001). The dynamics of team formation. *HMS Beagle: The BioMedNet Magazine*. Retrieved from http://www.nasw.org/users/RobWallace/team_dynamics.pdf

Workman, M. (2007). The effects from technology- mediated interaction and openness in virtual team performance measures. *Behaviour & Information Technology, 26*(5), 355–365. doi:10.1080/01449290500402809

Zakaria, N., Amelinckx, A., & Wilemon, D. (2004). Working together apart? Building a knowledgesharing culture for International teams. *Creativity and Innovation Management, 13*(1), 15–29. doi:10.1111/j.1467-8691.2004.00290.x

KEY TERMS AND DEFINITIONS

Collectivism: People in collectivist cultures define themselves and choose their actions based upon the expectations and norms of a group. Such defining groups may include the family, the church, or a national culture. In collectivistic cultures, an emphasis is placed on those actions and attributes that support the interests of the group.

Contextual Communication: The meaning of messages may or may not depend on the context in which the message originated. High context information is more reliant on an unstated or assumed context for part of its meaning whereas low context communication carries its meaning within the message itself.

Individualism: People in individualistic cultures tend to define themselves apart from a group and display individual characteristics and choices. In an individualistic culture, an emphasis is placed on those actions and attributes that support individual freedoms and choices.

Intra-Team Trust: The extent to which the members of a team regard each other as capable of contributing to the team's goals and likely to act in a way that supports the interests of the team.

Power Distance: Power distance is the extent to which individuals within a culture recognize and are comfortable with the distance between themselves and those that they regard as superiors in position or status. Individuals from high power distance cultures accept the fact that privileges have been afforded to those who have been placed in positions regarded as having more importance. Those from low power distance cultures tend to expect a more egalitarian power-sharing structure.

Pseudocommunity: Pseudocommunity is a term that has been used to refer to a team in its early formation stages where the members are cordial to one another and personal and cultural differences are not overtly recognized or valued. Community, over all other concerns, is the priority at this point and individual differences are minimized. Teams will progress from pseudocommunity to chaos, then emptiness, and finally to true community.

Uncertainty Avoidance: The extent to which the members of a community experience and attempt to avoid anxiety that results from uncertainty defines that community's level of uncertainly avoidance. Communities that experience high uncertainty avoidance will seek to establish clearly defined rules and processes to guide their decisions and actions. Those with lower levels of uncertainty avoidance are more comfortable if rules and process are less clearly defined and if actions and decisions are more spontaneous.

Chapter 22

Communication:
The Role of the Johari Window on Effective Leadership Communication in Multinational Corporations

Ben Tran
Alliant International University, USA

ABSTRACT

Based on previous research, leadership appears to be enacted through communication in such a way that it contains a relational (affective) and task (content) component. Additionally, when leaders communicate effectively, their followers experience greater levels of satisfaction. Thus, the purpose of this chapter is on communication, specifically, the role of the Johari Window (JW) on effective leadership communication in multinational corporations (MNCs). In regards to the JW, many researchers did not question, and even more practitioners did not realize is that, the JW is created based on a domestic paradigm, and not necessarily applicable to a multinational environment where intercultural and multicultural communication are at play for multinational environment within MNCs. Nevertheless, the JW has continuously been applied to cross cultural studies, without a paradigm shift, utilizing a domestic paradigm (no international cultural factors at play) within a multinational environment (various international cultural factors at play), issue at hand persists.

INTRODUCTION

According to Tran (2016), Scott (2005) defined communication as sending, receiving, and understanding information and meaning. Scott (2005) claimed that receiving and understanding are the most important operations in the communication process, since the response of the receiver defines whether the communication attempts are successful or not. Scott (2005) further defined two categories of communication that are related to workplace communication: effective communication and efficient communication. Effective communication is when the message of the sender has a successful decoding from the receiver and efficient communication is when the communication is done effectively at a low cost. Furthermore, Guo and Sanchez (2005) defined communication as the creation or exchange of thoughts, ideas, emotions, and understanding between sender(s) and receiver(s). Guo and Sanchez (2005) found a strong relationship among communication and

DOI: 10.4018/978-1-4666-9970-0.ch022

the efficient and effective performance of the organization.

Hence, communication process is the procedure where a sender and a receiver communicate. This scheme incorporates the encoding-decoding operations and describes the usual transfer of the message. McShane and Von Glinow (2003) have illustrated this process by adding feedback and communication barriers: environment and personal (factors). Furthermore, there are three types of communication: verbal, non-verbal (Moreau, 2013), and gendered (which will not be covered in this chapter). Therefore, the purpose of this chapter is on communication, specifically, the role of the Johari Window on effective leadership communication in multinational corporations (MNCs). The chapter will cover the meaning of multinational corporations (MNCs), intercultural communication, and multicultural communication in MNCs, as well as language and diversity, and the roles that language and diversity play in MNCs. The purpose of this chapter is *not* on the development of a new model of leader communication for MNCs and it is *not* on advocating for an existing model of leader communication for MNCs.

MULTINATIONAL CORPORATIONS (MNCs) AND COMMUNICATION

According to Tran (2016), due to globalization, MNCs, commonly defined as a corporation consisting of a parent organization (headquarters) and at least one subsidiary organization in a foreign country, have made communication ever inevitable. As such, effective cross cultural management within an MNC requires communication skills, especially communication skills in intercultural communication and multicultural communication. Such communication skills are derived from, historically, three different fields of studies: communication, business, and psychology. Communication is paramount, particularly within any country of immigrants, and it is critical for the country to promote cultural diversity and appreciate different cultural heritages (Dong, 1995). Ethnocentrism is viewed as lacking acceptance of cultural diversity and intolerance for outgroups (Berry & Kalin, 1995).

As the world becomes a global village and more and more people with diverse cultural backgrounds interact with each other constantly, it is imperative to investigate what factors could help overcome ethnocentrism, especially as multinational corporations (MNCs) are expanding overseas. One of the challenges facing those MNCs is the increased diversity of the workforce and similarly complex prospective customers with disparate cultural backgrounds. After all, language barriers, cultural nuances, and value divergence can easily cause unintended misunderstandings and how low efficiency in internal communication in a multinational environment. It leads to conflict among employees and profit loss in organizational productivity. Therefore, effective communication by people from different cultures stands out significantly to American MNCs who want to make inroads into international markets, take advantage of multiculturalism, and avoid possible side effects (Tran, 2016).

In the field of communication (academic degrees and researches), according to Tran (2016), foci are commonly (and traditionally dominant) on rhetoric and interpersonal communication, and some higher educational institutions will offer business communication (commonly known as workplace communication), and fewer higher educational institutions will offer intercultural and international (business) communication. In the field of business, on the other hand, foci are commonly (and traditionally dominant) on administration, accounting, economics, finance, management, and marketing. Thereafter, advertising and public relations, business information systems, corporate management, entrepreneurship, human resources management, operations and enterprise resource management, real estate management, and supply chain management started to make its presence in academics and research. The last to join the business field are industrial relations and organizational behavior (with ties to psychology). In the field of psychology, however, foci are commonly (and traditionally dominant) on clinical psychology: clinicians, therapists, and counseling. Thereafter, common nonclinical psychology made its presence: abnormal, cognitive, developmental, social, and personality. The last to join the psychology field are industrial and organizational psychology [along with organization development (with ties to business)] and human factor [engineering psychology (with ties to engineering)]. Hence, the field of communication, and the practice of communication more often than not, becomes rhetorical and subject to interpretation on what communication is and what communication is not, not to mention *effective communication* (practices).

COMMUNICATION

Communication can be defined as the process of transmitting information and common understanding from one person to another (Keyton, 2011). The word communication is derived from the Latin word, *communis*, which means *common*. The definition underscores the fact that unless a common understanding results from the exchange of information, there is no communication. The two elements in every communication exchange are the sender and the receiver. The *sender* initiates the communication. The *receiver* is the individual to whom the message is sent. The sender *encodes* the idea by selecting words, symbols, or gestures with which to compose a message. The *message* is the outcome of the encoding, which takes the form of oral or written verbal and nonverbal symbols. The message is sent through a *medium* or channel, which is the carrier of the communication. The medium can be a face-to-face conversation,

telephone call, e-mail, a written report, or text (via a cell phone). The receiver *decodes* the received message into meaningful information. Noise is anything that distorts the message. Different perceptions of the message, language barriers, interruptions, emotions, and attitudes are examples of noise. *Feedback* occurs when the receiver responds to the sender's message by returning the message to the sender. Feedback allows the sender to determine whether the message has been received and understood. The elements in the communication process determine the quality of communication. A problem, commonly known as a *barrier* (Lunenburg, 2010), in any one of these can reduce communication effectiveness (Keyton, 2011). There are numerous barriers that negatively affect effective communication, of which, the following barriers are detrimental to leaders: emotional barriers, physical barriers, semantic barriers, and psychological barriers.

Emotional Barriers

Emotional barriers may be present in either the sender or the receiver. People base their encoding or transmitting of information on their personal experiences and expectations. A subordinate who expects to be rejected or belittled for making a suggestion or comment will not send one's message. The need to preserve our self-esteem is universal. Individuals with low self-esteem use certain patterns when attempting to communicate (Lynch, 1970). Some use tag questions at the end of a sentence—for example, "This is an interesting case, isn't it?" Other people with low self-esteem use qualifiers or disclaimers in everyday speech. Qualifiers include *sort of* and *perhaps*, whereas disclaimers include such statements as, "I really don't think this is a good idea" (Wallace & Robertson, 2009, p. 49). Other emotional barriers that cause communication to break down range from simple depression to complex psychological problems. However, with emotional barriers aside, a less, but equally detrimental, is physical barriers, that also play a part in causing miscommunication.

Physical Barriers

Physical barriers are the aspects of an environment that make communication more difficult. Any number of physical distraction, according to Lunenburg, 2010), can interfere with the effectiveness of communication, including a telephone call, drop-in visitors, walls, and static during a conversation. People often take physical barriers for granted, but sometimes they can be removed. For example, an inconveniently positioned wall can be removed. Interruptions such as telephone calls and drop-in visitors can be removed by issuing instructions to an administrative assistance. An appropriate choice of media can overcome distance barriers between people.

Semantic (Cultural) Barriers

Semantic can pose as a form of communication barrier. Strictly speaking, *semantics* is the study of the development and meaning of words. Semantic problems, however, can be defined as "the inability to agree on the meaning of certain terms, with a resulting loss in the ability to communicate clearly" (Wallace & Robertson, 2009, p. 49). For example, the words we choose, how we use them, and the meaning we attach to them causes many communication barriers. These communication barriers are known as semantic, or the meaning of the words we use. The same word may mean different things to different people. Words and phrases such as *efficiency*, *increased productivity*, *management prerogatives*, and *just cause* may mean one thing to one person and something entirely different to another person (Lunenburg, 2010). Technology also plays a part in semantic barriers to communication.

Verbal Communication. Global leaders, according to Chuang (2013), need cross-cultural negotiation skills to maintain international competitiveness (Okoro, 2012; Tran, 2008; Tran, 2014a, 2014b). Global leaders need to be able to ask questions and exchange messages effectively because of diverse personalities and characteristics, also known as soft skills or the Other Characteristic (O) in [knowledge, skills, abilities, and other characteristics {KSAOs (Tran, 2008; Tran, 2013; Tran, 2015a, 2015b)}], can easily cause misunderstanding and misinterpretation. Words and tone must be used carefully in order to deliver the message accurately while maintaining a good relationship. Thus, global leaders who receive training in interpersonal relationship and group communication competence (Okoro, 2012; Tran, 2008) will communicate better.

Nonverbal Communication. Actions speak louder than words. The global managers must be cognizant of their nonverbal language and be aware of acceptable behaviors as well as restrict behaviors in different cultures. For example, according to Chuang (2013), when a Japanese businessperson gives a gift, it normally means a gift to welcome or for appreciation rather than a bribe, and returning a gift is considered polite (Lussier, 2005). In some cultures, such as Brazil, kisses and hugs are the norm of greeting while other countries, such as China, nodding heads and smiling or shaking hands are used greeting (Chuang, 2013). Due to such cultural differences, people have various perceptions of personal space, touching, eye contact, and the like. Global leaders need to fully understand what these nonverbal behaviors are and the messages they represent.

Written (Semantic) Communication. According to Carston (2008), Kent Bach has argued in favor of a view of the semantic component of an utterance ('what is said', as Bach uses this term) as consisting of that information which it provides *independent of the speaker's communicative intention* (Bach, 1987, pp. 180-181; Bach, 2001, p. 22). This is congruent to the first level Carston (2008) advocates, that is linguistically encoded meaning (LEM), or standing linguistic meaning, Kaplan's semantic character, Grice's *formal* signification, Perry's *meaning*. Semantics, on Bach's view, then, includes not only encoded linguistic information, but also any context-given values of shifting from context to context that arise independently of processes (inferences) geared to the recovery of speaker meaning (so employing pragmatic maxims or principles of some sort). This way of drawing the semantics/pragmatics distinction rests on two other distinctions:

1. A distinction between pronouns which refers semantically ('pure' indexicals) and those which refer pragmatically (demonstrative indexicals). For example, according to the Stanford Encyclopedia of Philosophy (2015), the pronouns 'he', 'she', 'his', and 'hers' appear to have three different types of use: indexical uses (sometimes called deictic or demonstrative uses), bound variable uses, and unbound anaphoric uses (Cappelen & Dever, 2014; Carroll, 1999; Giorgi, 2010; Kaplan 1989, pp. 489–90; Partee 1989; Perry, 2015).

2. A distinction between two kinds of context narrow (or semantic) and broad (or pragmatic, or cognitive). For example, Jeffrey King (2012) argues that the semantic value of a demonstrative in a context is the object such that (a) the speaker intends it to be the demonstrative's semantic value and (b) an attentive hearer would take it to be the speaker's intended semantic value (Cappelen & Dever, 2014; Carroll, 1999; Giorgi, 2010; Littlejohn, 1996; Perry, 2015; The Stanford Encyclopedia of Philosophy, 2015).

With regard to the second of these, Bach (1997) says the following: "There are two sorts of contextual information, one is much more restricted in scope than the other. Information that plays the limited role of combining with linguistic information to determine content [in the sense of fixing (or repairing) it] is restricted to a short list

of variables, such as the identity of the speaker and the hearer and the time and place of an utterance. Contextual information in the broad sense is anything that the hearer is to take into account to determine (in the sense of ascertain) the speaker's communicative intention" (p. 39).

Hence, pronouns that refer semantically are those whose referent is a simply function of narrow (semantic) context. Pronouns that refer pragmatically are those whose referents are a function of broad context (and so are a matter of the speaker's communicative, specifically referential, intention). The following examples, discussed in Bach (1987, p. 176), make the distinction very clear. The semantic ('what is said') of (1a) and (1b) is given by (2a) and (2b), respectively (Carroll, 1999; Littlejohn, 1996):

01a. I am ready to go now.
01b. He was ready to go then.
02a. a is ready to go at t
02b. A certain male was ready to go at a certain time period to the time of utterance.

The proposition in (01a) is the result of applying a standard Kaplanian semantics for *I* and *now* to a narrow context in which a is that parameter which corresponds to the speaker and t is the time if utterance parameter. Narrow context does not provide any objective parameters as referents for *he* and *then*, so their referents have to be pragmatically inferred, using broad context and maxims or principles geared to the recovery of speaker meaning.

Psychological Barriers

Three important concepts are associated with psychological and social barriers: fields of experience, filtering, and psychological distance (Antos, 2011). *Fields of experience* include people's backgrounds, perceptions, values, biases, needs, and expectations. Senders can encode and receivers decode messages only in the context of their fields of experience. When the sender's field of experience overlaps very little with the receiver's, communication becomes difficult. *Filtering* means that more often than not, we see and hear what we are emotionally tuned in to see and hear. Filtering is caused by our own needs and interests, which guide our listening (Lunenburg, 2010). Psychological barriers often involves a psychological distance between people that is similar to actual physical distance. With that said, let's take a closer look at the Johari Window.

JOHARI WINDOW

In cross-cultural communication, there are barriers to employees of different cultural backgrounds. To eliminate these barriers, one should first recognize the cultural differences that exist, given that cultures are perhaps the most indeterminate in the world (Qing & Jia, 2011). The model of the *Johari Window* offers a perspective in cultural awareness within cross-cultural communication. The Johari Window has provided an in-depth insight of various personalities. The *Johari Window* was created by Joseph Luft and Harry Ingham in 1955 in the United States (Tandon, 2013; Tran & Taing, 2013). This model was first published in the proceedings of the Western Training Laboratory in group Development by University of California, Los Angeles (UCLA) Extension Office in 1955, and was later expended by Joseph Luft (Tandon, 2013; Tran & Taing, 2013). This model is also referred to as a *disclosure/feedback* model of self-awareness where some people call it an *information processing tool* (Tandon, 2013). It is a communication model or a technique that can be used to understand the personality of the people. The four regions of the Johari Window are: (1) Open Area or the Arena Qualities, (2) Blind Area or Blind Spot Qualities, (3) Hidden Area or Façade Qualities, and (4) Unknown Area or Unknown Self Qualities (Qing & Jia, 2011; Tandon, 2013; Tran & Taing, 2013). According

to the Johari Window, individuals can understand the personality of a person by working upon these four areas.

Increasing mutual understanding through feedback and disclosure allows individuals to increase the open area and reduce the blind, hidden, and unknown areas of oneself (McShane & Von Glinow, 2003). In the Johari Window, Luft (1984) argues for increasing the open area so that the individual, and one's co-workers are aware of one's limitations. This is done by receiving more feedback from others and decreasing one's blind area (windowpane 2) and reducing the hidden area (windowpane 3) through disclosing more about oneself. The combination of feedback and disclosure may also help to produce more information in the unknown area (windowpane 4). The Johari Window can be used for opening the channels of communication. Open communication is important for improving employee morale and increasing worker productivity. Open communication allows supervisors and subordinates to openly discuss organization-related issues such as goals and conflicts. Nevertheless, Luft (1984) is cautions on the use of the Johari Window for all situations. Luft (1984) offers several guidelines for the appropriateness of self-disclosure. Luft (1984) recommends that self-disclosure is a function of an ongoing relationship. Timing and extent of disclosure are critical. A competent communicator knows when, with whom, and how much to disclose. For example, leaders in MNCs often make personal and strategic decision regarding the sharing of information with others.

The Four Regions of Knowledge

Joseph Luft and Harry Ingham created a communication model and named it after themselves. They combined their names and called the model the Johari Window (Luft, 1969, 1970). This model has four regions, or areas, that represent basic areas of knowledge or information held by the leader and others. The four panes, or windows, represent relevant information about the manager's ability to interact with other persons effectively. The Johari window has two basic aspects of communication: exposure and feedback. The *exposure* aspect concerns the ability of the individual to express feelings and ideas in an open method. This aspect basically represents the leader's ability to transmit information. The *feedback* aspect involves the ability of the subordinates to receive information from the leader. The Johari window panes are distinct regions that encompass the following characteristics that expand or contract depending on the type of interpersonal communication patterns that leader adopts (Wallace & Robertson, 2009):

Area 1: The area 1 pane is known as the *free area*, or *arena*. It represents the portion of a leader's communication ability that allows him or her to freely share and receive information with and from others. The leader's ability is the key to a successful interpersonal relationship in an organization (Hall, 1974). Therefore, the larger this pane, or region, is in relational to the other panes, the more effective the leader is in dealing with superior and subordinates.

Area 2: The area 2 pane is known as the *blind area*, or *blind spot*. This area represents information known by others—supervisors, peers, or subordinates—that is not known to the leader. The larger this pane, the more information is being withheld from the leader.

Area 3: The area 3 pane is known as the *hidden area*, or the *façade*. This area represents how much information the leader keeps private. Everyone makes conscious or unconscious decisions to withhold certain information from others. This information may relate to personal habits or professional knowledge. When a leader withholds information, area 1—the free area, or arena—is prevented from expanding. Although withholding a portion of ourselves from others is normal and healthy, a problem arises when an indi-

vidual withholds information to the extent that it prevents a free, honest interchange of knowledge.

Area 4: The area 4 pane is called the *unknown area*. This area represents the amount of information that is unknown to both the leader and his or her superiors, and to his or her subordinates. As the free area, or arena, grows through effective communication, the unknown area shrinks. As one area (the unknown) shrinks, other areas (1, 2, and/or expands) as the individual becomes more aware of oneself and one's shortcomings.

The Four Basic Types of Communication Patterns

The Johari Window establishes four basic types of communication patterns in relation to the process of exposure and feedback (Wallace & Robertson, 2009). It is this process of exposure and feedback that helps and allows the individual to be more aware of one's strengths and weaknesses.

Type A: A leader who uses the type A communication pattern provides little feedback or exposure. The person who is typified by this communication style does not communicate with subordinates or supervisors. This type of individual withdraws from the decision-making process and is not willing to take risk by making a decision. He or she is more concerned with self-protection than with functioning effectively. The unknown area is the dominating factor with this type of leader, while the free area, or arena is correspondingly smaller.

Type B: A leader who uses type B communication pattern does not transmit information to supervisors, subordinates, or peers, but will accept some interaction and feedback from them. This type of individual does not trust fellow leaders but must receive information from them as a survival technique. This

411

type of person constantly asks for opinions or thoughts but is hesitant to reciprocate by telling others what he or she believes or feels. The model for this type of leader has a larger hidden area, or façade.

Type C: A leader who uses the type C communication pattern is characterized by continual self-expression and refusal to accept feedback from others. In this situation, the model shows an increase in exposure with a corresponding decrease in feedback. Individuals in this category have egos so large that they believe they have all the correct answers and strive to emphasize their authority and dominance over other leaders. Friends and colleagues soon come to believe that these individuals do not value the opinions of others or will tolerate only feedback that confirms their own beliefs or position. The Johari Window for this type of leader is characterized by a large blind spot.

Type D: A leader who uses the type D communication pattern is the kind of individual who shows outstanding leadership. He or she emphasizes open lines of communication and accepts feedback from superiors and subordinates alike. Unfortunately, many leaders are not accustomed to dealing with this type of person and may distrust such communication techniques at hand. The model for this type of leader has a large free area, or arena. However, the Johari Window is just one of several communication models often utilized, and considered popular to utilize to analyze an individual. There exist other communication models that are less known and infrequently utilized in the field and practice of communication.

Other Communication Models

Several other models, according to Wallace and Robertson (2009), deal with the dynamics of communication. All these models or theories seek to explain how the communication process works. Wilbur Lang Schramm and Harold Dwight Lasswell were two of the early pioneers in the field of communication. Both of these leaders established communication models that are still viable. The following are other communication models and a brief descriptions for those inquiring minds. An elaborate coverage of these other communication models will not be provided in this chapter.

Wilbur Lang Schramm's Model. Wilbur Lang Schramm (1907-1987) introduced a model that illustrated the importance of interpersonal communication (Schramm, 1955). Schramm is coined by many people to be the father of the study of communication, and Schramm played a critical role in the development of communication research (Rogers, 1994). Schramm was the first academic professional to identify himself as a communication scholar, created the first academic degree in communication, and trained the first generation of communication scholars. Schramm founded research institutes at the University of Iowa, the University of Illinois, and Stanford University, and published numerous texts and articles dealing with the dynamics of communication (Wallace & Robertson, 2009). From 1948 to 1977, Schramm produced almost a book a year dealing with the study of communication (McAnany, 1988), in addition to the articles, conference papers, and high-quality academic reports that Schramm turned out during this period. Schramm also wrote several influential texts, including Mass Media and National Development (Schramm, 1964). This book was an international best-seller, studied by people throughout the world. Schramm established a model of communication that attempts to explain the problems inherent in human communication. Schramm's model evolved in stages. It proceeded from relatively simple individual form of communication to a complex model involving interaction between two parties.

According to Wallace and Robertson (2009), in the first stage of Schramm's model, a source sends a message through an encoder, and the message is received by a decoder and transmitted to its designation. The *source* is the mind of the person starting the communication process. The *encoder* is the process by which ideas are converted to symbols for transmission to another person. The *decoder* is the process by which symbols are received and converted into ideas by the person receiving the information. The *signal* is symbols that are produced and transmitted. In the second stage of Schramm's model, Schramm slowly modified his first-stage model to include the concept that only the information that is shared in the respective parties' fields of experience is actually communicated. This is the only portion of the information that is communicated because it is the only shared portion of the signal that both parties understand. Schramm's contribution to communication theory included the concept that each person has a field of experience that controls both the encoding and decoding of information and determines the meanings of this information. In the third stage of the Schramm's model, communication is viewed as an interaction in which both parties actively encode, interpret, decode, transmit, and receive signals. This model includes the feedback of continuously shared information.

Harold Dwight Lasswell's Model. Harold Dwight Lasswell (1902-1978) published more than six million words during his lifetime. The theme of his doctoral dissertation, *Propaganda Techniques in the World War*, was the effect of propaganda on people during World War I (Lasswell, 1971, 1972, 1938). Lasswell defined propaganda as "the management of collective attitudes by the manipulation of significant symbols". Lasswell did not consider propaganda good or bad, to him, that determination depended on the sender's and receiver's viewpoint and the truthfulness of the messages (Rogers, 1994). Hence, Lasswell is best known for one sentence: "Who says what in which channel to whom with what effects?" In one of his early classic works, Lasswell identified five common variables in the communication process (Lasswell, 1948). These variables are the build-

ing blocks for his well-known sentence. Lasswell stated that one way to analyze the act of communication is to answer the following questions (Wallace & Robertson, 2009):

1. *Who?* When scholars analyze the *who* component, they look at factors that initiate and guide the act of communication. This is called *control analysis.*
2. *Says what?* Scholars who examine this aspect of the communication process engage in *content analysis.*
3. *In which channel?* Scholars who look at the method or ways information travels engage in *data analysis.* They look at radio, press, film, and other channels of communication.
4. *To whom?* Scholars who investigate the person reached by the media engage in *audience analysis.*
5. *With what effects?* Scholars who are concerned about the impact of the information on audiences study *effect analysis.*

Claude Elwood Shannon's Mathematical Model. One schematic model of a communication system emerged in the late 1940s, based on the work of mathematical Claude Elwood Shannon. The simplicity of Shannon's model, its clarity, and its surface generality proved attractive to many students of communication in a number of disciplines. As originally conceived, Shannon's model contained five elements (Wallace & Robertson, 2009):

1. An *information* source, which produces a message;
2. A *transmitter*, which operates on the message to create a signal that can be sent through a channel;
3. A *channel*, which is the medium over which the signal, carrying the information that comprises the message, is sent;
4. A *receiver*, which transforms the signal back into the message intended for delivery; and

5. A *destination*, which can be a person or a machine, for whom or which the messages is intended.

Hence, when it comes to communication, when elements are arranged in linear order, communication travel along this path, to be changed by the transmitter, and to be reconstituted into intelligible language by the receiver. In time, the five elements of the model were renamed to specify components for other types of communication transmitted in various manners. The information source was split into its components to produce a wider range of applicability. The six elements of the revised model are: 1) a source, 2) an encoder, 3) a message, 4) a channel, 5) a decoder, and 6) a receiver (Wallace & Robertson, 2009). These six fundamental elements are paramount to implementing effective communication for leaders in MNCs.

LEADERSHIP

Leadership, according to Giltinane (2013), is complex, comprising many definitions and qualities (Grimm, 2010). One definition of leadership is "a multifaceted process of identifying a goal, motivating other people to act, and providing support and motivation to achieve mutually negotiated goals" (Porter-O'Grady, 2003). Although the practice of leadership has changed considerably over time, the need for leaders and leadership has not (Abu-Tineh, Khasawneh, & Omary, 2009; Bass, 1990; Kouzes & Posner, 1995). A review of the leadership literature reveals an evolving series of *schools of thought* from *Great Man* and *Trait* theories to *Transformational* leadership. While early theories tend to focus upon the characteristics and behaviors of successful leaders, later theories begin to consider the role of followers and the contextual nature of leadership (Tran, 2014c). Hence, there are thirteen different types of leadership styles, divided into four different

categories: the *classics* (autocratic, authoritative, democratic, and laisser-faire), the *traditional* (transactional, transformational, situational, and charismatic), the *modern* (affiliative, coaching, exemplary, and visionary/inspirational), and the *innovative* (servant-leadership).

The link between leadership and competent communication has received limited attention by business and communication scholars alike (Madlock, 2008). According to Holladay and Coombs (1993), leadership is a behavior enacted through communication. Specifically, Holladay and Coombs suggested that communication shapes the perceptions of a leader's charisma, and communication can be divided into the content of the leader's messages and the presentation of those messages. Similarly, messages sent by leaders are considered to contain both affective and cognitive strategies (Hall & Lord, 1995), and when leaders effectively communicate their vision, they win the confidence of followers, which in turn aids in communication satisfaction between the leader and follower (Pavitt, 1999).

The Trait Approach to Leadership. The trait approach arose from the Great Man theory as a way of identifying the key characteristics of successful leaders. It was believed that through this approach critical leadership traits could be isolated and that people with such traits could then be recruited, selected, and installed into leadership positions. This approach was common in the military and is still used as a set of criteria to select candidates for commissions. The problem with the trait approach lies in the fact that almost as many traits as studies undertaken were identified. After several years of such research, it became apparent that no consistent traits could be identified. Although some traits were found in a considerable number of studies, the results were generally inconclusive. Some leaders might have possessed certain traits but the absence of them did not necessarily mean that the person was not a leader. Although there was little consistency in the results of the various trait studies, however, some traits did appear more frequently than others, including: technical skills, friendliness, task motivation, applications to task, group task supportiveness, social skill, emotional control, administrative skill, general charisma, and intelligence (Bolden, Gosling, Marturano, & Dennison, 2003).

The Behavioral School Approach to Leadership. The results of the trait studies, according to Bolden et al. (2003), were inclusive. Traits, amongst other things, were hard to measure. After the publication of the late Douglas McGregor's classic book, *The Human Side of Enterprise* in 1960, attention shifted to *behavioral theories*. McGregor was a teacher, researcher, and consultant whose work was considered to be on the cutting edge of managing people. McGregor influenced all the behavioral theories, which emphasize focusing on human relationships, along with output and performance.

Communicator (Leaders' Communication) Competence

Harris and Cronen's (1979) research indicated that competent individuals must not only achieve their goals (be effective) but also do so appropriately. In following with this notion, communication competence has been conceptualized to encompass elements of knowledge, motivation, skills, behavior, and effectiveness (Spitzberg, 1983). Spitzberg and Cupach (1981) stated, "competent interaction can be viewed as a form of interpersonal influence, in which an individual is faced with the task of fulfilling communicative functions and goals (effectiveness) while maintaining conversational and interpersonal norms (appropriateness)" (p. 1). Cushman and Craig (1976) argued that communicator competence involves the ability of individuals to display competencies in areas such as listening and negotiating. Furthermore, Salacuse (2007) indicated that as a result of changing work environments in which employees are more educated and intelligent than past generations, leaders are now required to lead by negotiation. Specifically, Salacuse (2007) noted that in order for leaders to persuade people to follow their vision, they need to communicate effectively by appealing to the interests of the followers. In that competent communicators must employ communicative resources such as language, gestures, and voice (Stohl, 1984), and in order for supervisors to be perceived as competent communicators, they must share and respond to information in a timely manner, actively listen to other points of view, communicate clearly and succinctly to all levels of the organization, and utilize differing communication channels (Shaw, 2005).

Despite the vast amount of research focused on competent communication, there appears to be a lack on prior research directly examining the relationship between supervisor communicator competence and supervisor task and relational leadership styles. However, there does appear to be a limited amount of research examining the influence of supervisors' communicator competence on employee outcomes. One such study was that of Berman and Hellweg (1989), whose findings indicated that the perceived communicator competence of a supervisor was related to their subordinate's satisfaction with that supervisor. Another example was a study by Myers and Kassing (1998), who examined the relationship between subordinate perceptions of their supervisor's communication skills, including communicator competence, and the subordinate's level of organizational identification. Myers and Kassing's findings indicated that supervisor communication competence was a significant predicator of subordinate organizational identification. Yet, another example was a study of Sharbrough, Simmons, and Cantrill (2006), who examined the impact of motivational language on a number of outcomes. Specifically, Sharbrough et al. (2006), found positive relationships between a leader's use of motivational language and their perceived effectiveness, their communication competence, and their subordinates' job and communication satisfaction. The more communication satisfaction perceived by subordinates', the willingness to be led increases, and the more productive the subordinates become.

Communication Satisfaction between Leaders and Subordinates

Employee satisfaction has been an area examined by business and communication scholars primarily because satisfaction has been positively related to job performance (Gruneberg, 1979). A conceptualization of communication satisfaction was offered by Crino and White (1981), who argued that organizational communication satisfaction involves an individual's satisfaction with various aspects of the communication occurring in the organizations, whereas Putti, Aryee, and Phua (1990) demonstrated that organizational members; communication satisfaction is associated with the amount of information available to them. Although communication provides employees with information that clarifies work tasks and may contribute to communication satisfaction, Anderson and Martin (1995) found that employees engage in communication interactions with coworkers and supervisors to satisfy interpersonal needs of pleasure and inclusion. Thus, employee communication satisfaction appears to involve a task and relational dimension. Furthermore, prior research indicates that interpersonal interactions involving the exchanging of information and affect between coworkers and between employees and their supervisors can have significant effects on the employees' psychological job outcomes, including job satisfaction, organizational commitment, and burnout (e.g., Pincus, 1986; Postmes, Tanis, & de Wit, 2001; Ray & Miller, 1994). Generally, as employees experience more positive communication relationships, they also experience more positive job outcomes such as job satisfaction.

Job Satisfaction Due to Communication

The most common factors leading to worker stress and dissatisfaction are those emanating from the nature of the job itself, within which interpersonal relationships between employees and supervisors take place (Barnett & Brennan, 1997; Rodwell, Kienzle, & Shadur, 1998). According to Korte and Wynne (1996), a deterioration of relationships in organization settings resulting from reduced interpersonal communication between workers and supervisors negatively influences job satisfaction and sometimes leads to employees leaving their jobs. Hence, according to Madlock (2008), early work by Taylor (1970) suggested that worker satisfaction may be attributed to the highest possible earnings with the least amount of fatigue, whereas Locke (1976) defined job satisfaction from an employees' standpoint as "a pleasurable or positive emotional state from the appraisal of one's job or experiences" (p. 1297). Taylor's classical theory prompted a number of studies that revealed differing factors behind job satisfaction. Some of these factors found to mediate job satisfaction include supervisors' displays of nonverbal immediacy (Madlock, 2006a; Richmond & McCroskey, 2000), humor (Avrgis & Taber, 2006), communication satisfaction (Hilgerman, 1998), effects of gender (Madlock, 2006b), and supervisors' communication style (Richmond, McCroskey, Davis, & Koontz, 1980).

CULTURAL BARRIERS IN COMMUNICATION

Cultural prejudice refers to the formation of opinion on certain members of the group grounded on the previous perception, attitude, and viewpoint of the group, heedless of the particular characteristic of the individual (Zhang & Xu, 2007). Cultural prejudice is also commonly known as ethnocentrism, which means that "a tendency exists within individual to view his or her own culture as intrinsically better than other cultures" (Victor, 2001, p. 36). As such, in intercultural communication, people often reply on their first impressions and assumptions, drawing on previous knowledge of the common features of a culture to make conclusions about an individual instead of analyzing behaviors specifically. As a result, it is not uncommon to hear comments such as "you are from China, so you must never have had human rights", or "as an American, you must never feel safe to go outside at night since everyone is allowed to have guns" (Li, 2010, p. 121). These conclusions are easy to make since they require little effort in observation and eliminate the need to process a large amount of information. Although it is true that it speeds up message processing, improves communication efficiency, and provides timely convenience, cultural prejudice also ossifies into rigid patterns and colors our perspectives, which are difficult to then change or update. Consequently, it prevents meaningful and openhearted communication between people with divergent backgrounds. Moreover, another insidious, harmful side is that after repeating and emphasizing this cultural mindset, the fixed prejudice is likely to become "the eternal verities", which take root in people's minds and further hinder future communication.

Intercultural (Cross-Cultural) Communication

Culture according Tran (2013, 2014d, 2014e), is "the manifold ways of perceiving and organizing the world that are held in common by a group of people and passed on interpersonally and inter-generationally" (Yuan, 2006, p. 5). According to David Victor, it is "the part of behavior that is at once learned and collective", and therefore, "taught rather than instinctive or innate" (2001, p. 30). Starting at birth, "the infant mind is somewhat like a blank tape, waiting to be filled", culture plays a large part "in the recording process" (Fisher,

1988, p. 45). Handed down from members within the larger community, it is gradually reinforced and imprinted into an individual's mind as time progresses. Culture directly influences the way in which people within the context communicate, and the way in which they perceive each other (Victor, 2001). As a result, one organization's conduct, developed in a particular environment and reflecting the local staff's cultural identity, may not be applicable to another culture (Tran 2016). Hence, cross-cultural communication, also known as intercultural communication and trans-cultural communication, indicates the exchange of ideas, emotions, and information by means of language, words, and body language between people from different cultural backgrounds (Xu, 2007).

Multicultural Communication

Multicultural communication is also commonly known as multilingualism or bilingualism. The term bilingualism became common in the 50s and 60s to indicate an individual's ability to use two (or more) languages (Tran, 2016). However, the term has become key for a great number of works describing different educational programs for ethnically and culturally diverse societies. Modern concepts of multi-cultural, multi-ethnic, and cross-cultural, cultural pluralism, and anti-racist education presuppose the setting for and solution to the problem of linguistic variety. According to Dong, Day, and Collaço (2014), "Immigration has been one of the most persistent and pervasive influences of the United States" (Dong, 1995, p. 9). Due to immigration, globalization and ethnic diversification, multiculturalism is a pronounced characteristic of the United States. Multicultural ideology refers to "overall evaluation of the majority group addressing the degree to which they possess positive attitudes toward immigrants and cultural diversity" (Arends-Tóth & Van De Vijver, 2002, p. 252). When individuals hold a positive overall evaluation they tend to appreciate cultural diversity and cultural maintenance of ethnic groups. Arends-Tóth and Van De Vijver (2002) suggested that one main principle of multiculturalism is to focus on cultural diversity which, however, is perceived differently by majority and minority group members.

DIMENSIONS OF LANGUAGE IN (LANGUAGE) DIVERSITY

Before attempting to consider language management strategies, according to Tran (2016), companies will have to evaluate the magnitude of the language barrier confronting them and in doing so they will need to examine it in three dimensions. The first dimension is the number of different languages the company has to manage (the Language Diversity). The second is the number of functions and the number of levels within those functions that are engaged in cross-lingual communication (the Language Penetration) and the third is the complexity and refinement of the language skills required (the Language Sophistication).

Language Diversity

The first dimension, according to Tran (2016), is the language diversity, and the level of language diversity may depend on the extent of the company's global network of subsidiaries, customers, supplies and joint ventures, though even the most international of enterprises will embrace only a minute fraction of the world's 5,000 plus languages (Feely & Harzing, 2002). Global giants such as Microsoft have strategies to manage around 80 different languages. However, this is likely to be an unrealistic target for most companies. More typically global enterprises will be able to manage their global networks provided they establish capabilities in the leading European languages, including some from Eastern Europe, in Japanese, Chinese, Arabic and selected Asian languages notably Malay, Urdu, Hindi, and Bengali. An elucidate study identified the top dozen

or so language priorities for European companies (Hagen, 1999). This number is suggested also by the Engco model (Graddol, 1997) which uses population, demographic and economic data to position languages on a scale according to Global Influence. Beyond the leading 15 or so languages on this scale none can really be claimed to have any significant global influence (Feely & Harzing, 2002).

Language Penetration

The second dimension, according to Tran (2016), is the level of language penetration will depend on the number of functional areas within an MNC that have to operate across linguistic boundaries. There may have been a time when cross-lingual communication could have been channeled through a small and exclusive band of language specialists. For example, Finance (Global Treasury), R&D (Co-design), Production Engineering (Concurrent Engineering), Logistics (Supply Chain Management), Sales (Global Account Management), Purchasing (Global Sourcing), Human Resources (Global Management Development), and MIS (Global Systems Integration) are all directly tasked with coordinating activities that span national and linguistic boundaries. Furthermore, corporate level functions such as Legal and Public Relations require the same linguistic versatility to be able to support them (Feely & Harzing, 2002).

Language Sophistication

The third dimension, according to Tran (2016), is clearly the complexity, refinement and type of the language skills required vary from post holder to post holder, within an organization. A receptionist will require essentially speaking-listening proficiency and might suffice with the limited skills necessary to recognize requests and to exchange pleasantries. A logistics clerk will need to have a greater foreign language capability including reading and writing, but will at least have the benefit of being able to operate with a limited vocabulary. An engineer working as part of an international design team represents a further progression in language sophistication. They will be required to evolve concepts and resolve design problems in both spoken and written form without language being a barrier. With that said, at the pinnacle of the scale comes the international manager, who will need excellent language proficiency embracing the full range of rhetorical skills such as negotiation, persuasion, motivation, and humor. At this level the capability level might well exceed that of a typical masters' level graduate in modern languages (Feely & Harzing, 2002).

Measuring the Language Barrier Dimensions

The tool for measuring these three language barrier dimensions are provided by Linguistic Auditing (Reeves & Wright, 1996). The methodology is designed to enable international companies to evaluate their foreign language requirements and to benchmark these against their capabilities thereby identifying areas of strength and weakness. It goes on to assess the company's language training and recruitment needs and evaluates the efficacy of these programs (Tran, 2008). Finally it provides the means to match the organization's foreign language capability against its strategic aspirations. Unfortunately, research suggest that Linguistic Auditing has not been widely adopted (Randlesome & Myer, 1998) and that most companies have yet to develop language strategies (Hagen, 1999; Tran, 2008).

Arguably, according to Feely and Harzing (2002), the problem is the fact that a full audit is a costly and time-consuming process requiring extensive support from external language assessors. So, to combat this criticism, a simpler and less costly system called Language Check-up has been developed as a front-end to the Audit methodology (Reeves & Feely, 2001). Although lacking the rigor and reliability of the full Linguistic Audit,

the check-up offers some notable advantages. It is self-administered avoiding the cost of external language specialists, it generates results quickly and it embraces a wider range of language issues than the audit. Specifically, it evaluates the status of Corporate Language standardization, the availability of computer systems, publications and web sites with multiple language interfaces, the capabilities and controls on external language resources and the usage of machine translation tools (Tran, 2016).

FUTURE RESEARCH

With the Johari Window, what Luft (1984) did not mentioned, and many researchers did not question, and even more practitioners did not realize is that, the Johari Window is created based on a domestic paradigm, and not necessarily applicable to multinational environments where intercultural and multicultural communication are at play for multinational environment within MNCs. For example, based on the Johari Window, from a micro perspective, when practiced within a local environment, there are communication barriers that will already have come into play (Tran & Taing, 2013). Furthermore, take into consideration, if the Johari Window is to be taken from the micro perspective (within a local environment), into the macro perspective, and practiced the Johari Window within an international environment, the types of communication barriers that will come (or have already and continuously come) into play. Hence, there exists a gap in literature, regarding the role of the Johari window on effective leadership communication in MNCs.

Granted, Geert Hofetede is infamously known for his work in and with dimensions of national cultures, which may correlate with communication, but not specifically on and about the roles and effectiveness of communication within dimensions of national cultures in regards to the Johari Window. Nevertheless, the Johari Window has continuously been applied to cross cultural studies, without a paradigm shift. Due to the lack of paradigm shift, utilizing a domestic paradigm (no international cultural factors at play) within a multinational environment (various international cultural factors at play), issue at hand persists. Hence, future researches are detrimental in the understanding of the role of the Johari window on effective leadership in MNCs in regards to the usage of communication.

CONCLUSION

Communication is a major constituent in any multinational corporations (MNCs). In MNCs, the importance of well-functioning (international) communication from an effect leader of any MNCs, is even more vital than in any domestic corporations, due to the fact that, among other things, its units are dispersed across national borders. At the same time as the complexity that MNC requires from an effective internal communication channel, more detrimental is an effective leader in MNCs with good communication skills that compounds the complexity, that making it difficult to accomplish. Hence, most of the difficulties in achieving an effective internal communication within an MNC are, first of all, consequences of the nature and characteristics of the MNC and, second of all, they are interrelated with the Johari Window. Such that, one of the difficulties in MNCs when it comes to effective leaders and their communication skills are, cross-cultural communication due to employees of different cultural backgrounds.

To eliminate these barriers, one should first recognize the cultural differences that exist, given that cultures are perhaps the most indeterminate in the world. The model of Johari Window offers a perspective in cultural awareness within cross-cultural communication. Johari Window has provided an in-depth insight of various personalities. However, in regards to the Johari Window, many researchers did not question, and

even more practitioners did not realize is that, the Johari Window is created based on a domestic paradigm, and not necessarily applicable to a multinational environment where intercultural and multicultural communication are at play for multinational environment within MNCs. Nevertheless, the Johari Window has continuously been applied to cross cultural studies, without a paradigm shift, utilizing a domestic paradigm (no international cultural factors at play) within a multinational environment (various international cultural factors at play), issue at hand persists. Hence, MNCs need to evaluate and train their MNCs' leaders on their communication skills, often known as *soft skills*, or commonly known as their *other characteristics* in KSAOs (Al-Ababneh & Lockwood, 2010; Chen, Wang, & Chu, 2011; Ghafoor, Khan, Idrees, Javed, & Ahmed, 2011; Hsieh, Lin, & Lee, 2012; Joshua-Gojer, 2012; Okpara & Kabongo, 2011; Tran, 2008; Tran, 2013; Rozkwitalska, 2012; Tran, 2014a, Tran, 2015a, 2015b, Tran, 2016; Tsai, Zeng, Lan, & Fang, 2012).

REFERENCES

Abu-Tineh, A. M., Khasawneh, S. A., & Omary, A. A. (2009). Kouzes and Posner's transformational leadership model in practice: The case of Jordanian schools. *Journal of Leadership Education*, 7(3), 265–283. doi:10.12806/V7/I3/RF10

Al-Ababneh, M., & Lockwood, A. (2010). *The influence of managerial leadership style on employee job satisfaction in Jordanian resort hotels*. The 28th EuroCHRIE Annual Research Conference, Amsterdam, Netherlands.

Anderson, C. M., & Martin, M. M. (1995). The effects of communication motives, interaction involvement, and loneliness on satisfaction: A model of small groups. *Small Group Research*, 26(1), 118–137. doi:10.1177/1046496495261007

Antos, P. (2011). *Handbook of interpersonal communication*. The Hague, The Netherlands: Mouton De Gruyter.

Arends-Tóth, J., & Van De Vijver, F. J. R. (2002). Multiculturalism and acculturation: View of Dutch and Turkish-Dutch. *European Journal of Social Psychology, 33*(2), 249–266. doi:10.1002/ejsp.143

Avtgis, T. A., & Taber, K. R. (2006). "I laughed so hard my side hurts, or is that an ulcer?" The influence of work humor on job stress, job satisfaction, and burnout among print media employees. *Communication Research Reports, 23*(1), 13–18. doi:10.1080/17464090500535814

Bach, K. (1987). *Thought and reference*. Oxford, UK: Clarendon Press.

Bach, K. (1999). The semantics-pragmatics distinction: What it is and why it matters. In K. Turner (Ed.), *The semantics-pragmatics interface from different points of view* (pp. 65–84). Oxford, UK: Elsevier.

Bach, K. (2001). You don't say. *Synthese, 128*(1/2), 15–44. doi:10.1023/A:1010353722852

Barnett, R., & Brennan, R. (1997). Change in job conditions, change in psychological distress, and gender: A longitudinal study of dual-earner couples. *Journal of Organizational Behavior, 18*(3), 253–274. doi:10.1002/(SICI)1099-1379(199705)18:3<253::AID-JOB800>3.0.CO;2-7

Bass, B. M. (1990). From transactional to transformational leadership: Learning to share the vision. *Organizational Dynamics, 18*(3), 19–31. doi:10.1016/0090-2616(90)90061-S

Berman, S. J., & Hellweg, S. A. (1989). Perceived supervisor communication competence and supervisor satisfaction as a function of quality circle participation. *Journal of Business Communication, 26*(2), 103–122. doi:10.1177/002194368902600202

Berry, J., & Kalin, R. (1995). Multicultural and ethnic attitudes in Canada: An overview of the 1991 national survey. *Canadian Journal of Behavioural Science, 27*(3), 301–320. doi:10.1037/0008-400X.27.3.301

Bolden, R., Gosling, J., Marturano, A., & Dennison, P. (2003). *A review of leadership theory and competency frameworks: Edited version of a report for Chase consulting and management standards centre*. Centre for Leadership Studies at University of Exeter.

Cappelen, H., & Dever, J. (2014). *The inessential indexical: On the philosophical insignificance of perspective and the first person: Context and content*. Oxford University Press.

Carroll, D. W. (1999). Psychology of language (3rd ed.). Brooks/Cole Publishing Company.

Carston, R. (2008). Linguistic communication and the semantics/pragmatics distinction. *Synthese, 165*(3), 321–345. doi:10.1007/s11229-007-9191-8

Chen, Y. C., Wang, W. C., & Chu, Y. C. (2011). A case study on the business performance management of Hilton hotels corp. *International Business Research, 4*(2), 213–218. doi:10.5539/ibr.v4n2p213

Chuang, S. F. (2013). *Essential skills for leadership effectiveness in diverse workplace development*. Retrieved on May 29, 2015, available at http://www.scribd.com/doc/266987534/Essential-Skills-for-Leadership-Effectiveness#scribd

Crino, M. E., & White, M. C. (1981). Satisfaction in communication: An examination of the Downs-Hazen measure. *Psychological Reports, 49*(3), 831–838. doi:10.2466/pr0.1981.49.3.831

Dong, D., Day, K. D., & Collaço, C. M. (2014). Overcoming ethnocentrism through developing intercultural communication sensitivity and multiculturalism. *Human Communication: A Publication of the Pacific and Asian Communication Association, 11*(1), 27-38.

Dong, Q. (1995). *Self, identity, media use and socialization: A student of adolescent Asian immigrants to the United States.* (Unpublished doctoral dissertation). Washington State University, Pullman, WA.

Feely, A. J., & Harzing, A. W. (2002). Language management in multicultural companies. *Cross-Cultural Management: An International Journal, 10*(2), 37–52. doi:10.1108/13527600310797586

Fisher, G. (1998). *Mindsets: The role of culture and perception in international relations.* Yarmouth, ME: Intercultural Press.

Ghafoor, S., Khan, U. F., Idrees, F., Javed, B., & Ahmed, F. (2011). Evaluation of expatriates performance and their training on international assignments. *Interdisciplinary Journal of Contemporary Research in Business, 3*(5), 335-351.

Giltinane, C. L. (2013). Leadership styles and theories. *Nursing Standard, 27*(41), 35–39. doi:10.7748/ns2013.06.27.41.35.e7565 PMID:23905259

Giorgi, A. (2010). About the speaker: Towards a syntax of indexicality. Oxford University Press.

Graddol, D. (1997). *The future of English.* London: The British Council.

Grimm, J. W. (2010). Effective leadership: Making the difference. *Journal of Emergency Nursing: JEN, 36*(1), 74–33. doi:10.1016/j.jen.2008.07.012 PMID:20109788

Gruneberg, M. M. (1979). *Understanding job satisfaction.* New York: John Wiley. doi:10.1007/978-1-349-03952-4

Guo, L. C., & Sanchez, Y. (2005). Workplace communication. In N. Borkowski (Ed.), *Organizational behavior in health care* (pp. 77–110). Jones & Bartlett Learning.

Hagen, S. (1999). *Business communication across borders: A study of language use and practice in European companies.* London: Languages National Training Organisation.

Hall, J. (1974). Interpersonal styles and the communication dilemma: Management implications of the Johari awareness model. *Human Relations, 27*(4), 381–399. doi:10.1177/001872677402700404

Hall, R. J., & Lord, R. G. (1995). Multi-level information-processing explanations of followers' leadership perceptions. *The Leadership Quarterly, 6*(3), 265–281. doi:10.1016/1048-9843(95)90010-1

Harris, L., & Cronen, V. E. (1979). A rules-based model for the analysis and evaluation of organizational communication. *Communication Quarterly, 27*(1), 12–28. doi:10.1080/01463377909369320

Hilgerman, R. H. (1988). *Communication satisfaction, goal setting, job satisfaction, concertive control, and effectiveness in self-managed teams.* (Unpublished doctoral dissertation). University of Maine.

Holladay, S. J., & Coombs, W. T. (1993). Communication visions: An exploration of the role of delivery in the creation of leader charisma. *Management Communication Quarterly, 6*(4), 405–427. doi:10.1177/0893318993006004003

Hsieh, S. C., Lin, J. S., & Lee, H. C. (2012). Analysis on literature review of competency. *International Review of Business and Economics, 2*, 25–50.

Joshua-Gojer, A. E. (2012). Cross-cultural training and success versus failure of expatriates. *Learning and Performance Quarterly, 1*(2), 47–62.

Kaplan, D. (1989). Demonstratives. In J. Almog, P. Perry, H. K. Wettstein, & D. Kaplan (Eds.), *Themes from Kaplan* (pp. 481–563). Oxford University Press.

Keyton, J. (2011). *Communication and organizational culture: A key to understanding work experience*. Thousand Oaks, CA: Sage.

King, J. C. (2012). Anaphora. In G. Russell & D. G. Fara (Eds.), *The Routledge companion to the philosophy of Language*. Routledge.

Korte, W. B., & Wynne, R. (1996). *Telework Penetration, potential and practice in Europe*. Amsterdam: Ohmsha Press.

Kouzes, J. M., & Posner, B. Z. (1995). *The leadership challenge: How to keep getting extraordinary things done in organizations*. San Francisco, CA: Jossey-Bass.

Lasswell, H. D. (1927). *Propaganda techniques in the world war*. New York: Knopf.

Lasswell, H. D. (1938). *Propaganda techniques in the world war*. New York: Peter Smith.

Lasswell, H. D. (1948). The structure and function of communication is society. In L. Bryson (Ed.), *The new communication of ideas* (pp. 37–51). New York: Harper & Brothers.

Lasswell, H. D. (1971). *Propaganda techniques in the world war*. Cambridge, MA: The MIT Press.

Li, Y. (2010). Cross-cultural communication within American and Chinese colleagues in multinational organizations. *Proceedings of the 68th New York State Communication Association*.

Littlejohn, S. W. (1996). *Theories of human communication* (5th ed.). Wadsworth Publishing Company: An International Thomson Publishing Company.

Locke, E. A. (1976). The nature and causes of job satisfaction. In M. D. Dunnette (Ed.), *Handbook of industrial and organizational psychology* (pp. 1297–1349). Chicago: Rand McNally.

Luft, J. (1969). *Of human interaction*. Palo Alto, CA: National Press Book.

Luft, J. (1970). *Group processes: An introduction to group dynamics*. Palo Alto, CA: Mayfield.

Luft, J. (1984). *Group processes: An introduction to group dynamics* (3rd ed.). Palo Alto: Mayfield.

Lunenburg, F. C. (2010). Communication: The process, barriers, and improving effectiveness. *Schooling, 1*(1), 1–11.

Lynch, M. D. (1970). Stylistic analysis. In P. Emmert & W. D. Brooks (Eds.), *Method of research in communications* (pp. 315–342). New York: Houghton Miffin.

Madlock, P. E. (2006a). *Supervisor' nonverbal immediacy behaviors and their relationship to subordinates' communication satisfaction, job satisfaction, and willingness to collaborate*. Paper presented at the National Communication Association Convention, San Antonio, Texas.

Madlock, P. E. (2006b). Do difference in displays of nonverbal immediacy and communication competence between male and female supervisors affect subordinates, job satisfaction. *Ohio Communication Journal, 44*, 61–78.

Madlock, P. E. (2008). The link between leadership style, communicator competence, and employee satisfaction. *Journal of Business Communication, 45*(1), 61–78. doi:10.1177/0021943607309351

McAnany, E. (1988). Wilbur Schramm, 1907-1987: Roots of the past, seeds of the present. *Journal of Communication, 38*(4), 109–122. doi:10.1111/j.1460-2466.1988.tb02073.x

McShane, S. L., & Von Glinow, M. A. (2003). *Organizational behavior: Emerging realities for the workplace revolution* (2nd ed.). Boston, MA: McGraw-Hill.

Moreau, R. (2013). *The value of foreign languages in business communication.* Retrieved on May 1, 2015, available at http://scholarsarchive.jwu.edu/cgi/viewcontent.cgi?article=1016&context=mba_student

Myers, S. A., & Kassing, J. W. (1998). The relationship between perceived supervisory communication behaviors and subordinate organizational identification. *Communication Research Reports, 15*(1), 71–81. doi:10.1080/08824099809362099

Okoro, E. (2012). Cross-cultural etiquette and communication in global business: Toward a strategic framework for managing corporate expansion. *International Journal of Business and Management, 7*(16), 130–138. doi:10.5539/ijbm.v7n16p130

Okpara, J. O., & Kabongo, J. D. (2011). Cross-cultural training and expatriate adjustment: A study of western expatriate in Nigeria. *Journal of World Business, 46*(1), 22–30. doi:10.1016/j.jwb.2010.05.014

Partee, B. (1989). Binding implicit variables in quantified contexts. In C. Wiltshire, B. Music, & R. Graczyk (Eds.), *Papers from Chicago Linguistic Society (CLS) 25* (pp. 342–365). Chicago: Chicago Linguistic Society.

Pavitt, C. (1999). Theorizing about the group communication-leadership relationship: Input-process-output and functional models. In L. R. Frey, D. S. Gouran, & M. S. Poole (Eds.), *The handbook of group communication theory and research* (pp. 313–334). Thousand Oaks, CA: Sage.

Perry, J. (2015). *The problem of the essential indexical and other essays: Extended edition.* Center for the Study of Language and Information.

Pincus, J. D. (1986). Communication satisfaction, job satisfaction and job performance. *Human Communication Research, 12*(3), 395–419. doi:10.1111/j.1468-2958.1986.tb00084.x

Porter-O'Grady, T. (2003). A different age for leadership, part 1: New context, new content. *The Journal of Nursing Administration, 33*(2), 105–110. doi:10.1097/00005110-200302000-00007 PMID:12584463

Postmes, T., Tanis, M., & de Wit, B. (2001). Communication and commitment in organizations: A social identity approach. *Group Processes & Intergroup Relations, 4*(3), 227–246. doi:10.1177/1368430201004003004

Putti, J. M., Aryee, S., & Phua, J. (1990). Communication relationship satisfaction and organizational commitment. *Group & Organization Studies, 15*(1), 44–52. doi:10.1177/105960119001500104

Qing, L., & Jia, Z. (2011). On effective communication of cross-cultural enterprises. *Proceedings of the 8th International Conference on Innovation & Management.*

Randlesome, C., & Myers, A. (1998). Cultural fluency: The United Kingdom versus Demark. *European Business Journal, 10*(4), 184–194.

Ray, E. B., & Miller, K. I. (1994). Social support, home/work stress and burnout: Who can help? *The Journal of Applied Behavioral Science, 30*(3), 357–373. doi:10.1177/0021886394303007

Reeves, N., & Feely, A. (2001). Suspected language problems: Your company needs a language check-up. *Aston Business School Doctoral Working Paper, 37.*

Richmond, V. P., & McCroskey, J. C. (2000). The impact of supervisor and subordinate immediacy on relational and organizational outcomes. *Communication Monographs, 67*(1), 85–95. doi:10.1080/03637750009376496

Richmond, V. P., McCroskey, J. C., Davis, L. M., & Koontz, K. A. (1980). Perceived power as a mediator of management styles and employee satisfaction: A preliminary investigation. *Communication Quarterly*, *28*(4), 37–46. doi:10.1080/01463378009369380

Rodwell, J., Kienzle, R., & Shadur, M. (1998). The relationships among work-related perceptions, employee attitudes, and employee perceptions and employee performance: The integral role of communication. *Human Resource Management*, *37*(3/4), 277–293. doi:10.1002/(SICI)1099-050X(199823/24)37:3/4<277::AID-HRM9>3.0.CO;2-E

Rogers, E. M. (1994). *A history of communication study*. New York: Free Press.

Rozkwitalska, M. (2012). Staffing top management positions in multinational subsidiaries—a local perspective on expatriate management. *Journal of Global Science & Technology Forum (GSTF). Business Review (Federal Reserve Bank of Philadelphia)*, *2*(2), 50–56.

Salacuse, J. W. (2007). *Real leaders negotiate*. Retrieved on May 26, 2015, available at https://hbr.org/2008/02/real-leaders-negotiate-1.php

Schramm, W. (1955). How communications works. In W. Schramm (Ed.), *The process and effects of mass communications*. Urbana, IL: University of Illinois Press.

Schramm, W. (1964). *Mass media and national development*. Stanford, CA: Stanford University Press.

Scott, T. J. (2005). *The concise handbook of manager: A practitioner's approach*. USA: The Haworth Press.

Sharbrough, W. C., Simmons, S. A., & Cantrill, D. A. (2006). Motivating language in industry: Its impact on job satisfaction and perceived supervisor effectiveness. *Journal of Business Communication*, *43*(4), 322–343. doi:10.1177/0021943606291712

Shaw, K. (2005). Getting leaders involved in communication strategy: Breaking down the barriers to effective leadership communication. *Strategic Communication Management*, *9*, 14–17.

Spitzberg, B. H. (1983). Communication competence as knowledge, skill, and impression. *Communication Education*, *32*(3), 323–329. doi:10.1080/03634528309378550

Spitzberg, B. H., & Cupach, W. R. (1981). *Self-monitoring and relational competence*. Paper presented at the Speech Communication Association Convention, Anaheim, CA.

Stohl, C. (1984). *Quality circle and the quality of communication*. Paper presented at the Speech Communication Association Convention, Chicago, IL.

Tandon, R. (2013). New area in Johari Window. *International Journal of Engineering and Innovative Technology*, *3*(2), 83–85.

Taylor, F. W. (1970). What is scientific management? In H. F. Merrill (Ed.), *Classics in management* (pp. 67–71). New York: American Management Association.

The Stanford Encyclopedia of Philosophy. (2015). *Indexicals*. Stanford's Center for the Study of Language and Information. Retrieved on September 24, 2015, available at http://plato.stanford.edu/entries/indexicals/

Tran, B. (2008). *Expatriate selection and retention* (Published Dissertation). California School of Professional Psychology at Alliant International University.

Tran, B. (2013). Industrial and organizational (I/O) psychology: The roles and purposes of I/O practitioners in global business. In B. Christiansen, E. Turkina, & N. Williams (Eds.), Cultural and technological influences on global business (pp. 175-219). Hershey, PA: Business Science Reference/IGI Global.

Tran, B. (2014a). The human element of the knowledge worker: Identifying, managing, and protecting the intellectual capital within knowledge management. In M. A. Chilton & J. M. Bloodgood (Eds.), Knowledge management and competitive advantage: Issues and potential solutions (pp. 281-303). Hershey, PA: Information Science Reference/IGI Global.

Tran, B. (2014b). The construction of knowledge management: The foundation of organizational learning based on learning organization. In F. Soliman (Eds.), Learning models for innovation in organizations: Examining the roles of knowledge transfer and human resources Management (pp. 89-110). Hershey, PA: Business Science Reference/IGI Global.

Tran, B. (2014c). The origin of servant leadership: The foundation of leadership. In R. Selladurai & S. Carraher (Eds.), Servant leadership: Research and practice (pp. 262-294). Hershey, PA: Business Science Reference/IGI Global.

Tran, B. (2014d). Ethos, pathos, and logos of doing business abroad: Geert Hofstede's five dimensions of national culture on transcultural marketing for incremental & radical innovation. In B. Christiansen, S. Yildiz, & E. Yildiz (Eds.), Transcultural marketing for incremental & radical innovation (pp. 255-280). Hershey, PA: Business Science Reference/IGI Global.

Tran, B. (2014e). The psychology of consumerism in business and marketing: The macro and micro behaviors of Hofstede's cultural consumers. In H. R. Kaufmann & M. F. A. K. Panni (Eds.), Handbook of research on consumerism in business and marketing: Concepts and practices (pp. 286-308). Hershey, PA: Business Science Reference/IGI Global.

Tran, B. (2015a). The next generation of leaders: Women in global leaderships in hotel management industry. In J. Feng, S. Stocklin, & W. Wang (Eds.), *Educational strategies for the next generation leaders in hotel management* (pp. 16–42). Hershey, PA: IGI Global.

Tran, B. (2015b). Expatriate selection and retention: Identifying and assessing the other characteristics beyond knowledge, skills, and abilities. In A. A. Camillo (Ed.), *Handbook of research on global hospitality and tourism management* (pp. 468–492). Hershey, PA: Premier Reference Source/IGI Global. doi:10.4018/978-1-4666-8606-9.ch023

Tran, B. (2016). Communication (intercultural and multicultural) at play for cross cultural management within multinational corporations (MNCs). In N. Zakaria, A. N. Abdul- Talib, & N. Osman (Eds.), Handbook of research on impacts of international business and political affairs on the global economy. Hershey, PA: IGI Global.

Tran, B., & Taing, C. (2013). *Leadership: Team building and the communication within.* Workshop given at the California State University, Sacramento's Student Organizations & Leadership's Fall 2013 SO&L Leadership Conference (SO&L). California State University, Sacramento.

Tsai, H. L., Zeng, S. Y., Lan, C. H., & Fang, R. J. (2012). The impacts of expatriate selection criteria on organizational performance in subsidiaries of transnational corporate: Recent Researches in Applied Computers and Computational Science. In *Proceedings of the 11ᵗʰ WSEAS International Conference on Applied Computer and Applied Computational Science.*

Victor, D. A. (2001). A cross-cultural perspective on gender. In L. Arliss & D. Borisoff (Eds.), Women and men communicating: Challenges and change (2nd ed.; pp. 65-77). Long Grove: Waveland Press.

Wallace, H., & Robertson, C. (2009). *Written and interpersonal communication: Methods for law enforcement* (4th ed.). Prentice Hall.

Xu, Y. (2007). Strategic analysis on cross-cultural human resources management. *Market Modernization, 19*, 274–275.

Yuan, W. (2006). *Intercultural communication and conflict between American and Chinese colleagues in China-based multinational organizations.* (Unpublished doctoral dissertation). University of Kentucky.

Zhang, J., & Xu, M. (2007). Study of cross-cultural communication management in global competition. *Economic and Managerial Study, 9*, 77–81.

ADDITIONAL READING

Aggarwa, R. (2011). Developing a global mindset: Integrating demographics, sustainability, technology, and globalization. *Journal of Teaching in International Business, 22*(1), 51–69. doi:10.10 80/08975930.2011.585920

Amagoh, F. (2009). Leadership development and leadership effectiveness. *Management Decision, 47*(6), 989–999. doi:10.1108/00251740910966695

Baird, J. W., & Stull, J. B. (1981). Communication effectiveness in multinational organizations: Developing universal intercultural skills. Paper presented at the *31ˢᵗ Annual Meeting of the International Communication Association,* Minneapolis, Minnesota.

Barrett, D. (2013). *Leadership communication* (4th ed.). McGraw-Hill Education.

Byrd, M. (2007). Educating and developing leaders of racially diverse organizations. *Human Resource Development Quarterly, 18*(2), 275–279. doi:10.1002/hrdq.1203

Eisenberg, E. M., Goodall, H. L., & Trethewey, A. (2013). *Organizational communication: Balancing creativity and constraint* (7th ed.). Bedford: St. Martin's.

Ely, R. J., Ibarra, H., & Kolb, D. M. (2011). Taking gender into account: Theory and design for women's leadership development programs. *Academy of Management Learning & Education, 10*(3), 474–493. doi:10.5465/amle.2010.0046

Gilbert, R. M., & Gilbert, R. (1992). *Extraordinary relationships: A new way of thinking about human interactions.* Wiley.

Gutierrez, B., Spencer, S. M., & Zhu, G. (2012). Thinking globally, leading locally: Chinese, Indian, and Western leadership. *Cross Cultural Management: An International Journal, 19*(1), 67–89. doi:10.1108/13527601211195637

Hackman, M. Z., & Johnson, C. E. (6th ed.) (2013). Leadership: A communication perspective. Waveland Press, Inc.s

Harris, C. A., & Leberman, S. I. (2012). Leadership development for women in New Zealand universities: Learning from the New Zealand women in leadership program. *Advances in Developing Human Resources, 14*(1), 28–44. doi:10.1177/1523422311428747

Harteis, C. (2012). When workplace learning fails: Individual and organizational limitations? Exemplarily demonstrated by the issue of responsibility in work life. *International Journal of Human Resources Development and Management, 12*(1), 92–107. doi:10.1504/IJHRDM.2012.044202

He, R., & Liu, J. (2010). *Barriers of cross cultural communication in multinational firms: A case styudy of Swedish company and its subsidiary in China.* Retrieved on May 29, 2015, available at http://hh.diva-portal.org/smash/get/diva2:344618/FULLTEXT01.pdf

Holt, K., & Seki, K. (2012). Global leadership: A developmental shift for everyone. *Industrial and Organizational Psychology: Perspectives on Science and Practice, 5*(2), 196–215. doi:10.1111/j.1754-9434.2012.01431.x

Lovvorn, A. S., & Chen, J. S. (2011). Developing a global mindset: The relationship between an international assignment and cultural intelligence. *International Journal of Business and Social Science, 2*(9), 275–282.

Munter, M. M. (2011). *Guide to managerial communication* (9th ed.). Prentice Hall.

O'Rourke, J. S. (2012). *Management communication: A case-analysis approach* (5th ed.). Prentice Hall.

Ragir, S., & Brooks, P. J. (2012). The key to cultural innovation lies in the group dynamic rather than in the individual mind. *Behavioral and Brain Sciences, 35*(4), 237–238. doi:10.1017/S0140525X11002081 PMID:22697424

Rochstuhl, T., Seiler, S., Ang, S., Dyne, L., & Annen, H. (2011). Beyond general intelligence (IQ) and emotional intelligence (EQ): The role of cultural intelligence (CQ) on cross-border leadership effectiveness in a globalized world. *The Journal of Social Issues, 67*(4), 825–840. doi:10.1111/j.1540-4560.2011.01730.x

Rothwell, J. D. (2012). *In mixed company: Communicating in small groups* (8th ed.). Wadsworth Publishing.

Roy, S. R. (2012). Digital mastery: The skills needed for effective virtual leadership. *International Journal of e-Collaboration, 8*(3), 56–66. doi:10.4018/jec.2012070104

Schein, E. H. (2013). *Humble inquiry: The gentle art of asking instead of telling.* Berrett-Koehler Publishers.

Takahashi, K., Ishikawa, J., & Kanai, T. (2012). Qualitative and quantitative studies of leadership in multinational settings: Meta-analytic and cross-cultural reviews. *Journal of World Business, 47*(4), 530–538. doi:10.1016/j.jwb.2012.01.006

Ulrich, D., & Smallwood, N. (2012). What is leadership? In W. H. Mobley, Y. Wang, & M. Li (Eds.), *Advances in global leadership* (Vol. 7, pp. 9–36). Emerald Group Publishing Limited. doi:10.1108/S1535-1203(2012)0000007005

Wang, V. C. (2011). E-Leadership in the new century. *International Journal of Adult Vocational Education and Technology, 2*(1), 50–59. doi:10.4018/javet.2011010105

Zhu, Q. Z. Y. (1991). *Johari Window communication method: Deep psychology of communication channels.* China Electric Power Press.

KEY TERMS AND DEFINITIONS

Communication: Sending, receiving, and understanding information and meaning, or, communication can be defined as the process of transmitting information and common understanding from one person to another.

Decoder: The process by which symbols are received and converted into ideas by the person receiving the information.

Emotional Barriers: Barriers that are emotional in nature and lessen the effectiveness of the communication.

Encoder: The process by which ideas are converted to symbols for transmission to another person.

Feedback: the process that allows persons transmitting information to correct and adjust messages to adapt to the receiver.

Group: A number of person gathered or classified together.

Interpersonal Communication: The sharing of information between two persons.

Johari Window (JW): A technique created in 1955 by two American psychologists, Joseph Luft and Harrington Ingham, and used to help people better understand their relationship with self and others.

Leadership: A multifaceted process of identifying a goal, motivating other people to act, and providing support and motivation to achieve mutually negotiated goals.

Multinational Corporations (MNCs): A corporation consisting of a parent organization (headquarters) and at least one subsidiary organization in a foreign country, have made communication ever inevitable.

Physical Barriers: The aspects of an environment that make communication more difficult.

Propaganda: The management of collective attitudes by the manipulation of significant symbols.

Semantic Barriers: The inability to agree on the meaning of certain terms, with a resulting loss in the ability to communicate clearly.

Semantic: The study of the development and meaning of words.

Signal: Symbols that are produced and transmitted.

Source: The mind of the person starting the communication process.

Chapter 23
Credible Negotiation Leadership:
Using Principled Negotiation to Improve International Negotiation

Larry W. Long
Illinois State University, USA & International Academy of Public Safety, USA

Mitch Javidi
North Carolina State University, USA & International Academy of Public Safety, USA

L. Brooks Hill
Trinity University, USA

Anthony H. Normore
California State University Dominguez Hills, USA & International Academy of Public Safety, USA

ABSTRACT

The purpose of this chapter is to integrate credible leadership into the authors' previous work in principled negotiation. After the introduction, international negotiation is conceptualized with an in-depth description of the process. This is followed by description of negotiation styles and eight propositions for credible negotiation leadership that are predicated upon intercultural communication study. The conclusion is an application of Credible Negotiation Leadership with recommendations.

INTRODUCTION

In 1994, "Principled Negotiation" (Hill, Long, & Javidi, 1994) was proposed as an approach to peaceful international negotiation and conflict management. Two decades ago, the authors noted that:

The increasing interdependence among peoples and nations is a double edged sword: on the one hand, it compels attention to differences and thus fosters conflict; on the other hand, it provides a wonderful prospect for development of the ability to resolve our differences and conflicts. Despite the promising opportunities presented by this interdependence and an amazing technology the world is a boiling cauldron of conflicts which threaten harmony and the social fabric of many nations and regions of the world. Instead of using the available potential constructively, people are so blinded by self-interest that they engage in destructive actions which sacrifice mutual development. Unfortunately, these episodes are common throughout the world. (Hill, Long, & Javidi, 1994, p. 194)

DOI: 10.4018/978-1-4666-9970-0.ch023

Although this observation was made in the 1990's, there is evidence that these circumstances still exist and will continue in the foreseeable future. Projections for the years 2010 to 2030 suggest that leading nations, such as G-20 (the 20 major world economies), will not develop and implement appropriate policies to manage international weapons proliferation, deal with increasingly bitter socio-economic divisions, and adjust global environmental constraints (Rogers, 2004). These circumstances underscore the importance of leadership to effectively use negotiation as a key tool for international conflict management now and for the future (Creede, Fisher-Yoshida, & Gallegos, 2012; Hackman & Johnson, 2013; Normore & Erbe, 2013). Recent negotiations (August, 2015) to avoid escalation of military conflict between North and South Korea are a case in point. Furthermore, conflict projections for the future provide justification for revisiting and expanding the concept of "principled negotiation" to include elements of leadership and credibility.

In the latter portion of the Twentieth Century, experts studied the international negotiation process from diverse viewpoints. Much of this was likely motivated by the peace imperative or concern as to whether or not persons with diverse backgrounds (to include gender, age, ethnicity, ideology, geography, religion, language, etc.) can coexist peacefully (Martin & Nakayama, 2008). Clearly, many scholars have been motivated with the hope that people might settle disputes peacefully (Paupp, 2014; Pruitt & Kim, 2004). This body of literature draws heavily upon communication, education, psychology, sociology, political science, management, and other disciplines to discover and create concepts, principles, and best practices that will lead to effective negotiation outcomes (e.g., see Lewicki, Saunders, & Barry, 2006 & 2015; Watkins, 2002; Kolb & Williams, 2003). Regardless of scholarly orientation, no one can contest the centrality of communication in local, national, and international negotiation arenas (Oetzel & Ting-Toomey, 2013).

During the past two decades, scholars and negotiation experts have given more attention to the role of communication, in which credibility plays an important role, as fundamental in the negotiation process. For example, one of the most widely used books about negotiation is Lewicki, Saunders, and Barry's *Negotiation* (2006, 5th Ed. & and 2015, 7th Ed.). For several years and across different editions, the authors have devoted an entire chapter to communication, referring to it as one of the four main negotiation subprocesses (other subprocesses include perception/cognition/emotion, power, and influence). While basically an introductory overview of the communication process, inclusion of the chapter was important recognition of the critical role played by communication during negotiations. In their chapter about influence, Lewicki, et al discuss the impact and importance of source credibility. They provide a three page discussion of the credibility construct (Lewicki, Saunders, Barry, 2006, pp. 215-218), noting how it directly influences the perception of whether or not a negotiator's messages are believed and the consequence for negotiation outcomes. As a result, communication and credibility have become recognized as essentials of negotiation.

Interestingly, however, negotiation process descriptions rarely recognize the negotiator as a leader. Yet, a review of the published negotiation literature will yield numerous research articles and books elaborating on concepts like leading and managing, power, influence, relationships, teams, interpersonal trust, conflict management, problem solving, managing crises, etc., (Kriesberg, 1998; Pearce & Pearce, 2000). These concepts are also deeply rooted in communication and leadership literature (Bryman, 2013). Leadership and negotiation are often spoken of and written about together, yet infrequently integrated except in a very general way (Hackman & Johnson, 2013). Often, it is assumed that good leaders are good negotiators and are normally effective in "getting their way" and effective at persuasion. This chapter's depiction of international negotiation (see

Figure 1) places the negotiator in the prominent role of leader, recognizing the inherent processes of that role, including perceptions of credibility, add significantly to the nature of negotiation outcomes (Watkins, 2002).

While international and intercultural negotiation complexity demands insight from many perspectives, a pragmatic communication and credible leadership perspective guides us more directly to useful negotiation guidelines. Consequently, this chapter will elaborate the sometime neglected dimensions of leadership, credibility, and intercultural communication (see Erbe, 2011; Normore & Erbe, 2013) as applied to the nego-

Figure 1. International negotiation process

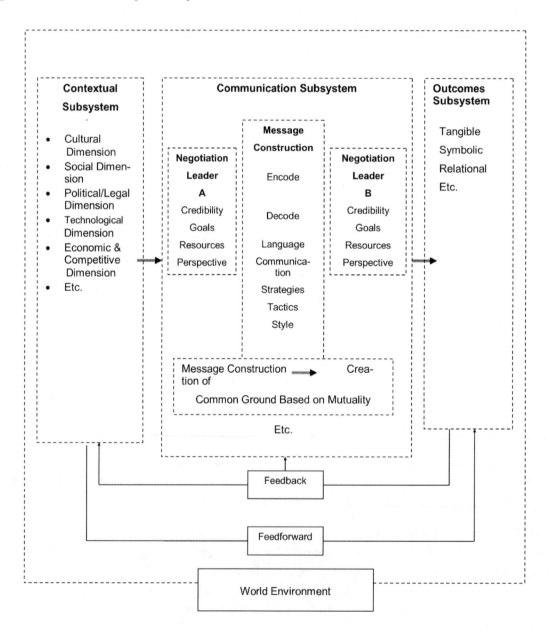

tiation process. Specifically, the last part of this chapter will offer a communication perspective based upon principled negotiation and credible negotiation leadership.

As was the case when "principled negotiation" was introduced two decades ago, one troublesome use of words needs to be mentioned. The term "international" will be used in such a way as to include "intercultural," even though situation may exist when international negotiation could occur between two or more people of the same culture; nations and cultures typically do not coincide, although instances to the contrary may be found.

The first section of this chapter highlights international negotiation complexities as it defines, provides a model, and analyzes/explains component parts of this process. Notably, this model has been modified with inclusion of the concepts of leadership and credibility. Within this conceptual framework, a general review of negotiation styles lays the groundwork for credible negotiation leadership which is couched in principled negotiation. A final section examines potential application of this position about international negotiation in order to achieve greater intercultural effectiveness.

CONCEPTUALIZATION OF INTERNATIONAL NEGOTIATION

This section provides a more comprehensive description of international negotiation, than presented originally, with the inclusion of leadership and credibility constructs. After initial definitions of international negotiation, a model of the process is presented. Finally, the major elements in the model are examined. The concepts and terms described here provide a foundation for understanding credible negotiation leadership and principled negotiation, its application, and the distinctiveness of an intercultural communication perspective.

Definition of International Negotiation

International negotiation is a communication function of international relations that is used for the purpose of mutual adaptation in order to' accomplish specific goals. This definition has several implications: First, international negotiation occurs when two or more persons from different nations (usually possessing different world views and representing different self-interests) lead (through communication) in order to achieve a particular outcome or goal. Since participants "represent" a position, the presumption of a vested interest supporting the position being represented by the negotiator normally exists. Also, the potential for misinterpretation and misattribution is much greater than in those circumstances where negotiators share a similar culture, experiences, and psychological frame-of-reference.

Second, this definition emphasizes mutual adjustment through communication between or among negotiators. Mutual adjustment is a two-way process in which all parties participate. When mutual adjustment is absent, negotiation actually does not exist. Rather, the relationship is one-way, based upon taking or winning at the other's expense. When, for example, a country uses its power to impose pre-determined outcomes, the negotiation becomes a sham, differences are only temporarily displaced, and they are likely to resurface later.

Third, goal attainment for all participants is the assumed outcome of negotiation. This does not imply that all parties realize complete gains without experiencing concessions. However, the process begins with the assumption that both parties can experience satisfying, productive outcomes that outweigh losses. If not, the negotiation process is compromised and relations between the groups represented may deteriorate.

Contrary to self-serving conceptions of international negotiations, the credible negotiation leadership presumes that effective negotiations, like effective communication, entail mutual achievement and relational development, rather than short-term winning or losing. This approach requires objective focus on the goals of all parties, development of trust, complete collaboration, and emphasis on mutually beneficial outcomes (Austin, 2010).

Model of International Negotiation

Effective international negotiation requires awareness, understanding, and appreciation of elements that interact when people representing different nations and cultures negotiate (Trompenaars & Hampden-Turner, 2012). Models of international relations cannot capture all aspects of negotiation. However, the model depicted in Figure 1 was an effort to be comprehensive by combining several communication, social change, and other process models. Advantages of this model include a communication orientation, emphasis on important external influences, the inclusion of an outcomes subsystem, and the central feature of mutuality accentuated with credible leadership. This model can enables the reader to analytically consider each element of the process and, through simultaneous consideration of all elements, gain an appreciation of their dynamic interaction in the international environment. For scholars, the model provides a template for understanding, explaining, and developing theories about negotiation.

The *world environment* influences negotiation processes between and among nations. The broken lines representing the world environment and surrounding the negotiation process and its subsystems mean that the subsystems are open to information and other kinds of influence that move in and out of the boundaries. Within this world environment are three subsystems. From a systems theory perspective they represent the input, throughput, and output. The *contextual subsystem* (input) contains at least five major dimensions which collectively constrain and

direct the negotiators who interact directly in the *communication subsystem* (throughput). The results of the actual negotiation are represented in the *outcomes subsystem* (output) which may through *feedback* impact on continuing interaction between the negotiators and may also impact on the *context*. The arrows represent likely directions of influence among the subsystems and highlight the ongoing, dynamic nature of the overall process.

COMPONENTS OF INTERNATIONAL NEGOTIATION: WORLD ENVIRONMENT

The twenty-first century provides the international negotiator with new challenges in realizing long-term stability and peace while contributing to the world economy and enhancing the standard of living for all mankind. The past century has contained incomparable wars, devastation of resources, and the consequences of technology; the current century is dealing with that aftermath, particularly those challenges listed earlier by Rogers (2005) and his prognostications for 2010 through 2030. Despite the challenges, when leadership and credibility concepts are combined into the international negotiation model there is additional knowledge to aid the prospects for peace, improving the global environment, and economic growth (Paupp, 2014). Thus, the current model provides a more in-depth analysis and synthesis of negotiating.

No longer can negotiators perceive their actions to be narrowly focused on the issues at hand. Actions taken in one specific instance may directly affect people in many other parts of the world. The fluctuations in the world wide stock markets during the latter part of August 2015 are testimony supporting that contention. Consider also, the process of trade talks between nations and their indigenous industries. In nearly every instance of negotiation about products and the policies regarding their manufacture and distribution will concern other nations. If, for example, If China opens its markets to allow a given technology more opportunity, how will this action impact on other producers of a similar technology in other parts of the world? If, for example, the USA tightens its restrictions on importation of automobile parts, then how might the Japanese or Koreans' response affect its production facilities in other countries? On an even broader scale, what are the possible ramifications of the policies of other nations which place tight control on economic relations because of human rights violations and past relations? The world environment contains all acts of negotiations between and among nations, and the environment and negotiation outcomes mutually influence each other.

Components: Contextual Subsystem

The model classifies five dimensions of the immediate context (derived from Hazelton & Long, 1988) which impact on the negotiators and their negotiations. The model includes et cetera which suggests the need to be alert for unforeseen influences. Each of the dimensions is explained and illustrated.

- **Cultural Dimension:** Culture is the behaviors and underlying values, motives, beliefs, knowledge, meanings, ethics, patterns of interaction, etc., that identify a specific "cultural" group and also differentiates it from other cultures. Culture may be related to physical appearance, the way a person dresses, and the manner in which a person communicates. But, culture is more than observable characteristics. It contains the underlying values, motives, beliefs, and ethics that stimulate a negotiator's behavior. Culture provides the negotiator with a dominant frame-of-reference that influences the nature and evolution of the negotiator's relationships and communication (Oetzel & Ting-Toomey, 2013). For example, cultures vary in emphasizing the self or the group. When developing a relationship with members of Western societies, it is most effective to stimulate the Westerner's self-interest and encourage participation. In contrast, Eastern cultures emphasize the group and social identity. Thus, it is more effective to develop congenial social relations and focus on relationship, rather than self-interest. Consequently, understanding culture provides the initial template for negotiators to use in developing international relations (Pearce, 2007).

- **Social Dimension:** Growing out of the cultural dimension, social values, norms, rules, and roles are one of the greatest sources of influence on human behavior. Culture and cultural influence as learned phenomena has long assumed a role of importance in understanding human communication. Consequently, an understanding the social environment is a necessary precondition to effective international negotiation because rules of appropriate "social" conduct largely determine communication strategies and tactics that should or should not be used. The social dimension also contains significant individuals and groups, who often serve to lead and influence negotiations more strongly, such as consumers, suppliers, opinion leaders, government, or any group that possesses the potential to influence other dimensions (Pearce, 2007).

- **Political/Legal Dimension:** International treaties and law set limits for negotiation; they constrain behavior and often designate the extent to which concessions can be made. Essentially, the political/legal dimension is comprised of formal rules which govern organizational, governmental, national conduct. It also operationalizes methods for creating rules and methods for rule enforcement. Understanding the political/legal dimension requires consideration of any electoral or position appointment practices, executive or administrative influence, and adjudication processes. Since international agreements are often vague, there is opportunity for self-serving negotiators to insinuate their best interests, skillfully rationalized in terms of the treaties or agreements. Resolution of these conflicts requires consideration of the reason(s) the agreements were originally made, along with the laws and principles of the nations/organizations negotiating.

- **Technological Dimension:** The technological dimension highlights a concern for methods and tools used to accomplish tasks; for purposes of this chapter, this dimension emphasizes transportation and communication/information technologies. A technological innovation spreads quickly as other nations attempt to duplicate or to acquire rights to use it themselves. The transportation and information revolutions have made isolationist doctrines impractical for any nation. Physical proximity to another culture is, at most, 24 hours away. Information transfer across the globe is instantaneous. However, instantaneous information transfer can mean instant communication or miscommunication. Thus, international relations are inevitable and must be effectively managed. The technological development represented by a negotiator sets limits to the amount and type of available resources during negotiation. Likewise, technology may indirectly impact on negotiations through other dimensions. For example, the presence or absence of computer technology and internet access, medical technology, sophisticated robotic systems, etc., will influence social and economic conditions for a nation or culture.

- **Economic/Competitive Dimension:** Social and technological influences have stimulated economic conditions and created international competitive situations. These have, in turn, influenced and have been influenced by political and legal realities. Adoption of North American Free Trade Agreement (NAFTA) by the United States in 1994 is a case in point. NAFTA had both positive and negative effects, with modest positive economic benefit for Mexico, the United States, and Canada; on the other hand, many Canadian companies were taken over by citizens of other countries, corn prices in Mexico fell while internal demand exceeded supply, and in the United States organized labor blamed the agreement for sending 700,000 jobs from the U.S. to Mexico. Clearly, global changes in patterns of competition and economic relations cannot be ignored. The competitive aspects of this dimension consist of all individuals, groups, organizations, nations, or entities who possess goals that may stimulate competition for resources, markets or alliances. Government trade agreements, for example, with respect to electronic technologies were the result of intense competition for international consumer market share and have been invoked to reduce negative aspects of the intense competition. Many international negotiation situations occur among businesses and governments because of economic competition and pressures for market expansion (Ahmad, Francis, & Zairi, 2007; Erbe, 2011). The economic aspects of this dimension influence the availability of resources. In particular, the economic environment directly defines the nature and extent of financial resources which influences the cost of physical, human, and information resources.

- **Contextual Dimensions Applied:** Cultural, social, political/legal, technological, and economic/competitive conditions

define, constrain, and guide the use of resources available to negotiators – these contextual elements are inputs that influence
negotiators. The negotiators' contextual
frames-of-reference are reflected by symbols used to produce messages; messages
influence the initiation, maintenance, and
termination of negotiation relationships.
Consequently, before any negotiation episode begins, application of this model requires that specific questions be answered
about the party with which an individual
may negotiate. Using the dimensions as a
template, and incorporating credible leadership concepts, questions were generated
for the Hill, Long, Javidi (1994) model:

- **Culture:**
    - What are the dominant values,
      beliefs, and attitudes expressed
      by members of the culture?
    - How does language in this cul-
      ture differ from mine?
    - How easy are translations of
      language and culture accom-
      plished without loss or distor-
      tion of meaning?
    - How is the culture similar or dif-
      ferent from mine?
    - How might differences affect
      the negotiation relationship?
    - How might differences affect
      perceptions of my credibility;
      perceptions of my trustworthi-
      ness and expertise?
- **Society:**
    - What norms, rules, and expecta-
      tions exist among members of
      the society?
    - How would members of this so-
      ciety define the negotiation role
      and what type of outcome would
      they accept?
    - How is the society similar or
      different from mine?
    - How might differences in the
      society affect the negotiation
      relationship?
    - What primary groups are influ-
      encing negotiator choices?
    - What is the society's preferred
      leadership negotiation style?
- **Political and Legal Processes:**
    - What international treaties,
      laws, and agreements must be
      observed by members of the
      nation?
    - What laws and accepted princi-
      ples for conducting negotiations
      are followed by members of the
      nation?
    - How are laws created, interpret-
      ed, and enforced among mem-
      bers of the nation?
    - How are political and legal pro-
      cesses in this nation similar or
      different from mine?
    - How might differences in politi-
      cal and legal processes influence
      outcomes?
- **Technology:**
    - What level of consumer techno-
      logical sophistication exists for
      this nation?
    - What level of technological de-
      velopment in transportation and
      information management exists
      in this nation?
    - Is technological development
      similar or different from mine?
    - How might differences in tech-
      nological development affect
      the negotiation relationship?
- **Competitive and Economic
  Conditions:**
    - What are the primary contribu-
      tors to the economy of this
      nation?

- How sound is this nation's economy? How volatile are its markets?
- What competitive pressure does this nation face?
- Are competitive and economic conditions of all parties compatible or are they incompatible?
- How might differences in competitive and economic conditions affect the negotiation relationship?

Possessing answers to these and other implied questions allows each person the information necessary to overcome many barriers to successful negotiation outcomes.

Components: Communication Subsystem

The communication subsystem is the throughput dynamic of the negotiation process that contains the negotiators and messages. Within this subsystem communication occurs. As the model suggests, each negotiator is influenced by contextual dimensions which, in turn, influence outcomes. Success or failure often results from how effectively the negotiators can use or adapt to the language(s), select appropriate communication strategies, and create an overall, credible style that may provide common ground on which to achieve mutually beneficial results.

- **Negotiator as Leader:** Earlier, international negotiation was defined as a communication function of international relations that is used for the purpose of mutual adaptation in order to accomplish specific goals. This perspective empowers the international negotiator to be a leader in a process that contains elements of influence across fluctuating circumstances with a desired end-result of realizing mutually satisfying goals. Thus, negotiation leadership in this model is defined from the perspective articulated by Tannenbaum, Weschler, & Massarik (1961) as interpersonal influence, exercised in a situation, and directed, through the communication process, toward the attainment of a specified goal or goals. An important element in this definition is communication which is a primary subprocess used by negotiators. Communication is influenced by a follower's/negotiator's perception of the leader's/negotiator's credibility.

  - **Credibility:** Credibility is one of the most studied areas of communication; for this chapter, it is one negotiator's perception of the other negotiator's levels of trustworthiness and expertise. Credibility is a most significant communication variable because a negotiator's of believability is influenced by the perceived level of their credibility. Writings about the construct date back over twenty centuries, occurring, most notably when Aristotle discussed the concept of *ethos* and how an audience's perceptions of a speaker's character would influence the believability of what the speaker said. Other notable scholars of the day, such as Plato and Cicero, raised similar issues. The concept was pretty straight-forward – the greater a speaker's credibility, the more believable the message or speech; the lower the credibility, the less believable the message. For Aristotle and his contemporaries, credibility consisted of a speaker's character, intelligence, and good will.

Contemporary scholars across several disciplines have thoroughly researched the area, producing definitions of credibility roughly similar to those expressed by Aristotle. For example, psychologists Hovland, Janis, and Kelley (1951) determined that credibility possessed three dimensions – trustworthiness, expertness, and intention. James McCroskey, one of the most prolific credibility researchers in communication, and Thomas Young (1981) ultimately concluded that perceptions of an individual's character and competence are the primary determinants of credibility, with intention being a part of character. For our purpose here, we will use the terms trust and expertise to refer to the two dimensions of credibility.

Credible negotiation leaders are those perceived as possessing enduring qualities of trust and expertise. What does this mean? In order to be wholly credible, a negotiation leader must be viewed as possessing the requisite knowledge and information to make decisions, solve problems, and move the negotiation process and the negotiators' relationship in the direction of mutual goal attainment. Furthermore, the negotiation leader must be perceived to be a person of integrity, well-intended, and desiring to move in the direction of doing the most good possible for all involved. Anything less renders communication effectiveness less than optimal because decreasing credibility induces decreasing levels of negotiator believability.

A credible negotiation leader's *expertise* is a function of the skill or knowledge possessed for effectively and efficiently achieving an objective or goal given a particular set of circumstances. Often, personal accomplishments like achieving advanced training or diplomas in a specific field will bestow expertise upon a leader. Similarly, having knowledge that the leader has successfully achieved these or similar goals in the past will heighten perceptions of expertise. It is common for associations, for example, to recognize person's competence in an area by bestowing credentials upon them when they demonstrate they have particular skills and knowledge. For example, the Public Relations Society of America grants an APR (Accredited in Public Relations) recognition to public relations professionals upon successful completion of the APR exam; the bar association grants a lawyer the right to practice law when they pass the bar exam. The logic here is obvious – if you are APR or a bar accredited professional, you more likely to produce a better public relations campaign or defend a client more effectively than those who do not possess the credentials.

Trust is the most important component of being a credible negotiation leader – trusted negotiators are more likely to be believed. Regardless of one's level of expertise, if you are not trusted, you cannot be a credible negotiation leader. As a major portion of ethical leader behavior, trust consistently occupies a high level concern across many circumstances. Current news stories about business and international leaders often reflect a lack of trust and violations of ethical expectations. It is common that during political campaigns across the world, opponents initially attack one another's credibility by exposing breaches of trust, implying the candidate is not worthy of election to office because they cannot be trusted. For example, in the United States' 2015 Presidential race Hillary Clinton was attacked by opponents for using a private server to conduct Department of State business during the period of time she was the U.S. Secretary of State. Her opponents were implying that she was hiding information, suggesting her intentions were dishonest and therefore she cannot be trusted to be an honest President. Negotiators and leaders aim to achieve ends through development of trust (Diddams & Chang, 2012). This is a key ingredient in establishing and maintaining healthy relationships. Furthermore, when negotiators perceive genuine trust in each other, the negotiation climate is more likely to be non-defensive, messages and actions are more consistent, participants have increased self-determination, there is greater focus on others' issues and less preoccupation with one's own circumstance, and there is emphasis on mutual benefit (Diddams & Chang, 2008)

The International Negotiation Process model recognizes that each negotiator is a human reflection of a set of goals, resources and perspectives that are symbolized in the messages transmitted and decoded. Consequently, any study of negotiation must to consider the contextual subsystem impact on the negotiator, its impact on message encoding/decoding, and the influence of perceptions of the negotiators' credibility.

- **Goals:** Time orientation provides an effective way to differentiate among different types of goals. From this perspective, goals can be categorized as short-term, intermediate, and long-term. Each type of goal has a unique emphasis. Short-term goals tend to focus on effectiveness, efficiency, productivity, and individual satisfaction. Attainment of short-term goals is often measured in terms of economic growth through competitive success, technological superiority, and high levels of morale experienced by being successful. Short-term goal emphasis, however, results in outcomes being defined as a win or a loss and ignores the consequences of "winning the battle, while losing the war." Although short-term issues are important considerations, excessive emphasis on the short-run is often characterized by limited problem definition, restricted solution alternatives, and neglect of broader implications. Negotiators who primarily emphasize short-term goals often tend to reduce negotiation relationships to exercises in power.

In contrast, intermediate goals are characterized by longer time orientation. Intermediate goals assume a greater level of awareness about the environment and all parties involved in negotiation as they emphasize development and adaptation. Consequently, negotiators at this level become concerned with cultural, social, political/ legal, competitive/ economic, and technological adaptation. From this perspective, all parties are collaborators and compromisers in order to survive and mutually coexist for a time period beyond the short-term. Thus, relational maintenance and mutual concern for each other's needs become strategy for intermediate goal attainment. Intermediate goal emphasis assumes that the goals of all negotiators are important and leads to longer-lasting relationships among negotiators and the groups they represent.

Long-term goals emphasize survival and reflect sensitivity to the world environment. Long-term goal attainment goes beyond accommodation and emphasizes collaboration beyond the short-term and intermediate time period with an interdependent, broader description of the negotiation problem and potential solutions. The emphasis here is on discovering how all negotiators, as well as unrepresented groups, can realize success from the negotiation. Here, the philosophy is "winning the war, and losing the battles when necessary."

- **Resources:** The international negotiations environment contains four basic resources: physical, capital, human, and symbolic. Negotiators are likely to possess varying levels of each. Physical resources are the tangible items a negotiator brings into the negotiation process. These can include raw materials, objects, or products. An abundance or scarcity of physical resources will influence a negotiator's level of capital resources and often reflects the form and nature of the technological dimension of the environment. Capital resources reflect the amount of money or tokens available to a negotiator. Of course, capital resources impact on other resource levels. Conceptualizations of the world as an economic marketplace underscore the importance of this resource at an international level. A negotiator's desire to acquire capital or financial resources determines the extent to which competitive and economic incentives will play a dominant role in negotiations. The nature and type of human resources available to a negotiator are a function of the cultural, social, and political/legal dimensions of the environment. Characteristics of the human resource interact with capital and physical resources. All of these resources are reflected in the symbols used by the negotiators. These symbolic representations are the reality of the negotiator, but like many symbols may be misinterpreted by other negotiators. This is especially true when the negotiators have different interpretations of the resources and underestimate or overestimate the relative power of their counterpart. Thus, symbols become obvious resources, but are often misunderstood indicators of negotiators' relative strengths and weaknesses.

- **Perspective:** The negotiator's perspective represents the unique integration of all influences into a negotiation style. Later this chapter will examine general styles of negotiation as broad approaches to negotiation. Here, however, the focus is on individual interpretation of diverse pressures and their integration with a distinctive perspective toward the negotiation. This perspective may or may not serve best the interests of the people represented, and this is why the selection of negotiator becomes a crucial decision in relation to the ultimate outcome.

Consider one prominent ingredient of perspective among typical negotiators from Japan and the USA. Because the USA is primarily a horizontal, individualistic culture, one might expect a negotiator to be independent and interact more informally. In contrast, Japan is primarily a vertical society wherein self-concept plays a less significant role, congeniality is emphasized, and interactions are more formal. Thus, negotiators from the USA with their more informal structure would predictably treat others informally and more directly while minimizing differences in building relations. The Japanese negotiator would predictably operate within a more formal structure and would emphasize titles, status, and rank as aids in building relations. Within these cultural frames the potential negotiator would develop his or her style. For some, little adjustment may be possible; for others, greater adjustment could facilitate better understanding and opportunity for mutually satisfying relationships (Oetzel & Ting-Toomey, 2013).

- **Message Construction:** Message construction is a primary component of the communication subsystem and provide focus on the interaction of negotiators as they encode and decode their intentions and information in the process of constructing messages which, in turn, may create a common ground for mutual achievements. Message construction is an outcome of the language(s) and symbol system employed, the communication strategies and tactics chosen, and the communication style of the negotiator.
  - **Language:** In many cases language becomes a major hurdle to cross for effective communication. Choice of language may be a major influence on the entire negotiating process. If the other party permits the primary use of your language, express your sincere appreciation, but then follow-up with increased patience, tolerance, and repetition necessary to permit discussion with someone using a second or third language skill. Translators are crucial whenever negotiators have different languages, but are essential if both parties use their own language.

Whenever possible use a translator well versed in your own perspective and who is sufficiently knowledgeable about the cultures involved to express the subtleties of the messages. Whatever language is used, recognize that everything one says or does has potential symbolic value and may be misinterpreted. This may require frequent requests for interpretations and restatements. Although time consuming and sometimes laborious, understanding the message well is essential to using the message to construct a basis for mutual success. Westerners must learn that the symbolic exchanges are crucial to longer-term relationships which are constructed in small increments.

○ **Communication Strategies and Tactics:** The word strategy refers to general goals and purposes, general organization of ideas and information, and the plan of action. Tactics are the specific techniques for use in the implementation of strategy. Examples of these techniques might include words chosen to express an idea, support selected for position, as well as non-verbal behavior used in the presentation of self and position. Despite the great variety of available strategies and tactics for any communication, a few basic guidelines can help avoid unnecessary problems.

▪ The selection of strategy must complement the goals, the other negotiations, and your ability.

▪ If one has a modest request and uses an overwhelming strategy, the inconsistency will reduce the likelihood of successful use of strong strategies later.

▪ Effective communication requires adaptation to those being addressed; so, strategy and tactics must fit the person or people with whom you are dealing. This may require a slow, time consuming beginning as negotiators come to know each other and better adapt.

▪ Personality constrains the range of choices. Some options are beyond an individual's ability. This reality directs each person to know themselves well (especially others' perceptions of one's credibility), and be able to choose wisely among strategies and tactical options. (Hill, Long, Javidi, 1994)

Negotiators must be flexible and be prepared to alter a strategy or tactic when feedback indicates it is not working well. Such flexibility is essential to achieving a mutually desirable basis for successful outcomes.

● **Style:** Each person develops a general communication style. Style is an outgrowth of language (verbal and non-verbal), patterns of communication strategies and tactics we normally use, and a reflection of our culture and personality (Trompenaars & Hampden-Turner, 2012). Collectively these parts create a distinctive style which others may recognize more readily than we can identify. One needs to understand their stylistic tendencies; once recognized, communication style can be monitored during interaction. This is important because the communication behavior of others is strongly influenced by their perception of our behavior, which, in turn, leads to assessments of credibility. As mentioned above, remain flexible whenever possible;

this permits one to keep options open and requires careful monitoring of the interaction.

- **Mutuality:** The central function of communication is to create a common ground. Throughout this chapter the authors are emphasizing the value of communication in the development of positive relations which can assist in the achievement of longer-term goals and objectives. Mutuality is essential to this approach, and is continually dependent upon establishing and maintaining trust. Mutually beneficial results are key to building relations and enhanced interdependence among peoples and nations.

Components: Outcomes Subsystem

Interaction between people produces effects or outcomes. For the present discussion, three categories of outcomes are considered: tangible, symbolic, and relational results. Although these categories are examined independently, they are not mutually exclusive. Sometimes, one specific negotiation outcome of may have tangible, symbolic, and relational consequences. More often than not, however, the effects of human interaction are encompassed by these three categories so that a negotiator can identify primary effects in one and separate the primary from secondary effects in a different category.

- **Tangible Outcomes:** These effects are closely aligned with the "bottom line" of negotiations and include increased profits, a contract extension, or better import-export quotas. Unfortunately too many negotiators become so focused on these tangibles that success becomes "reified." The notion of reification comes from the Latin word which loosely means to make an abstraction, such as success, into a thing or tangible object, such as a bottom line

result. Negotiators with exclusive focus on tangible outcomes are often captured by short-term goals and naively believe themselves to be very successful. Even though tangible results may be a primary concern of any negotiation, failure to acknowledge the symbolic and relational effects is unwise.

- **Symbolic Outcomes:** These effects are often perceived by the negotiators as secondary and thus seem to represent a lower level of achievement. In other words, one negotiator may not gain as much as desired, but receives some face-saving symbol of achievement which will have value with his or her constituents. While this sequence is often true, negotiators may ignore the more significant occasions when the symbolic effects are greater than tangible outcomes. For example, in trade negotiations success may be perceived solely in terms of concessions and gains in trade when, in fact, the most important consequences may be in attitudinal concessions regarding human rights, in mutual respect between the nations represented, or in moral principles set for future negotiators.

- **Relational Outcomes:** Cultural difference often impacts on the relative value assigned to relational outcomes of human interactions. For example, in some cultures, especially western, the relationship between negotiators is less important than in eastern cultures. With their short-term orientation, western negotiators neglect the fundamental human relations involved in successful interaction. Even though raised in western traditions, the authors of this chapter believe strongly in the more eastern orientation to relational development between negotiators. Once relations are established the negotiators are situated far better to understand the perspectives of their counterparts and to adapt more flexibly their communication strategies and tactics (Trompenaars & Hampden-Turner, 2012). Regardless of the initial attitudes of negotiators regarding relational development, no one can deny that the act of negotiation impacts on the relations of the negotiators and this impact will have consequences for them as well as others who may later negotiate.

Components: Process Dynamics

Just as the three categories of outcomes influence each other, nearly all parts of the negotiation process influence each other. Several features of this model suggest these interrelations. The broken lines indicate permeability of boundaries so that influences may move from outside the negotiation process into it or effects of the process may anywhere impact on elements outside of it. The arrows also suggest likely patterns of influence. Feedback from the outcomes subsystem may cause changes on the communication subsystem even while the negotiation is in process. Outcomes can also influence the context, especially as constituents learn the effects of the negotiation. The contextual subsystem can impact on how anyone perceives the results of the negotiation. For example, ongoing media coverage informs constituents who, in turn, respond and thereby influence subsequent interpretation of the effects and the negotiations generating those effects. This "public diplomacy" is also manipulated during negotiations as negotiators "test the waters" for the symbolic value of their tangible results. Elsewhere in the model the arrows suggest the most prominent directions of the movement of influence. Hence, credible negotiation leadership occurs in a dynamic, continuous, world environment with unceasing component interaction.

Communication provides an international boundary-spanning function among the different environments, governments, and businesses represented by negotiators. Despite the centrality of basic communication to all negotiations, the literature provides very few systematic attempts to directly apply symbolic resources and communication insights into international relations. Without question, governments and industry have used communication concepts and principles while pursuing personal goals in the international relations environment. Yet, this application and practice are very limited in nature and scope. With rare exceptions, such as the work of Glenn Fisher (1980 and 1988) and Hamid Mowlana (1986), communication has been neglected in treatments of international relations, and international communication as an area is often reduced to comparative media studies with minimal regard for people.

Because of limitations in prior treatments of international communication applications during negotiation, the remainder of this chapter will be devoted to elaborating and developing a concept called Credible Negotiation Leadership. This is an expansion of the authors' earlier work on "principled negotiation" and is different than the concept described by R. Fisher and W. Ury in 1988. This distinctiveness is derived from the use of the previously described international negotiation model which emphasizes leadership, credibility, intercultural communication concepts, principles, and orientations beyond Fisher and Ury's original approach. As such, the emphasis on communication or symbolic resources, and its corollaries in leadership and trust (Northouse, 2013), complement previous ideas and expands the potential for international negotiation effectiveness. Based on this comprehensive model of international negotiation, the next section examines negotiation styles.

Negotiation Styles

In *Mindsets* (1988) Glenn Fisher defined international negotiation basically as a communication process across cultural boundaries (p. 4). Despite the apparent emphasis on communication, this book emphasized social psychological variables, but did not draw upon communication theory and research sufficiently to reinforce the emphasis reflected in the definition. These omissions by Fisher and other authors prompted development of the earlier international negotiation model, which was needed to integrate intercultural communication theory and research with practical experience. Except for Glenn Fisher's work, few have attempted to relate communication to international negotiation. The expansiveness of the topic, the closed doors of the negotiation process, and the almost proprietary nature of training and preparation in government and industry have, no doubt, contributed to this oversight.

Compared with relevant communication research, the literature about negotiation and conflict resolution is far more extensive (e.g., Kriesberg, 1998), but is narrowly focused in a distinctively western bias and characterized by the readily marketable jargon of trainers and quick-fix artists. Since research and too much of the literature merely "follow the dollar," this overview should come as no surprise. Among these marketable commodities, the substance which underlies the gimmickry sometimes surfaces. Such is the case in Getting to Yes by R. Fisher and W. Ury (1988). According to them, a negotiator's style of conflict management and decision-making influences negotiation outcomes. From this perspective, these authors examine outcomes of "soft" and "hard" negotiators. Intent to overcome weaknesses of each, they settle for an alternative style they call "principled negotiation." For Fisher and Ury, this seemed to provide an interesting vehicle capable of carrying far more weight than the authors may have anticipated.

Soft Negotiating Style

To Fisher and Ury a "soft" negotiator is one who emphasizes the importance of relational initiation and maintenance, while not caring too much about accomplishing the negotiation goals and purposes. These negotiators would approach the process by overly accommodating other peoples'

goals and objectives. Buckholz, Lashbrook, and Wenburg (1976) described several social styles that emerged during conflict negotiations. One particular style was labeled as "amiable." This social style is indicative of "soft" negotiators. Amiable or "soft" negotiators are low in assertiveness, yet responsive. They are accommodative, seeking to satisfy the other party's concerns while neglecting their own needs and negotiation goals. The "soft" negotiator's philosophy is to avoid conflict; in other words, they use a non-confrontational style, and may even sacrifice productive outcomes in order to avoid confrontation. Consequently, a "soft" negotiator's communication behavior consists of a denial of the existence of differing positions. These negotiators actively deny the existence of conflict and direct conversation, often ambiguously, by shifting topics of discussion away from disagreement. This type of negotiator is most often agreeable and ingratiating. In addition, they may be conforming, unsure, dependable, awkward, supportive, respectful, and willing.

Since keeping other persons happy is an objective of the "soft" negotiator, this person is often characterized as being tentative in their communication behaviors. The "soft" negotiator will infrequently advocate a specific position on controversial issues; this person will tend to equivocate. As a consequence, this negotiator will produce messages that are ambiguous and difficult to understand. Comments are abstract, often containing inconsistent information. In fact, these persons learn to make decisions appear compatible with the person they are talking to at the time. The result is confusion and unclear perceptions among other negotiators. "Soft" negotiators prefer compromise strategies. When possible, these negotiators will allow persons in conflict to work out differences and remain uninvolved. For the "soft" negotiator, differing positions are "bad" and considered as evidence of dissatisfaction. Often, this negotiator will attempt to keep other people happy by distributing grief, or by following a course of avoidance.

"Hard" Negotiating Style

From the "hard negotiator's" perspective other people are viewed as adversaries and "victory" is the primary concern. This style uses what are referred to as "hardball tactics" (Lewicki, Saunders, and Barry, 2006). "Hard" negotiators make threats and apply pressures to get what they want. This style of negotiation is very common among Americans, especially in the corporate environment, since the number of wins provides a culturally-defined index of negotiation effectiveness. Buckholz, Lashbrook, and Wenburg's (1976) "driver" social style is very much like the "hard" negotiator. A "driver" is low in responsiveness to others, but is highly assertive. The driver seeks to win at the expense of the other negotiators. This behavior results from a heightened interest and desire for competition. The driver is pushy, severe, tough, dominating, harsh, strong-willed, independent, practical, decisive, and efficient. The "hard" negotiator will tend to use tactics that include threats, shouting, physical aggression, insults, hostility, and blaming other parties. For the "hard" negotiator, there is minimal concern for establishing trust or maintaining the relationship in the future.

"Hard" and "soft" negotiation styles were considered undesirable by Fisher and Ury. As was evident in the above descriptions, both styles result in short-term accommodations and deny efficient movement toward intermediate and long-term goal attainment. For example, soft negotiators may misrepresent truth and reality in their effort to maintain harmony. This action inevitably leads to future problems, along with lowered perceptions of credibility. In addition, humans naturally tend to resent those who predominantly use a hard, power-driven style. Eventually, these persons may experience a "boomerang" effect when the power differential changes. Cummings, Long, and Lewis (1986) described such a circumstance that occurred at a major American university:

A department chairperson operated as a highly authoritarian manager. Nothing seemed to get done unless the chairperson was there to see that faculty members did as they were told. One particularly unproductive faculty member was threatened with punishment: assignment to undesirable courses, no merit raise, and delays in promotion. This heavy-handed procedure was based upon a continual use of power. The faculty member became a life-long enemy and decided to lie in wait for retaliation. Eventually the opportunity arose. The faculty member became a Dean — that same chairperson's boss. The loser didn't stay a loser; the winner didn't stay a winner.

Determining whether a hard or soft negotiation style is the result of individual preference or the result of environmental influence is often difficult. In reality, it is probably a function of both influences. Since much of the previous work in this area has emphasized social-psychological influence, consideration of socio-cultural elements as sources of influence is warranted. Eastern and western conflict negotiation strategies provide examples of cultural influence on style selection. For example, western organizations often use formal confrontation meetings as a method to help manage conflicts during negotiations (Gibson, Ivancevich, Donnelly, and Konopaske, 2011). The purpose of such meetings is to provide various individuals and groups an opportunity to air their differences. Some Japanese companies have also used this intensive confrontation training to prepare their people to handle conflict situations. In both cases, it is assumed an open, direct avenue of interaction among negotiators will assist in increased understanding, awareness, and resolution of differences. Both presume, however, a limited and stereotypic conception of western negotiation practices.

Eastern organizational members negotiate differences quite differently than their western counterparts. Michael Yoshino (1968) has indicated that Japanese culture encourages the avoidance of open conflict expression. The reason for overt conflict avoidance behavior is to maintain flexibility in making adjustments in positions. Eastern culture tends to view open conflict as "public," and shifts in position cannot occur once a public position is stated. Thus, conflicts are low-key. Members of eastern decision-making groups also tend to be more sensitive than western decision-makers to subtle communication cues. In general, eastern cultures apparently believe that the less public confrontation accompanying conflict negotiation the less polarized and more flexible the parties in conflict tend to be (Long, 2003; Martin & Nakayama, 2008).

Credible Negotiation Leadership and Principled Negotiation Style

Principled negotiation is "designed to produce wise outcomes efficiently and amicably" (Fisher & Ury, 1988, p. 10-11). Essentially, this approach separates people from the problem first by focusing on interests rather than on bargaining positions. Principled negotiation generates a variety of possibilities and insists that the results be based on some objective standards. Thus, principled negotiation focuses on effective problem-solving through an initial understanding of cultural diversity and interpersonal sensitivity. This assumes at least a minimal level of interpersonal communication competence on behalf of all participants. It also presumes that negotiators lead in the process of establishing trust, i.e., credibility, for one another at the onset of negotiation relationship development.

From a human relations development perspective, credible negotiation leaders (CNL) can be characterized as avid users of conflict management tactics as described by Cummings, Long, and Lewis (1986):

- **Focus and Containment:** CNLs determine the location of differences; i.e., are they related to people or positions, individual negotiators or environmental conditions?
- **Control Threat Levels:** CNLs avoid "hard" styles and work actively to insure that perceptions of threat by others are reduced.
- **Clarify Communication Rules:** CNLs are concerned with reducing uncertainty and adverse emotions that may result; they actively consider cultural influences on the interpretation of messages and inferred motives underlying behavior.
- **Early Conflict Identification:** CNLs monitor differences that occur during negotiations and endeavor to insure that these differences do not result in debilitating, personal conflict that damages the relationship.
- **Balance Dependencies:** CNLs endeavor to insure that people perceive one another as relational equals; they are aware that perceived imbalances generate mistrust and suspicion. Development and maintenance of mutual dependence is a preferred strategy.

Credible Negotiation Leaders emphasize satisfying all participants. Parties do not advocate. Negotiators search comprehensively to define and solve problems in the short, intermediate, and long terms. Although these basic strategies are generally accepted methods for managing human relations, Credible Negotiation Leadership, as proposed in this chapter, embraces more than the human relationship; concern for spanning cultural boundaries and developing cultural relations in negotiation is the emphasis.

Propositions for Credible International Negotiation Leadership

The missing ingredient of principled negotiation is a set of universally applicable standards. Typically, a list of do's and don'ts with insufficient regard for foundations is provided. This void provides a strong potential contribution for intercultural communication and credible leadership applications. Based on Hill, Long, and Javidi's (1994) original formulation, previous propositions were modified and the list expanded with the inclusion of credible negotiation leadership, resulting in eight interrelated and progressively cumulative propositions. Each identifies a common feature of study or application which is either minimized or neglected in international negotiation literature. For each proposition, a brief explanation and application is provided.

Proposition 1: Intercultural communication and leadership study urges negotiators to recognize cultural differences as primary variables. Too often the presumption of similarity misleads negotiation. Because of an eagerness to succeed, individuals selectively reinforce apparent similarities thereby displacing objectivity with subjective desires. This self-fulfilling cycle leads to inappropriate selection of interaction strategies and confused results, often undermining attempts to establish trust and, ultimately, believability of messages generated in the process. Environmental conditions, characteristics of negotiators, and the nature of communication in the international negotiation model underscore the influence of cultural differences. For example, a significant amount of leadership literature and models have an inherent western bias. Intercultural communication study calls for all negotiators to consider leadership approaches and perspectives that may be outside their cultural comfort zone. Such introspective processes can lay the foundation for creative alternative solutions not easily recognized when only proceeding within one's comfort zone (Cummings, Long, and Lewis, 1986).

Proposition 2: Credible negotiation leadership study urges negotiators to establish and maintain highest levels of trust throughout the international negotiation process and supports maintenance of a positive negotiation environment. Establishment of a positive negotiation environment is a precondition to realizing efficient and effective outcomes. "Hard" and "soft" styles do not contribute to positive environments. Clearly, a "soft" style does not lead to a desirable outcome; "hard" styles typically fail (Lewicki, Saunders, and Barry, 2006). Rather than experience the down-side of "hard" and "soft" negotiation styles, credible leader study emphasizes the need for honesty and consistency during negotiations. Providing less triggers skepticism, disbelief, and an unhealthy negotiation environment.

Proposition 3: Credible negotiator leader study generates a variety of possibilities and insist that the results be based on some objective standards. Beginning with a focus on effective problem-solving through an initial understanding of cultural diversity and interpersonal sensitivity, the credible negotiator seeks to acquire the requisite information to make decisions, solve problems, and manage conflicts with intent of achieving mutual adaptation and goal attainment. This approach is concerned with moving in a direction that does the most good for all involved.

Proposition 4: The naturalistic bent of intercultural communication study should sensitize one to the situational variables and facilitate relationship development guidelines. Variable analytic studies emphasizing statistical or empirical differences between cultures are limited in presenting a holistic grasp of the intercultural endeavor. The overwhelming complexity of intercultural relations often requires naturalistic study that accentuates situational constraints and factors. This emphasis furthers the authors' concern for variations and differences.

Proposition 5: The intercultural communication perspective places people in the most central position of negotiation. Unlike business approaches with an obsessive task focus, intercultural communication study is at its core humanistic. The person and the relationship become more prominent than task, not necessarily to the disregard of the task, but in better perspective. Glenn Fisher's Mindsets (1988) contributes valuably to the understanding of these social-psychological aspects that play an important part of establishing a solid foundation for Credible Negotiation Leadership.

Proposition 6: The intercultural communication perspective presumes flexibility, adaptability, and accommodation to constantly changing circumstances. The focus on cultural variables, people, and the natural situation creates a permanent awareness of accommodation and adaptation. Whereas adjusting ideas to people and people to ideas is a way of life in communication studies, negotiators are often so focused on task that they neglect the essentiality of adaptation and how the process of getting to the results becomes part of the results for most cultures.

Proposition 7: Intercultural communication theory has a more pragmatic slant on research which makes the participant both a subject and a researcher, thereby fostering a unique and productive pattern of theory-research-application development. The prior propositions underscore the pragmatic concern for how negotiators can achieve symbolic congruence and ideological synchrony; one cannot focus on people and the situation without developing a repertory of skills to help cope. The skills are not merely applied, but can mutually support research, theory, and application skills.

Proposition 8: The intercultural perspective forces one to confront the basically ethical nature of human interaction and its associated components of character and good will. The results may not necessarily be desirable within a specific ethical frame, but the framework will be explicit, personal, and shared.

Beyond these propositions, credible leadership in principled negotiation implies the development of cross-cultural understanding in order to achieve long-term negotiation effectiveness. Also implied is that long-term, cross-cultural understanding occurs through the development of interpersonal relations which, in turn, grow out of mutual recognition of varied perceptions, values, norms, rules, and information processing, i.e., variations in the negotiators' respective environments. This relational development allows negotiators to penetrate each other's cultural boundaries and understand how each person reflects a different cultural and logical structure, strongly contributing to an environment of trust where negotiators share in "leading" the negotiation process.

Credible Negotiation Leadership strongly recommends Altman and Taylor's social penetration theory (1983): an orderly development of communication among negotiators that progresses from unintimate/formal to more intimate/informal. That is, negotiators interact to experience each other's world view and bottom line, to intensify communication and negotiation, to integrate cultural understanding and empathy, to develop bonds, to search for mutual solutions, and to come to agreement. Although this approach may seem as obvious as it is important, the literature discussing principled negotiation has fallen short of asking the negotiators to study the underlying presumptions of cultural interaction and to learn about their own culture. This is a prerequisite of long-term credibility and relational development.

Collectively, these propositions and other general concerns comprise an intercultural communication perspective on negotiation that integrates concepts from leadership and credibility. When combined, the international negotiation model and its propositions for intercultural communication and credible negotiation leadership provide a holistic approach that requires analysis of environmental conditions prior to development of the negotiation relationship, a separation of goals and people, and an emphasis on cultural variables at all times. An application of the model and propositions in a Japanese-American negotiation setting highlights potential outcomes and consequences for principled international negotiators.

Application of Credible Negotiation Leadership

Using Japanese and American interactions, Hill, Long, and Javidi (1994) illustrated the potential of Credible Negotiation Leadership. Perhaps even more importantly, the approach illustrated how negotiation in other cultures is more informed by an interculturally sensitive perspective than those of the more "short-termed" Americans.

Japanese Negotiators

Harmonious social relations are central to Japanese negotiations. Japanese negotiators tend to relate to one another on a vertical axis. For the Japanese, self-concepts play a relatively insignificant role in a negotiation situation. Enhancement of the group is much more important than satisfaction of personal needs. Loyalty plays an important factor in the way one negotiates, while a formal style of communication is strongly preferred. Japanese also tend to use go-betweens to assure smoothness in social relations and in all kinds of dealing and negotiating. Disagreement in public is distasteful (Pearce, 2007).

American Negotiators

In contrast to the Japanese, Americans view "negotiation sessions as problem-solving exercises" (Fisher, 1988, p. 18). The negotiation process for Americans takes place on a horizontal axis, while in most eastern cultures negotiation occurs on a vertical axis. More specifically, Americans tend to view people as independent, carrying to the negotiation tables a sense of who they are, what they should do, and what they want to accomplish from the negotiation. Americans focus on self-concept primarily in terms of self-awareness, self-image, self-esteem, self-identity, self-reliance, self-assistance, self-actualization, self-expression, and self-determination. Americans accentuate informal communication skills and tend to avoid the use of formal codes of conduct, titles, honorifics, and ritualistic manners. Often, negotiators are equalized in language or symbol selection, regardless of differences in age, sex, status, or rank.

Uncertainty Reduction

Reducing uncertainty during the international negotiation process also influences relationship development and negotiation outcome. Thus, negotiators need to understand how uncertainty is reduced across cultural boundaries (See Gudykunst and Kim, 1992). Japanese negotiators, characterized as vertical, homogeneous, collectivistic, and culturally "tight," reduce uncertainties by utilizing less verbal and more non-verbal means than do Americans. The Japanese focus on indirect and subjective forms of communication. Americans are products of a heterogeneous society. American negotiators reduce uncertainty through verbal codes and focus on direct, objective forms of communication.

The Japanese are also interested in gathering background (demographic) information such as what high school or university a person attended, his or her home town, the company for which he or she works, father's occupation, and religious background. This helps the Japanese negotiators reduce uncertainty and obtain a higher level of accuracy in predicting other negotiators' behaviors by making reasonable inferences from this information. The background information, therefore, allows people in high-context cultures to determine whether or not someone is indeed unknown.

Americans are not able to reduce uncertainty to the same degree by using background information. In contrast, they seek information on others' attitudes and values, such as: What kind of food do they like? What kind of books do they like to read? What movies do they usually watch? This often becomes small talk used to "break the ice" before getting to the "real stuff." Consequently, Americans tend to make fewer inferences from the information gathered in those preliminary conversations.

When the two contrasting styles, as somewhat superficially reflected here, are examined more carefully, the neglect of some very fundamental communication concerns from the American negotiator can be seen. Americans may be presumptuous to the level of boorishness; for example, implications of the immediate negotiation are neglected to the detriment of long-term relational development. Individual interaction is not placed in the broader framework of social harmony. In other words, Americans neglect the negative aspects of their culturally distinctive style while attempting to adjust to intercultural realities. If the eight propositions were now reexamined, the neglect of the fundamentals of intercultural relations reflected in this one Japanese-American comparison could be perceived. Perhaps one great advantage of an intercultural communication and credible leadership approach to international negotiations is the prospect that people representing different cultures might truly learn from each other (Trompenaars & Hampden-Turner, 2012).

Recommendations for International Negotiators

Restated, international negotiation is a form of communication across cultures in which participants come into contact with each other for the purpose of mutually desirable outcomes. Most individuals, however, usually see only two ways to negotiate: soft or hard. The soft negotiator wants to avoid personal and/or national conflict and so makes concessions readily in order to reach agreement. The hard negotiator, on the other hand, sees every situation as a contest of wills in which the side that has the most extreme positions and holds out longer fares better. Despite the occasional lure of hard negotiations, the authors strongly recommend the long-term results of credible negotiation leadership and principled negotiation which is neither hard nor soft, but rather is both soft and hard. The use of intercultural communication as a primary source of the principles is more strongly recommended.

This approach looks for mutual gains whenever possible, based on common and equitable standards independent of the will of either side. In addition, application of the international negotiation model continually requires that the negotiators monitor variables that influence each other's interactions and corollary information exchanges. This method is hard on merits, but soft on people. It employs the important aspects of intercultural bonding and trust to establish effective, believable communication among participants without any tricks or posturing. This method argues for culturally sensitive negotiation across cultures which is based on improvements of intercultural bonding and relations.

On the world scene many activities illustrate the strengths of this approach to international negotiation. In the trade negotiations between Japan and the USA, the contrast of short-term and long-term strategies regularly complicates relationships. On the one hand, the USA focuses on numerical quotas as a tangible outcome of such importance that the overemphasis threatens long-term relations. For example, US Senator Bradley indicted this behavior – "President Clinton's hardline on Japan trade policy was 'gratuitous brinkmanship' that puts the United States' long-term economic and strategic interests at risk in pursuit of domestic political gains" (quoted by Purdum, 1994). This firm position also threatened the political stability of Prime Minister Hosokawa's government. With similar imprudence, however, the Japanese negotiators did not assess accurately the political circumstances pressing President Clinton. Similar circumstances threatened public support for U.S. Secretary of State John Kerry and President Obama in 2015 as they negotiated in Vienna with other nations and Iran to seal an agreement that would limit Iran's uranium enrichment capabilities; critics argued that Iran would use billions of dollars after sanctions were lifted to beef up its military power. The ultimate significance of this stressful behavior is difficult to predict. Rather than publicly squabble over the particulars, however, the negotiators should recognize the need to strengthen ties through economic relations, especially when the post-Communist world will require innovative, credible leadership from its most powerful nations.

As a final note, the position provided in this chapter complements well other approaches (Erbe, 2011, 2014) to international negotiation. With the enrichment of intercultural communication and credible leadership some of the following principles assume even greater prominence. Examine them within the perspective of the prior discussion.

- *Do not bargain over positions.* Instead, try to understand the positions as you come to know the individuals involved. Arguing over positions produces unwise agreements. Arguing over positions is inefficient. Arguing over positions endangers an ongoing relationship. When there are many parties, positional bargaining is even worse. Being nice also is no simple answer.
- *Separate people from the task and overcome people problems as an entree to task achievement.* Negotiators are people first. Face the problem, not the people. Every negotiator has two kinds of interests, relationship and substance. Balance and proportion the emphasis wisely.
- *Avoid presumptions of similarity.* Try to learn the other culture as much as possible. Learn about environmental, cultural,

socio-cultural, and psychological factors influencing your negotiation.

- *Empathize or put yourself within the other negotiator's frame of reference.* Do not deduce another's intentions from your fears. Do not blame another negotiator for your problem. Negotiators should discuss each other's' perceptions.
- *Recognize and understand emotions through self-analysis and analysis of the other person.* Allow negotiators an opportunity to let off steam. Do not react to emotional outbursts. Listen actively and acknowledge what is being said. Speak for a purpose and speak clearly to be understood.
- Remember that Credible Negotiation Leadership, when the above principles are observed, becomes a shared activity, leading to longer term relationships and outcomes that are acceptable to all.

In summary, build a working relationship which is not only effective, but interculturally beneficial as well. For each of the do's and don'ts, many more reasons and pitfalls could be elaborated. But, that is the challenge for credible negotiation leaders as they work to enhance the world environment.

REFERENCES

Ahmad, A., Francis, A., & Zairi, M. (2007). Business process reengineering: Critical success factors in higher education. *Business Process Management Journal, 13*(3), 451–469. doi:10.1108/14637150710752344

Altaian, I., & Taylor, D. A. (1983). *Social penetration: The development of interpersonal relationships.* New York: Holt, Rhinehart, and Wilson.

Austin, J. (2010). *The collaboration challenge: How nonprofits and businesses succeed through strategic alliances.* San Francisco, CA: Jossey-bass.

Bryman, A. (2013). *Leadership and organizations*. London, UK: Routledge.

Buckholz, S., Lashbrook, W., & Wenburg, J. (1976). *Toward the measurement and processing of social styles*. Paper presented at the International Communication Association, Portland, OR.

Creede, C., Fisher-Yoshida, B., & Gallegos, P. (Eds.). (2012). *The reflective, facilitative, and interpretive practices of the coordinated management of meaning: making lives, making meanings*. Teaneck, NJ: Fairleigh Dickinson Press.

Cummings, H. W., Long, L., & Lewis, M. (1986). *Managing communication in organizations*. Scottsdale, AZ: Gorsuch-Scarisbrick.

Diddams, M., & Chang, G. C. (2012). Only human: Exploring the nature of weakness in authentic leadership. *The Leadership Quarterly*, *23*(3), 593–603. doi:10.1016/j.leaqua.2011.12.010

Erbe, N. (2011). *Negotiation alchemy: global skills inspiring and transforming diverging worlds*. Berkeley, CA: Public Policy Press.

Erbe, N. (2014). *Approaches to managing organizational diversity and innovation*. Hershey, PA: IGI Global Press. doi:10.4018/978-1-4666-6006-9

Fisher, G. (1980). *International negotiation: A cross cultural perspective*. Yarmouth, ME: Intercultural Press.

Fisher, G. (1988). *Mindsets*. Yarmouth, ME: Intercultural Press.

Fisher, R., & Ury, W. (1986). *Getting to yes: Negotiating agreement without giving in*. Bergenfield, NJ: Penguin.

Gibson, J., Ivancevich, J., Donnelly, J., & Konopaske, R. (2011). *Organizations: Behaviors, structures, and processes* (14th ed.). New York, NC: McGraw-Hill Education.

Gudykunst, W. B., & Kim, Y. Y. (1992). *Communicating with strangers: An approach to intercultural communication* (2nd Ed., revised). New York: McGraw-Hill.

Hackman, M., & Johnson, C. (2013). *Leadership: A communication perspective* (6th ed.). Long Grove, Ill: Wave Land Press.

Hazelton, V., & Long, L. (1988). Concepts for public relations education, research, and practice: A communication point of view. *Central States Speech Journal*, *39*(2), 77–87. doi:10.1080/10510978809363239

Hill, L. B., Long, L. W., & Javidi, M. (1994). Principled Negotiation: Achieving Intercultural Effectiveness. In N. Honna, L. Hill, B. Hoffer, & Y. Tokeshita (Eds.), Organizational behaviors in cross-cultural settings: Intercultural Understanding and Communication (vol. 2). Tokyo: Sanshuusha Publishers.

Hovland, C., Janis, I., & Kelley, H. (1953). *Communication and persuasion*. New Haven, CT: Yale University Press.

Kolb, D. M., & Williams, J. (2003). *Everyday negotiation: Navigating the hidden agendas in bargaining*. San Francisco: Jossey-Bass.

Kriesberg, L. (1998). *Constructive conflicts: From escalation to resolution*. Lanham, MD: Rowman and Littlefield.

Lewicki, R. J., Saunders, D. M., & Barry, B. (2006). *Negotiation* (5th ed.). Boston: McGraw-Hill Irwin.

Lewicki, R. J., Saunders, D. M., & Barry, B. (2015). *Negotiation* (7th ed.). Boston: McGraw-Hill Irwin.

Long, L., & Hazelton, V. (1984). *Assessing communication behavior: An application within the public relations profession. Journal of Applied Communication Martin, J., & Nakayama, T. (2008). Experiencing intercultural communication: An introduction* (3rd ed.). Boston: McGraw-Hill.

Long, L. W. (2003). Mapping Organizational Culture: An Integration of Communication and Organizational Design. *Intercultural Communication Studies, 12*(2), 127–142.

McCroskey, J. & Young, T. (1981). Ethos and credibility: the construct and its measurement after three decades. *Central States Speech Journal, 32*(981), 24-34.

Mowlana, H. (1986). *Global information and world communication*. White Plains, NY: Longman.

Normore, A., & Erbe, N. (2013). *Collective efficacy: interdisciplinary perspectives on international leadership*. Bingley, UK: Emerald Group Publishing.

Northouse, P. (2013). *Leadership: theory and practice* (6th ed.). Thousand oaks, CA: Sage.

Oetzel & Ting-Toomey, S. (2013). The handbook of communication. Thousand Oaks, CA: Sage.

Paupp, T. (2014). *Redefining human rights in the struggle for peace and development*. New York, New York: Cambridge University Press.

Pearce, B. (2007). *Making social worlds: a communication perspective*. London: Blackwell.

Pearce, B., & Pearce, K. (2000). Extending the theory of the coordinated management of meaning ("CMM") through a community dialogue process. *Communication Theory, 4*(4), 405–423. doi:10.1111/j.1468-2885.2000.tb00200.x

Pruitt, D., & Kim, S. (2004). *Social conflict: escalation, stalemate and settlement*. New York: McGraw-Hill.

Purdum, T. S. (1994, February 24). Bradley rebukes Clinton on Japan. *The New York Times*, pp. C1-C2.

Rogers, P. (2004). Trends *in conflict 2010-2030*. Centre for Humanitarian Dialogue Mediators Retreat, Oslo, Norway.

Tannenbaum, R., Weschler, I. R., & Massarik, F. (1961). *Leadership and organizations*. New York: McGraw-Hill.

Trompenaars, F., & Hampden-Turner, C. (2012). *Riding the waves of culture*. New York, N.Y.: McGraw Hill.

Watkins, M. (2002). *Breakthrough business negotiation*. San Francisco: Jossey-Bass.

Yoshino, M. (1968). *Japan's managerial system: Tradition and innovation*. Cambridge, MA: MIT Press.

ADDITIONAL READING

Kim, Y. Y. (2001). *Becoming intercultural: An integrative theory of communication and cross-cultural adaptation*. Thousand Oaks, CA: Sage.

Kouzes, J., & Posner, B. (2011). *Credibility: How leaders gain and lose it*. San Francisco, CA: Jossey-Bass. doi:10.1002/9781118983867

Lewicki, R., Barry, B., & Saunders. (2006). *Negotiation: readings, exercises, cases*. New York: Irwin/McGraw-Hill.

Northouse, P. (2010). *Leadership: Theory and practice*. Los Angeles, CA: Sage.

Samovar, L. A., & Porter, R. E. (2004). *Communication between cultures* (4th ed.). Belmont, CA: Wadsworth Press.

Starkey, B. (2009). *International negotiation in a complex world*. Lanham, MD: Rowman & Littlefield.

Vroom, V. (2000). Leadership and the decision making process. *Organizational Dynamics, 28*(4), 82–94. doi:10.1016/S0090-2616(00)00003-6

Weber, M. (2004). *Politics as a vocation* (D. Owen & T. Strong, Trans.). Indianapolis, IN: Hackett Publishing.

Winslade, J., & Monk, G. (2000). *Narrative mediation: a new approach to conflict resolution.* San Francisco, CA: Jossey-Bass.

KEY TERMS AND DEFINITIONS

Communication Subsystem: The throughput dynamic of the negotiation process that contains the negotiators and messages.

Contextual Subsystem: The input dynamic of the negotiation process that contains cultural, social, political/legal, technological, and economic/competitive dimensions.

Credibility: Perceptions of an individual's trustworthiness and expertise; one's level of believability during communication is influenced by the perceived level of their credibility.

Cultural Dimension: Concern for the behaviors and underlying values, motives, beliefs, knowledge, meanings, ethics, patterns of interaction, etc., that identify a specific "cultural" group and also differentiates it from other cultures.

Economic/Competitive Dimension: Concern for acquisition and management of financial resources; competitive aspects of this dimension consist of individuals, groups, organizations, nations, or entities who possess goals that may stimulate competition for resources, markets or alliances.

Intercultural Communication: Communication (creation and consumption of messages) among individuals from different cultures who often possess differing social norms and rules, as well as different languages, experiences, and world views.

International Negotiation: A communication function of international relations that is used for the purpose of mutual adaptation in order to' accomplish specific goals.

Leadership: Interpersonal influence, exercised in a situation, and directed, through the communication process, toward the attainment of a specified goal or goals (Tannenbaum, Weschler, & Massarik, 1961).

Outcomes Subsystem: Concern for interaction between people and consequent effects or outcomes; three categories of outcomes are considered tangible, symbolic, and relational results.

Political/Legal Dimension: Concern for formal rules which govern organizational, governmental, national conduct; methods of creating rules/laws/policy and methods for rule enforcement; electoral or position appointment practices, executive or administrative influence, and adjudication processes.

Social Dimension: Concern for the values, norms, rules, and roles; one of the greatest sources of influence on human behavior, emanating from the cultural dimension.

Technological Dimension: Concern for methods and tools used to accomplish tasks; for purposes of this chapter, this dimension emphasizes transportation and communication/information technologies.

Chapter 24
The Link between Communicative Intelligence and Procedural Justice:
The Path to Police Legitimacy

Renée J. Mitchell
University of Cambridge, UK & Sacramento Police Department, USA

Kendall Von Zoller
Sierra Training Associates, USA

ABSTRACT

The public's perception of police legitimacy is viewed through the lens of procedural justice (Tyler, 2003). Legitimacy it is a perception held by an audience (Tankebe & Liebling, 2013). Tyler (2006, p. 375) defines legitimacy as "a psychological property of an authority, institution, or social arrangement that leads those connected to it to believe that it is appropriate, proper, and just." Four aspects of the police contact that affects a citizen's view: active participation in the decision-making, the decision-making is neutral and objective, trustworthy motives, and being treated with dignity and respect (Tyler, 2004). Accordingly an officer should act in a way that supports citizen's active participation, conveys an air of neutrality, and enhances dignity and respect. One way an officer can transmit his intent is through communicative intelligence. Communicative intelligence is a communication theory based on five capabilities (Zoller, 2015). These authors intend to link communicative intelligence to behaviors officers should engage in to enhance PJ and improve PL.

INTRODUCTION

As a society there are social norms that prescribe process and outcome and when these are violated, we object (Tyler, 1990). When dealing with the criminal justice system, citizens encounter

processes when interacting with officer. That encounter defines a citizen's sense of procedural justice. Tyler (1990) asserts that "the justice of the procedures through which outcomes are distributed and decisions made" is procedural justice. The outcomes and decisions made influ-

DOI: 10.4018/978-1-4666-9970-0.ch024

ence the public's perception of police legitimacy (Mazerolle, Sargeant, Cherney, Bennett, Murphy, Antrobus, & Martin, 2014) Police legitimacy is the belief that police are a legitimate authority that the public will defer to and obey (Sunshine & Tyler, 2003b). Police legitimacy allows society to function smoothly. The authors assert that during this encounter, the citizen's experience with the officer defines the level of procedural justice, which in turn, creates the degree of police legitimacy.

America was founded on a citizen's right to procedural due process in regards to "life, liberty, or property". This belief was well founded in common law even before the constitution codified it in the Fifth and Fourteenth Amendments (Orth, 2003). These Amendments ensure fair treatment of an offender when charged with a legal violation. There are three essential features of due process: adequate notice, a fair hearing, and judgment based on evidence (Fogler, Konovsky, & Cropanzano, 1992). Citizens contacted by police officers over a potential violation are at the mercy of the police that they have a fair hearing and a judgment based on unbiased evidence. Officers collect evidence at the scene of the crime, take eyewitness testimony, and often provide testimony themselves. If citizens view the officer as incapable or unwilling to conduct the investigation in fair and equitable manner the citizen will view the encounter as a violation of their procedural due process or procedural justice. By definition, policing is procedural justice. The police make the initial decisions about which procedures and outcomes are distributed to the public (Tyler, 1990). All police/citizen contacts involve procedure and outcomes so every police contact will involve a modicum of procedural justice.

Enforcing the law is one of the fundamental duties of a police officer. To do this an officer must make contact with a citizen and communicate the violation that has occurred. And although they have discretion in their enforcement, often they are required to make arrests or administer citations due to policy or legal concerns. There

are four aspects of the police contact that affects a citizen's view: active participation in the decision-making, the decision-making is neutral and objective, trustworthy motives by the officer, and being treated with dignity and respect (Tyler, 2004). "Quality of treatment" and the "quality of decision making process" are the two overarching themes by which the public judges the officer's interaction (Reisig et al., 2007, p.1006). Whether the outcome for the citizen was positive or negative, it is the treatment by the officer that had an effect on the citizen's satisfaction with the police (Tyler, 1990). It is the treatment received by the citizen from the officer that shapes the citizen's perception of police legitimacy. Legitimacy according to Tyler (1990) is "a quality possessed by an authority, a law, or an institution that leads others to feel obligated to obey its decision and directives".

We posit that the level of fairness a citizen has of the treatment by the officer is significantly influenced by how the officer communicates with the citizen. Therefore officers who enhance their communication and build rapport through the development of their communicative intelligence (CI) can have more positive perceptions of procedural justice by the citizen. CI is the integration of cognitive and emotional resources with behavioral abilities that creates experiences and develops relationships to solve problems, catalyze change, and create new meaning (Zoller, 2008). According to Zoller (2015):

CI focuses on the cognitive and emotional elements of communication. It is behaviorally demonstrated through verbal and nonverbal channels. At its foundation, CI can be used to initiate and maintain rapport. Rapport is a foundation with which to build relationships (p. 305).

Officers may not have total control over the outcome of a police/citizen contact, but they do have control over the type of treatment the citizen receives from them. As such an officer needs to act in a way that supports citizen's active participation, conveys an air of neutrality, and enhances dignity and respect. Research is limited as to what actions officers should take to convey those principles, but we know the foundation of policing and procedural justice is communication (Tankebe & Liebling, 2014). One way an officer can transmit his intentions are through his verbal skills and body language. The author's assert that officers adept in communicative skills have higher levels of procedural justice and police legitimacy than officers who do not possess adept communication skills. To assert communication skills are a foundational to procedural justice and police legitimacy a framework of communication is introduced and described. When mastered, CI supports the ability of officers to communicate with greater consciousness and strategic purpose so they can be proactive with their communicative strategies while at the same time evaluating their communicative interactions with the citizen.

Communicative intelligence is a communication theory based on five capabilities: interdependence, consciousness, craftsmanship, efficacy, and flexibility (Zoller, 2105). The five capabilities were first defined by Costa and Garmston (2002, 2015). The theory of CI integrates both emotional capabilities with behavioral actions to give officers skills to nimbly adjust their approach to any citizen contact. These minor adjustments within communication skills can influence the citizen's perception so the citizen feels heard, listened to, and treated in a respectful neutral manner, keeping their dignity intact.

Improving the relationship between the police and the community (*interdependence*) requires the ability to recognize yourself and others' interactions and influences on each other (*consciousness*), having the knowledge that you can succeed (*efficacy*) by deploying an array of skills (*craftsmanship*) in an unpredictable and ever changing environment (*flexibility*) will result in better officer safety and improve the quality of the relationship with the community. CI consists of over fifty-five

patterns of verbal and physical behaviors officers can engage in to enhance procedural justice and improve police legitimacy. The framework linking CI to police legitimacy and procedural justice is supported in the following discussion on motivation theory and communicative intelligence.

BACKGROUND

Why Is Procedural Justice Important to the Police?

There are two types of motivation -instrumental and social. Instrumental motivation comes from the outside – it is the incentives, sanctions or punishment we might receive from performing or refraining from an act (Sunshine & Tyler, 2003a). Citations and jail are two forms of instrumental motivation. People are motivated by self-interest, but when citizens are engaged in a group or community they will begin to view the interest of the group as being aligned with their own interests (DeCremer & Tyler, 2005). Instrumental motivation would have a stronger effect if people were more motivated by self-interest. Instrumental motivation requires the sanctioning body (police) to be present. Of the two types of motivation, social motivation lasts when the sanctioning authority isn't around (Mcluskey, 2003). If people are only instrumentally motivated they will resume illegal activity when authorities are not around. This is true for employees and employers, civilians, and also those who enforce the law. Social motivation comes from within (Tyler, 1990). Social motivation is comprised of attitudes, values, identity, motive based trust and procedural justice.

There are three things that influence people's willingness to cooperate or obey the law, procedural fairness, legitimacy, and instrumental concerns (Tyler, 2003). When people obey the law out of concern for instrumental motivation they weigh the risk of getting caught for a crime, the ability of the police to combat crime, and how the law is enforced in the community (Tyler, 2003). Instrumental motivation supports the theory of deterrence, that citizens are rational beings and will weigh the costs and benefits of committing crime (Nagin, 1998). General deterrence can occur through police contact, police visibility and word of mouth about police activity on the street (Sherman, 1990). For policing to have an effect on crime and disorder an offender must have the perception that there is a high risk of swift and severe reaction by the police and then refrain from committing the act (Erickson et al., 1977). The challenge to this approach in policing is that the amount of resources necessary to create greater police visibility is expensive (Bayley, 1996). Often reduction in crime and social disorder is temporary and may not last longer than two hours after the appearance (Koper, 1995). The ability of the police to combat crime and how the law is enforced is also tenuously linked to police presence as the public will cooperate with the police inasmuch they believe the police can keep crime and disorder at bay (Tyler, 2003). Sanctions are an external motivator. When motivation is external people tend to hide their behavior so resources are consumed to monitor people (Tyler, 2010). The ability for a police department to allocate this high level of resources might be impossible.

Alternatives to allocating these expensive resources must be identified and social motivation may be one alternative. Because social motivation is internal it is a cheaper motivator than external. It is social motivation that originates from attitudes, values and beliefs about the world and our institutions (Tyler, 2010). Attitudes, values and beliefs are not represented by budget line items an as much are therefore more cost effective than external motivators. Additionally, of the two types of motivations, social motivation lasts when the sanctioning authority isn't around (McCluskey, 2003). Treating a citizen in a procedurally just manner taps into their social motivation and will have longer lasting effects on behavior than

instrumental motivation. It is the internal motivation, driven by police action that contributes to procedural justice.

Police tactical and communicative actions contribute to and define procedural justice. If the definition of procedural justice is "the justice of the procedures through which outcomes are distributed and decisions made" then by definition policing is procedural justice (Tyler, 2010, p. 42). The police officer distributes outcomes and makes decisions that affect the public. This means officers can control their actions and have influence on a citizen's perception of procedural justice. Officers can influence the public's perception of the police even when the outcome is not in favor of the citizen (Tyler, 1990). Tyler further asserts a citizen's treatment during a police contact carries slightly greater weight in their perception of an authority than the outcome of their contact. The treatment matters more than the law that is being enforced (Tyler, 1990). This is because there is an unwritten social contract that an authority figure will "act in the interests of those for whom she exercises authority," that they can trust them (Tyler, 1990). People trust that even when the outcome is negative the officer made the decision for the good of the people. Tom Tyler (2010) described it this way:

If people are allowed to present their concerns to a neutral authority, they are more likely to trust it. Further, when people feel treated with dignity and respect they are more trusting. Authorities can facilitate these beliefs by justifying their decisions in ways that make clear that they have considered the arguments raised and either can or cannot accept those arguments. It is also important for authorities to make clear that they are sincerely interested in the well-being of the parties involved – for example, through acknowledging the needs of those involved the difficulties they may be operating under, and/or their efforts to act in good faith (p. 106).

Public cooperation is imperative to an officer's ability to enforce laws. Although the public does not always cooperate; the majority of them do. The police often need cooperation from the very people least likely to give it, those whose freedoms are about to be taken away by virtue of the authority of the officer. Cooperation from a suspect or violator is one facet to procedural justice. Another facet to cooperation is that a suspect or violator may also be a witness. This duality of identity adds complexity to the paradigm of cooperation. Tankebe & Liebling (2013) suggest that there is "unpredictability" in communication because of the interactive nature of dialogue (p. 66).

The people involved in crime can also be the witnesses of crime. And all civilians (even suspects) are more likely to comply with a legal authority when they view the authority as legitimate. Legitimacy according to Tyler & Huo (2002) is "a quality possessed by an authority, a law, or an institution that leads others to feel obligated to obey its decision and directives" (p. 201). When the public views the police as "legitimate" they are more willing to cooperate because they view law enforcement values as congruent with or the same as their values (Sunshine & Tyler, 2003a). When viewed as legitimate people do not renege on their agreements and still heed an officer's advice even when the officers leave the area (Mastrofski et al. 1996, p. 283). Legitimacy leads to cooperation, cooperation leads to following the law even when sanctions are not imminent, and cooperation makes the police more effective in fighting crime (National Research Council, 2004). Summarizing Sunshine, Tyler, Mastrofski and National Research Council, treating citizens with dignity and respect, allowing citizens to have active participation in the decision-making process, making decisions that are neutral and objective, and ensuring the officer's motives are trustworthy are all necessary components of a procedurally just police contact. And although it is unknown which of these components is the strongest conveyor of procedural justice communication underlies each of the four

elements of procedural justice (Mazerolle et al., 2014) Thus, we suggest the mastery of CI will strengthen all four components of procedural justice no matter which of the four is the greater predictor of police legitimacy.

How Does Communicative Intelligence Relate to Procedural Justice?

Communicative Intelligence (Zoller, 2015) is a theory merging cognition and action when communicating. It is presented here as a way of influencing procedural justice. We call the cognitive elements of Communicative Intelligence the *5 Capabilities of CI* (modified from Costa & Garmston, 2002). They are capabilities in that they are future directed, can be developed, and contribute to the ability to think and problem solve. How do these *five capabilities* accomplish all that? To begin to make sense of these *five capabilities*, consider each a mental discipline representing a unique perspective of mental focus. Refining mental capabilities require focus on the mental processes you follow before you speak, gesture, or pause. A mental focus that has clarity increases energy and confidence when thinking and problem solving. The five capabilities of CI can be thought of as how you think about communication. If one of the capabilities is weak or missing you cannot master communication, the goal is to master communication and use it as an intelligence when making decisions and thinking critically. The 5 Capabilities are interdependence, consciousness, efficacy, craftsmanship, and flexibility.

The 5 Capabilities appears a little daunting at first glance as a way to think about communication, but when broken apart it emerges as a strategic and attainable approach to communicating with deliberate intention. Interdependence is the ability to recognize that your verbal and non-verbal communication has a symbiotic effect on those around you. When you speak or move, people around you respond to the inflection of your voice, the movement of your hand, the direction of your gaze, and the pattern of your breathing. We are in tune with each other when we are communicating or sometimes we are not in tune and miscommunication occurs. Being in tune is considered rapport. Rapport is part of the foundation of trust in relationships and a significant component of social intelligence (Goleman, 2006), whether the relationships are professional, interpersonal, or in this case, initiated by an officer.

Consciousness is the ability to step outside of yourself as you are speaking to see the interaction as though from a balcony. According to Costa and Garmston (2015) "the function of consciousness in humans is to represent information about what is happening outside and inside the body in such a way that it can be evaluated and acted upon by the body" (p. 117). Consciousness includes being cognizant of how your speech tones, inflections, and pauses have an effect on those you are speaking to. Consciousness is also having awareness of the skills of communication intelligence readily available to your actions. Consciousness is about knowing what you know and also being able to process what you see. High consciousness is not only about understanding what you see and hear it is also about what to do when you see and hear what you perceive.

Efficacy is the ability to have confidence in your communication skills, to know what speech patterns to engage in to achieve the response you are looking for (Costa & Garmston, 2002, 2015). Efficacy is a belief and as such is a source of energy when navigating communication and it "is grounded in the confidence that a person can effectively and appropriately respond and react to people when communicating" (p. 308). Efficacy is an internal drive emerging from the belief a person has about their ability to influence and positively impact a situation (Zoller, 2015). A collateral outcome of efficacy is confidence. High efficacy is a characteristic needed to be mindful and resourceful when communicating. People with "robust efficacy are likely to expend more

energy in their work, persevere longer, set more challenging goals, and continue in the face of barriers or failure" (Costa & Garmston, 2002, p. 127). According to Garmston and Wellman (2015) "the main purpose of the brain is survival" (p. 110) and "efficacy is a determining factor in the resolution of complex problems" (p. 110). Survival and resolution to complex problems are foundational to policing. It is a mindfull state independent of ego. It is a feeling of being competent even if you do not understand the problem completely or have all the answers. Efficacy is an energy source that generates effort. It is a trigger for everything else.

Craftsmanship is the repertoire of skills of communication, knowing what technique or speech pattern you are going to use and then having the ability to execute it. "Excellence is the soul of craftsmanship" (Costa & Garmston, 2015, p. 121). Craftsmanship is the process of mastering a practice. Craftsmanship in CI is the *what* of communication skills driven by the desire to seek precision, refinement, and specificity when communicating (Costa & Garmston, 2015). Craftsmanship is the foundation essential to support flexibility. Craftsmanship is the driver of continuous learning, refinement, and excellence leading to mastery (Costa & Garmston, 2002). By having a variety of skills at your disposal you can execute from multiple pathways. Craftsmanship includes several elements of communication; voice tone, speech pace, voice volume, gestures, breathing, eye contact duration, points of reference, and proxemics. It emerges from our yearning to be precise. Human beings do not advance when in a tensionless state; it is only when working between our threshold of learning and our limit of tolerance do we enter into a productive state of stress. It is this state, this striving, that our capacity for craftsmanship is created. Craftsmanship is fed by our desire to achieve our own self-imposed goals. The disciplined craftsman is never satisfied with the existing state. They know improvements are just beyond reach and with focus and work, will soon be in reach and successfully achieved. Like a great athlete, those high in craftsmanship live in a world of perpetual tension between the satisfactions of knowing you achieved while at the same time knowing the level is possible. We seek out officers that are high in craftsmanship because we trust they will lead us in the right direction, show us the correct way, or effectively demonstrate how something can be accomplished. Craftsmanship leads to trustworthiness. Within the framework of CI there are more than 50 verbal and nonverbal patterns found in a variety of languages and cultures (Poyatos, 2002a; Zoller, 2008; Zoller & Landry, 2010). One set of patterns that can be used to influence rapport and thus procedural justice are the four points of reference (Grinder, 2008).

There are four points of reference (Grinder, 2008) that can be used when communicating. Officers can deploy these reference points to be of influence on the citizen's perceptions of how they are being treated. First point is when the speaker refers to self. Two-point communication is between people when present and in real time. Third point is a visual reference between people when they are present. Third point can be a paper, easel, projector screen or any object the speaker can point to when talking to a person or group of people. Fourth point is a reference outside the people talking. It is most often represented by gestures directed outside the group. It is a reference to someone or something that is not present to the people communicating. These four points of reference are used to direct the attention of those listening to the speaker and contribute to increasing congruence between the speaker's intention and the listener's perception.

Flexibility includes the ability to see from multiple perspectives. According to Costa and Garmston (2015) we "are a unique form of life because [we] can perceive from multiple perspectives and can deliberately change, adapt, expand, and control [our] repertoire of response patterns" (p. 114). It is the ability to recognize when a communication approach is not working to a speaker's satisfaction and as such can seamlessly move to

a different approach. The confidence emerging from high efficacy constitutes the resourcefulness of flexibility. Human communication is wickedly complex and unpredictable. Unpredictable does not mean without pattern. It is true that communicating with people is like "a combination tap dance, shuffle, and tango to a syncopated rhythm produced by unpredictable humans" (Doyle & Strauss, 1976, p. 89). Yet, like dance, there are patterns. These patterns are repeating elements when we communicate. It is the patterns that make us recognizable. When officers can more quickly recognize the patterns of communication in people they contact, the more readily they can establish rapport. Since rapport is an element of trust and trust is an element of procedural justice, officers who develop rapport with contacts are more likely to establish higher levels of procedural justice than officers who do not establish rapport efficiently. Establishing rapport is dependent on flexibility. It is flexibility that drives the ability to match and mirror the patterns with those you speak to – matching, and mirroring are foundations of rapport. Zoller (2008) posits that conscious application of mirroring is a basic building block to establishing and maintaining rapport. Conscious attempts at mirroring include matching breathing patterns, voice tone, pace, and inflection, and body movements, including gestures. The greater the degree of mirroring coherence, the higher the level of rapport gained and is consistent with descriptions from Kendon (1990) and McCafferty (2002). Classrooms with higher levels of rapport most likely have students with lower distress levels; in turn, lower distress levels correlate to lower cortisol levels that increase neuron growth and integration from the hippocampus (Goleman, 2006,) (pp. 135-136).

Although the research reported above focused in classrooms, the findings are consistent across multiple contexts as indicated in the references within the above quote. The essence of this assertion of the need for flexibility in PJ and PL is that the underpinning of trust of rapport. A foundation of rapport is the ability to be flexible in your communication style to match and mirror who you are talking to so that person feels listened to and understood. With the framework of Flexibility in CI are at least 3 patterns: mirroring, pacing, and leading.

Mirroring is the deliberate matching of a person's gestures and posture. It is not simultaneous, a situation that would appear as aping. Rather is it is slightly delayed mirroring, about 3 to 5 seconds. Pacing is mirroring with the addition of matching the speaker's breathing pattern, tone of voice, and energy of their emotional state. When pacing, you are following the other person. Leading is when you (the officer) leads the other person with a pattern that may include breathing, tone of voice, or pace of speech. Successful leading is when the other person shifts to the officer's pattern. The result is often a reduction of conflict and energy. These 3 patterns are techniques an officer can deploy to "make clear" that they are "sincerely interested" as Tyler (2010) suggests are ways of increasing the public's perception of police legitimacy (p.106).

The following story describes the interactions between a citizen and two officers. The story provides an example of the influence of rapport on the perception of being understood.

During a class given by Mitchell and Zoller a police student described an attempt to build rapport with a distressed women. He was assisting another officer, as a cover officer, on a disturbance call. The contact officer was speaking with an angry woman when the cover officer arrived on scene. The woman was breathing high, pacing, and yelling at the officers. She told the officer she allowed friends of hers to move into her house. She described how they were now taking advantage of her kindness, not paying rent, staying up late, and eating all of her food. She spoke loudly and quickly. Her breathing was high in the chest. She told the officer, "I want them out of my house!"

The contact officer told the woman, "I understand you are upset but there is nothing we can do. We cannot throw the tenants out of your house. You have to give them a thirty-day notice." She then began screaming and yelling profanities at the officer ending the rant with "You are worthless!"

The contact officer kept saying, "Calm down ma'am, just calm down" to no avail. Each time the officer said to calm down, she became more agitated and loud. A second officer decided to try and build rapport with her, based on the training from the class he was experiencing. His goal was to get her to shift her emotion to a lower energy state so she was more receptive to police direction. He thought about her fear, frustration, and disappointment and in a voice volume that matched hers as well as gestures that mirrored her, he said, "You are so frustrated right now. Your friends have taken advantage of you and when you call the very people who are supposed to help you, the police, you find out that that we can't even help you." She stopped pacing, turned to the officer, taking a deep breath, she snarled with a significant decrease in volume, "That's right mutha fucka!"

The officer mirrored and paced her to get her to become open to police direction. And although this was not a conventional reaction she did shift emotionally for the officer and began to listen.

Interdependence is the sense and awareness of community. As Costa and Garmston assert (2015), "interdependence means knowing that we will benefit from participating in and contributing to work (p. 125). Zoller (2015) posits that Interdependence is a willingness to influence and be influenced by others and it includes a desire to contribute (p. 310). The link between interdependence and PJ/PL is cooperation. Relationships with high levels of interdependence have high levels of cooperation (Costa & Garmston, 2015) Interdependence creates trust and people are more likely to cooperate when they trust the other person (Tyler, 2010) Social motivation is stronger than instrumental motivation (Tyler, 1990). *Interdependence* is deeply human; it is our drive to be connected to others and to know we are part of a larger whole. We contribute to the whole and if we are missing (not connected) there is a hole in the community. Our personal relationships bring deep levels of purpose and meaning. Our professional interdependence increases our safety, social purpose, and courage. As social beings in need of reciprocity and community, we grow and nurture relationships with others. Besides communication the other aspect of policing that we are involved with one hundred percent of the time is our community whether it is a neighborhood, a district, a street, a precinct or a whole agency. These social facets are inter-connected through complex relationships. The healthy community is one where interdependence thrives. We are dependent on each other at various levels at different times of the day and different days of the week. To become exceptional police officers we have to understand our interdependence with each other and among layers of factions that make up our community. Cooperation is a socially motivated attribute that will continue even when a supervising entity is removed. Citizens cooperate when they are socially interdependent. An officer who understands interdependence will influence the public to obey the law (Tyler, 2010). A person with high levels of interdependence has wider perspectives that contribute to making smarter choices.

As previously stated, at first glance these 5 Capabilities may seem overwhelming and yet, once you begin learning each piece and see how they fit together you realize it is what we already do as human beings every day, we are now just going to do it with consciousness. Consciousness gives us the ability to deliberate and strategic, two elements essential to offices that wish to bolster a contact's sense of procedural justice. And one way of influence and officer can make difference is in making the contact feel listened to and understood.

Communicating using CI allows officers to actively engage in conversations with the public that support procedural justice and improve police legitimacy. Mastering the *five capabilities* allows a police officer to consciously and proactively evaluate their interactions with the community, which includes suspects. Small adjustments to an officer's behavior can improve community relations. Improving the relationship between officers and the community (*interdependence*) requires the ability to recognize yourself and others' interactions and influences on each other (*consciousness*), having the knowledge that you can succeed (*efficacy*) by deploying an array of skills (*craftsmanship*) in an unpredictable and ever changing environment (*flexibility*) will result in better office safety and improve the quality of the relationship with the community.

From about the time human beings are four years old they begin to think about other people's beliefs, called Theory of Mind. This theory explains and predicts behavior by making inferences about their internal state of mind (Bering, 2003). Observing what another person says and how they say it allows us to make inferences about their states of mind. This allows a communication loop between two people to develop with both sides adjusting to what the other person says and does. An officer's nonverbal and verbal behavior has a direct and observable effect on another's behavior and with practice can be adjusted in milliseconds to gain a citizen's cooperation and increase the safety of a situation. This thinking ability to consciously and deliberately make small adjustments in behavior in an instant is why mastering EVERY component of the five states capabilities is so important. Mastering the five capabilities has a direct effect on an officer's ability to interact with their community in a fair and respectful manner. This skill is similar to drawing your weapon; you need to practice the non-verbal behaviors so that when needed in an instant they flow seamlessly into place just as when your gun appears in your hand in milliseconds when required.

The Triad: What Is Procedural Justice, Police Legitimacy and Communicative Intelligence

To recognise always that the power of the police to fulfill their functions and duties is dependent on public approval of their existence, actions and behaviour, and on their ability to secure and maintain public respect – Peelian principle

Without legitimacy the police could not exist. If the public does not give the police permission to monitor their behavior we would return to a feudal system. Even in remote tribes, the chief resolved disputes between members and before there was organized police departments local constables settled matters (Williams & McShane, 1998). Today the United Kingdom actively promotes policing by consent. It has become part of their national agenda that unless the public approves of the police force as a whole they will not be able to carry out their function as law enforcers. Just like beauty, police legitimacy lies in the eye of the beholder. The citizen's perception of the police officer is what determines the citizen's view of

the police (Tyler, 1990). And the citizen's view is based on the four components of procedural justice. Figure 1 visually demonstrates how the relationship between the two ideas flow.

Procedural justice emerges from the officer's action in that they convey due process to a citizen. We believe the skills of communicative intelligence can provide officers with a greater flexibility when communicating to increase the probability of a positive citizen-police contact. If a citizen believes that they will not receive a fair and impartial outcome from the officer/citizen contact they will leave the interaction with a lowered perception of police legitimacy. In order for the citizen to perceive their interaction as procedurally just they must feel they were an active participate in the decision-making, the decision-making was neutral and objective, the officer's motives are trustworthy, and they were treated with dignity and respect (Tyler, 2004). The only way to convey these four components of PJ is through communication or a dialogue (Tankebe & Liebling, 2013). We can leave things the way they currently are believing that since humans communicated through body language and speech

Figure 1.

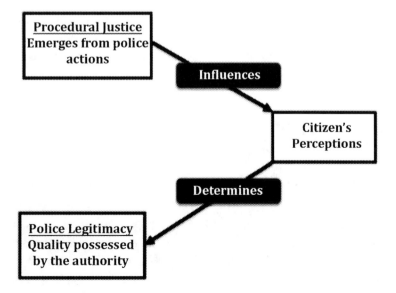

from infancy we all know what we are doing and we effectively communicate or we can begin to teach more effective communication to a profession which communication is the foundation. If we all effectively communicate on a daily basis then why is there miscommunication?

CI aims to break communication down into behaviors and patterns that can be learned and practiced in order to communicate exactly what is intended and to make a positive influence on the citizen. In this case it is important for officers to become skilled in CI as the public's perception of their communication skills affect the public's view of the police department as a whole (Mazerolle, Antrobus, & Bennett, 2012b). Officers who can become conscious of their influence on others can become a powerful force for police legitimacy. They will be able to influence how another perceives a whole profession. With that ability comes great responsibility and they will have to learn *Duco pro bono publico*, which is Latin for Influence for the benefit of the public or Influence for the greater good. The intent of CI is not to manipulate for self-serving reasons but to influence for the greater good, to settle someone down so an officer can get information or to get someone to understand someone else's point of view. To calm someone who is frightened. To successfully conduct a death investigation interview with awareness of cultural and religious beliefs. CI is a powerful tool that when used with integrity can improve a citizen's perception of police legitimacy.

THE FOUR COMPONENTS OF PROCEDURAL JUSTICE: VOICE, RESPECT AND DIGNITY, FAIR AND IMPARTIAL TREATMENT, AND NEUTRALITY

Tyler asserts Procedural Justice has four components and when these four components are fully developed, fairness emerges (Tyler, 2004).

Because Procedural Justice is a perception and communication influences perception, we assert CI can be used to influence the perceptions of PJ - the judgment one makes in reference to fairness. Fairness is an important trait to human beings. In a policing context procedural justice is the perception of fairness when a citizen has legal contact with an authority (Tyler, 1988) The determination of fairness is made by the way the legal decisions that affect the person are made (Tyler, 1988). Procedural justice is the "fairness of the process through which the police make decisions and exercise authority" (Sunshine & Tyler, 2003, p.514). There are two procedural elements citizens consider when determining fairness; the quality of the decision making and the quality of the treatment in the interaction (Tyler, 2003). In game theory if a player is being treated unfairly they will respond with vindictiveness and if treated fairly will respond in kind (Rabin, 1993). When people are treated kindly they respond with friendliness, when treated with hostility they will often respond at a heightened level even more nasty and even brutal at times (Fehr & Gaechter, 2000). The two procedural elements the quality of decision making and the quality of treatment are made up of four underlying foundational pieces; being treated with dignity and respect, having a voice in the decision making process, neutrality and the outcomes are made in a fair and impartial and manner (Mazerolle et al., 2014). When officers demonstrate behavior that supports these processes citizens view them as a legitimate authority and will follow their direction. It is still unknown which of the four processes is the strongest predictor of the perception of police legitimacy (Mazerolle et al., 2014). Although there is some support that voice does play a strong role in reducing citizen noncompliance (Dai, Frank, & Sun, 2011). Whether subjects are given a voice before or after a decision they will view a decision as more fairly than a decision where the subject was given no voice (Lind et al., 1990). Allowing a citizen to have input in the decision making process was found to be one of the strongest indicators for citizen cooperation (Dai et al., 2011). Giving the citizen voice is not sufficient. The citizen also needs to believe they have been listened to and understood. Communicative Intelligence offers skills officers can use to increase the probability a citizen will feel listened to and understood. The primary skill is paraphrasing (Zoller & Landry, 2010).

Paraphrasing is a listening skill demonstrated by matching the energy and nonverbal elements of the person who wishes to be listened to. Paraphrasing is not summarizing. Summarizing is repeating the information to ensure clarity from the listener not the speaker. The paraphrase contains not just the essence of the words spoken it also conveys the emotions and nuances beneath the words. The following is a story that demonstrates the use of paraphrasing a feeling without mimicking the words the speakers.

One of the authors, Renée, worked as an active patrol officer. She responded to a disturbance call between a boyfriend and girlfriend. When she got to the house the two were in a heated argument over domestic issues, who cleaned the house more, who fed the baby more, who was getting more time doing individual activities, etc. Both the male and the female each told Renée their side of the story. They each defended their actions claiming that they were putting in time for the relationship, claiming that they worked harder than the other, and claiming they were the righteous ones. Rather than taking sides or paraphrasing the feelings concerning the fight Renée asked, "Do you love each other?" Both the male and the female visibly relaxed. They took a breath, made eye contact with each other, and relaxed their shoulders. They both said, "Yes". Once they were in a receptive state Renée helped them talk through a plan to support each other in the relationship. With a new baby in the house they were struggling with making ends meet and still having the individual activities they used to have before the baby came.

Rather than paraphrasing the surface emotion which was fear and anger, Renée paraphrased the underlying emotion of love. She could hear that their argument was about not getting enough time together which meant they still felt love towards each other. Paraphrasing the positive emotion helped them shift their perceptual focus from defending their position to thinking about their love for the other person. The paraphrase used by the officer in the above story is an example of a paraphrase that attempts to shift conceptual focus (Garmston & Wellman, 2013). This type of paraphrase directs mental attention to the big idea underlying the verbal message.

HOW PROCEDURAL JUSTICE INFLUENCES A PERSON'S WILLINGNESS TO COOPERATE

Tyler (2004) asserts that citizens who have a positive sense of being treating fairly (high procedural justice) will cooperate. Sir Robert Peel maintained the following when establishing the first police force in 1829, "The ability of the police to perform their duties is dependent upon *public approval* of police existence, actions, behavior and the ability of the police to secure and maintain *public respect*" (Sir Robert Peel's Principles of Law Enforcement, 2015, p.1). Citizen cooperation is the goal of any police/citizen contact so encouraging and creating processes for officers that allow increased citizen cooperation should be a priority for every police department (Tyler & Huo, 2002). Research has demonstrated that people cooperate when they are treated in a procedurally just manner in both their work place and when interacting with a public official (Tyler, 2010). The perceptions of fairness citizens have of a police officer have an effect on the citizen's reaction to the officer (Dai, et al. 2011). Citizen/police interaction begins with unequal status, an imbalance of power (Sykes & Clark, 1975). The imbalance of power requires the officer to set the tone and context for the contact to put the citizen at ease. When citizens are in a position of disadvantage, as they are during a police contact, they view procedures that favor them as more fairly than a procedure that advantages the officer (Thibaut et al., 1973). Because the officer is in a role where he is being paid to represent the city or state, it is incumbent on him to adjust his approach to the citizen and not the other way around. The officer has control over their own behavior, not that of the citizen. If citizens perceive the officer is treating them with disrespect this affects their social identity and they will respond with treatment in kind (Dai et al., 2011). But if officers engage in respectful policing and allow the citizen to participate in decision-making the citizen will be more compliant and be more likely to follow the law even when officers are not around (Tyler, 1990).

Communication Is the Foundation of Procedural Justice

Thus far we have argued procedural justice is grounded in CI. Procedural justice is a perception that influences cooperation (Tyler, 2010). The common theme across these sociological frameworks is communication. Developing an officer's ability to communicate is grounded in understanding a framework of communication. CI offers the framework in both intellectual and actionable fields. Establishing an environment where the citizen feels listened to and understood requires communication strategies that engage the citizen at an emotional level. If this can be accomplished it will result in higher levels of respect for the police and improved perceptions of police legitimacy. Communication is not just about the words that fall from a person's mouth. It's about which words you choose, the speed at which you say them, the way you hold your head, purse your lips, and breathe, communication ultimately is about the micro-level processes that symphonize to create meaning. If the goal of procedural justice is to make a citizen feel as

though they were treated with dignity and respect and as though they had a voice in the process, then officers must understand the micro-processes that create those feelings (Tyler, 1990). The five capabilities of communicative intelligence offer a path to understanding.

Communicative intelligence and the five foundational capabilities is the foundation for procedural justice. The five capabilities provide an officer with the ability to perceive and respond to situations with greater effectiveness. The five states capabilities are the tools we use to make choices and take action. Unlike thinking styles, the *five capabilities* are at once innate to human processing and at the same time developmental and can be learned and refined. Through the lens of police legitimacy, craftsmanship is the drive to hone a skill to perfection to ensure the police officer's safety and the citizen's perception of procedural justice. Efficacy is the knowledge and belief that the officer can overcome any obstacle. Or in this case, any variation of communication the citizen takes such that the officer knows what to do. Flexibility is the ability of the officer to change their approach when talking to a citizen and the conversation shifts based on the citizen's response or participation. Consciousness is the ability of the officer to understand how their emotions influence thinking and decision making when communicating – to recognize their triggers. Consciousness is also the officer's ability to recognize, name and assess what is being said by the citizen while simultaneously having awareness of the available communication skills that when deployed will have the most successful outcomes. Interdependence is when the officer knows how their actions contribute to the greater whole of an organization, a community, or to the public. The five capabilities create an atmosphere of procedural justice through officers understanding that effective communication requires all five capabilities in order to seamlessly move a citizen from a reactive emotional state to an accepting emotional state.

THE FOUR ABILITIES: THE BEHAVIORAL ELEMENTS OF COMMUNICATIVE INTELLIGENCE

The *Four Abilities* comprise the behavioral elements of the CI model. Drawing from the fields of behavioral psychology, linguistics, and biology (Kendon, 1997; McNeill, 1992; Poyatos, 2002b) the four abilities of CI define specific patterns of communication that can be used to be of influence. In real time communication the patterns of communication identified in the four abilities are not distinct and isolated. The patterns as intertwined and complex, nuanced by subtle changes in breathing, eye gaze, and speed of deployment. Communication is dynamic and complex and looks and sounds differently in each culture.

Although deployment of a pattern may be culturally unique, the patterns are universal in their appearance in communication. Some common nonverbal skills across cultures include gestures, voice tones, and pausing (Poyatos, 2002a, 2002b; Kendon, 1997, 2004). What is relevant about CI in police legitimacy is that nonverbal skills provide meaning beyond the words (Beattie & Shovelton, 1999; Bevalas, Chovil & Row, 1995; Burgoon, Byuller, Hale & deTurck, 1984; Goldin-Meadow, 1997, 1999, 2002) and can be used to influence perceptions. CI is a model that officers can use to increase their deliberate and conscious use of verbal and nonverbal skills. The four abilities of CI are comprised of verbal and nonverbal patterns of communication.

Receptivity

Four important skills of receptivity are credible voice tone, stance, mirroring, and paraphrasing. These skills have influence on the emotional and cognitive receptivity of the listener. Furthermore, the skills of receptivity can be influential even when the message challenges a person's knowledge, abilities, values and beliefs. Receptivity is recognized by the presence of abdominal levels

of breathing (Grinder, 2008). An officer can use the patterns of receptivity to attempt to increase the citizen's state of receptivity for the message the officer is attempting to send.

Receptivity is enhanced by rapport. According to Zoller and Landry (2010), rapport is "a short-term psychological state in which the lines of communication are wide open" (p. xxiv). Forming relationships is dependent on the ability to develop rapport (Milgram, Dunn, & Price, 1993) and mirroring the gestures of a speaker when listening contributes to rapport (Valdesolo & DeSteno, 2011). Officers can more quickly get into rapport by knowing these skills and knowing when best to use them to achieve the desired outcomes of the citizen contact. When citizens are in rapport they are more likely to be receptive and more likely to leave the conversation with the officer with a more positive attitude. This positive attitude is a direct measure of procedural justice. The authors taught a course on Communicative Intelligence and Procedural Justice at a large Northwestern Police Department. The officers were taught specifics skills on voice, stance, gestures and how to use these behaviors to get into rapport with citizens. One of the students described a contact with an overwrought teenager and how he used the skills taught in the course to build rapport with a female student:

One of the students at the high school had brought her IPhone to school and it was stolen. She was hysterical. She was crying uncontrollably, taking in large gulps of air, and was unable to calm herself down enough to explain to the officer what had happened. The school counselor kept telling the student that she broke the rules by bringing the IPhone to school and if she would have made better decisions she wouldn't have this problem. The counselor said, "I'm sorry you lost your phone but there is nothing we can do about it now." The officer had been listening to the student talk about how her deceased grandmother's photos were on the phone. There were multiple pictures of the two of them together. The officer matched her stance and gestures stating, "So what you are really upset about is losing the photos of your grandmother." The student took a breath, wiped her eyes, and nodded her head. She continued to breathe deeply taking deep breaths to settle herself down and began telling the officer exactly what happened.

The preceding story illustrates an example of a clarifying paraphrase (Garmston & Wellman, 2013). In this story the paraphrase was used to acknowledge the specificity of the girl's emotional focus. Once she felt understood, she shifted her breathing and got into rapport with the officer.

A third component to receptivity is credibility. Credibility is the listener's perception the speaker is worth listening to. This is important to police legitimacy because to have high levels of legitimacy the citizen needs to believe the officer is capable of doing the job. The perception of credibility is enhanced through the use of voice tone, pausing, and stance (Poyatos, 2002; Zoller, 2008; Zoller & Landry, 2010). A narrow voice tone is perceived as more credible than a rhythmic voice tone. The pause is a naturally occurring pattern in communication. Pausing to influence credibility is best accomplished by standing still at the same time while simultaneously breathing abdominally (Zoller, 2008).

Receptivity is influenced by the patterns of rapport. People engaged in conversation are in rapport when they can be observed mirroring each other. Valdesolo & DeSteno (2011) found higher levels of receptivity when mirroring was present than when these behaviors were not evidenced. In addition to rapport, empathy contributes to procedural justice by making the citizen feel they have been heard and understood from their perspective.

Empathy

Empathy is a state of awareness in others where they feel they are understood contextually and emotionally. When there is empathy, trust emerges.

With trust, a sense of procedural justice emerges. Empathy is dependent on effectively establishing rapport. According to Goleman (2006), what makes empathy unique from rapport is that the person being spoken to feels understood beyond their words. Goleman (1996, 2006) further asserted that empathy and rapport form the foundations of social intelligence and emotional intelligence.

When a person feels understood, they display a shift in their breathing so more abdominal breaths and often the blood pressure and tensions lower (Grinder, 2008). An officer can create that moment by effectively paraphrasing the citizen. When the paraphrase is delivered in a way that matches the energy and meaning of what the other person initially said, empathy emerges. Tyler (2010) suggested officers need to "make clear" they are "sincerely interested" to improve legitimacy, when empathy emerges citizens will feel heard. Garmston and Wellman (1999, 2013) assert that paraphrasing is a listening skill as opposed to being a language skill. The paraphrase is used to convey to the citizen they are understood by their works and also understood at an emotional level. Understanding a citizen is important when conveying the officer has considered the citizen's argument (Tyler, 2010). When empathy is conveyed, the potential for defensiveness is reduced. With reduced defensiveness comes increasing receptivity and increased cooperation (Dai et al., 2011).

Agility

Agility is the ability to move quickly and easily with nimbleness. Human interactions are complex and unpredictable (Zoller, 2015). Officers with high levels of agility have flexibility and can react quickly. Consciousness and flexibility are the energy sources for agility. To be agile is to simultaneously recognize culturally specific patterns among individual's unique patterns and the influences. In policing this means an officer engaging a citizen must be able to read the nonverbal patterns of the citizen, assess the situation, and choreograph a response congruent with their intended goal. Agility requires the ability to see from the citizen's perspective. This is called the allocentric perspective (Garmston & Wellman, 2013). Being allocentric is evidenced by expressing empathy. Agility is the ability to see or respond to the unique patterns and behaviors during a citizen contact. Dynamic presence is the ability to respond in ways that maintain receptivity and empathy with a citizen in the hopes of establishing a positive sense of procedural justice. A citizen who feels listened to and understood as well as empathized should hold high levels of police legitimacy.

Dynamic Presence

Doyle and Strauss (1976) equate human interactions as an "impromptu, syncopated dance with unpredictable humans" (p. 89). This view is consistent with the situations officers face during citizen contacts. To navigate this state of unpredictability with dynamic presence an officer relies on sensory acuity and the CI patterns that support receptivity and empathy. The energy states supporting dynamic presence include consciousness, because consciousness is necessary to acknowledge and process incoming data, as well as craftsmanship and flexibility. To process the incoming data accurately and thoroughly the officer must go beyond the words and respond also to emotions.

WHY IS COMMUNICATIVE INTELLIGENCE IMPORTANT TO PROCEDURAL JUSTICE?

At the heart of procedural justice is the citizen's perception of fair treatment. We hear our young children cry out, "That's not fair" when they feel someone else is getting something better, bigger, or more valuable than they are. Fairness is a value that runs deep within all societies. Officers trained in Communicative Intelligence will gain skills that allow them to be more responsive to the public's need for fairness. When treated in a procedurally just way citizens are more likely to cooperate and have improved opinions of the police officers in general (Mazerolle, Bennett, Antrobus, & Eggins, 2012a; Tyler, 2010). Suspects recidivate less in domestic violence situations when treated in a procedurally just manner (Paternoster et al., 1997). These two areas alone cooperation and reduction of continuing spousal assault are reasons enough for officers to trained in specific behaviors that improve a citizen's perception of the police.

What Are the Skills of Communicative Intelligence?

Ultimately the skills of CI are about building rapport with another human being through receptivity, empathy, and dynamic presence. Becoming skilled at CI gives an officer the agility and dynamic presence to seamlessly move in rhythm with a citizen in a way that establishes that rapport. Once officers have the skills needed to engage with the public in this way it then becomes about choice. An officer must choose to build rapport through CI. And most importantly if officers are tasked with treating the public in a procedurally just manner then they must choose to use CI when interacting with all of the public, not just the public they feel deserve their efforts to use CI.

How Does Communicative Intelligence Influence Procedural Justice?

The skills of CI are the undercurrent of human communication. Just as a river can look smooth and slow moving on the surface but have fast moving eddies of water that can pull you to your death, so too does communication look smooth on the surface unless you are trained to observe the undercurrent of communication. CI skills give officers this tool. Citizens want to be treated in a procedurally just way by any person or institution that has power over them (Tyler, 2010). When they are not treated in this manner they become angry and/or frustrated and may lash out (Dai et al., 2011). CI gives skills that when used properly can assist a citizen in becoming more receptive to a negative outcome (Engel et al, 2005). Officers generally are called when something is not going in a positive direction. Through CI officers can influence how the citizens views the outcome of the situation. By using receptivity, empathy, and dynamic presence in an agile manner the officer can create an atmosphere of procedural justice.

How Can Police Officers Use Communicative Intelligence?

Officers respond to a variety of situations on a daily basis that upon arrival can change in a moment's notice. Officers need skills that allow them to shift rapidly from one approach to another, from one weapon to another, from one verbal tactic to another. The nature of policing requires an officer to have the agility and dynamic presence to shift in flap of a hummingbird's wing to a new approach. Officers develop these skills anecdotally by their fifth year on the street. They pick up cues from other officers or citizens on the street that create micro-adjustments over time to their own communication techniques. Often officers that are smooth out on the street cannot articulate what it is they do that puts a citizen at ease, they just know that it comes naturally and easily to them. CI training gives the vocabulary to the officer so they can teach others how to get a citizen to relax and become receptive. CI training can decrease the amount of time a new officer takes to become adept at speaking to people during tense situations. CI skills allow officers the awareness of what it is about their body language that is either increasing a citizen's receptivity to direction or decreasing it. By being aware of which skills they are engaging and the reaction of the citizen the officer will be more adept at consciously choos-

ing which techniques to engage in with different types of citizens.

Procedural Justice + Communicative Intelligence = Police Legitimacy

Police legitimacy is in the eye of the beholder. Legitimacy is a quality held by an authority that determines whether a citizen will obey its decisions and directions (Tyler, 2006). The citizen's perception of legitimacy is influenced by their sense of procedural justice. When citizens feel as though they have been treated impartially, respectfully, fairly, and were listened to they will acquiesce to the decisions and directions of the police (Tyler, 2010). CI allows officers to choose which skills they will employ when trying to build rapport with a citizen, which skills when they are trying to show empathy, and which skills when breaking rapport in a gentle manner is needed. Understanding the components of procedural justice and the skills of CI allow officers to determine what level of legitimacy a citizen walks away with. Without both sets of skills officers will continue to use trial and error to learn communication skills that work on the street.

How Does Communicative Intelligence Impact the Public?

Police decisions impact people's lives on a daily basis. Police officers have been imbued with the power to seize property, seize people, and take lives. The communication that is exchanged before any of these measures are taken are imperative to the outcome of those situations. Giving officers tangible skills that can be practiced and measured is a significant step towards creating a more procedurally just approach to police/citizen contacts. Improving perceptions of police legitimacy can lead to lower incidents in use of force (Dai et al, 2011). Officers often escalate situations when citizen's first communication is one of disrespect and vice versa citizens will escalate if officer's first communication is one of disrespect (Dai et al., 2011). This seems like common sense. When someone feels disrespected it diminishes their social identity and they react to feeling "less than" by showing they cannot be coerced (Dai et al., 2011). Making officers aware of CI they can make conscientious decisions about how their first communication will be made. They can consciously decide to be approachable or credible, whether to build or break rapport. CI allows officers to influence a situation to maintain officer safety. Additionally, CI allows officers to reduce the stress of the police/citizen interactions for both the officer and the citizen. By maintaining a dynamic presence officers can consciously keep both themselves and the citizen in a receptive state. Remaining in a receptive state allows citizens to feel understood and heard, to remain calm in the face of adversity and to walk away from a situation feeling as though the best outcome was decided.

SOME OF THE CURRENT BARRIERS TO INTRODUCING POLICE TO COMMUNICATIVE INTELLIGENCE: COMMAND PRESENCE VERSUS DYNAMIC PRESENCE

Command presence is a concept without a universal definition. The term is discussed in the academy from the first day as a recruit and as a trainee out in the field, but the definition is a vague combination of body language, voice projection, and professionalism. Chief Ron Richards described command presence in *Command presence: Feeding your own self confidence* as, "essentially presenting yourself as someone in authority, trusted and respected." He goes on to say that you need to walk with intent and your head up, project an air of "I am in charge of the situation", speak clearly, groom yourself neatly and behave professionally to project command presence. Command presence presents a challenge when measuring because it is a subjective measure.

How do you walk with intent? What projects an air of being in charge? It is a concept without a concrete set of behaviors that can be taught and then measured.

Dynamic presence on the other hand is based on patterns of CI. These patterns can be taught and measured in the field when officers are in training. They can be reinforced. Dynamic presence teaches that an officer can control a situation by influencing the officer/citizen interaction through rapport and empathy rather than coercive means. Dynamic presence feels more like respectful negotiation between an authority and a citizen rather than a forceful directive. CI is tangible whereas command presence is ambiguous. Officers when dealing with divergent situations multiple times a day need skills they can practice and then artfully master to deal with the ever-changing society around them.

FUTURE RESEARCH

The current literature articulates what procedural justice is and how engaging in procedural justice practices improve the public's perception of police legitimacy. Researchers are still unclear on which components of procedural justice are the strongest indicators of police legitimacy (Mazerolle et al., 2014). We do not have a clear understanding of whether respect and dignity influences police legitimacy more strongly than having a voice. We also do not understand what components of an officer's actions influence the public's perception. Dai & Sun (2011) demonstrated that "disrespect" by an officer leads to disrespectful behavior by a citizen. It still needs to be determined what conveys "disrespect" to a citizen, is it the tone an officer takes, a look of contempt, the words the officer uses, or does social status create a skewed lens from which the citizen views the officer.

Communicative Intelligence accords the officers specific skill sets to learn, practice, and master. Training in communicative intelligence allows an officer to become agile in the reciprocal exchange that occurs between officers and citizens. Having specific skill and patterns in CI allows for definitive research to take place on whether the patterns have influence on a citizen's perception. Engel (2005) demonstrated that citizen's perceptions change based on whether they receive a traffic citation or not. Studies like this make evident the possibility that studies can be designed to test the effectiveness of CI patterns on the public's perception.

CONCLUSION

Police attitudes and behaviors are at the forefront of a negative national conversation about policing. Police are given relatively little training on communication when compared to shooting, arresting, and driving techniques. Communication training when given is often taught within a control framework. Teaching officer how to use command presence to control people and to use communication techniques that benefit the officer over the citizen. Communicative Intelligence affords officers the opportunity to learn specific patterns of behavior to influence a citizen's attitude and behavior in a subtle way that supports police legitimacy. Training officers in dynamic presence to create rapport within the framework of procedural justice offers a flexibility that tactical communication techniques do not. Communicative Intelligence as a police practice is an approach that is in need of greater development and study.

REFERENCES

Bavelas, J. B., Chovil, N., & Roe, L. (1995). Gestures specialized for dialogue. *Personality and Social Psychology, 21*(4), 394–405. doi:.10.1177/0146167295214010

Bayley, D. H. (1996). *Police for the Future.* Oxford, UK: Oxford University Press.

Beattie, G., & Shovelton, H. (1999). Iconic hand gestures that accompany spontaneous speech. *Journal of Language and Social Psychology, 18*(4), 438–463. doi:10.1177/0261927X99018004005

Bering, J. J. (2003). Towards a cognitive theory of existential meaning. *New Ideas in Psychology, 21*(2), 101–120. doi:10.1016/S0732-118X(03)00014-X

Burgoon, J. K., Byuller, D. B., Hale, J. L., & deTurck, M. A. (1984). Relational message associated with nonverbal behaviors. *Human Communication Research, 10*(3), 351–378. doi:10.1111/j.1468-2958.1984.tb00023.x

Costa, A. L., & Garmston, R. J. (2002). *Cognitive coaching: A foundation for renaissance schools.* Norwood, MA: Christopher-Gordon.

Costa, A. L., & Garmston, R. J. (2015). *Cognitive coaching: Developing self-directed learners and leaders.* Lanham, MD: The Rowan & Littlefield Publishing Group, Inc.

Dai, D., Frank, J., & Sun, I. (2011). Procedural justice during police-citizen encounters: The effects of process-based policing on citizen compliance and demeanor. *Journal of Criminal Justice, 39*(2), 159–168. doi:10.1016/j.jcrimjus.2011.01.004

Dai, M., & Nation, D. (2009). Understanding non-coercive, procedurally fair behavior by the police during encounters. *International Journal of Law, Crime and Justice, 37*(4), 170–181. doi:10.1016/j.ijlcj.2009.10.002

De Cremer, D., & Tyler, T. R. (2005). Managing group behavior: The interplay between procedural justice, sense of self, and cooperation. *Advances in Experimental Social Psychology, 37*, 151–218. doi:10.1016/S0065-2601(05)37003-1

Doyle, M., & Straus, D. (1976). *How to make meetings work*. New York, NY: Berkeley Publishing Group.

Engel, R. S. (2005). Citizens' perceptions of distributive and procedural injustice during traffic stops with police. *Journal of Research in Crime and Delinquency*, *42*(4), 445–481. doi:10.1177/0022427804272725

Erickson, M. L., Gibbs, J. P., & Jensen, G. F. (1977). The deterrence doctrine and the perceived certainty of legal punishments. *American Sociological Review*, *42*(2), 305–317. doi:10.2307/2094607 PMID:860865

Fehr, E. & Gaechter, S. (2000). *Fairness and Retaliation: The economics of reciprocity*. Academic Press.

Folger, R., Konovsky, M. A., & Cropanzano, R. (1992). A due process metaphor for performance appraisal. *Research in Organizational Behavior*, *14*, 129–129.

Garmston, R., & Wellman, B. (1998). *The adaptive schools sourcebook*. Norwood, MA: Christopher- Gordon.

Garmston, R., & Wellman, B. (2013). *The adaptive schools sourcebook*. Lanham, MD: Rowman & Litchfield Publishers, Inc.

Goldin-Meadow, S. (1997). When gestures and words speak differently. *Current Directions in Psychological Science*, *6*(5), 138–143. doi:10.1111/1467-8721.ep10772905

Goldin-Meadow, S. (2002). *Hearing gestures: How our hands help us think*. Cambridge, MA: Belknap Press.

Goldin-Meadow, S., Kim, S., & Singer, M. (1999). What the teacher's hands tell the student's mind about math. *Journal of Educational Psychology*, *91*(4), 720–730. doi:10.1037/0022-0663.91.4.720

Goleman, D. (1996). *Emotional intelligence*. New York, NY: Bantam Books.

Goleman, D. (2006). *Social intelligence*. New York, NY: Bantam Books.

Grinder, M. (2008). *The elusive obvious*. Battle Ground, WA: Michael Grinder and Associates.

Hinds, L., & Murphy, K. (2007). Public satisfaction with police: Using procedural justice to improve police legitimacy. *Australian and New Zealand Journal of Criminology*, *40*(1), 27–42. doi:10.1375/acri.40.1.27

Kendon, A. (1990). *Conducting interaction: Patterns of behavior in focused encounters*. New York, NY: Cambridge University Press.

Kendon, A. (1997). Gesture. *American Review of Anthropology*, *26*, 109–128.

Kendon, A. (2004). *Gesture: Visible action as utterance*. Cambridge, England: Cambridge University Press; doi:10.1017/CBO9780511807572

Koper, C. S. (1995). Just enough police presence: Reducing crime and disorderly behavior by optimizing patrol time in crime hot spots. *Justice Quarterly*, *12*(4), 649–672. doi:10.1080/07418829500096231

Lind, E. (1990, November). Allan; Kanfer, Ruth; Earley, P. Christopher. (1990) Voice, control, and procedural justice: Instrumental and noninstrumental concerns in fairness judgment. *Journal of Personality and Social Psychology*, *59*(5), 952–959. doi:10.1037/0022-3514.59.5.952

Mastrofski, S. D., Snipes, J. B., & Supina, A. E. (1996). Compliance on demand: The public's response to specific police requests. *Journal of Research in Crime and Delinquency*, *33*(3), 269–305. doi:10.1177/0022427896033003001

Mazerolle, L., Antrobus, E., Bennett, S., & Tyler, T. R. (2012b). Shaping citizens perceptions of police legitimacy: A randomized field trial of procedural justice. *Criminology*, *51*(1), 33–64. doi:10.1111/j.1745-9125.2012.00289.x

Mazerolle, L., Bennett, S., Antrobus, E., & Eggins, E. (2012a). Procedural Justice, routine encounters, and citizen perceptions of police: Main findings from the Queensland Community Engagement Trial (QCET). *Journal of Experimental Criminology*, *8*(4), 343–367. doi:10.1007/s11292-012-9160-1

Mazerolle, L., Bennett, S., Davis, J., Sargeant, E., & Manning, M. (2013). Procedural Justice and police legitimacy: A systematic review of the research evidence. *Journal of Experimental Criminology*, *9*(3), 245–274. doi:10.1007/s11292-013-9175-2

Mazerolle, L., Sargeant, E., Cherney, A., Bennett, S., & Murphy, K. (2014). *Antrobus, E., and Martin, P*. Procedural Justice and Police Legitimacy in Policing.

McCafferty, S. G. (2002). Gesture and Creating Zones of Proximal Development for Second Language Learning. *Modern Language Journal*, *86*(2), 192–203. doi:10.1111/1540-4781.00144

McCluskey, J. D. (2003). *Police requests for compliance: Coercive and procedurally just tactics*. LFB Scholarly Pub.

McNeill, D. (1992). Hand and mind: What gestures reveal about thought (1st ed.). Chicago, IL: Chicago University Press.

Milgram, R. M., Dunn, R., & Price, G. E. (Eds.). (1993). *Teaching and counseling gifted and talented adolescents: An international learning style perspective*. Westport, CT: Praeger.

Nagin, D. S. (1998). Criminal deterrence research at the outset of the twenty-first century. *Crime and Justice*, *23*, 1–42. doi:10.1086/449268

Orth, J. V. (2003). *Due process of law: A brief history*. University Press of Kansas.

Paternoster, R., Brame, R., Bachman, R., & Sherman, L. W. (1997). Do fair procedures matter? The effect of procedural justice on spouse assault. *Law & Society Review*, *31*(1), 163–204. doi:10.2307/3054098

Poyatos, F. (2002a). *Nonverbal communication across disciplines* (1st ed., Vol. 1). Philadelphia, PA: John Benjamins.

Poyatos, F. (2002b). *Nonverbal communication across disciplines. Paralanguage, kinesics, silence, personal and environmental interaction* (Vol. 2). Philadelphia, PA: John Benjamins; doi:10.1075/z.ncad2

Rabin, M. (1993). Incorporating fairness into game theory and economics. *The American Economic Review*, 1281–1302.

Reisig, M. D., Bratton, J., & Gertiz, M. G. (2007). The construct validity and refinement of process-based policing measures. *Criminal Justice and Behavior*, *34*(8), 1005–1028. doi:10.1177/0093854807301275

Reiss, A. J. (1971). *The police and the public*. New Haven, CT: Yale University Press.

Richards, R. (n.d.). *Command presence: Feeding your own self confidence*. Retrieved from the internet August 30, 2015, http://www.withthecommand.com/2004-May/PA-Richards-commandpresence.html

Sherman, L. W. (1990). Police crackdowns: Initial and residual deterrence. *Crime and Justice*, *12*, 1–48. doi:10.1086/449163

Sir Robert Peel's Principles of Law Enforcement. (n.d.). Retrieved on October 12, 2015 from https://www.durham.police.uk/AboutUs/Documents/Peels_Principles_Of_Law_Enforcement.pdf

Skogan, W. G., Van Craen, W., & Hennessy, C. (2014). Training police for procedural justice. *Journal of Experimental Criminology, 4*, 1–16. doi:10.1007/s11292-014-9223-6

Sunshine, J., & Tyler, T. (2003a). Moral solidarity, identification with the community, and the importance of procedural justice: The police as prototypical representatives of a group's moral values. *Social Psychology Quarterly, 66*(2), 153–165. doi:10.2307/1519845

Sunshine, J., & Tyler, T. R. (2003b). The role of procedural justice and legitimacy in shaping public support in policing. *Law & Society Review, 37*(3), 513–548. doi:10.1111/1540-5893.3703002

Sykes, R. E., & Clark, J. P. (1975). A theory of deference exchange in police-civilian encounters. *American Journal of Sociology, 81*(3), 584–600. doi:10.1086/226109

Tankebe, J., & Liebling, A. (2013). *Legitimacy and criminal justice: An international exploration.* OUP Oxford. doi:10.1093/acprof:oso/9780198701996.001.0001

Thibaut, J., Walker, L., LaTour, S., & Houlden, P. (1973). Procedural justice as fairness. *Stanford Law Review, 26*(6), 1271. doi:10.2307/1227990

Tyler, T. R. (1988). What is procedural justice? Criteria used by citizens to assess the fairness of legal procedures. *Law & Society Review, 22*(1), 103–135. doi:10.2307/3053563

Tyler, T. R. (1990). *Why people obey the law.* Princeton University Press.

Tyler, T. R. (2003). Procedural justice, legitimacy, and the effective rule of law. In M. Tonry (Ed.), *Crime and justice: A review of research* (Vol. 30, pp. 431–505). Chicago: University of Chicago Press. doi:10.1086/652233

Tyler, T. R. (2004). Enhancing police legitimacy. *The Annals of the American Academy of Political and Social Science, 593*(1), 84–99. doi:10.1177/0002716203262627

Tyler, T. R. (2010). *Why people cooperate: The role of social motivations.* Princeton University Press. doi:10.1515/9781400836666

Tyler, T. R., & Huo, Y. (2002). *Trust in the law: encouraging public cooperation with the police and courts through.* Russell Sage Foundation.

Valdesolo, P., & DeSteno, D. (2011). Synchrony and the social tuning of compassion. *Emotion (Washington, D.C.), 11*(2), 262–266. doi:10.1037/a0021302 PMID:21500895

Well, W. (2007). Type of contact and evaluations of police officers: The effects of procedural justice across three types of police-citizen contacts. *Journal of Criminal Justice, 35*(6), 612–621. doi:10.1016/j.jcrimjus.2007.09.006

Williams, F. P., & McShane, M. D. (1998). Criminology Theory: Selected Classic Readings (2nd ed.). Cincinnati, OH: Anderson Publishing Co.

Zoller, K. (2008). Nonverbal patterns of teachers from 5 countries: Results from the TIMSS-R video study. *Dissertation Abstracts International. A, The Humanities and Social Sciences, 68*(9-A), 154.

Zoller, K. (2015). The Philosophy of Communicative Intelligence. In Cross-Cultural Collaboration and Leadership in Modern Organizations. IGI Global.

Zoller, K., & Landry, C. (2010). *The choreography of presenting: the 7 essential abilities of effective presenters.* Thousand Oaks, CA: Corwin Press.

ADDITIONAL READING

Gottman, J. M. (1982). Emotional responsiveness in marital conversations. *Journal of Communication, 32*(3), 108–120. doi:10.1111/j.1460-2466.1982.tb02504.x

Harper, R. G., Wiens, A. N., & Matarazzo, J. D. (1978). *Nonverbal communication: The state of the art.* John Wiley & Sons.

Hinde, R. A. (1972). *Non-verbal communication.* Cambridge University Press.

Knapp, M., Hall, J., & Horgan, T. (2013). *Non-verbal communication in human interaction.* Cengage Learning.

Lind, E. A., & Tyler, T. R. (1988). *The social psychology of procedural justice.* Springer Science & Business Media. doi:10.1007/978-1-4899-2115-4

Meško, G., & Tankebe, J. (Eds.). (2014). *Trust and Legitimacy in Criminal Justice: European Perspectives.* Springer.

Molm, L. D., Peterson, G., & Takahashi, N. (2003). In the eye of the beholder: Procedural justice in social exchange. *American Sociological Review, 68*(1), 128–152. doi:10.2307/3088905

Rosenbaum, D., & Lawrence, D. (2012). *Teaching respectful police-citizen encounters and good decision-making: results of a randomized control trial with police recruits. National Police Research Platform Report.* Washington: National Institute of Justice.

Tyler, T. R., & Blader, S. L. (2000). *Cooperation in groups: Procedural justice, social identity, and behavioral engagement.* Psychology Press.

Van den Bos, K., Wilke, H. A. M., & Lind, E. A. (1998). When do we need procedural fairness? The role of trust in authority. *Journal of Personality and Social Psychology, 75*(6), 1449–1458. doi:10.1037/0022-3514.75.6.1449

Wheller, L., Mills, A., & Quinton, P. 2013. The Greater Manchester Police procedural justice training experiment. Available from: www.college.police.uk/en/20840.htm [Accessed 18 November 2013].

KEY TERMS AND DEFINITIONS

Command Presence: Essentially presenting yourself as someone in authority, trusted and respected.

Communicative Intelligence: The integration of cognitive and emotional resources with behavioral abilities that creates experiences and develops relationships to solve problems, catalyze change, and create new meaning.

Consciousness: The ability to step outside of yourself as you are speaking to see the interaction as though from a balcony.

Craftsmanship: The repertoire of skills of communication, knowing what technique or speech pattern you are going to use and then having the ability to execute it.

Efficacy: The ability to have confidence in your communication skills, to know what speech patterns to engage in to achieve the response you are looking for.

Police Legitimacy: A psychological property of an authority, institution, or social arrangement that leads those connected to it to believe that it is appropriate, proper, and just.

Procedural Justice: The justice of the procedures through which outcomes are distributed and decisions made.

Chapter 25
Effective Engagement and Communication between First–Line Police Supervisors and Police Officers

Brian Ellis
Sacramento Police Department, USA

Anthony H. Normore
California State University Dominguez Hills, USA & International Academy of Public Safety, USA

ABSTRACT

Leadership is the act of influencing others whereby power comes from things such as referent and reward bases and "have an ethical responsibility to attend to the needs and concerns of followers" (Northouse, 2010, p. 4). In this chapter, the authors highlight the extant literature on organizational leadership and its role in effective communication and engagement processes. The authors focus on first-line supervisors and the impact of communication and engagement on people under their supervision. Employee trait, state, and behavioral constructs coupled with the culture of emotional connection between police officers and the police organization are explored. Further, the authors examine the principles of empowerment including meaningfulness, competence, choice, and impact and its applicability to police leadership. The outcome of the relationship between effective leadership and employee engagement is directly linked to innovation, participation, teamwork, accountability, and the ability to face challenges. Conclusions and recommendations for future research are discussed.

INTRODUCTION

While there are many organizations studying the implications of employee engagement, minimal information exists in the study of employee engagement within police organizations. In western policing, the profession has seen many standards of performance, with regards to the training

and readiness of their police forces in the field. Unfortunately, little is required to supervise this new workforce. In California for instance, while a police academy offers approximately 664 hours of instruction, only 80 hours of training is mandated to become a supervisor (www.post.ca.gov). To complicate the issue of training, the higher an officer promotes in a police organization, the

DOI: 10.4018/978-1-4666-9970-0.ch025

less education is required. In a hierarchical setting such as police organizations, it remains essential that leaders within those organizations have the competency necessary to enhance performance, and make police organizations vibrant places where officers remain highly engaged to deliver great customer service. This occurs through the ability of leaders to understand what drives employees to do excellent work, and how to better attach employees to organization values.

Like any other professional, police officers have signature strengths. Those strengths are seen as traits or interests that allow officers to flourish in some environments and become frustrated in others (Buckingham & Coffman, 1999; Seligman & Csikszentmihalyi, 2000). It becomes central for leaders to identify the needs of each individual, which may include their individual traits, behaviors, and work setting to maximize their abilities (Macey & Schneider, 2008). Furthermore, police leaders must be effective at utilizing empowerment. Empowerment stems from understanding and proper application of the numerous sources of empowerment: *meaningfulness*, where employees attach themselves to the work itself by understanding how the work makes a difference; *competence,* the ability to become proficient at a job, where one feels they have mastery of a role or task; *choice,* or the ability for one to do work in a fashion that compliments them; and *impact,* which is knowing that the work they complete is making a difference (Yukl & Becker, 2006). Finally, for police leaders to deliver the next generation of best practices, they need an understanding of all who are positively impacted by an engaged employee. Within this context, the authors argue that there are positive impacts for the police employee, the organization, and the public they serve and protect. We further argue that engagement and communication lead police employees to improved teamwork, creativity and innovation, accountability, and the ability to more effectively deal with any potential organizational adversity (Lakshmi, 2012).

This chapter will expand on the above-mentioned concepts (i.e., engagement, communication, leadership) and its applicability within police agencies. In understanding the process of effectively engaging employees (e.g. police officers), the leaders (e.g., first-line police supervisors) must first focus on social processes (e.g. cultural, personal, professional, and organizational). Northouse (2010) asserts that leadership is the act of influencing others where most power comes from things such as referent and reward bases and "have an ethical responsibility to attend to the needs and concerns of followers" (Northouse, 2010, p. 4). Towards this end, we will highlight the extant literature on organizational leadership and its pivotal role in effective communication and engagement processes. First, we provide examples of employee trait, state, and behavioral constructs (e.g., Mark & Schneider, 2008; Seligman & Csikszentmihalyi, 2000) as seen in police organizations. Then, we discuss the culture of emotional connection between police officers and the police organization (Tomlinson, 2010). Next, we highlight the synergistic effect of the four principles of effective empowerment including *meaningfulness, competence, choice, and impact* (Yukl & Becker, 2006) and its applicability to effective police leadership. We articulate the outcomes of effective leadership (Gladwell, 2008) and employee engagement (Chughtai, Buckley & Finian, 2008; Harter, Schmidt, & Hayes, 2002) and how employee engagement has direct links to innovation, participation, teamwork, accountability, and the ability to face challenges (e.g., Lakshmi, 2012). Conclusions and future research directions are articulated.

LEADERSHIP AND THE FIRST-LINE POLICE SUPERVISOR

Leadership has a critical role within any police agency, and is often considered the key element in determining a division o department's success or failure. The leadership of the chief of police and the command staff down through the ranks (e.g., middle management of captains and lieutenants) to first-line supervisors (sergeants) to the patrol officer often acts as a catalyst for promoting or devaluing the goals and objectives of a police department (Waters, 2004). Although "every position within a police agency presents leadership challenges - the role of the first-line supervisor is often the most crucial" (Waters, para.1).

According to research on police supervisors (e.g., Baker, 2000; Tully, 2002; Waters, 2004) the first-line supervisor is considered the backbone of any police agency. The leadership - or lack of leadership - shown by a sergeant "can have a dramatic effect on how the agency is perceived by the community…upper management can have the most well thought-out strategic planning initiatives, but without the first-line supervisor's leadership ability to move his or her subordinates toward the implementation of those goals, they will remain just ideas" (para.15). According to Baker (2000), "Sergeants must be able to organize, plan and evaluate their officers to reach department objects. Frustrated police personnel can lead to negative productivity." (p. 89). The first-line supervisor has to be able to "quickly identify potential problems and seek remedies that will promote growth for the department and the affected employee" (para. 15). Of equal importance, they are expected to provide opportunities for officer engagement, motivate subordinates, and communicate effectively (Baker, 2000).

COMMUNICATION AND ENGAGEMENT IN POLICING CONTEXT

A police organization benefits from communication and engagement as people become more connected to an agency's strategies that lead to positive outcomes (Harter, Schmidt, & Hayes). Engaged police officers leads to better service,

thereby positively impacting customer satisfaction (Crabb, 2011). Further, the engagement-oriented police leader looks for ways to impact people that not only make a social impact for their people, organizations, and communities, but show the moral responsibility to their followers (Northouse, 2010). From an extant review of literature one can find numerous reasons to pay attention to employee engagement. Based on the work by Mone and London (2009), engaged employees produce more for their organizations. They feel more involved, committed, and empowered in their workplace. It is important to understand the desired outcomes, but to also understand that influential positive behavior of first-line police supervisors, managers, and anyone in a police leader role is a path to more engagement. When the aforementioned groups fail to communicate with their employees, fail to provide them with learning and development opportunities, and fail to recognize good work, subsequent positive engagement is thwarted (Mone & London 2009). This should help send a message to leaders that communication is essential to maximize the workplace.

There are layers of the communication process which can impede the flow of information depending on the number of layers (Buckingham & Coffman, 1999). Based on these authors research there is a universal understanding of the technical process of communication. For example, when we tell a story around a campfire, that story is likely to be very different from how it began. That is why leaders must ensure that the message carries the same force within each layer of our organization. Otherwise it becomes diluted. Leaders can do this by over- communicating simple messages and using various mediums to communicate. Finally, Buckingham and Coffman (1999) indicated that far too often supervisors and managers look at employees' weaknesses and not their strengths.

If organizations want the best out of employees, they should identify their strengths and bring the best out of them while simultaneously managing their weaknesses. In turn, leaders create opportunities to reduce resistance, reflect on the presence of irritants, and build motivation and commitment in a manner consistent with being credible, authentic, deliberate, and intentional (Keis & Javidi, 2014). In police work, there are myriad assignments to choose from such as fugitive apprehension team, traffic, investigations, Special Weapons and Tactics (SWAT), or school resource officer. Officers gravitate towards assignments that are aligned with their current or emerging identity, while the organization sends the message that in order to promote, officers need to be well rounded. Yet, there are many who promote through the ranks with limited experience.

Keis and Javidi assert that employee well-being and job satisfaction are the desires of the individual, while commitment and performance are that of the organization. Consequently, it is paramount that leaders understand how to balance individual and organizational needs for maximum performance. Communication is expected to be simple, yet there are times where it is the pitfall that stands in the way of organizational effectiveness. Many times when supervisors communicate the message, it is derailed by the negative message that is delivered, whether intended or not. The "don't do that", "not on my watch", or "look what you have done this time" are negative messages that impede the essential communication that rallies effective engagement, happiness and optimism (Keis & Javidi, 2014).

Seligman and Csikszentmihalyi (2000) explored the enablers of happiness and traits (e.g., optimism) in the relation to how these enablers affect health. Through their personal discoveries and life lessons, these authors found that people often ignore the needs of others out of selfishness, a behavior that leads to chaos and despair. The authors argued that people cannot be excluded from organizational culture because of their poor attitudes but rather a need exists to develop and reinforce positive attitudes. Positive attitudes such as optimism lead to a great deal of preventative measures while increasing strengths and capacities

for interpersonal skills, honesty, and hope. They further articulated that people with high optimism levels tend to have better moods, to be more preserving and successful, and to experience better physical health. Developing positive attitudes in police agencies not only develops the relationship between supervisor and subordinate, but also between the police officer and community member.

Seligman and Csikszentmihalyi (2000) also noted that peak performance is a product of people using their signature strength. This is a process where one knows and understands their work and feels they have excellent skills in completing the task at hand. As a result, leaders create opportunities for employees to recommit to their work and become re-motivated in the work place while the organization enjoys the benefits of maximizing resources. To do otherwise, leaders can create an atmosphere of resentment, hostility, and excuses. We argue that police leadership must strive to have a talent pool greater than the number of specialty jobs available. Tomlinson (2010) asserts that the hopes of employee engagement is to create a culture of emotional connection between the employees and the organization. This in turn leads to perpetual commitment and attachment to the company.

To return to the key findings from the Gallup organization (2010) pertaining to employee engagement, it is clear that engagement is critical for any organization's success. In their meta-analysis of over 199 research studies across over 152 organizations, and reaching over 950,000 employees, Gallup concluded that organizational leadership is desperately in need of a more engaging atmosphere. Key findings revealed that only 11% of the workforce is engaged; 62% is unengaged; and 27% are actively disengaged.

Similar studies (e.g., Kahn, 1990; Macey & Schneider, 2008) have been completed by both larger and smaller companies where the engagement numbers are similar. Even police departments and cities have completed similar studies, both pointing for a need of more employee recognition and a need to better understand the metrics that assist in creating engagement.

ELEMENTS OF ENGAGEMENT: TRAIT, STATE, AND BEHAVIORAL

Kahn described engagement as,

The simultaneous employment and expression of a person's "preferred self" in task behaviors that promote connectedness to work and to others, personal presence (physical, cognitive, and emotional), and active, full role performances. To employ such dimensions is to drive personal energies into physical, cognitive, and emotional labors. People who are personally engaged keep their selves within a role, without sacrificing one for the other. People become physically involved in tasks, whether alone or with others, cognitively vigilant, and empathically connected to others in the service of the work they are doing in ways that display what they think and feel, their creativity, their beliefs and values, and their personal connections to others (p. 700).

Researchers (e.g., Macey & Schneider, 2008; Yukl & Becker, 2006) suggest that employee engagement is a complex system, which has *trait*, *state*, and *behavioral* constructs under an umbrella of work conditions that may facilitate behavioral and state engagement. We now explain these three elements and include our own professional examples of how these are recognized in police agencies.

Trait

Trait engagement deals with personality attributes of the individual such as being positive and energetic about work (Macey & Schneider, 2008). These attributes are considered the inner personal process of being a proactive person. In policing, discovering past work products in an employee's

background might tell supervisors a great deal about the trait aspects of a person. Police leaders have many opportunities to understand their workforce. From checking employees personnel files and/or to talking to past supervisors. In addition, leadership must set unambiguous goals and strategies that are reinforced and checked on frequently. Police organizations are filled with many people who show high trait value, as seen in the many alpha personalities who want to be better. As great of a quality that is, it can also hinder success of these people who do not have the humility, as they can potentially resist leadership movement. We contend that leadership is about making all people in the organization as successful as possible, not just the highest performers. We further assert that when leaders play favorites or make excuses such as not having enough time in rank, or needing more experience while concurrently giving opportunities to others who have limited qualifications, is a potential failure of leadership.

Great trait qualities can be seen in police overachievers. Unfortunately, all over-achievers do not always have good organizational reputations. From our own experience, perceptions of other sergeants and managers can be that these people have an air of arrogance or insecurity about who they are as people and/or as officers and as a result are threatened by the stellar performance of some. This can, and has led to some over-achievers being blind-sided in their careers, which subsequently leads to unengagement and underperformance. For example, we have experienced situations where patrol officers want to spend their shift apprehending criminals. As a rule, this could be considered an admirable quality and directly aligned with the protection of community members. There is, however, much more to being an effective problem solver in the community being served. Our best employees often create much extra work for supervisors. Great employees are involved in a lot of police work; therefore supervisors have additional paperwork through the checks and balances (e.g., use of force reports, pursuit reports, injured on duty forms, etc.). The last thing first-line police leaders want is for employees to apologize for doing great work because it makes work for the boss. To curb these behaviors, leaders should make it a priority to provide opportunities for each team member to show signature strengths in the workplace.

Unfortunately, some sergeants and managers get caught up in the "numbers game" and rely on those who are well known throughout the agency to produce. Sadly, the reward for doing a good job is usually recognized in the form of more work assigned. Supervisors and managers get bogged down in work that they simply want to give it to people who will get it done, while shying away from developing others along the way. Essentially, this type of leadership buries top performers and creates a lack of development opportunities within the organization. Police officers can be very mission-focused and lose sight of all the processes that garner better leverage for the organization. When leadership continues to throw large loads onto an employee, sooner or later, they take on too much and are burdened by an overwhelming amount of work, and might not accomplish anything at all, or simply burn out.

State

State engagement is associated with work setting where a person can have feelings of energy, dedication, enthusiasm, and pride (Yukl & Becker, 2008). This happens through an attitude created by factors, which happen at work such as being valued by your supervisor, or company value programs. Leaders can learn more about this from their people with well-crafted employee surveys that question organizational pride, advocacy, overall satisfaction, and commitment. This connects largely with the intrinsic rewards to which leaders align their people (Ellis & Normore, 2015).

One of the more effective ways to create new energy within a team is to create small wins for team members early (Macey & Schneider, 2008).

Police leaders need to first look at the work setting and remove all of the irritants possible prior to engaging a team towards a new mission. For example, officers may be frustrated with working conditions or processes that can be easily fixed or removed. If officers do not have a clear understanding of purpose that drives these practices they may feel buried with endless work expectations with no real concrete outcome. First-line police leaders cannot expect people to be effective in their daily workspace if leaders are not making workspaces that are full of energy and user friendly.

Creating "wins" for employees assists efforts of change (Macey & Schneider, 2008). Changes to policies and procedures that are either not relevant anymore or complicate the process create easy victories for leaders. As long as they are not detrimental to customer service in the long run, they are worth exploring. Research indicates that the best way to start this process is to reach out to trusted sources and ask for feedback about these irritants existence in the workplace (Yukl & Becker, 2006). Some of the frustration comes from the very way policies are created and updated. Often our police leaders and managers are tasked with writing and/or updating policies and often rely on the way they "use to do it" and/or collaborating with other managers to rewrite the policy rather than asking for line-level opinions. We contend that in order to be a good police agency leader it means having the ability to reach out to line-level troops and frequently ask, "What do you think?"

Behavioral

The behavioral component of employee engagement is an adaptive process that can describe a range of behaviors such as doing more and/or something different (Macey & Schneider, 2008). In police work, officers have to be comfortable with change. It is an essential part of the criminal justice system. This is where an employee's willingness to work towards the organizations values appears. For example, for a police department, its values are demonstrated by the way an officer acts in an effort to enhance customer service. Police leaders must frequently align the work of employees with organizational values (Ellis & Normore, 2015). It's our experience that when police leaders weave individual officer's values into organizational values it allows officers to see how their work directly reflects on their personal values while simultaneously empowering the officer to achieve satisfaction on both personal and professional levels. This type of engagement between police officer and police leader is then representative of the organizational conditions that enhance relationships, or introduces additional behavioral engagement (Ellis & Normore, 2014; Macey & Schneider, 2008) through the effective use of empowerment within the police agency

EMPOWERMENT PRINCIPLES: MEANINGFULNESS, COMPETENCE, CHOICE, AND IMPACT

In their work, *Effective Empowerment in Organizations*, Yukl and Becker (2006) suggest that engagement is directly related to empowerment. These researchers assert that when employees believe they can adjust their work roles to accomplish assignments, engagement naturally happens. Further, they theorize that empowerment comes from four independent principles that have a synergistic effect when used in combination: *meaningfulness, competence, choice, and impact*. The following section provides an overview of the principles of empowerment with professional examples added for purposes of understanding how these translate into practice.

Meaningfulness

Meaningfulness is the attachment an employee makes with the work itself. This is described by Yukl and Becker (2006) as the "engine" of empowerment. In police work, officers are very

attached to their identity as police officers. This is reinforced through various mechanisms - namely being a police officer 24-7, personal values, and shift work which tends to isolate officers to only socialize with other officers. When work is in line with an individual's values, there is a greater attachment to the work being completed (Yukl & Becker, 2006). While one might think the policing profession does this well, there are still several issues to be considered. An officer's work can be very meaningful. However, when all of the moving parts of the criminal justice system are not collaborating, the balance becomes chaotic (Bone, Normore, Javidi, 2015).

There are many instances where police agencies, District Attorney's offices, probation/parole Departments, and the courts find themselves in conflict with the same cases they have been assigned. For example, an officer makes what he/she believes to be a great arrest on a chronic offender. Upon filing the criminal charges at the DA's office, the case is referred to parole due to the status of the individual. With parole being inundated with the large percentage of recidivism of offenders, sentences are often shortened. The officer sees the same career criminal on the street just a few months later reoffending. Upset, the officer looks to see that there were never any charges filed on the last case. After a while, this officer begins to ask himself/herself why he/she should work as hard as he/she does to keep criminals off the street. Subsequently, he/she finds himself/herself in an ethical dilemma related to his/her discretion such as reducing their number of self-initiated stops. That same officer now begins to heavily monitor all future cases and can become very cynical about the system to the point where he/she does not put forth the same effort as before. The officer feels like it is a personal attack on him/her, when in fact it is a system simply trying to survive on its individual set of rules.

The saturation of the criminal justice system puts all of the cogs in positions in order to be selective of the work they do. It begs the question if society should gage a DA's office, the court system, or police investigators on conviction/clearance rates, or rather how much the entire system disrupts crime in a region? Perhaps this is where regionalization can finally make its mark on the criminal justice system? What does this mean for law enforcement leaders? What are the fixes to the problem? Does this lie with providing officers with more training so that their cases are better suited to get filed? Or is it an issue related to unrealistic dispositions for criminal cases? The answer is complicated and maybe the best answer is "it depends." The real nexus to leadership in these moments is to identify when these actions happen and attempt to stay abreast of them. Policing in today's world is the act of problem solving. Problem solving has internal (workplace) and external (community) components. We assert that when the synergistic effects of the criminal justice system fall out of balance it has consequences for the overall organization in that the organizations will inevitably lose a great deal of employee engagement. It is up to first-line supervisors to properly monitor and identify events to ensure they are raised up on the correct flagpole for executives to fine-tune the system.

A second area where police leadership can better attach meaningfulness is to be more mindful to express gratitude and appreciation to officers for a job well done. By publically acknowledging and celebrating the good work of officers, leaders create a culture of recognition therefore enhancing meaningfulness. This could be done by simply reading a citizen's thank you letter in a police roll call. At the same time, leaders create responsibility and accountability. Accountability comes from officers knowing that leaders are paying attention to their work (Ellis & Normore, 2015).

Competence

The *competence* component from Yukl and Becker's work is derived from the notion that people like to complete skills of which they have

a personal mastery. This is the self-belief of employees of successfully completing tasks (Ellis & Normore, 2015). To illustrate with an example, prior to graduation night from the police academy one of the academy staff expressed to the class, "Congratulations, you are now all police officers. It will take you five years on the job to become cops." In retrospect, the academy staff was right in many ways. There is a real difference between the two. Police officers are the people who wear a badge, whereas cops are the intellectual property of people who are passionate about their purpose and provide value each and every minute for their organizations and the citizens they serve. The hopes of any leader are to have an organization of cops. People like to play their strengths. Personal mastery is a link to those strengths that police leaders should use to get officers excited about their work by linking them to the things for which they have a passion (Bone & Normore, 2015; Keis & Javidi, 2014).

Mastery

Mastery is about the personal experiences and life lessons on the job. Personal mastery allows for what Peter Senge (1990) calls the difference between what's important, what we want, and where we are now, which produces "creative tension." Creative tension is generated and maintained through the forces of personal mastery (Anderson, Gisborne, & Holliday, 2012). When reflecting about mastery and an appropriate example to share with the reader, we chose to look at a particular job skill over the course of one author's career to see how it has changed. We decided to look at the "name game," a staple of deception within policing. It is universally agreed that most cops are familiar with the "name game" but for those who are unfamiliar with it, it is arguably one of the more thought-provoking experiences in police work – especially for a detective or a patrol officer. This is a game of wits where an officer intellectually jousts with some of society's "slipperiest" people. In the early stages of his career, Brian found himself dealing with a seasoned criminal. In retrospect, he wonders how many criminals were so successful in playing this deception game. Fast forward years later, and the name game has now become easy due to experience. Yet, Brian is not always certain as to why that is. He understands there are some tell-tale signs in the interaction, but there is also that certain feeling an officer confronts when he has played the game repeatedly. To more fully understand the nuances of the "name game" we offer a sample scenario below between a cop and a criminal:

An officer makes a contact, either via an enforcement stop or a consensual contact someone in public. The officer drums up some conversation with the subject and then asks for some identification. Yet, most criminals do not carry their identification with them for fear of being identified. While all of the content is not here, the essence of it situation is paraphrased in the following:

COP: *What's your name?*

BAD GUY: *What's my name? (Or some other kind of stall tactic like "what?", "huh", "what did you say?")*

COP: *What is your date of birth?*

BAD GUY: *(Quietly and anxiously provides a birth date, usually a few numbers off, or a birthdate other than his own that he easily remember, such as a sibling.)*

COP: *How old does that make you? (Now it becomes a game of math. Trying to play deception math on the fly is difficult and this is where the game can fall apart, or another early sign of deception appears.)*

BAD GUY: *Uh, 39. (Now if the numbers do not add up, the cop has him. Note however, the cop probably had him prior to that - based upon body language, eye movement such as looking for potential escape routes, and overall nervousness).*

COP: *That birth date you gave me would make you 41. Why are you lying to me?*

BAD GUY: *Sorry boss, I am just nervous and have problems with numbers (or a number of other excuses for not getting it right).*

This process continues from one lie to another. Some cops will extend this game even when they already know they have caught the subject in a lie. As officers engage in this "name game" over a period of time their skills become more and more refined. An officer will gain much confidence that upon the first set of deception, he puts a criminal on notice and because the officer carries so much conviction about it, the offender comes clean. This is mastery. In retrospect, the scenario draws parallels to Malcolm Gladwell's (2008) 10,000 Rule. Gladwell suggests it takes 10,000 hours to become great at anything. The leadership lesson here is for leaders to empower employees with opportunities that will enhance their skills at tasks they find meaningful and to subsequently provide them with the tools to master those skills.

Choice

The third empowerment principle introduced by Yukl and Becker is choice whereby the employee chooses to complete a task in a manner of his/her choice. This is the individual's sense of having a choice of initiating the work that he/she is planning to do. Police work is filled with choice. Officers often ask themselves, Should I stop this violator or that one? Should I give this person a ticket? How do I best mediate this neighborhood dispute so I do not have to return? Then there is the choice of assignments: Patrol, detectives, SWAT, and other various specialized units.

One would think that police work is filled with so much choice that this is an easy win for policing. However, supervisors and managers have their work to do here as well. An important skill needed early in leadership is the ability to properly delegate. Delegation is a critical piece of being a leader. Learning to let go becomes a critical piece of this process, and one that most leaders find challenging. It requires people to be a little vulnerable and to give up control. According to Enter (2006), everyone faces burnout if leadership tries to shoulder the load. Leaders also miss valuable educational opportunities for themselves and their staff (Enter, 2006). Being "in charge" is not about having all of the answers but rather being as resourceful as possible for those under one's leadership. For choice to be meaningful, leaders have to identify problems with employees and ask for their input, then facilitate teaching and learning opportunities to the same employees so they can solve problems on their own, or as a collective (Enter, 2006).

Impact

The final principle of empowerment is the role of impact. Impact is the sphere of "making a difference." (Yukl & Becker, 2006, p. 229). Police work is replete with opportunities to make a difference such as the search for the criminal element that victimizes society and subsequently bring justice to the incident that unfolded within a community. Furthermore, there are the personal opportunities such as the ability to make a difference in someone's life. There are, however, instances where police work is not about impactful work. An illustration of this is the false alarm call or a non-injury vehicle accident where there is no opportunity to impact events in others lives. Yet, as first responders, police officers have a duty to do this work. They are law enforcers, guardians, counselors, and numerous other trades weaved within their roles. While all of these forces create impactful work, police leaders must recognize those instances where impact is affected and/or non-existent. In those instances, the challenge is to find ways to create impactful work from those reactive forces. It is also an opportunity to challenge the forces that stand in the way of great work such as the disequilibrium in the criminal justice system mentioned earlier. One way of doing this is to realign officers to the statements they made

upon entering the profession. Most applicants when asked during the hiring process as to why they choose to do this kind of work will respond with "to help people." Along the way, they get to chase "bad guys". They are assigned other types of autonomous duties which create conflicting desires about what the officer feels needs to be done.

One author is aware of these types of conflicts because he was once considered his effectiveness by the sheer number of trips he took to jail (e.g., arrests). Many other parts of the job created obstacles that he needed to quickly "jump" through in order to create another opportunity to jail another criminal or make another arrest. In that time, people can short-cut calls and undermine an officer's other duties. What was learned about the enforcement aspect of his job could be compared to the importance of primary needs such as food and water. On one hand arresting offenders might fill up an officer's emotional appetite for a short while, it offers very little long-term sustenance. On the other hand, opportunities for organizational problem solving has potential for a healthy officer and a healthy agency. Metaphorically stating, these problem-solving instances fills the belly, the heart, and the mind all the while being filled with action-oriented processes. Still, problem solving can be challenging for officers because they are action-oriented individuals.

Police leaders need to reinforce why the work officers do has an impact and makes a difference. Policing is filled with all kinds of styles and communities would benefit from officers assigned to specific work they do best. For example, it stands to reason that a police leader would not want to assign an officer who he/she depends on to arrest criminals to work instead a traffic complaint, or in parking enforcement. There is a school of thought that every officer is a leader (see Anderson et al., 2012) and needs to be well rounded. While we mostly agree with this statement we also argue that the health of any police agency (or any organization in general) would benefit more from leaders who take the initiative and care to ensure assignments are delegated to those who have special knowledge and training in specific areas. When the leader assigns a task to someone on the team for the sake of well-roundedness and is unsuited for the task, we question the level of communication and positive engagement the employees are in fact receiving.

OUTCOMES OF ENGAGEMENT: FUTURE RESEARCH DIRECTIONS

There are quite a number of outcomes of employee engagement that range from direct benefits to the employee, to the organization and customer benefits. Studies point to a relationship between trust and work engagement, which ultimately leads to additional performance (Chughtai, Buckley & Finian, 2008). In a research project, the Gallup organization teamed up with the University of Iowa and the U.S. Department of Immigration and Naturalization (Harter, Schmidt, & Hayes, 2002) to examine the relationship between satisfaction, employee engagement, and business outcomes. In their meta-analysis of over 7,900 business units in 36 companies, Gallup findings revealed a substantial relation between individual job satisfaction and individual performance. Researchers concluded that employee satisfaction and engagement are related to meaningful outcomes at such a magnitude that organizations should take a closer examination. Other research (e.g., Lakshmi, 2012) concluded that employee engagement has been linked to innovation, participation, teamwork, accountability, and the ability to face challenges. Furthermore, Crabb (2011), a senior consultant with A&DC, a leading talent management consultancy company in the UK linked engagement to elevated levels of customer satisfaction.

We now propose several research directions concerning the significance of potential positive influence of leadership, engagement, communication, and empowerment on an organization's health and well-being. For our purpose, we reflect on these processes as they pertain to police agencies, first-line police supervisors, and police officers. Future research directions made as a result of the findings suggest that police agencies need to conduct further research on the impact of supervisor and officer engagement as a key component for improving an agency's performance. With such positive attributes as those listed in earlier research (see above), it is undoubtedly a force-multiplier for police agencies, and therefore every attempt should be taken to understand and develop engagement opportunities tailored to supervisor and officer workspace as well as for the entire agency.

From Kahn's studies in the early 90's to present time (2015), academics and organizational personnel have continued to research employee engagement in search of the link between communication, engagement and organizational performance. A large amount of useful information has resulted from the studies while organizations still find the same problem of a mostly disengaged workforce. It stands to reason that more qualitative research is warranted in this area to determine why police agencies and their police supervisory leaders continue to miss the mark in leading their agencies forward to a healthy space in time.

In understanding the process of engaging employees, Northouse (2010) asserts that organizational leaders must first focus on social processes. Northouse reiterates that leadership is the act of influencing others where most power springs from organizational culture such as referent and reward bases. Consequently, leaders "have an ethical responsibility to attend to the needs and concerns of followers" (Northouse, 2010, p. 4). To this end, we suggest longitudinal study is necessary on the professional and organizational leadership socialization processes of police supervisors, and the self-efficacy of officers while in the training academy, and subsequently during the promotional processes. Such a study could help determine what factors play a role in the understanding of leadership versus management, the reasons for entering the police force, job satisfaction, employee engagement, communication forms (e.g., lateral, top-down, bottom-up), and the dynamics of creating an agency's institutional culture.

There appears to be no viable system which police agencies could put into action whereby the success of every officer is guaranteed. Still, police leaders should strive to connect with as many officers as possible. The organizational and individual values ought to be aligned for any process to succeed. At the very least, the organizational goals of formal and informal leaders within the organization need to be aligned with the organizational direction. Unfortunately, this is not the usual way in police agencies. If the circle of power, or the sphere of influence, excludes organizational input from all its members, there is a likelihood that some members will not be valued despite their high productivity level. We argue for the maximizing of "wins" in order to understand that every department has those people who have "street credibility" with their peers. These people are at times distractions for organizational movement because they can be seen as cynical (Anderson et al., 2012). Leadership is often about reducing resistance and removing irritants. If leaders can at the very least remove irritants in order to build credibility, they could most likely leverage the trust of new allies to reduce resistance to future programs and productivity levels. If leaders ignore or attempt to forcefully move these key allies within departments, it will be futile. Police leaders need energy and drive that officers possess in order to create an impact. The old formula of "strength plus speed equals power" helps to illustrate how a leader's power cannot live up to that leader's potential without rallying layers of informal leaders throughout the agency. Informal leaders could likely provide speed to the cause. We propose further research in the area of organizational health so police

leaders and officers are provided opportunities to share real-time input concerning the respect of the agency's values, philosophy, and long-term vision. Such a study could reveal the factors that lead to organizational cynicism.

It is common in community-oriented policing events for police officers to push the community to engage with their neighbors (Ellis & Normore, 2014) where officers preach the old adage of "strength in numbers". Leaders, however, sometimes forget how compelling such an external relationship is for building internal organizational health and work satisfaction. As noted earlier, employee well-being and job satisfaction are the desires of the individual, while commitment and performance are that of the organization (Keis & Javidi, 2014). It is paramount that leaders understand how to balance individual and organizational needs for maximum performance.

CONCLUSION

Leadership holds the key to the ability to create force multipliers and it is the action that is necessary to move this momentous stone. Think about it in terms of physical fitness. When you have been hitting the gym hard, you reap the rewards of feeling and looking great. Then life gets in the way with one thing or another and you find yourself a little out of shape. It is really the same with the engagement process? If we are not developing relationships at all times and doing authentic actions that make people feel they are a part of the team, we will find those relationships will atrophy. When you get back into any routine, the hardest part is the beginning. After awhile you adapt to the new workload and actually crave more. This is the very process we are chasing. We must take action towards the sometimes unquantifiable processes that build trust. It is here that we will find employee engagement.

REFERENCES

Anderson, T., Gisborne, K. D., & Holliday, P. N. (2012). *Every officer is a leader: Coaching leadership, learning, and performance in justice, public safety, and security organizations.* Trafford Publishing. Retrieved from www.trafford.com

Baker, T. (2000). *Effective police leadership.* New York, NY: Looseleaf Law Publications, INC.

Bone, D., & Normore, A. H. (2014). Progressive law enforcement leaders effectively manage departmental risk. *Law Enforcement Today (LET): The Law Enforcement Community.* Retrieved from, http://www.lawenforcementtoday. com/2014/07/13/striving-for-educational-excellence-in-law-enforcement-leadership-the-case-of-jefferson-parish-sheriffs-office/

Bone, D., Normore, A.H., & Javidi, M. (2015). Human factors: police leaders improving safety while developing meaningful public trust. *FBI Law Enforcement Journal.*

Buckingham, M., & Coffman, C. (1999). *First, break all the rules: What the world's greatest managers do differently.* New York, NY: Simon & Schuster.

Chughtai, A., Buckley, & Finian. (2008). *Work engagement and its relationship with state and trait trust: A conceptual analysis.* Retrieved from, http://findarticles.com/p/articles/mi_qa5335/ is_200809/ai_n29493978/?tag=content;col1

Ellis, B., & Normore, A. H. (2014). Police leadership: Connecting with communities through a partnership initiative. *Peace Officers Research Association of California Law Enforcement.* Retrieved from, http://porac.org/

Ellis, G., & Normore, A. H. (2015). Performance management strategies for effective leadership in law enforcement: An accountability process. *FBI Law Enforcement Bulletin.* Available [online]: http://leb.fbi.gov/2015/february/performance-management-strategies-for-effective-leadership-an-accountability-process

Gallup, Inc. (2010). *The state of the global workplace: A worldwide study of employee engagement and wellbeing.* Retrieved from, http://www. gallup.com

Gladwell, M. (2008). *Outliers: The story of success.* New York, NY: Little, Brown & Company.

Harter, J., Schmidt, F., & Hayes, T. (2002). Business-united-level relationship between employees satisfaction. *The Journal of Applied Psychology,* 87(2), 268–279. doi:10.1037/0021-9010.87.2.268 PMID:12002955

Kahn, W. A. (1990). Psychological conditions of personal engagement and disengagement at work. *Academy of Management Journal,* 33(4), 692–724. doi:10.2307/256287

Keis, K., & Javidi, M. (2014). *Deliberate leadership: Creating success through personal style.* Vancouver, BC: CRG Publishing.

Lakshmi, K. (2012). Employee engagement- A corporate boon. 10 ways for effective engagement. *Advances in Management Journal,* 5(2), 64–65.

Macey, W., & Schneider, B. (2008). The meaning of employee engagement. *Industrial and Organizational Psychology: Perspectives on Science and Practice,* 1(1), 3–30. doi:10.1111/j.1754-9434.2007.0002.x

Mone, E., & London, M. (2009). *Employee engagement: Through effective performance management.* New York, NY: Taylor-Francis Group.

Northhouse, P. (2010). *Leadership: Theory and practice* (5th ed.). Thousand Oaks, CA: Sage.

Seligman, M., & Csikszentmihalyi, M. (2000). Positive psychology: An introduction. *The American Psychologist, 55*(1), 5–14. doi:10.1037/0003-066X.55.1.5 PMID:11392865

Senge, P. (1990). *The fifth discipline: The art & practice of the learning organization*. New York, NY: Doubleday.

Tomlinson, G. (2010). Building a culture of high employee engagement. *Strategic HR Review, 9*(3), 25–31. doi:10.1108/14754391011040046

Tully, E. (2002, May). The slippery slope. *National Executive Institute Associates, Major Cities Chiefs Association and Major County Sheriff's Association Leadership Bulletin,* 1-11.

Waters, M. (2004). The leadership role of the first-line supervisor in police operations. *Florida Police Chief Magazine.* Retrieved from, http://www.clearwaterpolice.org/articles/waters.asp

Yulk, G., & Becker, W. (2006). Effective empowerment in organizations. *Organizational Management Journal, 3*(3), 210–231. doi:10.1057/omj.2006.20

ADDITIONAL READING

Ellis, B., & Normore, A. H. (2015). Has the term law enforcement run its course in police agencies? *Law Enforcement Today (LET): The Law Enforcement Community.* Available [Online]: http://www.lawenforcementtoday.com

Harari, O. (2002). *The leadership secrets of Colin Powell*. New York, NY: McGraw – Hill.

Kruse, K.E. (2012). *Employee engagement 2.0: How to motivate your team for high performance (A real-world guide for busy managers).* An Amazon.com Company: CreateSpace Independent Publishing Platform

Marciano, P. T. (2010). *Carrots and sticks don't work: Build a culture of employee engagement with the principles of RESPECT.* McGraw-Hill.

Murrell, K., & Meredith, M. (2000). *Empowering employees.* New York, NY: McGraw- Hill.

Normore, A. H., Javidi, M., & Anderson, T. (2015). Developing future police leaders. *Blue Line: Canada;s National Law Enforcement Magazine.* Available [Online]: http://blueline.ca/

Normore, A. H., Javidi, M., Anderson, T., Normand, N., Scott, W., & Hoina, C. (2014). *Moral compass for law enforcement professionals.* Holly Springs, NC: International Academy of Public Safety.

Starhawk (2011). *The empowerment manual: A guide for collaborative groups.* Gabriola Island, BC, Canada: New Society Publishers.

Tully, E. (1997, December). Misconduct, corruption, abuse of power-what can the chief do? *National Executive Institute Associates, Major Cities Chief's Association and Major County Sheriff's Association Leadership Bulletin,* 1-8.

Watt, R., Javidi, M., & Normore, A. H. (2015). Identifying and combatting organizational leadership toxicity. *California Peace Officer. Journal of California Law Enforcement, 49*(2).

Werder, E. (1996, January). The great sergeant! *National Executive Institute Associates, Major Cities Chief's Association and Major County Sheriff's Association Leadership Bulletin,* 1-9.

KEY TERMS AND DEFINITIONS

Communication: The process of exchanging information, both verbal and non-verbal, within an organization. An organization may consist of employees from different parts of the society. In order to unite the activities of all employees, communication is crucial. Communicating necessary information to the entire workforce becomes necessary.

Empowerment: Sharing information, rewards, and power with employees so that they can take initiative and make decisions to solve problems and improve service and performance. Empowerment is based on the idea that giving employees skills, resources, authority, opportunity, motivation, as well holding them responsible and accountable for outcomes of their actions, will contribute to their competence and satisfaction.

Engagement: Emotional connection an employee feels toward his or her employment organization, which tends to influence his or her behaviors and level of effort in work related activities. The more engagement an employee has with his or her company, the more effort they put forth.

First-Line Police Supervisor: Produces the police departmental product/service to the citizens of the community. Usually a sergeant who accomplishes this task by having direct contact with the officers he or she supervises to ensure accountability and performance objectives. Because of the first-line supervisor's close interaction with the patrol officers, they are the key element in identifying and reducing potential misconduct incidents within police organizations.

Chapter 26
Communicating across the Generations:
Implications for Higher Education Leadership

Carolyn N. Stevenson
Kaplan University, USA

ABSTRACT

Today's workplace is composed of four generational groups of employees, each with varying degrees of technological expertise, career expectations, and professional experience. As such, higher education administrators need to identify differences among generations of workers and develop a strategic plan for managing and motivating across the generations. This case study addresses the following question: "How do higher education administrators lead and motivate multi-generational employees and online students?" An understanding of the common characteristics of each generational group is the first step for developing a strategy for motivating all employees and students in higher education. Communication, mentoring programs, training, respect, and opportunities for career advancement are components valued by all. It is important for higher education administrators to understand the values, work ethic, and communication style of the different generations. The implications for higher education administrators lie in establishing an organizational culture that promotes satisfaction for all individuals in the higher education setting.

INTRODUCTION

As more individuals are delaying retirement and working several years past the retirement age, it is important for higher education administrators to be knowledgeable about the different generations working in various capacities in the higher education setting. College administrators, such as department chairs or other administrators responsible for training and hiring faculty members, also need to

be aware of the differences across the generations. This is especially true for online instructors who do not meet face-to-face with students.

According to Ferri-Reed, J. (2013), "A mixture of the mature generation, baby boomers, generation X, and generation Y (or millennials) can be found working side by side. For the most part, the members of varying generations are capable of working well with one another, but there are generational differences that can create friction

DOI: 10.4018/978-1-4666-9970-0.ch026

and, in some cases, cause open conflict," (p.12). As such, the topic of engaging and managing the multi-generational workforce calls for further research. Educational leaders at all levels are challenged with leading various generations. This has had a major impact on higher education administration in terms of retention, recruitment, motivation, and productivity. Faculty members also need to be aware of the differences between multi-generational students, especially in the online classroom, and establish communication models where all students are motivated to perform at the highest level.

At the present time, there are four generational groupings of employees in the workplace and in the higher education classroom. According to Friesner (2015) the four multi-generational groups in the workplace are:

- **The Traditional Generation:** Born pre-1945;
- **Baby Boomers:** Born 1946-1964;
- **Generation X:** Born 1965-1980;
- Generation Y or Millennials.

In the very near future, there will be five generational groupings of employees in the workforce and in the online classroom at the same time. As individuals are working well into their late 60's or early 70's, higher education administrators need to adapt their leadership styles to effectively manage, motivate, and retain employees from various generations. Additionally, the flexibility of online learning promotes many adults to return to college. Students across generations have different communication styles and study habits. Online instructors need to be mindful of these generational differences and adapt a teaching style that promotes success for all students in the online classroom.

The diversity of generational workers and students impacts motivation and retention of employees. Additionally, higher education administrators, such as department chairs, need to train instructors

on communicating with multi-generational students. This is especially imperative in the online classroom where nonverbal cues are absent. As such, college administrators and instructors need to be knowledgeable of the differences across generations and leverage the strengths of each group. "When communicating across generations most likely it isn't just one. Most of us are trying to reach a mix of individuals, but how does each generation like to be reached and how do we combine them," (Aalgaard, 2015, p.1).

While higher education administrators and instructors may be aware of the various generations in their institutions and classrooms, implications for motivating and managing across the generations may not have been considered. "Research indicates that people communicate based on their generational backgrounds. Each generation has distinct attitudes, behaviors, expectations, habits and motivational buttons. Learning how to communicate with the different generations can eliminate many major confrontations and misunderstandings in the workplace and the world of business,"(Hammill, 2015).

While the core values are similar, college administrators need to take a different approach when attempting to meet the needs of multi-generational employees. "The key is to be able to effectively address and take advantage of the differences in values and expectations of each generation. But experts say managers must be careful not to follow blanket stereotypes," (*Wall Street Journal,* 2011). Online instructors also need to be mindful of these differences in the classroom and adjust communication styles to meet the needs of the diverse generational groupings of the students.

This chapter discusses the differences in communication, motivation, and work styles of multi-generational workers and students. Having an understanding of the different characteristics of multi-generational employees in the higher education setting will assist in motivating all employees. Regardless of the generational group, employees value a positive work environment, fun environment, respect, and appropriate benefits. Higher education leaders need to acknowledge the differences among the generations, keep communication lines open, and develop an environment where all employees are motivated to perform their best. College administrators also need to train instructors on communicating with multi-generational students in the online classroom. While students may have the desire to succeed, learning styles are also different across the generations.

Following is a case study discussing the issues related to leading across generations. It is important to note that the differences discussed are generalizations. While each individual is unique, there are commonalities that exist among members of all the generational groupings.

CASE DESCRIPTION

The Organization

The organization selected for this case study was a two-year college in a suburb near a large metropolitan city in the United States. Students may take classes in the traditional classroom format, online, or through a hybrid option. All courses are taught via the learning management system BlackBoard.

For this case study, four full-time faculty members were selected. Each faculty member teaches in both the online and face-to-face format. The four faculty members are of different academic rank and represent each of the four generational groupings. All of the participating faculty members agreed to discuss their experience working with administrators and other faculty members from different generational groupings. Each participant, as well as the official name of the college was changed to ensure confidentiality of the institution and the faculty members. Due to space limitations, highlights of the interviews are represented in the vignettes that follow. Participants did go into

greater detail and responded to eight interview questions. The passages were selected based on the relevance to the topic.

Statement of the Problem

Literature and observation reveal that there are workplace differences in work ethic, leadership styles, communication styles, and preferred method for communication among the four generations in the workplace. Additionally, differences exist in factors which motivate individuals from the various groups to perform responsibilities to their best abilities. Some researchers argue that there really is no difference between the four generations. It is simply the time in their lives in which the groups exist. Others are concerned that educational and organizational need to recognize these differences to promote an organizational culture that fosters success and job satisfaction among all employees. This is especially important for college administrators whose employees have a direct impact on student success. The findings of the research illustrate there is a need for both college administrators and faculty to understand differences among generations in their institution and develop a plan for enhanced communication and job satisfaction at the institution.

It is reasonable to suggest there is a need for higher education administrators to identify differences among the generations of workers and develop a strategic plan for managing and motivating across the generations. This is a topic of interest for many higher education administrators as well as faculty members. College administrators are faced with a number of factors concerning creating a positive institutional culture among multi-generational workers.

Firstly, deans, faculty members, and other college administrators must employ strong leadership skills as well as knowledge of the generational differences of the individual. Communicating effectively across the generations is challenging and college administrators must be able to motivate others to see the value each generation brings to the institution. College administrators must be open to suggestions from others regarding changes within the institution. A basic knowledge of generational differences is also needed to guide deans, faculty members, and other college administrators in understanding the workplace values of the different generations and establishing an organizational culture that promotes motivation for all employees.

Secondly, college administrators and faculty members must re-think teaching methods and curriculum design for online courses. Four generations of learners are in the online classroom. Assignments, projects, and discussion board questions should foster critical thinking, collaboration, and creativity for all students. Market demands often influence the decision as well. Oftentimes institutions attempt to keep abreast with the competition without reflecting on the needs of the individual institution and the student population specific to the organization. In addition, teaching methods must also be considered. Online learning allows for flexible approaches for students to actively gain knowledge, but also requires instructors to guide students in learning course material through individual learning styles. Inclusion of experiential learning opportunities also allow for a holistic approach to teaching and learning.

Lastly, identifying differences among the generations of workers and developing a strategic plan for managing and motivating across the generations involves attention to a future vision and establishment of specific policies and procedures. Training for all employees at the institution needs to be designed and implemented. The institution must be committed to investing in designing online curriculum that will motivate students from all generations. College administrators must also be committed to continual training as new generations of employees and students enter the institution. While the diversity of generations continues to increase, college administrators

need to cautiously develop appropriate policies, but must quickly devise new guidelines regarding motivating and retaining employees and students across generations.

Based on these facts, it is reasonable to assume that college administrators, faculty members, and other employees at the institution have a different perspective on leading and motivating across generations. Additionally, college administrators are challenged with addressing a number of issues associated with retaining quality employees and students. The problem presented in this study is to investigate and determine the perspectives of faculty members on communicating and leading students and other faculty members across the generations. Findings from this case study will assist higher education administrators in leading and motivating multi-generational employees.

Purpose of the Study

The purpose of this study was to describe and explain selected faculty member perspectives on working with multi-generational administrators, students, and faculty. The results may assist higher education administrators in three areas.

The findings of the study will inform higher education administrators, faculty members, and other college administrators of the generation differences of individuals and students at the institution. The findings will also inform current and future college administrators and faculty members of the ways to motivate and retain employees, faculty, and students in the institution. The study will provide the basis for greater understanding of the leadership needed in educational settings that both want and have an interest in communicating, motivating, and training multi-generational employees, faculty, and students.

Research Question

The purpose of this study was to describe and explain selected faculty member perspectives on working with multi-generational administrators, students, and faculty. The exploratory questions that guided the study were:

1. What elements constitute this perspective in for working with multi-generational colleagues?
2. What variables influence this perspective working with multi-generational colleagues?
3. What beliefs do these faculty members hold which support or negate this perspective?

Methodology

The decision to conduct a qualitative study was influenced by the characteristics of qualitative design discussed by Janesick (2011). She describes research as being alive and active. It is a way of looking at the world and interpreting the world. This study focused on qualitative methods as means to understand the multiple complexities existing in the social world (Janesick, 2011).

Qualitative research involves passion for the work. The qualitative researcher is interactive in the sense used by John Dewey (1934) when writing about artists:

An *"expression of the self in and through a medium, constituting the work of art, is itself a prolonged interaction issuing from self with objective conditions, a process in which both of them acquire form and order they did not first possess" (p. 65).*

This immersion into the research process actively involves the qualitative researcher in the quest for gaining a deeper understanding of the social phenomena. A case study was selected for this study. Case studies involve an in-depth study of this bounded system and rely on a number of data collection materials. The cases used in this study were four faculty members teaching in an online format from four generation. The study sought to gain understanding of the perspectives

of faculty members on working with multigenerational employees and students.

Presentation of the individual cases provides the reader the opportunity to gain understanding of the views, observations, and opinions of the individual participant perspectives on working with multi-generational administrators, students, and faculty. Direct quotes from the participants were used in the case studies as an attempt to portray the participant as an individual entity.

Data Collection

Interviews, researcher reflective journal, observations, researcher field notes, documents, artifacts, and transcripts were collected. At least two in-depth interviews were conducted with the participants. In an attempt to gather the rich, descriptive information required for qualitative research, semi-structured interviews with open-ended questions were used. The first step in the data collection process was conducting interviews with the study participants. The information qualitative researchers seek to gain is rich, thick descriptions of the participants in their social setting. Thus, open-ended questions were used to elicit the most complete and thorough responses from the participants.

The nature of qualitative research is flexible, as participants are being studied in their social setting. While variables in the social world cannot be controlled, the researcher can follow a format to help ensure items such as equipment are functioning.

In addition to interviews, participant observation was used to supplement the data collected in the interviews. Janesick (2011) alludes to observation as the immersion into the social setting which allows the researcher to begin to experience the experiences of the participants. The researcher observed each participant at least one time. Settings for potential observations included faculty in their offices, department meetings, and faculty interaction with others at the institution.

Observations also provided a check as to the credibility of the other data collected. Observations do require a series of planned steps. There are limitations as to the amount of information individuals reveal in the interview. Observations served as a means for verifying that the participants' actions match their words.

Document and artifact analysis, researcher field notes, and a researcher reflective journal also served as other sources of data for this case. The researcher gathered documents and artifacts from all participants as an attempt to further understand selected faculty member perspectives on working with multi-generational administrators, students, and faculty. Field notes consisted of supporting interview and observation notes. Format for the field notes collected during interviews and observations followed suggestions provided by Janesick (2011). A researcher's reflective journal was also kept as another means of data collection. The reflective journal served as means for the researcher to express emotions, ideas, and reactions to the study. During the data analysis stage, the reflective journal provided another resource for identifying emerging themes and sub themes.

Participant Selection

Four faculty members from a two-year college in a large suburb in the U.S. were interviewed individually regarding their perspective on working with multi-generational administrators, students, and faculty. The four faculty members taught in an online format only. Each faculty member represented a member of the four generations in the workplace and online classroom: one Traditionalist, one Baby Boomer, one Generation Xer, and one Millennial. Following the recommendations of Janesick (2011), the researcher relied on collection and analysis of various forms of data. Each online faculty member was interviewed at least two times for a total of eight formal and informal interviews. The online faculty members were audiotaped for the formal interviews. Data were also collected from three observations, thirteen documents and artifacts, and nineteen researcher reflective journal entries.

The online faculty members were selected because of the representation of the four generational groupings, their willingness to talk about their experiences, and their ability to provide different perspectives. Each participant had been at the institution for at least three years, had first-hand experience working with higher education administrators, other faculty members, and other administrators at the institution.

Mike was the only male involved in this study. This was not intentional but due to the fact that the other online faculty members willing to participate in the study were female. Jane was selected because of her dual role of faculty member and her extensive administrative responsibilities at the institution. Kayla and Kendra were selected because of their willingness to participate in the study, their role as faculty member for the college for at least three years, and their interaction with other college administrators. Each participant, as well as the official name of the college was changed to ensure confidentiality of the institution and the faculty members. Table 1 shows the basic profile of each participant.

Table 1. Case ordered matrix, participant characteristics

Faculty Member	Gender	Position	Years at College	Time in Position
Mike	Male	Dean, General Studies	18 years	13 years
Jane	Female	Professor, Philosophy	11 years	8 years
Kayla	Female	Associate Professor of Communications	7 years	6 years
Kendra	Female	Assistant Faculty, Composition	3 years	3 years

Each participant discussed his or her perspective on working with colleagues from different generational groupings. A summary of the responses follows.

Mike: The Traditionalist

Mike was the oldest member of the participants and has also been at the college the longest. He is nearing retirement, but remains in his position because he enjoys working in higher education. In addition to his administrative role, he also teaches one online class. When asked why is does not wish to retire he responded, "I love what I do." Prior to working in higher education he worked as a Certified Public Accountant for several years. He began teaching part-time and decided he enjoyed teaches so much, he made it his career. Additionally, he stated, "It is a great way to share my experience with others."

When asked about working with different generational groupings, he described his experience as the following:

I enjoy working with all people. One of the benefits of being the oldest kid on the block is that I hold a wealth of experience—both in the classroom and in the boardroom. However, it is difficult at times working with younger individuals who try and rush through decisions without following procedure. I also wish younger faculty would seek out my experience more often.

When asked about the preferred method of communication, Mike responded:

I prefer a phone call for a complex issue or a face-to-face meeting. There are bi-monthly meetings with my full-time faculty members and semester meetings with my part-time faculty members. It is important to sit around the table and discuss student issues, university issues, changes in policy, and other topics.

When asked about what motivates him at work, Mike responded:

The students motivate me. I enjoy when they have an 'ah-ha' moment. You know, when the light goes on in their head and they really understand the concept. Also, in my administrative role as department chair, I enjoy being part of the decision-making process. In this role, I have the opportunity to meet with a number of administrators across the College. The sharing of ideas is what makes my department and the College run smoothly.

Jane: The Baby Boomer

Jane is a full-time faculty member that teaches both in the traditional classroom setting and in an online. She enjoys teaching in both formats but prefers the face-to-face classroom because of "the connection she can make with the students." Jane started her career working as a librarian. She enjoyed the work but wanted to challenge herself professionally. She went back to college to earn her Ph.D. in Philosophy later in life and completed her degree when she was 47 years old. She began teaching for the College part-time and then accepted a full-time position. She also is a member of the College Assessment Committee and interacts with individuals various departments at the College.

When asked about working with different generational groupings, she described her experience as the following:

The diversity of individuals promotes fresh ideas. When you work with a variety of age groups, people bring experience and creativity to the table. One of the challenges I have is when new faculty complain about the amount of work involved in teaching. It is not just teaching but service to the College, service to academic community, and research. At times, younger faculty complain that there is no mentorship program to help them with their research. I never had a mentor. You have to work hard in academia—both in the classroom as well as in fostering professional development. It is part of your job, but you need to be self-motivated.

When asked about the preferred method of communication, Jane responded:

I prefer a phone call or a meeting when working with faculty members or administrators. Email is essential for the online instructor, but I also encourage students to call during my office hours. It can be easier to explain things with a phone rather than going back and forth on email. Face-to-face meetings are also important when discussing important issues as well as for keeping in touch with your colleagues.

When asked about what motivates her at work, Jane responded:

I love my job and I love to work with both students and administrators. Research is also something I value and effort is made to stay on top of changes in my field. Conference attendance and participation are very important and I am motivated by new ideas presented by scholars in the field. Going into higher education was a choice because I enjoy helping students understand the historical and practical applications of philosophy. There is nothing better than reviewing student evaluations and seeing how much they enjoyed the Introduction to Philosophy class and how much they learned.

Kayla: The Generation Xer

Higher education was a second career choice for Kayla. After graduating college, she began her career in publishing. She worked for a major college textbook publisher for three years and then two years for a medical publisher. She began her master's program immediately after undergraduate school and completed her master's degree in communication within two years. Like many of her friends, she changed companies frequently

the first ten years. There was a saying that they were part of the "job of the year club." She also worked in the insurance industry and as a technical consultant. After moving to the city, she began working part-time nights for a junior college and discovered a passion for teaching. After getting married and thinking about a family, she realized that a 9-5 job would not be conducive to raising a family. She found a full-time job in teaching and was able to balance raising children and working full-time.

When asked about working with different generational groupings, she described her experience as the following:

I never really thought about the age differences of my colleagues. Reflecting on that point, there are obvious differences, especially when it comes to communication. My department chair is older and likes to hold face-to-face meetings. Meetings are appropriate when there is a critical issue to discuss. However, meeting just to meet is frustrating for me. I would rather do my work during office hours then talk, talk, talk without an agenda or an action item. It also seems like some younger co-workers need a lot of hand-holding on projects. My work style is just to give me a project and let me go. I'll ask questions when needed. However, some of the younger workers need constant reassurance.

When asked about the preferred method of communication, Kayla responded:

Email is the communication method I prefer. It is a quick and easy way to send and receive information. For my online students, it is the only form of communication. Also, with my iPhone I can check email anytime anywhere. However, phone calls or meetings are appropriate to ensure communication of complex issues occurs. On a person level, I would rather text for short, simple messages rather than make a phone call.

When asked about what motivates her at work, Kayla responded:

I love my job and am self-motivated. Being an instructor, especially teaching online, provides a great deal of flexibility. This creates a more balanced life, especially spending time with my family. Also, I enjoy working with my colleagues on research projects. When you work with a talented, experienced group of individuals, it creates a sense of motivation for the project as well as a feeling of being engaged with ther members of the College. But most of all, my students motivate me. Working with a large percentage of adult learners, especially online, really has opened my eyes to their dedication. The way the students balance work, family, school, and social issues is amazing. They inspire me every day. Yes---I do cry at graduation when I see how proud they are of themselves and how proud their family is for their accomplishments. It is such a wonderful feeling to know that I played a role in helping them achieve their dream of graduating college.

Kendra: The Millennial

Kendra always knew she wanted to be a college professor. Both of her parents were college professors and she loves the higher education setting. Upon completing her Ph.D., she was fortunate to land a full-time job and the College. She did have an opportunity to teach one part-time class prior to obtaining the full-time position. She enjoys working at the College and the fact the College in the suburb where her friends and family also live.

When asked about working with different generational groupings, she described her experience as the following:

Since I am the youngest faculty member in my department, it can be frustrating at times. Although I don't have the experience like many other faculty, I have creative ideas. At times it feels like my voice is not heard. Also, I thought that I would be able

to get more direction and mentorship when being at the College. I am new to teaching and really wished someone could have had mentored me my first year. On the positive side, the different age groups does allow to learn from the information shared at meetings. There are also a number of younger workers at the College that work in other departments and we do go to lunch every day which is enjoyable.

When asked about the preferred method of communication, Kendra responded:

I prefer social networking tools like Facebook or Twitter. Email is used for almost all communication with my students. However, I like working in groups on special projects and prefer to meet face-to-face with my team members on these special projects. Group work for me is enjoyable, especially when talented and creative people can share ideas openly. When we can support each other, it can be a positive experience.

When asked about what motivates her at work, Kendra responded:

It is motivating to teach others. I have always wanted to be a college professor and I enjoyed working with the students. I am also motivated by projects that allow me to express by ideas. Last spring I was able to re-design a course which made it much more current to today's students. I do wish there was more recognition for great teacher evaluation or work done on a project.

Major Themes

The themes of engagement, motivation, and mentorship were major themes from the interviews. While the participants varied in age group, all faculty members were motivated by their students. There was a major difference in the preferred form of communication. The Traditionalist and Baby Boomer preferred phone calls or face-to-face meetings, while the Generation Xer and Millennial preferred electronic forms of communication. The preferred communication style was also consistent with the literature. Another important theme was that of mentorship. The Traditionalist spoke about enjoying his work, and wanting to share his experience. The Millennial has a strong desire for a mentor.

SOLUTIONS AND RECOMMENDATIONS

Since the four generations of workers have very different viewpoints about job satisfaction in the workplace, college administrators need to find ways to meet these needs. The older generations of workers, specifically the Traditionalists and Baby Boomers, need to feel valued in the workplace. Online students share the same need in the classroom. Since these two groups have the most workplace experience, there is an expectation that their experience is valued by other employees. "Veteran workers are seen as loyal and steadfast employees that an organization can count on to get specific tasks done. Baby Boomers are seen as hard, eager workers, well-suited to be brought back as consultants or for individual projects after their retirement," (Burke, 2004, p. 9).

Generation Xer's can be motivated by assigning workplace projects that allow for their sense of independence and problem solving to utilized to their fullest potential. "Generation X workers can be counted on in situations where conditions are fluid or not well defined," (Burke, 2004, p.9). This group will be motivated by challenging projects with little or no supervision. By allowing Generation Xer's the freedom to work on alternative solutions to problems, a high sense of job satisfaction will be achieved (Burke 2004). In the online classroom, students enjoy projects where creativity can be applied. Online students also enjoyed being challenged to go deeper into discussion board posts.

Millennials will shortly hold the title of the largest generation of employees in the workplace. As more Baby Boomers retire, there will be more leadership opportunities within organizations for this group. The smaller number of Generation Xer's will not be sufficient to fulfill these vacant leadership roles. As such, managers need to mentor and channels the talents of the Millennial group. Generation Y are highly expressive, over-confident and relatively self-absorbed risk-taking group who can move an institution forward with their creativity, innovation, global perspective, inclusiveness and immediacy. These are powerful energies to harness and transform (Paul, 2011). In the online classroom, this group enjoys collaboration and creative projects. By encouraging creativity in assignments and discussion posts, students of this group will perform their best. Students new to online learning would also benefit by have a peer mentor during their first term of classes.

It is essential that open, honest communication occurs among the generations. As described in an article by *New Zealand Management* (2012), "The future of our society is dependent upon a respectful and constructive interaction between the generations. We need many more such conversations to grow in focus and diversity; this was just a beginning," (p.23). According to the American Management Association (2015), "A leader's primary responsibility is to ensure that everyone in the organization understands that "working together" is not negotiable. Create a respectful, open and inclusive environment where workers of all ages and cultural backgrounds can share who they are without fear of being judged, "fixed," or changed," (p.1). As such, leaders in higher education need to actively pursue ways to encourage communication among generational groups.

The differences between the generations are often easy to see in the workplace. However, it's important to recognize their similarities as well. Successful organizations are ensuring that company leaders not only understand these similarities, but create work environments that support them. According to recent research conducted by Randstad and the Center for Creative Leadership, employees across the generations agree that:

- Work is a vehicle for personal fulfillment and satisfaction, not just for a paycheck.
- Workplace culture is important.
- Being trusted to get the job done is the number one factor that defines job satisfaction.
- They need to feel valued by their employer to be happy in the job.
- They want flexibility in the workplace.
- Success is finding a company they can stay with for a long time.
- Career development is the most valued form of recognition, even more so than pay raises and enhanced titles (Raines, 2015, p.1).

College administrators, such as Department Chairs, should offer training for online faculty working with multigenerational groups. Additionally, Student Services should provide resources promoting academic success and career development. The following suggestions are suggestions for motivating and retaining online students from all generations:

- Offer peer mentoring opportunities for all first-term students. The mentoring program would allow leadership skills to be exercised by all generations.
- Provide a strong Career Services department. Students from all generations need resources for current and future career searches.
- Offer new student orientation webinars to prepare students for the world of online learning.
- Provide set policies and clear expectations in course syllabi.
- Require instructors to keep virtual office hours at a set time.

- Encourage all students to share personal and professional experience in discussion board responses.

Employee recognition is important for all generations. *The Wall Street Journal* (2011), "Even simple gestures like a pat on the back or positive email congratulations can help boost productivity with Gen Xers. Boomers may seek status so may respond best to an office-wide memo that announces that they are meeting or exceeding their goals. Millennials may seek validation and approval so will appreciate increased responsibility and additional training opportunities. To this end, Millennials may also prefer more frequent employee reviews," (2011).

IMPLICATIONS FOR LEADERS

While placing categories of workers or students into categories based on a set of characteristics can be seen as stereotyping, it is important for college administrators and online instructors to be aware of some of the common traits. As Fox (2011) states, "A stereotype is an oversimplified characterization and therefore doesn't apply to every person of a group at all times in all situations. However, people fall back on stereotypes related to age, physical appearance or gender when interacting. So, real or imagined, stereotypes play a role in how people are judged and how their actions and words are perceived," (Fox, 2011, p.1).

There are personal and lifestyle characteristics common among the generations. A summary of these personal and lifestyle characteristics by generations described by Hammill (2015) are summarized as follows:

- Traditionalists have core values characterized by respect for authority, conforming, and discipline. The preferred communication media are landline phones, one-on-one meetings, and written memos.

- Baby Boomers have core values characterized by optimism and involvement. The preferred communication medium is phone with a "call me anytime" attitude.
- Generation Xers have core values characterized by skepticism, fun, and informality. The preferred communication media is cell phone (call me only at work) or email.
- Millennials have core values characterized by realism, confidence, extreme fun, and highly social. The preferred communication media is social media (such as Facebook and Twitter), Smartphones, and email.

According to the research, there are also workplace characteristics that are common among the generations. A summary of these workplace characteristics by generations described by Hammill (2005) are summarized as follows:

- Traditionalists have work ethics characterized by hard work, respect for authority, sacrifice, duty before fun, and adherence to rules. Work is considered an obligation. The leadership style is directive and command and control. The feedback and reward system is "no news is good news" and "satisfaction in a job well done." The message that motivates is that your experience is valued.
- Baby Boomers have work ethics characterized by being workaholics, working efficiently, crusading causes, desiring quality, and questioning authority. Work is considered an exciting adventure. The leadership style is consensual and collegial. The feedback and reward system is "don't appreciate it." The message that motivates is time and money.
- Generation Xers have work ethics characterized by being direct, being self-reliant, demanding structure, and being skeptical. Work is considered a challenge and a con-

tract. The leadership style is everyone is the same, challenge others, and ask why. The feedback and reward system is "sorry to interrupt, but how am I doing?" and "freedom is the best reward." The message that motivates is forget the rules and do it your way.
- Millennials have work ethics characterized by multitasking, tenacity, tolerant, and goal-oriented. The leadership style is collaborative. The feedback and reward system is "whatever I want, at the push of a button" and meaningful work. The message that motivates is you working with other bright, creative people.

Working with multi-generational employees is not a new phenomenon. Traditionalists, Baby Boomers, and Generation Xer's have all worked side by side for several years. The same is true for online students. Due to the flexible nature of online learning, adult learners of all ages have been drawn to the virtual classroom for many years. However, this is the first time four generations will be in the workforce and online classroom at the same time. Each generation has brought a set of core values, beliefs, and technological aptitude in the workplace. However, these qualities do change over time as work/life priorities shift and change. According to Baltierra (2005), "Generational differences are unique in that all of us tend to forget that our perspectives change over time and that each of us has a unique set of life experiences and expectations. Therefore, it is important to be able to find ways that we can 'connect' with each other and see the things that really drive us at work," (p.1). Since the generations work in various positions, creating a collaborative work environment is needed to ensure both the success of the individual as well as the institution.

In an effort to develop a strategic plan for managing, recruiting, retaining, and motivating employees across generations, an understanding of the common characteristics is needed. Several factors impact the common traits of the various generations. Societal issues, economics, and technology all impact the values and ethics of the workers. "Members of the Silent Generation, or Traditionalists, grew up during the devastation of the Great Depression and came of age under the sacrifices of World War II. They witnessed the growth of the federal government as Social Security programs created jobs and safety nets for the poor and the elderly. Therefore, Traditionalists' values in the workplace tend to be frugality, adherence to rules, loyalty to employers, and a deep sense of responsibility and sacrifice for the good of the organization," (Fox, 2011). Although Traditionalists make up a smaller percentage of the workforce, their work ethics and values are very much aligned with traditional corporate structure. "The culture they created is fiscally conservative, rewards tenure and loyalty, is rules-focused, and measures performance based on the number of hours worked," (Fox, 2011).

The Baby Boomers represent the largest number of workers in the workforce. "Independence and social consciousness are Baby Boomers' bedrock values. They marched against 'the establishment' to bring about equal rights and an end to the Vietnam War. Competitive and independent, Baby Boomers are workaholics, with identities closely aligned to their professions," (Fox, 2011).

Generation X is often considered the "lost generation," since this is the smallest group in the workforce. Growing up, members of this group were often latchkey children, with both parents working outside the home or divorced. "This generation saw the invention of the personal computer, a deregulated airline industry, and multiple recessions. They became technologically astute, more mobile and highly educated, as they went back to school when they couldn't find jobs. Self-management, pragmatism, and cynicism are traits associated with Generation X," (Fox, 2011).

The impact of the economic, social, and technical advancement had an impact on the way this group views corporate loyalty. "Their value

set is focused on gaining transferable skills so that they can be ready when the rug is pulled out from under them—as it has throughout their lives. All the major institutions fell apart around them—marriage, family, corporations and the economy. Their attitude is, 'You've never done anything for me. Why should I do something for you?' "(Fox, 2011).

Millennials have been raised around technology. This group also is a heavy user of social media such as Twitter and Facebook. This sense of creating a collaborative network also translates into the Millennials' work preference for working in teams. As children of Baby Boomers, they were raised with the "Everyone Gets a Trophy Mentality." This group had been characterized in the research as needing constant praise and views career advancement based on work performance rather than seniority, (John & Johnson, 2010). "Raised by Baby Boomers who desired peer-like relationships with their children, Millennials have been constantly coached, praised and encouraged for participation—rather than for accomplishments," (Fox, 2011).

While Generation Xer's seek to find a work/life balance, "Millennials view work as a key part of life, not a separate activity that needs to be 'balanced' by it. For that reason, they place a strong emphasis on finding work that is personally fulfilling. They want work to afford them the opportunity to make new friends, learn new skills, and connect to a larger purpose," (Meister & Willyerd, 2010). This characteristic is important to job satisfaction of this group. Employers need to be aware of the high standards that Millennials set for themselves and their employers and seek out ways to motivate and retain this group.

College administrators should also acknowledge the challenges faced by employees when younger members of the institution serve as a supervisor for an older worker. In a 2010 survey conducted by Career Builder, more than half (53 percent) of workers ages 45 and up said they have a boss younger than them, followed by 69 percent of workers ages 55 and up. According the survey CareerBuilder (2010), workers reported that there are a variety of reasons why working for someone younger than them can be a challenge, including:

- They act like they know more than me when they don't.
- They act like they're entitled and didn't earn their position.
- They micromanage.
- They play favorites with younger workers.
- They don't give me enough direction (CareerBuilder, 2010, p.1).

CareerBuilder (2010) offers the following suggestions for older generations with younger supervisors:

- **Understand Others' Point of View:** Different generations tend to have differing opinions on a variety of topics, from management style to pop culture. Put yourself in others' shoes to better understand where they're coming from.
- **Adapt Your Communication:** Younger workers tend to favor communicating frequently using technology, such as e-mail and instant messenger. Older workers may prefer more face-to-face contact. Both parties should take this and other communication differences into consideration when interacting.
- **Keep an Open Mind:** Try not to make assumptions about those who are of a different age group than you. All workers have different skill sets and strengths, so see what you can learn from others rather than making judgments based on their age (CareerBuilder, 2010, p.1).

The suggestions offered by CareerBuilder (2015) are useful for both college administrators as well as online faculty members. Administrators can use the suggestions for training faculty to be

aware of the ways older students may communicate with younger students and younger instructors. Being aware of generational differences, without stereotyping individuals, can assist in creating more satisfying work and classroom environments.

FUTURE RESEARCH DIRECTIONS

The study findings and review of the literature raise interest related to the diversity of multi-generational workers in higher education settings. This is a trend that will continue to increase both on a national and international level as more of the Millennials enter the workplace and take on leadership roles in higher education. The research also shows that members of the Millennial group require mentoring and are looking for growth in their career in an environment that fosters collaboration and creativity.

The field of higher education is competitive on a global scale. With the number of online for-profit institutions and traditional on-ground institutions all competing for the same students, it is imperative that higher education administrators recruit and retain the best employees in an environment that fosters growth. This covers individuals across the institution: financial aid, student services, faculty, advising, and admissions.

Once hired at the institution, it is important that higher education administrators keep these employees. With four generations of workers in the institution, each group needs to feel valued and respected in their individual role. College administrators can leverage this diversity by channeling into the factors that motivate the different groups. For example, the Millennial group often seeks mentorships. Mentors can be provided from older workers to coach new employees or faculty.

Online faculty members need to be aware of the multi-generational groups of students in the classroom. This may be difficult because unless students self-disclose this information on a discussion board or in a webinar, there is no way to track the age of the student. Since the majority of online students are adult learners, faculty need to be trained on communication styles for all the generations. While Millennials may send numerous emails and ask for sample projects, a Baby Boomer may ask for a phone call to ask questions about a project. Setting clear expectations in the course syllabus is important for students of all generations. Well-defined rubrics are also important in outlining the expectations for the students.

Higher education administrators may consider reviewing other case studies established by corporations that address multigenerational concerns. Businesses can provide a viable model for implementing a strategy for creating a collaborative spirit in the educational environment. At times, there may be a tendency to view higher education as an entity separate from business. However, the mission to provide a service to individuals is the same. As such, there is a common need to create an environment in which people want to work, be it a corporate or educational setting.

Many businesses have done extensive studies on ways to create a cohesive multi-generational workplace. Higher education administrators can use the experience from these corporations to also address multi-generational concerns and remain competitive in a global economy. For example, Cisco is one company that can be used as a model for higher education administrators charged with enhancing motivation, leadership, and communicating across multi-generational workers and faculty.

Delong & Associates (2009) prepared a case study that describes the importance of enhancing engagement across generations at the company. Higher education administrators can also apply these guidelines for supporting employee collaboration and engagement across the generations to the educational institution. According to Delong & Associates (2009), five key practices stand out in shaping Cisco's work environment:

- **Continually Communicating the Big Picture:** Employees of every generation need to understand how their jobs fit into the organization's overall mission. Making sure all employees and managers know how their efforts are directly connected to the firm's larger mission is essential for creating a sense of purpose, giving work greater meaning, and increasing engagement.

- **Creating Structures that Increase Collaboration and Engagement:** Working together to create strategy and direction means people are incredibly engaged in execution. Strong emphasis on career and leadership development. Keeping employees engaged in growth opportunities can mean international assignments, rotational assignments, or working on high-visibility projects. Keeping employees engaged in growth opportunities can mean international assignments, rotational assignments, or working on high-visibility projects.

- **Maximize Work-Life Integration and Flexible Work Options:** The company recognizes that one of the primary sources of disengagement for employees is health problems. So they have invested heavily in wellness programs designed to meet a wide range of employee needs. The company has also adopted an optional flexible work schedule. However, one challenge is creating programs, which may include telecommuting, part-time work, and sabbaticals, that are appealing to all generations.

- **Leveraging the Benefits of Social Networking Tools:** Leaders actively promote the use of new social networking technologies to build relationships, increase collaboration, and enhance employee engagement. Research shows that employees who feel personally connected to their co-workers are more likely to stay with the organization (Delong & Associates, 2009).

Organizations succeed when they create a work culture that encourages people from all generations to contribute to their fullest potential. According to Raines, 2015), these organizations:

- *Know their company demographics—internally and externally.* They gather data about their current customers and target where they want to increase market share. They gather data and learn about their employees and consider how well their staff mirrors current and projected customers.
- *Are intentional about creating and responding to generational diversity.* They identify needed skill sets within the company and recruit new staff from across the generations. They seek out individuals from under-represented generations for work teams, boards and advisory groups.
- *Build on strengths.* The most effective mixed-generation work teams recognize the unique strengths of each individual. Successful companies find ways to bring out those strengths and help each individual develop his or her talents so they can reach their own potential and contribute in their own ways.
- *Offer options.* They recognize that people from a mix of generations have differing needs and preferences and design their human resources strategies to meet varied employee needs. They offer a variety of benefits, flexible schedules, and an array of opportunities for professional growth and advancement.
- *Develop an understanding of and appreciation for generational differences and strengths.* They find ways to learn about their employees' needs, perspectives and interests and share that learning across the organization. They structure opportunities for less experienced employees from each generation to learn from their more experienced and knowledgeable colleagues.

- *Train people to communicate effectively across generations.* Communication styles and levels of comfort with varied technologies differ from one generation to the next. Successful companies recognize those differences, employ an array of communication methods and teach employees how to reach out effectively to their colleagues and insure that their communication approaches are inclusive and welcoming (p.1).

There are several opportunities for further research based on themes that emerged from the research and review of the literature. Higher education administrators may wish to conduct studies from the students' perspective. Understanding how multi-generational students learn in the online classroom would benefit the institution and promote student success. Additional research on the perspectives of higher education administrators would also call for further study. Specially, researching the ways multi-generational leaders promote engagement from all employees across the institution. Additional information from the faculty perspective calls for further research. The faculty members who participated from this study were from one institution. Drawing opinion from online, traditional settings, for-profit, and not-for-profit institutions would offer a more diverse perspective. Finally, the research should be done on a global scale. This study was limited to the U.S. higher education administrators would benefit from the global perspective.

CONCLUSION

In summary, the findings of this study and review of the literature conclude that higher education administrators must assess the challenges and benefits associated with working with multigenerational employees. The Millennial group is the largest generational grouping since the Baby Boomer era and will soon hold more leadership roles at institutions of higher learning. More junior-level faculty will also be from this generational grouping and higher education administrators need to develop a plan to motivate and retain this group of individuals.

There have been numerous studies outlining ways to communicate, motivate, engage, and retain multi-generational employees and higher education faculty. Yet there have been few studies that describe and explain from the students' perspective ways to engage and motivate multi-generational peers in the online classroom. Gaining a better understanding of the faculty members' perspective on working with multi-generational peers had led to the identification of major themes and sub-themes related to mentorship, engagement, leadership, and motivation. These findings may be useful to future researchers who investigate educational leadership, communication, and diversity issues. Additionally, higher education administrators who are responsible for making hiring decisions may also utilize the findings in this study to enhance their understanding of the need to train and mentor new employees and faculty members on ways to work in a multi-generational college setting.

The findings of the research questions presented here, if conducted, may help to further understand the questions about working with multi-generational employees and faculty in higher education on an international level, faculty resistance and administrative pressure related to change, and the impact of student demographics and socioeconomic status on student success in online learning courses. As the student population of higher education is becoming more diverse in terms of gender, race, demographics, and sexual orientation, gaining an understanding of the ways to motivate and retain students because a critical issue. In an era of a rapidly changing landscape in higher education, higher education administrators need to look at the value the multi-generational groupings bring to the institution and assess ways to motivate and retain quality faculty members, administrators, other institutional employees, and students.

REFERENCES

Aalgaard, J. (2015). *Communicating Across the Generations*. Retrieved from http://gettingsmart.com/2015/01/communicating-across-generations/

American Management Association. (2015). *Leading the Four Generations at Work*. Retrieved from http://www.amanet.org/training/articles/Leading-the-Four-Generations-at-Work.aspx

Baltierra, E. (2005). SHRM Case Study: Generational differences. *Society of Human Resource Management*. Retrieved August 30, 2012 from: http://www.shrm.org/TemplatesTools/Toolkits/Documents/CMS_011553.pdf

Burke, M. E. (2004). Generational differences survey report. *Society of Human Resource Management*. Retrieved from: http://www.shrm.org/hr-disciplines/benefits/Documents/Generational%20Differences%20Survey%20Report.pdf

CareerBuilder. (2010). *More than four-in-ten workers over the age of 35 currently work for a younger boss, finds new CareerBuilder survey*. Retrieved from http://www.careerbuilder.com/share/aboutus/pressreleasesdetail.aspx?id=pr554&sd=2/17/2010&ed=12/31/2010&siteid=cbpr&sc_cmp1=cb_pr554

Delong & Associates. (2009). *Driving collaboration in a multi-generational environment*. Retrieved from: http://www.cisco.com/web/about/ac49/ac55/DeLong-CiscoCollaborativeCulture-Case3-09.pdf

Dewey, J. (1934). *Art as experience*. New York: Minton, Malach, and Co.

Ferri-Reed, J. (2013). Quality, Conflict, and Communication Across the Generations. *Journal for Quality and Participation, 35*(4), 12–14.

Fox, A. (2011). Mixing it up. *Society of Human Resource Management, 56*(5). Retrieved from http://www.shrm.org/Publications/hrmagazine/EditorialContent/2011/0511/Pages/0511fox.aspx

Friesner, T. (2015). *The Six Living Generations in America*. Retrieved from http://www.marketingteacher.com/the-six-living-generations-in-america/

Hammill, G. (2015). Mixing and matching four generations of generations of employees. *FDU Magazine Online*. Retrieved from: http://www.fdu.edu/newspubs/magazine/05ws/generations.htm

Janesick, V. J. (2011). *Stretching exercises for qualitative researchers* (3rd ed.). Thousand Oaks: Sage.

John, L., & Johnson, M. (2010). *Getting the most from an age-diverse workforce*. Retrieved from http://www.generationsincbook.com

Management, N. Z. (2012). A conversation across the generations. *New Zealand Management*, *59*(6), 21.

Meister, J. C., & Willyerd, K. (2010). Mentoring millennials. *Harvard Business Review*, (May): 1–5. PMID:20429252

Raines, C. (2015). *4GenR8tns: Succeeding with colleagues, cohorts & customers*. Retrieved from http://www.generationsatwork.com/articles_succeeding.php

Society for Human Resource Management. (2009). The multi- generational workforce: opportunity for competitive success. *Research Quarterly*. Retrieved from: http://www.shrm.org/Research/Articles/Articles/Documents/09- 0027_RQ_March_2009_FINAL_no%20ad.pdf

Wall Street Journal. (2011). *How to Manage Different Generations*. Retrieved from: http://guides.wsj.com/management/managing-your-people/how-to-manage-different-generations/

ADDITIONAL READING

Alvesson, M., & Karreman, D. (2000). Varieties of discourse: On the study of Organizations through discourse analysis. *Human Relations*, *53*(9), 1125–1149. doi:10.1177/0018726700539002

Armour, S. (2005). Generation Y: They've arrived at work with a new attitude. *USA Today*. Retrieved from http://www.usatoday.com/money/workplace/2005-11-06-geny_x.htm

Ashcraft, K. L. (2005). Feminist organizational communication studies: Engaging gender in public and private. In S. May & D. K. Mumby (Eds.), *Engaging organizational communication theory* (pp. 141–169). Thousand Oaks, CA: Sage. doi:10.4135/9781452204536.n7

Ashcraft, K. L., & Mumby, D. K. (2004). *Reworking gender: A feminist communicology Of organization*. Thousand Oaks, CA: Sage.

Brinckerhoff, P. C. (2007). *Generations: The challenge of a lifetime for your nonprofit*. Saint Paul, MN: Fieldstone Alliance.

Buzzanell, P. M. (1995). Reframing the glass ceiling as a socially constructed process: Implications for understanding and change. *Communication Monographs*, *62*(4), 327–354. doi:10.1080/03637759509376366

Buzzanell, P. M., & Liu, M. (2005). Struggling with maternity leave policies and practices: A post-structuralist feminist analysis of gendered organizing. *Journal of Applied Communication Research*, *33*(1), 1–25. doi:10.1080/0090988042000318495

Coleman Gallagher, V., & Fiorito, J. (2005). Generational differences in attitudes about unions: A segmented dispositional marketing approach. *Southern Business Review*, *31*, 35–49.

Cordeniz, J. A. (2002). Recruitment, retention, and management of Generation X: A focus on nursing professionals. *Journal of Healthcare Management, 47,* 237–250. PMID:12221745

Dausien, B., Hanses, A., Inowlocki, L., & Riemann, G. (2008). The analysis of Professional practice, the self-reflection of practitioners, and their way of doing things: Resources of biography analysis and other interpretive approaches. *Forum Qualitative Sozial Forschung, 9.* Retrieved from http://www.qualitative-research.net/index.php/fqs/article/view/312

Dodson, L., & Schmalzbauer, L. (2005). Poor mothers and habits of hiding: Participatory Methods in poverty research. *Journal of Marriage and the Family, 67*(4), 949–959. doi:10.1111/j.1741-3737.2005.00186.x

Dou, W., Wang, G., & Zhou, N. (2006). Generational and regional differences in media Consumption patterns of Chinese Generation X consumers. *Journal of Advertising, 35*(2), 101–110. doi:10.1080/00913367.2006.10639230

Durkin, D. (2008). Youth movement. *Communication World, March-April,* 23-25.

Eckman, E. W. (2002). Women high school principals: Perspectives on role conflict, role commitment, and job satisfaction. *Journal of School Leadership, 12,* 57–77.

Elmore, C. (2009). Turning points and turnover among female journalists: Communication Resistance and repression. *Women's. Studies in Communications, 32,* 232–254.

Faber, B. D. (2001). Gen/ethics? Organizational ethics and student and instructor conflicts in workplace training. *Technical Communication Quarterly, 10*(3), 291–317. doi:10.1207/s15427625tcq1003_4

Fairhurst, G., & Sarr, R. (1996). *The art of framing: Managing the language of leadership.* San Francisco, CA: Jossey-Bass.

Fishbein, J. (2008, June 9). Balancing work and life. *Bloomberg Businessweek.* Retrieved From http://www.businessweek.com/magazine/content/08_34/b4097000492024.htm

Fletcher, J. K. (1999). *Disappearing acts: Gender, power, and relational practice at work.* Cambridge: MIT Press.

Gross, J. (2006, March 25). As parents age, baby boomers and business struggle to cope. *The New York Times.* Retrieved from http://www.nytimes.com/2006/03/25/national/25care.html?_r=1

Harding, S. (1991). *Whose science? Whose knowledge? Thinking from women's lives.* Ithaca, NY: Cornell University Press.

Harwood, J. (1998). Young adults' cognitive representations of intergenerational conversations. *Journal of Applied Communication Research, 26*(1), 13–31. doi:10.1080/00909889809365489

Holmes, J. (1995). *Women, men and politeness.* London, England: Longman.

Holmes, J., & Marra, M. (2004). Relational practice in the workplace: Women's talk or Gendered discourse? *Language in Society, 33*(03), 377–398. doi:10.1017/S0047404504043039

Holmes, J., & Stubbe, M. (2003). *Power and politeness in the workplace: A Sociolinguistic analysis of talk at work.* Harlow, England: Pearson.

Jayson, S. (2006). Companies slow to adjust to work-life balance concerns Of Gen Y. *USA Today.* Retrieved from http://www.usatoday.com/news/nation/2006-12-06-gen-next-life-work-balance_x.htm

Jorgenson, J. (2000). Interpreting the intersections of work and family: Frame conflicts in women's work. *Electronic Journal of Communication/La Revue Electronique de Communication, 10.* Retrieved from http://www.cios.org/www/ejc/v10n3400.htm#Dois

Kirby, E. L. (2000). Should I do as you say, or do as you do? Mixed messages about work and family. *La Revue Electronique de Communication, 10*. Retrieved from http://www.cios.org/www/ejc/v10n3400.htm#Dois

Kirby, E. L., Golden, A. G., Medved, C. E., Jorgenson, J., & Buzzanell, P. M. (2003). An Organizational communication challenge to the discourse of work and family research: From problematics to empowerment. In P. J. Kalbfleisch (Ed.), *Communication yearbook 27* (pp. 1–43). Thousand Oaks, CA: Sage. doi:10.1207/s15567419cy2701_1

Kirby, E. L., & Krone, K. J. (2002). "The policy exists but you can't really use it": Communication and the structuration of work-family policies. *Journal of Applied Communication Research, 30*(1), 50–77. doi:10.1080/00909880216577

Kirby, E. L., Wieland, S., & McBride, M. C. (2006). Work-life communication. In J. Oetzel & S. Ting-Toomey (Eds.), *Handbook of conflict communication* (pp. 327–357). Thousand Oaks, CA: Sage.

Leavy, P. L. (2007). The practice of feminist oral history and focus group interviews. In S. Nagy Hesse-Biber & P. L. Leavy (Eds.), *Feminist research practices: A primer* (pp. 149–186). Thousand Oaks, CA: Sage. doi:10.4135/9781412984270.n6

Lindlof, T. R., & Taylor, B. C. (2002). *Qualitative communication research methods* (2nd ed.). Thousand Oaks, CA: Sage.

Martin, C. A., & Tulgan, B. (2006). *Managing the generation mix: From urgency to Opportunity* (2nd ed.). Amherst, MA: HRD Press.

Martin, J. (1990). Deconstructing organizational taboos: The suppression of gender conflict in organizations. *Organization Science, 1*(4), 339–359. doi:10.1287/orsc.1.4.339

McCann, R. M., Dailey, R. M., Giles, H., & Ota, H. (2005). Beliefs about Intergenerational communication across the lifespan: Middle age and the roles of age stereotyping and respect norms. *Communication Studies, 56*(4), 293–311. doi:10.1080/10510970500319286

McCann, R. M., & Giles, H. (2006). Communication with people of different ages in the workplace: Thai and American data. *Human Communication Research, 32*(1), 74–108. doi:10.1111/j.1468-2958.2006.00004.x

Medved, C. E., & Kirby, E. L. (2005). Family CEOs: A feminist analysis of corporate Mothering discourses. *Management Communication Quarterly, 18*(4), 435–478. doi:10.1177/0893318904273690

Miller, S. (2004, August). *SHRM Survey: Generations hold differing views on work/life balance.* Alexandria, VA: Society for Human Resource Management.

Mullany, L. (2006). "Girls on tour": Politeness, small talk, and gender in managerial Business meetings. *Journal of Politeness Research, 2*(1), 55–77. doi:10.1515/PR.2006.004

Parker, K. (2011, March 14). Born-again feminism: How a movement that's grown stale in America can draw new inspiration from its abaya-clad sisters in the Middle East. *Newsweek*, pp. 11-12.

Perlow, L. A. (1997). *Finding time: How corporations, individuals, and families can Benefit from new work practices.* Ithaca, NY: Cornell University Press.

Rapoport, R., & Bailyn, L. (1996). *Relinking life and work: Toward a better future.* New York, NY: Ford Foundation.

Sacks, D. (2006, January/February). Scenes from the culture clash. *Fast Company*. Retrieved from http://www.fastcompany.com/magazine/102/culture-clash.html

Trethewey, A. (1997). Resistance, identity, and empowerment: A postmodern feminist Analysis of clients in a human service organization. *Communication Monographs*, *64*(4), 281–301. doi:10.1080/03637759709376425

Twenge, J. (2006). *Generation me: Why today's young Americans are more confident, assertive, entitled—and more miserable than ever before.* New York, NY: Free Press.

KEY TERMS AND DEFINITIONS

Baby Boomers: Individuals born between 1946 and 1964. Work ethic and values for this group include being a workaholic and a high level of personal fulfillment.

Collaborative Learning: This term is used to refer to students working on a computer-based learning program that requires them to collaborate by, for example, taking different roles, operating different controls, etc.

Experiential Knowledge/Learning: This term describes knowledge gained through experience/learning through experience. Contrasts, and moreover conflicts, with academic knowledge and learning through instruction.

Generation Xer's: Individuals born between 1965 and 1980. Work ethic and value for individuals in this group include wanting structure and direction. This group was the first focus on work/life balance.

Holistic: This term is used to describe an integrated knowledge structure or an approach to learning that recognizes that knowledge needs to be integrated.

Mentoring Programs: Formal or informal programs in which more experienced individuals assist individual with limited experience. Mentor programs can occur in the workplace as well as the classroom.

Millennials: Individuals born between 1965 and 1980. Work ethic and value for individuals in this group include questioning what is next and multitasking. This group also has a high interest in creating work/life balance.

Multi-Generational Work Groups: The representative of four generations in the workplace. This includes Traditionalists, Baby Boomers, Gen Xer's, and Millennials.

Traditionalists: Individuals born pre-1945. Work ethic and values for individuals in this group include sacrifice and completion of tasks before personal enjoyment.

Virtual Teams: Groups of individuals working in a professional or academic setting set out to achieve comma goals or completion of a project. Communicating is not face-to-face but occurs via electronic format.

Work/Life Balance: Creating a balance between achievement and enjoyment. Work can also refer to tasks that need to be completed in the household in addition to a formal place of employment.

Chapter 27
The Role of Leadership and Communication:
Re-Conceptualizing Graduate Instruction Online

Heather M. Rintoul
Nipissing University, Canada

ABSTRACT

This chapter explores concerns and challenges associated with the transition to online graduate instruction from the traditional face-to-face format. The author discusses several catalysts for the transition to virtual teaching; the ethics of being present; impediments to learning and communication online; and participant concerns. The chapter also considers online knowledge and meaning-making, online communities and associated uncertainties. Finally, considerations for leadership and communication moving forward are addressed.

INTRODUCTION

The pursuant exponential expansion of virtual instruction offers an appropriate opportunity to reflect about the effectiveness of this medium from a leadership and communication perspective as it compares to the traditional face-to-face experience. Conceptual in nature, in this chapter I examine the role of faculty as instructional leaders of graduate online teaching and learning. I first consider two significant pieces of the backstory leading to the implementation of online instruction. Next, I speak to concerns regarding the ethics of 'being present' in the graduate seminar tradition, specifically: instructor presence, interpersonal (social) presence, and cognitive presence while discussing some supplementary perceived impediments to authentic leadership, communication, and learning online. I then consider the (re)-conceptualising of online knowledge acquisition and meaning-making, understandings around the idea of communities and perceptions of relationships online, as well as on-going uncertainties about online instruction and learning. Finally, I envisage possible pathways for instructional leadership and communication moving forward in the virtual realm.

DOI: 10.4018/978-1-4666-9970-0.ch027

BACKGROUND

The Synergy of Two Catalysts

As economic difficulties related to the recent recession continue to be a challenging global phenomenon, universities in Ontario, Canada have not been exempt from associated financial woes. At the most basic level, financial resources have not kept pace with escalating expenditures, compelling universities to do substantially more with substantially less (Metcalfe, Fisher, Gingras, Jones, Rubenson, & Snee, 2010). The latest victim of diminishing fiscal resources appears to be a heretofore untouchable- the graduate seminar (of Masters and Doctoral programs). In recent years, venues at-a-distance have been on the increase as colleges and universities seek to broaden their student base and their financial bottom line by expanding student access to their programs (Dobbins, 2009). Serving these distant centres with traditional face-to-face graduate seminars, however, has necessarily incurred significant auxiliary expenses for institutions, for example: rental of off-site venues, travel expenses (hotel/meals/gasoline for faculty), and loss of considerable faculty work hours unavoidably spent in travel. As a consequence, in an effort to stem the financial bleeding, many universities initially thought to replace much (and in some cases, all) of their face-to-face graduate teaching with an on-line model (Chau, 2010). Was the purpose and rationale of the new technology-based on-line model for graduate teaching driven by an ever-strengthening economic component in that graduate education was being viewed as a standardized commodity, with keeping expenses in check emerging as a primary university goal (Power & Vaughan, 2010)? Would such a strategy represent a permanent divergence from the ideological and towards more pragmatic ends- that of servicing a university's bottom line (Braddock, Mahony, & Taylor, 2006)? If so, how could faculty reconcile the experience of on-line teaching and learning as authentic if academic freedom was subjugated to the vagaries of increasingly aggressive fiscal influences? In the short term, this conversion to online appeared to accomplish the desired economic goal in that it reined in faculty expenses (Rich, 2015). There was, however, an equally significant and perhaps unforeseen circumstance that was soon to enter the expenditures fray that would signal an unanticipated consequence.

Lifestyles today have become increasingly demanding and multifaceted. A key component of that complexity appears to rest with the explosion of interest in social media (Facebook, Twitter, and Instagram, for example) and the Internet. No longer tethered by telephone lines, a vast array of revolutionary cordless devices now offer the facility and flexibility to contact anyone from anywhere at any time. Interactive electronic devices and their ever-expanding resources permit instant access to the Internet, not only to keep in touch with others but to search and acquire information on a broad variety of topics: travel mapping, meal options, online purchasing, music, health care, and even the acquisition of a university/college degree. Indeed, almost anything anyone can dream up, can be searched and utilized, all from the comfort of home or, from any place, at any time. The limitless capacity of the electronic world as the leading interactive information highway of people, places, and things now seems as intrinsic to life as breathing, especially so for our younger generation (Dobbins, 2009), our 'digital natives' (Prensky, 2006), who have known only an intensifying cordless world- the one of sophisticated cell phones, progressive electronic devices, and seemingly unlimited data and information exchanges available via the Web, online and the Internet.

With the explosion of the virtual world, computer programs for teaching graduate and other coursework (for e.g. undergraduate massive open online courses, MOOC, Prensky, 2014) began to be widely accessible with students clamoring for a virtual learning experience (VLE) which, from their perspective, adapted more easily to their hectic lifestyles (Johnson, Stewart & Bachman, 2015). Initially, universities saw online learning as a two-pronged positive: a means to satisfy student demand for online instruction as well as an opportunity to reduce expenses associated with travelling faculty. Unfortunately, graduate online programs, for example, 'Elluminate' (synchronous) and 'Blackboard' (asynchronous) themselves come with considerable continuing expenditures. The programs are cost-significant to purchase initially, with on-going annual fees, and of necessity, the availability of specialized teams with technical expertise to upgrade the technology of the program in maintaining its current status, and to help faculty and students when online challenges manifest. While student maximums for face-to-face graduate seminars have risen, in many instances to an academic grouping of 30 or even 35, it has become apparent that online graduate instruction best supports a maximum of 20 individual participants; otherwise, managing the experience becomes unwieldy to the detriment of knowledge-building within the learning community (Rich, 2015). What was initially conceived as a viable option to satisfy much-needed university fiscal re-structuring (Braddock, et al, 2006) has arguably become another significant financial drain on university coffers (Rich, 2015).

THE GRADUATE TEACHING TRADITION: THE ETHICS OF BEING PRESENT

Instructional, Interpersonal, and Cognitive Presence: Do They Matter?

As leaders of learning, many instructional faculty leaders and facilitators of all graduate learning are struggling to make sense and to decipher the intricacies of the new online model. Chief among their concerns is instructional presence. How can faculty instructors, notwithstanding, effectively communicate ethical purpose and simultaneously

model an ethical environment for their online participants when they are not actually physically present with their students (Garrison, Anderson, & Archer, 2000; Rintoul, 2011)? Assuming that the main aspiration of graduate teaching continues to be the nurturing and support of graduate students in an authentic way, how can we construe this new online standard to achieve the stated goal? Where and who are our faculty models for conceptualizing and/or contextualizing content and for facilitating authentic interactive communication in the new online convention? Where are the faculty role models who set high standards and enforce the discipline needed to achieve these benchmarks when students are associating only with their online peers? Should online learners themselves be re-conceptualized within this new environment? Specifically, what criteria should be considered in this re-conceptualization and who should make this determination? Current faculty, mostly digital immigrants (Prensky, 2006), who struggle to navigate the new medium may themselves become the leader models for a new generation of graduate instructors. If so, the necessity and burden for faculty to 'get it right' for current students, as well as for present and future instructors alike, seems even more acute.

Those who teach graduate education have honed their craft by experiencing graduate education first as students, learning from and being guided by professor mentors as they, in turn, hypothesized and made meaning of their own graduate teaching. Customarily, it has been the task of faculty, as instructional leaders and facilitators, to model an ethical purpose, to develop new scholars to their full potential, and to authentically support each individual's connection to learning (Leonard & Rintoul, 2010; Metcalfe et al., 2010). This graduate model has historically been defined largely as face-to-face academic nurturing, with faculty and students interacting, often on a daily basis, as learners master the content and methods necessary to become the new trailblazers and intellectuals in their field. The graduate class itself, a significant cornerstone of this connection piece, has traditionally been conceptualized as a small aesthetic seminar of about 15 to 20 individuals engaged in the immediacy of intelligent, face-to-face conversational exchanges, scholarly discussions, lively debates and workshops, all in an ethical learning environment (Leonard & Rintoul, 2010). The face-to-face interaction model of both faculty and students has generally been considered largely successful within the stated aims and goals of graduate education, and as such has been a fundamental characteristic of graduate seminar instruction for decades, perhaps even centuries. This practice has been refined over time with considerable dedication and skill by each instructor to become the authentic learning experience each believes her/his present standard to be. With the transition to on-line graduate teaching and learning, however, some might speculate how and whether we can replicate genuine student/instructor rapport if we are sublimating what we currently understand as authentic pedagogy to the purpose and goal of (as yet unproven) financial viability.

With virtual instruction (VLE), there continues to be much talk about the new 'global village/community' with unlimited access to resources and individuals using the latest technological advancements and engaging in the social construction of information to enhance scholarly achievements (Hibbert & Rich, 2006; Li, 2009). But, what does this new community look like? We have always understood that the one constant of the traditional graduate model has included faculty and students physically together in a seminar room. Perversely, the current online model appears to be that of a solitary individual in front of a computer, often counties, countries, and even continents apart engaging in *some form* of self-directed learning. The phrase '*some form*' is significant because, as faculty, we have no way of truly understanding what *form* that self-direction takes. Tech-savvy graduate students are communicating and networking constantly it seems, skipping along the surface of one website to another, but valuable intellectual pursuits of an in-depth nature may not necessarily be part of that agenda. Darting impulsively from one website after another like hummingbirds sampling flowers may ultimately be counter-productive to the graduate experience by promoting a type of intellectual superficiality, an inability and unwillingness to concentrate (Flaherty, 2010). A virtual world rife with numerous jolts of astounding information bytes available in seconds does not appear to bode well for instructors attempting to engage participants in higher-level thinking, nor perhaps does it augur well for the patience and dedication required for reading academic tomes and thinking intensely about complex scholarly content. Even so, there are strong advocates of virtual instruction for 'digital natives' suggesting the banning of paper books at university altogether in favour of online technology (Prensky, 2011).

Many individuals may comfortably embrace self-directed learning and autonomy while others may seem adrift, anxious, and unable to experience quality education without the nurturing presence of the instructor. Neither is self-directed learning without its challenges. Although the instructor-centric model has changed, at least online, to a learner-centric view (Rosenberg, 2003), even those individuals who are comfortable with autonomous learning may require, from time to time, some degree of support, affirmation, and even re-direction. When the instructor is not physically present to guide and mentor, students who ostensibly appear to be contributing online, may be treating course content cursorily much like skimming websites or just responding to the online discussion without even bothering to read the preparatory documents. Faculty have long been aware that students enter graduate school with differing levels of expertise, ability and motivations. Without the presence of strong instructional leadership these discrepancies may be widening such that the triangle of instructor, learner, and course content may not be as intellectually vigorous with the current online paradigm as it is with the traditional face-to-face format wherein skilled instructors are available to assess, scaffold and re-direct as necessary. Further, how can we as graduate learner leaders and course facilitators be assured and trust that students are actually acquiring, reading, and engaging with the content of the prescribed course pack or text? Even more troubling, from an ethical perspective, how is it possible to guide online behaviour and guarantee the authenticity of online responses when we really do not know our graduate students or have a personal relationship with them?

To further compound the complexity of the problem, students are subscribing to online courses in record numbers (DeCosta, Berquist, & Holbeck, 2015) but their reasons for doing so, in many instances, may not necessarily be pedagogically sound. Even key courses described as 'degree required,' which initially were reserved for the traditional face-to-face format, are now commonly available online to allow access for the maximum number of students, culturally diverse, from a wide variety of locations, both nearby and at a distance. Although the reasons for enrolling might not be always pedagogically pure, the burgeoning number of students embracing the online format has perhaps served to strengthen the case that online is the desired learning format of students (DeCosta, et al., 2015). What is not clear is whether the perceived demands of students regarding course format should supercede the beliefs and considerations of experienced faculty, arguably a form of professional de-skilling. Nonetheless, online offerings are on the increase. Required courses available online typically have long waiting lists, sometimes necessitating a parallel course offering. Is there some way forward to manage the authenticity of the face-to-face teaching/learning traditional paradigm attendant with the new online learning model, a model which appeared, at least initially, to be so financially expedient and the preferred choice of students? To confound thinking even further, studies have revealed that face-to-face graduate modes of instruction scored significantly better on 2 of 3 measures of evaluation (see Ferguson

& Tryjankowski, 2009) as well as on preference, performance and pass rates for White and minority Master's students (Richardson, 2012).

Learning and training are not the same. Learning involves a process of translating information into knowledge, a very intimate and human activity, whereas training is a means to facilitate this pursuit (Rosenberg, 2003). The processes around managing and presenting course content has traditionally been the purview of faculty, but with no tutoring other than that associated with program practicalities, the urgency to make meaning of this new format and to render the experience a quality one for graduate learners have also become matters of on-going concern. Content itself is rather one-dimensional and flat but comes alive with on-going exchanges of discovery, questioning, interaction and debate. To merely offer content online as flat information (Malamed, 2009) seems antithetical to the graduate experience which historically has created dimension by challenging theory, urging us to examine our own beliefs and practices and thereby, through interactive discussion, put substance to that which is flat. Is it possible for faculty to nurture meta-cognitive thinking and put flesh on flat content from a distance? If so, how is this actuality to be accomplished? Are faculty presently satisfied that they are able to adequately provide an achievable interpersonal dimension to these 'flat' conversational threads online (Garrison, et al., 2000; Hauser, Paul, Bradley, & Jeffrey, 2012)? More importantly, how can faculty adjudicate such viability in a medium when we are not there in person to investigate and make a coherent and ultimately crucial determination?

Most learning builds on that which is known and slowly incorporates that which is unknown and unfamiliar (Malamed, 2009). It seems reasonable then that faculty, in preparing online graduate courses, quite naturally would begin with what they believe constitutes quality graduate education, an experience probably both comfortable and familiar, and '*somehow*' translate it to the new and relatively unknown online milieu. But some may question the wisdom of such a plan. To assume that the simplified understanding of one mode (face-to-face) may be transferable and even applicable to another (online) seems ingenuous and myopic at best, yet, what else is currently available, tested and successful? Although graduate investigation in particular, has tended to endorse and encourage self-directed inquiry, faculty were always present as buttressing assistance to facilitate and re-direct. There may be specific literacies, certain competencies, and abilities essential to comfortable online learning which would enable students to make the most of their electronic environment. Are graduate faculty confident that they have facility with these essential literacies and competencies for competent online learning and able to intercede effectively when appropriate and imperative? Without the scaffolding physical presence of the instructor, are isolated participants feeling able to safely negotiate the dynamics of the asynchronous platform in terms of meaning-making and knowledge-building (Kop, 2011)? If struggling students are not communicating their difficulties, how are we, as instructors-at-a-distance, able to know, intervene and mediate?

Online learning (and this includes graduate learning) is socially-constructed through the practicality of the social community or, as Hibbert and Rich (2006) identify –communities of practice, but the traditional supportive 'in-the-flesh' *relationship* component is absent online. Information shared online, by definition, lacks authentic interpersonal depth because participants are not physically present with each other. Many online contributors use the same 'personal paragraph' to share from one graduate course to the next, much like a desultory form letter summarizing their likes, dislikes, and current activities, with this superficial introductory paragraph somehow posturing as the initial stage of an 'authentic' interpersonal connection. When we are physically together, 'in-the-flesh' so to speak, interpersonal activities abound: visual cue exchanges, eye contact, perhaps dining/shopping together, chatting

about the trivialities of daily life, sharing and exchanging beliefs, ideas, and innermost thoughts. It is this intensely intimate interactive interchange that begins to weave our personal 'fabric' with that of another, shaping and crafting a kind of 'interpersonal quilt' we can describe as a *relationship*. When an interpersonal relationship develops and becomes established, meaning-making becomes authentic, caring, and more in-depth, rather than casual and perfunctory (Noddings, 2012).

Similarly, there is the possibility too, that online graduate discussions can become mere assemblages of existing information, a rather cursory activity, rather than processes of knowledge-building in a thought-filled meta-cognitive way that being physically present with others seems to actively inspire. Similarly, there is on-going concern about the perceived tone of online conversations. Considerable skill is required in crafting online commentary that stimulates cutting edge thinking and dynamic conversational dialogue but does not read to others as abrasive, abrupt and even rude. In face-to-face conversation, tone of voice is a powerful motivator, but is absent with online. Electronic words are inanimate with no apparent soul until a meaning, rightly or wrongly, is placed upon them by another. Rather than risk being accused of online rudeness or even bullying and harassment, participants may 'play it safe' and not push the conversational boundaries, thus eliminating the possibility of engaging in higher level reasoning and learning. Faculty can pose questions that encourage meta-cognitive thinking and debate but the impersonal nature of online coupled with inherent time delays and fears of being labelled a bully (Clark, Werth & Ahten, 2012) may relegate the potential for profound discussion to languish among the myriad of other unremarkable posting dialogues. On the other hand, when the potential interaction has at its foundation a personal affiliation and vested interest, such as is commonly found in face-to-face communication, the presence of strong interpersonal relationship capital is perhaps much more likely to inspire authentic high level conversational engagement (Major, 2014).

Student-centred learning is not new, but in an online paradigm students are different regionally, demographically, ethnically, as well as in motivation and expectations. In face-to-face learning graduate participants have to make a significant commitment: driving to the venue, setting aside time to attend, preparing academically by pre-reading, perhaps engaging individuals to care for their children, and a myriad of other obligations. Online graduate learning can be 'attended' at a level of marginal preparation and contribution-a participant may be simply fulfilling minimal program requirements with course credit as the primary goal. As a consequence, there is a legitimate concern that online courses may be increasingly limited to cognitive learning, just the acquisition of knowledge/credentials- a form of reductionism. Other learner participants who really want authentic meta-cognitive interaction may be anxious (Hauser, et al, 2012), feeling that their course is being 'watered down' by the lack of dynamic and stimulating online graduate-level discussions. If graduate online learning is conceived as an interactive process, a convergence of inquiry, debate and discovery with 'present' individuals forming a learning community, what, then, ensues if one or more individuals fail to attend online in a timely manner? Starratt (2005) proposes an expectation of interdependence on each other, such that if one partner is not fully engaged "the mutuality of presence is diminished" (p.403). This interdependence underscores that online courses are *not* usually conceived as an isolationist experience, but rather as an interactive community of learning and knowledge-building (Hibbert & Rich, 2006; Nicol, Minty, & Sinclair, 2003). The participant may be sitting alone but any contribution, like a strand of a double helix, is inextricably generated as part of the knowledge-building collective (Garrison, Anderson, & Archer, 2010). Graduate online group work though does not necessarily appear to be a satisfactory answer for increasing

communication as participants may feel there are fewer channels for communication than available with face-to-face (Smith, Sorensen, Gump, Caris, Heindel & Martinez, 2011).

Online (graduate) exchanges are typically featured as non-spontaneous dialogue and interactive responses with individuals able to carefully contemplate and edit their involvement before posting online as they attempt to move the conversation forward. Once a posting is available online, it is ready to be interpreted, perhaps differently by each individual reader, with the originating author having little occasion for elucidation unless queried directly. Likewise, the graduate instructor has no immediate opportunity to pose clarifying questions until some misdirection becomes obvious. All posting, reading, and questioning by participants takes considerable time, with responses and any remediation, especially in the instance of perceived online harassment, delaying the consolidation of learning and knowledge-building within the online graduate community even further. Additionally, are individual participants able, and perhaps more importantly, *should* they be willing to place their trust with unknown members of their online learning cohort?

Conceptualizing Knowledge-Acquisition and Meaning-Making

Traditionally, universities and their libraries were repositories of scholarly collections, contributed by learned men and women. Tangible works were gathered over decades and centuries since the beginning of the written and printed word: books, periodicals, newsprint, film, documents, microfiche and the like, were accessed by students, researchers and scholars physically on site browsing, searching and gathering information from material available in the library stacks. Most of this early information along with the most recent is now readily available online as university libraries have also embraced the virtual world by acquiring their current (and even past) collections making them available for learner acquisition online as virtual electronic 'paper'. As a natural consequence of electronic media and internet advances in the virtual world, access to the electronic 'information highway' requires only a few taps of an electronic device that heretofore required hours, days, weeks and sometimes months to search, procure, and print information from paper-based libraries. In the current academic environment, seminar participants no longer need to be physically present on campus to 'browse' the library stacks. They can do their browsing virtually with an electronic device and an Internet connection from places as far-flung as world travel and connectivity will allow.

Online Environment Apprehension: Potential Impediments to Authentic Communication and Learning

Were faculty leaders commonly consulted when computer-supported online programs were in the design phase? If so, who were they? There appears to be no discussion around these technically generic inventions regarding any consideration for pedagogical soundness and instructional individuation, nor is there necessarily any alignment with current academic programming and practices. These feats of technical origination are simply created by those with specialised electronic expertise to be adapted as, arguably, a means of educational convenience, purchased at considerable expense, and made available to faculty as 'fait accompli' programs ready-for-use. Universities can then claim they are up-to-date and in line with current educational experiences as they proudly showcase these costly virtual accommodations. Any personalization of the online template must be undertaken by faculty instructors, who perhaps have little or no facility with the practicalities of the online paradigm. With any new instructional instrument, especially those that are computer-based, there is considerable new up-front and in-progress learning necessary to acquire the technical competency for navigating

and trouble-shooting the online program and its latest revisions, as well as the online medium itself. Skill acquisition and a high level of comfort are essential for faculty whom students immediately consult as their 'technical' expert and leader when electronic issues manifest. Any failure by faculty to resolve electronic difficulties promptly has immediate negative implications for the smooth progression of learning within the practising learning community. Regrettably, when on-going electronic issues become the focus, all leadership, communication, and learning are negatively affected and in-course knowledge-building quickly falls into disarray or is truncated completely until the issue is resolved. Faculty and students are no longer physically in the same room to attempt a temporary solution together, nor is technical staff always immediately available. This frustrating and interruptive gap in the pragmatic aspects of the virtual learning instrument further complicates the resolution of any but the most elementary of electronic glitches.

As a tentative step into these uncharted online waters, faculty, at first, often utilized a combination of synchronous and asynchronous learning strategies. Synchronous learning (for example, using Skype or Elluminate) more closely models the traditional face-to-face experience, in that, students are required to log on and participate at the same time as their cohort members. One difficulty quickly became apparent. Although online connectivity reduced geographical barriers, location actually *does* matter in synchronous learning. Time differences among remote locations around the world meant that some students had to log on in the middle of the night or, as is common for adult student income earners, during an inopportune time of their workday, just to be in the 'virtual class' with their cohort. In an attempt to alleviate this challenge, synchronous attendance with the instructor was allowed at different times, but regrettably, the goal of all participants attending together was rarely achievable. As a consequence, synchronous learning was/is not always the best option. Enter the asynchronous learning environment whereby students logged in at times that were most convenient for them.

Leaping into the Abyss: Troubling Practicalities and Possibilities

With the asynchronous on-line experience, it seems reasonable to speculate too, about who is teaching and what is being taught/learned online when graduate faculty are not a constant presence to guide and mentor. The context for ethical communication and authenticity appears to have changed with the on-line environment perhaps, because unlike much of face-to-face teaching and learning interaction, online communication is time-delayed with deliberately-planned 'written' dialogue and non-spontaneous interaction. As a corollary, faculty may speculate about who is actually doing the learning? Are graduate students actually who they say they are and how can faculty verify that course work is being completed by the registered student? This latter concern seems especially troubling.

When first introduced, the use of online instruction was left to individual faculty choice, many feeling apprehensive about purpose and content, as well as the teaching and learning processes of this relatively untested electronic medium. Adjunct graduate instructors were the most frequent consumers of the online paradigm, while many site-based university faculty resisted online instruction, mentioning course quality as a major concern. The university, initially placing their faith in online as a means to address both financial strife and student interest; and students, enrolling in significant numbers (Johnson, et al., 2015), seemed to be conspiring against the traditional norm (and excellence perhaps?) of graduate education. Face-to-face graduate seminars began to be cancelled for want of sufficient enrolment, signalling a necessary shift in thinking by apprehensive mainstream faculty who reluctantly began to sample the online prototype (Rintoul,

2011). For their part, graduate students wholeheartedly embraced the ability to learn from the comfort of their home, or indeed, from anywhere in the world, at any time (Parry, 2010). Rejoicing in the freedom and flexibility this mode of learning afforded, student enrolment ballooned exponentially (DeCosta, et al., 2015).

There remain, however, many reservations and uncertainties to contemplate, consider and confront. As efficiency is gained (and this has by no means been confirmed), have interpersonal connections and instructional practices as we know them been subjugated by online standardization? Graduate students continue to endorse the virtual learning environment, ranking it enthusiastically as their favourite mode of learning (Johnson, et al., 2015), but numerous questions remain. A significant number of students clamoring enthusiastically for online graduate courses have themselves never experienced instruction via a face-to-face model (Rintoul, 2011). One might query whether those who have only been exposed to one delivery mode, that of online, are even qualified to make such arbitration? Should faculty concerns about the authenticity of online instruction be trumped by student demands for ease of access to virtual course instruction? Do these changes to satisfy format demands from students with scant regard for the quality of courses represent a trend toward de-skilling of university instructors (Flaherty, 2010)? Further, is this change, although seemingly significant, merely an essential re-tooling to keep abreast of current trends and practices or could there be something much more fundamental happening to contemporary instructional practices?

The pragmatics of the new technology, perhaps of necessity, has been put in place first, but little else, as we leap blindly into the abyss of the virtual world. While many have embraced the virtual teaching/learning milieu (Prensky, 2014), others may cautiously argue that there has not been enough time to appreciate, comprehend and assess the nuances of the on-line graduate experience. Is this new milieu redefining interactive behaviour in seminars- and if so, in what way(s)? Does the explanation lie with the re-design of graduate courses or is it our understandings that must change- or both? How then should online courses to be crafted, led and assessed? Should the parameters for interaction and appraisal of participants' work be somehow parachuted from the face-to-face experience (Topper, 2007) or is it now appropriate and necessary to initiate new philosophies and practices styled specifically for the new literacy of electronic instruction and online interaction? What are these new philosophies and new practices and who should undertake these significant decisions?

Attempting to manage the technology of online, while simultaneously fostering a fulfilling and appropriate learning experience for individuals of unknown personas, has generated significant trepidation and a litany of concerns for faculty (Rintoul, 2011). Some might question whether the allure of innovative technology mechanisms itself might interfere and obfuscate the true reason for schooling- learning to think. In the transition to technology-based online graduate seminars, faculty have strong resources available for university-sponsored programs such as 'Blackboard,' but that assistance, although necessary and helpful, is more of a pragmatic and practical nature dealing with the functioning and navigating of the online milieu. Resources do not offer, nor are they intended as, assistance regarding (re) conceptualizing and (re)contextualizing content, re-considering online leadership/communication, and perhaps most significantly, appraisal practices appropriate for the new literacy of online learning. Preliminary discussions comparing face-to-face and online graduate course evaluations have begun (e.g. see Berk, 2013; Topper 2007) but certainly more qualitative study would be helpful. Many faculty remain unclear and unconvinced about the viability of virtual learning and may not feel predisposed to undertake these momentous decisions, however, there appears to be no one else with the scholarly acumen to do so.

RECOMMENDATIONS

Trending Uncertainties: Re-Conceptualizing and Re-Designing – Some Considerations for Moving Forward

The new digital literacy for our learning society has emerged as an essential and energizing aspect of our social phenomenology- both practical and intellectual (Florica, Mozelius, Shabalina, Balan, Malliarakis, Miller & Jones, 2013; Pendlebury & Enslin, 2000). The virtual door has been opened wide and wholly embraced universally as we move forward at lightning speed (with)in the virtual realm. Perhaps it is now expedient to embrace this new paradigm as an innovative stimulating adventure with the capacity to support a quality, yet discrete, experience that can be as meaningful and satisfying for both leaders and learners as the more traditional modes of discovery and interaction, IF prepared thoughtfully and administered well (Hauser et al., 2012). Instructing graduate faculty must find a way to comfortably navigate the new medium and uncover imaginative techniques to offer students the stimulating and scholarly graduate course experience they have come to expect, all while continuing to maintain high standards. As lifelong learner leaders, the path for graduate instructors to accomplish this task will, of necessity, be fraught with uncertainty, trepidation, trials, successes, and even disheartening setbacks. The successful instructional learner leader must now not only understand course content and the nuances of the ever-changing technology, but also comprehend the synergy of these two aspects working together to support authentic learning opportunities (Karchmer-Klein & Shinas, 2012; Moten, Fitterer, Brazier, Leonard, & Brown, 2013) for a vast array of participants with disparate experiences and motivation, from diverse cultures, beliefs, and locales.

The online dynamic is dissimilar from face-to-face in many key aspects as I have noted throughout this chapter yet faculty goals to achieve an authentic learning experience within a quality learning environment must continue (Armstrong & Thornton, 2012). Displaying ethical sensitivity and moral erudition together with care-filled reasoning, graduate instructors, in my view, must navigate a path that facilitates a re-conceptualization of online as a contemporary and provocative scholarly and social community in a medium for progressive communication and learning, not instead of face-to-face learning, but as another viable mode of graduate knowledge-building and interaction. I suggest that this path must of necessity include online conversation with lively discussion as a significant component facilitating discovery, learning and erudition. The key to robust student engagement and spirited participation online may well lie in the structure (Prensky, 2005/2006) and precision of the details: the thoroughness and clarity of course design outlining the purpose(s) and outcomes of learning and collaborative conversational interaction, together with timely, detailed, and thoughtful instructor feedback. Such strategies are not new as these particulars were, and continue to be, the benchmark of a quality face-to-face graduate experience. Unlike undergraduate teaching, most graduate seminars have long ago moved from lecturing to a conversation-driven experience, therefore, the transition to online, arguably, may be more seamlessly achieved. Another favorable aspect moving forward is that graduate students, for the most part, seem wholly engaged with virtual learning and the online environment as a key component of daily learning and communication.

A new dimension with innovative abbreviated language has permeated casual online communication, for example, the blurring of words, numerals, letters and symbols to convey meaning and emotions (the latter pictorials are termed 'emoticons') and this language has seeped into graduate online participation. There are many of these letter/symbol mixes but even their con-

notations are not universally consistent, probably because this new language is still in its infancy- for example 'lol' at last count (August, 2015) has 111 suggested meanings on Google. Although some may consider this online 'street' language the wave of the future, as even now it occasionally finds its way into scholarly papers submitted for grading, graduate instructors may be concerned that students' competence with traditional writing and grammatical structure to convey meaning clearly and eloquently is on the wane. There is a plethora of troubling examples: the use of the pronoun 'this' without a discernable antecedent, the use of 'then' for 'than,' to offer but two. While these grammatical errors of structure and syntax may, from a cursory view, seem relatively minor, complexity and complication occurs when intended meaning becomes obscured through lack of precision in writing. Sentence comprehension, at the graduate level certainly, should not be reduced to a guessing game of 'what's the intended meaning'? As a consequence, it may be that graduate faculty will feel it necessary to re-imagine online seminar conversation as an exercise in promoting and strengthening writing skills through a variety of purposive and purposeful writing experiences.

In traditional graduate instruction/learning, the rhythm of a dynamic and vibrant energy among cohort members sitting across from one another in seminar passionately and spontaneously debating an issue verbally has been the standard of excellence by which all graduate teaching has been compared. Such free-wheeling, real time interactive conversation suddenly seems to have gone the way of the dinosaur, leaving in its wake an online literacy model of physical isolation and potential ambiguity as participants sit solitarily struggling to make meaning of the written word, both their own and that of others. This new literacy appears to be socially constructed and conceptualized as an on-going written dialogue of ideas and knowledge-building that may not always read or flow well, subject to the vagaries of posting times as well as the whims and commitment of seminar participants, if they even seize the online conversational mantle at all!

Alternatively, when participants take the time to contemplate and craft their responses carefully, online collaboration can lead to complex knowledge-building by these virtual communities (Hibbert & Rich, 2006). In consideration of this new online reality, it seems even more imperative that students acquire and demonstrate effective writing and thinking skills to convey their viewpoints, philosophies, and responses both concisely and clearly. Taking extra care with the composition of written posts may help alleviate the necessity for endless queries regarding intended meaning as well as accusations of bullying (Clark, at al., 2012; Park, Na, & Kim, 2014). The latter is a very real concern as individuals read and place their own interpretation on written posts, with those opaquely constructed being especially vulnerable to misunderstanding. Interpersonal skills have taken on a new meaning as online participants struggle to write their conversational postings intelligently and scholarly yet in a sensitive interpersonally-mindful way. Consistent and helpful instructor feedback on writing mechanics, both scholarly and ethically sensitive, as well as suggestions of books offering advice on grammatical structure and syntax may be initial steps to assist individuals in their quest to become better online writers. The challenge for instructors may lie in our ability, or lack thereof, to inspire participants to take extra care with their writing *before* posting, especially when we are not physically present to assist, support, and re-direct.

Online structure seems to be of critical importance (Hauser, et al, 2012). To promote care-filled writing and as a catalyst to robust engagement, instructors may deem it necessary to be more prescriptive and to apply certain parameters to regulate the frequency and length of online responses. The goal of such strategies is not only for participants to show they are attempting to move the dialogue and debate forward

by posting at least a minimum number of times within a sessional time frame, but also to prevent never-ending quantities of 'empty' text within each post. The latter tends rather quickly to disengage reader-participants. Posting individuals will be required to 'say what they need to say' succinctly and unambiguously within the given parameters, with the course syllabus clearly and succinctly outlining the requirements. Of necessity, participants will have to learn to edit their work carefully to improve their 'conversational' writing competencies in order to avoid negative feedback (clarity and intended meaning issues) from their cohort members and, of consequence, a lower participation grade from the instructor. Control over posting, in some respects, may seem antithetical to the free-flowing process of typical face-to-face graduate student interactive involvement, but for online participation, doing so may assist in prompting the highly-valued reciprocity that is associated with, and is intensely valued in, spontaneous oral conversation. After all, online postings are part of a continuing social dialogue, not meant to simply remain inert and nebulous but rather to actively supplement meaning and to engage the learner in the facilitation of thinking and discovery; and to shape understandings as individuals react and counter, join and riposte, expanding theory and the knowledge base of the practicing learning community. To facilitate this atmosphere of continuing dialogue, it may be appropriate that sessions will close at the end of a prescribed time frame such that participation cannot be 'made up.' Participants have been known to forget about posting sessions and then email the instructor their posts in a non-contextualized electronic lump (Rintoul, 2011). Clearly, the interaction aspect of postings should be considered a significant part of the participation grade and directly stated as such in the course outline. Even though participants are not actually together in the same physical space, online dialogue is an inherent part of the social learning and knowledge-building experience of the online graduate community.

In an effort to offer a more (w)holistic experience and to supplement what appears to be a rather solitary graduate experience, it seems appropriate to consider team-prepared activities and presentations online such as interactive workshops, critiques of individual short writing assignments online (instructor graded), as well as the availability of an ungraded online Lounge or Bistro where individuals can 'chat' about topics not necessarily related to course materials or to expand on a theme that particularly resonated with them in the graded and posting dialogue of the course. The ungraded portions are always available for all to utilize as little or as often as time and inclination permit. These team-prescribed assignments, both arbitrary (graded) and the ungraded Lounge or Bistro may encourage more interpersonal familiarity, thus helping to promote stronger interactive connections which generally may serve to enhance the comfort of the online milieu while easing some misgivings and trust among cohort members. It is worth noting, though, that there is often less satisfaction associated with online group work and its fewer channels of communication to resolve logistical difficulties than group work done in a face-to-face setting (Smith, et al., 2011).

FUTURE RESEARCH DIRECTIONS

It may be that graduate instruction has moved from the philosophical and scholarly and toward the more practical and pragmatic with acquisition of graduate degrees for individuals and financial viability for institutions as the main goals. Alternatively, it may be that virtual learning is at the threshold of a revolution in the phenomenology of knowledge-building. Certainly, online graduate education is 'of the moment' and the wave of the future. Opportunities for future research and consideration of this dynamic and innovative paradigm might include more in-depth study of the evaluation and content viability of online graduate programs as contextualized by both instructional faculty and our graduate participants.

CONCLUSION

Graduate faculty, especially digital immigrants, may be struggling to keep abreast of the exploding advances of the virtual universe and this whole process may at times feel a bit messy, clumsy and laborious but, in many respects, a slower pace allows for careful re-thinking, re-tooling and refinement of strategies moving forward- what works, what doesn't and especially, what needs to be re-conceptualized, re-contextualized and how stated goals might be achieved. I would argue that ultimately, it remains the role of faculty, the learner leaders, as the final guardians of scholarly instruction, communication and course facilitation to ensure that online graduate teaching still inspires meta-cognitive thinking in an intellectually stimulating environment that enriches and strengthens graduate learning and knowledge-building of our burgeoning future scholars in their various fields of study.

REFERENCES

Armstrong, A., & Thornton, N. (2012). Incorporating Brookfield's discussion techniques synchronously into asynchronous online courses. *The Quarterly Review of Distance Education*, *13*(1), 1–9.

Berk, R. (2013). Face-to-face versus online course evaluations: A 'consumer's guide' to seven strategies. *Journal of Online Teaching and Learning*, *9*(1), 140–148.

Braddock, R., Mahony, P., & Taylor, P. (2006). Globalisation, commercialism, managerialism and internationalisation. *International Journal of Learning*, *13*(8), 61–67.

Chau, P. (2010). Online higher education commodity. *Journal of Computing in Higher Education*, *22*(3), 177–191. doi:10.1007/s12528-010-9039-y

Clark, C., Werth, L., & Ahten, S. (2012, July/August). Cyberbullying and incivility in the online learning environment, Part I: Addressing faculty and student perceptions. *Nursing Educator*, *37*(4), 150–156. doi:10.1097/NNE.0b013e31825a87e5 PMID:22688872

DeCosta, M., Berquist, E., & Holbeck, R. (2015, July). A desire for growth: Online full-time faculty's perception of evaluation processes. *The Journal of Educators Online*, *13*(2), 73–102.

Dobbins, K. (2009). Feeding innovation with learning lunches: Contextualising academic innovation in higher education. *Journal of Further and Higher Education*, *33*(4), 411–422. doi:10.1080/03098770903272495

Ferguson, J., & Tryjankowski, A. (2009, August). Online versus face to face learning: Looking at modes of instruction in Master's level courses. *Journal of Further and Higher Education*, *33*(3), 219–228. doi:10.1080/03098770903026149

Flaherty, J. (2010 October/November). Bridging the digital divide: A non-technical approach to the use of new technology in post-secondary teaching and learning. *Academic Matters Journal of Higher Education*, 21-26.

Florica, T., Mozelius, P., Shabalina, O., Balan, O., Malliarakis, C., Miller, C., & Jones, P. (2013). An international approach to creative pedagogy and students' preferences of interactive media. *Proceedings of the International Conference on E-Learning*, 479- 487.

Garrison, D., Anderson, T., & Archer, W. (2000). Critical inquiry in a text-based environment: Computer conferencing in higher education. *The Internet and Higher Education*, *2*(2-3), 87–105. doi:10.1016/S1096-7516(00)00016-6

Garrison, D., Anderson, T., & Archer, W. (2010). The first decade of the community of inquiry framework: A retrospective. *The Internet and Higher Education*, *13*(1/2), 5–9. doi:10.1016/j.iheduc.2009.10.003

Hauser, R., Paul, R., Bradley, J., & Jeffrey, L. (2012). Computer self-efficacy, anxiety and learning in online versus face to face medium. *Journal of Information Technology Education*, *11*, 141–154.

Hibbert, K., & Rich, S. (2006). Virtual communities of practice. In J. Weiss, J. Hunsinger, & J. Trifonas (Eds.), *The international handbook of virtual learning environments* (pp. 563–579). The Netherlands: Springer. doi:10.1007/978-1-4020-3803-7_22

Johnson, R., Stewart, C., & Bachman, C. (2015, August). What drives students to complete online courses? What drives faculty to teach online? Validating a measure of motivation orientation in university students and faculty. *Interactive Learning Environments*, *23*(4), 528–543. doi:10.1080/10494820.2013.788037

Kop, R. (2011). The challenges to connectivist learning on open online networks: Learning experiences during a massive open online course. *International Review of Research in Open and Distance Learning*, *12*(3), 19–37.

Leonard, P., & Rintoul, H. (2010). An international collaboration: Examining graduate educational leadership in Louisiana and Ontario. In A. Normore (Ed.), *Advances in educational administration, 11. Global perspectives on educational leadership reform: The development and preparation of leaders of learning and learners of leadership* (pp. 301–321). Emerald Group Publishing Limited. doi:10.1108/S1479-3660(2010)0000011018

Li, Q. (2009). Knowledge building in an online environment: A design-based research study. *Journal of Educational Technology Systems, 37*(2), 195–216. doi:10.2190/ET.37.2.f

Major, W. (2014, Fall). Contagion in the classroom: The need for physical and emotional connectedness for deep learning classrooms offering social experience. *Liberal Education, 100*(4), 66–69.

Malamed, C. (2009). *10 ways to organize instructional content.* E-Learning podcast 2.0.

Metcalfe, A., Fisher, D., Gingras, Y., Jones, G., Rubenson, K., & Snee, I. (2010 October/November). How influential are faculty today? Responses from the Canadian Professorate. *Academic Matters Journal of Higher Education*, 16-20.

Moten, J., Fitterer, A., Brazier, E., Leonard, J., & Brown, A. (2013). Examining online college cyber cheating methods and preventative measures. *The Electronic Journal of E-Learning, 11*(2), 139–146.

Nicol, D., Minty, I., & Sinclair, C. (2003). The social dimensions of online learning. *Innovations in Education and Teaching International, 40*(3), 270–280. doi:10.1080/1470329032000103807

Noddings, N. (2012). *Philosophy of education* (3rd ed.). Boulder, CO: Westview Press.

Park, S., Na, E., & Kim, E. (2014, July). The relationship between online activities, netiquette and cyberbullying. *Children and Youth Services Review, 42*, 74–81. doi:10.1016/j.childyouth.2014.04.002

Parry, M. (2010). Tomorrow's college. *Chronicle of Higher Learning, 57*(11), 84–86.

Pendlebury, S., & Enslin, P. (2000). Lifelong learning for a new society. In J. Field & M. Leicester (Eds.), *Lifelong learning: Education across the lifespan* (pp. 149–157). New York: Routledge Falmer.

Power, M., & Vaughan, N. (2010). Redesigning online learning for international graduate seminar delivery. *Journal of Distance Education, 24*(2), 19–38.

Prensky, M. (2005 December. (2006, January). Listen to the natives. *Educational Leadership, 63*(4), 8–13.

Prensky, M. (2011). In the 21st century university, let's ban (paper) books. *The Chronicle of Higher Education, 58*(13), 309.

Prensky, M. (2014, January/February). Innovation experiementation and courage in the education of students for the future. *Educational Technology, 54*(1), 64.

Rich, S. (2015, May 27). *Personal email communication.* Associate Vice President, (Academic). Nipissing University, Ontario Canada.

Richardson, J. (2012). Face to face versus online tuition: Preference, performance and pass rates in White and ethnic minority students. *British Journal of Educational Technology, 43*(1), 17–27. doi:10.1111/j.1467-8535.2010.01147.x

Rintoul, H. (2011). *Transforming educational practices. The online graduate experience: Concerns, challenges and dilemmas.* Paper presented at the annual meeting of the Center for the Study of Leadership and Ethics in Education, Victoria, Canada.

Rosenberg, M. (2003, March). Redefining e-learning. *Performance Improvement, 42*(3), 38–41. doi:10.1002/pfi.4930420307

Smith, G., Sorensen, C., Gump, A., Heindel, A., Caris, M., & Martinez, C. (2011, March). Over-coming student resistance to group work: Online versus face to face. *The Internet and Higher Education, 14*(2), 121–128. doi:10.1016/j.iheduc.2010.09.005

Starratt, R. (2005). Cultivating the moral character of learning and teaching: A neglected dimensions of educational leadership. *School Leadership & Management, 25*(4), 399–411. doi:10.1080/13634230500197272

Topper, A. (2007, December). Are they the same? Comparing the instructional quality of online and face-to-face graduate education courses. *Assessment & Evaluation in Higher Education, 32*(6), 681–691. doi:10.1080/02602930601117233

ADDITIONAL READING

Benton, S., & Cashin, W. (2012). *Student ratings of teaching: A summary of research and literature*. Manhattan, KS: The IDEA Center.

Berk, R. (2010). The secret to the 'best' ratings from any evaluation scale. *Journal of Faculty Development, 24*(1), 37–39.

Del Barrio-Garcia, S., Arquero, J., & Romero-Frias, E. (2015, July). Personal learning environments acceptance model: The role of need for recognition, e-learning satisfactions and students' perceptions. *Journal of Educational Technology & Society, 18*(3), 129–141.

Rothman, T., Romeo, L., Brennan, M., & Mitchell, D. (2011). Criteria for assessing student satisfaction with online courses. *International Journal for e-Learning Security, 1*(1-2), 27-32.

Taylor, P., Parker, K., Lenhart, A., & Moore, K. (2011). *The digital revolution and higher education*. Washington, D.C: Pew Internet & American Life Project.

KEY TERMS AND DEFINITIONS

Asynchronous Program: A program whereby participants attend online at different times, e.g. Blackboard.

Digital Immigrant: A person who became familiar with computers as a young adult or later in life.

Digital Native: A person who has been familiar with computers, the Internet, and other digital technology from a very young age.

E-Learning: Learning conducted via electronic media, typically on the Internet.

Graduate Programs: These programs include both Masters and Doctoral seminars.

MOOC: Massive open online courses.

Self-Directed Learning: Each individual takes responsibility and accountability for his/her own learning.Synchronous Program: A program facilitating all participants attending face-to-face together online at the same time, e.g. Elluminate, Skype.

Virtual Learning Environment: Web-based platform for the digital aspects of course study.

Chapter 28
CAMES:
An Approach to Project Management Based on Action Research and the Ideal Speech Situation

Peter Smith
University of Liverpool, UK

Olaf Cames
University of Liverpool, UK

ABSTRACT

The majority of IT Projects are not successful and fail for non-technical reasons, despite the fact that numerous project management methodologies exist in the marketplace and are now in common use in organisations. As the CHAOS report from Standish Group documents, this remains an important and current issue (Dominguez, 2009; The Standish Group International Inc., 2013). The fact is that for more than 20 years the majority of IT projects have failed; largely as a result of human factors and communication issues. This leads to enormous economic issues for organisations in the public and private sector. This chapter proposes a new approach to project management which addresses the human factor and issues of communication. The proposed approach is novel and applies principles drawn from philosophy and action research to produce an approach which has the potential to radically change the way in which projects are managed. The approach is discussed in terms of practice and the academic literature and is applied to two project simulations.

INTRODUCTION

Current project management methods are based upon predefined best-practices and a predetermined understanding of an enterprise's management information system. They will usually represent project management as a simple,

straightforward linear problem and as a series of events, which can be represented and modelled in a Gantt chart, or within a software package. The Standish Group (2013) report a slight increase in projects being considered successful, and attribute this to a more fine grained, non-linear solution approach; considering a multiplicity

DOI: 10.4018/978-1-4666-9970-0.ch028

of success factors, which are linked in complex dynamic and networked way. This is contrary to most methods which consider the golden triangle of triple constraints of time, cost and quality to be the predominant success criteria. This chapter will further explore the possibility of considering the rich complexity and multiplicity of project management as a nonlinear problem.

The proposal presented here is rooted in philosophy and sets out to use the concept of the "ideal speech situation" as proposed by Habermas (1990, 2002, 2014). Habermas argued that an ideal speech situation is found when communication between individuals is governed by basic, implied rules. In an ideal speech situation, participants are able to evaluate each other's assertions solely on the basis of reason and evidence in an atmosphere completely free of any non-rational "coercive" influences, including both physical and psychological coercion. Furthermore, all participants are motivated solely by the desire to obtain a rational consensus. The "ideal speech" situation operates in an ideal world, and sets a series or rules for communication between people. The approach proposed within this chapter sets out to use these rules to enhance and improve communication within the context of project management, and to recognise and act on any departures from these rules.

The rationale for this new approach is that current best practice, expressed in modern project management methodologies does not handle the "wicked problems" which are often caused by humans during the management of projects. A "wicked problem" is one which is difficult or even impossible to solve, as a result of complex, incomplete, contradictory, and dynamic requirements, and often as a result of human factors. The phrase "wicked problem" was introduced in 1967 by Churchman (1967). Handling "wicked problems" is not part of the formal education or training of project managers. This results in the constant re-application of procedures and strategies which have been shown time and again to fail, which also prolongs the number of failing or challenged projects.

BACKGROUND

This chapter presents an alternative approach to project management, named CAMES (Corporate Action Methodology for Enterprise Systems). CAMES offers project managers an alternative approach to managing complex projects and decision making. It starts from the premise that the really important issues of project management lie within the human factors domain; that projects fail because of issues of communication, politics and emotion.

Projects run into problems because of how people act, how they feel about the project and the way it is progressing; and because of what they say (or don't say) to other team members. How often have we seen emotion enter the arena of project implementation, with team members debating and arguing issues which on reflection, in the cooler light of day, seem trivial? Yet how often have we seen such emotionally charged conversations take the project to a place of no return, to the edge of chaos, and to a point where the project partners can no longer work together? The CAMES approach sets out to recognise and flag up the early signs of such emotionally charged communication, using simple conversational analysis to recognise when danger approaches. It will then highlight these issues to the project manager, at an early stage while there is still time to intervene, change direction and "save" the project. The proposed system will offer the project team an online environment which supports all project communication, monitors that communication and, in simple terms, "measures" the "heat" in project communications.

LITERATURE REVIEW

The purpose of this section is to critique current academic and practitioner perspectives on project management related issues, and methods and reasons for project failure, particularly with regard to human factors. The review covers the issues surrounding linear and non-linear methods of project management, and also discusses the principle of Habermas which lie behind the conceptual framework, and quantum computing which is the chosen technology for implementing the system and which provides the massive computational power needed to address these complex issues.

Current project management methods are based upon pre-defined notions of best practice, pre-determined understandings of management systems (Dillard & Yuthas, 2006) and they tend to represent project management as a simplified linear problem (Curlee & Gordon, 2010). The Standish Group report a slight increase in projects being considered successful, and attribute this to a more fine grained, non-linear solution approach considering a multiplicity of success factors (Standish Group International Inc., 2013). This is contrary to most methods which consider the golden triangle of triple constraints of time, cost and quality to be the predominant success criteria (Cicmil et al., 2009).

Most project management methods are entirely process driven (Curlee & Gordon, 2010) and consider only a limited set of factors. But real project management is not as simple as this. The authors are both experienced project managers, and have observed the success and failure of many projects over the years. Reflecting on these experiences has made them realise that the majority of projects fail for non-technical reasons. Rather, the failure of projects is often a result of:

- **Political Factors:** Staff working on the projects have their own political agendas. These may relate to their own organisa-

tional objectives, or they may relate simply to their own personal agendas, preferences and prejudices.

- **Communication Issues:** Team members often do not communicate as often, as clearly, or as much as needed. Things are said and misunderstood, things are not said that need to be said.

- **Emotional Issues:** Project team members becoming emotionally linked to their particular part of the project, and take particular positions. They become entrenched in those positions and will not move, even when it is obvious that they need to do so for the benefit of the project.

- **Not Wishing to Admit Failure:** Sometimes the fact that the project is not progressing well is obvious; yet team members continue to work along the same path. Rather than admit failure, learn from it, change and move on, they continue along a path which is never going to lead to a successful result.

- **Lack of Objectivity:** Team members become so connected to the project, they can no longer be objective

- **Different World Views:** Team members see the project through their own lens

- **Cultural Issues**.

All of the above can be termed "human factors" or the "people factor". What is urgently needed is a paradigm change towards consideration of unpredictable situations of uncertainty, conditions dominated by instability and an increased awareness of the non-sequential, and non-linearity of the management process (Curlee & Gordon, 2010; Horkheimer, 1974; Cicmil et al., 2009). Processes that cannot be explained by a linear operation, (e.g. human systems), are often wrongly handled as background noise. This misunderstanding of the problem on the part of the project practitioner results in inappropriate handling of situations.

Pathological forms of communication leave clearly identifiable traces in IT projects. Power struggles between discourse protagonists as well as organizational power struggles (Gul, 2012) can be observed, traced and learnt from. Hamdan, Belkhouche and Smith (2008) argue that culture and leadership impact significantly upon the operation of an organization, and play an important part in the success or otherwise of projects. The quality of the project team, including the capabilities of the project manager and the project team members is a major factor in determining the cost and quality of the output from a project.

The more complex the project the more likely that it can become endangered, challenged or fail (Standish Group International Inc., 2013). Sadly, these situations are likely to occur and reoccur. The very same individuals who do not understand these issues, and have managed failed projects, now possess software systems which give them dashboard controls and access to key performance indicators which aim to standardize every process (Curlee & Gordon, 2010) and encourage and almost eliminate the need for the manager to understand non-linear activities (Dillard & Yuthas, 2006). Such systems, although appearing advanced and sophisticated do not solve the real issues, but cause an 'the Emperor's New Clothes' effect (Andersen, 1837) which lead to further project failures (Masuch, 1985; Pozzebon, Titah & Pinsonneault, 2006).

No guidelines exist for practitioners as to how to pursue reasoning under uncertainty, and this often results in project failure. But this need not be the case. Academic research offers us logical formal mathematical notations which can be used to handle the entangled linear and non-linear system states which can occur in a project. Philosophy, in the form of the work of Habermas, offers us a critical and practical analysis methodology which can be used to address the human discourse issues. Habermas also prescribes a specific way to apply his arguments and defines this as a "simultaneous

empirical discourse analysis" (Habermas, 2002; Cukier et al., 2009). Action research can offer us a practical way of learning from experience. This chapter proposes an approach which draws from all three: mathematics, philosophy and action research.

Habermas is a contemporary philosopher. One of his well-known concepts is "communicative action", in which people seek to reach a common understanding through reasoned argument, consensus, and cooperation rather than pursing a strategic action in pursuit of their own goals (Habermas, 1987a, p. 86). This collaborative approach sits well within the framework of project management. Within the concept of communicative action; Habermas has developed the "ideal speech situation", which proposes environmental parameters for distortion free communication. Habermas provides a set of formal rules through the application of which communication problems pathologies can be identified and diagnosed (Rich & Craig, 2012; Lawless & Schwartz, 2002; Searle, 2007).

People must adhere to these rules for an "ideal speech situation" to occur (Habermas, 1987a, 1987b, 1990):

1. *Every subject with the competence to speak and act is allowed to take part in a discourse.*
2a. *Everyone is allowed to question any assertion whatever.*
2b. *Everyone is allowed to introduce any assertion whatever into the discourse.*
2c. *Everyone is allowed to express their attitudes, desires and needs without any hesitation.*
3. *No speaker may be prevented, by internal or external coercion, from exercising his rights as laid down in (1) and (2).*

The approach proposed here builds on the work of Habermas by applying his rules to aid in the communication and human issues of project management, as part of a decision support environment. The authors propose that in doing so, the system provide opportunities to identify and address issues of communication and other human factors before they become significant and are likely to lead to system failure.

Quantum computing is at the forefront of the next generation of decision support systems, and provides the basis for autonomous artificial intelligence solutions and the optimization of machine learning systems (Standish Group, 2013). Quantum models will greatly improve decision support systems to solve problems of high complexity and enable new and exciting business models. The radical new architecture of quantum computing enable fast processing of massive data sets, such as that which will be assembled when collecting conversational data from a project management system(Lawless & Schwartz, 2002; Lorenz, 2007; Nielsen & Chuang, 2010).

To summarise the system proposed and discussed in this chapter, draw from practitioner experience and the literature in the following ways:

- It recognises that many project fail because of human factors and communication issues. This is substantiated by practitioner experience and the literature on project management

- It suggests that the majority of modern project management practices and software packages are based on a linear model which is not realistic. Again the literature supports this view.

- The published and established philosophical concepts of Habermas can be applied to help analyse issues in communication within projects.

- Quantum computing is becoming available and provides the power t to analyse the complex data sets and which will be needed to construct a working version of the proposed system.

METHODOLOGY

The approach taken has been that of action research, which is a process of problem solving whereby the researcher collaborates with others in their community of practice to address issues and solve problems. The authors chose to use the participatory collaborative method of action research (Coghlan & Brannick, 2014). The project has been through a number of cycles, as is normal for an action research project, with reflection and refinement after each cycle. The cyclic process is discussed below.

Cycle 1: The initial concept was developed based on the review of the literature as discussed above. This was at this stage a simple conceptual module of the system. This conceptual model (Cames & Smith, 2015a) was presented as a poster paper at ICDSST 2015, the International Conference on Decision Support System Technology "Big Data Analytics for Decision-Making" in Belgrade, Serbia in May 2015. The concept was well received by conference delegates, and a number of practical suggestions were made which resulted in refinements to the conceptual model, and to the technological platform on which the system is developed and implemented. In particular, it became clear that what is required is a cloud-based system which can be made widely available to project managers.

Cycle 2: In order to collect feedback from the project management community, one of the authors attended ProjMAN, the International Conference on Project MANagement which was held in the Algarve, Portugal (Cames & Smith, 2015b). The concept and its applications within project management were presented as a poster paper. The concept was well received and a number of participants agreed to take part in the testing of the system.

Cycle 3: The next cycle was scenario testing of the system. This involved applying the principles of the systems to a series of project management scenarios. Two of these scenarios are presented in a later section of this chapter.

Cycle 4: The CAMES project is currently in the final cycle which is the experimental phase. The authors have built an experimental prototype system and are undertaking a series of experiments to test the validity of the concept. These experiments are being carried out with a sample of experienced project managers from the domain of IT (Information Technology). The experiments are based on a set of simulated project case studies, designed to raise issues and conflict. The project participants are required to role play the parts of team members of varying levels of responsibility and seniority, thus trying as far as is possible to replicate a real live project management experience. The participants are encouraged to play a full part in the simulation, and to enter into the debate in an authentic manner. In this way we are trying to replicate the type of heated debates which often take place during the life cycle of real world projects.

Ethics

The study raised a number of ethical issues and required approval by a Research Ethics Committee. The initial plan was to test the system on a series of actual projects. However, on discussion and reflection, it became clear that this was neither practicable nor ethical. The Ethics Committee also, quite correctly, insisted that the authors did not use any existing clients as subjects for the study, thus eliminating the potential for conflict of interest. Also a clear distinction has been made between the current prototype experimental system and the possible commercialism of any system in the future. All of these issues were fully discussed and cleared by the Ethics Committee.

The current study follows a protocol designed within the principles of informed consent. That is, all participants have entered the study voluntarily, have been fully informed of the nature and implications of their participation and can withdraw at any point without penalty. Further, their identity will be confidential and qualitative data obtained during the study, such a project dialogue and conversations, will be fully anonymised in any subsequent reports, such as this chapter.

THE CAMES SYSTEM

The CAMES system implements a series of presuppositions based on the idealized speech (Habermas, 1973, 2014). These are implemented as computer enforced technical controls:

Presupposition 1: If controversial issues are raised during a session, such issues must be made visible to all participants so that there can be open and inclusive debate about the issue. This presupposition is implemented by searching for issues in language (that is, language which suggests a problem or issue has arisen), and, when an issue is discovered, every participant is informed so that they can be aware of the issue and join the discussion in order to help resolve that issue. This will prevent project participants pursuing their own agenda, without the knowledge of other participants.

Presupposition 2: No-one will be excluded from a session or from raising or discussing a controversial issue. The CAMES system will ensure open and inclusive communication in an environment where participants feel able to raise and discuss issues with each other. The environment will not only assume this, but it will ensure it happens using powerful data searching and analysis.

Presupposition 3: Every participant had equal rights to engage in communication. There will be no hierarchy in the system, no hidden areas. Everything will be open and viewable by all. There will be free and inclusive communication.

Presupposition 4: Every participant will have access to the same technical controls. Project participants will be trained in the use of the system and the way in which it collects data and controls communication. This will be open to all, and everyone will be aware exactly how the system operates. Furthermore, participants will also be able to raise issues themselves, and use the system controls to flag these issues to other participants.

Presupposition 5: Any deception will automatically become the subject of discussion by all. If any participants attempt to deceive others, this will be identified by the system and that deception will be highlighted to all as a point of issue and discussion. Furthermore, if a participant thinks they have observed deceit on the part of another participant, they will be able to raise this, anonymously, as a point of issue for discussion by all. In such a way, all issues will be raised and open for discussion by all within a safe and inclusive environment.

Presupposition 6: Communication within the system will be continually observed, traced and tracked in order to detect issues or problems, and possible deceit or coercion.

Project participants will be made aware of the above presuppositions, and will be trained in the use of the system. They will be asked to agree to theses presuppositions, and to the collection and analysis of all communications. The authors believe that the very fact that the participants know that all communications are being tracked and analysed will in itself improve inclusivity and the ethics of communication.

CAMES consists of three separate systems: an online chat discussion board, an access panel and the analysis suite. Each of these systems is built on three distinct access components: a storage mechanism, an application and a database. All components are embedded in a token accessed based eco-system requiring three identities to match up in order to decrypt data at rest, data in motion, and data in memory and transform only machine and eco-system readable data into human readable data. No personal data are held in the database.

The CAMES system is primarily a cloud solution with a data management layer that manages the data collected from project participants on a 24/7 basis, an enrichment layer for data discovery, refinement, and data quality and an analytics layer that supports real-time analytics. It will be hosted in a Microsoft Azure data center to serve project participants across the globe, providing a 24/7 available user interfaces. Key to the system will be that data are visualized via graphical displays which will provide real-time visualization on the fly sourced from the underlying big data platform.

The CAMES system has four elements:

- An online environment which provides full project management, messaging, discussion and communication facilities
- A data collection function which collects the content of discussions for analysis
- A data analysis function analyses the textual communications which have been taking place within the online environment
- A dashboard which display the current status of the project in terms of the communication which is going on within the project.

The online environment uses standard software to provide the user with a full project management environment which includes everything that a project manager or project team member would expect to have when working on a project. There are normal project management tools for controlling and reporting on a project, and a full online messaging system so that participants can discuss the project in an open and inclusive manner. There are also tools for the storage and manipulation of documents and other project artefacts.

The data collection function collects all communication data in real time, and at all times. The project participants will be aware of, and will have agreed to this. The data will be stored in a secure, cloud-based, database.

The data analysis function uses software based on the principles of graph theory to compare the content, structure and patterns of communication going on within the project. Underlying the analysis are the concepts of Habermas and the five presuppositions outlined above. The software has algorithms which analyse the patterns of communication and measure the difference between those patterns and the ideal situation as proposed by Habermas. Significant deviation from ideal communication situations will be reported through the monitoring dashboard.

The monitoring dashboard can report at three levels:

- **Green:** All communications are open and positive and all appears to be progressing well with the project.
- **Amber:** The communications within the project signal that there are some aspects of concern which warrant further investigation and possible intervention.
- **Red:** The communications within the project suggest that there are significant issues and/or areas for concern, which warrant immediate intervention.

As well as reporting through the dashboard, the system will also flag up issues to all participants. The system will thus monitor and address the human factors and communication issues in several different ways, and at different levels:

- The system will first train the project team members in the inclusive communication approach, based on Habermas principles. This training in itself will raise the

openness, authenticity and inclusivity of communication.

- The system will encourage users to raise issues and will provide tools to help them to do so in a safe and inclusive manner.
- The system will continually observe and monitor communication with the agreement of all, and will flag any issues.
- Issues will be raised to all, and will become the subject of open inclusive communication, until they are resolved. This resolution process will itself be the subject of monitoring and analysis. Further issues may be raised during the resolution process. These will also be raised as issues and become the subject of a resolution process.
- The overall state of the project will be flagged as green, amber or red. This status will be flagged to the project manager, but will also, according to the principles of CAMES, be visible to all.
- Team members will have agreed to the principles, monitoring and analysis.

SCENARIO TESTING OF THE PRINCIPLES

The principles within CAMES have been tested against two project management scenarios.

Scenario A: Software Development Company

This is based on a real project. Details have been changed substantially for ethical reasons.

The company won a government funded research grant with their local university. The grant monies were to be used to fund a software development project with the requirement that the company and the university appointed a graduate student on a two year contract to work on the project and develop a prototype software system. The company also had to contribute a proportion of the funding to the project. The graduate associate was to be employed by the university, would register for a Master's degree by research and would spend most of the time working at the company. The university and the company formed a joint interview panel and held a day of interviews where they met five candidates. One of the candidates, we will call Tony, was already known by the company who recommended him strongly and pushed for his appointment. He was an experienced software developer; however his academic qualifications were not strong. In the end the interview panel member from the university was persuaded by his colleague from the company to appoint John, perhaps against his better judgement. John started work on the project and was soon making good progress on development of the software system. The university supervisor, who we will call Dr Forest, would go to the company every week to meet John and his industrial supervisor, who we will call Mrs Kindly. At first things appeared to be going well. After some time, probably six months, there were signs that things were not going well. John was often not at work, and Mrs Kindly was reporting to Dr Forest that John's work was not to standard. Dr Forest would meet with John and Mrs Kindly separately. John would tell Dr Forest that he was being asked to do private work for the company, which was outside of the scope of the project. He said that he was starting to refuse to do so. Mrs Kindly was denying that she was asking John to do any work which was not part of the project, and also raised issues with John's attendance and with the standard of his work.

One day Dr Forest received a phone call from John to say that he had been dismissed by the company and that they would not allow him back on the premises. Dr Forest went to the company and Mrs Kindly confirmed that she did not want John back. She said he was difficult to work with, would not do what was required and that they wished to terminate the project. The University tried to persuade the company to continue with the project but they would not do so. John worked at the university for a few months and then left to start another job. He did not complete his Master's degree.

Scenario A: Issues

Dr Forest never did get to the bottom of what went wrong with this project. What is clear is that the relationship between John and Mrs Kindly broke down to the extent that it became irreparable, and the issues became irresolvable. There were clear issues of communication with John and Mrs Kindly giving very different accounts of what was happening. John's view was that the company were using him to do menial day to day work tasks, which were not related to the project and when he started to refuse to do so, that was the start of things going downhill. He also believed that the company had lost interest in the project and wanted a way out so that they did not have to continue to pay their share of the funding.

Scenario A: Application of the CAMES Approach

In a CAMES world, the interactions between John and Mrs Kindly would be visible and the language used would begin to flag up warnings. CAMES would also compare the communication between John and Mrs Kindly with that between Dr Forest and Mrs Kindly and inconsistencies would be tracked and flagged. The emotionally charged discussions about "refusal" to do certain tasks and the disagreements would all result in project alerts at the highest level. These would be highlighted to an overall project manager, perhaps a senior member of staff at the university, who would then be able to step in and resolve issues. At the same time the communication issues between John, Dr Forest and Mrs Kindly would be raised and they would be required to discuss these in an open and inclusive manner in order to resolve them.

Scenario B: Replacing a Major Software System

An organisation was upgrading a major software system. There were three possible ways forward. The first was to stay with their existing system, which was due a major upgrade and an increase in annual licence fee. The second was to move to a free open source solution. This appeared attractive; however, any open source solution would require significant redesign and tailoring which would take much time, cost and effort. The third option was to purchase a completely new system. The organisation set up a project team chaired by the head of IT services, and comprising representation from all major stakeholder groups. The project team hired the services of an external facilitator. The group set about seeing each possible system and having presentations from all vendors. The facilitator arranged these and ran the project team sessions. It became clear that the facilitator, rather than remaining neutral, had strong views about the possible choice, and was beginning to favour the purchase of a new system from one particular supplier. It also became clear to the project team that the facilitator "had the ear" of the head of IT services. The project team became split, with one section (about half) supporting the view of the facilitator (perhaps for political reasons, as they wished to be seen to be on the same side as the head of IT services), and the rest preferring to either stay with the existing supplier or go with an open source solution. The latter group raised many objections to the suggestion of the facilitator, but in the end that view was carried, and the new system was purchased from the external supplier. The system was not a success, and has not satisfied stakeholder requirements. There remains much bad feeling about the entire exercise.

Scenario B: Issues

The whole running of the project became highly political. There were clear issues of communica-tion with camps forming and each camp having very different views of how best to move forward. The facilitator and head of IT services domi-nated the discussions in project meetings and the "against" camp were never really allowed to put their views forward, no matter how much they tried.

Scenario B: Application of the CAMES Approach

In a CAMES world, the interactions within the project team would be visible and the language used would begin to flag up warnings. The team would be required to discuss the options in an open and inclusive manner, with each member being allowed to their say and an agreed way of resolving issues would be found.

FUTURE RESEARCH DIRECTIONS

The next stages in the study are to undergo full experimentation of the CAMES software tool, using a number of real world project scenarios. If these prove to be successful the following stage will be to try the system out on real project cases.

CONCLUSION

This chapter has presented a new approach to proj-ect management. Humans operate non-linearly, yet the process and project management systems used in organizations tend to be linear. The authors propose a new system, CAMES, which provides a computerized method to improve system process management that accounts for the non-linearity of human behavior. The development of CAMES was stimulated by Habermas' position that an ideal speech situation is found when communication between individuals is governed by basic, implied rules. In an ideal speech situation, participants are able to evaluate each other's assertions solely on the basis of reason and evidence in an atmosphere completely free of any non-rational "coercive" influences, including both physical and psychological coercion. CAME will encouraged support and implement these rules and in doing so, create an ideal speech situation.

CAMES is a cloud-based system which uses quantum models of computing to produce an early warning and intervention system for practitioners, based on big data principles: aimed to lower the rate of project failure. CAMES is currently at a conceptual stage, and an experimental prototype of the system is under development. The system will be tested in a series of simulated scenarios to explore the possibilities which the concept could offer to IT practitioners and project managers. The authors offer this concept for critique and comment, which will further inform the next stages of this study

The authors have through reflection on their own experience and review of the relevant literature demonstrated that project failure remains a critical issue for organisations throughout the world. They have also shown how human factors, emotion, political issues and communication are the root cause of many project failures. They propose the use of Habermas' principles of communication as a solution to the problem. The promise of the approach has been demonstrated through application of the principles to a real project management scenario. The authors are now extending their approach to a software implementation, called CAMES. A prototype software system has been constructed and this is now the subject of a series of ongoing experiments which are using experienced project managers as subjects to further validate the concept and to test the system. Results to date are promising and will be reported in a future publication.

REFERENCES

Andersen, C. (1837). *The Emperor's New Clothes*. Copenhagen, Denmark.

Cames, O., & Smith, P. (2015a). CAMES (Corporate Action Methodology for Enterprise Systems): Decision Management through Improved Communication. *Proceedings of ICDSST 2015: International Conference on Decision Support System Technology "Big Data Analytics for Decision-Making"*.

Cames, O., & Smith, P. (2015b). *CAMES: a system to transform project management interactions*. Algarve, Portugal.

Churchman, C. (1967). Wicked Problems. *Management Science, 14*(2).

Cicmil, S., Cooke-Davies, T., Crawford, L., & Richardson, K. (2009). *Exploring the complexity of projects: Implication of Complexity Theory For Project Management Practice*. Newtown Square, PA: PMI.

Coghlan, D., & Brannick, T. (2014). *Doing action research in your own organization* (4th ed.). London: Sage.

Cukier, W., Ngwenyama, O., Bauer, R., & Middleton, C. (2009). A critical analysis of media discourse on information technology: Preliminary results of a proposed method for critical discourse analysis. *Information Systems Journal, 19*(2), 175–196. doi:10.1111/j.1365-2575.2008.00296.x

Curlee, W., & Gordon, R. (2010). *Complexity Theory and Project Management*. Wiley.

Dillard, J., & Yuthas, K. (2006). Enterprise resource planning systems and communicative action. *Critical Perspectives On Accounting, 17*, 202-223 doi:10.1016/j.cpa.2005.08.003

Dominguez, J. (2009). *The Curious Case of the CHAOS Report 2009*. Available from: http://www.projectsmart.co.uk/the-curious-case-of-the-chaos-report-2009.html

Gul, S., (2012). *The role of conflict & negotiation in the complexity of projects*. British Library EThOS

Habermas, J. (1987a). The Theory of Communicative Action: Vol. 1. *The Critique of Functionalist Reason*. London: Heinemann.

Habermas, J. (1987b). The Theory of Communicative Action: Vol. 2. *The Critique of Functionalist Reason*. London: Heinemann.

Habermas, J. (1990). *Moral Consciousness and Communicative Action*. Cambridge, MA: MIT Press.

Habermas, J. (2002). *On the Pragmatics of Social Interaction: Preliminary Studies in the Theory of Communicative Action*. Cambridge, MA: MIT Press.

Habermas, J. (2014). *Between Naturalism and Religion: Philosophical Essays*. Academic Press.

Habermas, J., & Lenhardt, C. (1973). A postscript to 'knowledge and human interests'. *Philosophy of the Social Sciences*, *3*(1), 157–185. doi:10.1177/004839317300300111

Hamdan, K., Belkhouche, B., & Smith, P. (2008). The Influence of Culture and Leadership on Cost Estimation. In *Software Process and Product Measurement* (pp. 223–232). Springer Berlin Heidelberg. doi:10.1007/978-3-540-89403-2_19

Horkheimer, M. (1974). *Eclipse of Reason* (Vol. 1). New York: Bloomsbury Publishing.

Khrennikov, A. (2010). *Ubiquitous Quantum Structure*. Springer. doi:10.1007/978-3-642-05101-2

Lawless, W., & Schwartz, M. (2002). The social quantum model of dissonance: From social organization to cultural evolution. *Social Science Computer Review*, *20*(4), 441–450. doi:10.1177/089443902237321

Lorenz, E. (2007). *The essence of chaos. Taylor and Francis CRC ebook account*. Kindle Edition.

Masuch, M. (1985). Vicious circles in organizations. *Administrative Science Quarterly*, *30*(1), 14–33. doi:10.2307/2392809

Nielsen, M., & Chuang, I. (2010). Quantum Computation and Quantum Information. Cambridge University Press. doi:10.1017/CBO9780511976667

Pozzebon, M., Titah, R., & Pinsonneault, A. (2006). Combining social shaping of technology and communicative action theory for understanding rhetorical closure in IT. *Information Technology & People*, *19*(3), 244–271. doi:10.1108/09593840610689840

Rich, M., & Craig, R. (2012). Habermas and Bateson in a World Gone M.A.D.: Metacommunication, Paradox, and the Inverted Speech Situation. *Communication Theory*, *22*(4), 383–402. doi:10.1111/j.1468-2885.2012.01412.x

Searle, J. (2007). Neuroscience, Intentionality and Free Will: Reply to Habermas. *Philosophical Explorations*, *10*(1), 69–76. doi:10.1080/13869790601170169

Standish Group International Inc. (2013). *Chaos Manifesto 2013 - Think Big*. Act Small.

Wilde, M. (2013). *Quantum Information Theory*. Cambridge University Press. doi:10.1017/CBO9781139525343

ADDITIONAL READING

Adams, N. (1996). Eschatology and Habermas' Ideal Speech Situation. *Modern Believing*, *37*(2), 3–10. doi:10.3828/MB.37.2.3

Aerts, D. (2009). Quantum structure in cognition. *Journal of Mathematical Psychology*, *53*(5), 314–348. doi:10.1016/j.jmp.2009.04.005

Anderson, P. (1999). Complexity theory and organization science. *Organization Science*, *10*(3), 216–232. doi:10.1287/orsc.10.3.216

Axelrod, R. (1976). *Structure of Decision. The Cognitive Maps of Political Elites*. Princeton, New Jersey: Princeton University Press.

Baines, P. (2013). Lorenz, E.N, 1963: Deterministic nonperiodic flow. Journal of the atmospheric sciences 20, 130-41. *Alternative Law Journal*, *38*(4), 475–480.

Barker, J. R. (1993). Tightening the iron cage: Concertive control in self-managing teams. *Administrative Science Quarterly*, *38*(3), 408–437. doi:10.2307/2393374

Bazerman, M. (2012). Judgment in Managerial Decision Making, 8th Edition. Wiley. Kindle Edition.

Bazerman, M. H., & Samuelson, W. F. (1983). 'I won the auction but don't want the prize'. *The Journal of Conflict Resolution*, *27*(4), 618–634. doi:10.1177/0022002783027004003

Bisconti, C., Corallo, A., Fortunato, L., & Gentile, A. (2014). A Quantum-BDI Model for Information Processing and Decision Making. *International Journal of Theoretical Physics*, 710–726.

Bowman, J., & Rehg, W. (2007). *Jürgen Habermas*. Stanford Encyclopaedia of Philosophy.

Busemeyer, J., & Bruza, P. (2012). *Quantum Models of Cognition and Decision*. Cambridge University Press. doi:10.1017/CBO9780511997716

Chen, C., & Zhang, C. (2014). Data-intensive applications, challenges, techniques and technologies: A survey on Big Data. *Information Sciences*, *275*, 314–347. doi:10.1016/j.ins.2014.01.015

Drummond, H. (2001). *The Art of Decision-making: Mirrors of Imagination, Masks of Fate*. Chichester: Wiley.

Easterby-Smith, M., Thorpe, R., & Jackson, P. (2012). *Management research* (4th ed.). London: Sage.

Ezzamel, M., Willmott, H., & Worthington, F. (2001). Power, control, and resistance in the factory that time forgot. *Journal of Management Studies*, *38*(8), 1053–1079. doi:10.1111/1467-6486.00272

Fisher, K. (2000). The role of the team leader. In *Leading self-directed work teams: a guide to developing new team leadership skills* (pp. 121–135). New York: McGraw-Hill.

Galbraith, J. R. (1982). *Designing Complex Organizations*. Reading: Addison-Wesley.

Gross, A. (2006). Habermas, Systematically Distorted Communication, and the Public Sphere. *Rhetoric Society Quarterly*, 3.

Johnson, P., & Duberley, J. (2000). *Understanding Management Research: An Introduction to Epistemology* (p. 95). Kindle Edition.

Khrennikov, A., & Haven, E. (2013). *Quantum Social Science*. Cambridge University Press.

Mechanic, D. (1962). Sources of power of lower participants in complex organizations. *Administrative Science Quarterly*, *7*(3), 349–364. doi:10.2307/2390947

Myers, M. (1994). 'A disaster for everyone to see: An interpretive analysis of a failed IS project', Accounting. *Management And Information Technologies*, *4*(4), 185–2. doi:10.1016/0959-8022(94)90022-1

Paraskevas, A. (2006). Crisis management or crisis response system?: A complexity science approach to organizational crises. *Management Decision*, *44*(7), 892–907. doi:10.1108/00251740610680587

Pearson, C. M., & Clair, J. A. (1998). Reframing crisis management. *Academy of Management Review*, *23*(1), 59–76.

Radder, H. (2012). *The Material Realization Of Science. From Habermas To Experimentation And Referential Realism, n.p.* Dordrecht: Springer.

Reason, P., & Bradbury, H. (2008). *Handbook of Action Research* (2nd ed.). London: Sage. doi:10.4135/9781848607934

Robinson, I., Webber, J., Eifrem, E., (2013). Graph Databases. O'Reilly Media. Kindle Edition.

Ross, A., & Chiasson, M. (2011). Habermas and information systems research: New directions. *Information and Organization*, *21*(3), 123–141. doi:10.1016/j.infoandorg.2011.06.001

Sandberg, F., & Wallo, A. (2013, June 01). The interactive researcher as a virtual participant: A Habermasian interpretation. *Action Research*, *11*(2), 194–212. doi:10.1177/1476750313484503

Tannenbaum, R., & Schmidt, W. H. (1973). How to choose a leadership pattern. *Harvard Business Review*, *51*(3), 162–180.

Theiler, J., & Eubank, S. (1993). Don't bleach chaotic data. *Chaos (Woodbury, N.Y.)*, *3*(4), 771–782. doi:10.1063/1.165936 PMID:12780079

Volberda, H. W., & Lewin, A. Y. (2003). Co-evolutionary dynamics within and between firms: From evolution to co-evolution. *Journal of Management Studies*, *40*(8), 2111–2136. doi:10.1046/j.1467-6486.2003.00414.x

Wheatley, Margaret J. (2000-11-29). Leadership and the New Science: Discovering Order in a Chaotic World Revised. Berrett-Koehler Publishers

KEY TERMS AND DEFINITIONS

Action Research: A collaborative approach to problem solving which involves taking action, and then evaluated the impact of that action, reflecting of it, taking further modified action. Usually takes place in cycles of action with data collection, evaluation and reflection between each cycle.

Cloud Computing: A network of remote servers hosted on the Internet which can store, manage, and process data, rather than using a local server or a personal computer.

Habermas: A contemporary philosopher who presented theories relating to human communication.

Human Factors: Those factors or organisational issues which relate to, and are the results of, the actions of, people; also known as the people factor.

Project Management: A formalised approach to the management of activities, including a series of procedures and possibly supported by software. The application of processes, methods, knowledge, skills and experience to achieve the project objectives.

Project: A unique endeavour, undertaken to achieve planned objectives, which can be defined in terms of outputs, outcomes or benefits.

Quantum Computing: A new approach to computing which is based on a new model of computer. Quantum computers are different from digital computers. Whereas digital computers require data to be encoded into binary digits, each of which is always in one of two definite states (0 or 1), quantum computation uses quantum bits, which can be in different states. A quantum computer is much faster than traditional computers.

Chapter 29
Mobile Communication in Hospitals:
Is It Still a Problem?

Terje Solvoll
University Hospital of North Norway, Norway

ABSTRACT

The work setting in hospitals is communication intensive and can lead to significant difficulties related to interruptions from co-workers. Physicians often need information fast, and any delay between the decision made and the action taken could cause medical errors. One suggested solution for this problem is to implement wireless phone systems. However, psychological theory and empirical evidence, both suggest that wireless phones have the potential of creating additional problems related to interruptions, compared to traditional paging systems. The fact that hospital workers prefer interruptive communication methods before non-interruptive methods, amplifies the risk of overloading people when phones are widely deployed. This challenge causes some hospital staff to resist the diffusion of wireless phones, and one key is how to handle the balance between increased availability, and increased interruptions. In this chapter we will present solutions based on context aware communication systems which aims to reduce interruptions.

INTRODUCTION

We know from earlier studies within health care that physicians in hospitals are interrupted unnecessary by mobile devices in situations where such interruptions should be avoided (Scholl, Hasvold, Henriksen, & Ellingsen, 2007; T. Solvoll & Scholl, 2008; Terje Solvoll, Scholl, & Hartvigsen, 2010, 2013). Unnecessary interruptions can cause concentration difficulties and disturb the activity performed (Hersh et al., 2002). Unwanted interruptions should be minimized in order to avoid distraction that can lead to intolerable action or decisions, especially during surgery or patient examinations. This is a problem in today's hospital settings, and a solution to reduce such unnecessary interruptions from mobile devices is needed and wanted (T. Botsis, T. Solvoll, J. Scholl, P. Hasvold, & G. Hartvigsen, 2007; Scholl, et al., 2007; T. Solvoll & Scholl, 2008; Terje Solvoll, et al., 2013). A lot of research has been done within this area, some of this work will be presented in the next

DOI: 10.4018/978-1-4666-9970-0.ch029

sections, but we cannot see that the situation has changed to the better. In this chapter, which is an update of the earlier chapter (T. Solvoll, 2013), we will present some earlier work on context sensitive systems for mobile communication in hospitals (internal communication systems, not including public networks (GSM/3G)) that aims to improve the communication situation, reduce interruptions, but at the same time include smartphone functionality and 3 party applications.

BACKGROUND

Physicians' working conditions rely on mobility. They move frequently between in-patient ward, out-patient ward, emergency ward, operating theatres, etc., and often do not stay more than a few minutes in the same location. High mobility requires mobile communication systems, which enables physicians to communicate with colleges at any time and place, to avoid any delay between the decision made and action taken. Such delays could result in medical errors (Hersh, et al., 2002), and mobile communication systems have been suggested as a solution to improve communication in hospitals (Coiera & Tombs, 1998). The challenge when deploying mobile communication systems is to handle the balance between the increased availability and possible interruptions (Scholl, et al., 2007; T. Solvoll & Scholl, 2008; Terje Solvoll, et al., 2010, 2013). Most hospitals still rely on a mobile communication infrastructure with dedicated devices for each role, where pagers are the most dominant mobile communication device.

Pagers provide a cheap and reliable way for contacting staff. They are ubiquitous and several physicians carry numerous pagers simultaneously to cover the various work roles they have been assigned. Pagers suffer from a number of problems due to their simplicity. The most obvious limitation is that it requires the staff to locate a telephone (landline or wireless) in order to respond to a page. This might cause unnecessary delays and

communication overhead, since the person placing the page is not always near the phone when the page is returned (Spurck, Mohr, Seroka, & Stoner, 1995). Pagers also create a large amount of unnecessary interruptions (Blum & Lieu, 1992; Katz & Schroeder, 1988), which is unpleasant and can cause medical errors (Hersh, et al., 2002).

The most intuitive solution to improve the communication situation in hospitals is to provide physicians with wireless phones. However, phones can be even more interruptive than pagers (Scholl, et al., 2007; T. Solvoll & Scholl, 2008; Terje Solvoll, et al., 2010, 2013). In (Scholl, et al., 2007) a physician states that; "with a pager you just have to glance down at your coat pocket to see who is paging, while with a phone, you have to pick it up from your pocket to see who is calling. Having done that, it is easier just answering and explaining that you are busy" (T. Solvoll & Scholl, 2008). However, today the trend is that healthcare workers also bring their own private mobile phone to work. The device is sometimes used for contacting other health care workers, or to answer a page, but at the same time also for medical applications, i.e. Medical references and so on.

Preliminary studies points at a diversity of potential benefits from wireless phones in hospital settings, using both mobile text and voice services (Acuff, Fagan, Rindfleisch, Levitt, & Ford, 1997; Eisenstadt et al., 1998; Minnick, Pischke-Winn, & Sterk, 1994 ; Spurck, et al., 1995). These studies also reveal potential technological limitations that can explain some of the challenges of gaining acceptance. Text-chat is a less obtrusive medium than other forms of workplace communication (Bradner, Kellogg, & Erickson, 1999). It is therefore unlikely that mobile text-messaging creates the same amount of interruptions as mobile voice services. Improved asynchronous communication systems have in fact been recommended for improving hospital communication practices (Coiera & Tombs, 1998). In addition to mobile synchronous communication systems, mobile text-messaging systems are therefore an interesting medium to explore in hospitals settings.

However, the current generation of mobile-text messaging systems seems ill suited for hospital environments. Studies of mobile text-messaging usage in hospitals have revealed difficulties related to small screen size (Eisenstadt, et al., 1998), and problems related to forcing doctors to carrying an additional device (Acuff, et al., 1997). It has to be taken into account that these studies are some years old. Today displays and keyboards are significantly improved, which might have changed the situation. A continual problem with mobile text messaging is that senders often need an acknowledgement that an asynchronous message has been read by the receiver (Coiera & Tombs, 1998). The acknowledgement challenge could be solved by a forced feedback when the message has been opened. Actually, there are several messaging systems available today that offers feedback if a message has been delivered and opened. The question is if these systems are suitable for hospital use. Another solution that may ease the difficulties with text messaging, is automatic suggestions for replies. It has been reported that predefined messages can meet up to 90% of the mobile text-messaging needs for some hospital workers (Jakob E. Bardram & Hansen, 2004).

Mobile communication systems for hospitals, is an important research area since hospitals are noted to suffer from poor communication practices. The combination of wireless phones and fact that hospital workers prefer interruptive communication methods before non-interruptive methods (Blum & Lieu, 1992; Coiera & Tombs, 1998; Katz & Schroeder, 1988) and often exhibit "selfish" interruptive communication practices, may result in unnecessary interruptions for conversations that otherwise would' not occur (Parker & Coiera, 2000). This amplifies the risk of overloading limited resources with special knowledge, experience, and the power of taking medical decisions. The balance between getting immediate access to

resources and causing interruptions in moments where it is not appropriate, has similarities with the classical problems regarding collaboration and sharing of resources, such as of disparity in work and benefit, "prisoner's dilemma" and "the tragedy of the commons" (Grudin, 1994). A critical issue for voice services is the potential of make people "fatally available" (Spurck, et al., 1995), which cannot be overlooked, since health care is a knowledge intensive activity where consulting colleagues or senior staff members is a necessity in many situations (Coiera, 2000). One way of attacking this problem is to provide the caller with context information from the receiver's situation. Context information could be any kind of information which helps to decide if the receiver is available or not, such as; location, activity, surrounding noise, role, etc. In a study by (Avrahami, Gergle, Hudson, & Kiesler, 2007) they revealed that if the caller is provided with context information about the receiver's situation, it reduces the mismatch between the caller's decision and the receiver's desires.

To address the conflict between physicians' needs for mobile communication and the interruptions from mobile devices in hospitals, we have been looking at context sensitive (also called context aware) systems for mobile communication first in general and then in hospital settings. A number of studies have focused on context-sensitive systems for hospitals; however, a lot of this work has focused on scopes not covered by this chapter, including issues related to mobile learning and privacy, accessing clinical data, or on multimedia communication at terminals with fixed locations (Mitchell, Spiteri, Bates, & Coulouris, 2000).

CONTEXT SENSITIVE COMMUNICATION SYSTEMS

There have been many suggestions on how to reduce interruptions from mobile devices during the years. In this chapter we will focus on context sensitive/aware communication systems that aims to reduce interruptions, first in general, and then within hospital settings. But first of all we need to define context sensitive/aware systems. We will use the terms context aware and context sensitive as equal terms during this chapter.

Identifying Context Sensitive Systems

A system is a set of interacting or interdependent components forming an integrated whole. The behaviour of this whole has observable Inter-Process Communications. Further, to define what we mean by context, we had to look into some of the definitions defined during the years by the research community (Bisgaard, Heise, & Steffensen, 2004; Lieberman & Selker, 2000; Schilit, Adams, & Want, 1994), and came up with (Abowd et al., 1999) as the most suitable definition for this chapter:

Context is any information that can be used to characterize the situation of an entity. An entity is a person, place, or object that is considered relevant for the interaction between a user and an application, including the user and applications themselves.

This definition highlights the importance of which information that is relevant or not in a context sensitive system. A Context sensitive system could therefore be defined as a system allowing interactions between multiple entities using relevant information. Abowd, et al., (1999) states; "a system is context-aware if it uses context to provide relevant information and/or services to the user, where relevancy depends on the user's task". This definition shows that a context-aware system can change its behaviour and send some relevant information according to the context, which reflects our view. So, what is relevant information? What are the most common types

of contextual information used by context aware applications? (Mizzaro, Nazzi, & Vassena, 2008) identified some common types of information:

- Spatial,
- Temporal,
- Social situation,
- Resources that are nearby,
- Physiological measurements,
- Schedules and agendas,
- Activities,
- Identity.

Only a small number of these crucial information types are applied in existing applications. Only the information that satisfies the requirements of the targeted application, technology available, and environmental constraints, is used. The trend has been to offer the user as much information as possible in order to provide more sophisticated and useful services, and at the same time making the users more available. A preliminary study on the Aware Media system by Jakob E. Bardram, Hansen, & Soegaard (2006), presented in this book, they suggest a classification that splits the above listed information along three main axes:

- **Social Awareness:** 'Where a person is', 'activity in which a person is engaged on', 'self-reported status'.
- **Spatial Awareness:** 'What kind of operation is taking place in a ward', 'level of activity', 'status of operation and people present in the room'.
- **Temporal Awareness:** 'Past activities', 'present and future activities' that is significant for a person.

This classification describes social aspects regarding knowledge about a person, spatial aspects regarding information about a specific place, and temporal aspects describing information about history and future plans of a subject.

The adoption of context-aware services based on these definitions is growing in a variety of domains, as mention in (Hristova, 2008):

- **Smart Homes:** Context aware applications provide useful services to the residents in order to increase their quality of life and help disabled or elderly people to be more independent, such as; supervising health care functions to monitor the person's biomedical functions: glucose levels, blood pressure, heartbeats or provide reminders about daily medication.

- **Airports:** Context-aware solutions are used to identify possible threats or emergency conditions providing automatic mechanisms aimed at delivering immediate security notification to the appropriate department such as maintenance, fire department or police. Services linked to passenger's behaviour have been developed as well. Most of them are able to send information to passengers' mobile devices about shopping zones, exits, gates, arrivals and departures delay according to their location.

- **Travel/Entertainment/Shopping:** Information provided, typically on mobile phone, is about nearby restaurants, theatres, festivals, events, shops, sales and other data related to the area where the user is located.

- **Museum:** Context aware applications are often used to detect user's position within a building, in order to guide visitors through a predefined path. Typically, these applications are developed on suitable portable devices able to sense the location and capable to provide video/audio information relating paintings, statues and other objects within a museum.

- **Offices:** Context-aware systems are usually aimed at monitoring the status of equipment and providing better allocation of human resources by changing the shift schedules considering location and activity performed by the workers.

Spatial information is perhaps the most frequently used type of contextual information, pertaining to user location. It can be as simple as knowing whether a user is at home or at work or more precise, by specifying which office floor for their current location. The benefits of using this kind of information is obvious. Trying to find someone is a lot easier when you know which building. In addition, if a user uses a context aware system in order to find someone, the system can inform the user that the person they are looking for is currently in a meeting, and thereby not available.

Temporal information can be of high value when collecting contextual data, and several different ways of presenting the information has been proposed (Omar, A., et al., 2007; Steve B Cousins and Michael G Kahn, 1991; Robert Wu et al., 2011). An example of how to use temporal information is to use it to check for colliding or overlapping events in calendars and schedulers. Other example uses involve combining temporal data with, as an example, sales data, and looking for connections between time of day and sales of certain items. Horvitz et al., (2002) presents a system allowing for setting of thresholds regarding alerts on desktop and mobile, depending on urgency, availability, and other factors, including temporal data.

Knowing which resources are available nearby can be used in order to help the users in a variety of situations. This could be as simple as; informing the user that a meeting room is now available, or where the closest available projector is located. However, taking this to the next level, then the system might recognise that a user currently located in a meeting room is about to make a presentation due to an event in the user's schedule, and as a result it automatically connects the users laptop to the projector and speaker system located in the room.

Having access to the users schedule can include a lot of information. Knowing when people are attending meetings, seeing their doctor, or taking vacation, can be very useful for providing relevant information without the user having update this themselves. An example of using this kind of information: The interaction between Google's services, Gmail offers functionality that automatically import event data to your calendar. Many applications also exist in which automatically puts your phone in silent mode during meetings and other events, by checking your calendar. Similarly, a phone system can note that a callee is in a meeting, and thereby inform the caller when it is appropriate to call back, or it can present the caller with a set options as to what to do depending on the context of the callee, as presented in Chihani et al. (2011).

The identity of the user, as well as those attempting to contact them or contacted by them, is also useful to know in terms of context. We mentioned earlier that a context aware system could be used in order to reduce the availability of the user if they were in a meeting, but what if the one calling is someone with an urgent need to contact the user, an acute situation? The fact is that people are often willing to be interrupted if the responsible party has a valid reason for it (Daniel Massaguer et al. 2009). Identity can also be used in order to tailor the users' surroundings. A user might have his office set up as the lighting is adjusted based on the time of day, or having the temperature turned down and the lights turned off when they aren't there. Chen et al. (2000) features more examples of how various contextual information can be utilized.

While the term context aware was first used to describe a system in 1994 (Bill N Schilit, David M Hilbert, and Jonathan Trevor, 2002), the concept had already been in use for years. Bill N Schilit and Marvin M Theimer (1994) and Albrecht Schmidt et al. (1999) gives a good overview of some earlier systems, the usage of context-aware systems, and design objectives that they believe should be considered.

One of the first system developed was the Active Badge System first deployed at Cambridge early 1990 (Roy Want et al., 1995; Andy Harter and Andy Hopper, (1994). The system used light-

weight badges, carried by the users. These badges used infrared (IR) communication in order to send a short signal that could be picked up by network sensors, which were placed around the building. The information gathered by these sensors could be presented on a standard PC display showing users' name, location, and the probability of the given location. The probability of a user being in their last location were based on whether the system noticed that the user have been moving around recently. The system was primarily used by receptionists who used the presented information in order to forward phone calls. Though some were sceptical towards the system at first, it quickly became a useful tool, and many praised the system for making their lives easier in regards to responding to people trying to reaching them, though they wanted more control over when calls were forwarded (Roy Want et al., 1995).

Another early system that used similar techniques was the PARCTAB system develop at Xerox PARC in the early nineties (Norman Adams et al., 1993; Mark Weiser, 1991). PARCTAB was a Personal Digital Assistant (PDA) whose applications mostly ran on remote machines and was primarily meant for use in buildings. Like the Active Badge System (Roy Want et al., 1995) it uses IR communication in order to communicate with these applications. While the Active Badge System had network sensors, which only picked up signals from the badges, the PARCTAB system used a series of transceivers.

More recently, some businesses and retail stores have started to take advantage of the possibilities offered by context-aware systems. As an example, Estimote (www.estimote.com), a company that produces lightweight Blue Tooth (BT) beacons, which can be used for location tracking. They promotes the idea of combining BT beacons with an application on the consumer's phone, which can notify the user of sales and other deals going on when the application detects that the consumer is in close range to the store. In addition, the application can also show the consumer where in the store the desired product is located. These kinds of systems can be categorised as continuation of guidance systems like Cyberguide as (Sue Long et al., 1996) introduces. Similarly the aptly named recommendation systems, systems that try to predict the users interest in an area, product, or event, have also begun using contextual information in order to offer better information to their users (Roy Want et al., 1992; Julie Parker and Enrico Coiera, 2000; Gediminas Adomavicius and Alexander Tuzhilin, 2011).

Context aware system's also share similarities with another concept known as ubiquitous computing, a term initially introduced in the late eighties at Xerox PARC (Johanna I Westbrook et al., 2011; Mark Weiser, Rich Gold, and John Seely Brown, 1999). The general concept is the idea of computers being everywhere and adapting to our presence and surroundings, without the users necessarily realising or having to think about it. An example of how ubiquitous computing is becoming more widespread is that more and more devices and items are connected to Internet. This collection of devices is often referred to as the Internet of Things (IoT), and is often used when presenting ubiquitous devices. IoT consists of billions of devices, and increases every day. Cisco features a device counter on their site, which keeps track of the number of devices connected to the Internet, and estimates that the IoT will count more than 50 billion units by 2020, if the growth continues at its current rate.

While the use of context aware system's can potentially offer a lot of functionality, some people are still sceptical. Some context aware systems often gather large amounts of personal data used to offer additional utilities, which for many users do not outweigh the loss of privacy that the system generates. As a result, privacy is often referred to as the biggest concern when talking about context aware systems (Jason I Hong and James A Landay, 2004). We will not focus on privacy issues. Privacy is a large field and needs more investigation than we will be able cover in this chapter.

Context Sensitive Communication Systems to Control Interruptions

One approach for generalizing context aware communication systems that aims to reduce interruptions, is to divide them into two categories (Ashraf Khalil & Connelly, 2006). The first category includes systems where the phone automatically changes configuration (Ashraf Khalil & Connelly, 2005; Nelson, Bly, & Sokoler, 2001; Schmidt, Takaluoma, & Mäntyjärvi, 2000; Siewiorek et al., 2003). This includes quiet calls where the receiver could negotiate with the caller through text or pre-recorded audio messages (Nelson, et al., 2001), which will not reduce personal interruptions due to the user is supposed to act upon the received call. SenSay (Siewiorek, et al., 2003) is an interesting context-aware mobile phone that adapts to dynamically changing environmental and physiological states. It combines information from several different sensors to catch the user's context, and adapt the ringer volume, the vibration and the feedback to the caller based on the phones context. It also makes call suggestion to users when they are idle. Contextual information is gathered by using 3-Axis accelerometers, Bluetooth, ambient microphones, and light sensors, mounted on different part of the user's body. A central hub mounted on the waist is the central component that receives and distributes data coming from the sensors to the decision logic module. The decision logic module analyzes the collected data and changes the state of the phone. The system provides four states: Uninterruptible, Idle, Active and Normal state. A number of settings on the phone are automatically changed within the different states. The uninterruptible state turns off the ringer and turn on the vibration only if the light level is below a certain threshold. This state is entered when the user is involved in a conversation (recognized by the environmental microphone) or is involved in a meeting recognized from the phones calendar. In this state, all incoming calls are blocked and with feedback messages sent to the caller. The caller does have an option to force the call in case of emergency. When high physical activity or high ambient noise level are detected by the accelerometer or microphones, the active state is entered. This means that the ringer is set to high and the vibration is turned on. When there activity level is low and the detected sounds of the surroundings are very low, the idle state is entered. In this state the phone reminds the user of pending calls. As the name indicates, the normal state will configure the ringer and vibration to default values. Figure 1 shows the overall architecture of the SenSay system, from sensor box to platform, to mobile phone. In another system presented in (Schmidt, et al., 2000), they use wireless application protocols (WAP) to automatically change the phones setting based on the recognized context, and in (Ashraf Khalil & Connelly, 2005) they use calendar information with the users scheduled activity stored, to automatically configure the phone.

The second category (Ashraf Khalil & Connelly, 2006) deals with systems that gives the caller information about the receivers context and thereby helps the caller to make decisions when it is appropriate to make the call (Milewski & Smith, 2000; Pedersen, 2001; Tang et al., 2001). In one study by (Avrahami, et al., 2007), they revealed that if they provided the caller with context information about the receiver's situation, it reduces the mismatch between the caller's decision and the receivers desires. In (Milewski & Smith, 2000) they provide information about the receiver's presence using the phone book and location, like the "buddy list" in instant messenger services. An interaction web-page that gives caller information about the receivers' situation and the available communication channels is used in (Pedersen, 2001), and in (Marmasse, Schmandt, & Spectre, 2004) they formed some kind of member-list combined with a prototype of a wristwatch that captures the user's context and share it to the members of the list, which use the information to check the availability before calling.

Figure 1. SenSay; from sensor box, to platform, to mobile phone; this is a simplified version of the overall system architecture.
(Siewiorek, et al., 2003).

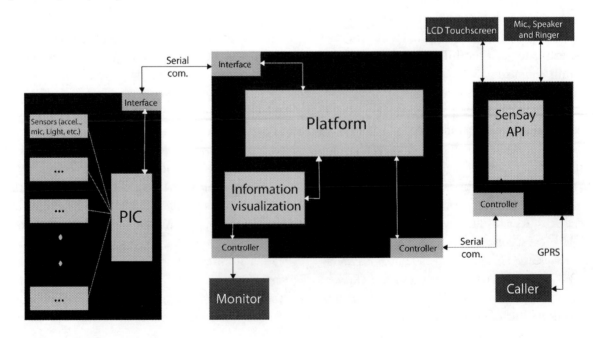

Context Sensitive Communication Systems for Hospitals

Context aware systems for hospitals are a promising application domain. Hospitals are dependent of a wide and reliable communication infrastructure for exchanging different kinds of data, such as patient reports, lab tests and working shifts, together with text, voice and alarm services. This means that the security needs to be on a certain level. The management of this information is difficult and requires considering a wide variety of problems that should be avoided in order to properly meet the needs of hospital professionals. Context-aware applications for mobile communication seem to be a valid solution, which also can be used to move parts of the workers activities over to computers. While the society outside of hospitals have embraced mobile phones (GSM/3G), have health care only shown limited use of the technology. This is mainly due to a possible interference with medical equipment. However, some earlier studies showed that the benefits from this technology could outweigh the risk of interference (Kidd, Sharratt, & Coleman, 2004; Myerson & Mitchell, 2003). This has been challenged by Van Lieshout et al., (2007), which in 2007 classified incidents of electromagnetic interference (EMI) by mobile phones (GSM/3G) on critical care medical equipment. Latest years, the introduction of smartphones and medical applications available, has also made smartphones interesting for hospital communication, despite the fair for interference and the fatal available issues.

Several other studies have been carried out within hospital settings, with improved communication and interruption reduction in mind (Acuff, et al., 1997; Coiera & Tombs, 1998; Eisenstadt, et al., 1998; Minnick, et al., 1994 ; Sammon, Karmin, Peebles, & Seligmann, 2006; Spurck, et al., 1995). In (Coiera & Tombs, 1998) they recommend a variety of approaches to improve communication, including support and asynchronous communication with acknowledge-ment. Different kind of text messaging systems for hospitals has also been revealed as positive (Acuff, et al., 1997; Eisenstadt, et al., 1998), but also showed concerns for character limits, small displays, and yet another device to carry. Of course, a lot have been improved within text messaging systems and mobile devices, regarding small displays and keyboards, since these studies were carried out, which may obliterate these concerns. The introduction of Smartphones has probably changed this. Other studies have shown positive results when providing nursing teams with wireless phones (Spurck, et al., 1995), wearable radio transmitters (Minnick, et al., 1994), and wireless hands-free headsets which interfaces the phone system (Sammon, et al., 2006). The feedback was; quicker updates to patient information, easier to locate nursing staffs, and reduced noise levels, but also concerns about being too available.

PDA have been used by (Munoz, Rodriguez, Favela, Martinez-Garcia, & Gonzalez, 2003) in a contextual message exchange system. This solution, developed at IMSS General Hospital in Ensenada Mexico, uses handheld devices that allow users to specify when and where they want to send messages and/or data to other colleagues. Physicians' can, for example; specify who will be the recipient of a patient's lab test result, and thereby automatically send it when it is ready. Moreover, within this system it is enabled that physicians can send messages without knowing the names of the recipients. This is done by sending the lab tests to any physician in charge for the next shift, or to the first doctor who enters a specified room the next day. In another system by Holleran et al. (2003), they used PDAs for simple text services.

PDA's with built in mobile phones, web-browsers, electronic versions of commonly used UK medical reference text books, drug interactions compendium, anatomy atlases, International Classification of Diseases – 10 (ICD-10), guidelines, and medical calculators, has been used by (Aziz et al., 2005) to enrich communication between health care workers. The purpose of this study, carried out at the Academic Surgical Unit at St. Mary's Hospital (London), was to verify whether PDAs with built-in phones, could be an efficient solution to improve communication between hospital workers. This solution was also compared with pagers. During the assessment phase, Palm Tungsten PDAs were given to a surgical team. The information used to evaluate the communication efficiency gained with these devices, was the time clinicians needed to respond to a call. After 6 weeks of tests and questionnaires filled out by the involved participants, the results were encouraging. It showed a general benefit in replacing pagers with the new advanced PDA devices. In a study described in (Mendonca et al., 2004) they used PDA's with access to patent data and with virtual white boards, which allows health care workers assigned to the same patient know about each other's work progress.

In (Skov & Høegh, 2006) they evaluated a context-aware solution based on mobile phones capable to give nurses patient information. The provided information included the nurse's daily tasks, timing constraints and positions. Moreover, the mobile devices could also be used to insert collected data during the daily work, and to view previously stored patient's information in order to monitor changes. After the development, an assessment phase was conducted. The identified problems mainly concerned the complexity of the automatic update mechanism of the devices: Some subjects did not understand how to navigate between the different interfaces and they felt forced to undergo the information displayed on the phone. Others felt confused when the system suddenly changed the interface while they were reading the information displayed. Some of the nurses also expressed uncertainties about the validity of the data previously entered into the system, and they were not sure if the information was saved properly when using the device.

Intelligent Hospital, QoS Dream Platform, is an application proposed by (Mitchell, et al., 2000).

It is based on wired touch-sensitive terminals ubiquitously scattered throughout the hospital. These terminals makes is possible for clinicians, after an authentication process, to request a video call with a colleague without knowing the location of the person they want to contact. The call is routed to the nearest terminal of the recipient, who can choose to accept the call, or refuse it. The user's location is tracked by an active badge system worn by the clinicians. The application is used for: Remote consultation between doctors (e.g. discussions regarding patients and their treatments), and consultation of patient's data enabled by an event notification infrastructure that allows pushing clinical data directly into the terminal's display. The Intelligent Hospital application was built to demonstrate a real application within the QoS Dream middleware platform. This platform supports context aware, event driven applications, and solutions based on multimedia contents where user mobility is a predominant factor. It is based on four main conceptual components: Operating system with resource management and overall control functionality, a dynamic multimedia streaming component based on the DJINN platform used to re-route video streaming contents according to the movement of the participants, an event-based infrastructure based on the HERALD architecture, and a set of APIs for building applications using the technologies within the system.

Other systems like the AwareMedia and the AwarePhone systems to Bardram et al. (Jakob E. Bardram & Hansen, 2004; Jakob E. Bardram, et al., 2006), supports context aware communication. Figure 2 shows the AWARE system architecture divided into four layers: the Client layer, the Awareness layer, the Context layer, and the Monitor and Actuator layer (Jakob E. Bardram & Hansen, 2010). It was developed in centre for Pervasive Health care at the University of Aarhus in Denmark. These systems in combination, forms a complete communication system for clinicians in a surgical ward. The tracking system is tracking clinicians in selected areas, using Bluetooth tags/

Figure 2. The AWARE system; this is a simplified version of the AWARE overall system architecture (Jakob E. Bardram & Hansen, 2010).

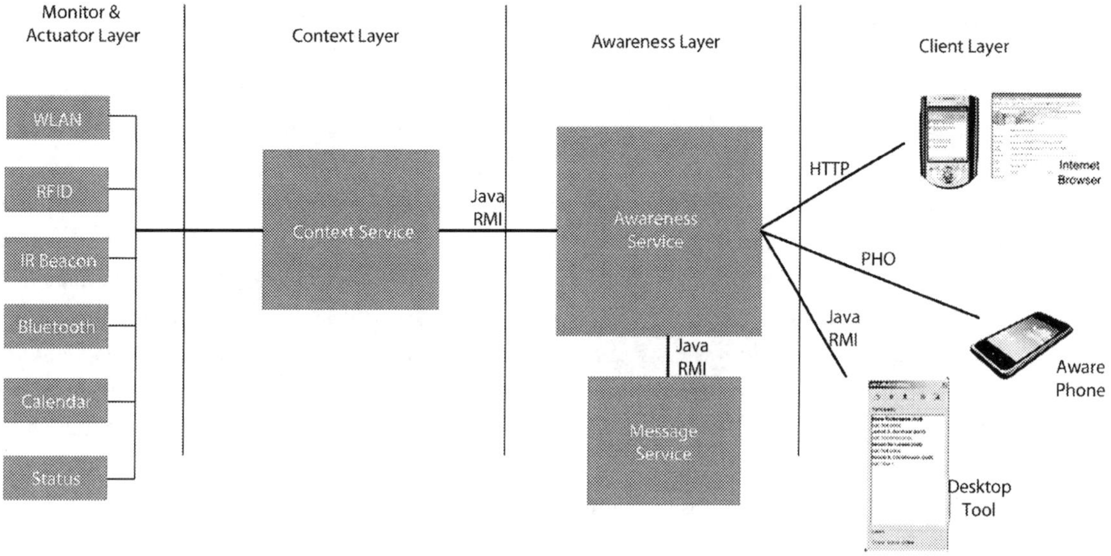

FUTURE RESEARCH DIRECTIONS

devices worn by the clinicians. The AwareMedia shows information on a number of large interactive touch screen displays scattered throughout the hospital. The information includes; location from the tracking system along with the clinician's schedule, what kind of operation is currently performed at a specific ward, status of the operation, which physicians present in the room, actual stage of the operation through dynamic colored bars, and status of the work schedule (e.g. delays or cancellations) provided by displaying visual signs and text messages. Further, in a dedicated area of the display, the application shows the status on other physicians' activities, their location, status, and future schedules. The AwarePhone system is an application running on a mobile phone (GSM/3G), which allows clinicians to call or send a message to a person in an operating theatre. Messages sent directly to the room, is shown to all people presented in that room through the AwareMedia Screen. The feedback from the use of these systems focusing on privacy issues as one of the big drawbacks deploying a system like this.

A number of studies have focused on context-sensitive systems for hospitals. Much of this work has focused on scopes not covered by this chapter, including issues related to mobile learning and privacy, accessing clinical data, or on multimedia communication at terminals with fixed locations (Mitchell, et al., 2000). The work done on context-sensitive mobile communication within hospital settings has identified some important elements of context, including location, role, delivery timing and artifact location, and user state (Munoz, et al., 2003). As presented in the previous sections, this model has been applied to an instant messaging system based on PDAs enabling contact based on these contextual elements. This approach, however, requires workers to carry additional mobile devices in order to support voice and paging services, since it is not compatible with existing hospital communication infrastructure. Another issue, by our knowledge not covered in previous work on role-based contact, is how to design interaction forms that allow users to easily switch work roles.

A variety of models for detecting interruptability have been created for stationary (Fogarty et al., 2005; Eric Horvitz & Apacible, 2003; E. Horvitz, Koch, Kadie, & Jacobs, 2002) and mobile settings (Bernstein, Vorburger, & Egger, 2005; Sawhney & Schmandt, 2000; Siewiorek, et al., 2003). In general, these models focused on office workers and social settings, and used information such as a user's calendar, interactions with computing devices, switches to determine if doors are open, accelerometers, microphones and motion sensors. Accuracy rates of approximately 80% to 90% have been reported for directly predicting interruptability and user state, such as "standing" or "walking", and social context, such as "lecture", "conversation" etc. None of these models, by our knowledge, has been explored in health care settings, and there are several factors that suggest the development of new health care relevant models is needed. First; studies on context aware communication for hospitals suggest information not included in these interruptability models, such as work role, are critical for detecting proper context in health care settings (Munoz, et al., 2003). Second; another issue is elements such as location and social relationships are inherently different within health care, and needs to be accounted for in health care appropriate models. For example, scenarios such as "visiting patients", "in surgery" etc. needs to be considered in combination with the work roles of the person initializing the contact and the contacted person.

In addition, appropriate forms for user-interaction with these interruptability models also needs to be investigated. It has been reported that users tend to use the information provided about a person's availability for communication, as a presence indicator instead of using it to control interruptions. This suggests that automatic configuration of devices may be the most appropriate approach (Fogarty, Lai, & Christensen, 2004). As previous presented in this chapter, the "SenSay"

context-aware mobile phone (Siewiorek, et al., 2003) uses a hybrid approach that automatically blocks calls, and also generates text messages notifying the caller that their call have been blocked. Then they are allowed to override the blocking by calling back within a predetermined number of minutes from the same phone number. This problem needs to be reinvestigated in health care settings, since there are some situations where certain calls should not be blocked (such as those for a specific role) whereas other calls may need to be restricted. Thus, the context of both the caller and person being called will need to be considered.

The use of semi-structured messages has shown to be particularly useful for work coordination (Malone, Grant, Lai, Rao, & Rosenblitt, 1987). Preliminary studies have estimated that up to 90% of mobile text-messages used by hospital workers could be met by the use of such messages (Jakob E. Bardram & Hansen, 2004). However, we have not been able to find any published work on the style and function of such messages, nor any studies that demonstrate if they would actually be adopted, or if they would have any effect during real work practice. The possibility to create automatic replies, and suggestions for replies, is also an advantage when using predefined messages, but the appropriate replies have not been studied in the context of mobile-text messaging. This could be particularly useful within health care settings, since such replies actually offers acknowledgement when a message has been read (Coiera & Tombs, 1998).

During the latest years, the industry has started to develop and launch systems for health care that in different levels controls the communication, and introduces smartphones for internal hospital communication. These systems are not presented in this chapter since we have not been able to find any research on the effectiveness or usage of the systems. Vocera (www.vocera.com), Ascom (www.ascom.com), Cisco (www.cisco.com) are examples of such companies/systems.

CONCLUSION

We know from earlier studies within health care, but also from our own studies (Scholl, et al., 2007; T. Solvoll & Scholl, 2008; Terje Solvoll, et al., 2010, 2013) that physicians in hospitals are interrupted unnecessary by mobile devices in situations where such interruptions should be avoided. This is a problem in today's hospital settings, and a solution to reduce such unnecessary interruptions from mobile devices is needed and wanted. A lot of work, as presented in the previous sections, has been done within the area during the years, but we cannot see that the situation has changed. The introduction of systems like Vocera, could have changed this, but we have not been able to find any research on this. We believe that one of the problems that is applicable to most of the earlier systems developed, it that they requires both new devices and infrastructure, and/or is based on public networks like GSM/3G, which in both cases requires considerable investments. A system based on existing infrastructure and devices used in hospitals, would be much cheaper,

and will probably require less training and maybe less resistance from health care workers when introduced. This is important since early studies shows that over half of medical informatics systems fail because of user and staff resistance (Anderson, 1993). However, this is an old study, but the situation does not seems to have changed a lot. We believe that; by knowing and understanding the physicians' work situation, the nature of unnecessary interruptions, and also by involving the participants in the design process, it is possible to build a system suited for their communication patterns and work situations, on top of an existing communication infrastructure, using devices already in use at hospitals. Our studies (Taxiarchis Botsis, Terje Solvoll, Jeremiah Scholl, Per Hasvold, & Gunnar Hartvigsen, 2007; Scholl, et al., 2007; T. Solvoll & Scholl, 2008; Terje Solvoll, et al., 2010) contributes to such knowledge, and were used as input in when we designed and developed a context sensitive system for mobile communication in hospitals, CallMeSmart. Figure 3 presents the overall system architecture of the system developed. The system aims to reduce

Figure 3. CallMeSmart overall system architecture

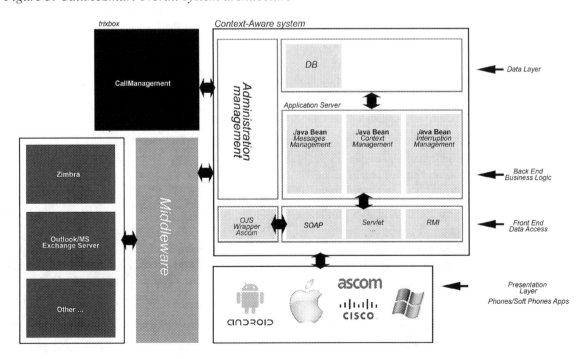

unnecessary interruptions from mobile devices in situations where interruptions should be avoided, like; when involved in a surgery (dressed in sterile clothing), doing patient examination at the outpatient clinic, having serious conversations with patients/relatives in conversation rooms, etc.

The system focuses on context sensitive interfaces, middleware, and new interaction forms for mobile devices that support multi-modal communication in hospitals. These devices supports media such as voice services, text-messaging and paging services, in an efficient and non-interruptive manner, as well as enable support for individual and role-based contact on a single device. That is, the user only need to carry one device for both personal and role based communication, which enables other users to, for example, contact someone assigned as "on-call" duties at a specific department, even if they do not know who that person is. At the same time, it aims to balance between availability and interruptions, while it enables acute calls and alarms forced through. Currently, by our knowledge, similar devices are not generally available for internal communication systems in hospitals.

CallMeSmart senses the context automatically from different sensors, calendar information, work schedule, etc., to change the physicians'/health care workers availability and the phones profile, according to the collected context information. At the same time, the caller is given feedback about the physicians'/health care workers availability, and thereby it is possible for the caller to force through an emergency call, or forward the call to another physician/health care worker at the same level, that is available. The system is based on the ideas from earlier studies on interruptions in combination with the ideas from (T. Botsis, et al., 2007; Terje Solvoll, Fasani, Ravuri, Tiemersma, & Hartvigsen, 2010; T. Solvoll & Scholl, 2008; Terje Solvoll et al., 2011, 2013; Talaei-Khoei, Solvoll, Ray, & Parameshwaran, 2011, 2012). A first version of the system is ready, and has been tested in lab-settings with physicians/nurses as test users. The tests were performed as scenarios observed from real situations. The feedback was mostly positive and has been used as input for improvement and further development of the system moving from prototype to production (Solvoll, T., Gironi, L., & Hartvigsen, G., 2013; Solvoll, T., Gironi, L., Giordanengo, A., & Hartvigsen, G., 2013). The overall system architecture is presented in Figure 3, and the system is ready for testing in clinical settings and a small pilot was started at the University Hospital of North Norway during May 2014, and a full size pilot is planned in a smaller hospital in northern part of Norway during the fall of 2015. The results from the pilots will be published in international journals.

CallMeSmart supports several forms of communication between users in the form of calling, messaging, and the ability to send out and answer alarms. Differing from many other alarm systems, which will alert all users when sending out an alarm, CallMeSmart uses contextual information in order to only send alarms to relevant users. Calls are performed using Session Initiation Protocol (SIP). The differences from a ordinary phone system comes from the context aware services of the system that decides what action to take, depending on the availability setting of the user receiving the call. Messaging works similar to regular Short Messages Services (SMS), but in CallMeSmart the user is also getting feedback when a message has been delivered to a phone, and when the user has opened the message. This helps the user to know if an important message has been received and read.

REFERENCES

Abowd, G. D., Dey, A. K., Brown, P. J., Davies, N., Smith, M., & Steggles, P. (1999). *Towards a Better Understanding of Context and Context-Awareness.* Paper presented at the 1st international symposium on Handheld and Ubiquitous Computing, Karlsruhe, Germany. doi:10.1007/3-540-48157-5_29

Acuff, R. D., Fagan, L. M., Rindfleisch, T. C., Levitt, B. J., & Ford, P. M. (1997). *Lightweight, Mobile E-Mail for Intra-Clinic Communication.* Paper presented at the 1997 AMIA Annual Fall Symposium, Nashville, TN.

Adams, N., & Gold, R. (1993). An infrared network for mobile computers. In *Proceedings USENIX Symposium on Mobile & Location-Indendent Computing* (vol. 10).

Alonso, O., Gertz, M., & Baeza-Yates, R. (2007) On the value of temporal information in information retrieval. *SIGIR Forum, 41*(2), 35-41. doi:10.1145/1328964.1328968

Anderson, J. G. (1993). *Evaluating Health Care Information Systems: Methods and Applications.* Sage Publications, Inc.

Avrahami, D., Gergle, D., Hudson, S. E., & Kiesler, S. (2007). Improving the match between callers and receivers: A study on the effect of contextual information on cell phone interruptions. *Behaviour & Information Technology, 26*(3), 247–259. doi:10.1080/01449290500402338

Aziz, O., Panesar, S., Netuveli, G., Paraskeva, P., Sheikh, A., & Darzi, A. (2005). Handheld computers and the 21st century surgical team: A pilot study. *BMC Medical Informatics and Decision Making, 5*(1), 28. doi:10.1186/1472-6947-5-28 PMID:16109177

Bardram, J. E., & Hansen, T. R. (2004). *The AWARE architecture: supporting context-mediated social awareness in mobile cooperation.* Paper presented at the 2004 ACM Conference on Computer Supported Cooperative Work, Chicago, IL. doi:10.1145/1031607.1031639

Bardram, J. E., & Hansen, T. R. (2010). Context-Based Workplace Awareness. *Computer Supported Cooperative Work, 19*(2), 105–138. doi:10.1007/s10606-010-9110-2

Bardram, J. E., Hansen, T. R., & Soegaard, M. (2006). *AwareMedia: A shared interactive display supporting social, temporal, and spatial awareness in surgery.* Paper presented at the 2006 20th anniversary conference on Computer supported cooperative work, Banff, Canada. doi:10.1145/1180875.1180892

Bernstein, A., Vorburger, P., & Egger, P. (2005). *Direct Interruptablity Prediction and Scenario-based Evaluation of Wearable Devices: Towards Reliable Interruptability Predictions.* Paper presented at the First International Workshop on Managing Context Information in Mobile and Pervasive Environments MCMP-05.

Bill, N. (2002). Context-aware communication. *Wireless Communications, IEEE, 9*(5), 46–54.

Bisgaard, J. J., Heise, M., & Steffensen, C. (2004). *How is Context and Context-awareness Defined and Applied? A Survey of Context-awareness.* Department of Computer Science, Aalborg University.

Blum, N. J., & Lieu, T. A. (1992). Interrupted care. The effects of paging on pediatric resident activities. *American Journal of Diseases of Children, 146*(7), 806–808. doi:10.1001/archpedi.1992.02160190038016 PMID:1496947

Botsis, T., Solvoll, T., Scholl, J., Hasvold, P., & Hartvigsen, G. (2007). Context-aware systems for mobile communication in healthcare - A user oriented approach. *Proceedings of the 7th Wseas International Conference on Applied Informatics and Communications*, (pp. 69-74).

Bradner, E., Kellogg, W. A., & Erickson, T. (1999). *The adoption and use of; a field study of chat in the workplace.* Paper presented at the Sixth European conference on Computer supported cooperative work, Copenghagen, Denmark.

Chen, Kotz, et al. (2000). *A survey of context-aware mobile computing research*. Technical Report TR2000-381. Dept. of Computer Science, Dartmouth College.

Chihani, B., Bertin, E., Jeanne, F., & Crespi, N. (2011) Context-aware systems: a case study. In Digital Information and Communication Technology and Its Applications (pp. 718-732). Springer. doi:10.1007/978-3-642-22027-2_60

Coiera, E. (2000). When Conversation Is Better Than Computation. *Journal of the American Medical Informatics Association, 7*(3), 277–286. doi:10.1136/jamia.2000.0070277 PMID:10833164

Coiera, E., & Tombs, V. (1998). Communication behaviours in a hospital setting: An observational study. *BMJ (Clinical Research Ed.), 316*(7132), 673–676. doi:10.1136/bmj.316.7132.673 PMID:9522794

Cousins, S. B., & Kahn, M. G. (1991). The visual display of temporal information. *Artificial Intelligence in Medicine, 3*(6), 341–357. doi:10.1016/0933-3657(91)90005-V

Eisenstadt, S. A., Wagner, M. M., Hogan, W. R., Pankaskie, M. C., Tsui, F. C., & Wilbright, W. (1998). Mobile workers in healthcare and their information needs: Are 2-way pagers the answer? *Proc AMIA Symp., 1998,* 135–139. PMID:9929197

Fogarty, J., Hudson, S. E., Atkeson, C. G., Avrahami, D., Forlizzi, J., Kiesler, S., & Yang, J. et al. (2005). Predicting human interruptibility with sensors. *ACM Transactions on Computer-Human Interaction, 12*(1), 119–146. doi:10.1145/1057237.1057243

Fogarty, J., Lai, J., & Christensen, J. (2004). Presence versus availability: The design and evaluation of a context-aware communication client. *International Journal of Human-Computer Studies, 61*(3), 299–317. doi:10.1016/j.ijhcs.2003.12.016

Gediminas Adomavicius and Alexander Tuzhilin. (2011). Context-aware recommender systems. In *Recommender systems handbook* (pp. 217–253). Springer. doi:10.1007/978-0-387-85820-3_7

Grudin, J. (1994). Groupware and social dynamics: Eight challenges for developers. *Communications of the ACM, 37*(1), 92–105. doi:10.1145/175222.175230

Harter, A., & Hopper, A. (1994). A distributed location system for the active office. *IEEE Network, 8*(1), 62–70. doi:10.1109/65.260080

Hersh, W., Helfand, M., Wallace, J., Kraemer, D., Patterson, P., Shapiro, S., & Greenlick, M. (2002). A systematic review of the efficacy of telemedicine for making diagnostic and management decisions. *Journal of Telemedicine and Telecare, 8*(4), 197–209. doi:10.1258/135763302320272167 PMID:12217102

Holleran, K., Pappas, J., Lou, H., Rubalcaba, P., Lee, R., & Clay, S. et al.. (2003). Mobile Technology in a Clinical Setting. *AMIA... Annual Symposium Proceedings / AMIA Symposium. AMIA Symposium, 2003.* PMID:14728368

Hong & Landay. (2004) An architecture for privacy-sensitive ubiquitous computing. In *Proceedings of the 2nd international conference on Mobile systems, applications, and services.* ACM.

Horvitz, E., & Apacible, J. (2003). *Learning and reasoning about interruption.* Paper presented at the 5th international conference on Multimodal interfaces, Vancouver, Canada. doi:10.1145/958432.958440

Horvitz, E., Koch, P., Kadie, C. M., & Jacobs, A. (2002). *Coordinate: Probabilistic forecasting of presence and availability.* Paper presented at the 18th Conference in Uncertainty in Artificial Intelligence (UAI'02).

Hristova, A. (2008). *Conceptualization and Design of a Context-aware platform for user centric Applications. Master of Science in Communication Technology.* Trondheim: Norwegian University of Science and Technology.

Katz, M. H., & Schroeder, S. A. (1988). The sounds of the hospital. Paging patterns in three teaching hospitals. *The New England Journal of Medicine, 319*(24), 1585–1589. doi:10.1056/NEJM198812153192406 PMID:3200267

Khalil, A., & Connelly, K. (2005). Improving Cell Phone Awareness by Using Calendar Information. Human-Computer Interaction - INTERACT 2005 (pp. 588-600).

Khalil, A., & Connelly, K. (2006). *Context-aware Telephony: Privacy Preferences and Sharing Patterns.* Paper presented at the CSCW'06, Banff, Alberta, Canada. doi:10.1145/1180875.1180947

Kidd, A. G., Sharratt, C., & Coleman, J. (2004). Mobile communication regulations updated: how safely are doctors' telephones used? *Qual Saf Health Care, 13*(6), 478. doi: 10.1136/qhc.13.6.478

Lieberman, H., & Selker, T. (2000). Out of context: Computer systems that adapt to, and learn from, context. *IBM Systems Journal, 39*(3-4), 617 - 632. doi: 10.1147/sj.393.0617

Long, S., Aust, D., Abowd, G., & Atkeson, C. (1996). Cyberguide: Prototyping context-aware mobile applications. In *Conference Companion on Human Factors in Computing Systems, CHI '96* (pp. 293–294). New York, NY: ACM.

Malone, T. W., Grant, K. R., Lai, K.-Y., Rao, R., & Rosenblitt, D. (1987). Semistructured messages are surprisingly useful for computer-supported coordination. *ACM Transactions on Information Systems, 5*(2), 115–131. doi:10.1145/27636.27637

Marmasse, N., Schmandt, C., & Spectre, D. (2004). WatchMe: Communication and Awareness Between Members of a Closely-Knit Group. UbiComp 2004: Ubiquitous Computing (pp. 214-231).

Massaguer, D., Hore, B., Diallo, M. H., Mehrotra, S., & Venkatasubramanian, N. (2009) Middleware for pervasive spaces: Balancing privacy and utility. In *Proceedings of the 10th ACM/I- FIP/ USENIX International Conference on Middleware.* New York, NY: Springer-Verlag New York, Inc. doi:10.1007/978-3-642-10445-9_13

Mendonca, E. A., Chen, E. S., Stetson, P. D., McKnight, L. K., Lei, J., & Cimino, J. J. (2004). Approach to mobile information and communication for health care. *International Journal of Medical Informatics, 73*(7), 631–638. doi:10.1016/j.ijmedinf.2004.04.013 PMID:15246044

Milewski, A., & Smith, T. (2000). *Providing presence cues to telephone users.* Paper presented at the 2000 ACM conference on Computer supported cooperative work. doi:10.1145/358916.358978

Minnick, A., Pischke-Winn, K., & Sterk, M. B. (1994). Introducing a two-way wireless communication system. *Nursing Management, 25*(7), 42–47. doi:10.1097/00006247-199407000-00011 PMID:8044475

Mitchell, S., Spiteri, M. D., Bates, J., & Coulouris, G. (2000). *Context-aware multimedia computing in the intelligent hospital.* Paper presented at the 9th workshop on ACM SIGOPS European workshop: beyond the PC: new challenges for the operating system, Kolding, Denmark. doi:10.1145/566726.566730

Mizzaro, S., Nazzi, E., & Vassena, L. (2008). *Retrieval of context-aware applications on mobile devices: how to evaluate?* Paper presented at the second international symposium on Information interaction in context, London, UK. doi:10.1145/1414694.1414710

Munoz, M. A., Rodriguez, M., Favela, J., Martinez-Garcia, A. I., & Gonzalez, V. M. (2003). Context-aware mobile communication in hospitals. *Computer, 36*(9), 38–46. doi:10.1109/MC.2003.1231193

Myerson, S. G., & Mitchell, A. R. J. (2003). Mobile phones in hospitals. *BMJ (Clinical Research Ed.), 326*(7387), 460–461. doi:10.1136/bmj.326.7387.460 PMID:12609917

Nelson, L., Bly, S., & Sokoler, T. (2001). *Quiet calls: talking silently on mobile phones.* Paper presented at the SIGCHI conference on Human factors in computing systems. doi:10.1145/365024.365094

Parker, J., & Coiera, E. (2000). Improving Clinical Communication: A View from Psychology. *Journal of the American Medical Informatics Association, 7*(5), 453–461. doi:10.1136/jamia.2000.0070453 PMID:10984464

Pedersen, E. R. (2001). *Calls.calm: enabling caller and callee to collaborate.* Paper presented at the CHI '01 extended abstracts on Human factors in computing systems, Seattle, WA. doi:10.1145/634067.634207

Sammon, M. J., Karmin, L. S. B., Peebles, E., & Seligmann, D. D. (2006, 2006-09-29). *MACCS: Enabling communications for mobile workers within healthcare environments.* Paper presented at the MobileHCI'06.

Sawhney, N., & Schmandt, C. (2000). Nomadic radio: Speech and audio interaction for contextual messaging in nomadic environments. *ACM Transactions on Computer-Human Interaction, 7*(3), 353–383. doi:10.1145/355324.355327

Schilit, B., Adams, N., & Want, R. (1994). *Context-aware computing applications.* Paper presented at the Mobile Computing Systems and Applications, 1994.

Schilit & Theimer. (1994). Disseminating active map information to mobile hosts. *Network, IEEE, 8*(5), 22-32.

Schmidt, A., Aidoo, K. A., Takaluoma, A., Tuomela, U., Van Laerhoven, K., & Van de Velde, W. (1999). Advanced interaction in context. In *Handheld and ubiquitous computing* (pp. 89–101). Springer. doi:10.1007/3-540-48157-5_10

Schmidt, A., Takaluoma, A., & Mäntyjärvi, J. (2000). Context-Aware telephony over WAP. *Personal and Ubiquitous Computing, 4*(4), 225–229.

Scholl, J., Hasvold, P., Henriksen, E., & Ellingsen, G. (2007). *Managing Communication Availability and Interruptions: A Study of Mobile Communication in an Oncology Department.* Pervasive Computing.

Siewiorek, D., Smailagic, A., Furukawa, J., Krause, A., Moraveji, N., Reiger, K.,.... (2003). *SenSay: a context-aware mobile phone.* Paper presented at the Wearable Computers, 2003. doi:10.1109/ISWC.2003.1241422

Skov, B., & Høegh, T. (2006). Supporting information access in a hospital ward by a context-aware mobile electronic patient record. *Personal and Ubiquitous Computing, 10*(4), 205–214. doi:10.1007/s00779-005-0049-0

Solvoll, T. (2013). Mobile Communication in Hospitals: What is the Problem? In C. Rückemann (Ed.), *Integrated Information and Computing Systems for Natural, Spatial, and Social Sciences* (pp. 287–301). Hershey, PA: Information Science Reference; doi:10.4018/978-1-4666-2190-9.ch014

Solvoll, T., Fasani, S., Ravuri, A. B., Tiemersma, A., & Hartvigsen, G. (2010, August 23-24, 2010). *Evaluation of an Ascom/trixbox system for context sensitive communication in hospitals.* Paper presented at the 8th Scandinavian Conference on Health Informatics, Copenhagen, Denmark.

Solvoll, T., Gironi, L., Giordanengo, A., & Hartvigsen, G. (2013). CallMeSmart: A VoIP Softphone on Android Based Mobile Devices Using SIP eTELEMED 2013. *The Fifth International Conference on eHealth, Telemedicine, and Social Medicine* (Vol. 15, pp. 198-203). International Academy, Research and Industry Association (IARIA).

Solvoll, T., Gironi, L., & Hartvigsen, G. (2013). *CallMeSmart: An Ascom/Trixbox Based Prototype for Context Controlled Mobile Communication in Hospitals*. Paper presented at the Information Science and Applications (ICISA), 2013 International Conference on Information Science and Applications. doi:10.1109/ICISA.2013.6579344

Solvoll, T., & Scholl, J. (2008). Strategies to reduce interruptions from mobile communication systems in surgical wards. *Journal of Telemedicine and Telecare, 14*(7), 389–392. doi:10.1258/jtt.2008.007015 PMID:18852324

Solvoll, T., Scholl, J., & Hartvigsen, G. (2010). Physicians interrupted by mobile devices – relations between devices, roles and duties. *Studies in Health Technology and Informatics, 160*, 1365.

Solvoll, T., Scholl, J., & Hartvigsen, G. (2013). Physicians Interrupted by Mobile Devices in Hospitals: Understanding the Interaction Between Devices, Roles, and Duties. *Journal of Medical Internet Research, 15*(3), e56. doi:10.2196/jmir.2473 PMID:23470528

Solvoll, T., Tiemersma, A., Kerbage, E., Fasani, S., Ravuri, A. B., & Hartvigsen, G. (2011). *Context-sensitive Communication in Hospitals: A User Interface Evaluation and Redesign of Ascom Wireless IP-DECT Phones*. eTELEMED 2011, The Third International Conference on eHealth, Telemedicine, and Social Medicine, Gosier, Guadeloupe, France.

Spurck, P. A., Mohr, M. L., Seroka, A. M., & Stoner, M. (1995). The impact of a wireless telecommunication system on time efficiency. *The Journal of Nursing Administration, 25*(6), 21–26. doi:10.1097/00005110-199506000-00007 PMID:7776003

Talaei-Khoei, A., Solvoll, T., Ray, P., & Parameshwaran, N. (2011). Policy-based Awareness Management (PAM): Case study of a wireless communication system at a hospital. *Journal of Systems and Software, 84*(10), 1791–1805. doi:10.1016/j.jss.2011.05.024

Talaei-Khoei, A., Solvoll, T., Ray, P., & Parameshwaran, N. (2012). Maintaining awareness using policies; Enabling agents to identify relevance of information. *Journal of Computer and System Sciences, 78*(1), 370–391. doi:10.1016/j.jcss.2011.05.013

Tang, J. C., Yankelovich, N., Begole, J., Kleek, M. V., Li, F., & Bhalodia, J. (2001). *ConNexus to awarenex: extending awareness to mobile users*. Paper presented at the SIGCHI conference on Human factors in computing systems, Seattle, WA. doi:10.1145/365024.365105

van Lieshout, E., van der Veer, S., Hensbroek, R., Korevaar, J., Vroom, M., & Schultz, M. (2007). Interference by new-generation mobile phones on critical care medical equipment. *Critical Care (London, England), 11*(5), R98. doi:10.1186/cc6115 PMID:17822524

Want, R., Schilit, Adams, Gold, Petersen, Goldberg, … Weiser. (1995). An overview of the parctab ubiquitous computing experiment. Personal Communications, IEEE, 2(6), 28-43.

Want, R., Hopper, A., Falcao, V., & Gibbons, J. (1992). The active badge location system. *ACM Transactions on Information Systems, 10*(1), 91–102. doi:10.1145/128756.128759

Weiser, M. (1991). The computer for the 21st century. *Scientific American*, *265*(3), 94–104. doi:10.1038/scientificamerican0991-94 PMID:1675486

Weiser, M., Gold, R., & Brown, J. S. (1999). The origins of ubiquitous computing research at parc in the late 1980s. *IBM Systems Journal*, *38*(4), 693–696. doi:10.1147/sj.384.0693

Westbrook, Woods, Rob, Dunsmuir, & Day. (2011). Association of interruptions with an increased risk and severity of medication administration errors. *Archives of Internal Medicine*, *170*(8), 683-690.

Wu, R., Rossos, P., Quan, S., Reeves, S., Lo, V., Wong, B., & Morra, D. et al. (2011). An evaluation of the use of smartphones to communicate between clinicians: A mixed-methods study. *Journal of Medical Internet Research*, *13*(3), e59. doi:10.2196/jmir.1655 PMID:21875849

Section 5
Ethic of Managerial Communication and Electronic Surveillance of Employees

Chapter 30
The Ethics of Strategic Managerial Communication in the Global Context

Angelo A. Camillo
Woodbury University, USA

Isabell C. Camillo
Brock University, Canada

ABSTRACT

Managerial Communication, in today's hyper communicative global business, is integral to business related disciplines such as strategic management, leadership, strategic marketing, and business ethics, etc. However, within the context of global strategic management, Managerial Communication follows under the broad umbrella of "Business Communication". Communication with internal and external stakeholders demands careful – ethical considerations, regardless of the industry. Having an inclusive – ethical strategic managerial communication policy in place, allows for strategic information dissemination as well as the protection of transmission of confidential data. This chapter discusses the topic of communication in general with emphasis on ethical managerial communication within the global context. The result of the study confirm that effective – ethical communication strategies and appropriate communications policy implementation is conducive to the firm's success. Within the framework of managerial leadership effectiveness, ethical managerial communication refers solely to managerial communication within the context of ethical global business management and not media communication.

INTRODUCTION

Within the framework of strategic managerial communication, we define business ethics as "a set of moral rules and principles to protect the interest of all stakeholders including but not limited to, employers, employees, customers, society, business associates, and the industry as a whole, while communicating with others."

Within the context of communication, trying to persuade what is ethical and what is not may influence the management's ability to communicate ethically and effectively.

The "inability" communicative with full transparency within the company and with stakeholders outside the company may lead to complex problems. Consequently, managerial decisions must be taken which could lead to unintended

DOI: 10.4018/978-1-4666-9970-0.ch030

consequences. For example, an expatriate managing a family owned enterprise may discover that a relative working in management is embezzling company money. Should the expatriate manager communicate the problem to the ownership? If so, how? Will they believe him/ her? Will they understand and support the expatriate, or will the owners retailed again him/her? If there is no clear communication policy in place, the expatriate will have to make a tough decision:

1. Say nothing;
2. Communicate the discovery in an ethical manner to the ownership;
3. Contact the embezzler first and explain and inform him/her about the responsibility to inform the owners; or
4. Consult a legal counsel first.

Obviously there are no easy answers unless an inclusive - strategic communication plan has been implemented for all stakeholders, regardless of the role or responsibility.

The current global business environment is characterized by an explosion in information technology, globalization of the economies, localized - acute economic crisis, and increased pressure from consumers, organized labor, and government regulations. It is clear that communicating freely and ethically becomes challenging. As a result, managers often chose "silence" over communication, in the hope that bad things will just go away, instead problems only escalate the majority of times. Ethical managers can create a certain image (positive or negative) of the organization, both within the company, and in the community and society. Therefore, considering that global corporations are becoming bigger and more powerful, there is a need for managers to communicate in an ethical and socially responsible manner. Lately, there has been an overwhelming interest by scholars on the importance of socially responsible communication. Social scientists are dynamically engaging in the much-discussed topic

of "micro aggression in managerial communication" and ethics in communication (Makau, 2009; Sue, 2010).

In a broad sense, Managerial Communication today is an integral component of many business related disciplines (strategic management, leadership, strategic marketing, international negotiation, business ethics, etc.). Cross-cultural communication, however, encompasses every area of communication including interpersonal communication (Lustig & Koester, 2010). This topic is usually integrated in courses under the discipline of Media Communication, which does not fall within the scope of this chapter.

A global search on the topic of cross-cultural communication within the global business context reveals that the discipline is under-researched. In fact, since 2010, UNESCO (United Nations Education Scientific and Cultural Organization) has been running a multilingual program called Transcultural Communication in the Digital Age (UNESCO, 2010). Its scope is to strengthen research in the field of multilingual and transcultural communication, including multilingual computing methods, e-learning, multilingual web content management, and related methods; to promote the development of a multilingual social web, harnessing semantic web technologies and strengthening transcultural communication patterns using a wide range of language resources and technologies; and multilingual computing methods, multilingual e-learning and cultural diversity management procedures (UNESCO).

However, within the global business management context and to a certain extent, Managerial Communication falls under the broad umbrella of "Business Communication", which is at the core of this chapter. In fact, when researching global competitive advantage, a major research question comes to mind: Why are some competitors more successful than others? Further, why do some executives consistently make the right decisions while others invariably fail? This chapter provides an explanation by asserting that one of the most significant attributes to global managerial success is *effective and ethical managerial communication*. In an attempt to exploit the true meaning of managerial communication, we theorize that when humans interact they create relationships. We base our theories and applications on a polycentric approach by thinking of *communication* as being more universal in nature than ethnocentric based. And, because we are different in nature, different people act and react differently. Since we are actively interacting, we adapt and learn the rules of the surroundings which condition the interaction, whether it is at the work place, at school, or on the golf course. By interacting, we acquire each other's culture and integrate our exchanged behavior, knowledge, experience, etc., thus becoming multicultural. Consequently, we adapt to the way we interact and communicate, and according to each given situation. Hence, when adaptation is not possible, we fail.

Indeed, failure due to lack of effective communication with all stakeholders leads to lower productivity, lower profitability, and short-term survivorship. Increased managerial communication effectiveness, however, enables practitioners at all management levels to realize the benefits of proper communication. In order to achieve effective communication, a firm must have well defined communication policies and plans in place. Communication policies are designed to enable a member of an organization to understand the finer points of internal communication with employees and external communication with business associates (Stevens, 2005). Through appropriate training and effective policy implementation, companies aim to develop communication skills, which can be applied to all levels of the organization, especially at middle to upper management levels.

However, policies and plans can only be developed and implemented with effective and continuous training, by using new and more efficient supporting tools such as developing communication technologies, and by having effective and ethical communication leadership.

To support this objective, certain fundamental elements are necessary. The management must have the ability to manage and deliver what it promises, and must possess a high level of communication competence - including but not limited to - ethical communication skills, language proficiency, cross-cultural awareness, intelligence, expertise, adaptability, and understanding (Hammer, 1989 pp. 247-261; Cushner & Brislin, 1996; Earley & Ang, 2003; Arasaratnam & Doerfel, 2005; Abbe, Gulick, & Herman, 2007).

Within this framework, Managerial Communication can be described as "an integrative theory-practice methodology that enables the management to sensibly apply the knowledge acquired to any situations, within the perspective of business communication." In other words, it is the process that interconnects knowledge with competent practice (Ting-Toomey, 1999). Furthermore, Managerial Communication can be interpreted as "the skill to efficiently communicate activities/messages to stimulate an anticipated reaction in a specific situation and without offending anyone in the process." Specifically, competent management needs to master the art of interaction and apply it efficiently with the people and the environment, and at the same time fulfil its own communication goals using this capability (Chen & Starosta, 1998: pp. 241–2).

BACKGROUND

Meaning and Application of Ethical Managerial Communication

Scholastically, managerial communication, within the framework of applied business communication, is considered a discipline (Gross, 2011) and a research topic in the field of social sciences (Calhoun, 2011), which has reached the classroom of many business schools around the globe. In fact, many graduate business programs now include managerial communication and also strategic managerial communication in their curriculum. Strategic communication is instructed as a foundational management competence instrumental in amplifying general performance at personal, company, financial, and strategic strata. It is applied to key managerial fields of study, which include crisis management, multicultural leadership, ethical communication, informational vs. persuational leadership, and team building, amongst others. Practitioners have long seen the necessity of effective communication.

In early 1980s, the topic of managerial communication engaged scholars in finding its clear definition. In 1986, Henderson proposed "A Conceptual Explication and Model for Guiding Future Research" (Henderson, 1986). Since then many definitions have emerged. To a certain extent, managerial communication today can be defined as *the communication between manager and subordinates.* In a broader sense, it can also include external stakeholders, including but not limited to customers and suppliers (Ellis & Hopkinson, 2010). However, Managerial Communication is considered an applied and essential discipline that continues to engage scholars in research, and has become one of the most important elements of concern within the context of global management.

Nevertheless, the goal of communication within the global business context is comprehensive in that it intends to develop and disseminate relevant knowledge, which will increase the effectiveness and efficiency of managers and employees in the contemporary multicultural and diverse business environment. Transcultural communication is still in the developmental stage today. The scope, however, is to integrate it within the area of managerial communication, which already expands beyond the walls of the global organization. It involves interaction between two or more diverse individuals who must communicate in a business situation, whether it is Manager to Employee (M2E), Business to Business (B2B), Business to Customer/Guest (B2CG), or in a "non-verbal" and "impersonal setting" such as social media across

the globe (MIT, 2009; Monash University, 2010; Cornell University, 2011). Good communication practices in the working environment are developed over time through experience and education. Too often, miscommunication can lead to create conflict. It is important, therefore, that firms not only have communication training and manuals at their disposal, but also that they master the art of "ethical managerial communication."

In an ideal world, a message sender could easily predict how others will perceive his or her message. In such a world, television commercials would be optimally placed, and no one would be offended by an inter-office email. In such a world, there would be no language barriers, no political, religious, gender, or cultural constraints. Unfortunately, the business world does not deal with such utopias, and consequently business leaders must be organized and prepared with well-formulated communication policies in place to avoid possible pitfalls.

Communicating strategically involves several basic elements: Purpose, Message Sender (Encoder), Message Configuration, Message Receiver (Decoder), Channel of Communication, and Expected Outcome. When properly applied, communication should be an easy task to accomplish. However, all too frequently, we hear that a company's major hurdle to success is communication. Consequently, talented managers with expertise in their field often fail in their duties simply because they lack the ability to communicate effectively. They also run the risk of delegating ineffectively because of their own inability to communicate effectively. A marketing manager who has innovative ideas about how to capture more customers, for instance, will be passed over if he/she is unable to make his/her suggestions clear and compelling. Many strategic plans may never be implemented if there is lack of communication ability (Thatam, 2008). Having a well defined policy is, therefore, key. Such a plan will have one goal in mind: to communicate a request, an idea, accomplishment, event, or even a failure. In other words, effective communication is neither a function of trial and error nor is it a matter of doing what comes naturally. Effectiveness in managerial communication requires managers to establish clear goals and then apply principles and insights to make wise choices about language and behavior in the communication process.

This chapter describes general ethical communication with real-life examples on how prominent companies have a communications policy in place, and how they use the results to raise awareness about the criticality of communication issues within organizational settings, especially during this current era of dynamic interconnectivity due to IT evolution. It also addresses the responsibility of executives who manage complex international businesses, and have a need to communicate effectively with diverse cultures in foreign lands. Therefore, the focus is on the importance of effective and ethical communication, both oral and written, while emphasizing the criticality of culture and cultures in business communication. Overall, it explores ways in which intrapersonal, interpersonal, intercultural, group, and organizational communication is experienced within both companies and cultures.

From a practitioner's perspective, the International Association of Business Communicators has established very clear and concise standards in their communication's policies (IABC, 2015):

The Global standard is defined by communication professionals around the world embracing a shared career purpose and six core Principles as the building blocks of their work. Informed by a passion for engaging audiences with strategic communication, the purpose and Principles focus our work and form a global standard.

Their organization's six principles are *Ethics, Consistency, Context, Analysis, Strategy, and Engagement.* Their members' day-to-day communication includes cultural values, compli-

ance with the law, and truthful, fair and accurate representation of the organization, and mutual respect and understanding. They communicate with sensitivity to cultural values and beliefs, act without deception and in accordance with the law, represent the organization truthfully, fairly and accurately, enable mutual understanding and respect, and adhere to the "IABC Code of Ethics for Professional Communicators and the Code of Ethics for Communication Professionals" (IABC, 2015).

Past, Present, and Future Applicability of Ethical Managerial Communication

Interest has been shown in the art of communication since the classical age. The Greeks developed specific communication methods and techniques that conferred it the status of a science. In the contemporary age, the communication theory has experienced an impressive growth, becoming a major preoccupation for many specialists in extremely different domains (psychology, philosophy, marketing and public relations, management, etc.). Managerial communication today has a special status, derived from an organizational framework simply known as *business communications* in which it is performed, from its goals, purpose and role (Gheorghe et al., 2009). For example, Carlson's (1951) classic study was based upon nine senior Scandinavian managers recording the details of each activity they engaged in. Subsequent researchers have empirically documented the volume, hierarchical direction, and purposes of managerial communication (Landsberger, 1961; Kelly, 1964; Horne & Lupton, 1965; Stinchcombe, 1974). Lawrence and Lorsch (1967) found that managerial communications and influence from lower and middle levels of management increased the quality of the decision making process. Also, Vroom and Yetten (1973) have investigated managerial communication and decision-making among managers, and their impact on the quality of decision making and implementation. Vroom (1964), in his studies of both autocratic and participative decisions, found that communication amongst diverse work groups required a greater investment of time, but produced a higher acceptance of decisions and increased the probability that the decision would be executed efficiently. Astley and Zammuto (1992) more explicitly centralize managerial communication in the sense-making processes that both create and disseminate managerial knowledge, thereby making and shaping communities and organizations. For them, "managers espouse their own theories about the way their world works, and the conceptual language they use establishes a context within which organizational life is constructed and reconstructed."

Weick (1995) argues that the basis of managerial action is not the world as objectively given but rather the world as people understand it to be. Rejecting traditional approaches to management scholarship that assume objectivity and rationality as human characteristics, Weick (1995) considers interpretation of communication in general as the underpinning of human nature. Several empirical studies of communication during mergers have provided support for the positive effects of managerial communication on employee attitudes and behaviours, especially in relationship with diverse work groups (Covin et al., 1996; Schraeder, 2001; Zorn et al., 2000).

Other researchers have provided empirical support for the positive effects of communication on organizational performance. For example, Miller, Johnson, and Grau (1994) found that communication was a significant factor in reducing employees' anxiety and increasing their willingness to participate in planned activities. Similarly, Wanberg and Banas (2000) examined the role of communication in a longitudinal study of government reorganization. They found that

employees who received adequate information about the organization plan demonstrated more positive attitudes toward the organization. More recent organizational researchers have suggested that communication is particularly important in organizational change processes (Zorn et al., 2000; Armenakis & Harris, 2002).

The role of organizational communication in a change context is generally defined as a process through which companies announce, explain, or prepare employees for change (Armenakis & Harris, 2002). This process perspective suggests that when employees receive sufficient and appropriate communication in a change context (i.e., appropriate justification for, and information about, the change and timely feedback), they will have more favourable attitudes towards the change which, in turn, should result in positive organizational outcomes (Goodman & Truss, 2004).

Effective communication within an organization has also been identified as a significant factor in helping employees understand the need for change, as well as the personal effects of a proposed change (Armenakis & Harris, 2002). This becomes even more critical in a global organization operating in any given host country. Increasing employees' understanding of the change process may also reduce the level of uncertainty and resistance toward the change and, thus, help promote employees' involvement in and acceptance of the change (Goodman & Truss, 2004). The importance of effective communication is noted also by Weick, Sutcliffe and Obstfeld (2005) who argue that it is talk that brackets action and thus gives meaning. Harvard Busines School focused on the meaning and application of effective communication, and emphasized that "Face-to-Face Communication" be used for clarity and impact by the "Results-Driven Manager" (HBS, 2004).

However, over time, the concept of managerial communication and specifically Ethical Managerial Communication has been ascribed numerous and varied meanings. Its exact meaning is still intensely debated. There are several definitions of managerial communication:

1. It is an applied, interdisciplinary field focusing on language and behavior within an organizational context (Brownell, 2003);
2. It focuses on cross-cultural communication across various contexts: interpersonal, group, organizational and, in some instances, mediated (Kraut et al., 1982; Kraut et al., 2002);
3. It includes all relevant forms and channels of communication that managers may select in accomplishing their purposes, including written, oral, nonverbal, and mediated (Cornelissen, 2004); and
4. Its research supplies the principles and insights that help practitioners to apply knowledge derived from all other disciplines as they seek to increase their effectiveness (Clampitt, 2005).

In an organizational approach, ethical managerial communication represents the decisive means by which the manager fulfils his/her tasks and duties, and employs the competences and skills pertaining to his/her role in the company and in relation to business partners (Gheorghe et al., 2009) - all interactions within an appropriate and ethical manner. The manager sends information to the members of an organization and its business partners, and their response influences his/her subsequent decisions and behavior. The quality of communication channels depends on the functionality of the communication system. This system needs to be conceived as a dynamic organism, capable of adapting to the information needs of the company at any moment, at any level, responding to any problems that may influence and condition its normal functioning (Johansson & Heide, 2008; Gheorghe et al., 2009).

Within a company, the individual and the group performance of the employees largely depends on the quality and ethical delivery of managerial communication. The manager communicates for the purpose of sending and receiving information, triggering adequate answers, and implicitly, influencing the receptors' decisions and their response to the transmitted messages. The efficient and ethical management of communication is a weighty responsibility for any manager, and the way he/she fulfils it is fundamental to business success. Managers need to inform all employees of company missions and goals, and related costs and targets. However, a manager is also interested in conveying information on task fulfilment, and suggestions and opinions on the well-being of the company, as seen by employees; hence, micro aggression of any kind must be avoided to achieve optimal success. At the same time, the members of the managerial team must also exchange information with regard to any technical, economic, and social problems affecting the company in a mutually ethical manner. Within the global business framework and the scope of this chapter, managerial communication becomes an important element of the interaction between all players. Thus, a system of reciprocal cooperation is created, facilitating the fundamental objectives of the company.

Published literature (Dance, 1970; Campbell & Level Dale, 1985; Clampitt, 2005; Stefanescu & Popa, 2008) emphasizes many modes of communication. However, two modes stand out as the most important: formal and informal. Formal communication can be defined as a set of rules that all stakeholders in the organization strictly adhere to. It is a structured flow of information formally conveyed to members within and outside the organization. The structure enables the flow of communication in a way that guarantees the transfer of a specific knowledge effectively, effortlessly, precisely, timely, and confidentially. In other words, the structure is the only formal channel of communication. Formal communication within the organization includes but is not limited to: departmental meetings, conferences, telephone calls, emails, text messages, company news releases, media interviews and specialist publications.

Informal communication cannot be as readily defined since its content is derived from unplanned events that may occur under specific circumstances. Informal communication is based on the realization that individuals or group members cannot be effective without personal interaction amongst its members. Therefore, informal communication is personal, unofficial, and mostly verbal. While it is unplanned for, past experience shapes informal communication. Accordingly, it is mostly through *informal communication* that unethical communication behaviour may occur. Because managers may be unprepared for what is not planned, and because the communication may be sudden and spontaneously, the necessity to communicate in any way or means available may cause the message to lose its meaning, while unethical components may carry more weight and micro aggression toward employees may become inevitable.

When formal communication is non-existent, informal communication occurs organically between individuals and within a team. When a crisis occurs, key players who have not been trained in communication develop and sporadically implement an immediate communication plan based on successful past experiences. When emergencies happen, a manager is able to promptly begin communicative interactions, fostering effective crisis management (McKinney et al., 2005).

Managerial communication acts as an integrated relationship with those inside the company as well as those outside the company. Competitive companies have understood this, and have promoted communicative ethical competence as a philosophy assumed by management and the organization as a whole. In many companies, communication is considered to be, and is used as, one of the most valuable instruments of strategic management. Conversely, the defective transmission of information, communication breakdowns,

and lack of transparency and honesty frequently account for business failures.

Examples of the criticality of using managerial communication are prevalent in the international political arena. The online version of The Hill Times, a Canadian weekly newspaper, reports that the current Prime Minister of Canada, Stephen Harper, has taken communiqués to a new level. The Hill Times reports that Mr. Harper's office and departments employ approximately 1,500 communications staffers (Ryckewaert, 2011). Quite a high number considering that Canada's population is about one tenth of that of the USA.

Approaches to Managerial Communication

Over time, multiple approaches to communication have been built. According to literature (Dance, 1970; Campbell & Level Dale, 1985; Clampitt, 2005; Copley, 2004; Stefanescu & Popa, 2008), there are four approaches that are the most significant and prevalent in managerial practice: the one-way communication model, the circuit communication model, the interactive communication model, and the behavioural model.

The one-way communication approach is a classic model (Schramm, 1955; Campbell & Dale Level, 1985). Managers who choose this approach (from transmitter to receptor or from encoder to decoder), which Clampitt (2005) called "the arrow approach" (p. 1), start from the presupposition that the receptor's feedback is not needed as long as the information and decisions transmitted were clearly formulated, in a language that is adequate and unambiguous. This idea relies on the belief that if the message is clear for the transmitter, it must be equally clear to the receptor. The latter will act in complete accordance with the content of the message received. By adopting this type of communication, the manager considers that, by using a clear and precise language, the decision he/she transmits will be correctly understood and complied with by the receiver, without any feedback required. This type of communication is a model that proves defective, as it generates problems at the organizational level. Employees often complain about the lack of information or about the fact that the information reaches them distortedly. In the absence of a response, this sort of information can no longer be corrected. The inadequate distribution of the information from the upper level of management to the lower levels was critiqued by Peter Drucker (1993) - when taking up the one-way communication model, a manager invariably ignores the receptor.

Communication is incomplete if information is misunderstood. Many theorists consider that we may speak of communication only when the receiver gives feedback. Under the conditions of the ever-increasing complexity of company activities, the efficiency of managerial communication process is not fully sustained by adopting a one-way communication model. Organizational practice has shown that efficient managerial communication relies on a plurality of factors. Among them, employee feedback to messages received from management attests to communication comprehension, and makes possible the adaptation of employee behavior to managerial expectations. Overlooking employee responses can have negative effects upon the success of the communication process and, consequently, upon the company in general.

Another approach of managerial communication is circuit communication, which supposes the existence, in all cases, of the receptor's response (reaction) to the received message. Unlike the *arrow approach*, this type of communication starts from the presupposition that the manager must know all problems facing subordinates are facing in fulfilling assigned tasks, and all their opinions and views on activities they carry within the company. The success of this type of managerial approach depends on the manager's skills in psychology and of his/her ability to stimulate the employee devotion towards the company. The disadvantage

of approaching this sort of communication comes from the large amount of time spent in discussions and debates, which may negatively reflect on the effectiveness and efficacy of the company.

Interactive communication is yet another way of approaching communication. Interactive communication supposes an exchange of ideas between those who communicate, each having in turn, the role of receptor and transmitter. This model of communication is particularly characteristic of organizations in which employees' creative skills are appreciated and their participation in problem solving is stimulated. Interactive communication relies on group creativity, the valorisation of proposals, and suggestions and ideas expressed by members of the organization. Its aim is to identify solutions generated by the exchange of ideas. The effectiveness of this type of communication is conditioned by the compatibility of those who communicate their shared level of knowledge, experience, values, and behaviours.

In 1985, Campbell and Level proposed a more complex model of communication – the behavioural model. The two researchers analyzed the managerial communication process by studying transmitter expectations of receptor reactions to a message. The anticipation of likely employee responses to a message helps the manager structure and adapt the message in order to illicit a positive response. The determination of the receiver's behavior subsequent to the communication must be, in the two researchers' view, the transmitter's first goal. He/she should also take into account the outside interferences that might occur and prejudice the communication process.

Although companies have gone through massive changes with respect to the way they approach managerial communication, none of the models presented above are remotely close to perfection. Each has, as shown, both advantages and disadvantages. In essence, any communication must be approached in a manner that best suits the set purpose and the communication competence of all concerned. He/she must ensure the smooth transit of the communication process through all channels, both formal and informal, and both inside and outside the company.

Development of the Managerial Communication Competence

Although communication may at first glance appear simple and uncomplicated, it is in fact a complex undertaking. Clampitt (2005) argues that communication within the firm is an important skill for all managers, irrespective of their seniority. Effective communication requires training and development. Often, organizations do not invest sufficient money, time, and effort in developing effective communication skills that in turn results in communication failure.

Many researchers have placed communicational competence at the very core of managerial success. Reflecting on the qualities that underpin managerial success, Maxwell (2002) ranks the manager's ability to communicate efficiently first in importance, with a rating of 38% (p. 101). It is notable that Maxwell gives other components a markedly lower grade: creativity – 31%, management knowledge – 19%, relationships – 12% (2002). In turn, Drucker (1977) urges managers to improve their communicative competence, so that they may be noted for their "ability to communicate with people and to introduce to them their own thoughts and ideas in such a way as to get them to understand and be persuaded" (p. 262). Furthermore, "this ability to express oneself may be the most important aptitude one can have" (Drucker, 1977).

A manager's ability to constantly improve his/her communication skills is fundamental to the operation of any company. In the process, the true understanding of *managerial communication* and its application becomes most critical for any manager. The result is a positive-communicative aptitude that fosters a climate of open mindedness

and trust, and repels conflict and tension. Additionally, the ability to convey unpleasant news or information with diplomacy, to divert conflict tactfully, and to solve problems with authority is a key aspect of effective communication.

Published literature (Johansson & Heide, 2008; Gheorghe et al., 2009) shows that too often communication by managers fail because of lack of proper training, lack of follow-up and follow through, and lack of consequence for those who do not perceive the communication to be relevant or important. Accordingly, managers often abdicate the responsibility for communicating effectively with their internal communication department, and lack the confidence to facilitate discussion within their teams (Clampitt, 2005). Communication is far from simple, and experienced communicators recognize, therefore, the need to be persistent until their messages have been clearly received, understood, and dealt with accordingly. The results of an investigation into persistent and redundant communication revealed that clarity in messaging was not the goal for redundant communication (Girard, 2011). Even if a powerful manager is clear and direct with an employee-team member, it is still the redundancy that counts in order to get the core of the message delivered as intended.

Strategic communication, policy-making, and guidance for consistent information activity, both internally and externally, are of increased interest to researchers. It is key that sensitive information be safeguarded effectively. E.g. computer hackers are now able to use social media to gain competitive advantage. WikiLeaks (Johnson, 2011) provides a vivid example of a seemingly weaker social media stakeholder empowered to compel concessions from an apparently stronger adversary (Castells, 2007). Certainly, companies ignore the power of social media within the context of communication at their peril. Top management, however, should be rather concerned that leaks can be detrimental to any company, and therefore the need to be prepared should be a priority.

The Role of Information Technology in Contemporary Communication Practice

Advances in information technology are allowing organizations to:

1. Distribute information at increased rates of speed;
2. Make more information available than ever before;
3. Allow broader and more immediate access to this information;
4. Encourage participation in the sharing and use of information; and
5. Integrate systems and functions in unprecedented ways.

The political tumult since 2011 in the Middle East has illustrated the key role of social media. Similarly, global corporations are using social media to disseminate all manner of information, whether marketing related or human resources related (Shah, et al. 2005). The most popular social media outlets such as Facebook, Twitter, and various other Web 2.0 technologies, are being used to communicate with individuals internally and externally across the globe.

Although using social media to communicate can be challenging, executives often use it effectively to stay in touch with all concerned in a timely and effective fashion (Lenhart & Fox, 2006). Oracle's CEO Jonathan Benoit, http://blogs.oracle.com/jonathan (Oracle, 2011), Bill Marriott Chairman & CEO of Marriott International http://www.blogs.marriott.com/, and John Mackey Whole Foods CEO http://www2.wholefoodsmarket.com/blogs/jmackey/ use internal and external blogs. The phenomenon delivers measurable benefits to all stakeholders (Drezner & Farrell, 2004). Internal blogs can, for example, facilitate the collation of workplace data. This information can be used to aid performance evaluations and many other applications. Data collected on external

parties such as guests/customers can be used in the application of competitive analytics, Customer Relations Management (CRM), Customer Experience Management (CEM), and other marketing related applications. With unparalleled access to stakeholders, IT communication must avoid any breach of privacy and unlawful collection of personal information.

New Developments in Ethical Communication

With the evolution of social media, there has been an increased interest by people in launching blogs, becoming members of online platforms that profile business people, and having personal websites as a tool for personal branding. This evolution has allowed business people to be positively exposed yet also criticized. Accordingly, anything said can be voice or video recorded, and can be used against the person being put in the spotlight. Therefore, communicating ethically in this ever-increasing interconnected and overexposed world has become one the most feared factor for many managers.

In 2007, Alex Brigham, an expert in the field of ethics and compliance, founded the Ethisphere Institute with a website and magazine. Its scope is to explore, examine, and circulate best practices through Ethisphere's proprietary research and rating system (Ethisphere, 2015). The Institute publishes a yearly report ranking the 100 most ethical global companies, 100 most influential - ethical business people, and a report on lawyers that matter. Ethisphere is not unique in rating and exposing the best ethical people and companies. Similarly, the Dow Jones Sustainability Indices publishes a yearly review of the most globally sustainable companies (DJ, 2015). A company that is publicly traded having a low DJ sustainability index score may not be attractive to investors; therefore, the manager must make any effort in ensuring that the index score's high. How the manager communicates this strategic goal and inspires all stakeholders to buy into it becomes a highly ethical and challenging task. This is to demonstrate that businesses and business leaders around the world are being watched, closely evaluated, and criticized (whether negatively of positively) around the clock. Therefore, the business landscape has and continues to transition into a new era of self-policing and carefully dealing in all business related endeavors in order to stay ethically – business viable. Accordingly, the way managers communicate, what they communicate, and how they use communication, has become an integral component in business strategy and in striving to achieve competitive advantage. As a result, companies and management are compelled not only to participate but also anticipate and prevent what could be detrimental to the company's future success. By saying even one wrong word, not only the going concern of the business may be in jeopardy but also the lives of all stakeholders involved could change forever. In sum, considering that we now live in the era of hi-tech evolution with no point of return, communicating in the best ethical way will be one of the most important key success factors for business managers and the companies they work with.

Use of Effective Communication to Create Competitive Advantage

Earlier in the chapter we discussed that when researching competitive advantage, some major research questions come to mind: why are some competitors more successful than others? Why do some executives consistently make the right decisions while others invariably fail? Studies in the field of managerial communication reveal that failure to effectively communicate leads to lower productivity, lower profitability, and short-term survivorship. In response to continuous failure, Fortune 500 companies have been hiring experts in the field of corporate communication in order to gain competitive advantage. A global search for job opportunities in *Corporate Communication* revealed that most job descriptions include

some common themes: "Identifying, anticipating, and prioritizing communication needs; providing strategic insight and direction for organizational communication within the organization; developing a concerted stakeholder engagement effort, especially among business leaders - complete with metrics and aligned with the company's *change management* program; partnering with the company's leadership team at a strategic level - coaching and counselling them; influencing leadership thinking in communication outreach; developing executive communications strategies for members of the company's leadership team; leading, developing, and executing internal organizational and employee communication programs to engage employees and heighten their level of commitment to the new operating model's goals and objectives; and managing issues and crisis situations that may arise, in coordination with senior management" (Johnson & Johnson, 2011).

Even the most talented managers, who attempt to lead an organization without effective communication especially without the concept of managerial communication, will ultimately fail while their more communicatively astute counterparts succeed. Many strategic plans may never be implemented due to lack of communication from managers. Increased managerial communication effectiveness enables practitioners at all management levels to realize the benefits of proper communication (Munter, 2011). In response to companies' demand for improved communication, institutions are now incorporating new disciplines into executive training on the topic of communication. One such discipline is *Emotional Intelligence* (EI) to improve communication (UC Berkeley, 2015). Through the concept of EI, managers can reflect on their own behaviour in order to improve their communication, thus acting ethically and successfully. Key components/ factors in such executive training include:

- Reading own emotional state and understanding how it affects the ability to im-

- prove interactions with co-workers and management.
- Interpreting co-workers' emotions and the situations that could result in different emotions, feelings and moods.
- Comprehending the importance of effective co-worker relationships that consider all parties' emotions.
- Understanding the positive and negative impacts that emotions can have on management and leadership.

A QUALITATIVE FIELD INVESTIGATION ON MANAGERIAL COMMUNICATION

Methodology of the Study

In support of the criticality of managerial communication discussed earlier in the chapter, we present and discuss the findings of a qualitative study on the topic of communication in general. The study uses philosophical and ethnographic research methodology to investigate and assess the status-quo of contemporary managerial communication policy implementation within firms. The study applies qualitative methodology using interpretative techniques to analyze the non-intrusive collection of data. This data is obtained from a convenience sample of companies across industries listed in the Fortune 500 directory, and from companies that provide communication related services.

The methodology uses the techniques of coding and frequency, and trend and pattern analysis. Coding is an analytical process in which data is categorized to facilitate the detailed analysis of critical variables which have variety, richness, and individual character. Coding is also used to distinguish between a set of variables followed by an additional in-depth interpretive coding in which more specific trends and patterns can be interpreted. Thus, coding allows for summarizing the prevalence and relevance of codes, discussing similarities and differences among them. In addition, it uses recursive abstraction, a methodology where datasets are summarized. Those summaries are then further summarized until a subset of useful data is obtained (Denzin & Lincoln, 2005; Loseke & Cahil, 2007; Holliday, 2007).

Data Collection

Data from previous studies was extrapolated principally from published scholarly literature and partially from practitioners' trade literature. The qualitative data was obtained from previously arranged semi-structured phone interviews, and face-to-face structured interviews with participants. Information was assessed accurately and consistently by asking all subjects the same questions, and from referring to company websites. Like personal interviews, telephone interviews enable a researcher to gather information rapidly, and they allow for personal contact between the interviewer and the respondent. During the interview, participants also had the opportunity to answer open-ended questions that allowed them to contribute their personal point of view.

About 100 firms representing America's largest and most successful corporations listed in the Fortune 500 directory were selected and contacted via email and by phone to participate in the study (CNN, 2014). We specifically selected companies based on their success, which in turn infers competitive advantage, and that *communication* in general may be an integral part of their strategic planning. We determined that a convenience sample of 100 firms was appropriate for this exploratory study. From the sample, 27 representatives agreed to participate. Participants were asked a set of questions that included whether their company had a communications policy in place, the policy content, and to what extent the policy was implemented - for example, at the corporate level or at other levels of the organization chart; whether a communications plan was effectively implemented; and if they had information they could freely provide.

RESULTS

Summary from Published Literature

The synthesis of the findings from published literature revealed that firms across industries cannot neglect the importance of a well formulated and implemented communication policy when operating in this century of high-tech evolution. A well-executed communication policy has a direct correlation with a company's success. Furthermore, the implementation of a managerial communication plan allows for maximum efficiency of information dissemination as well as the protection of confidential and highly sensitive data, which is vital to maintaining advantage over a competitor. Also of key importance is the methodology in which data is disseminated, and the degree of confidentiality as to who should receive the information and what to do with it. For example, using company blogs, Facebook, intranet, internet mail, written internal memorandum, etc. Table 1 shows the factors a firm should consider in the formulation of a managerial communication plan identified in an earlier study on Managerial Communication for an industry specific investigation (Camillo & Di Pietro, 2011).

Once the factors to be considered in the formulation of a communication plan have been identified, a logistics of the critical components must be developed (see Table 2).

Much debate pervades the education sector on managerial communication. Since it was first introduced in the classroom, academicians have argued about whether the subject should be catalogued and taught as a discipline, or be part of the social sciences, or simply regarded as an integral tool for the practitioner in the field. In addition,

scholars and practitioners in the field have yet to agree on a convention about the definition, distinction, meaning, and application of various terms used almost interchangeably within the context of managerial communication (see introduction section in this chapter for additional highlights). Nevertheless, top business schools today offer communication classes, both general and specific, as a requisite for those majoring in journalism or mass communication, and as an elective for those students enrolled in MBA programs.

Regardless of prevailing managerial communication debates, published literature and recent events (including that of the WikiLeaks release of sensitive U.S. Department of Defence documents) (Johnson, 2011) offer compelling evidence that not only is there a need for companies to implement

Table 1. Factors a firm should consider in the formulation of a managerial communications plan

Factors (Not Rank Specific)
Good communication skills and proper etiquette by managers are essential
The value of learning about culture and cultures
Effectively practicing Managerial Communication
Must have a communication plan in place
Defining the scope and the goal of the plan
Deciding on the critical components of the communication plan
Who should be in charge of disseminating what information
Who should receive the information
What should the content of the information include
The criticality of the timing on when information should be released
What methodology should be used to relay the information
Determining how to store, track, retrieve, and if necessary delete the disseminated information
Planning for unintended consequences and how to deal with them
Implementing an effective control mechanism that can monitor all company information to avoid distortion, tempering, and manipulation of the original information by intruders
Clear the Managerial Communication initiative with legal department before implementing the final plan.

Table 2. Critical components and logistics of a communication plan

Who Is Responsible for the Plan and Dissemination of Information?	What Should the Plan Include?	When Should the Plan Be Implemented?	How Should the Plan Be Developed?	Where – through Which Channel Should the Information Be Disseminated?	Who Are the Stakeholders?
Management-appointed spokes person	Policy and plan type of communication: internal-external, how much and level of confidentiality	At inception or by timely adoption, specific timing, frequency, ongoing	Self developed, hiring an expert, adoption from parent company, research	At specified location, either with public access or private, at all designated physical locations and in cyber space, directly via memo, email, presentation, or indirectly accessible on intranet, website, or personal by relaying to others in person, or in writing - electronically, voice and video recording, or by other means such as witness observation and taking notes	All management, employees and customers, all persons as appointed by management

an effective communication policy support by a dynamically updated training plan, but there is also a need to formulate a policy that is effective in protecting confidential data.

Summary from Structured Interviews

Data obtained from the structured interviews was transcribed, coded, and analyzed for frequency and pattern. Results were synthesized applying recursive abstraction, then summarized, tabulated, and are presented below. The first questions participants were asked was: Does your company have a communication department? If yes, does it have a communication policy in place? What are the most important factors included in your communication policy? Does your policy cover internal and external communication? Please provide an example of what your internal and external communication policy, e.g. a meeting (internal) or a press release (external), includes? Table 3 lists the most essential elements participants believed a firm should consider in policy creation.

Communication policies require efficient practicality and compelled adherence by all stakeholders. Not only must everything be recorded at any time for any given situation, but the rules must be followed without exception. Table 4 shows the outline of an actual meeting agenda that highlights the importance of producing a record about anything concerning an important company meeting. In this scenario a financial matter is discussed. A lot is at stake before the final financial results can

Table 3. Essential elements to consider when creating a communication policy

Essential Elements of Communication
Purpose
Message Sender (Encoder)
Message Configuration (timing, content, level of confidentiality)
Message Receiver (Decoder)
Channel of Communication (electronic, type written, in person)
Expected Outcome

Table 4. Sample communication meeting schedule regarding quarterly performance results

Q1-Quarterly Meeting – North America Division

• **Purpose:** Quarterly performance results and strategic planning review.
• **Date and Time:** April 16ˢᵗ. 20xx.
• **Venue:** Head Office Executive Boardroom.
• **Present:** VP Finance, Divisional Managers.
• **Participants Excused:** (List all absentees).
• **In Attendance:** (List all attendees).
• **Agenda Items:**
    o Approval of previous meeting minutes
    o Discussion of matters pending or arising from previous meeting
    o Discussion of agenda items in order of priority:
        ■ As planned by the meeting chair
        ■ As submitted by meeting attendees
        ■ As submitted by absentees
        ■ Items from the Board of Directors, Shareholders, other Executives/Stakeholders
    o Financial performance review
    o Sales and Marketing Strategies feedback
    o New Business Development
    o Divisional Activities at regional and Strategic Business Unit (SBU) Level
    o Production – Inventory – Backlog, etc…
    o Logistics and Distribution
    o Quality Assurance Report
    o New Projects – R&D report
    o Ethics report
    o CSR (Corporate Social Responsibility) Report
    o Human Resources Issues
    o Union Issues (if applicable)
    o Communications and Media Relations report
    o Other Business Issues
    o Date of next meeting and deadline for submitting new agenda items
    o Time meeting was adjourned
    o Signed: Minutes taken by…

be communicated to all stakeholders: the company stock value, the effect of the financial performance results will have on customers, employees, and business associates outside the company. (In order to protect the identity of the company and the identity of the meeting participants the names have been omitted).

Participants indicated several internal factors that are critical to management in the formulation and implementation of a communication policy and plan (see Table 5). The results in Table 5 concur with the industry specific factors determined in previous study. See Table 1.

Summary of the Results

In this era of rapid-fire technological advances, managers must understand the complexity of ethical managerial communication, and must decide to what extent a communication policy should be implemented. In the case of a company that operates globally, there is a need to change and adapt the communication policy to reflect the diversity and local culture of the host country's nationals. Hence, education and continuous training programs have to be in place, especially if firms operate as multinationals or conglomerates. One must also consult with legal experts to ensure that no potential legal infringements exist. In the case

Table 5. Factors a firm should consider in the formulation of a managerial communications policy

Factors
• Management responsible for the policy must possess good communication skills • Effective practicing of managerial communication • Understand the demographics of the stakeholders: different cultures and beliefs, diversity • Understand for whom the policy is being developed: employees, customers • Demonstrate good ethics • Must have an effective and well formulated communications policy and plan in place • Decide who should be in charge of developing and implementing the policy and plan • Define the scope and the goal of the policy and plan • Determine what the policy and plan should include • Decide who should be in charge of disseminating what information • Determine who the stakeholders are • When should be the information disseminated • What is the information about and what should the information include • What channel of communication should be used • How should the information be filed, stored, tracked, retrieved, classified, or deleted • Have a contingency plan for unexpected response or action against the firm • Have an effective monitoring system in place for accurate feed-back and corrective action if necessary • Be ready to • Prepare to counter negative criticism and take action for "Damage Control" • Always consult with the legal representative before implementing a policy, a plan or before responding to negative criticism or action by stakeholders.

of an international or multinational company, both countries' host and home-countries' legal aspects must be considered before a policy can be freely implemented. The findings from companies that have a communication policy in place reveal six common elements they value the most before a plan is implemented (see Table 4). These elements revolve around the information that needs to be disseminated as highlighted below:

- **Purpose:** Define the purpose of the policy and determine whether messages disseminated based on this policy will be clearly understood by all stakeholders. Assess the decoder's perception about the creditability of your company and the validity of the message being sent.

- **Message Sender (Encoder):** Encoding means translating information into a message in the form of symbols that represent ideas or concepts into the coded message that will be communicated. Encoding involves the use of specific language, types of words, and graphic, visual or auditory representations. Thus, encoding translates ideas into messages that others can interpret and understand. When encoding a message, the sender decides what to transmit based on what he/she believes about the receiver's (decoder's) knowledge and assumptions, along with additional information he/she wants the receiver (decoder) to have. It is important for the sender to use symbols that are familiar to the intended receiver. The sender should always create a scenario to mentally visualize the communication from the receiver's point of view (Munter, 2011).

- **Message Configuration:** Strategic formulation of the message being disseminated. What is the message? Is it negative, positive, informative, persuasive, or reinforcing? Does it raise awareness about something new or something to be concerned

about? Does the message carry a further message to a sub-audience? Does the encoder require feedback? What is the level of confidentiality? Is this the right timing?

- **Channel of Communication:** A communication channel is the means used to convey a message. Channels can be oral, written, visual, auditory, electronic, internal or external mail distribution, or via telephone. Various media such as television, websites, blogs, radio, etc. also exist. The effectiveness of each channel fluctuates depending on the characteristics of the communication. For example, when immediate feedback is necessary, oral communication channels are more effective because any uncertainties can be corrected instantaneously. In a situation where the message must be delivered to a wider audience, other channels should be considered.

- **Message Receiver (Decoder):** The receiver is the individual (or individuals) by whom the message is intended to be received. Once the message is received, examined, and interpreted, the decoder assigns some type of meaning to it. Successful communication takes place when the receiver correctly decodes and interprets the sender's message. The extent to which the decoder comprehends the message will depend on several factors: familiarity with the topic, the creditability of the sender, validity of the message based on prior relationship, and trust. The receiver's interpretation of the message is influenced by his/her experiences, attitude, knowledge, skills, perception, and culture. It is, in a way, the reverse of what the encoder attempts to determine before a message is disseminated.

- **Expected Outcome, Feedback:** These are important components of the communication process. Feedback and expected outcome are crucial in the evaluation of the effectiveness of the message. Feedback provides an opportunity for the sender to determine if the message correctly served its purpose. Did it produce the expected outcome and does corrective action need to be taken to reduce or eliminate confusion? Misunderstandings and eventual failure to ethically and effectively communicate is caused by several factors: inappropriate channel of communication, incorrect grammar, offensive language, micro aggression, words that may be misconstrued, misstranslation, etc. Regardless of the policy in place, communication within an organization can only be successful and effective if the communication process is flawlessly implemented and carried out. Ineffective communication can be averted if the organization thinks of communication as a process of continuous improvement. The results of this qualitative investigation offer useful insights into the criticality of having a communications policy and plan in effect at all levels of the organizational chart. The section below highlights this study's findings, and proposes useful recommendations for the practitioner in the field, for educators who wish to include the critical components of a managerial communications policy into their curriculum, and for graduating business major students about to join the workforce.

SOLUTIONS AND RECOMMENDATIONS

Ethical managerial communication is a vast field of study, which affects every individual who works within the organization. Despite its unstable or non-standardized position in the academic world, research in the field of communication is of great importance. The need for a solid communication infrastructure within an organization is key at every level. Having a communication department contributes to the overall competitive strategy of the company. Not only is good managerial communication dependent on the communication adroitness of individual managers, it also pivots on the response of subordinates. However, the problem will continue to persist until an agreement for a solution can be mitigated in regards to the criticality and complexity of ethical communication in general. Specifically, scholars and practitioners in the field should agree whether the subject should be catalogued and taught as a discipline, be part of the social sciences, or simply regarded as an integral tool for the practitioner in the field. Furthermore, the definition, distinction, meaning, and application of various terms used almost interchangeably within the context of managerial communication must be discussed and agreed upon "conventionally" in order to have common understanding of the application across the board (see introduction section in this chapter for additional highlights). The results will be mutually beneficial to all stakeholders. In this way, a communication plan will be taught, learned in the classroom, and applied in the field the same as a budget or any other component of the strategic planning. Therefore, a communication plan can be described as a tool that helps an individual, such as a manager, decide how he/she intends to have the organization understand the team's plans, strategies, and operations objectives. In an era of advanced technological innovation, we can relay a message in person, by email, by texting, over social network sites such as Facebook and Twitter, or simply indirectly through gossip. Too often messages reach unintended audiences. Consequences derived from miscommunication can be detrimental to an entire organization, especially in the international arena. Yet, incidents such as this do happen on a regular basis. It is also worth noting that once electronic messages have been sent, they can be stored by anyone in perpetuity. In sum, future studies should audit the effectiveness of communication policies by applying measurement matrices, surveys, and focus groups especially in relationship to evolution of information technology. The development of a model for global standardization of corporate communication would be beneficial to the entire international business community. Business schools should require that managerial communication be included in their curriculum at undergraduate and graduate levels, in required disciplines such as journalism, and in related disciplines such as marketing, accounting, finance, management, and leadership.

LIMITATIONS OF THE STUDY

To conduct this study, about 100 companies listed in the Fortune 500 directory on CNN.com (CNN, 2014) were contacted. There were several challenges. Ironically, as the study was about communication, the main challenge was finding the right department or person who could confirm if the company had a communication policy in place. Although several firms' representatives had agreed to participate in the interviews, eventually they could not due to company proprietary-confidentiality policies. Nevertheless, we were able to determine that most companies had a communication link or sub-page on their corporate website, dedicated to various audiences. E.g. shareholders, employees, customers, etc. Usually this was established through public relations departments. Although several attempts were made to communicate using electronic mail, no personalized reply was ever received; instead, only automated email responses were received. This confirms that the complexity and criticality of communication in the modern era will remain a hot topic for discussion. Company information can be received (pushed) as deemed worthy and necessary; however, it cannot be received (pulled) by simply contacting a communication's department or individual. Clearly this is an area companies can improve upon.

CONCLUSION

An extensive review of the literature and data obtained from selected companies provided valuable information about the status-quo of contemporary communication. In sum, effective and ethical managerial communication is a vital skill for everyone in business today, especially for managers at all levels of global companies. Great communicators have a key advantage in building managerial influence especially while starting their careers. Knowing how to communicate ethically and effectively in every business situation is not only important but critical to business success. From sensitively articulated employee feedback to persuasive announcements to customers, today's executive must be a frontline communicator.

In order to master the art of communication, a manager has to apply the following proficiencies:

- Understand the optimal 'medium' to present information.
- Learn the best timing to deliver key messages.
- Master the art of self-editing.

Grasping the best timing for *bad news* is paramount in the business world, especially during economic downturns when employees face job loss. Knowing when to communicate forthcoming layoffs is a tricky task. With a comprehensive communication policy in place, many scenarios can be planned for making it easier for management to deliver grave tidings.

This study is a subsequent study of an industry specific one (Camillo & Di Pietro, 2011), which investigates managerial communication cross-nationally and across-industries, and contributes to extant business research by raising awareness about the criticality of managerial communication. It illustrates the need for further study of this discipline in business schools, and provides useful insights regarding the factors and logistics needed to create and implement a communication policy and plan.

REFERENCES

Abbe, A., Gulick, L. M. V., & Herman, J. L. (2007). *Cross-cultural competence in Army leaders: A conceptual and empirical foundation.* Washington, DC: U.S. Army Research Institute.

Ali, M. (2011). *Chartis Launches Reputation-Guard®, Reputational Risk Insurance.* Retrieved from http://www.chartisinsurance.com/searchresults/search_295_195443.html

Allen, J. (2011). $16 muffins, $8 coffee served in Justice Audit. *Reuters Online Edition.* Accessed from the Web site: http://www.reuters.com/article/2011/09/21/us-usa-justice-muffins-idUSTRE78J7B020110921

Arasaratnam, L. A., & Doerfel, M. L. (2005). Intercultural communication competence: Identifying key components from multicultural perspectives. *International Journal of Intercultural Relations, 29*(2), 137–163. doi:10.1016/j.ijintrel.2004.04.001

Armenakis, A., & Harris, S. (2002). Crafting a change message to create transformational readiness. *Journal of Organizational Change Management, 1*(2), 169–183. doi:10.1108/09534810210423080

Astley, W. G., & Zammuto, R. F. (1992). Organization science, managers and language games. *Organization Science, 3*(4), 443–460. doi:10.1287/orsc.3.4.443

Berkeley, U. C. (2015). *Using Emotional Intelligence to Improve Communication.* UC Berkeley Extension. Retrieved June 25, 2015 from http://extension.berkeley.edu/search/publicCourseSearchDetails.do?method=load&courseId=8939289&gclid=CI2akq7Cq8YCFUGTfgod5lwAdw

Brownell, J. (2003). Applied Research in Managerial Communication. *The Cornell Hotel and Restaurant Administration Quarterly, 44*(2), 39–49. doi:10.1016/S0010-8804(03)90017-6

Calhoun, C. (2011). Communication as Social Science (and More). *International Journal of Communication, 5,* 1479–1496.

Camillo, A. A., & Di Pietro, L. (2011). The Importance of Managerial Communication for Hospitality Organizational Settings in the Era of High-Tech Evolution. *Hosteur, 20*(2), 19–27.

Campbell, D. P., & Level Dale, A. (1985). A Black Box Model of Communication. *Journal of Business Communication, 22*(3), 37–47. doi:10.1177/002194368502200304

Carlson, S. (1951). *Executive Behavior.* Stockholm: Strombergs.

Castells, M. (2007). Communication, power and counter-power in the network society. *International Journal of Communication, 1*(1), 238–266.

Chen, G. M., & Starosta, W. J. (1998). *Foundations of Intercultural Communication.* Boston: Allyn and Bacon.

Clampitt, P. (2005). *Communicating for Managerial Effectiveness.* New York: Sage Publications.

CNN. (2011). *Money, Annual Ranking of America's Largest Corporations. Fortune 500 companies.* Available from the Web site: http://money.cnn.com/magazines/fortune/fortune500/2011/full_list/

Copley, P. (2004). *Marketing Communications Management. Concepts and Theories, Cases and Practices.* Oxford, UK: Elsevier.

Cornelissen, J. (2004). *Corporate communications. Theory and Practice.* London: Sage Publications Ltd.

Cornell University. (2011). *Managerial Communication. An introduction to key library resources for Hotel Administration.* Available from the Web site: http://guides.library.cornell.edu/HADM3365

Covin, T., Sightler, K., Kolenko, T., & Tudor, R. (1996). An investigation of post-acquisition satisfaction with the merger. *The Journal of Applied Behavioral Science, 32*(2), 125–141. doi:10.1177/0021886396322001

Cushner, K., & Brislin, R. W. (1996). *Intercultural interactions: A practical guide*. Thousand Oaks, CA: Sage.

Dance, F. (1970). The concept of communication. *Journal of Communication, 20*(2), 201–210. doi:10.1111/j.1460-2466.1970.tb00877.x

Denzin, N. K., & Lincoln, Y. S. (2005). *The Sage Handbook of Qualitative Research*. Thousand Oaks, CA: Sage.

DJ. (2015). *Dow Jones Sustainability Indices*. Accesses June 24, 2015 at http://www.sustainability-indices.com/review/industry-group-leaders-2014.jsp

Drezner, D., & Farrell, H. (2004). *The power and politics of blogs*. Paper presented at the American Political Science Association Conference, Chicago, IL.

Drucker, P. (1977). *People and Performance*. New York: Harper`s College Press.

Drucker, P. (1993). *Inovatia si sistemul antreprenorial*. Editura Enciclopedica, Bucaresti.

Earley, P. C., & Ang, S. (2003). *Cultural intelligence: Individual interactions across cultures*. Stanford, CA: Stanford University Press.

Ellis, N., & Hopkinson, G. (2010). The construction of managerial knowledge in business networks: Managers' theories about communication. *Industrial Marketing Management, 39*(3), 413–424. doi:10.1016/j.indmarman.2007.08.011

Ethisphere. (2015). Research, rating and certification of corporate and institutional ethics, anti-corruption and sustainability. *The Ethisphere Institute History*. Retrieved June 25, 2015 from http://ethisphere.com/about/history/

Gheorghe, P., Gardan, D., & Geangu, P. (2009). *The Importance of Managerial Communication in Establishing the Company Marketing Communication*. Paper presented at the International Conference on Administration and Business, ICEA – FAA, Faculty of Business and Administration, University of Bucharest, Bucharest, Romania.

Girard, K. (2011). *It's Not Nagging-Why Persistent, Redundant Communication Works*. Paper presented at the Research and Ideas, Working Knowledge Conference, Harvard Business School, UK.

Goodman, J., & Truss, C. (2004). The medium and the message: Communicating effectively during a major change initiative. *Journal of Change Management, 4*(3), 217–229. doi:10.1080/1469701042000255392

Gross, L. (2011). Communication as the Discipline of the 21st Century. *International Journal of Communication, 5*, 1497–1498.

Hall Edward, T. (1959). *The Silent Language*. New York: Doubleday.

HBS. (2004). *Face-to-Face Communications for Clarity and Impact by the Results-Driven Manager*. Harvard Business School Press.

Henderson, L. S. (1986). Unraveling the Meaning of Managerial Communication: A Conceptual Explication and Model for Guiding Future Research. *Academy Of Management Best Papers Proceedings,* 219-223.

Holliday, A. R. (2007). *Doing and Writing Qualitative Research*. London, UK: Sage Publications.

Horne, J., & Lupton, T. (1965). The work activities of middle managers: An exploratory study. *Journal of Management Studies*, *1*(21), 14–33. doi:10.1111/j.1467-6486.1965.tb00563.x

IABC. (2015). *The six principles of the profession*. The Global Standard of the Profession. International Association of Business Communicators. Retrieved June 24, 2015 from https://www.iabc.com/global-standard-2/

Johansson, C., & Heide, M. (2008). Speaking of change: Three communication approaches in studies of organizational change. *Corporate Communications: An International Journal*, *13*(3), 288–305. doi:10.1108/13563280810893661

Johnson, C. (2011, August). Case Against Wiki Leaks Part Of Broader Campaign. *NPR News*. Accessed from the Web site: http://www.npr.org/2011/05/11/136173262/case-against-wikileaks-part-of-broader-campaign

Johnson & Johnson. (2011, December). *Director, Corporate Communications Job, Health Care Systems Inc*. Accessed from the Web site: http://www.careers.jnj.com/region

Kelly, J. (1964). The study of executive behavior by activity sampling. *Human Relations*, *17*(3), 277–287. doi:10.1177/001872676401700310

Kraut, R. E., Egido, C., & Galegher, J. (2002). Patterns of contact and communication in scientific research collaboration. In J. Galegher & R. Kraut (Eds.), *Intellectual Teamwork: Social and technological foundations of group work*. Hillsdale, NY: Lawrence Earlbaum Associates.

Kraut, R. E., Lewis, S. H., & Swezey, L. W. (1982). Listener responsiveness and the coordination of conversation. *Journal of Personality and Social Psychology*, *43*(4), 718–731. doi:10.1037/0022-3514.43.4.718

Landsberger, H. (1961). Horizontal Dimension in Bureaucracy. *Administrative Science Quarterly*, *6*(3), 299–322. doi:10.2307/2390705

Lawrence, P. R., & Lorsch, J. W. (1967). *Organization and Environment: Managing Differentiation and Integration*. Cambridge, MA: Harvard University Press.

Leeds-Hurwitz, W. (1990). Notes in the History of Intercultural Communication: The Foreign Service Institute and the Mandate for Intercultural Training. *The Quarterly Journal of Speech*, *76*(3), 262–281. doi:10.1080/00335639009383919

Lenhart, A., & Fox, S. (2006). *Bloggers: A portrait of the Internet's new story tellers*. Washington, DC: Pew Internet & American Life Project.

Loseke, D. R., & Cahil, S. E. (2007). Publishing qualitative manuscripts: Lessons learned. In C. Seale, G. Gobo, J. F. Gubrium, & D. Silverman (Eds.), *Qualitative Research Practice: Concise Paperback Edition* (pp. 491–506). London: Sage.

Lustig, M. W., & Koester, J. (2010). *Intercultural competence: interpersonal communication across cultures*. Boston: Pearson/Allyn & Bacon.

Makau, J. (2009). Ethical and unethical communication. In W. Eadie (Ed.), 21st century communication: A reference handbook. (pp. 435-444). Thousand Oaks, CA: SAGE Publications, Inc. doi:10.4135/9781412964005.n48

Maxwell, J. C. (2002). *Cele 21 de legi supreme ale liderului*. Editura Amaltea, Bucaresti.

Mckinney, E. H. Jr, Barker, J. R., Davis, K. J., & Smith, D. (2005). How Swift Starting Action Teams Get off the Ground: What United Flight 232 and Airline Flight Crews Can Tell Us About Team Communication. *Management Communication Quarterly*, *19*(2), 198–237. doi:10.1177/0893318905278539

Miller, V., Johnson, J., & Grau, J. (1994). Antecedents to willingness to participate in a planned organizational change. *Journal of Applied Communication Research, 22*(1), 59–80. doi:10.1080/00909889409365387

MIT Massachusetts Institute of Technology. (2009, August). *Advanced Managerial Communication*. Accessed from the Web: http://ocw.mit.edu/courses/sloan-school-of-management/

Monash University. (2010, January). *Managerial Communication*. Retrieved from http://www.monash.edu.au/

Munter, M. (2011). *Guide to Managerial Communication* (8th ed.). Prentice Hall Publisher.

Oracle. (2011, August). *Oracle CEO Blog*. Retrieved from http://blogs.oracle.com/jonathan/

Ortiz, F. (2012). In *Encyclopædia Britannica*. Retrieved June 27, 2012 from: http://www.britannica.com/EBchecked/topic/848801/Fernando-Ortiz

Rogers, E. M., Hart, W. B., & Miike, Y. (2002). Edward T. Hall and the History of Intercultural Communication: The United States and Japan. *Keio Communication Review, 24*, 1–5.

Rogers Everett, M., & Steinfatt Thomas, M. (1999). *Intercultural Communication*. Prospect Heights, IL: Waveland Press.

Ryckewaert, L. (2011, November). PM Harper takes communications strategy to new level. *Hill Times News Online*. Retrieved from http://www.hilltimes.com/news/2011/11/21/pm-harper-takes-communications-strategy-to-new-level/28868

Schraeder, M. (2001). Identifying employee resistance during the threat of a merger: An analysis of employee perceptions and commitment to an organization in a pre-merger context. *The Mid-Atlantic Journal of Business, 37*(4), 191–204.

Schramm, W. (1955). *The Process and Effects of Mass Communication*. Urbana, IL: University of Illinois Press.

Shah, D. V., Cho, J., Eveland, W. P., & Kwak, N. (2005). Information and expression in a digital age: Modelling Internet effects on civic participation. *Communication Research, 32*(5), 531–565. doi:10.1177/0093650205279209

Starbucks. (2011, November). *Starbucks to Present at Morgan Stanley Global Consumer Conference*. Starbucks Coffee Company Investor Relations. Retrieved from http://investor.starbucks.com/phoenix.zhtml?c=99518&p=irol-irhome

Stefanescu, C., & Popa, L. (2008, February). *Managerial Communication, Paper No. 7172*. Retrieved from http://mpra.ub.uni-muenchen.de/7172/

Stevens, B. (2005). What communication skills do employers want? Silicon Valley recruiters respond. *Journal of Employment Counseling, 42*(1), 2–9. doi:10.1002/j.2161-1920.2005.tb00893.x

Stinchcombe, A. L. (1974). *Creating Efficient Industrial Administration*. New York: Academic Press.

Thatam, S. A. (2008). *Strategic Communication: A Primer*. Advanced Research and Assessment Group.

Ting-Toomey, S. (1999). *Communicating across cultures*. New York: Guilford.

UNESCO. (2010). *Transcultural Communication in the Digital Age*. http://www.unesco.org/en/university-twinning-and-networking/access-by-region/europe-and-north-america/austria/unesco-chair-in-multilingual-transcultural-communication-in-the-digital-age-902/

Vicini, J. (2011). Government did not pay $16 for muffins after all. *Reuters Online Edition*. Retrieved from http://www.reuters.com/article/2011/09/30/us-usa-justice-muffins-idUS-TRE78T54220110930

Vroom, V. H. (1964). *Work and Motivation*. Willey New York.

Vroom, V. H., & Yetton, P. W. (1973). *Leadership and decision making*. Pittsburgh, PA: University of Pittsburgh Press.

Wanberg, C. R., & Banas, J. T. (2000). Predictors and outcomes of openness to changes in a reorganizing workplace. *The Journal of Applied Psychology*, *85*(1), 132–142. doi:10.1037/0021-9010.85.1.132 PMID:10740964

Weick, K., Sutcliffe, K. M., & Obstfeld, D. (1995). Sensemaking in organizations. *Sage (Atlanta, Ga.)*.

Weick, K., Sutcliffe, K. M., & Obstfeld, D. (2005). Organizing and the process of sensemaking. *Organization Science*, *16*(4), 409–421. doi:10.1287/orsc.1050.0133

Whiting, J. W. M. (1986). George Peter Murdock (1897–1985). *American Anthropologist*, *88*(3), 682–686. doi:10.1525/aa.1986.88.3.02a00120

Wholefoods. (2011, August). *John Mackey's Blog*. Retrieved from http://www2.wholefoodsmarket.com/blogs/jmackey/

Wing, D. W. (2010). Microaggressions in Everyday Life: Race, Gender, and Sexual Orientation. Hoboken, NJ: John Wiley & Sons.

Zorn, T., Page, D., & Cheney, G. (2000). Nuts about change: Multiple perspectives on change-oriented communication in a public sector organization. *Management Communication Quarterly*, *13*(4), 515–566. doi:10.1177/0893318900134001

ADDITIONAL READING

Edfelt, R. B. (2010). *Global comparative management: A functional approach*. Thousand Oaks, CA: Sage.

Hamlin, S. B. (1989). The Art of Q & A. In *How to Talk So People Listen: The Real Key to Job Success*. New York, NY: Harper Paperbacks.

Hattersley, M., & McJannet, L. J. (1996). Giving and Receiving Feedback. In *Management Communication: Principles and Practice*. New York, NY: McGraw-Hill.

Mclean, S. (2010). *Business communication for success*. Flatworld Knowledge Publishing.

Munter, M. (1995). Consult/Join Meetings. In *Guide to Managerial Communication: Effective Business Writing and Speaking* (5th ed.). Upper Saddle River, NJ: Prentice Hall.

Schein, E. (1988). *The Process of Building and Maintaining a Group*. Upper Saddle River, NJ: Prentice Hall.

KEY TERMS AND DEFINITIONS

Communication Plan: The art and science of reaching target audiences using marketing communication channels such as advertising, public relations, experiences, or direct mail, for example. It is concerned with deciding who to target, when, with what message, and how. The communication plan serves as a guide to the communication efforts throughout the duration of the project. It is a living and working document, and is updated periodically as audience needs change.

Communication Policy: Strategic information dissemination and a protection of transmission of confidential data.

Communication: The use of available resources to convey information, to move, to inspire, to persuade, to enlighten, to connect—is an inherently ethical undertaking. Regardless of context, communication involves choice, reflects values, and has consequences. These three key elements of communication form the basis of its ethical makeup.

Electronic Communication: Communication by advanced technologies.

Ethics: The study of values, of what is more or less important, of the "good," of behavioral guidelines and norms. Ethics provides frameworks and tools for recognizing and assessing available options and for differentiating between more or less morally justified pathways in any given situation. Ethics is a choice. An individual or group has options available in any given situation while being morally responsible.

Information Technology: A term that encompasses all forms of technology used to create, store, exchange, and use information in its various forms (business data, voice conversations, still images, motion pictures, multimedia presentations, and other forms, including those not yet conceived). It's a convenient term for including both telephony and computer technology in the same word.

Managerial Communication: Decisive means by which the manager fulfils his/her tasks and duties, and employs the competences and skills pertaining to his/her role in the company and in relation to business partners. The manager sends information to the members of an organization and its business partners, and their response influences his/her subsequent decisions and behavior.

Chapter 31
Surveillance of Electronic Communications in the Workplace and the Protection of Employees' Privacy

Ioannis Inglezakis
Aristotle University of Thessaloniki, Greece

ABSTRACT

The use of Information and Communication Technologies in the workplace is constantly increasing, but also the use of surveillance technology. Electronic monitoring of employees becomes an integral part of information systems in the workplace. The specific software which is used for monitoring electronic communications is, however, intrusive and infringes upon the employees' right to privacy. The issue of surveillance of employees' electronic communications is subject to different approaches in various jurisdictions. The most comprehensive protection to employees is afforded in the EU, and it would be enhanced once the General Data Protection Regulation is passed.

INTRODUCTION

The penetration of Internet technology in the workplace is constantly increasing, as almost every office today is equipped with computer systems and Internet connections. The low cost and high efficacy of computers and electronic communications are important factors that make the use of Information and Communication Technologies (ICTs) in the workplace inescapable (Kierkegaard, 2005, p. 226). However, this ever growing trend has also its drawbacks, due to the fact that it raises privacy risks for employees, since employers are taking advantage of surveillance technology in order to monitor employees' e-mail and internet usage. In addition, monitoring of electronic communications increases working stress and generates discomfort amongst employees.

The monitoring of workers in the workplace is not a new phenomenon. Employers have used various methods to control the performance of employees and their behavior at work on the past and they continue to do so. Yet, there were limits to the amount of information that could be collected and used for monitoring purposes with traditional means (Fraser, 2005, p. 227).

DOI: 10.4018/978-1-4666-9970-0.ch031

Nowadays, new technologies provide more advanced possibilities for monitoring of employees and in more particular, of their surfing activities and the electronic communications that they use, such as e-mail, instant messaging, etc. Other aspects of workplace monitoring include drug testing, closed-circuit video monitoring, phone monitoring, location monitoring, personality and psychological testing and keystroke logging.

The particular subject which will be addressed in this chapter concerns workplace monitoring in relation to employees' electronic communications. This issue constitutes a specific aspect of the more general topic of electronic workplace surveillance, i.e. the use of information technology to monitor the activities and work performance of workers (Godfrey, 2001). Our attention will be drawn at the surveillance of electronic communications at work, that is, the use of monitoring devices in order to gain access to employees' e-mail communications and to data revealing their online activities.

The use of electronic communications by employees and of the Internet in big businesses is very high, while in medium and small-sized businesses it is also constantly rising. Besides the benefits of the wide use of e-mails, this brings about serious issues for companies, such as the dissemination of illegal or offensive material and the leak of trade secrets by disappointed employees to third parties (Mitrou & Karyda, 2006). Additionally, a great number of employees are wasting their working time surfing on the Net and sending private e-mails (so-called "cyberslacking"), whereas this may give rise to termination of employment contracts.

For those reasons employers consider as their right to control the online activities of their employees. Certainly, employers have a legitimate interest in monitoring the behavior of their employees in order to secure the acceptable performance of employees and maximize productive use of their computer systems, to prevent the leak of sensitive company information, to prevent or even detect unauthorized use of said systems for criminal activities and ensure security of computer systems,

to avoid sexual harassment in the workplace and discrimination, and monitor employees' compliance with employment workplace policies related to use of ICT (EPIC; Lasprogata et al., 2004, pp. 2-3). However, such monitoring may have as a consequence the intrusion into the private life of employees and an infringement of their rights to respect of privacy and confidentiality of communications.

1. MONITORING METHODS OF ELECTRONIC COMMUNICATIONS AND MONITORING DEVICES

New technologies not only provide unlimited access to information, which becomes available to employees, but also effective means for their surveillance. Specific software applications exist, which facilitate the interception of communications and real time surveillance of surfing behavior. Such applications provide central control over software on individual PCs, meaning that programs can be remotely modified or suspended, while e-mail traffic and surfing activities can be read and analyzed (Davies, 1999). Companies are making extensively use of such software, which is affordable and widely available. In a survey carried out by the American Management Association and the ePolicy Institute in 2007, it was determined that employers were concerned over inappropriate use of the Internet in a great extent and as a result, they proceeded into monitoring of e-mail and Internet activities. Pursuant to the survey, 66% of employers monitor Internet connections and 65% block connections to unauthorized Internet sites (Survey, 2007).

In particular, according to this survey, intrusion into employee's communications takes the following forms:

- 45% of employers track content, keystrokes, and time spent at the keyboard;
- 43% store and review computer files;

- 12% monitor the blogosphere to see what is being written about the company; and
- 10% monitor social networking sites.

Another interesting finding of the survey is that of the 43% of companies that monitor e-mail, 73% use technology tools to automatically monitor e-mail and 40% assign an individual to manually read and review e-mail. Furthermore, blocking access to the Internet concerned adult sites, games sites, social networking sites, shopping/auctions sites, sport sites and external blogs.

E-mail and Internet misuse resulted into termination of employment relationship. A 28% of employers fired workers for e-mail misuse and 30% for Internet misuse. The reasons cited by employers were violation of company police, inappropriate or offensive language, excessive personal use and breach of confidentiality for e-mail related termination, whereas Internet related termination relied upon viewing, downloading or uploading of inappropriate or offensive content, violation of company police and excessive personal use.

Other workplace surveillance methods include monitoring of telephone and voice mail, whereas 45% of companies monitored time spent and numbers called, 16% recorded phone conversations and 9% monitored employees' voicemail message. In accordance with the survey, 48% of the companies surveyed used video monitoring to address theft, violence and sabotage, and a small percentage used global satellite positioning technology for employee surveillance.

Monitoring of employees' electronic communications is assisted by specific software, for which there is a vast market, since companies install such software in their computer systems that they appreciate as very useful in the modern work environment. Software packages monitoring e-mail offer varying services, ranging from full e-mail monitoring to programs that only record the employee name, the date and the time at which the employees pick up their e-mails (Ciocchetti, 2001, p. 26).

There exists also software that intercepts e-mail messages, on the basis of keywords which the employer specify that constitute offensive language, and block web pages, which are off-limits for employees, because they have been characterized as inappropriate by employers. Such software can be set to alert employers or the person appointed by them when employees websites which are barred. Other computer programs intercept emails of a private nature, in order to discover possible leakage of company information (Mitrou & M. Karyda, 2009). As it is obvious, monitoring software allows in a great extent covert interception of emails and control of web pages visited by employees, which are exceedingly intrusive (Kierkegaard, 2005, p. 229).

Such practices raise, therefore, risks for employees' rights, as it has been mentioned above, particularly, in the modern information society where the boundaries between professional and private life are blurred.

2. THE LEGAL FRAMEWORK

2.1. Constitutional Protection of the Right to Privacy

Intrusions into the private life of workers may infringe their right to privacy and in more particular, their right to information privacy.[1] The latter concerns a specific aspect of the more general right to privacy, i.e. the protection of the personal information with regard to their processing. It should be noted that, in our understanding, privacy is more than the right "to be let alone", as it is traditionally defined by Warren and Brandeis (Warren & Brandeis, 1890). Information privacy is conceived as the freedom of the individual to determine whether one's personal information is communicated to other member of society (Westin, 1967; Gormley, 1992).

Privacy is recognized as a fundamental right in most jurisdictions, with the exception of U.S.A. It is enshrined in international law treaties such as the Universal Declaration of Human Rights, which states in Article 12 that "no one shall be subjected to arbitrary interference with his privacy, family, home or correspondence, nor to attacks upon his honour and reputation. Everyone has the right to the protection of the law against such interference or attacks". With the same formulation it is also included in the International Covenant on Civil and Political Rights, in Article 17.

However, there are convergences concerning the approach followed as regards the constitutional status of privacy worldwide. In the U.S. privacy is not explicitly derived by the Constitution, but has been developed by jurisprudence[2], which recognized a right to privacy, but a limited one. The right to privacy, in particular, applies only against government intrusion and where the individual has a reasonable expectation of privacy (Kesan, 2002, p. 294).

In Europe, privacy is elevated at the status of a fundamental right, which stems from the principle of human dignity and is either enshrined as a specific right (e.g., Belgium, Spain, Portugal, Greece) or as a right deriving from other constitutional principles (e.g., Germany). The European Convention for the Protection of Human Rights and Fundamental Freedoms (ECHR), laid down by the Council of Europe, establishes the right to privacy in Article 8.[3] The Charter of Fundamental Rights of the European Union also includes this right[4] and a more specific right for data protection[5], but this legal text does not have a binding nature.

The right to privacy, however, is not an absolute right and it may be subject to restrictions that are based on other rights or the interests of others or the society. Such restrictions are provided for in Article 8 ECHR, stating that no public authority should interfere with the exercise of the right to privacy except such as is in accordance with the law and is necessary in a democratic society in the interests of national security, public safety or the economic well-being of the country, for the prevention of disorder or crime, for the protection of health or morals, or for the protection of the rights and freedoms of others. It is evident that in the case concerning workplace monitoring, the right to information privacy has to be balanced against the legitimate interests of the employers. It has to be examined, therefore, whether the law provides for salient solutions, taking into account the need to respect of employees' privacy and the interests of employers.

2.2. International Regulations

On international level, a notable instrument concerning data protection of employees is the "Code of Practice on the Protection of Workers' Personal Data" from 1997. The Code purports to providing guidance on the protection of workers' personal data. It does not have binding force, but rather contains principles, which can be used in the development of legislation, regulations, collective agreements, work rules, policies and practical measures at enterprise level.

The Code contains general principles, such as that personal data should be processed lawfully and fairly, and only for reasons directly relevant to the employment of the worker (Section 5.1); also, it states that personal data collected in connection with technical or organizational measures to ensure the security and proper operation of automated information systems should not be used to control the behaviour of workers (Section 5.4) and further, that personal data collected by electronic monitoring should not be the only factors in evaluating worker performance (Section 5.6).

It also contains provisions on collection, storage, use and communication of personal data, and on individual and collective rights. Concerning monitoring it provides the following in Section 6.14:

1. *If workers are monitored they should be informed in advance of the reasons for monitoring, the time schedule, the methods and techniques used and the data to be collected, and the employer must minimize the intrusion on the privacy of workers.*
2. *Secret monitoring should be permitted only: (a) if it is in conformity with national legislation; or (b) if there is suspicion on reasonable grounds of criminal activity or other serious wrongdoing.*
3. *Continuous monitoring should be permitted only if required for health and safety or the protection of property.*

Furthermore, in section 12.2 it is provided that:

The workers' representatives, where they exist, and in conformity with national law and practice, should be informed and consulted:

1. *Concerning the introduction or modification of automated systems that process worker's personal data;*
2. *Before the introduction of any electronic monitoring of workers' behaviour in the workplace; (…)*

Apparently, monitoring of employees is not prohibited, but underlies specific requirements. Particularly, secret monitoring is permitted exceptionally where there are reasonable grounds of criminal activity or if national legislation so permits. In addition, it is provided for collective protection, since representatives of workers should be informed and consulted before the introduction of electronic monitoring systems.

Furthermore, the Council of Europe issued a Recommendation on the Protection of Personal Data used for Employment Purposes.[6] This recommendation does not include provisions regulating the legitimacy of monitoring, but address this issue only with regard to information and collective protection of workers. In Section 3.1. it is stated that:

In accordance with domestic law or practice and, where appropriate, in accordance with relevant collective agreements, employers should, in advance, fully inform or consult their employees or the representatives of the latter about the introduction or adaptation of automated systems for the collection and use of personal data of employees. This principle also applies to the introduction or adaptation of technical devices designed to monitor the movements or productivity of employees.

A legal obligation to introduce monitoring practices in the workplace is foreseen in the Cybercrime Convention of Council of Europe, which lays down in Article 12 that criminal liability may be inflicted upon corporations, if they allow the commission of illegal acts through lack of supervision or control. In particular, it is stated that:

1) Each Party shall adopt such legislative and other measures as may be necessary to ensure that legal persons can be held liable for a criminal offence established in accordance with this Convention, committed for their benefit by any natural person, acting either individually or as part of an organ of the legal person, who has a leading position within it, based on: a) a power of representation of the legal person; b) an authority to take decisions on behalf of the legal person; c) an authority to exercise control within the legal person. 2) In addition to the cases already provided for in paragraph 1 of this article, each Party shall take the measures necessary to ensure that a legal person can be held liable where the lack of supervision or control by a natural person referred to in paragraph 1 has made possible the commission of a criminal offence established in accordance with this Convention for the benefit of that legal person by a natural person acting under its authority."

This provision might be interpreted so as to encourage businesses to introduce electronic surveillance measures in order to make sure that their employees do not commit illegal acts and more precisely, any activities which constitute cybercrimes or other offences such as copyright infringement, pornography, etc. (Kierkegaard, p. 232).

In the EU, besides the General Data Protection Directive, there is no specific legal instrument regulating privacy of employees. The EU Data Protection Working Party has set down general principles applying to email and internet monitoring in the Working Document on the surveillance of electronic communications in the workplace[7], which is complementary to Opinion 8/2001[8]. The Working Party lays down general principles and rules that implement the EU Privacy Directive in the specific circumstances of the employment relationships.

In particular, this document stresses out that employees should not be denied their right to privacy and data protection in the workplace. On the contrary, it should be recognized that they have a legitimate expectation of a certain degree of privacy as they develop a significant part of their relationships with other human beings within the workplace. This right should, however, be balanced with other legitimate rights and interests of the employer and this requires taking certain principles into account.

The following questions summarize principles underlying privacy protection of workers:

- Is the monitoring activity transparent to the workers?
- Is it necessary? Could not the employer obtain the same result with traditional methods of supervision?
- Is the processing of personal data proposed fair to the workers?
- Is it proportionate to the concerns that it tries to ally?

Furthermore, the Article 29 Working Party is of the opinion that prevention is better than detection, meaning that the interest of the employer is better served when preventing Internet misuse rather than detecting it. It also highlights the fact a general ban on the personal use of the Internet by employees is not reasonable and fails to acknowledge the importance of Internet for employees.

The opinion of the Article 29 Working Party rightfully points out that it is essential that the employer informs the worker of the presence, use and purpose of any detection equipment and/or apparatus activated with regards to his/her working station and any misuse of the electronic communications detected (e-mail or the Internet), unless important reasons justify the continuation of the secret surveillance, which is not normally the case.

As a practical advice, the Article 29 Working Party suggests that employers should consider providing workers with two email accounts: a) one for professional use only, in which monitoring would be possible and b) another account for private use, which may not be subjected to monitoring, unless security measures should be taken and which would be checked for abuse in exceptional cases.

3.3. The Provisions of the EU Draft Data Protection Regulation on Employees' Privacy

In 2012 the European Commission presented the proposal for a Regulation on the protection of individuals with regard to the processing of personal data and on the free movement of such data (General Data Protection Regulation, GDPR).[9] Once it is adopted, this regulation will replace the existing Directive 95/46/EC, which is the basic EU legal act in the field of data protection and its replacement will have important repercussions in the legislations of EU member states (Hert et al, 2012). Particularly, the choice of a regulation will result in the full harmonization of the EU member states' legislation and ensure a consistent and high level of protection. The objective of the European legislator with this proposal is to substantially reduce fragmentation, administrative burden and cost and to provide clear rules that will simplify the legal environment.[10]

The Regulation also has an impact on the protection of employees' data protection. In particular, substantial reforms such as the introduction of the principle of transparency and accountability enhance the level of data protection in the workplace and create specific obligations for employers. Notably, according to Article 11, data controllers are under the obligation to provide transparent information and communication relating to the processing of personal data to the data subject, i.e., the employee. Thus, surveillance of electronic communications should be defined in a policy document. The principle of accountability for data controllers imposes the obligation to implement specific measures in order to ensure that data protection principles are complied with. Such measures include, inter alia, performing a data protection assessment or designating a data protection officer, etc.[11]

A novel requirement is the designation of a data protection officer, according to Article 35 GDPR. This should take place at the discretion of the controller or processor or where this is required by Union or member state law.[12] The role of the data protection officer is very important, as this person shall act independently and assist the controller or processor to monitor internal compliance with the GDPR.

The conditions for consent do not exclude workers' data, however, it is foreseen in Article 7 (4) GDPR that it shall not provide a legal basis for the processing, where there is a significant imbalance between the position of the data subject and the controller. As explained in Recital Nr. 34, this is the case others, where personal data are processed by the employer of employees' personal data in the employment context.

Finally, it should be mentioned that the GDPR includes in Article 82 a delegation to member states to adopt specific laws in the employment sector.

The delegation is very broad, as it includes many aspects of the working relationship. The European Parliament adopted an amendment, which provides that the legal provisions of member states in accordance with para. 1 shall include minimum standards, including:

(d) whether and to what extent the use of telephone, e-mail, internet and other telecommunications services shall also be permitted for private use may be regulated by collective agreement. Where there is no regulation by collective agreement, the employer shall reach an agreement on this matter directly with the employee. In so far as private use is permitted, the processing of accumulated traffic data shall be permitted in particular to ensure data security, to ensure the proper operation of telecommunications networks and telecommunications services and for billing purposes.

Notwithstanding the third sentence, Member States may, by law, provide for the admissibility of this practice, by setting appropriate deadlines for the deletion of data, providing there exists a suspicion based on factual indications that must be documented that the employee has committed a crime or serious dereliction of duty in the employment context, providing also the collection of data is necessary to clarify the matter and providing finally the nature and extent of this data collection are necessary and proportionate to the purpose for which it is intended. The privacy and private lives of employees shall be protected at all times. The investigation shall be carried out by the competent authority;

2.4. Review of the Legality of Employees' Electronic Communications Monitoring

In USA and in Europe there are different approaches concerning the issue at stake, i.e. the surveillance of employees' electronic communications. Generally speaking, US law and jurisprudence afford minimal protection to employees, whereas in Europe the principles for a balanced approach have been elaborated. However, also in Europe there is no straightforward answer to the question whether surveillance of private e-mails could be permitted and to which extend.

Privacy of electronic communication under federal US law is afforded by the Electronic Communications Privacy Act, which prohibits unauthorized access to communications in electronic storage. Although this act applies to workplace surveillance of electronic communications, it includes many exceptions, which result in excluding employee protection (Kesan; Lasprogata). The jurisprudence also adopts a restrictive stance, taking into account the public nature of the workplace, which leads to denial of employee privacy. Courts in the USA apply the "tort of intrusion of seclusion" (Restatement of Torts § 652B, 1976)[13] and upheld that monitoring of employees' Internet use is not an invasion of privacy, since employees have no reasonable expectation of privacy for communications voluntarily transmitted on an employer's network, and that, even if there were such an expectation, the intrusion upon seclusion is not highly offensive (Fazekas, 2004, p. 15).

In *Smyth v. Pillsbury Co.*[14], the court held that an employee has no reasonable expectation of privacy, although the employee had been assured that the content of monitored emails would remain confidential and would not be used against employees for termination or reprimand. In this case the employee was terminated for abusing the email privilege by sending too many emails, which were reviewed by the employer and it was found that they contained offensive material about the employer. The court applied the tort of intrusion upon seclusion and it held that the plaintiff - employees' right to privacy was not infringed because "once plaintiff communicated the alleged unprofessional comments to a second person over an e-mail system which was apparently utilized by the entire company, any reasonably expectation of privacy was lost".

In *McLaren v. Microsoft Corp.*[15], McLaren accused Microsoft of privacy invasion, for it accessed and distributed the email stored in his personal folder on his computer. McLaren had been suspended pending an investigation following accusations of sexual harassment and "inventory questions". McLaren's email messages in his personal folder were read by Microsoft, which fired him based on their contents. In this case the court held that the employee did not have a reasonable expectation of privacy, since the e-mails were transmitted over the company's network and were at some point accessible to a third-party. It was stressed that although the plaintiff used a password to access his messages and he stored them in his personal folder, the messages were not McLaren's personal property, but were merely an inherent part of the office environment. The court cited Smyth v. Pillsbury and it came to the conclusion that the employers' "interest in preventing inappropriate and unprofessional comments, or even illegal activity, over its e-mail system would outweigh McLarens's claimed privacy interest in those communications" (Desrochers & Roussos, 2001).

In Europe, a different approach is adopted, as already mentioned. Namely, it is recognized that employees have a legitimate expectation of privacy in the workplace, but this right has to be balanced with other legitimate rights and interests of the employer, who is the owner of the facilities in his business and, in principle, can decide whether to allow employees private use of Internet and e-mail or not. The employee has the right to manage his business efficiently and to protect himself from the liability or harm caused by employees' actions.[16]

The differences in the expectations of privacy in USA and in Europe are primarily reflected in the jurisprudence of courts, particularly in those of the European Court of Human Rights (ECtHR). The ECtHR ruled in *Niemitz v. Germany* that no distinction can be made between private life and professional life regarding the protection of the right to privacy. This case concerned the search by a government authority of the law office of the complainant. The latter alleged, inter alia, that the search had violated his right to respect for his home and correspondence, guaranteed by Article 8 of the Convention. The argument of the government was that Article 8 did not afford protection against the search of someone's office, since "the Convention drew a clear distinction between private life and home, on the one hand, and professional and business life and premises, on the other".

The Court rejected this argument and pointed out that it would be too restrictive to limit the notion of "private life" – enshrined in Article 8 ECHR – to an "inner circle", in which the individual would live his own personal life as he chooses and to exclude therefrom entirely the outside world. On the contrary, it held that respect for private life must also comprise to a certain degree the right to establish and develop relationships with other human beings. Accordingly, it found that there is no reason to exclude activities of a professional or business nature from the notion of private life, particularly because the majority of people have a significant, if not the greatest, opportunity of developing relationships with the outside world in the course of their working lives. This argument is also supported by the view that it is not always possible to distinguish clearly which of an individual's activities form part of his professional or business life and which do not.

The ECtHR dealt with the monitoring of telephone and e-mail communications more precisely in two cases. In the case of *Halford v. the United Kingdom* the Court decided that interception of employees' phone calls at work constituted a violation of Article 8 ECHR. In more particular, the complainant, Ms Halford was provided with her own office two telephones, one of which was for private use, and these telephones were part of the police internal telephone network. The complainant alleged that calls made from her home and her office telephones were intercepted and this interception amounted to unjustifiable interferences with her rights to respect for her private life and freedom of expression, etc. The Government was of the opinion that telephones made by Ms Halford from her workplace fell outside the protection of Article 8, because she could have no reasonable expectation of privacy in relation to them. The Court, however, found that "telephone calls made from business premises as well as from the home may be covered by the notions of "private life" and "correspondence" within the meaning of Article 8 paragraph 1". It also noted that "there is no evidence of any warning having been given to Ms Halford, as a user of the internal telecommunication system that calls made on that system would be liable to interception. She would, the Court considers, have had a reasonable expectation of privacy for such calls…"

In the case of *Copland v. the United Kingdom*, the ECtHR found that a College that monitored an employee's e-mail, Internet usage and telephone calls infringed her right to privacy. This monitoring took place in order to ascertain whether the applicant was making excessive use of College facilities for personal purposes. The Government alleged that there has been no monitoring of content data, but that only an analysis of automatically generated information, i.e. of traffic data. Therefore, this case differed from the case of *Halford v. the United Kingdom*, where the applicant's telephone calls were intercepted. The Court held that e-mails sent from work and information derived from the monitoring of personal Internet usage is protected under Article 8, likewise as telephone calls. As the applicant had been given no warning that her communications were subject to monitoring, she held a reasonable expectation as to the privacy of calls made from her work telephone and to her e-mail and Internet usage. The Court also held that "the collection and storage of personal information relating to the applicant's telephone, as well as to her e-mails and Internet usage, without her knowledge, amounted to an interference with her right to respect for her private life and correspondence without the meaning of Article 8." Thus, it was irrelevant that the data held by the college were not disclosed or used against the applicant in disciplinary proceedings.

The jurisprudence of the ECtHR in the case of *Niemitz v. Germany* and in other cases did have a considerable impact upon the jurisprudence of national courts in Europe. In *Onof v. Nikon France*[17], the French Supreme Court held that an employee enjoyed the right to respect for his private life under Article 8 of the Convention in the workplace, and this right extended to private e-mails received at work, although the employer had prohibited on professional use of the computer facilities. The Court noted that an employer cannot read personal e-mail messages of an employee without violating the right of privacy and the right to respect of confidentiality of communications.

It is notable that the EU Data Protection Working Party attaches great significance upon the jurisprudence of the ECtHR and that, although they concern government action, the findings of the Court, as well as Article 8 of the Convention apply in a private action, also. This view is supported by the fact that in Europe under the concept of *Drittwirkung*, fundamental rights can be directly applied against private bodies by the courts.[18] The Working Party states three principles, which derive from the jurisprudence in relation to Article 8 ECHR:

1. Workers have a legitimate expectation of privacy at the workplace, which is not overridden by the fact that workers use communication devices or any other business facilities of the employer. However the provision of proper information by the employer to the worker may reduce the workers legitimate expectation of privacy.
2. The general principle of secrecy of correspondence covers communications at the workplace. This is likely to include electronic e-mail and related files attached thereto.
3. Respect for private life also includes to a certain degree the right to establish and develop relationships with other human beings. The fact that such relationships, to a great extent, take place at the workplace puts limits to employer's legitimate need for surveillance measures.

More specific criteria for assessing when monitoring of employees' communications may be lawful could be derived from the data protection legislation and in more particular, from the EU Data Protection Directive.[19] The legitimacy of monitoring can be based on Article 7 (f) of the Directive; accordingly, a monitoring activity should be necessary for the purposes of the legitimate interests pursued by the controller and it must not infringe upon the interests for fundamental rights and freedoms of employees, including the secrecy of communications.

Another legal basis for the legitimacy of monitoring could be the employee's consent. However, this stumbles upon the fact that e-mails contain personal data of both the sender and the recipient, and therefore, with the exception of inter-staff correspondence, this possibility is very limited (WP 55, p. 21). Besides that, due to the nature of employment relationship, in which there is an inherent asymmetry of power, employees would not have the possibility to make a free choice for monitoring. (Mitrou & Karyda, 2006). The Working Party has stressed out in this particular regard that "reliance on consent should be confined to cases where the worker has a genuine free choice and is subsequently able to withdraw the consent without detriment." (WP 2001, p. 23),

In case, however, the rules for monitoring of e-mail and Internet use are agreed between the employer and the employees' works council, this would amount to consent, pursuant to Article 7 (a) of the Directive.

General principles derived by the Directive also apply to e-mail and Internet monitoring. These are the principles of necessity, finality, transparency, proportionality and accuracy and limited storage of data (WP 55, p. 13). In accordance with the principle of necessity, the employer must check if monitoring is absolutely necessary for a specified purpose before introducing any such activity. Under the principle of finality, data must be collected for a specified, explicit and legitimate purpose and not further processed in a way incompatible with those purposes.

Furthermore, the principle of transparency means that an employer must be clear and open about his activities. Hence, covert e-mail monitoring would not be allowed, except in those cases where it is necessary for the investigation, detection of criminal offences, committed by employees, or for the protection of the rights and freedom of others and in particular, where sensitive company information should be protected.[20] Thus, there should be suspicion on reasonable grounds of criminal activity and monitoring should be permitted if it is in conformity with national legislation.[21] Moreover, the principle of transparency necessitates the obligation to provide information to the data subject and this entails the need to establish an e-mail/Internet policy within the policy, and an obligation to notify supervisory authorities.

The principle of proportionality means that personal data must be adequate, relevant and not excessive in relation to the purposes for which they are collected and/or further processed. As the Working Party points out (WP 55, p. 17), the application of this principle would prohibit blanket monitoring of individual e-mails and Internet use of all staff other than where necessary for the purpose of ensuring the security of the system. This also implies that monitoring of e-mail should be limited to traffic data and not extend to the content of communications.

The principle of accuracy and limited storage of data obliges employers to store only data from employees' e-mail accounts or concerning use of the Internet, which are accurate and kept up to date and not kept for longer than necessary.

3. CONCLUSION

In accordance with the general principles and rules which derive from the Data Protection Directive and the jurisprudence of the ECtHR, final conclusions which are arrived at, are the following:

Concerning e-mail monitoring, a distinction should be made between monitoring of company and private e-mails (Däubler, 2002, p. 100-101). Monitoring of company e-mails would be permitted without restrictions, but where an e-mail company address has a personal character (e.g. employee@company.com) the principles of necessity, finality, transparency, proportionality and accuracy and limited storage of data should be applied.

Where private use of the Internet is permitted and private e-mail accounts are provided to employees, monitoring of private e-mails would be permitted only in limited cases. This would be the case, for example, where it is necessary for the purposes of the legitimate interest pursued by the controller or by the third party or parties to whom the data are disclosed (Article 7 (f) of Directive 95/46/EC). This requirement would not be applied for monitoring the work performance of employees, since in this case the employee's right to privacy would be overridden. Furthermore, where sensitive personal data are concerned, monitoring of electronic communications would not be permitted, since Article 8 of the Directive does not provide for an equivalent with Article 7 (f) provision.

Concerning monitoring of Internet access, it should be underlined that allowing the personal use of the Internet lies at the discretion of the employer. However, a ban on the use of Internet for private purposes seems unrealistic in our information society. Thus, a reasonable use of the Internet appears to be more suitable (Bouchet. 2002). Monitoring of Internet use may also be regarded lawful in restricted cases and for security reasons or for the control of access. Such control may be exercised through filtering mechanisms and this would be less intrusive. It would also be less intrusive to exercise a posteriori control of Internet use of more general nature and not an individualized, personal control of accessed sites, which may reveal users preferences pertaining to sensitive data, such as political opinions, etc. (Bouchet, op. cit.).

In relation with monitoring of e-mail and Internet access, employees should be informed about monitoring. It is recommended to draft a company policy defining the rules for the use of the Internet and the standards to e-mail monitoring (WP 55, p. 25; Bouchet, p. 15). In addition, it is recommended to inform and consult workers' representatives before introducing monitoring systems.[22]

These requirements for an effective protection of employees' electronic communications are enshrined in the GDPR, which is under discussion; thus, a successful outcome of the reform process in the EU will have a positive effect on such protection.

REFERENCES

Article 29 Data Protection Working Party, Opinion 8/2001.

Article 29 Data Protection Working Party, Working document on the surveillance of electronic communications in the workplace, adopted on 29 May 2002, 5401/01/EN/Final, WP 55.

Bouchet, H. (2002). *Cyber-Surveillance in the Workplace*. Report adopted by the CNIL. Available at: http://www.cnil.fr/fileadmin/documents/uk/CNIL-cybersurveillance-feb2002-VA.pdf

Ciocchetti, C. A. (2001). Monitoring Employee e-mail: Efficient Workplaces vs. Employee Privacy. *Duke law & Technology Review*.

Costa, L., & Poullet, Y. (2012). Privacy and the regulation of 2012. *CLSR, 28*, 254–262.

Däubler, W. (2002). *Gläserne Belegschaften? Datenschutz in Betrieb und Dienststelle, 4.* Aufl.

Davies, S. (1999). *New Techniques and Technologies of Surveillance in the Workplace*. MSF Information 596 Professionals Association, London School of Economics. Available at: http://www.amicustheunion.org/pdf/surveillencetechniques.pdf

Desrochers, S., & Roussos, A. (2001). The Jurisprudence of Surveillance: a Critical Look at the Laws of Intimacy. *Lex Electronica, 6*(2). Available at: http://www.lex-electronica.org/articles/v6-2/desroussos.htm

Electronic Monitoring & Surveillance Survey. (2007). Retrieved from http://www.amanet.org/movingahead/editorial.cfm?Ed=697

EPIC. (n.d.). *Workplace Privacy*. Available at: http://epic.org/privacy/workplace

Fazekas, C. P. (2004). 1984 is still fiction: Electronic Monitoring in the Workplace and U.S. Privacy Law. *Duke Law & Technology Review, 15*. Available at: http://www.law.duke.edu/journals/dltr/articles/pdf/2004dltr0015.pdf

Fraser, J. (2005). Telecommunications (Lawful Business Practice) (Interception of Communications) Regulations 2000 Workplace Surveillance, Privacy and New Technologies. In L. Edwards (Ed.), The New Legal Framework for E-Commerce in Europe (pp. 277-291). Academic Press.

Godfrey, B. (2001). Electronic Work Monitorung: An Ethical Model. In *Proc. Selected papers from the 2nd Australian Institute of Computer Ethics Conference (AICE2000)*. ACS.

Gormley, K. (1992). One Hundred Years of Privacy. *Wisconsin Law Review*, 1335–1441.

Hert, P. D. (2012). The proposed data protection regulation replacing Directive 95/46/EC: A sound system for the protection of individuals. *CLSR, 28*, 130–142.

International Labour Organization (ILO). (1997). *Protection of workers' personal data*. An ILO code of practice. ILO.

Kesan, J.P. (2002). Cyber-Woring or Cyber-Shrinking? A First Principles Examination of Electronic Privacy in the Workplace. *Florida Law Review*, (54).

Kierkegaard, S. (2005). Privacy in electronic communication. Watch your e-mail: Your boss is snooping! *CLSR*, (pp. 226-236).

Lasprogata, G., King, N. J., & Pillay, S. (2004). *Regulation of Electronic Employee Monitoring: Identifying Fundamental Principles of Employee Privacy through a Comparative Study of Data Privacy Legislation in the European Union*. Stanford Technology Law Review.

Mitrou, L., & Karyda, M. (2009). Bridging the Gap between Employee Surveillance and Privacy Protection. In M. Gupta & R. Sharman (Eds.), *Social and Human Elements of Information Security: Emerging Trends and Countermeasures*. doi:10.4018/978-1-60566-036-3.ch016

Mitrou, L. & Karyda, M. (2006). Employees' privacy vs. employers' security: Can they be balanced?. *Telematics and Informatics*, *23*(3), 164-178.

Warren, S., & Brandeis, L. (1890). The right to privacy. *Harvard Law Review*, *4*(4), 193–220. doi:10.2307/1321160

Westin, A. (1967). *Privacy and Freedom*. Academic Press.

Mitrou, E., & Karyda, M. (2006). Employees' Privacy vs. Employers' Security: Can they be balanced? *Telematics and Informatics Journal*, 23(3), 2006, 164 – 178.

Moukiou, Ch. (2003). The European Legal Frame and its Effectiveness in Greek Reality – The Special Issue of Digital Signature. In D. Politis & N. Papasteriadou (Eds.), *Recent Advances in Court Computerisation and Legal Databases – First Steps towards e-Justice*. Athens: A.N. Sakkoulas Publications.

Schwartz, P., & Reidenberg, J. (1996). *Data Privacy Law*. Charlottesville.

Simitis S., Reconsidering the Premises of Labour Law: Prolegomena to an EU Regulation on the Protection of Employees' Personal Data, European Law Journal, Vol. 5 1/1999, 45-62.

Simitis S. Reviewing Privacy in an Information Society, University of Pennsylvania Law Review 135 (1987), 707 ff.

Theoharidou, M., Kokolakis, S., Karyda, M., & Kiountouzis, E. (2005). The insider threat to Information Systems and the effectiveness of ISO 17799. *Computers and Security Journal*, *24*(6), 472–484. doi:10.1016/j.cose.2005.05.002

Watson, G. E-mail surveillance in the UK workplace – a management consulting case study, in: Aslib Proceedings, MCB UP Ltd. 54 (1), 23-40.

ADDITIONAL READING

Delbar, C., Mormont, M., & Schots, M. New technology and respect for privacy at the workplace. MSF Information Professionals' Association, London School of Economics, London. Available from: <http://www.eiro.eurofund.eu.int/print/2003/07/study/TN0307101S.html>

KEY TERMS AND DEFINITIONS

Informational Privacy: The protection of the personal information with regard to collection and processing of data relating to an individual.

Lawful Interception: The interception of electronic communications by law enforcement agencies and other government services, in accordance with national legislation and after following due process and receiving proper authorization from competent authorities.

Right to Private Life: The right of the individual to continue its life privately, without government interference, respecting the rights of other people.

Secrecy of Communications: The right to protection of the secrecy of communications, which derives from the classic right to secrecy of correspondence. It protects the content of the communication, but also the information on when and to whom any messages (if any) have been sent.

Workplace Surveillance: The use of information technology by businesses in the course of employees' communications and work in order to monitor their activities. This includes, inter alia, telephone, PC monitoring and also, e-mail and Internet surfing monitoring.

ENDNOTES

[1]   The right to privacy includes many aspects; the most important ones are i) information privacy, i.e. the right of protection of private information, ii) physical privacy, which refers to respect of a person and the surrounding environment and iii) decisional privacy, referring to respect of one's personal decisions; see Lasprogata et al., op. cit., p. 4.

[2]   See, e.g., Griswold v. Connecticut, 381 U.S. 479 (1965); Olmstedt v. United States, 277 U.S. 438 (1928).

[3]   "Everyone has the right to respect for his private and family life, his home and correspondence".

[4]   Article 7 (Respect for private and family life): "Everyone has the right to respect for his or her private and family life, home and communications".

[5]   Article 8 (Protection of personal data): "1. Everyone has the right to the protection of personal data concerning him or her. 2. Such data must be processed fairly for specified purposes and on the basis of the consent of the person concerned or some other legitimate basis laid down by law. Everyone has the right of access to data which has been collected concerning him or her, and the right to have it rectified. 3. Compliance with these rules shall be subject to control by an independent authority."

[6]   Recommendation No R (89) 2, 1989.

[7]   Article 29 Data Protection Working Party, Working document on the surveillance of electronic communications in the workplace, adopted on 29 May 2002, 5401/01/EN/Final, WP 55.

[8]   Article 29 Data Protection Working Party, Opinion 8/2001 on the processing of personal data in the employment sector, adopted on 13 September 2001, 5062/01/EN/Final, WP 48.

[9]   COM(2012) 11 final.

[10]   Commission Communication, Safeguarding Privacy in a Connected World: A European Data Protection Framework for the 21st Century, COM(2012) 9 final, p. 2, 8, 12.

[11]   See Article 22 GDPR.

[12]   See, e.g., § 4f of the German data protection law.

[13]   "One who intentionally intrudes, physically or otherwise, upon the solitude or seclusion of another or his private affairs or concerns, is subject to liability to the other for invasion of his privacy, if the intrusion would be highly offensive to a reasonable person."

[14]   914 F. Supp. 97 (E.D. Pa. 1996).

[15]   No 05-97-00824-CV.

[16]   See WP 55, p. 4.

[17]   See: www.courdecassation.fr

[18]   The European Court of Human Rights recognized this concept in the case of *X and Y v. the Netherlands*.

[19]   Directive 95/46/EEC of the European Parliament and of the Council of 24 October 1995 on the protection of individuals with regard to the processing of personal data and on

the free movement of such data, L 281/31, 23.11.1995.

[20]   The EU Data Protection Working Party refers to Article 13 of the Directive, which states that: "Member States may adopt legislative measures to restrict the scope of the obligations and rights provided for in Articles 6 (1), 10, 11 (1), 12 and 21 when such a restriction constitutes a necessary measures to safeguard: (a) national security; (b) defence; (c) public security; (d) the prevention, investigation, detection and prosecution of criminal offences, or of breaches of ethics for regulated professions;

(e) an important economic or financial interest of a Member State of the European Union, including monetary, budgetary and taxation matters; (f) a monitoring, inspection or regulatory function connected, even occasionally, with the exercise of official authority in cases referred to in (c), (d) and (e); (g) the protection of the data subject or of the rights and freedoms of others."

[21]   See ILO Code of Practice.

[22]   See Council of Europe, Recommendation No R(89)2, Article 3.1; ILO, Code of Practice on the protection of workers' personal data, Sections 5.8, 12.2, 5.11.

Chapter 32

Dataveillance and Information Privacy Concerns:
Ethical and Organizational Considerations

Regina Connolly
Dublin City University, Ireland

Grace Kenny
Dublin City University, Ireland

ABSTRACT

Information privacy research historically focuses on exploring individuals' concerns in the transaction environment. However, the recent growth of technology-enabled workplace surveillance is raising many concerns over employees' privacy. Employee surveillance practices are becoming increasingly prevalent, ranging from monitoring internet and email activities to capturing employees' interactions with customers and employees' personal health and fitness data using wearable health devices. Individuals may understand that employers can monitor their activities, but may not the potential uses or the repercussions of such monitoring. Moreover, employees may not feel they have the ability to opt-out of this monitoring. This chapter explores the privacy and ethical issues surrounding emerging means of workplace surveillance. The chapter considers both employee and employer perspectives and poses many questions to consider when deciding when does legitimate monitoring become an invasion of employee privacy?

INTRODUCTION

Privacy has been an issue of enduring concern across a wide variety of disciplines and throughout history with discussions spanning back to the writings of Aristotle. In recent decades privacy has grown exponentially in prominence, in terms of increased research activity in many disciplines, the introduction of more stringent legislation in many countries and attracting regular attention in media and societal discussions. Despite the continually growing interest in privacy, a widely agreed upon encompassing, unambiguous definition of privacy remains lacking. It can be argued that the absence of one universally, accepted definition can be attributed to the multidisciplinary nature of privacy, which has generated debate in disciplines such as Law, Marketing, Manage-

DOI: 10.4018/978-1-4666-9970-0.ch032

ment Information systems (MIS), Economics and Psychology (Pavlou, 2011). The contrasting conceptualisations of privacy across, and often within disciplines, has led to a fragmented body of privacy literature replete with inconsistent, underdeveloped, and partially validated concepts (Smith, Dinev & Xu, 2011). Thus the generalisability of the conclusions reached from privacy research is often constrained by the conceptual lens applied by the researcher to examine privacy and the context of the study.

The confusion surrounding the privacy construct is also apparent in efforts to determine what is and what is *not* considered privacy. Numerous similar concepts such as secrecy, anonymity and security have are often discussed interchangeably with privacy despite representing separate constructs. However, recently progress has been made to both, distinguish privacy from similar concepts and to organise and categorise the competing perspectives of privacy. For example, Smith, Dinev & Xu (2011) reviewed the varying conceptualisations of privacy across a number of academic disciplines and derived two broad views of privacy; cognate based views and the value based views. While the work of Smith, Dinev & Xu (2011) provides a means of classifying privacy, Dinev *et al.,* (2013) call for the integration of these differing perspectives to build a more rigorous, empirically testable framework of privacy and its closely associated correlates, which have often been confused with privacy.

The need to disentangle the labyrinthine privacy construct is driven by fact that information privacy is an issue of increasing concern to many stakeholders, including citizens, employers, privacy activists, researchers and policy makers. The growing prevalence of Internet-based technologies partly drives concerns across these parties. While these technologies can yield a bounty of benefits for organisations, employees, government bodies, and citizens, they also facilitate the collection, collation and analysis of vast quantities of personal information, often unbeknownst to the person the

information pertains to. Such practices used by organisations to collect information on consumers, competitors, and even employees foster privacy concerns. In recent years, there has been a massive surge in the application of pervasive monitoring technologies in the workplace. Activities such as employee email and Internet monitoring unsurprisingly generates privacy concerns amongst employees. Employees' expectation of privacy in the work environment conflicts with the aim of all organisations to operate efficiently. The motivation behind organisations' use of technology-enabled monitoring is understandable and arguably a legitimate means to ensure productivity. However, it can also be argued that organisations' entitlement to engage in some monitoring must be balanced with maintaining some element of privacy for employees.

Technology-enabled monitoring of employees has grown exponentially in recent years, and this growth is forecast to prevail. According to Garner, 60% of organisations will implement a formal digital monitoring policy in 2015 (Garner, 2012). Such monitoring activities as noted tend to include email activity, internet and external social media use but, may also take the form of indisputably invasive keystroke logging, and more recently, sociometric badges that record face to face employees' interactions with fellow employees and customers. Another emerging form of monitoring relates to wearable fitness devices, often used by individuals to track their personal activity and fitness. Employers have begun offering these devices through company wellness programs to monitor employees' physical activities. With technology enabled monitoring shifting towards invasive practices such as sociometric badges and crossing boundaries from work-related activities only to monitoring employees' health, more questions arise regarding how far organisations' right to monitor extends before it impeaches on individuals' right to privacy. The aim of this chapter therefore is to outline some of the major issues associated with technology-enabled workplace surveillance, to discuss the resultant employee information privacy concerns, as well as managements' motivation to employ monitoring technologies in the workplace. The chapter explores the ethical impact of emerging monitoring practices and the murkiness surrounding the boundaries between monitoring employees to improve efficiency, as is the company's right, and the employees' right to some level of privacy.

INFORMATION PRIVACY

As noted the history of the privacy concept spans centuries, yet the concept remains beset by conceptual and operational confusion. The fact privacy attracts interest from various academic disciplines such as Law, Psychology, Sociology, Marketing and Management Information systems contributes to the lack of clarity surrounding the concept. Conceptualisations of privacy vary not only from one discipline to another, and within each discipline, but views of what privacy means can vary from one individual to another (Jourard, 1964; Sheehan & Hoy, 1998). When discussing privacy, it is important at the outset to distinguish between physical privacy and information privacy. Physical privacy, the earliest form of privacy, relates to an individual's physical environment and privacy violations of a physical nature. Aristotle described two spheres of physical activity that humans engage in, the public sphere and the private sphere, with the former representing activities performed in the public forum and the latter concerns activities that are performed alone or with family (DeCew, 2002). This view of privacy as the separation of one's life into public and private matters echoes the meaning of the word *privacy*, which stems from the Latin word *privare*, meaning to separate (Zheng *et al.* 2010). While early conversations focused on an individual's private physical space, it is information privacy which forms the focus of this chapter and indeed privacy conversations today. Information privacy relates to access to an individual's information and is considered to be a subset of the overall privacy concept (Bélanger & Crossler, 2011).

The emergence of interest in information privacy in the form of conversations among members of the public, increased presence in government policy and research can be traced back to the 1960s (Regan *et al.,* 2013). In recent decades, information privacy has continued to attract a great deal of attention. Despite the plethora of studies this interest has generated, various contrasting conceptualisations of information privacy frequent the literature. As noted, Smith, Dinev & Xu (2011) grouped these conceptualisations into value based views and cognate based views. Value based views include contrasting perspectives of privacy as a right and privacy as a commodity. Definitions of privacy as a right of individuals to '*be let alone*' free from surveillance, date back to Warren & Brandeis' 1890 Harvard Law review article. While their focus was physical surveillance, privacy as a right of individuals has been cited in the literature in various disciplines. More recently in the privacy economics literature the view of privacy as a commodity emerged, which states that individuals will often trade their private information in return for benefits (Smith, Dinev & Xu, 2011). Cognate views comprise of privacy as a state of limited access to a person, and privacy as controlling access to oneself (Westin, 1967; Altman, 1975).

Two observations can be made regarding these differing perspectives of privacy. Firstly, each view of privacy has limitations. For instance, an individual's right to privacy is difficult to define and must always be balanced with the needs of the organisation or society. Secondly, no view of privacy is completely distinct from other views. Each view has evolved and influenced subsequent conceptualisations. For example, privacy as a state was originally viewed in terms of selective access to an individual (Altman, 1975), this view has adapted to the increasing prevalence of information technologies and now views privacy as a state of limited access to an individual's information. Many earlier definitions of privacy placed control at the centre, assuming individuals could control access to them and to information about them (Westin, 1967). With the growing pervasiveness of information technologies, it is widely agreed that individuals cannot fully control what information is collected about them, or how this information is subsequently used. In response, definitions now discuss information privacy as an individual's desire to exercise some level of control over how their personal information is used (Clarke, 1999; Bélanger & Crossler, 2011). This illustrates how information privacy literature is influenced by other disciplines and external forces.

In the context of workplace surveillance, the relevance of all views of privacy is easily identifiable. Privacy could be viewed as maintaining a balance between individuals' right to some level of privacy and the organisations' need to operate effectively and efficiently. Similarly, the privacy economics view is relevant in cases when employee monitoring activities result in potential benefits such as rewards for productive employees. Many employees may willingly partake in monitoring activities when incentives are offered. In addition, as employers are entitled to engage in monitoring of email or Internet use, it can be argued that the use of email or the internet in the work environment involves forfeiting the privacy of this information. Under the commodity view, employees would rationally compare their desire to engage in these activities with the value the place on the privacy of their information. Privacy as a state of limited access relates to individuals' reasonable assumption that they have some level of privacy in the work environment. It can be contended that employee monitoring has the potential to infringe on this privacy. Lastly, in line with the privacy as control perspective, it can be argued that employees desire greater control over how personal information their employer collects is subsequently used. It is evident that all views of what privacy means

need to be considered when discussing the role of privacy in employee monitoring programs.

Confusion surrounding privacy extends beyond conceptualisations to efforts to measure individuals' information privacy concerns. The multidimensionality of the information privacy construct is empirically supported and undisputed (Xu *et al.,* 2011; Hong & Thong, 2013). However, little agreement has been reached with regards to what dimensions capture information privacy. The existing literature has generated a bounty of different measures of privacy concern, each presenting a different combination of dimensions and factor structure. Six dimensions are repeatedly included in these measures which, allowing for varying naming conventions, are; unauthorised secondary use, improper access, errors, collection, control and awareness (Hong & Thong, 2013). The first four of these dimensions represent the Concern for Information Privacy (CFIP) measure proposed by Smith, Milberg, & Burke (1996), while the last three dimensions comprise the Internet Users' Information Privacy Concerns (IUIPC) measure developed by Malhotra, Kim and Agarwal (2004). CFIP and IUIPC are considered the most popular measures of information privacy concern and have been applied in a number of studies across various contexts (Bélanger & Crossler, 2011). Recently, Hong & Thong (2013) amalgamated these two measures to develop the Internet Privacy Concerns (IPC) measure which encompasses all six dimensions.

It is argued that these six dimensions are pertinent when exploring how workplace monitoring influences employees' information privacy concern. Collection relates to individuals' concerns that organisations are collecting a great deal of information about them (Smith, Milberg & Burke, 1996). It is likely that monitoring of email and Internet activities for example would foster concerns among employees regarding the volume of information collected. Unauthorised secondary use relates to individuals' fears that data is collected for one purpose and subsequently used for another without their permission (Smith, Milberg & Burke, 1996). A Pew Internet survey showed that 85% of adults considered it to be very important that they could control access to their personal information (Madden, Fox, Smith, & Vitak, 2007). Therefore, it is plausible that employees would express concern regarding how data collected in the workplace might be subsequently used. Improper access is described as individuals' concerns that organisations do not have the measures in place to prevent unauthorised individuals accessing the data (Smith, Milberg & Burke, 1996). Employees are likely to be concerned about who within and outside the organisation might access information about them. Errors relates to concerns that organisations don't have the measures in place to prevent and correct errors in data (Smith, Milberg & Burke, 1996). The potential for information about employees to be misinterpreted is likely to incite concerns. Control pertains to individuals' concern that they cannot exercise control over how their data is used (Malhotra, Kim & Agarwal, 2004). In a recent European wide study, a mere 26% of social network users and 18% of online shoppers felt they could control how their data was used (Eurobarometer, 2011). It is extremely probable that employees will be frustrated with their lack of control over their information collected and collated by employers. Lastly, awareness involves concerns over individuals' lack of awareness of how their information is used and protected (Malhotra, Kim & Agarwal, 2004). It is widely argued that individuals lack an understanding of how information they disclose is used. Thus, if employees feel unaware of how their information is and can be used, they are likely to be concerned.

The role context plays in determining the importance of privacy and the relevant dimensions of information privacy concern cannot be understated. Individuals tend limit the information they disclose based on the context and the relevance of the information, often disclosing large volumes of information such as personal pictures on Facebook, but not information related to religion or politics (Hoadley *et al.,* 2010). Individuals are more concerned about the privacy of information they deem to be personal and sensitive. In a recent report conducted on behalf of the European Commission, over 26,700 citizens were interviewed across 27 European Union member states. When asked what information they viewed as personal, 75% said financial information and 74% said medical information such as patient records and health data (Eurobarometer, 2011). Various studies have found that individuals express high concerns about the privacy of their health information (Chhanabhai & Holt, 2007; Angst and Agarwal, 2009; Lafky & Horan, 2011; Li & Slee, 2014). It is likely that individuals will view certain types of information as relevant to the work environment, while considering other information types as irrelevant and private. Employees may express greater privacy concerns regarding the collection of sensitive information such as health data in the workplace.

SURVEILLANCE: AN EMPLOYEE PERSPECTIVE

The exponential growth of Internet-based technologies has empowered organisations to collate vast quantities of information from consumers and in some cases employees. Dataveillance describes the systematic monitoring of the actions or communications of individuals (Clarke, 1988). Modern technologies provide the opportunity for constant observation and continuous data collection ensuring that surveillance is employed through an individual not over them. The monitoring of employees' computer-related interactions has previously been described as an 'electronic whip' used unfairly by management (Tavani, 2004) where employees can be observed by an electronic supervisor who never leaves the office (Wen *et al.,* 2007). In some cases individuals may be conscious that they are being monitored, they are just not sure of the extent and detail of that monitoring. Neither are they aware of how that collated information is being used by the monitoring body. As such it is clear that there are two distinct issues relating to surveillance – one relating to the actual act of monitoring or surveillance itself, the second relating to how the collated information can be used.

Technology has enabled an invasion of employee privacy on a hitherto unimagined scale. For example, a 2005 study carried out by AMA found that as many as 55% of US firms not only retain, but also review an employee's email messages, a figure which has risen 8% since 2001. Managements' ability to monitor employee actions also stretches to use of the Internet within the workplace. AMA (2005) further revealed that 76% of organisations monitor an employee's Internet usage, 65% of which are blocking access to particular websites highlighting Web surfing as a primary concern for many organisations. It is now estimated that as many as 80% of organisations monitor employee activities in the workplace – a figure which has doubled since 1997 (AMA, 2001; D'Urso, 2006). While the speed and productivity benefits of email are immense from an organisational perspective, the placing of stringent controls by management on the use of email systems may also jeopardise an employee's privacy.

Moreover, this monitoring is not limited to email surveillance. In a drive to reduce costs and improve efficiency, companies are employing an increasing array of tracking and monitoring technology to allow them to view what their employees are doing at all times. Companies such as StealthGenie specialise in monitoring employees' mobile phones, Inland Empire requires its employees to carry scanning devices that show how quickly they are moving boxes and the outcomes of such tracking is subject to performance reviews, whilst employees at the Unified Grocers warehouse in the US wear headsets which tell them what to do and how much time they have to do it. Such tracking is used extensively in call centres with companies such as Paychez tracking the duration of

phone calls and time between phone calls at their call centre. However, tracking has also pervaded the health service delivery industry with nurses at Mills-Peninsula Health services hospital in California having to wear tracking devices so that the hospital can see where they are at all times. Such metrics may show increased productivity, but they come at a cost to employees. For example, micromanagement control systems increase employee stress and break the psychological trust contract between employee and employer. As Connolly (2013) (in Semuels; 2013) notes, the technology is being used to satisfy the needs of the employer, but is being leveraged against the employee. Thus the playing field is being tilted in favour of the industry against the employee with employees having little say on how the tracking data are used. The information can be used to justify pay cuts, to pay people piecemeal or to fire people outrights. In short, it provides employers with an increasing array of data to use to justify changes in the workplace. Workplace privacy is becoming highly comprised by technology as the knowledge power dynamic in the workplace shifts in favour of the employer.

Despite the fact that management are entitled to monitor employee behaviour primarily for 'business-related reasons' a study carried out by McParland and Connolly (2009) found that only 45% of employees surveyed knew their actions could be monitored by management while in the workplace. From this, only 22% believed that their actions were monitored on a regular – such as daily or weekly – basis. Interestingly however a significant number of respondents indicated a strong degree of privacy concerns in relation to managements' ability to monitor their email interactions in the workplace, despite the fact that many were unsure of whether or not such activities actually occurred. For example, 35% were concerned that employers could log into and record their personal emails, 42% were concerned that they could access their emails without their knowledge and 45% were concerned with how management would or could use information obtained from their personal emails. Employees indicated a stronger level of concern regarding the monitoring of personal emails they receive (32%) as opposed to those they send themselves from their work email account (12%) confirming the notion that control is an important aspect in relation to privacy issues.

The concept and art of surveillance is based on the notion that one is 'under watch' or being observed in some way. However based on the fundamental principles of the 'Hawthorne Effect' it is reasonable to assume that if one is aware they are under observation they may alter their actions according. For example, McParland and Connolly (2009) found that 84% of employees surveyed were careful about the type of information they would send in an email while in the workplace with only 32% sending a personal email if they thought their employer could not see them. Furthermore 57% sent emails from their own personal (yahoo, gmail) account in order to prevent management from tracking their behaviour with only 54% of the overall sample accepting managements' right to monitor staff email interactions in the workplace.

While it is apparent that employees often alter or modify their behaviour in response to management monitoring activities, it is important to note that the use of such techniques may result in other more worrying outcomes. For example, many workers experience high degrees of stress because their activities and interactions can be monitored by employers (Tavani, 2004). Once again based on the fundamental principles of panopticism the question can be raised as to whether it is the presence of the 'invisible supervisor' that generates or in part fuels this distress. Ironically however, it is the computer-based information worker whose work is dependent upon the use of computer systems that is often the one most subjected to this form of monitoring. In a study carried out by McParland and Connolly (2009) it was found that many individuals felt extremely uncomfortable being under watch by management expressing

explicit concerns, questioning how the information collated is used and in some instances even translating it into a failing performance or lack of ability on their behalf. This obvious negative impact that such surveillance techniques have on employee morale is a serious issue and one which must be addressed. In fact, the use of electronic surveillance in the workplace has been compared to that of a work environment tantamount to an 'electronic sweatshop' in some instances (Tavani, 2004).

Workplace surveillance clearly raises many ethical and social issues. However in order to adequately address many of these issues we must first consider the motivations behind managements decision to employ monitoring technologies in the first place.

MONITORING EMPLOYEES' HEALTH AND PRIVACY

Individuals are increasingly engaging in personal monitoring or tracking, with a huge rise in the use of technology to track one's health. For instance, 19% of adults in the United States used some form of mobile health application in 2012 (Fox and Duggan, 2012). These applications offer many monitoring capabilities such as diet, physical activity, sleep and medication management to name but a few. Mobile health applications are forecast to grow in popularity and will be used by 500 million people worldwide according to the Privacy Rights ClearingHouse (2013). In addition to these applications, wearable health tracking devices such provided by companies such as Fit-Bit or Jawbone, are gaining huge traction. These devices worn by the user track everything from steps taken and calories burnt to sleep quality, and enable individuals to monitor these indicators using a dashboard based mobile application. By 2013, 17 million wearable devices has been sold, a Tractica report estimates that this will reach 187 million by 2020 (Mottl, 2015). The emergence of wearable devices offers employers a new avenue to monitor employees to derive productivity and monetary gains. Such practices fall under employer wellness programs which traditionally meant physical assessments or medicals. With wearable devices, employers can monitor employees' physical activity and offer rewards to employees if targets are reached. Under the Affordable Care Act in the United States, employers can offer incentives for healthy behaviours (Olson, 2014).

While benefits are effective in incentivising employees to partake in these programmes and reach targets, there is the potential to use punishment to incentivise employees further. StickK, a US start-up offers software to analyse wearable device data and promotes the introduction of charges on health insurance premiums of employees for engaging in unhealthy behaviours such as smoking (Olson, 2014). Such practices are likely to be met with objection from employees, due to the potential discrimination of individuals with health conditions. Recently, Penn State University introduced a monthly charge of $100 for employees who didn't complete various health activities. Due to outcry from staff, they were forced to remove this charge (Murphy & Lucey, 2014). This case illustrates the influence employees can have when they feel monitoring activities infringe on their privacy and the importance of balancing employer goals with employees' desire for privacy. However, it is likely we have just seen the beginning of employers' use of technology to monitor employees' health. A recent study conducted by PwC of 2,000 adults in the UK found that 40% would be willing to wear a health tracking device if it was offered by their employer in return for benefits. This highlights the transactional form privacy can often take, but this doesn't deduct from individuals' moral right for some level of privacy and some degree of control. Indeed, employees did express privacy concerns, but willingness rose to 56% when individuals were informed that the data collected would be use to improve employee wellbeing, illustrating the importance of awareness and ensuring no unauthorised use of data takes place. Furthermore, individuals felt more comfortable if data would be anonymised and analysed on an aggregate level as opposed to individual level (PwC, 2015). This study illustrates the relevance of privacy in the workplace surveillance sphere, and the need to educate employees and provide some control in terms of anonymising data.

There are many ethical questions surrounding the use of health tracking devices, regardless of what benefits are offered to employees, or what reasons employers have for their use. For example, due to the power imbalance between employees and their employers, some may feel pressure to participate in monitoring programmes (O'Connor, 2015). Thus, does consent ever conform to EU Data Protection legislation? In addition, the use of health devices raises significant questions over the boundaries between information needed for the organisation to operate productively, and information pertinent to employees' personal lives. Of course, in some occupations, physical fitness is extremely important to fulfil the job's requirements and organisations can always argue that having healthy employees results in reduced healthcare costs, and may even make benevolent claims for engaging in such monitoring. However, the sensitive and personal nature of health data cannot be underestimated. Furthermore, much work remains to be done to make employees are fully cognizant of how health data gathered is used, to ensure employers don't use this data for any secondary purposes, and most of all ensure individuals have some control over the level of data that is collected and the ability to opt-in or out of such programmes.

SURVEILLANCE: A MANAGEMENT PERSPECTIVE

While many reports emphasis the risks faced by the employee, it is reasonable to assume that in some instances management may have legitimate reasons to monitor their employee's actions. For example, profit driven organisations aim to manage their business in an efficient and productive manner and as such it may be unreasonable to expect that such companies would not avail of methods or employ technologies to ensure that their employees are completing the job they are being paid to do. Furthermore and perhaps more notably, organisations continually face the risk of adverse publicity resulting from offensive or explicit material circulating within the company and as such many employ monitoring technologies to protect themselves from costly litigation claims (Laudon & Laudon, 2001). The Internet has increased the possible threat of hostile work environment claims by providing access to inappropriate jokes or images that can be transmitted internally or externally at the click of a button (Lane, 2003). In fact, a study carried out in 2000 concluded that 70% of the traffic on pornographic Websites occurs during office hours, with Com-Score networks reporting 37% of such visits actually taking place in the office environment (Alder, Noel, & Ambrose, 2006).

Moreover, the risks to organisations stretch also to the abuse of the email system, with virtually all the respondents in an AMA (2003) survey reporting some sort of disruption resulting from employee's email use. For example, 33% of the respondents experienced a computer virus, 34% reporting business interruptions and 38% of which had a computer system disabled for some time as the result of a bogus email. In a similar vein, Jackson, Dawson, and Wilson (2001) conducted a study to investigate the cost management endure as a result of such email interruption. The study indicated that it took the average employee between 1 and 44 seconds to respond to a new email when the icon or pop up box appeared on their screen. 70% of these mails were reacted to within 6 seconds of them appearing and a further 15% were reacted to within a 2 minute time period. Overall the study found that it took on average 64 seconds for an employee to return to a productive

state of work for every one new mail sent. Other practitioner reports also identify the potential cost of email usage with as many as 76% reporting a loss of business time due to email problems, 24% of which estimating a significant two day loss of company time (AMA, 2003). These statistics are not so surprising given the amount of time the average employee spends online. The survey further reported that the average employee spends 25% of his or her working day solely on their emails, with a further 90% admitting to sending and receiving personal mails during company time.

Whilst the need to improve productivity is a common rationale for employee monitoring, other motivations such as minimising theft and preventing workplace litigation can be considered equally justifiable in the eyes of management seeking to protect the interests of the organisation. The former motivation is particularly understandable as research shows that employees stole over 15 billion dollars in inventory from their employers in the year 2001 alone (Lane, 2003). In addition, the seamless integration of technology into the workplace has increased the threat of internal attacks with Lane (2003) noting the ease at which sensitive corporate data and trade secrets can be downloaded, transmitted, copied or posted onto a Web page by an aggrieved employee. Internal attacks typically target specific exploitable information, causing significant amounts of damage to an organisation (IBM, 2006). Management need to ensure that their employees use their working time productively and are therefore benefiting the organisation as a whole (Nord, McCubbins, & Horn Nord, 2006). It is apparent however, that tensions will remain constant between both parties unless some form of harmony or balance between the interests of both the employer and employee is achieved.

In order to balance this conflict of interests however it is vital that clearly defined rules and disciplinary offences are implemented into the workplace (Craver, 2006). The need for structure becomes all the more apparent when one considers the differing views and tolerance levels certain managers may hold (Selmi, 2006). For example, if an employee is hired to work, then technically they should refrain from sending personal emails or shopping online during working hours. However, as a general rule, most management will overlook these misdemeanours as good practice or in order to boost worker morale. The situation becomes more serious however when the abuse of Internet privileges threatens to affect the company itself, be it through loss of profits or adverse publicity for the company. Furthermore, the problem increases as boundaries in the modern workplace begin to blur and confusion between formal and informal working conditions arise (Evans, 2007). For example by allowing an employee to take a company laptop into the privacy of their own home, management could be sending out a message that the computer can be used for personal use which may lead to the employee storing personal data on management's property. Legally, the employer would have claims over all of the data stored on the computer and could use it to discipline or even terminate an employee. In fact, it is this apparent lack of natural limit in regards what is acceptable or indeed unacceptable relating to workplace privacy which makes the task of defining appropriate principles all the more difficult to comprehend (Godfrey, 2001).

ORGANIZATIONAL JUSTICE AND WORKPLACE SURVEILLANCE

The recent surge in the use of communication monitoring technologies within the computer-mediated work environment has further brought the issues of justice and fairness centre stage in the literature. In fact, justice and fairness are often cited as key drivers in managing the ethical and privacy concerns of employees who are subjected to monitoring practices within the computer-mediated work environment (Stanton, 2000a, 2000b; Zweig & Webster, 2002). Organisational

justice is an overarching term used to describe individuals' perceptions of what is fair and just within the workplace. For researchers such as Stanton (2000b) justice theories thus provide researchers with a solid framework to help predict the perceived fairness of specific organisational procedures, outcomes and actions.

Justice perceptions for the main are separated into three specific forms notably (1) procedural justice, (2) distributive justice, and (3) interactional justice. The first of these antecedents, procedural justice centres around an individuals' perception that the organisational decision-making process will produce fair and just outcomes (Barrett-Howard & Tyler, 1986; Stanton, 2000b; Hauenstein, McGonigle, & Flinder, 2001). In this way, procedural justice act as a critical factor for understanding the relations between the supervisors' social power and the employees' subsequent reactions to it whereby they perceive positive outcomes in a more favourable light (Mossholder, Bennett, Kemery, & Wesolowski, 1998). Distributive justice refers to the distribution of outcomes, measuring the extent to which employees feel recognised and therefore appropriately rewarded for their efforts within the workplace (Stanton, 2000b; Cohen-Charash & Spector, 2001; Hauenstein *et al.*, 2001). In this way management are required to treat employees who are similar in respect to a certain outcome in the same manner, as opposed to basing decisions on arbitrary characteristics (Daft, 2000). According to Cohen-Charash and Spector (2001) if a distributive injustice is perceived, it will affect an employee's emotions, cognitions and their overall behaviour. The final facet of organisational justice, interactional justice stems from the interpersonal communications of the workplace, examining the quality of the interpersonal treatment employees experience at the hands of the company power-holders (Bies & Moag, 1986; Cohen-Charash & Spector, 2001). More specifically it examines the extent to which employees' believe they have been treated with dignity, sincerity and respect during the distribution of outcomes as well as the process undertaken to achieve them by company decision-makers (Stanton, 2000b; Helne, 2005). Consequently if an employee perceives interpersonal injustice they are more likely to act negatively towards their direct supervisor as opposed to the organisation or the injustice in question (Cohen-Charash & Spector, 2001).

Organisational justice theories have been linked to research on performance monitoring – specifically electronic performance monitoring (EPM) in the literature (Stanton & Barnes-Farrell, 1991; Stanton, 2000a, 2000b). EPM differs from traditional (non-electronic) forms of monitoring in that it can be carried out on a continuous, large scale basis recording multiple dimensions of a single workers performance (Stanton, 2000a). The ubiquitous nature of these monitoring technologies contributes to the employees' ethical concerns relating to loss of personal privacy in the workplace.

Trust and risk perceptions also play an important role in the issue of workplace surveillance. For example studies on trust – in particular relating to trust in leaders - are becoming increasingly prominent in the literature. Mayer, Davis, and Schoorman (1995) for example developed a model that suggested that integrity, benevolence and ability were major factors that had the potential to affect an individual's perception of trustworthiness in a leader. Similarly, a study carried out by Robinson and Rousseau (1994) found that as many as 55% of respondents reported a reduced level of trust in an employer as a result of management violating a psychological contract with them. The seamless integration of communication-monitoring technologies into the workplace can influence an employee's perception of the risks they face working in the computer-mediated environment. Therefore, it is conceivable that an employees' attitude towards the technology will act as an important determinant in the implementation process of communication-monitoring technologies into the workplace.

Furthermore it is apparent that risk perceptions can affect how an individual makes specific decisions, subsequently influencing their behaviour. In fact studies show that when an employee is aware they are under surveillance, they modify their behaviour accordingly. For example, a recent study carried out by SHRM in 2005 found that as many as 75% of employees display a certain degree of caution in relation to what they write in emails due to possible monitoring by the organisation. Similarly, the study showed that 47% are equally cautious in relation to telephone conversations while in the workplace environment. Studies show however that the degree of risk perceived by an individual can be reduced if trust exists in a particular situation (So & Sculli, 2002). In this way the significance of trust within studies on risk perception cannot be understated. In fact, an individuals' need to trust often relates directly to the risks involved in a given situation and consequently the pervasive nature of communication-monitoring practices within the computer-mediated organisation hold risks that are unique to that context (Mayer *et al.,* 1995). In order for trust to be engendered however, employees must feel confident that the boundaries between what is acceptable and unacceptable in relation to information monitoring are clearly and openly stated. Those companies that are successful at building that trust and managing the uncertainty associated with communication monitoring practices will benefit from increased employee confidence.

It is becoming increasingly apparent that there is a significant disparity between management and employee perspectives on the issue of workplace surveillance. The uncertainty and lack of control related to the use of these communication monitoring technologies in the workplace reflects the significant asymmetry that exists in terms of what they mean to management versus the employee. While it is apparent that technology has created better, faster and cheaper ways for individuals to satisfy their own needs, the capability to leverage this technology is far higher for companies than for the employee. Because unequal forces, leading to asymmetric information availability, tilt the playing field significantly in favour of industry, such technologies do not create market benefit to all parties in an equitable manner (Prakhaber, 2000). As such one of the major tasks facing the computer-mediated organisation is that of identifying the factors to improve employees' attitudes and behavioural reactions towards surveillance in the workplace. There is a distinct need for clear measures to be implemented, that govern the effective and fair use of communication technologies in the workplace allowing management to monitor their staff in a reasonable and rational manner. Management should consider the ethical and social impacts that surveillance techniques may have within the workplace and employ specific policies which may both minimise the negative implications associated with the use of such technology as well as helping to improve employee receptiveness overall.

WORKPLACE SURVEILLANCE ETHICS

Organisations looking for ways in which to balance this conflict of interest between management and employees are focusing towards the use of workplace policies, many of which are framed on established or predefined codes of ethics. For example, Marx and Sherizen (1991) argue that employees should be made aware in advance of any monitoring practices conducted in the workplace before it actually occurs. In this way the individual can electively decide whether or not he or she wishes to work for that particular organisation. Furthermore the authors suggest that the employee should have the right to both view information collated on them and challenge inaccurate information before it can be used against them. This idea of 'transparency' in relation to surveillance methods is commonly supported by

privacy advocates however it can be argued that it goes against fundamental principles of the act of surveillance. Similarly we can once again note the impact of the 'Hawthorne Effect' in that individuals will alter their behaviour if they believe they are being observed in some way. In this way management need to have clearly defined sanctions in place within the organisation informing employees of the depth and detail of monitoring practices in the company whilst deterring them from abusing workplace systems.

Other ethical strategies focus solely on how management use the information collated on employees in the workplace. Again we can note that the scope of surveillance is generally divided into two main components - one relating to the actual act of monitoring or surveillance itself, the second relating to how the collated information can be used. In some cases it is reasonable to assume that employees may not fear the act of surveillance but more so how the information could be used and whether or not employers will make subsequent judgments about them (Introna, 2001). For example, McParland and Connolly (2009) found that 33% of employees they surveyed were concerned that their employers would react negatively to their use of personal email in the workplace however 24% still thought it was reasonable to use work email to chat freely with their friends and colleagues. Once again the lines regarding what are acceptable or indeed unacceptable forms of behaviour begin to blur.

In order to alleviate much of this confusion other researchers such as Turban, King, Lee, Liang, and Turban (2010) apply the basic ethical principles to information collected in an online environment. It is apparent however that these basic ethical principles can also be applied to the use of communication-monitoring technologies in the workplace environment thus providing a solid framework to guide management in their efforts to monitor employees in a fair and effective manner. The basic principles include the following;

- **Notice or Awareness:** Employees should be made aware of the extent and detail of monitoring techniques, prior to the collection or use of personal information.

- **Choice or Consent:** Employees should be made aware of how the collated information can be used and consent must be granted by the employee by signing a workplace policy or notification which outlines the companies monitoring practices.

- **Access or Participation:** Employees should be able to access certain information on them and challenge the validity of the data.

- **Integration or Security:** Employees should be assured that their personal information is kept secure within the organisation and cannot be used in a way which was not intended.

- **Enforcement or Redress:** Employees must be made aware of organisational sanctions set in place such that a misuse of workplace systems will be detected and punished by management. Otherwise there is no deterrent or indeed enforceability to protect privacy.

Effective workplace policies need to protect the interests of all parties involved, ergo a code needs to be developed that protects the interests of both the employee and the employer. Little progress can be made in this area however unless the current privacy legislation is addressed.

THE ROLE OF PRIVACY LEGISLATION

Privacy legislation differs considerably between Europe and the United States. While both Europe and the United States define privacy in a similar way, it is the fundamental objective of their information privacy laws that signifies the major difference between the two. For example, in Europe privacy protection is considerably stronger than in the United States as it focuses on controlling and regulating managements' collection and use of employee data. While the European Directive is based on the Fair Information Doctrine of the United States it extends the level of control an individual can exercise over their own personal information (Laudon & Traver, 2010). In this way European law lends itself more to the protection of data – and therefore the individual – compared to the United States which focuses more on the use and collection of data. Any country that is a member state of the European Union [EU] must comply with the legislation that is passed by any one of its major institutions as well as any national laws or regulations set in place. Furthermore, under the Directive 95/46/EC and Article 29 WP55 all monitoring in the organisation must pass a number of specified criteria before being implemented into the workplace.

Under current EU legislation, the employer must prove that electronic observation is a necessary course of action for a specific purpose before engaging in it. In this way, management are encouraged to consider traditional and less intrusive measures of observation before resorting to electronic means (Directive 95/46/EC). For the purpose of Internet or indeed email surveillance, it is likely that some form of electronic monitoring would be enlisted, however in such instances the employer by law can only keep the data in question no longer than necessary for the specific monitoring action. In a similar vein, the second principal of finality denotes that any data collected, must be used for an explicit purpose and therefore cannot be processed or used for any other purpose than initially intended (Directive 95/46/EC).

Under EU law, management must also be clear and open regarding the surveillance practices of the organisation and are therefore obliged to provide employees with information regarding organisational monitoring policies. In this way employees are advised of improper procedures and disciplinary offences that justify the scope of invasive monitoring techniques (Directive 95/46/EC). Furthermore details of the surveillance measures undertaken are also provided so as the employee will know who is monitoring them, how they are being monitored as well as when these actions are taking place. This principal of transparency also provides individuals with access rights to personal data processed or collated by management, allowing them to request its rectification or deletion where appropriate (Directive 95/46/EC).

The fourth criterion, legitimacy is similar to that of necessity in so far as data can only be obtained for a justifiable purpose and must not contravene an employee's fundamental or inherent right to privacy. Under this element of the legislation however, data of a very sensitive nature can be deemed too personal to collect and collection therefore must be specifically authorised by a national law in extreme circumstances (Directive 95/46/EC). Organisations must also comply with the notion of proportionality, using the most non-intrusive or least excessive action in order to obtain the desired information. For example the monitoring of emails should if possible focus on the general information such as the time and transmission as opposed to the content if the situation permits. If however viewing of the email content is deemed necessary then the law presides that the privacy of those outside of the organisation should also be taken into account and that reasonable efforts be made to inform the outside world of any monitoring practices (Directive 95/46/EC).

Any data that is collated on an employee must only be retained for as long as is necessary under this European law and data that is no longer needed should then be deleted. Management should specify a particular retention period based on their business needs so as employees are constantly aware of the ongoing process (Directive 95/46/EC). Furthermore, provisions should be set in place to ensure that any data that is held by the employer will remain secure and safe from any form of intrusion or disturbance. The employer is also required to protect the technological medium from the threat of virus as a further means of protecting the personal data (Directive 95/46/EC).

It is apparent that the central concept of the European Directive relates to the processing and flow of information (Elgesem, 1999). As a result researchers such as Evans (2007) note how the existence of these European laws that favour the employee are consequently putting considerable pressure on the United States to adopt similar laws. In fact, it has been previously suggested that the various proposals and directives – or at least the relevant aspects of them - should be combined into one robust comprehensive model (Tavani, 2004). While such a model combining the interests of both the organisation and the employee would appear to be a sensible solution however for Wang, Lee and Wang (1998) it poses 'one of the most challenging public policy issues of the information age.' In the United States, citizens have a general right to privacy, however California is the only State at present with legal protection for employees' privacy (Yerby, 2013). However, it is often suggested that until legislation catches up with technology, employers utilising monitoring technologies regardless of geographic location, should ensure they abide to the more stringent European Data Protection Laws (Madan *et al.* 2009).

FUTURE RESEARCH DIRECTIONS

The increasing of scope workplace surveillance is accompanied with an increasing murkiness surrounding what constitutes a legitimate cause for surveillance. Employee monitoring is moving beyond social media and email towards the keystroke monitoring programs which provide employers with reports of every key the employee presses (Yerby, 2013). Future research should explore whether employees are aware of these activities and how they are affected. As noted, employee monitoring is also evolving to encompass the tracking of employees' health using wearable devices. However, many questions persist over this practice and it is unlikely to become widespread unless employers consider the privacy concerns of employees. Studies have shown that employee participation in wellness and productivity programmes is low, partly due to the fact that many health issues such as mental health are still thwarted by stigma (Towers Watson, 2015). Future research could further explore the types of health information individuals are willing to share with employers and their fears and concerns over the potential misuse of this information or potential ramifications that may arise from this sharing of information. This type of research can help navigate the path employers should follow when educating employees on health monitoring programmes. In addition to research focused on employees' issues and concerns, there is room for comprehensive studies focusing on employers aims, employees' understanding of monitoring in terms of data collected and subsequent uses for data, and their perceptions towards these activities, and attempting to reach some level of harmony between both parties. As repeated throughout this chapter, educating employees on monitoring programmes is imperative. Thus, there is also significant scope for studies to test the efficacy of different means of educating employees to reach conclusions on what methods work best to ensure employees are informed of how their behaviour is monitored and of the level of privacy that exists in the workplace. Educated employees can then alter their behaviours to conform to employers' expectations.

These suggestions represent a small sample of the potential avenues future research in workplace surveillance could explore. Further research into these avenues and the many more associated with workplace surveillance will be of great significance and interest to practitioners. Employees are the lifeblood of any organisation and only by understanding the behavioural outcomes of such individuals can we begin to understand the factors that predict the perceptions, attitudes and beliefs

that are generated through the implementation of various different monitoring technologies in the work environment. Consequently future research into some of these major issues will have significant and important consequences for aiding businesses in successfully employing these ever emerging monitoring technologies.

CONCLUSION

Technology-enabled surveillance and tracking of employees in increasing both in terms of pervasiveness and sophistication. The primary objective of this chapter was to address the issue of electronic monitoring in the computer-mediated work environment and emerging trends of monitoring. This paper explored the ethical impact of monitoring in the computer-mediated work environment, addressing whether management's ability to monitor employee actions in workplace represents good business practice or constitutes an invasion of privacy. Broadly speaking, there are three main reasons behind employers' decision to engage in employee monitoring namely; to improve productivity, to protect the company's brand and to mitigate potential legal liabilities (Ball, 2010). However, at what point do these monitoring activities infringe on employee privacy? Furthermore, arguments can be made that excessive monitoring and ensuing feelings of *constant observation* can lead to stress and dips in employee morale and productivity, thus having an opposite effect on employee productivity than intended. This further strengthens calls to balance striving to achieve employer goals with appeasing employee information privacy concerns.

The type of information employers are collecting is extending beyond the realm of information disclosed when using company computers to send emails, to the implementation of wearable health tracking devices. There is a great need for empirical research in the realm of these emerging trends in workplace surveillance. Such research can aid employers in educating employees to a level that they can comprehend what data is collected and how it is used but also how it could be potentially used. The dimensions of IPC outlined earlier in the chapter, can also be addressed by employers in efforts to educate employees and appease privacy concerns. These dimensions provide a starting point for understanding the privacy issues associated with employee monitoring. In the context of increasingly pervasive monitoring of employees extending from social media use to physical activity, other context-specific privacy issues may emerge. Employers should address potential employee concerns prior to introducing invasive monitoring programmes, and intermittently following their implementation to ensure all issues are addressed. In addition to these educational efforts, there is a broader need for specific legislation and ethical guidelines for employee monitoring that can transcend industry and international boundaries.

ACKNOWLEDGMENT

The author would like to acknowledge Cliona McParland for her contribution to the research on which this work is based.

REFERENCES

Alder, G. S., Noel, T. W., & Ambrose, M. L. (2006). Clarifying the effects of Internet monitoring on job attitudes: The mediating role of employee trust. *Information & Management*, *43*(7), 894–903. doi:10.1016/j.im.2006.08.008

Altman, I. (1975). *The environment and social behaviour: Privacy, personal space, territory, and crowding*. Monterey, CA: Brooks/Cole.

Angst, C. M., & Agarwal, R. (2009). Adoption of Electronic Health Records in the Presence of Privacy Concerns: The Elaboration Likelihood Model and Individual Persuasion. *Management Information Systems Quarterly*, *33*(2), 339–370.

Ball, K. (2010). Workplace surveillance: An overview. *Labor Review*, *51*(1), 87–106.

Barrett-Howard, E., & Tyler, T. R. (1986). Procedural justice as a criterion in allocation decisions. *Journal of Personality and Social Psychology*, *50*(2), 296–304. doi:10.1037/0022-3514.50.2.296 PMID:3746613

Bélanger, F., & Crossler, R. E. (2011). Privacy in the digital age: A review of information privacy research in information systems. *Management Information Systems Quarterly*, *35*(4), 1017–1041.

Bies, R. J., & Moag, J. F. (1986). Interactional justice: Communication criteria of fairness. In R. J. Lewicki, B. H. Sheppard, & M. H. Bazerman (Eds.), *Research on negotiations in organisations* (Vol. 1, pp. 43–55). Greenwich, CT: JAI Press.

Chhanabhai, P., & Holt. (2007). Consumers are ready to accept the transition to online and electronic records if they can be assured of the security measures. *Medscape General Medicine*, *9*(1), 8.

Clarke, R. (1999). Internet privacy concerns confirm the case for intervention. *Communications of the ACM*, *42*(2), 60–67. doi:10.1145/293411.293475

Clarke, R. A. (1988). Information technology and dataveillance. *Communications of the ACM*, *31*(5), 498–512. doi:10.1145/42411.42413

Cohen-Charash, Y., & Spector, P. E. (2001). The role of justice in organizations: A meta-analysis. *Organizational Behavior and Human Decision Processes*, *86*(2), 278–321. doi:10.1006/obhd.2001.2958

Craver, C. B. (2006). Privacy issues affecting employers, employees and labour organizations. *Louisiana Law Review, 66,* 1057–1078.

D'Urso, S. C. (2006). Who's watching us at work? Toward a structural-perceptual model of electronic monitoring and surveillance in organisations. *Communication Theory, 16*(3), 281–303. doi:10.1111/j.1468-2885.2006.00271.x

Daft, R. L. (2000). *Management* (5th ed.). Hinsdale, IL: The Dryden Press.

DeCew, J. (2002). *Privacy.* Retrieved from http://plato.stanford.edu/entries/privacy/

Dinev, T., Xu, H., Smith, J. H., & Hart, P. (2013). Information privacy and correlates: An empirical attempt to bridge and distinguish privacy-related concepts. *European Journal of Information Systems, 22*(3), 295–316. doi:10.1057/ejis.2012.23

Elgesem, D. (1999). The structure of rights in Directive 95/46/EC on the protection of individuals with regard to the processing of personal data and the free movement of such data. *Ethics and Information Technology, 1*(4), 283–293. doi:10.1023/A:1010076422893

Eurobarometer. (2011) *Attitudes on Data Protection and Electronic Identity in the European Union,* Retrieved from: http://ec.europa.eu/public_opinion/archives/ebs/ebs_359_en.pdf

European Union. (2002). *Directive 95/46/EC: Article 29 WP55.* Retrieved from http://ec.europa.eu/justice_home/fsj/privacy/docs/wpdocs/2002/wpss_en.pdf

Evans, L. (2007). Monitoring technology in the American workplace: Would adopting English privacy standards better balance employee privacy and productivity? *California Law Review, 95,* 1115–1149.

Fox, S., & Duggan, M. (2012). Mobile Health. *Pew Internet* Research. Retrieved from http://www.pewinternet.org/files/old-media//Files/Reports/2012/PIP_MobileHealth2012_FINAL.pdf

Garner. (2012). *Gartner Says Monitoring Employee Behavior in Digital Environments is Rising.* Retrieved from: http://www.gartner.com/newsroom/id/2028215

Godfrey, B. (2001). Electronic work monitoring: An ethical model. In *Selected Papers from the Second Australian Institute Conference on Computer Ethics* (pp. 18-21). Academic Press.

Harris Interactive. (2003). *Poll.* Retrieved from http://www.harrisinteractive.com/harris_poll/index.asp?PID=365

Hauenstein, N. M. A., McGonigle, T., & Flinder, S. W. (2001). A meta-analysis of the relationship between procedural justice and distributive justice: Implications for justice research. *Employee Responsibilities and Rights Journal, 13*(1), 39–56. doi:10.1023/A:1014482124497

Helne, C. A. (2005). Predicting workplace deviance from the interaction between organizational justice and personality. *Journal of Managerial Issues, 17*(2), 247–263.

Hoadley, C. M., Xu, H., Lee, J. J., & Rosson, M. B. (2010). Privacy as information access and illusory control: The case of the Facebook News Feed privacy outcry. *Electronic Commerce Research and Applications, 9*(1), 50–60. doi:10.1016/j.elerap.2009.05.001

Hong, W., & Thong, J. (2013). Internet Privacy Concerns: An Integrated Conceptualisation and four empirical studies. *Management Information Systems Quarterly, 37*(1), 275–298. Retrieved from http://pewresearch.org/pubs/663/digital-footprints

IBM. (2006). *Stopping insider attacks: How organizations can protect their sensitive information*. Retrieved from http://www-935.ibm.com/services/us/imc/pdf/gsw00316-usen-00-insider-threats-wp.pdf

Introna, L. D. (2001). Workplace surveillance, privacy and distributive justice. In R. A. Spinello & H. T. Tavani (Eds.), *Readings in cyberethics* (pp. 519–532). Sudbury, MA: Jones and Barlett.

Jackson, T., Dawson, R., & Wilson, D. (2001). The cost of email interruption (Item No. 2134/495). Loughborough, UK: Loughborough University Institutional Repository. Retrieved from http://km.lboro.ac.uk/iii/pdf/JOSIT%202001.pdf

Jourard, S. (1964). Some Psychological Aspects of Privacy. *Law and Contemporary Problems*, *31*(2), 307–318. doi:10.2307/1190673

Lafky, D. B., & Horan, T. A. (2011). Personal health records: Consumer attitudes toward privacy and security of their personal health information. *Health Informatics Journal*, *17*(1), 63–71. doi:10.1177/1460458211399403 PMID:25133771

Lane, F. S. (2003). *The naked employee: How technology is compromising workplace privacy*. New York, NY: AMACOM.

Laudon, K. C., & Laudon, J. P. (2001). *Essentials of management information systems: Organisation and technology in the networked enterprise* (4th ed.). Upper Saddle River, NJ: Prentice Hall.

Laudon, K. C., & Traver, C. G. (2010). *E-Commerce 2010 – Business. Technology. Society* (6th ed.). Upper Saddle River, NJ: Prentice Hall.

Li, T., & Slee, T. (2014). The effects of information privacy concerns on digitizing personal health records. *Journal of the Association for Information Science and Technology*, *65*(8), 1541–1554. doi:10.1002/asi.23068

Louis Harris and Associates. (1999). *Poll.* Retrieved from http://www.natlconsumersleague.org/FNLSUM1.PDF

Madan, A., Waber, B., Ding, M., Kominers, P., & Pentland, A. (2009). Reality Mining: The End of Personal Privacy. In *Proceedings of 1st Engaging Data Forum*.

Madden, M., Fox, S., Smith, A., & Vitak, J. (2007). *Digital footprints: Online identity management and search in the age of transparency*. Academic Press.

Malhotra, N. K., Kim, S. S., & Agarwal, J. (2004). Internet Users' Information Privacy Concerns (IUIPC): The Construct, the Scale and a Causal Model. *Information Systems Research*, *15*(4), 336–355.

Marx, G., & Sherizen, S. (1991). Monitoring on the job: How to protect privacy as well as property. In T. Forester (Ed.), *Computers in the human context: Information technology, productivity, and people* (pp. 397–406). Cambridge, MA: MIT Press.

Mayer, R. C., Davis, J. D., & Schoorman, F. D. (1995). An integrative model of organisational trust. *Academy of Management Review*, *20*(3), 709–734.

McParland, C., & Connolly, R. (2009). *The role of dataveillance in the organsiation: Some emerging trends*. Paper presented at the Irish Academy of Management Conference, Galway, Ireland.

Mossholder, K. W., Bennett, N., Kemery, E. R., & Wesolowski, M. A. (1998). Relationships between bases of power and work reactions: The mediational role of procedural justice. *Journal of Management*, *24*(4), 533–552. doi:10.1177/014920639802400404

Mottl, J. (2015). Reports: Wearables primed for big growth, with Apple Watch driving adoption. *FierceMobile Healthcare.* Retrieved from: http://www.fiercemobilehealthcare.com/story/reports-wearables-primed-big-growth-apple-watch-driving-adoption/2015-02-22

Murphy, T., & Lucey, C. (2014). Wellness programs grow more popular with employers. *Mercury News.* Retrieved from: http://www.mercurynews.com/health/ci_25639907/wellness-programs-grow-more-popular-employers

Nord, G. D., McCubbins, T. F., & Horn Nord, J. (2006). Email monitoring in the workplace: Privacy, legislation, and surveillance software. *Communications of the ACM, 49*(8), 73–77.

O'Connor, S. (2015). Wearables at work: the new frontier of employee surveillance. *Financial Times.* Retrieved from: http://www.ft.com/intl/cms/s/2/d7eee768-0b65-11e5-994d-00144feab-dc0.html#axzz3cesjiVgY

Olson, P. (2014). Wearable Tech Is Plugging Into Health Insurance. *Forbes.* Retrieved from: http://www.forbes.com/sites/parmyolson/2014/06/19/wearable-tech-health-insurance/

Pavlou, P. (2011). State of the Information Privacy Literature: Where are we now and Where Should we Go? *Management Information Systems Quarterly, 35*(4), 977–989.

Prakhaber, P. R. (2000). Who owns the online consumer? *Journal of Consumer Marketing, 17*(2), 158–171. doi:10.1108/07363760010317213

Privacy Rights Clearinghouse. (2013). *Mobile Health and Fitness Apps: What Are the Privacy Risks?* Retrieved from: https://www.privacyrights.org/mobile-medical-apps-privacy-alert

PWC. (2015). Half of people would use a workplace smartwatch. *PWC.* Retrieved from: http://pwc.blogs.com/press_room/2015/04/half-of-people-would-use-a-workplace-smartwatch-pwc-research.html

Regan, P. M., FitzGerald, G., & Balint, P. (2013). Generational views of information privacy? *Innovation: The European Journal of Social Science Research, 26*(1-2), 81–99.

Robinson, S. L., & Rousseau, D. M. (1994). Violating the psychological contract: Not the exception but the norm. *Journal of Organizational Behavior, 15*(3), 245–259. doi:10.1002/job.4030150306

Selmi, M. (2006). Privacy for the working class: Public work and private lives. *Louisiana Law Review, 66*, 1035–1056.

Semuels, A. (2013). Monitoring upends blance of power at workplace some say. *Los Angeles Times.* Available at http://www.latimes.com/business/money/la-fi-mo-monitoring-upends-balance-of-power-at-workplace-20130408,0,7425573.story

Sheehan, K. B., & Hoy, M. G. (1998). Flaming, Complaining, Abstaining: How Online Users Respond to Privacy Concerns. *Journal of Advertising, 28*(3), 37–51. doi:10.1080/00913367.1999.10673588

SHRM. (2005). *Workplace privacy – Poll findings: A study by the Society for Human Resource Management and CareerJournal.com.* Retrieved from http://www.shrm.org/Research/SurveyFindings/Documents/Workplace%20Privacy%20Poll%20Findings%20-%20A%20Study%20by%20SHRM%20and%20CareerJournal.com.pdf

Smith, H. J., Dinev, T., & Xu, H. (2011). Information privacy research: An interdisciplinary review. *Management Information Systems Quarterly, 35*(4), 989–1015.

Smith, H. J., Milberg, J. S., & Burke, J. S. (1996). Information privacy: Measuring individuals' concerns about organizational practices. *Management Information Systems Quarterly, 20*(2), 167–196. doi:10.2307/249477

So, M. W. C., & Sculli, D. (2002). The role of trust, quality, value and risk in conducting e-business. *Industrial Management & Data Systems, 102*(9), 503–512. doi:10.1108/02635570210450181

Stanton, J. M. (2000a). Reactions to employee performance monitoring: Framework, review, and research directions. *Human Performance, 13*(1), 85–113. doi:10.1207/S15327043HUP1301_4

Stanton, J. M. (2000b). Traditional and electronic monitoring from an organizational justice perspective. *Journal of Business and Psychology, 15*(1), 129–147. doi:10.1023/A:1007775020214

Stanton, J. M., & Barnes-Farrell, J. L. (1996). Effects of electronic performance-monitoring on personal control, satisfaction and performance. *The Journal of Applied Psychology, 81*(6), 738–745. doi:10.1037/0021-9010.81.6.738

Survey, A. M. A. (2001). *Workplace monitoring and surveillance*. Retrieved from http://www.amanet.org/research/pdfs/ems_short2001.pdf

Survey, A. M. A. (2003). *Email rules, policies and practices survey*. Retrieved from http://www.amanet.org/research/pdfs/email_policies_practices.pdf

Survey, A. M. A. (2005). *Electronic monitoring and surveillance survey*. Retrieved from http://www.amanet.org/research/pdfs/ems_summary05.pdf

Tavani, H. T. (2004). *Ethics and technology: Ethical issues in an age of information and communication technology*. Chichester, UK: John Wiley & Sons.

Towers Watson. (2015). *Prioritising Employee Wellness*. Retrieved from: http://www.towerswatson.com/en/Insights/IC-Types/Reprints/2015/Prioritising-Employee-Wellness

Turban, E., King, D., Lee, J., Liang, T. P., & Turban, D. (2010). *Electronic commerce 2010: A managerial perspective* (6th ed.). Upper Saddle River, NJ: Pearson.

Turban, E., Leidner, D., McClean, E., & Wetherbe, J. (2006). *Information technology for management – Transforming organisations in the digital economy* (5th ed.). New York, NY: John Wiley & Sons.

Wang, H., Lee, M. K. O., & Wang, C. (1998). Consumer privacy concerns about internet marketing. *Communications of the ACM, 41*(3), 63–70. doi:10.1145/272287.272299

Warren, S., & Brandeis, L. (1890). The Right to Privacy. *Harvard Law Review, 4*(5), 193–220. doi:10.2307/1321160

Wen, H. J., Schwieger, D., & Gershuny, P. (2007). Internet usage monitoring in the workplace: Its legal challenges and implementation strategies. *Information Systems Management, 24*(2), 185–196. doi:10.1080/10580530701221072

Westin, A. (1967). *Privacy and Freedom*. New York: Athenbaum.

Xu, H., Dinev, T., Smith, J. H., & Hart, P. (2011). Information privacy concerns: Linking individual perceptions with institutional privacy assurances. *Journal of the Association for Information Systems, 12*(12), 798–824.

Yerby. (2013). Legal and ethical issues of employee monitoring. *Online Journal of Applied Knowledge Management, 1*(2), 44-55.

Zheng, S., Shi, K., Zeng, Z., & Lu, Q. (2010). The Exploration of Instrument of Users' Privacy Concerns of Social Network Service. *2010 IEEE International Conference on Industrial Engineering and Engineering Management* (pp. 1538-1542). doi:10.1109/IEEM.2010.5674165

Zweig, D., & Webster, J. (2002). Where is the line between benign and invasive? An examination of psychological barriers to the acceptance of awareness monitoring system. *Journal of Organizational Behavior*, 23(5), 605–633. doi:10.1002/job.157

Compilation of References

De Long, D. W., & Fahey, L. (2000). Diagnosing cultural barriers to knowledge management. The Academy of Management Executive, 14(4),

Hyypiä, M., & Pekkola, S. (2011). Interaction challenges in leadership and performance management in developing a network environment. *Journal of Advances in Management Research, 8*(1), 85–98. doi:10.1108/09727981111129318

14. Urban Outfitters Controversies. (2015, February). *The Week*. Retrieved from http://theweek.com/articles/480961/14-urban-outfitters-controversies

Aalgaard, J. (2015). *Communicating Across the Generations*. Retrieved from http://gettingsmart.com/2015/01/communicating-across-generations/

Aarons, G., & Sawitzky, A. (2006). Organizational climate partially mediates the effect of culture on work attitudes and staff turnover in mental health services. *Administration and Policy in Mental Health, 33*(3), 289–301. doi:10.1007/s10488-006-0039-1 PMID:16544205

Abbe, A., Gulick, L. M. V., & Herman, J. L. (2007). *Cross-cultural competence in Army leaders: A conceptual and empirical foundation*. Washington, DC: U.S. Army Research Institute.

Abeysekera, N., & Jayakody, J. K. (2011). Relationship marketing perspective in salesperson's transformational leadership behavior effect. *Contemporary Management Research, 7*(2), 143–156. doi:10.7903/cmr.3602

Abowd, G. D., Dey, A. K., Brown, P. J., Davies, N., Smith, M., & Steggles, P. (1999). *Towards a Better Understanding of Context and Context-Awareness*. Paper presented at the 1st international symposium on Handheld and Ubiquitous Computing, Karlsruhe, Germany. doi:10.1007/3-540-48157-5_29

Abraham, R. (2000). The role of job control as a moderator of emotional dissonance and emotional intelligence-outcome relationships. *The Journal of Psychology, 134*(2), 169–184. doi:10.1080/00223980009600860 PMID:10766109

Abu Elanain, H. M. (2014). Leader-member exchange and intent to turnover. *Management Research Review, 37*(2), 110–129. doi:10.1108/MRR-09-2012-0197

Abu Lughod, A. (2000). Palestinian higher educaion: National identity, liberation and globalization. *Boundary, 27*(1), 75–95. doi:10.1215/01903659-27-1-75

Abu-Tineh, A. M., Khasawneh, S. A., & Omary, A. A. (2009). Kouzes and Posner's transformational leadership model in practice: The case of Jordanian schools. *Journal of Leadership Education, 7*(3), 265–283. doi:10.12806/V7/I3/RF10

ACA. (2015). *Affordable Care Act and Title X Program*. Retrieved October 8, 2015, from http://www.hhs.gov/opa/affordable-care-act/index.html

Acuff, R. D., Fagan, L. M., Rindfleisch, T. C., Levitt, B. J., & Ford, P. M. (1997). *Lightweight, Mobile E-Mail for Intra-Clinic Communication*. Paper presented at the 1997 AMIA Annual Fall Symposium, Nashville, TN.

Adams, D., Acedo, C., & Popa, S. (2012). In Search of Quality Education. In C. Acedo, D. Adams, & S. Popa (Eds.), *Quality and Qualities: Tensions in Higher Education* (pp. 1–22). Rotterdam: Sense Publishers. doi:10.1007/978-94-6091-951-0_1

Adams, M., Bell, L. A., & Griffin, P. (Eds.). (2007). *Teaching for diversity and social justice* (2nd ed.). New York, NY: Routledge.

Adams, M., Blumenfeld, W., Casteñeda, C. R., Hackman, H., Peters, M., & Zúñiga, X. (2010). *Readings for diversity and social justice* (2nd ed.). New York, NY: Routledge.

Adams, N., & Gold, R. (1993). An infrared network for mobile computers. In *Proceedings USENIX Symposium on Mobile & Location-Indendent Computing* (vol. 10).

Adler, M. J., & Ghadar, E. (2003). Strategic human resource management. New York: Routledge Publications.

Ahmad, F., Mohamad, O., & Ibrahim, H. (2013). Effect of organizational culture on individual absorptive capacity: Evidence from Malaysian electrical and electronic sector. Researchers World –Journal of Arts, Science & Commerce, 4(1), 66–76.

Ahmad, A., Francis, A., & Zairi, M. (2007). Business process reengineering: Critical success factors in higher education. *Business Process Management Journal, 13*(3), 451–469. doi:10.1108/14637150710752344

Ahmed-Kristensen, S., & Vianello, G. (2015). A model for reusing service knowledge based on an empirical case. *Research in Engineering Design, 26*(1), 57–76. doi:10.1007/s00163-014-0184-6

Aier, S. (2014). The role of organizational culture for grounding, management, guidance and effectiveness of enterprise architecture principles. *Information Systems and e-Business Management, 12*(1), 43–70.

Akcigit, U. (2009). *Firm Size, Innovation Dynamics and Growth. In 2009 Meeting Papers (No. 1267).* Society for Economic Dynamics.

Al Dabbagh, M. (2009). The context for intergroup leadership: Women's groups in Saudi Arabia. In T. Pittinsky (Ed.), *Crossing the divide: Intergroup leadership in a world of difference.* Boston, MA: Harvard Business School Publishing Corporation.

Al-Ababneh, M., & Lockwood, A. (2010). *The influence of managerial leadership style on employee job satisfaction in Jordanian resort hotels.* The 28th EuroCHRIE Annual Research Conference, Amsterdam, Netherlands.

Alavi, M., Kayworth, T. R., & Leidner, D. E. (2005). An empirical examination of the influence of organizational culture on knowledge management practices. *Journal of Management Information Systems, 22*(3), 191–224. doi:10.2753/MIS0742-1222220307

Alavi, M., & Leidner, D. E. (1999). Knowledge management system: Issues, challenges, and benefits. *Communications of the AIS, 1*(7), 1–37.

Alcobia, P. (2001). Atitudes e satisfação no trabalho. In J. M. Ferreira, J. Neves, & A. Caetano (Eds.), *Manual de psicossociologia das organizações.* Lisboa: McGraw-Hill.

Alder, G. S., Noel, T. W., & Ambrose, M. L. (2006). Clarifying the effects of Internet monitoring on job attitudes: The mediating role of employee trust. *Information & Management, 43*(7), 894–903. doi:10.1016/j.im.2006.08.008

Ali, M. (2011). *Chartis Launches ReputationGuard®, Reputational Risk Insurance.* Retrieved from http://www.chartisinsurance.com/searchresults/search_295_195443.html

Allen, J. (2011). $16 muffins, $8 coffee served in Justice Audit. *Reuters Online Edition.* Accessed from the Web site: http://www.reuters.com/article/2011/09/21/us-usa-justice-muffins-idUSTRE78J7B020110921

Allen, N., & Meyer, P. (1990). Organizational socialization tactics: A longitudinal analysis of links to newcomers' commitment and role orientation. *Academy of Management Journal, 33*(4), 1–18. doi:10.2307/256294

Almintisir, A., Akeel, A., & Devi Subramainiam, I. (2013). The role of transformational leadership style in motivating public sector employees in Libya. *Australian Journal of Basic & Applied Sciences, 7*(2), 99–108.

Alonso, O., Gertz, M., & Baeza-Yates, R. (2007) On the value of temporal information in information retrieval. *SIGIR Forum, 41*(2), 35-41. doi:10.1145/1328964.1328968

ALS Association. (2015). *What is ALS?* Retrieved from http://www.alsa.org/about-als/what-is-als.html

Altaian, I., & Taylor, D. A. (1983). *Social penetration: The development of interpersonal relationships.* New York: Holt, Rhinehart, and Wilson.

Altman, I. (1975). *The environment and social behaviour: Privacy, personal space, territory, and crowding.* Monterey, CA: Brooks/Cole.

Amabile, T. M. (1988). A model of creativity and innovation in organizations. In B. M. Stew & L. L. Cummings (Eds.), *Research in organizational behavior* (pp. 123–167). Greenwich, CT: JAI.

American Association State Colleges and Universities (AASCU). (2005). *Strengthening the science and mathematics pipeline for a better America.* Washington, DC: American Association of State Colleges and Universities. Retrieved from http://www.aascu.org

American Management Association. (2015). *Leading the Four Generations at Work.* Retrieved from http://www.amanet.org/training/articles/Leading-the-Four-Generations-at-Work.aspx

American National Standard ANSI/ASQC A3-1978. (1978). *Quality Systems Terminology.* Milwaukee, WI: American Society for Quality Control.

Amit, R., Glosten, L., & Muller, E. (1993). Challenges to theory development in entrepreneurship research. *Journal of Management Studies*, *30*(5), 815–834. doi:10.1111/j.1467-6486.1993.tb00327.x

Amstrong, A., & Hagel, J. (2000). The real value of online communities. In E. L. Lesser & M. Fontaine (Eds.), *Knowledge and communities* (pp. 85–98). Boston: Butterworth-Heinemann. doi:10.1016/B978-0-7506-7293-1.50009-3

Anand, A., Kant, R., Patel, D. P., & Singh, M. D. (2015). Knowledge management implementation: A predictive model using an analytical hierarchical process. *Journal of the Knowledge Economy*, *6*(1), 48–71. doi:10.1007/s13132-012-0110-y

Anand, R., & UdayaSuriyan, G. (2010). Emotional intelligence and its relationship with leadership practices. *International Journal of Business and Management*, *5*(2), 65–76.

Andersen, C. (1837). *The Emperor's New Clothes.* Copenhagen, Denmark.

Anderson, T., Gisborne, K. D., & Holliday, P. N. (2012). *Every officer is a leader: Coaching leadership, learning, and performance in justice, public safety, and security organizations.* Trafford Publishing. Retrieved from www.trafford.com

Anderson, C. M., & Martin, M. M. (1995). The effects of communication motives, interaction involvement, and loneliness on satisfaction: A model of small groups. *Small Group Research*, *26*(1), 118–137. doi:10.1177/1046496495261007

Anderson, J. G. (1993). *Evaluating Health Care Information Systems: Methods and Applications.* Sage Publications, Inc.

Anderson, L., & Stillman, J. (2013). Student teaching's contribution to preservice teacher development: A review of research focused on the preparation of teachers for urban and high-needs contexts. *Review of Educational Research*, *83*(1), 3–69. doi:10.3102/0034654312468619

Andreescu, V., & Vitio, G. F. (2010). An exploratory study on ideal leadership behavior: The opinions of American police managers. *International Journal of Police Science & Management*, *12*(4), 567–583. doi:10.1350/ijps.2010.12.4.207

Angelino, L. M., Williams, F. K., & Natvig, D. (2007). Strategies to engage online students and reduce attrition rates. *The Journal of Educators Online*, *4*(2), 1–14.

Angst, C. M., & Agarwal, R. (2009). Adoption of Electronic Health Records in the Presence of Privacy Concerns: The Elaboration Likelihood Model and Individual Persuasion. *Management Information Systems Quarterly*, *33*(2), 339–370.

Antonakis, J., Cianciolo, A. T., & Sternberg, R. J. (Eds.). (2004). *The nature of leadership.* Thousand Oaks, CA: Sage Publications.

Antonelli, C. (1999). The evolution of the industrial organization of the production of knowledge. *Cambridge Journal of Economics*, *23*(2), 243–260. doi:10.1093/cje/23.2.243

Antos, P. (2011). *Handbook of interpersonal communication.* The Hague, The Netherlands: Mouton De Gruyter.

Anyon, J. (2014). *Radical possibilities: Public policy, urban education, and a new social movement.* New York, NY: Routledge.

Anzaldúa, G. (1999). *Borderlands/la frontera: The new Mestiza* (2nd ed.). San Francisco, CA: Aunt Lute Books.

APA Practice Organization. (2014). *The Health Information Technology For Economic and Clinical Health Act* (HITECH Act). Retrieved September 1, 2015, from http://www.apapracticecentral.org/advocacy/technology/hitech-act.aspx

Arasaratnam, L. A., & Doerfel, M. L. (2005). Intercultural communication competence: Identifying key components from multicultural perspectives. *International Journal of Intercultural Relations, 29*(2), 137–163. doi:10.1016/j.ijintrel.2004.04.001

Archer, A. (2006). A Multimodal Approach to Academic 'Literacies': Problematising the Visual/Verbal Divide. *Language and Education, 20*(6), 449–462. doi:10.2167/le677.0

Arends-Tóth, J., & Van De Vijver, F. J. R. (2002). Multiculturalism and acculturation: View of Dutch and Turkish-Dutch. *European Journal of Social Psychology, 33*(2), 249–266. doi:10.1002/ejsp.143

Argote, L., McEvily, B., & Reagan, R. (2003). Managing knowledge in organizations: An integrative framework and review of emerging themes. Management Science, 49(4), 571–582.

Argyris, C. (1958). Some problems in conceptualizing organizational climate: A case study of a bank. *Administrative Science Quarterly, 2*(4), 501–520. doi:10.2307/2390797

Armenakis, A., & Harris, S. (2002). Crafting a change message to create transformational readiness. *Journal of Organizational Change Management, 1*(2), 169–183. doi:10.1108/09534810210423080

Armistead, C., & Machin, S. (1997). Implications of business process management for operations management. *International Journal of Operations & Production Management, 17*(9), 886–898. doi:10.1108/01443579710171217

Armstrong, A., & Thornton, N. (2012). Incorporating Brookfield's discussion techniques synchronously into asynchronous online courses. *The Quarterly Review of Distance Education, 13*(1), 1–9.

Arnison, L., & Miller, P. (2002). Virtual teams: A virtue for the conventional team. *Journal of Workplace Learning, 14*(4), 166–173. doi:10.1108/13665620210427294

Arthur Andersen Business Consulting and APQC. (1996). *The knowledge management assessment tool: External benchmarking version.* Houston, TX: The American Productivity and Quality Center.

Arthur Andersen Business Consulting. (1999). *Zukai knowledge management.* Tokyo, Japan: Keizai Inc.

Arthur, W. B. (2011, October). The Second Economy. *McKinsey Quarterly.* Retrieved 11/10/2011, at https://www.McKinseyquarterly.com/The_second_economy_2853

Article 29 Data Protection Working Party, Opinion 8/2001.

Article 29 Data Protection Working Party, Working document on the surveillance of electronic communications in the workplace, adopted on 29 May 2002, 5401/01/EN/Final, WP 55.

Aryee, S., Walumbwa, F. O., Zhou, Q., & Hartnell, C. A. (2012). Transformational leadership, innovative behavior, and task performance: Test mediation and moderation processes. *Human Performance, 25*(1), 1–25. doi:10.1080/08959285.2011.631648

Asha, C. S., & Jyothi, P. (2013). Internal branding: A determining element of organizational citizenship behavior. *The Journal of Contemporary Management Research, 7*(1), 37–57.

ASHE-ERIC. (2003). Understanding and facilitating organizational change in the 21st century: Recent research and conceptualizations. Washington, DC: John Wiley Inc.

Associated Press. (2011a, April 19). A timeline of Tressel's NCAA troubles. *USA Today.* Retrieved August 28, 2015 from http://usatoday30.usatoday.com/sports/college/football/2011-04-19-2215755358_x.htm

Associated Press. (2011b, May 30). Jim Tressel resigns as Ohio State's coach. *CBS News.* Retrieved August 28, 2015 from http://www.cbsnews.com/news/jim-tressel-resigns-as-ohio-states-coach/

Association for the Study of Higher Education. (2001). *Theories and models of organizational change (ASHE-- ERIC Higher Education Report).*Washington, DC: John Wiley Inc.; doi:10.1002/ache.2804

Astley, W. G., & Zammuto, R. F. (1992). Organization science, managers and language games. *Organization Science, 3*(4), 443–460. doi:10.1287/orsc.3.4.443

Asunda, P. (2010). Productivity, social networks and net communities in the workplace. *Techniques: Connecting Education and Careers, 85*(5), 38–41.

Atkinson, R., & Flint, J. (2001). Accessing hidden and hard-to-reach populations: Snowball research strategies. *Social Research Update, 33.* Retrieved from http://sru.soc.surrey.ac.uk/SRU33.pdf

Aud, S., Rathbun, A., Flicker-Wilkinson, S., & Kristapov-ich, P. Wang, Zhang, J., & Notter, L. (2013). The Condition of Education. Annual Report for the National Center for Education Statistics (NCES), Institute of Education Sciences. Washington, DC: U.S. Department of Education.

Aurum, A., Jeffery, R., Wohlin, C., & Handzic, M. (2003). *Managing software engineering knowledge.* Berlin, Germany: Springer–Verlag. doi:10.1007/978-3-662-05129-0

Austin, J. (2010). *The collaboration challenge: How nonprofits and businesses succeed through strategic alliances.* San Francisco, CA: Jossey-bass.

Australian Commission on Safety and Quality in Health Care (ACSQHC). (2010). *Patient-Centered Care: Improving Quality and Safety by Focusing Care on Patients and Consumers.* Discussion Paper. Retrieved September 2, 2015, from http://www.safetyandquality.gov.au/wp-content/uploads/2012/01/PCCC-DiscussPaper.pdf

Autor, D. H., & Dorn, D. (2013). The Growth of Low-Skill Service Jobs and the Polarization of the US Labor Market. *American Economic Review, 103*(5), 1553-97. Retrieved on 03/17/2014 from http://ideas.repec.org/s/aea/aecrev.html

Avery, G. C. (2004). *Understanding leadership: Paradigms and cases.* London, UK: Sage.

Avery, G. C. (2005). *Understanding leadership.* London: Sage Publications.

Avolio, B. J., Waldman, D. A., & Einstein, W. O. (1988). Transformational leadership in a management game simulation: Impacting the bottom line. *Group & Organization Studies, 13*(1), 59–80. doi:10.1177/105960118801300109

Avrahami, D., Gergle, D., Hudson, S. E., & Kiesler, S. (2007). Improving the match between callers and receivers: A study on the effect of contextual information on cell phone interruptions. *Behaviour & Information Technology, 26*(3), 247–259. doi:10.1080/01449290500402338

Avruch, K. (2002). *Culture and negotiation pedagogy.* Available at www.pon.harvard.edu

Avtgis, T. A., & Taber, K. R. (2006). "I laughed so hard my side hurts, or is that an ulcer?" The influence of work humor on job stress, job satisfaction, and burnout among print media employees. *Communication Research Reports, 23*(1), 13–18. doi:10.1080/17464090500535814

Awadh, A. M., & Saad, A. M. (2013). Impact of organizational culture on employee performance. *International Review of Management and Business Research, 2*(1), 168–175.

Axelrod, B. (2015, July 28). How Urban Meyer has Ohio State set up for a long-term dynasty. *The Bleacher Report.* Retrieved July 29, 2015 from http://bleacherreport.com/articles/2533002-how-urban-meyer-has-ohio-state-set-up-for-a-long-term-dynasty

Axtell, C. M., Holman, D. J., Unsworth, K. L., Wall, T. D., Waterson, P. E., & Harrington, E. (2000). Shopfloor innovation: Facilitating the suggestion and implementation of ideas. *Journal of Occupational and Organizational Psychology, 73*(3), 265–285. doi:10.1348/096317900167029

Ayoko, O. B., & Konrad, A. M. (2012). Leaders' transformational, conflict, and emotion management behaviors in culturally diverse workgroups. *Equality, Diversity and Inclusion. International Journal (Toronto, Ont.), 31,* 694–724. doi:10.1108/02610151211277581

Azizan, H., & Lee, Y. M. (2011, April 12). Minding our language. *The Star.*

Aziz, O., Panesar, S., Netuveli, G., Paraskeva, P., Sheikh, A., & Darzi, A. (2005). Handheld computers and the 21st century surgical team: A pilot study. *BMC Medical Informatics and Decision Making, 5*(1), 28. doi:10.1186/1472-6947-5-28 PMID:16109177

Bach, K. (1987). *Thought and reference.* Oxford, UK: Clarendon Press.

Bach, K. (1999). The semantics-pragmatics distinction: What it is and why it matters. In K. Turner (Ed.), *The semantics-pragmatics interface from different points of view* (pp. 65–84). Oxford, UK: Elsevier.

Bach, K. (2001). You don't say. *Synthese, 128*(1/2), 15–44. doi:10.1023/A:1010353722852

Baehler, K., & Bryson, J. (2008). Stress, Minister: Government policy advisors and work stress. *International Journal of Public Sector Management, 21*(3), 257–270. doi:10.1108/09513550810863169

Bagnoli, C., & Vedovato, M. (2014). The impact of knowledge management and strategy configuration coherence on SME performance. *Journal of Management & Governance, 18*(2), 615–647. doi:10.1007/s10997-012-9211-z

Baker, G. (2002). The effects of synchronous collaborative technologies on decision making: A study of virtual teams. *Information Resources Management Journal, 15*(4), 79–93. doi:10.4018/irmj.2002100106

Baker, T. (2000). *Effective police leadership.* New York, NY: Looseleaf Law Publications, INC.

Bakker, M., Leenders, R. T. A. J., Gabbay, S. M., Kratzer, J., & Van Engelen, J. M. L. (2006). Is trust really social capital? Knowledge sharing in product development projects. *The Learning Organization, 13*(6), 594–605. doi:10.1108/09696470610705479

Bakshy, E., Rosenn, I., Marlow, C., & Adamic, L. (2012). The Role of Social Networks in Information Diffusion. *International World Wide Web Conference,* Lyon, France. doi:10.1145/2187836.2187907

Ball, K. (2010). Workplace surveillance: An overview. *Labor Review, 51*(1), 87–106.

Baltierra, E. (2005). SHRM Case Study: Generational differences. *Society of Human Resource Management.* Retrieved August 30, 2012 from: http://www.shrm.org/TemplatesTools/Toolkits/Documents/CMS_011553.pdf

Banathy, B. H., & Jenks, C. L. (1990, April). *The transformation of education: By design.* Paper presented at the Annual Meeting of the American Educational Research Association, Boston, MA. Retrieved from http://files.eric.ed.gov/fulltext/ED323660.pdf

Banathy, B. H. (1991). *Systems Design of Education: A Journey to Create the Future.* Englewood Cliffs, NJ: Educational Technology Publications.

Baramki, G. (2009). Peaceful Resistance: Building a Palestinian University under Occupation. London: Pluto Press.

Barbeira, M. R., & Franco, M. J. (2009). Um sistema de gestão do conhecimento como fomentador de redes estratégicas interorganizacionais. *Revista Ibero-Americana de Estratégia, 8*(2), 5–29.

Bardram, J. E., & Hansen, T. R. (2004). *The AWARE architecture: supporting context-mediated social awareness in mobile cooperation.* Paper presented at the 2004 ACM Conference on Computer Supported Cooperative Work, Chicago, IL. doi:10.1145/1031607.1031639

Bardram, J. E., Hansen, T. R., & Soegaard, M. (2006). *AwareMedia: A shared interactive display supporting social, temporal, and spatial awareness in surgery.* Paper presented at the 2006 20th anniversary conference on Computer supported cooperative work, Banff, Canada. doi:10.1145/1180875.1180892

Bardram, J. E., & Hansen, T. R. (2010). Context-Based Workplace Awareness. *Computer Supported Cooperative Work, 19*(2), 105–138. doi:10.1007/s10606-010-9110-2

Barkema, H. G., Chen, X. P., George, G., Luo, Y., & Tsui, A. (2015). West meets east: New concepts and theories. *Academy of Management Journal, 58*(2), 460–479. doi:10.5465/amj.2015.4021

Barmeyer, C., & Franklin, P. (Eds.). (forthcoming). *Intercultural Management: European Case Studies - Achieving Synergy from Diversity.* London: Palgrave McMillan.

Barnard, C. (1938). *The functions of the executive* (2nd ed.). Harvard University Press.

Barnatt, C. (2008). Higher Education 2.0. *International Journal of Management Education, 7*(3), 47–56.

Barnett, D. (2004). School leadership preparation programs: Are they preparing tomorrow's leaders? *Education, 125*, 121–129.

Barnett, R., & Brennan, R. (1997). Change in job conditions, change in psychological distress, and gender: A longitudinal study of dual-earner couples. *Journal of Organizational Behavior, 18*(3), 253–274. doi:10.1002/(SICI)1099-1379(199705)18:3<253::AID-JOB800>3.0.CO;2-7

Barnwell, D., Nedrick, S., Rudolph, E., Sesay, M., & Wellen, W. (2014). Leadership of international and virtual project teams. *International Journal of Global Business, 7*(2), 1–8.

Barrett-Howard, E., & Tyler, T. R. (1986). Procedural justice as a criterion in allocation decisions. *Journal of Personality and Social Psychology, 50*(2), 296–304. doi:10.1037/0022-3514.50.2.296 PMID:3746613

Barth, R. S. (1986). Principal centered professional development. *Theory into Practice, 25*(3), 156–160. doi:10.1080/00405848609543218

Barthwal, S., & Som, A. J. (2012). Emotional intelligence as a measure of an employee's overall effectiveness. *Drishtikon: A Management Journal, 3*, 140-176.

Bashouri, J., & Duncan, G. (2014). Communities of practice: Linking knowledge management and strategy in creative firms. *The Journal of Business Strategy, 35*(6), 49–57. doi:10.1108/JBS-08-2013-0072

Bass, B. M. (1985). *Leadership and performance beyond expectations*. New York: Free Press.

Bass, B. M. (1990). *Bass & Stogdill's handbook of leadership: Theory, research & managerial applications*. New York, NY: The Free Press.

Bass, B. M. (1990). From transactional to transformational leadership: Learning to share the vision. *Organizational Dynamics, 18*(3), 19–31. doi:10.1016/0090-2616(90)90061-S

Bass, B. M. (1997). Does the transactional-transformational leadership paradigm transcend organizational and national boundaries? *Journal of American Psychologist, 52*(2), 130–139. doi:10.1037/0003-066X.52.2.130

Bass, B. M. (1999). On the taming of charisma: A reply to Janice Beyer. *The Leadership Quarterly, 10*(4), 541–554. doi:10.1016/S1048-9843(99)00030-2

Bass, B. M. (2007). From transactional to transformative leadership: Learning to share the vision. In R. P. Vecchio (Ed.), *Leadership: Understanding the dynamics of power and influence in organizations* (pp. 302–317). Notre Dame, IN: University of Notre Dame Press.

Bass, B. M., & Avolio, B. J. (1990). *Manual: The multifactor leadership questionnaire*. Palo Alto, CA: Consulting Psychologists Press.

Bass, B. M., & Avolio, B. J. (1994). *Improving organizational effectiveness through transformational leadership*. Thousand Oaks, CA: Sage.

Bass, B. M., & Avolio, B. J. (1995). *The multifactor leadership questionnaire*. Palo Alto, CA: Mind Garden.

Basu, S., Andrews, J., Kishore, S., Panjabi, R., & Stuckler, D. (2012). Comparative Performance of Private and Public Healthcare Systems in Low- and Middle-Income Countries: A Systematic Review. *PLoS Medicine, 9*(6), e1001244. doi:10.1371/journal.pmed.1001244 PMID:22723748

Bau, I. (2011). Connected for health: The potential of health information and communications technologies to reduce health care disparities. *National Civic Review, 100*(3), 15-18. doi:10.1002/ncr.20064

Bavelas, J. B., Chovil, N., & Roe, L. (1995). Gestures specialized for dialogue. *Personality and Social Psychology, 21*(4), 394–405. doi:.10.1177/0146167295214010

Bayley, D. H. (1996). *Police for the Future*. Oxford, UK: Oxford University Press.

Beattie, G., & Shovelton, H. (1999). Iconic hand gestures that accompany spontaneous speech. *Journal of Language and Social Psychology, 18*(4), 438–463. doi:10.1177/0261927X99018004005

Beck, M., Brannon, S., Dracos, G., Junnarkar, P., Katz, R., Malik, A., . . . Sonavane, S. (2011). Working in a virtual world: Establishing highly effective virtual teams on information technology projects. *Deloitte*. Retrieved September 15, 2012 from http://www.deloitte.com/assets/Dcom-UnitedStates/Local%20Assets/Documents/us_consulting_WorkingwithaVirtualWorld_080911.pdf

Bélanger, F., & Crossler, R. E. (2011). Privacy in the digital age: A review of information privacy research in information systems. *Management Information Systems Quarterly*, *35*(4), 1017–1041.

Belderbos, R., & Somers, D. (2015). Do Technology Leaders Deter Inward R&D Investments? Evidence from regional R & D location Decisions in Europe. In Regional Studies. Carfax.

Bell, B. S., & Kozlowski, S. W. J. (2002). A typology of virtual teams: Implications for effective leadership. *Group & Organization Management*, *27*(1), 14–49. doi:10.1177/1059601102027001003

Bengtson, M., & Solvell, O. (2004). Climate of competition, clusters, and innovative performance. *Scandinavian Journal of Management*, *20*(3), 225–244. doi:10.1016/j.scaman.2004.06.003

Benner, M. J., & Veloso, F. M. (2008). ISO 9000 practices and financial performance: A technology coherence perspective. *Journal of Operations Management*, *26*(5), 611–629. doi:10.1016/j.jom.2007.10.005

Bennett, S., Bishop, A., Dalgarno, B., Waycott, J., & Kennedy, G. (2012). Implementing Web 2.0 technologies in higher education: A collective case study. *Computers & Education*, *59*(2), 524–534. doi:10.1016/j.compedu.2011.12.022

Benoit, W. (1995). *Accounts, excuses, and apologies: A theory of image restoration*. State University of New York Press.

Benoit, W. (2014). *Accounts, excuses, and apologies: Image repair theory and research*. State University of New York Press.

Benson, V., Filippaios, F., & Morgan, S. (2010). Online social networks: Changing the face of business education and career planning. *International Journal of Business and Management*, *4*(1), 20–33.

Bentkover, J. D. (2012). *Leadership is Central to Healthcare System Reform*. Retrieved September 2, 2015, from http://www.beckershospitalreview.com/hospital-management-administration/leadership-is-central-to-healthcare-system-reform.html

Bering, J. J. (2003). Towards a cognitive theory of existential meaning. *New Ideas in Psychology*, *21*(2), 101–120. doi:10.1016/S0732-118X(03)00014-X

Berjano, E., Sales-Nebot, L., & Lozano-Nietoc, A. (2013). Improving professionalism in the engineering curriculum through a novel use of oral presentations. *European Journal of Engineering Education*, *38*(2), 121–130. doi:10.1080/03043797.2012.745829

Berkeley, U. C. (2015). *Using Emotional Intelligence to Improve Communication*. UC Berkeley Extension. Retrieved June 25, 2015 from http://extension.berkeley.edu/search/publicCourseSearchDetails.do?method=load&courseId=8939289&gclid=CI2akq7Cq8YCFUGTfgod5lwAdw

Berkowitz, S. (2013, May 2). NCAA had record $71 million surplus in fiscal 2012. *USA Today*. Retrieved March 17, 2014 from http://www.usatoday.com/story/sports/college/2013/05/02/ncaa-financial-statement-surplus/2128431/

Berk, R. (2013). Face-to-face versus online course evaluations: A 'consumer's guide' to seven strategies. *Journal of Online Teaching and Learning*, *9*(1), 140–148.

Berlew, D. E. (1974). Leadership and organizational excitement. In D. A. Kolb, I. M. Rubin, & J. Mc Intyre (Eds.), *Organizational psychology: A book of readings* (2nd ed., pp. 265–277). Englewood Cliffs, NJ: Prentice Hall.

Berman, S. J., & Hellweg, S. A. (1989). Perceived supervisor communication competence and supervisor satisfaction as a function of quality circle participation. *Journal of Business Communication*, *26*(2), 103–122. doi:10.1177/002194368902600202

Bernhardt, V. (2013). *Translating data into information to improve teaching and learning*. New York: Routledge.

Bernstein, A., Vorburger, P., & Egger, P. (2005). *Direct Interruptablity Prediction and Scenario-based Evaluation of Wearable Devices: Towards Reliable Interruptability Predictions*. Paper presented at the First International Workshop on Managing Context Information in Mobile and Pervasive Environments MCMP-05.

Berry, G. (1997). Leadership and the development of quality culture in schools. *International Journal of Educational Management*, *11*(2), 52–65. doi:10.1108/09513549710163943

Berry, J., & Kalin, R. (1995). Multicultural and ethnic attitudes in Canada: An overview of the 1991 national survey. *Canadian Journal of Behavioural Science*, *27*(3), 301–320. doi:10.1037/0008-400X.27.3.301

Betts, F. (1992, November). How Systems Thinking Applies to Education. *Educational Leadership*, *50*(3), 38–41. Retrieved from http://search.proquest.com/docview/224857527?accountid=12528

Bhalla, P., & Nazneen, A. (2013). A study of organizational culture in Indian organized retail sectors. *International Journal of Retail Management and Research*, *3*(1), 1–6.

Bhasin, K. (2012, February). 13 epic Twitter fails by big brands. *Business insider*. Retrieved from http://www.businessinsider.com/13-epic-twitter-fails-by-big-brands-2012-2?op=1

Bhattacharyya, E., & Sargunan, R. A. (2009). *The technical oral presentation skills and attributes in engineering education: Stakeholder perceptions and university preparation in a Malaysian context*. Paper presented at the 20th Australasian Association for Engineering Education Conference, University of Adelaide.

Bien, L. (2014, November). A complete timeline of the Ray Rice assault case. *SB Nation*. Retrieved from http://www.sbnation.com/nfl/2014/5/23/5744964/ray-rice-arrest-assault-statement-apology-ravens

Bies, R. J., & Moag, J. F. (1986). Interactional justice: Communication criteria of fairness. In R. J. Lewicki, B. H. Sheppard, & M. H. Bazerman (Eds.), *Research on negotiations in organisations* (Vol. 1, pp. 43–55). Greenwich, CT: JAI Press.

Bilich, F., & Neto, A. A. (1997). Strategic total quality management. *Total Quality Management*, *8*(2-3), 88–89. doi:10.1080/0954412979767

Bill, N. (2002). Context-aware communication. *Wireless Communications, IEEE*, *9*(5), 46–54.

Bisgaard, J. J., Heise, M., & Steffensen, C. (2004). *How is Context and Context-awareness Defined and Applied? A Survey of Context-awareness*. Department of Computer Science, Aalborg University.

Blackburn, R., Furst, S., & Rosen, B. (2003). Building a winning virtual team. In C. B. Gibson & S. Cohen (Eds.), *Virtual teams that work: Creating conditions for virtual team effectiveness* (pp. 95–120). San Francisco, CA: Jossey-Bass.

Blake, R. R., & Mouton, J. S. (1964). *The Managerial Grid*. Houston: Gulf Publishing Company.

Blaney, J. R., Lippert, L. R., & Smith, J. S. (2013). Repairing the athlete's image. Lanham, MD: Lexington Books (Rowman & Littlefield).

Blase, J., & Blase, J. (2000). Effective instructional leadership. *Journal of Educational Administration*, *38*(2), 130–141. doi:10.1108/09578230010320082

Blauth, C., McDaniel, J., Perrin, C., & Perrin, P. B. (2011). *Age-Based Stereotypes: Silent Killer of Collaboration and Productivity*. Tampa, FL: AcheiveGlobal.

Blavin, J. H., & Cohen, L. G. (2002). Gore, Gibson, and Goldsmith: The Evolution of Internet Metaphors in Law and Commentary. *Harvard Journal of Law & Technology*, 16.

Bliese, P. D. (2000). Within-group agreement, non-independence, and reliability: Implications for data aggregation and analysis. In K. Klein & S. Kozlowski (Eds.), *Multilevel theory, research, and method in organizations* (pp. 349–381). San Francisco, CA: Jossey–Bass.

Bloland, P., Simone, P., Burkholder, B., Slutsker, L., & De Cock K. M. (2012). The Role of Public Health Institutions in Global Health System Strengthening Efforts. *PLoS Med*, *9*(4), e1001199. doi:10.1371/journal.pmed.1001199

Blumenthal, D. (2010). Launching HITECH. *The New England Journal of Medicine*.

Blum, N. J., & Lieu, T. A. (1992). Interrupted care. The effects of paging on pediatric resident activities. *American Journal of Diseases of Children, 146*(7), 806–808. doi:10.1001/archpedi.1992.02160190038016 PMID:1496947

Boal, K., & Hooijberg, R. (2001). Strategic leadership research: Moving on. *The Leadership Quarterly, 11*(4), 515–549. doi:10.1016/S1048-9843(00)00057-6

Bock, G. W., & Kim, Y. G. (2002). Breaking the myths of rewards: An exploratory study of attitudes about knowledge sharing. *Information Resources Management Journal, 15*(2), 14–21. doi:10.4018/irmj.2002040102

Bock, G. W., Zmud, R. W., Kim, Y. G., & Lee, J. N. (2005). Behavioral intention formation in knowledge sharing: Examining the roles of extrinsic motivators, social-psychological factors, and organizational climate. *Management Information Systems Quarterly, 29*(1), 87–111.

Boerema, A. J. (2011). Challenging and supporting new leader development. *Educational Management Administration & Leadership, 39*(5), 554–567. doi:10.1177/1741143211408451

Bogliacino, F., Piva, M., & Vivarelli, M. (2012). R&D and Employment: An application of the LSDVC Estimator using European Microdata. *Economics Letters, 116*, 56–59.

Bok, D. (2006). *Our underachieving colleges: A candid look at how much students learn and why they should be learning more.* Princeton, NJ: Princeton University Press.

Bolden, R., Gosling, J., Marturano, A., & Dennison, P. (2003). *A review of leadership theory and competency frameworks: Edited version of a report for Chase consulting and management standards centre.* Centre for Leadership Studies at University of Exeter.

Boler, M., & Zembylas, M. (2003). Discomforting truths: The emotional terrain of understanding difference. In P. Trifonas (Ed.), *Pedagogies of difference: Rethinking education for social change* (pp. 110–136). New York, NY: Routledge.

Bolman, L. G., & Deal, T. E. (2003). *Reframing organizations: Artistry, choice and leadership.* San Francisco, CA: Jossey Bass, Inc.

Bone, D., & Normore, A. H. (2014). Progressive law enforcement leaders effectively manage departmental risk. *Law Enforcement Today (LET): The Law Enforcement Community.* Retrieved from, http://www.lawenforcementtoday.com/2014/07/13/striving-for-educational-excellence-in-law-enforcement-leadership-the-case-of-jefferson-parish-sheriffs-office/

Bone, D., Normore, A.H., & Javidi, M. (2015). Human factors: police leaders improving safety while developing meaningful public trust. *FBI Law Enforcement Journal.*

Bone, D. (1996). Quality management is collegiate management: Improving practice in a special school. In P. Lomax (Ed.), *Quality Management in education: Sustaining the vision through Action Research* (pp. 19–46). London: Routledge and Hyde Publications.

Bonstingl, J. J. (1992). The quality revolution in education. *Educational Leadership, 50*(3), 4–9.

Bonstingl, J. J. (1993). The quality movement: What's it really about? *Educational Leadership, 51*(1), 66–70.

Boomer, J. (2004). Finding out what knowledge management is – and isn't. *Accounting Today, 18*(14), 9–22.

Boren, C. (2011, July 15). Report: Ohio State's Jim Tressel had history of compliance violations. *The Washington Post.* Retrieved October 18, 2015 from https://www.washingtonpost.com/blogs/early-lead/post/report-ohio-states-jim-tressel-had-history-of-compliance-violations/2011/07/15/gIQAJjbFGI_blog.html

Bortree, D. S., & Seltzer, T. (2009). Dialogic strategies and outcomes: An analysis of environmental advocacy groups' Facebook profiles. *Public Relations Review, 35*(3), 317–319. doi:10.1016/j.pubrev.2009.05.002

Borzillo, S., Schmitt, A., & Antino, M. (2012). Communities of practice: Keeping the company agile. *Journal of Business Strategy, 33*(6), 22-30.

Botan, C. (1993). A human nature approach to image and ethics in international public relations. *Journal of Public Relations Research, 5*(2), 71–81. doi:10.1207/s1532754xjprr0502_02

Botan, C. (1997). Ethics in strategic communication campaigns: The case for a new approach to public relations. *Journal of Business Communication, 34*(2), 188–202. doi:10.1177/002194369703400205

Botsis, T., Solvoll, T., Scholl, J., Hasvold, P., & Hartvigsen, G. (2007). Context-aware systems for mobile communication in healthcare - A user oriented approach. *Proceedings of the 7th Wseas International Conference on Applied Informatics and Communications*, (pp. 69-74).

Bottaffi, G., Bacalentri, R., Braham, P., & Gindro, S. (2002). *Dictionary of race ethnicity, & culture.* New York, NY: Sage Publications.

Bouchet, H. (2002). *Cyber-Surveillance in the Workplace.* Report adopted by the CNIL. Available at: http://www.cnil.fr/fileadmin/documents/uk/CNIL-cybersurveillance-feb2002-VA.pdf

Boulos, M. N., & Wheeler, S. (2007). The emerging Web 2.0 social software: An enabling suite of sociable technologies in health and health care education. *Health Information and Libraries Journal, 24*(1), 2–23. doi:10.1111/j.1471-1842.2007.00701.x PMID:17331140

Bouygues UK Ltd v. Dahl Jensen UK Ltd, (1999).

Bowers, C. P. (1996). Courts, Contracts, and the Appropriate Discount Rate: A Quick Fix for the Legal Lottery. *The University of Chicago Law Review. University of Chicago. Law School, 63*(3), 1099–1137. doi:10.2307/1600250

boyd, d. m., & Ellison, N. B. (2007). Social network sites: Definition, history, and scholarship. *Journal of Computer-Mediated Communication, 13*(1), 210-230.

Boyd, D., Grossman, P., Ing, M., Lankford, H., Loeb, S., & Wyckoff, J. (2011). The influence of school administrators on teacher retention decisions. *American Educational Research Journal, 48*(2), 303–333. doi:10.3102/0002831210380788

Bozarth, J., Chapman, D. D., & LaMonica, L. (2004). Preparing for distance learning: Designing an online student orientation course. *Journal of Educational Technology & Society, 7*, 87–106.

Braddock, R., Mahony, P., & Taylor, P. (2006). Globalisation, commercialism, managerialism and internationalisation. *International Journal of Learning, 13*(8), 61–67.

Bradley, W. E., & Vozikis, G. S. (2004). Trust in virtual teams. In S. H. Godar & S. P. Ferris (Eds.), *Virtual and collaborative teams: Process, technologies, and practice* (pp. 99–113). Hershey, PA: Idea Group Publishing. doi:10.4018/978-1-59140-204-6.ch006

Bradner, E., Kellogg, W. A., & Erickson, T. (1999). *The adoption and use of; a field study of chat in the workplace.* Paper presented at the Sixth European conference on Computer supported cooperative work, Copenghagen, Denmark.

Brandt, R. (2003). Is this school a learning organization? 10 ways to tell. *Journal of Staff Development, 24*(1), 10–16. Retrieved from http://search.proquest.com/docview/211520094?accountid=12528

Brazeal, L. M. (2008). The image repair strategies of Terrell Owens. *Public Relations Review, 34*(2), 145–150. doi:10.1016/j.pubrev.2008.03.021

Brinson, S. L., & Benoit, W. L. (1999). The tarnished star: Restoring Texaco's damaged public image. *Management Communication Quarterly, 12*(4), 483–519. doi:10.1177/0893318999124001

Bristow, D., & Vasilopoulous, R. (1995). The New CCDC 2: Facilitating Dispute Resolution of Construction Projects. *Constitutional Law Journal (Newark, N.J.), 11*(2), 95–117.

Brockman, J., & Matson, K. (Eds.). (1995). How Things Are: a Science Tool-Kit for the Mind. London: Phoenix.

Bronfman, V. S. (2002). Comunidades de práctica. Paper presented at the Workshop GEC S.A., Barcelona, Spain.

Brooks, J., & Normore, A. (2010). Educational leadership and globalization: Literacy for a glocal perspective. *Educational Policy, 24*(1), 52–82. doi:10.1177/0895904809354070

Brown, S. L., & Eisenhardt, K. M. (1995). Product development: Past research, present findings, and future directions. Academy of Management Review, 20(2), 343–378. doi: 10.2307/258850

Brown, S. P., & Leigh, T. W. (1996). A new look at psychological climate and its relationship to job involvement, effort, and performance. Journal of Applied Psychology, 81(4), 358–368. doi:10.1037/0021-9010.81.4.358 PMID:8751453 doi:10.1037/0021-9010.81.4.358 PMID:8751453

Brownell, J. (2003). Applied Research in Managerial Communication. *The Cornell Hotel and Restaurant Administration Quarterly, 44*(2), 39–49. doi:10.1016/S0010-8804(03)90017-6

Browning Leadership Model. (2013). Leading at the Strategic Level: The Browning Leadership Model. Designed by Jen Russell for The Browning Strategic Leadership Model. *Stratified Systems Theory*. Retrieved September 2, 2015, from http://www.browningleadershipmodel.org/Stratified_Systems_Theory.pdf

Brown, J. F., & Marshall, B. L. (2008). Continuous quality improvement: An effective strategy for improvement of program outcomes in a higher education setting. *Nursing Education Perspectives, 29*(4), 205–211. PMID:18770948

Brown, J. S., & Duguid, P. (1991). Organizational learning and communities of practice: Towards a Unified View of working, learning and innovation. *Organization Science, 2*(1), 40–57. doi:10.1287/orsc.2.1.40

Bruce, T., & Tini, T. (2008). Unique crisis response strategies in sports public relations: Rugby league and the case for diversion. *Public Relations Review, 34*(2), 108–115. doi:10.1016/j.pubrev.2008.03.015

Brunelle, E. (2012). Virtuality in work arrangements and affective organizational commitment. *International Journal of Business and Social Science, 3*(2), 56–62.

Bryman, A. (2013). *Leadership and organizations*. London, UK: Routledge.

Brynjolfsson, E., & McAfee, A. (2011). *Race against the machine: How the digital revolution is accelerating innovation, driving productivity, and irreversibly transforming employment and the economy*. Digital Frontier Press.

Buang, Z., Elangsegaran, R., Jano, Z., Ahmad, S., & Husain, K. (2003). *An investigation on the nature of spoken English among engineers in Malaysian industry*. Kolej Universiti Teknikal Kebangsaan Malaysia.

Buchanan, D., & Huczynski, A. (1997). *Organizational Behaviour*. Harlow: Prentice Hall.

Buckholz, S., Lashbrook, W., & Wenburg, J. (1976). *Toward the measurement and processing of social styles*. Paper presented at the International Communication Association, Portland, OR.

Buckingham, M., & Coffman, C. (1999). *First, break all the rules: What the world's greatest managers do differently*. New York, NY: Simon & Schuster.

Buckley, P. J., & Carter, M. J. (2000). Knowledge management in global technology markets. *Long Range Planning, 33*(1), 55–71. doi:10.1016/S0024-6301(99)00102-8

Bühring-Uhle, C., Kirchhoff, L., & Scherer, G. (2006). *Arbitration and mediation in international business*. New York: Kluwer Law International.

Bulca, M., & Safaeib, L. A. (2013). Public presentation: Who fears? *Procedia: Social and Behavioral Sciences, 70*, 574–579. doi:10.1016/j.sbspro.2013.01.095

Bunt, G. G., Wittek, R. P., & Klepper, M. C. (2005). The evolution of intra-organizational trust networks. *International Sociological Association, 20*(3), 339–369. doi:10.1177/0268580905055480

Burgoon, J. K., Byuller, D. B., Hale, J. L., & deTurck, M. A. (1984). Relational message associated with nonverbal behaviors. *Human Communication Research, 10*(3), 351–378. doi:10.1111/j.1468-2958.1984.tb00023.x

Burke, M. E. (2004). Generational differences survey report. *Society of Human Resource Management*. Retrieved from: http://www.shrm.org/hrdisciplines/benefits/Documents/Generational%20Differences%20Survey%20Report.pdf

Burke, W. W. (2010). *Organization change: Theory and practice. Foundations for Organizational Science*. Thousand Oaks, CA: Sage Publications, Inc.

Burns, J. M. (1978). *Leadership*. New York, NY: Harper & Row; doi:10.1177/1742715005049347

Burton, J. W. (1990). *Conflict Resolution and Prevention*. New York: St. Martin's Press.

Burton, J. W. (1993). Conflict Resolution as Political Philosophy. In H. van der Merwe & D. J. Sandole (Eds.), *Conflict Resolution Theory and Practice: Integration and Application* (pp. 55–64). Manchester, UK: Manchester University Press.

Burton, J. W. (1997). *Violence Explained: The Sources of Conflict, Violence and Crime and Their Prevention*. Manchester, UK: Mancherster University Press.

Burton, J. W. (1998). Conflict Resolution: The Human Dimension. *International Journal of Peace Studies*, *3*(1), 4.

Buscaglia, E. (1996). Corruption and Judicial Reform in Latin America. *Policy Studies*, *17*(4), 273–285. doi:10.1080/01442879608423713

Buscaglia, E., & Stephan, P. B. (2005). An Empirical Assessment of the Impact of Formal Versus Informal Dispute Resolution on Poverty: A Governance-Based Approach. *International Review of Law and Economics*, *25*(1), 89–106. doi:10.1016/j.irle.2004.06.004

Cabrera, E. F., & Cabrera, A. (2005). Fostering knowledge sharing through people management practices. *International Journal of Human Resource Management*, *16*(5), 720–735. doi:10.1080/09585190500083020

Cahill, D. (1995). The managerial implications of the learning organization: A new tool for internal marketing. *Journal of Services Marketing*, *9*(4), 43–51. doi:10.1108/08876049510094513

Caldwell, B. (2005). *School-based management. Education Policy Series. International Academy of Education and International Institute for Educational Planning*. UNESCO.

Caldwell, B. (2007). *Self managing schools and improved learning outcomes*. Canberra: Department of Employment, Education, Training and Youth Affairs.

Calhoun, C. (2011). Communication as Social Science (and More). *International Journal of Communication*, *5*, 1479–1496.

Cameron, K. S., & Freeman, S. J. (1991). Cultural congruence, strength, and type: Relationships to effectiveness. *Research in Organizational Change and Development*, *5*(2), 23–58.

Cameron, K. S., & Quinn, R. E. (2006). *Diagnosing and changing organizational culture*. San Francisco, CA: John Wiley Inc.

Cames, O., & Smith, P. (2015a). CAMES (Corporate Action Methodology for Enterprise Systems): Decision Management through Improved Communication. *Proceedings of ICDSST 2015: International Conference on Decision Support System Technology "Big Data Analytics for Decision-Making"*.

Cames, O., & Smith, P. (2015b). *CAMES: a system to transform project management interactions*. Algarve, Portugal.

Camillo, A. A., & Di Pietro, L. (2011). The Importance of Managerial Communication for Hospitality Organizational Settings in the Era of High-Tech Evolution. *Hosteur*, *20*(2), 19–27.

Campbell, C. R. (2007). On the journey toward wholeness in leader theories. *Leadership and Organization Development Journal*, *28*(2), 137–153. doi:10.1108/01437730710726831

Campbell, D. J. (2000). The proactive employee: Managing workplace initiative. *The Academy of Management Executive*, *14*(3), 52–66. Retrieved from http://amp.aom.org/content/14/3/52.short

Campbell, D. P., & Level Dale, A. (1985). A Black Box Model of Communication. *Journal of Business Communication*, *22*(3), 37–47. doi:10.1177/002194368502200304

Campbell, J. L., & Göritz, A. S. (2014). Culture corrupts! A qualitative study of organizational culture in corrupt organizations. *Journal of Business Ethics*, *120*(3), 291–311. doi:10.1007/s10551-013-1665-7

Campbell, J. P. (1990). Modeling the performance prediction problem in industrial and organizational psychology. In M. Dunnette & L. Hough (Eds.), *Handbook of industrial and organizational psychology* (pp. 687–732). Palo Alto, CA: Consulting Psychologists Press.

Campbell, J. P., & Campbell, R. J. (1988). *Productivity in organizations: New perspectives from industrial and organizational psychology*. San Francisco, CA: Jossey–Bass.

Canavan, D., Scott, P. S., & Mangematin, V. (2013). Creative professional service firms: Aligning strategy and talent. *The Journal of Business Strategy, 34*(3), 24–32. doi:10.1108/JBS-10-2012-0058

Canen, A. G., & Canen, A. (2008). Multicultural leadership. *The International Journal of Conflict Management, 19*(1), 4–19. doi:10.1108/10444060810849155

Cappelen, H., & Dever, J. (2014). *The inessential indexical: On the philosophical insignificance of perspective and the first person: Context and content.* Oxford University Press.

CareerBuilder. (2010). *More than four-in-ten workers over the age of 35 currently work for a younger boss, finds new CareerBuilder survey.* Retrieved from http://www. careerbuilder.com/share/aboutus/pressreleasesdetail.asp x?id=pr554&sd=2/17/2010&ed=12/31/2010&siteid=cb pr&sc_cmp1=cb_pr554

Carlson, J. R., George, J. F., Burgoon, J. K., Adkins, M., & White, C. H. (2004). Deception in computer-mediated communication. *Group Decision and Negotiation, 13*(1), 5–28. doi:10.1023/B:GRUP.0000011942.31158.d8

Carlson, S. (1951). *Executive Behavior.* Stockholm: Strombergs.

Carneiro, A. (2000). How does knowledge management influence innovation and competitiveness? *Journal of Knowledge Management, 4*(2), 87–98. doi:10.1108/13673270010372242

Carnevale, P. J., & Pruitt, D. G. (1992). Negotiation and Mediation. *Annual Review of Psychology, 43*(1), 531–582. doi:10.1146/annurev.ps.43.020192.002531

Carroll, D. W. (1999). Psychology of language (3rd ed.). Brooks/Cole Publishing Company.

Carston, R. (2008). Linguistic communication and the semantics/pragmatics distinction. *Synthese, 165*(3), 321–345. doi:10.1007/s11229-007-9191-8

Carter, K. (2004). Online training: What's really working? *Technology & Learning, 24*(10), 32–36.

Cascio, W. F., & Shurygailo, S. (2003). E-leadership and virtual teams. *Organizational Dynamics, 31*(4), 362–376. doi:10.1016/S0090-2616(02)00130-4

Casimir, G., & Yong Ngee, K. N. (2010). Combinative aspects of leadership style and the interaction between leadership behaviors. *Leadership and Organization Development Journal, 31*(6), 501–517. doi:10.1108/01437731011070005

Castells, M. (2007). Communication, power and counter-power in the network society. *International Journal of Communication, 1*(1), 238–266.

Castilla, E. J. (2005). Social networks and employee performance in a call center. *American Journal of Sociology, 110*(5), 1243–1283.

Castro, A. J. (2010). Themes in the research on preservice teachers' views of cultural diversity: Implications for researching millennial preservice teachers. *Educational Researcher, 39*(3), 198–210. doi:10.3102/0013189X10363819

Cater, J. J., Michel, N., & Varela, O. E. (2012). Challenges of online learning in management education: An empirical study. *Journal of Applied Management and Entrepreneurship, 17*(4), 76–96.

Cavusgil, S. T., Calantone, R. J., & Zhao, Y. (2003). Tacit knowledge transfer and firm innovation capability. *Journal of Business and Industrial Marketing, 18*(1), 6–21. doi:10.1108/08858620310458615

Census, U. S. (2013). *Profile on America's workforce demographics.* Retrieved September 6, 2013, from http:// quickfacts.census.html.

Center for Creative Leadership. (2015). *Nearly 70% of all change efforts fail. We can do better.* Retrieved October 14, 2015, from http://www.ccl.org/leadership/landing/ leadingContinousChange.aspx?gclid=CjwKEAjw1_Kw-BRDEz_WvncL4jGwSJAAEym0dYf9Q_XkbWnD-4Nodhy-8vtzE_yQDuk0gEf6Kio6uPnBoC7kTw_ wcBhttp://www.ldihealtheconomist.com/he000023.shtml

Center for Health Leadership. (2015). *Developing public health leaders, creating change, and reducing health inequities.* Retrieved October 7, 2015, from http://www. healthleadership.org/

Centers for Medicare and Medicaid Services. (2013). *Medicare Data for Dual Eligible for States.* Retrieved October 1, 2015, from https://www.cms.gov/Medicare-Medicaid-Coordination/Medicare-and-Medicaid-Coordination/Medicare-Medicaid-Coordination-Office/MedicareDataforStates.html

Chang, H., & Dodd, T. (2001). International perspectives on race & ethnicity: An annotated bibliography. *Electronic Magazine ofMulticultural Education.*

Chang, C.-S., & Chang, H.-H. (2007). Effects of internal marketing on nurse job satisfaction and organizational commitment: Example of medical centers in southern Taiwan. *The Journal of Nursing Research*, *15*(4), 265–274. doi:10.1097/01.JNR.0000387623.02931.a3 PMID:18080971

Chang, H. H., Hung, C. J., & Hsieh, H. W. (2014). Virtual teams: Cultural adaptation, communication quality, and interpersonal trust. *Total Quality Management & Business Excellence*, *25*(11/12), 1318–1335. doi:10.1080/14783363.2012.704274

Chathoth, P. K., & Olsen, M. D. (2002, April-September). Organizational Leadership and Strategy in the Hospitality Industry. *Journal of Service Research*, *2*(1).

Chatman, J. A., Caldwell, D. F., O'Reilly, C. A., & Doerr, B. (2014). Parsing organizational culture: How the norm for adaptability influences the relationship between culture consensus and financial performance in high-technology firms. *Journal of Organizational Behavior*, *35*(6), 785–808. doi:10.1002/job.1928

Chau, P. (2010). Online higher education commodity. *Journal of Computing in Higher Education*, *22*(3), 177–191. doi:10.1007/s12528-010-9039-y

Chemers, M. M. (1997). *An integrative theory of leadership.* Mahwah, NJ: Lawrence Erlbaum Associates.

Chen, Kotz, et al. (2000). *A survey of context-aware mobile computing research.* Technical Report TR2000-381. Dept. of Computer Science, Dartmouth College.

Chen, C. J. (2004). The effects of knowledge attribute, alliance characteristics, and absorptive capacity on knowledge transfer performance. *R & D Management*, *34*(3), 311–321. doi:10.1111/j.1467-9310.2004.00341.x

Chen, C. J., & Huang, J. W. (2007). How organizational climate and structure affect knowledge management: The social interaction perspective. *International Journal of Information Management*, *27*(2), 104–118. doi:10.1016/j.ijinfomgt.2006.11.001

Chen, C. J., & Lin, B. W. (2004). The effects of environment, knowledge attribute, organizational climate, and firm characteristics on knowledge sourcing decisions. *R & D Management*, *34*(2), 137–146. doi:10.1111/j.1467-9310.2004.00329.x

Chen, G. M., & Starosta, W. J. (1998). *Foundations of Intercultural Communication.* Boston: Allyn and Bacon.

Chen, G., Chittoor, R., & Vissa, B. (2015). Modernizing without westernizing: Social structure and economic actions in the Indian financial sector. *Academy of Management Journal*, *58*(2), 511–537. doi:10.5465/amj.2012.1039

Cheng, Y. C. (2003). Quality assurance in education: Internal, interface, and future. *Quality Assurance in Education*, *11*(4), 202–213. doi:10.1108/09684880310501386

Cheng, Y. C., & Tam, W. M. (1997). Multi-models of quality in education. *Quality Assurance in Education*, *5*(1), 22–31. doi:10.1108/09684889710156558

Chen, Y. C., Wang, W. C., & Chu, Y. C. (2011). A case study on the business performance management of Hilton hotels corp. *International Business Research*, *4*(2), 213–218. doi:10.5539/ibr.v4n2p213

Chesebro, J. W., McCroskey, J. C., Atwater, D. F., Bahrenfuss, R. M., Cawelti, G., Gaudino, J. L., & Hodges, H. (1992). Communication apprehension and self-perceived communication competence of at-risk students. *Communication Education*, *41*(4), 345–360. doi:10.1080/03634529209378897

Cheung, M. K. C., Chiu, P.-Y., & Lee, M. K. O. (2011). Online social networks: Why do students use facebook? *Computers in Human Behavior*, *27*(4), 1337–1343. doi:10.1016/j.chb.2010.07.028

Cheung, S. O., Suen, H. C., & Lam, T. I. (2002). Fundamentals of Alternative Dispute Resolution Processes in Construction. *Journal of Construction Engineering and Management*, *128*(5), 409–417. doi:10.1061/(ASCE)0733-9364(2002)128:5(409)

Chhanabhai, P., & Holt. (2007). Consumers are ready to accept the transition to online and electronic records if they can be assured of the security measures. *Medscape General Medicine, 9*(1), 8.

Chia, J. (2005). *Measuring the immeasurable*. Retrieved from http://praxis.massey.ac.nz/fileadmin/Praxis/Files/Journal_Files/Evaluation_Issue/CHIA_ARTICLE.pdf#search=%22%20joy%20chia%20measuring%20the%20immeasurable%22

Chickering, A. W., & Potter, D. (1993). TQM and quality education: Fast food or fitness center. *The Educational Record, 74*(2), 35–36.

Chihani, B., Bertin, E., Jeanne, F., & Crespi, N. (2011) Context-aware systems: a case study. In Digital Information and Communication Technology and Its Applications (pp. 718-732). Springer. doi:10.1007/978-3-642-22027-2_60

Chin, W., Marcolin, B., & Newsted, P. (2003). A partial least squares latent variable modeling approach for measuring interaction effects: Results from a Monte Carlo simulation study and an electronic-mail emotion/adoption study. *Information Systems Research, 14*(2), 189–217. doi:10.1287/isre.14.2.189.16018

Chizmar, J. F. (2000). Total quality management of teaching and learning. *The Journal of Economic Education, 25*(2), 1–8. doi:10.1080/00220485.1994.10844828

Cho, T., & Korte, R. (2014). Managing knowledge performance: Testing the components of a knowledge management system on organizational performance. *Asia Pacific Education Review, 15*(2), 313–327. doi:10.1007/s12564-014-9333-x

Christie, A., Barling, J., & Turner, N. (2011). Pseudo-transformational leadership: Model specification and outcomes. *Journal of Applied Social Psychology, 41*, 2943-2984. doi:10.1111/j. 1559-1816.2011.00858.x

Chu, A., & Chu, R. (2011). The intranet's role in newcomer socialization in the hotel industry in Taiwan – technology acceptance model analysis. *International Journal of Human Resource Management, 22*(5), 1163–1179. doi:10.1080/09585192.2011.556795

Chuang, S. F. (2013). *Essential skills for leadership effectiveness in diverse workplace development*. Retrieved on May 29, 2015, available at http://www.scribd.com/doc/266987534/Essential-Skills-for-Leadership-Effectiveness#scribd

Chubbuck, S. (2010). Individual and structural orientations in socially just teaching: Conceptualization, implementation and collaborative effort. *Journal of Teacher Education, 61*(3), 197–210. doi:10.1177/0022487109359777

Chughtai, A., Buckley, & Finian. (2008). *Work engagement and its relationship with state and trait trust: A conceptual analysis*. Retrieved from, http://findarticles.com/p/articles/mi_qa5335/is_200809/ai_n29493978/?tag=content;col1

Chu, M. T., Kumar, P., Kumar, K., & Khosla, R. (2014). Mapping knowledge sharing traits to business strategy in knowledge based organization. *Journal of Intelligent Manufacturing, 25*(1), 55–65. doi:10.1007/s10845-012-0674-1

Chung-Kai, L., & Chia-Hung, H. (2009). The influence of transformational leadership on workplace relationships and job performance. *Social Behavior & Personality: An International Journal, 37*(8), 1129–1142. doi:10.2224/sbp.2009.37.8.1129

Churchman, C. (1967). Wicked Problems. *Management Science, 14*(2).

Cicmil, S., Cooke-Davies, T., Crawford, L., & Richardson, K. (2009). *Exploring the complexity of projects: Implication of Complexity Theory For Project Management Practice*. Newtown Square, PA: PMI.

Cincera, M., & Veugelers, R. (2012). Young leading innovators and the EU's R&D intensity gap. *Economics of Innovation and New Technology*, 1-22.

Ciocchetti, C. A. (2001). Monitoring Employee e-mail: Efficient Workplaces vs. Employee Privacy. *Duke law & Technology Review*.

Ciriaci, D., Moncada-Paternò-Castello, P., & Voigt, P. (2013). *Innovation and Employment: A sustainable relation?*. IPTS Working Papers on Corporate R&D and Innovation series - European Commission – No. 01/2013 – EUR 25807.

Ciribelli, M. (2003). *Como realizar uma dissertação de mestrado através da pesquisa científica*. Rio de Janeiro: Viveiros de Castro Editora.

Civil Evidence Act, (1995).

Clampitt, P. (2005). *Communicating for Managerial Effectiveness*. New York: Sage Publications.

Clapp-Smith, R., Vogelgesang, G. R., & Avey, J. B. (2009). Authentic leadership and positive psychological capital: The mediating role of trust at the group level of analysis. *Journal of Leadership & Organizational Studies*, *15*(3), 227–240. doi:10.1177/1548051808326596

Clark, C. (2005a, Spring). Intergroup dialogue as pedagogy across the curriculum. *Multicultural Education*, *12*(3), 51–61.

Clark, C. (2005b, Fall). People of color coming "out" and being "out" on campus: A conversation with Mark Brimhall-Vargas, Sivagami Subbaraman, and Robert Waters. *Multicultural Education*, *13*(1), 45–59.

Clark, C., & Gorski, P. (2002). Multicultural education and the digital divide: Focus on gender. *Multicultural Perspectives*, *4*(1), 30–40. doi:10.1207/S15327892MCP0401_6

Clark, C., & O'Donnell, J. (Eds.). (1999). *Becoming and unbecoming white: Owning and disowning a racial identity*. Westport, CT: Greenwood Publishing Group, Inc., Bergin & Garvey.

Clark, C., Werth, L., & Ahten, S. (2012, July/August). Cyberbullying and incivility in the online learning environment, Part I: Addressing faculty and student perceptions. *Nursing Educator*, *37*(4), 150–156. doi:10.1097/NNE.0b013e31825a87e5 PMID:22688872

Clarke, R. (1999). Internet privacy concerns confirm the case for intervention. *Communications of the ACM*, *42*(2), 60–67. doi:10.1145/293411.293475

Clarke, R. A. (1988). Information technology and dataveillance. *Communications of the ACM*, *31*(5), 498–512. doi:10.1145/42411.42413

Clark, M. (2002). The relationship between employees' perceptions of organizational climate and customer retention rates in a major UK retail bank. *Journal of Strategic Marketing*, *10*(2), 93–113. doi:10.1080/09652540210125260

Clawson, J. G. (2012). *Level three leadership: Getting below the surface*. Upper Saddle River, NJ: Pearson Education.

Clayton, M. (1995). Encouraging the kaizen approach to quality in a university. *Total Quality Management*, *6*(5/6), 593–601. doi:10.1080/09544129550035242

Clutterbuck, D. (2004). *The challenge of the virtual team*. Training Journal.

CNN. (2011). *Money, Annual Ranking of America's Largest Corporations. Fortune 500 companies*. Available from the Web site: http://money.cnn.com/magazines/fortune/fortune500/2011/full_list/

Coad, A., & Hölzl, W. (2010). *Firm growth: empirical analysis (No. 1002)*. Papers on Economics and Evolution.

Coakes, E., Smith, P. A. C., & Alwis, D. (2011). Sustainable innovation and right to market. *Information Systems Management*, *28*(1), 30–42. doi:10.1080/10580530.2011.536110

Coate, L. E. (1990). TQM on campus: Implementing total quality management in a university setting. *Business Officer*, *24*(5), 26–35.

Cochran-Smith, M. (2010). Toward a theory of teacher education for social justice. In M. Fullan, A. Hargreaves, D. Hopkins, & A. Lieberman (Eds.), *The international handbook of educational change* (2nd ed., pp. 445–467). New York, NY: Springer. doi:10.1007/978-90-481-2660-6_27

Cockburn, T., Jahdi, K. S., & Wilson, E. (2012). Ethical capital and the culture of integrity: 3 cases in UK and NZ. In W. Amann & A. Stachowicz-Stanusch (Eds.), *Business Integrity in Practice – insights from international case Studies*. New York, NY: Business Expert Press.

Cockburn, T., Jahdi, K., & Wilson, E. (Eds.). (2015). *Responsible governance: International perspectives for the new era*. New York, NY: Business Expert Press.

Cockburn, T., & McKie, D. (2004). Imagining uncertainty: Creative tales of corporate and global futures. *Global Business & Economic Review Journal*, *6*(1), 92–106. doi:10.1504/GBER.2004.006222

Cockburn, T., Treadwell, P., & Wootten, C. (2001). The politics of community: Challenges in digital education. *Campus-Wide Information Systems*, *18*(5), 187–194. doi:10.1108/10650740110408517

Cocklin, B. (1999). Gumly Gumly Public School as a learning community. In J. Retallick, B. Cocklin, & K. Coombe (Eds.), *Learning Communities in Education* (pp. 265–286). London: Routledge.

Cogburn, D. L., & Levinson, N. S. (2008). Teaching globalization globally: A 7-year case study of South Africa – U.S. virtual teams. *Informational Technologies and International Development*, *4*(3), 75–89. doi:10.1162/itid.2008.00018

Coghlan, D., & Brannick, T. (2014). *Doing action research in your own organization* (4th ed.). London: Sage.

Cohen, D., & Prusak, L. (2001). In Good Company: How Social Capital Makes Organizations Work. Harvard Business Press.

Cohen-Charash, Y., & Spector, P. E. (2001). The role of justice in organizations: A meta-analysis. *Organizational Behavior and Human Decision Processes*, *86*(2), 278–321. doi:10.1006/obhd.2001.2958

Cohen, S. G., & Gibson, C. B. (2003). Introduction. In C. B. Gibson & S. G. Cohen (Eds.), *Virtual teams that work: Creating conditions for virtual team effectiveness* (pp. 59–86). San Francisco: Jossey-Bass.

Cohn, J. (2012 June 13). Obamacare, Good for the Economy. *The New Republic*. Retrieved October 10, 2015, from http://www.newrepublic.com/article/104035/romney-republicans-say-affordable-care-act-will-kill-jobs-best-available-evidence

Coiera, E. (2000). When Conversation Is Better Than Computation. *Journal of the American Medical Informatics Association*, *7*(3), 277–286. doi:10.1136/jamia.2000.0070277 PMID:10833164

Coiera, E., & Tombs, V. (1998). Communication behaviours in a hospital setting: An observational study. *BMJ (Clinical Research Ed.)*, *316*(7132), 673–676. doi:10.1136/bmj.316.7132.673 PMID:9522794

Cole, B. M. (2015). Lessons from a martial arts dojo: A prolonged process model of high-context communication. *Academy of Management Journal*, *58*(2), 567–591. doi:10.5465/amj.2012.0986

Coll, C. (2001). Las comunidades de aprendizaje y el futuro de la educación: el punto de vista del forum universal de las culturas. Simposio Internacional Sobre Comunidades de Aprendizaje, Barcelona, Spain.

Coll, C. (2004). Una experiencia educativa con futuro. *Trabajadores de la enseñanza,* 249, enero 2004, 12-13. Retrieved February 2, 2009, from http://www.fe.ccoo.es/publicaciones/TE/249/249pdf

Colquitt, J. A., Noe, R. A., & Jackson, C. L. (2002). Justice in teams: Antecedents and consequences of procedural justice climate. *Personnel Psychology*, *55*(1), 83–109. doi:10.1111/j.1744-6570.2002.tb00104.x

Combe, I., & Bostchen, G. (2004). Strategy paradigms for the management of quality: Dealing with complexity. *European Journal of Marketing*, *38*(5), 500–523. doi:10.1108/03090560410529187

Combs, G. M., Milosevic, I., Jeung, W., & Griffith, J. (2012). Ethnic identity and job attribute preferences: The role of collectivism and psychological capital. *Journal of Leadership & Organizational Studies*, *19*(1), 5–16. doi:10.1177/1548051811433359

Commission of the European Communities. (2004). *European Innovation Scoreboard 2004: comparative analysis of innovation performance.* Author.

Commission of the European Communities. (2005). *Report on the implementation of the European Charter for Small Enterprises, (COM(2005) 30 final).* Author.

Committee for the Study of the Future of Public Health IoM. (1988). *The future of public health.* Washington, DC: National Academy Press.

Commonwealth Of Australia. (2008). *Quality education: The case for an education revolution in our schools* Retrieved from http://apo.org.au/files/Resource/deewar_quality-education_2008.pdf

Cone, J. H. (2002). Liberation theology and multicultural community. Border Crossing Speaker Series Keynote Address. University of Maryland, College Park, MD.

Conlin, J., Langford, D., & Kennedy, P. (1996). *The Relationship Between Construciton Procurement Strategies and Construction Contract Disputes*. Paper presented at the CIB W92 North Meets South, Durban, South Africa.

Connaughton, S. L., & Daly, J. A. (2003). Long distance leadership: Communicative strategies for leading virtual teams. In D. Pauleen (Ed.), *Virtual teams: Projects, protocols and processes* (pp. 116–144). Hershey, PA: Idea Group.

Connaughton, S. L., & Daly, J. A. (2004). Leading from afar: Strategies for effectively leading in virtual teams. In S. Godar & S. P. Ferris (Eds.), *Virtual and collaborative teams: Projects, protocols and processes* (pp. 49–75). Hershey, PA: Idea Group. doi:10.4018/978-1-59140-204-6.ch004

Connor, K. R., & Prahalad, C. K. (1996). A resource-based theory of the firm: Knowledge versus opportunism. *Organization Science*, *7*(5), 477–501. doi:10.1287/orsc.7.5.477

Cooil, B., Aksoy, L., Keiningham, T. M., & Maryott, K. M. (2009). The relationship of employee perceptions of organizational climate to business-unit outcomes: An MPLS approach. *Journal of Service Research*, *11*(3), 277–294. doi:10.1177/1094670508328984

Cook, J., & Wall, T. (1980). New work attitude measures of trust, organizational commitment and personal need non-fulfillment. *Journal of Occupational Psychology*, *53*(1), 39–52. doi:10.1111/j.2044-8325.1980.tb00005.x

Coombs, W. T. (1995). Choosing the right words: The development of guidelines for the selection of "appropriate" crisis response strategies. *Management Communication Quarterly*, *8*(4), 447–476. doi:10.1177/0893318995008004003

Coopers, P. W. (2013). *Corporate Choices in International Arbitration*. Academic Press.

Copley, P. (2004). *Marketing Communications Management. Concepts and Theories, Cases and Practices*. Oxford, UK: Elsevier.

Cornelissen, J. (2004). *Corporate communications. Theory and Practice*. London: Sage Publications Ltd.

Cornell University. (2011). *Managerial Communication. An introduction to key library resources for Hotel Administration*. Available from the Web site: http://guides.library.cornell.edu/HADM3365

Cortes, C. E. (2000). Minorities Insinuating Images Influence Perceptions. Making the Media Work for You. *Media & Values*.

Costa, A. L., & Garmston, R. J. (2002). *Cognitive coaching: A foundation for renaissance schools*. Norwood, MA: Christopher-Gordon.

Costa, A. L., & Garmston, R. J. (2015). *Cognitive coaching: Developing self-directed learners and leaders*. Lanham, MD: The Rowan & Littlefield Publishing Group, Inc.

Costa, L., & Poullet, Y. (2012). Privacy and the regulation of 2012. *CLSR*, *28*, 254–262.

Costley, D. L., & Howell, J. P. (2006). *Understanding behaviors for effective leadership*. Upper Saddle River, NJ: Pearson Education.

Cousins, S. B., & Kahn, M. G. (1991). The visual display of temporal information. *Artificial Intelligence in Medicine*, *3*(6), 341–357. doi:10.1016/0933-3657(91)90005-V

Covin, T., Sightler, K., Kolenko, T., & Tudor, R. (1996). An investigation of post-acquisition satisfaction with the merger. *The Journal of Applied Behavioral Science*, *32*(2), 125–141. doi:10.1177/0021886396322001

Cox, T. H., & Blake, S. (1991). Managing cultural diversity: Implications for organization competitiveness. *Journal of Management Executive*, *5*(3).

Cranston, N. (2000). The impact of school-based management on primary school principals: An Australian Perspective. *Journal of School Leadership*, *10*(3), 214–232.

Cranston, N. C. (2001). Collaborative decision-making and school-based management: Challenges, rhetoric and reality. *Journal of Educational Enquiry*, *2*(2), 1–26.

Craver, C. B. (2006). Privacy issues affecting employers, employees and labour organizations. *Louisiana Law Review*, *66*, 1057–1078.

Crawford, L. E. D., & Shutler, P. (1999). Total quality management in education: Problems and issues for the classroom teacher. *International Journal of Educational Management, 13*(2), 67–72. doi:10.1108/09513549910261122

Creede, C., Fisher-Yoshida, B., & Gallegos, P. (Eds.). (2012). *The reflective, facilitative, and interpretive practices of the coordinated management of meaning: making lives, making meanings.* Teaneck, NJ: Fairleigh Dickinson Press.

Creswell, J. W. (2013). *Qualitative inquiry & research design: Choosing among five approaches* (3rd ed.). Thousand Oaks, CA: Sage.

Crino, M. E., & White, M. C. (1981). Satisfaction in communication: An examination of the Downs-Hazen measure. *Psychological Reports, 49*(3), 831–838. doi:10.2466/pr0.1981.49.3.831

Crosling, G., & Ward, I. (2002). Oral communication: Workplace needs and uses of business graduates employees. *English for Specific Purposes, 21*(1), 41–57. doi:10.1016/S0889-4906(00)00031-4

Crossman, A., & Lee-Kelley, L. (2004). Trust, commitment and team working: The paradox of virtual organizations. *Global Networks, 4*(4), 375–390. doi:10.1111/j.1471-0374.2004.00099.x

Cuevas, H. M., Fiore, S. M., Salas, E., & Bowers, C. A. (2004). Virtual teams as sociotechnical systems. In S. Godar (Ed.), *Virtual and collaborative teams* (pp. 1–16). Hershey, PA: Idea Group. doi:10.4018/978-1-59140-204-6.ch001

Cukier, W., Ngwenyama, O., Bauer, R., & Middleton, C. (2009). A critical analysis of media discourse on information technology: Preliminary results of a proposed method for critical discourse analysis. *Information Systems Journal, 19*(2), 175–196. doi:10.1111/j.1365-2575.2008.00296.x

Cummings, H. W., Long, L., & Lewis, M. (1986). *Managing communication in organizations.* Scottsdale, AZ: Gorsuch-Scarisbrick.

Curlee, W., & Gordon, R. (2010). *Complexity Theory and Project Management.* Wiley.

Currie, W. (1999). Revisiting management innovation and change programmes: Strategic vision or tunnel vision? *Omega, 27*(6), 647–660. doi:10.1016/S0305-0483(99)00023-7

Curseu, P. L., Schalk, R., & Wessel, I. (2008). How do virtual teams process information? A literature review and implications for management. *Journal of Managerial Psychology, 23*(6), 628–652. doi:10.1108/02683940810894729

Cushner, K., & Brislin, R. W. (1996). *Intercultural interactions: A practical guide.* Thousand Oaks, CA: Sage.

Czarnitzki, D., & Delanote, J. (2012). *Young innovative companies: The new high-growth firms?* ZEW Discussion.

Czarnitzki, D., & Delanote, J. (2013). Young innovative companies: The new high-growth firms? *Industrial and Corporate Change, 22*(5), 1315–1340. doi:10.1093/icc/dts039

D'Aprix, R. (2009). *The Credible Company.* San Francisco: Jossey-Bass.

D'Urso, S. C. (2006). Who's watching us at work? Toward a structural-perceptual model of electronic monitoring and surveillance in organisations. *Communication Theory, 16*(3), 281–303. doi:10.1111/j.1468-2885.2006.00271.x

Daft, R. L. (2000). *Management* (5th ed.). Hinsdale, IL: The Dryden Press.

Daft, R. L. (2005). *The leadership experience.* Vancouver, Canada: Thomson–Southwestern.

Dahlgaard, J. J., Kristensen, K., & Kanji, G. K. (1995). Total quality management and education. *Total Quality Management, 6*(5), 445–456. doi:10.1080/09544129550035116

Dai, D., Frank, J., & Sun, I. (2011). Procedural justice during police-citizen encounters: The effects of process-based policing on citizen compliance and demeanor. *Journal of Criminal Justice, 39*(2), 159–168. doi:10.1016/j.jcrimjus.2011.01.004

Dai, M., & Nation, D. (2009). Understanding non-coercive, procedurally fair behavior by the police during encounters. *International Journal of Law, Crime and Justice, 37*(4), 170–181. doi:10.1016/j.ijlcj.2009.10.002

Dalkir, K. (2005). *Knowledge management in theory and practice.* Oxford, UK: Elsevier Butterworth–Heinemann.

Damaskopoulos, T., Gatautis, R., & Vitkauskaitë, E. (2008). Extended and dynamic clustering of SMEs. *Engineering Economics*, *1*(56), 11–21.

Dance, F. (1970). The concept of communication. *Journal of Communication*, *20*(2), 201–210. doi:10.1111/j.1460-2466.1970.tb00877.x

Daniels, H., & Warmington, P. (2007). Analyzing third generation activity systems: Labour power, subject, position and personal transformation. *Journal of Workplace Learning*, *19*(6), 377–391. doi:10.1108/13665620710777110

Darroch, J. (2003). Developing a measure of knowledge management behaviors and practices. *Journal of Knowledge Management*, *7*(5), 41–54. doi:10.1108/13673270310505377

Dash, S., Magidin de Kramer, R., O'Dwyer, L. M., Masters, J., & Russell, M. (2012). Impact of online professional development or teacher quality and student achievement in fifth grade mathematics. *Journal of Research on Technology in Education*, *45*(1), 1–26. doi:10.1080/15391523.2012.10782595

Däubler, W. (2002). *Gläserne Belegschaften? Datenschutz in Betrieb und Dienststelle, 4.* Aufl.

Davenport, T. H., De Long, D. W., & Beers, M. C. (1998). Successful knowledge management projects. *MIT Sloan Management Review*, *39*(2), 43–57.

Davenport, T. H., & Prusak, L. (1998). *Working knowledge: Managing what your organization knows*. Boston, MA: Harvard Business Review Press.

Davies, S. (1999). *New Techniques and Technologies of Surveillance in the Workplace*. MSF Information 596 Professionals Association, London School of Economics. Available at: http://www.amicustheunion.org/pdf/surveillencetechniques.pdf

Davis, C. H. F. III, Deil-Amen, R., Rios-Aguilar, C., & Canche, M. S. G. (n.d.). Social Media in Higher Education: A literature review and research directions. *The Center for the Study of Higher Education at The University of Arizona And Claremont Graduate University*.

Davis, D. D. (2004). The Tao of leadership in virtual teams. *Organizational Dynamics*, *33*(1), 47–62. doi:10.1016/j.orgdyn.2003.11.004

Dawnays Ltd v FG Minter Ltd (2 All ER 1389; [1971] 1 WLR 1205 1971).

Dawson, J. F., Gonzalez-Roma, V., Davis, A., & West, M. A. (2008). Organizational climate and climate strength in UK hospitals. *European Journal of Work and Organizational Psychology*, *17*(1), 89–111. doi:10.1080/13594320601046664

De Bussy, N., Ewing, M., & Pitt, L. (2004). Stakeholder theory and internal marketing communications: A framework for analyzing the influence of new media. *Journal of Marketing Communications*, *9*(3), 147–161. doi:10.1080/1352726032000129890

De Cremer, D., & Tyler, T. R. (2005). Managing group behavior: The interplay between procedural justice, sense of self, and cooperation. *Advances in Experimental Social Psychology*, *37*, 151–218. doi:10.1016/S0065-2601(05)37003-1

De Grauwe, A. (2005). Improving quality of education through school-based management: Learning from international experiences. *International Review of Education*, *51*(4), 269–287. doi:10.1007/s11159-005-7733-1

De Pillis, E., & Furumo, K. (2007). Counting the cost of virtual teams: Studying the performance, satisfaction, and group dynamics of virtual and face-to-face teams. *Communications of the ACM*, *50*(12), 93–95. doi:10.1145/1323688.1323714

De Stricker, U. (2014). *Knowledge management Practice in Organizations*. Hershey, PA: IGI Global. doi:10.4018/978-1-4666-5186-9

Deal, T. E., & Kennedy, A. A. (1982). *Corporate cultures: The rites and rituals of corporate life*. Harmondsworth, UK: Penguin Books.

DeCew, J. (2002). *Privacy*. Retrieved from http://plato.stanford.edu/entries/privacy/

DeCosta, M., Berquist, E., & Holbeck, R. (2015, July). A desire for growth: Online full-time faculty's perception of evaluation processes. *The Journal of Educators Online*, *13*(2), 73–102.

Dellar, G. B. (1998). School Climate, School Improvement and Site-based Management. *Learning Environments Research*, *1*(3), 353–367. doi:10.1023/A:1009970210393

Deloitte Core Beliefs and Culture Survey. (2013). Retrieved from http://www.deloitte.com/assets/Dcom-UnitedStates/Local%20Assets/Documents/us_leadership_2013corebeliefs&culturesurvey_051613.pdf, August 6, 2013.

Delong & Associates. (2009). *Driving collaboration in a multi-generational environment.* Retrieved from: http://www.cisco.com/web/about/ac49/ac55/DeLong-CiscoCollaborativeCultureCase3-09.pdf

Delpit, L. (2006). *Other people's children: Cultural conflict in the classroom.* New York, NY: The New Press.

Deng, F. M. (1996). Identity in Africa's internal conflicts. *The American Behavioral Scientist, 40*(1), 45–46. doi:10.1177/0002764296040001007

Deng, F. M. (1997). Ethnicity: An African predicament. *The Brookings Review, 15*(3), 28–31. doi:10.2307/20080749

Denison, D. R. (1996). What is the difference between organizational culture and organizational climate? A native's point of view on a decade of paradigm wars. *Academy of Management Review, 21*(3), 619–654. doi:10.2307/258997

Denison, D. R., Haaland, S., & Goelzer, P. (2004). Corporate culture and organizational effectiveness: Is Asia different from the rest of the world? *Organizational Dynamics, 33*(1), 98–109. doi:10.1016/j.orgdyn.2003.11.008

Denzin, N. K., & Lincoln, Y. S. (2005). *The Sage Handbook of Qualitative Research.* Thousand Oaks, CA: Sage.

DeRosa, D. M., Hantula, D. A., Kock, N., & D'Arcy, J. (2004). Trust and leadership in virtual teamwork: A media naturalness perspective. *Human Resource Management, 43*(2-3), 219–232. doi:10.1002/hrm.20016

Dervitsiotis, K. N. (2007). On becoming adaptive: The new imperative for survival and success in the 21st century. *Total Quality Management, 18*(1-2), 21–38. doi:10.1080/14783360601043005

Dervojeda, K., Verzijl, D., Nagtegaal, F., Lengton, M. & Rouwmaat, E. (2013). *Big Data -Artificial Intelligence.* Business Innovation Observatory.

Desimone, L. M. (2009). Improving impact studies of teachers' professional development: Toward better conceptualizations and measures. *Educational Researcher, 38*(3), 181–199. doi:10.3102/0013189X08331140

Desjardins, C., & Obara, Y. (1993). From Québec to Tokyo: Perspectives on TQM. *Educational Leadership, 51*(1), 68–69.

Desrochers, S., & Roussos, A. (2001). The Jurisprudence of Surveillance: a Critical Look at the Laws of Intimacy. *Lex Electronica, 6*(2). Available at: http://www.lex-electronica.org/articles/v6-2/desroussos.htm

Dess, G., & Shaw, J. (2001). Voluntary turnover, social capital and organizational performance. *Academy of Management Review, 26*(3), 446–456.

Dever, J. T. (1997). Reconciling educational leadership in the learning organization. *Community College Review, 25*(2), 37–63. doi:10.1177/009155219702500205

Devi, S. I., & Shahnaz, F. F. (2008). Oral communication apprehension and communicative competence among electrical engineering undergraduate in UTeM. *Journal of Human Capital Development, 1*(1), 1–10.

Dewey, J. (1934). *Art as experience.* New York: Minton, Malach, and Co.

Diana, M. L., Harle, C. A., Huerta, T. R., Ford, E. W., & Menachemi, N. (2014). Hospital Characteristics Associated With Achievement of Meaningful Use. *Journal of Healthcare Management, 59*(4), 272–284. PMID:25154125

Dickson, M. W., Resick, C. J., & Hanges, P. J. (2006). When organizational climate is unambiguous, it is also strong. *The Journal of Applied Psychology, 91*(2), 351–364. doi:10.1037/0021-9010.91.2.351

Diddams, M., & Chang, G. C. (2012). Only human: Exploring the nature of weakness in authentic leadership. *The Leadership Quarterly, 23*(3), 593–603. doi:10.1016/j.leaqua.2011.12.010

Diekmann, J., Girard, M., & Abdul-Hadi, N. (1994). *Disputes Potential Index: A study into the Predictability of Contract Disputes.* Academic Press.

Diggins, P. B. (1997). Reflections on leadership characteristics necessary to develop and sustain learning school communities. *School Leadership & Management, 17*(3), 413–425. doi:10.1080/13632439769953

Dillard, J., & Yuthas, K. (2006). Enterprise resource planning systems and communicative action. *Critical Perspectives On Accounting, 17,* 202-223 doi:10.1016/j.cpa.2005.08.003

Dinev, T., Xu, H., Smith, J. H., & Hart, P. (2013). Information privacy and correlates: An empirical attempt to bridge and distinguish privacy-related concepts. *European Journal of Information Systems, 22*(3), 295–316. doi:10.1057/ejis.2012.23

Dingsoyr, T., & Conradi, R. (2002). A survey of case studies of the use of knowledge management in software engineering. *International Journal of Software Engineering and Knowledge Engineering, 12*(4), 391–414. doi:10.1142/S0218194002000962

DiPietro, R. A. (1993). TQM: Evolution, scope and strategic significance for management development. *Journal of Management Development, 12*(7), 11–18. doi:10.1108/02621719310044910

DiSanza, J. R., & Legge, N. J. (2003). *Business and Professional Communication: Plans, Processes and Performance.* Boston, MA: Allyn & Bacon.

DJ. (2015). *Dow Jones Sustainability Indices.* Accesses June 24, 2015 at http://www.sustainability-indices.com/review/industry-group-leaders-2014.jsp

DMHC. (2015). *DMHC regulates Health Plans and Helps health plan members and providers.* Retrieved October 6, 2015, from http://www.dmhc.ca.gov/

Dobbins, K. (2009). Feeding innovation with learning lunches: Contextualising academic innovation in higher education. *Journal of Further and Higher Education, 33*(4), 411–422. doi:10.1080/03098770903272495

Doherty, G. D. (1993). Towards total quality management in higher education: A case study of the University of Wolverhampton. *Higher Education, 25*(3), 321–339. doi:10.1007/BF01383857

Dohrmann, G., & Epstein, D. [2] (2011, May 30). SI investigation reveals eight-year pattern of violations under Tressel. *Sportsillustrated.com.* Retrieved June 14, 2011 from http://www.si.com/more-sports/2011/05/30/jim-tressel

Dolphin, R. R. (2005). Internal communications: Today's strategic imperative. *Journal of Marketing Communications, 11*(3), 171–190. doi:10.1080/1352726042000315414

Domine, V. (2011). Building 21st century teachers: An intentional pedagogy of media literacy education. *Action in Teacher Education, 33*(2), 194–205. doi:10.1080/01626620.2011.569457

Dominguez, J. (2009). *The Curious Case of the CHAOS Report 2009.* Available from: http://www.projectsmart.co.uk/the-curious-case-of-the-chaos-report-2009.html

Donaldson, E., Ensher, E. A., & Grant-Vallone, E. J. (2000). Longitudinal examination of mentoring relationships on organizational commitment and citizenship behavior. *Journal of Career Development, 26*(4), 233–248. doi:10.1177/089484530002600401

Donavan, D., Brown, T., & Mowen, J. (2004). Internal benefits of service-worker customer orientation: Job satisfaction, commitment and organizational citizenship behaviors. *Journal of Marketing, 68*(1), 128–146. doi:10.1509/jmkg.68.1.128.24034

Doney, P. M., Cannon, J. P., & Mullen, M. R. (1998). Understanding the influence of national culture on the development of trust. *Academy of Management Review, 23,* 491–512. doi:10.2307/259297

Dong, D., Day, K. D., & Collaço, C. M. (2014). Overcoming ethnocentrism through developing intercultural communication sensitivity and multiculturalism. *Human Communication: A Publication of the Pacific and Asian Communication Association, 11*(1), 27-38.

Dong, Q. (1995). *Self, identity, media use and socialization: A student of adolescent Asian immigrants to the United States.* (Unpublished doctoral dissertation). Washington State University, Pullman, WA.

Donnelly, R. (2008). The management of consultancy knowledge: An internationally comparative analysis. *Journal of Knowledge Management, 12*(6), 71–83. doi:10.1108/13673270810875877

Dougherty, D., & Hardy, C. (1996). Sustained product innovation in large, mature organizations: Overcoming innovation-to-organization problems. *Academy of Management Journal, 39*(5), 1120–1153. doi:10.2307/256994

Doyle, M., & Straus, D. (1976). *How to make meetings work*. New York, NY: Berkeley Publishing Group.

Drago-Severson, E. (2012). The need for principal renewal: The promise of sustaining principals through principal-to-principal reflective practice. *Teachers College Record, 114*, 1–56. PMID:24013958

Dreher, S. (2014). Social media and the world of work. *Corporate Communications. International Journal (Toronto, Ont.), 19*(4), 344–356.

Drezner, D., & Farrell, H. (2004). *The power and politics of blogs*. Paper presented at the American Political Science Association Conference, Chicago, IL.

Driskell, J. E., Radtke, P. H., & Salas, E. (2003). Virtual teams: Effects of technological mediation on team performance. *Group Dynamics, 7*(4), 297–323. doi:10.1037/1089-2699.7.4.297

Driskill, G. W., & Brenton, A. L. (2005). *Organizational culture in action: A cultural analysis workbook*. Sage Publications, Inc.

Drucker, P. (1977). *People and Performance*. New York: Harper's College Press.

Drucker, P. (1993). *Inovatia si sistemul antreprenorial*. Editura Enciclopedica, Bucaresti.

Drucker, P. (2001). *The Essential Drucker*. London: Harper.

Drucker, P. F. (1993). *Post-capitalist society*. New York, NY: Harper Business.

Drury, A., & Absolom, R. (2012). *Multi-market BYOD Survey Results: The Management gap*. Retrieved on 03/22/2014 from *http://ovum.com/research/multi-market-byod-survey-results-the-byod-management-gap/*

Drysdale, L., Goode, H., & Gurr, D. (2009). An Australian model of successful school leadership. *Journal of Educational Administration, 47*(6), 697–708. doi:10.1108/09578230910993087

Du Rausis, M. P., Manyika, J., Hazan, E., Bughin, J., Chui, M., & Said, R. (2011). *Internet matters: The net's sweeping impact on growth, jobs and prosperity*. McKinsey Global Institute.

Dube, L., & Pare, G. (2001). International teams: Recent interviews with GVT leaders and members offer critical advice from the trenches regarding the challenges and coping strategies for collaborating on a global scale. *Communications of the ACM, 44*(12), 71–73.

Duckett, H., & Macfarlane, E. (2003). Emotional intelligence and transformational leadership in retailing. *Leadership and Organization Development Journal, 24*(6), 309–317. doi:10.1108/01437730310494284

Dulewicz, V., & Higgs, M. (2005). Assessing leadership dimensions, styles and organizational context. *Journal of Managerial Psychology, 20*(2), 105–123. doi:10.1108/02683940510579759

Duncan-Howell, J. (2010). Teachers making connections: Online communities as a source of professional learning. *British Journal of Educational Technology, 41*(2), 324–340. doi:10.1111/j.1467-8535.2009.00953.x

Dunnette, M. (Ed.). (1976). *Handbook of Industrial and Organizational Psychology*. Chicago: Rand McNally.

Dunn, M. W., Dastoor, B., & Sims, R. L. (2012). Transformational leadership and organizational commitment: A cross-cultural perspective. *Journal of Multidisciplinary Research, 4*, 45–60.

Eagle, L., & Brennan, R. (2007). Are students customers? TQM and marketing perspectives. *Quality Assurance in Education, 15*(1), 44–60. doi:10.1108/09684880710723025

Earley, P. C., & Ang, S. (2003). *Cultural intelligence: Individual interactions across cultures*. Stanford, CA: Stanford University Press.

Earley, P. C., & Mosakowski, E. (2004). Toward culture intelligence: Turning cultural differences into a workplace advantage. *The Academy of Management Executive, 18*(3), 151–157.

Eckel, P., & Hartley, M. (2008). Developing academic strategic alliances: Reconciling multiple institutional cultures, policies and practice. American Council on Education. *The Journal of Higher Education*, *79*(6), 613–637. doi:10.1353/jhe.0.0023

Economist Intelligence Unit. (2009). Managing virtual team: Taking a more strategic approach. *The Economist*. Retrieved September 15, 2012 from http://graphics.eiu.com/upload/eb/NEC_Managing_virtual_teams_WEB.pdf

Edelman Trust Barometer. (2013). Retrieved on 8/21/13 from http://www.edelman.com/insights/intellectual-property/trust-2013/

Edelman Trust Barometer. (2014). Retrieved on 1/22/14 from http://www.edelman.com/insights/intellectual-property/2014-edelman-trust-barometer/

Edwards, C., Edwards, A., Spence, P. R., & Shelton, A. K. (2014). Is that a bot running the social media feed? Testing the differences in perceptions of communication quality for a human agent and a bot agent on Twitter. *Computers in Human Behavior*, *33*, 372–376. doi:10.1016/j.chb.2013.08.013

Eisenstadt, S. A., Wagner, M. M., Hogan, W. R., Pankaskie, M. C., Tsui, F. C., & Wilbright, W. (1998). Mobile workers in healthcare and their information needs: Are 2-way pagers the answer? *Proc AMIA Symp.*, *1998*, 135–139. PMID:9929197

Eissa, G., Fox, C., Webster, B. D., & Kim, J. (2012). A framework for leader effectiveness in virtual teams. *Journal of Leadership. Accountability and Ethics*, *9*(2), 11–22.

Eker, M., Eker, S., & Pala, F. (2008). The effects of job satisfaction on organizational commitment among Turkish health care staff: An empirical study. *Journal of Academic Studies*, *10*(36), 46–68.

Electronic Monitoring & Surveillance Survey. (2007). Retrieved from http://www.amanet.org/movingahead/editorial.cfm?Ed=697

Elgesem, D. (1999). The structure of rights in Directive 95/46/EC on the protection of individuals with regard to the processing of personal data and the free movement of such data. *Ethics and Information Technology*, *1*(4), 283–293. doi:10.1023/A:1010076422893

Elizabeth, S. K., & Wolff, S. B. (2008). Emotional intelligence competencies in the team and team leader. *Journal of Management Development*, *27*(1), 55–75. doi:10.1108/02621710810840767

Ellis, B., & Normore, A. H. (2014).Police leadership: Connecting with communities through a partnership initiative. *Peace Officers Research Association of California Law Enforcement*. Retrieved from, http://porac.org/

Ellis, G., & Normore, A. H. (2015). Performance management strategies for effective leadership in law enforcement: An accountability process. *FBI Law Enforcement Bulletin*. Available [online]: http://leb.fbi.gov/2015/february/performance-management-strategies-for-effective-leadership-an-accountability-process

Ellis, N., & Hopkinson, G. (2010). The construction of managerial knowledge in business networks: Managers' theories about communication. *Industrial Marketing Management*, *39*(3), 413–424. doi:10.1016/j.indmarman.2007.08.011

Else, S. (2003). Practicing Knowledge Communities. *Knowledge Management*. Retrieved February 2, 2009, from http://www.destinationkm.com/articles/default.asp?ArticleID=1044

Emstad, A. B. (2011). The principal's role in the post-evaluation process. How does the principal engage in the work carried out after the schools self-evaluation? *Educational Assessment, Evaluation and Accountability*, *23*(4), 271–288. doi:10.1007/s11092-011-9128-0

Engelen, A., Flatten, T. C., Thalmann, J., & Brettel, M. (2014). The effect of organizational culture on entrepreneurial orientation: A comparison between Germany and Thailand. *Journal of Small Business Management*, *52*(4), 732–752. doi:10.1111/jsbm.12052

Engel, R. S. (2005). Citizens' perceptions of distributive and procedural injustice during traffic stops with police. *Journal of Research in Crime and Delinquency*, *42*(4), 445–481. doi:10.1177/0022427804272725

Engeström, Y. (2001). Expansive learning at work: Toward an activity theoretical reconceptualization. *Journal of Education and Work*, *14*(1), 133–156. doi:10.1080/13639080020028747

Engeström, Y., & Glaveanu, V. (2012). On third generation activity theory: Interview with Yrjö Engeström. *Europe's Journal of Psychology, 8*(4), 515–518. doi:10.5964/ejop. v8i4.555

Engineering Accreditation Council. (2007). *Engineering Programme Accreditation Manual.* Kuala Lumpur: Board of Engineers Malaysia.

Enterline, S., Cochran-Smith, M., Ludlow, L., & Mitescu, E. (2008). Learning to teach for social justice: Measuring change in the beliefs of teacher candidates. *New Educator, 4*(4), 267–290. doi:10.1080/15476880802430361

EPIC. (n.d.). *Workplace Privacy.* Available at: http://epic. org/privacy/workplace

Erbe, N. (2011). *Negotiation alchemy: global skills inspiring and transforming diverging worlds.* Berkeley, CA: Public Policy Press.

Erbe, N. (2014). *Approaches to managing organizational diversity and innovation.* Hershey, PA: IGI Global Press. doi:10.4018/978-1-4666-6006-9

Erickson, M. L., Gibbs, J. P., & Jensen, G. F. (1977). The deterrence doctrine and the perceived certainty of legal punishments. *American Sociological Review, 42*(2), 305–317. doi:10.2307/2094607 PMID:860865

Ethisphere. (2015). Research, rating and certification of corporate and institutional ethics, anti-corruption and sustainability. *The Ethisphere Institute History.* Retrieved June 25, 2015 from http://ethisphere.com/about/history/

Eurobarometer. (2011) *Attitudes on Data Protection and Electronic Identity in the European Union,* Retrieved from: http://ec.europa.eu/public_opinion/archives/ebs/ ebs_359_en.pdf

European Commission. (2002). *Regional Innovation Strategies under the European Regional Development Fund Innovative Actions 2000-2002.* Author.

European Commission. (2013). *Share of Business enterprise expenditures on R&D (BERD) to the gross value added (GVA) – Unpublished calculations by DG Research and Innovation/Economic Analysis Unit based on OECD.* Eurostat and DG Enterprise and Industry.

European Union. (2002). *Directive 95/46/EC: Article 29 WP55.* Retrieved from http://ec.europa.eu/justice_home/ fsj/privacy/docs/wpdocs/2002/wpss_en.pdf

Evans, D. (2007). An exploratory review of global leadership: The example of French and British leadership styles. *The Journal of Leadership Studies, 1*(1), 28–33. doi:10.1002/jls.20005

Evans, L. (2007). Monitoring technology in the American workplace: Would adopting English privacy standards better balance employee privacy and productivity? *California Law Review, 95,* 1115–1149.

Evans, S. (2013). "Just wanna give you guys a bit of an update": Insider perspectives on business presentations in Hong Kong. *English for Specific Purposes, 32*(4), 195–207. doi:10.1016/j.esp.2013.05.003

Fairlie, R. W., & Robinson, J. (2012). *Experimental evidence on the effects of home computers on academic achievement among schoolchildren* (No. w19060). National Bureau of Economic Research. Retrieved from http://www.sole-jole.org/12192.pdf

Fan, K. T., Chen, Y. H., Wang, C. W., & Chen, M. (2014). E-leadership effectiveness in virtual teams: Motivating language perspective. *Industrial Management & Data Systems, 114*(3), 421–437. doi:10.1108/IMDS-07-2013-0294

Farrey, T.[3] (2011, May 30). Timeline: Jim Tressel's fall. *ESPN.com.* Retrieved July 19, 2011 from http://sports. espn.go.com/ncf/news/story?id=6607982

Fazekas, C. P. (2004). 1984 is still fiction: Electronic Monitoring in the Workplace and U.S. Privacy Law. *Duke Law & Technology Review, 15.* Available at: http://www. law.duke.edu/journals/dltr/articles/pdf/2004dltr0015.pdf

Feely, A. J., & Harzing, A. W. (2002). Language management in multicultural companies. *Cross-Cultural Management: An International Journal, 10*(2), 37–52. doi:10.1108/13527600310797586

Fehr, E. & Gaechter, S. (2000). *Fairness and Retaliation: The economics of reciprocity.* Academic Press.

Felstiner, W. L., Abel, R. L., & Sarat, A. (1980). The Emergence and Transformation of Disputes: Naming, Blaming, Claiming..... *Law & Society Review, 15,* 631.

Fenn, P. (2006). Conflict Management and Dispute Resolution. In D. Lowe & R. Leiringer (Eds.), *Commercial Management of Projects: Defining the Discipline* (pp. 234–269). Blackwell Publishing. doi:10.1002/9780470759509. ch11

Fenn, P., Lowe, D., & Speck, C. (1997). Conflict and Dispute in Construction. *Construction Management and Economics*, *15*(6), 513–518. doi:10.1080/014461997372719

Ferguson, J., & Tryjankowski, A. (2009, August). Online versus face to face learning: Looking at modes of instruction in Master's level courses. *Journal of Further and Higher Education*, *33*(3), 219–228. doi:10.1080/03098770903026149

Fernandes, V. M. (2013) *The Effectiveness of Total Quality Management as a School Improvement Process.* (Doctoral dissertation). Monash University Theses Collection, Melbourne, Australia. Retrieved from http://arrow.monash.edu.au/hdl/1959.1/871750

Fernandez, W. D. (2003). Trust and the trust placement process in metateam projects. In D. Pauleen (Ed.), *Virtual teams: Projects, protocols and processes* (pp. 57–69). Hershey, PA: Idea Group.

Ferri-Reed, J. (2013). Quality, Conflict, and Communication Across the Generations. *Journal for Quality and Participation*, *35*(4), 12–14.

Ferris, G. R., Frink, D. D., Galang, M. C., Zhou, J., Kacmar, M. K., & Howard, J. L. (1996). Perceptions of organizational politics: Prediction, stress-related implications, and outcomes. *Human Relations*, *49*(2), 233–266. doi:10.1177/001872679604900206

Fisher, G. (2001). Communities of interest: learning through the Interaction of Multiple Knowledge Systems. *Proceedings of the 24thIRIS Conference.* Ulvik, Department of Information Science, Bergen.

Fisher, G. (1980). *International negotiation: A cross cultural perspective.* Yarmouth, ME: Intercultural Press.

Fisher, G. (1988). *Mindsets.* Yarmouth, ME: Intercultural Press.

Fisher, G. (1998). *Mindsets: The role of culture and perception in international relations.* Yarmouth, ME: Intercultural Press.

Fisher, R., & Ury, W. (1986). *Getting to yes: Negotiating agreement without giving in.* Bergenfield, NJ: Penguin.

Flaherty, J. (2010 October/November). Bridging the digital divide: A non-technical approach to the use of new technology in post-secondary teaching and learning. *Academic Matters Journal of Higher Education*, 21-26.

Flick, U. (2004). Design and process in qualitative research. In U. Flick, E. von Kardorff, & I. Steinke (Eds.), *A companion to qualitative research* (pp. 146–152). Thousand Oaks, CA: Sage.

Florica, T., Mozelius, P., Shabalina, O., Balan, O., Malliarakis, C., Miller, C., & Jones, P. (2013). An international approach to creative pedagogy and students' preferences of interactive media.*Proceedings of the International Conference on E-Learning*, 479- 487.

Fogarty, J., Hudson, S. E., Atkeson, C. G., Avrahami, D., Forlizzi, J., Kiesler, S., & Yang, J. et al. (2005). Predicting human interruptibility with sensors. *ACM Transactions on Computer-Human Interaction*, *12*(1), 119–146. doi:10.1145/1057237.1057243

Fogarty, J., Lai, J., & Christensen, J. (2004). Presence versus availability: The design and evaluation of a context-aware communication client. *International Journal of Human-Computer Studies*, *61*(3), 299–317. doi:10.1016/j.ijhcs.2003.12.016

Folger, R., Konovsky, M. A., & Cropanzano, R. (1992). A due process metaphor for performance appraisal. *Research in Organizational Behavior*, *14*, 129–129.

Fonseca, F. (2012, February). Navajo nation sues Urban Outfitters over goods. *Associated Press.* Retrieved from http://www.nbcnews.com/id/46574519/ns/business-retail/t/navajo-nation-sues-urban-outfitters-over-goods/#.Vd-wTLS_uTA

Forde, P. (2011, May 30). Tressel's end fits with saga's pattern. *ESPN.com.* Retrieved June 14, 2011 from http://espn.go.com/espn/print?id=6607408&type=story

Ford, E. W., Menachemi, N., Huerta, T. R., & Yu, F. (2010). Hospital IT Adoption Strategies Associated with Implementation Success: Implications for Achieving Meaningful Use. *Journal of Healthcare Management*, *55*(3), 175–188. PMID:20565034

Forehand, G. A., & Gilmer, B. V. (1964). Environmental variation in studies of organizational behavior. *Psychological Bulletin*, *62*(6), 228–240. doi:10.1037/h0045960 PMID:14242590

Forkosh-Baruch, A., & Hershkovitz, A. (2012). A Case Study of Israeli Higher-Education Institutes Sharing Scholarly Information with the Community via Social Networks. *The Internet and Higher Education*, *15*(1), 56–68. doi:10.1016/j.iheduc.2011.08.003

Forst, B. (1984). Overburdened Courts and Underutilized Information Technology: A Modern Prescription for a Chronic Disorder. *Judicature*, *68*, 30.

Fortunato, J. A. (2008). Restoring a reputation: The Duke University lacrosse scandal. *Public Relations Review*, *34*(2), 116–123. doi:10.1016/j.pubrev.2008.03.006

Foster, M. K., Francescucci, A., & West, B. C. (2010). Why users participate in online social networks. *International Journal of Business and Management*, *4*(1), 3–19.

Foucault, M. (1995). *Discipline and punish: The birth of the prison* (2nd ed.). New York, NY: Vintage.

Fox, A. (2011). Mixing it up. *Society of Human Resource Management*, *56*(5). Retrieved from http://www.shrm.org/Publications/hrmagazine/EditorialContent/2011/0511/Pages/0511fox.aspx

Fox, S., & Duggan, M. (2012). Mobile Health. *Pew Internet* Research. Retrieved from http://www.pewinternet.org/files/old-media//Files/Reports/2012/PIP_Mobile-Health2012_FINAL.pdf

Frampton, S., Guastello, S., Brady, C., Hale, M., Horowitz, S., & Bennett-Smith, S. (2008). *The Patient-Centered Care Improvement Guide*. The Planetree Association and The Picker Institute.

Fraser, J. (2005). Telecommunications (Lawful Business Practice) (Interception of Communications) Regulations 2000 Workplace Surveillance, Privacy and New Technologies. In L. Edwards (Ed.), The New Legal Framework for E-Commerce in Europe (pp. 277-291). Academic Press.

Freel, M. S. (2000). Strategy and structure in innovative manufacturing SMEs: The case of an English region. *Small Business Economics*, *15*(1), 27–45. doi:10.1023/A:1012087912632

Freidman, T. L. (2006). *The world is flat: A brief history of the 21ˢᵗ century*. New York, NY: Farrar, Straus and Giroux.

Freire, P. (1970). *Pedagogy of the oppressed*. New York, NY: Continuum.

Frey, C. B., & Osborne, M. A. (2013). *The Future of Employment: How susceptible are jobs to computerisation?* Academic Press.

Friedman, A., & Becker, N. (2012). *Understanding the Individual Mandate's SCOTUS Pivot Points*. Retrieved September 2, 2015, from http://www.ldihealtheconomist.com/he000023.shtml

Friend, T. (2011, May). Maurice Clarett tells his side. *ESPN.com*. Retrieved October 24, 2015 from http://sports.espn.go.com/ncf/news/story?id=1919246

Friesner, T. (2015). *The Six Living Generations in America*. Retrieved from http://www.marketingteacher.com/the-six-living-generations-in-america/

Furst, S. A., Reeves, M., Benson, R., & Blackburn, R. S. (2004). Managing the life cycle of virtual teams. *The Academy of Management Executive*, *18*(2), 6–20. doi:10.5465/AME.2004.13837468

Gaan, N. (2012). Collaborative tools and virtual team effectiveness: An inductively derived approach in India's software sector. *Decision*, *39*(1), 5–27.

Gallo, G., & Yan, Ch. (2015). The Effects of Reputational and Social Knowledge on Cooperation. *Proceedings of the National Academy of Sciences of the United States of America*, *112*(12), 3647–3652. PMID:25775544

Gallup, Inc. (2010). *The state of the global workplace: A worldwide study of employee engagement and wellbeing*. Retrieved from, http://www.gallup.com

Gammage, D. T. (2008). Three decades of implementation of school-based management in the Australian Capital Territory and Victoria in Australia. *International Journal of Educational Management*, *22*(7), 664–675. doi:10.1108/09513540810908575

Garbutt, S. (1996). The transfer of TQM from industry to education. *Education + Training*, *38*(7), 16–22. doi:10.1108/00400919610130736

Gardner, J. W. (1990). *On leadership*. New York, NY: The Free Press.

Gardner, L., & Stough, C. (2002). Examining the relationship between leadership and emotional intelligence in senior level managers. *Leadership and Organization Development Journal*, *23*(2), 68–78. doi:10.1108/01437730210419198

Gardner, W. L., Lowe, K. B., Moss, T. W., Mahoney, K. T., & Cogliser, C. C. (2010). Scholarly leadership of the study of leadership: A review of The Leadership Quarterly's second decade, 2000–2009. *The Leadership Quarterly*, *21*, 922–958.

Garg, A. K., & Ramjee, D. (2013). The relationship between leadership styles and employee commitment at a Parastatal company in South Africa. *The International Business & Economics Research Journal*, *12*, 1411–1472.

Garmon, M. A. (2005). Six key factors for changing preservice teachers' attitudes/beliefs about diversity. *Educational Studies*, *38*(3), 275–286. doi:10.1207/s15326993es3803_7

Garmston, R., & Wellman, B. (1998). *The adaptive schools sourcebook*. Norwood, MA: Christopher- Gordon.

Garner. (2012). *Gartner Says Monitoring Employee Behavior in Digital Environments is Rising*. Retrieved from: http://www.gartner.com/newsroom/id/2028215

Garrison, D., Anderson, T., & Archer, W. (2000). Critical inquiry in a text-based environment: Computer conferencing in higher education. *The Internet and Higher Education*, *2*(2-3), 87–105. doi:10.1016/S1096-7516(00)00016-6

Garrison, D., Anderson, T., & Archer, W. (2010). The first decade of the community of inquiry framework: A retrospective. *The Internet and Higher Education*, *13*(1/2), 5–9. doi:10.1016/j.iheduc.2009.10.003

Gediminas Adomavicius and Alexander Tuzhilin. (2011). Context-aware recommender systems. In *Recommender systems handbook* (pp. 217–253). Springer. doi:10.1007/978-0-387-85820-3_7

Geier, B. (2015, March). Why this Starbucks PR exec deleted his Twitter account. *Fortune*. Retrieved from http://fortune.com/2015/03/19/starbucks-vp-twitter-delete/

Gelb, B. D., & Rengarajan, D. (2014). Employee contributions to brand equity. *California Management Review*, *56*(2), 95–112. doi:10.1525/cmr.2014.56.2.95

George, J. M., & Brief, A. P. (1992). Feeling good-doing good: A conceptual analysis of the mood at work-organizational spontaneity relationship. *Psychological Bulletin*, *112*(2), 310–329. doi:10.1037/0033-2909.112.2.310 PMID:1454897

Geroski, P., & Machin, S. (1992). Do Innovating Firms Outperform Non-Innovators? *Business Strategy Review*, *3*(2), 79–90. doi:10.1111/j.1467-8616.1992.tb00030.x

Ghafoor, S., Khan, U. F., Idrees, F., Javed, B., & Ahmed, F. (2011). Evaluation of expatriates performance and their training on international assignments. *Interdisciplinary Journal of Contemporary Research in Business*, *3*(5), 335-351.

Gheorghe, P., Gardan, D., & Geangu, P. (2009). *The Importance of Managerial Communication in Establishing the Company Marketing Communication*. Paper presented at the International Conference on Administration and Business, ICEA – FAA, Faculty of Business and Administration, University of Bucharest, Bucharest, Romania.

Ghorbanhosseini, M. (2013). The effect of organizational culture, teamwork and organizational development on organizational commitment: The mediating role of human capital. *Tehnički vjesnik*, *20*(6), 1019–1025.

Gibson, C. B., & Manuel, J. A. (2003). Building trust: Effective multicultural communication process in virtual teams. In C. B. Gibson & S. G. Cohen (Eds.), *Virtual teams that work: Creating conditions for virtual team effectiveness* (pp. 59–86). San Francisco: Jossey-Bass.

Gibson, C. B., & Vermeulen, F. (2003). A healthy divide: Subgroups as a stimulus for team learning behavior. *Administrative Science Quarterly*, *48*(2), 202–239. doi:10.2307/3556657

Gibson, J., Ivancevich, J., Donnelly, J., & Konopaske, R. (2011). *Organizations: Behaviors, structures, and processes* (14th ed.). New York, NC: McGraw-Hill Education.

Giddens, A. (2009). *Sociology* (6th ed.). Cambridge: Polity Press.

Gillberg, C., & Vo, L. C. (2014). Contributions from pragmatist perspectives towards an understanding of knowledge and learning in organisations. *Philosophy of Management*, *13*(2), 33–51. doi:10.5840/pom201413210

Gillespie, M. A., Denison, D. R., Haaland, S., Smerek, R. E., & Neale, W. S. (2008). Linking organizational culture and customer satisfaction: Results from two companies in different industries. *European Journal of Work and Organizational Psychology*, *17*(1), 112–132. doi:10.1080/13594320701560820

Gilson, L. L., & Shalley, C. E. (2004). A little creativity goes a long way: An examination of teams' engagement in creative processes. *Journal of Management*, *30*(4), 453–470. doi:10.1016/j.jm.2003.07.001

Giltinane, C. L. (2013). Leadership styles and theories. *Nursing Standard*, *27*(41), 35–39. doi:10.7748/ns2013.06.27.41.35.e7565 PMID:23905259

Giorgi, A. (2010). About the speaker: Towards a syntax of indexicality. Oxford University Press.

Girard, K. (2011). *It's Not Nagging-Why Persistent, Redundant Communication Works*. Paper presented at the Research and Ideas, Working Knowledge Conference, Harvard Business School, UK.

Giroux, H. A. (1996). *Fugitive cultures: Race, violence, and youth*. New York, NY: Routledge.

Gladwell, M. (2008). *Outliers: The story of success*. New York, NY: Little, Brown & Company.

Gleitman, H. (1981). *Basic Psychology*. New York: Norton.

Glisson, C., & James, L. R. (2002). The cross-level effects of culture and climate in human service teams. *Journal of Organizational Behavior*, *23*(6), 767–794. doi:10.1002/job.162

Glueck, M. (Ed.). (2006). *Work the Net: a Management Guide for Formal Networks*. New Delhi: GTZ.

Gluesing, J. C., Alcordo, T. C., Baba, M. L., Britt, D., Wagner, K. H., & McKether, W. (2003). The development of International teams. In C. B. Gibson & S. G. Cohen (Eds.), *Virtual teams that work: Creating conditions for virtual team effectiveness* (pp. 95–120). San Francisco: Jossey Bass.

Glynn, M. A. (1996). Innovative genius: A framework for relating individual and organisational intelligences to innovation. *Academy of Management Review*, *21*(4), 1081–1111.

Gnyawali, D. R., & Park, B.-J. R. (2006). Impact of co-opetition on firm competitive behavior: An empirical examination. *Journal of Management*, *32*(4), 507–530. doi:10.1177/0149206305284550

Godfrey, B. (2001). Electronic work monitoring: An ethical model. In *Selected Papers from the Second Australian Institute Conference on Computer Ethics* (pp. 18-21). Academic Press.

Godfrey, B. (2001). Electronic Work Monitorung: An Ethical Model. In *Proc. Selected papers from the 2nd Australian Institute of Computer Ethics Conference (AICE2000)*. ACS.

Goetsch, D. L., & Davis, S. B. (2000). *Quality management: Introduction to total quality management for production, processing and services* (3rd ed.). Prentice-Hall International Inc.

Gold, A. H., Malhora, A., & Segars, A. H. (2001). Knowledge management: An organizational capabilities perspective. *Journal of Management Information Systems*, *18*(1), 185–214.

Goldin-Meadow, S. (1997). When gestures and words speak differently. *Current Directions in Psychological Science*, *6*(5), 138–143. doi:10.1111/1467-8721.ep10772905

Goldin-Meadow, S. (2002). *Hearing gestures: How our hands help us think*. Cambridge, MA: Belknap Press.

Goldin-Meadow, S., Kim, S., & Singer, M. (1999). What the teacher's hands tell the student's mind about math. *Journal of Educational Psychology*, *91*(4), 720–730. doi:10.1037/0022-0663.91.4.720

Goleman, D. (1995). *Emotional intelligence: Why EQ can matter more than IQ*. New York: Bantam Books.

Goleman, D. (1996). *Emotional intelligence*. New York, NY: Bantam Books.

Goleman, D. (1998). *Working with emotional intelligence*. New York, NY: Bantam.

Goleman, D. (2006). *Social intelligence*. New York, NY: Bantam Books.

Goleman, D., Boyatzis, R., & McKee, A. (2002). *Primal leadership: Realizing the power of emotional intelligence*. Boston, MA: Harvard Business School Press.

Golembliewski, R. T. (1993). *Approaches to planned change: Orienting perspectives and micro-level interventions*. New Brunswick, NJ: Transaction Publishers.

González, J., & Garazo, T. (2006). Structural relationships between organizational service orientation, contact employee job satisfaction and citizenship behavior. *International Journal of Service Industry Management*, *17*(1), 23–50. doi:10.1108/09564230610651561

Goodard, J. T. (2010). Toward Glocality: Facilitating leadership in an age of diversity. *Journal of School Leadership*, *20*, 37–56.

Goodman, J., & Truss, C. (2004). The medium and the message: Communicating effectively during a major change initiative. *Journal of Change Management*, *4*(3), 217–229. doi:10.1080/1469701042000255392

Goos, M., Manning, A., & Salomons, A. (2009). Job polarization in Europe. *The American Economic Review*, *99*(2), 58–63. doi:10.1257/aer.99.2.58

Gordon, E., Ponticelli, R., Morgan, R. R., & Donaldson, C. (2009). *Closing the literacy gap in American business*. Westport, CT: Qutarum Books.

Gordon, G. G., & DiTomaso, N. (1992). Predicting corporate performance from organizational culture. *Journal of Management Studies*, *29*(6), 783–798. doi:10.1111/j.1467-6486.1992.tb00689.x

Gormley, K. (1992). One Hundred Years of Privacy. *Wisconsin Law Review*, 1335–1441.

Grabner-Kraeuter, S. & Waiguny, M. (2011).Why users stay in online social networks: perceptions of value, trust, subjective norm and the moderating influence of duration of use. *American Marketing Association*, *22*(1), 240-249.

Graddol, D. (1997). *The future of English*. London: The British Council.

Graham, C. M., Daniel, H., & Doore, B. (2015). Millennial leadership: The Oppositional relationship between leadership type and the quality of database system's development in virtual environments. *International Journal of e-Collaboration*, *11*(3), 29–48. doi:10.4018/ijec.2015070103

Graham, J. (1991). An essay on organizational citizenship behavior. *Employee Responsibilities and Rights Journal*, *4*(4), 249–270. doi:10.1007/BF01385031

Grant, R. M. (1996). Toward a knowledge-based theory of the firm. *Strategic Management Journal*, *17*(7), 109–122. doi:10.1002/smj.4250171110

Gratton, L., & Truss, C. (2003). The three-dimensional people strategy: Putting human resources policies into action. *The Academy of Management Executive*, *17*(3), 74–86. doi:10.5465/AME.2003.10954760

Greenberg, J., & Baron, R. A. (2003). *Behavior in organizations* (8th ed.). Upper Saddle River, NJ: Prentice Hall.

Greenhow, C. (2011). Online social networks and learning. *On the Horizon*, *19*(1), 4–12. doi:10.1108/10748121111107663

Green, M., & Cifuentes, L. (2011). The effects of follow-up and peer interaction on quality of performance and completion of online professional development. *Journal of Interactive Learning Research*, *22*, 85–109.

Greeno, J. G. (1998). The situativity of knowing, learning, and research. *The American Psychologist*, *53*(1), 5–26. doi:10.1037/0003-066X.53.1.5

Greenwood, M. S., & Gaunt, H. J. (1994). *Total quality management for schools*. London: Cassell.

Griffin, R. W. (2012). *Fundamentals of Management*. Mason, OH: South–Western Cengage Learning.

Griffith, D. A., & Harvey, M. G. (2001). Executive insights: An intercultural communication model for use in global interorganizational networks. *Journal of International Marketing*, *9*(3), 87–103. doi:10.1509/jimk.9.3.87.19924

Griffith, J. (2006). A compositional analysis of organizational climate-performance relation: Public schools as organizations. *Journal of Applied Social Psychology*, *36*(8), 1848–1880. doi:10.1111/j.0021-9029.2006.00085.x

Griffith, T. L., Mannix, E. A., & Neale, M. A. (2003). Conflict in virtual teams. In C. Gibson & S. Cohen (Eds.), *Virtual teams that work: Creating conditions for virtual team effectiveness* (pp. 335–352). San Francisco, CA: Jossey-Bass.

Grimm, B. L., Johansson, P., Nayar, P., Apenteng, B. A., Opoku, S., & Nguyen, A. (2015). *Assessing the Education and Training Needs of Nebraska's Public Health Workforce.* doi:10.3389/fpubh.2015.00161

Grimm, J. W. (2010). Effective leadership: Making the difference. *Journal of Emergency Nursing: JEN*, *36*(1), 74–33. doi:10.1016/j.jen.2008.07.012 PMID:20109788

Grinder, M. (2008). *The elusive obvious.* Battle Ground, WA: Michael Grinder and Associates.

Grissom, J. (2011). Can good principals keep teachers in disadvantaged schools? Linking principal effectiveness to teacher satisfaction and turnover in hard-to-staff environments. *Teachers College Record, 113*, 2552–2585.

Grissom, J. A., & Loeb, S. (2011). Triangulating principal effectiveness: How perspectives of parents, teachers, and assistant principals identify the central importance of managerial skills. *American Educational Research Journal, 48*(5), 1091–1123. doi:10.3102/0002831211402663

Grissom, J. A., Loeb, S., & Master, B. (2013). Effective instructional time use for school leaders: Longitudinal evidence from observations of principals. *Educational Researcher, 42*(8), 433–444. doi:10.3102/0013189X13510020

Grodnitzky, G. (2005, March). Forcing conflict as a leadership style. *Leaders, Teams, Profits.* Retrieved 29 May 2013, from http://www.drgustavo.com/LTP/Issue34.pdf

Grosse, C. U. (2002). Managing communication within virtual intercultural teams. *Business Communication Quarterly, 65*(4), 22–38. doi:10.1177/108056990206500404

Gross, L. (2011). Communication as the Discipline of the 21st Century. *International Journal of Communication, 5*, 1497–1498.

Gross, S. R., & Syverud, K. D. (1992). Getting to No: A Study of Settlement Negotiations and the Selection of Cases for Trial. *Michigan Law Review, 90*, 323–373. PMID:10115793

Grudin, J. (1994). Groupware and social dynamics: Eight challenges for developers. *Communications of the ACM, 37*(1), 92–105. doi:10.1145/175222.175230

Grumdahl, C. R. (2010). *How schools can effectively plan to meet the goal of improving student learning.* (Doctoral dissertation). University of Minnesota. Retrieved from:https://conservancy.umn.edu/bitstream/handle/11299/59567/Grumdahl_umn_0130E_10969.pdf?sequence=1

Gruneberg, M. M. (1979). *Understanding job satisfaction.* New York: John Wiley. doi:10.1007/978-1-349-03952-4

Gudykunst, W. B., & Kim, Y. Y. (1992). *Communicating with strangers: An approach to intercultural communication* (2nd Ed., revised). New York: McGraw-Hill.

Guerci, M., Radaelli, G., Siletti, E., Cirella, S., & Shani, A. B. R. (2015). The impact of human resource management practices and corporate sustainability on organizational ethical climates: An employee perspective. *Journal of Business Ethics, 126*(2), 325–342. doi:10.1007/s10551-013-1946-1

Guetzkow, H., Forehand, G. A., & James, B. J. (1962). An evaluation of educational influence on executive judgment. *Administrative Science Quarterly, 6*(4), 483–500. doi:10.2307/2390727

Guille, A., Hacid, H., Favre, C., & Zighed, D. A. (2013). Information Difusion in Online Social Networks: A Survey. *Association for Computing Machinery, 42*(2), 17–28.

Gul, S., (2012). *The role of conflict & negotiation in the complexity of projects.* British Library EThOS

Gunderson, G., Hellesøy, B. T., & Raeder, S. (2012). Leading international project teams: The effectiveness of transformational leadership in dynamic work environments. *Journal of Leadership & Organizational Studies, 19*(1), 46–57. doi:10.1177/1548051811429573

Guo, L. C., & Sanchez, Y. (2005). Workplace communication. In N. Borkowski (Ed.), *Organizational behavior in health care* (pp. 77–110). Jones & Bartlett Learning.

Gupta, V. (2014). The Business System of India. Academic Press.

Gupta, J., & Sharma, S. (2004). *Creating knowledge based organization*. Boston, MA: Idea Group Publishing. doi:10.4018/978-1-59140-162-9

Gurin, P., Dey, E. L., Hurtado, S., & Gurin, G. (2002). Diversity and higher education: Theory and impact on educational outcomes. *Harvard Educational Review*, *72*(3), 330–366. doi:10.17763/haer.72.3.01151786u134n051

Gurteen, D. (2012). *Leading Issues in Social Knowledge Management. A collection of important Social Knowledge Management papers*. Academic Publishing International.

Habermas, J. (2014). *Between Naturalism and Religion: Philosophical Essays*. Academic Press.

Habermas, J. (1987a). The Theory of Communicative Action: Vol. 1. *The Critique of Functionalist Reason*. London: Heinemann.

Habermas, J. (1990). *Moral Consciousness and Communicative Action*. Cambridge, MA: MIT Press.

Habermas, J. (2002). *On the Pragmatics of Social Interaction: Preliminary Studies in the Theory of Communicative Action*. Cambridge, MA: MIT Press.

Habermas, J., & Lenhardt, C. (1973). A postscript to 'knowledge and human interests'. *Philosophy of the Social Sciences*, *3*(1), 157–185. doi:10.1177/004839317300300111

Hackett, J. (2000). *Construction Claims: Current Practice and Case Management*. London: LLP Professional Publishing.

Hackman, M., & Johnson, C. (2013). *Leadership: A communication perspective* (6th ed.). Long Grove, Ill: Wave Land Press.

Hackman, R., & Oldham, G. (1975). Development of the Job Diagnostic Survey. *The Journal of Applied Psychology*, *60*(2), 150–170. doi:10.1037/h0076546

Hackman, R., & Oldham, G. (1976). Motivation through the design of work: A test of a theory. *Organizational Behavior and Human Performance*, *16*(2), 250–279. doi:10.1016/0030-5073(76)90016-7

Hagen, S. (1999). *Business communication across borders: A study of language use and practice in European companies*. London: Languages National Training Organisation.

Håkansson, H. (1987). Product development in networks. In H. Håkansson (Ed.), *Technological development: A network approach* (pp. 84–128). New York: Croom Helm.

Hale, R., & Whitlam, P. (1997). *Towards the virtual organization*. London: The McGraw-Hill Co.

Hall Edward, T. (1959). *The Silent Language*. New York: Doubleday.

Hallinger, P. (2005). Instructional leadership and the school principal: A passing fancy that refuses to fade away. *Leadership and Policy in Schools*, *4*(3), 221–239. doi:10.1080/15700760500244793

Hallinger, P., & Heck, R. H. (2011). Exploring the journey of school improvement: Classifying and analyzing patterns of change in school improvement processes and learning outcomes. *School Effectiveness and School Improvement*, *22*(1), 1–27. doi:10.1080/09243453.2010.536322

Hallinger, P., & Murphy, J. F. (2013). Running on empty? Finding the time and capacity to lead learning. *NASSP Bulletin*, *97*(1), 5–21. doi:10.1177/0192636512469288

Hall, J. (1974). Interpersonal styles and the communication dilemma: Management implications of the Johari awareness model. *Human Relations*, *27*(4), 381–399. doi:10.1177/001872677402700404

Hall, J. T. (1976). *Beyond culture*. New York: Doubleday.

Hall, R. (1993). A framework linking intangible resources and capabilities to sustainable competitive advantage. *Strategic Management Journal*, *14*(8), 607–618. doi:10.1002/smj.4250140804

Hall, R. J., & Lord, R. G. (1995). Multi-level information-processing explanations of followers' leadership perceptions. *The Leadership Quarterly*, *6*(3), 265–281. doi:10.1016/1048-9843(95)90010-1

Hamdan, K., Belkhouche, B., & Smith, P. (2008). The Influence of Culture and Leadership on Cost Estimation. In *Software Process and Product Measurement* (pp. 223–232). Springer Berlin Heidelberg. doi:10.1007/978-3-540-89403-2_19

Hammer, M. (2007a). The 7 deadly sins of performance measurement. *MIT Sloan Management Review*, *48*(3), 19–28.

Hammer, M. (2007b). The process audit. *Harvard Business Review, 85*(4), 111–123. PMID:17432158

Hammill, G. (2015). Mixing and matching four generations of generations of employees. *FDU Magazine Online*. Retrieved from: http://www.fdu.edu/newspubs/magazine/05ws/generations.htm

Hanapi, Z., & Nordin, M. S. (2014). Unemployment among Malaysia graduates: Graduates' attributes, lecturers' competency and quality of education. *Procedia: Social and Behavioral Sciences, 112*, 1056–1063. doi:10.1016/j.sbspro.2014.01.1269

Handy, C. (1993). *Understanding Organisations*. Harmondsworth: Penguin.

Handy, C. (1995). Trust and virtual organization: How do you manage people whom you do not see. *Harvard Business Review, 73*(3), 40–50.

Hansbrough, T. (2012). The construction of a transformational leader: Follower attachment and leadership perceptions. *Journal of Applied Social Psychology, 42*(6), 1533–1549. doi:10.1111/j.1559-1816.2012.00913.x

Hargadon, A. (2003). *How Breakthroughs Happen*. Boston, MA: Harvard Business School Press.

Harris Interactive. (2003). *Poll*. Retrieved from http://www.harrisinteractive.com/harris_poll/index.asp?PID=365

Harris, A. (2011). Distributed leadership: Implications for the role of the principal. *Journal of Management Development, 31*(1), 7–17. doi:10.1108/02621711211190961

Harris, A., & Spillane, J. (2008). Distributed leadership through the looking glass. *Management in Education, 22*(1), 31–34. doi:10.1177/0892020607085623

Harris, L., & Cronen, V. E. (1979). A rules-based model for the analysis and evaluation of organizational communication. *Communication Quarterly, 27*(1), 12–28. doi:10.1080/01463377909369320

Harrison, A. G. (2013). Engagement Ring: Building connections between employees and strategy. *Public Relations Tactics, 20*(5), 16.

Harrisson, T. R. (2003). Victims, Targets, Protectors, and Destroyers: Using Disputant Accounts to Develop a Grounded Taxonomy of Disputant Orientations. *Conflict Resolution Quarterly, 20*(3), 307–329. doi:10.1002/crq.27

Harter, A., & Hopper, A. (1994). A distributed location system for the active office. *IEEE Network, 8*(1), 62–70. doi:10.1109/65.260080

Harter, J., Schmidt, F., & Hayes, T. (2002). Business-united-level relationship between employees satisfaction. *The Journal of Applied Psychology, 87*(2), 268–279. doi:10.1037/0021-9010.87.2.268 PMID:12002955

Hartman, H. (2014). *Food & the New Community, How the Internet changes Food Culture*. Retrieved on 03/14/2014 from http://www.hartman-group.com/news/press-releases/eating-alone-is-the-new-norma-reports-the-hartman-group

Hart, R. K., & McLeod, P. L. (2003). Rethinking team building in geographically dispersed teams: One message at a time. *Organizational Dynamics, 31*(4), 352–361. doi:10.1016/S0090-2616(02)00131-6

Harvey, M., Mcintyre, N., Moeller, M., & Sloan, H. Hanover Research Council. (2012). Managerial self-concept in a global context: An integral component of cross-cultural competencies. *Journal of Leadership & Organizational Studies, 19*(1), 115–125. doi:10.1177/1548051811431826

Hasegawa, H., & Noronha, C. (Eds.). (2014). *Asian Business And Management Systems: Theory, Practice and Perspectives* (2nd ed.). Basingstoke: Palgrave Macmillan.

Hashemi, M., & Hokmabadi, M. (2011). Effective English Presentation and Communication in an International Conference. *Procedia: Social and Behavioral Sciences, 30*, 2104–2111. doi:10.1016/j.sbspro.2011.10.409

Hauenstein, N. M. A., McGonigle, T., & Flinder, S. W. (2001). A meta-analysis of the relationship between procedural justice and distributive justice: Implications for justice research. *Employee Responsibilities and Rights Journal, 13*(1), 39–56. doi:10.1023/A:1014482124497

Hauschild, S., Licht, T., & Stein, W. (2001). Creating a knowledge culture. *The McKinsey Quarterly, 74*(1), 74–82.

Hauser, R., Paul, R., Bradley, J., & Jeffrey, L. (2012). Computer self-efficacy, anxiety and learning in online versus face to face medium. *Journal of Information Technology Education, 11*, 141–154.

Hawley, W. D., & Valli, L. (2000). Learner-centered professional development. *Phi Delta Kappa Center for Evaluation, Development, and Research, 27*, 7–10.

Hayashi, A., & Ewert, A. (2006). Outdoor leaders' emotional intelligence and transformational leadership. *Journal of Experimental Education, 28*(3), 222–242. doi:10.1177/105382590602800305

Hayes, D., Christie, P., Mills, M., & Lingard, B. (2004). Productive leaders and productive leadership: Schools as learning organisations. *Journal of Educational Administration, 42*(4/5), 520–538. doi:10.1108/09578230410554043

Hayes, M., & Walsham, G. (2003). Knowledge sharing and ICTs: A relational perspective. In M. Easterby-Smith & M. Lyles (Eds.), *The Blackwell handbook of organizational learning and knowledge management* (pp. 54–27). Malden, MA: Blackwell.

Hazelton, V., & Long, L. (1988). Concepts for public relations education, research, and practice: A communication point of view. *Central States Speech Journal, 39*(2), 77–87. doi:10.1080/10510978809363239

HBS. (2004). *Face-to-Face Communications for Clarity and Impact by the Results-Driven Manager.* Harvard Business School Press.

HDR. (2014). Sustaining Human Progress: Reducing Vulnerabilities and Building Resilience. In *United Nations Development Report, explanatory note on the 2014 Human Development Report composite indices: Palestine, State of*. New York: United Nations.

HealthyPeople.gov. (2010). *Public Health Infrastructure*. Retrieved September 2, 2015, from http://www.healthypeople.gov/2020/topics-objectives/topic/public-health-infrastructure

Heath, B., Hills, B., & Berry, M. (1994). *The Origin of Conflict within the Construction Process.* Paper presented at the First Plenary Meeting of TG15, The Netherlands.

Heidemann, J., Klier, M., & Probst, F. (2012). Online social networks: A survey of a global phenomenon. *Computer Networks, 56*(18), 3866–3878. doi:10.1016/j.comnet.2012.08.009

Heller, J. I., Daehler, K. R., Wong, N., Shinohara, M., & Miratrix, L. W. (2012). Differential effects of three professional development models on teacher knowledge and student achievement in elementary science. *Journal of Research in Science Teaching, 49*(3), 333–362. doi:10.1002/tea.21004

Hellriegel, D., & Slocum, J. W. (2008). Organizational Behavior (12th ed.). Cincinnati, OH: South-Western College Publishing (Thomson Learning).

Helne, C. A. (2005). Predicting workplace deviance from the interaction between organizational justice and personality. *Journal of Managerial Issues, 17*(2), 247–263.

Heminway, M. A., & Smith, C. A. (1999). Organizational climate and occupational stressors as predictors of withdrawal behaviors and injuries in nurses. *Journal of Organizational Psychology, 72*(3), 285–299. doi:10.1348/096317999166680

Hemmelgarn, A. L., Glisson, C., & Dukes, D. (2001). Emergency room culture and the emotional support component of family-centered care. *Children's Health Care, 30*(2), 93–110. doi:10.1207/S15326888CHC3002_2

Hemmelgarn, A. L., Glisson, C., & James, L. (2006). Organizational culture and climate: Implications for services and interventions research. *Clinical Psychology: Science and Practice, 13*(1), 73–89. doi:10.1111/j.1468-2850.2006.00008.x

Hemphill, C. F., & Vanneman, A. (2011). *Achievement gaps: How Hispanic and White students in public schools perform in mathematics & reading on the National Assessment of Educational Progress (NCES 2011-459), National Center for Educational Statistics, Institute of Education Sciences*. Washington, D. C: U.S. Department of Education.

Hemsworth, D., Muterera, J., & Baregheh, A. (2013). Examining Bass's transformational leadership in public sector executives: A psychometric properties review. *Journal of Applied Business Research, 29*, 853–862.

Henderson, L. S. (1986). Unraveling the Meaning of Managerial Communication: A Conceptual Explication and Model for Guiding Future Research. *Academy Of Management Best Papers Proceedings*, 219-223.

Henderson, J. C., & Lee, S. (1992). Managing I/S design teams: A control theories perspective. *Management Science*, *38*(6), 757–777. doi:10.1287/mnsc.38.6.757

Hensley, N., & Blau, R. (2015, March). Starbucks ends 'Race Together' coffee cup campaign, continues push for forums and new stories. *NY Daily News*. Retrieved from http://www.nydailynews.com/news/national/starbucks-ends-race-coffee-cup-campaign-article-1.2158755

Hernandez, J. R., Jr. (2001). *Total quality management in education: The application of TQM in a Texas school district.* (Unpublished doctoral dissertation). University of Texas, Austin, TX. Retrieved November 3, 2008, from Dissertations & Theses: Full Text (Publication No. AAT 3034546).

Hersh, W., Helfand, M., Wallace, J., Kraemer, D., Patterson, P., Shapiro, S., & Greenlick, M. (2002). A systematic review of the efficacy of telemedicine for making diagnostic and management decisions. *Journal of Telemedicine and Telecare*, *8*(4), 197–209. doi:10.1258/135763302320272167 PMID:12217102

Hertel, G., Konradt, U., & Orlikowski, B. (2004). Managing distance by interdependence: Goal setting, task interdependence, and team-based rewards in virtual teams. *European Journal of Work and Organizational Psychology*, *13*(1), 1–28. doi:10.1080/13594320344000228

Hert, P. D. (2012). The proposed data protection regulation replacing Directive 95/46/EC: A sound system for the protection of individuals. *CLSR*, *28*, 130–142.

HHS.gov. (2014). *Regulations*. Retrieved September 22, 2015, from: http://www.hhs.gov/regulations

Hibbert, K., & Rich, S. (2006). Virtual communities of practice. In J. Weiss, J. Hunsinger, & J. Trifonas (Eds.), *The international handbook of virtual learning environments* (pp. 563–579). The Netherlands: Springer. doi:10.1007/978-1-4020-3803-7_22

Higgs, M. J. (2003). How can we make sense of leadership in the 21st century? *Leadership and Organization Development Journal*, *24*(5), 273–284. doi:10.1108/01437730310485798

Hilgerman, R. H. (1988). *Communication satisfaction, goal setting, job satisfaction, concertive control, and effectiveness in self-managed teams.* (Unpublished doctoral dissertation). University of Maine.

Hill, L. B., Long, L. W., & Javidi, M. (1994). Principled Negotiation: Achieving Intercultural Effectiveness. In N. Honna, L. Hill, B. Hoffer, & Y. Tokeshita (Eds.), Organizational behaviors in cross-cultural settings: Intercultural Understanding and Communication (vol. 2). Tokyo: Sanshuusha Publishers.

Hill, P. W., Rowe, K. J., Holmes-Smith, P., & Russell, V. J. (1996). The Victorian Quality Schools Project: A study of school and teacher effectiveness (Report, Volume 1). Centre for Applied Educational Research: University of Melbourne.

Hillman, A. J., & Keim, G. D. (2001). Shareholder value, stakeholder management and social issues: What's the bottom line? *Strategic Management Journal*, *22*(2), 125–139. doi:10.1002/1097-0266(200101)22:2<125::AID-SMJ150>3.0.CO;2-H

Hinds, L., & Murphy, K. (2007). Public satisfaction with police: Using procedural justice to improve police legitimacy. *Australian and New Zealand Journal of Criminology*, *40*(1), 27–42. doi:10.1375/acri.40.1.27

Hinterhuber, H. H. (1995). Business process management: The European approach. *Business Change & Reengineering*, *2*(4), 63–73.

Hirt, M., & Willmott, P. (2014). Strategic principles for competing in the digital age. *McKinsey Quarterly*. Retrieved from http://www.mckinsey.com/insights/strategy/strategic_principles_for_competing_in_the_digital_age

Hizwari, S., Ahmad, I., Hifzurrahman, A., & NorHaizar, W. (2008). *Second language anxiety among diploma students in Technical University (Universiti Malaysia Perlis).* Paper presented at the International Conference on the Roles of the Humanities and Social Sciences in Engineering 2008 (ICOHSE08). Accessed online on 10 March 2014 from http://hdl.handle.net/123456789/5831

Hoadley, C. M., Xu, H., Lee, J. J., & Rosson, M. B. (2010). Privacy as information access and illusory control: The case of the Facebook News Feed privacy outcry. *Electronic Commerce Research and Applications, 9*(1), 50–60. doi:10.1016/j.elerap.2009.05.001

Hoang, H., & Antoncic, B. (2003). Network-based research in entrepreneurship: A critical review. *Journal of Business Venturing, 18*(2), 165–187. doi:10.1016/S0883-9026(02)00081-2

Hobson, M. (2015, March). Starbucks board member Mellody Hobson: Let's be color brave. *Starbucks Newsroom.* Retrieved from https://news.starbucks.com/news/starbucks-board-member-mellody-hobson-lets-be-color-brave

Hoch, J. E., & Kozlowski, S. W. J. (2014). Leading virtual teams: Hierarchical leadership, structural supports, and shared team leadership. *The Journal of Applied Psychology, 99*(3), 390–403. doi:10.1037/a0030264 PMID:23205494

Hodgkinson, M., & Brown, G. (2003). Enhancing the quality of education: A case study and some emerging principles. *Higher Education, 45*(3), 337–352. doi:10.1023/A:1022680504729

Hodgkinson, M., & Kelly, M. (2007). Quality management and enhancement processes in UK business schools: A review. *Quality Assurance in Education, 15*(1), 77–91. doi:10.1108/09684880710723043

Hoffman, N. A. (2011). The Requirements for Culturally and Linguistically Appropriate Services in Health Care. *Journal of Nursing Law, 14*(2), 49–57.

Hofstede, G. (1984). *Culture's consequences: International differences in Work-related Values.* London: Sage.

Hofstede, G. (2001). *Culture's Consequences.* London: Sage.

Hofstede, G. H. (1985). The interaction between national and organizational value systems. *Journal of Management Studies, 22*(4), 347–357. doi:10.1111/j.1467-6486.1985.tb00001.x

Hofstede, G. H., & Hofstede, G. J. (2005). *Cultures and organizations: Software of the mind* (2nd ed.). New York: McGraw Hill.

Hofstede, G., Neuijen, B., Ohayv, D. D., & Sanders, G. (1990). Measuring organizational cultures: A qualitative and quantitative study across twenty cases. *Administrative Science Quarterly, 35*(2), 286–316. doi:10.2307/2393392

Holladay, S. J., & Coombs, W. T. (1993). Communication visions: An exploration of the role of delivery in the creation of leader charisma. *Management Communication Quarterly, 6*(4), 405–427. doi:10.1177/0893318993006004003

Hollander, D. P., & Mihaliak, C. E. (2002). Tech helps deliver innovation in claims. *National Underwriter, 106*(48), 26–27.

Holleran, K., Pappas, J., Lou, H., Rubalcaba, P., Lee, R., & Clay, S. et al.. (2003). Mobile Technology in a Clinical Setting. *AMIA ... Annual Symposium Proceedings / AMIA Symposium. AMIA Symposium,* 2003. PMID:14728368

Holliday, A. R. (2007). *Doing and Writing Qualitative Research.* London, UK: Sage Publications.

Holness, G. V. R. (2001). Achieving quality using TQM and ISO. *ASHRAE Journal, 43*(1), 195–199.

Holt, M. (1993a). Dr. Deming and the improvement of schooling: No instant pudding. *Journal of Curriculum and Supervision, 9*(1), 6–23.

Holt, M. (1993b). The educational consequences of W. Edwards Deming. *Phi Delta Kappan, 74*(5), 382–388.

Hong & Landay. (2004) An architecture for privacy-sensitive ubiquitous computing. In *Proceedings of the 2nd international conference on Mobile systems, applications, and services.* ACM.

Hong, W., & Thong, J. (2013). Internet Privacy Concerns: An Integrated Conceptualisation and four empirical studies. *Management Information Systems Quarterly, 37*(1), 275–298. Retrieved from http://pewresearch.org/pubs/663/digital-footprints

Hong, Y., Catano, V. M., & Liao, H. (2011). Leader emergence: The role of emotional intelligence and motivation to lead. *Leadership and Organization Development Journal, 32*(4), 320–343. doi:10.1108/01437731111134625

Horkheimer, M. (1974). *Eclipse of Reason* (Vol. 1). New York: Bloomsbury Publishing.

Horne, J., & Lupton, T. (1965). The work activities of middle managers: An exploratory study. *Journal of Management Studies*, *1*(21), 14–33. doi:10.1111/j.1467-6486.1965.tb00563.x

Horvitz, E., & Apacible, J. (2003). *Learning and reasoning about interruption.* Paper presented at the 5th international conference on Multimodal interfaces, Vancouver, Canada. doi:10.1145/958432.958440

Horvitz, E., Koch, P., Kadie, C. M., & Jacobs, A. (2002). *Coordinate: Probabilistic forecasting of presence and availability.* Paper presented at the 18th Conference in Uncertainty in Artificial Intelligence (UAI'02).

Horwitz, E. K., Horwitz, M. B., & Cope, J. (1986). Foreign language classroom anxiety. *Modern Language Journal*, *70*(2), 125–132. doi:10.1111/j.1540-4781.1986.tb05256.x

Horwitz, F. M., Bravington, D., & Silvis, U. (2006). The promise of virtual teams: Identifying key factors in effectiveness and failure. *Journal of European Industrial Training*, *30*(6), 472–494. doi:10.1108/03090590610688843

Hossain, L. W., & Wigand, R. T. (2004). ICT enabled virtual collaboration through trust. *Journal of Computer-Mediated Communication*, *10*(1). Retrieved from http://jcmc.indiana.edu/vol10/issue1/hossain_wigand.html

House, R. J., Spangler, W. D., & Woycke, J. (1991). Personality and charisma in the US presidency: A psychological theory of leadership effectiveness. *Administrative Science Quarterly*, *36*(3), 374–396. doi:10.2307/2393201

Hovland, C., Janis, I., & Kelley, H. (1953). *Communication and persuasion.* New Haven, CT: Yale University Press.

Howley, A., Chadwick, K., & Howley, C. (2002). *Networking for the nuts and bolts: The ironies of professional development for rural principals.* Paper presented at the Annual Meeting of the American Educational Research Association, New Orleans, LA.

Hristova, A. (2008). *Conceptualization and Design of a Context-aware platform for user centric Applications. Master of Science in Communication Technology.* Trondheim: Norwegian University of Science and Technology.

Hsieh, S. C., Lin, J. S., & Lee, H. C. (2012). Analysis on literature review of competency. *International Review of Business and Economics*, *2*, 25–50.

Hsin-Kuang, C., Chun-Hsiung, L., & Dorjgotov, B. (2012). The moderating effect of transformational leadership on knowledge management and organizational effectiveness. *Social Behavior & Personality: An International Journal*, *40*(6), 1015–1024. doi:10.2224/sbp.2012.40.6.1015

Hubbard, S., & Menzel, S. (1995). Mt. Edgecumbe High School case study report. In S. Hubbard & S. Menzel (Eds.), *The Study of School-to-Work Reform Initiatives. Volume II: Case Studies* (pp. 5-55). Studies of Education Reform Series. Academy for Educational Development, Washington, DC. National Inst. for Work and Learning. Retrieved from http://files.eric.ed.gov/fulltext/ED397551.pdf

Huddleston, T. (2014, November). Urban Outfitters' profits and shares tumble. *Fortune.* Retrieved from http://fortune.com/2014/11/17/urban-outfitters-shares-dip-as-namesake-brand-weighs-down-same-store-sales/

Hudson Highland Group. (2004). *The Case for diversity: Attaining global competitive advantage.* The Hudson Highland Group Thought Series.

Hughes, J. (2010). What teacher education programs can do to better prepare teachers to meet the challenges of educating students living in poverty. *Action in Teacher Education*, *32*(1), 54–64. doi:10.1080/01626620.2010.10463542

Hughes, P. (Ed.). (1988). *The challenge of identifying and marketing quality in education.* Sydney, Australia: The Australian Association of Senior Educational Administrators.

Huhtala, M., Tolvanen, A., Mauno, S., & Feldt, T. (2015). The associations between ethical organizational culture, burnout, and engagement: A multilevel study. *Journal of Business and Psychology*, *30*(2), 399–414. doi:10.1007/s10869-014-9369-2

Humphrey, R. H. (2002). The many faces of emotional leadership. *The Leadership Quarterly*, *13*(5), 493–504. doi:10.1016/S1048-9843(02)00140-6

Hunt, J. G., Schriescheim, C. A., & Sekaran, U. (Eds.). (1982). *Leadership: Beyond establishment views.* Carbondale, IL: Southern Illinois University Press.

Hurlbert, J. S. (2001). Social networks, social circles and job satisfaction. *Work and Occupations*, *18*(4), 415–430. doi:10.1177/0730888491018004003

Hurtado, S. (2001). Linking diversity with educational purpose: How the diversity impacts the classroom environment and student development. In G. Orfield (Ed.), *Diversity challenged: Legal crisis and new evidence* (pp. 143–174). Cambridge, MA: Harvard Publishing Group.

Hvannberg, E. T. (2015). Identifying and explicating knowledge on method transfer: A sectoral system of innovation approach. *Universal Access in the Information Society, 14*(2), 187–202. doi:10.1007/s10209-013-0340-1

Hydle, K., Kvalshaugen, R., & Breuning, K. (2014). Transnational practices in communities of task and communities learning. *Management Learning, 45*(5), 609–629. doi:10.1177/1350507613500881

Hylton, K. N. (1990). The influence of litigation costs on deterrence under strict liability and under negligence. *International Review of Law and Economics, 10*(2), 161–171. doi:10.1016/0144-8188(90)90021-K

Hyypia, M., & Parajanen, S. (2013). Boosting creativity with transformational leadership in fuzzy front-end innovation processes. *Interdisciplinary Journal of Information. Knowledge & Management, 8*, 821–841.

I F R. (2012). *World robotics 2012*. Tech. Rep. International Federation of Robotics.

IABC. (2015). *The six principles of the profession*. The Global Standard of the Profession. International Association of Business Communicators. Retrieved June 24, 2015 from https://www.iabc.com/global-standard-2/

IBM. (2006). *Stopping insider attacks: How organizations can protect their sensitive information*. Retrieved from http://www-935.ibm.com/services/us/imc/pdf/gsw00316-usen-00-insider-threats-wp.pdf

Idrus, H., & Salleh, R. (2008). Perceived self-efficacy of Malaysian ESL Engineering and Technology students on their speaking ability and its pedagogical implications. In B. H. Tan, K. E. Tan & P. Nair (Eds.), The English Teacher (Vol. 31, pp. 61-75). Selangor: Malaysian English Language Teaching Association (MELTA).

Idrus, N. (1995). Empowerment as a manifestation of total quality: A study in three countries. *Total Quality Management, 6*(5 & 6), 603–612. doi:10.1080/09544129550035251

Idrus, N. (1996). Towards total quality management in academia. *Quality Assurance in Education, 4*(3), 34–40. doi:10.1108/09684889610125850

Iles, P., & Hayers, P. K. (1997). Managing diversity in transnational project teams: A tentative model and case study. *Journal of Managerial Psychology, 12*(2), 95–117. doi:10.1108/02683949710164190

IMRhelp. (2015). *Independent medical review*. Retrieved October 8, 2015, from http://www.dir.ca.gov/dwc/IMR.htm

Index, B. G. (n.d.). Retrieved from https://www.boardsource.org/eweb/dynamicpage.aspx?webcode=GovernanceIndex

Innovaro. (2014). *Technology Foresight*. Retrieved from http://www.trendsandforesight.com/uploads/TF%20 2013%2039%20Experience%20API.pdf

International Labour Organization (ILO). (1997). *Protection of workers' personal data. An ILO code of practice*. ILO.

Introna, L. D. (2001). Workplace surveillance, privacy and distributive justice. In R. A. Spinello & H. T. Tavani (Eds.), *Readings in cyberethics* (pp. 519–532). Sudbury, MA: Jones and Barlett.

Isaksen, S. G., & Ekvall, G. (2007). *Assessing the context for change: A technical manual for the situational outlook questionnaire*. Orchard Park, NY: The Creative Problem Solving Group.

Ismail, R., Yussof, I., & Lai, W. S. (2011). Employers' perceptions on graduates in Malaysian services sector. *International Business Management, 5*(3), 184–193. doi:10.3923/ibm.2011.184.193

Issa Lahera, A., Mendoza, M., & McManus, H. (2015). Developing authentic non-traditional principals to lead underserved student populations: The case of charter and autonomous school leadership academy. Journal of Authentic Leadership in Education, 4(2), 1-8.

Issa Lahera, A., Holzman, S., & Robinson, P. (2014). Ready to lead: Creating a pathway that ensures readiness. In A. H. Normore, K. Hamdan, & A. I. Lahera (Eds.), *Pathways to excellence: Developing and cultivating leaders for the cassroom and beyond* (pp. 117–137). Bingley, UK: Emerald Group Publishing. doi:10.1108/S1479-366020140000021017

Ittner, C. D., & Larcker, D. F. (1997). The performance effects of process management techniques. *Management Science*, *43*(4), 522–534. doi:10.1287/mnsc.43.4.522

Jackson, B., & Robertson, L. (2011 January 7). A 'Job-Killing' Law?. FactCheck. Retrieved October 10, 2015, from http://www.factcheck.org/spindetectors/about/

Jackson, K. (2013). East Asian Management: An Overview. Academic Press.

Jackson, K., Arshynnikova, O., Gasser, N., & Harasyuk, R. (forthcoming) Lynchpin: from diversity to discord and synergy to (near) derailment of a Japanese-Ukrainian infrastructure project. Academic Press.

Jackson, T., Dawson, R., & Wilson, D. (2001). The cost of email interruption (Item No. 2134/495). Loughborough, UK: Loughborough University Institutional Repository. Retrieved from http://km.lboro.ac.uk/iii/pdf/JOSIT%20 2001.pdf

Jackson, B., & Parry, K. (2011). *A very short, fairly interesting and reasonably cheap book about studying leadership*. Los Angeles, CA: Sage Publications.

Jackson, D. S. (2000). The School Improvement Journey: Perspectives on leadership. *School Leadership & Management Development*, *20*(1), 61–78. doi:10.1080/13632430068888

Jackson, K. (forthcoming). Education. In *The Encyclopedia of Social Theory*. New York: John Wiley. doi:10.7208/chicago/9780226389394.001.0001

Jacob, B. A. (2007). The challenges of staffing urban schools with effective teachers. *The Future of Children*, *17*(1), 129–153. doi:10.1353/foc.2007.0005 PMID:17407926

Jacobs, T., & Clement, D. (2013). *Contributions of Stratified Systems Theory to Military Leader Development and Organization Redesign in the US Army*. Retrieved September 2, 2015, from http://dmcodyssey.org/wp-content/uploads/2013/09/part-three-chapter-4-p197-209.pdf

James, J. R., Choi, C. C., Ko, C. H., McNeil, P. K., Minton, M. K., Wright, M. A., & Kim, K. (2008). Organizational and psychological climate: A review of theory and research. *European Journal of Work and Organizational Psychology*, *17*(1), 5–32. doi:10.1080/13594320701662550

Janesick, V. J. (2011). *Stretching exercises for qualitative researchers* (3rd ed.). Thousand Oaks: Sage.

Janz, B. D., & Prasarnphanich, P. (2003). Understanding the antecedents of effective knowledge management: The importance of a knowledge-centered culture. *Decision Sciences*, *34*(2), 351–384. doi:10.1111/1540-5915.02328

Jarvenpaa, S. L., Knoll, K., & Leidner, D. E. (1998). Is anybody out there? Antecedents of trust in global virtual teams. *Journal of Management Information Systems*, *14*(4), 29–64. doi:10.1080/07421222.1998.11518185

Jarvenpaa, S. L., & Leidner, L. E. (1999). Communication and trust in global virtual teams. *Organization Science*, *10*(6), 791–815. doi:10.1287/orsc.10.6.791

Jarvenpaa, S. L., Shaw, T. R., & Staples, D. S. (2004). Toward contextualized theories of trust: The role of trust in global virtual teams. *Information Systems Research*, *15*(3), 250–267. doi:10.1287/isre.1040.0028

Jehn, K. A. (1994). Enhancing effectivenes: An investigation of advantages and disadvantages of value-based intragroup conflict. *The International Journal of Conflict Management*, *5*(3), 223–238. doi:10.1108/eb022744

Jehn, K. A., & Mannix, E. A. (2001). The dynamic nature of conflict: A longitudinal study of intragroup conflict and group performance. *Academy of Management Journal*, *44*(2), 238–251. doi:10.2307/3069453

Jenkins, S. (2013, January 20). NCAA touts amateurism rules over open market, but which is more corrupt. *The Washington Post*. Retrieved January 22, 2014 from http://www.washingtonpost.com/sports/colleges/ncaa-touts-amateurism-rules-over-open-market-but-which-is-more-corrupt/2013/09/20/511e18ea-2204-11e3-a358-1144dee636dd_story.html

Jerome, A. M. (2008). Toward prescription: Testing the rhetoric of atonement's applicability in the athletic arena. *Public Relations Review, 34*(2), 124–134. doi:10.1016/j.pubrev.2008.03.007

Jerome, A. M., & Rowland, R. C. (2009). Organizational apologia: The rhetoric of inter-organizational conflict. *Western Journal of Communication, 73*, 395–417. doi:10.1080/10570310903279059

Jha, A. K., DesRoches, C. M., Campbell, E. G., Donelan, K., Rao, S. R., Ferris, T. G., & Blumental, D. et al. (2009). Use of electronic health records in U.S. hospitals. *The New England Journal of Medicine, 360*(16), 1628–1638. doi:10.1056/NEJMsa0900592 PMID:19321858

Jimenez, L. (2014). Media, Diversity and Negative Perceptions and Assumptions. *Diversity Journal.*

Jin, Y. (2010). Emotional leadership as a key dimension of public relations leadership: A national survey of public relations leaders. *Journal of Public Relations Research, 22*(2), 159–172. doi:10.1080/10627261003601622

Johannessen, J. A., Olsen, B., & Olaisen, J. (1999). Aspects of innovation theory based knowledge management. *Journal of International Management, 19*(2), 121–139.

Johansson, C., & Heide, M. (2008). Speaking of change: Three communication approaches in studies of organizational change. *Corporate Communications: An International Journal, 13*(3), 288–305. doi:10.1108/13563280810893661

John, L., & Johnson, M. (2010). *Getting the most from an age-diverse workforce.* Retrieved from http://www.generationsincbook.com

John, M. I., Robert, K., & Konopaske, M. T. (2008). *Organizational behavior and management.* Boston, MA: McGraw–Hill/Irwin.

Johnson & Johnson. (2011, December). *Director, Corporate Communications Job, Health Care Systems Inc.* Accessed from the Web site: http://www.careers.jnj.com/region

Johnson, C. (2011, August). Case Against Wiki Leaks Part Of Broader Campaign. *NPR News.* Accessed from the Web site: http://www.npr.org/2011/05/11/136173262/case-against-wikileaks-part-of-broader-campaign

Johnson, R., Stewart, C., & Bachman, C. (2015, August). What drives students to complete online courses? What drives faculty to teach online? Validating a measure of motivation orientation in university students and faculty. *Interactive Learning Environments, 23*(4), 528–543. doi:10.1080/10494820.2013.788037

Jones, T. L. (2009). *Virtual team communication and collaboration in Army and corporate applications.* Retrieved September 15, 2012 from http://www.dtic.mil/cgi-bin/GetTRDoc?AD=ADA502091

Jones, J. P., & Seraphim, D. (2008). TQM implementation and change management in an unfavourable environment. *Journal of Management Development, 27*(3), 291–306. doi:10.1108/02621710810858614

Jones, K. R. (2013). Developing and implementing a mandatory online student orientation. *Journal of Asynchronous Learning Networks, 17*, 43–45.

Jones, M. (2006). Which is a better predictor of job performance: Job satisfaction or life satisfaction? *Journal of Behavioral and Applied Management, 8*(1), 20–42.

Joreskog, K. G., & Sorbom, D. (1993). *LISREL 8: User's reference guide.* Chicago, IL: Scientific Software International.

Joshua-Gojer, A. E. (2012). Cross-cultural training and success versus failure of expatriates. *Learning and Performance Quarterly, 1*(2), 47–62.

Jourard, S. (1964). Some Psychological Aspects of Privacy. *Law and Contemporary Problems, 31*(2), 307–318. doi:10.2307/1190673

Judge, T., Parker, S., Colbert, A., Heller, D., & Remus, I. (2001). Job satisfaction: a cross-cultural review. In N. Anderson, D. Ones, H. Sinangil, & C. Viswesvaran (Eds.), *Handbook of Industrial, Work and Organizational Psychology* (Vol. 2, pp. 25–52). London: Sage Publications.

Kahn, L. (2015). *Leadership in Health Care for the 21st Century.* Retrieved September 2, 2015, from http://www.amjmed.com/article/S002-9343(14)00287-3/pdf

Kahn, R. L. (1964). Introduction. In R. L. Kahn & E. Boulding (Eds.), *Power and Conflict in Organizations* (pp. 1–7). Basic Books.

Kahn, W. A. (1990). Psychological conditions of personal engagement and disengagement at work. *Academy of Management Journal*, *33*(4), 692–724. doi:10.2307/256287

Kaiser Family Foundation. (2013). *The Uninsured: A Primer - Key Facts about Health Insurance on the Eve of Coverage Expansions*. Retrieved September 2, 2015, from http://kff.org/uninsured/report/the-uninsured-a-primer-key-facts-about-health-insurance-on-the-eve-of-coverage-expansions/

Kakepoto, I., Habil, H., Omar, N. A. M., & Said, H. (2012). Factors that Influence Oral Presentations of Engineering Students of Pakistan for Workplace Environment. *Information and Knowledge Management*, *2*(7), 70–78.

Kalla, H. K. (2005). Integrated internal communications: A multidisciplinary perspective. *Corporate Communications*, *10*(4), 302–314. doi:10.1108/13563280510630106

Kanai, T. (2000). Shin no leadership wa leader to follower no aida ni aru [The real leadership lies between the leader and the followers]. *Hanbai no Hito*, (109), 8-12.

Kankanhalli, A., Tan, B. C. Y., & Wei, K.-K. (2007). Conflict and performance in global virtual teams. *Journal of Management Information Systems*, *23*(3), 237–274. doi:10.2753/MIS0742-1222230309

Kanter, R. B. (1983). *The change masters: Innovation and entrepreneurship in the American corporations*. New York, NY: Simon and Schuster.

Kanter, R. M. (1983). *The change masters: Innovation for productivity in the American corporation*. New York: Simon & Schuster.

Kaplan, S. (2014, September). #WhyIStayed: She saw herself in Ray Rice's wife, Janay, and tweeted about it. So did thousands of others. *The Washington Post*. Retrieved from http://www.washingtonpost.com/news/morning-mix/wp/2014/09/09/whyistayed-she-saw-herself-in-ray-rices-wife-janay-and-tweeted-about-it-so-did-thousands-of-others/

Kaplan, A. M., & Haenlein, M. (2011). The early bird catches the news: Nine things you should know about micro-blogging. *Business Horizons*, *54*(2), 105–113. doi:10.1016/j.bushor.2010.09.004

Kaplan, D. (1989). Demonstratives. In J. Almog, P. Perry, H. K. Wettstein, & D. Kaplan (Eds.), *Themes from Kaplan* (pp. 481–563). Oxford University Press.

Kaplan, R. S., & Norton, D. P. (1996). Linking the balanced scorecard to strategy. *California Management Review*, *39*(1), 53–79. doi:10.2307/41165876

Kasemsap, K. (2014a). Strategic innovation management: An integrative framework and causal model of knowledge management, strategic orientation, organizational innovation, and organizational performance. In P. Ordóñez de Pablos & R. Tennyson (Eds.), *Strategic approaches for human capital management and development in a turbulent economy* (pp. 102–116). Hershey, PA: IGI Global. doi:10.4018/978-1-4666-4530-1.ch007

Kasemsap, K. (2014b). The role of knowledge sharing on organisational innovation: An integrated framework. In L. Al-Hakim & C. Jin (Eds.), *Quality innovation: Knowledge, theory, and practices* (pp. 247–271). Hershey, PA: IGI Global. doi:10.4018/978-1-4666-4769-5.ch012

Kasemsap, K. (2015a). Developing a framework of human resource management, organizational learning, knowledge management capability, and organizational performance. In P. Ordoñez de Pablos, L. Turró, R. Tennyson, & J. Zhao (Eds.), *Knowledge management for competitive advantage during economic crisis* (pp. 164–193). Hershey, PA: IGI Global. doi:10.4018/978-1-4666-6457-9.ch010

Kasemsap, K. (2015b). The role of data mining for business intelligence in knowledge management. In A. Azevedo & M. Santos (Eds.), *Integration of data mining in business intelligence systems* (pp. 12–33). Hershey, PA: IGI Global. doi:10.4018/978-1-4666-6477-7.ch002

Kassim, H., & Ali, F. (2010). English communicative events and skills needed at the workplace: Feedback from the industry. *English for Specific Purposes*, *29*(3), 168–182. doi:10.1016/j.esp.2009.10.002

Katz, D., & Kahn, R. (1987). Psicologia social das organizações (3ª ed.). São Paulo: Editora Atlas.

Katz, M. H., & Schroeder, S. A. (1988). The sounds of the hospital. Paging patterns in three teaching hospitals. *The New England Journal of Medicine*, *319*(24), 1585–1589. doi:10.1056/NEJM198812153192406 PMID:3200267

Kauffman, S. (1995). *At home in the universe - the search for laws of self-organization and complexity.* New York, NY: Oxford University Press.

Kaur, S., & Lee, S. H. (2006). Analysing workplace oral communication needs in English among IT graduates. *English for Specific Purposes World.* Accessed online on 20 April 2010 from http://www.esp-world/info

Kayworth, T. R., & Leidner, D. E. (2001-2002). Leadership effectiveness in global virtual teams. *Journal of Management Information Systems, 18*(3), 7–41.

Keis, K., & Javidi, M. (2014). *Deliberate leadership: Creating success through personal style.* Vancouver, BC: CRG Publishing.

Kelemen, M., & Papasolomou, I. (2007). Internal Marketing: A Qualitative Study of Culture Change in the UK Banking Sector. *Journal of Marketing Management, 23*(7-8), 745–767. doi:10.1362/026725707X230027

Kelloway, E., Turner, N., Barling, J., & Loughlin, C. (2012). Transformational leadership and employee psychological well-being: The mediating role employee trust in leadership. *Work and Stress, 26*(1), 39–55. doi:10.1080/02678373.2012.660774

Kelly, J. (1964). The study of executive behavior by activity sampling. *Human Relations, 17*(3), 277–287. doi:10.1177/001872676401700310

Kendon, A. (1990). *Conducting interaction: Patterns of behavior in focused encounters.* New York, NY: Cambridge University Press.

Kendon, A. (1997). Gesture. *American Review of Anthropology, 26,* 109–128.

Kendon, A. (2004). *Gesture: Visible action as utterance.* Cambridge, England: Cambridge University Press; doi:10.1017/CBO9780511807572

Kesan, J.P. (2002). Cyber-Woring or Cyber-Shrinking? A First Principles Examination of Electronic Privacy in the Workplace. *Florida Law Review,* (54).

Kess, P., & Haapasalo, H. (2002). Knowledge creation through a project review process in software production. *International Journal of Production Economics, 80*(1), 49–55. doi:10.1016/S0925-5273(02)00242-6

Kets de Vries, M. F. R. (1993). *Leaders, fools and imposters: Essays on the psychology of leadership.* San Francisco, CA: Jossey-Bass.

Keyes, A. (2014). Striking out ALS: Ice Bucket Challenge brings floods of donations. *NBC News.* Retrieved from http://www.nbcnews.com/feature/making-a-difference/striking-out-als-ice-bucket-challenge-brings-flood-donations-n177896

Keyton, J. (2011). *Communication and organizational culture: A key to understanding work experience.* Thousand Oaks, CA: Sage.

Khalil, A., & Connelly, K. (2005). Improving Cell Phone Awareness by Using Calendar Information. Human-Computer Interaction - INTERACT 2005 (pp. 588-600).

Khalil, A., & Connelly, K. (2006). *Context-aware Telephony: Privacy Preferences and Sharing Patterns.* Paper presented at the CSCW'06, Banff, Alberta, Canada. doi:10.1145/1180875.1180947

Khan Academy. (2012). *A free world class education for anyone anywhere.* Retrieved September 15, 2012 from http://www.khanacademy.org/about

Khanna, P. (2011). *How to run the world: Charting a course to the next renaissance.* New York, NY: Random House.

Khoury, G., & Analoui, F. (2010). How Palestinian managers cope with stress. *Journal of Management Development, 29*(3), 282–291. doi:10.1108/02621711011025795

Khoury, G., & Khoury, M. (Eds.), *Cases on Management and Organizational Behavior in An Arab Context.* Hershey, PA: IGI Global. doi:10.4018/978-1-4666-5067-1

Khoury, G., & McNally, B. (2014). Under pressure: The role of the external context in creating internal tensions - A case study of a Palestinian University. In G. C. Khoury & M. C. Khoury (Eds.), *Cases on Management and Organizational Behavior in an Arab Context* (pp. 128–145). Hershey, PA, USA: IGI Global. doi:10.4018/978-1-4666-5067-1.ch008

Khrennikov, A. (2010). *Ubiquitous Quantum Structure.* Springer. doi:10.1007/978-3-642-05101-2

Kidd, A. G., Sharratt, C., & Coleman, J. (2004). Mobile communication regulations updated: how safely are doctors' telephones used? *Qual Saf Health Care, 13*(6), 478. doi: 10.1136/qhc.13.6.478

Kierkegaard, S. (2005). Privacy in electronic communication. Watch your e-mail: Your boss is snooping! *CLSR,* (pp. 226-236).

Kikrman, B. L., Rosen, B., Tesluk, P. E., & Gibson, C. B. (2004). The impact of team empowerment on virtual team performance: The moderating role of face-to-face interaction. *Academy of Management Journal, 47*(2), 175–192. doi:10.2307/20159571

Kim, S. B. (2014). Impacts of knowledge management on the organizational success. *KSCE Journal of Civil Engineering, 18*(6), 1609–1617. doi:10.1007/s12205-014-0243-6

King, J. (2002). Preparing EFL learners for oral presentations. *Dong Hwa Journal of Humanistic Studies, 4*, 401–418.

King, J. C. (2012). Anaphora. In G. Russell & D. G. Fara (Eds.), *The Routledge companion to the philosophy of Language*. Routledge.

Kirkpatrick, A. (2010). *English as a lingua franca in ASEAN. A multilingual model*. Hong Kong, China: Hong Kong University Press. doi:10.5790/hongkong/9789888028795.001.0001

Kirsch, I., Brown, H., & Yanamoto, K. (2007). *America's perfect storm: Three forces changing our nation's future. Education Testing Service.* Washington, DC: U. S. Department of Education.

Kirschner, P. A., & Van Bruggen, J. (2004). Learning and understanding in virtual teams. *Cyberpsychology & Behavior, 7*(2), 135–139. doi:10.1089/109493104323024401 PMID:15140357

Kisamore, J. L., Jawahar, I. M., Liguori, E. W., Mharapara, T. L., & Stone, T. H. (2010). Conflict and abusive workplace behaviors: The moderating effects of social competencies. *Career Development International, 15*(6), 583–600. doi:10.1108/13620431011084420

Klein, H. J., Noe, R., & Wang, C. (2006). Motivation to learn and course outcomes: The impact of delivery mode, learning goal orientation, and perceived barriers and enablers. *Personnel Psychology, 59*(3), 665–702. doi:10.1111/j.1744-6570.2006.00050.x

Klein, M. (1957). *Envy and gratitude: A study of unconcious sources*. London: Tavistock.

Klidas, A., van den Berg, P. T., & Wilderom, C. P. M. (2007). Managing employee empowerment in luxury hotels in Europe. *International Journal of Service Industry Management, 18*(1), 70–88. doi:10.1108/09564230710732902

Kodama, M. (2005). New knowledge creation through dialectical leadership: A case of IT and multimedia business in Japan. *European Journal of Innovation Management, 8*(1), 31–55. doi:10.1108/14601060510578565

Koene, B. A., Vogelaar, A. L., & Soeters, J. L. (2002). Leadership effects on organizational climate and financial performance: Local leadership effect in chain organizations. *The Leadership Quarterly, 13*(3), 193–215. doi:10.1016/S1048-9843(02)00103-0

Koeszegi, S., Vetschera, R., & Kersten, G. (2004). National cultural differences in the use and perception of Internet-based NSS: Does high or low context matter? *International Negotiation, 9*(79), 79–109. doi:10.1163/1571806041262070

Kohlbacher, M. (2009). *The perceived effects of business process management*. Paper presented at the IEEE Toronto International Conference, Toronto, Canada. doi:10.1109/TIC-STH.2009.5444467

Kohlbacher, M. (2010). The effects of process orientation: A literature review. *Business Process Management Journal, 16*(1), 135–152. doi:10.1108/14637151011017985

Kohlbacher, M., & Gruenwald, S. (2011). Process ownership, process performance measurement and firm performance. *International Journal of Productivity and Performance Management, 60*(7), 709–720. doi:10.1108/17410401111167799

Kohn, A. (1993). Turning learning into a business: Concerns about total quality management. *Educational Leadership, 51*(1), 58–61.

Kolb, D. M., & Williams, J. (2003). *Everyday negotiation: Navigating the hidden agendas in bargaining*. San Francisco: Jossey-Bass.

Kolb, D., & Bartunek, J. M. (Eds.). (1992). *Hidden Conflict in Organizations: Uncovering Behind-the-Scenes Disputes*. Newbury Park, CA: Sage. doi:10.4135/9781483325897

Koles, B., & Kondath, B. (2015). Organizational climate in Hungary, Portugal, and India: A cultural perspective. *AI & Society*, *30*(2), 251–259. doi:10.1007/s00146-013-0507-6

Konovsky, M., & Organ, D. (1996). Dispositional and contextual determinants of organizational citizenship behavior. *Journal of Organizational Behavior*, *17*(3), 253–266. doi:10.1002/(SICI)1099-1379(199605)17:3<253::AID-JOB747>3.0.CO;2-Q

Koper, C. S. (1995). Just enough police presence: Reducing crime and disorderly behavior by optimizing patrol time in crime hot spots. *Justice Quarterly*, *12*(4), 649–672. doi:10.1080/07418829500096231

Kop, R. (2011). The challenges to connectivist learning on open online networks: Learning experiences during a massive open online course. *International Review of Research in Open and Distance Learning*, *12*(3), 19–37.

Korte, W. B., & Wynne, R. (1996). *Telework Penetration, potential and practice in Europe*. Amsterdam: Ohmsha Press.

Kostner, J. (2001). *Bionic e-teamwork: How to build collaborative virtual teams at hyperspeed*. Chicago, IL: Dearborn Trade.

Kotkin, J. (2010). *The Next hundred million: American 2050*. New York, NY: Penguin Press.

Koudal, P., & Coleman, G. C. (2005). coordinating operations to enhance innovation in the global corporation. *Strategy and Leadership*, *33*(4), 20–32. doi:10.1108/10878570510608013

Kouzes, J. M., & Posner, B. Z. (1995). *The leadership challenge: How to keep getting extraordinary things done in organizations*. San Francisco, CA: Jossey-Bass Publishers.

Kovacs, J. (2009). Facilitating Change in Australian Schools: Applying a Business Quality Improvement Model. Unpublished Doctoral dissertation. Melbourne, Australia: Swinburne University of Technology. Retrieved from http://researchbank.swinburne.edu.au/vital/access/manager/Repository/swin:14100

Kovacs, J., & King, M. (2005). Studying the Impact of the Quality in Schools and Quality and Improvement in Schools and Preschools Initiatives: 1997-2003. *Quality Learning and Improvement in Schools and Preschools Summary Report*, November 2005 [Electronic Version]. Melbourne: Quality Learning Australia Pty Ltd. Retrieved from http://www.qla.com.au/pathtoitems/QLA_QISP_Report.pdf

Kraut, R. E., Egido, C., & Galegher, J. (2002). Patterns of contact and communication in scientific research collaboration. In J. Galegher & R. Kraut (Eds.), *Intellectual Teamwork: Social and technological foundations of group work*. Hillsdale, NY: Lawrence Earlbaum Associates.

Kraut, R. E., Lewis, S. H., & Swezey, L. W. (1982). Listener responsiveness and the coordination of conversation. *Journal of Personality and Social Psychology*, *43*(4), 718–731. doi:10.1037/0022-3514.43.4.718

Krebs, S., Hobman, E. V., & Bordia, P. (2006). Virtual team and group member dissimilarity: Consequences for the development of trust. *Small Group Research*, *37*, 721–741. doi:10.1177/1046496406294886

Kress, N. (2005). Engaging your employees through the power of communication. *Workspan*, *48*(5), 26–36.

Kriesberg, L. (1998). *Constructive conflicts: From escalation to resolution*. Lanham, MD: Rowman and Littlefield.

Kritzer, H. M., Sarat, A., Trubek, D. M., Bumiller, K., & McNichol, E. (1984). Understanding the Costs of Litigation: The Case of the Hourly-Fee Lawyer. *Law & Social Inquiry*, *9*(3), 559–581. doi:10.1111/j.1747-4469.1984.tb00020.x

Krohe, J. (2011). How much do you know? Too much and not enough. *The Conference Board Review*. Retrieved November 10, 2011, from http://www.tcbreview.com/summer_2011.aspx

Kruse, N. W. (1981). Apologia in team sport. *The Quarterly Journal of Speech, 67*(3), 270–283. doi:10.1080/00335638109383572

Kukulska-Hulme, A. (2012). How should the higher education workforce adapt to advancements in technology for teaching and learning? *The Internet and Higher Education, 15*(4), 247–254. doi:10.1016/j.iheduc.2011.12.002

Kumaraswamy, M. M. (1997). Conflicts, Claims and Disputes in Construction. *Engineering Construction & Architectural Management, 4*(2), 95-111. 10.1046/j.1365-232X.1997.00087.x

Kung, P., & Hagen, C. (2007). The fruits of business process management: An experience report from a Swiss bank. *Business Process Management Journal, 13*(4), 477–487. doi:10.1108/14637150710763522

Küpers, W., & Weibler, J. (2006). How emotional is transformational leadership really? *Leadership and Organization Development Journal, 27*(5), 368–383. doi:10.1108/01437730610677972

Kuppusamy, J., Ganesan, J., & Rosada, S. (2010). Leadership styles and management techniques: An analysis of Malaysian women entrepreneurs. *Communications of the IBIMA,* 1-10. doi:.10.5171/2010.817881

Kwan, P. Y. K. (1996). Application of total quality management in education: Retrospect and prospect. *International Journal of Educational Management, 10*(5), 25–35. doi:10.1108/09513549610146114

Lafky, D. B., & Horan, T. A. (2011). Personal health records: Consumer attitudes toward privacy and security of their personal health information. *Health Informatics Journal, 17*(1), 63–71. doi:10.1177/1460458211399403 PMID:25133771

Lakis, J. (2009). Social conflicts and the culture of co-operation in transitional society. *Baltic Journal of Management, 4*(2), 206–220. doi:10.1108/17465260910958818

Lakshmi, K. (2012). Employee engagement- A corporate boon. 10 ways for effective engagement. *Advances in Management Journal, 5*(2), 64–65.

Landsberger, H. (1961). Horizontal Dimension in Bureaucracy. *Administrative Science Quarterly, 6*(3), 299–322. doi:10.2307/2390705

Lane, F. S. (2003). *The naked employee: How technology is compromising workplace privacy.* New York, NY: AMACOM.

Lasprogata, G., King, N. J., & Pillay, S. (2004). *Regulation of Electronic Employee Monitoring: Identifying Fundamental Principles of Employee Privacy through a Comparative Study of Data Privacy Legislation in the European Union.* Stanford Technology Law Review.

Lassey, W. R., & Sashkin, M. (1983). Theories of leadership: A review of useful research. In W. R. Lassey & M. Sashkin (Eds.), *Leadership and social change* (pp. 91–106). San Diego, CA: United Associates.

Lasswell, H. D. (1927). *Propaganda techniques in the world war.* New York: Knopf.

Lasswell, H. D. (1948). The structure and function of communication is society. In L. Bryson (Ed.), *The new communication of ideas* (pp. 37–51). New York: Harper & Brothers.

Latham, J., & Vinyard, J. (2008). *Organization, diagnosis, design, and transformation.* Monfort Institute: University of North Carolina.

Laudon, K. C., & Laudon, J. P. (2001). *Essentials of management information systems: Organisation and technology in the networked enterprise* (4th ed.). Upper Saddle River, NJ: Prentice Hall.

Laudon, K. C., & Traver, C. G. (2010). *E-Commerce 2010 – Business. Technology. Society* (6th ed.). Upper Saddle River, NJ: Prentice Hall.

Lave, J., & Wenger, E. (1991). *Situated Learning: Legitimate Peripheral Participation.* Cambridge, UK: Cambridge University Press. doi:10.1017/CBO9780511815355

Lavelle, J., Brockner, J., Konovsky, M., Price, K., Henley, A., Taneja, A., & Vinekar, V. (2008). Commitment, procedural fairness, and organizational citizenship behavior: A multifoci analysis. *Journal of Organizational Behavior, 30*(3), 337–357. doi:10.1002/job.518

Lawler, E. E., Hall, D. T., & Oldman, G. R. (1974). Organizational climate: Relationship to organizational structure, process and performance. *Organizational Behavior and Performance*, *11*(1), 139–155. doi:10.1016/0030-5073(74)90010-5

Lawless, W., & Schwartz, M. (2002). The social quantum model of dissonance: From social organization to cultural evolution. *Social Science Computer Review*, *20*(4), 441–450. doi:10.1177/089443902237321

Lawrence, K. (2013). *Developing Leaders in a VUCA environment*. UNC-Kenan-Flagler Business School Whitepaper.

Lawrence, C. R. III. (2005). Forbidden conversations: On race, privacy, and community (A continuing conversation with John Ely on racism and democracy). *The Yale Law Journal*, *114*, 1353–1403.

Lawrence, P. R., & Lorsch, J. W. (1967). *Organization and Environment: Managing Differentiation and Integration*. Cambridge, MA: Harvard University Press.

Lax, D., & Sebenius, J. (1986). *The Manager as Negotiator*. New York: Free Press.

Leeds-Hurwitz, W. (1990). Notes in the History of Intercultural Communication: The Foreign Service Institute and the Mandate for Intercultural Training. *The Quarterly Journal of Speech*, *76*(3), 262–281. doi:10.1080/00335639009383919

Lee, I. (2011). Overview of emerging Web 2.0-based business models and web 2.0 applications in business: An ecological perspective. *International Journal of E-Business Research*, *7*(4), 1–16. doi:10.4018/jebr.2011100101

Lee-Kelley, L. (2002). Situational leadership: Managing the virtual project team. *Journal of Management Development*, *21*, 461–476. doi:10.1108/02621710210430623

Lee, O. (2002). Cultural differences in e-mail use of virtual teams: A critical social theory perspective. *Cyberpsychology & Behavior*, *5*, 227–232. doi:10.1089/109493102760147222 PMID:12123245

Lee, Y. R., & Lazarus, H. (1993). Uses and criticisms of total quality management. *Journal of Management Development*, *12*(7), 5–10. doi:10.1108/02621719310044901

Leinonen, P., Järvelä, S., & Häkkinen, P. (2005). Conceptualizing the awareness of collaboration: A qualitative study of a International team. *Computer Supported Cooperative Work*, *14*(4), 301–322. doi:10.1007/s10606-005-9002-z

Leithwood, K. (1994). Leadership for school restructuring. *Educational Administration Quarterly*, *30*(4), 498–518. doi:10.1177/0013161X94030004006

Leithwood, K., & Menzies, T. (1998). A review of research concerning the implementation of site-based management. *School Effectiveness and School Improvement*, *9*(3), 233–285. doi:10.1080/0924345980090301

Lenhart, A., & Fox, S. (2006). *Bloggers: A portrait of the Internet's new story tellers*. Washington, DC: Pew Internet & American Life Project.

Leonard-Barton, D., & Sensiper, S. (1998). The role of tacit knowledge in group innovation. *California Management Review*, *40*(3), 112–132. doi:10.2307/41165946

Leonard, D., & McAdam, R. (2003). An evaluative framework for TQM dynamics in organisations. *International Journal of Operations & Production Management*, *23*(5/6), 652–677. doi:10.1108/01443570310476663

Leonardi, P. M., Jackson, M., & Marsh, N. (2004). The strategic use of "distance" among virtual team members: A multi-dimensional communication model. In S. Godar (Ed.), *Virtual and collaborative teams* (pp. 156–171). Hershey, PA: Idea Group. doi:10.4018/978-1-59140-204-6.ch009

Leonard, P., & Rintoul, H. (2010). An international collaboration: Examining graduate educational leadership in Louisiana and Ontario. In A. Normore (Ed.), *Advances in educational administration, 11. Global perspectives on educational leadership reform: The development and preparation of leaders of learning and learners of leadership* (pp. 301–321). Emerald Group Publishing Limited. doi:10.1108/S1479-3660(2010)0000011018

Lerman, R. I., & Schmidt, S. R. (1999). *An overview of economic social and demographic trends affecting the U. S. labor market*. Report J-9-M-0048 prepared for the US Department of Labor, Office of the Assistant Secretary for Policy. Washington, DC: Urban Institute.

Lesmerises, D. (2011, June 7). Ohio State President Gordon Gee: "Flurry of activity" led to Jim Tressel resignation. *Cleveland.com.* Retrieved October 27 from http://www.cleveland.com/osu/index.ssf/2011/06/ohio_state_president_gordon_ge.html

Lesmerises, D. (2014a, June 3). Gordon Gee: 'I think everyone won'-closing the book on the Ohio State tattoo scandal. *Cleveland.com.* Retrieved October 27 from http://www.cleveland.com/osu/index.ssf/2014/06/gordon_gee_i_think_everyone_wo.html

Lesmerises, D. (2014b, June 5). Urban Meyer: 'I can tell you there is nothing behind door no. 2'-Closing the book on the Ohio State football scandal. *Cleveland.com.* Retrieved October 28, 2015, 2015 http://www.cleveland.com/osu/index.ssf/2014/06/urban_meyer_i_can_tell_you_the.html

Lesmerises, D. (2014c, June 11). Gene Smith: 'We moved forward a long time ago"- Closing the book on the Ohio State football scandal. *Cleveland.com.* Retrieved October 27 from http://www.cleveland.com/osu/index.ssf/2014/06/gene_smith_our_kids_are_much_f.html

Lesser, E. L., & Storck, J. (2001). Communities of practice and organizational performance. *IBM Systems Journal, 40,* 4. Retrieved February 2, 2009, from http://www.research.ibm.com/journal/sj/404lesser.html

Levine, T. R., Sun Park, H. S., & Kim, R. K. (2007). Some Conceptual and Theoretical Challenges for Cross Cultural Communication Research in the 21st Century. *Journal of Intercultural Communication Research, 36*(3), 205–221. doi:10.1080/17475750701737140

Lewicki, R. J., Saunders, D. M., & Barry, B. (2006). *Negotiation* (5th ed.). Boston: McGraw-Hill Irwin.

Li, Y. (2010). Cross-cultural communication within American and Chinese colleagues in multinational organizations. *Proceedings of the 68th New York State Communication Association.*

Lieberman, H., & Selker, T. (2000). Out of context: Computer systems that adapt to, and learn from, context. *IBM Systems Journal, 39*(3-4), 617 - 632. doi: 10.1147/sj.393.0617

Lind, E. (1990, November). Allan; Kanfer, Ruth; Earley, P. Christopher. (1990) Voice, control, and procedural justice: Instrumental and non-instrumental concerns in fairness judgment. *Journal of Personality and Social Psychology, 59*(5), 952–959. doi:10.1037/0022-3514.59.5.952

Lindell, M. K., & Brandt, C. J. (2000). Climate quality and climate consensus as mediators of the relationship between organizational antecedents and outcomes. *The Journal of Applied Psychology, 85*(3), 331–348. doi:10.1037/0021-9010.85.3.331

Linvill, D. L., McGee, S. E., & Hicks, L. K. (2012). Colleges' and universities' use of Twitter: A content analysis. *Public Relations Review, 38*(4), 636–638. doi:10.1016/j.pubrev.2012.05.010

Lipiainen, H., Karjaluoto, H., & Nevalainen, M. (2014). Digital channels in the internal communication of a multinational corporation. *Corporate Communications. International Journal (Toronto, Ont.), 19*(3), 275–286.

Lipnack, J., & Stamps, J. (2000). *Virtual teams: People working across boundaries with technology* (2nd ed.). New York: Wiley.

Li, Q. (2009). Knowledge building in an online environment: A design-based research study. *Journal of Educational Technology Systems, 37*(2), 195–216. doi:10.2190/ET.37.2.f

Lisak, A., & Erez, M. (2015). Leadership emergence in multicultural teams: The power of global characteristics. *Journal of World Business, 50*(1), 3–14. doi:10.1016/j.jwb.2014.01.002

Li, T., & Slee, T. (2014). The effects of information privacy concerns on digitizing personal health records. *Journal of the Association for Information Science and Technology, 65*(8), 1541–1554. doi:10.1002/asi.23068

Littlejohn, S. W. (1996). *Theories of human communication* (5th ed.). Wadsworth Publishing Company: An International Thomson Publishing Company.

Liu, J., Siu, O., & Shi, K. (2010). Transformational leadership and employee well-being: The mediating role of trust in the leader and self-efficacy. *Applied Psychology, 59*(3), 454–479. doi:10.1111/j.1464-0597.2009.00407.x

Liu, X. J., & Wang, Y. L. (2015). Semantic-based knowledge categorization and organization for product design enterprises. *Journal of Shanghai Jiaotong University (Science)*, *20*(1), 106–112. doi:10.1007/s12204-015-1596-9

Liu, X., Magjuka, R. J., & Lee, S. L. (2008). The effects of cognitive thinking styles, trust, conflict management on online students' learning and virtual team performance. *British Journal of Educational Technology*, *39*(5), 829–846. doi:10.1111/j.1467-8535.2007.00775.x

Locke, E. (1968). *What is job satisfaction?* Washington, DC: American Psychological Association.

Locke, E. A. (1976). The nature and causes of job satisfaction. In M. D. Dunnette (Ed.), *Handbook of industrial and organizational psychology* (pp. 1297–1349). Chicago: Rand McNally.

Locke, E. A. (1976). The nature and causes of job satisfaction. In M. D. Dunnette (Ed.), *Handbook of Industrial and Organizational Psychology* (pp. 297–350). Chicago, IL: Prentice Hall.

Locke, E., Latham, G., & Erez, M. (1988). The determinants of goal commitment. *Academy of Management Review*, *13*(1), 23–39.

Logicalis. (2014). Compilation of reports and white papers. *Employee Behaviour and Attitudes toward Mobile Device Usage at Work*. Logicalis.

Lo, M.-C., & Ramayah, T. (2009). Dimensionality of organizational citizenship behavior (OCB) in a multicultural society: The case of Malaysia. *International Business Research*, *2*(1), 48–55. doi:10.5539/ibr.v2n1p48

Long, D. D. (1997). *Building the knowledge-based organizations: How culture drives knowledge behaviors*. Cambridge, MA: Center for Business Innovation, Ernst & Young LLP.

Long, L. W. (2003). Mapping Organizational Culture: An Integration of Communication and Organizational Design. *Intercultural Communication Studies*, *12*(2), 127–142.

Long, L., & Hazelton, V. (1984). *Assessing communication behavior: An application within the public relations profession. Journal of Applied Communication Martin, J., & Nakayama, T. (2008). Experiencing intercultural communication: An introduction* (3rd ed.). Boston: McGraw-Hill.

Long, S., Aust, D., Abowd, G., & Atkeson, C. (1996). Cyberguide: Prototyping context-aware mobile applications. In *Conference Companion on Human Factors in Computing Systems, CHI '96* (pp. 293–294). New York, NY: ACM.

Lorenz, E. (2007). *The essence of chaos. Taylor and Francis CRC ebook account*. Kindle Edition.

Loseke, D. R., & Cahil, S. E. (2007). Publishing qualitative manuscripts: Lessons learned. In C. Seale, G. Gobo, J. F. Gubrium, & D. Silverman (Eds.), *Qualitative Research Practice: Concise Paperback Edition* (pp. 491–506). London: Sage.

Louis Harris and Associates. (1999). *Poll*. Retrieved from http://www.natlconsumersleague.org/FNLSUM1.PDF

Lovejoy, K., Waters, R. D., & Saxton, G. D. (2012). Engaging stakeholders through Twitter: How nonprofit organizations are getting more out of 140 characters or less. *Public Relations Review*, *38*(2), 313–318. doi:10.1016/j.pubrev.2012.01.005

Lowes, S., Lin, P., & Wang, Y. (2007). Studying the effectiveness of the discussion forum in online professional development courses. *Journal of Interactive Online Learning*, *6*(3), 181–210.

Luft, J. (1969). *Of human interaction*. Palo Alto, CA: National Press Book.

Luft, J. (1970). *Group processes: An introduction to group dynamics*. Palo Alto, CA: Mayfield.

Lundvall, B.-Å. (1992). *National Systems of Innovation: Towards a Theory of Innovation and Interactive Learning*. London: Pinter.

Lunenburg, F. C. (2010). Communication: The process, barriers, and improving effectiveness. *Schooling*, *1*(1), 1–11.

Lustig, M. W., & Koester, J. (2010). *Intercultural competence: interpersonal communication across cultures*. Boston: Pearson/Allyn & Bacon.

Lynch, M. D. (1970). Stylistic analysis. In P. Emmert & W. D. Brooks (Eds.), *Method of research in communications* (pp. 315–342). New York: Houghton Miffin.

Macey, W., & Schneider, B. (2008). The meaning of employee engagement. *Industrial and Organizational Psychology: Perspectives on Science and Practice, 1*(1), 3–30. doi:10.1111/j.1754-9434.2007.0002.x

Madan, A., Waber, B., Ding, M., Kominers, P., & Pentland, A. (2009). Reality Mining: The End of Personal Privacy. In *Proceedings of 1st Engaging Data Forum.*

Madden, M., Fox, S., Smith, A., & Vitak, J. (2007).*Digital footprints: Online identity management and search in the age of transparency.* Academic Press.

Madhavan, R., & Griver, R. (1998). From embedded knowledge to embodied knowledge: New product development as knowledge management. *Journal of Marketing, 62*(4), 1–12. doi:10.2307/1252283

Madjeski, M., Johnson, M., & Bellovin, S. M. (2011). *The Failure of Online Social Network Privacy Settings.* Columbia University Computer Science Technical Reports.

Madlock, P. E. (2006a). *Supervisor' nonverbal immediacy behaviors and their relationship to subordinates' communication satisfaction, job satisfaction, and willingness to collaborate.* Paper presented at the National Communication Association Convention, San Antonio, Texas.

Madlock, P. E. (2006b). Do difference in displays of nonverbal immediacy and communication competence between male and female supervisors affect subordinates, job satisfaction. *Ohio Communication Journal, 44*, 61–78.

Madlock, P. E. (2008). The link between leadership style, communicator competence, and employee satisfaction. *Journal of Business Communication, 45*(1), 61–78. doi:10.1177/0021943607309351

Madu, C. N., Aheto, J., Kuei, C., & Winokur, D. (1994). Adoption of strategic total quality management philosophies: Multi-criteria decision analysis model. *International Journal of Quality & Reliability Management, 13*(3), 57–72. doi:10.1108/02656719610116081

Madu, C. N., & Kuei, C. (1993). Dimensions of quality teaching in higher institutions. *Total Quality Management, 4*(3), 325–338. doi:10.1080/09544129300000046

Magnusson, P., Schuster, A., & Taras, V. (2014). A process-based explanation of the psychic distance paradox: Evidence from global virtual teams. *Management International Review, 54*(3), 283–306. doi:10.1007/s11575-014-0208-5

Mahalinga Shiva, M. M., & Suar, D. (2012). Transformational leadership, organizational culture, organizational effectiveness, and programme outcomes in non-governmental organizations. *Voluntas: International Journal of Voluntary & Nonprofit Organizations, 23*(3), 684–710. doi:10.1007/s11266-011-9230-4

Major, W. (2014, Fall). Contagion in the classroom: The need for physical and emotional connectedness for deep learning classrooms offering social experience. *Liberal Education, 100*(4), 66–69.

Makau, J. (2009). Ethical and unethical communication. In W. Eadie (Ed.), 21st century communication: A reference handbook. (pp. 435-444). Thousand Oaks, CA: SAGE Publications, Inc. doi:10.4135/9781412964005.n48

Making Light of Domestic Violence. (n.d.). *Adweek.* Retrieved from http://www.adweek.com/adfreak/digiorno-really-really-sorry-about-its-tweet-accidentally-making-light-domestic-violence-159998

Malamed, C. (2009). *10 ways to organize instructional content.* E-Learning podcast 2.0.

Malhotra, N. K., Kim, S. S., & Agarwal, J. (2004).Internet Users' Information Privacy Concerns (IUIPC): The Construct, the Scale and a Causal Model. *Information Systems Research, 15*(4), 336–355.

Mali, F. (2005). Global-Local Dialectics in the Process of European Scientific Integration. Institute for Advanced Studies on Science, Technology and Society.

Malik, M., Nawab, S., Naeem, B., & Danish, R. Q. (2010). Job satisfaction and organizational commitment of University teachers in public sector of Pakistan. *International Journal of Business and Management, 5*(6), 17–26. doi:10.5539/ijbm.v5n6p17

Mallak, L. A., Lyth, D. M., Olson, S. D., Ulshafer, S. M., & Sardone, F. J. (2003). Culture, the built environment, and healthcare organizational performance.*Managing Service Quality, 13*(1), 27–38. doi:10.1108/09604520310456690

Malmberg, A., & Maskell, P. (2002). The elusive concept of localization economies: Towards a knowledge-based theory of spatial clustering. *Environment & Planning A, 34*(3), 429–449. doi:10.1068/a3457

Malone, T. W., Grant, K. R., Lai, K.-Y., Rao, R., & Rosenblitt, D. (1987). Semistructured messages are surprisingly useful for computer-supported coordination. *ACM Transactions on Information Systems, 5*(2), 115–131. doi:10.1145/27636.27637

Management, N. Z. (2012). A conversation across the generations. *New Zealand Management, 59*(6), 21.

Mangold, W. G., & Faulds, D. J. (2009). Social media: The new hybrid element of the promotion mix. *Business Horizons, 52*(4), 357–365. doi:10.1016/j.bushor.2009.03.002

Manso, J. (1996). Estatística descritiva e previsão (2ª ed.). Covilhã: Universidade da Beira Interior.

Maritz, D. (1995). Leadership and mobilizing potential. *Human Resource Management, 10*(1), 8–16.

Markow, D., Macia, L., & Lee, H. (2013). *The MetLife survey of the American teacher: Challenges for school leadership*. New York, NY: Metropolitan Life Insurance Company.

Marks, H. M., & Printy, S. M. (2003). Principal leadership and school performance: An Integration of Transformational and Instructional Leadership. *Educational Administration Quarterly, 39*(3), 370–397. doi:10.1177/0013161X03253412

Marmasse, N., Schmandt, C., & Spectre, D. (2004). WatchMe: Communication and Awareness Between Members of a Closely-Knit Group. UbiComp 2004: Ubiquitous Computing (pp. 214-231).

Maroco, J. (2007). Análise Estatística com utilização do SPSS (3ª ed.). Lisboa: Edições Sílabo.

Maroco, J., & Garcia-Marques, T. (2006). Qual a fiabilidade do alfa de Cronbach? Questões antigas e soluções modernas? *Laboratório de Psicologia, 4*(1), 65–90.

Marr, B. (2013). *How Big Data Will Change People Management Forever*. Retrieved from http://smartdatacollective.com

Marshall, A. (2011, March 8). Ohio State football coach Jim Tressel suspended 2 games, fined $250,000 in aftermath of Yahoo report. *Cleveland.com*. Retrieved June 14, 2011 from http://www.cleveland.com/osu/index.ssf/2011/03/post_36.html

Marshall, B., Choi, J., El-Shinnaway, M. M., North, M., Svensson, L., Wang, S., & Valenzuala, J. P. et al. (2009). Online and offline social ties of social network website users: An exploratory study in eleven societies. *Journal of Computer Information Systems, 50*(1), 54–64.

Martins, L. L., Gilson, L. L., & Maynard, M. T. (2004). Virtual teams: What do we know and where do we go from here? *Journal of Management, 30*, 805–835. doi:10.1016/j.jm.2004.05.002

Maruping, L. M., & Agarwal, R. (2004). Managing team interpersonal processes through technology: A task–technology fit perspective. *The Journal of Applied Psychology, 89*, 975–990. doi:10.1037/0021-9010.89.6.975 PMID:15584836

Marx, G., & Sherizen, S. (1991). Monitoring on the job: How to protect privacy as well as property. In T. Forester (Ed.), *Computers in the human context: Information technology, productivity, and people* (pp. 397–406). Cambridge, MA: MIT Press.

Massaguer, D., Hore, B., Diallo, M. H., Mehrotra, S., & Venkatasubramanian, N. (2009) Middleware for pervasive spaces: Balancing privacy and utility. In *Proceedings of the 10th ACM/I- FIP/USENIX International Conference on Middleware*. New York, NY: Springer-Verlag New York, Inc. doi:10.1007/978-3-642-10445-9_13

Massey, A. P., Montoya-Weiss, M., Hung, C., & Ramesh, V. (2001). Cultural perceptions of task-technology fit: Acknowledging cultural differences helps companies build the strongest International teams and determine the strongest tool they need. *Communications of the ACM, 44*(12), 83–84. doi:10.1145/501317.501353

Massingham, P. (2015). Knowledge sharing: What works and what doesn't work: A critical systems thinking perspective. *Systemic Practice and Action Research, 28*(3), 197–228. doi:10.1007/s11213-014-9330-3

Masters, G. N. (2010). *Teaching and learning school improvement framework. Melbourne: Australian Council for Educational Research (ACER)*. Brisbane: Department of Education and Training.

Mastrofski, S. D., Snipes, J. B., & Supina, A. E. (1996). Compliance on demand: The public's response to specific police requests. *Journal of Research in Crime and Delinquency, 33*(3), 269–305. doi:10.1177/0022427896033003001

Masuch, M. (1985). Vicious circles in organizations. *Administrative Science Quarterly, 30*(1), 14–33. doi:10.2307/2392809

Mavender, K., & Shamsudin, S. (2012). Writing professional discourse: The challenges faced by Malaysian engineers. *The Asian ESP Journal, 8*(4), 125–161.

Maxwell, J. C. (2002). *Cele 21 de legi supreme ale liderului*. Editura Amaltea, Bucaresti.

Mayer, J. D., & Salovey, P. (1997). *What is Emotional Intelligence?*. Retrieved September 2, 2015, from http://www.unh.edu/emotional_intelligence/EI%20Assets/Reprints...EI%20Proper/EI1997MSWhatIsEI.pdf

Mayer, M. D., Caruso, C. R., & Salovey, P. (2004). Emotional Intelligence Meets Traditional Standards for an Intelligence. *Intelligence, 27*(4), 267-298.

Mayer, R. C., Davis, J. D., & Schoorman, F. D. (1995). An integrative model of organisational trust. *Academy of Management Review, 20*(3), 709–734.

Mazerolle, L., Antrobus, E., Bennett, S., & Tyler, T. R. (2012b). Shaping citizens perceptions of police legitimacy: A randomized field trial of procedural justice. *Criminology, 51*(1), 33–64. doi:10.1111/j.1745-9125.2012.00289.x

Mazerolle, L., Bennett, S., Antrobus, E., & Eggins, E. (2012a). Procedural Justice, routine encounters, and citizen perceptions of police: Main findings from the Queensland Community Engagement Trial (QCET). *Journal of Experimental Criminology, 8*(4), 343–367. doi:10.1007/s11292-012-9160-1

Mazerolle, L., Bennett, S., Davis, J., Sargeant, E., & Manning, M. (2013). Procedural Justice and police legitimacy: A systematic review of the research evidence. *Journal of Experimental Criminology, 9*(3), 245–274. doi:10.1007/s11292-013-9175-2

Mazerolle, L., Sargeant, E., Cherney, A., Bennett, S., & Murphy, K. (2014). *Antrobus, E., and Martin, P.* Procedural Justice and Police Legitimacy in Policing.

Mc Dermott, R. (1999). Nurturing Three Dimensional communities of Practice: How to get the most out of human networks. *Knowledge management Review*. Retrieved February 2, 2009, from http://www.co-i-l.com/coil/knowledge-garden/cop/dimensional.shtml

McAdam, R., Leonard, D., Henderson, J., & Hazlett, S. A. (2006). A grounded theory research approach to building and testing TQM theory in operations management. *International Journal of Management Sciences, 36*, 825–837. doi:10.1016/j.omega.2006.04.005

McAnany, E. (1988). Wilbur Schramm, 1907-1987: Roots of the past, seeds of the present. *Journal of Communication, 38*(4), 109–122. doi:10.1111/j.1460-2466.1988.tb02073.x

McCafferty, S. G. (2002). Gesture and Creating Zones of Proximal Development for Second Language Learning. *Modern Language Journal, 86*(2), 192–203. doi:10.1111/1540-4781.00144

McCauley, C. (2006). *Developmental assignments: Creating learning experiences without changing jobs*. Greensboro, NC: N.C. Center for Creative Leadership Press.

McCluskey, J. D. (2003). *Police requests for compliance: Coercive and procedurally just tactics*. LFB Scholarly Pub.

McCormack, K. P. (2001). Business process orientation: Do you have it? *Quality Progress, 34*(1), 51–60.

McCormack, K. P. (2007). *Business process maturity: Theory and application*. Raleigh, NC: DRK Research.

McCormack, K. P., & Johnson, W. C. (2001). *Business process orientation: Gaining the e-business competitive advantage*. Boca Raton, FL: St. Lucie Press. doi:10.1201/9781420025569

McCormack, K. P., Johnson, W. C., & Walker, W. T. (2003). *Supply chain networks and business process orientation*. Boca Raton, FL: St. Lucie Press.

McCroskey, J. & Young, T. (1981). Ethos and credibility: the construct and its measurement after three decades. *Central States Speech Journal, 32*(981), 24-34.

McCroskey, J. C., & McCroskey, L. L. (1988). Self-report as an approach to measuring communication competence. *Communication Research Reports, 5*(2), 108–113. doi:10.1080/08824098809359810

McDermott, R. (1999). Why Information Technology Inspired But Cannot Deliver Knowledge Management. *California Management Review, 41*(3), 103–117. doi:10.2307/41166012

McDermott, R., & O'Dell, C. (2001). Overcoming cultural barriers to sharing knowledge. *Journal of Knowledge Management, 5*(1), 76–85. doi:10.1108/13673270110384428

McEvers, K. (2015, March). Starbucks' 'Race Together' campaign begins. *NPR*. Retrieved from http://www.npr.org/2015/03/21/394517431/starbucks-race-together-campaign-begins

McFadzean, E., O'Loughlin, A., & Shaw, E. (2005). Corporate entrepreneurship and innovation part 1: The missing link. *European Journal of Innovation Management, 8*(3), 350–372. doi:10.1108/14601060510610207

McGovern, F. E. (1996). *Beyond efficiency: A bevy of ADR justifications (An unfootnoted summary)*. Dispute Resolution Magazine, 3.

McGregor, D. (1967). *The professional manager*. New York, NY: McGraw–Hill.

McKimm, J. (2003). Assuring quality and standards in teaching. In H. Fry, S. M. Ketteridge, & S. Marshall (Eds.), *A Handbook for Teaching and Learning in Higher Education* (2nd ed., pp. 182–199). London: Kogan Page.

Mckinney, E. H. Jr, Barker, J. R., Davis, K. J., & Smith, D. (2005). How Swift Starting Action Teams Get off the Ground: What United Flight 232 and Airline Flight Crews Can Tell Us About Team Communication. *Management Communication Quarterly, 19*(2), 198–237. doi:10.1177/0893318905278539

McKinsey Global Institute. (2013). *Disruptive technologies: Advances that will transform life, business, and the global economy*. Technical Report.

McLaren, P. (2000). *Ché Guevara, Paulo Freire, and the pedagogy of revolution*. Lanham, MD: Rowman & Littlefield.

McLarty, J., & McCartney, D. (2009). The nurse manager the neglected middle. *Healthc Financ, 63*(8), 74.

McLaughlin, S., Paton, R. A., & Macbeth, D. K. (2008). Barrier impact on organizational learning within complex organizations. *Journal of Knowledge Management, 12*(2), 107–123. doi:10.1108/13673270810859550

McNamara, R. S. (1995). *In Retrospect: The Tragedy and Lessons of Vietnam*. New York: Random House, Inc.

McNeill, D. (1992). Hand and mind: What gestures reveal about thought (1st ed.). Chicago, IL: Chicago University Press.

McParland, C., & Connolly, R. (2009). *The role of dataveillance in the organisation: Some emerging trends*. Paper presented at the Irish Academy of Management Conference, Galway, Ireland.

McPhail, M. L. (2003). Race and the (im)possibility of dialogue. In R. Anderson, L. Baxter, & K. Cisna (Eds.), *Dialogue: Theorizing difference in communication studies* (pp. 209–224). Thousand Oaks, CA: Sage Publications.

McShane, S. L., & Von Glinow, M. A. (2003). *Organizational behavior: Emerging realities for the workplace revolution* (2nd ed.). Boston, MA: McGraw-Hill.

McSweeney, B. (2002). Hofstede's model of national cultural differences and their consequences: A triumph of faith - a failure of analysis. *Human Relations, 55*(1), 89–118. doi:10.1177/0018726702055001602

Means, B., Bakia, M., & Murphy, R. (2014). *Learning online: What research tells us about whether, when and how*. New York, NY: Routledge.

Mehra, S., & Ranganathan, S. (2008). Implementing total quality management with a focus on enhancing customer satisfaction. *International Journal of Quality & Reliability Management, 25*(9), 913-927. doi: 02656710810908070

Mehra, S., Hoffman, J., & Sirias, D. (2001). TQM as a management strategy for the next millenia. *International Journal of Operations & Production Management, 21*(6), 855–877. doi:10.1108/01443570110390534

Meisel, Z., & Oldham, J. (2011, May 24). Ray Small tells all: Ex-Buckeye says he sold memorabilia, some players don't 'think about' rules. *The Lantern.* Retrieved October 14, 2015 from http://thelantern.com/2011/05/ray-small-tells-all-ex-buckeye-says-he-sold-memorabilia-some-players-dont-think-about-rules/

Meister, J. C., & Willyerd, K. (2010). Mentoring millennials. *Harvard Business Review*, (May): 1–5. PMID:20429252

Mendonca, E. A., Chen, E. S., Stetson, P. D., McKnight, L. K., Lei, J., & Cimino, J. J. (2004). Approach to mobile information and communication for health care. *International Journal of Medical Informatics*, *73*(7), 631–638. doi:10.1016/j.ijmedinf.2004.04.013 PMID:15246044

Men, L. R., & Stacks, D. (2014). The effects of authentic leadership on strategic internal communication and employee-organization relationships. *Journal of Public Relations Research*, *26*(4), 301–324. doi:10.1080/1062726X.2014.908720

Metcalfe, A., Fisher, D., Gingras, Y., Jones, G., Rubenson, K., & Snee, I. (2010 October/November). How influential are faculty today? Responses from the Canadian Professorate. *Academic Matters Journal of Higher Education*, 16-20.

Metcalfe, B. (2009). *Developing women's capability in the public sector in Middle East.* Paper presented at the International Conference on Administrative Development: Towards Excellence in the Public Sector, Riyadh, Saudi Arabia.

Meyer, E. (2010). Leadership: The four keys to success with virtual teams. *Forbes.* Retrieved August 1, 2012 from http://www.forbes.com/2010/08/19/virtual-teams-meetings-leadership-managing-cooperation.html

Meyer, J. P., & Allen, N. J. (1997). *Commitment in the workplace.* Thousand Oaks, CA: Sage.

Meyer, J. P., Stanley, D. J., Hescovitch, L., & Topolnytsky, L. (2002). Affective continuance and normative commitment to the organization: A meta-analysis of antecedents, correlates and consequences. *Journal of Vocational Behavior*, *61*(1), 20–52. doi:10.1006/jvbe.2001.1842

Meyer, J., & Herscovitch, L. (2001). Commitment in the workplace: Toward a general model. *Human Resource Management Review*, *11*(3), 299–326. doi:10.1016/S1053-4822(00)00053-X

Meyers, J. D. (2012). *What Is Emotional Intelligence (EI)?* Retrieved September 2, 2015, from http://www.unh.edu/emotional_intelligence/ei%20What%20is%20EI/ei%20fourbranch.htm

Milewski, A., & Smith, T. (2000). *Providing presence cues to telephone users.* Paper presented at the 2000 ACM conference on Computer supported cooperative work. doi:10.1145/358916.358978

Milgram, R. M., Dunn, R., & Price, G. E. (Eds.). (1993). *Teaching and counseling gifted and talented adolescents: An international learning style perspective.* Westport, CT: Praeger.

Miller, D., & Shamsie, J. (1996). The resource-based view of the firm in two environments: The Hollywood firm studios from 1936 to 1965. *Academy of Management Journal*, *39*(3), 519–543. doi:10.2307/256654

Miller, V., Johnson, J., & Grau, J. (1994). Antecedents to willingness to participate in a planned organizational change. *Journal of Applied Communication Research*, *22*(1), 59–80. doi:10.1080/00909889409365387

Mills, P. K., & Ungson, G. (2003). Reassessing the limits of structural empowerment: Organizational constitution and trust as controls. *Academy of Management Review*, *28*(1), 143–153.

Milton, N., Shadbolt, N., Cottman, H., & Hammersley, M. (1999). Towards a knowledge technology for knowledge management. *International Journal of Human-Computer Studies*, *51*(3), 615–641. doi:10.1006/ijhc.1999.0278

Mind Tools Ltd. (2015). *Leadership Styles: Choosing the Right Approach for the Situation.* Retrieved September 2, 2015, from http://www.mindtools.com/pages/article/newLDR_84.htm

Minnick, A., Pischke-Winn, K., & Sterk, M. B. (1994). Introducing a two-way wireless communication system. *Nursing Management*, *25*(7), 42–47. doi:10.1097/00006247-199407000-00011 PMID:8044475

Min, P. G. (1992). A comparison of the Korean minorities in China and Japan. *International Migration Review, 26*(1), 4–21. doi:10.2307/2546934 PMID:12285045

Mirabella, L. (2014, October). Starbucks teams with city to address community problems. *Baltimore Sun.* Retrieved from http://www.baltimoresun.com/business/bs-bz-starbucks-baltimore-youth-employment-20141020-story.html

Mishra, A. K., & Spreitzer, G. M. (1998). Explaining How Survivors Respond to Downsizing: The Roles of Trust, Empowerment, Justice and Work Redesign. *Academy of Management Review, 23*(3), 567-588.

Mishra, K. E., & Boynton, L. (2009). *Talk-the-Talk: Using InternalCommunication to Build Trust with Employees.* International Public Relations Research Conference, Miami, FL.

Mishra, K. E., & Schwarz, G. M. (2011). The Evolution of Trust and Control as Seen through an Organization's Human Resources Practices. In R. Searle (Eds.), Trust and Human Resource Management. Cheltenham, UK: Edward Elgar.

Mishra, K. E., Walker, K., & Mishra, A. K. (2014). Employee Use of Social Media in the Workplace: How "Lenovo Central" brings employees together. In I. Lee (Ed.), Integrating Social Media into Business Practice, Applications, Management, and Models. Academic Press.

Mishra, A. K. (1996). Organizational responses to crisis: The centrality of trust. In R. Kramer & T. Tyler (Eds.), *Trust in organizations* (pp. 261–287). Newbury Park, CA: Sage. doi:10.4135/9781452243610.n13

Mishra, A. K., & Mishra, K. E. (1994). The role of mutual trust in effective downsizing strategies. *Human Resource Management, 33*(2), 261–279. doi:10.1002/hrm.3930330207

Mishra, A. K., & Mishra, K. E. (2013). *Becoming a Trustworthy Leader: Psychology & Practice.* Routledge Press.

Mishra, K. E., Boynton, L., & Mishra, A. K. (2014). Driving Employee Engagement: The Expanded Role of Internal Communications. *Journal of Business Communication, 51*(2), 183–202. doi:10.1177/2329488414525399

MIT Massachusetts Institute of Technology. (2009, August). *Advanced Managerial Communication.* Accessed from the Web: http://ocw.mit.edu/courses/sloan-school-of-management/

Mitchell, S., Spiteri, M. D., Bates, J., & Coulouris, G. (2000). *Context-aware multimedia computing in the intelligent hospital.* Paper presented at the 9th workshop on ACM SIGOPS European workshop: beyond the PC: new challenges for the operating system, Kolding, Denmark. doi:10.1145/566726.566730

Mitra, S., & Dangwal, R. (2010). Limits to self-organising systems of learning - The Kalikuppam experiment. *British Journal of Educational Technology, 41*(5), 672–688. doi:10.1111/j.1467-8535.2010.01077.x

Mitroff, I. I. (1998). *Smart thinking for crazy times: The art of solving the right problems.* San Francisco: Berrett-Koehler.

Mitrou, L. & Karyda, M. (2006). Employees' privacy vs. employers' security: Can they be balanced?. *Telematics and Informatics, 23*(3), 164-178.

Mitrou, L., & Karyda, M. (2009). Bridging the Gap between Employee Surveillance and Privacy Protection. In M. Gupta & R. Sharman (Eds.), *Social and Human Elements of Information Security: Emerging Trends and Countermeasures.* doi:10.4018/978-1-60566-036-3.ch016

Mizzaro, S., Nazzi, E., & Vassena, L. (2008). *Retrieval of context-aware applications on mobile devices: how to evaluate?* Paper presented at the second international symposium on Information interaction in context, London, UK. doi:10.1145/1414694.1414710

Modell, S. (2009). Bundling management control innovations: A field study of organisational experimenting with total quality management and the balanced scorecard. *Accounting, Auditing & Accountability Journal, 22*(1), 59-90. doi: 09513570910923015

Moffitt, M. L., & Bordone, R. C. (Eds.). (2005). *The Handbook of Dispute Resolution.* San Francisco, CA: Jossey-Bass.

Moldenhauser-Salazar, R. (1999). *Visions and missions: A case study of organizational change and diversity in higher education* (Doctoral Dissertation, University of Michigan). Retrieved from ProQuest Dissertations and Theses Databases (UMI: 9959824).

Moliner, C., Martinez-Tur, V., Peiro, J. M., Ramos, J., & Cropanzano, R. (2005). Relationships between organizational justice and burnout at the work-unit level. *International Journal of Stress Management, 12*(2), 99–116. doi:10.1037/1072-5245.12.2.99

Molinet, J. (2015, April). Back to school! Starbucks offers baristas free college tuition in landmark deal with Arizona State University. *New York Daily News*. Retrieved from http://www.nydailynews.com/news/national/starbucks-offers-baristas-free-college-tuition-article-1.2175742

Molinsky, A., & Hahn, M. (2015a, April6). Learning the language of indirectness. *Harvard Business Review*.

Molinsky, A., & Hahn, M. (2015b, April8). Building relationships in cultures that don't do small talk. *Harvard Business Review*.

Moll, L., Amanti, C., Neff, D., & González, N. (1992). Funds of knowledge for teaching: Using a qualitative approach to connect homes and classrooms. *Theory into Practice, 31*(2), 132–141. doi:10.1080/00405849209543534

Monash University. (2010, January). *Managerial Communication*. Retrieved from http://www.monash.edu.au/

Moncada-Paternò-Castello, P. (2011). The growth of companies in the EU: the case for a more sophisticated research and innovation policy. IPTS Policy Briefs Series.

Moncada-Paternò-Castello, P., & Voigt, P. (2013). *The effect of innovative SMEs' growth to the structural renewal of the EU economy-a projection to 2020*. Academic Press.

Moncada-Paternò-Castello, P., Ciupagea, C., Smith, K., Tübke, A., & Tubbs, M. (2010, April). Does Europe perform too little corporate R&D? A comparison of EU and non-EU corporate R&D performance. *Research Policy, 39*(4), 523–536. doi:10.1016/j.respol.2010.02.012

Mone, E., & London, M. (2009). *Employee engagement: Through effective performance management*. New York, NY: Taylor-Francis Group.

Montecinos, C., Madrid, R., Fernández, M. B., & Ahumada, L. (2014). A goal orientation analysis of teachers' motivations to participate in the school self-assessment processes of a quality assurance system in Chile. *Educational Assessment, Evaluation and Accountability, 26*(3), 241–261. doi:10.1007/s11092-014-9190-5

Montes, F. J., Moreno, A. R., & Fernandez, L. M. (2004). Assessing the organizational climate and contractual relationship for perceptions of support for innovation. *International Journal of Manpower, 25*(2), 167–180. doi:10.1108/01437720410535972

Montoya-Wiess, M. M., Massey, A. P., & Song, M. (2001). Getting it together: Temporal coordination and conflict management in global virtual teams. *Academy of Management Journal, 44*, 1251–1263. doi:10.2307/3069399

Moore, C. (1989). *The Mediation Process*. San Francisco: Jossey Bass.

Moore, C. W. (2014). *The mediation process: Practical strategies for resolving conflict*. New York, NY: John Wiley & Sons.

Moore, M. (2010). *Capitalism: A love story*. Beverly Hills, CA: Anchor Bay Entertainment.

Moorman, R. H. (1991). Relationship between organizational justice and organizational citizenship behaviors: Do fairness perceptions influence employee citizenship? *The Journal of Applied Psychology, 76*(6), 759–776. doi:10.1037/0021-9010.76.6.845

Mor Barack, M. E. (2010). *Managing diversity toward a global Inclusive workplace* (2nd ed.). Thousand Oaks, CA: Sage Publications.

Moran, E. T., & Volkwein, J. F. (1992). The cultural approach to the formation of organizational climate. *Human Relations, 45*(1), 19–47. doi:10.1177/001872679204500102

Moran, M., Seaman, J., & Tinti-Kane, H. (2011). *Teaching, Learning, and Sharing: How Today's Higher Education*. Boston: Pearson Learning Solutions.

Moreau, R. (2013). *The value of foreign languages in business communication*. Retrieved on May 1, 2015, available at http://scholarsarchive.jwu.edu/cgi/viewcontent.cgi?article=1016&context=mba_student

Morell, T. (2015). International conference paper presentations: A multimodal analysis to determine effectiveness. *English for Specific Purposes, 37*, 137–150. doi:10.1016/j.esp.2014.10.002

Morgan, L., Paucar-caceres, A., & Wright, G. (2014). Leading effective global virtual teams: The consequences of methods of communication. *Systemic Practice and Action Research, 27*(6), 607–624. doi:10.1007/s11213-014-9315-2

Morrison, E. W. (1994). Role definitions and organizational citizenship behavior: The importance of the employee's perspective. *Academy of Management Journal, 37*(6), 1543–1567. doi:10.2307/256798

Morrison, T. (2007). *The bluest eye.* New York, NY: Vintage International.

Mossholder, K. W., Bennett, N., Kemery, E. R., & Wesolowski, M. A. (1998). Relationships between bases of power and work reactions: The mediational role of procedural justice. *Journal of Management, 24*(4), 533–552. doi:10.1177/014920639802400404

Moten, J., Fitterer, A., Brazier, E., Leonard, J., & Brown, A. (2013). Examining online college cyber cheating methods and preventative measures. *The Electronic Journal of E-Learning, 11*(2), 139–146.

Motowidlo, S. J., & Borman, W. C. (1978). Relationships between military morale, motivation, satisfaction, and unit effectiveness. *The Journal of Applied Psychology, 63*(1), 47–52. doi:10.1037/0021-9010.63.1.47

Mottl, J. (2015). Reports: Wearables primed for big growth, with Apple Watch driving adoption. *FierceMobile Healthcare.* Retrieved from: http://www.fiercemobilehealthcare.com/story/reports-wearables-primed-big-growth-apple-watch-driving-adoption/2015-02-22

Moulaert, F., & Nussbaumer, J. (2005). Beyond the Learning Region: the Dialectics of Innovation and Culture in Territorial Development. In R. A. Boschma & R. C. Kloosterman (Eds.), *Learning from Clusters: A Critical Assessment* (pp. 89–109). Netherlands: Springer. doi:10.1007/1-4020-3679-5_5

Mouly, S., & Sankaran, J. (2002). The enactment of envy within organizations. Insights from a New Zealand academic department. *The Journal of Applied Behavioral Science, 38*(1), 36–56. doi:10.1177/0021886302381003

Mounter, P. (2003). Global internal communication: A model. *Journal of Communication Management, 7*(3), 3. doi:10.1108/13632540310807412

Mowday, R. T., Porter, L. W., & Dubin, R. (1974). Unit performance, situational factors and employee attitudes in spatially separate work units. *Organizational Behavior and Human Performance, 12*(2), 231–248. doi:10.1016/0030-5073(74)90048-8

Mowlana, H. (1986). *Global information and world communication.* White Plains, NY: Longman.

Mowry, D. (2005, December 2). Cultural competence: Oregon style. *Oregon Catalyst.com.* Retrieved October 11, 2009, from http://www.oregoncatalyst.com/index.php/archives/20-Cultural-Competence;-Oregon-Style.html

Mueller, J. (2015). Formal and informal practices of knowledge sharing between project teams and enacted cultural characteristics. *Project Management Journal, 46*(1), 53–68. doi:10.1002/pmj.21471

Mulford, B. (2008) The leadership challenge improving learning in schools. Australian Education Review. Melbourne: Australian Council for Educational Research (ACER).

Mullen, J. E., & Kelloway, E. (2009). Safety leadership: A longitudinal study of the effects of transformational leadership on safety outcomes. *Journal of Occupational and Organizational Psychology, 82*(2), 253–272. doi:10.1348/096317908X325313

Mullin, J., Adam, R. M., Halliwell, J. E., & Milligan, L. P. (1999). *Science, technology, and Innovation in Chile, International Development Research Centre.* Canada: IDRC Books.

Muna, F. A. (2011). Contextual Leadership: A Study of Lebanese Executives Working in the Lebanon, the GCC Countries, and the United States. *Journal of Management Development, 30*(9), 865–881. doi:10.1108/02621711111164349

Muna, F. A., & Khoury, G. C. (2012). *The Palestinian Executive: Leadership Under Challenging Conditions.* Farnham: Gower.

Muna, F. A., & Zennie, Z. A. (2011). *Developing Multicultural Leaders: The Journey to Leadership.* Basingstoke: Palgrave Macmillan. doi:10.1057/9781137104649

Muna, F., & Khoury, G. (2012). *The Palestianian executive: Leadership under challenging conditions.* Farnham, UK: Gower Publishing Ltd.

Munoz, M. A., Rodriguez, M., Favela, J., Martinez-Garcia, A. I., & Gonzalez, V. M. (2003). Context-aware mobile communication in hospitals. *Computer*, *36*(9), 38–46. doi:10.1109/MC.2003.1231193

Munter, M. (2011). *Guide to Managerial Communication* (8th ed.). Prentice Hall Publisher.

Murgatroyd, S., & Morgan, C. (1993). *Total quality management and the school.* Buckingham, UK: Open University Press.

Murphy, T., & Lucey, C. (2014). Wellness programs grow more popular with employers. *Mercury News.* Retrieved from: http://www.mercurynews.com/health/ci_25639907/wellness-programs-grow-more-popular-employers

Murphy, J., & Vriesenga, M. (2006). Research on school leadership preparation in the United States: An analysis. *School Leadership & Management*, *26*(2), 183–195. doi:10.1080/13634230600589758

Murphy, L. R., & Sauter, S. L. (2003). The USA perspective: Current issues and trends in the management of work stress. *Australian Psychologist*, *38*(2), 151–158. doi:10.1080/00050060310001707157

Mustafa, R., & Zain, S. N. M. (2009). Language anxiety in a remedial English language course: What teachers need to know. *Journal of Linguistics Studies*, *2*(1), 56–68.

Myerson, S. G., & Mitchell, A. R. J. (2003). Mobile phones in hospitals. *BMJ (Clinical Research Ed.)*, *326*(7387), 460–461. doi:10.1136/bmj.326.7387.460 PMID:12609917

Myers, S. A., & Kassing, J. W. (1998). The relationship between perceived supervisory communication behaviors and subordinate organizational identification. *Communication Research Reports*, *15*(1), 71–81. doi:10.1080/08824099809362099

Naami, A., & Asadi, P. (2011). Study on the mediating role of innovative climate in the relationship between transformational leadership style and innovative behavior of an industrial company workers in Khoozestan. *Australian Journal of Basic & Applied Sciences*, *5*, 861–866.

Nagda, B. A., Gurin, P., & López, G. E. (2003). Transformative pedagogy for democracy and social justice. *Race, Ethnicity and Education*, *6*(2), 165–191. doi:10.1080/13613320308199

Nagda, B. A., Kim, C. W., & Truelove, Y. (2004). Learning about difference, learning with others, learning to transgress. *The Journal of Social Issues*, *60*(1), 195–214. doi:10.1111/j.0022-4537.2004.00106.x

Nagda, B. A., & Zúñiga, X. (2003). Fostering meaningful racial engagement through intergroup dialogues. *Group Processes & Intergroup Relations*, *6*(1), 111–128. doi:10.1177/1368430203006001015

Nagin, D. S. (1998). Criminal deterrence research at the outset of the twenty-first century. *Crime and Justice*, *23*, 1–42. doi:10.1086/449268

Nahapiet, J., & Ghoshal, S. (1998). Social capital, intellectual capital, and organizational advantage. *Academy of Management Review*, *23*(2), 242–266. doi:10.2307/259373

Nakata, C., Zhu, Z., & Izberk-Bilgin, E. (2011). Integrating marketing and information services functions: A complementarity and competence perspective. *Journal of the Academy of Marketing Science*, *39*(5), 700–716. doi:10.1007/s11747-010-0236-z

National Academies of Science (NAS). (2007). *Rising Above the Gathering Storm: Energizing and Employing America for a Brighter Economic Future.* Retrieved from http://books.nap.edu/catalog/11613.html

National Commission on Adult Literacy. (2008, June). *Reach Higher America: Overcome Crisis in the U. S. Workforce. Report of the national Commission on Adult Literacy.* Retrieved from Council of Advancement for Adult Literary: www.nationalcommissionadultliterarcy.org

National Defense University. (1997). *Strategic Leadership and Decision Making Part One: The Environment of Strategic Leadership and Decision Making.* Retrieved September 21, 2015, from http://www.au.af.mil/au/awc/awcgate/ndu/strat-ldr-dm/pt1ch1.html

National Network of Public Health Institutes. (2010). *What is a Public Health Institute?* Retrieved September 21, 2015, from http://www.nnphi.org/about/what-is-a-public-health-institute

Navaratnam, K. K. (1997). Quality management in education must be a never-ending journey. In K. Watson & S. Modgol (Eds.), *Educational dilemma: Debate and diversity; VI: Quality in education.* London: Cassell.

NCAA. (2010, December 23). *NCAA Requires Loss of Contests for Six Ohio State Football Student-Athletes.* Retrieved August 29, 2015 from http://www.dispatch.com/content/stories/sports/2010/12/23/text-of-ncaa-press-release.html?sid=101

Neelam, N., Bhattacharya, S., Sinha, V., & Tanksale, D. (2015). Organizational culture as a determinant of organizational commitment: What drives IT employees in India? *Global Business and Organizational Excellence, 34*(2), 62–74. doi:10.1002/joe.21594

Negroponte, N. (1996). *Being Digital.* New York, NY: Vintage.

Nelson, L., Bly, S., & Sokoler, T. (2001). *Quiet calls: talking silently on mobile phones.* Paper presented at the SIGCHI conference on Human factors in computing systems. doi:10.1145/365024.365094

Nelson, J. (1984). The defense of Billie Jean King. *Western Journal of Speech Communication, 48*(1), 92–102. doi:10.1080/10570318409374144

Nelson, R. R. (Ed.). (1993). *National Innovation Systems: A Comparative Study.* Oxford: Oxford University Press.

Nelson, R. R., & Winter, S. G. (1982). *An evolutionary theory of economic change.* Cambridge, MA: Harvard Business School Press.

Newhall, S. (2011). Preparing our leaders for the future. *Strategic HR Review, 11*(1), 5–12. doi:10.1108/14754391211186250

Ngware, M. W., Wamukuru, D. K., & Odebero, S. O. (2006). Total quality management in secondary schools in Kenya: Extent of practice. *Quality Assurance in Education, 14*(4), 339–362. doi:10.1108/09684880610703947

Nicol, D., Minty, I., & Sinclair, C. (2003). The social dimensions of online learning. *Innovations in Education and Teaching International, 40*(3), 270–280. doi:10.1080/1470329032000103807

Nielsen, M., & Chuang, I. (2010). *Quantum Computation and Quantum Information.* Cambridge University Press. doi:10.1017/CBO9780511976667

Nielsen, K., Randall, R., Yarker, J., & Brenner, S. (2008). The effects of transformational leadership on followers' perceived work characteristics and psychological well-being: A longitudinal study. *Work and Stress, 22*(1), 16–32. doi:10.1080/02678370801979430

Nierenberg, D. (2014). *Article.* Retrieved on Monday 10 March 2014 from http://www.theguardian.com/

Nilsen, T. R. (1974). *Ethics of speech communication* (2nd ed.). Indianapolis, IN: Bobbs-Merrill.

Noddings, N. (2012). *Philosophy of education* (3rd ed.). Boulder, CO: Westview Press.

Nonaka, I., & Takeuchi, H. (1995). *The knowledge-creating company.* New York, NY: Oxford University Press.

Nord, G. D., McCubbins, T. F., & Horn Nord, J. (2006). Email monitoring in the workplace: Privacy, legislation, and surveillance software. *Communications of the ACM, 49*(8), 73–77.

Normore, A., & Erbe, N. (2013). *Collective efficacy: interdisciplinary perspectives on international leadership.* Bingley, UK: Emerald Group Publishing.

Norrgren, F., & Schaller, J. (1999). Leadership style: Its impact on cross-functional product development. *Journal of Product Innovation Management, 16*(4), 377–384. doi:10.1016/S0737-6782(98)00065-4

Northhouse, P. (2007). *Leadership: Theory and practice.* Thousand Oaks, CA: Sage Publications.

Northouse, P. (2013). *Leadership: theory and practice* (6th ed.). Thousand oaks, CA: Sage.

Northouse, P. G. (2015). *Leadership: Theory and Practice.* New York: Sage.

Nunamaker, J. F. Jr, Reinig, B. A., & Briggs, R. O. (2009). Principles for effective virtual teamwork. *Communications of the ACM, 52*(4), 113–117. doi:10.1145/1498765.1498797

Nutini, H. G. (1997). Class and ethnicity in Mexico: Somatic and racial considerations. *Ethnology, 36*(3), 227–238. doi:10.2307/3773987

O'Connor, S. (2015). Wearables at work: the new frontier of employee surveillance. *Financial Times.* Retrieved from: http://www.ft.com/intl/cms/s/2/d7eee768-0b65-11e5-994d-00144feabdc0.html#axzz3cesjiVgY

O'Dell, C., & Grayson, J. (1999). Knowledge transfer: Discover your value proposition. *Strategy and Leadership, 27*(2), 10–15. doi:10.1108/eb054630

O'Reilly, C. A., & Chatman, J. A. (1996). Culture as social control: Corporation, cults, and commitment. In B. Staw & L. Cummings (Eds.), *Research in organizational behavior* (pp. 157–200). Greenwich, CT: JAI Press.

OECD. (2012). *Entrepreneurship at a Glance 2012.* OECD Publishing; doi:10.1787/entrepreneur_aag-2012-en

Oetzel & Ting-Toomey, S. (2013). The handbook of communication. Thousand Oaks, CA: Sage.

Oetzel, J., & Ting-Toomey, S. (2003). Face concerns in interpersonal conflict: A cross-cultural empirical test of the face negotiation theory. *Communication Research, 30*(6), 599–624. doi:10.1177/0093650203257841

Ohio State football players sanctioned. (2010, December 26). *ESPN.com News Service.* Retrieved August 29, 2015 from http://sports.espn.go.com/ncf/news/story?id=5950873

Ohio State players, alums stand behind Tressel. (2011, May 31). *Sportsillustrated.com.* Retrieved June 1, 2011 http://sportsillustrated.cnn.com/2011/football/ncaa/05/30/tressel-reaction.ap/index.html

Ohio State Buckeyes-2014 NCAA Football Champions. (2014). Retrieved July 29, 2015 from http://www.ohio-statebuckeyes.com/sports/m-footbl/2014-championship.html

Ohlheiser, A. (2014, September). Urban Outfitters apologizes for its blood-red-stained Kent State sweatshirt. *The Washington Post.* Retrieved from http://www.washingtonpost.com/news/morning-mix/wp/2014/09/15/urban-outfitters-red-stained-vintage-kent-state-sweatshirt-is-not-a-smart-look-this-fall/

Okoro, E. (2012). Cross-cultural etiquette and communication in global business: Toward a strategic framework for managing corporate expansion. *International Journal of Business and Management, 7*(16), 130–138. doi:10.5539/ijbm.v7n16p130

Okpara, J. O., & Kabongo, J. D. (2011). Cross-cultural training and expatriate adjustment: A study of western expatriate in Nigeria. *Journal of World Business, 46*(1), 22–30. doi:10.1016/j.jwb.2010.05.014

Olaniran, B. (2004). Computer-mediated communication in cross-cultural virtual teams. *International and Intercultural Communication Annual, 27,* 142–166.

Olaniran, B. A., Scholl, J. C., Williams, D. E., & Boyer, L. (2012). Johnson and Johnson phantom recall: A fall from grace or a re-visit of the ghost of the past. *Public Relations Review, 38*(1), 153–155. doi:10.1016/j.pubrev.2011.08.001

Olaniran, B., & Williams, D, (2001). Anticipatory model of crisis management. In R. Heath (Ed.), *Handbook of public relations* (pp. 487–500). Thousand Oaks, CA: Sage. doi:10.4135/9781452220727.n41

Oliver, R. L., & Anderson, E. (1994). An empirical test of the consequences of behavior-and outcome-based sales control systems. *Journal of Marketing, 58*(4), 53–67. doi:10.2307/1251916

Olson, P. (2014). Wearable Tech Is Plugging Into Health Insurance. *Forbes*. Retrieved from: http://www.forbes.com/sites/parmyolson/2014/06/19/wearable-tech-health-insurance/

Olson, J. D., Appunn, F. D., McAllister, C. A., Walters, K. K., & Grinnell, L. (2014). Webcams and virtual teams: An impact model. *Team Performance Management, 20*(3/4), 148–177. doi:10.1108/TPM-05-2013-0013

Omar, W., & Hussin, F. (2013). Transformational leadership style and job satisfaction relationship: A study of structural equation modeling (SEM). *International Journal of Academic Research In Business & Social Sciences, 3,* 346–365.

Onrubia, J. (2004). Las aulas como comunidades de aprendizaje. *Trabajadores de la enseñanza, 249,* 14-15. Retrieved February 2, 2009, from http://www.fe.ccoo.es/publicaciones/TE/249/249pdf

Oracle. (2011, August). *Oracle CEO Blog.* Retrieved from http://blogs.oracle.com/jonathan/

Organ, D. (1977). A reappraisal and reinterpretation of the satisfaction-causes-performance hypothesis. *Academy of Management Review, 2*(1), 46–53.

Organ, D. W. (1988). *Organizational citizenship behavior: The good soldier syndrome.* Lexington, MA: Lexington Books.

Organ, D., & Lingl, A. (1995). Personality, satisfaction and organizational citizenship behaviors. *The Journal of Social Psychology, 135*(3), 339–250. doi:10.1080/00224545.1995.9713963

Organ, D., & Moorman, R. (1993). Fairness and organizational citizenship behavior: What are the connections? *Social Justice Research, 6*(1), 5–18. doi:10.1007/BF01048730

Orlikowski, W. J. (2000). Using technology and constituting structures: A practice lens for studying technology in organizations. *Organization Science, 11*(4), 404–428. doi:10.1287/orsc.11.4.404.14600

Ortega-Argilés, R., & Brandsma, A. (2010). EU-US differences in the size of R&D intensive firms: Do they explain the overall R&D intensity gap? *Science & Public Policy, 37*(6), 429–441. doi:10.3152/030234210X508633

Orth, J. V. (2003). *Due process of law: A brief history.* University Press of Kansas.

Ortiz, F. (2012). In *Encyclopædia Britannica.* Retrieved June 27, 2012 from: http://www.britannica.com/EB-checked/topic/848801/Fernando-Ortiz

Ostroff, C. (1993). The effects of climate and personal influences on dividual behavior and attitudes in organizations. *Organizational Behavior and Human Decision, 56*(1), 56–90. doi:10.1006/obhd.1993.1045

OSU Athletic Director Gene Smith on timeline of events. (2010, December 23). *WEWSNewsChannel5.* Retrieved August 29, 2015 from https://www.youtube.com/watch?v=aJ3z7_oM5W0

OSU coach Jim Tressel on suspensions. (2010, December 23). *WEWSNewsChannel5.* Retrieved August 29, 2015 from https://www.youtube.com/watch?v=OuqH3PVQJAg

Ouchi, W. G. (1981). *Theory Z: How American business can meet the Japanese Challenge.* Reading, MA: Addison-Wesley Publishing Co.

Palmer, B., Wallis, M., Burgess, Z., & Stough, C. (2001). Emotional intelligence and effective leadership. *Leadership and Organization Development Journal, 22*(1), 5–10. doi:10.1108/01437730110380174

Palos, A. (Dir.) (2011). *Precious knowledge* [DVD]. United States: Dos Vatos Films.

Panning, R. (2014). Healthcare Reform 101. *Clinical Laboratory Science, 27*(2), 107–111. Retrieved from http://www.bing.com/search?q=Panning,+R.+(2014).+Healthcare+Reform+101&form=MSSEDF&pc=MSE1 PMID:25000654

Paprock, K. E. (2006). National human resource development in transitioning societies in the developing world: Introductory overview. *Advances in Developing Human Resources, 8*(1), 12 -27.

Paris, J. (2012). Culturally sustaining pedagogy: A needed stance, terminology, and practice. *Educational Researcher, 41*(3), 93–97.

Parker, J., & Coiera, E. (2000). Improving Clinical Communication: A View from Psychology. *Journal of the American Medical Informatics Association*, 7(5), 453–461. doi:10.1136/jamia.2000.0070453 PMID:10984464

Park, H., & Reber, B. (2008). Relationship building and the use of Websites: How Fortune 500 companies use their Websites to build relationships. *Public Relations Review*, 34(4), 409–411. doi:10.1016/j.pubrev.2008.06.006

Park, S., Na, E., & Kim, E. (2014, July). The relationship between online activities, netiquette and cyberbullying. *Children and Youth Services Review*, 42, 74–81. doi:10.1016/j.childyouth.2014.04.002

Parry, M. (2010). Tomorrow's college. *Chronicle of Higher Learning*, 57(11), 84–86.

Partee, B. (1989). Binding implicit variables in quantified contexts. In C. Wiltshire, B. Music, & R. Graczyk (Eds.), *Papers from Chicago Linguistic Society (CLS) 25* (pp. 342–365). Chicago: Chicago Linguistic Society.

Paternoster, R., Brame, R., Bachman, R., & Sherman, L. W. (1997). Do fair procedures matter? The effect of procedural justice on spouse assault. *Law & Society Review*, 31(1), 163–204. doi:10.2307/3054098

Patterson, K. A. (2005). *Leadership practices*. Virginia Beach, VA: Regent University Law School Admissions.

Patterson, M. G., West, M. A., Schackleton, V. J., Dawson, J. F., Lawthom, R., Maitlis, S., & Wallsace, A. M. et al. (2005). Validating the organizational climate measure: Links to managerial practices, productivity and innovation. *Journal of Organizational Behavior*, 26(4), 379–408. doi:10.1002/job.312

Pauleen, D. J. (2003-2004). An inductively derived model of leader-initiated relationship building with virtual team members. *Journal of Management Information Systems*, 20, 227–256.

Pauleen, D. J., & Yoong, P. (2001a). Facilitating virtual team relationships via internet and conventional communication channels. *Internet Research*, 11, 190–202. doi:10.1108/10662240110396450

Pauleen, D. J., & Yoong, P. (2001b). Relationship building and the use of ICT in boundary-crossing virtual teams: A facilitator's perspective. *Journal of Information Technology*, 16, 205–220. doi:10.1080/02683960110100391

Paul, S., Samarah, I. M., Seetharaman, P., & Mykytyn, P. P. (2004-2005). An empirical investigation of collaborative conflict management style in group support system-based global virtual teams. *Journal of Management Information Systems*, 21, 185–222.

Paulus, T. M., Bichelmeyer, B., Malopinsky, L., Pereira, M., & Rastogi, P. (2005). Power distance and group dynamics of an international project team: A case study. *Teaching in Higher Education*, 10(1), 43–55. doi:10.1080/1356251052000305525

Paupp, T. (2014). *Redefining human rights in the struggle for peace and development*. New York, New York: Cambridge University Press.

Pavitt, C. (1999). Theorizing about the group communication-leadership relationship: Input-process-output and functional models. In L. R. Frey, D. S. Gouran, & M. S. Poole (Eds.), *The handbook of group communication theory and research* (pp. 313–334). Thousand Oaks, CA: Sage.

Pavlou, P. (2011). State of the Information Privacy Literature: Where are we now and Where Should we Go? *Management Information Systems Quarterly*, 35(4), 977–989.

Pawanchik, S. (2006). Improving Students Proficiency in English. In The 2006 European College Teaching & Learning Conference, Florence, Italy.

Pawar, B. S. (2003). Central conceptual issues in transformational leadership research. *Leadership and Organization Development Journal*, 24(7), 397–406. doi:10.1108/01437730310498596

Pearce, B. (2007). *Making social worlds: a communication perspective*. London: Blackwell.

Pearce, B., & Pearce, K. (2000). Extending the theory of the coordinated management of meaning ("CMM") through a community dialogue process. *Communication Theory*, 4(4), 405–423. doi:10.1111/j.1468-2885.2000.tb00200.x

Pearlson, K. E., & Saunders, C. S. (2010). *Managing and Using Information Systems*. Hoboken, NJ: John Wiley & Sons, Inc.

Peck, M. S. (1987). *A different drum: Community making and peace*. New York: Touchstone.

Pedersen, E. R. (2001). *Calls.calm: enabling caller and callee to collaborate.* Paper presented at the CHI '01 extended abstracts on Human factors in computing systems, Seattle, WA. doi:10.1145/634067.634207

Pendlebury, S., & Enslin, P. (2000). Lifelong learning for a new society. In J. Field & M. Leicester (Eds.), *Lifelong learning: Education across the lifespan* (pp. 149–157). New York: Routledge Falmer.

Penrose, E. (1959). *The theory of the growth of the firm*. Oxford, UK: Oxford University Press.

Penuel, W. R., Fishman, B. J., Yamaguchi, R., & Gallagher, L. P. (2007). What makes professional development effective? Strategies that foster curriculum implementation. *American Educational Research Journal, 44*(4), 921–958. doi:10.3102/0002831207308221

Perez, A. D., & Hirschman, C. (2009). The changing racial and ethnic composition of the US population: Emerging American identities. *National Institutes of Health, 35*(1), 1-51. doi: 10.1111/j.1728-4457.2009.00260.x

Perryer, C., & Jordan, C. (2005). The influence of leader behaviors on organizational commitment: A study in the Australian public sector. *International Journal of Public Administration, 28*(5/6), 379–396. doi:10.1081/PAD-200055193

Perry, J. (2015). *The problem of the essential indexical and other essays: Extended edition*. Center for the Study of Language and Information.

Peterson, P., Park, N., Hall, N., & Seligman, M. E. P. (2009). Zest at work. *Journal of Organizational Behavior, 30*(2), 161–172. doi:10.1002/job.584

Peters, T. J., & Waterman, R. H. (1982). *In search of excellence – Lessons from America's best run company*. New York, NY: Harper & Row.

Petrie, N. (2014). *Future Leadership Trends*. Retrieved September 21, 2015, from http://insights.ccl.org/wp-content/uploads/2015/04/futureTrends.pdf

Pew Global Research Report. (2014). *Emerging and Developing Nations Want Freedom on the Internet-Young Especially Opposed to Censorship*. Retrieved 03/21/2014 from http://www.pewglobal.org/2014/03/19/emerging-and-developing-nations-want-freedom-on-the-internet/

Pfahl, M. E., & Bates, B. R. (2008). This is not a race, this is a farce: Formula One and the Indianapolis Motor Speedway tire crisis. *Public Relations Review, 34*, 135–144.

Pfeffer, N., & Coote, A. (1991). Is Quality Good for You? A Critical Review of Quality Assurance. In *Welfare Services. Social Policy Paper No. 5*. London: Institute for Public Policy Research.

Piccoli, G., Powell, A., & Ives, B. (2004). Virtual teams: Team control structure, work processes, and team effectiveness. *Information Technology & People, 17*(4), 359–379. doi:10.1108/09593840410570258

Pickavance, K. (2007). *Construction Law and Management*. London: Routledge.

Picower, B. (2011). Learning to teach and learning to learn: Supporting the development of new social justice educators. *Teacher Education Quarterly, 38*(4), 7–24.

Pinar, T., Zehir, C., Kitapçi, H., & Tanriverdi, H. (2014). The relationships between leadership behaviors team learning and performance among the virtual teams. *International Business Research, 7*(5), 68–79. doi:10.5539/ibr.v7n5p68

Pinchot, G. (1985). *Intrapreneuring*. New York: Harper & Row.

Pincus, D. J., Rayfield, R. E., & Cozzens, M. D. (1991). The Chief Executive Officer's internal communications role: A benchmark program of research. In L. A. Grunig & J. E. Grunig (Eds.), *Public Relations Research Annual* (Vol. 3, pp. 1–36). Hillsdale, NJ: Lawrence Earlbaum Associates.

Pincus, J. D. (1986). Communication satisfaction, job satisfaction and job performance. *Human Communication Research, 12*(3), 395–419. doi:10.1111/j.1468-2958.1986.tb00084.x

Pitsillides, A., Pitsillides, B., Dikaiakos, M., Christodoulou, E., Andreou, P., & Georgiadis, D. (2006). DITIS: A collaborate virtual medical team for home healthcare of cancer patients. *Topics in Biomedical Engineering, II,* 247–266. doi:10.1007/0-387-26559-7_18

Piyachat, B., Chanongkorn, K., & Panisa, M. (2014). The mediate effect of employee engagement on the relationship between perceived employer branding and discretionary effort. *DLSU Business & Economics Review, 24*(1), 59–72.

Podsakoff, P., & MacKenzie, S. (1993). Citizenship behavior and fairness in organizations: Issues and directions for future research. *Employee Responsibilities and Rights Journal, 6*(3), 257–269. doi:10.1007/BF01419449

Podsakoff, P., & MacKenzie, S. (1997). Impact of organizational citizenship behavior on organizational performance: A review and suggestions for future research. *Human Performance, 10*(2), 133–151. doi:10.1207/s15327043hup1002_5

Podsakoff, P., MacKenzie, S., Paine, J., & Bachrach, D. (2000). Organizational citizenship behaviors: A critical review of the theoretical and empirical literature and suggestions for future research. *Journal of Management, 26*(3), 513–563. doi:10.1177/014920630002600307

Ponte, L. M. (2001). Broadening traditional ADR notions of disclosure: Special considerations for posting conflict resolution policies and programs on e-business Web sites. *Ohio State Journal of Dispute Resolution, 17,* 321.

Poon, I., & Rowley, C. (2011). Leadership Development. Academic Press.

Porter-O'Grady, T. (2003). A different age for leadership, part 1: New context, new content. *The Journal of Nursing Administration, 33*(2), 105–110. doi:10.1097/00005110-200302000-00007 PMID:12584463

Postmes, T., Tanis, M., & de Wit, B. (2001). Communication and commitment in organizations: A social identity approach. *Group Processes & Intergroup Relations, 4*(3), 227–246. doi:10.1177/1368430201004003004

Potter, R. E., & Balthazard, P. A. (2002). Virtual team interaction styles: Assessment and effects. *International Journal of Human-Computer Studies, 56,* 423–443. doi:10.1006/ijhc.2002.1001

Potter, R. E., & Balthazard, P. A. (2004). Understanding composition and conflict in virtual teams. In S. Godar (Ed.), *Virtual and collaborative teams* (pp. 35–47). Hershey, PA: Idea Group. doi:10.4018/978-1-59140-204-6.ch003

Powell, A., Piccoli, G., & Ives, B. (2004). Virtual teams: A review of current literature and directions for future research. *The Data Base for Advances in Information Systems, 35*(1), 6–36. doi:10.1145/968464.968467

Power, M., & Vaughan, N. (2010). Redesigning online learning for international graduate seminar delivery. *Journal of Distance Education, 24*(2), 19–38.

Powers, E. (2006, June 6). A spirited disposition debate. *Inside Higher Ed.* Retrieved November 10, 2009, from http://www.insidehighered.com/news/2006/06/06/disposition

Poyatos, F. (2002a). *Nonverbal communication across disciplines* (1st ed., Vol. 1). Philadelphia, PA: John Benjamins.

Poyatos, F. (2002b). *Nonverbal communication across disciplines. Paralanguage, kinesics, si- lence, personal and environmental interaction* (Vol. 2). Philadelphia, PA: John Benjamins; doi:10.1075/z.ncad2

Pozzebon, M., Titah, R., & Pinsonneault, A. (2006). Combining social shaping of technology and communicative action theory for understanding rhetorical closure in IT. *Information Technology & People, 19*(3), 244–271. doi:10.1108/09593840610689840

Prakhaber, P. R. (2000). Who owns the online consumer? *Journal of Consumer Marketing, 17*(2), 158–171. doi:10.1108/07363760010317213

Prensky, M. (2005 December. (2006, January). Listen to the natives. *Educational Leadership, 63*(4), 8–13.

Prensky, M. (2011). In the 21st century university, let's ban (paper) books. *The Chronicle of Higher Education, 58*(13), 309.

Prensky, M. (2014, January/February). Innovation experiementation and courage in the education of students for the future. *Educational Technology, 54*(1), 64.

Pretorius, M., & le Roux, I. (2011). A reality check for corporate leaders: When managers don't respect their bosses. *Strategy and Leadership*, *40*(1), 40–44. doi:10.1108/10878571211191693

Priest, G. L., & Klein, B. (1984). The Selection of Disputes for Litigation. *The Journal of Legal Studies*, *12*, 1–55.

Printy, S. M., Marks, H. M., & Bowers, A. J. (2009). Integrated Leadership: How Principals and Teachers Share Transformational and Instructional Influence. *Journal of School Leadership*, *19*(5), 504–532.

Pritchard, R. D., & Karasick, B. W. (1973). The effect of organizational climate on managerial job performance and job satisfaction. *Organizational Behavior and Human Performance*, *9*(1), 126–146. doi:10.1016/0030-5073(73)90042-1

Privacy Rights Clearinghouse. (2013). *Mobile Health and Fitness Apps: What Are the Privacy Risks?* Retrieved from: https://www.privacyrights.org/mobile-medical-apps-privacy-alert

Pruett, M., & Thomas, H. (1996). Thinking About Quality and its Links with Strategic Management. *European Management Journal*, *14*(1), 37–46. doi:10.1016/0263-2373(95)00045-3

Pruitt, D., & Kim, S. (2004). *Social conflict: escalation, stalemate and settlement*. New York: McGraw-Hill.

Purdum, T. S. (1994, February 24). Bradley rebukes Clinton on Japan. *The New York Times*, pp. C1-C2.

Putti, J. M., Aryee, S., & Phua, J. (1990). Communication relationship satisfaction and organizational commitment. *Group & Organization Studies*, *15*(1), 44–52. doi:10.1177/105960119001500104

PWC. (2015). Half of people would use a workplace smartwatch. *PWC*. Retrieved from: http://pwc.blogs.com/press_room/2015/04/half-of-people-would-use-a-workplace-smartwatch-pwc-research.html

Pyle, E., & Ludlow, R. (2011, July 16). *Ohio State football: Tressel had early history of warnings*. Retrieved October 14, 2015 from http://www.dispatch.com/content/stories/local/2011/07/16/tressel-had-early-history-of-warnings.html

Qing, L., & Jia, Z. (2011). On effective communication of cross-cultural enterprises. *Proceedings of the 8th International Conference on Innovation & Management*.

QSR. (2014, April). *Starbucks kicks off 4th annual global month of service*. Retrieved from http://www.qsrmagazine.com/news/starbucks-kicks-4th-annual-global-month-service-0

Quick, J. C., & Nelson, D. L. (2013). *Principles of organizational behavior: Realities and challenges* (International ed.). South Western Cengage Publishing.

Quinn, T., & Meiners, E. (2007). Do ask, do tell: What's professional about taking social justice and sexual orientation out of classrooms? *Rethinking Schools Online*. Retrieved September 30, 2009, from http://www.rethinkingschools.org/archive/21_04/ask214.shtml

Quinn, R. E., & Cameron, K. (1983). Organizational life cycles and sifting criteria of effectiveness: Some preliminary evidence. *Management Science*, *29*(1), 33–51. doi:10.1287/mnsc.29.1.33

Quirke, B. (2008). *Making the connections: Using internal communication to turn strategy into action*. Burlington, VT: Gower.

Qureshi, S., & Vogel, D. (2001). Adaptiveness in virtual teams: Organisational challenges and research directions. *Group Decision and Negotiation*, *10*(1), 27–46. doi:10.1023/A:1008756811139

Rabin, M. (1993). Incorporating fairness into game theory and economics. *The American Economic Review*, 1281–1302.

Radick, S. (2011). *The power of social networks: Reviving the intranet*. Public Relations Tactics.

Radzuan, N. R. M. (2013). *An analysis of technical oral presentation anxiety among engineering students in Universiti Malaysia Pahang*. (Unpublished PhD Thesis).

Radzuan, N. R. M., Ali, F., Kassim, H., Hashim, H., Osman, N., & Abid, R. (2008). Developing Speaking Skills Module for Engineering Students. *The International Journal of Learning.*, *14*(11), 61–70.

Radzuan, N. R. M., & Kaur, S. (2011). Technical Oral Presentations in English: Qualitative Analysis of Engineering Students' Sources of Anxiety. *Procedia: Social and Behavioral Sciences, 29,* 1436–1445. doi:10.1016/j.sbspro.2011.11.383

Rahim, M. A. (1986). *Managing Conflict in Organizations.* New York, NY: Praeger.

Rahim, M. A. (2002). Toward a theory of managing organizational conflict. *The International Journal of Conflict Management, 13*(3), 206–235. doi:10.1108/eb022874

Raines, C. (2015). *4GenR8tns: Succeeding with colleagues, cohorts & customers.* Retrieved from http://www.generationsatwork.com/articles_succeeding.php

Ramirez, J. C., & Silva Lira, I. (2008). Globalization and regional development: The economic performance of Chile's regions, 1990-2002. *CEPAL Review, 95*(Aug), 103–123.

Ramon, S., Campbell, J., Lindsay, J., McCrystal, P., & Baidoun, N. (2006). The impact of political conflict on social work: Experiences from Northern Ireland, Israel and Palestine. *British Journal of Social Work, 36*(3), 435–450. doi:10.1093/bjsw/bcl009

Rampa, S. H. (2005). The Relationship between Total Quality Management and School Improvement. Unpublished doctoral dissertation. Pretoria, South Africa: University of Pretoria; Retrieved from http://repository.up.ac.za/bitstream/handle/2263/23595/Complete.pdf?sequence=5

Randlesome, C., & Myers, A. (1998). Cultural fluency: The United Kingdom versus Demark. *European Business Journal, 10*(4), 184–194.

Rands, M., Levinger, G., & Mellinger, G. D. (1981). Patterns of Conflict Resolution and Marital Satisfaction. *Journal of Family Issues, 2,* 297–321.

Rasheed, R. K. J. (2014). Communication, culture and discord: A case study of avoidable leadership failure in a European-Palestinian NGO. Academic Press.

Ravasi, D., & Schultz, M. (2006). Responding to organizational identity threats: Exploring the role of organizational culture. *Academy of Management Journal, 49*(3), 433–458. doi:10.5465/AMJ.2006.21794663

Ravindran, S., & Iyer, G. S. (2014). Organizational and knowledge management related antecedents of knowledge use: The moderating effect of ambiguity tolerance. *Information Technology Management, 15*(4), 271–290. doi:10.1007/s10799-014-0190-4

Rawlins, B. (2006). Prioritizing stakeholders for public relations. *Institute for Public Relations.* Retrieved October 18, 2015 from http://pdfcast.org/pdf/prioritizing-stakeholders-for-public-relations

Ray, E. B., & Miller, K. I. (1994). Social support, home/work stress and burnout: Who can help? *The Journal of Applied Behavioral Science, 30*(3), 357–373. doi:10.1177/0021886394303007

Raykov, T., & Grayson, D. (2003). A test for change of composite reliability in scale development. *Multivariate Behavioral Research, 38*(2), 143–159. doi:10.1207/S15327906MBR3802_1

Reddy, S. (2007). *SCHOOL QUALITY: Perspectives from the Developed and Developing Countries.* Azim Premji Foundation. Retrieved from http://www.azimpremjifoundation.org/pdf/ConsolidatedSchoolQualityreport.pdf

Redmond, R., Curtis, E., Noone, T., & Keenan, P. (2008). Quality in higher education: The contribution of Edward Deming's principles. *International Journal of Educational Management, 22*(5), 432–441. doi:10.1108/09513540810883168

Reed, G. E. (2006 May-June). *Leadership and Systems Thinking.* Defense AT&L. Retrieved September 2, 2015, from http://www.au.af.mil/au/awc/awcgate/dau/ree_mj06.pdf

Reed, S. E. (2011). *The Diversity Index: The Alarming Truth about Diversity in Corporate America.* New York, NY: American Management Association.

Reeves, N., & Feely, A. (2001). Suspected language problems: Your company needs a language check-up. *Aston Business School Doctoral Working Paper, 37.*

Reeves, T. D., & Li, Z. (2012). Teachers' technological readiness for online professional development: Evidence from the US e-Learning for Educators initiative. *Journal of Education for Teaching, 38,* 389–406.

Regan, P. M., FitzGerald, G., & Balint, P. (2013). Generational views of information privacy? *Innovation: The European Journal of Social Science Research, 26*(1-2), 81–99.

Rego, A. (2002). *Comportamentos de cidadania nas organizações*. Lisboa: McGraw-Hill.

Rego, A., Ribeiro, N., & Cunha, M. (2010). Perceptions of organizational virtuousness and happiness as predictors of organizational citizenship behaviors. *Journal of Business Ethics, 93*(1), 215–235. doi:10.1007/s10551-009-0197-7

Reichers, A. E., & Schneider, B. (1990). Climate and culture: An evolution of constructs. In B. Schneider (Ed.), *Organizational climate and culture* (pp. 5–39). San Francisco, CA: Jossey–Bass.

Reid, A., Cranston, N., Keating, J., & Mulford, B. (2010). *Exploring the Public Purposes of Education in Australian Primary Schools*. Report on an ARC-Linkage Project conducted in partnership with the Australian Government Primary Principals Association (AGPPA) and the Foundation for Young Australians. Retrieved from: http://www.agppa.asn.au/index.php?option=com_content&view=article&id=28&Itemid=18

Reijers, H. A. (2006). Implementing BPM systems: The role of process orientation. *Business Process Management Journal, 12*(4), 389–409. doi:10.1108/14637150610678041

Reisig, M. D., Bratton, J., & Gertiz, M. G. (2007). The construct validity and refinement of process-based policing measures. *Criminal Justice and Behavior, 34*(8), 1005–1028. doi:10.1177/0093854807301275

Reiss, A. J. (1971). *The police and the public*. New Haven, CT: Yale University Press.

Ren, S., Wood, R., & Zhu, Y. (2015). *Business Leadership Development in China*. Abingdon: Routledge.

Renzl, B. (2007). Language as a vehicle of knowing: The role of language and meaning in constructing knowledge. *Knowledge Management Research & Practice, 5*(1), 44–53. doi:10.1057/palgrave.kmrp.8500126

Resick, C. J., Gillian, S. M., Keating, M. A., Dickson, M. W., Kwan, H. K., & Peng, C. (2011). What ethical leadership means to me: Asian, American, and European perspectives. *Journal of Business Ethics, 101*(3), 435–457. doi:10.1007/s10551-010-0730-8

Rhys Jones, S. (1994). How Constructive is Construction Law? *Constitutional Law Journal (Newark, N.J.), 10*(1), 28–38.

Rice, T., Rosenau, P., Unruh, L. Y., Barnes, A. J., Saltman, R. B., & van Ginneken, E. (2013). United States of America: Health system review. *Health Systems in Transition, 15*(3), 1–431. PMID:24025796

Rich, S. (2015, May 27). *Personal email communication*. Associate Vice President, (Academic). Nipissing University, Ontario Canada.

Richards, R. (n.d.). *Command presence: Feeding your own self confidence*. Retrieved from the internet August 30, 2015, http://www.withthecommand.com/2004-May/PA-Richards-commandpresence.html

Richardson, J. (2012). Face to face versus online tuition: Preference, performance and pass rates in White and ethnic minority students. *British Journal of Educational Technology, 43*(1), 17–27. doi:10.1111/j.1467-8535.2010.01147.x

Rich, M., & Craig, R. (2012). Habermas and Bateson in a World Gone M.A.D.: Metacommunication, Paradox, and the Inverted Speech Situation. *Communication Theory, 22*(4), 383–402. doi:10.1111/j.1468-2885.2012.01412.x

Richmond, V. P., & McCroskey, J. C. (1998). *Communication: Apprehension, Avoidance and Effectiveness* (5th ed.). Boston: Allyn and Bacon.

Richmond, V. P., & McCroskey, J. C. (2000). The impact of supervisor and subordinate immediacy on relational and organizational outcomes. *Communication Monographs, 67*(1), 85–95. doi:10.1080/03637750009376496

Richmond, V. P., McCroskey, J. C., Davis, L. M., & Koontz, K. A. (1980). Perceived power as a mediator of management styles and employee satisfaction: A preliminary investigation. *Communication Quarterly, 28*(4), 37–46. doi:10.1080/01463378009369380

Rintoul, H. (2011). *Transforming educational practices. The online graduate experience: Concerns, challenges and dilemmas.* Paper presented at the annual meeting of the Center for the Study of Leadership and Ethics in Education, Victoria, Canada.

Robbins, S. (2005). Organizational Behavior. Eaglewood Cliffs: Prentice Hall.

Robbins, S. (2012). *Organizational Behavior.* New York: Pearson.

Robbins, S. P. (2001). *Organizational behavior* (9th ed.). Upper Saddle River, NJ: Prentice-Hall.

Robinson, B. M. (1996). *Total quality management in education: The empowerment of a school community.* (Unpublished doctoral dissertation). University of Nebraska, Lincoln, NE.

Robinson, W. (2002). The Effects of the Human Rights Act 1998 on Arbitration. *Amicus Curiae,* (42).

Robinson, S. L., & Rousseau, D. M. (1994). Violating the psychological contract: Not the exception but the norm. *Journal of Organizational Behavior, 15*(3), 245–259. doi:10.1002/job.4030150306

Robotics-VO. (2013). *A Roadmap for US Robotics. From Internet to Robotics.* Robotics in the United States of America.

Robson, P., & Tourish, D. (2005). Managing internal communication: An organizational case study. *Corporate Communications, 10*(3), 213–222. doi:10.1108/13563280510614474

Rockland, D. B. (2014). *Why internal communications is a business driver.* Tactics.

Rodwell, J., Kienzle, R., & Shadur, M. (1998). The relationships among work-related perceptions, employee attitudes, and employee perceptions and employee performance: The integral role of communication. *Human Resource Management, 37*(3/4), 277–293. doi:10.1002/(SICI)1099-050X(199823/24)37:3/4<277::AID-HRM9>3.0.CO;2-E

Roebuck, D., Brock, S., & Moodie, D. (2004). Using a simulation to explore the challenges of communicating in a virtual team. *Business Communication Quarterly, 67,* 359–367. doi:10.1177/1080569904268083

Rogers Everett, M., & Steinfatt Thomas, M. (1999). *Intercultural Communication.* Prospect Heights, IL: Waveland Press.

Rogers, P. (2004). Trends *in conflict 2010-2030.* Centre for Humanitarian Dialogue Mediators Retreat, Oslo, Norway.

Rogers, E. M. (1994). *A history of communication study.* New York: Free Press.

Rogers, E. M., Hart, W. B., & Miike, Y. (2002). Edward T. Hall and the History of Intercultural Communication: The United States and Japan. *Keio Communication Review, 24,* 1–5.

Rojo-Laurilla, M. A. (2007). English for maritime purposes: Communication apprehension and communicative competence among maritime students in the Philippines. *Reflections on English Language Teaching, 6*(2), 39–58.

Ronson, J. (2015, February). How one stupid tweet blew up Justine Sacco's life. *The New York Times.*

Rose, A. T. (2002, November). Improving student skills in multimedia presentations. In *Frontiers in Education Conference* (Vol. 2, pp. F1F-8). doi:10.1109/FIE.2002.1158134

Rosenberg, M. (2003, March). Redefining e-learning. *Performance Improvement, 42*(3), 38–41. doi:10.1002/pfi.4930420307

Rosenfeld, L. B., Grant, C. H. III, & McCroskey, J. C. (1995). Communication apprehension and self-perceived communication competence of academically gifted students. *Communication Education, 44*(1), 79–89. doi:10.1080/03634529509378999

Rothman, L. (2014, September). Urban Outfitters: 'We understand how our sincerity may be questioned'. *TIME.* Retrieved from http://time.com/3387566/urban-outfitters-sweatshirt-apology/

Rought-Brooks, H., Duaibis, S., & Hussein, S. (2010). Palestinian women: Caught in the crossfire between occupation and patriarchy. *Feminist Formations, 22*(3), 124–145. doi:10.1353/ff.2010.0018

Rouse, M. (2015). *Systems Thinking Definition.* Retrieved September 22, 2015, from http://searchcio.techtarget.com/definition/systems-thinking

Roush, P. E., & Atwater, L. E. (1992). Using the MBTI to understand transformational leadership and self perception accuracy. *Military Psychology*, *4*(1), 17–34. doi:10.1207/s15327876mp0401_2

Rowland, R. C., & Jerome, A. M. (2004). On organizational apologia: A reconceptualization. *Communication Theory*, *14*(3), 191–211. doi:10.1111/j.1468-2885.2004.tb00311.x

Rowley, C., & Jackson, K. (Eds.). (2011). *Human Resource Management: The Key Concepts*. Abingdon: Routledge.

Rowley, C., & Ulrich, D. (2012). *Leadership in the Asia Pacific, Asia Pacific Business Review Special Issue*. Abingdon: Routledge.

Rozkwitalska, M. (2012). Staffing top management positions in multinational subsidiaries—a local perspective on expatriate management. *Journal of Global Science & Technology Forum (GSTF). Business Review (Federal Reserve Bank of Philadelphia)*, *2*(2), 50–56.

Rubin, J. (2014). The learning strategy prism: Perspectives of learning strategy experts. *System*, *43*(1).

Rubin, R. B., Graham, E. E., & Mignerey, J. T. (1990). A longitudinal study of college students' communication competence. *Communication Education*, *39*(1), 1–14. doi:10.1080/03634529009378783

Ruettimann, L. (2011). HR: You're doing it wrong. The culture myth. *The Conference Board Review*. Retrieved November 19, 2011 from http://www.tcbreview.com/summer_2011.aspx

Ruppel, C. P., & Harrington, S. J. (2001). Sharing knowledge through intranets: A study of organizational culture and intranet implementation. *Professional Communication*, *44*(1), 37–52. doi:10.1109/47.911131

Rus, D. (2015). The Robots Are Coming. How Technological Breakthroughs Will Transform Everyday Life. *Foreign Affairs*. Retrieved from https://www.foreignaffairs.com/articles/2015-06-16/robots-are-coming

Rus, I., & Lindvall, M. (2002). Knowledge management in software engineering. *IEEE Software*, *19*(3), 26–38. doi:10.1109/MS.2002.1003450

Rybalko, S., & Seltzer, T. (2010). Dialogic communication in 140 characters or less: How Fortune 500 companies engage stakeholders using Twitter. *Public Relations Review*, *36*(4), 336–341. doi:10.1016/j.pubrev.2010.08.004

Ryckewaert, L. (2011, November). PM Harper takes communications strategy to new level. *Hill Times News Online*. Retrieved from http://www.hilltimes.com/news/2011/11/21/pm-harper-takes-communications-strategy-to-new-level/28868

Saari, L., & Judge, T. (2004). Employee attitudes and job satisfaction. *Human Resource Management*, *43*(4), 395–407. doi:10.1002/hrm.20032

Sabherwal, R., Hirschheim, R., & Goles, T. (2001). The dynamics of alignment: Insights from a punctuated equilibrium model. *Organization Science*, *12*(2), 179–197. doi:10.1287/orsc.12.2.179.10113

Saddi, J., Sabbagh, K., & Sheddiac, R. (2011). Measures of Leadership. *Strategy + Business*. Retrieved October 20, 2011 at http://www.strategy-business.com/article/10203?gko=64f7f&cid= enews20100720

Sahaya, N. (2012). A learning organization as a mediator of leadership style and firms' financial performance. *International Journal of Business and Management*, *7*(14), 96–113. doi:10.5539/ijbm.v7n14p96

Said, E. (1978). *Orientalism: Western Conceptions of the Orient*. Harmondsworth: Penguin.

Saks, A. M. (2006). Antecedents and consequences of employee engagement. *Journal of Managerial Psychology*, *21*(7), 600–619. doi:10.1108/02683940610690169

Salacuse, J. W. (2007). *Real leaders negotiate*. Retrieved on May 26, 2015, available at https://hbr.org/2008/02/real-leaders-negotiate-1.php

Salazar, P. S. (2007). The professional development needs of rural high school principals: A seven-state study. *Rural Educator*, *28*(3), 20–27.

Salleh, L. M. (2008). Communication competence: A Malaysian perspective. *Human Communication A Journal of the Pacific and Asian Communication Association*, *11*(3), 303-312.

Sallis, E. (1993). *Total quality management in education*. London: Kogan Page Ltd. doi:10.4324/9780203417010

Salovey, P., & Mayer, J. D. (1990). Emotional intelligence. *Imagination, Cognition and Personality, 9*(3), 185–211. doi:10.2190/DUGG-P24E-52WK-6CDG

Samad, S. (2005). Unraveling the organizational commitment and job performance relationship: Exploring the moderating effect of job satisfaction. *Business Review (Federal Reserve Bank of Philadelphia), 4*(2), 79–84.

Sammon, M. J., Karmin, L. S. B., Peebles, E., & Seligmann, D. D. (2006, 2006-09-29). *MACCS: Enabling communications for mobile workers within healthcare environments.* Paper presented at the MobileHCI'06.

Sanchez, R. (1996). *Strategic learning and knowledge management.* Chichester, UK: John Wiley & Sons.

Sanders, S. (2015, March). Starbucks will stop putting the words "race together" on cups. *The two-way: Breaking news from NPR.* Retrieved from http://www.npr.org/sections/thetwo-way/2015/03/22/394710277/starbucks-will-stop-writing-race-together-on-coffee-cups

Sandman, P. (2012). *Responding to community outrage: Strategies for effective risk communication.* American Industrial Hygiene Association.

Santos, V., Goldman, A., & de Souza, C. R. B. (2015). Fostering effective inter-team knowledge sharing in agile software development. *Empirical Software Engineering, 20*(4), 1006–1051. doi:10.1007/s10664-014-9307-y

Sanz, S. (2009). Comunitats de pràctica o l'aprenentatge compartit. *Revista Guix.*

Saraph, J. V., & Sebastian, R. J. (1993). Developing a quality culture. *Quality Progress, 26*(9), 73–78.

Sarudin, I., Zubairi, A. M., & Ali, A. M. (2009). *A comparative analysis of engineering students' problem in speaking and writing.* Paper presented at the 2nd International Conference of Teaching and Learning, INTI University College, Malaysia.

Sauner-Leroy, J. B. (2004). Managers and productive investment decisions: The impact of uncertainty and risk aversion. *Journal of Small Business Management, 42*(1), 1–18. doi:10.1111/j.1540-627X.2004.00094.x

Sawhney, N., & Schmandt, C. (2000). Nomadic radio: Speech and audio interaction for contextual messaging in nomadic environments. *ACM Transactions on Computer-Human Interaction, 7*(3), 353–383. doi:10.1145/355324.355327

Schacful, P. (2008). Cultural diversity, information, and communication: Today's impact on global virtual teams: An explanatory study. *Journal of Global Information Management, 45*(2), 131–142. doi:10.1016/j.im.2007.12.003

Schauber, A. C. (1999). *Assessing organizational climate: First step in diversifying an organization.* Doctoral Dissertation, Union Institute, UMI: 9945517

Schawbel, D. (2013). 10 Ways Millennials Are Creating The Future Of Work. *Forbes.* Retrieved from http://onforb.es/18QL7p3

Scheel, C. (2007). Why the Latin American region has not succeeded in building world-class industrial clusters. In *KGCM Proceedings.* Winter Garden, FL: International Institute of Informatics and Systems.

Schein, E. (1992). *Organizational Culture and Leadership.* New York: Jossey Bass.

Schein, E. H. (1984). Coming to a new awareness of organizational culture. *MIT Sloan Management Review, 25*(2), 3–16.

Schein, E. H. (1985). How culture forms develops and changes. In R. H. Kilmann & M. J. Saxton (Eds.), *Gaining Control of Corporate Structure.* San Francisco, CA: Jossey Bass.

Schein, E. H. (1992). *Organizational culture and leadership: A dynamic view* (2nd ed.). San Francisco, CA: Jossey-Bass Publishers.

Schein, E. H. (1992). The role of the CEO in the management of change. In T. A. Kochan & M. Usteem (Eds.), *Transforming Organizations.* New York, NY: Oxford University Press.

Schelling, T. C. (1957). Bargaining, Communication, and Limited War. *The Journal of Conflict Resolution, 1*(1), 19–36. doi:10.1177/002200275700100104

Schilit & Theimer. (1994). Disseminating active map information to mobile hosts. *Network, IEEE, 8*(5), 22-32.

Schilit, B., Adams, N., & Want, R. (1994). *Context-aware computing applications*. Paper presented at the Mobile Computing Systems and Applications, 1994.

Schlenkrich, L., & Upfold, C. (2009). A guideline for virtual team managers: The key to effective social interaction and communication. *The Electronic Journal of Information Systems Evaluation*, *12*(1), 109–118.

Schmidt, A., Aidoo, K. A., Takaluoma, A., Tuomela, U., Van Laerhoven, K., & Van de Velde, W. (1999). Advanced interaction in context. In *Handheld and ubiquitous computing* (pp. 89–101). Springer. doi:10.1007/3-540-48157-5_10

Schmidt, A., Takaluoma, A., & Mäntyjärvi, J. (2000). Context-Aware telephony over WAP. *Personal and Ubiquitous Computing*, *4*(4), 225–229.

Schmid, W., & Kern, E. M. (2014). Integration of business process management and knowledge management: State of the art, current research and future prospects. *Journal of Business Economics*, *84*(2), 191–231. doi:10.1007/s11573-013-0683-3

Schmoker, M., & Wilson, R. B. (1993). Adapting total quality doesn't mean "turning learning into a business". *Educational Leadership*, *51*(1), 62–63.

Schneider, B., Salvaggio, A. N., & Subirats, M. (2002). Climate strength: A new direction for climate research. *The Journal of Applied Psychology*, *87*(2), 220–229. doi:10.1037/0021-9010.87.2.220

Scholl, J., Hasvold, P., Henriksen, E., & Ellingsen, G. (2007). *Managing Communication Availability and Interruptions: A Study of Mobile Communication in an Oncology Department*. Pervasive Computing.

Schraeder, M. (2001). Identifying employee resistance during the threat of a merger: An analysis of employee perceptions and commitment to an organization in a pre-merger context. *The Mid-Atlantic Journal of Business*, *37*(4), 191–204.

Schramm, W. (1955). How communications works. In W. Schramm (Ed.), *The process and effects of mass communications*. Urbana, IL: University of Illinois Press.

Schramm, W. (1955). *The Process and Effects of Mass Communication*. Urbana, IL: University of Illinois Press.

Schramm, W. (1964). *Mass media and national development*. Stanford, CA: Stanford University Press.

Schultz, J. R. (2014). *Four-cornered Leadership: A Framework for Making Decisions*. CRC Press, Taylor & Francis Group.

Schumpeter, J. A. (1942). Capitalism, Socialism and Democracy. Harper & Brothers.

Schuster, D., Jentsch, F., & Shumaker, R. (2011, May). *Robots as team members*. In Information Systems and Technology Panel Symposium on Emerged and Emerging "disruptive" Technologies. Symposium conducted at the meeting of the North Atlantic Treaty Organization (NATO), Madrid, Spain.

Schuster, D., Ososky, S., Jentsch, F., Phillips, E., Lebiere, C., & Evans, A. W. (2011). A research approach to shared mental models and situation assessment in future robot teams.*Proceedings of the Human Factors and Ergonomics Society Annual Meeting*. Santa Monica, CA: Human Factors and Ergonomics Society. doi:10.1177/1071181311551094

Schyve, P. M. (2009, Winter). *Leadership in healthcare organizations: A Guide to Joint Commission Leadership Standards*. San Diego, CA: A Governance Institute White Paper.

Schyve, P., M. (2007). Language Differences as a Barrier to Quality and Safety in Health Care: The Joint Commission Perspective. *Journal of General Internal Medicine*, *22*(Suppl 2), 360–361. doi:10.1007/s11606-007-0365-3

Scott, M. B., & Lyman, S. M. (1968). Accounts. *American Sociological Review*, *33*(1), 46–62. doi:10.2307/2092239 PMID:5644339

Scott, T. J. (2005). *The concise handbook of manager: A practitioner's approach*. USA: The Haworth Press.

Scott, W. R., & Davis, G. F. (2007). *Organizations and organizing: Rational, natural and open system perspectives*. Upper Saddle, NJ: Pearson Prentice Hall.

Searle, J. (2007). Neuroscience, Intentionality and Free Will: Reply to Habermas. *Philosophical Explorations*, *10*(1), 69–76. doi:10.1080/13869790601170169

Seeger, M. W. (2006). Best practices in crisis communication: An expert panel process. *Journal of Applied Communication Research, 34*(3), 232–244. doi:10.1080/00909880600769944

Seidler-de Alwis, R., & Hartmann, E. (2008). The use of tacit knowledge within innovative companies: Knowledge management in innovative enterprises. *Journal of Knowledge Management, 12*(1), 133–147. doi:10.1108/13673270810852449

Selamat, N., Samsu, N. Z., & Kamalu, N. S. (2013). The impact of organizational climate on teachers' job performance. *Educational Research, 2*(1), 71–82.

Seligman, M., & Csikszentmihalyi, M. (2000). Positive psychology: An introduction. *The American Psychologist, 55*(1), 5–14. doi:10.1037/0003-066X.55.1.5 PMID:11392865

Selmi, M. (2006). Privacy for the working class: Public work and private lives. *Louisiana Law Review, 66,* 1035–1056.

Selwyn, N. (2012). Social Media in Higher Education. In *The Europa World of Learning* (62nd ed.). Routledge.

Semple, C., Hartman, F., & Jergas, G. (1994). Construction Claims and Disputes: Causes and Cost/Time Overruns. *Journal of Construction Engineering and Management, 120*(4), 785–795. doi:10.1061/(ASCE)0733-9364(1994)120:4(785)

Semuels, A. (2013). Monitoring upends blance of power at workplace some say. *Los Angeles Times.* Available at http://www.latimes.com/business/money/la-fi-mo-monitoring-upends-balance-of-power-at-workplace-20130408,0,7425573.story

Senge, P. M., & Drucker, P. (2006). Strategies for change leaders. Executive Forum. *Leadership Institute.* Retrieved from http://www.mendeley.com

Senge, P. (1990). *The fifth discipline: The art & practice of the learning organization.* New York, NY: Doubleday.

Senge, P. (1990). *The Fifth Discipline: The Art and Practice of the Learning Organisation.* New York: Doubleday.

Senge, P. M. (2006). *The fifth discipline: The art and practice of the learning organization.* New York, NY: Doubleday, Random House Inc.

Senior, B., & Swailes, S. (2012). *Organizational Change.* London: FT-Pearson.

Serenko, A., & Bontis, N. (2004). Meta-review of knowledge management and intellectual capital literature: Citation impact and research productivity rankings. *Knowledge and Process Management, 11*(3), 185–198. doi:10.1002/kpm.203

Service, R. W., & Fekula, M. J. (2008). Beyond emotional intelligence: The EQ matrix as a leadership imperative. *Business Renaissance Quarterly, 3*(2), 23–57.

Shadur, M. A., Kienzle, R., & Rodwell, J. J. (1999). The relationship between organizational climate and employee perceptions of involvement. *Group & Organization Management, 24*(4), 479–503. doi:10.1177/1059601199244005

Shah, D. V., Cho, J., Eveland, W. P., & Kwak, N. (2005). Information and expression in a digital age: Modelling Internet effects on civic participation. *Communication Research, 32*(5), 531–565. doi:10.1177/0093650205279209

Shahhosseini, M., Daud Silong, A., & Arif Ismaill, I. (2013). Relationship between transactional, transformational leadership styles, emotional intelligence and job performance. *Researchers World: Journal of Arts. Science & Commerce, 4*(1), 15–22.

Shamir, B., Zakay, E., Breinin, E., & Popper, M. (1998). Correlates of charismatic leader behavior in military units: Subordinates' attitudes, unit characteristics and superior's appraisal of leader performance. *Academy of Management Journal, 41*(4), 387–438. doi:10.2307/257080

Sharbrough, W. C., Simmons, S. A., & Cantrill, D. A. (2006). Motivating language in industry: Its impact on job satisfaction and perceived supervisor effectiveness. *Journal of Business Communication, 43*(4), 322–343. doi:10.1177/0021943606291712

Sharma, M. (2014). English and Communication Skills for the 21st Century Engineers. *International Journal of Research in Advent Technology,* 86-89.

Sharma, R. S., & Djiaw, V. (2011). Realising the strategic impact of business intelligence tools. *VINE: The Journal of Information and Knowledge Management Systems, 41*(2), 113–131. doi:10.1108/03055721111134772

Shaw, B. (2001, March 9). What, Gee worry? OSU president's lack of concern over the Tressel scandal will likely raise some with the NCAA: Bud Shaw's sports spin. *Cleveland.com.* Retrieved October 27, 2015 from http://www.cleveland.com/budshaw/index.ssf/2011/03/what_gee_worry_osu_presidents.html

Shaw, E., O'Loughlin, A., & McFadzean, E. (2005). Corporate entrepreneurship and innovation part 2: A role- and process-based approach. *European Journal of Innovation Management, 8*(4), 393–408. doi:10.1108/14601060510627786

Shaw, K. (2005). Getting leaders involved in communication strategy: Breaking down the barriers to effective leadership communication. *Strategic Communication Management, 9,* 14–17.

Sheehan, K. B., & Hoy, M. G. (1998). Flaming, Complaining, Abstaining: How Online Users Respond to Privacy Concerns. *Journal of Advertising, 28*(3), 37–51. doi:10.1080/00913367.1999.10673588

Shepard, K., Gray, J. L., Hunt, J. G., & McArthur, S. (2005-2007). *Senior Fellow of the Global Organization Design Society Former GO Society Board Member.* Retrieved October 10, 2015, from http://globalro.org/index.php/sig/1619-julian-fairfield-page

Sherman, L. W. (1990). Police crackdowns: Initial and residual deterrence. *Crime and Justice, 12,* 1–48. doi:10.1086/449163

Shewart, W. A. (1931). *Economic Control of Quality of Manufactured Product.* New York: Van Nostrand.

Shin, Y., Sung, S. Y., Choi, J. N., & Kim, M. S. (2015). Top management ethical leadership and firm performance: Mediating role of ethical and procedural justice climate. *Journal of Business Ethics, 129*(1), 43–57. doi:10.1007/s10551-014-2144-5 PMID:26430288

Shooshtarian, Z., Ameli, F., & Aminilari, M. (2013). The effect of labor's emotional intelligence on their job satisfaction, job performance and commitment. *Iranian Journal of Management Studies, 6*(1), 29–45A.

Shrestina, L. B., & Hesler, E. J. (2011). *The Changing Demographic Profile of the United States.* CRS Report #RL32701 for United States Congress.

SHRM. (2005). *Workplace privacy – Poll findings: A study by the Society for Human Resource Management and CareerJournal.com.* Retrieved from http://www.shrm.org/Research/SurveyFindings/Documents/Workplace%20Privacy%20Poll%20Findings%20-%20A%20Study%20by%20SHRM%20and%20CareerJournal.com.pdf

Siebdrat, F., Hoegl, M., & Ernst, H. (2009). How to manage virtual teams. *MIT Sloan Management Review, 50*(4), 63–68.

Siegall, M., & Gardner, S. (2000). Contextual factors of psychological empowerment. *Personnel Review, 29*(6), 703–722. doi:10.1108/00483480010296474

Siegel, P. (2000). Using Baldridge to improve education: A rationale based on results. *Training & Development, 54*(2), 66–67.

Siemieniuch, C., & Sinclair, M. (2002). On complexity, process ownership and organizational learning in manufacturing organizations, from an ergonomics perspective. *Applied Ergonomics, 33*(5), 449–462. doi:10.1016/S0003-6870(02)00025-X PMID:12236654

Siewiorek, D., Smailagic, A., Furukawa, J., Krause, A., Moraveji, N., Reiger, K., ... (2003). *SenSay: a context-aware mobile phone.* Paper presented at the Wearable Computers, 2003. doi:10.1109/ISWC.2003.1241422

Silins, H. (1994). Leadership Characteristics and School Improvement. *Australian Journal of Education, 38*(3), 268–281. doi:10.1177/000494419403800306

Silins, H., & Mulford, B. (2002). Schools as learning organisations: The case for system, teacher and student learning. *Journal of Educational Administration, 40*(5), 425–446. doi:10.1108/09578230210440285

Silins, H., Mulford, B., Zarins, S., & Bishop, P. (2000). Leadership for Organizational Learning in Australian Secondary Schools. In K. Leithwood (Ed.), *Understanding Schools as Intelligent Systems* (pp. 267–291). Stamford, CT: JAI Press; doi:10.1080/03057640302041

Silins, H., Zarins, S., & Mulford, B. (2002). What characteristics and processes define a school as a learning organisation? Is this a useful concept to apply to schools? *International Education Journal, 3*(1), 24–32.

Sim, K. L., & Rogers, J. W. (2009). Implementing lean production systems: Barriers to change. *Management Research News*, *32*(1), 37–49. doi:10.1108/01409170910922014

Simonin, B. L. (1999). Ambiguity and the process of knowledge transfer in strategic alliances. *Strategic Management Journal*, *20*(7), 595–623. doi:10.1002/(SICI)1097-0266(199907)20:7<595::AID-SMJ47>3.0.CO;2-5

Sims, R. R., & Quatro, S. A. (2005). *Leadership: Succeeding in the private, public and not-for-profit sectors*. Armonk, NY: M.E. Sharpe.

Singh, S. (2013, March 8). Muhyiddin: English a compulsory pass subject as early as 2016. *The Star*.

Singh, P. (2013). Influence of leaders' intrapersonal competencies on employee job satisfaction. *The International Business & Economics Research Journal*, *12*, 1289–1302.

Sir Robert Peel's Principles of Law Enforcement. (n.d.). Retrieved on October 12, 2015 from https://www.durham.police.uk/AboutUs/Documents/Peels_Principles_Of_Law_Enforcement.pdf

Sisler, H. E. (2015). Crisis of man to crisis of men: Ray Rice and the NFL's transition from crisis of image to crisis of ethics. *TopSCHOLAR*. Retrieved October 18, 2015 from http://digitalcommons.wku.edu/theses/1520/

Skogan, W. G., Van Craen, W., & Hennessy, C. (2014). Training police for procedural justice. *Journal of Experimental Criminology*, *4*, 1–16. doi:10.1007/s11292-014-9223-6

Skok, W., & Goldstein, B. (2007). Managing organizational knowledge: Developing a strategy for a professional services company. *Strategic Change*, *16*(7), 327–339. doi:10.1002/jsc.805

Skov, B., & Høegh, T. (2006). Supporting information access in a hospital ward by a context-aware mobile electronic patient record. *Personal and Ubiquitous Computing*, *10*(4), 205–214. doi:10.1007/s00779-005-0049-0

Sledgianowski, D., & Kulviwat, S. (2009). Using social network sites: The effects of playfulness, critical mass and trust in a hedonic context. *Journal of Computer Information Systems*, *49*(4), 74–83.

Smircich, L. (1983). Concepts of culture and organizational effectiveness. *Administrative Science Quarterly*, *28*(3), 339–358. doi:10.2307/2392246

Smirich, L. (1985). Concepts of culture and organizational analysis. *Science Quarterly*, *28*, 39-58. Retrieved from http://www.jstor.org/stable/2392246

Smith, E. (2011, December 20). Ohio State hit with bowl ban, Tressel gets show-cause penalty. *USA Today*. Retrieved March 8, 2011 from USAToday.com.

Smith, P.A.C. (2005). Knowledge Sharing and Strategic Capital: The Importance and Identification of Opinion Leaders. *The Learning Organization*, *12*(6), 563 – 574.

Smith: Tressel's speech to team "eloquent". (2011, May 30). *USA Today*. Retrieved August 28, 2015 from http://usatoday30.usatoday.com/sports/college/football/2011-05-30-4107396395_x.htm

Smith, G., Sorensen, C., Gump, A., Heindel, A., Caris, M., & Martinez, C. (2011, March). Over-coming student resistance to group work: Online versus face to face. *The Internet and Higher Education*, *14*(2), 121–128. doi:10.1016/j.iheduc.2010.09.005

Smith, H. J., Dinev, T., & Xu, H. (2011). Information privacy research: An interdisciplinary review. *Management Information Systems Quarterly*, *35*(4), 989–1015.

Smith, H. J., Milberg, J. S., & Burke, J. S. (1996). Information privacy: Measuring individuals' concerns about organizational practices. *Management Information Systems Quarterly*, *20*(2), 167–196. doi:10.2307/249477

Smith, P., & Cockburn, T. (2013). *Dynamic Leadership Models for Global Business: Enhancing Digitally Connected Environments*. IGI Global. doi:10.4018/978-1-4666-2836-6

Smith, P., & Cockburn, T. (Eds.). (2014). *Impact of Emerging Digital Technologies on Leadership in Global Business*. IGI Global. doi:10.4018/978-1-4666-6134-9

Smith, R. A. (1962). Question of Arbitrability-The Role of the Arbitrator, the Court, and the Parties. *Southwestern Law Journal*, *16*(1).

Society for Human Resource Management (SHRM). (2015). *Leadership Competencies*. Retrieved September 2, 2015, from http://www.shrm.org/research/articles/articles/pages/leadershipcompetencies.aspx

Society for Human Resource Management. (2009). The multi-generational workforce: opportunity for competitive success. *Research Quarterly*. Retrieved from: http://www.shrm.org/Research/Articles/Articles/Documents/09-0027_RQ_March_2009_FINAL_no%20ad.pdf

Solis, B. (2011). *The end of business as usual: Rewire the way you work to succeed in the consumer revolution.* New York: John Wiley & Sons.

Solomon, J. (2013, August 6). Jay Bilas uses NCAA store to highlight Johnny Manziel scandal. *AL.com.* Retrieved September 16, 2014 from www.al.com

Solomon, C. M. (2001). Managing virtual teams. *Workforce, 80*(6), 60–64.

Solvoll, T., Fasani, S., Ravuri, A. B., Tiemersma, A., & Hartvigsen, G. (2010, August 23-24, 2010). *Evaluation of an Ascom/trixbox system for context sensitive communication in hospitals.* Paper presented at the 8th Scandinavian Conference on Health Informatics, Copenhagen, Denmark.

Solvoll, T., Gironi, L., & Hartvigsen, G. (2013). *CallMeSmart: An Ascom/Trixbox Based Prototype for Context Controlled Mobile Communication in Hospitals.* Paper presented at the Information Science and Applications (ICISA), 2013 International Conference on Information Science and Applications. doi:10.1109/ICISA.2013.6579344

Solvoll, T., Gironi, L., Giordanengo, A., & Hartvigsen, G. (2013). CallMeSmart: A VoIP Softphone on Android Based Mobile Devices Using SIP eTELEMED 2013. *The Fifth International Conference on eHealth, Telemedicine, and Social Medicine* (Vol. 15, pp. 198-203). International Academy, Research and Industry Association (IARIA).

Solvoll, T., Tiemersma, A., Kerbage, E., Fasani, S., Ravuri, A. B., & Hartvigsen, G. (2011). *Context-sensitive Communication in Hospitals: A User Interface Evaluation and Redesign of Ascom Wireless IP-DECT Phones.* eTELEMED 2011, The Third International Conference on eHealth, Telemedicine, and Social Medicine, Gosier, Guadeloupe, France.

Solvoll, T. (2013). Mobile Communication in Hospitals: What is the Problem? In C. Rückemann (Ed.), *Integrated Information and Computing Systems for Natural, Spatial, and Social Sciences* (pp. 287–301). Hershey, PA: Information Science Reference; doi:10.4018/978-1-4666-2190-9.ch014

Solvoll, T., & Scholl, J. (2008). Strategies to reduce interruptions from mobile communication systems in surgical wards. *Journal of Telemedicine and Telecare, 14*(7), 389–392. doi:10.1258/jtt.2008.007015 PMID:18852324

Solvoll, T., Scholl, J., & Hartvigsen, G. (2010). Physicians interrupted by mobile devices – relations between devices, roles and duties. *Studies in Health Technology and Informatics, 160,* 1365.

Solvoll, T., Scholl, J., & Hartvigsen, G. (2013). Physicians Interrupted by Mobile Devices in Hospitals: Understanding the Interaction Between Devices, Roles, and Duties. *Journal of Medical Internet Research, 15*(3), e56. doi:10.2196/jmir.2473 PMID:23470528

So, M. W. C., & Sculli, D. (2002). The role of trust, quality, value and risk in conducting e-business. *Industrial Management & Data Systems, 102*(9), 503–512. doi:10.1108/02635570210450181

Sorge, A. (2005). *The Global and the Local: Understanding the Dialectics of Business Systems.* Oxford: Oxford University Press. doi:10.1093/acprof:oso/9780199278909.001.0001

Sosa, E. (2010). The Epistemology of Disagreement. *His Armchair Philosophy.*

Sosik, J. J., & Jung, D. I. (2002). Workgroup characteristics and performance in collectivistic and individualistic cultures. *The Journal of Social Psychology, 142*(1), 5–23. doi:10.1080/00224540209603881 PMID:11913835

Sousa, R. (2003). Linking Quality Management to Manufacturing Strategy: An Empirical Investigation of Customer Focus Practices. *Journal of Operations Management, 21*(1), 1–18. doi:10.1016/S0272-6963(02)00055-4

Sousa, R., & Voss, C. (2002). Quality Management Re-visited: A Reflective Review and Agenda for Future Research. *Journal of Operations Management, 20*(1), 91–109. doi:10.1016/S0272-6963(01)00088-2

Spanbauer, S. J. (1989). *Measuring and Costing Quality in Education*. Appleton, WI: Fox Valley Technical College Foundation.

Spanneut, G., Tobin, J., & Ayers, S. (2012). Identifying the professional development needs of public school principals based on the interstate school leader licensure consortium standards. *NASSP Bulletin, 96*, 67–88. doi:10.1177/0192636512439230

Sparrow, P. R., & Gaston, K. (1996). Generic climate maps: A strategic application of climate survey data. *Journal of Organizational Behavior, 17*(6), 679–698. doi:10.1002/(SICI)1099-1379(199611)17:6<679::AID-JOB786>3.0.CO;2-M

Sperber, D. (1995). How do we communicate? Academic Press.

Sperber, D. (Ed.). (2000). *Metarepresentations*. Oxford: Oxford University Press.

Spicker, P. (2012). Leadership: A perniciously vague concept. *International Journal of Public Sector Management, 25*(1), 34–47. doi:10.1108/09513551211200276

Spillane, J. P. (2006). *Distributed leadership*. San Francisco, CA: Jossey-Bass.

Spitzberg, B. H., & Cupach, W. R. (1981). *Self-monitoring and relational competence*. Paper presented at the Speech Communication Association Convention, Anaheim, CA.

Spitzberg, B. H. (1983). Communication competence as knowledge, skill, and impression. *Communication Education, 32*(3), 323–329. doi:10.1080/03634528309378550

Spreitzer, G. M., & Mishra, A. K. (1999). Giving Up Control Without Losing Control: Trust and Its Substitutes' Effects on Managers' Involving Employees in Decision Making. *Group & Organization Management, 14*(2), 155–187. doi:10.1177/1059601199242003

Spurck, P. A., Mohr, M. L., Seroka, A. M., & Stoner, M. (1995). The impact of a wireless telecommunication system on time efficiency. *The Journal of Nursing Administration, 25*(6), 21–26. doi:10.1097/00005110-199506000-00007 PMID:7776003

Stacey, R. D. (2001). *Complex Responsive Processes in Organizations*. London: Routledge.

Stam, R. (1997). *Tropical multiculturalism: A comparative history of race in Brazilian cinema and culture*. Durham, NC: Duke University Press.

Standish Group International Inc. (2013). *Chaos Manifesto 2013 - Think Big*. Act Small.

Stanton, J. M. (2000a). Reactions to employee performance monitoring: Framework, review, and research directions. *Human Performance, 13*(1), 85–113. doi:10.1207/S15327043HUP1301_4

Stanton, J. M. (2000b). Traditional and electronic monitoring from an organizational justice perspective. *Journal of Business and Psychology, 15*(1), 129–147. doi:10.1023/A:1007775020214

Stanton, J. M., & Barnes-Farrell, J. L. (1996). Effects of electronic performance-monitoring on personal control, satisfaction and performance. *The Journal of Applied Psychology, 81*(6), 738–745. doi:10.1037/0021-9010.81.6.738

Staples, A. (2011, May 30). Tressel tries to take brunt of NCAA wrath with Ohio State resignation. *Sportsillustrated.com*. Retrieved June 1, 2011 from http://www.si.com/more-sports/2011/05/30/jim-tresselosu

Staples, D. S., & Cameron, A. F. (2004). Creating positive attitudes in virtual team members. In S. Godar (Ed.), *Virtual and collaborative teams* (pp. 76–113). Hershey, PA: Idea Group. doi:10.4018/978-1-59140-204-6.ch005

Staples, D. S., Wong, I. K., & Cameron, A. F. (2004). Best practices for virtual team effectiveness. In S. Godar (Ed.), *Virtual and collaborative teams* (pp. 160–185). Hershey, PA: Idea Group. doi:10.4018/978-1-59140-166-7.ch007

Staples, D. S., & Zhao, L. (2006). The effects of cultural diversity in virtual teams versus face-to-face teams. *Group Decision and Negotiation, 15*(4), 389–406. doi:10.1007/s10726-006-9042-x

Starbucks. (2011, November). *Starbucks to Present at Morgan Stanley Global Consumer Conference*. Starbucks Coffee Company Investor Relations. Retrieved from http://investor.starbucks.com/phoenix.zhtml?c=99518&p=irol-irhome

Starbucks. (2014, December). *A conversation with Starbucks partners about race in America.* Retrieved from https://news.starbucks.com/news/schultz-begins-a-conversation-with-starbucks-partners-about-racial-issues

Starbucks. (2015a, March 16). *What race together means for Starbucks partners and customers.* Retrieved from https://news.starbucks.com/news/what-race-together-means-for-starbucks-partners-and-customers

Starbucks. (2015b, March 20). *Video of the 2015 annual shareholders meeting.* Retrieved from https://news.starbucks.com/news/an-unprecedented-conversation-about-race-in-America

Starratt, R. (2005). Cultivating the moral character of learning and teaching: A neglected dimensions of educational leadership. *School Leadership & Management, 25*(4), 399–411. doi:10.1080/13634230500197272

Staw, B. (1986). Organizational psychology and the pursuit of the happy/productive worker. *California Management Review, 28*(4), 40–53. doi:10.2307/41165214

Stefanescu, C., & Popa, L. (2008, February). *Managerial Communication, Paper No. 7172.* Retrieved from http://mpra.ub.uni-muenchen.de/7172/

Sternberg, R. (2000). *Handbook of Intelligence.* Cambridge, UK: Cambridge University Press. doi:10.1017/CBO9780511807947

Sterrett, A. S. (2000). *The manager's pocket guide to emotional intelligence.* Boston, MA: HRD Press.

Stevens, B. (2005). What communication skills do employers want? Silicon Valley recruiters respond. *Journal of Employment Counseling, 42*(1), 2–9. doi:10.1002/j.2161-1920.2005.tb00893.x

Stevens, J., Beyer, J., & Trice, H. (1978). Assessing personal role and organizational predictors of managerial commitment. *Academy of Management Journal, 21*(3), 380–396. doi:10.2307/255721 PMID:10246524

Steyn, G. M. (2000). Applying Principles of TQM to a learning process: a case study. *SAJHE/SATHO, 14*(1), 11-14. Retrieved from http://hdl.handle.net/10500/242

Stinchcombe, A. L. (1974). *Creating Efficient Industrial Administration.* New York: Academic Press.

Stohl, C. (1984). *Quality circle and the quality of communication.* Paper presented at the Speech Communication Association Convention, Chicago, IL.

Stone, P. W., Larson, E. L., Mooney-Kane, C., Smolowitz, J., Lin, S. X., & Dick, A. W. (2006). Organizational climate and intensive care unit nurses' intention to leave. *Critical Care Medicine, 34*(7), 1907–1912. doi:10.1097/01.CCM.0000218411.53557.29 PMID:16625126

Subramaniama, G. K. J., & Harun, R. N. S. R. (2012). Marketing students' perceptions and their experiences during industrial training on English oral communication skills. *Procedia: Social and Behavioral Sciences, 66*, 283–289. doi:10.1016/j.sbspro.2012.11.270

Su, C., & Contractor, N. (2011). A Multidimensional Network Approach to Studying Team Members' Information Seeking From Human and Digital Knowledge Sources in Consulting Firms. *Journal of the American Society for Information Science and Technology, 62*(7), 1257–1275. doi:10.1002/asi.21526

Sullivan, P. (1998). *Profiting from intellectual capital: Extracting value from innovation.* New York: John Wiley and Sons Inc.

Sunindijo, R. Y. (2012). Integrating emotional intelligence, political skill, and transformational leadership in construction. *Civil Engineering Dimension, 14*, 182–189. doi:10.9744/CED.14.3.182-189

Sunshine, J., & Tyler, T. (2003a). Moral solidarity, identification with the community, and the importance of procedural justice: The police as prototypical representatives of a group's moral values. *Social Psychology Quarterly, 66*(2), 153–165. doi:10.2307/1519845

Sunshine, J., & Tyler, T. R. (2003b). The role of procedural justice and legitimacy in shaping public support in policing. *Law & Society Review, 37*(3), 513–548. doi:10.1111/1540-5893.3703002

Survey, A. M. A. (2001). *Workplace monitoring and surveillance.* Retrieved from http://www.amanet.org/research/pdfs/ems_short2001.pdf

Survey, A. M. A. (2003). *Email rules, policies and practices survey.* Retrieved from http://www.amanet.org/research/pdfs/email_policies_practices.pdf

Survey, A. M. A. (2005). *Electronic monitoring and surveillance survey*. Retrieved from http://www.amanet.org/research/pdfs/ems_summary05.pdf

Svensson, M., & Klefsjö, B. (2006). TQM-based self-assessment in the education sector: Experiences from a Swedish Upper Secondary School Project. *Quality Assurance in Education, 14*(4), 299–323. doi:10.1108/09684880610703929

Sykes, J. (1996). Claims and Disputes in Construction. *Constitutional Law Journal (Newark, N.J.), 12*(1), 3–13.

Sykes, R. E., & Clark, J. P. (1975). A theory of deference exchange in police-civilian encounters. *American Journal of Sociology, 81*(3), 584–600. doi:10.1086/226109

Sztajn, P. (1992). A matter of metaphors: Education as a handmade process. *Educational Leadership, 50*(3), 35–37.

Szulanski, G. (1996). Exploring internal stickiness: Impediments to the transfer of best practice within the firm. *Strategic Management Journal, 17*(S2), 27–43. doi:10.1002/smj.4250171105

Tacit. (2014). *The Impact of Tacit Knowledge on Perceived Performance of Doctors in a Chinese Hospital*. Retrieved October 8, 2015, from http://trap.ncirl.ie/1793/contactsatnocost

Talaei-Khoei, A., Solvoll, T., Ray, P., & Parameshwaran, N. (2011). Policy-based Awareness Management (PAM): Case study of a wireless communication system at a hospital. *Journal of Systems and Software, 84*(10), 1791–1805. doi:10.1016/j.jss.2011.05.024

Talaei-Khoei, A., Solvoll, T., Ray, P., & Parameshwaran, N. (2012). Maintaining awareness using policies; Enabling agents to identify relevance of information. *Journal of Computer and System Sciences, 78*(1), 370–391. doi:10.1016/j.jcss.2011.05.013

Taminiau, Y., Smit, W., & De Lange, A. (2009). Innovation in management consulting firms through informal knowledge sharing. *Journal of Knowledge Management, 43*(1), 42–55. doi:10.1108/13673270910931152

Tandon, R. (2013). New area in Johari Window. *International Journal of Engineering and Innovative Technology, 3*(2), 83–85.

Tang, J. C., Yankelovich, N., Begole, J., Kleek, M. V., Li, F., & Bhalodia, J. (2001). *ConNexus to awarenex: extending awareness to mobile users*. Paper presented at the SIGCHI conference on Human factors in computing systems, Seattle, WA. doi:10.1145/365024.365105

Tang, H. K. (1999). An inventory of organizational innovativeness. *Technovation, 19*(1), 41–51. doi:10.1016/S0166-4972(98)00077-7

Tan, H. H., & Quek, B. C. (2001). An exploratory study on the career anchors of educators in Singapore. *The Journal of Psychology, 135*(5), 527–545. doi:10.1080/00223980109603717 PMID:11804006

Tankebe, J., & Liebling, A. (2013). *Legitimacy and criminal justice: An international exploration*. OUP Oxford. doi:10.1093/acprof:oso/9780198701996.001.0001

Tannenbaum, R., Weschler, I. R., & Massarik, F. (1961). *Leadership and organization: A behavioral science approach*. New York, NY: McGraw-Hill Book Company.

Tavani, H. T. (2004). *Ethics and technology: Ethical issues in an age of information and communication technology*. Chichester, UK: John Wiley & Sons.

Taylor, F. W. (1970). What is scientific management? In H. F. Merrill (Ed.), *Classics in management* (pp. 67–71). New York: American Management Association.

Technologies, T. D. K. (2015). *Key Components of Organizational Leadership*. Retrieved September 2, 2015, from http://www.tdktech.com/tech-talks/key-components-of-organizational-leadership

Teece, D. J. (1998). Capturing value from knowledge assets: The new economy, markets for know-how and intangible assets. *California Management Review, 40*(3), 55–79. doi:10.2307/41165943

Temple, P., & Wragg, C. (2000). Virtual teamwork (or the magnificent seven ride again). *Perspectives, 4*(2), 1–3.

Temponi, C. (2005). Continuous improvement framework: Implications for academia. *Quality Assurance in Education, 13*(1), 17–36. doi:10.1108/09684880510578632

Temtime, Z. T. (2003). The Moderating Impacts of Business Planning and Firm Size on the Total Quality Management Practices. *The TQM Magazine, 15*(1), 52–60. doi:10.1108/09544780310454457

Terry, P. M. (1996). *Using Total Quality Management Principles to Implement School-Based Management.* Paper presented at the 14th Annual International Conference of the International Association of Management, Toronto, Canada. Retrieved from http://files.eric.ed.gov/fulltext/ED412590.pdf

Tess, P. A. (2013). The role of social media in higher education classes (real and virtual) – A literature review. *Computers in Human Behavior, 29*(5), A60–A68. doi:10.1016/j.chb.2012.12.032

Thatam, S. A. (2008). *Strategic Communication: A Primer.* Advanced Research and Assessment Group.

The Channel Tunnel Group Ltd v. Balfour Beatty Construction Ltd, (1993).

The Ohio State University. (2011, December 20). *Statement on NCAA sanctions.* Retrieved August 28, 2015 from http://www.ohiostatebuckeyes.com/genrel/122011aab.html

The Power of Transformational Leadership. (2013). *Professional Safety, 58*(1), 19.

The Stanford Encyclopedia of Philosophy. (2015). *Indexicals.* Stanford's Center for the Study of Language and Information. Retrieved on September 24, 2015, available at http://plato.stanford.edu/entries/indexicals/

The Week. (2015, February). 14 Urban Outfitters controversies. Retrieved from http://theweek.com/articles/480961/14-urban-outfitters-controversies

Theobald, P. (2005). Urban and rural schools: Overcoming lingering obstacles. *Phi Delta Kappan, 87*(2), 116–122. doi:10.1177/003172170508700207

Therkelsen, D. J., & Fiebich, C. L. (2003). The supervisor: The linchpin of employee relations. *Journal of Communication Management, 8*(2), 120–129. doi:10.1108/13632540410807592

Thibaut, J., Walker, L., LaTour, S., & Houlden, P. (1973). Procedural justice as fairness. *Stanford Law Review, 26*(6), 1271. doi:10.2307/1227990

Thomas, M., Hawkins, A., Christian, F., Merlene, M., & de Meyrick, C. (2011). *Independent Review of the School Based Management Report. Summary Report (October 2011).* Department of Education and Communities, NSW: ARTD Consultants. Retrieved from: https://www.det.nsw.edu.au/media/downloads/about-us/statistics-and-research/key-statistics-and-reports/irsb-management-pilot-sr.pdf

Thomas, K. (1976). Conflict and conflict management. In *Managing Across Diverse Cultures in Asia: Issues and Challenges in a Changing World.* London: Routledge.

Thompsen, J. A. (2000). Effective leadership of virtual project teams. *Futurics, 24*(3/4), 85–91.

Thompson, J. (2012). Transformational leadership can improve workforce competencies. *Nursing Management-UK, 18*(10), 21-24. doi: 10.7748/nm2012.03.18.10.21.c8958

Thornberry, N. (2001). Corporate entrepreneurship: Antidote or oxymoron? *European Management Journal, 19*(5), 526–533. doi:10.1016/S0263-2373(01)00066-4

Tidd, J. (2001). Innovation management in context: Environment, organization and performance. *International Journal of Management Reviews, 3*(3), 169–183. doi:10.1111/1468-2370.00062

Timmerman, C. E., & Scott, C. R. (2006). Virtually working: Communicative and structural predictors of media use and key outcomes in virtual work teams. *Communication Monographs, 73*(1), 108–136. doi:10.1080/03637750500534396

Ting-Toomey, S. (1994). Managing intercultural conflicts effectively. In L. Samovar & R. Porter (Eds.), *Intercultural communication: A reader* (7th ed.; pp. 360–372). Belmont, CA: Wadsworth.

Ting-Toomey, S. (1999). *Communicating across cultures.* New York: Guilford.

Tjosvold, D. (2008). The conflict-positive organization: It depends upon us. *Journal of Organizational Behavior, 29*(1), 19–28. doi:10.1002/job.473

Toffler, A., & Toffler, H. (2006). *Revolutionary wealth.* New York, NY: Knopf.

Tomlinson, G. (2010). Building a culture of high employee engagement. *Strategic HR Review*, 9(3), 25–31. doi:10.1108/14754391011040046

Tompkins, T. C. (1995). Role of diffusion in collective learning. *The International Journal of Organizational Analysis*, 3(1), 69–85. doi:10.1108/eb028824

Topper, A. (2007, December). Are they the same? Comparing the instructional quality of online and face-to-face graduate education courses. *Assessment & Evaluation in Higher Education*, 32(6), 681–691. doi:10.1080/02602930601117233

Tordera, N., Gonzalez-Roma, V., & Peiro, J. M. (2008). The moderator effect of psychological climate on the relationship between leader-member exchange (LMX) quality and role overload. *European Journal of Work and Organizational Psychology*, 17(1), 55–72. doi:10.1080/13594320701392059

Torres, C. A., & Antikainen, A. (2003). Introduction to a sociology of education: Old dilemmas in a new century? In C. A. Torres & A. Antikainen (Eds.), *The International Handbook on the Sociology of Education: An International Assessment of New Research and Theory* (pp. 1–18). Lanham, MD: Rowman & Littlefield.

Towers Watson Study. (2013). Retrieved from http://www.towerswatson.com/en/Insights/IC-Types/Survey-Research-Results/2013/05/Infographic-2013-Change-and-Communication-ROI-Study

Towers Watson. (2015). *Prioritising Employee Wellness*. Retrieved from: http://www.towerswatson.com/en/Insights/IC-Types/Reprints/2015/Prioritising-Employee-Wellness

Tracey, J. B., & Hinkin, T. R. (1998). Transformational leadership or effective managerial practices? *Group & Organization Studies*, 23(3), 220–236. doi:10.1177/1059601198233002

Tran, B. (2008). *Expatriate selection and retention* (Published Dissertation). California School of Professional Psychology at Alliant International University.

Tran, B. (2013). Industrial and organizational (I/O) psychology: The roles and purposes of I/O practitioners in global business. In B. Christiansen, E. Turkina, & N. Williams (Eds.), Cultural and technological influences on global business (pp. 175-219). Hershey, PA: Business Science Reference/IGI Global.

Tran, B. (2014a). The human element of the knowledge worker: Identifying, managing, and protecting the intellectual capital within knowledge management. In M. A. Chilton & J. M. Bloodgood (Eds.), Knowledge management and competitive advantage: Issues and potential solutions (pp. 281-303). Hershey, PA: Information Science Reference/IGI Global.

Tran, B. (2014b). The construction of knowledge management: The foundation of organizational learning based on learning organization. In F. Soliman (Eds.), Learning models for innovation in organizations: Examining the roles of knowledge transfer and human resources Management (pp. 89-110). Hershey, PA: Business Science Reference/IGI Global.

Tran, B. (2014c). The origin of servant leadership: The foundation of leadership. In R. Selladurai & S. Carraher (Eds.), Servant leadership: Research and practice (pp. 262-294). Hershey, PA: Business Science Reference/IGI Global.

Tran, B. (2014d). Ethos, pathos, and logos of doing business abroad: Geert Hofstede's five dimensions of national culture on transcultural marketing for incremental & radical innovation. In B. Christiansen, S. Yildiz, & E. Yildiz (Eds.), Transcultural marketing for incremental & radical innovation (pp. 255-280). Hershey, PA: Business Science Reference/IGI Global.

Tran, B. (2014e). The psychology of consumerism in business and marketing: The macro and micro behaviors of Hofstede's cultural consumers. In H. R. Kaufmann & M. F. A. K. Panni (Eds.), Handbook of research on consumerism in business and marketing: Concepts and practices (pp. 286-308). Hershey, PA: Business Science Reference/IGI Global.

Tran, B. (2016). Communication (intercultural and multicultural) at play for cross cultural management within multinational corporations (MNCs). In N. Zakaria, A. N. Abdul- Talib, & N. Osman (Eds.), Handbook of research on impacts of international business and political affairs on the global economy. Hershey, PA: IGI Global.

Tran, B., & Taing, C. (2013). *Leadership: Team building and the communication within.* Workshop given at the California State University, Sacramento's Student Organizations & Leadership's Fall 2013 SO&L Leadership Conference (SO&L). California State University, Sacramento.

Tran, B. (2015a). The next generation of leaders: Women in global leaderships in hotel management industry. In J. Feng, S. Stocklin, & W. Wang (Eds.), *Educational strategies for the next generation leaders in hotel management* (pp. 16–42). Hershey, PA: IGI Global.

Tran, B. (2015b). Expatriate selection and retention: Identifying and assessing the other characteristics beyond knowledge, skills, and abilities. In A. A. Camillo (Ed.), *Handbook of research on global hospitality and tourism management* (pp. 468–492). Hershey, PA: Premier Reference Source/IGI Global. doi:10.4018/978-1-4666-8606-9.ch023

Trauth, E. M., Beehr, T. A., & Haiyan, H. (2009). Retaining women in the US IT workforce: Theorizing the influence of organizational factors. *European Journal of Information Systems, 18*(5), 476–497. doi:10.1057/ejis.2009.31

Tressel Resignation: A Timeline of Quotes. (2011, May 30). *The Columbus Dispatch.* Retrieved August 28, 2015 from http://www.dispatch.com/content/stories/sports/2011/05/30/timeline-in-quotes.html

Tressel, J. (2011, March 8). Jim Tressel press conference 3/8/11. *Eleven Warriors.* Retrieved from http://www.youtube.com/watch?v=_wyQwtXvCC4

Trice, H. M., & Beyer, M. R. (1993). *The culture of work organizations.* Upper Saddle, NJ: Prentice Hall.

Triebs, T., & Kumbhakar, S. (2012b). *Management Practice in Production.* Ifo Working Paper Series Ifo Working Paper No. 129. Ifo Institute for Economic Research at the University of Munich.

Triebs, T., Saal, D. S., Arocena, P., & Kumbhakar, S. C. (2012a). *Estimating Economies of Scale and Scope with Flexible Technology.* Ifo Working Paper Series Ifo Working Paper No. 142. Ifo Institute for Economic Research at the University of Munich.

Trompenaars, F., & Hampden-Turner, C. (2012). *Riding the waves of culture.* New York, N.Y.: McGraw Hill.

Tsai, H. L., Zeng, S. Y., Lan, C. H., & Fang, R. J. (2012). The impacts of expatriate selection criteria on organizational performance in subsidiaries of transnational corporate: Recent Researches in Applied Computers and Computational Science. In *Proceedings of the 11th WSEAS International Conference on Applied Computer and Applied Computational Science.*

Tuckman, B. W. (1965). Developmental sequence in small groups. *Psychological Bulletin, 63*(6), 384–399. doi:10.1037/h0022100 PMID:14314073

Tully, E. (2002, May). The slippery slope. *National Executive Institute Associates, Major Cities Chiefs Association and Major County Sheriff's Association Leadership Bulletin,* 1-11.

Turban, E., King, D., Lee, J., Liang, T. P., & Turban, D. (2010). *Electronic commerce 2010: A managerial perspective* (6th ed.). Upper Saddle River, NJ: Pearson.

Turban, E., Leidner, D., McClean, E., & Wetherbe, J. (2006). *Information technology for management – Transforming organisations in the digital economy* (5th ed.). New York, NY: John Wiley & Sons.

Turner, R., & Lloyd-Walker, B. (2008). Emotional intelligence (EI) capabilities training: Can it develop EI in project teams? *International Journal of Managing Projects in Business, 1*(4), 512–534. doi:10.1108/17538370810906237

Twitter. (2015). *About Twitter: Fact sheet.* Retrieved from https://about.twitter.com/company

Tyler, T. R. (1988). What is procedural justice? Criteria used by citizens to assess the fairness of legal procedures. *Law & Society Review, 22*(1), 103–135. doi:10.2307/3053563

Tyler, T. R. (1990). *Why people obey the law.* Princeton University Press.

Tyler, T. R. (2003). Procedural justice, legitimacy, and the effective rule of law. In M. Tonry (Ed.), *Crime and justice: A review of research* (Vol. 30, pp. 431–505). Chicago: University of Chicago Press. doi:10.1086/652233

Tyler, T. R. (2004). Enhancing police legitimacy. *The Annals of the American Academy of Political and Social Science*, *593*(1), 84–99. doi:10.1177/0002716203262627

Tyler, T. R. (2010). *Why people cooperate: The role of social motivations*. Princeton University Press. doi:10.1515/9781400836666

Tyler, T. R., & Huo, Y. (2002). *Trust in the law: encouraging public cooperation with the police and courts through*. Russell Sage Foundation.

Tyran, K. L., Tyran, C. K., & Shepherd, M. (2003). Exploring emerging leadership in virtual teams. In C. Gibson & S. Cohen (Eds.), *Virtual teams that work: Creating conditions for virtual team effectiveness* (pp. 183–195). San Francisco, CA: Jossey-Bass.

U.S. Department of Health and Human Services. (2011). *Quality Improvement*. Retrieved September 2, 2015, from http://www.hrsa.gov/quality/toolbox/508pdfs/qualityimprovement.pdf

U.S. Department of Health and Human Services. (2014). *Regulations*. Retrieved September 2, 2015, from http://www.hhs.gov/regulations

Ullrich, C., Tan, X., Borau, K., Shen, L., Luo, H., & Shen, R. (2008). Why Web 2.0 is good for learning and for research: principles and prototypes. *Proceedings of the 17 th International World Wide Web Conference*. doi:10.1145/1367497.1367593

Ulmer, R. R., Seeger, M. W., & Sellnow, T. L. (2007). Post-crisis communication and renewal: Expanding the parameters of post-crisis discourse. *Public Relations Review*, *33*(2), 130–134. doi:10.1016/j.pubrev.2006.11.015

Ulmer, R. R., Sellnow, T. L., & Seeger, M. W. (2009). Post-crisis communication and renewal: Understanding the potential for positive outcomes in crisis communication. In R. L. Heath & D. H. O'Hair (Eds.), *Handbook of Risk and Crisis Communication*. New York: Routledge.

Ulmer, R. R., Sellnow, T. L., & Seeger, M. W. (2015). *Effective crisis communication: Moving from crisis to opportunity* (3rd ed.). Thousand Oaks, CA: Sage.

UNESCO. (2010). *Transcultural Communication in the Digital Age*. http://www.unesco.org/en/university-twinning-and-networking/access-by-region/europe-and-north-america/austria/unesco-chair-in-multilingual-transcultural-communication-in-the-digital-age-902/

United Nations Commission on International Trade Law. (2015). *UNCITRAL Model Law on International Commercial Arbitration*. Retrieved from http://www.uncitral.org/uncitral/en/uncitral_texts/arbitration/1985Model_arbitration_status.html

University of Toronto. (2013). *Higher Emotional Intelligence leads to better decision-making*. Retrieved September 2, 2015, from https://www.rotman.utoronto.ca/Connect/MediaCentre/NewsReleases/20131119.aspx

USA Time Zones Map with Current Local Time. (2009). Retrieved August 11, 2009, from http://www.worldtimezone.com/time-usa12.php

Uselac, S. (1993). *Zen Leadership: The Human Side of Total Quality Team Management*. Loudonville, OH: Mohican.

Vala, J., Monteiro, M., Lima, L., & Caetano, A. (1995). *Psicologia social das organizações: estudos em empresas portuguesas*. Oeiras: Celta Editora.

Valdesolo, P., & DeSteno, D. (2011). Synchrony and the social tuning of compassion. *Emotion (Washington, D.C.)*, *11*(2), 262–266. doi:10.1037/a0021302 PMID:21500895

Vallaster, C., & deChernatony, L. (2004). Internal brand building and structuration: The role of leadership. *European Journal of Marketing*, *40*(7/8), 761–784.

Van de Ven, A. H., & Poole, M. S. (1995). Explaining development and change in organizations. *Academy of Management Review*, *20*(3), 510. doi:10.2307/258786

Van de Ven, A. H., & Sun, K. (2012). Breakdowns in Implementing Models of Organizational Change. *Academy of Management Journal*, *50*(58-63).

Van Dyne, L., Graham, J., & Dienesch, R. (1994). Organizational citizenship behavior: Construct redefinition, measurement and validation. *Academy of Management Journal*, *37*(4), 765–802. doi:10.2307/256600

van Lieshout, E., van der Veer, S., Hensbroek, R., Korevaar, J., Vroom, M., & Schultz, M. (2007). Interference by new-generation mobile phones on critical care medical equipment. *Critical Care (London, England)*, *11*(5), R98. doi:10.1186/cc6115 PMID:17822524

Van Rijmenam, M. (2014). *How Big Data Analytics Will Affect Your Company Culture*. Retrieved from http://smartdatacollective.com/bigdatastartups/180176/how-big-data-analytics-will-affect-your-company-culture

Van Rijmenam, M. (2014). *Is Artificial Intelligence About To Change Doing Business Forever?* Retrieved from http://www.bigdata-startups.com/the-big-data-trends/

Van Vught, F. A., & Westerheijden, D. F. (1992). *Quality Management and Quality Assurance in European Higher Education: Methods and Mechanics.* Center for Higher Education Policy Studies, University of Twente.

Vanneman, A., Hamilton, L., Baldwin-Anderson, J., & Rahman, T. (2009). *Achievement Gaps: How Black and White Students in Public Schools Perform in Mathematics and Reading on the National Assessment of Educational Progress, (NCES 2009-455). National Center for Education Statistics, Institute of Education Sciences.* Washington, DC: U.S. Department of Education.

Varner, I., & Beamer, L. (1995). *Intercultural Communication in the Global Workplace.* Chicago, IL: Irwin Publishing Co.

Veletsianos, G. (2011). Higher education scholars' participation and practices on Twitter. *Journal of Computer Assisted Learning*, *28*(4), 336–349. doi:10.1111/j.1365-2729.2011.00449.x

Venkatraman, N., & Ramanujam, V. (1986). Measurement of business performance in strategy research: A comparison of approaches. *Academy of Management Review*, *11*(4), 801–814. doi:10.5465/AMR.1986.4283976

Vicini, J. (2011). Government did not pay $16 for muffins after all. *Reuters Online Edition*. Retrieved from http://www.reuters.com/article/2011/09/30/us-usa-justice-muffins-idUSTRE78T54220110930

Victor, D. A. (2001). A cross-cultural perspective on gender. In L. Arliss & D. Borisoff (Eds.), Women and men communicating: Challenges and change (2nd ed.; pp. 65-77). Long Grove: Waveland Press.

Viswesvaran, C. (2001). Assessment of individual job performance: a review of the past century and a look ahead. In N. Anderson, D. Ones, H. Sinangil, & C. Viswesvaran (Eds.), *Handbook of Industrial, Work and Organizational Psychology* (Vol. 1, pp. 110–126). London: SAGE Publications. doi:10.4135/9781848608320.n7

Vladimirov, R. (2014). *Website.* Retrieved from http://www.technologyreview.com/news/519051/is-samsungs-galaxy-gear-the-first-truly-smart-watch/

Von Hippel, E. (1988). *The Sources of Innovation.* New York: Oxford University Press.

Vrasidas, C., & Zembylas, M. (2004). Online professional development: Lessons from the field. *Education + Training*, *46*, 326–334. doi:10.1108/00400910410555231

Vrba, M. (2007). Emotional intelligence skills and leadership behaviour in a sample of South African first-line managers. *Management Dynamics*, *16*(2), 25–35.

Vroom, V. H. (1964). *Work and Motivation.* Willey New York.

Vroom, V. H., & Yetton, P. W. (1973). *Leadership and decision making.* Pittsburgh, PA: University of Pittsburgh Press.

Wager, K. A., Lee, F. W., & Glaser, J. P. (2013). *Health Care Information Systems: A Practical Approach for Health Care Management.* Hoboken, NJ: John Wiley & Sons.

Walker, D. (2010, December 23). Ohio State Buckeyes: Why Terrelle Pryor and others should sit out the Sugar Bowl. *The Bleacher Report*. Retrieved October 27, 2015 from http://bleacherreport.com/articles/551973-bad-buckeyes-why-terrell-pryor-and-others-should-sit-out-the-sugar-bowl

Walker, A., & Byrd, R. (2010). *The world has changed: Conversations with Alice Walker.* New York, NY: The New Press.

Walker, A., & Qian, H. (2015). Review of research on school principal leadership in mainland China, 1998-2013: Continuity and change. *Journal of Educational Administration, 53*(4), 467–491. doi:10.1108/JEA-05-2014-0063

Wall Street Journal. (2011). *How to Manage Different Generations*. Retrieved from: http://guides.wsj.com/management/managing-your-people/how-to-manage-different-generations/

Wallace, R. W. (2001). The dynamics of team formation. *HMS Beagle: The BioMedNet Magazine.* Retrieved from http://www.nasw.org/users/ RobWallace/team_dynamics.pdf

Wallace, H., & Robertson, C. (2009). *Written and interpersonal communication: Methods for law enforcement* (4th ed.). Prentice Hall.

Wallach, E. (1983). Individuals and organizations: The cultural match. *Training and Development Journal, 37*(2), 29–36.

Walpole, M., & Noeth, R. J. (2002). *The Promise of Baldrige for K-12 Education.* ACT Policy Report: ACT Policy Research Inc. Retrieved from https://www.act.org/research/policymakers/pdf/baldrige.pdf

Wan Ismail, W., & Al-Taee, F. (2012). Integrating gender, traits and transformational leadership style as viewed from human resource management. *International Journal of Academic Research, 4*, 16–20.

Wanberg, C. R., & Banas, J. T. (2000). Predictors and outcomes of openness to changes in a reorganizing workplace. *The Journal of Applied Psychology, 85*(1), 132–142. doi:10.1037/0021-9010.85.1.132 PMID:10740964

Wang, H., Lee, M. K. O., & Wang, C. (1998). Consumer privacy concerns about internet marketing. *Communications of the ACM, 41*(3), 63–70. doi:10.1145/272287.272299

Want, R., Schilit, Adams, Gold, Petersen, Goldberg, … Weiser. (1995). An overview of the parctab ubiquitous computing experiment. Personal Communications, IEEE, 2(6), 28-43.

Want, R., Hopper, A., Falcao, V., & Gibbons, J. (1992). The active badge location system. *ACM Transactions on Information Systems, 10*(1), 91–102. doi:10.1145/128756.128759

Wardak, A. (2003). *Jirga: a traditional mechanism of conflict resolution in Afghanistan.* Retrieved from Glamorgan: http://unpan1.un.org/intradoc/groups/public/documents/apcity/umpan017434.pdf

Ware, B. L., & Linkugel, W. A. (1973). They spoke on defense of themselves: On the generic criticism of apologia. *The Quarterly Journal of Speech, 59*(3), 273–283. doi:10.1080/00335637309383176

Warren, S., & Brandeis, L. (1890). The right to privacy. *Harvard Law Review, 4*(4), 193–220. doi:10.2307/1321160

Warr, P. (2006). Differential activation of judgments in employee well-being. *Journal of Occupational and Organizational Psychology, 79*(2), 225–244. doi:10.1348/096317905X52652

Warschauer, M. (2011). *Learning in the Cloud.* New York, NY: Teachers College Press.

Warschauer, M., Cotten, S. R., & Ames, M. G. (2011). One laptop per child birmingham: Case study of a radical experiment. *International Journal of Learning, 3*(2), 61–76. doi:10.1162/ijlm_a_00069

Washington State Office of Administrative Hearings. (2015). Glossary for Administrative Hearings.

Wasko, M. M., & Faraj, S. (2005). Why should I share? Examining social capital and knowledge contribution in electronic networks of practice. *Management Information Systems Quarterly, 29*(1), 35–57.

Waters, M. (2004). The leadership role of the first-line supervisor in police operations. *Florida Police Chief Magazine.* Retrieved from, http://www.clearwaterpolice.org/articles/waters.asp

Waters, R. D., & Jamal, J. Y. (2011). Tweet, tweet, tweet: A content analysis of nonprofit organizations' Twitter updates. *Public Relations Review, 37*(3), 321–324. doi:10.1016/j.pubrev.2011.03.002

Watkins, M. (2002). *Breakthrough business negotiation.* San Francisco: Jossey-Bass.

Watson Wyatt White Paper. (2008/2009). *Driving business results through continuous engagement.* Retrieved on 29 August from http://www.watsonwyatt.com/research/pdfs/2008-US-0232.pdf

Webster, F. (2002). A genre approach to oral presentation. *The Internet TESL Journal, 8*(7), 1-5. Retrieved online on 13 March 2010 from http://iteslj.org/Techniques/Webster-OralPresentation.html

Webster, M. (2014). *Regulation*. Retrieved September 2, 2015, from http://www.merriam-webster.com/dictionary/regulation

Weick, K. E. (2000). Quality Improvement: A Sensemaking Perspective. In R. E. Cole & W. R. Scott (Eds.), *The Quality Movement & Organization Theory* (pp. 155–172). Thousand Oaks, CA: Sage Publications Inc.

Weick, K., Sutcliffe, K. M., & Obstfeld, D. (1995). Sensemaking in organizations. *Sage (Atlanta, Ga.)*.

Weick, K., Sutcliffe, K. M., & Obstfeld, D. (2005). Organizing and the process of sensemaking. *Organization Science, 16*(4), 409–421. doi:10.1287/orsc.1050.0133

Weinberger, L. A. (2002). Emotional intelligence: Its connection to HRD theory and practice. *Human Resource Development Review, 1*(2), 215–243. doi:10.1177/15384302001002005

Weiser, M. (1991). The computer for the 21st century. *Scientific American, 265*(3), 94–104. doi:10.1038/scientificamerican0991-94 PMID:1675486

Weiser, M., Gold, R., & Brown, J. S. (1999). The origins of ubiquitous computing research at parc in the late 1980s. *IBM Systems Journal, 38*(4), 693–696. doi:10.1147/sj.384.0693

Wei, Y., Samiee, S., & Lee, R. P. (2014). The influence of organic organizational cultures, market responsiveness, and product strategy on firm performance in an emerging market. *Journal of the Academy of Marketing Science, 42*(1), 49–70. doi:10.1007/s11747-013-0337-6

Welch, M., & Jackson, P. R. (2007). Rethinking internal communication: A stakeholder approach. *Corporate Communications, 12*(2), 177–198. doi:10.1108/13563280710744847

Weller, L. D. (1998). Unlocking the culture for quality schools: Reengineering. *International Journal of Educational Management, 12*(6), 250–259. doi:10.1108/09513549810237959

Well, W. (2007). Type of contact and evaluations of police officers: The effects of procedural justice across three types of police-citizen contacts. *Journal of Criminal Justice, 35*(6), 612–621. doi:10.1016/j.jcrimjus.2007.09.006

Welsh-Huggins, A. (2013, June 5). Ohio State President Gordon Gee resigns. *The Boston Globe*. Retrieved October 25, 2015 from https://www.bostonglobe.com/sports/2013/06/05/ohio-president-gee-resigns/ifaooLYgKU6YAiqkjzOaSK/story.html

Wenger, E., McDemortt, R., & Snyder, W. (2002). Cultivating Communities of practice. Boston: Harvard Business Scholl Press.

Wenger, E. (1998). *Communities of practice: Learning, meaning, and identity*. Cambridge, UK: Cambridge University Press. doi:10.1017/CBO9780511803932

Wenger, E., & Snyder, W. (2000). Communities of practice: The organizational frontier. *Harvard Business Review*, (January-February), 139–145.

Wen, H. J., Schwieger, D., & Gershuny, P. (2007). Internet usage monitoring in the workplace: Its legal challenges and implementation strategies. *Information Systems Management, 24*(2), 185–196. doi:10.1080/10580530701221072

Wenying, W. (2005). Role of Conciliation in Resolving Disputes: A PRC Perspective. *The Ohio State Journal on Dispute Resolution, 20*(421).

Westbrook, Woods, Rob, Dunsmuir, & Day. (2011). Association of interruptions with an increased risk and severity of medication administration errors. *Archives of Internal Medicine, 170*(8), 683-690.

Western, S. (2013). *Leadership. A Critical Text* (2nd ed.). London: Sage.

Westin, A. (1967). *Privacy and Freedom*. Academic Press.

Westin, A. (1967). *Privacy and Freedom*. New York: Athenbaum.

Whipp, J. L. (2013). Developing socially just teachers: The interaction of experiences before, during, and after teacher preparation in beginning urban teachers. *Journal of Teacher Education, 64*(5), 454–467. doi:10.1177/0022487113494845

Whitehead, P. (2001). Team building and culture change: Well–trained and committed teams can successfully roll out culture change programs. *Journal of Change Management, 2*, 184–193. doi:10.1080/714042495

Whiting, J. W. M. (1986). George Peter Murdock (1897–1985). *American Anthropologist, 88*(3), 682–686. doi:10.1525/aa.1986.88.3.02a00120

Wholefoods. (2011, August). *John Mackey's Blog.* Retrieved from http://www2.wholefoodsmarket.com/blogs/jmackey/

Wiewiora, A., Murphy, G., Trigunarsyah, B., & Brown, K. (2014). Interactions between organizational culture, trustworthiness, and mechanisms for inter-project knowledge sharing. *Project Management Journal, 45*(2), 48–65. doi:10.1002/pmj.21407

Wiewiora, A., Trigunarsyah, B., Murphy, G., & Coffey, V. (2013). Organizational culture and willingness to share knowledge: A competing values perspective in Australian context. *International Journal of Project Management, 31*(8), 1163–1174. doi:10.1016/j.ijproman.2012.12.014

Wiig, K. M. (1997). Knowledge management: An introduction and perspective. *Journal of Knowledge Management, 1*(1), 6–14. doi:10.1108/13673279710800682

Wilde, M. (2013). *Quantum Information Theory.* Cambridge University Press. doi:10.1017/CBO9781139525343

Williams, F. P., & McShane, M. D. (1998). Criminology Theory: Selected Classic Readings (2nd ed.). Cincinnati, OH: Anderson Publishing Co.

Williams, L. J., & Anderson, S. E. (1991). Job satisfaction and organizational commitment as predictors of organizational citizenship and in-role behaviors. *Journal of Management, 17*(3), 601–617. doi:10.1177/014920639101700305

Willmott, H., & Alvesson, M. (Eds.). (1994). *Critical Management Studies.* London: Sage.

Wilson, D. (2000). Metarepresentation in linguistic communication. Academic Press.

Wilson, M. (2014, September). Urban Outfitters CEO to employees: Kent State sweatshirt sale an 'unfortunate occurrence'. *PR Daily.* Retrieved from http://www.prdaily.com/Main/Articles/Urban_Outfitters_CEO_to_employees_Kent_State_sweat_17280.aspx

Wilson, A. M. (2001). Understanding organizational culture and the implication for corporate marketing. *European Journal of Marketing, 35*(3/4), 353–367. doi:10.1108/03090560110382066

Winchel, B. (2014, September). Urban Outfitters offends with red-stained 'vintage' Kent State sweatshirt. *PR Daily.* Retrieved from http://www.prdaily.com/Main/Articles/17261.aspx

Wing, D. W. (2010). Microaggressions in Everyday Life: Race, Gender, and Sexual Orientation. Hoboken, NJ: John Wiley & Sons.

Winslade, J., & Monk, G. (2000). *Narrative Mediation: A New Approach to Conflict Resolution.* San Francisco: Jossey-Bass Publishers.

Woodrow, L. (2006). Anxiety and speaking English as a second language. *RELC Journal, 37*(3), 308–328. doi:10.1177/0033688206071315

Woolf, L. (1998). *Access to Justice: Interim and Final Reports by Lord Woolf to the Lord Chancellor.* Academic Press.

Workman, M. (2007). The effects from technology-mediated interaction and openness in virtual team performance measures. *Behaviour & Information Technology, 26*(5), 355–365. doi:10.1080/01449290500402809

Worland, J. (2014, November). Here's what's happening with the Ice Bucket Challenge money. *TIME.* Retrieved from http://time.com/topic/als-ice-bucket-challenge-2/

Wu, E. (2015). *SB853 Bill Health care language assistance.* Retrieved October 6, 2015, from: http://cpehn.org/policy-center/cultural-and-linguistic-competency/sb-853-health-care-language-assistance-act

Wu, F. Y. (2009). The relationship between leadership styles and foreign English teachers' job satisfaction in adult English cram schools: Evidences in Taiwan. *Journal of American Academy of Business, Cambridge, 14*(2), 75–82.

Wu, R., Rossos, P., Quan, S., Reeves, S., Lo, V., Wong, B., & Morra, D. et al. (2011). An evaluation of the use of smartphones to communicate between clinicians: A mixed-methods study. *Journal of Medical Internet Research*, *13*(3), e59. doi:10.2196/jmir.1655 PMID:21875849

Xiaowei, L. (2006). A test on the systematic fuzzy measures of the key degree for the core employees' performance traits. *Canadian Social Science*, *2*(5), 38–43.

Xu, H., Dinev, T., Smith, J. H., & Hart, P. (2011).Information privacy concerns: Linking individual perceptions with institutional privacy assurances. *Journal of the Association for Information Systems*, *12*(12), 798–824.

Xu, Y. (2007). Strategic analysis on cross-cultural human resources management. *Market Modernization*, *19*, 274–275.

Yamane, T. (1970). *Statistics: An introductory analysis.* Tokyo, Japan: John Weatherhill.

Yammarino, F. J., & Dubinsky, A. J. (1994). Transformational leadership theory: Using levels of analysis to determine boundary conditions. *Personnel Psychology*, *47*(4), 787–811. doi:10.1111/j.1744-6570.1994.tb01576.x

Yang, M. (2012). Transformational leadership and Taiwanese public relations practitioners' job satisfaction and organizational commitment. *Social Behavior & Personality: An International Journal*, *40*(1), 31–46. doi:10.2224/sbp.2012.40.1.31

Yankelovich, D., & Immerwahr, J. (1983). *Putting the work ethic to work.* New York: Public Agenda Foundation.

Yasin, A. Y. M., Shaupil, W. M. H. W. M., Mukhtar, A. M., Ab Ghani, N. I., & Rashid, F. (2010). The Englisg Proficiency of Civil Engineering Students at a Malaysian Polytechnic. *Asian Social Science*, *6*(6), 161. doi:10.5539/ass.v6n6p161

Yerby. (2013). Legal and ethical issues of employee monitoring. *Online Journal of Applied Knowledge Management, 1*(2), 44-55.

Yi-Feng, Y. (2009). An investigation of group interaction functioning stimulated by transformational leadership on employee intrinsic and extrinsic job satisfaction: An extension of the resource-based theory perspective. *Social Behavior & Personality: An International Journal*, *37*(9), 1259–1277. doi:10.2224/sbp.2009.37.9.1259

Yin, R. K. (2013). *Case Study Research: Design and Methods* (5th ed.). London: Sage.

Yin, R. K. (2014). *Case study research: Design and methods* (5th ed.). Thousand Oaks, CA: Sage.

Yoshino, M. (1968). *Japan's managerial system: Tradition and innovation.* Cambridge, MA: MIT Press.

Yosso, T. J. (2005). Whose culture has capital? A critical race theory discussion of community cultural wealth. *Race, Ethnicity and Education*, *8*(1), 69–91. doi:10.1080/1361332052000341006

Young, K. (2011). Social ties, social networks and the Facebook experience. *International Journal of Emerging Technologies and Society*, *9*(1), 20–34.

Youngs, P., & King, M. B. (2002). Principal leadership for professional development to build school capacity. *Educational Administration Quarterly*, *38*(5), 643–670. doi:10.1177/0013161X02239642

Yousef, R., Jamil, H., & Razak, N. (2013). Willingness to Communicate in English: A Study of Malaysian Pre-Service English Teachers. *English Language Teaching*, *6*(9), 205–216. doi:10.5539/elt.v6n9p205

Yuan, W. (2006). *Intercultural communication and conflict between American and Chinese colleagues in China-based multinational organizations.* (Unpublished doctoral dissertation). University of Kentucky.

Yuan, B. C., Wan-Lung, H., Jia-Horng, S., & Kuang-Pin, L. (2012). Increasing emotional intelligence of employees: Evidence from research and development teams in Taiwan. *Social Behavior & Personality: An International Journal*, *40*(10), 1713–1724. doi:10.2224/sbp.2012.40.10.1713

Yukl, G. (2002). *Leadership in organizations* (5th ed.). Upper Saddle River, NJ: Prentice Hall.

Yukl, G. (2005). *Leadership in Organizations* (6th ed.). New York: Pearson.

Yukl, G. (2009). Leading organizational learning: Reflections on theory and research. *The Leadership Quarterly*, *20*(1), 49–53. doi:10.1016/j.leaqua.2008.11.006

Yulk, G., & Becker, W. (2006). Effective empowerment in organizations. *Organizational Management Journal*, *3*(3), 210–231. doi:10.1057/omj.2006.20

Yung-Shui, W., & Tung-Chun, H. (2009). The relationship of transformational leadership with group cohesiveness and emotional intelligence. *Social Behavior & Personality: An International Journal, 37*(3), 379–392. doi:10.2224/sbp.2009.37.3.379

Yusoff, M. (2010). Analysing communication competence in oral presentations: Engineering students' experiences. *Journal of Human Capital Development, 3*(1), 99–117.

Zaccaro, S. (2001). The Nature of Executive Leadership: A Conceptual and Empirical Analysis of Success. Washington, DC: American Psychological Association

Zaccaro, S. J. (2007). Trait-based perspectives of leadership. *The American Psychologist, 62*(1), 6–16. doi:10.1037/0003-066X.62.1.6 PMID:17209675

Zaccaro, S. L., & Bader, P. (2003). E-leadership and the challenges of leading e-teams: Minimizing the bad and maximizing the good. *Organizational Dynamics, 31*, 377–387. doi:10.1016/S0090-2616(02)00129-8

Zahra, S. A. (1985). Corporate entrepreneurship and financial performance: The case of management leveraged buyouts. *Journal of Business Venturing, 10*(3), 225–24. doi:10.1016/0883-9026(94)00024-O

Zakaria, N., Amelinckx, A., & Wilemon, D. (2004). Working together apart? Building a knowledge–sharing culture for global virtual teams. *Creativity and Innovation Management, 13*(1), 15–29. doi:10.1111/j.1467-8691.2004.00290.x

Zeffane, R., Tipu, S. A., & Ryan, J. C. (2011). Communication, Commitment & Trust: Exploring the Triad. *International Journal of Business and Management, 6*(6), 77–87. doi:10.5539/ijbm.v6n6p77

Zhang, J., & Xu, M. (2007). Study of cross-cultural communication management in global competition. *Economic and Managerial Study, 9*, 77–81.

Zhao, D., & Rosson, M. B. (2009, May). How and why people Twitter: the role that micro-blogging plays in informal communication at work. In *Proceedings of the ACM 2009 international conference on supporting group work* (pp. 243-252). New York: ACM. doi:10.1145/1531674.1531710

Zheng, S., Shi, K., Zeng, Z., & Lu, Q. (2010). The Exploration of Instrument of Users' Privacy Concerns of Social Network Service. *2010 IEEE International Conference on Industrial Engineering and Engineering Management* (pp. 1538-1542). doi:10.1109/IEEM.2010.5674165

Zigurs, I. (2003). Leadership in virtual teams: Oxymoron or opportunity? *Organizational Dynamics, 31*, 339–351. doi:10.1016/S0090-2616(02)00132-8

Zivick, J. (2012). Mapping global virtual team leadership actions to organizational roles. *Business Review (Federal Reserve Bank of Philadelphia),19*(2), 18–25.

Zolin, R., Hinds, P. J., Fruchter, R., & Levitt, R. E. (2004). Interpersonal trust in cross-functional, geographically distributed work: A longitudinal study. *Information and Organization, 14*(1), 1–26. doi:10.1016/j.infoandorg.2003.09.002

Zoller, K. (2015). The Philosophy of Communicative Intelligence. In Cross-Cultural Collaboration and Leadership in Modern Organizations. IGI Global.

Zoller, K. (2008). Nonverbal patterns of teachers from 5 countries: Results from the TIMSS-R video study. *Dissertation Abstracts International. A, The Humanities and Social Sciences, 68*(9-A), 154.

Zoller, K., & Landry, C. (2010). *The choreography of presenting: the 7 essential abilities of effective presenters.* Thousand Oaks, CA: Corwin Press.

Zorn, T., Page, D., & Cheney, G. (2000). Nuts about change: Multiple perspectives on change-oriented communication in a public sector organization. *Management Communication Quarterly, 13*(4), 515–566. doi:10.1177/0893318900134001

Zúñiga, X., & Nagda, B. A. (1993). Dialogue groups: An innovative approach to multicultural learning. In D. Schoem, L. Frankel, X. Zúñiga, & E. Lewis (Eds.), *Multicultural teaching in the university* (pp. 233–248). Westport, CT: Praeger.

Zúñiga, X., Nagda, B. A., & Sevig, T. D. (2002). Intergroup dialogues: An educational model for cultivating engagement across differences. *Equity & Excellence in Education, 35*(1), 7–17. doi:10.1080/713845248

Zuñiga, X., & Sevig, T. D. (1997). Bridging the "us/them" divide through intergroup dialogues and peer leadership. *Diversity Factor*, 6(2), 23–28.

Zweig, D., & Webster, J. (2002). Where is the line between benign and invasive? An examination of psychological barriers to the acceptance of awareness monitoring system. *Journal of Organizational Behavior*, 23(5), 605–633. doi:10.1002/job.157

About the Contributors

Anthony H. Normore holds a Ph.D from the University of Toronto and is currently a Professor of Educational Leadership, and Department Chair of Graduate Education at California State University Dominguez Hills. His other leadership experiences include Chair of Special Education; Co-Chair of Teacher Education; visiting professor at Seoul National University; Director of Doctoral Programs at California Lutheran University; visiting professor at Guelph/Humber; and a graduate professor for the Summer Leadership Academy at Teachers College-Columbia University. His 30+ years of professional experiences has taken him throughout the world. His research focusses on urban school leadership development in the context of ethics and social justice in which he has authored and edited of numerous books including *Inclusive practices and social justice leadership for special populations in urban settings* (2015, Information Age Publishing); and *Cross-cultural collaboration and leadership in modern organizations* (2015, IGI Global). He has published a litany of book chapters and peer-reviewed articles in numerous leading leadership journals, and law enforcement venues. Dr. Normore was named the 2013 recipient of the *Bridge People Award* with the American Educational Research Association, and more recently the recipient of 2015 Donald Willower Award of Excellence in Research at Penn State University. He serves as the Chairman of the Criminal Justice Commission for Credible Leadership Development at the International Academy of Public Safety.

Larry W. Long holds a Ph.D in Communication from the University of Oklahoma and is Professor and Director Emeritus of the School of Communication at Illinois State University. Currently, he serves as Executive Director of the Criminal Justice Commission for Credible Leadership Development. Dr. Long is a retired artillery and infantry officer who completed 21 years of honorable service with the Army National Guard and is an honorary member of the U.S. Army Special Forces, Fort Bragg, North Carolina. He received numerous decorations including the Army Commendation Medal and the Oklahoma Army National Guard Commendation Medal. He has experience overseeing international programs in France and Korea and has served as visiting professor for Novancia Grande école de commerce in Paris, France.. In addition, he received the honor of being named as the 1998-99 "Person of the Year" by the National Society of Accountants for his work in developing their strategic plan and process decision making systems. Dr. Long has been qualified as an expert witness in product liability litigation, particularly in the areas of warning label efficacy and research methodology. He has published over 40 books, book chapters and articles in national and international journals. He has presented over 100 research reports at national and international meetings. He has received special recognition and awards for teaching, service, and scholarship from the College of Humanities and Social Sciences at North

Carolina State University, Illinois State University, Central States Communication Association, and the National Communication Association.

Mitch Javidi holds a Ph.D. from the University of Oklahoma. He is currently the founder and the president of the International Academy of Public Safety (IAPS), the Institute for Credible Leadership Development (ICLD) and the Criminal Justice Commission on Credible Leadership Development (CJCCLD). Mitch is an envisioneer with over 30 years of practical and hands-on business experience in diverse industries including but not limited to Academia, Automotive, Banking, Insurance, Government, Military, Law Enforcement, Retail, Logistics, Oil & Chemical, Pharma, Procurement, Supply Chain, and Technology. As a globally recognized leader, Mitch has trained at the Joint Special Operations Command "JSOC" and the US Army Special Operations Command "USASOC." He was awarded the Honorary Member of the United States Army Special Operations Command in 1999 and Honorary Sheriff by the National Sheriffs Association in 2015. He served as a tenured Associate Professor at NC State University for 16 years before taking an early retirement but continues to serve as an Adjunct professor without pay at both NC State and Illinois State Universities. He is a member of the "Academy of Outstanding Teachers and Scholars" at NC State University and the Distinguished 2004 Alumni of the University of Oklahoma. Mitch has published significant number of articles and presented over 890 presentations worldwide. Mitch was the recipient of prestigious "Person of the Year" award by the National Society of Accountants ~ Senator William Victor "Bill" Roth, Jr. "Roth IRA" received the award in the following year.

* * *

Katherine Bergethon grew up in Bloomington-Normal, IL. She has an undergraduate degree in 3D Art and Design from Illinois Wesleyan University. After undergrad, she continued her education in Graphic Communications for two years before completing her Masters in Project Management with a focus in Leadership Communication at Illinois State University. Currently, Katherine is expanding her experience in IT and Organizational Projects, as well as continuing research and writing on Leadership Communication. Katherine's personal interests include: Art and Design such as photography, sculpture, painting, functional found furniture restoration; Cooking flavorful dishes that utilize local produce, traditional and innovative techniques; Eclectic music collection and classically trained violinist; Outdoor and athletic interests including rock climbing, triathlons, cycling, weight training, swimming, camping and hiking; Lucky to be supported by a loving group of friends and family; Dedicated to being a caring, supportive, honest and strong human being.

Olaf Cames, MSc with Distinction is SME Owner of German Quantum High Tech Startup 'IAQS Institute for Applied Quantum Information Science GmbH' (Source) and CEO of US based Quantum High Tech Startup Virtual Broadcasting Information Center (VBIC) LLC (Source). He received MSc degree in IT with Distinction (Information Security), and is in the Thesis phase of his Doctorate degree in Business Administration – University of Liverpool (UK). His research interests are focused on quantum information science, design of augmented intelligence decision support systems and Global Data Privacy Compliance (www.eu-security.us).

Angelo A. Camillo, PhD, is Associate Professor of Strategic Management at Woodbury University in Burbank California, and is Adjunct Professor at Sonoma State University, Sonoma, USA. He has over 35 years of international hospitality industry management experience and has worked and lived in ten countries and four continents. He holds a degree from Heidelberg Hotel Management School Germany, a MBA from San Francisco State University, and a PhD from Oklahoma State University and Executive Education Certificates from Cornell University. He teaches courses in Strategic Management, Global Enterprise Management, Entrepreneurship, Management Consulting, Hospitality Management and Business Development. He is also hospitality business consultant to major international corporations.

Isabell C. Camillo is an adjunct instructor at the Goodman School of Business, Brock University in St. Catharines, Canada. She teaches courses in Business Communication and Human Relations. Her cross-disciplinary research areas of interest are Intercultural Business Communication, Wine Business, and Hospitality and Tourism Management. Her industry experience spans 27 years. She received a Bachelor's Degree in Modern Languages, a certificate in Adult Education teaching ESL, and a Master's in Linguistics from Brock University, and holds certifications in Business Management and Leadership from Niagara College Canada. She is the Principal of Aeris Language Solutions, a multilingual business language service and consulting firm based in Niagara Falls, Canada.

Vera Silva Carlos has a Ph.D. in Business and taught Electronic Commerce and Web Marketing at the University of Beira Interior, in Portugal. Currently, she teaches Project Management and New Product Development to master students at the University of Aveiro. She is also a researcher at the Research Centre on Enterprise Science (NECE – Núcleo de Estudos em Ciências Empresariais). Her research interests are mainly focused on Digital Marketing and on Internal marketing and its influence on the individual's attitudes and behavior at work. Specifically, her research is focused on the context of Higher Education.

Edward T. Chen is a professor of Management Information Systems of Operations and Information Systems Department in the Manning School of Business at University of Massachusetts Lowell. Dr. Chen has published over sixty refereed research articles in scholarly journals and chapters in reference books. Dr. Chen has served as vice-president, board director, track chair, and session chair of many professional associations and conferences. Professor Chen has also served as journal editor, editorial reviewer, and ad hoc reviewer for various academic journals. Dr. Chen has received the Irwin Distinguished Paper Award at the Southwestern Federation of Administrative Disciplines conference and the Best Paper Award at the International Conference on Accounting and Information Technology. His main research interests are in the areas of Social Media, Project Management, Knowledge Management, and Software Development.

Christine Clark is Professor of Curriculum and Instruction, Senior Scholar for Multicultural Education, and Founding Vice President for Diversity and Inclusion at the University of Nevada, Las Vegas. She coordinates masters and doctoral level specialization programs in multicultural education in the Department of Teaching and Learning/College of Education. She is lead co-editor of *Occupying the Academy: Just How Important is Diversity Work in Higher Education?* (2012, with Brimhall-Vargas and Fasching-Varner, Rowman & Littlefield), an invited chapter co-author for *Leadership for Increasingly Diverse Schools* (2015, with Horsford, and co-edited by Theoharis & Scanlan, Routledge) and an invited entry author for *Multicultural America: A Multimedia Encyclopedia* (Cortés, 2013, Sage) and the *Encyclopedia of Diversity in Education* (Banks, 2012, Sage). Clark was a member of the Board of Directors of the National Association for Multicultural Education (NAME) for seven years and has served on the Editorial Board for the organization's journal, *Multicultural Perspectives*, since 1998. In 2014, NAME awarded Clark the G. Pritchy Smith National Multicultural Educator of the Year Award. In 2010 and 2013, Clark was appointed/reappointed to the National Advisory Committee of the National Conference on Race and Ethnicity (NCORE). Clark is also the Associate Editor for the Higher Education section of *Multicultural Education* (since 2002), serves on the Editorial Board for *Equity & Excellence in Education* (since 2014), and served on the Editorial Board of the *Journal of Praxis in Multicultural Education* (from 2005-2009); she is also a regular reviewer for the *Journal of Diversity in Higher Education*, the *Journal of Educational Philosophy and Theory*, the *Journal of Negro Education*, *Action in Teacher Education*, the *National Association for Bilingual Education (NABE) Journal of Research and Practice*, and *Multicultural Education Review (MER)*, the Journal of the Korean Association for Multicultural Education (KAME).

Tom Cockburn obtained his first degree with honors from Leicester University, England, Postgraduate Cert. Ed., in Wolverhampton,England and both his MBA and Doctorate were gained at Cardiff University, Wales. Tom was elected an Associate Fellow of the New Zealand Institute of Management in 2010 and is currently director(policy) for the Center for Dynamic Leadership Models in Global Business and a senior associate of The Leadership Alliance Inc., headquartered in Canada.

Regina Connolly specialises in Management Information Systems at Dublin City University Business School, Dublin, Ireland. She received her PhD from Trinity College Dublin. Her research interests include eCommerce trust and privacy issues, website service quality evaluation, eGovernment and IT value evaluation in the public sector. Dr. Connolly has served on the expert eCommerce advisory group for Dublin Chamber of Commerce, which has advised national government on eCommerce strategic planning.

Doris E. Cross received a Ph.D. in management with a specialty in Organizational Leadership. She is currently the CEO and Principal Consultant at Organizational Change & Development Company (OCDC) in Lancaster, Pennsylvania. An organizational leadership consultant, Dr. Cross has over 20 years of experience working with diverse workplace environments. She has experience in organizational diagnosis and the design, and facilitation of large scale events and workforce development activities. Her knowledge base includes higher education institutions, profit and non-profit businesses, and government agencies. Dr. Cross is proficient in communicating effectively at all organizational levels and building relationships of trust among high performing teams. Other areas of expertise include organizational cultural analysis, needs assessment, focus group facilitations, executive coaching, leadership assessment and development, diversity training, program development and a host of other OD skills. She is a member of American Society for Training and Development (ATSD), the Organizational Development Network (ODN), and the National Speakers Association.

Daniel Cochece Davis joined Illinois State University as an assistant professor in the School of Communication in 2012. He holds an A.A. in General Education with an emphasis and certificate in Speech Communication from Santa Rosa Junior College, a B.A. in Communication Studies from San Francisco State University, an M.A. in Speech Communication from San Diego State University, and both an M.A. and Ph.D. in Communication Theory from University of Southern California. His teaching, research and consulting interests include organizational, leadership, group/team, intercultural, and nonverbal communication, examining the neuro-cultural dialectic across all types and contexts of human communication. He specializes in sustainable organizations.

Brian Ellis is an 18-year veteran with the Sacramento Police Department.Lieutenant Ellis has worked in a number of specialized assignments including with the Problem Oriented Policing Unit, Parole Intervention and Career Criminal Apprehension Teams, Narcotics and Robbery/Burglary divisions. He is currently a watch commander for the East Command. Brian earned his undergraduate degree in Criminal Justice from California State, Sacramento and has a MS in Organizational Leadership from National University. He is a contributor to *Cross-cultural collaboration and leadership in modern organizations* (2015, IGI Global), and some of his publications appear in *Law Enforcement Today, Peace Officers Research Association of California, PoliceOne, and The Journal of California Law Enforcement*. Brian serves as a commissioner for the Criminal Justice Commission for Credible Leadership and Development at the International Academy of Public Safety. Follow him on Twitter at @BrianEllis10.

Venesser Fernandes is a Lecturer – Educational Leadership Studies in the Faculty of Education, Monash University, Melbourne, Australia. She currently teaches courses in the Master of Leadership Studies, Masters in Education and Masters in International Development programs offered at Monash University. Her areas of teaching and research interest include: Leadership and Organisational Development Studies; School Leadership; School Accountability and Improvement Systems, Data-Driven Decision-making Processes; Change Management Systems; Globalisation and Social Justice in Education and, Educational Policy Analysis and Development. Venesser has been involved with the Principal Preparation Program team that runs in partnership with Monash University, the DE&T, Victoria and Bastow Institute of Educational Leadership which focuses on the leadership development of aspiring principals within state schools around Victoria. Venesser also works as a School Reviewer for the DE&T schools in Victoria and researches in this space as an Early Career Researcher. In her role as a Professional Experience Educator, Venesser works with aspiring teachers at the undergraduate level in developing their core understanding around teaching and learning and in engaging them productively through their professional experience practicuums within schools. Venesser has also worked previously as an educational consultant with schools helping them in developing whole school continuous improvement systems.

Saleem Gul has several years of field experience in projects spread across countries such as USA, Canada, Guyana, and Pakistan. In addition, he is a British Council Certified Corporate Trainer and has been conducting the Project Management Institute's (PMI) Project Management Professional (PMP) exam preparation training for the last 9 year. During the time this training has been running over 3500 individuals have been trained; these trainings have been conducted in Pakistan and UK. He holds a PhD in the Management of Complex Projects from the University of Southampton, UK. His research interests include: conflict and negotiations, complexity theory, modelling and simulation, qualitative techniques, and research philosophy. Presently, Dr. Gul is an Assistant Professor at the Institute of Management Sciences, Peshawar Pakistan.

Joyce Marie Hawkins is a full-time faculty member in the Office Administration Department of Wake Tech Community College, in Raleigh, North Carolina. She is also affiliated with the college's Workforce Continuing Education Department as an Information Technology Instructor. She has participated in the higher education arena at several major institutions which include Cornell University, State University of New York, Ferris State University, Grand Rapids Community College, and Johnston Community College. At these institutions she headed successful departments which include human resource development, benefits and compensation, staffing services, single parent/displaced homemaker services, sex equity services, cosmetology/cosmetic arts education and continuing education - information technology. She has written over six cosmetic arts training manuals and two teacher education training manuals. Joyce enjoys the classroom and facilitating student learning experiences.

L. Brooks Hill is Professor and Head Emeritus of the Department of Human Communication and Theatre at Trinity University, having devoted 25 of his 40 years in academe at that institution. He served three two-year terms as President of the International Association for Intercultural Communication Studies, working with academic and business professionals throughout the world. He is an internationally known expert and published author in areas including intercultural communication and negotiation. He has provided counsel to several government and private business organizations on topics that include interpersonal communication, cross-cultural relations, leadership, and organizational communication.

Ioannis Iglezakis is an Assistant Professor of Computers & Law at the Faculty of Law in the Aristotle University in Thessaloniki (Greece) and attorney-at-law at the Thessaloniki Bar Association. He graduated from the Faculty of Law of Aristotle University (Thessaloniki). After completing master degrees in the Universities of Thessaloniki (1990) and the University of Hannover (1993), he received his Ph.D. from the University of Thessaloniki in 2000. He was scientific collaborator in the postgraduate programme 'Single European Legal Space: Sector of New Technologies and Law', in the University of Thessaloniki (2002–2003) and Visiting Lecturer in the same University (2003–2009). He is the author of seven books related to I.C.T. (in Greek) and has various publications in Greek, German and English legal reviews, on issues related to I.T. law, public, economic and EU law. He is also the co-author of Cyber law (Greece), Kluwer Law Editions, and Legal and Socioeconomic Aspects of Intrusion, IGI editions.

Keith Jackson (PhD, MBA, MA, BA, CIPD, CMI) was born near Liverpool and is an author, researcher and consultant-practitioner in professional mentoring, leadership development and cross-cultural management communications. Based at SOAS, University of London, Keith designs and delivers courses in international management (Asia & Africa) and business research methods. Keith is currently engaged as a Professor in sustainable human resource management at Doshisha University in Kyoto, Japan.

Angela M. Jerome (Ph.D., University of Kansas, 2002) is an Associate Professor and the Graduate Program Coordinator in the Department of Communication at Western Kentucky University. The majority of her research focuses on organizational image repair, particularly in the athletic arena. She also does work on the communication of female athletes and school crisis communication.

Kijpokin Kasemsap received his BEng degree in Mechanical Engineering from King Mongkut's University of Technology Thonburi, his MBA degree from Ramkhamhaeng University, and his DBA degree in Human Resource Management from Suan Sunandha Rajabhat University. He is a Special Lecturer at Faculty of Management Sciences, Suan Sunandha Rajabhat University based in Bangkok, Thailand. He is a Member of International Association of Engineers (IAENG), International Association of Engineers and Scientists (IAEST), International Economics Development and Research Center (IEDRC),

International Association of Computer Science and Information Technology (IACSIT), International Foundation for Research and Development (IFRD), and International Innovative Scientific and Research Organization (IISRO). He also serves on the International Advisory Committee (IAC) for International Association of Academicians and Researchers (INAAR). He has numerous original research articles in top international journals, conference proceedings, and book chapters on business management, human resource management, and knowledge management published internationally.

Sarjit Kaur is Professor and Programme Chairperson of the English Language Studies Section at the School of Humanities, Universiti Sains Malaysia. Widely published, her research areas include Teaching English to Speakers of Other Languages (TESOL), workplace literacies, postgraduate education and policy research in higher education. Her recent co-edited books include Quality Assurance and University Rankings in Higher Education in the Asia Pacific: Challenges for Universities and Nations (USM Press, 2010) with Morshidi Sirat & William G. Tierney, Globalisation and Internationalisation of Higher Education in Malaysia (2008), Governance and Leadership in Higher Education (2008) and a monograph on Contemporary Issues in the Global Higher Education Marketplace: Prospects and Challenges (2010).

Lauren (Oliver) Keil currently serves as Business Development Manager for Advisory Board Consulting and Management in Nashville, Tennessee, where she manages the team responsible for preparing all Engagement Letters and project budgets, as well as tracking and reporting firm revenue. She received her Master of Arts in communication from Western Kentucky University, where she received the Top Paper in Public Relations and Debut Paper Award from the Central States Communication Association annual conference. She received her Bachelor of Science in organizational communication from the University of Evansville. Mrs. Keil's related interests include organizational identification, image repair and public relations, especially in the media, sports, popular business and health care industries.

Grace Kenny is a doctoral research student at Dublin City University Business School. Her research focuses on citizen privacy concerns and the impact of those concerns on intention and behavioural outcome in a variety of contexts.

Grace Khoury currently the dean of the business school and is an associate professor of management and has been the Director of MBA Program at Birzeit University in Palestine. She has over twenty five years of experience as a university professor, administrator, students' career advisor, researcher, management trainer and consultant at private and public organizations. She holds an MBA from Suffolk University, USA, and PhD in human resource management from Bradford University, UK. Dr Khoury is the marketing director at Taybeh Brewing Company, a family-owned business. She obtained certificates in project management and customer relationship management. She has published a number of management case studies and research articles in several academic journals. She is co-editor of a case book titled "Rising to the Digital Challenge: Lessons from Mediterranean Enterprises" (2005). She is co-author of "The Palestinian Executive: Leadership under Challenging Conditions" (2012). She is also a co-editor of "Cases on Management and Organizational Behavior in an Arab Context" (2014).

Kurt Kirstein is the Associate Provost of City University of Seattle. He is also serving as the Dean of School of Management and, in the past, has served as a faculty member and Program Director in business and technology. Dr. Kirstein has led several projects to create and revise business and technology programs and has led the effort to expand the level of internationalization and social responsibility that is infused into all of CityU's programs. Dr. Kirstein has published a number of chapters and articles focused on internationalization of higher education and, more recently, strategies for teaching social and environmental responsibility to business students both in the US and abroad. He also served as the lead editor of three collected volumes on adult education and online training. Prior to his time at CityU, Dr. Kirstein spent 20 years managing technical teams for organizations in the telecommunications and pharmaceutical industries. He holds a BS from The Evergreen State College, an MA in Adult Education from Seattle University, and a doctorate in Organizational Leadership from Nova Southeastern University.

D. Israel Lee, Ph.D., CDE. Visiting Professor at Southern Illinois University and Professor at the University of Phoenix. I have more than 12 years of research expertise in the field of Adult Education and Research Methodology, coupled with more than 27 years of classroom instruction in the military and postsecondary arenas. Additionally, I am a Certified Diversity and Inclusion Executive where I have a wealth of expertise in the enhancement of C-Suites for high performing organizations.

Blanca Martins (PhD) is a Public Accountant by the University of Uruguay, M.A. in Management Sciences by the COPPEAD-Federal University of Rio de Janeiro and PhD in Business Administration by the UPC. She worked for an economic-and-financial consultancy firm, acting in both the private and public sector. In 2001 she moved to Spain where she gained her doctoral degree. Since 2005 she is part of the research staff of the Dept. of Business Administration of the UPC. She was project manager and senior researcher in CADIC and InCaS FP projects. She is member of the scientific committee of IFKAD and reviewer for several business journals. Her current research interests are in sustainability and business model innovation in SMEs, SME collaborative arrangements, and clusters' management.

Beverley McNally is an assistant professor at Prince Mohammad Bin Fahd University in Kingdom of Saudi Arabia. She has a PhD in Management from Victoria University of Wellington, New Zealand and an MBA from Henley Management School in the UK. Beverley is an experienced educator working in both the contact and distance tertiary environments. She has worked for over twenty years in the tertiary education sector in New Zealand including Victoria University of Wellington and Massey University and the Open Polytechnic of New Zealand. Her research interests include leadership, human resource management, and organizational behavior. Prior to entering the education profession she spent a number of years in various management roles in the insurance and finance sector in New Zealand. Dr. McNally has also held board and governance roles in the NGO sector as well as mentoring roles for young women in business.

Aneil Mishra is the Thomas D. Arthur Distinguished Professor of Leadership at the East Carolina University College of Business.

Karen Mishra is an assistant professor at Meredith College where she teaches global corporate communications.

Renée J. Mitchell has served in the Sacramento Police Department for seventeen years and is currently a Police Sergeant. She holds a Bachelor of Science in Psychology from the University of California, Davis, a Master of Arts in Counseling Psychology from the University of San Francisco, a Master of

Business Administration from the California State University, Sacramento, and a Juris Doctorate from the University of the Pacific, McGeorge School of Law, where she was awarded an academic scholarship. She was the 2009/2010 Fulbright Police Research Fellow where she attended the University of Cambridge Police Executive Program and completed research in the area of juvenile gang violence at the London Metropolitan Police Service. She is a Police Foundation Fellow and is currently a Jerry Lee Scholar in the Institute of Criminology, at the University of Cambridge where she is completing a PhD. Her doctoral dissertation is based on a 15 minute high visibility intermittent random patrol hot spot policing program conducted in Sacramento, CA with the Sacramento Police Department. Sergeant Mitchell's hot spot study won the 2012 International Association of Chiefs of Police Excellence in Law Enforcement Research Silver Award. She is also the President of the newly organized American Society of Evidence-Based Policing. Her two latest projects are randomized control studies at the Portland Police Bureau. The first is procedural justice/communication course studying the effects of the training on officer's beliefs and the public's perception of police legitimacy. The second is a hot spot study on the effects of community engagement in hot spots of crime. Renée's primary research interests are place-based policing, procedural justice, police legitimacy, police training, communication, and evidence-based policing. She has lectured internationally on evidence-based policing, hot spot policing, crime analysis, procedural justice, police legitimacy, police training, and police leadership.

Mario Pérez-Montoro holds a PhD in Philosophy and Education from the University of Barcelona (Spain) and a Master in Information Management and Systems from the Polytechnic University of Catalonia (Spain). He studied at the Istituto di Discipline della Comunicazione at the Università di Bologna (Italy) and has been a Visiting Scholar at the Center for the Study of Language and Information (CSLI) at Stanford University (California, USA) and at the School of Information at UC Berkeley (California, USA). He is a Professor in the Department of Information Science and Media Studies at the University of Barcelona (Spain). His work has focused on information architecture and visualization.

Andrew Pyle is assistant professor of strategic communication at Clemson University in Clemson, SC. His research focuses on the intersection of crisis, culture, and communication technologies.

Noor Raha Mohd Radzuan is a senior lecturer at the Centre for Modern Languages and Human Sciences, Universiti Malaysia Pahang, Malaysia. She receives her Doctoral degree from Universiti Sains Malaysia, a Masters Degree in English Language Teaching from the University of Nottingham, United Kingdom and a Bachelor Degree in TESL from Universiti Kebangsaan Malaysia, Malaysia. She has presented a number of papers in both local and international conferences held around the globe. Previously, she was the Head of Modern Languages Department at the Centre for Modern Languages and Human Sciences, Universiti Malaysia Pahang. Her research interests include technical oral presentations, communication competence, second language anxiety, issues in engineering education and English for Professional Purposes.

Heather Rintoul received her PhD. from the University of Toronto and is Associate Professor of Graduate Education at the Schulich School of Education Nipissing University, graduate education. She is Director of the Nipissing University Centre for the Study of Leadership and Ethics in Education and Editor of the Journal of Authentic Leadership in Education. Her writing can be found in periodicals: Educational Management, Administration and Leadership, Values, Ethics and Educational Administration and in recent books: Examining the Assistant Principalship, Pathways to Excellence, and Global Perspectives on Educational Leadership Reform.

Ricardo Gouveia Rodrigues has a Ph.D. in Business and teaches Marketing Research, Entrepreneurial Marketing and Data Analysis to undergraduate, master and doctoral students at the University of Beira Interior, Portugal. He is also a researcher at the Research Centre on Enterprise Science (NECE – Núcleo de Estudos em Ciências Empresariais). His main research interests are Entrepreneurial Marketing and Entrepreneurship Education, but he's also interested in studying the impact of marketing efforts on themes such as physical activity, children behavior, online gaming addiction, and happiness. Ricardo Gouveia Rodrigues has published several books and book chapters, as well as peer reviewed papers in international journals.

T. Ray Ruffin retired from the United States Navy and currently teaches face-to-face classes during the day, evening, and online as full time and adjunct faculty. Affiliated colleges and universities include school include: University of Phoenix since 2012, School of Advanced Studies (SAS) Faculty Member and Dissertation Chair for the University of Phoenix, focus on the Doctoral Proposal for approval. Dr. Ruffin has received five Honorarium Awards and one Excellent in Publishing Award. Affiliate in Charlotte, North Carolina for the University of Phoenix Research Center for Workplace Diversity. Colorado Technical University since 2103, were Dr. Ruffin received two Adjunct Faculty Funding Awards. Rounding out the list with the University of Mount Olive since 2008 and Wake Technical Community College since 2010 was instrumental in course and syllabus development along with submitting grants or Faculty Honorarium Awards. Member of North Carolina Community College Faculty Association (NCCCFA) and North Carolina Computer Instruction Association (NCCIA), serving on the Leadership Team as Project Leader for Health Information Technology and Health Information Management. Has over twenty years of management (including financial management), and information technology experience. Dr. Ruffin's educational background has spawned and spans a Bachelor of Business Administration from Northwood University and the completion of four graduate degrees, Master of Arts in Organizational Leadership, Master of Science in Human Resources, Master of Health Administration all from Chapman University, and lastly Doctorate of Business Administration with a concentration in Information Systems from Argosy University. Additionally, Dr. Ruffin is currently, working toward a Post Doctorate Certificate in Healthcare Management and Leadership from Colorado Technical University. His research interest includes technology and leadership on all levels with a specialty for health information technology. Additionally, he is a reviewer for IGI Global and for the Journal of Emerging Trends in Healthcare Administration with Wyvern Publishing Group (WPG).

Sandra Sanz-Martos is a Lecturer at the Faculty of Information Sciences and Communication of the UOC Co-director of graduate studies in Social Media Content: Community Manager and Content Curator. She has a Degree in Hispanic Studies from the University of Barcelona (1995) and Degree of Information Science from the University of Granada (1998). Doctor Knowledge and Information Society by the Open University of Catalonia (2010). Author of the first book on communities of practice in Spanish, Comunidades de práctica: el valor de aprender de los pares (2012). Researcher at GAME (Learning, Media and Entertainment). Member of the Research Network Communities and Culture Network CCN +. Communities and social activism. ThinkEPI group member.

Nancy Scaffidi-Clark joined Mount Saint Mary College as the Associate Director of Admissions in 2008. Nancy graduated from Marlboro High School, and has a bachelor's degree from SUNY Albany and a Master of Arts in Communications from Marist College. She is now the Director of Admissions.

Peter A. C. Smith since 1990, as President of The Leadership Alliance Inc. (TLA, www.tlainc.com), Peter Smith has maintained a worldwide consulting practice assisting leading public and private sector organizations boost their performance by enhancing their leadership and innovation capabilities and addressing VUCA issues. The breadth of Peter's previous practical hands-on management experience with Exxon has proven invaluable in ensuring that he continues to relate to the problems and pressures faced by organizations in today's complex and ambiguous global environments, and is fundamental to framing his research interests which include complexity leadership, global business drivers, organizational strategy, socio-digital technology, sustainability, innovation, knowledge management, organizational learning, and related emerging paradigms. Peter is Managing Editor of the *Journal of Knowledge Management Practice*, Past Consulting and Special Issues Editor *The Learning Organization*, and Associate Editor (Practitioners) *International Journal of Sociotechnology & Knowledge Management*. Peter has published over sixty scholarly papers and is in demand internationally as a speaker, workshop leader and conference chair.

Peter Smith is a doctoral thesis tutor at University of Liverpool. He received his Doctorate in 1981. Since then he has held several teaching, research and management positions. He has published over 250 papers, and supervised and examined over 100 doctoral candidates at Universities in the UK, Europe and Hong Kong. Peter is a Fellow of the British Computer Society and the Higher Education Academy. He has published extensively on a range of subjects including computing, management, and doctoral studies, particularly in relation to Professional Doctorates.

Terje Solvoll started his career as a researcher in Telenor R&D early in 2001 as a Cand. Scient within computer science. Here he worked mainly with mobile phones and mobile technology. He managed projects developing interactive real time multiplayer games for mobile phones using PDA's and WiFi to simulate smartphones and UMTS, or 3G networks before 3G was available. In this project, he collaborated with Compaq R&D department in Huston USA. He worked further with tracking within WiFi, Bluetooth, GSM and low frequency radio networks, sending positions from sheep's and signals from medical sensors attached to the animal to the farmer, using GSM networks. In this project, he collaborated with MIT Media lab in Boston Massachusetts USA, center for Things That Think. In 2003, Terje Solvoll left Telenor and started to work with in the commercial industry and satellite communications. He worked as a Systems Supervisor for a company called Dualog, which delivers ship-shore IT services to the ships and electronic reporting systems to fishing vessels through satellite communication. He worked here until 2006, and after several hospital stays, he decided to go back to research, and mainly research within telemedicine. In April 2006, he started at NST as a project manager for an eczema-counselling project, where parents of children suffering of atopic eczema could have counselling using Internet to communicate with dermatologist to treat the patients, and avoid hospitalization. In 2007, he started to work with his PhD, within mobile communication for hospitals, which he finished in 2013. During this time, he has been involved in several other projects, which involves professional networks for dentists, stroke diagnosing and treatment in rural areas using High Definition video conferencing systems through dedicated networks guaranteeing quality, decision-making systems, medical sensors, and more.

Carolyn Stevenson holds a Master of Arts degree in Communication, Master of Business Administration, and Doctor of Education with an emphasis in Higher Education. Prior to pursuing a career in higher education, she worked in the publishing field and served as a technical writing consultant. She currently serves as committee member for the American Educational Research Association's Division D: Research Methods for the Early Career Award; Associate Editor for the International Journal of Technologies and Educational Marketing (IJTEM), published by IGI-Global; Editorial Board Member and Reviewer for the Journal of Education and Learning published by the Canadian Center of Science and Education; and Membership Committee Member for the Qualitative Research Special Interest Group (AERA). Recent publications include a chapter entitled: "Leading across Generations: Issues for Higher Education Administrators" published in the Handbook of Research on Transnational Higher Education Management, by IGI Global and Technical Writing: A Comprehensive Resource for Technical Writers at all Levels, (Martinez, Hannigan, Wells, Peterson and Stevenson) Revised and Updated Edition, Kaplan Publishing and Building Online Communities in Higher Education Institutions: Creating Collaborative Experience with an anticipated publication date of February 2014. She is a full-time faculty member for OC@KU (Kaplan University).

Ben Tran received his Doctor of Psychology (Psy.D) in Organizational Consulting/Organizational Psychology from California School of Professional Psychology at Alliant International University in San Francisco, California, United States of America. Dr. Tran's research interests include domestic and expatriate recruitment, selection, retention, evaluation, & training, CSR, business and organizational ethics, organizational/international organizational behavior, knowledge management, and minorities in multinational corporations. Dr. Tran has presented articles on topics of business and management ethics, expatriate, and gender and minorities in multinational corporations at the Academy of Management, Society for the Advancement of Management, and International Standing Conference on Organizational Symbolism. Dr. Tran has also published articles and book chapters with the Social Responsibility Journal, Journal of International Trade Law and Policy, Journal of Economics, Finance and Administrative Science, Financial Management Institute of Canada, and IGI Global.

Ramon Salvador Valles has developed his academic and professional career in the area of business management and information systems for over thirty years, giving lectures, tutorials and carrying out research at the Technical University of Catalonia (UPC) – BarcelonaTech. He is currently working at its Engineering Faculty of Barcelona. He has authored and coauthored books and book chapters, technical reports and journal articles on information systems, knowledge management, e-government as well as business management. He has been working in projects and performing as adviser for private companies as well as public institutions.

Khaner Walker is the Senior Manager Communications at Lenovo where he manages the internal communications team. This team plans comprehensive campaigns for multiple global business groups and the company as a whole.

Doron Zinger is a doctoral student in education at the University of California, Irvine. A former high school science teacher and administrator, Doron's research focuses on teacher learning and thinking, and the use of online learning environments for teachers and administrators.

Kendall Zoller (Ed.D.) is an author, researcher, educator, and speaker. He co-authored The Choreography of Presenting (Corwin-Press, 2010) and has over a dozen peer reviewed articles and chapters on education and leadership. He was a guest author in Bob Garmston's Presenter's Fieldguide. As president of Sierra Training Associates, Inc., he provides seminars and keynotes on communicative intelligence, adaptive leadership, and facilitation/presentation skills to schools, districts, universities, state agencies, and corporations across the United States and internationally. He is a curriculum designer, trainer, and presenter for law enforcement training thought the California Peace Officers Standards. His international research focuses on identifying nonverbal patterns in the learning environment and their influences on thinking, memory, and learning. He introduced Nonverbal Communicative Intelligence (2007) and Communicative Intelligence (2014). His extensive experience includes training corporate executive level, sales teams, senior managers, university faculty and staff, law enforcement leaders, administrators, and teachers. He is a Cohort I Fellow and mentor to the National Academy for Science and Mathematics Education Leadership.

Index

Become an IRMA Member

Members of the **Information Resources Management Association (IRMA)** understand the importance of community within their field of study. The Information Resources Management Association is an ideal venue through which professionals, students, and academicians can convene and share the latest industry innovations and scholarly research that is changing the field of information science and technology. Become a member today and enjoy the benefits of membership as well as the opportunity to collaborate and network with fellow experts in the field.

IRMA Membership Benefits:

- **One FREE Journal Subscription**

- **30% Off Additional Journal Subscriptions**

- **20% Off Book Purchases**

- Updates on the latest events and research on Information Resources Management through the IRMA-L listserv.

- Updates on new open access and downloadable content added to Research IRM.

- A copy of the Information Technology Management Newsletter twice a year.

- A certificate of membership.

IRMA Membership $195

Scan code to visit irma-international.org and begin by selecting your free journal subscription.

Membership is good for one full year.

Printed in the United States
By Bookmasters